THE PENGUIN BIOGRAPHICAL DICTIONARY OF WOMEN

THE PENGUIN
BIOGRAPHICAL DICTIONARY OF
WOMEN

PENGUIN BOOKS

PENGUIN BOOKS

Published by the Penguin Group
Penguin Books Ltd, 27 Wrights Lane, London W8 5TZ, England
Penguin Putnam Inc., 375 Hudson Street, New York, New York 10014, USA
Penguin Books Australia Ltd, Ringwood, Victoria, Australia
Penguin Books Canada Ltd, 10 Alcorn Avenue, Toronto, Ontario, Canada M4V 3B2
Penguin Books (NZ) Ltd, 182–190 Wairau Road, Auckland 10, New Zealand

Penguin Books Ltd, Registered Offices: Harmondsworth, Middlesex, England

First published 1998
1 3 5 7 9 10 8 6 4 2

Printed in England by Clays Ltd, St Ives plc

A

Abakanowicz, Magdalena (1930–)
Polish weaver and sculptor

Abakanowicz is known both for her unique woven sculptures and for her brooding figurative sculptures made from sacking.

Born in Falenty, Poland, she trained at the Warsaw Academy of Fine Arts (1950–55). In 1956 she married Jan Kosmowski and began to work as an artist. Her early works concentrated on hanging forms constructed of fibres and woven material, but in the 1960s she achieved international recognition with her three-dimensional woven structures, which were monumental and abstract in form. She later moved on to work with sacking, clay, and wood.

In 1965 Abakanowicz started teaching at the State College of Arts in Poznań, where she served as a professor from 1979 until 1990. Her work has been widely acclaimed in Poland and in the West. She has held one-woman exhibitions in several countries, and her many awards include the Grand Prize of the World Crafts Council, New York (1974). Pieces of her work hang in many major galleries, including the Museum of Modern Art, New York, and the Pompidou Centre, Paris.

Abbott, Berenice (1898–1991) *American photographer*

> Photography can never grow up if it imitates some other medium. It has to walk alone; it has to be itself.
>
> "It Has to Walk Alone," *Infinity* (1951)

Abbott is best known for her dynamic and detailed photographic record of New York City in the 1930s, which was published as her first book, *Changing New York* (1939). (This was reissued as *New York in the Thirties* in 1973.) She pioneered a realism in photography with her dramatic images of the urban environment.

Born in Springfield, Ohio, and educated at schools in Columbus, Ohio, and at Ohio State University, in 1921 she went to Europe and worked in Paris for a time as a darkroom assistant to the American surrealist artist Man Ray. It was during this period that she discovered the work of the little-known French photographer Eugène Atget. Abbott arranged exhibitions of his work and bought some of his prints. After Atget's death she acquired his archives, which she classified and maintained until they were bought by New York's Museum of Modern Art in 1968.

Abbott was also interested in the technical aspects of photography and wrote two books, *A Guide to Better Photography* (1941) and *The View Camera Made Simple* (1948), as well as numerous articles on the subject. She taught in New York at the New School for Social Research from 1935 to 1958, then moved to Boston, to the Physical Science Study Commission of Educational Services, Inc., where she developed photographic techniques to solve scientific problems.

Her work has been exhibited throughout the world and she was known for offering every encouragement to women wishing to take up photography as a profession.

Abbott, Diane (Julie) (1953–)
British Labour politician

In 1987 Diane Abbott became a nationally known figure when she was elected as Britain's first black woman MP.

The daughter of middle-class parents of West Indian origin, Abbott was raised in north London, where she attended Harrow County Girls' School. After graduating from Newnham College, Cambridge, in 1975 she began a career in the civil service but was dismayed by the racism and sexism she encountered in the Home Office. She subsequently found more congenial employment as race relations officer for the National Council for Civil Liberties and as a researcher for independent television.

An active member of the Labour Party since her teenage years, Abbott became increasingly involved in local government during the 1980s. She worked as a press officer for the Greater London Council during its left-wing heyday under Ken Livingstone and was also a member of Westminster City Council (1982–86). In 1987 Diane Abbott was elected to parliament for the safe Labour seat of Hackney North and Stoke Newington. Although her outspoken statements on racial and sexual matters have often caused controversy in the press, Abbott is widely respected as a hardworking and able MP. She was elected to Labour's National Executive Committee (NEC) in 1994.

Abigail (10th century BC) *Old Testament heroine*

Abigail was the beautiful and wise wife of the churlish Nabal, a rich sheep farmer at Carmel. She later became the wife of King David and the mother of his son Chileab, or Daniel. Her story appears in I Samuel 25.

While David was hiding in the wilderness of Paran from King Saul, he sent some of his men to Nabal, who was shearing his sheep at Carmel. Their mission was to ask for provisions in return for the kindness and hospitality David had previously shown Nabal's shepherds. When Nabal refused, David marched towards Carmel with a large troop of his men. However, Abigail received advanced warning of the impending attack and intercepted David's troops herself, bringing gifts of food and wine. Ten days later Nabal was dead ("his heart died within him and he became as a stone"), and David married Abigail.

Abigail was later abducted during a raid by the Amalekites but was rescued by David.

Abzug, Bella (1920–) *American lawyer and politician*

> Our time has come. We will no longer content ourselves with leavings and bits and pieces of the rights enjoyed by men...we want our equal rights, nothing more but nothing less. We want an equal share of political and economic power.
>
> —Quoted by Jill Johnston in *Gullible's Travels* (1974)

Known as "Battling Bella" because of her ferocious campaigning style, Bella Abzug has worked tirelessly for civil rights, is prominent in the women's movement, and is a member of many committees and pressure groups, including NOW (National Organization of Women), the American Civil Liberties Union, and Americans for Democratic Action.

Born into a Russian-Jewish émigré family in New York City and educated there, she married Daniel Abzug in 1944 and received her LLB the following year. Admitted to the New York Bar in 1947, she practised law in New York until 1970. During the McCarthy witch-hunts of the 1950s she defended writers accused of un-American activities, also taking on civil rights cases in the South. In the 1960s she played an active part in the peace, antinuclear, and women's movements, founding Women Strike for Peace (1961) and the National Women's Political Caucus.

In 1971 Abzug won a seat in the House of Representatives and campaigned there for six years on many welfare issues as well as for aid to Israel. She campaigned unsuccessfully to win a seat in the Senate (1976) and to become mayor of New York (1977). Returning to her law practice in 1980, she has continued to be involved in politics.

Bella Abzug's writings include many articles of political commentary and on women's issues, as well as a column in *Ms.* magazine. She is the author of *Bella! Ms. Abzug Goes to Washington* (1972) and *Gender Gap: Bella Abzug's*

Guide to Political Power for American Women (1984). She was inducted into the U.S. National Women's Hall of Fame in 1994.

Achurch, Janet (1864–1916) *British actress*

Janet Achurch is best known for being the first British actress to perform Ibsen, when in 1889 she played Nora in *A Doll's House* in a production at the Novelty Theatre, London. George Bernard Shaw was so impressed with her performance that he saw it five times.

Janet Achurch made her theatrical debut in 1883 and then joined Frank Benson's touring company, mainly playing Shakespearean leads. Following her pioneering role in *A Doll's House*, which was directed by her husband, the actor Charles Carrington, she herself produced Ibsen's *Little Eyolf* in 1896, playing the leading role of Rita. In 1900 she took the title role in *Candida*, which Shaw had written especially for her, also playing Lady Cecily Wayneflete in his *Captain Brassbound's Conversion* the same year. Shaw thought her a tragic actress of genius. She also toured widely with her husband until she retired from the stage in 1913.

Acton, Eliza(beth) (1799–1859) *British cookery writer*

Eliza Acton is remembered as the author of a pioneering cookery book, *Modern Cookery*, which was first published in 1845 and went through five editions in two years. Its success was due to its attention to cooking details and the summary of ingredients given for each recipe.

The daughter of a brewer, she grew up in Suffolk and spent some time abroad because of ill health. In Paris she became engaged to a French army officer, but the marriage never took place. Returning to England, she began her literary career by writing poetry, some of which was published in the 1820s and 1830s. By the early 1840s she was living at Tonbridge, Kent, keeping house for her mother, and her publishers suggested that a cookery book might be more commercially successful than poetry. Accordingly, *Modern Cookery* appeared in 1845, when it became an instant bestseller; it remained in print until 1914, being used as a basis for many cookery books of that period. Her last book, *The English Bread Book*, was published in 1857.

Adams, Abigail (1744–1818) *American political figure, letter writer, and feminist*

> Men of Sense in all Ages abhor
> those customs which treat us only as
> the vassals of your Sex.
> —Letter to John Adams, March 31,
> 1776

The wife of John Adams, the second president of the United States, and the mother of the sixth president, John Quincy Adams, Abigail Adams is best known for her shrewd observations in the many letters she wrote to her husband while he was away from home during his long public career.

She was the second of four children of the Reverend William Smith and his wife Elizabeth, a member of the influential Quincy family. Because of her delicate health as a child she was educated largely by her maternal grandmother at Mount Wollaston, Massachusetts. In 1764 she married the young lawyer John Adams, with whom she had five children. John Adams's opposition to the Stamp Act of 1765 brought him into the political sphere; while he was away in Philadelphia and later in Europe on diplomatic missions, Abigail ran the family farm at Braintree, Massachusetts, and brought up her four surviving children. Her long and vivid letters to him describe the ups and downs of their daily life. Her independence led her to support the education of women and the rights of wives within marriage.

In 1784 she joined her husband in Paris for eight months and then spent three years in London, where he was the American representative. Many of her letters from Europe contain frank and caustic comments on the politicians and diplomats she met. After returning to the United States, Adams was elected vice president in 1787 and president in 1797. During these years he shared many of his official duties with his wife, who is thought to have had a strong influence on his thinking, as she later did on that of her son during his political career. Her letters during this period contain many references to current politics: as she was a staunch Federalist, they are somewhat partisan. As the contemporary American statesman Albert Gallatin observed: "Mrs. President not of the United States but of a faction."

In 1800 the White House was completed; Abigail lived there as First Lady for just a year before John Adams was defeated. They then retired to the family home at Quincy (formerly part of Braintree), where she was able to resume her role as a farmer while continuing to act as an informal political adviser. In 1803 her son John Quincy Adams became a senator; he was elected president in 1824. Her letters continued until her death from typhoid fever at the age of 74.

Adams, Maude (1872–1953) *American actress*

A great stage star in the early 20th century, Maude Adams is best remembered for her performance in J. M. Barrie's *Peter Pan*, which she first played in 1906.

The daughter of a leading lady in a repertory company, she was born in Salt Lake City, Utah. Taking her mother's maiden name (her family name was Kiskadden), she first appeared on the stage while still a child. At 16 she joined the E. H. Sothern Company in New York, later becoming the leading lady of the Charles Frohman Stock Company. Projecting an elfin quality that was especially suited to the plays of J. M. Barrie, she appeared as Lady Babbie in his *The Little Minister* (1897, 1905, 1916), to great critical acclaim. After her success as Peter Pan she went on to star in Barrie's other plays, *Quality Street* (1902) and *What Every Woman Knows* (1908).

After retiring for 13 years, she made a comeback as Portia in *The Merchant of Venice* (1931) and as Maria in *Twelfth Night* (1934). She headed the drama department at Stephens College, Columbia, Missouri, from 1937 to 1943, then taught part-time at the college.

Adamson, Joy (1910–1980) *Austrian-born British conservationist, writer, and artist*

> How could she [Elsa the lioness] know that it needed all the strength of my love for her to leave her now and give her back to nature.
> —*Born Free* (1960)

Best known for helping a tame lioness, Elsa, return to the wild in Kenya, Joy Adamson was also a dedicated conservationist and started the World Wildlife Fund in the United States in 1962.

Brought up in Vienna, Joy Gessner originally studied for a career as a concert pianist. When she did not succeed, she turned to bookbinding and drawing and became interested in archaeology. She married Victor von Klarwill in 1935, but two years later, while travelling in Kenya, she met Peter Bally, a botanist, and they were married, after her divorce, in 1938. Together they went on field trips, and she painted over 700 studies of flowers, trees, and shrubs. This marriage also ended in divorce, and in 1943 she married George Adamson, a game warden in the North Frontier District.

Joy Adamson then began painting both animals and people, securing a commission from the British Colonial Government of Kenya to paint portraits of members of the 22 tribes whose culture was fast disappearing. This collection of some 600 paintings now belongs to the National Museum of Kenya.

Her association with the lioness Elsa began in 1956. Her book *Born Free* (1960), a worldwide best-seller and later a film, describes how she raised Elsa from a cub and helped her return to the wild. *Living Free* (1961) and *Forever Free* (1962) continue the tale of Elsa and her cubs. In 1964 she retrained a cheetah, Pippa, later describing the experience in *The Spotted Sphinx* (1969). In 1980 Joy Adamson was found dead, supposedly mauled by a lion, in northern Kenya. A man was later charged with her murder.

Addams, Jane (1860–1935) *American social reformer and feminist*

> Civilization is a method of living, an attitude of equal respect for all men.
>
> —Speech, Honolulu, 1933

> She had compassion without condescension. She had pity without retreat into vulgarity. She had infinite sympathy for common things without forgetfulness of those that are uncommon. That, I think, is why those who have known her say she was not only good, but great.
>
> —Walter Lippman, *American Heroine, The Life and Legend of Jane Addams*

Jane Addams was awarded the Nobel Peace Prize in 1931. A noted supporter of pacifism, racial equality, and feminism, she founded Hull House, the Chicago social welfare centre, in 1889 and was president of the Women's International League for Peace and Freedom (1919–35).

Born in Cedarville, Illinois, and brought up by her widowed father, a prosperous banker and friend of Abraham Lincoln, she was educated at the Rockford Female Seminary (now Rockford College), graduating in 1881. While travelling in Europe during the 1880s she was greatly affected by the urban poverty she saw and impressed by the social reform movement in England, particularly Toynbee Hall in London, the first university settlement.

In 1889, with her college classmate Ellen Starr, she founded Hull House in a Chicago slum. It was an immediate success, initiating reforms in many areas, including housing, education, and child labour, as well as providing a safe haven in the alienating city, particularly for newly arrived immigrants. By 1893 Hull House was running 40 local clubs, including a nursery, a dispensary, and a boarding house. In 1895 the *Hull House Maps and Papers* were published; this detailed study of local conditions was instrumental in initiating social reforms, both locally and nationally.

In 1910 Jane Addams became the first woman president of the National Conference of Charities and Corrections, and in 1911 she founded the National Federation of Settlements, of which she was president (1911–35). She fought for prohibition and women's suffrage, being vice president of the National American Women Suffrage Alliance from 1911 until 1914, and in 1912 she campaigned for the Progressive Party.

A lifelong pacifist, at the outbreak of World War I she became chair of the Woman's Peace Party and president of the first Women's Peace Congress at The Hague. She canvassed for the war to be ended by mediation, arousing hostility by speaking out against American involvement. In 1919 she presided over the second Women's Peace Congress in Zurich and raised funds for war victims. In 1920 she became a founder member of the American Civil Liberties Union, continuing to campaign tirelessly against civil injustices, including racial and social inequality, until her death.

Addams wrote ten books, including *Democracy and Social Ethics* (1902), *The Spirit of Youth and the City Streets* (1909), and the well-known *Twenty Years at Hull House* (1910), as well as over 400 articles.

See also BALCH, EMILY GREENE.

Adelaide, Saint (931–999) *Wife of the Holy Roman Emperor Otto I*

Adelaide (Adelheid in German) wielded great influence during three successive reigns of Holy Roman Emperors. Also noted for her piety, she was a lifelong supporter of the Cluniac (reformed Benedictine) monastic order.

The daughter of King Rudolf II of Burgundy, Adelaide became the wife of King Lothair II of Italy in 947. After his death in 950 she was imprisoned by his successor for a year until Otto I of Germany, who later became the Holy Roman Emperor, rescued her and married her. In 962 she was crowned empress with him and was very influential in helping to shape the policies of the Holy Roman Empire; she retained her power after the death of her husband (973), during the rules of both her son Otto II (reigned 973–983) and her grandson Otto III (reigned 983–996). Towards the end of her life she devoted herself to religious works, founding many monasteries, convents, and churches. She died at her monastery at Selz, in Alsace, which became a place of pilgrimage; she was canonized in 1097.

Adie, Kate (1945–) *British television reporter*

Kate Adie's reports about conflicts and disasters from around the globe have made her one of the BBC's most respected news journalists.

An adopted child, Adie was brought up in Sunderland, northeast England. After graduating from Newcastle University with a degree in Scandinavian studies, she began a career in BBC radio, working first as a technician and then as a producer. In the late 1970s she moved to local television and began to appear on screen as a reporter. She made her debut on BBC national news in 1979.

During the 1980s Adie became a household name in Britain with her frontline coverage of wars, revolutions, and natural disasters from around the world – a type of reporting previously considered a male province. Her reports, which are often made in circumstances of great difficulty or danger, are characterized by a coolly authoritative manner that inspires absolute trust in the viewer. Adie has received numerous honours and awards for her work, including the Monte Carlo International TV News Award (1981, 1990) and the prestigious Richard Dimbleby Award (1989). She became the BBC's chief news correspondent in 1989 and was appointed OBE in 1993.

Aelgifu (*c.* 1010–1040) *Anglo-Saxon noblewoman and tyrannical regent of Norway*

The daughter of a nobleman of Northamptonshire (then part of the Anglo-Saxon kingdom of Mercia), Aelgifu became the mistress of Canute of Denmark when he came to England with an invasion party as a young man. She remained Canute's companion all his life, and they had two sons, in spite of his marriage to EMMA, the widow of Aethelred (II) "the Un-ready," whom Canute succeeded as king of England in 1017. Aelgifu's eldest son, Sweyn, was made king of Norway in 1029, and Canute appointed Aelgifu as regent. She became a tyrant, notorious for her cruelty. Eventually her despotic behaviour provoked an uprising in 1035, during which she was deposed. After Canute's death that same year Aelgifu returned to England and supported her second son, Harold Harefoot, who was acting as regent of England, in his claim to the throne. Her efforts were rewarded in 1037 when Harold was recognized as Canute's legal heir instead of his legitimate son, Hardecanute.

Aethelflaed (died *c.* 918) *Anglo-Saxon princess*

Known as Lady of the Mercians, Aethelflaed (or Ethelfleda) was a powerful ruler who commanded armies, planned campaigns, and built fortresses; her fame lived on until the Renaissance. The dramatist Thomas Heywood included her as one of his "viragos" in his *Nine Books of Various History Concerning Women* (1624), and in 1697 the diarist John Evelyn put her on his list of people worthy of receiving a medal.

The daughter of Alfred the Great, king of Wessex, Aethelflaed married Aethelred, the ruler of West Mercia, in about 880 and governed with him until his death in 912. Ruling alone as Lady of the Mercians, she helped her brother Edward, king of Wessex, to overcome the Vikings in eastern England. She fortified the important trade centres of Warwick and Stafford and repaired the walls at Chester. In 917 she and her brother planned a major attack on the Danes, and she led her conquering armies into Derby and Leicester. She also won authority in parts of Wales and Northumbria. After her death Edward took over her kingdom. It is believed that at the time of her death she was planning further campaigns in the north and east of England.

Aethelthryth, Saint (*c.* 630–679) *Queen, by marriage, of Northumbria*

Founding abbess of Ely, Aethelthryth had a reputation for asceticism and chastity that earned her a high place in the catalogue of saints.

Aethelthryth was one of four sainted daughters of Anna, king of the East Angles. After the death of her first husband, Tonbert, prince of the fen countrymen of South Cambridgeshire, she married Egfrid, the 14-year-old heir to the throne of Northumbria. Following his accession she fled to Ely to avoid consummating the marriage. She became a nun in about 672 and founded a monastery for monks and nuns at Ely in 673. The date of her death, June 23, became her feast day, and Ely cathedral, of which she is patron saint, was built over her grave.

Her name is also recorded as Ætheldreda and Etheldreda, which was contracted to Audry. The word "tawdry" is derived from St. Audry's lace, a type of lace that was sold as cheap finery at St. Audry's fair.

Agassiz, Elizabeth (1822–1907)
American naturalist and first president of Radcliffe College for Women

Born into a wealthy Boston family, Elizabeth Carey married the Swissborn naturalist Jean Louis Agassiz in 1850. Although she had received no formal training, she helped her husband to establish a marine laboratory on Penikese Island in Buzzard's Bay, Massachusetts, and shared in his work. She published two manuals, *Actaea: A First Lesson in Natural History* (1859) and *Seaside Studies in Natural History* (1865).

In 1856 Elizabeth established the Agassiz School for Girls in Cambridge, Massachusetts, which she ran for eight years. She then accompanied her husband on an expedition to Brazil (1865–66), during which she kept detailed records that were published as *A Journey in Brazil* in 1867. After two further voyages along the Pacific and Atlantic coasts of America she wrote articles about deep-sea dredging; subsequently she became involved in the development of the Natural History Museum at Cambridge.

In 1879 Elizabeth Agassiz cofounded the institution that later became Radcliffe College in Cambridge, Massachusetts (now affiliated to Harvard University). Although she was not in favour of co-education, she thought women should have the same opportunities for education as men and travelled to Britain to view the universities at Oxford and Cambridge in search of inspiration. She was president of Radcliffe College from 1894 to 1903, where a scholarship and a student hall are named after her.

Agatha, Saint (died *c.* 251) *Sicilian Christian martyr*

The only recorded fact about St. Agatha is that she was martyred in the port of Catania, eastern Sicily, but many legends surround her death. She is thought to have been a virgin who suffered torture and martyrdom because she rejected the amorous attentions of a Roman consul.

St. Agatha, whose feast day is February 5 (the date of her death), has been venerated as a saint since the 5th century. Her intercession is invoked against fire and lightning, possibly because – according to one legend – Mount Etna erupted on the day she was due to be burnt at the stake. The patron saint of Catania, she was depicted by artists as bearing a tray holding her breasts, which were said to have been cut off during her torture. These were often mistaken for bells; hence she is also the patron saint of bell founders.

Agnes, Saint (*c.* 292–*c.* 304) *Christian martyr*

Thought to have been born into a wealthy family, Agnes lived in Rome during the reign of the Emperor Diocletian. According to legend she was condemned to be burnt at the stake for refusing to renounce her Christian faith and marry the son of the magistrate, choosing instead to dedicate her virginity to Christ. When the flames would not burn her, she was beheaded.

St. Agnes's feast day is January 21; her emblem – a symbol of purity – is a lamb. Every year on her feast day the wool of two lambs is blessed in the church of St. Agnes in Rome before being made into the mantles worn by the pope and every archbishop.

The poem *The Eve of St. Agnes* by John Keats is based on the legend that a girl might dream of her lover if she fasted and observed the rituals of St. Agnes's Eve.

Agnesi, Maria (1718–1799) *Italian mathematician and philosopher*

Maria Agnesi is particularly remembered for her study of the versed sine curve in trigonometry, which became known in English as the "witch of Agnesi" – a mistranslation of the Latin *versiera* (curve) as witch. It was, in fact, a relatively minor part of her work.

Born into a wealthy and cultured Milanese family, Maria was the eldest of 21 children and recognized as a child prodigy. At the age of five she spoke French, and at nine, Latin, Greek, and Hebrew as well as some modern languages. When only nine she delivered an hour-long speech in Latin to a learned gathering on a woman's right to education. She studied mathematics as a teenager while tutoring her brothers and keeping house for her father; in 1738 she published *Propositiones philosophicae*, essays on science and philosophy. By that time she had already begun *Istituzioni analitiche*, published in 1748 in two volumes – one on algebra and geometry, the other on calculus. This was to be her major achievement, a work of great scholarship that broke new ground in mathematics.

In 1749 Agnesi was elected to the Bologna Academy of Sciences, and in 1750 Pope Benedict XIV instructed that she be appointed professor of mathematics at Bologna University (although there is no evidence that she took the post). After the death of her father in 1752 Agnesi turned her house into a hospital and devoted the rest of her life to the sick. From 1771 until her death she ran the Pio Instituto Trivulzio, a charitable institute in Milan for the sick.

Agnodice (4th century BC) *Greek gynaecologist*

Agnodice attended the medical classes of the famous Greek doctor Herophilus (*c.* 335–*c.* 280 BC), but in order to do so she had to dress as a man since at that time only men were allowed to practise medicine. Practis-ing as a gynaecologist, also in disguise, she soon antagonized her fellow doctors who, jealous of her fame, accused her of corrupting women. In court she revealed her femininity to save her life, incurring a new charge of practising medicine illegally, of which she was acquitted.

Agoult, Marie, Comtesse d' (1805–1876) *French writer*

Madame d'Agoult is remembered as the companion and lover of the composer and pianist Franz Liszt. Her Paris salon, which was a favourite gathering place of the leading thinkers, writers, and musicians of the day, was famous throughout the 1840s.

Marie Catherine Sophie de Flavigny was born in Frankfurt am Main, Germany. In 1827 she married Charles, Comte d'Agoult, but after several years she left him to live and travel with Liszt, by whom she had three children. Her daughter became Cosima WAGNER, the wife of the composer Richard Wagner.

In 1839 Madame d'Agoult left Liszt and went to Paris, where, using the pen name Daniel Stern, she began to write. Her novel *Nélida* (1846) is largely an autobiographical account of her relationship with Liszt. A good friend of George SAND, she is "Arabella" in Sand's *Lettres d'un voyageur*. Her other writings include works on history, politics, and philosophy: *Lettres républicaines* (1848), *Esquisses morales et politiques* (1849), and *Histoire de la révolution de 1848* (3 vols., 1850–53). Her volumes of memoirs (1877, 1927) provide a contemporary view of French society of the period 1806–54.

Agrippina the Elder (*c.* 13 BC–33 AD) *Roman noblewoman*

A high-minded and courageous woman, Vipsania Agrippina, known as Agrippina the Elder, played a major role in the power struggles that took place during the later stages of the reign of Emperor Tiberius.

The daughter of the Roman general Marcus Agrippa and JULIA THE ELDER (the daughter of Emperor Augustus), she married Germanicus, the popular adopted son of Tiberius, in about 5 AD. Although she bore him nine children (including the future Emperor Caligula and AGRIPPINA THE YOUNGER), she managed to accompany him on many of his military expeditions. When Germanicus, who had been appointed governor of Rome's eastern provinces, died mysteriously at Antioch in 19 AD, Agrippina returned to Rome and publicly accused Tiberius of being responsible. Political intrigue followed as she attempted to have her sons named as heirs to the empire, a move that was opposed by Sejanus, Tiberius's adviser. In 29 she was banished by Tiberius to Pandateria, where she starved to death.

Agrippina the Younger (c. 15–59 AD) Roman noblewoman

> No philosophy, my son [Nero]; it is of no use to an emperor.
>
> —Quoted by Maximilian Schele de Vere in *The Great Empress, A Portrait* (1870)

Julia Agrippina, known as Agrippina the Younger, was the ruthless and ambitious mother of Nero.

The eldest daughter of AGRIPPINA THE ELDER and Germanicus, Agrippina the Younger grew up in an atmosphere of political intrigue. In 28 AD she married her cousin Domitius Ahenobarbus; their son Nero, the future emperor, was born in 37. During the reign of her brother Caligula (37–41) she was involved in a conspiracy against him; as a result he accused her of treason and adultery, banishing her from Rome. After the assassination of Caligula and the accession of her uncle Claudius, Agrippina was allowed to return. She then married the wealthy Crispus Passienus. In 48 Claudius's scheming wife, Valeria MESSALINA, was executed for treason and adultery; Agrippina seized the opportunity to court Claudius, who in 49 agreed to marry her despite the general opinion that such a marriage was incestuous. She was then in a position to persuade Claudius to name her son Nero as his heir, even though he had a son, Britannicus, by his previous marriage. Eventually Agrippina destroyed all Nero's possible rivals and is even thought to have been responsible for Claudius's

death in 54 by feeding him poisoned mushrooms.

In the first years of Nero's reign Agrippina was a powerful influence behind the throne. However, in 59, because of her constant intrigues and interferences in affairs of state, she was murdered at Baiae on Nero's instruction.

Aguilar, Grace (1816–1847) Anglo-Hebrew writer

Although she wrote poetry and books about the Jewish faith, it is for her sentimental novels that Grace Aguilar is best known.

Born into a family of Sephardic Jews (Jews from Spain and Portugal) in London, she was always sickly and therefore educated at home. The family moved to Devon in 1828. Aguilar began to write at an early age, and her first volume of poems, *Magic Wreath*, appeared in 1835. After her father's death she took up writing professionally, producing *The Spirit of Judaism*, which attacked the formalism of contemporary Judaism, in 1842. *The Women of Israel* (1845) and *The Jewish Faith* (1846) provide an accessible account of Judaism.

Home Influence (1847) was Aguilar's only novel that was published in her lifetime. The others, including *A Mother's Recompense* (1850), *Woman's Friendship* (1851), and *The Days of Bruce* (1852), were edited and published after her death by her mother. She died during a visit to Frankfurt, and is buried in the Jewish cemetery there.

Aidoo, Ama Ata (1942–) Ghanaian writer

> Women allow them [men] to behave the way they do instead of seizing some freedom themselves.
>
> —*No Sweetness Here* (1970)

The author of plays, short stories, and poems, Aidoo is considered one of the finest living African women writers.

She was born at Abeadzi Kyiakor, in central Ghana, and educated at Wesley Girls' School, Cape Coast. Graduating from the University of Ghana in 1964, she went to Stanford University, California, to study creative writing.

While there Aidoo began to write short stories that were published in magazines. Returning to Ghana, she lectured at Cape Coast University (1970–73) and has served as a consultant at various academic institutions in Africa, the United States, and Europe.

The theme of Aidoo's work is the clash of cultures – the conflict between the traditional and the new in African society: typically, as in her semiautobiographical novel *Our Sister Killjoy* (1976), one of the main characters is a "been-to" (an African educated abroad) or a woman with feminist ideas. In her first play, *The Dilemma of a Ghost* (1965), a "been-to" returns to Africa with a black American wife and watches the modern world confront the traditional African ways; in the end the dilemma is resolved through the triumph of traditional African hospitality. In the play *Anowa* (1970), set in the 19th century, a feminist woman marries a conventional man of whom her parents disapprove. Backed by her ambition and resourcefulness, he becomes a successful trader. However, material achievement fails to bring happiness. The differences in their backgrounds and in their sense of values tragically lead them both to commit suicide.

Aidoo's other published works include the novel *Changes: A Love Story* (1991), the collection of poems *Someone Talking to Sometime* (1985), and the short-story collections *No Sweetness Here* (1970) and *The Chicken and Other Stories* (1987).

Aimée, Anouk (1932–) *French film actress*

Anouk Aimée is best known for her starring role in Claude Lelouch's international film success *A Man and a Woman* (1966), for which she received an Oscar nomination, the BAFTA (British Academy Film and Television Arts) Award, and the Golden Globe Award for Best Actress.

Born Françoise Sorya Dreyfus in Paris into an acting family, she studied dance at the Marseilles Opéra before going on to drama school in Britain. She made her film debut at the age of 14 in Henri Calef's *La Maison sous la mer* (1947; *The House Beneath the Sea*) after she was spotted by the director walking along the street with her mother. Her international reputation developed from her appearances in André Cayatte's *The Lovers of Verona* (1948) and Nico Papatakis's *The Golden Salamander* (1950). She married the first of her four husbands, Edouard Zimmermann, in 1949, divorcing him to marry Papatakis in 1950. During the 1950s her career in Europe thrived with such films as *Forever My Heart* and *The Journey*. Acclaim followed in 1960 with Fellini's *La Dolce Vita*, in which she played Madalena, and for the title role in Jacques Demy's *Lola*. She appeared in Fellini's *8½* (1963) and, after the success of *A Man and a Woman*, worked in Hollywood, starring in George Cukor's *Justine* (1969) and Sidney Lumet's *The Appointment* (1969).

After her fourth marriage (1970–75) to the actor Albert Finney, during which time she did not work, Aimée returned to France where she has made such films as Lelouch's *Si c'était à refaire* (1978; *Second Choice*) and *A Man and a Woman: Twenty Years Later* (1986), *Docteur Norman Bethune* (1992), and *Prêt-à-porter* (1995).

A'isha (*c.* 614–678) *Third and favourite wife of the Prophet Mohammed*

A'isha became an important influence on Muslim thought after the death of Mohammed. Her religious teachings contributed to the emergence of the Sunni Muslims.

Her father, 'Abu Bakr, was Mohammed's chief adviser and A'isha became Mohammed's child bride in about 624, after the battle of Bakr, when he was about 50 years old. They had no children, but she was always his favourite: as he grew older and death approached, he preferred her company to that of any of his other eight wives. After his death in 632 he was buried in her chamber.

As the widow of the Prophet, A'isha was not allowed to remarry; during the rule of her father (632–34) and of 'Umar I (634–44) she took no part in politics either, maintaining her position of authority through her intelligence and learning. She emerged as a powerful leader after the murder of the third Muslim ruler in 656 and the civil war that followed, opposing the succession of Ali, Mohammed's son-in-law. However, she was captured at the Battle of the Camel (656), so called because the fiercest fighting took place around the camel carrying her litter. She was only released on condition that she renounce political life; A'isha, therefore, lived the rest of her life quietly in Medina.

See also KHADIJAH

Akhmadulina, Bella (1937–) *Russian poet*

Known for her lyrical poems of city life, Akhmadulina is of mixed Tatar and Italian descent. She was born in Moscow and educated at the Gorky Literary Institute. Her first poetry collection, *Struna* (1962; String), attracted great attention in the Soviet literary world, and she went on to publish many other volumes, including *Uroki muzyki* (1969; The Lessons of Music) and *Strikhi* (1975; Poems). One of her collections has been published in English – as *Fever and Other New Poems* (1970). Her more recent volumes include *The Mystery* (1983), *The Garden* (1987), and *The Seaboard* (1991). Akhmadulina has given readings of her poems throughout Europe and is also known as a translator, especially of Georgian poetry. She has been married four times; her first husband, whom she married in 1958, was the Russian poet Yevgenii Yevtushenko.

Akhmatova, Anna (1889–1967) *Russian poet*

O great language we love:
It is you, Russian tongue, we must
                save, and we swear
We will give you unstained to the
                sons of our sons;
You shall live on our lips, and we
                promise you – never
A prison shall know you, but you
                shall be free Forever.
                —"Courage" (1942)

Akhmatova is widely regarded as Russia's greatest 20th-century woman poet. Her fine poems are notable for their economy of words and unusual rhythms.

She was born Anna Andreyevna Gorenko in Odessa but took the pen name "Akhmatova" when she began publishing poetry in 1907. In 1910 she married Nikolai Gumilev, the founder of the "acmeist" literary movement, which sought to reaffirm Russian romantic traditions in the face of contemporary symbolism. This style is represented in Akhmatova's early collections *Evening* (1912), *The Rosary* (1913), and *The White Flock* (1917), which are full of vivid evocations of landscapes and emotions. Her marriage ended in 1918 and in 1921 Gumilev was shot for counter-revolutionary activity.

The publication in 1921 of her collection *Anno Domini MCMXXI*, with its religious and mystical themes, aroused official disapproval, and she published nothing further until 1940, when some of her work began appearing in Leningrad (now St. Petersburg) magazines. In 1946 her poetry was again banned and she was expelled from the Union of Soviet Writers. Although she was reinstated after Stalin's death, she did not immediately find favour, and her great works *Poems without a Hero* and *Requiem* (for the victims of Stalinism) were first published abroad. Akhmatova received an honorary degree from Oxford University in 1965.

Alacoque, Saint Margaret Mary (1647–1690) *French nun*

Saint Margaret Mary Alacoque is remembered for initiating public devotion to the Sacred Heart of Jesus.

Born in Lauthecour, she suffered from the early death of her father and joined the Visitation order at Paray-le-Monial in 1671. Noted for her piety, she experienced a vision in which Christ appeared to her, urging that special honour be given to His Sacred Heart on the first Friday of each month and on the feast of the Sacred Heart. Devotion to the Sacred Heart had been practised since the 11th century, and St. Jean Eudes (1601–80) had incorporated it in the liturgy; but after

Margaret Mary revealed her vision to her confessor, Father Claude de la Colombière, it became widespread. In 1856 Pope Pius IX raised the feast to major rank. Margaret Mary died at Paray-le-Monial and was canonized in 1920. Her feast day is October 17.

Alboni, Marietta (1823–1894) *Italian opera singer*

Acclaimed as one of the greatest contraltos of her era, Alboni was especially known for singing the contralto roles in Rossini's operas.

Alboni first attracted Rossini's attention while she was studying at Bologna, and he later taught her the principal contralto roles in his operas. (This was a great honour as he took on only a few exceptional pupils.) She made her debut in Pacini's *Saffo* at Bologna in 1842, first appearing at La Scala, Milan, in Rossini's *Le Siège de Corinthe* (*The Siege of Corinth*) that same year. She went on to tour widely: her most acclaimed performances took place in Paris and London, singing in Rossini's *Semiramide*, and in 1852 she was extremely successful in the United States. Alboni retired in 1866. When Rossini died in Paris in 1868, she and Adelina PATTI sang one of the duets from his *Stabat mater* at the funeral.

Albright, Madeleine Korbel (1937–) *Czech-born American politician*

> She is a unique blend of the skilled diplomat and the compassionate humanitarian, a woman of brilliant thought, deep conviction, and grace under pressure.
>
> —General John Shalikashvili, quoted in *The Guardian*, December 6, 1996

Albright is the first woman to hold the office of U.S. Secretary of State, to which she was appointed in December 1996 after four years as the United States Permanent Representative to the United Nations.

The daughter of Joseph Korbel, a Czech diplomat who had been ambassador to Belgrade (1945–48), Marie Jana Korbel was born in Prague but spent the years of World War II in London, where she learned to speak English with a British accent. In 1948 she came to the United States with her family when her father sought asylum from the Communists who had seized power in Czechoslovakia. After high school she attended Wellesley College, Massachusetts, from which she graduated in 1957 with a BA in political science. A period at the School of Advanced International Studies at Johns Hopkins University was followed by a number of years at Columbia University, where she studied under Zbigniew Brzezinski, being awarded a PhD in Russian history in 1976. She subsequently served in various senior capacities under several leading Democrats, including Adlai Stevenson, Edmund Muskie, and Jimmy Carter. She was also resident professor of international affairs at Georgetown University.

When Dr. Albright was appointed as the U.S. representative to the UN, she was the first foreign-born holder of the post. As an academic, rather than a career diplomat, she quickly established a reputation for plain speaking. The then UN secretary-general, Boutros Boutros-Ghali, is said to have described her in a fit of pique as an "East European peasant with American crassness." She is probably best remembered at the UN for her strong commitment to U.S. intervention in Bosnia. As Secretary of State she took a generally hawkish line in the crisis that erupted in early 1998 over Iraq's refusal to allow full UN monitoring of its alleged weapons of mass destruction.

Dr. Albright was married to the journalist Joseph Albright, with whom she had three daughters; although the marriage was dissolved in 1980, she has retained her married name. In 1997 it was disclosed that the Korbel family was Jewish and that three of Dr. Albright's grandparents and other family members were murdered by the Nazis in the Holocaust. Her father converted to Roman Catholicism as the German army approached Prague. Dr. Albright was subsequently raised as a Catholic but later converted to Episcopalianism.

Alcott, Louisa May (1832–1888) *American writer*

I believe that it is as much a right and a duty for women to do something with their lives as for men.

—*Rose in Bloom* (1876)

Best known as the author of *Little Women*, the children's classic, Louisa May Alcott was the daughter of the philosopher Bronson Alcott, from whom she received almost all of her early education. This was later supplemented by instruction from Henry David Thoreau, Ralph Waldo Emerson, Theodore Parker, and Nathaniel Hawthorne, who were all family friends.

After the failure in 1843 of her father's vegetarian community Fruitlands, the family lived in great poverty and Alcott contributed to their income with schoolteaching and domestic service. She also began to write, producing stories for magazines; her first book, which was published in 1854, was *Flower Fables*, a collection of stories originally written for Emerson's daughter Ellen. By 1860 both her poems and stories began to appear in the prestigious Boston journal *Atlantic Monthly*.

During the American Civil War she was a nurse in a Union hospital in Georgetown, D.C., and her letters home from this period (1862–63) were published as *Hospital Sketches* (1863). Her first novel, *Moods*, a passionate tale of doomed love, appeared in 1864, and in 1867 she became editor of the children's magazine *Merry Museums*. In 1868 she achieved enormous success with *Little Women*, a novel of childhood and family life that was largely autobiographical.

Alcott now became her family's sole earner, writing copiously and producing a huge number of novels, short stories, and poems, including the sequels to *Little Women*: *Good Wives* (1869), *Little Men* (1871), and *Jo's Boys* (1886). Her other works include *Eight Cousins* (1875), *A Modern Mephistopheles* (1877), *Under the Lilacs* (1879), and *A Garland for Girls* (1888). A passionate supporter of racial equality and women's suffrage, Alcott worked on a feminist novel that was published in 1873 as *Work: A Story of*

Experience. She died in Boston on the day of her father's funeral.

Alexandra (1844–1925) *Wife of King Edward VII of the United Kingdom*

Alexandra is best known for founding Queen Alexandra's Imperial (now Royal) Army Nursing Corps in 1902 and for setting up, in 1912, the Alexandra Rose Day in aid of hospitals.

Alexandra was born in Copenhagen, the eldest daughter of Prince Christian, later King Christian IX of Denmark, and Louise, the daughter of Prince William of Hesse-Cassel. In 1863 she married Edward, then Prince of Wales, and in the same year her father became king of Denmark and her brother king of Greece. Her sister was married to Tsar Alexander III.

In 1868, because of Queen VICTORIA's seclusion following the death of Prince Albert, Alexandra began to take a more active part in public life. In 1901 Edward became king: he and Alexandra were crowned together in Westminster Abbey on August 9, 1902. After the death of her husband in 1910 and the accession of her second son as George V (her first son, Albert, died in 1892) Alexandra lived at Marlborough House in London.

Alexandra Fyodorovna (1872–1918) *Wife of Tsar Nicholas II*

Alexandra's dominance over her husband and later her fanatical religious beliefs made her extremely unpopular at court and played a fatal part in the overthrow of the Russian monarchy.

Alexandra, a German princess, was the daughter of Louis IV, Grand Duke of Hesse-Barmstadt; her mother, Alice Maud Mary, was a daughter of Queen VICTORIA. Alexandra was married to Nicholas in 1894, a few weeks before he became tsar.

When her son Alexis was found to be suffering from the hereditary blood disease haemophilia, she turned to the "holy man" Rasputin for help. Rasputin was thus able to exert considerable influence over her and the already corrupt government. During World War I, while Nicholas was away as supreme commander of the Russian forces, Rasputin's domination of

Alexandra led to her being accused, wrongly, of being a German agent. Nicholas was unable to salvage the situation on his return; after the October Revolution in 1917 the Bolsheviks arrested and shot the royal family at Yekaterinburg on July 17, 1918.

See also ANASTASIA.

Allen, Florence Ellinwood (1884–1966) *American judge*

In 1922 Florence Allen became the first woman in the world to be appointed a judge in a court of last resort (i.e., the highest court of a state); in 1934 she was the first woman to sit as a judge in the U.S. Circuit Court of Appeals.

Born in Salt Lake City, Utah, she graduated from Western Reserve University in Cleveland, Ohio, in 1904 and went on to study music in Berlin. Returning to Cleveland in 1906, she became interested in civic affairs, joining the New York League for the Protection of Immigrants in 1910. She then turned her attention to law, which she studied at Chicago and New York universities; she began to practise law in Cleveland in 1914 and was elected judge of the Supreme Court of Ohio in 1922.

Throughout her career Florence Allen was highly respected, both as a judge and as an assiduous advocate of women's rights. Retiring from active service in 1959, she assumed the title of senior judge of the Court of Appeals of the Sixth Circuit.

Allen, Gracie (1895–1964) *American comedy actress*

Gracie Allen was famous as part of a comedy double act with her husband George Burns (1896–1996); their show-business career lasted more than three decades and spanned vaudeville, radio, films, and television.

Born Grace Ethel Cecile Rosalie Allen, she came from a San Francisco show-business family and made her vaudeville debut with her sisters. In 1922 she met George Burns; married four years later, they formed a double act called "Sixty-Forty," in which he played the cigar-chewing straight-man to her crazy chatterbox. They had their own radio show, *The Adventures of Gracie*, which ran from 1932 until

they transferred to television with *The Burns and Allen Show* (1950–57). Burns and Allen appeared in 13 films together, including *The Big Broadcast* (1932), *Love in Bloom* (1935), and *Two Girls and a Sailor* (1944). Gracie also appeared without Burns in *The Gracie Allen Murder Case* (1939) and *Mr. and Mrs. North* (1941). In 1940 she ran for president on the Surprise Party ticket. She retired because of ill health in 1958.

Allende, Isabel (1942–) *Chilean writer*

> I think of my great-grandmother, of my clairvoyant grandmother, of my own mother, of you [her daughter Paula], of my granddaughter who will be born in May, a strong female chain going back to the first woman, the universal mother.
>
> —*Paula* (1995)

Best known for her first novel, published in English as *The House of the Spirits* (1985) and later made into a film, Allende weaves mythical elements into realistic fiction in her writing. Her work has been compared to that of Gabriel García Márquez and Octavio Paz. She is one of the few Latin-American writers whose name is internationally known, her work having been translated into 25 languages.

Born in Lima, Peru, she is the niece and goddaughter of the former president of Chile, Salvador Allende. In 1973, after the overthrow of the Chilean government and the assassination of her uncle, Isabel, together with her first husband and their children, fled to Venezuela, where they lived for several years. *The House of the Spirits* arose out of this exile and her estrangement from her family (and particularly her grandfather) who remained in Chile. In 1987 she emigrated to the United States with her second husband, William Gordon, a lawyer. They live outside San Francisco.

English translations of her other works of fiction are *Of Love and Shadows* (1987), *Eva Luna* (1988), *The Stories of Eva Luna* (1991), and *The Infinite Plan* (1993). In 1995 Allende published a nonfiction work, *Paula*, written in the form of a letter to her daughter, who was in a coma for a year as a result of a hereditary blood disease; Paula died in 1992.

Amalsuntha (498–535) *Queen of the Ostrogoths*

The daughter of Theodoric the Great, king of the Ostrogoths who ruled Italy, Amalsuntha (also spelt Amalasuentha or Amalaswintha) was married in 515 to the Ostrogoth noble Eutharic, by whom she had two sons. On the death of Theodoric in 526 Amalsuntha, by now a widow, became regent during the minority of her son Athalaric; she retained this position until his death on October 2, 534, when she became queen. When she invited her cousin Theodahad to share the throne, he became her second husband.

Amalsuntha's appreciation of Roman and Byzantine learning made her unpopular with her Gothic subjects. Moreover, Theodahad accused her of plotting to hand over the kingdom to the Byzantine emperor Justinian. He therefore imprisoned her in a castle on Lake Bolsena, near Viterbo in Italy, and had her strangled.

Anastasia (1901–1918) *Youngest daughter of Tsar Nicholas II*

Although few now question that Anastasia was killed by the Bolshevik revolutionaries with the rest of the Romanov royal family at Yekaterinburg in Russia on July 17, 1918, for many years there was some doubt about her fate. During this time several women claimed to be Anastasia and, therefore, the heir to the Romanov fortune held in Swiss banks. These women maintained that Anastasia had survived the firing squad and managed to escape from Russia. One such claimant, a Mrs. Anna Anderson (died 1984), upheld her story from 1920 until it was officially rejected in 1961. In 1991 the bones of Nicholas II and three of his children were discovered near Yekaterinburg; subsequent DNA tests established that Anna Anderson could not have been related to the family.

A play called *Anastasia*, based on these claims, was written by Marcelle Maurette and adapted by Guy Bolton in 1954; this play was made into a film (1956) starring Ingrid BERGMAN.

See also ALEXANDRA FYODOROVNA.

Anderson, Elizabeth Garrett (1836–1917) *British physician*

Elizabeth Garrett Anderson is remembered for her pioneering work in opening up the medical profession to women, becoming the first woman to qualify as a medical practitioner in Britain (1865) and the first female member of the British Medical Association (1873–92).

She was born in Whitechapel, London, but moved with her family, at the age of five, to Aldeburgh, Suffolk. Her medical training began in 1859 when she became a nurse at the Middlesex Hospital, London, as a means of gaining access to the operating theatre there. The following year, refused admission by the medical schools because it was their policy not to train women as doctors, she began to study medicine privately, under some of the country's leading physicians; at times she was forced to dissect cadavers in her own room because she was forbidden to use hospital facilities. In 1865 she qualified as a medical practitioner by passing the examination of the Society of Apothecaries, and the following year she founded the St. Mary's Dispensary for Women in London. This dispensary later became the New Hospital for Women and Children, the first hospital in England to be staffed by women and to provide medical courses for women. In 1918, after her death, it was renamed the Elizabeth Garrett Anderson hospital.

In 1870 Anderson finally received recognition of her status when she was awarded an MD from the University of Paris. She became a lecturer at the London School of Medicine for Women, where she served as dean for 20 years. Anderson was also connected to the women's suffrage movement through her sister Millicent FAWCETT. In 1908 she became the first woman mayor in England when she was elected to that post at Aldeburgh, her childhood home.

Anderson, Dame Judith (1898–1992) *Australian actress*

In a career on stage and screen that lasted over 70 years Judith Anderson was acclaimed for the dramatic intensity of her interpretations of both modern and classical roles. She was best known for her portrayal of evil characters, notably Mrs. Danvers, the sinister housekeeper in the film *Rebecca* (1940).

Born in Adelaide, Judith Anderson made her stage debut in Sydney in 1915 and moved to the United States in 1918. Continuing her work in the theatre, her first major success was in *Cobra* in New York City in 1924. She then took leading roles in Eugene O'Neill's *Strange Interlude* (1928) and *Mourning Becomes Electra* (1932) and – in London – in John Gielgud's productions of *Hamlet* (1936; as Gertrude) and *Macbeth* (1937; as Lady Macbeth). Her portrayal of the title role in Robinson Jeffers's *Medea* in 1947 was particularly memorable.

Anderson's films include *Laura* (1944), *The Ten Commandments* (1956), *Cat on a Hot Tin Roof* (1958), and *A Man Called Horse* (1970), and she starred in the television productions of *Macbeth* (1960), for which she won an Emmy Award, and *The Chinese Prime Minister* (1974). She was created a DBE in 1960, and in 1984 a Broadway theatre was named after her. Between 1984 and 1987 she appeared as a domineering matriarch in the U.S. soap opera *Santa Barbara*.

Anderson, Marian (1897–1993)
American singer

Marian Anderson was the first African-American soloist to appear with the Metropolitan Opera in New York. However, she was best known as a concert singer, her rich and versatile contralto voice being equally suited to Schubert's songs and African-American spirituals.

Born into a poor family in Philadelphia, she began singing with the local Union Baptist Church at the age of six in order to raise money for singing lessons. After high school she studied with Giuseppe Boghetti in New York, winning, in 1925, first prize in a competition of 300 entrants held by the New York Philharmonic. In 1930 Anderson began a series of tours in Europe to study and perform, giving recitals in London, Scandinavia, and Germany for which she received wide acclaim: the conductor Arturo Toscanini remarked: "a voice like hers comes only once in a century."

Returning to the United States in 1935, Anderson gave a highly praised recital in New York, which was followed by a series of other successful engagements. However, in 1939 the Daughters of the American Revolution (DAR) refused to allow her to use its Constitution Hall in Washington D.C. for a concert because of her race. Eleanor ROOSEVELT resigned from the DAR in protest and helped to organize a separate concert at the Lincoln Memorial, where Anderson sang for 75,000 people (with millions more listening over the radio). In 1955 she made her debut with the Metropolitan Opera, playing Ulrica in Verdi's *A Masked Ball*; the same year she sang at the White House. She resumed her concert career in 1957, singing around the world and giving her last concert in 1965, at New York's Carnegie Hall.

Anderson worked for the civil rights movement and was a delegate to the 13th General Assembly of the United Nations in 1958. Much honoured with degrees and awards, she received the Presidential Medal of Freedom (1963), the first Eleanor Roosevelt Human Rights Award (1984), and the National Medal of Art (1986). She established the Marian Anderson Fellowship for young artists in 1972. Her autobiography, *My Lord, What a Morning*, was published in 1956.

Anderson, Mary Antoinette (1859–1940) *American actress*

Noted for her flexible voice and extraordinary beauty, Mary Anderson was acclaimed for her performances in both the United States and England.

Born in Sacramento, California, she made her theatrical debut in Louisville, Kentucky, at the age of 16 as Shakespeare's Juliet. Her New York debut came three years later, after which she made several successful tours of the United States as the star of her own company. In 1883 she played in London and at Stratford-on-Avon, where she portrayed the Shakespearean heroines Rosalind, Hermione, Perdita, and Lady Macbeth. Sir William S. Gilbert wrote the play *Comedy and Tragedy* for her. In 1889, when she was not yet 30, Anderson was forced to retire from the stage after a nervous breakdown. A year later she married Antonio F. de Navarro, an American lawyer, and the couple settled in England, where she lived until her death. Although she never returned to the professional theatre, she gave some charity concerts. Anderson wrote two books of reminiscences, *A Few Memories* (1896) and *A Few More Memories* (1936), and with Robert Hichens dramatized his novel *The Garden of Allah*.

Andrews, Julie (1935–) *British actress and musical comedy star*

> She has that wonderful British strength that makes you wonder why they lost India.
>
> —Remark by Moss Hart

Julie Andrews is best known for her starring roles in Disney's *Mary Poppins* (1964), for which she won an Oscar, and *The Sound of Music* (1965), which broke box-office records. Both films together established the star's reputation as a wholesome and reliable young woman of great charm and integrity.

Born Julia Elizabeth Wells in Walton-on-Thames, Surrey, Julie Andrews made her stage debut at the age of 12 as a singer at the London Hippodrome. She went on to appear in the stage musicals *The Boy Friend* (1954) and *My Fair Lady* (1956) on Broadway, re-creating the latter role of the cockney flower seller in London two years later to wide criticial acclaim. Following her success in *The Sound of Music*, after which her costar Christopher Plummer remarked: "Working with her is like being hit over the head with a Valentine's Card," she starred in Alfred Hitchcock's *Torn Curtain* (1966) with Paul Newman. Subsequent films include *Thoroughly Modern Millie* (1967), *Star!* (1968), and *Darling Lili* (1969).

Her American TV series *The Julie Andrews Hour* (1972–73) won an Emmy as best variety series; her subsequent cabaret act brought out her talent as a comedienne. In the 1980s, under the direction of Blake Edwards, her second husband, Andrews attempted to move away from her goody-goody image in such films as *S.O.B.* (1981), *Victor/Victoria* (1982), and *That's Life* (1986), but the enduring image of Julie Andrews is of Mary Poppins. She later starred in the short-lived sitcom *Julie* (1992).

Angelou, Maya (1928–) *American writer, educator, performer, and feminist*

> The fact that the adult American Negro female emerges a formidable character is often met with amazement, distaste and even belligerence. It is seldom accepted as an inevitable outcome of the struggle won by survivors, and deserves respect if not enthusiastic acceptance.
>
> —*I Know Why the Caged Bird Sings* (1970)

A powerful and inspiring figure with great presence, Angelou became internationally known with the publication of the first volume of her autobiography, *I Know Why the Caged Bird Sings* (1970), which portrays unsparingly, but with humour, the hardships of her early years, including the trauma of rape by her mother's lover; it was nominated for a U.S. National Book Award.

She was born Marguerite Johnson in St. Louis and nicknamed "Maya" by her brother; her surname is an adaptation of that of her first husband. After moving to San Francisco when she was 16, Angelou studied music, dance (with Martha GRAHAM and others), and drama. In her twenties she toured Europe and Africa in a production of *Porgy and Bess* sponsored by the U.S. Department of State (1954–55) before settling in Harlem, where she became a member of the Writers' Guild while working as a nightclub singer and entertainer. During the 1950s she became involved in the civil rights movement, serving as northern coordinator of the Southern Christian Leadership Conference in 1959–60, a post for which she was chosen by Martin Luther King, Jr. Between 1963 and 1966 she was an administrator at the University of Ghana as well as editor of the *African Review*.

After the success of *I Know Why the Caged Bird Sings*, four more volumes of autobiography were published – *Gather Together in My Name* (1974), *Singin' and Swingin' and Getting Merry Like Christmas* (1976), *The Heart of a Woman* (1981), and *All God's Children Need Travelling Shoes* (1986). *Wouldn't Take Nothing for My Journey Now* (1993) tells of her journey from obscurity to fame as a performer and civil rights activist. Angelou has also written much poetry – her first book of poems, *Just Give Me A Cool Drink of Water 'Fore I Die* (1971), was nominated for a Pulitzer Prize. She has also made numerous television appearances, being nominated for an Emmy Award for her portrayal of Nyo Boto in *Roots* (1977). In addition, she has directed films and plays (in 1988 she directed Errol John's black classic *Moon on a Rainbow Shawl* in London), composed music, and served as writer-in-residence and lecturer at several universities. Since 1981 she has been Reynolds Professor of American Studies at Wake Forest University, North Carolina. She read her poem "On the Pulse of the Morning: The Inaugural Poem" (1992) at the inauguration of President Bill Clinton.

Anguissola, Sofonisba (*c*.1535–1625) *Italian painter*

The first internationally recognized Italian woman artist, Anguissola was the best-known woman portrait painter of the 16th century.

Born in Cremona, the eldest of six daughters of a nobleman, she was recognized as a child prodigy and apprenticed to the painter Bernardo Campi from 1546 until 1549. She then taught painting to three of her sisters, all of whom became talented artists. (This was encouraged by their father, who thought they ought to be able to support themselves if their dowries proved inadequate.) Michelangelo took an interest in her work, which was brought to the attention of the Spanish court by the Duke of Alba. Consequently, in 1559, Sofonisba became court painter to Philip II of Spain in Madrid, where she remained until her marriage to a Sicilian nobleman and their return to Palermo in 1580. After her husband's death in 1584, she married Orazio Lomellino, the captain of the ship on which she was travelling to northern Italy.

Although much of Anguissola's work is now lost, at least 50 of her paintings are displayed in museums and private collections, including some court studies, such as *Philip II*; family studies, such as *Husband and Wife* and *Three Sisters Playing Chess*; and many self-portraits.

Anna Comnena (1083–*c*. 1148) *Byzantine historian*

Anna Comnena is famous as the author of the *Alexiad*, an outstanding work of Byzantine history that covers the First Crusade (1095–99).

The daughter of the Byzantine emperor Alexius I (reigned 1081–1118), the founder of the Comnenian dynasty, Anna married Nicephorus Bryennius (*c*. 1062–1137) in 1097. With her mother, the empress Irene, she attempted to persuade Alexius to disinherit his son, John II (1088–1143), in favour of her husband. After her father's death Anna conspired to depose her brother, but the plot was revealed, her property was forfeited, and she retired to a convent. Here she began working on the *Alexiad*, a history celebrating the achievements of her father's reign. Written in Greek, it covers the period 1069–1118 and is a valuable source of information about religious and intellectual life at that time.

Anna Ivanovna (1693–1740) *Empress of Russia*

Anna's reign was noted for its cruelty and for the persecution of thousands who were either exiled to Siberia or executed.

A niece of Peter the Great, Anna was born in Moscow, the second daughter of Tsar Ivan V; in 1710 she married Frederick William, Duke of Courland, who died almost immediately after the wedding. She was elected to the throne by the Supreme Privy Council on the death of Tsar Peter II in 1730 on the condition that she accepted a number of provisions restricting her authority. With the help of some friends Anna overthrew the council and appointed a three-man cabinet. The real power, however, was held by Anna's favourite, Ernst Johann Biron, who had no official position in the government. Her foreign policy was successful: it ensured the accession of the Russian-sponsored August III as king of Poland in the War of the Polish Succession (1733–35), and Russia regained Azov when Anna joined Austria in the war against Turkey in the Crimea (1736, 1739).

Anna Leopoldovna (1718–1746) *Regent of Russia*

A niece of the Russian empress ANNA IVANOVNA, Anna Leopoldovna was born in Rostock, Germany; her father was the Duke of Mecklenburg-Schwerin. In 1739 she married Prince Anthony Ulrich of Brunswick, a nephew of Emperor Charles VI of the Holy Roman Empire. Their first child, Ivan, was born in August 1740. In October 1740 the childless Anna Ivanovna named Ivan as her successor, to be known as Ivan VI, and designated Ernst Johann Biron as regent for the child. In November 1740, after Anna Ivanovna's death, Biron was deposed and Anna Leopoldovna was appointed regent.

Anna's regency (1740–41) was a period of indecision. The court was ruled by a group of German aristocrats who cared nothing for domestic affairs and advised a disastrous foreign policy. Anna was overthrown on December 6, 1741, and her son was deposed. ELIZABETH, daughter of Peter the Great, was then proclaimed empress; Anna was exiled to Siberia, where she died in childbirth.

Anne (1665–1714) *Queen of Great Britain and Ireland*

> I have changed my Ministers, but I have not changed my measures; I am still for moderation and will govern by it.

> —Speech to the new Tory government, 1711

Ascending to the throne as queen of England, Scotland, and Ireland in 1702, Anne became the first monarch of Great Britain and Ireland after the union of England and Scotland in 1707. She was the last Stuart sovereign, and her reign brought to an end more than 75 years of political instability.

Anne was the second daughter of James, Duke of York (who became King James II in 1685), and his first wife, Anne Hyde. Although James became a Roman Catholic in about 1670, Anne was educated a Protestant and became a loyal member of the Church of England. In 1683 she married Prince George of Denmark, a devout Anglican. In 1688 Anne supported the Glorious Revolution, which deposed her father because of his religion and put Anne's sister MARY II and her husband William of Orange on the throne. The Declaration of Rights of the following year ensured Anne's succession if William and Mary left no children.

In 1702 Anne succeeded to the throne and appointed Tories as ministers, but her friendship with John Churchill, Duke of Marlborough, and his wife Sarah, Duchess of MARLBOROUGH, led her to abandon her Tory loyalties and support the rival Whigs and their involvement in the War of the Spanish Succession. However, in 1710, after a quarrel with the Marlboroughs and because the Whig government was proving to be so unpopular with the country, she appointed a Tory ministry.

Anne became pregnant 18 times, but only five of her children were born alive and none of them survived childhood. She therefore agreed to the Act of Settlement (1701), which provided for Anne to be succeeded by the heirs of SOPHIA, electress of Hanover (who was a granddaughter of King James I). Sophia's son became King George I on Anne's death.

Anne, the Princess Royal (1950–) *Daughter of Queen Elizabeth II of the United Kingdom*

Don't irritate Princess Anne by asking questions about women's hats. Although she will be receptive to chat about tanks and submachine guns.

—*Life*

When I appear in public people expect me to neigh, grind my teeth, paw the ground and swish my tail — none of which is easy.

—"Sayings of the Week,"
The Observer, May 22, 1977

One of the most respected and hardworking members of the Royal Family, Princess Anne is patron of over 80 charities and has worked tirelessly for the Save the Children Fund, of which she has been president since 1971. She has visited many developing countries on its behalf and is now an expert on the administration of international aid. She was granted the title Princess Royal by the Queen in 1987 in recognition of her charitable work.

The only daughter of the Queen and the Duke of Edinburgh, Princess Anne Elizabeth Alice Louise was educated at Benenden School before taking up her public duties. Her skills as a horsewoman were recognized in 1975, when she won a silver medal in the Individual European Three-Day Event, and the following year she was a member of the British equestrian team at the Montreal Olympics. Also interested in horse racing, Princess Anne won her first steeplechase in 1987, successfully competing in the United States as well as in Europe. She is president of the British Olympic Association and, since 1981, chancellor of London University.

Princess Anne married Captain Mark Phillips in 1973; they had two children, Peter and Zara, before divorcing in 1992. She has been married to Commander Timothy Laurence since 1992.

As a young woman the Princess Royal was known for her abrasive attitude towards the press, but later her hard work and her discretion led her to become one of the most popular members of the Royal Family.

Anne of Austria (1601–1666) *Regent of France*

As regent for her son, Louis XIV, Queen Anne wielded enormous power jointly with her lover, Cardinal Mazarin.

The daughter of Philip II of Spain and Margaret of Austria, Anne was married in 1615 to Louis XIII of France. The unhappiness of this marriage was largely due to the king's chief minister, Cardinal de Richelieu, who was hostile to the new Austrian influence at court. All but separated from Louis since 1620, on his death in 1643 Anne became regent for her son Louis XIV and ruled with the help of her chief minister, Cardinal Mazarin, who was also her lover.

Their rule was challenged in 1648 by the Fronde rebellion (so called because the rebels used slingshots, or *frondes*), which protested against excessive tax demands. The rebellion was led by bourgeois legislators of the Paris parliament and suppressed by General Condé leading the royal army in 1649. The second outbreak in 1650, however, was led by Condé himself. Although forced to leave Paris for a time, there was an upsurge of support for the monarchy, and Anne and Mazarin were able to subdue the nobles. They continued to rule the country together after 1651, when Louis XIV technically came of age. In 1661 Mazarin died and Louis XIV assumed full power, while Anne retired to a convent at Val-de-Grâce, where she lived until her death.

Anne of Bohemia (1366–1394) *Wife of King Richard II of England*

Born in Prague, the daughter of the Holy Roman Emperor Charles IV (who was also king of Bohemia) and Elizabeth of Pomerania, Anne was the first wife of Richard II. Her father was not a wealthy or powerful ruler, and the arranged marriage, which took place in 1382 after a delay caused by the Peasants' Revolt led by Wat Tyler, was regarded with hostility and as of little advantage to England. However, Anne's gentleness and piety soon won the affection of her subjects; Richard himself was devoted to her. Queen Anne founded and patronized several religious houses before her early death from the plague; she left no children.

Anne of Brittany (1476–1514)
Duchess of Britanny and, by marriage, Queen of France

Throughout her life Anne sought to maintain the independence of Brittany within the French kingdom.

The daughter of Duke Francis II of Brittany and Marguerite de Foix, Anne became Duchess of Brittany in 1488 when her father died without leaving a male heir. France, to which Brittany had feudal obligations, then tried to secure Brittany in order to extend its territory. To counter this threat Anne married Maximilian I of Austria (later emperor) by proxy in 1490, but France had this marriage annulled the following year. That same year the French regent, ANNE OF FRANCE, invaded Brittany and forced Anne to surrender and marry Charles VIII of France. In 1498 Charles died and Anne married his successor, Louis XII. Anne insisted that Brittany's rights and privileges should be maintained and that the duchy should be inherited separately from France – by the eldest daughter or second son of her marriage to Louis. She devoted the rest of her life to the administration of Brittany.

Despite Anne's efforts Brittany formally became part of France in 1532 when Francis, Duke of Angoulême, who had married Anne's daughter Claude, became King Francis I of France.

Anne of Cleves (1515–1557) *Fourth wife of King Henry VIII of England*

Anne's marriage to King Henry lasted for only six months. Anne was the daughter of John, Duke of Cleves in Germany. The marriage was arranged to enable Henry to establish an alliance with her brother William, Duke of Cleves, who was then leader of German Protestants. Henry, advised by his minister Thomas Cromwell, believed that the Roman Catholic Holy Roman Empire and France were about to launch an attack on Protestant England.

Before her betrothal to Henry the king had never seen Anne, although he had admired a portrait of her by Holbein. When the planned alliance turned out to be unnecessary, Henry was doubly disappointed to find his new bride plain and graceless. Nevertheless, he reluctantly made Anne his fourth wife in January 1540, five days after their first meeting. The following July he obtained an annulment from Parliament, alleging that the marriage had never been consummated: there were certainly no children. Thomas Cromwell, for his part in arranging the marriage, was beheaded on July 28 – the day Henry secretly married his fifth wife, Catherine HOWARD. Anne remained in England, supported by the crown and on good terms with the king (who referred to her as his "beloved sister") until her death in London.

Anne of Denmark (1574–1619) *Wife of King James VI of Scotland (later James I of England)*

Anne of Denmark was best known for her fun-loving nature, taste for extravagant finery, and heavy expenditure on building and court entertainments. The daughter of Frederick II, king of Norway and Denmark, she was married to James by proxy in 1589 when he was James VI of Scotland but not yet king of England. In 1603 he succeeded to the English throne as James I, and James and Anne were crowned together at Windsor Castle. However, they had few interests in common and lived separately after 1606. An enthusiastic patron of the arts, Anne frequently took part herself in entertainments staged at court. Her second son became king as Charles I after his father's death in 1625.

Anne of France (1461–1522) *Regent of France*

As regent for her younger brother, Charles VIII, from 1483 to 1491, Anne succeeded in maintaining the stability of the kingdom during the early difficult years of his reign.

Also known as Anne of Beaujeu, she was the eldest daughter of King Louis XI and Charlotte of Savoy and wife of Pierre de Beaujeu, who became Duke of Bourbon in 1488 following the death of his elder brother. After the death of Louis XI in 1483 Anne – with her husband's help – ably governed France. She appeased powerful nobles who had suffered under Louis, defeated rebellious lords in the "Silly War" (*la guerre folle*) in 1485, and suppressed an uprising in Brittany (1487). She was responsible for arranging the marriage between Charles VIII and ANNE OF BRITTANY, which took place in 1490 and eventually led to Brittany becoming part of the kingdom of France.

After Charles assumed control of France in 1491, Anne was less influential, although she remained politically active. Following the death of her husband in 1503, she continued to rule the Bourbon lands, which belonged to her daughter.

Anning, Mary (1799–1847) *British fossil collector*

One of the foremost 19th-century women palaeontologists, Mary Anning came from a family who were all enthusiastic about fossils: her father, a carpenter by trade, sold fossils to visitors to the coastal resort of Lyme Regis where they lived. In 1811 Mary discovered the complete remains of a marine reptile, a 10 meter (30-foot)-long Ichthyosaurus, which is now in the Natural History Museum in London. Further important discoveries followed: another marine reptile, a Plesiosaurus (1821); and a flying reptile – a pterodactyl (1828). She supplied museums with her finds, also continuing her father's fossil trade after his death. Her fame was such that the tongue-twister "she sells seashells on the seashore" is said to refer to her. A learned authority on her subject, despite her lack of formal education, Mary Anning received a small government grant for her work and was made an honorary member of the Geological Society of London before she died.

Anthony, Susan B(rownell) (1820–1906) *American reformer and advocate of women's rights*

> There never will be complete equality until women themselves help to make laws and elect lawmakers.
>
> —"The Status of Women, Past, Present and Future," *The Arena*, May 1897

A teacher, writer, and editor of the pioneering women's-suffrage journal *Revolution*, Susan Anthony made her greatest contributions to the cause of women's suffrage by direct action: she organized the International Council of Women (1888) and was president (1892–1900) of the National American Woman Suffrage Association.

Born into an old colonial Quaker family in Massachusetts, Anthony became a teacher – the only profession then open to women – before managing the family farm and working for the temperance and antislavery movements. In 1848 she attended the first women's rights convention at Seneca Falls. Rebuffed by the male temperance workers, she was instrumental in forming the Woman's State Temperance Society of New York in 1852. The president of this society was Elizabeth Cady STANTON, who became her lifelong friend and collaborator.

Throughout the 1850s Anthony continued her antislavery and temperance work, while demanding equal voting rights and equal pay in the New York State Teachers' Association. She also campaigned throughout the country for the right of women to vote, to control their own property, and to have guardianship of children after divorce. By bombarding officials with thousands of petitions demanding action, very gradually she persuaded several states to give women some legal status.

From 1868 to 1870 Anthony and Stanton co-edited *Revolution*, with its motto "Men their rights and nothing more; women their rights and nothing less." The magazine incurred debts, which Anthony paid off by undertaking, until 1876, extensive speaking tours of the Midwest and West Coast. In 1869, with Stanton, she formed the National Woman's Suffrage Association, although some of her views on black suffrage and the Association's tactics caused splits in the movement. Their campaign focused on obtaining amendments to the U.S. Constitution rather than on challenging state legislation. In 1872 Anthony was arrested after leading a group of women to the polls in Rochester to test the right of women to vote. Convicted of violating the voting laws, she refused to pay the fine. From 1892 to 1900 she served as president of the newly united National and American movements – the National American Woman Suffrage Association. In 1889 she played a part in the inauguration of the International Council of Women in London, and in 1904, with Carrie CATT, she founded the International Woman Suffrage Alliance in Berlin.

From 1881 to 1886 Anthony compiled the four-volume *History of Woman Suffrage* with Stanton and Matilda Gage.

See also MOTT, LUCRETIA COFFIN; STONE, LUCY BLACKWELL.

Aquino, Corazon (1933–) *Philippine stateswoman*

Mrs. Aquino was the first woman president of the Philippines (1986–92), having led the opposition that brought about the overthrow of the corrupt President Ferdinand Marcos in a virtually bloodless "people's revolution."

Corazon Cojuangco was the daughter of prominent sugar plantation owners in Tarlac province; her grandfather had been a senator, her father a congressman. She was educated in the United States, graduating from Mount St. Vincent College, New York, in 1953. In 1954 she returned to the Philippines and married the political journalist Benigno Aquino (1933–83), who also came from an influential family in Tarlac.

With Corazon's help and support Aquino became leader of the opposition Liberal Party in 1967 and the main challenge to the regime of President Marcos. In 1972 Marcos assumed dictatorial powers and imprisoned rivals, including Benigno Aquino, issuing a death sentence on him in 1977. Following international protest, the death sentence was commuted, and Aquino was allowed to travel to the United States to undergo heart surgery. In 1983 the Aquinos returned to the Philippines to enable Benigno to contest the presidential elections. He was shot dead on arriving at Manila airport, and the ensuing acquittal of the 26 government defendants indicted in the murder led Mrs. Aquino to challenge government corruption at mass protest rallies, demanding Marcos's resignation.

In 1986 she stood in place of her husband against Marcos in the presidential elections. Although Marcos was declared the winner, independent observers charged the government with fraud, and Mrs. Aquino's followers proclaimed her president. Marcos fled to the United States.

Initially expecting only to be in power until a new election could be arranged, Mrs. Aquino went on to end the repression and corruption of the Marcos years. She introduced a new constitution on February 2, 1987. Although considered slow to introduce land reforms, she was able to withstand continuing problems from communist insurgents as well as sections of the military who mounted unsuccessful coups in 1986, 1987, and 1990. She remained in office until June 30, 1992, when she was succeeded by a longtime supporter, Fidel Ramos.

See also MARCOS, IMELDA.

Arber, Agnes (1879–1960) *British botanist*

The first woman botanist to be made a fellow of the Royal Society – Britain's oldest and most important scientific society – Agnes Arber received the Gold Medal of the Linnean Society in 1948.

Interested in botany since her schooldays in London, Agnes Robertson was educated at London and Cambridge universities. She studied comparative plant anatomy at University College, London, from 1903 until 1909, when she married the palaeobotanist Edward Arber; after her marriage she worked largely alone. Her first book, *Herbals: Their Origin and Evolution*, published in 1912 and rewritten in 1938, became a standard textbook of the period. Her later works were *Water Plants: A Study of Aquatic Angiosperms* (1920), *Monocotyledons* (1925), and *The Gramineae: A Study of Cereal, Bamboo and Grass* (1934). Arber also wrote, between 1902 and 1957, numerous articles on comparative anatomy.

Arbus, Diane (1923–1971) *American photographer*

Denounced at first for her candid black-and-white photographs of people on the fringe of society, such as transvestites and midgets, Diane Arbus is now recognized as one of the most influential artists of her generation.

Diane Nemerov was born into a prosperous Jewish family who owned a Fifth Avenue fashion house in New York. At the age of 18 she married Allan Arbus, by whom she had two daughters; together they worked as fashion photographers from 1946 until 1957, when Diane became disenchanted with fashion. She then began to pursue her own studies, encouraged by the photographer Lisette MODEL. She separated from her husband in 1960, the year that her first nonfashion photographs appeared in *Esquire* magazine. She undertook assignments for other magazines in the United States and Britain and received Guggenheim Fellowships in 1963 and 1966. In 1965 her work appeared in an exhibition at the Museum of Modern Art in New York – the only showing of more than a few of her photographs during her lifetime. Her disconcertingly honest portraits of children and ordinary people, as well as misfits, were radical in their approach, compelling the attention of the viewer.

Arbus taught photography at the Parsons School of Design (1965–66), the Cooper Union (1968–69) in New York, and at the Rhode Island School of Design (1970–71) in Providence. She finally divorced her husband in 1969 and committed suicide in 1971. In July 1972 she became the first American photographer to be exhibited at the Venice Biennale. That same year the Museum of Modern Art in New York organized a retrospective exhibition of her work, which travelled through the United States and Europe for seven years.

Arden, Elizabeth (1884–1966) *Canadian beautician and businesswoman*

> Elizabeth Arden was a pioneer in an industry which was backward and insanitary when she entered it, and prosperous, modern and a real contribution to human happiness when she died.
>
> —Anne Scott-James, *1000 Makers of the 20th Century*

Born Florence Graham in Ontario, she was the youngest of five children of a Scottish grocer. Moving to New York, she worked in a cosmetic shop and then became a partner in a beauty salon before changing her name and opening her own premises on Fifth Avenue in 1909. In 1918 Arden married Thomas Lewis, who was her business manager until their divorce in 1935, when he went to work for her rival Helena RUBINSTEIN. From 1942 until 1944 she was married to Prince Michael Evlonoff. Elizabeth Arden built up an empire of more than 100 exclusive salons across the United States and Europe and manufactured an expensive range of over 300 cosmetics.

Also a well-known owner of racehorses, she is said to have "treated her women like horses and her horses like women," insisting that the horses be treated with her own beauty preparations. She was also famous for always dressing in shades of pink.

Arendt, Hannah (1906–1975) *German-born American political philosopher*

One of the most influential philosophers of the 20th century, Arendt was born into a Jewish family in Hanover and studied at the foremost German universities – Marburg, Freiburg, and Heidelburg. Taught there by Edmund Husserl, Martin Heidegger, and Karl Jaspers, she became interested in existentialism and in 1928 completed her doctorate on St. Augustine's concept of love.

Following the rise of Nazism, Arendt became involved in German Zionism and in 1933 fled to Paris, where she worked for various Zionist organizations; in 1936 she led a group of French-Jewish children to Palestine, then under British mandate. In 1940 she married a philosophy professor, Heinrich Bluecher, and was interned in a camp for German refugees. Securing her release, she emigrated to the

United States, where she was actively involved with various Jewish organizations and worked as a publisher's editor. After the publication of her first major work, *The Origins of Totalitarianism* (1951), Arendt held positions at major American academic institutions, including Princeton (where she became the first woman professor in 1959), the University of Chicago, and the New School for Social Research, in New York.

In *The Origins of Totalitarianism* Arendt traced the rise of Nazi and Communist theories back to the nationalism, imperialism, and racialism of the 19th century. She believed that in the "mass society" typical of the modern age individuals become preoccupied with material advancement and indifferent to the world they share, allowing themselves to be dominated by bureaucratic states and ideological manipulators. She also deplored the separation of moral thought from political action and saw how this could lead to scientists developing weapons over which they could have no control.

Arendt explored these themes further in *The Human Condition* (1958). Sent to Israel to cover Eichmann's trial, she wrote *Eichmann in Jerusalem: A Report on the Banality of Evil* (1963), which outraged some Zionists with its portrayal of Eichmann as a typically thoughtless banal modern man rather than a profoundly evil one. She suggested that the passivity of the Jewish leaders in Eastern Europe had in part facilitated the extermination of Jews in World War II. Her later works, *On Revolution* (1963) and *On Violence* (1970), stress the idealistic nature of social change. She left a three-volume work, *The Life of the Mind*, unfinished at the time of her death. Two volumes, *Thinking* and *Willing*, were edited and published in 1978 by her friend and literary executor, Mary MCCARTHY.

Argentina, La (*c.* 1890–1936) *Spanish dancer*
Famous for her skill with the castanets in her performance of regional Spanish dances, La Argentina is credited with reviving interest in Spanish dance as a classical art form.

She was born Antonia Mercé in Buenos Aires, Argentina, hence her stage name. A child prodigy, she studied operatic ballet with her father and made her debut at the Royal Opera House in Madrid at the age of nine; two years later she was prima ballerina. However, at the age of 14 she gave up classical ballet to study native Spanish dances, performing these at first in Spanish music halls and cafés and later on international tours, to great acclaim. La Argentina formed her own company in 1928. Using traditional and modern Spanish music, she popularized the works of such contemporary Spanish composers as Manuel de Falla, Isaac Albéniz, and Julián Bautista: her interpretation of Falla's *El amor brujo* was particularly impressive. She also produced a series of one-act ballets.

Arletty (1898–1992) *French actress*
A legendary star of the French cinema in the 1930s and 1940s, Arletty is best known for her role as the enigmatic courtesan Garance in Marcel Carné's film *Les Enfants du paradis* (1945).

Born Arlette-Léonie Bathiat, the daughter of a miner, she worked as a secretary and as an artist's model (she sat for Matisse, among others) before turning to acting. After her screen debut in *Un Chien qui rapporte* (1930), Arletty had minor roles in other films – being typically cast as a "woman of the world" – until her first taste of fame in Carné's *Hôtel du nord* (1938). She went on to star in other Carné films – *Le Jour se lève* (1939; *Daybreak*) and *Les Visiteurs du soir* (1942; *The Devil's Own Envoy*) – before her memorable appearance in *Les Enfants du paradis*. Made with great difficulty during the Nazi occupation of France, this movie came to symbolize the unquenchable spirit of the country.

After World War II Arletty was condemned to death by a tribunal in Algiers because of her affair with a German officer during the war. The sentence was eventually commuted to two months in prison. This had a drastic effect on her career: she was reduced to taking supporting roles during the late 1940s and 1950s, although she did star as Blanche in Jean Cocteau's stage production of Tennessee Williams's *A Streetcar Named Desire* in 1949 and appeared in the film *Huis Clos* (1954; *No Exit*). During the 1960s Arletty had several stage roles and in 1962 appeared in her only English-language film, *The Longest Day*; however, because of an accident that left her almost blind, her roles were small. Arletty wrote two volumes of memoirs: *La Défense* (1971) and *Je suis comme je suis* (1987).

Armatrading, Joan (1950–) *West Indian-born British singer and songwriter*

> To talk about making more "commercial music" is misleading. But I would like millions of people to buy what I do rather than ten people.
>
> —Interview, 1979

Reaching the peak of her popularity in the early 1980s, Joan Armatrading has been internationally acclaimed for her soulful blending of rock, reggae, and folk.

Born on the island of St. Kitts in the West Indies, she emigrated to Birmingham with her family in 1958. Unsettled by the move, she preferred to stay at home playing her guitar rather than mixing with other children. In her teens she joined a Jamaican group giving performances, sometimes of her own songs, in Birmingham's black neighbourhoods. Still a teenager, she accepted a part in the chorus of the musical *Hair* and toured England with the company for 18 months. Beginning her career as a songwriter in 1972, in collaboration with the lyricist Pam Nestor, Armatrading signed with A&M records the following year to record her first album, *Whatever Is for Us*. Although a critical success, it did not sell well and marked the end of her partnership with Nestor. She then recorded *Back to the Night* (1975), but it was not until the release of her third album, *Joan Armatrading* (1976), that she finally received recognition. From this album came "Love and Affection," a widely acclaimed hit single. Her greatest successes came with her albums of the early 1980s: these include *Me, Myself, and I* (1980), *Walk Under Ladders* (1981), and *The Key* (1983). During her career this immensely popular singer has earned 28 gold discs in seven countries.

Armstrong, Gillian (1950–) *Australian film director*

A leading exponent of the Australian "New Wave" movement of the 1970s and 1980s, Gillian Armstrong was the first woman to direct an Australian feature film, *My Brilliant Career* (1978), since the early 1930s. This movie, about an unconventional young woman with literary ambitions in late 19th-century Australia, won seven Australian Film Institute Awards, including Best Picture and Best Director, as well as the British Critics' Award for Best Newcomer.

Originally intending to be a film editor, in 1973 she moved from her native Melbourne to Sydney to attend the Australian Film and Television School, where she was encouraged to try directing. Among her earliest work is *Smokes and Lollies* (1975), the first of a rights-of-passage trilogy of short documentaries. Her short film *The Singer and the Dancer* (1976), which she also produced, won an award at the Sydney Film Festival. After the success of *My Brilliant Career* Armstrong directed the rock opera *Starstruck* (1982) in Australia before making her Hollywood debut with the period drama *Mrs. Soffel* (1984). She returned to Australia to direct *High Tide* (1987) and *The Last Days of Chez Nous* (1992). After disowning her next Hollywood film, *Fires Within* (1991), because MGM recut it to place more emphasis on the sex scenes, Armstrong returned there to make a new version of Louisa M. ALCOTT's *Little Women* (1994), starring Susan SARANDON and Winona RYDER.

Arnim, Bettina von (1785–1859) *German writer*

A key figure in the German literary Romantic movement, Bettina von Arnim is best known as the author of *Goethe's Correspondence with a Child*, a fanciful blend of fact and fiction based on her correspondence with the poet Goethe.

The daughter of an Italian merchant, she was born Elisabeth Brentano at Frankfurt am Main. In 1811 she married the poet and novelist Achim von Arnim; with her brother, the writer Klemens Brentano, the von Arnims were at the centre of the German Romantic movement. Bettina first met Goethe in 1807, in Weimar, and her letters to him date from around that period. She idolized the poet, who was 35 years her senior, and the correspondence continued over a four-year period, until Bettina's rudeness to Goethe's wife caused him to end the friendship in 1811. When Goethe died in 1832, Bettina's letters were returned, and in 1835 she published from that material *Goethes Briefwechsel mit einem Kinde*; Bettina herself translated the work into English as *Goethe's Correspondence with a Child* (1837). For many years the authenticity of the correspondence was doubted, and it was not until the publication of Goethe's actual letters to Bettina in 1879 that her book was shown to be based on fact, although greatly romanticized.

Her other works include two additional correspondences that mix fact and fiction: an exchange of letters with the poet Karoline von Günderode was published in 1840, and one with her brother in 1844. Her *Dies Buch gehört dem König* (1843; This Book Belongs to the King) was a plea to King Frederick William IV of Prussia for various reforms. Bettina's works were collected in 11 volumes in 1853.

Arnold, Eve (1913–) *American photojournalist*

A versatile photographer, Arnold is known equally for her photo-essays on peoples and cultures and her sensitive portraits.

Eve Arnold was born in Philadelphia, the daughter of Russian immigrant parents. As a young woman she trained for a medical career but in 1947 she began to study photography at the New School for Social Research in New York. In 1951 she became the first woman to work for the celebrated Magnum Photos agency, becoming a full member in 1957. During this period she became a friend and disciple of the great French photographer Henri Cartier-Bresson.

Although Arnold was based mainly in London during the 1960s and 1970s, she also undertook an ambitious programme of travel in order to find new subject matter. She was a frequent visitor to the communist and Muslim world, travelling to the Soviet Union on several occasions as well as to Afghanistan and China. Her work, which appeared regularly in *Life* magazine and *The Sunday Times* among other publications, shows a particular interest in the role of women in society. Arnold also excelled as a portraitist, with subjects that ranged from celebrities (most notably Marilyn Monro) to the poor and unknown. Her work has been published in such volumes as *The Un-retouched Woman* (1976) and *All in a Day's Work* (1989). She also directed the documentary film *Behind the Veil* (1973), about the lives of veiled women in the Middle East.

Arsinoë II (316–271 BC) *Queen of Egypt*

A powerful figure in the ancient world, Arsinoë II was ruthless, ambitious, and capable, taking an active part in politics, war, and administration.

The daughter of Ptolemy I Soter of Egypt and BERENICE I, Arsinoë was married, in about 300 BC, to Lysimachus, king of Thrace, and had three sons by him: Ptolemaeus, Lysimachus, and Philip. Determined that her children should succeed to the throne, she persuaded her husband to put to death Agathocles, his son from his first marriage. However, Lysandra, the murdered prince's wife, then fled with her children to Seleucus I Nicator of Syria, who took up arms on her behalf, killed Lysimachus, and conquered his kingdom (281 BC).

Arsinoë fled to Macedonia, but that too was overrun by the Syrian army until Seleucus was assassinated by Arsinoë's half-brother Ptolemy Keraunos. Arsinoë, who held the Macedonian city of Cassandreia (Potidaea), was then persuaded by the promise of marriage to allow her half-brother to enter the city, but no sooner had he been admitted than he had two of her sons murdered in front of her. Exiled to Samothrace, Arsinoë managed to escape to Egypt, and in 276 BC she became the second wife of her brother Ptolemy II Philadelphus, who had banished his first wife, Arsinoë I, to Coptos. Until her death Arsinoë II ruled Egypt jointly with her brother: their union set a precedent for marriages between brother and sister that were to become common among the Greek rulers of Egypt.

After Arsinoë's death Ptolemy II, who had been devoted to his wife, named an Egyptian province (Arsinoïtis) after her as well as several cities. His own death, and that of his architect, prevented the planned building of a temple in her honour.

Arteaga, Rosalia (1956–) *Ecuadorian politician*

Vice president of Ecuador since 1996, Rosalia Arteaga briefly became the country's first woman leader when she was elected interim president in February 1997.

Dr. Arteaga originally trained to be a journalist but later became a teacher in a secondary school. She was appointed a provincial governor in 1986. Since then she has assiduously climbed the political ladder, being elected vice-minister of culture in 1992 and minister of education in 1994. In 1996 she formed her own political party of the centre right, the Independent Movement for an Authentic Republic. In July of the same year she was elected vice president of Ecuador. When President Bucarám (known as "El Loco" – the madman) was dismissed by Congress in February 1997, Dr. Arteaga won a congressional vote, in competition with the speaker (Fabián Alarcón), to become temporary head of state. A few days later, however, Alarcón was appointed president and she resumed her post of vice president.

Artemisia I (early 5th century BC) *Queen of Halicarnassus*

> I was not the least brave of those who fought at Euboea, nor were my achievements there among the meanest.

—Remark (*c.* 480 BC) to Xerxes, quoted by Herodotus in *The Persian Wars* (*c.* 450 BC)

Ruler of Helicarnassus, an ancient Greek city (now Bodrum in Turkey), and several of the Dodecanese Islands, Artemisia is distinguished by being the first woman naval commander. She accompanied Xerxes I of Persia on his invasion of Greece and fought bravely in the disastrous naval battle near Salamis in 480 BC, which she had prophesied would fail. Distressed by her unrequited love for a younger man, she is alleged to have committed suicide by jumping from a high cliff.

Artemisia II (died *c.* 350 BC) *Queen of Caria*

Artemisia II is best known for building the Mausoleum of Halicarnassus, one of the Seven Wonders of the World.

She succeeded to the throne of Caria, in Asia Minor, in 352 BC, following the death of her husband and brother, King Mausolus. In 363–361 she erected a magnificent tomb in his memory at her capital, Halicarnassus (now Bodrum in Turkey). The building, designed by Pythius, was probably similar to a standard temple in form, with adorning sculptures. It is known that Bryaxis, Scopas, Leochares, Timotheus, and possibly Praxiteles were among the sculptors who worked on its decoration. Raised on a high base and with a stepped pyramid-like roof, it was known as the Mausoleum, giving its name to all future memorial tombs.

Arundell, Blanche (1583–1649) *English heroine*

Lady Blanche is remembered for her defiant defence of the family castle during the Civil War (1642–46).

The daughter of the Earl of Worcester, Lady Blanche was married to Thomas, Lord Arundell of Wardour, Wiltshire. When the Civil War broke out in 1642, her husband joined the royalist forces. In 1643, while Lord Arundell was fighting with the royalists at Oxford, Lady Blanche defended Wardour Castle against the parliamentary soldiers, withstanding the seige for nine days. After two mines were set off under the castle, she was obliged to surrender. The defenders were spared, but the castle and grounds were ruined. Her son, Henry Arundell (*c.* 1606–94), regained the castle in 1644 but did not retain it or take up residence there.

Arzner, Dorothy (1900–1979) *American film director*

The only female film director from Hollywood's golden era of the 1930s, Dorothy Arzner was at that time listed as one of the top ten American directors. Her films are notable for their strong-minded independent heroines – role models for the feminist movement.

Arzner first came into contact with the film world when she was a waitress in her father's Hollywood restaurant. An ambulance driver during World War I, she subsequently became a shorthand typist and began cutting and then editing at a subsidiary of Paramount Pictures. Her imaginative editing of Rudolph Valentino's important silent film *Blood and Sand* (1922), in which she also shot some of the bullfight sequences, gained the attention of director James Cruze; she then edited Cruze's *The Covered Wagon* (1923) and wrote or co-wrote scripts for several of his other westerns.

Arzner's first directing assignment was *Fashions for Women* (1927). Her subsequent films include *The Wild Party* (1929), with Clara BOW; *Honour Among Lovers* (1931), with Claudette COLBERT; *Christopher Strong* (1933), with Katharine HEPBURN; *The Bride Wore Red* (1937), with Joan CRAWFORD; and *Dance Girl Dance* (1940). Arzner's last film, *First Comes Courage*, was made in 1943, after which she retired because of ill health. She later started a film-making course at the Pasadena Playhouse and taught film at the University of California, Los Angeles during the 1960s; at the same time, she produced over 50 TV commercials for Pepsi, with Joan Crawford. In 1975 she received a special award from the Directors' Guild of America.

Ashby, Dame Margery Corbett (1882–1981) *British feminist*

Margery Ashby played a major role in the international movement for women's rights: she was president of the International Women's Suffrage Alliance for 23 years.

The daughter of a Liberal member of Parliament, Margery Corbett was born in Sussex, and educated first at home and then at Newnham College, Cambridge, where she studied classics. Taught at home by French and German governesses, she was fluent in both these languages, going on to learn Italian and Turkish so that she could act as translator at international conferences. She attended the first International Suffrage Conference in Berlin in 1904; three years later she became secretary of the National Union of Women's Suffrage Societies. After her marriage to the lawyer Arthur Ashby in 1910, Margery continued to work for the women's movement, representing the International Woman Suffrage Alliance in the deputation to the Peace Conference at Versailles (1919–20) after World War I. She was instrumental in securing equality of the sexes in the constitutions of the International Labour Organization. In 1920 she became secretary of the International Woman Suffrage Alliance and in 1923 its president. She toured widely, lecturing and campaigning for women's rights, being particularly concerned with the problems of women in developing countries. In the 1930s she served as a British delegate to the disarmament conference in Geneva. Resigning from the Alliance after World War II, Margery nevertheless continued until she was 80 to travel all over the world giving lectures on pacifism and feminism.

Awarded an honorary LLD by Mount Holyoke College, Massachusetts, she was made a DBE in 1967.

Ashcroft, Dame Peggy (1907–1991) *British actress*

Described by J. B. Priestley as "the best all-round actress on the English-speaking stage," Peggy Ashcroft played every major Shakespearean heroine except Lady Macbeth, many opposite John Gielgud. Her Desdemona to Paul Robeson's Othello in

1930 and her Juliet in Gielgud's 1935 production of *Romeo and Juliet* were considered among the greatest of modern times.

Born Edith Margaret Emily Ashcroft in Croydon, she made her debut at the Birmingham Repertory Theatre in 1926 in J. M. Barrie's play *Dear Brutus*. The following year she gained national recognition for her performance in Feuchtwanger's *Jew Süss* in London. In 1937 she made her Broadway debut in Maxwell Anderson's *High Tor*, returning to London for Gielgud's 1937–38 season, during which she played several roles including Irina in Chekhov's *Three Sisters*. Just before World War II Ashcroft appeared in Gerhart Hauptmann's *Before Dawn* with the German actor Werner Krauss. His appearance on stage brought boos from the audience and the curtain came down. Ashcroft then appeared on stage and asked the audience to respect the company's privilege in being able to perform with such a distinguished artist. The play went on to receive a great ovation and excellent reviews.

Of her role as Cecily in the 1942 production of Oscar Wilde's *The Importance of Being Earnest*, *The Times* wrote that she was like "a jewel changing colour with the light, now innocently olive-green, now an audacious pink." Her 1954 performance of the title role in Ibsen's *Hedda Gabler* was a sensation; repeating the part a year later in Oslo, she was awarded King Haakon's Gold Medal. During the 1950s Ashcroft began to take roles in contemporary plays, including the 1956 production of Enid Bagnold's *The Chalk Garden*: that same year she was made a DBE.

A founding member of the Royal Shakespeare Company in 1961, she later became a director. Her roles with the company included Queen Margaret in Peter Hall's *Wars of the Roses* cycle (1963–64). Her later stage successes included Beckett's *Happy Days* (1974), HELLMAN's *Watch on the Rhine* (1980), and *All's Well That Ends Well* (1982).

Ashcroft also won acclaim as a screen actress, notably in the 1984 TV series *Jewel in the Crown* and in the film *A Passage to India* (1984), for which she won an Academy Award as Best Supporting Actress. Her other films include *The Nun's Story* (1959) and *Sunday Bloody Sunday* (1971). In 1962 a 700-seat theatre in Croydon was named after her.

Ashley, Laura (1925–85) *British designer and businesswoman*

> She knew what was right and wrong in fabrics just the same as she did in life, there were no grey areas.
> —Lynda Kee-Scott in Ann Sebba's
> *Laura Ashley – A Life* (1990)

Known as the "Earth Mother of the Alternative Society," Laura Ashley became famous in the late 1960s for her women's clothes, typically flowing floral prints and high-necked blouses in traditional cottons, which were based on Victorian and Edwardian styles. By the time of her death her business had expanded into an international chain of shops selling women's clothes and home furnishings.

Born in South Wales and educated in London, Laura Mountney worked for the War Office, the Women's Royal Naval Service, and then for the National Federation of Women's Institutes after leaving school. In 1949 she married Bernard Ashley. During her first pregnancy she began printing fabric with a home-made silkscreen in her kitchen, making it up into scarves, which she sold to a department store in London. They sold immediately, and the store ordered more. The scarves were so successful that in 1953 the Ashleys set up a company producing scarves and household items to her designs. By 1961 Laura had branched out into designing and making dresses and blouses, using prints inspired by 18th- and 19th-century fabric patterns; in 1967 the first Laura Ashley boutique opened in fashionable Kensington. In 1963 the Ashleys had taken over a disused railway station in Carno, Wales, which became the international headquarters for their fast-growing business. During the 1970s and 1980s they opened shops all over Britain, Europe, and the United States, expanding into furnishing fabrics, wallpapers, and decor.

The Ashleys maintained, at Laura's insistence, a simple lifestyle, and she always wore her own designs. After her death Bernard Ashley became chairman of the company: her son David developed the business in North America, while her son Nicholas and daughter Jane design for the collections.

Ashrawi, Hanan (1946–   ) *Palestinian politician and academic*

Hanan Ashrawi achieved worldwide recognition as spokeswoman for the Palestinian Delegation in the peace talks with Israel (1991–93).

She was born Hanan Mikhail in Nablus, Palestine (now in the West Bank), into a wealthy middle-class family: her father, a physician, was an atheist with a Christian background, while her mother was an Anglican. Raised in Ramallah, in the West Bank, Hanan was studying at the American University of Beirut when the Arab-Israeli Six-Day War broke out in June 1967. Because she was away from home at the outbreak of the war, she was classified as an "absentee"; as such, she had no legal existence and was unable to return home. She therefore supported herself in Beirut before going to the United States, where she studied medieval literature at the University of Virginia.

Allowed by the Israeli authorities to resettle in Ramallah in 1973, Hanan returned to the West Bank and became chairwoman of the English Studies department at the Anglican Teachers' College, Birzeit. In 1975 she married Emile Ashrawi, a photographer; the couple now have two daughters.

At this time Hanan Ashrawi became involved in Palestinian politics. Joining the mainstream Fatah faction of the PLO (Palestine Liberation Organization), she became an articulate spokeswoman for the Palestinians in their quest for self-government. In 1991 Yasser Arafat, chairman of the PLO, appointed her official spokeswoman for the Palestinian Delegation in the peace talks with Israel. A peace accord was signed in Oslo in September 1993. Although a tough and skilful negotiator, as a nonpractising Angli-can with a wealthy background Ashrawi was regarded with some suspicion by Muslim Palestinians, many of whom felt that their interests had not been adequately represented in the peace agreement.

Ashrawi resigned as Palestinian spokeswoman in December 1993. Refusing a post in the Palestinian National Authority (PNA), set up in 1995 to administer the West Bank and Gaza Strip, she founded the Palestinian Independent Commission to monitor human rights in areas under the jurisdiction of the PNA. In 1996 she became a member of the Palestinian Legislative Council.

Ashrawi has meanwhile continued her academic career, becoming professor of English literature at Birzeit University. Her publications include *This Side of Peace* (1995), her personal account of the Palestinian struggle.

Askew, Anne (1521–1546) *English Protestant martyr*

Born into a well-to-do family of Lincolnshire, Anne Askew was highly educated and always interested in theological debate. Leaving her husband, Thomas Kyme, because of her growing adherence to the Protestant faith, she travelled to London, possibly to obtain a divorce. Here she became an attendant at the court of Henry VIII's last wife, Catherine PARR, and moved among circles sympathetic to Protestantism.

Because her religious views were regarded as heretical at that time, Anne was questioned by the authorities in 1545 and refused to assert that she believed in transubstantiation (the Catholic doctrine that the whole substance of the bread and wine of the Eucharist are transformed into the substance of the body and blood of Christ), which countered Henry's Act of the Six Articles. Rearrested the following year, she was tortured on the rack in an attempt to implicate the queen and certain nobles in her beliefs: "they did put me on the rack because I confessed no ladies or gentlemen to be of my opinion...till I was nigh dead." Steadfast in her refusal both to abandon her faith and to incriminate oth-

ers, Anne was finally condemned to be
burned to death at the stake in July
1546: by this time she was so weak that
she had to be carried there on a chair.
Her great courage and calm throughout this ordeal earned Anne Askew a
high rank among the Protestant mar-
tyrs.

Asquith, Margot (1864–1945) *British society leader*

> If instead of birth control every one
> would preach drink control, you
> would have little poverty, less
> crime, and fewer illegitimate chil-
> dren.
>
> —*Places and Persons* (1925)

> The affair between Margot Asquith
> and Margot Asquith will live as one
> of the prettiest stories in all litera-
> ture.
>
> —Dorothy Parker, quoted by Robert
> Drennan (ed.) in *Wit's End*

Famous for her wit, Margot Asquith
was an influential figure in London society. As the second wife of Liberal
politician Henry Herbert Asquith, who
was prime minister from 1908 to 1916,
she became a renowned political hostess.

Born Emma Alice Margaret Tennant
in Scotland, she was the 11th child of
Sir Charles Tennant. Despite the lack
of a formal education – she was taught
at home before briefly attending a
finishing school in London – Margot
Tennant had considerable literary and
artistic abilities. In 1881 she "came
out" into fashionable London society,
in which her combination of talents
and wit ensured her instant success.
With her sister Laura, she became the
centre of a group of young intellectuals who advocated greater freedom of
expression for women. Over the years
her circle also included William Gladstone, the theologian Benjamin Jowett,
Virginia WOOLF, and Alfred, Lord
Tennyson.

In 1894 Margot married Herbert
Asquith, who was then home secretary, and began to give her famous political dinner parties, noted for the
brilliance and wit of the conversation.
It was considered an honour to be invited, but Margot's love of intrigue

and flamboyance also made her enemies.

In 1906 Asquith became chancellor
of the exchequer, being appointed
prime minister two years later: he resigned in 1916 because of the unsat-
isfactory progress of World War
I. Margot continued entertaining
throughout the war and after it began
to write her memoirs: her *Autobiography* was published in 1922. Notorious
for its indiscretions, it was followed by
two further volumes: *More Memories*
(1933) and *Off the Record* (1943). She
was also the author of a travel book,
Lay Sermons (1927), and an autobiographical novel, *Octavia* (1928). The
Asquiths had seven children, five of
whom died in infancy.

See also BONHAM CARTER, VIOLET.

Astell, Mary (1668–1731) *English feminist*

> If Absolute Sovereignty be not nec-
> essary in a State, how comes it to be
> so in a family?
>
> —*Some Reflections upon Marriage*
> (1700)

In her *Serious Proposal to the Ladies
for the Advancement of Their True and
Greatest Interest*, published anonymously in 1694, Mary Astell made the
first demand in England for higher education for women.

The daughter of a merchant, she was
born in Newcastle upon Tyne. After
the deaths of her parents she moved to
London and by 1695 was established
among a group of women and clergymen supporting the cause of women's
education. In the first part of her *Serious Proposal* Astell stated the problem:
"Women are from their very infancy
debarr'd those advantages with the
want of which they are afterwards reproached, and nursed up in those vices
with which will here after be upbraided
them." As a solution, she proposed the
establishment of a female academic
community – a "Place of Religious Retirement" where women could receive
a liberal education to develop their intellectual and spiritual resources. In
Part II, which was published in 1697,
she laid out the proposed subjects for
study. Her proposals were almost
taken seriously, but in the end the

ridicule of figures in the religious Establishment, published in influential journals of the day, swayed public opinion against her. She continued, however, to put forward her ideas on the importance of education for women, especially as a defence against unwanted marriages. In her tract *Some Reflections upon Marriage* (1700) she argued that well-educated women could arrange their marriages more wisely and become happier and more efficient wives and mothers. Astell also contributed articles to the philosophical and religious debates of the time, including *The Christian Religion, as professed by a Daughter of the Church of England, 1705*.

Astor, Mary (1906–1987) *American film actress*

A prolific and versatile actress, whose roles ranged from innocent maidens to kindly matriarchs, Mary Astor was best known for her portrayal of bitchy women, as in *The Great Lie* (1941), for which she won an Oscar.

Born Lucille Vasconcellos Langhanke, in Quincy, Illinois, she made her film debut at 15, but it was not until she appeared with her lover John Barrymore in *Beau Brummel* (1924) that she found fame. She was highly acclaimed in *Red Dust* (1932), in which she starred with Jean HARLOW and Clark Gable.

However, in 1936 Astor was at the centre of a Hollywood scandal when her diary, containing details of her love affairs, was used as evidence in a court case over the custody of her daughter. She claimed later that her role as the dignified wife in *Dodsworth* (1936) helped her through the ordeal of the custody battle, during which her lover, the playwright George S. Kaufman, was arrested for forging a version of her diary that excluded him. Surprisingly, her career did not seem to be affected by the case: in 1941 she costarred with Humphrey Bogart in *The Maltese Falcon* and with Bette DAVIS in *The Great Lie*, for which she received an Academy Award for Best Supporting Actress.

As she grew older, Astor played gentle, more motherly women, as in *Meet Me in St. Louis* (1944) and *Little Women* (1949). She reverted however, to her more familiar form in *Act of Violence* (1948) and *Hush, Hush, Sweet Charlotte* (1964). She also appeared in *Youngblood Hawke* as a faded Hollywood star in 1964. Married four times, she struggled against a heart condition, which forced her into semiretirement during the 1950s. She also had a problem with alcoholism and once attempted suicide.

Astor, Nancy, Viscountess (1879–1964) *American-born British politician*

> The penalty of success is to be bored by people who used to snub you.
>
> —Quoted in the *Sunday Express*, January 12, 1956

In 1919 Nancy Astor attracted international attention by becoming the first woman member of Parliament in Britain to take her seat in the House of Commons.

Nancy Witcher Langhorne was born in Greenwood, Virginia, one of five daughters of a wealthy tobacco auctioneer. In 1897 she married Robert Gould Shaw, a Bostonian, but the couple were divorced in 1903. Nancy then travelled to England, where in 1906 she married Waldorf Astor, the son of an American millionaire who had been made a lord. Nancy became an influential society hostess, presiding at the Astors' country home at Cliveden, Buckinghamshire, until 1910, when Waldorf was elected as a Conservative member of Parliament and they moved to his constituency of Plymouth. In 1919, when Waldorf inherited his father's title and entered the House of Lords, Nancy was elected to his Plymouth seat and – until 1921 – was the only woman to sit in the House of Commons (Constance MARKIEWICZ, elected in 1918, had chosen not to take her seat). Lady Astor worked hard crusading for stricter temperance laws and was a champion of women's and children's rights; she was, however, vehemently opposed to socialism. In 1914 she became a Christian Scientist: a reflection of her strict moral code. Her political popularity began to wane in the 1930s, when she supported appeasement of Germany, but she deplored Nazism, vociferously attacking German policy in 1939. Regarded with affection by her constituents in Plymouth, whom she continued to visit during the heaviest bombing in the war, she retired from politics in 1945. Although deeply opposed to Communism, she spoke out against the McCarthy witch-hunts in the United States in the 1950s.

Nancy Astor was one of the wittiest and most colourful figures in British public life; her book, *My Two Countries*, was published in 1923.

Athaliah (died 837 BC) *Queen of Judah*

The only recorded queen of Judah, Athaliah ruthlessly secured her position by slaughtering the male heirs to the throne.

The daughter of King Ahab of Israel and his wife JEZEBEL, she was married to Jehoram, king of Judah. After the death of her son, King Ahaziah, in 843 BC Athaliah seized power and ruled alone for six years, having killed all the males in the royal family. However, her stepdaughter Jehosheba had managed to rescue Ahaziah's infant son, Joash, hiding him away from Athaliah in the Temple. During her reign Athaliah supported the worship of the fertility god Baal, which went against the law of the Ten Commandments. Therefore, when Joash was seven, the priest Jehoiada, who was Jehosheba's husband, revealed the identity of the boy to the chiefs and the rulers of the army and organized a coup to overthrow Athaliah. The coup was successful, Joash was placed on the throne, and Athaliah was killed. Her story is told in II Kings 11 and II Chronicles 22.

Atherton, Gertrude (1857–1948) *American writer*

Gertrude Atherton is best known for her novels. Many of these reflect her experience of foreign travel; others portray heroines of the American West.

Born Gertrude Franklin Horn, in San Francisco, she was educated at private schools in California and Kentucky. In 1876 she married George Henry Bowen Atherton, by whom she had two children. Her literary career began after her husband's death in 1887, when she travelled widely and started to write novels. These are set in a wide variety of countries, including ancient Greece, France, Germany, and the West Indies, as well as in California.

Her most popular books are *The Conqueror* (1902), a fictional biography of the American statesman Alexander Hamilton, for which she went to his birthplace in the West Indies to gather information; and *Black Oxen* (1923), a novel about rejuvenation inspired by her own experience with the Steinach method. Among her other novels are *The Doomswoman* (1892), featuring a Californian heroine in 1840; *Senator North* (1900); *Rezanov* (1906); *The Immortal Marriage* (1927), set in ancient Greece; *Dido, Queen of Hearts* (1929); and *The Horn of Life* (1942), a novel of San Francisco. She also published collections of short stories: *Before the Gringo Came* (1894) and *The Bell in the Fog* (1905). *Adventures of a Novelist* (1932) is an autobiography in which she revealed her dislike for the conventional, and *My San Francisco* (1946) comprises her reminiscences. She is also the author of two histories of her native California – *California, An Intimate History* (1914) and *Golden Gate Country* (1945). In 1925 Mrs. Atherton was appointed to the Legion of Honour for her relief work in France during World War I. In 1947 she received a gold medal from the city of San Francisco. She was also awarded honorary degrees by the University of California and by Mills College, Oakland.

Atkins, Eileen (1934–) *British actress and writer*

Atkins's versatility has embraced leading roles in Shakespeare, Shaw, and many contemporary playwrights.

Eileen Atkins was born in Birmingham and trained at the Guildhall School of Music and Drama, London. After making her West End debut in 1953, she became a member of the Shakespeare Memorial Theatre, Stratford on Avon, in 1957 and the Bristol Old Vic in 1959.

Atkins first came to prominence with her performance as the lesbian Childie in Frank Marcus's *The Killing of Sister George* (1961); the play earned her an Evening Standard Drama Award and later transferred to Broadway. During the 1960s she took major roles in plays by Peter Nichols and David Storey amongst other contemporary playwrights. Another career highlight was the role of Elizabeth I in Robert Bolt's *Vivat! Vivat Regina!*, which earned her a Variety Award in 1970.

In the early 1970s Atkins was involved in a prolonged campaign to stage an English version of Marguerite DURAS's *Suzanna Andler*, about the anguish of a middle-aged woman contemplating an affair. Her own production of the play, in which she also starred, appeared to widespread acclaim in 1973. Other major roles of the 1970s included Rosalind in *As You Like It* (RSC, 1973) and the title role in Shaw's *Saint Joan* (National Theatre, 1977). More recent triumphs have included an Olivier Award for the unpromising role of the Queen in Shakespeare's *Cymbeline* (1988) and her performance in Ibsen's *John Gabriel Borkman* (1996). Her rare work for the cinema includes supporting roles in *Equus* (1974), *The Dresser* (1984), and *Wolf* (1994); she has also made frequent appearances on British television.

In 1994 Atkins fulfilled a long-cherished ambition when she produced the script for *Vita and Virginia*, a play about the relationship between Vita SACKVILLE-WEST and Virginia WOOLF. This was produced successfully in both London and New York, with Atkins and her great friend Vanessa RED-GRAVE in the title roles. Three years later she supplied the screenplay for a film version of Woolf's *Mrs Dalloway*, which also starred Vanessa Redgrave. Eileen Atkins was appointed CBE in 1990.

Attwell, Mabel Lucie (1879–1964)
British artist and illustrator of children's books.

Attwell's pictures of angelic curly-haired children became hugely popular in the 1920s and helped to define the image of childhood for several generations.

Mabel Lucie Attwell was born in the East End of London, the daughter of a butcher. Having shown an early talent for drawing, she attended various London art schools and began to contribute sketches to magazines while still in her teens. This led to a series of commissions from book publishers in the years before World War I. Much of her best work dates from the 1910s, when she produced imaginative illustrations for *Alice in Wonderland* (1910), the stories of Hans Christian Andersen (1913), and *The Water Babies* (1915).

In 1908 Attwell married the artist and illustrator Harold Earnshaw, with whom she had three children. After Earnshaw lost his drawing arm in World War I, it fell to Attwell to support the family. Accordingly she greatly increased her productivity and concentrated on the idealized images of children that proved her most saleable work. She also diversified into such media as toys, postcards, calendars, and decor for nurseries. Her instantly recognizable style made her a household name in the 1920s and had a noticeable influence on the dress and hairstyles imposed on young children at this time. Among her most popular productions was the *Lucie Attwell Annual*, which appeared without a break from 1922 until 1974, having been taken over by her daughter in the 1960s. Although Attwell's work is too sentimental for most modern tastes, her illustrated books are now sought by collectors.

Atwood,   Margaret   (Eleanor)
(1939–   ) *Canadian writer*

> Margaret Atwood is the quiet Mata Hari, the mysterious, violent figure…who pits herself against the ordered, too-clean world like an arsonist.
>
> —Michael Ondaatje

The author of poetry, novels, short stories, and literary criticism, Margaret Atwood is regarded by many as Canada's most important contemporary writer.

Born in Ottawa, Margaret Atwood was brought up in the wilds of northern Ontario and Quebec, where her father ran forest stations studying insects. After graduating from the University of Toronto, where she won a Woodrow Wilson Fellowship, and taking a master's degree from Radcliffe College, Atwood travelled widely, holding teaching positions at various Canadian universities. She also began to make a reputation for herself as a poet: her collection *The Circle Game* (1966) won the Governor General's Award. She has since published numerous collections, including *Power Politics* (1971), *You Are Happy* (1974), *Interlunar* (1988), and *Morning in the Burned House* (1995). A prolific writer, she has also produced short stories, children's books, and literary criticism, including the controversial *Survival: A Thematic Guide to Canadian Literature* (1972). Atwood's work as a critic and editor has played an important role in defining Canadian literature as a distinctive tradition. Since the 1970s she has also been active in Amnesty International and anticensorship campaigns.

However, it is as a novelist that Atwood is best known. Her fiction covers a wide spectrum of subjects, ranging from the nature of time and memory to the state of modern marriage and the problems of Canada's equivocal relationship with the United States; a recurring theme is modern woman's painful search for self-realization. Despite the serious issues addressed, her novels are characterized by acerbic wit and tongue-in-cheek humour. Her early novels include *The Edible Woman* (1969), *Surfacing* (1972), *Lady Oracle* (1976), and *Bodily Harm* (1981). *The Handmaid's Tale* (1985) is a futuristic story about a state in which women are totally subordinated to their reproductive role; a worldwide bestseller, it was made into a film in 1990. This book was also shortlisted for the Booker Prize, as were her later novels *Cat's Eye* (1988) and *Alias Grace* (1996). Other works include the novel *The Robber Bride* (1993) and the collection of stories *Wilderness Tips* (1991).

Augusta (1811–1890) *Wife of William I, king of Prussia and emperor of Germany*

The daughter of Charles Frederick, Grand Duke of Saxe-Weimar, Marie Luise Katharina Augusta was born in Weimar, and educated at the court there, where she became acquainted with Goethe.

In 1829 she married William, then crown prince of Prussia, who became king of Prussia in 1861 and emperor of Germany in 1871. Their son, Frederick William, eventually became Emperor Frederick III, and Louise, their daughter, married Frederick I, Grand Duke of Baden. Augusta was bitterly opposed to the German chancellor, Otto von Bismarck, who tried (unsuccessfully) to persuade her husband to abdicate in favour of their son, the young Frederick William, whom Bismarck could then control. A friend of Queen VICTORIA, Augusta was sympathetic towards liberals and Roman Catholics.

Aulnoy, Comtesse d' (*c.* 1650–1705) *French writer*

Madame d'Aulnoy is best known as the author of charming fairy tales (including "Goldilocks"), which were published as *Contes de fées* (1697; Fairy Tales) and *Contes nouvelles ou les fées à la mode* (1698; New Tales, or the Fancy of the Fairies).

Born Marie Catherine Le Jumel de Barneville, at Barneville in Normandy, she married Comte d'Aulnoy (also spelled Aunoy) in 1666. After she and her mother were discovered in a plot to bring charges of treason against the count, they were forced to leave France. For the next 15 years Marie travelled around Europe, living in England, the Netherlands, and (from 1679) Spain. Eventually she was allowed to return to France as a reward for secret services rendered to the government; for the rest of her life the countess lived mainly in Paris.

Madame d'Aulnoy was the mother of five children, which probably prompted her to write the famous fairy tales. Her other works were inspired by her travels. They include *Mémoires de la cour d'Espagne* (1690; published in English as *Memoirs from the Court of Spain*, 1692), an account of life in the Spanish court covering the years 1679–81; *Relation du voyage d'Espagne* (1691; published in English as *,Travels into Spain*, 1692), written in the form of letters; and historical romances, such as *L'histoire d'Hippolyte, comte de Douglas* (1690; published in English as *Hippolitus, Earl of Douglas*, 1708).

Austen, Jane (1775–1817) *British novelist*

> That young lady has a talent for describing the involvements and feelings and characters of ordinary life which is to me the most wonderful thing I ever met with.
>
> —Sir Walter Scott, *Journals*, March 14, 1826

> More can be learnt from Miss Austen about the nature of the novel than from almost any other writer.
>
> —Walter Allen, *The English Novel* (1954)

Jane Austen's novels explore the manners and customs of one small section of English society – the rural gentry – with brilliant wit and great formal elegance. She herself acknowledged the limited range of her art (as well as its fine precision) by writing of "the little bit (two inches wide) of Ivory on which I work with so fine a brush." However, as new generations of readers discover, her work goes beyond social comedy to address enduring moral dilemmas (notably the relationship between the sensitive individual and his or her society) with great insight.

Austen's life was outwardly uneventful. Born at Steventon, Hampshire, she was one of seven children of a country clergyman. She grew up in a genteel and cultivated environment, read widely the works of 18th-century English novelists, and was herself encouraged to write. Although she had several suitors, she never married. The family spent five years (1801–06) living in the fashionable centre of Bath and then moved to Southampton on the death of her father.

From 1809 she lived in Chawton, Hampshire, with her mother and her favourite sister, Cassandra, until a few months before her death, when she moved to Winchester to be near her doctor.

Austen's earliest surviving works, which date from her teenage years, include several lively skits on the then-fashionable gothic melodramas of Mrs. RADCLIFFE and others. Her first completed novel, *Northanger Abbey* (begun in about 1798 but published after her death), provides a more serious criticism of popular women's fiction by examining its effect on a susceptible young heroine. From this period also date the earliest drafts of what became *Sense and Sensibility* (1811), her first published novel. In this mature work Austen contrasts the behaviour of two sisters, the impetuous Marianne and the self-controlled Elinor, to criticize the contemporary cult of "sensibility," which emphasized emotion and spontaneity. Austen's next novel, *Pride and Prejudice* (1813), was another extensively rewritten version of an early work. This has always been the most popular of her books, owing mainly to its sparkling wit and its attractive spirited heroine, Elizabeth Bennet. By contrast *Mansfield Park* (1814), a rather sombre novel with an off-puttingly virtuous heroine, has proved relatively unpopular. *Emma* (1816), the last of Austen's works to appear during her lifetime, describes the painful moral education of Emma Woodhouse, a clever but self-satisfied young woman. It is often considered Austen's most perfect work. She completed one other novel, *Persuasion*, a tender story about an interrupted love affair that was published in 1818, after her death. Unlike her other novels, which had been published anonymously, this appeared with a biographical note from her brother, Henry Austen. During her final months of ill health she had begun to write *Sanditon*, of which a fragmentary draft survives.

During her lifetime Austen received very little recognition or reward for her work (she was apparently much delighted with £150 "clean profit" on *Sense and Sensibility*). Despite this, her novels found discerning admirers from the start. The Prince Regent is said to have kept a set of her complete works at each of his residences, while Sir Walter Scott, the most successful novelist of the day, was also full of praise for her novels.

Although her reputation was eclipsed slightly during the Victorian era, when she was thought to lack "passion," 20th-century critics have praised her combination of sharp wit with moral seriousness. In recent years her popularity has risen to new heights owing mainly to a series of film and television adaptations; these include films of *Sense and Sensibility* and *Emma* (both 1996) and the TV serial *Pride and Prejudice* (1995).

Avellaneda y Arteaga, Gertrudis Gómez de (1814–1873) *Spanish writer*

Avellaneda y Arteaga is best known as the author of sensitive poems on the theme of love, both human and divine, that she published under the pen name "La Peregrina" ("The Pilgrim").

She was born in Camagüey, Cuba, but after 1836 lived for the rest of her life in Spain except for the years 1859–63, when she returned to Cuba. In addition to her poetry she also wrote novels and plays; with grandiose themes typical of 19th-century Romanticism, these works were highly thought of in her time but now seem dated. They include the novels *El Mulato Sab* (1839), *Espatolino* (1844), and *Guatimozín* (1845) and historical and biblical dramas, such as *Alfonso Munio* (1844), *Saúl* (1950), and *Baltasar* (1858). She also wrote the comic play *Errores del corazón* (1852; Mistakes of the Heart).

Ayer, Harriet Hubbard (1849–1903) *American businesswoman and journalist*

Best known for being the first of many women to make a fortune in the cosmetics industry, Harriet Ayer also published a bestseller, *Harriet Hubbard Ayer's Book: A Complete and Authentic Treatise on the Laws of Health and Beauty* (1899).

Born and educated in Chicago, she married Herbert Crawford Ayer when she was 16. She became a society hostess and patron of the arts, but her pursuit of these interests led to a separation from her husband in 1882,

when she moved to New York. The following year her husband's business failed, and she supported herself by working in prestigious furniture shops. The couple were divorced in 1886.

In 1886 Ayer began to make face cream from a recipe she claimed to have found in Paris, and which – according to her inspired publicity – had been used by the famous salon hostess Madame RÉCAMIER, a great beauty. Ayer's business was extremely successful, but she lost everything when a feud developed between herself and one of her sponsors, her daughter Harriet's father-in-law. Claiming that she was too unstable to run a business, he managed, in 1893, to have her committed to a lunatic asylum. Her lawyer obtained her release, but it took 14 months, by which time her business had gone.

In 1896 Ayer began a new career as a journalist, writing a beauty advice column in the *New York World*. She continued with this until her death, when her daughter Margaret took it over.

Aylward, Gladys (1903–1970) *British-born Chinese missionary*

Known as "the small woman" (she was only five feet tall), Gladys Aylward devoted her life to her mission in China. This was made famous by the film *The Inn of the Sixth Happiness* (1958), in which Aylward was played by Ingrid BERGMAN.

Born in London, she had always wanted to be a missionary. Leaving school at 14, she worked as a parlourmaid in order to save enough money to buy a train ticket to China. In 1930 she travelled to Tientsin in north China and joined the Scottish missionary Jeannie Dawson at Yangzheng in southern Shanxi. There they worked together to establish "The Inn of the Sixth Happiness," where they hoped to teach the gospels to passing travellers. They established good relations with the local Chinese, learning their language. Gladys was then appointed the area's official foot inspector, with the job of enforcing the new law forbidding the ancient custom of binding women's feet. In 1931 she took Chinese citizenship. In 1938 the war between Japan and China reached Yangzheng, and the province was overrun. Gladys led 100 children on the now legendary journey to freedom over treacherous mountain terrain. She then joined the Nationalists and travelled from village to village, attending to the sick. In 1948 she returned to Britain to preach and lecture, but in 1953 settled in Taiwan, heading an orphanage for refugee children.

Ayres, Gillian (1930–) *British painter*

Gillian Ayres has become internationally known for her colourful and exuberant abstract paintings.

Ayres was born in Barnes, southwest London, and educated at St. Paul's Girls' School. From the age of 16 she studied at the Camberwell School of Art, where she grew discontented with the realist style that dominated its teaching. After leaving Camberwell in 1950 she developed a personal style of abstraction that relied on colour to make a direct sensuous appeal. She gave her first one-woman show in 1957 and in 1960 contributed to "Situation," an important exhibition of British abstract painters.

During the 1960s and 1970s Ayres taught at various art schools, including the Winchester School of Art, where she was head of painting (1979–81). It was during this period that she developed her mature style, which is characterized by rich colouring and a highly expressive and tactile use of oil paint. Following a move to North Wales in 1981, her work became still more lyrical, incorporating shapes suggestive of flowers, mountains, and seascapes. She now lives and works in Cornwall.

A retrospective exhibition of Ayres's work in 1983 established her reputation as one of Britain's leading painters. She was appointed OBE in 1986 and a Royal Academician in 1991, but later resigned from the Academy as a protest over several matters, including the controversial "Sensation" exhibition of 1997. Ayres has two sons by her marriage (later dissolved) to the painter Henry Munday.

B

Bacall, Lauren (1924–) *American actress*

Lauren Bacall is known for her distinctively husky voice and sultry manner, and for her romance, on- and off-screen, with the actor Humphrey Bogart.

Born Betty Joan Perske in New York, she trained to be a dancer and stage actress. In 1943 she came to the attention of film director Howard Hawks, who hired her to play opposite Humphrey Bogart in the adventure film *To Have and Have Not* (1944). Bacall and Bogart were married the following year and stayed together until his death in 1957. Their notable collaborations on screen include *The Big Sleep* (1946) and *Key Largo* (1948).

Bacall's film career was at its height during the late 1940s and early 1950s. Her performance in *How to Marry a Millionaire* (1953) revealed that she also had a talent for comic parts. Thereafter she appeared on screen only infrequently. She returned to Broadway in the late 1960s, winning a Tony Award for her role in *Applause* (1970). From 1961 to 1969 she was married to the actor Jason Robards, Jr.

Bacall's later films have included *Murder on the Orient Express* (1974), *The Shootist* (1976), and *Misery* (1990). In 1997 her performance in *The Mirror Has Two Faces* earned her an Oscar nomination for Best Supporting Actress. Her autobiography, *Lauren Bacall*, was published in 1978.

Bacewicz, Grazyna (1909–1969) *Polish composer and violinist*

Grazyna Bacewicz became accomplished on both violin and piano in her youth. She studied in her native country (at Lodz and Warsaw) and also

under the renowned music teacher Nadia BOULANGER in Paris. She was acclaimed as a performer and a composer, but increasingly concentrated on writing her own works. In 1951 her fourth string quartet was awarded first prize in the International Composers' Competition. Her compositions are principally neoclassical in style; they include four symphonies and seven violin concertos.

Bacewicz taught at the Lodz conservatory before and after World War II. She later took up a post at the Warsaw Academy, working there until her death.

As well as her musical compositions, Bacewicz wrote several novels and short stories.

Bachmann, Ingeborg (1926–1973) *Austrian writer*

Although she only concentrated on poetry for a few years in the 1950s, this work established Ingeborg Bachmann as one of the most influential German-language poets of the postwar era.

Bachmann was brought up in the south Austrian city of Klagenfurt and went on to study law and philosophy at the universities of Innsbruck, Graz, and Vienna. She wrote a doctoral dissertation on the work of Martin Heidegger in 1950. After staying for a time in Italy and the United States, she was appointed to a professorship at the University of Frankfurt when only 33 years old.

Bachmann's writings include poetry, radio plays, and prose works. Her first collection of poems, *Die gestundete Zeit* (Time by the Hour), was published in 1953 and widely acclaimed by her contemporaries. Her short stories *Das dreissigste Jahr* (1961; The Thirtieth Year) were also highly successful. In her work she focused on the manipulation of women in a male-dominated society.

In addition to her literary output Bachmann also wrote the librettos for Hans Werner Henze's operas *Der Prinz von Homburg* (1960; The Prince of Homburg) and *Der junge Lord* (1965; The Young Lord).

Bachmann was killed in a fire at her home in Rome.

Baden-Powell, Dame Olave (1889– 1977) *British promoter of the Girl Guides*

Born Olave Soames, the daughter of a wealthy brewery owner, she inherited from her father a restless spirit and taste for travel. Accompanying him on a visit to the West Indies in 1912, she met on board the ship Robert Baden-Powell, hero of the Boer War and founder of the Boy Scout movement. Despite the difference in their ages (he was 32 years her senior), they were married later that year, spending their honeymoon under canvas in the Algerian desert.

Following war work in France during World War I, Olave became interested in the Girl Guides. The Guides had been established in 1910 but – administered half-heartedly by committee – they had remained in the shadow of the Scouts. In 1916 Olave became Chief Commissioner of the Guides, later retitled Chief Guide, and travelled around Britain seeking suitable people to organize local Guide troops. During the war years she also had a son and two daughters.

Lady Baden-Powell was elected Chief Guide of the World in 1930, and over the next 40 years she travelled an estimated 487,777 miles to broaden the movement. On these journeys she was received by heads of state as well as ordinary Guide troops, her warmth and charisma generating much favourable publicity. Her work helped the movement to overcome religious and ethnic differences; on her personal insistence there was no racial segregation of the Guides during apartheid in South Africa.

Olave Baden-Powell received numerous international awards for her work, including the Order of the White Rose

(Finland), the Order of the Sun (Peru), and the DBE.

Baez, Joan (1941–   ) *American folksinger and political activist*

> Instead of getting hard ourselves and trying to compete, women should try and give their best qualities to men – bring them softness, teach them how to cry.
> —Quoted in *The Los Angeles Times*, May 26, 1974

With her pure soprano voice Joan Baez not only contributed greatly to the revival of folk music during the 1960s and 1970s but also spoke for a generation opposed to American involvement in the Vietnam War.

Baez was born in New York City, the daughter of a Mexican-born physicist and academic. While her father was teaching at Harvard, she learned from folksinger friends in Boston to play the guitar and to perform a wide repertoire of folk songs, ballads, blues numbers, and spirituals. Her voice, though untrained, has a range of more than three octaves.

After occasional performances in Boston coffeehouses, Baez was invited to appear at the 1959 Newport music festival in Rhode Island. She also appeared at the festival the following year and released her first album, entitled simply *Joan Baez*. It was an immediate bestseller, and she subsequently became one of the most popular female folksingers in the United States. There followed a series of extensive tours in the 1960s and 1970s, some of which were conducted jointly with Bob Dylan, whose songs she helped popularize (notably on the double album *Any Day Now*). Baez appeared at the Woodstock free festival in upstate New York in 1969. Her many recordings include *Gracias a la Vida* (1974), *Diamonds and Rust* (1975), *Gulf Winds* (1976), *Play Me Backwards* (1992), and *Gone From Danger* (1997). She was awarded a gold disc for her version of 'The Night They Drove Old Dixie Down', a song first popularized by Dylan's backing group, The Band.

A committed pacifist, Baez began a campaign of civil disobedience in 1964 by refusing to pay what she called "war taxes," and she was arrested in 1967 for participating in demonstrations opposing the draft for the Vietnam War. She founded Humanitas, the International Human Rights Commission in 1979, and has been a member of the advisory council of Amnesty International since 1974. In April 1993 she did a benefit tour of Bosnia. Since the early 1990s she has reduced her political commitments in order to concentrate on a successful musical comeback.

Baez is the author of the memoir *Daybreak* (1968), cowritten with her former husband, the student activist David Harris, and *And a Voice to Sing With* (1987).

Bagnold, Enid (1889–1981) *British novelist and playwright*

> Whoever the author may be, he is one of the cleverest of contemporary writers.
>
> —Joseph Wood Krutch, on Bagnold's anonymous novel *Serena Blandish* (1924)

Edith Bagnold is best known as the author of *National Velvet*, a horseracing saga made into a highly successful film (1945) starring Elizabeth TAYLOR.

Bagnold was born in Rochester, Kent, and educated in Switzerland and France. At the outbreak of World War I she volunteered as a nurse and worked in a London hospital. Her candid account of this experience, *Diary Without Dates* (1917), was so critical of hospital discipline that it led to her dismissal by outraged military authorities. In the final year of the war she joined another voluntary unit, serving as a driver for the French army.

In 1920 Enid Bagnold married the head of the Reuters news agency, Sir Roderick Jones. Four years later she published anonymously the light novel *Serena Blandish: or, The Difficulty of Getting Married*, which was received with acclaim. This was followed by the commercially successful *National Velvet* (1935), a novel about a girl who acquires a horse on which she wins the Grand National. Her other novels include *The Loved and Envied* (1951).

Bagnold's greatest theatrical success came at the age of 66, when her drama *The Chalk Garden*, rejected by British producers, opened in New York City in 1955 and enjoyed instant popularity. The following year it was performed in London. Her other plays include *Lottie Dundass* (1943), *The Chinese Prime Minister* (1964), and *A Matter of Gravity* (1975).

Bailey, Pearl (1918–1990) *American singer and actress*

Pearl Bailey, a preacher's daughter, was born in Newport News, Virginia. After winning an amateur contest, she began her career as a nightclub singer and dancer at the age of 15. She toured with various popular bands and jazz groups, working frequently with drummer Louie Bellson, whom she married in 1952, and arranger Don Redman. However, it is for her work in stage musicals, films, and TV that she is best known.

Bailey made her Broadway debut in *St. Louis Woman* (1946) and her film debut in *Variety Girl* (1947). Her other films include *Carmen Jones* (1955), *St. Louis Blues* (1958), and *Porgy and Bess* (1959). Her greatest success came with the Tony Award she received for the title role in the all-black production of *Hello, Dolly!* on Broadway in 1967. She continued in nightclub engagements in the United States and Britain, and in 1971 she hosted her own TV variety show. Pearl Bailey retired from show business in 1975. She was later appointed to the U.S. delegation to the United Nations.

Baillie, Dame Isobel (1895–1983) *British soprano*

> Isobel…was, and abides still, a part of this century's musical history. Age has no power to disturb or modify that fact – its only relevance is in our abiding affection and admiration for the beauty of her singing, and for her greatly-loved self.
>
> —Herbert Howells, tribute to Isobel Baillie on her 80th birthday in 1975

Singing mainly in oratorios and operas, Isobel Baillie was praised for the purity and clarity of her tone. She is particularly remembered as a soloist in Handel's *Messiah*, which she is reputed to have performed over 1,000 times.

Isobel Baillie was born at Hawick in southern Scotland, the youngest child of a master baker and his wife. She was a typical "Scottish lass," with red hair and a fair complexion. Showing early musical talent, she had singing lessons from the age of nine and won a scholarship to the High School in Manchester, where her family had settled.

Isobel gave her first performance of the *Messiah* at the age of 15. In 1917 she made a wartime marriage to Henry Leonard Wrigley; the couple had one daughter. In 1921 she was invited to appear with Manchester's Hallé orchestra, and she made her first, highly successful, London appearance in 1923. During 1925–26 Isobel studied with Guglielmo Somma in Milan.

She was now well established as a singer of the *Messiah* and of other choral works, notably Haydn's *Creation*, Mendelssohn's *Elijah*, and Brahms's *German Requiem*. In 1933 she became the first British performer to sing in the Hollywood Bowl in California. Although she did not regard herself as an operatic singer, her performances of Gluck's *Orpheus* and Gounod's *Faust* were very popular. She was also noted for her renderings of British music, including Vaughan Williams's *Serenade to Music*, Elgar's *The Kingdom*, and Howells's *Hymnus Paradisi*.

Isobel Baillie taught at the Royal College of Music in London (1955–57, 1961–64), and in 1960–61 she was a visiting professor at Cornell University in the United States. She continued to give lectures and recitals after her retirement and in 1978 was made a DBE. Her autobiography, *Never Sing Louder than Lovely*, was published in 1982, the year before her death.

Baillie, Joanna (1762–1851) *Scottish poet and writer of verse plays*

Baillie's plays are noted for their simple but forceful language and her characterization of women.

The daughter of a Presbyterian minister, Joanna Baillie was born in Bothwell, near Glasgow. In 1783 she moved to London, where she published the first of her three-volume *Plays on the Passions* (1798). This series of ten plays attempted to reveal the nature of human passions through both tragedies and comedies. Although these plays were not ideally suited to stage production, they assured Baillie's literary reputation. The second volume in the series appeared in 1802, and a third in 1812. *Volumes of Miscellaneous Plays* were published in 1804 and 1836, and a complete edition of her dramatic works in 1850.

Several of Baillie's plays were performed during her lifetime. The tragedy *De Monfort*, on the subject of hatred, was staged by John Kemble in 1800, with Kemble and Sarah SIDDONS in the leading roles; in a later production, the celebrated tragedian Edmund Kean played the title role. Sir Walter Scott, a friend of Baillie who greatly admired her work, financed the production of her tragedy *Family Legend* in 1810. She died in London.

Baker, Dame Janet (Abbott) (1933–) *British opera singer*

Janet Baker is a versatile mezzo-soprano renowned for her opera performances and her recitals of songs.

After studying in England at the Royal College of Music and at the Mozarteum in Salzburg, Janet Baker made her operatic debut in 1956 as Roza in Smetana's *The Secret*. At an early stage she began to specialize in the Renaissance and Baroque repertoire, singing the works of such composers as Purcell, Handel, and Monteverdi. However, she also appeared regularly in the operas of Benjamin Britten. Her debut at London's Covent Garden opera house was in Britten's *A Midsummer Night's Dream*, in 1966; the composer wrote the part of Kate Julian especially for her in his work *Owen Wingrave*. Baker has made many other notable appearances, for example in Mozart's *Così fan tutte*, Berlioz's *The Trojans*, and Strauss's *Der Rosenkavalier*. Her final operatic performances took place in 1982.

Janet Baker has performed and made recordings of numerous song cycles, including the songs of Schubert and those of Gabriel Fauré, as well as arias by a variety of early Italian composers.

She was honoured by her country with the title of DBE in 1976. In 1982 she retired and published her autobiography, *Full Circle*.

Baker, Josephine (1873–1945) *American physician and public-health worker*

Josephine Baker was born in New York City; in defiance of the wishes of her family, she trained to become a doctor, graduating from the New York Infirmary Medical College in 1898. She immediately secured a post in the city's Department of Health, where she set about combating the spread of disease among the poor immigrant families who had settled in the overcrowded and insanitary Lower East Side.

In 1908 Josephine Baker founded the Bureau of Child Hygiene in an attempt to stem New York's high infant mortality rate; her efforts succeeded in reducing the rate to the lowest of any American or European city. Among the measures she introduced were accredited midwives and free milk clinics. As well as advancing healthcare facilities, Baker was concerned to champion the causes of women's suffrage and education; she lobbied President Woodrow Wilson to extend voting to women and was instrumental in changing New York University's bar on accepting postgraduate women students.

Baker, Josephine (1906–1975) *American singer and dancer*

Baker lived most of her life in France, where she came to be regarded as the personification of the "Jazz Age" for her revue dancing.

She was born Freda Josephine McDonald to a black mother and Jewish father in the slums of St. Louis, Missouri. In 1923, aged only 17, she joined the chorus line of the all-black Broadway musical *Shuffle Along*.

After a brief period working in theatre and nightclub productions, in 1925 Baker took a leading dancing role in *La Revue Nègre*, an American show produced in Paris by Caroline Dudley. Within a short time she joined the Folies-Bergère, where she received star billing – and gained notoriety for a suggestive dance in which she wore a skirt of bananas. Although she was most famous for her "danse sauvage" (primitive dance), Baker was a multi-talented entertainer who became a blues singer of international repute. She also featured in films during the 1920s and 1930s.

Baker took French citizenship in 1937 and aided the French Resistance movement during World War II, for which she was rewarded after the war by being appointed to the Legion of Honour. In the 1950s she adopted 12 orphans of various racial origins – she called them her "Rainbow Tribe" – and lived with them at Les Milandes, her château in Bergerac, southwestern France. Baker died in 1975, in Paris, where she had just given two triumphant performances.

Balch, Emily Greene (1867–1961) *American pacifist and feminist*

Emily Balch was joint recipient of the Nobel Peace Prize in 1946 (with John R. Mott) for her lifetime's work in promoting peace in many areas.

Balch was born in Jamaica Plain, Massachusetts. After graduating as one of the first class of students at Bryn Mawr College, Pennsylvania, in 1889, she devoted herself to women's rights, helping to found the Denison House Settlement in Boston and the Women's Trade Union League. In 1890–91 her research on poverty in Paris led to the publication of her study *The Poor in France*. She helped draft the first minimum-wage bill put before a state legislature. In 1896 she joined the faculty of Wellesley College, Massachusetts, where she taught economics and political science, becoming departmental head in 1913.

During World War I Emily Balch and her fellow labour activist Jane ADDAMS formed a small group of pacifists that later became the Women's International League for Peace and Freedom. When she outspokenly opposed the entry of the United States into the war in 1917, she was dismissed from her professorship at Wellesley. In *Women at The Hague* (1915) and other books she wrote extensively about the peace movement; she also held important posts in several pacifist organizations, including acting as secretary of the Women's International League for Peace and Freedom at Geneva, Switzerland (1912–22). This organization later named her honorary international president.

Baldwin, Monica (c. 1896–1975)
British nun and writer

> Nearly 400 years ago my ancestor Thomas Baldwin of Diddlesbury leaped to freedom from behind the walls of the Tower of London...His name...can still be seen where he carved it on the wall of his cell.
> —*I Leap Over the Wall* (1950)

Monica Baldwin is known for her book *I Leap Over the Wall: Contrasts and Impressions after Twenty-Eight Years in a Convent* (1950), which describes her experiences of the outside world after spending many years as a nun.

A niece of the prime minister Stanley Baldwin, she entered a convent in 1914 and remained a nun until 1941. The book she wrote after leaving reflects on and compares life in a convent with that of wartime Britain. Its title was based on the Baldwin family motto, "Per Deum meum transilio murum" ("Through my God I leap over the wall"), which was itself taken from Psalm 18. The book is also of interest for the character sketch of Stanley Baldwin that it contains. Monica Baldwin wrote only two other books: *The Called and the Chosen*, about religious vocation, and *Goose over the Jungle*.

Ball, Lucille (1911–1989) *American actress and television producer*

> What could I do? I couldn't dance. I couldn't sing. I could *talk*.
> —Quoted by David Shipman (editor) in *Movie Talk* (1988)

Lucille Ball is best known for her starring role in the early television comedy *I Love Lucy*, one of the most popular television shows of all time.

Ball was born in Jamestown, New York. Her career in show business began with a bit part in Eddie Cantor's musical farce *Roman Scandals* (1933).

Although she continued to appear in films throughout the 1930s and 1940s, she achieved her greatest success in radio comedy.

While working on the movie *Too Many Girls* (1940), Ball met and married Desi Arnaz, a Cuban bandleader. Together they formed the TV production company Desilu Productions in 1950. Their first venture was *I Love Lucy*, starring themselves, which first went on air in 1951. The show and the production company enjoyed immediate success. Although the last episode of *I Love Lucy* was broadcast in 1957, the programme continued to be shown around the world for decades afterwards. After Ball and Arnaz divorced in 1960, she took full control of Desilu but later sold the company and started her own venture, Lucille Ball Productions.

Ball won four Emmys for her television work, which also included *The Lucy Show* (1962–68) and *Here's Lucy* (1968–74). She died in Los Angeles.

Bancroft, Anne (1931–) *American actress*

A highly respected actress, Anne Bancroft has worked in television, the cinema, and the theatre. Her most famous role was that of Mrs. Robinson in the 1967 film *The Graduate*.

Born Anna Maria Italiano in New York City, Bancroft began her acting career in television drama in the late 1940s. She made her Hollywood debut in 1952, but her early film appearances were unremarkable. While in Hollywood, she adopted her stage name.

In 1958 Bancroft had her first stage role in *Two for the Seesaw*, in which she portrayed a Jewish girl from the Bronx. This performance won her the Antoinette Perry (Tony) Award. She immediately followed this success with a second Tony (and the New York Drama Critics' Circle Award) for her role as Anne Sullivan MACY, teacher of Helen KELLER, in the play *The Miracle Worker*. Her reprise of the role on screen in 1962 won her the 1963 Academy Award for Best Actress. Bancroft's Broadway appearances include *Mother Courage* (1963), *The Devils* (1965), *Golda* (1977–78), and *Duet for*

One (1981). She won an Emmy for the 1970 television special *Annie: The Woman in the Life of Men*; other television performances include the title roles in the 1994 movies *Oldest Living Confederate Widow Tells All* and *The Mother*. In addition, she has made notable contributions to the films *The Pumpkin Eater* (1964), *The Slender Thread* (1965), *The Prisoner of Second Avenue* (1975), *The Turning Point* (1977), *The Elephant Man* (1980), *Garbo Talks* (1984), *Agnes of God* (1985), *'Night Mother* (1986), *84 Charing Cross Road* (1987), *Torch Song Trilogy* (1988), and *Point of No Return* (1993). Although she usually plays serious parts, Bancroft took comic roles in two films directed by her husband, Mel Brooks: *Silent Movie* (1976) and *To Be or Not To Be* (1983).

Bandaranaike, Sirimavo (Ratwatte Dias) (1916–) *Sri Lankan politician*

Sirimavo Bandaranaike made history in 1960 when she became the world's first woman prime minister.

She was born into an influential Sri Lankan family, many of whose members had been involved in politics. In 1940, in an arranged marriage, she wed the politician Solomon Bandaranaike, who was 17 years her senior. Her husband, as head of a socialist–nationalist coalition, was elected prime minister in 1951, but Mrs. Bandaranaike did not take a prominent political role herself at this time. However, when Solomon Bandaranaike was assassinated by a Buddhist extremist in 1959, she campaigned to succeed him and won the ensuing election (1960). Three years later her power was consolidated when her Sri Lanka Freedom Party (which had been founded by her husband) won an overall majority.

Her second term of office began in 1970, after she had spent five years in opposition. Her domestic policies of nationalization and social welfare proved popular with her Sinhalese compatriots, as did the creation of a Sri Lankan republic in 1972. Yet the attempt to make Sinhalese the island's official language – long a goal of her husband – alienated the Tamil minority population. Economic difficulties

and charges of corruption caused her downfall in 1977.

In 1980 Sirimavo Bandaranaike was convicted of abuse of power during her term as prime minister and debarred from office. However, she made a remarkable comeback from the political wilderness in August 1994, when she once again occupied the post of prime minister, left vacant by her daughter Chandrika KUMARATUNGE when she was elected president.

Bankhead, Tallulah Brockman (1903–1968) *American actress*

Bankhead's unique husky voice and extravagant style made her one of the most colourful personalities of stage, screen, and broadcasting.

Bankhead was born in Huntsville, Alabama. Her father, the politician William Brockman Bankhead, supported her theatrical ambitions, and she moved to New York while still in her teens. In the 1920s she became part of the "Algonquin set," a group of wits named after their meeting place, the Hotel Algonquin. This group included the critics Alexander Woolcott, Heywood Broun, and Dorothy PARKER.

Bankhead made her New York stage debut in *Squab Farm* (1918) and in the same year appeared in her first film. She rose to stardom after the celebrated London production of *The Dancers* in 1923. Her Broadway successes included Lillian HELLMAN's *The Little Foxes* (1939), Thornton Wilder's *The Skin of Our Teeth* (1942), and the 1956 revival of Tennessee Williams's *A Streetcar Named Desire*.

She appeared in several films, most notably Alfred Hitchcock's *Lifeboat* (1943). Her memoirs, *Tallulah: My Autobiography*, were published in 1952.

Bara, Theda (1890–1955) *American film actress*

The first star to be created and heavily promoted by a studio, Theda Bara was the most renowned "vamp" of silent films.

Bara was born Theodosia Goodman, the daughter of a Jewish tailor, in Cincinnati, Ohio. Her first screen role was as a sultry temptress in *A Fool There Was* (1915), a film based on

Rudyard Kipling's poem *The Vampire* (origin of the term "vamp"). Her studio's publicity campaign claimed she was the daughter of a French artist and an Arabian princess and that her name was an anagram of the phrase "Arab death." In fact, her first name was a shortened form of Theodosia, while Bara was a family name. She contributed to the myth of her exotic origins by living in decadent splendour in Hollywood. From 1915 until her retirement in 1920 Bara appeared in about 40 films, making one film a month at the height of her career. Her most famous performance was as Cleopatra in a film of the same name. She made her only stage appearance in *The Blue Flame* in 1920, retiring from show business shortly afterwards.

Barbauld, Anna Letitia (1743–1825)
British poet, essayist, and critic

Anna Letitia Aikin was born in Kibworth, Leicestershire, into a family of religious dissenters. In 1774 she married the nonconformist clergyman Rochemont Barbauld, an unstable man who would commit suicide in 1808. Her popular *Hymns in Prose for Children* (1781) was written for the pupils of the boarding school that she and her husband established in a Suffolk village. In 1802 the family moved to Stoke Newington (now part of London). Here she became a prominent member of radical London literary circles. Her most ambitious literary venture was to edit and annotate *British Novelists* (1810), a 50-volume set of English novels.

Her earliest poetry is contained in *Poems* (1773). Her most substantial verse work, *Eighteen Hundred and Eleven*, was a sombre poem that foretells the decline of Britain and the rise of America. She also wrote challenging essays on religious toleration and other radical causes. The volume *Miscellaneous Pieces of Prose* (written with her brother, John Aikin) contains two of her finest essays, "Inconsistency in our Expectations" and "On Romances." Admirers of her literary style included Samuel Johnson and William Wordsworth. Her collected works were published in two volumes in 1825.

Bardot, Brigitte (1934–) *French actress*

> I'm a woman who has undoubtedly made a success of her career but not of her life. The myth of Bardot is finished, but Brigitte is me.
>
> —Quoted on her 40th birthday in *TV Times*, October 20, 1983

Best known as a sex symbol of the late 1950s and 1960s, Brigitte Bardot retired from acting in 1973 to concentrate on championing animal welfare.

She was born Camille Javal, in Paris, the daughter of a prominent industrialist. At the age of seven she began to study dancing and at 13 she won an award from the Paris Conservatory. At 14 Bardot became a model in her mother's dress shop and two years later posed for the cover of the French fashion magazine *Elle* using her assumed name, abbreviated to "BB," or "Bébé." She was promptly talent-spotted by the film director Marc Allegret and was soon playing small roles in films such as *Le Trou Normand* (1952; *Crazy for Love*) and the U.S. production *Helen of Troy* (1956).

Bardot's international fame as a "sex kitten" arose from her starring role in her husband Roger Vadim's film *Et Dieu créa la femme* (1956; *And God Created Woman*); by portraying her as sexually uninhibited, this film provoked outrage in conservative circles. Later films include *Une Parisienne* (1957), *Babette s'en va-t-en guerre* (1959; *Babette Goes to War*), *Viva Maria!* (1965), and *Don Juan* (1973). During this period her personal life was in turmoil. Divorce from Vadim was followed by two further failed marriages.

Bardot subsequently repudiated her film career and devoted herself to charitable causes. She established the Foundation for the Prote ction of Distressed Animals in 1976. Now married to the extreme right-wing politician Bernard d'Ormale, she has caused much controversy in France with her anti-immigrant views. She published her memoirs in 1996.

Barnes, Djuna (Chappell) (1892–1982) *American writer*

Djuna Barnes was born in Cornwall-on-Hudson, New York State. After studying art, she embarked on a career in journalism, acting as a writer and illustrator on several New York magazines. Her literary endeavours also began at this time, with the publication of several one-act plays, poems, and stories, such as *Book of Repulsive Women* (1915) and *A Book* (1923).

Barnes's heyday was in the 1920s and 1930s. She lived in Paris for much of this period, where she encountered the avant-garde American writer Gertrude STEIN and the erotic novelist Anaïs NIN. Her *Ladies' Almanack* appeared anonymously in 1928; in this controversial work she parodied the style of 18th-century lesbian writers and socialites. Her most famous novel, *Nightwood* (1936), portrayed a nightmarish vision of horror and decadence in a cosmopolitan setting. One admirer of its highly crafted poetic language was T. S. Eliot. Despite its success she published little after the 1930s.

Barnes's other works include the novel *Ryder* (1928) and the verse tragedy *The Antiphon* (1958); a volume of *Selected Works* appeared in 1962.

Barnes, Dame Josephine (1921–)
British obstetrician and gynaecologist

Alice Josephine Mary Taylor Barnes was the first woman president of the British Medical Association (1979–80), having devoted her distinguished medical career to the promotion of women's medicine.

The daughter of a Methodist minister and a musician, she grew up in Oxford, where she studied physiology at the university. She completed her clinical training at University College Hospital, London, in 1937 and held a series of posts in obstetrics, gynaecology, and surgery at hospitals in London and Oxford. During World War II she delivered babies and performed operations during the bombing of London, and later ran an obstetrics "flying squad" from University College Hospital, an experience which convinced her that babies should be born in hospital. She became the head of the obstetric unit at this hospital (1947–52) and surgeon to the Marie Curie Hospital (1947–67). In 1942 she married another doctor, Sir Brian Warren, with whom she had a son and two daughters. The marriage was dissolved in 1964.

Barnes has served in several official medical positions, notably with the Royal Society of Medicine, the Royal College of Obstetrics and Gynaecology, and the National Association of Family Planning Doctors, in addition to being president of the BMA. She has also been appointed to many national and international committees, work that reflects her interest in infant mortality, cancer screening for women, and abortion. She has been labelled "pro-abortion," but believes that the decision as to when to terminate a pregnancy must be left with doctors. She has been awarded several honorary degrees and fellowships and was created a DBE in 1974.

Barnett, Dame Henrietta Octavia (Weston) (1851–1936) *British philanthropist and social reformer*

A Christian socialist, Henrietta Barnett worked in the poorest districts of London for over 30 years. She was a founder of Toynbee Hall, the first university settlement, and later took the lead in creating Hampstead Garden Suburb.

Henrietta Rowland was born in Clapham, London, the daughter of a wealthy businessman. As a young woman she developed both strong religious beliefs and a highly independent and assertive character. Moved by the squalor and poverty of mid-Victorian London, in 1871 she joined the housing reformer Octavia HILL at her project in Marylebone. While working there she met Samuel Barnett, a young curate with socialist views, whom she married in 1873.

That same year Samuel Barnett was appointed to a deprived parish in the East End of London. For the next 33 years Henrietta supported him in his often controversial attempts to improve the lives of his parishioners. In particular, she was actively involved in the founding of Toynbee Hall, a project that brought Oxford academics to lecture and work in the East End. Henrietta was also involved in various projects of her own, mainly involving the welfare of children. She was the manager of a local charity school, sat on a government education committee, and set up a fund to provide poor city children with holidays in the country. She was also a founder of Whitechapel Art Gallery.

In 1906 Samuel Barnett was appointed a canon of Westminster and the couple moved to the leafy suburb of Hampstead. The contrast between her new and her former surroundings inspired Henrietta with the idea of creating a model suburb in which decent housing, open spaces, and recreational amenities would be available to people of modest income. Under her guidance, Hampstead Garden Suburb began to take shape in the years after 1907. When completed the development featured special housing for the old and disabled, modern schools, and new churches of all major denominations. She herself founded The Henrietta Barnett School for Girls in 1911. This remains a prestigious selective voluntary-aided school in Hampstead Garden Suburb.

Henrietta Barnett was appointed CBE in 1917 and became a Dame of the British Empire in 1924. Her publications include *Practicable Socialism* (1885; with her husband).

Barney, Natalie (1876–1972) *American literary hostess and writer*

Natalie Barney was the daughter of Alice Pike Barney, a playwright, designer, and painter. She grew up in Washington, D.C., and Maine. When her mother went to Paris to study painting Natalie accompanied her. She was educated there by a French governess and then at boarding school at Fontainebleau, near Paris, where she became totally bilingual. She later toured Europe, where she studied the violin in Germany, but returned to Paris in 1898 attracted by its artistic activity and apparent moral freedom.

A noted society beauty, Barney became engaged to a string of eligible men. However, instead of marrying she made a frank declaration that she was a lesbian. The notoriety this brought her overshadowed her work as a writer, as she became the centre of a lesbian group whose affairs were widely publicized.

Barney is perhaps best remembered as the hostess of a salon in the Rue Jacob, Paris, which was frequented by Ezra Pound, T. S. Eliot, Jean Cocteau, COLETTE, Gertrude STEIN, and Djuna BARNES among others and became extremely influential. To encourage new women writers, she gave a prize in honour of Renée Vivien, a poet with whom she had had a tempestuous affair. She also established an Académie des Femmes in 1920.

Although much of her literary output, mostly written in French, remains in manuscript form, Barney published limited editions sporadically throughout her life. In recent years her work has attracted attention from feminist critics, most notably *The One Who is Legion, or AD's Afterlife* (1930), in which she examined Western ideas on femininity.

Barry, Elizabeth (1658–1713) *English actress*

Barry was the first celebrated actress of the English stage. Launched on her theatrical career by the patronage of the Earl of Rochester, her lover, she specialized in tragedy, frequently playing opposite the greatest actor of the age, Thomas Betterton. She appeared in more than 100 roles, including those of Monimia in Thomas Otway's *The Orphan* and Belvidera in his *Venice Preserv'd*; Otway fell in love with Barry and courted her unsuccessfully. Having retired from the stage in 1710, she died shortly afterwards, in London.

Barrymore, Ethel (1879–1959) *American actress*

Ethel Barrymore, a member of the famous Barrymore family of actors, was known as "the first lady of the American theatre."

Born in Philadelphia, she was the daughter of the British actor and playwright Maurice Barrymore and the actress Georgiana Drew; her brothers were the stage and screen actors Lionel and John Barrymore, whose caustic sense of humour she shared.

Ethel made her debut at the age of 15 with her uncle John Drew, the foremost actor of his time. In 1897–98 she had a great West End success with Sir Henry Irving in *The Bells*. She took her first Broadway starring role in 1900 in *Captain Jinks of the Horse Marines*. Her many other acclaimed stage performances included *Trelawney of the Wells* (1911), *The Second Mrs. Tanqueray* (1924), *Whiteoaks* (1938), and *The Corn is Green* (1942). A New York theatre was named after her in 1928.

Ethel also made over 30 films, her first being *The Nightingale* (1914). Although she was one of the early screen stars, between 1919 and 1944 she made only one film, *Rasputin and the Empress* (1933), in which she gave a remarkable performance as the Tsarina ALEXANDRA FYODOROVNA. This was the only film to feature all three Barrymores. In 1944 she received an Academy Award for Best Supporting Actress in *None but the Lonely Heart*, with Cary Grant, playing his dying mother. Her later roles were mostly small character parts. She published an autobiography, *Memories*, in 1956, and died three years later in Hollywood.

Bartoli, Cecilia (1966–) *Italian opera singer*

Cecilia Bartoli, who first came to prominence in her native country in 1986, has since achieved international fame as a rising operatic star.

Bartoli was born into a musical family in Rome; both her mother and her father were opera singers. After private voice tuition by her mother, Cecilia undertook formal musical training at the Academia Santa Cecilia in Rome. Her performance of an aria and a duet on a television programme showcasing musical talent was an instant success. She subsequently made a number of recordings, including Rossini's *The Barber of Seville*.

Her first performance in the United States was a song recital at the Lincoln Center in New York. This was followed by opera roles in Houston, Texas, in 1993 and her Metropolitan Opera debut in 1995.

Barton, Clara (1821–1912) *American humanitarian*

> It is...a wise benevolence that makes preparation in the hour of peace for assuaging the ills that are sure to accompany war.
> —*A Story of the Red Cross* (1904)

Clarissa Harlowe Barton is renowned as the founder of the American Red Cross. Born in North Oxford, Massachusetts, she was forced to give up her career as a schoolteacher because of a throat ailment; from 1854 to 1861 she worked as a clerk in the Patent Office in Washington, D.C. Following the outbreak of the American Civil War, she began independently to organize medical supplies and to nurse battlefield casualties. She quickly became known as the "Angel of the Battlefield," dividing her time between tending the wounded and cooking for them. Late in the war she was accredited as superintendent of nurses with the Army of the James.

When the war ended in 1865, Barton persuaded President Lincoln to allow her to gather information on missing Union soldiers. This resulted in the identification of thousands of war dead, particularly those who had fallen victim to the appalling conditions of the notorious Andersonville Prison in Georgia. At the same time, her public lectures on the war brought her national prominence; however, her exertions affected her health to such an extent that in 1869 she took a trip to Europe to recuperate.

While in Switzerland Barton learnt of the International Red Cross, established in 1864 by Jean Henri Dunant. Enrolling as a volunteer in this organization, within two years she was helping to organize relief for casualties of the Franco-Prussian War.

On her return to the United States in 1873 she settled in Washington as a lecturer. In 1877 the Red Cross invited her to organize an American branch, which was incorporated as the American Association of the Red Cross in 1881. In 1882 the United States became a signatory to the Geneva Convention of 1864, which established Red Cross principles in international law.

Barton was elected president of the American Red Cross.

Barton was instrumental in having relief for victims of major peacetime disasters added to the programme of the Red Cross; she personally led many aid expeditions into regions devastated by forest fires, floods, and hurricanes. At the age of 77 she was again active as a nurse and supply organizer during the Spanish-American War of 1898. By 1900 growing criticism of Barton's style of active personal leadership without delegation led the U.S. Congress to demand reforms, such as the production of an annual financial report. However, Barton remained as president until 1904.

Clara Barton won many honours and medals for her tireless work as a philanthropic pioneer. Her publications include *A Story of the Red Cross* (1904) and *Story of My Childhood* (1907).

Barton, Elizabeth (*c.* 1506–1534)
English mystic

Barton, or the "Maid of Kent," as she came to be called, gained fame and notoriety for her prophecies, supposedly uttered when she was in a trancelike state. She figured in a political and religious controversy during the reign of King Henry VIII.

Barton was born at Aldington in Kent, and took employment as a servant in Canterbury. Prone to hysterical fits, perhaps brought on by epilepsy, she claimed to have religious revelations and made prophecies, some of which came true. Her growing fame attracted the attention of the archbishop of Canterbury, who ordered an investigation. Meanwhile, Henry VIII delegated Thomas More to make inquiries. More regarded her utterances as nonsense, but Edward Bocking, Canterbury's investigator, used her to further his own political ends. On his suggestion Barton became a nun and began to offer increasingly political prophecies. She warned Henry VIII that if he divorced CATHERINE OF ARAGON to marry Anne BOLEYN, he would die within six months; when this marriage proceeded without mishap, she claimed that he would be shunned

by his subjects. Henry promptly had Barton arrested for treason and examined before the Star Chamber. Under interrogation she confessed that the trances had been feigned. She was condemned without trial and hanged. Bocking and four others also were executed.

Controversy still surrounds Elizabeth Barton. The validity of documents confirming her confession has been questioned. In the absence of trial records it is impossible to judge whether she was a conspirator, a visionary, or the victim of mental illness.

Bashkirtseff, Marie (1859–1884)
Russian painter and diarist

Bashkirtseff is best known for her autobiographical *Journal*, which presents a vivid psychological self-portrait of a young artist. Born Maria Konstantinovna Bashkirtseva, near Poltava, Ukraine, she travelled widely with her mother from an early age. In Italy she started training as a singer, but from 1877, after her voice failed, she studied painting in Paris, where she was a pupil of Joseph-Nicolas Robert-Fleury and Jules Bastien-Lepage. Adept at paintings showing everyday domestic life and pastel portraits, she exhibited with the Académie Julian between 1881 and 1884.

Bashkirtseff began her *Journal* on August 6, 1872, when she was 13 years old, and continued it until the time of her death. Like Jean Jacques Rousseau's *Confessions*, the work claimed to be an absolutely candid expression of personal experience. But the manuscript was severely cut by her mother before its publication in Paris. The diary was first translated into English in 1890. Her letters, consisting of her correspondence with the writer Guy de Maupassant, were published in 1891. She died of tuberculosis in Paris, at the early age of 24.

Bateman, Hester (1709–1794) *British silversmith*

Hester Bateman is now regarded as one of the finest silversmiths of the 18th century. Little is known about her early life. Born Hester Needham, she received no formal education. Her husband, John Bateman, worked in gold and silver, specializing in making watch chains. They had five children.

On the death of her husband in 1760 Hester took over his business with the assistance of two of her sons, John and Peter, and an apprentice, registering her hallmark, "H.B.," in 1761. She produced work for other silversmiths for some years, but eventually her shop became renowned for fine-quality household silver, particularly tea and coffee pots, cutlery, and other tableware, such as a fine silver cruet stand (now in the Victoria and Albert Museum). With its elegant, simple lines and decoration, it is the quality of this work, produced mainly in the 1780s, upon which Bateman's reputation rests, although she also produced presentation pieces and church silver. She retired in 1790 but her business, run by her son Peter and her widowed daughter-in-law Anne, continued to enjoy success for many years.

Batten, Jean (1909–1982) *New Zealand aviator*

Together with the U.S. aviator Amelia EARHART and the British flyer Amy JOHNSON, Jean Batten was a pioneering woman pilot renowned for her solo endurance flights made in the 1930s. Unlike them, however, she survived her adventures to reach old age.

Jean Batten was born at Rotorua, on the North Island of New Zealand. Enthralled by flight from an early age, she cherished a dream of making the solo journey by aeroplane from England to New Zealand. At the age of 20 she went to England, joined a flying club, and became a fully qualified pilot in three years.

After successfully seeking sponsorship, Batten flew solo from England to Australia in 1934, following two failed attempts. Her journey time of 13 days took 4 days off the previous record, set by Amy Johnson in 1930. In 1935 Batten became the first solo woman to complete the journey in the opposite direction. Her longstanding dream was realized shortly afterwards, when she flew from London to New Zealand, setting a record that remained unbroken for 44 years.

Batten's other notable flights included a crossing of the south Atlantic, from England to Brazil, in record time, and the fastest crossing of the Timor Sea.

Battle, Kathleen (1948–) *American opera singer*

A popular soprano, Battle is one of the most successful American opera stars to rise to prominence without first acquiring experience in Europe.

Kathleen Deanna Battle was born in Portsmouth, Ohio. Studying at the College-Conservatory of Music at the University of Cincinnati, she received bachelor's (1970) and master's (1971) degrees in music education. She taught music for a short time in an inner-city Cincinnati elementary school. However, she soon came to the attention of the conductor James Levine, who took her on as his protégée and presented her at concerts in Ohio. In October 1975 she was well received in a Broadway production of Scott Joplin's jazz opera *Treemonisha*.

After appearances at the New York City and San Francisco operas, Battle made her debut at the Metropolitan Opera in 1977 as the Young Shepherd in Wagner's *Tannhäuser*. At the "Met" and in Europe she progressed to playing leading roles in works by Mozart, Richard Strauss, Handel, and Rossini. From 1980 onwards she frequently performed at the Salzburg Festival.

Battle's bright and crisp vocal style proved effective in roles such as Pamina in Mozart's *The Magic Flute* and Adina in Donizetti's *L'Elisir d'amore* (with Luciano Pavarotti), both of which she recorded and filmed on video. In her prime in the 1980s, she excelled in her smooth rendering of melodic lines and displayed a pert comic presence in opera.

In concerts and recordings Battle has explored a diversity of musical forms, including spirituals, jazz, and popular music. André Previn's jazz-influenced *Honey and Rue*, setting poems by Toni MORRISON, was composed for Battle in 1991. She received four honorary doctorates and won Grammy Awards in 1987 and 1989. In February 1994 increasingly public rumours of temperamental behaviour backstage culminated in Battle's dismissal from the Metropolitan Opera during rehearsals for Donizetti's *La Fille du regiment*. Despite this setback Battle remained a very popular artist, continuing to perform in recitals, concerts, recordings, and on television.

Baum, Vicki (1888–1960) *Austrian-born American writer*

Baum was born in Vienna and studied at the Vienna Conservatory of Music and the Performing Arts. After an early unsuccessful marriage, she became harpist of an orchestra in Darmstadt, Germany, and in 1916 married Richard Lert, its conductor. From 1926 she worked as a magazine editor at the Ullstein publishing house, which published her first stories and novels.

When her highly successful play *Grand Hotel* opened in New York in 1931, she and her family emigrated to the United States. The play was subsequently made into a Hollywood film. In 1932 Baum moved to Los Angeles, where she worked on film scripts, becoming an American citizen in 1938. She died in Hollywood.

Vicki Baum was a prolific writer; her novels include *Shanghai* (1939), *Hotel Berlin* (1943), *Headless Angel* (1948), and *Theme for Ballet* (1958). All were written in German and translated into English.

Bausch, Pina (1940–) *German choreographer and director*

As director of the Wuppertal Dance Theater, Pina Bausch has become well known for her innovative and emotionally charged choreography.

Pina Bausch was born in the industrial town of Solingen, where her parents were proprietors of a restaurant patronized by local artists and musicians. After initial dance training at a local academy Bausch progressed to the performing arts school in the nearby city of Essen in 1955. Four years later she was awarded a scholarship to study at the world-famous Juilliard School of music and dance in New York. While in the United States she danced with the New American and Metropolitan Opera ballet companies.

In 1962 Bausch returned to Germany, where she renewed acquaintance with her former teacher Kurt Jooss, whose company she danced with and later began to choreograph for. In 1972 she staged Wagner's opera *Tannhäuser* for the Wuppertal Opera Company, an engagement that led to the establishment in 1973 of the Wuppertal Dance Theater under her direction. She proceeded to establish a reputation with her radical reworkings of classic plays and operas, such as Goethe's *Iphigenie* and Gluck's *Orfeo ed Euridice*. In 1975 she won great acclaim for her new choreography to Stravinsky's *The Rite of Spring*. Later works, such as *Bluebeard* (1977), *The Legend of Chastity* (1979), *Nelken* (1982), and *Nur Du* (1996; *Only You*) explore themes of isolation and emotional violence with disturbing power. She is recognized as one of the leading lights of contemporary dance.

Baylis, Lilian (1874–1937) *British theatre manager*

Lilian Baylis was born in London. After being trained as a musician, she appeared in London concerts as a child prodigy, toured England and South Africa as a violinist and music teacher, and returned to London in 1898 to take up the post of assistant manager (under her aunt, Emma Cons) of the Royal Victoria Theatre, a music and lecture hall for workers founded on the principle of temperance. After her aunt's death in 1912, she became manager of the theatre, which was popularly known as the "Old Vic," transforming it into a venue for opera and, only incidentally, drama.

After Shakespearean drama became established as the Old Vic's main repertoire between 1914 and 1923, Lilian Baylis purchased the derelict Sadler's Wells Theatre in London and by 1931 had turned it into a celebrated showcase for opera and ballet productions. She hired Ninette DE VALOIS, who developed the Sadler's Wells ballet company (later the Royal Ballet) into one of the world's leading dance ensembles. Baylis, who was renowned for her tireless promotion of all forms of theatrical entertainment, died in London.

Beach, Amy Marcy (1867–1944)
American pianist and composer

The leading woman composer of her
time, Beach was one of the first American composers to train almost exclusively in the United States. Born Amy
Marcy Cheney in Henniker, New
Hampshire, she studied piano with
Ernst Perabo and Carl Baermann,
making her professional debut in
Boston in 1883. The following year she
performed as a soloist with the Boston
Symphony Orchestra. She married Dr.
Henry H. A. Beach, a Boston surgeon,
in 1885.

After her marriage Beach withdrew
from the concert stage and devoted
herself to composing. In 1892 she was
commissioned to write a *Festival Jubi-
late* for the opening of the World's
Columbian Exposition in Chicago.
Her *Gaelic Symphony* (1893) was the
first symphony composed by an American woman to be performed in the
United States. Her other works include a mass in E flat (1892), a chorale
composed for the Omaha Exposition
of 1898, and an opera (*Cabildo*, 1932).

After her husband's death in 1910,
she returned to performing. She toured
Europe for four years (1911–14), playing her own compositions under the
professional name Mrs. H. H. A.
Beach. She died in New York.

Beach, Sylvia (Woodbridge) (1887–
1962) *American publisher*

Beach's reputation rests principally on
her publication, in France, of the first
edition of James Joyce's *Ulysses*.

She was born in Baltimore and educated in Switzerland, Germany, and
France. In 1907 she resolved to live in
France, where her father, a Presbyterian minister, was a pastor to American
students at the time. Between 1919 and
1941 she ran Shakespeare and Company in Paris, a combined bookshop,
lending library, and avant-garde publishing house.

A friend of many intellectuals and
writers, most notably James Joyce, she
accepted his novel *Ulysses* in 1922,
after its alleged pornographic passages
had led several other publishers to re-
ject it. The book was later acknowledged as a literary masterpiece and

published by major companies in the
United States, England, Germany, and
France. Copies of the original Shakespeare and Company edition became
highly valued as collectors' items. In
1941 the German occupying powers in
Paris closed the company down and
briefly interned Sylvia Beach. Her autobiography, *Shakespeare and Company*, was published in 1959. She died
in Paris.

Beale, Dorothea (1831–1906) *British
feminist and educational pioneer*

> Miss Buss and Miss Beale
> Cupid's darts do not feel.
> How different from us,
> Miss Beale and Miss Buss.
>
> —Anonymous

Dorothea Beale was born in London
and educated there at the newly
opened Queen's College for Ladies in
Harley Street, where she later became
teacher of mathematics and headmistress. In 1858 she was appointed
principal of the first private girls'
school in England, Cheltenham Ladies' College (founded in 1854). She
devoted her life to building up the college, adding a nursery school and reforming the curriculum. When she
became principal, the enrolment was
69; by 1912 it had risen to 1,000.

Miss Beale also promoted higher education for women. She helped to
found two teacher training colleges for
women – St. Hilda's College, Cheltenham (1885), and St. Hilda's, Oxford
(1892). In 1894 she succeeded her associate Frances Mary BUSS as president
of the Association of Headmistresses.
She wrote several reports on girls' education and was an active suffragist.
She died at Cheltenham.

Beale, Mary (1633–99) *English
painter*

A prolific portrait painter, Mary Beale
was England's first professional woman artist.

Mary Craddock was born in Suffolk,
the daughter of a Puritan minister. She
was educated at home and learned to
draw and paint from her father, a keen
amateur artist. At the age of 19 she
married Charles Beale, a landowner

and manufacturer with artistic interests, who encouraged her talent.

During the 1650s the couple lived in London and Mary seems to have received some training from the portraitist Robert Walker. She also met and was influenced by the leading English portrait painter of the day, Sir Peter Lely: indeed, a number of her best works were later mistakenly attributed to him. In the later 1650s Charles Beale acquired a post at the Patent Office and the couple moved into spacious official lodgings, where Mary was able to set up her first studio. By her 25th birthday she had already acquired a reputation as one of London's leading portraitists.

In about 1670 the fortunes of the Beale family altered when Charles lost his government post and Mary was obliged to become the breadwinner. Accordingly, she set up as a full-time portrait painter to London society and maintained a prodigious output throughout the 1670s. Her two sons assisted her in the studio, while her husband mixed her colours and dealt with administration: the detailed records he kept provide a valuable insight into the workings of a painter's studio at that time.

Although most critics have found Mary Beale's work rather pedestrian and derivative, a few have praised her handling of colour. Her sitters included prominent figures from the court, including King Charles II, writers and intellectuals such as the poets Cowley and Milton, and leading clergymen, including Archbishop Tillotson. Demand for her work seems to have fallen off considerably with the change of taste that followed Lely's death in 1680: at the same time this freed her to produce some of her more original work. Mary Beale's name remained well known for a century after her death but then fell into obscurity: her work was not rediscovered until the mid-1970s.

Beard, Mary Ritter (1876–1958)
American historian and social activist

Mary Ritter Beard is widely credited with establishing women's history as an academic discipline.

She was born Mary Ritter in Indianapolis, Indiana, the daughter of a schoolteacher mother and a lawyer father. She graduated from DePauw University in 1897 and married Charles Austin Beard in 1900. As keen proponents of women's and workers' rights, the couple moved to England, where Mary Beard became involved in the PANKHURSTS' militant suffragist activities, while Charles helped found a college for trade unionists – Ruskin Hall in Oxford. On their return to the United States in 1902, Mary Beard pursued graduate studies at Columbia University for two years. She then devoted herself to labour and suffragist movements and edited *The Woman Voter* from 1910 to 1912.

Beard's support for protective legislation for working women led her to oppose the suggested Equal Rights Amendment to the Constitution. Her attempts in the 1930s to establish a World Centre for Women's Archives ultimately failed. Mary Beard collaborated with her husband on several highly successful American history surveys and textbooks. Her work *On Understanding Women* (1931) and in particular *Woman as a Force in History* (1946) re-evaluated women's role in history, rejecting the view that women had always been dominated by men. After her husband's death Mary Beard moved to Arizona; she died in Phoenix.

Beatrice (1266–1290) *Italian noblewoman*

Beatrice is the fictional name given by the poet Dante Alighieri to the woman who inspired his genius; her real name was Bice Portinari (Dante chose "Beatrice" to signify her "beatitude," or blessed nature). Beatrice is the object of Dante's great love in his autobiographical work, *La vita nuova*, and in the "Paradiso" section of the *Divine Comedy* she acts as his guide through the spheres of heaven to a vision of God. Beatrice probably met Dante only once or twice, first when she was eight and he was nine years old. There is little doubt that she remained unaware of her significance for him.

Sometime before 1287 Bice Portinari

married Simone dei Bardi. She died in Florence at the early age of 24; Dante was stricken with grief at news of her death.

Beatrix (1938–) *Queen of the Netherlands*

Princess Beatrix Wilhelmina Armgard succeeded to the throne of the Netherlands on the abdication of her mother, Queen JULIANA, on April 30, 1980.

She was born at Soestdijk Palace in Baarn, near Amsterdam, the first child of Juliana and Prince Bernhard. During World War II she lived in exile with her parents in Britain and Canada. Returning to the Netherlands at the end of the war, she attended elementary and grammar schools, and went on to obtain a law degree at the University of Leiden in 1961.

Her marriage in 1966 to Claus-Georg von Amsberg, a German nobleman, provoked rioting in Amsterdam because of his service in the German army in World War II. (After being cleared of having Nazi sympathies by an Allied postwar court, he had taken Dutch citizenship.) They had three sons; the eldest, Willem-Alexander, became heir to the throne. Further rioting broke out on Beatrix's accession to the throne.

Beaufort, Lady Margaret (1443–1509) *English noblewoman*

Lady Margaret Beaufort, Countess of Richmond and Derby, is remembered principally as a patron of education, endowing colleges and professorships at Oxford and Cambridge.

The daughter of John Beaufort, 1st Duke of Somerset, and the great-granddaughter of John of Gaunt, fourth son of King Edward III , she was married three times. Her first husband was Edmund Tudor, Earl of Richmond. Their son Henry Tudor, Earl of Richmond, was born shortly before Margaret's fourteenth birthday, in the same year that his father died (1457). He later became King Henry VII of England, basing his claim to the English throne on his mother's descent from Edward III. Margaret's second and third husbands were Henry Stafford, son of the Duke of Buckingham, and Thomas Stanley,

Earl of Derby and a minister of Edward IV ; she had no more children.

A generous patron, Lady Margaret Beaufort founded Christ's College, Cambridge, and St. John's College, Cambridge, as well as endowing two divinity professorships. She also promoted the work of the early English printers William Caxton and Wynkyn de Worde.

Beauharnais, Hortense de (1783–1837) *French noblewoman*

Hortense de Beauharnais was the wife of Napoleon's brother Louis Bonaparte, becoming queen of Holland when Louis was given the Dutch throne. She was born in Paris, the daughter of the revolutionary general Alexandre de Beauharnais and of JOSÉPHINE, later the wife of Napoleon Bonaparte.

After Napoleon married Joséphine in 1796, Hortense became closely associated with the Bonaparte family, marrying Louis at Napoleon's request in 1802. The marriage was a deeply unhappy one and only endured because Napoleon wished it to appear stable. Hortense became queen of Holland in 1806 when Napoleon placed Louis on the Dutch throne. Louis relinquished the crown in 1810 after a dispute with Napoleon; in the same year the emperor finally allowed Louis and Hortense to separate.

Hortense bore Louis three sons; however, there is suspicion that a lover fathered the third, the future Emperor Napoleon III. In 1811 she had a fourth son, the future Duke of Morny, by the Count of Flahaut. Despite her separation, Hortense remained a loyal adherent to the Bonapartist cause, and her support of Napoleon after his return from exile on Elba in 1815 led to her banishment from France after his final defeat. After travelling in Germany and Italy, Hortense bought the château of Arenenberg in the Swiss canton of Thurgau, where she died.

Beauvoir, Simone de (1908–1986) *French writer, feminist, and philosopher*

> If you live long enough, you'll see that every victory turns into a defeat.
>
> —*All Men Are Mortal* (1955)

Simone de Beauvoir was one of the leaders of The post-war existentialist movement as well as a major exponent of women's rights.

Born into a middle-class Parisian family, she graduated from the Sorbonne in 1929 and taught philosophy at several women's colleges from 1931 to 1943, when she began her writing career. She had met the existentialist philosopher Jean-Paul Sartre at the Sorbonne, and they remained companions and professional associates until his death in 1980.

In the 1940s de Beauvoir and Sartre together formulated the principles of a modern existentialist philosophy; this theory stressed the importance of personal experience in a meaningless godless universe. In the absence of an absolute moral law people create their own moral values and are thus responsible for their own actions. Many of de Beauvoir's novels reflect this viewpoint, including *The Blood of Others* (1948), *All Men Are Mortal* (1955), and *The Woman Destroyed* (1968). Another, *The Mandarins* (1954), satirized some leading writers of her generation and pointed to the dilemmas facing contemporary intellectuals.

A long commitment to improving the status of women gave rise to her highly popular and controversial book *The Second Sex* (1949), which traces women's oppression by male-dominated society, firmly rejecting the idea that women's inferior social position is conditioned by any biological or psychological factors. This work has had a profound effect on later feminist writers. Another concern, the worsening condition of the elderly, is explored in *The Coming of Age* (1972), in which de Beauvoir severely criticizes Western society for neglecting the aged.

Notable among de Beauvoir's other writings are four volumes of autobiography: *Memoirs of a Dutiful Daughter* (1958), *The Prime of Life* (1962), *Force of Circumstance* (1965), and *All Said and Done* (1974).

Beaux, Cecilia (1863–1942) *American portrait painter*

Beaux's paintings were very highly re-garded by her contemporaries and have been compared with those of the celebrated portraitist John Singer Sargent.

Beaux was born in Philadelphia, where she studied painting techniques under William Sartain. She later studied in Paris at the Académie Julian and the Lazar School. Her most outstanding works were portraits of women and children, including *Mother and Daughter*, *A New England Woman*, *Girl with the Cat*, *Portrait of Mrs. Dupont*, and *Sita and Sarita*. Famous people who sat for portraits by Beaux included Theodore Roosevelt and President Georges Clemenceau of France. In 1926 she won the Gold Medal of the American Academy of Arts and Letters. Her many other awards included the Gold Medal of the Philadelphia Art Club, the National Academy of Design Dodge Prize, the Carnegie Institute gold and bronze medals, and the Temple Gold Medal of the Pennsylvania Academy of Fine Arts. Her paintings are exhibited at the Metropolitan Museum of Art, New York City; the Corcoran Gallery, Washington, D.C.; the Uffizi Gallery, Florence; and the Luxembourg Palace, Paris.

Her autobiography, *Background with Figures*, was published in 1930. She died at Gloucester, Massachusetts.

Beckett, Margaret (Mary) (1943–)
British Labour politician

Margaret Beckett has sat on Labour's front bench for over 13 years. During the party's long period of opposition she was Labour's deputy leader (1992–94) and acting leader (1994).

Margaret Jackson was born in Ashton-under-Lyne near Manchester, the daughter of a carpenter father and a teacher mother. She was educated at an independent school in Norwich and the Manchester College of Science and Technology, where she trained as an engineer. After several years working as a metallurgist, she entered politics as Labour MP for Lincoln in 1974. Although she rose quickly to become a junior minister in the Callaghan government, she lost her seat in the 1979 general election. That same year she married Leo Beckett.

During the early 1980s Margaret Beckett worked as a television researcher while remaining active in the politics of the Labour Party: at this time she was known as a supporter of the left-wing maverick Tony Benn. After her re-election to parliament in 1983 she became increasingly prominent as opposition spokesman on health and social security (1984–89) and shadow chief secretary to the treasury (1989–92). In 1992 she was a surprise winner in the election to Labour's deputy leadership; for the next two years she combined this role with that of shadow Leader of the House. Despite her left-wing background, she was by this time fully identified with the modernizing tendency within the party.

Following the sudden death from a heart attack of John Smith in May 1994, Beckett became acting leader of the Labour party for several months. However, she performed poorly in the ensuing elections, losing the leadership to Tony Blair and the deputy leadership to John Prescott. She subsequently became opposition spokesman for health (1994–95) and for trade and industry (1995–97). Following Labour's victory at the general election of 1997, she was appointed to her first cabinet post, that of President of the Board of Trade.

Beecher, Catharine Esther (1800–1878) *American educator*

Beecher, the elder sister of writer Harriet Beecher STOWE, devoted her life to improving educational opportunities for women.

She was born at East Hampton, Long Island, New York State, the eldest of 13 children of a Congregational pastor, Lyman Beecher. The family moved to Litchfield, Connecticut, in 1810. When her mother died, Catharine – aged only 16 – effectively became responsible for looking after the family. After the death of her fiancé in 1823, Miss Beecher – who never married – established a young ladies' school in Hartford, Connecticut. She opened a similar school in Cincinnati, Ohio, in 1832.

Returning east in 1837, she campaigned to improve women's education, particularly in more remote states, as the United States began to expand westward toward the Pacific. She founded many women's colleges at this time. Unlike her liberal brother Henry Ward, however, Catharine was strongly opposed to the women's suffrage movement. Miss Beecher died at Elmira, New York State.

Beeton, Isabella Mary (1837–1865) *British cookery writer*

> There is no more fruitful source of family discontent than a housewife's badly cooked dinners and untidy ways.
>
> —*Book of Household Management* (1861)

Isabella Beeton, whose life was cut short by illness, achieved lasting fame as the author of *Mrs. Beeton's Book of Household Management*, one of the most celebrated and frequently republished cookery books in English.

Mrs. Beeton was born Isabella Mayson in Cheapside, London. She was an only child but became part of a large family of stepbrothers and stepsisters when her mother remarried after her father's death. She spent a happy childhood during which she learned French and German, and married Sam Beeton, a London publisher, at the age of 19. Beeton's firm produced the first popular magazine for women – *The English-woman's Domestic Magazine* – and it was in this journal, from 1859 onwards, that the recipes and articles that formed the basis of Isabella's cookery book began to appear. They were finally collected together in book form in 1861. As well as its 3,000 recipes, and articles on food preparation and other areas of household management, Mrs. Beeton's cookery book contained helpful advice on legal and medical matters relating to the home.

Isabella and Sam Beeton set up their home in Pinner and travelled extensively, but the family was plagued by financial difficulties and personal tragedy (the first two children both died young). Mrs. Beeton herself died of puerperal fever at the age of 28.

Behn, Aphra (c.1640–1689) English writer

> She was involved in an insurrection of slaves, thus going one better than Harriet Beecher Stowe, who merely preached abolitionism.
> —Anthony Burgess, *The Observer*, December 30, 1980

Behn is renowned not only for being the first woman in England to earn a living as a professional writer but also for her colourful life, which included a spell as a clandestine government agent. Described by the British critic Sir Edmund Gosse as "the George SAND of the Renaissance," she was the author of many popular plays but is chiefly remembered for her exotic novel *Oroonoko*.

The date and place of Aphra Behn's birth remain the subject of speculation. Some authorities maintain that her father was James Johnson, a barber of Canterbury; others, that she was the daughter of John and Amy Amis of Wye, Kent. What is known beyond question, however, is that Aphra (also spelled Afra and Ayfara) went with relatives to what is now Suriname (formerly Dutch Guiana), then an English possession, in 1663; on her return to England in the following year, she married a London merchant named Behn. When her husband died in 1666, she was left destitute. She sought favour at the court of Charles II and became an English secret agent in Antwerp during the Second Dutch War (1665–67), adopting the code name Astraea, which later became her nickname in literary circles. She received no payment from the English government for her espionage activities and on her return to England was forced to serve a term in a debtors' prison. Around 1670 she wrote her first play, *The Forc'd Marriage*, which was staged in London in 1671 and won great popular acclaim. Thereafter she earned her living as a playwright and led a Bohemian existence. She died in London and was buried in Westminster Abbey.

Aphra Behn's 15 plays are as witty and ribald as those of any male writer of the Restoration period. The most successful of them were the comedies *The Rover* (in two parts, 1677–81); *The Roundheads* (1682); *The City Heiress* (1682), which was based on Thomas Middleton's *A Mad World, My Masters* (1608); and *Sir Patient Fancy* (1678), with a plot taken from Molière's *Le Malade imaginaire*. Behn's novel *Oroonoko, or the History of the Royal Slave* (1688), which tells of a slave revolt in Suriname led by an African prince, influenced the development of prose fiction in England and anticipates the work of Daniel Defoe. She also wrote a volume of poetry, *Love Letters to a Gentleman*, published in 1696, after her death. Although she was accused during her lifetime of lewdness and depravity, later critics have acclaimed her as a pioneering woman writer.

Belgioioso, Cristina, Princess of (1808–1871) Italian patriot and writer

Princess Cristina was born into the distinguished Trivulzio family of Milan. She was married to the prince of Belgioioso d'Este at the age of 16. During the Austrian occupation of Milan in 1830 she moved to Paris, where she established a salon frequented by leading contemporary writers and musicians. Her writings, which promoted the cause of Italian liberation, include *Histoire de la maison de Savoie* (1860; History of the House of Savoy) and *Réflexions sur l'état actuel de l'Italie et sur son avenir* (1869; Reflections on the Current State of Italy and on its Future). When liberal–nationalist rebellions swept Europe in 1848, she returned to Italy and equipped several hundred volunteers for Charles Albert of Sardinia in his vain struggle against Austrian domination. Exiled again when conservative forces prevailed in 1849, she subsequently returned to Italy and founded the political journal *L'Italie* in Milan, where she later died.

Bell, Gertrude (Margaret Lowthian) (1868–1926) British traveller, archaeologist, and diplomat

Born in the county of Durham, Bell was educated at Queen's College for Ladies in London and then at Lady Margaret Hall, Oxford. When she graduated in 1888, she embarked on a series of travels that included a voyage around the world and several record-breaking mountain climbs in the Alps. Her fascination with the Middle East determined the course of her life; her interest in this area of the world was further stimulated by having relatives in the diplomatic service in Tehran. She taught herself Persian and later Arabic. Her courage was demonstrated on extensive Middle Eastern travels, some of which are recorded in *Safar Nameh* (1894; reprinted as *Persian Pictures*, 1928) and *Amurath to Amurath* (1911). Her account of Syria, *The Desert and the Sown* (1907), is considered one of the finest works in its field. On the subject of archaeology she produced *The Thousand and One Churches* (1909), a book on Byzantine architecture written in collaboration with W. M. Ramsay; and *The Palace and Mosque of Ukhaidir* (1914).

During World War I Bell first joined the Red Cross, specializing in tracing missing combatants, and then offered her services to the British government. She was assigned in 1915 to the Arab Intelligence Bureau in Cairo, where her extensive knowledge of Middle Eastern geography, languages, and personalities was of great value. She was especially useful in liaison work between Arab leaders and the British, which was intended to mobilize Arabs against the Ottoman empire. In 1917 she went to Baghdad as adviser to the British civil administrator of the Mesopotamian region (Iraq) and retained that position after the war. Like her friend T. E. Lawrence ("Lawrence of Arabia"), she believed passionately in political independence for the Arabs: she was influential in establishing the modern state of Iraq and in placing Faisal I on the throne as the state's first ruler in 1921. Bell then devoted herself to founding and directing the national archaeological museum in Baghdad, where she died.

Bell, Marie (1900–1985) *French actress and theatre manager*

Born Marie de Bellon, in Bordeaux, Bell studied at the drama conservatories of Bordeaux and Paris, winning a first prize for acting talent in Paris. In 1921 Bell joined the Comédie Française in Paris and played many of the young heroines of the French classic repertoire. Her most notable successes were in Molière's *Le Misanthrope*, Racine's *Phèdre* and *Bérénice*, Henri Becque's *Les Corbeaux* (*The Vultures*), Rostand's *Cyrano de Bergerac*, and Hugo's *Ruy Blas*. One of her most famous performances was in Claudel's *Le Soulier de satin* (*The Satin Slipper*) in 1943. Bell left the Comédie Française to form her own company, Compagnie de Marie Bell, in 1953. In 1955, as a guest with Jean-Louis Barrault's company, she was hailed for her magisterial Clytemnestra in the *Oresteia*. With her own company she performed in Jean Genet's *Le Balcon* (1960; *The Balcony*) and other contemporary plays.

Bell also acted in over 30 films, including the classics *Le Grand Jeu* (1934) and *Un Carnet de bal* (1937).

Bell, Vanessa (1879–1961) *British artist*

Vanessa Bell was born into an aristocratic family in London; her father was the critic and biographer Sir Leslie Stephen, and her younger sister was the writer Virginia WOOLF. Their mother died early, and on the death of their father in 1904, Vanessa, Virginia, and their two brothers set up home together at 46 Gordon Square, Bloomsbury. This address became a meeting place for fashionable artistic and intellectual circles; collectively the extended circle came to be known as the "Bloomsbury Group."

Vanessa was a central figure in this group. She had studied under the impressionist society painter John Singer Sargent at the Royal Academy from 1901 to 1904, but her style gradually changed from impressionism to abstraction under the influence of fellow painters and the art historian Clive Bell, whom she married in 1907 and by whom she had two sons. In her abstract period Vanessa Bell's paintings were characterized by clear simplified shapes – in this she was undoubtedly influenced by Henri Matisse. From 1913 to 1919 she worked with the art historian Roger Fry in his Omega Workshops, designing textiles, ceramics, and book illustrations (including the covers for her sister's novels).

From 1916 Bell lived apart from her husband, setting up a home in Sussex with the painter Duncan Grant, by whom she had a daughter. During the 1920s and 1930s Bell returned to figurative art. At this time her personal life was struck by tragedy; Fry, a devoted admirer, died in 1934, her son died fighting in the Spanish Civil War in 1937, and Virginia Woolf committed suicide by drowning in 1941.

Bell Burnell, (Susan) Jocelyn
(1943–   ) *British astronomer*

With her supervisor, Antony Hewish, Bell Burnell discovered the first pulsar, a type of small dense star that emits regular pulses of radiation.

Born in Belfast, the daughter of the architect who designed the Armagh planetarium, Jocelyn Bell developed an early interest in radioastronomy. She was advised by Professor Bernard Lovell, the noted radioastronomer, to study physics first and consequently found herself the only woman in a class of 50 physics students at Glasgow University. After graduating from Glasgow she moved to Cambridge, where she completed her PhD in 1968.

As part of her duties she visited the Mullard Radio Astronomy Laboratory each day; here the sky was scanned every four days by the large radio telescope, and with little computer power available at that time, the data had to be analysed by hand. One day she identified a strange signal. As it meant nothing to her, Bell simply put a question mark next to it. When she noticed it again, she drew it to the attention of Antony Hewish. But nothing more was seen for a month. Perhaps, Hewish suggested, it had been a one-time event, a flare that had been and gone.

But after a month it reappeared. On examination Bell found the signals were equally spaced out at intervals of about 1.3 seconds. It was soon established that the signal was coming from a source lying outside the solar system. Bell discovered a second signal coming

from a different part of the sky in December and a third and fourth the following month. Hewish made the discovery public in 1968. The name "pulsar" was soon coined for the source; shortly afterwards Thomas Gold proposed that the signals were emitted by a small and rapidly rotating neutron star. In an earlier age the first pulsar would have been known as "Bell's Star"; today it carries the number CP 1919. Bell's work helped Hewish to gain the 1974 Nobel Prize for physics.

In 1968 Bell married Martin Burnell (from whom she separated in 1989) and was appointed to a research fellowship at the University of Southampton, where she worked on gamma rays. In 1973 she moved to the Mullard Space Science Laboratory in London to work on x-ray astronomy. Bell moved again in 1982 to head the James Clerk Maxwell Telescope project at the Royal Observatory, Edinburgh. In 1991 she was appointed professor of physics at the Open University, Milton Keynes.

Benedict, Ruth (Fulton) (1887–1948)
American anthropologist

Mrs. Benedict's work was influential in discrediting theories of racial supremacy that were prevalent in the 1930s.

Ruth Fulton was born in New York City. Graduating from Vassar College in 1909, she moved to California to teach in girls' schools. After her marriage to the biochemist Stanley Benedict in 1914 she returned to New York, where she studied and later taught anthropology at Columbia University, eventually becoming a professor of anthropology there. Benedict's studies of primitive societies provided powerful evidence in favour of the doctrine of cultural relativity, which holds that every human culture, primitive or advanced, has its own very distinctive set of values. Accordingly, norms of behaviour in so-called "civilized" societies cannot be imposed on other cultures. In her most important work, *Patterns of Culture* (1934), Benedict analysed the basic structure and character of three primitive societies: the

Zuñi Indians of New Mexico – peaceful, traditional, and co-operative; the Dobuans of New Guinea – hostile, treacherous, and paranoid; and the Kwakiutl Indians of Vancouver and British Columbia – competitive and status-seeking. She noted that the specific traits of each of the three primitive societies were repeated in varying degrees among so-called advanced cultures.

Mrs. Benedict's other works include *Zuñi Mythology* (1935), *Race: Science and Politics* (1940), and *The Chrysanthemum and the Sword: Patterns of Japanese Culture* (1946). She died in New York City.

Benetton, Giuliana (1937–) *Italian fashion designer*

Together with her three brothers, Giuliana Benetton founded a company that has expanded to become the world's largest knitwear manufacturer.

Giuliana was born and raised in Treviso, northern Italy. Her father, a lorry-driver, died when she was eight, leaving her family so poor that she had to begin work at the age of 13 – as a skein winder in a knitting workshop. Later she produced her own brightly coloured sweaters on a home knitting machine. Her brother Luciano sold her sweaters to local stores, enabling her to start her own business, in 1955, with a collection of 18 pieces. By 1960 Benetton was able to employ a team of young women and to sell wholesale.

The first Benetton factory opened in Treviso in 1965; four years later the first Benetton store opened in nearby Belluno. Giuliana and her three brothers expanded the business throughout Italy in the 1970s, before taking on the rest of Europe and the world. By the mid 1990s there were some 7,000 Benetton stores in over 100 countries. The Benetton name, assisted by unusual and sometimes controversial advertising, is now an instantly recognized trademark throughout the world.

Bentley, Phyllis (1894–1977) *British novelist*

Bentley was born in Halifax, Yorkshire – the setting for her best-known works. Educated at the University of London, she taught in a boys' grammar school during World War I and later worked as a librarian before devoting her time to writing. Her first novel was *Environment*, a semi-autobiographical work published in 1922.

Phyllis Bentley's fiction is traditional in both form and content. Her best-known novels are family sagas set in her native Yorkshire. These include *Cat-in-the-Manger* (1923), *Carr* (1929), *Inheritance* (1932), *A Modern Tragedy* (1934), *Sleep in Peace* (1938), *The Rise of Henry Mor car* (1946), and *A Man of His Time* (1966). She also wrote historical fiction, such as *Freedom Farewell!* (1936), which charts the decline of republican ideals in ancient Rome.

Bentley lectured on literary topics in England and America and wrote several literary studies. Her particular interest lay in her fellow Yorkshire writers, the BRONTË sisters, about whom she wrote and lectured widely. Her autobiography, *O Dreams, O Destinations*, was published in 1962.

Berengaria (died 1231) *Wife of King Richard I of England*

The daughter of King Sancho VI of Navarre, Berengaria married Richard on May 12, 1191, at Limassol, Cyprus, during the Third Crusade. She accompanied the king to Acre, Palestine, where she stayed while he fought the Saracens for control of Jerusalem. From 1192 to 1194, while Richard was imprisoned in Germany, she lived in Poitou, France. This separation effectively ended their marriage; she became estranged from Richard soon after his release. In 1230 she founded a Cistercian monastery called Pietas Dei at Espau, near Le Mans, France. She died soon afterwards and was buried there.

Berenice (born 28 AD) *Judean princess*

Berenice, or Bernice, was the eldest daughter of Herod Agrippa I, king of Judea. Her first marriage was to Marcus, son of Alexander, head magistrate of the Jews in Alexandria. She later married her uncle, Herod of Chalcis. After his death in 48 she lived with her brother, Herod Agrippa II. This allegedly incestuous relationship led her to marry Polemon II, king of Olba in Cilicia, in order to quell rumours; however, she soon deserted Polemon and returned to her brother. She was with Agrippa at Caesarea when St. Paul was taken before the king for a hearing (Acts 25:13 to 26:32). Unable to suppress the Jewish revolt of 66, she and her brother were forced to flee to the Romans.

Titus, son of the Roman emperor Vespasian, took Berenice as his mistress during his stay in Judea. She followed him to Rome, but popular opinion forced him to send her away. She tried unsuccessfully to renew their relationship when Titus became emperor in 79, and she died sometime later. The French playwright Racine made the love between Titus and Berenice the subject of his tragedy *Bérénice* (1670).

Berenice I (*c*. 340–281 BC) *Third wife of King Ptolemy I of Egypt*
Berenice was a granddaughter of Cassander, King of Macedon. Her first husband was Philippus, a Macedonian officer in the service of Alexander the Great; their son, Magas, became king of Cyrene (in modern Libya). After the death of Philippus Berenice travelled to Egypt as part of the retinue of her aunt Eurydice, who became the second wife of King Ptolemy I. Berenice became the mistress of Ptolemy I and succeeded Eurydice as his wife in about 317 BC; Ptolemy made Berenice queen of Egypt in 290 BC. She was the mother of Ptolemy II and the formidable ARSINOË II.

Berenice II (*c*. 273–221 BC) *Wife of King Ptolemy III of Egypt*
Berenice II was the daughter of King Magas of Cyrene (in modern Libya); she married King Ptolemy III, thereby uniting Cyrene and Egypt. When her husband went to fight in Syria, she cut off her beautiful hair and dedicated it to Venus so that he might return safely. When the hair disappeared from the temple, the astronomer Conon of Samos declared that the gods had taken it up to the heavens as a constellation. From this legend arose the name of the northern constellation, Coma Berenices. Following her

husband's death, Berenice II became coruler of Egypt with her son, Ptolemy IV, who had Berenice put to death in 221 BC.

Berg, Patty (1918–) *American golfer*
Patty (Patricia Jane) Berg is one of the most successful women golfers of all time. In over 30 years of competition she won 83 tournaments (40 of them as an amateur) and held nearly every women's championship.

She was born in Minneapolis, Minnesota, and won her first golf title (the Minneapolis City championship) at the age of 16. A surprise runner-up in the women's national amateur matches in 1935 and 1937, she won the title in 1938 while a student at the University of Minnesota. She joined the national Curtis Cup squads in 1936 and 1938.

Patty Berg turned professional in 1940. After serving in the Marine Corps Women's Reserve during World War II, she won the first U.S. Women's Open in 1946. She won the Titleholders Tournament played in Augusta, Georgia and the Western Open seven times each and was awarded the Vare Trophy for the lowest average score on three occasions. The only honour to elude her was the Ladies' Professional Golfers' Association (LPGA) title, for which she was twice runner-up. She is a member of the LPGA Hall of Fame and those of the Professional Golfers' Association (PGA) and the International Women's Sports.

Berganza, Teresa (1935–) *Spanish opera singer*
Berganza has won especial praise for her portrayal of heroines in Rossini operas.

Born in Madrid, she studied piano and voice at the Madrid Conservatory, where she was awarded first prize for singing in 1954. She made her debut in Madrid in 1955 and performed in her first opera (as Dorabella, in Mozart's *Cosi fan tutte*) at the Aix-en-Provence Festival two years later. She first sang in England at Glyndebourne in 1958, making her U.S. debut the same year. In 1960 she played Rosina in Rossini's *The Barber of Seville* in her first performance at the Royal Opera House, Covent Garden, and in 1967 made her Metropolitan Opera debut as Cherubino in Mozart's *The Marriage of Figaro*. She subsequently appeared in most of the world's leading opera houses, being particularly renowned for the roles of Rosina and Cherubino.

Also an accomplished recitalist, Berganza made her Carnegie Hall debut in 1964. Her concert repertoire includes Spanish, French, German, and Russian songs. She has been admired for her expressive performance style, which combines technical virtuosity and musical intelligence with a beguiling stage presence.

Bergen, Candice (1946–) *American actress*

Daughter of the ventriloquist Edgar Bergen, Candice Bergen was born in Beverly Hills, California. She was briefly a model and attended the University of Pennsylvania before embarking on an acting career.

She made her screen debut in Sidney Lumet's *The Group* (1960), an adaptation of a Mary MCCARTHY novel, in which she played the lesbian Lakey Eastlake. This film made her an instant star; she subsequently appeared opposite Steve McQueen in the Chinese civil war epic *The Sand Pebbles* (1966) and as a fashion model in *Live for Life* (1967), with Yves Montand. In 1971 she starred with Jack Nicholson and Art Garfunkel in Mike Nichols's *Carnal Knowledge* (1971), an acerbically funny examination of the 1960s sexual "liberation."

Unfortunately, Bergen's talent for portraying determined, worldly-wise characters was ill-served by a series of poor films produced during the 1970s, including comedies, westerns, and melodramas, all of which failed both critically and at the box office. Her career did not revive until 1979, when she played a singer in Alan J. Pakula's *Starting Over* (1979) and was nominated for an Oscar as Best Supporting Actress. She was nominated for the same award in George Cukor's *Rich and Famous* (1981), in which she supported Jacqueline Bisset.

Following her marriage to the film director Louis Malle in 1980, Bergen's only significant film role has been that of the photojournalist Margaret BOURKE-WHITE in *Gandhi* (1982). Her portrayal of this character met with a mixed reception, and her career seemed to be over. However, in 1988 she was given the title role in the TV series *Murphy Brown*, portraying a witty, outspoken single mother. Murphy Brown became part of the political debate in the United States on the issue of single motherhood, and Bergen has won two Emmy Awards, in 1989 and in 1996, for the series.

Bergman, Ingrid (1915–1982) *Swedish actress*

> Keep it simple. Make a blank face and the music and the story will fill it in.
>
> —On the art of acting. *Time*, May 2, 1983

Bergman is best known for her performances in Hollywood films of the 1940s and 1950s – most famously *Casablanca* (1942), in which she starred opposite Humphrey Bogart.

Bergman was born in Stockholm. After attending the High School for Girls, she studied at the Royal Dramatic Theatre School in Stockholm in 1933–34. Her film career began with a small part in the Swedish film *The Count from the Monk's Bridge* in 1934. She quickly became a star in her native country. After she played the leading role in *Intermezzo* (1937), the American producer David O. Selznick signed her for a Hollywood version of the film, which was released in 1939. In the years following she starred in such Hollywood classics as *Casablanca* (1942); *Gaslight* (1944), for which she won an Academy Award; and *Spellbound* (1945).

In 1949, while working in Italy on the film *Stromboli*, she fell in love with its director, Roberto Rossellini. The following year she divorced her first husband, Dr. Peter Lindström, having already had a child by Rossellini. Her actions caused a furore in the United States; the scandal led to her condemnation in the U.S. Senate and her absence from Hollywood films for several years. Under Rossellini's direction she made a series of not-too-successful films in the early 1950s; their marriage was annulled in 1958. Bergman resumed her Hollywood career in 1957 with *Anastasia*, for which she won a second Academy Award and a New York Film Critics Award. Other films included *Inn of the Sixth Happiness* (1958), *Goodbye Again* (1961), *The Yellow Rolls-Royce* (1965), and *Murder on the Orient Express* (1974), for which she won an Academy Award as Best Supporting Actress.

Ingrid Bergman was also an accomplished stage actress, appearing in several theatrical successes in the United States: *Liliom* (1940), *Anna Christie* (1941), and *Joan of Lorraine* (1946). She died of cancer in London on her 67th birthday.

Beriosova, Svetlana (1932–)
Lithuanian-born British ballet dancer

Svetlana Beriosova was born in Biržai in Lithuania. In her youth she was trained by her father, a ballet dancer with the state company. The family emigrated to the United States, where Svetlana's ballet training continued. In 1947 she was engaged to dance by the Grand Ballet de Monte Carlo. However, guest appearances in London with the Metropolitan Ballet in the late 1940s led to her taking up residence in England and joining the Sadler's Wells Ballet Company in 1952. She was appointed its prima ballerina in 1955.

Beriosova was equally at home in both classical and modern ballet, appearing in the classics *Swan Lake*, *Giselle*, and *Cinderella*, as well as in George Balanchine's *Firebird* and Frederick Ashton's *Ondine*. Her dancing was famous for both technical brilliance and emotion, while her acting ability also drew praise. In 1975 she gave up dancing in order to concentrate on teaching.

Bernadette of Lourdes, Saint
(1844–1879) *French visionary*

St. Bernadette is the popular name given to St. Marie Bernarde, a French girl whose visions led to the founding of the world-famous shrine at Lourdes, France.

Born in Lourdes, Bernadette was the eldest of six children of François and Louise Soubirous. Her father, a poor miller, could afford little education for her. She suffered from asthma but had a happy childhood. On February 11, 1858, while gathering firewood near the rock of Massabielle, a cave on the River Gave, Bernadette had the first of a series of 18 visions in which a beautiful lady dressed in white and carrying a rosary appeared to her. On February 25 the lady instructed Bernadette to "drink and wash in the spring." Up to this time only a trickle of water flowed from the rock; afterwards the spring produced a steady flow of water. The local clergy, at first sceptical, were now convinced that these visions were genuine.

The lady, who subsequently identified herself to Bernadette as the Virgin Mary with the words "I am the Immaculate Conception," asked that a chapel be built on the site. Satisfied that Bernadette's visions were valid, the Roman Catholic Church authorized a basilica to be built. However, by the time it was consecrated in 1876, Bernadette had long since become a nun at the Convent of Notre-Dame at Nevers. She had sought only obscurity from the day of the lady's final appearance, July 16, 1858. Bernadette always regarded herself simply as a means by which Mary revealed herself to humanity. She once compared herself to a broom: "Our Lady used me. They have put me back in my corner. I am happy there." After serving as a nurse during the Franco-Prussian War of 1870–71, she died of tuberculosis at the convent of Nevers.

A larger church, dedicated to the Holy Rosary, was built at Lourdes in 1901 to cater for the many pilgrims who now arrived seeking cures from the waters of the spring. In 1907 Pope Pius X created the feast of the Appearances of Lourdes, which is celebrated on February 11. Bernadette was beatified in 1925 and canonized in 1933 as St. Marie Bernarde. Her feast day is April 16.

Bernauer, Agnes (died 1435) *German beauty*

The daughter of a commoner, reputedly a baker in Augsburg, Bavaria, Agnes Bernauer was secretly married to Duke Albert of Bavaria. This union, however, directly flouted the plans of the duke's father, who wished his son to marry Anne, daughter of the Duke of Brunswick. When Albert's marriage to Agnes became known, his father had her arrested and tried for witchcraft. Found guilty before a special tribunal, she was drowned on October 12, 1435, by being thrown into the Danube with her hands tied. In revenge Albert led an armed revolt against his father; however, the emperor Sigismund finally reconciled them.

The story of Agnes Bernauer was a favourite theme of German writers, the most notable dramatization being *Agnes Bernauer* (1855) by Friedrich Hebbel.

Bernhardt, Sarah (1844–1923) *French actress and theatre manager*

> For the theatre one needs long arms; it is better to have them too long than too short. An *artiste* with short arms can never, never make a fine gesture.
>
> —*Memories of My Life*

Sarah Bernhardt was one of the most renowned stage actresses of all time; she was celebrated in her own lifetime as "the Divine Sarah." Her flamboyant style, striking clear voice, and powerful emotional delivery suited her especially to tragic roles.

Bernhardt was born Henriette Rosine Bernard in Paris. Her mother was a Dutch Jew; little is known of her father, except that he took her from her maternal grandparents in Amsterdam when she was a girl, had her baptized as a Roman Catholic, and enrolled her in a French convent school. From 1858 to 1860 she studied at the Paris Conservatoire, and in 1862 made her debut at the Comédie Française, in the title role of Racine's *Iphigénie en Aulide* (Iphigenia at Aulis). Neither this nor her other early roles met with particular success.

In 1864 Bernhardt had an illegitimate son, Maurice, by Henri, prince de Ligne, whom she left soon after the birth. In 1866, after a much-publicized

fight with a fellow actress, Bernhardt was dismissed from the Comédie. Unemployed for some time, she was finally taken on by the prestigious Odéon, where she enjoyed her first popular success in the play *Kean*, a dramatic version of the life of the actor Edmund Kean, by Alexandre Dumas the Elder. Her performance in François Coppée's *Le Passant* (1869; The Passerby) was highly praised by theatre critics. In 1873, returning to the Comédie, she had another huge success, in Racine's *Phèdre*. Her performance in *Hernani*, by Victor Hugo, also won widespread acclaim. However, frustration at the restrictions at the Comédie led her to resign in 1879 – after her success with the company in London assured her future independence. While in London, she formed a long-lasting rivalry with another fine tragedienne, Eleanora DUSE.

She was invited to perform in the United States by Edward Jarrett, an American impresario. Although she had never played the role of Marguerite in the younger Dumas's *La Dame aux camélias*, she chose it for her American debut in 1880. It was an immediate sensation and she continued playing it until 1914.

In 1882 Bernhardt had a popular hit in Victorien Sardou's romantic play *Fédora*, the first of several highly successful melodramas that he wrote specifically for her. In the same year she married Jacques Damala, a Greek actor, but the marriage lasted only one year. Despite her physical beauty and the popular interest that her love life attracted, this was to be her only marriage.

In 1893 Bernhardt acquired a theatre of her own in Paris, the Théâtre de la Renaissance, which she ran for six years as actress-manager. Although this theatre was extremely popular, in 1899 she built her own Théâtre Sarah Bernhardt in Paris, which she owned and operated for the rest of her life. In its opening season she gave the first of her famous portrayals of Hamlet. The following year she took the role of Roxanne in Rostand's *Cyrano de Bergerac*, and in 1902 she played the title roles in Gabriele d'Annunzio's *Fran-*

cesca da Rimini and in a sensational stage adaptation of Alphonse Daudet's novel *Sapho*. In addition, she continued to play roles from the French classical repertoire.

In 1905 Bernhardt suffered a knee injury that left her lame for the rest of her life. Although her leg was amputated in 1914, she continued acting, taking seated parts until the year before her death, when she had her final success – as a young man in Louis Verneuil's *Daniel*. In 1914 she was made a Chevalier of the Legion of Honour, France's highest award. She died in Paris. Such was the extent of public adulation for Sarah Bernhardt that crowds massed at her magnificent funeral, and millions, either in person or by telegram and letter, mourned her passing.

As well as being a great actress, Bernhardt was an accomplished sculptor and a writer. Her writing talents were devoted mostly to autobiographical sketches and to "guiding" (and sometimes sharply revising) the work of playwrights who created roles especially for her. She was also adept at managing her own publicity. Her several love affairs excited and scandalized her public. However, in spite of both professional and personal shortcomings, she is still generally regarded as France's greatest actress.

Berry, Duchesse de (1798–1870) *French noblewoman*

The wife of Charles Ferdinand de Bourbon, Duc de Berry, whose father was King Charles X of France, the Duchesse de Berry was born Princess Caroline Ferdinande Louise in Palermo, Sicily; she was the eldest daughter of King Francis I of Naples. Shortly after the assassination of her husband in 1820, she bore his son, the future Comte de Chambord (1820–83). He was to be the last member of the elder branch of the Bourbon family, which had ruled France since the late 16th century.

After the revolution of 1830 in France, Madame de Berry followed the exiled Charles X to England, from whence she canvassed support for a counterrevolution. On returning to France in 1832, she attempted to organize a revolt to secure the throne for her son but was arrested at Nantes and imprisoned. Released after the birth of a daughter in May 1833, she retired to Italy and settled in Palermo, where she joined Count Ettore Lucchesi-Palli, to whom she had been secretly married. She died in Brunnensee, Switzerland.

The Comte de Chambord, pretender to the French throne, was referred to by his supporters as Henry V. He died without heirs in 1883.

Besant, Annie (1847–1933) *British social reformer and political campaigner*

> There is no birthright in the white skin that it shall say that wherever it goes, to any nation, amongst any people, there the people of the country shall give way before it, and those to whom the land belongs shall bow down and become its servants.
>
> —*Wake Up, India: A Plea for Social Reform* (1913)

For over 60 years Annie Besant was at the forefront of liberal reform movements demanding intellectual freedom, women's rights, and social justice. Besant combined boundless energy and a forceful presence with great charisma and beauty. George Bernard Shaw, a longtime friend and fellow socialist, considered her the greatest woman orator of the age.

Annie Wood was born in London into a family of Irish descent. Her father died when she was a child, and although he had left his wife and children well provided for, the family soon became impoverished as a result of financial mismanagement by their solicitor. Annie was taught privately by the progressive educator Ellen Marryat, sister of the popular writer Frederick Marryat, at Marryat's country estate. In her youth Annie was a devout member of the Anglican Church, reading widely in the Bible and religious literature. In 1867 she married Frank Besant, an Anglican clergyman several years her senior, but could not reconcile her free-thinking upbringing with his strict conventional standards.

At the same time, she began to entertain doubts about religious doctrine and to question her faith; this brought her into further conflict with her husband, and in 1873 they separated.

In 1874 she became acquainted with the radical thinker Charles Bradlaugh, a professed atheist, and was elected to the vice-presidency of the National Secular Society. Her writings and lectures made Mrs. Besant well known in Britain, and in 1877 her fame spread abroad as a defendant in a trial involving freedom of the press. She and Bradlaugh had reissued a pamphlet – *Fruits of Philosophy* – advocating birth control, which had been written some 45 years before by Charles Knowlton, an American physician. However, both were eventually acquitted of the charge of publishing immoral literature. Annie Besant also espoused the cause of socialism. She joined the socialist Fabian Society and contributed a major article to the influential collection *Fabian Essays* (1885), edited by George Bernard Shaw. In 1888 she helped organize the famous Match Girls' strike. Around this time she began to be influenced by the thinking of Madame BLAVATSKY, founder of the movement known as theosophy, a blend of Oriental and Christian thought that emphasizes the spiritual perfectibility of man. Besant wrote widely on the subject and became president of the Theosophical Society from 1907 until her death.

In 1893 Annie Besant took the sudden decision to go to India, where for the rest of her life she campaigned for Indian independence and helped organize the Central Hindu College at Benares (Varanasi) in 1898. A long-time associate of future president Jawaharlal Nehru, whom she had initiated into the Theosophical Society, she split with him over their conflicting approaches to independence – she rejected his methods of civil disobedience and passive resistance, and he considered her views too moderate. In 1913 her book *Wake Up, India: A Plea for Social Reform* was published. She died at Adyar, Madras, India.

Bethune, Mary McLeod (1875–1955) *American educator*

A leader of the African-American community, Mary Bethune also advised President Franklin D. Roosevelt on the problems of minority groups.

A child of former slaves, she was born in Mayesville, South Carolina. In between cotton-picking seasons she gained an education and won a scholarship to a seminary. She graduated from the Moody Bible Institute, Chicago, in 1895 and taught in mission schools in Georgia and South Carolina until 1903. In 1895 she met and married Albertus Bethune. Some nine years later she founded Daytona Normal and Industrial Institute for Girls, at Daytona Beach, Florida. The institute merged with Cookman Institute for men, located in Jacksonville, in 1923 to form Bethune-Cookman College. She was president of the college until 1942, by which time the school had grown from its original five members to over 1,000. In 1935 she founded the National Council of Negro Women.

President Roosevelt appointed Mary Bethune to head the Division of Negro Affairs of the National Youth Administration, which she directed from 1936 to 1943. During World War II she served as special assistant to the secretary of war for the selection of officer candidates for the Women's Army Corps. She was also a special adviser to the president on minority affairs and a vice president of the National Association for the Advancement of Colored People. She served as a consultant on interracial relations at the San Francisco Conference, which organized the United Nations in 1945.

For her public services Mary Bethune received the Spingarn Medal (1935), the Francis A. Drexel Award (1936), the Thomas Jefferson Award (1942), and the Italian Medal of Honour and Merit (1949). She died in Daytona Beach, Florida.

Bhutto, Benazir (1953–) *Pakistani politician*

As prime minister of Pakistan (1988–90, 1993–96), Benazir Bhutto was the first woman leader of a Muslim country in modern times.

She was born in Karachi. Her father,

a lawyer from a landowning family in the province of Sind, was Zulfikar Ali Bhutto, who founded the Pakistan People's Party (PPP) and became president and prime minister of the country in the 1970s. Benazir Bhutto received her higher education abroad, obtaining degrees from Radcliffe College (1973) in the United States and from Oxford (1976). While at Oxford, she was president of the Oxford Union. Shortly after her return to Pakistan in 1977, her father's government was toppled in a coup staged by General Muhammad Zia-ul-Haq. Zia had Zulfikar Ali Bhutto executed in 1979.

Leadership of the PPP was assumed by Bhutto's widow, Nusrat, but increasingly their daughter came to be regarded as his true political heir. She was held under house arrest by the military regime for most of the period between 1977 and 1984. She went into exile in 1985 but returned the following year. In an arranged marriage in 1987 she became the wife of a wealthy Sindhi, Asif Ali Zardari.

Benazir Bhutto campaigned vigorously against Pakistan's rulers and, following Zia's death in an air crash in August 1988, succeeded in making the PPP the largest single party in November elections. The next month she was able to form a coalition government. She was confronted with great difficulties as prime minister – a strong president, an influential military, and an entrenched political opposition that controlled Pakistan's largest province, Punjab. These problems eventually proved overwhelming, and in August 1990 President Ghulan Ishaq Khan, with army support, dismissed her government, charging her and Zardari with corruption, which both denied. In October, although she retained her seat in parliament, her party suffered a heavy defeat in the election.

Bhutto remained prominent in Pakistani politics and became the chairperson of the National Assembly's Standing Committee on Foreign Affairs in 1993. In October of the same year she regained office as prime minister, defeating former prime minister Nawaz Sharif. However, she was forced to resign amid renewed allegations of corruption in late 1996 and was heavily defeated in the general election in February 1997.

Bigelow, Kathryn (1952–) *American film director*

Kathryn Bigelow has specialized in directing slick and stylish thrillers, often with implausible plots.

Although she began her career as an artist, Bigelow changed direction after completing a course at the graduate film school of Columbia University, New York. As a director and screenwriter she enjoyed her first successes in the 1980s. In addition to cowriting the script for *The Loveless* (1981), she also codirected the film with Monty Montgomery. Paralleling the 1954 release *The Wild One*, it is a stylishly shot biker movie, featuring strong images of 1950s lifestyle – zipguns, sunglasses, and leather. In 1987 Bigelow coscripted and directed *Near Dark*, a bloodthirsty "vampire western," and the following year was given a retrospective exhibition at the Museum of Modern Art. She also cowrote her next film, *Blue Steel*, a political thriller that was released in the same year (1989) as her marriage to the director James Cameron. *Point Break* (1991) was an implausible thriller with a surfing and skydiving theme, while the lurid *Strange Days* (1995) is set in a violent Los Angeles on the eve of the new millennium.

Bijns, Anna (*c.*1494–1575) *Flemish poet*

Anna Bijns (also spelled Byns) is generally considered to be the foremost Dutch poet of the 16th century. Born in Antwerp (now in northern Belgium), she became a teacher there and, it is thought, also a lay nun. She was an ardent opponent of the Protestant Reformation and particularly of the ideas of Martin Luther, which were gaining popularity in Flanders. Her passionate lyric poetry reflected her devotion to the Roman Catholic Church. Known as the "SAPPHO of Brabant," Bijns is often credited with initiating the linguistic transition from Middle to Modern Dutch. Her verse was published in three volumes (1528, 1548, 1567). She died in Antwerp.

Bishop, Elizabeth (1911–1979) *American poet*

Noted for the penetrating and imaginative quality of her verse, Bishop was awarded the Pulitzer Prize for poetry in 1956.

Elizabeth Bishop was born in Worcester, Massachusetts. After her father died and her mother became mentally ill, she spent her childhood with her grandparents in the remote Canadian province of Nova Scotia and with her aunt in Boston. She graduated from Vassar College, Poughkeepsie, in 1934, travelled in Europe and North Africa in 1935–37, and lived briefly in Key West, Florida, and in Mexico. She held a Guggenheim fellowship in 1947 and in 1949–50 served as poetry consultant to the Library of Congress. For 15 years, between 1951 and 1969, she lived in Brazil. In her later years Bishop taught creative writing at Harvard University (from 1970) and at the Massachusetts Institute of Technology. Her short stories appeared in *The New Yorker* and other magazines and journals. She died in Boston.

Bishop's poems – intricate, dense, and witty – are to some extent influenced by the poetry of Marianne MOORE (a contemporary at Vassar) and Robert Lowell, both her close friends. Her first volume of poems, *North and South*, was published to great critical acclaim in 1946. Bishop was awarded the Pulitzer Prize for her second book of verse, *North and South – A Cold Spring* (1955), which was followed by *Questions of Travel* (1965) and *Geography III* (1977; National Book Critics Circle Award). Her *Collected Poems* (1970) earned her a National Book Award. The *Complete Poems, 1927–79* was published in 1983; her *Collected Prose* appeared in 1984.

Bishop, Isabella Bird (1831–1904) *British writer and explorer*

Bishop is particularly remembered for her travel writings. The daughter of an Anglican cleric, she was born Isabella Lucy Bird at Boroughbridge Hall in Yorkshire. By the end of her life she had circled the globe three times. Her first travel book, *An Englishwoman in America*, was written in 1856, after she had travelled to the United States for an operation. Her concern with the question of urban poverty in Britain led her to promote emigration schemes to Canada in the 1860s. In 1881, at the age of 49, she married Dr. John Bishop of Edinburgh. In 1892 she became the first woman to be elected a fellow of the Royal Geographical Society. She died in Edinburgh.

Isabella Bishop spent some time in Australia and New Zealand, and also worked as a medical missionary in India. However, she is best known for her travel writings and photography of the Far East, including *Unbeaten Tracks in Japan* (1880), *Journeys in Persia and Kurdistan* (1891), *Among the Tibetans* (1894), and *Chinese Pictures* (1900).

Blackadder, Elizabeth (Violet) (1931–) *Scottish artist*

Best known for her paintings of flowers and plants, Elizabeth Blackadder is the first woman painter to have been elected to both the Royal Scottish Academy (1972) and the Royal Academy (1977).

Born in Falkirk, central Scotland, Elizabeth Blackadder was educated at Edinburgh University and Edinburgh College of Art, where she later taught for nearly 25 years (1962–86). She held her first one-woman show in 1959 and her first London exhibition in 1965.

By the 1970s Blackadder had moved away from her early experiments in landscape painting to the highly individual still-lifes for which she is now best known. These create an unusual effect by placing detailed representations of ordinary household objects against an empty or stylized background. The influence of Japanese art is sometimes apparent. Since the late 1970s she has favoured a predominantly botanical subject matter. Her work first came to national attention with a touring retrospective exhibition in 1981: she was appointed OBE a year later.

As well as painting in oils and watercolour, Elizabeth Blackadder has made prints, lithographs, and tapestries. Her work in stained glass includes a window for the National Library of Scotland, commissioned in 1987. In 1994 she published a selection of her more recent work in the volume *Favourite Flowers* (text by Deborah Kellaway), which quickly established itself as a popular gift book.

Blackstone, Tessa (Ann Vosper), Baroness (1942–) *British sociologist, educationalist, and academic administrator*

Baroness Blackstone is known as a writer on educational and social issues, as a leading policy adviser to the Labour Party, and as the master of Birkbeck College, London.

Born into a middle-class family in the Suffolk village of Bures, Tessa Blackstone was educated at grammar school and the London School of Economics (LSE), where she earned a doctorate in sociology. She lectured on sociology at Enfield College of Technology (1965–66) and on social administration at the LSE (1966–75). An early marriage to Thomas Evans produced two children but was later dissolved.

A long-time supporter of the Labour Party, Tessa Blackstone became a member of the cabinet's Central Policy Review Staff (the 'Think Tank') during the Wilson and Callaghan governments of the 1970s. She has since worked chiefly in the field of educational administration, becoming a professor at the University of London's Institute of Education (1978–83), a director of education for the Inner London Education Authority (1983–87), and master of Birkbeck College (1987–97). Since 1988 she has been chairman of the Institute for Public Policy Research, a centre-left think tank. In 1987 she was awarded a life peerage, becoming Baroness Blackstone of Stoke Newington. She has taken an active role in the House of Lords, serving as Labour's frontbench spokesman on education and science (1988–92) and on foreign affairs (1992–97), and as a minister of state for education and employment (1997–). Tessa Blackstone's publications include *Social Policy and Administration in Britain* (1975) and *Prisons and Penal Reform* (1990), as well as various works written jointly with others.

Blackwell, Antoinette Brown (1825–1921) *American minister and reformer*

Mrs. Blackwell was the first ordained woman minister in the United States.

Born Antoinette Louisa Brown, in Henrietta, New York State, she began to speak publicly in the services of the local Congregational church from an early age. She graduated from Oberlin College in 1847 and completed a course at its theological seminary in 1850, though she was not granted her degree. (Oberlin later conferred on her an honorary MA in 1878 and a DD in 1908.) She was a Congregationalist pastor in South Butler, New York, for four years but was initially refused ordination because she was a woman; eventually she was ordained on September 15, 1853, but was dismissed in July 1854, apparently at her own request. She later became a Unitarian.

In 1856 Antoinette married Samuel C. Blackwell, whose brother had married her college friend Lucy STONE. The couple moved to New Jersey, and Mrs. Blackwell often preached in Unitarian and other liberal pulpits. She campaigned in her sermons and in her writing for many causes, especially women's rights, temperance, and the emancipation of slaves. She delivered her last sermon at the age of 90; her final book appeared three years later.

Blackwell, Elizabeth (1821–1910) *British-born American physician*

> I must have something to engross my thoughts, some object in life which will fill this vacuum, and prevent this sad wearing away of the heart.
>
> *—Pioneer Work for Women*

Elizabeth Blackwell's fame rests on her position as the first woman doctor of modern times. As the first woman to gain a medical degree in the United States, she also pioneered the education of women as physicians.

Elizabeth Blackwell was born in Bristol, the daughter of the liberal dissenters Samuel and Hannah Blackwell.

In 1832 the Blackwell family emigrated to the United States, settling first in New York City and later in Cincinnati, where Samuel Blackwell died.

In order to support the family, Elizabeth, together with her mother and sisters, ran a private school for several years, but in 1844 she decided to become a doctor. Medical schools in Philadelphia and New York refused to enrol her, so she studied privately until 1847, when she finally gained entrance to Geneva Medical School in Geneva, New York State. After being awarded her MD in 1849, she studied in London, at St. Bartholomew's Hospital, and in Paris, where exposure to a contagious disease left her with sight in only one eye.

After returning to the United States and trying unsuccessfully to gain a medical appointment at a hospital or clinic, Dr. Blackwell opened a dispensary and small hospital in New York City in 1853. This establishment was staffed entirely by women and later became known as the New York Infirmary. Here, during the American Civil War, she trained nurses for the Union (Northern) Army and in 1868, with the aid of her younger sister Emily BLACKWELL, opened the Women's Medical College of the New York Infirmary. She returned to England in 1857 and in 1875 helped to found the London School of Medicine for Woman. She died in Hastings, Sussex.

Blackwell, Emily (1826–1910) *British-born American physician*

Emily Blackwell was the younger sister of the pioneering woman physician Elizabeth BLACKWELL. Born in Bristol, Emily emigrated with her family to the United States when she was six.

Emily encountered the same prejudice from the medical establishment as her sister when she attempted to enrol for training as a physician. First accepted, then summarily rejected, by Rush Medical College in Chicago, she was eventually accepted for a course of medical study at Western Reserve University in Cleveland, Ohio. She graduated in 1854.

After postgraduate work in Europe from 1854 to 1856, Emily returned to help her sister establish the New York Infirmary. While Elizabeth specialized in promoting and lecturing on public health projects, Emily's particular talents lay in administration and in active surgery. She was principally responsible for the day-to-day operation of the infirmary for its first 40 years. She also trained many women student doctors in the infirmary's medical college; during her term of office as dean the college flourished, attracting many gifted students. She died, aged 74, the same year as her elder sister.

Blanche of Castile (*c.*1188–1252) *Wife of King Louis VIII of France*

As regent for her son King Louis IX, Blanche ruled France wisely and firmly.

Born at Palencia, in Castile, she was one of three daughters of King Alfonso VIII of Castile and Eleanor of England. In 1200 ELEANOR OF AQUITAINE escorted Blanche, her granddaughter, to France, where she was married to Louis as part of a short-lived peace settlement between her uncle, King John of England, and Philip II of France. In 1216–17 she supported her husband's vain attempt to invade England.

On the early death of Louis VIII in 1226, Blanche became regent for her 12-year-old son Louis IX. A coalition of powerful French barons saw the regency as their opportunity to rebel. In this crisis Blanche proved able and energetic, personally leading her forces into battle. With Church support she managed to defeat the great feudal lords and preserve recent royal gains. She was also adroit in diplomacy. A treaty in 1229 ended the crusade against the Cathars (a heretical sect in southern France) and provided for the marriage of Blanche's third son Alphonse to the heiress of the county of Toulouse. This important territory passed to the crown in 1271.

Blanche continued to support her son after he came of age in 1236, and Louis was much influenced by her piety (he was to become St. Louis). She died during his crusade to Egypt and Syria (1246–52), while once more acting as regent.

Blankers-Koen, Fanny (1918–)
Dutch athlete

Fanny Blankers-Koen, who achieved international success at the comparatively late age of 30, was one of the greatest all-round woman athletes of the 20th century.

She was born Francina Koen, at Baarn in the Netherlands. Although her father was a shot-putter and discus thrower, Fanny did not take up athletics until she was 16, when she met Jan Blankers, who became her trainer and subsequently her husband. She made her debut at 17 as a 800-metre runner, although between 1938 and 1951 she was to set world records in several separate events – the 100 yards, 100 metres, 220 yards, 80 metres hurdles, the high jump, long jump, and pentathlon.

Blankers-Koen reached her peak in the first postwar Olympic Games, held in London in 1948, which she dominated totally. She won four gold medals – in the 100 metres, 200 metres, 80 metres hurdles, and the 4 × 100 metres relay, an unprecedented achievement. To some extent she was spurred on to these successes by unflattering comments in the British press, suggesting that her age was against her. Before the most gruelling event, the 80 metres hurdles, in which she was competing against the British athlete Maureen Gardner, her husband said to her, "Don't forget, Fanny, you're too old"; this provided sufficient provocation to ensure her victory. The 1948 London Games were first to focus on the achievements of a woman.

Fanny competed in the 1952 Olympics in Helsinki, but her great successes were now behind her. Nevertheless, in 1956, at the age of 38, she was still able to run a wind-assisted 80 metres hurdles in 11.3 seconds, which compared favorably with the world record time of 11 seconds she had set some years earlier.

Blavatsky, Helena Petrovna (1831–1891) *Russian-born American founder of theosophy*

> This idea of passing one's whole life in moral idleness, and having one's hardest work and duty done by another – whether God or man – is most revolting to us, as it is most degrading to human dignity.
> —*The Key to Theosophy* (1889)

Born Helena von Hahn in Dnepropetrovsk, Russia, she was married briefly at the age of 17 to Nikifor Blavatsky. Many years after the breakup of her marriage she became interested in spiritualism and the occult, spending a considerable amount of time travelling around the world and finally moving to the United States in 1873. In 1875 she and Colonel Henry Steel Olcott founded the Theosophical Society, a mystical society dedicated to countering materialism and agnosticism and promoting research into the hidden laws of nature. As secretary of the new organization, she founded its journal, *The Theosophist*. Blavatsky became an American citizen, and in 1882 she accompanied Olcott to India, where they established the international centre of the Theosophical Society in Madras. There her philosophy was greatly influenced by Hindu mysticism and Buddhism. Madame Blavatsky's fame increased after reports that paranormal phenomena occurred in her presence. A report carried out by the Society of Psychical Research subsequently called these phenomena into doubt, but theosophists claimed that the report was based on insufficient evidence.

Helena Blavatsky was the author of *Isis Unveiled* (1877), *The Key to Theosophy* (1889), and *The Voice of Silence* (1889). Her most famous work, *The Secret Doctrine* (1888), has been widely translated. She died in London. Theosophy continued to gain adherents after Blavatsky's death; several artists and writers were influenced by the doctrine around the beginning of the 20th century.

Blessington, Countess of (1789–1849) *Irish writer*

Marguerite, Countess of Blessington, is remembered mainly for her association with Lord Byron and Comte d'Orsay. Of her large literary output little survives except her *Journal of Conversations with Lord Byron* (1834), in which, according to recent research, she exaggerated her intimacy with Byron.

She was born Margaret (later Marguerite) Power at Knockbrit, County Tipperary, the daughter of an Irish patriot, Francis Power. Graced with good looks, at the age of 14 she was, by her own account, sold into marriage to Captain Maurice St. Leger Farmer, a dissolute landowner who maltreated her. They soon separated, and, after a time as the mistress of various high-ranking men in Dublin, her beauty and charm captivated the rich widower Charles Gardiner, Viscount Mountjoy and 1st Earl of Blessington. With Lord Blessington, Marguerite moved to London, where she presided over one of the most fashionable salons of the time. In 1817 her husband died, and on February 16, 1818, she became Blessington's wife.

The handsome nobleman Alfred, Comte d'Orsay, first made her acquaintance in 1822, and soon he and the Blessingtons were living together in a love triangle. The same year they embarked on a tour of Italy and France; Marguerite became acquainted with Byron in 1823, during a two-month stay at Genoa. In 1827 d'Orsay married Lady Harriet Gardiner, Lady Blessington's 15-year-old stepdaughter, in order to secure her huge dowry, but by prearrangement between d'Orsay and Lady Blessington the marriage was never consummated.

After Blessington's death in 1829 his widow continued to live in great style with d'Orsay, even though her income from Blessington's estate was reduced and her debts were mounting. Returning to London in 1831, Lady Blessington started writing novels and editing fashionable "annuals" in order to support her sumptuous lifestyle. However, her earnings proved inadequate for her tastes. In 1849 d'Orsay fled to Paris to escape his creditors and she followed, dying there shortly afterwards.

Bloom, Claire (1931–) *British actress*

> She could not be more beautiful without upsetting the balance of nature.
>
> —Walter Kerr

Claire Bloom is renowned as an actress of great sophistication and elegance. Throughout her long and distinguished career, she has continued to work both in the theatre and in cinema.

She was born Claire Blume, the daughter of an advertising executive of German-Jewish descent, in the north London suburb of Finchley. Captivated by the idea of acting at an early age, she won a scholarship to the prestigious Guildhall School of Music and Drama in London during World War II. She studied at the Guildhall and at London's Central School of Speech and Drama before making her acting debut in 1946 at the Oxford Playhouse. In 1948 she was made a member of the Royal Shakespeare Company.

Although she appeared in several acclaimed theatre roles in London in the late 1940s, Claire Bloom first gained widespread recognition for her leading role in Charlie Chaplin's film *Limelight* (1951). Further screen performances in the 1950s included Lady Anne in Laurence Olivier's film of *Richard III* and Helena in an adaptation of John Osborne's *Look Back in Anger*. In 1959 she married the American actor Rod Steiger; since then, she has had two more unsuccessful marriages, including one to the American writer Philip Roth.

Throughout the 1960s Bloom continued to act in films. In the following decade, however, she made a return to the stage, winning particular praise for her performances in the Ibsen plays *A Doll's House* and *Hedda Gabler* and for the leading role of Blanche DuBois in Tennessee Williams's *A Streetcar Named Desire*. Bloom has also worked in television, notably in *Brideshead Revisited* (1981), *Shadowlands* (1985), and *Family Money* (1997). In 1996 she published a forthright memoir, *Leaving a Doll's House*.

Bloomer, Amelia Jenks (1818–1894) *American reformer and women's rights campaigner*

> In the minds of some people the short dress and women's rights were inseparably connected. With us, the dress was but an incident, and we

were not willing to sacrifice greater questions to it.

—Quoted by Charles N. Gattey in
The Bloomer Girls

Amelia Bloomer proposed a new form of dress for women, consisting of full Turkish trousers gathered at the ankles; this outfit rapidly came to be associated with her name, although it was actually created by Elizabeth Smith Miller.

She was born in Homer, New York State. In 1840 she married Dexter Chamberlain Bloomer, a Quaker newspaper editor and antislavery campaigner. Her own reforming zeal led her to contribute regularly to her husband's newspaper, and in 1849 she started her own temperance journal, *The Lily*, probably the first publication edited entirely by a woman. The magazine also championed women's rights (including the right to vote), opposed unjust marriage laws, and called for dress reform.

The "Bloomer costume," ridiculed by most observers, soon became a symbol of radicalism. Bloomer adopted this mode of dress for a time, as did her fellow townswomen Elizabeth Cady STANTON, Susan B. ANTHONY, and other leaders of the women's rights movement. However, they all abandoned the costume when it seemed to draw attention away from more fundamental aspects of the movement. Bloomer was a serious campaigner for equal rights, despite her perhaps misguided attempt to free women from the restrictions of traditional clothing. She died in Council Bluffs, Iowa.

Bloor, Ella Reeve (1862–1951) *American radical*

Bloor achieved international fame as "Mother Bloor" for her pursuit of libertarian ideals. In defiance of her conservative upbringing, she progressed from women's suffrage and temperance to promoting more radical causes, such as socialism and communism.

Born Ella Reeve in Staten Island, New York, she adopted the name "Bloor" while aiding the reformist writer Upton Sinclair's investigations of Chicago meat-packers in 1904. She was married twice, to Lucien Ware and Louis Cohen, both of which relationships ended in divorce, before she met and married Andrew Omholt, a communist. Two of her eight children, Harold Ware and Carl Reeve, also embraced communism. Ella Reeve began her political career as a Socialist Party organizer in 1902, participating in the Pennsylvania anthracite coal strike. She later took part in other labour disputes, notably those in Calumet, Michigan, in 1913 and Ludlow, Colorado, in 1914. She was also active in the women's rights movement, helping to found a group that in 1917 became the National Woman's Party. As a pacifist, she opposed U.S. intervention in World War I.

In 1919 "Mother Bloor" became a founder member of the U.S. Communist Party. A party official in state and national posts, she was also active in the unions and causes that the party fostered. She was instrumental in organizing labour in the steel and mining industries, and in the Great Depression worked with farmers in the Midwest as well as with the unemployed. Bloor visited the Soviet Union several times. *We Are Many*, her memoirs, was published in 1940. She died in Quakertown, Pennsylvania.

Blow, Susan Elizabeth (1843–1916)
American educator

Blow was the first person to open a public kindergarten in the United States. A profoundly religious woman, she was influenced by the idealist philosophy of Fichte and Hegel. She gained particular inspiration from the educational ideas of Friedrich Froebel, resolving to open a public kindergarten on the German model in her home town, St. Louis, Missouri. She was supported in this endeavour by superintendent of schools William T. Harris.

Blow's kindergarten opened its doors in 1873. The experiment proved so successful that she founded a training school for kindergarten teachers in the following year. She also translated Froebel's *Mother Play*, a book of songs and games for use in kindergartens. Her work in St. Louis and her activity in the National Education Association made her the chief spokesperson for the orthodox Froebelian movement in the United States. During the 1890s such educators as Patty Smith Hill began to call for less traditional methods in kindergarten teaching; however, Susan Blow opposed these liberal tendencies. She died in New York.

Blume, Judy (Sussman) (1938–) *American novelist*

Despite disapproval from some parents, and attempts to restrict the availability of her books, Judy Blume has become the most popular writer of fiction for teenagers in America.

Born in Elizabeth, New Jersey, she studied the education of young children at New York University and married while still at college. She did not begin her writing career until after the birth of her second child, publishing her first book in 1969. Her third novel, *Are You There, God? It's Me, Margaret* (1970), brought her to the attention of the public and established the formula that would become so successful with her teenage readership. Blume's honest handling of the problems faced by teenage girls, notably the onset of puberty, coping with parental divorce, adolescent sexual relationships, and the unpredictability of schoolfriends, were all expressed in a natural straightforward style and seemed to her readers to provide an accurate reflection of their own experiences. She has commented, "When I was growing up, I never had any books that showed the way I was. I wanted to write what I knew to be true and somehow kids relate to this." Her other fiction for teenagers includes *Then Again, Maybe I Won't* (1971), *It's Not the End of the World* (1972), *Blubber* (1974), and *Forever* (1975).

Although her explicit account of teenage life and her willingness to tackle previously taboo areas brought her a huge readership, Blume found herself under attack from some parents; indeed, heavy-handed attempts were made to restrict the circulation of her books. It is said that no other au-

thor has had to cope with such determined censorship in American schools and libraries.

Judy Blume has also written for adults. Her two most noteworthy novels, *Wifey* (1978) and *Smart Women* (1984), are concerned with the position of women within the structure of a traditional marriage.

Bly, Nellie (1867–1922) *American journalist*

Nellie Bly (whose real name was Elizabeth Seaman) acquired international fame in 1889–90, when she travelled around the world in 72 days, 6 hours, and 11 minutes, surpassing the feat of Phineas Fogg in Jules Verne's contemporary novel *Around the World in 80 Days* (1873). Her account of this trip was published as *Nellie Bly's Book: Around the World in 72 Days* (1890).

Born Elizabeth Cochrane, in Cochrane Mills, Pennsylvania, she took the pen name "Nellie Bly" from a popular song of the day. After an apprenticeship on the *Pittsburgh Dispatch*, she went to work in 1887 for Joseph Pulitzer's *World* in New York City. That same year, she sent a series of articles from Mexico on social conditions. A specialist in sensational exposés, she once feigned insanity to gain admittance to a city asylum. Her account of conditions there was published as *Ten Days in a Mad House* (1887). She also wrote undercover stories on crime, slums, and sweatshop working conditions. In 1895 she married Robert L. Seaman, an elderly magnate. She was a writer for the *New York Journal* at the time of her death, in New York City.

Blyton, Enid (1897–1968) *British children's author*

Enid Blyton is famous as the creator of Noddy, a small pixielike character, as well as being the writer of many other successful children's stories.

She was born in Beckenham, Kent, and had an unhappy childhood; her father left the family when Enid was 15 years old. Though she showed early promise as a musician, she embarked on a teachers' training course during World War I and eventually opened her own infants' school. Her writing career began at this stage, with her contribution of children's stories to magazines. In 1924 she married Hugh Pollack, by whom she had two daughters; this marriage ended in divorce in 1942, after which she married Kenneth Darrell, a surgeon.

During the 1920s and 1930s Enid Blyton divided her time between teaching, editing books on teaching, compiling a children's encyclopedia, and raising her daughters. In the early 1940s her first school stories for girls appeared and were an instant success. From then on her writing career flourished, and she produced over 400 titles before her death.

Apart from the *Noddy* series, her most widely read books were those of the two series *The Famous Five* and *The Secret Seven*. In these, as in all her works, the world depicted is one of middle-class white children. This embroiled her in controversy in her final years, as children's librarians sought to reflect an increasingly multicultural Britain in their purchases; in some cases Blyton's books were banned as reactionary and racist. She fought vigorously against this charge, but her powers were diminished by growing senility in the last two years of her life.

Nevertheless, Blyton's books have remained popular into the 1990s. They have been translated into almost 30 languages and sell eight million copies a year.

Boadicea (died 62 AD) *Ancient British queen*

> She [Boadicea] was very tall and her aspect was terrifying, for her eyes flashed fiercely and her voice was harsh. A mass of red hair fell down to her hips, and around her neck was a twisted gold necklace.
>
> —Dio Cassius, *Roman History*,
> Bk. 42, Vol. VIII

Boadicea (also called Boudicca) was queen of the Iceni, a British tribe whom she led in a rebellion against the Romans.

Boadicea's husband, Prasutagus, had allied his kingdom – which lay in modern East Anglia – with Rome and bequeathed half of it to the emperor Nero in the hope that the rest might be saved for his daughters. However, the Romans refused to honour the treaty after his death, brutally assaulting the royal family and confiscating their land. Accordingly, the tribe rose, joined forces with other rebels, and sacked the Roman colony at Camulodunum (Colchester). The Roman governor, Suetonius Paulinus, hurried back with his cavalry from a campaign in north Wales. Unable to save Londinium (London) or Verulamium (St. Albans) from destruction, he withdrew further northwest to join up with his infantry. Boadicea followed, and in an ensuing battle the Iceni were annihilated. Boadicea took poison when she saw her forces were defeated.

Boadicea's uprising was the last serious rebellion to confront the Romans in their conquest of Britain, where she is still regarded as a heroine.

Bogan, Louise (1897–1970) *American poet*

Influenced by the 17th-century English metaphysical poets, Louise Bogan's highly crafted poetry is characterized by its restrained lyrical treatment of strong emotions.

Bogan, who was born at Livermore, Maine, was educated at the Girls Latin School in Boston and at Boston University. From 1931 she was poetry critic of *The New Yorker* magazine. She held Guggenheim fellowships in 1933 and 1937 and was professor of poetry at the Library of Congress in 1945–46.

Her *Collected Poems 1923–1953* (published in 1954), her best-known work, was joint-winner (with Léonie Adams) of the 1955 Bollingen Prize for poetry. Bogan was elected a member of the American Academy of Arts and Letters (1968) and won the fellowship award of the Academy of American Poets (1959). She died in New York City.

Böhlau, Helene (1859–1940) *German novelist*

Böhlau was born in Weimar. While travelling in the Middle East she married her tutor, Friedrich Arndt, who had become a Muslim and adopted the name Omar al-Rashid Bey. They later settled in Munich.

Helene Böhlau gained her literary reputation with the publication of *Ratsmädelgeschichten* (1888; Tales of the Councillors' Daughters), which portrayed everyday life in her native town. Though realistically described, the events in her stories are also tinged with romanticism. Other works, with feminist themes, include *Halbtier* (1899; Half a Beast) and the autobiographical *Isebies* (1911). She died near Munich.

Boleyn, Anne (1507–1536) *Second wife of King Henry VIII of England*

> The King has been very good to me. He promoted me from a simple maid to be a marchioness. Then he raised me to be a queen. Now he will raise me to be a martyr.
>
> —Quoted by W. Abbot in *Notable Women in History*

Anne Boleyn was the mother of Queen ELIZABETH I. Her failure to produce a son for Henry led to her execution for alleged adultery.

Anne was the daughter of Sir Thomas Boleyn, who later became Earl of Wiltshire and Ormond; he was the grandson of Sir Geoffrey Boleyn, a prosperous merchant, who was lord mayor of London in 1457. Her mother was Elizabeth Howard, daughter of the Earl of Surrey, Sir Thomas Howard, who later became Duke of Norfolk. This maternal connection with the Howard family linked Anne Boleyn to a powerful faction at the court of Henry VIII.

With her older sister Mary, Anne Boleyn spent a portion of her childhood in France and returned there again in the early 1520s as an attendant to Queen Mary, wife of Louis XII. In 1522, with war looming, the Boleyn sisters returned to England, where Henry VIII made Mary one of his mistresses. Anne was also the subject of the king's attention during this period. She was courted by Piers Butler, Henry Percy, and the poet Sir Thomas Wyatt; however, these suitors all failed to win her hand in marriage and were most probably dissuaded by Henry from pursuing their claims. Certainly the king gave land to Anne's father at this time, possibly because of his interest in the two sisters.

In 1527 Henry began writing a series of passionate love letters to Anne in which he referred to a love that was already a year old, and, moreover, pledged devotion to her alone. Yet Anne steadfastly refused to become his mistress, insisting on the legality of marriage.

In 1527 Henry took the first steps towards divorcing his first wife, CATHERINE OF ARAGON, who had failed to bear a son. At the same time, he sought to gain permission from Pope Clement VII to marry Anne. However, the pope was reluctant to annul Henry's marriage and instructed his officials to delay proceedings; this situation continued over a period of six years, during which Henry's determination to divorce Catherine and marry Anne persisted. A stalemate ensued in which Henry brought pressure to bear on the pope by forcing parliament to reduce papal power in England, while the pope refused to yield. The situation was resolved in 1533, when Thomas Cranmer, the archbishop of Canterbury, stated that he was free to convene a court of his own to settle Henry's matrimonial affairs. At this court, in May of that same year, he declared the marriage of Henry and Catherine to be invalid.

In the meantime, Henry had already secretly married Anne, who was pregnant, in January 1533. Archbishop Cranmer proclaimed Anne to be Henry's lawful wife; she was accordingly crowned queen in Westminister Abbey on Whitsunday. On September 7, 1533, Anne gave birth to Elizabeth . The disappointment of another daughter, instead of a male heir, led to Henry's growing estrangement from Anne. This increased when Anne's further pregnancies in the next two years brought only miscarriage and a stillborn child.

In early 1536 rumours began to circulate at court of Anne's infidelity to Henry. These rumours soon became official charges. The king's lawyers accused Anne of committing adultery with four members of the royal household and of committing incest with her brother. Henry had Anne imprisoned in the Tower of London. At her subsequent trial she was found guilty, and on May 15, 1536, she was condemned to death by her own uncle, the Duke of Norfolk. On May 19 she was executed. Henry married Jane SEYMOUR only two weeks later. Throughout these events Anne displayed great dignity, protesting her innocence to the last.

See also ANNE OF CLEVES; HOWARD, CATHERINE; PARR, CATHERINE.

Bonaparte, Caroline (1782–1839)
French princess

Caroline Bonaparte, Napoleon's youngest sister, is said to have resembled him closely in personality. The contemporary politician and diplomat Charles Talleyrand referred to her as "The head of Cromwell on a pretty woman."

Born Maria Annunziata Buonaparte, she was married in 1800 to General Joachim Murat, later marshal of France, grand duke of Berg, and king of Naples (1808–15). As queen of Naples Caroline arranged that she should succeed Murat if he died before her; she encouraged Murat to promote Neapolitan interests, while pretending to Napoleon that she was acting on behalf of France. Meanwhile, in the interest of her sons she plotted to have Murat named as Napoleon's successor and opposed the emperor's second marriage to MARIE LOUISE of Austria. These machinations greatly displeased Napoleon and alienated him from Murat.

As Napoleon's power waned in 1813–14, Caroline persuaded her husband to betray him in order to save their own crown. In 1815, however, Murat was defeated by the Austrians and lost Naples. Caroline surrendered the kingdom and was taken to Vienna together with her two sons and two daughters. Murat attempted to regain power but was captured by Bourbon troops and executed.

Caroline soon married a Neapolitan general, Francisco Macdonald. She spent the rest of her life in Austria and Italy, dying in Florence.

Bonaparte, Elisa (1777–1820) *French princess*

Elisa was the eldest and most gifted of Napoleon's sisters. Born Maria Anna Buonaparte at Ajaccio, Corsica, Elisa married her countryman Felice Baciocchi in 1797. Napoleon made them Prince and Princess of Piombino (1805) and of Lucca (1806). He also conferred the title of Grand Duchess of Tuscany (1809) on Elisa.

Elisa ruled her domains in a humane and enlightened way. In Tuscany she made Florence a city of beauty to which artists and thinkers were drawn. She helped revive the Accademia della Crusca, which published, among other things, a Tuscan dictionary that formed the basis of the standardization of the Italian language.

In 1813–14 Elisa reluctantly allied herself with her brother-in-law Joachim Murat in his rebellion against Napoleon. As a result, she lost her crown. She died at Sant'-Andrea, near Trieste.

Bonaparte, Pauline (1780–1825)
French princess

Pauline was the second sister of Napoleon Bonaparte. Although lacking the political ambition of her sisters Caroline BONAPARTE and Elisa BONAPARTE, she was intelligent, witty, and graced with great physical beauty. Her personal life was fraught with scandal.

Born Maria Paola Buonaparte at Ajaccio, Corsica, she was married at the age of 16 to General Charles Leclerc. When he went to the Caribbean island of Santo Domingo in 1802 to suppress a slave revolt, she followed him there; however, he fell victim to fever and died. The following year she married the Italian nobleman Prince Camillo Borghese, whom she soon left for the freedom of life in Paris. In 1806 Napoleon made Pauline Duchess of Guastalla, in northern Italy. The sculptor Canova made a famous statue of her as a reclining nude at this time.

In 1814 Pauline went to Elba to comfort the exiled Napoleon. After 1815 she lived in Italy, suffering ill health for the rest of her life. She died in Florence.

Bondfield, Margaret Grace (1873–1953) *British trade union leader and politician*

In 1929 Bondfield became the first woman to be appointed a British cabinet minister.

Margaret Bondfield was born in Chard, Somerset, the daughter of a lacemaker with radical views. Her first job was as a shop assistant, but she soon became involved in labour organizations. From 1898 to 1908 she was assistant secretary of the Shop Assistants Union and from 1898 to 1938 served as a national official of the National Union of General and Municipal Workers. In 1923 she was elected to the chair of the Trades Union Congress and entered parliament as a Labour Party member. Bondfield was parliamentary secretary to the ministry of labour in 1924 during Ramsay MacDonald's short-lived first government; as minister of labour from 1929 to 1931 in MacDonald's second administration she was the first woman in Britain to become a cabinet minister. She retired from political life in 1931 and from her various union posts in 1938. She died in Sanderstead, Surrey.

Bonham Carter, (Helen) Violet, Lady Asquith (1887–1969) *British political figure*

Violet Bonham Carter was a leading figure in the inner circles of the Liberal Party for over 50 years.

Violet was the daughter of the Liberal politician H. H. Asquith and his first wife, Helen, who died when her children were still young. During Violet's youth her father rose through the cabinet ranks to become prime minister in 1908, when she was 21. In 1915 she married Asquith's principal private secretary, Maurice Bonham Carter.

As a young woman, Violet campaigned vigorously for her father and developed a considerable gift for oratory by speaking at meetings and rallies. She remained a staunch supporter during Asquith's ousting from the premiership in 1916 and the subsequent fragmentation and eclipse of the Liberal Party. Remaining at the forefront of Liberal politics after Asquith's death in 1927, she was a consistent supporter of libertarian and internationalist causes. Bonham Carter backed the formation of the National Government in 1931 but later withdrew her support in protest at its adoption of protectionism. She also argued for electoral reform and supported Eleanor RATHBONE's campaign for family allowances. During the 1930s she was a champion of the League of Nations and a leading critic of appeasement: in the latter cause she became an ally of Winston Churchill, of whom she later wrote a memoir. After the war she became a keen supporter of the idea of a United States of Europe.

Despite her skills as a speaker and campaigner, Violet Bonham Carter failed in both her attempts to enter parliament (1945, 1951). She was appointed DBE in 1953 and became a life peer in 1964. Several of her children and grandchildren have been active in politics and the arts: her daughter Laura married Jo Grimond, who became the Liberal leader in the 1950s, while her granddaughter Helena BONHAM CARTER is a well-known film actress.

See also ASQUITH, MARGOT.

Bonham Carter, Helena (1966–) *British actress*

Helena Bonham Carter is best known for her portrayal of young Englishwomen in movies set around the turn of the century.

She was born in London into a privileged background; her great-grandfather was the Liberal prime minister Herbert Henry Asquith (1852–1928), and her grandmother was Lady Violet BONHAM CARTER. Helena resolved to pursue a career in acting from her early teens; without any formal dramatic training she promoted herself in the theatrical press, and her independence of spirit and good looks soon secured her an agent.

Her film debut was in the role of Lady Jane GREY in the historical film *Lady Jane* (1984), which was not a critical or commercial success. However, the following year brought her stardom, when she played the part of a naive English girl who finds love with a compatriot during a visit to Italy, in the film of E. M. Forster's 1908 novel

A Room with a View. This performance began an association with director James Ivory and producer Ismail Merchant, which continued with the highly praised film *Howards End* (1992), another Forster adaptation.

Helena Bonham Carter has acted in a number of other films and appeared on the stage but, by her own admission, found it hard to escape being typecast as an innocent "English rose." In *Margaret's Museum* (1997), however, a bittersweet love story set in 1940s Nova Scotia, Bonham Carter departed from her previous image by playing a miner's daughter who becomes a serial murderer. That same year she starred as the unscrupulous Kate Croy in *The Wings of the Dove*, a performance that earned her an Oscar nomination as Best Actress.

Bonheur, Rosa (1822–1899) *French artist*

Bonheur was one of the most famous and significant women artists of her age. She was particularly known for her studies of animals, executed both in paint and as sculptures.

Marie Rosalie Bonheur was born in Bordeaux, the daughter of Raymond Bonheur, an amateur painter turned professional. She was the eldest of four children, all of whom followed their father's profession – her brother Auguste and her sister Juliette were painters, and her brother Isidore Jules became a sculptor. Although she was originally going to be a seamstress, Rosa insisted on receiving artistic training from her father, after which she studied with Léon Cogniet at the Ecole des Beaux-Arts in Paris.

Her interest in animal subjects began early. She studied them outside Paris in the Bois de Boulogne, some parts of which were then still quite wild. She began to exhibit at the Paris Salon in 1840 and won a first-class medal in 1848 for *Ploughing in the Nivernais*, which now hangs in the Louvre. Her fame was assured in 1853 when she exhibited *The Horse Fair* (now in the Metropolitan Museum of Art, New York City). This painting was instantly popular and admired by Queen VICTORIA, among others; it became known through engraved copies. Late in life Bonheur adopted the brilliant colour of the impressionists.

Rosa Bonheur was also one of the most successful of a group of French animal sculptors who flourished in mid-19th-century Paris. Among them were Antoine Louis Barye, Pierre Jules Mène, and Rosa's brother Isidore Jules.

Her father had encouraged Rosa to believe in female equality, and from her youth she showed an independence of spirit and a desire to be accepted on the same footing as the male artists of her time. She wore men's clothes from the early 1850s, yet also managed to win favour and patronage from the French Establishment. She was named a Chevalier of the Legion of Honour by the Empress EUGÉNIE in 1865 and was the first woman to receive the Grand Cross of the Legion.

Rosa Bonheur spent her last years at the estate she had bought in 1853 at By, near Fontainebleau, where she died; a monument to her, sculpted by her brother Isidore Jules, stands in the grounds of her house.

Bonner, Yelena (1923–) *Russian physician and dissident*

As the wife of the Russian dissident Andrei Sakharov – developer of the USSR's first hydrogen bomb and a leading protestor against Soviet human-rights abuses – Yelena Bonner came to prominence as she and her husband suffered growing persecution during the 1970s and 1980s.

Her awareness of the Soviet system's repressiveness began in her youth, when her parents, both staunch Communist Party members, were arrested in a Stalinist purge in 1937. Her father was executed by the authorities. She lived with relatives in Leningrad (now St. Petersburg) during her mother's long imprisonment, which only ended in 1954, after Stalin's death. During World War II Yelena Bonner sustained eye injuries while serving at the Front, but she still managed to qualify as a doctor in 1953.

She did medical aid work abroad before marrying Sakharov in 1971. Their criticism of the Soviet Union's failure to observe human rights agreements led to police surveillance and, ultimately, internal exile. Bonner was permitted to travel abroad for eye treatment and to collect Sakharov's 1975 Nobel Peace Prize; throughout this period she continued to work tirelessly to obtain her husband's freedom and reinstatement. The era of *glasnost* brought rehabilitation under President Gorbachev, but only Bonner was to witness the final collapse of the Soviet system in 1991, Sakharov having died in 1989.

Bonny, Anne (*c*.1700–?) *Irish-born pirate*

Following their capture and trial for piracy in 1721, Anne Bonny and her shipmate Mary Read became the subject of numerous romantic legends.

Anne Bonny was born near Cork, the illegitimate daughter of a wealthy lawyer and a serving maid. To avoid the scandal, Anne's father emigrated to America, taking mother and child with him. Anne grew up in the prosperous plantation society of South Carolina, where she seems to have developed a highly independent and self-willed character. In about 1718 she married James Bonny, a poor seaman, against the wishes of her father. When Anne was cast out without a penny, the couple headed for New Providence Island in the Bahamas, a well-known haunt of pirates and privateers.

Although the details are unclear, Anne Bonny subsequently became separated from her husband and formed a liaison with the famous pirate 'Calico' Jack Rackham, whose child she apparently bore. Wearing man's attire, she joined Rackham's crew and participated in various acts of piracy, including several attacks on Spanish ships in the Caribbean. In about 1719 Rackham's crew captured a sloop sailing from Providence, New England. Remarkably, the crew working this vessel included another female pirate, the English-born Mary Read (*c*.1690–1721). The two women became inseparable friends and may even have been lovers.

In 1720 Rackham's sloop was captured by a government ship off Jamaica. According to later accounts, which were almost certainly romanticized, Anne and Mary remained fighting boldly on deck long after Rackham and the male crew had retreated to the hold. At the subsequent trial both women were convicted of capital crimes but escaped with their lives by pleading pregnancy. Not having this option, Rackham and his men were hanged. Mary Read died in prison shortly after her reprieve, while of Anne Bonny nothing further has been recorded.

The image of Anne Bonny as a dashing witty adventurer was largely created by an account published in 1724, *A General History...of the Most Notorious Pyrates* by Charles Johnson (possibly a pseudonym for Daniel Defoe). The 20th century has seen several fictional treatments of her story, in which she and Mary Read emerge as feminist heroines.

Bonstelle, Jessie (*c*.1872–1932) *American theatre manager and actress*

Bonstelle was popularly known as the "Maker of Stars" because she helped launch the careers of several prominent performers, including Katharine CORNELL and Melvyn Douglas. She was also a leading light in promoting the development of "noncommercial" civic or community theatres in the United States.

Bonstelle was born Laura Justine Bonesteele in Greece, New York State. Her theatre career began with touring companies, and by the age of 19 she was manager of the theatre in Syracuse, New York. She later organized and acted in her own repertory companies in Buffalo and Rochester. In 1910 she leased the Garrick Theatre in Detroit and in 1925 opened her own theatre, the Bonstelle Playhouse, which she converted in 1928 into the Detroit Civic Theatre. She died in Detroit.

Booth, Catherine (1829–90) *British evangelist and social campaigner*

With her husband, Charles, Catherine Booth founded the Salvation Army in 1877. One of the first women preachers to become a national figure in Britain, she was an early advocate for the complete equality of women in the Christian Church.

Catherine Mumford was born in Ashbourne, Derbyshire, the daughter of a coachbuilder who was also a Wesleyan lay preacher. Owing to persistent ill health, which dogged her for all her life, she was educated mainly at home. In 1844 the family moved to Brixton, London, where Catherine experienced an intense religious conversion and became active in the Wesleyan Methodist Church. However, her sympathies for the reforming movement within Methodism led to her expulsion from the official church in 1851. Amongst those expelled with her was the young pastor Charles Booth, who became her husband in 1855.

For the first ten years of their married life Charles Booth worked as a preacher for the breakaway Methodist New Connection. Although they settled for a while in Gateshead, his role was largely itinerant and Catherine generally travelled with him, taking an increasingly active part at the large revivalist meetings he addressed. In 1859 she published *Female Ministry*, an eloquent defence of women's role in the church; the following year she herself stepped forward as a preacher – a role in which she soon became celebrated.

Prompted mainly by his wife, Charles Booth broke his remaining links with Methodism in 1865 and moved to London to work as an independent preacher amongst the capital's poor. The East End mission they founded together was restyled the Salvation Army in 1877. By preaching on street corners and pitching their appeal chiefly to society's outcasts – alcoholics, criminals, and prostitutes – the Booths initially incurred a good deal of hostility. However, thanks in part to Catherine's skill in cultivating wealthy sympathizers, the movement grew steadily in strength and respectability.

Catherine Booth's influence on the ethos and organization of the Salvation Army was second only to that of her husband. Its combination of military-style discipline with fervent emotionalism was very much a reflection of her own temperament. More specifically, she ensured that the movement gave a full role to women and was largely responsible for its radical teaching on the sacraments (which she regarded as inessential). Despite the onset of cancer in the 1880s, she continued to preach, write, and campaign, being particularly active in the movement to outlaw child prostitution. In her old age she was a firm supporter of women's suffrage. Weakened by illness, she finally retired in 1888. Her funeral was attended by an estimated 36,000 people.

Catherine Booth combined her public life with heavy family responsiblities: the Booths had eight children, all of whom became active in the Salvation Army. Their daughter Evangeline BOOTH became the Army's first female general in 1934.

Booth, Evangeline (1865–1950)
British-born American general of the Salvation Army

Evangeline Booth is remembered for her role as commander of the Salvation Army in Canada and the United States and later of the whole organization worldwide. She was a great speaker and also wrote a number of hymns.

Born on Christmas Day in the East End of London, Eveline Cory Booth was the seventh of eight children of William and Catherine BOOTH, founders of the Salvation Army. As an early indication of her religious ardour, she changed her name to Evangeline, loosely translated as "daughter of the Gospels." As a teenager helping the poor in the slums, she came to be known as the "White Angel."

Evangeline had a great talent for organization and publicity and at 15 was made a sergeant in the Army, becoming a captain two years later. After extensive work with the Army she became its commander in London.

In 1896 the Salvation Army appointed Evangeline Booth as its field commander in Canada. Following this, in 1904, she became national commander for the United States, where she served for 30 years and established the Army as a major welfare organization. During this period she also published some of her writings, including a volume of hymns, *Songs of the Evangel* (1927), and a collection of her sermons, *Towards a Better World* (1928).

From 1934 to 1939 Evangeline Booth served as the first woman general of the whole Salvation Army. Having taken U.S. citizenship in 1923, she settled in Hartsdale, New York State, after her retirement.

Booth, Shirley (1898–1992) *American actress*

After years of playing supporting roles on the stage, Shirley Booth became a Broadway star in 1950 playing Lola Delaney, the frumpy pathetic wife in William Inge's drama *Come Back, Little Sheba*.

Born Thelma Booth Ford in New York City, she had an unhappy childhood: her father was very severe and her mother terminally ill. To compensate for her loneliness, she created a world of theatrical make-believe. She first appeared on stage around 1920 with a repertory company in Hartford, Connecticut, in the thriller *The Cat and the Canary*. After acting with other repertory companies, Shirley Booth made her Broadway debut in *Hell's Bells* in 1925, playing opposite Humphrey Bogart. Her first major part on Broadway was as a gambler's girlfriend in the 1935 comedy hit *Three Men on a Horse*.

Shirley Booth's most memorable stage roles were in the comedies *The Philadelphia Story* (1939) and *My Sister Eileen* (1940); the dramas *Tomorrow the World* (1943) and *The Time of the Cuckoo* (1952); and the musical *A Tree Grows in Brooklyn* (1951). She repeated on film her original role in *Come Back, Little Sheba* (1953), winning an Academy Award. She also appeared as Miss Duffy in the radio series *Duffy's Tavern* in the 1940s and in the title role of the television series *Hazel* in the 1960s. She died in North Chatham, Massachusetts.

Boothroyd, Betty (1929–   ) *British Labour politician and first woman speaker of the House of Commons*

As speaker of the House of Commons Betty Boothroyd has become one of the most widely admired figures in British public life.

Betty Boothroyd was born in Dewsbury, Yorkshire, and educated at the College of Art and Commerce there. After several years as a dancer with the popular Tiller Girls troupe, she began a career as a secretary and political assistant in the mid-1950s. In this capacity she worked for five years at Labour Party headquarters in London, for two years in Washington D.C., and for over ten years (1962–73) as a personal assistant to Labour ministers during the era of Harold Wilson. During this period she also served as a councillor for the London borough of Hammersmith (1965–68) and made several unsuccessful attempts to enter parliament (from 1957).

In 1973 Betty Boothroyd was finally elected as the Labour MP for West Bromwich (West Bromwich West from 1974). She was also a member of the European Parliament from 1975 to 1977. At Westminster, she sat on several committees concerned with the administration of the House and became one of the three deputy speakers in 1987. Following the general election of 1992, she was elected speaker of the House of Commons with wide support from across the political parties. Owing largely to the televising of parliament (from 1989), Boothroyd has become a famous figure in Britain and abroad; she is widely popular for her good-humour, even-handedness, and no-nonsense manner, as well as for her evident ability to control the rowdy male-dominated House.

Bora, Katherina von (1499–1552) *Wife of the German Protestant reformer Martin Luther*

Katherina von Bora, whose Christian name is also spelt Katharina and Catherina, was born in Klein-Laussig, near Bitterfeld, Saxony, and entered a Cistercian nunnery in 1515. However, she became interested in the ideals of the Protestant Reformation and in 1523 was one of a group of nuns who renounced their vows and left the order. As her relatives refused to take her back, she lived for a time with the family of the mayor of Wittenberg, a stronghold of the Reformation.

While in Wittenberg, she met the re-

ligious reformer Martin Luther, whose
ideas had already inspired her. Their
relationship quickly developed, and
they were married in June 1525.
Throughout their marriage Katherina
supported and helped her husband in
his work; she also bore him six children. After Luther's death in 1540
Katherina moved to Torgau on the
River Elbe, where she died.

Borden, Lizzie Andrew (1860–1927)
American suspected murderess

> Lizzie Borden took an axe
> And gave her mother forty whacks;
> When she saw what she had done,
> She gave her father forty-one.
>
> —Anonymous rhyme

Lizzie Borden was charged with mur-
dering her father and stepmother with
an axe on August 4, 1892. The case
was one of the most celebrated in
American legal history. Although she
was legally acquitted, popular opinion
continued to regard her as guilty.

She was born in Fall River, Massachusetts, and never married; at the
time of the murders she was a Sunday
school teacher. She and the maid,
Bridget Sullivan, were both known to
have been on the premises when the
murders occurred, but only Lizzie was
arrested. She claimed to have been
outside in the barn at the time the
killings took place. After a 13-day trial
she was acquitted on June 20, 1893.

As a member of a wealthy Yankee
family, Lizzie Borden may have been
the victim of malicious rumour by
local mill workers; this may explain
why she was still reviled even after her
acquittal. Nevertheless, she refused to
yield to pressure and remained in Fall
River until her death. Interest in the
case was revived when Edmund Pearson proclaimed her guilty in *The Trial
of Lizzie Borden* (1937). But Pearson's
conclusions were challenged by Edward D. Radin in his re-examination
of the case, *Lizzie Borden: The Untold
Story* (1961). The Society of the
Friends of Lizzie Borden was organized after its publication. The case
has been the subject of a number of
plays, novels, a ballet, an opera, and a
musical revue.

Borgia, Lucrezia (1480–1519) *Italian noblewoman*

> The more I try to do God's will the
> more he visits me with misfortunes.
>
> —Quoted by Rachel Erlanger in
> *Lucrezia Borgia*

Lucrezia Borgia has become a symbol
of the moral corruption and violence
that characterized Renaissance Italy in
the late 15th century. Her advocates,
by contrast, regard her as an innocent
victim of circumstance.

Lucrezia was born in Subiaco, Italy,
the daughter of the Spanish cardinal
Rodrigo Borgia (who became Pope
Alexander VI in 1492) and his Roman
mistress Vanezza dei Catanei. Lucrezia
was thus born into a world of dynastic
ambition and political intrigue. Before
her 22nd birthday she was twice engaged to be married to Spanish noblemen and three times actually married
to Italian princes in order to further
her father's political advancement.

Her first marriage, in 1493, to Giovanni Sforza, lord of Pesaro, was annulled in 1497 when Alexander VI
changed his allegiance and aligned the
papacy with Spain and Naples against
France and the Sforza family of Milan.
A second marriage, in 1498, to Alfonso of Aragon, Duke of Bisceglie, illegitimate son of King Alfonso II of
Naples, ended with her husband's
murder in 1500 on the instructions of
Lucrezia's brother Cesare after the
Borgias had reached an agreement
with Louis XII of France. Finally,
with an undeserved reputation for
treachery and decadence, she was married in 1501 to Alfonso d'Este, son of
the Duke of Ferrara.

After the death of her father in 1503
Lucrezia ceased to be the political
pawn of her family and led a blameless
life in Ferrara. When her husband became duke in 1505, she made their
court a centre of patronage for men of
letters and artists, among them the
writers Ludovico Ariosto and Pietro
Bembo and the painters Dosso Dossi
and Titian. She died peacefully in Ferrara. However, she never managed entirely to rid herself of the scandal that
had accompanied her since her turbulent early life.

Bori, Lucrezia (1887–1960) *Spanish opera singer*

Lucrezia Bori was one of the great stars of the "golden age of opera" in the early 20th century.

Born Lucrecia Borja González de Riancho, in Valencia, she first sang on stage in Rome in 1908. In 1910, while the Metropolitan Opera Company of New York City was on tour in Paris, she won an audition to sing opposite Enrico Caruso in Puccini's *Manon Lescaut*. After two years at the famous opera house La Scala, in Milan, she joined the Metropolitan, where she remained until her retirement in 1936. Only an absence following throat surgery (1915–21) broke this continuity.

Her most celebrated roles included the title role in Massenet's *Manon*, Mélisande in Debussy's *Pelléas et Mélisande*, Mimi in Puccini's *La Bohème*, and Violetta in Verdi's *La Traviata*. She died in New York City.

Boulanger, Nadia (Juliette) (1887 –1979) *French music teacher and conductor*

Initially a composer, Nadia Boulanger turned increasingly to teaching, influencing a number of well-known composers, including Aaron Copland, Virgil Thomson, Marc Blitzstein, and Igor Markevitch.

Nadia Boulanger was born in Paris. After studying at the Paris Conservatory and in Italy, she taught musical composition at the Conservatory from 1909. She later taught at the Ecole Normale de Musique (1920–39), the American Conservatory at Fontainebleau (of which she was director after 1949), and, during World War II, in the United States – at Radcliffe and Wellesley colleges in Massachusetts as well as at the Juillard school in New York.

She visited the United States on lecture-concert tours in 1958 and 1962, becoming the first woman to conduct the Boston Symphony and New York Philharmonic. She was also the first woman to conduct a symphony orchestra in London in 1937. With Raoul Pugno she composed the music for *La Ville morte* (1911; The Dead City).

Boulanger also played a major role in the revival of Renaissance and Baroque music.

Bourignon, Antoinette (1616–1680) *Flemish religious reformer*

Antoinette Bourignon identified herself with the "woman clothed with the sun" of the Book of Revelations. Claiming to receive direct inspiration from Christ, she became an active critic of organized religion, attacking both the Protestant and the Roman Catholic Churches.

Bourignon was born in Lille, in northern France, and brought up a Roman Catholic. In 1636 she fled from home, lived for a while in a convent, and later supervised an orphanage. Her visionary zeal won over many converts to quietism, a form of religious mysticism involving complete submission to God's will.

She preached extensively throughout France, Belgium, and Holland, telling her listeners of Christ's distress that neither form of Christianity was upholding the true spirit of the Gospels. Bourignon's theology stressed internal emotions and supernatural impulses rather than doctrine or religious practices. She died at Franeker, Holland.

Bourignon wrote prolifically; her works were edited and published in 19 volumes (1679–86) by one of her disciples, Pierre Poiret. Her ideas were condemned by many Protestant churches, particularly the Church of Scotland, many of whose members defected to her. For its part, the Roman Catholic Church placed all her works on its list of banned books.

Bourke-White, Margaret (1906–1971) *American photographer*

Bourke-White captured on film many of the significant events of the first half of the 20th century. In choosing her professional name, she combined her own surname, White, with her mother's maiden name, Bourke.

Born in New York City, she graduated from Cornell University in 1927 and first practised as an architectural and industrial photographer. She took industrial photographs for *Fortune* magazine from 1929 to 1933 and also established herself as a freelance commercial photographer. At this time Bourke-White undertook the first of many photographic expeditions to the Soviet Union. In 1936 she began a life-long association with *Life* magazine. One early assignment for *Life* was to record the harrowing experience of the Great Depression in the American Midwest. During World War II she worked as an Army Air Force photographer. In the postwar years she travelled to India, where she photographed Gandhi in 1946, and to South Africa and Korea. She died in Stamford, Connecticut.

Bourke-White's volumes of photo-essays include *Eyes on Russia* (1931), *Shooting the Russian War* (1942), and *Halfway to Freedom: A Study of the New India* (1949). With novelist Erskine Caldwell, her husband from 1939 to 1942, she published her dossier of Depression photos, *You Have Seen Their Faces* (1937), as well as *North of the Danube* (1939) and *Say! Is This the U.S.A.?* (1941). Her autobiographical *Portrait of Myself* appeared in 1963.

Bow, Clara (1905–1965) *American film actress*

> Being a sex symbol is a heavy load to carry, especially when one is tired, hurt and bewildered.
>
> —Quoted by Clyde Jeavons and Jeremy Pascal in *A Pictorial History of Sex in the Movies*

Clara Bow was publicized as the "It" girl and came to personify glamor in the 1920s. On screen she was the model of the Jazz Age "flapper," a role that reflected her equally wild lifestyle off screen.

Clara Bow was born to poor parents in Brooklyn, New York. She went to Hollywood as a beauty contest winner in 1920 and first attracted attention in *Down to the Sea in Ships* (1925). Her fame grew with *The Plastic Age*, *Kid Boots*, and *Mantrap*, all released in 1926. The next year brought her spectacular success in *It*, based on the novel by Elinor GLYN. Although critics hated the film and were not at all impressed with Miss Bow's performance, *It* made her world famous.

Clara Bow, whose mother had suffered mental problems, was herself troubled by nervous disorders and physical illness. Unable to make the transition to sound films, she retired in 1931, spending much of the rest of her life in mental homes. She was married to Rex Bell, a star of Western films.

Bowen, Elizabeth (1899–1973) *Irish-born British novelist and short-story writer*

Elizabeth Bowen's works are noted for their delicate portrayal of the lives and dilemmas of upper middle-class characters. Many of her writings concern spinsters, widows, and lonely girls – sensitive and vulnerable women in search of elusive happiness. She has also been praised for her vivid depiction of life in Britain during World War II. Elizabeth Bowen's capacity to describe colours, light, and atmospheric effects may derive from an early wish to be an artist.

Born in Dublin, Elizabeth Dorothea Cole Bowen was brought up at Bowen's Court, County Cork, Ireland, and educated in Kent. At the age of 19 she began living part of the year in London and part in Italy; to help support herself she started her career as a writer. Her first published work, *Encounters*, a collection of short stories, appeared in 1923. In that year she married Alan Cameron, an educational administrator. Four years later she published her first novel, *The Hotel*. Throughout the 1930s and 1940s, her novels and short stories met with great critical approval. Among her best-known novels are *The House in Paris* (1935), *The Death of the Heart* (1938), *The Heat of the Day* (1949), *A World of Love* (1955), and *Eva Trout* (1969). *Seven Winters*, an early piece of autobiography, appeared in 1942, while *Pictures and Conversations* (1975) contains memories of her youth as well as essays of literary criticism. She also wrote radio and television scripts for the BBC.

Boyd, Belle (1844–1900) *American actress and spy*

Isabelle Boyd was born in Martinsburg, Virginia. According to her own account of her eventful early life, *Belle Boyd, in Camp and Prison* (1865), during the American Civil War she secretly gathered information from Union officers in Martinsburg and in Front Royal, Virginia, and passed it to the Confederate authorities. She was imprisoned twice for spying: in 1862, being released in a prisoner exchange, and in 1863, after which she was exiled to the South.

Boyd travelled to England in March 1864 with Confederate dispatches, but was arrested after the ship was captured by a Union warship, transported to Boston, and banished to Canada. She then sailed from Quebec to England, where in August 1864 she married Samuel Wylde Hardinge, Jr., the Union naval officer who had taken command of the rebel vessel on which she was earlier captured. They had a daughter, but Hardinge died before the war's end.

In 1866 Belle Boyd wrote her memoirs with the help of English journalist George Sala, who encouraged her to take up the profession of acting. Subsequently she played in the United States, touring the South, appearing in New York City in 1868 in the comedy *The Honeymoon*, and then working with several repertory companies. Retiring from the stage in 1869, she married John Swainston Hammond, a wealthy businessman, with whom she had four children. They divorced in 1884, and the next year Boyd married Nathanial Rue High, Jr., an actor. In 1886, again in order to support herself, she began what was to be a successful career as a public speaker, presenting dramatic recitals of her wartime experiences. *Belle Lamar*, a play by the Irish playwright Dion Boucicault, is said to be based on her life.

Boyle, Kay (1902–1992) *American writer*

Boyle is best known for her short stories, which display technical mastery and convey an incisive and sophisticated view of character and situation. Her writings are principally concerned with social and moral issues.

Born in St. Paul, Minnesota, Boyle spent much of her childhood abroad. She studied architecture at the Ohio Mechanics Institute and music at the Cincinnati Conservatory of Music,

after which, from 1922, she travelled around Europe with her first husband, living mostly in France. She returned to the United States in 1941. After World War II Boyle worked as a European correspondent for *The New Yorker* magazine. From 1963 until 1979 she taught at San Francisco State College.

Although Boyle wrote some essays and poetry, she was mainly a writer of fiction. Her stories won her numerous literary awards, including the O. Henry Memorial Award for "White Horses of Vienna" (1934) and "Defeat" (1941). Later works include the collections of stories *Smoking Mountain* (1951), *Nothing Ever Breaks Except the Heart* (1966), and *Fifty Stories* (1980) selected from over 40 years of writing. Boyle's novels include *Plagued by the Nightingale* (1931), which portrays the stifling atmosphere of conventionality in a French provincial family, and *His Human Majesty* (1949).

Bracegirdle, Anne (1663–1748) *English actress*

Anne Bracegirdle was one of the most celebrated actresses of her day. A lifelong companion of the fashionable playwright William Congreve, she specialized in playing comic parts.

Born into an impoverished family in the Midlands town of Wolverhampton, she was sent away from her natural parents, to be raised by the actors Thomas and Mary Betterton in London. There she discovered an aptitude for acting and began to appear in the comedies of manners that had become hugely popular since the Restoration of Charles II. These plays, by such writers as Congreve, Sir John Vanbrugh, and William Wycherley, were bawdy satires on contemporary sexual morality, and Bracegirdle excelled in the stock character of the innocent girl who is the subject of many men's attention. Famous roles included Belinda in Vanbrugh's *The Provok'd Wife* (1697) and Millamant in Congreve's *The Way of the World* (1700). Yet she was a versatile actress, who also had success playing Shakespearean tragedy.

After some ten years as London's most vaunted actress, her fame began to be eclipsed by the rising theatre star Anne Oldfield, and she retired from the stage in 1707. Such was her prominence, even at her death some 40 years later, that she was buried in Westminster Abbey.

Braddock, Bessie (1899–1970) *British Labour politician*

In her 25 years on the Labour backbenches Bessie Braddock became famous for her outspoken attacks on poverty and social injustice.

Elizabeth Margaret Bamber was born in Liverpool, the daughter of Harry Bamber, a skilled bookbinder, and his wife Mary, a trade-union organizer noted for her fiery platform speeches. It was from her parents that Bessie absorbed the radical socialist views that she retained to the end of her life. Although her own background was comfortable, she became aware at a young age of the grave social problems in her native city, which at that time had some of the worst housing and infant mortality rates in Western Europe.

In 1922 Bessie married Jack Braddock, a local politician who shared her ideals. The couple formed a successful working partnership and became well-known figures in the politics of Merseyside: Bessie served on the city council from 1930 to 1961 and as an alderman from 1955, while Jack went on to become leader of Liverpool city council. During her years in local government Bessie concentrated on campaigns to improve the city's housing.

In 1945 Bessie Braddock was elected to Westminster as the member for the Exchange Division of Liverpool. Although she would never hold office, her independent views and her forthright manner of expressing them made her one of the best-known parliamentarians of the day. She was often direct to the point of rudeness and treated her political opponents – including her own party leadership – with scant respect. A well-known story has her reproaching Winston Churchill at a dinner party in typically forthright style: "Winston you're drunk, horribly drunk." Churchill allegedly replied: "Bessie you're ugly, horribly ugly. But I shall be sober in the morning."

Bessie Braddock remained well-loved by her Liverpool constituents, whom she continued to represent until the year of her death.

Braddon, Mary Elizabeth (1837–1915) *British novelist*

Mary Braddon was the author of a series of melodramatic tales of crime and passion that were once highly popular but are seldom read today.

London-born, Mary had an unsettled childhood. Her father led a rootless life so, when Mary was only three years old, her mother took her away from the family home. At the age of 18 she began contributing to a Brighton newspaper (as well as performing on the stage under an assumed name to support herself and her mother), and in 1862 she published *Lady Audley's Secret*, the first of her many popular novels.

For several years Mary Braddon edited the magazine *Belgravia*, in which some of her sho
rt stories first appeared. She married John Maxwell, a well-known publisher, in 1874. Their son, William B. Maxwell (1866–1938), was also a prolific novelist.

Bradstreet, Anne (c. 1612–1672) *English-born American poet*

> If what I do prove well, it won't advance,
>   They'll say it's stolen, or else it was by chance.
>
> —'Prologue,' *Several Poems Compiled with Great Variety of Wit and Learning* (1678)

Anne Bradstreet was the first woman in the English colonies in America to win recognition for her poetry.

She is thought to have been born in Northampton, the daughter of Thomas Dudley, steward to the Earl of Lincoln. In 1628 she married the nonconformist Simon Bradstreet. Two years later she emigrated with her family to New England, where both her father and her husband later became governors of the Massachusetts Bay Colony. The Bradstreets, who had eight children, settled first in Boston. In 1634 they moved to Ipswich, and in 1644 to North Andover, where Mrs. Bradstreet died.

Anne Bradstreet's poetry was first published without her knowledge by her brother-in-law in London as *The Tenth Muse, Lately Sprung Up in America* (1650). *Several Poems Compiled with Great Variety of Wit and Learning*, published in Boston in 1678, after her death, contains improvements to the poems in the earlier volume, as well as new verses.

Anne Bradstreet was a devout Puritan; her poetry reflects the piety of her religious views. Although she occasionally sounds a feminist note, protesting that women are capable of reason, she is generally in full accord with the ideas and horizons of her contemporaries, who found nothing to criticize in her poems.

Braun, Eva (1912–1945) *German mistress of Adolf Hitler*

Eva Braun was born into a lower middle-class family in Simbach-am-Inn, Bavaria. She gained her education at a convent school run by English nuns. When Hitler met her in 1931, she was an assistant in the shop of Heinrich Hoffmann, Hitler's photographer. The following year she became his mistress, living with him in his house in Munich. Four years later she moved to the Berghof, Hitler's villa in the Bavarian Alps.

As Hitler's companion Braun adhered to his puritanical code; in his absence, she pursued her interests in English literature, sports, pets, cinema, and fashion. She was not permitted to appear with him in public or to join him in Berlin. With no particular intellectual gifts and no understanding of politics, she exerted no influence on political decisions. Hitler's indifference to her as he became totally preoccupied with affairs of state after 1933 led her to attempt suicide on several occasions.

In April 1945 Eva Braun defied Hitler's order and joined him at his bunker in Berlin, determined to be with him when the end came. In recognition of her "many years of loyal friendship," Hitler married her in a civil ceremony on April 29. On the following day she committed suicide with him. Their bodies were burned by Hitler's guard and have never formally been identified.

Bremer, Fredrika (1801–1865) *Swedish novelist*

Credited with introducing the "domestic" novel to Swedish literature, Bremer was also a strong advocate of women's rights. With her novel *Hertha* (1856), she influenced reforming legislation that advanced the status of women in Sweden.

Fredrika Bremer was born in Turku (Åbo), Finland. In 1804 her parents moved to a country estate near Stockholm, Sweden, where she spent most of her life. Her upbringing was strict in an orthodox Lutheran household. Between 1849 and 1851 she lived in the United States, an experience she portrays delightfully in her travel book *Hemmen i den nya världen* (3 vols., 1853–54), published in English as *Homes of the New World* (1853–54).

Grannarne (1837) and *Hemmet* (1839), published in English as *The Neighbours* (1842) and *The Home* (1843), respectively, are generally regarded as Fredrika Bremer's best novels. Both depict domestic situations with a gentle, wry humour. The Swedish Academy awarded her a gold medal for her work in 1844. *Familjen H-* (1829; English translation, *The H-Family*, 1844) was the first realistic novel in Swedish literature.

As well as pursuing her feminist interests, Bremer was also involved in promoting other reform and charitable movements, such as bringing aid to deprived city children. She died in Arsta, Sweden. Her collected works in Swedish were published in six volumes between 1868 and 1872. Her letters were issued in four volumes between 1915 and 1920.

Breshko-Breshkovskaya, Yekaterina Konstantinovna (1844–1934) *Russian revolutionary leader*

Breshko-Breshkovskaya is known by the nickname "Grandmother of the Russian Revolution."

She was born into an aristocratic

family in Chernigov province in south-western Russia. In 1873 she renounced her noble background and began to work as a Populist agitator among the common people. She was arrested for subversive activity in Kiev in 1874 and deported to Siberia, the first of several long exiles. After she was allowed to return to European Russia in 1896, Breshkovskaya joined the budding Socialist Revolutionary movement. She resumed her revolutionary activities, travelling through the countryside and spreading radical propaganda among the peasants. Though she confined herself to organizing and agitating, she endorsed revolutionary violence as a necessary measure to bring about the downfall of the Russian monarchy. Breshkovskaya visited the United States in 1904 to collect funds for the cause. Returning to Russia during the 1905 Revolution, she was arrested and again banished to Siberia, where she remained until the collapse of the tsar's regime in February 1917.

Breshkovskaya received a warm welcome when she returned to Petrograd (now St. Petersburg). She became a staunch supporter of Kerensky's Menshevik government (representing the more constitutional and moderate wing of the socialist party) and its war effort against Germany. When the Bolsheviks under Lenin seized power in October 1917, she bitterly opposed them and their withdrawal from the war. She eventually left her native country, dying in Prague at the age of 90.

Brice, Fanny (1891–1951) *American comedian and singer*

The vaudeville performer Fanny Brice was a highly popular entertainer in the early decades of the 20th century. Her mischievous eyes, half-moon mouth, and winning personality delighted audiences for nearly half a century. Her most famous comic creation was the badly behaved brat "Baby Snooks."

Brice was born Fannie Borach, the daughter of Jewish immigrant parents, in New York City. She made her stage debut when she was 13, performing at amateur nights in New York vaudeville houses. Within five years she became a favourite of burlesque audiences, at a time when burlesque was still family entertainment containing jokes, slapstick, and comic songs. In 1910 the impresario Florenz Ziegfeld saw her act in a run-down Brooklyn theatre and instantly offered her a part in his "Follies." She appeared in more editions of the Ziegfeld Follies than any other star.

In 1921 Brice gained an international reputation with her sentimental torch song "My Man." Her heartfelt delivery was influenced by her personal life, especially her unhappy marriage to Nicholas Arnstein, a Broadway gambler and speculator who spent several years in jail. Her marriages to Arnstein, by whom she had two children, and to the producer Billy Rose both ended in divorce.

Baby Snooks was a popular character on radio from the late 1930s until Brice's death, in Hollywood. The musical comedies *Funny Girl* (1964) and *Funny Lady* (1975), starring Barbra STREISAND, were based on her life.

Brico, Antonia (1902–1989) *Dutch-born American conductor and pianist*

Brico was among the very first women to enter the male stronghold of orchestral conducting.

She was born in Rotterdam but emigrated with her parents to the United States at the age of six. She began to learn the piano at an early age, and in her late teens gave recitals to help fund her course at the University of California at Berkeley. Following her graduation in 1923, she studied conducting in Berlin with Karl Muck.

Brico became the first woman to conduct the Berlin Philharmonic in 1930, the same year she made her U.S. debut with the Los Angeles Philharmonic. In 1933 she gave her first performance in New York conducting the Musicians' Symphony Orchestra, and in 1938 she became the first woman to conduct the New York Philharmonic. Despite such prestigious guest appearances, she was unable to find a resident conducting post. As a result, she founded the Women's Symphony Orchestra, which thrived from 1935 to 1939. Around 1940 she moved to Denver, Colorado, where she taught piano and led an orchestra that later came to be known as the Brico Symphony (1948–85). Her life was portrayed in *Antonia: Portrait of a Conductor*, a 1974 documentary film that brought her further renown.

Bridge, Ann (1889–1974) *British novelist*

Ann Bridge was born Mary Dolling Sanders, in Surrey; she was educated privately and at the London School of Economics. After her marriage in 1913 to the diplomat Sir Owen St. Clair O'Malley, she travelled extensively throughout the world; her husband's foreign service postings took them to China, Yugoslavia, Hungary, and Portugal. These travels provided background material for her novels, most of which contain exotic local colour. Because of her husband's prominent position, she wrote exclusively under the pen name Ann Bridge, concealing her true identity until he retired from the foreign service in 1947.

Bridge's first novel, *Peking Picnic* (1932), which described diplomatic life in China, won the Atlantic Monthly Prize. She also later won prizes from the Book Society in Britain and the Literary Guild in the United States. Her other novels included *Illyrian Spring* (1935), *Enchanter's Nightshade* (1937), *The Dark Moment* (1952), and *Portuguese Escape* (1958).

Bridget of Sweden, Saint (1303–1373) *Swedish visionary*

St. Bridget (Birgitta in Swedish) was a mystic who founded the religious Order of the Holy Saviour ("Brigittines") and became the patron saint of Sweden.

She was born at Finsta Gaard, near Uppsala, Sweden. Her father was the nobleman Birger Persson, governor of Uppland, and her family was related to the ruling house of Folkung. In 1316 she married Ulf Gudmarsson, a noble landowner, who was later named governor of Nercia. She bore him eight children. Bridget served as tutor to the young Queen Blanche of Namur from 1335 to 1337. Her husband died in 1344, a few months after he entered the Cistercian monastery of Alvastra.

On her husband's death, Bridget renounced the worldly life. She left her family and from 1345 to 1349 lived in penance and poverty near Alvastra. She had experienced visions and revelations since childhood, and these now became more frequent. For the next 30 years, she dictated to her secretary, who then translated Bridget's words into Latin. This work, which concerns Christ's sufferings, has come to be known as *Revelations*. In 1346 Bridget founded and wrote the rule for the Brigittines. Its first convent opened (1371–72) at Vadstena. St. CATHERINE OF SWEDEN, Bridget's daughter, was its abbess from 1374–75.

In 1349 Bridget moved to Rome, where she acted as an adviser and comforter to many ill and troubled people. She also petitioned civil and ecclesiastical authorities, criticizing abuses and urging reforms. Bridget's condemnation of the breakaway popes who had established a separate papal seat in Avignon, France, was extremely severe. However, her urgent recommendations that the rift be healed were not decisive in prompting Pope Urban V's eventual return to Rome in 1367.

Bridget died in Rome, shortly after returning from a pilgrimage to the Holy Land. She was canonized in 1391; her feast day is celebrated on July 23.

Bridgman, Laura Dewey (1829–1889) *American blind deaf-mute*

Laura Bridgman was the first known deaf-blind person to receive an education. An attack of scarlet fever at the age of two had left her with no sight, hearing, smell, and possibly no taste. By relying on and developing her remaining sense of touch, she learned to find her way around, and even to sew and knit. In 1837, aged seven, she came to the attention of Dr. Samuel Gridley Howe, the celebrated pioneer in work for the blind who was director of the Perkins Institution and Massachusetts Asylum for the Blind. She entered the Institution that same year.

Laura's teacher began by taking such everyday objects as a key, spoon, and knife, and pasting on each a label with the name of the object in embossed letters. By learning to recognize first the objects themselves and then the names for them, Laura was subsequently able to match a correct, unattached label with the appropriate object. Later she learned to arrange individual letters into words. At first she performed these tasks by rote, until she finally realized that each particular object had a name, and so became aware of the concept of communication through language. She was then given a set of metal types with raised letters at the end and a board with holes into which they would fit, so that they could be read with the finger. She never learned to speak, but was taught the manual alphabet of the deaf with words spelled into her hand. This became her primary means of communication. Using this method, she studied a variety of advanced subjects.

This remarkable achievement, publicized by the novelist Charles Dickens, brought Laura Bridgman fame – she received letters from all over the world. Dickens had published his account of meeting Laura in *American Notes*. She remained at the Perkins Institution until her death.

Bright Eyes (1854–1903) *Native American writer and lecturer*

Bright Eyes, through her writing and public speaking, was instrumental in ensuring that the U.S. government adopted a more humane attitude towards Native American peoples.

She was born in Nebraska, the daughter of the Omaha chief Inshtamaza ("Iron Eye"), or Joseph La Flesche, and was baptized Susette La Flesche. However, she used her Indian name Inshtatheamba ("Bright Eyes") in her public work. At an early age she displayed talent in the mission school on the reservation; she was therefore sent east to gain an education, returning to teach in the government school. Bright Eyes soon became the most renowned Native American woman of her day.

In violation of earlier treaties, a government order of 1877 had forcibly transferred the Ponca, a tribe related to the Omaha, from their Nebraska reservation to Oklahoma, where they were terribly afflicted by disease and starvation. In 1879 several Poncas, including Chief Standing Bear, attempted to return to Nebraska and were arrested. Thomas H. Tibbles, an editor on the *Omaha Herald* newspaper, took up the Poncas' case. Although those arrested and tried were acquitted and freed, there remained the problem of resettling the Ponca in Nebraska with the right to hold property as individuals. Concerned churchmen persuaded Bright Eyes and her brother Francis Le Flesche to travel east with Tibbles and Standing Bear and solicit public support by telling of the Poncas' plight.

Bright Eyes drew large crowds in Boston, Philadelphia, and Washington, and was praised in the U.S. Senate. Her influence brought about the termination of the policy of forcible relocation of Native peoples. Furthermore her efforts were rewarded by the passage of the Dawes Act of 1885, which, albeit under certain conditions, gave individual Indians the right to own land.

Bright Eyes and Tibbles, who were married in 1881, gave a series of lectures in Britain in 1886. Returning to the United States, they settled on the Nebraska reservation, where Bright Eyes wrote and illustrated stories of Indian life.

Brightman, Sarah (1959–) *British actress, singer, and dancer*

Sarah Brightman is the former wife of the composer and producer Andrew Lloyd Webber and starred in several of his hit musicals.

She was born in the coastal resort of Bournemouth. Her mother had been in show business and arranged dancing lessons for her three-year-old daughter. Thereafter she attended theatrical schools, making her first appearance on the London stage at the age of 13. Three years later she began dancing in television song-and-dance companies. The hallmark of the groups with which Brightman was involved – Pan's People and, especially, Hot Gossip – was energetic and suggestive choreography set to contemporary pop music.

After recording a hit single with Hot

Gossip, Brightman left to pursue a solo career and successfully auditioned for Lloyd Webber's new musical, *Cats*, in 1981. This long-running show was a box-office spectacular, from which she went on to star in several more of his works, including *Requiem* and *The Phantom of the Opera*. She married the composer in 1984. Although she is now divorced from him, she continues to appear in his musicals, most recently in *Aspects of Love*.

Brigid of Ireland, Saint (*c.* 460–*c.* 528) *Irish abbess*

St. Brigid, also known as Bride, Bridget, or Breeda, is famous for founding a number of monasteries in Ireland. Together with St. Patrick and St. Columba, she is regarded as one of the country's main patron saints. Much of her life is shrouded in uncertainty, and many myths and legends have grown up around her.

It is reasonably certain that Brigid was born in County Offaly, around 460. Her father, a petty king or chieftain, belonged to the Fotharta clan; her mother, a Christian, was one of his slaves. Brigid received some education and was trained in domestic duties. She persuaded her father, who had planned to marry her to the king of Ulster, to let her remain a virgin and devote her life to the service of God.

Brigid founded the famous convent and church at the "Church of the Oak," Cill Dara (Kildare). Her great generosity to the poor and afflicted undoubtedly influenced the many tales of miracles that surround her in Irish folklore. In her active aid to the poor she resembled a modern missionary sister, rather than a strictly cloistered medieval nun. She often travelled far from Cill Dara on charitable expeditions. She died in County Kildare around 528.

Soon after her death the people of Ireland began to honour her as a saint. Her great popularity is indicated by the many churches and places named after her. To her own people, she was the "Mary of Gael." As Irish missionaries spread the Gospel abroad, so they spread devotion to her in Britain and throughout Europe. Her feast is celebrated on February 1.

Brion, Friederike Elisabeth (1752–1813) *German muse of Goethe*

Friederike Brion was one of the first loves of the German writer Johann Wolfgang von Goethe.

Born at Niederrödern, Alsace, she first met Goethe in 1770, while he was studying law at Strasbourg and her father was serving as pastor at nearby Sesenheim. Goethe harboured an unrequited passion for her, alluding to her in many of his early works. She was probably the model for the virtuous characters Marie and Gretchen in *Götz von Berlichingen*, and *Faust*, respectively. Goethe also dedicated several early poems to her and wrote very fondly of her in his autobiography, *Dichtung und Wahrheit* (Poetry and Truth; 1811–30). She died, never having married, in Sesenheim.

Brittain, Vera Mary (1893–1970) *British writer, pacifist, and feminist*

> It is probably true to say that the largest scope for change still lies in men's attitude to women, and in women's attitude to themselves.
>
> —*Lady into Woman*

Vera Brittain is best known as the author of *Testament of Youth*, an autobiographical account of her early years, relating her struggle for education in a society hostile to women's learning; it also records her harrowing experiences in World War I.

She was born in Newcastle-under-Lyme, Staffordshire, the daughter of a wealthy paper manufacturer. Showing early promise of academic excellence, she progressed from school to a scholarship at Somerville College, Oxford. The outbreak of war in 1914 interrupted her studies, and she volunteered as a nurse, serving in London, France, and Malta. The war brought personal tragedy, taking both her fiancé and her brother from her.

At the end of the war Vera Brittain finished her degree and began a career in journalism. In 1925 she married the political philosopher George Catsin. Although she wrote prolifically from the 1920s onwards, it was her *Testa-*

ment (1933–57) trilogy that brought her most attention. She also wrote numerous scholarly studies on literary and feminist subjects.

Vera Brittain was always outspoken and forthright in her views, which she expounded in writing and through extensive lecture tours. She was tireless in her promotion of the pacifist cause and of women's rights.

Her daughter, Shirley WILLIAMS, rose to prominence as a leading social democrat politician and academic.

Brontë, Anne (1820–1849) British novelist

> A sort of literary Cinderella.
>
> —George Moore, describing Brontë, *Conversations in Ebury Street*

Anne Brontë was the youngest of the famous trio of literary sisters. Anne's literary endeavors, like those of Emily BRONTË, went unacknowledged in her brief lifetime.

Anne and her sisters were brought up by their strict authoritarian father Patrick Brontë, rector of Haworth in the bleak moorland of Yorkshire, and by their aunt Elizabeth Branwell. Their mother had died in 1821; Anne's infancy prevented her being sent with all her other sisters to boarding school in 1824, a harsh institution where the two eldest girls of the six original Brontë children fell ill and died.

In childhood Anne was especially close to her elder sister Emily , who returned home from boarding school with Charlotte BRONTË in 1825. Together they read extensively, inventing an imaginary world as a setting for their early poetry. After completing her education at home, Anne took employment as a governess to wealthy families from 1839 until 1845. Like her sisters' similar positions, this role proved a source of frustration and unhappiness. Their plan to establish a school together came to nothing, and all the sisters relied on literary work to make a living from home after 1845.

Anne's first work was a joint effort with her sisters, a volume of verse entitled *Poems, by Currer, Ellis and Acton Bell* (1846); these male pen names (Anne was "Acton Bell") were taken by the women to ensure publication.

Anne's novel *Agnes Grey* – the story of a governess, based on her own experiences – was published in 1847, but attracted no critical attention. Her second novel, *The Tenant of Wildfell Hall*, appeared the following year, this time under her own name. Its theme is the moral anguish of an innocent girl married to a brutal and dissipated drunkard who is dying and afraid of hellfire – a character based on Anne's brother Branwell. The novel shocked the reading public, but Anne was firm in what she saw as her duty to write about unpalatable truths.

Throughout this period, as well as striving to sustain themselves with their writing, Anne and her sisters were having to care for their dissolute, failed artist brother Branwell, who was addicted to drink and opium. His death, in September 1848, was closely followed first by that of Emily and then of Anne, who fell victim to tuberculosis.

Brontë, Charlotte (1816–1855) British novelist

> If these remarkable works are the productions of a woman we shall only say she must be a woman pretty nearly unsexed.
>
> —James Lorimer, *North British Review*, August 1849

Charlotte, the eldest of the literary Brontë sisters, was the only one to achieve recognition during her lifetime, for the novel *Jane Eyre* (1847).

Like her sisters Anne and Emily BRONTË, Charlotte was raised in Haworth, Yorkshire, where her father was appointed rector in 1820. At the age of five she was sent with her elder sisters Maria and Elizabeth and her younger sister Emily to the Clergy Daughters' School in Cowan Bridge. The severe regime there brought about the deaths of Maria and Elizabeth, and the two younger Brontë children were withdrawn from the school (which Charlotte later portrayed, in all its harshness, in the fictional Lowood Institution in *Jane Eyre*).

During their subsequent education at home, Charlotte and her brother Branwell collaborated in creating the imaginary world of "Angria," an exotic realm full of passion and tragedy. Many themes were to resurface in her mature fiction. From 1835 onwards Charlotte worked as a school teacher and as a governess for prosperous local families. Planning to set up a school together, she and her sister Emily spent some time, in 1842, in Brussels in order to learn languages. Here Charlotte fell hopelessly in love with the married head of the boarding school at which they were studying; her love was not reciprocated.

With her sisters and her brother Charlotte lived at home in Haworth from 1845 onwards. Deciding to abandon careers in teaching, the Brontë sisters began to pursue their literary ambitions. *Poems, by Currer, Ellis and Acton Bell* (1846) was published under male pen names (Charlotte was "Currer Bell"). Although Charlotte's first novel, *The Professor*, never found a publisher in her lifetime, the second, *Jane Eyre*, was immediately accepted and became widely popular. This novel follows the progress of a penniless orphan of great courage who succeeds in becoming a governess to a wealthy family. A passionate attachment to Mr. Rochester, the head of the family, almost ends in tragedy, but moral rectitude eventually triumphs and happiness ensues.

However, the increasing tragedy engulfing the Brontë's domestic situation meant that Charlotte could not enjoy her literary success. The death of all her remaining siblings left her alone after 1849 (the year in which her third novel, *Shirley*, appeared). Charlotte's final novel, *Villette* (1853), was based on her experiences in Brussels.

In 1854 she married her father's curate, Arthur Bell Nicholls, but died the following year in pregnancy.

Brontë, Emily (1818–1848) *British novelist and poet*

> Stronger than a man, simpler than a child, her nature stood alone.
>
> —Charlotte Brontë, Preface to *Wuthering Heights*

Emily was the middle sister of the famous Brontë novelists. She is best known as the author of *Wuthering Heights*, a novel renowned for its evo-

cation of the wild moorland landscape of west Yorkshire and its depiction of equally tempestuous human relationships.

Emily's first juvenile literary efforts were the poems written with her sister Anne BRONTË for the make-believe world of "Gondal," which they had created as children. Unlike her sisters, however, Emily continued to write Gondal poems into maturity, producing works of great imaginative intensity. Like her sisters, she spent time as a governess after completing her education but was desperately unhappy at being separated from the family home and the environment of Haworth.

When the sisters reassembled at Haworth in 1845 to live by their writing, Emily's poems were the impetus to the joint production *Poems, by Currer, Ellis and Acton Bell* (1846), after her elder sister Charlotte BRONTË had discovered Emily's verse and recognized its great quality. The *Poems* were published under male names – Emily was "Ellis Bell." *Wuthering Heights* – the story of an unrequited passion between Cathy Earnshaw, daughter of a landowner, and the orphan Heathcliff, whom he had adopted – was considered morbid and immoral by contemporaries on its publication in 1847. By contrast, it is now recognized as a masterpiece that goes far beyond the moral commonplaces of its day. Emily herself is regarded as the romantic visionary among the Brontë sisters, not least because of the sensitive and emotional approach to nature that pervades both her poems and the novel.

At the age of 30 Emily died of tuberculosis, brought on by a chill contracted at her brother Branwell's funeral three months earlier.

Brookner, Anita (1928–) *British art historian and writer*

> How to achieve love, how to be worthy of love, how to conduct love…The rules are really crude. The rules are: Who dares, wins. This is bad news for people who don't dare and who see others win.
>
> —Talking to *Publishers Weekly* about her novels, 1985

Brookner's experiences as an academic

have shaped the subject matter of her fiction. Praised for her graceful style and subtle insight, she has explored the emotional frustrations of intellectual women who struggle to reconcile reality with the expectations created by their education.

Anita Brookner was born in London into a family of Polish Jewish descent. After studying for her first degree at King's College, London, she took a PhD at the Courtauld Institute, London. She pursued a career as an art historian, lecturing at Reading and Cambridge universities and at the Courtauld Institute. In 1967 she became the first woman to hold the post of Slade Professor of Art at Cambridge. A Fellow of New Hall, Cambridge, and of King's College, London, Brookner has written several highly regarded books on French 18th- and 19th-century art, including *Watteau* (1968), *Greuze* (1972), and *Jacques-Louis David* (1980).

Brookner turned to fiction relatively late in her career but in the period 1981–97 had 17 novels published. Drawing on her own experiences, she explores issues of loneliness through women who are intellectually independent yet have a deep-seated yearning for romantic love. Though Brookner claims not to be a feminist, such works as *A Start in Life* (1981), *Providence* (1982), and *Look at Me* (1983) unmask the harm done by traditional literature and education in leading women to believe that meekness and self-effacement will be rewarded with happiness.

In 1984 Brookner won the Booker Prize for fiction for *Hôtel du Lac*, which explores the plight of an intelligent but unworldly woman who has rejected the security of marriage for the uncertainties of romantic love. A similar theme underlies *A Misalliance* (1986). Initially a rather introspective writer, Brookner has broadened her scope in later novels, which include *Latecomers* (1988), which has a Jewish theme, *Brief Lives* (1990), *A Private View* (1994), *Altered States* (1996), and *Visitors* (1997).

Brooks, Gwendolyn (1917–) *American poet and novelist*

Brooks was the first African-American writer to be awarded a Pulitzer Prize, which she won in 1950 for her verse collection *Annie Allen* (1949).

Born in Topeka, Kansas, Gwendolyn Brooks was raised in Chicago, where she spent most of her life. Brooks's first poem was published in the magazine *American Childhood* when she was aged 13; later in her teens she published more than 75 poems in an African-American newspaper, the *Chicago Defender*. Her first book of poetry, *A Street in Bronzeville*, was published in 1945 and well received critically. She was awarded an American Academy of Arts and Letters grant in 1946 and Guggenheim fellowships in 1946 and 1947.

Brooks's later volumes of verse include *The Bean Eaters* (1960), *In the Mecca* (1968), and *The Near Johannesburg Boy* (1987). She also wrote children's books. Her work is collected in *Selected Poems* (1963) and in *Blacks* (1987), which includes her first novel, *Maud Martha* (1953). Her memoirs, entitled *Report from Part One: An Autobiography*, were published in 1972. Brooks served as poetry consultant to the U.S. Library of Congress from 1985 to 1986.

Brough, Louise (1923–) *American tennis player*

Of the generation of women tennis players who emerged immediately after World War II, Louise Brough played a central role in establishing a new style of play – the serve and volley tactic.

Brough was born in Oklahoma. Her career is closely linked with that of her friend and doubles partner, Margaret Osborne du Pont. Although her singles record was impressive Brough won the U.S. doubles 12 times with Osborne, from 1942 to 1950 and from 1955 to 1957. They also won the Wimbledon competition five times and the French title three times. Brough was also successful in the mixed doubles at Wimbledon, winning in 1946–48 and 1950, and in the Wightman Cup, winning all 22 of her series of matches.

Brough won the U.S. singles only once, in 1947, losing the 1948 final to

Margaret Osborne. That year she underwent an operation for a back problem, which had affected her stamina after two sets. She won all three titles at Wimbledon in 1948, two of the three in 1949, and all three again in 1950, in which year she also took the Australian singles title. It was five years before she was able to win the Wimbledon singles again. By this time, now 32 years old, she beat Beverly Fleitz in the 1955 final in two sets.

Brown, Helen Gurley (1922–)
American journalist and writer

> You may marry or you may not. In today's world that is no longer the big question for women.
>   —*Sex and the Single Girl* (1962)

Helen Gurley Brown is responsible for the phenomenal success of *Cosmopolitan* magazine, of which she was editor-in-chief for over 30 years.

Helen Gurley was born in Green Forest, in the Ozark Mountains, and grew up in Little Rock, Arkansas. At 18 she began work as a secretary, later becoming an advertising copywriter. With the encouragement of her husband, Hollywood producer David Brown, whom she had married in 1959, she then decided to write a book.

Sex and the Single Girl, which appeared in 1962, caused a storm on both sides of the Atlantic. A manifesto of Western women's desire for independence from men and for the freedom to choose when and how to have sexual relationships, it anticipated the sexual revolution of the 1960s. The huge response Gurley Brown received from her readers, who found both her ideas and her language stimulating and liberating, prompted her to start a magazine. She and her husband therefore approached the Hearst newspaper empire for backing. In the event Hearst appointed her editor-in-chief of *Cosmopolitan*, an ailing literary magazine, which they gave her complete freedom to transform.

Her well-publicized first issue in 1965 sold 900,000 copies; with cover lines written by her husband, this issue established the formula that has made it one of the most popular women's magazines in the world. *Cosmopolitan*

encourages young women to be independent of men, to go out to work, and to be successful; it also provides advice on how to ensnare a man and keep him. Although this apparent contradiction has brought criticism from such leading feminists as Betty FRIEDAN, the formula with national variations has remained successful, with Gurley Brown seeing herself as the personification of "Cosmo Girl." She retired as American editor in 1997.

Brown, Trisha (1936–) *American choreographer*

Brown is one of the most significant "postmodern" choreographers. Her experimental innovative work has included silent dances and daredevil choreography in outdoor settings.

Trisha Brown was born in Aberdeen, Washington; as a teenager she learned acrobatics, tap, ballet, and show dancing. She went on to study at Mills College, California and Connecticut College School of Dance, where she was taught by Merce Cunningham. Becoming interested in improvisation, she moved to New York in 1961 and in 1962 became a member of the newly formed Judson Dance Theater.

After appearing in a number of productions, Brown began in 1968 to devise her own "equipment pieces," such as *Walking on the Wall* (1970), in which special apparatus was used to perform daring routines. In *Roof Piece* (1971) dancers had to relay movements from one building to another across the Manhattan skyline, while in *Spiral* (1974) they were required, by means of special apparatus, to walk down trees, perpendicular to the trunk.

Brown founded the Trisha Brown Dance Company in 1970 and belonged to the Grand Union improvisation group from 1970 to 1976. From the late 1970s she concentrated more on indoor work, such as *Glacial Decoy* (1979), which used a setting of black-and-white photographs by Robert Rauschenberg, and *Son of Gone Fishin'* (1981), with music by Robert Ashley. She evolved a more supple and sinuous dance style in the 1980s. Brown's more recent works include *Another Story:*

As in Falling (1993) and *If You Could See Me* (1994).

Browning, Elizabeth Barrett
(1806–1861) *British poet*

> I love thee with a love I seem to lose
> With my lost saints–I love thee with
>   the breath,
> Smiles, tears, of all my life!–and, if
>   God choose,
> I shall love thee better after death.
> —*Sonnets from the Portuguese*, XLII
>   (1850)

> Her physique was peculiar; curls
> like the pendant ears of a water
> spaniel and poor little hands–so
> thin that when she welcomed you
> she gave you something like the foot
> of a young bird.
> —Frederick Locker, *My Confidences*

During her lifetime Elizabeth Barrett Browning was widely regarded as England's greatest woman poet. Although her poetry has now fallen into disfavour, it shows individuality of style and rich imagination. Her works also reveal fascinating biographical details, notably her love for the poet Robert Browning, with whom she eloped.

Elizabeth Barrett was born at Coxhoe Hall, Durham, the eldest of 12 children of plantation owner Edward Moulton Barrett. Although a delicate child, she was intelligent beyond her years, spending her days at home studying languages, reading literature, philosophy, and history, and writing verse. In 1835, after her father had suffered financial setbacks, the family moved to London, where they eventually settled at their famous address, 50 Wimpole Street. In London she met John Kenyon, who brought her to the attention of leading literary figures. Although she had published verse from an early age, her first work to come to public attention was *The Seraphim, and Other Poems* (1838), which was generally praised by reviewers, who called its author the most promising contemporary young poet.

In 1838 Elizabeth went to the coastal resort of Torquay to recuperate from a serious illness. While there, her eldest and much-loved brother Edward was drowned, an accident that greatly affected her health. She returned to London in 1841, still in a delicate condition. However, she continued her literary work throughout this unhappy period; *Poems*, published in 1844, brought her wide fame.

Robert Browning, whose poetry Elizabeth had long admired, began a correspondence with her in 1845 at the urging of their mutual friend John Kenyon. Browning and Elizabeth soon met and fell in love, but – because of the jealousy of her tyrannical father – their courtship had to be conducted in secret. Finally in 1846 they were married without her father's knowledge and eloped to the Continent. Edward Barrett never forgave his daughter.

After a brief stay in France the Brownings moved to Italy, where they settled in Florence. A son was born to them in 1849. In 1850 Elizabeth published a second volume of *Poems*, which included the famous *Sonnets from the Portuguese*, recording her romance with Browning (the title refers to Browning's pet name for her – "my little Portuguese"). The extensive poetical novel *Aurora Leigh* (1856), a somewhat sentimental work, was praised for its breadth of sympathy and intellectual vitality, although most reviewers remarked on major flaws in its plot, characterization, and taste.

Elizabeth had always incorporated progressive social ideas in her poetry, and her work was now beginning to reflect an increasing interest in Italian politics. *Casa Guidi Windows* (1851), her first volume on Italian politics, was attacked as inconsistent and commonplace. Likewise a later overtly political volume, *Poems Before Congress* (1860), was not well received by her contemporaries.

Mrs. Browning's passionate interest in politics seemed adversely to affect her health. The death of the great Italian patriot Camillo Cavour in early June 1861 upset her immensely; later that month she died in Florence. Her *Last Poems* was published in 1862. Many volumes of her lively and engaging correspondence have been published since her death.

Brundtland, Gro Harlem (1939–)
Norwegian physician and stateswoman

A politician of unusual popularity, Gro Harlem Brundtland was Norway's first woman prime minister.

Born in Oslo, the daughter of a doctor who later became a cabinet minister, Gro Harlem studied medicine in Oslo and qualified as a physician. In 1960 she married Arne Olav Brundtland, a leader of the opposition Conservative Party; the couple have four children. Her particular interest in public health led her to take several appointments in the public medical service in Oslo in the 1960s. Becoming interested in politics from this experience, she joined the Labour Party in 1969. In 1974 she was appointed minister of the environment, a post she held until 1979, when she left the government to concentrate on party organization. In 1981, after the resignation of Prime Minister Nordli, Gro Harlem Brundtland became the first woman prime minister of Norway, leading a minority Labour government for nine months.

Brundtland was out of power during the early 1980s but became a member of the UN Commission on Disarmament and Security. She later chaired the World Commission on the Environment and Development, which produced the report *Our Common Future*. Her international work considerably raised the profile of Norway in world affairs and in 1988 she was awarded the Third World Foundation Prize for leadership on environment issues.

Brundtland became prime minister again in 1986, appointing a cabinet consisting of eight women and nine men, making it the most heavily female-dominated cabinet in history. She lost the 1989 election, but when the victorious centre-right coalition failed in 1990 she returned to power, winning another election in 1993. She remained prime minister until her resignation in 1996.

Brunhilde (died 613) *Wife of the Frankish King Sigebert*
Brunhilde was a Visigothic princess who became queen of Austrasia. For two generations she exerted great influence over political life in the Frankish kingdoms of Austrasia, Neustria, and Burgundy. She is not to be confused with the Brunhilde of Germanic and Norse legend, who appears in the *Nibelungenlied* (Song of the Nibelungs) and Wagner's *Ring* cycle.

Brunhilde married King Sigebert of Austrasia in 567, while her sister Galswintha married Sigebert's brother Chilperic, king of Neustria. Rivalry between the brothers developed into open war when Chilperic had Galswintha murdered and Brunhilde demanded that her sister's death be avenged. When Sigebert was assassinated on the orders of FREDEGUND, Chilperic's second wife, in 575, Chilperic claimed his lands. Brunhilde resisted this claim in the name of her son Childebert II. However, her nobles deserted her and she fled to Burgundy. Childebert remained in Austrasia and in 592 inherited Burgundy.

When Childebert died in 595, Brunhilde attempted to assert her control as regent over Burgundy and Austrasia, which her grandsons Theodoric II and Theodebert II had inherited. After successfully resisting attacks by Chilperic's heir Clotaire II, Brunhilde tried and failed to conquer Neustria in 600 and again in 603–04. In 612 Theodoric murdered his brother Theodebert at her instigation. Theodoric himself died in 613. When Brunhilde tried to make her great-grandson Sigebert II king, the nobles rebelled and acknowledged Clotaire as king. In the autumn of 613, near Dijon, France, Clotaire had both Sigebert and Brunhilde executed.

Bryher (1894–1983) *British novelist*
Bryher was the pen name of Annie Winifred Ellerman, whose novels were noted for their vividly authentic recreations of the past.

Born in Margate, Kent, the daughter of an industrialist, she took her pen name from one of the Scilly Isles, where she spent holidays.

Bryher's work was influenced by the psychologist and essayist Havelock Ellis, who focused on human sexual psychology. She began her career as an author by writing a series of articles and reviews from 1917. With her former husband Kenneth MacPherson, she published *Close Up*, a magazine on silent films, from 1927 to 1933. *Film Problems of Soviet Russia* appeared in 1929. Her historical novels include *Beowulf* (1948), *The Fourteenth of October* (1952), *The Player's Boy* (1953), *Roman Wall* (1954), *Gate to the Sea* (1958), *Ruan* (1960), *The Coin of Carthage* (1964), *Visa for Avalon* (1965), and *The Colours of Vaud* (1970). *The Days of Mars* (1972) is a memoir of her life during World War II. Her autobiography, *The Heart to Artemis*, was published in 1962.

Buck, Pearl S. (1892–1973) *American writer*

> I feel no need for any other faith than my faith in human beings.
>
> —*I Believe* (1939)

Pearl Sydenstricker Buck, winner of the Nobel Prize for literature in 1938, is best known for her novels about China.

The daughter of Presbyterian missionaries, she was born in Hillsboro, West Virginia. Her parents took her to Chinkiang, China, in her infancy and she was educated in Shanghai. Several of her sisters and brothers died during this harsh period in China. After graduating in 1914 from Randolph-Macon Woman's College in Virginia, she returned to China, where in 1917 she married the agriculturalist and missionary, John Lossing Buck. From 1921 to 1931 she taught in Nanking.

Her first novel, *East Wind, West Wind*, was published in 1930, but it was her second that gained her international fame. *The Good Earth* (1931) was a moving description of the struggle of a Chinese peasant and his wife for land and security. This novel won her the Pulitzer Prize for literature in 1932. The book was made into a successful film in 1937.

Buck resigned from the Presbyterian Board of Foreign Missions in 1933 after publishing an article critical of foreign missionary personnel. The next year she returned to the United States, where she divorced John Buck. In 1935 she married her publisher, Richard J. Walsh. Between 1932 and 1935 she wrote the novels *Sons* (1932) and *A House Divided* (1935), sequels to *The*

Good Earth. Her nonfiction includes biographies of her father (*Fighting Angel*, 1936) and her mother (*The Exile*, 1936), works that were in large measure responsible for her receiving the Nobel Prize. More than a dozen novels followed, in addition to short stories, children's stories, and further nonfiction, notably the autobiographical *My Several Worlds* (1954) and *A Bridge for Passing* (1962). Buck also used the pen name John Sedges.

Budd, Zola (1966–) *South African athlete*

> [Apartheid] began before I was born and will probably be resolved long after I die. In the meantime I want to run.
>
> —Comment in 1984

A slight teenager who ran barefoot, Zola Budd became notorious in 1984 as the white South African who took British nationality in order to compete in international athletics events.

Born in Bloemfontein, Orange Free State, Budd broke her first record at 13. Having abandoned her university education to concentrate on athletic training, in January 1984 she ran 5,000 metres in 15 minutes 1.83 seconds, 7 seconds faster than Mary DECKER's existing record. However, Budd's achievement could not be recognized as South Africa had been banned from international sporting events because of its policy of apartheid.

Determined to compete at the 1984 Olympics, Budd applied for British citizenship on the grounds that she had a British grandfather. Supported by the *Daily Mail* newspaper, her claim was rapidly granted, amid angry protests that her change of nationality had more to do with her sporting ambitions than with a genuine condemnation of apartheid. In any case, her hopes of an Olympic victory were dashed that summer when she bumped Decker in the 3,000 metres. Distressed, Budd continued but came in seventh.

In 1985 Budd won the European Cup 3,000 metres title and set a new world record of 14 minutes 48.07 seconds for the 5,000 metres. In addition to world cross-country titles in 1985–86 she set the world indoor record for the 3,000 metres in 1986. Banned from the Commonwealth Games that year as a result of continued controversy, she returned, disappointed, to South Africa in 1988.

After her marriage to Mike Pieterse in 1989, Budd returned to international competition, running under her married name. Although she competed in the 1992 Olympics, she failed to repeat her early success.

Bueno, Maria (1939–) *Brazilian tennis player*

Maria Bueno made headlines in 1959 when she became the first non-American woman to take both the Wimbledon and U.S. titles for 13 years. Slim and regal in appearance, Bueno was one of the most accomplished players of the game on all surfaces.

Maria Esther Audion Bueno was born in São Paulo, Brazil. Her singles titles included four U.S. championships (1959, 1963, 1964, and 1966), three Wimbledon titles (1959, 1960, and 1964), and the 1965 Italian championship. She is especially remembered for her brilliant performance in the final stages of her victory over the Australian Margaret Smith, who later became Margaret COURT, in the last of her U.S. championships in 1964.

Bueno also took the U.S. doubles title four times (in 1960 and 1962 with Darlene R. HARD, in 1966 with Nancy Richey, and in 1968 with Margaret Smith Court), and the Wimbledon doubles title five times (in 1958 with Althea GIBSON, in 1960 and 1963 with Miss Hard, in 1965 with Billie Jean KING, and in 1966 with Miss Richey). Her later victories were achieved despite her having suffered an attack of hepatitis in 1961.

Bumbry, Grace (Melzia) (1937–) *American opera singer*

Grace Bumbry's voice is noted for its richness and versatility, ranging from mezzo-soprano to high soprano.

Born in St. Louis, Missouri, she gained early singing experience in church and school choirs. She formally studied voice techniques with Lotte LEHMANN, among others. After making her London debut in 1959 she sang for the next few years with the Paris Opéra and the Basel Opera, touring Europe and Japan. In 1961 she was the first African-American singer to perform in the Wagner festival at Bayreuth, Germany.

Grace Bumbry made her New York debut in 1962. In the same year she was invited by the First Lady, Jacqueline Kennedy (see ONASSIS, JACQUELINE KENNEDY), to sing at the White House. She first performed at the Metropolitan Opera, New York City, in 1965 as Princess Eboli in *Don Carlos*. In 1966 she sang the title role in Bizet's *Carmen* at the Salzburg Festival, and in 1970 she appeared in her first soprano role, as Santuzza in Mascagni's *Cavalleria rusticana*. She continued to prove her mastery of voice styles by singing both Aïda and Amneris in Verdi's *Aïda* and both Venus and Elisabeth in Wagner's *Tannhäuser*.

Burbidge, (Eleanor) Margaret (1922–) *British astronomer*

Margaret Burbidge has done important work on quasars and on the synthesis of elements in stars.

Born Eleanor Margaret Peachey in Davenport, she studied physics at the University of London. After graduation in 1948 she joined the University of London Observatory, where she obtained her PhD and served as acting director (1950–51). She then went to the United States as a research fellow, first at the Yerkes Observatory of the University of Chicago (1951–53) and then at the California Institute of Technology (1955–57).

The period 1953–55 was spent in highly productive work at the Cavendish Laboratory in Cambridge, in collaboration with the theoretical physicist Geoffrey Burbidge (whom she had married in 1948) and astronomers Fred Hoyle and William Fowler. In 1957 they published a key paper on the synthesis of the chemical elements in stars. They later produced one of the first comprehensive works on quasars in their *Quasi-Stellar Objects* (1967). Margaret Burbidge had earlier recorded the spectra of a number of quasars and discovered that their spectral lines displayed different shifts, probably indicating the ejection of matter at very high speeds. The first accurate estimates of the masses of galaxies were based on Margaret Burbidge's careful observation of their rotation.

She returned to Yerkes in 1957, serving as associate professor of astronomy from 1959 to 1962, and then transferred to the University of California, San Diego, where she was professor of astronomy from 1964 until 1990 and emeritus professor from 1990. She also served (1979–88) as director of the Center for Astrophysics and Space Sciences.

Burbidge returned briefly to England in 1972 on leave of absence to become director of the Royal Greenwich Observatory, which was then situated at Herstmonceux Castle in Sussex. She declared her aim to be to strengthen optical astronomy in Britain. But as the 2.5-metre (98-inch) Isaac Newton telescope at Herstmonceux was only a few hundred feet above sea level and sited above a marsh, her opportunities for observation at the Royal Observatory were somewhat limited. A little over a year later, in October 1973, Burbidge resigned amid much speculation, declaring simply that she preferred "to return to her own research work rather than devote a major part of her time to administrative matters."

Burdett-Coutts, Angela Georgina, Baroness (1814–1906) *British philanthropist*

The daughter of the reformist politician Sir Francis Burdett, Angela Burdett-Coutts inherited the great banking fortune amassed by her grandfather, Thomas Coutts. Her humanitarian views were inherited from her father and reinforced by her close friendship with Charles Dickens. She supported a number of causes, including the housing and education of the poor, the relief of Irish distress following the potato famine, the rehabilitation of prostitutes, and the prevention of cruelty to children and animals.

She established youth clubs, sewing schools, a large toll-free market, and a factory to employ crippled girls in the East End of London. She supported "ragged schools" that brought rudimentary education to deprived children and instituted the Flower Girls Brigade for young flower sellers. A strong Anglican, she built several churches in England and endowed bishoprics in South Africa, Australia, and Canada.

Burdett-Coutts was a tall, dignified, and imposing person. She was also a fine public speaker and a capable businesswoman, whose charity was always marked by shrewd practicality. Her generosity and charitable work brought her into contact with most of the leading personalities of the age. Like Florence NIGHTINGALE, she demonstrated that public service was not a male preserve; her contribution to alleviating suffering in Victorian England was duly acknowledged in 1871, when she was given the title of baroness, the first time a woman had been ennobled for her own services. In 1881 she married William L. Ashmead-Bartlett (1851–1921), an American by birth, many years her junior. She died in London and was accorded the honor of being buried in Westminster Abbey.

Burnett, Frances Hodgson (1849–1924) *British-born American writer*

The author of novels and plays for adults and fiction for children, Frances Hodgson Burnett is best known for the children's novels *Little Lord Fauntleroy* and *The Secret Garden*.

Frances Eliza Hodgson was born in Manchester, the daughter of a hardware merchant who died when she was five years old. In 1865 the family emigrated to Tennessee, where she lived near Knoxville until her marriage to Dr. S. M. Burnett in 1873. Between the ages of 16 and 20 she wrote stories under her family name, Hodgson, for newspapers and magazines, including Godey's *Lady's Book* and *Scribner's*.

She gained her first success with *That Lass o'Lowries* (1877), a novel based on the harsh life of coal miners, of which she had had direct experience in England. Although she wrote many novels, it is her books for children that brought her fame. *Little Lord Fauntleroy* (1886), whose main character wore a velvet jacket and knickerbockers, set a fashion in clothes for boys. *The Secret Garden* (1911) tells the story of an orphaned girl who recovered from her grief by tending a neglected walled garden. It was made into a successful film in 1994 by the Polish director Agnieszka HOLLAND.

Of Mrs. Burnett's adult fiction, *Through One Administration* (1883), which deals with the love of a single man for a married woman in the setting of U.S. political society, received critical acclaim and brought her international recognition as a novelist.

Burney, Fanny (1752–1840) *British writer*

Fanny Burney was the most famous female novelist of the late 18th century. She was also known by her married name, Madame d'Arblay. Her novels departed from the rumbustious language and vulgar situations used by such earlier writers as Henry Fielding and Tobias Smollett, setting a trend towards more refined fiction as the 18th century drew to a close and the Victorian age dawned. Her diaries and letters, published after her death, remain an important source of information about many famous contemporaries.

Frances Burney was born in King's Lynn, Norfolk, the daughter of Dr. Charles Burney, a renowned organist and music historian. She educated herself at home, and when her father moved to London to teach music, she was introduced to his distinguished circle of friends, who included Dr. Samuel Johnson, Edmund Burke, and the painter Joshua Reynolds. She published her first novel, *Evelina, or A Young Lady's Entrance Into the World*, anonymously in 1778; when its authorship was revealed, she won a wide circle of admirers. Her fame increased with the appearance of *Cecilia, or Memoirs of an Heiress* (5 vols., 1782).

In 1786 Queen CHARLOTTE appointed Fanny Burney to the position of second keeper of the robes. Though prestigious, this office brought long hours of tedious attendance on the Queen. After five years Fanny's health declined and she was allowed to retire from court with a small pension.

Her health gradually improved and in 1793 she met and married General Alexandre Gabriel d'Arblay, one of the many aristocratic French émigrés escaping the French Revolution. After giving birth to a son she resumed her writing career to help support the family. From 1802 to 1812 she lived with her husband in France, where he was appointed to a government post under Napoleon. In 1812 the d'Arblays returned to England, where Fanny continued to write after her husband's death in 1818.

Fanny Burney was well acquainted with the taste of her reading public for sentiment, moralizing, and instruction in manners. She especially appealed to the growing number of women readers by providing examples of correct behaviour in society, in the manner of the etiquette books then fashionable. Her novels *Evelina* and *Cecilia* also skilfully satirize coarseness, show a capable handling of character (the heroines reflect the development of the author's own personality), and they have natural-sounding dialogue. However, in her two later novels, *Camilla, or A Picture of Youth* (5 vols., 1796) and *The Wanderer, or Female Difficulties* (5 vols., 1814), artistry gives way to unconvincing characters, excessive moralizing, and melodrama.

Fanny Burney was also a diarist and a great collector of letters; her fame may eventually rest on her vivid and often amusing memoirs. In 1832 she published the *Memoirs of Dr. Burney* (3 vols.). Two other important works, published after her death, were *The Diary and Letters of Madame d'Arblay* (7 vols., 1842–46) and *The Early Diary of Frances Burney* (2 vols., 1889). A number of her letters, as well as additional diaries, still remain unpublished.

Bush, Kate (1958–   ) *British singer and songwriter*

> How could you leave me
> When I needed to possess you?
> I hated you, I loved you too...
> Heathcliff, it's me, I'm Cathy, I've
>   come home
> And I'm so cold, let me in your win-
>   dow.
>
> —"Wuthering Heights" (1978)

Kate Bush is best known for her haunting song "Wuthering Heights" (1978), which reached number one in the British charts, and for her shrill expressive vocal style.

Born in Plumstead, near London, and brought up in Kent, Kate Bush taught herself to play the piano when she was nine; two years later she began to write songs. When she was 16, a family friend told Dave Gilmour, of the band Pink Floyd, about her extraordinary vocal range; Gilmour therefore funded a demonstration tape that won her a contract with EMI. While preparing her first album, *The Kick Inside* (1978), Bush studied mime, dance, and karate and had singing lessons to develop her individual style. Her first single, "Wuthering Heights," inspired by Emily BRONTË's novel, was an instant success and was followed by a concert tour.

Bush's next album, *Lionheart* (1978) earned her several awards and in 1980 its successor, *Never Forever,* went straight to number one in the charts. Among Bush's later songs and albums, some show the influence of "world music" and Peter Gabriel, on two of whose albums she guested (1980 and 1986). Her own bestselling album *Hounds of Love* (1985), which is usually considered her finest work, was followed by *The Sensual World* (1989) and *The Red Shoes* (1993).

Since the mid 1980s Kate Bush has adopted a fairly reclusive lifestyle: she does not tour and rarely gives interviews.

Buss, Frances (1827–1894) *British feminist and educational pioneer*

An early pioneer of women's education in Britain, Miss Buss was the first woman to call herself a headmistress.

Frances Mary Buss, one of five children, was the daughter of Robert Buss, a painter and etcher. Since her father earned very little, Frances's mother supported the family by running a school. Frances herself began teaching at the age of 14 and at 18 she took charge of the older children at her mother's new school in Kentish Town, London. In 1850, having gained a diploma from Queen's College after attending evening classes, Frances opened her own school, the North London Collegiate School for Ladies.

The school was to provide a high-quality education based on social and religious tolerance for a low fee; Miss Buss insisted that all her teachers should be highly qualified. It was a great success and is today one of London's most highly regarded independent girls' schools. In 1871 a lower school, Camden School, was opened by Buss.

By this time Miss Buss, together with other educational reformers, was attempting to extend university education to girls, supporting Emily DAVIES in the establishment of Girton College, Cambridge, in 1873. She continued to stress the importance, to pupils and parents alike, of further education, believing it to be vital to women's independence. In 1871, in accordance with Miss Buss's wishes, her schools were endowed with funds to secure their future. This opened her schools to girls from poorer families.

In 1874 Miss Buss established the Association of Headmistresses, serving as its president for 20 years. She was also a founder member of the Council for Teacher Training and helped to establish the Training College for Women Teachers in Cambridge in 1886. In addition, she supported the antislavery and temperance movements and the campaign for women's suffrage.

See also BEALE, DOROTHEA.

Butler, Elizabeth (1846–1933) *British painter*

> I never painted for the glory of war, but to portray its pathos and heroism.

In her complex and skilfully painted military scenes Elizabeth Butler proved that women artists could succeed with subjects that were traditionally regarded as "male". Her pictures were popular for their patriotism but also for the sympathy with which the heroic sacrifice of ordinary soldiers was depicted.

Born Elizabeth Thompson in Lausanne, Switzerland, she was the child of well-to-do and cultured parents.

With her sister, the poet Alice MEYNELL, she was taught by her father; in 1862 she began studying oil painting with William Standish in London. Elizabeth soon joined the South Kensington School of Art and, after an unhappy spell in the "elementary" class, flourished when she was allowed to attend the "antique" and life classes. Her skill at figure drawing improved still further by studying in Florence and Rome.

Elizabeth had developed an early interest in military subjects and horses. Having exhibited *Missing* at the Royal Academy in 1873, she caused a great stir with *Calling the Roll after an Engagement – the Crimea* in 1874, when crowds had to be held back from the canvas. Queen VICTORIA persuaded the original patron to let her buy the picture, which was shown to Florence NIGHTINGALE on her deathbed. In 1875 the chauvinistic critic John Ruskin was so impressed with *Quatre Bras*, depicting a scene at the Battle of Waterloo, that he changed his mind about women being unable to paint.

In 1877 Elizabeth married Colonel (later Sir) William Butler. Butler was one of the first painters to depict moving horses correctly; in *Scotland for Ever* (1881) she proved her skill in this respect by her handling of a throng of cavalry horses charging toward the viewer.

Warm-hearted and witty, Butler seems not to have resented the Royal Academy's refusal to elect her as a member in 1879. In her autobiography (1922) she gave a light-hearted account of her experiences. After a busy and well-travelled career, the Butlers retired to Bansha, Tipperary, Ireland, where Elizabeth continued to live and work after her husband's death in 1910. She died at her daughter's home in County Meath, 23 years later.

Butler, Josephine (1828–1906) *British social reformer and feminist*

The daughter of John Grey, a campaigner for agricultural reform and the abolition of slavery, and a cousin of Earl Grey, the future prime minister, Josephine Elizabeth Grey was born in Northumberland. Educated by her parents, she came to share their moral and religious values. In 1852 she married George Butler, a lecturer at Durham University, and later moved with him to Oxford.

The moral attitudes of her husband's colleagues at Oxford, who were all men, and their acceptance of double standards based on gender, appalled her. The contempt with which her own opinions were treated, together with the effects of an illness, meant that her time in Oxford was not very happy. The Butlers therefore decided to move to Cheltenham, where George took up a post at Cheltenham College, a boys' public school. By now the American Civil War was raging; the Butlers, who were strongly against slavery, were largely ostracized by their conservative Cheltenham colleagues, who favoured the South. In 1863 they experienced personal tragedy when their five-year-old daughter fell to her death before their eyes. After this disaster they moved to Liverpool, where Josephine attempted to bury her grief by working with the poor and destitute, taking particular interest in sick prostitutes. Both Butlers also campaigned for women's higher education, although Josephine believed in separate entrance examinations for women to avoid direct competition with men – a view that was not widely held.

In 1869 Josephine embarked on a national campaign against the Contagious Diseases Acts (1866–69). Passed to combat sexually transmitted disease among servicemen, these acts required that women in seaports or garrison towns who were thought to be prostitutes should submit to an (often humiliating) examination, invariably by a male doctor. Men were not examined. In 1886, after a long campaign in which she played a prominent part, the acts were repealed.

Josephine devoted the later part of her life to the problem of child prostitution and the "white slave traffic." Two of her fellow campaigners were imprisoned, but the public outcry at their treatment led to the age of consent in Britain being raised to 16.

Butler-Sloss, Dame Elizabeth (1933–) *British judge*

In 1987 she became the first female judge to serve in the Court of Appeal, as the Rt Hon. Lady Justice Butler-Sloss.

She was born Ann Elizabeth Oldfield Havers in Richmond, Surrey. At an early age she decided to enter the legal profession, following in the footsteps of her father, the High Court judge Sir Cecil Havers, and her elder brother Michael, who was to become the lawyer and politician Lord Havers. The British actor Nigel Havers is her nephew. Elizabeth was educated at Wycombe Abbey School and became a barrister in 1955. Three years later she married the barrister Joseph Butler-Sloss; in 1959, heavily pregnant with her first child, she tried to enter politics as the Conservative candidate for Lambeth. Having failed to win the seat, she continued to practise as a barrister while raising her family, becoming a divorce registrar in 1970.

In 1979 Butler-Sloss was appointed to the family division of the High Court; in the same year she was created a Dame of the British Empire. She found herself in the public eye in 1987–88, when she presided over the Cleveland sex abuse inquiry, a highly controversial case involving the alleged abuse of 120 children by members of their own families. Her report, published in July 1988, was highly critical of the police, the social services, and the doctors concerned. The vast majority of the children were returned to their families, who were exonerated of any wrongdoing.

Butt, Dame Clara (1873–1936)
British singer

Clara Ellen Butt was born at Southwick in Sussex. She studied at the Royal College of Music in London from 1890, and also in Paris and Berlin. Her professional debut, singing the part of Ursula in Sir Arthur Sullivan's cantata *The Golden Legend*, came in 1892.

Clara Butt was renowned for her rendering of ballads and oratorios, possessing a contralto voice of great range and power. A number of compositions were written especially for her, notably the song cycle *Sea Pictures*

(1899), by Sir Edward Elgar, who also acknowledged that she was the inspiration for the part of the angel in his oratorio *The Dream of Gerontius* (1900). She gave concerts in the United States in 1899 and toured the world in 1913 with her husband, the baritone R. Kennerley Rumford.

During World War I Clara Butt performed for war charities; she was particularly identified with Elgar's songs 'Land of Hope and Glory' and 'Spirit of England'. This war work contributed to her being created a DBE in 1920.

Byatt, A(ntonia) S(usan) (1936–)
British writer

> My novels are about habits of thought and imagination.
>
> —Comment in 1986

A. S. Byatt has achieved widespread acclaim for her novels, which contain an interesting use of symbolism as well as a wealth of literary and historical allusions. She has also produced important works of literary criticism.

Antonia Susan Drabble was born in Sheffield, the daughter of a judge. She and her younger sister, Margaret DRABBLE, attended the Mount School in York; both went on to study at Newnham College, Cambridge. After gaining a first-class degree, Antonia continued her education at Bryn Mawr College, Pennsylvania, and Somerville College, Oxford. In 1959 she married the economist Ian C. R. Byatt. Their marriage produced two children but was dissolved in 1969. The same year Antonia married Peter John Duffy, by whom she had two daughters.

From the early 1960s Byatt pursued an academic career as a lecturer in London. Her published works of literary criticism include two books on Iris MURDOCH (1965, 1976), who influenced her own fiction.

By 1964 Byatt had already written her first novel, *Shadow of a Sun*. Her second, *The Game* (1967), tells of the rivalry between two sisters, one an Oxford academic and the other a popular novelist; it undoubtedly reflects something of Byatt's feeling towards her younger sister's early success as a novelist. She found her own niche, however, with *The Virgin in the Garden* (1978), the first of an intended tetralogy symbolically charting the lives of two girls and their brother. The time of ELIZABETH II's coronation is seen through imagery from the first Elizabethan age. Its sequel, *Still Life* (1985), has a less successful structural formula linked to the visual arts. The sequence continued with *Babel Tower* (1996).

In 1990 Byatt's fame was assured when she was awarded the Booker Prize for her novel *Possession: A Romance*, a mysterious tale of two academics whose lives reflect those of the two Victorian poets they are studying. Byatt's subsequent works include the short-story collections *Sugar* (1987) and *The Matisse Stories* (1994), the book of essays *Passions of the Mind* (1991), and a pair of interlinked novellas, *Angels and Insects* (1992).

Byron, Augusta Ada, Countess of Lovelace (1815–1852) *British computer pioneer*

Ada Lovelace, the daughter of Annabella Millbanke and the poet Lord Byron, has been commemorated in the name of the high-level computer language ADA.

Ada's mother left Byron after a month of marriage, and Ada never saw her father. Born in London, she was educated privately, studying mathematics and astronomy in addition to the more traditional topics. She seems to have developed an early ambition to be a famous scientist. Her correspondence, however, with Mary SOMERVILLE and Augustus De Morgan, two of her informal teachers, shows

that her mathematical skills were very limited. De Morgan saw her as a talented beginner who could have become an original mathematician if given the chance to receive a rigorous Cambridge-style training. Such routes were not open to young women in the early 19th century.

In 1834 she heard Charles Babbage lecture on his famous "difference engine," which is often regarded as the prototype of the modern computer. She offered Babbage her support, and they became good friends. In 1842 she translated from French an account of Babbage's engine by the Italian engineer L. F. Manabrea. At Babbage's suggestion she added some explanatory notes. They constitute one of the primary sources of his work.

Other plans, such as a *Calculus of the Nervous System*, failed to mature – the obstacles in her way were simply too great. As a woman, for example, she was denied access to the Royal Society Library. Nor did her private life flourish. Her marriage in 1835 to Lord King, created the Earl of Lovelace in 1838, seemed merely to replace the guardianship of her titled mother with that of her titled husband. She began an affair in the 1840s with John Crosse, a gentleman who seemed to be as interested in her money as herself. She also took in later life to heavy gambling on horses, and by Derby Day 1851 she had run up losses of over £3,000. Worse was to come, however, as cancer of the womb had been diagnosed. She was buried beside her father's remains at Newstead Abbey, the family home in Nottinghamshire, having died, like him, at the age of 36.

C

Caballé, Montserrat (1933–)
Spanish opera singer

Caballé is considered to be one of the greatest operatic sopranos of the 20th century; she is also well known as a performer of Spanish songs.

Born into a musical family in Barcelona, from the age of nine she studied at the Conservatorio del Liceo in that city and then privately. She made her concert debut in 1954 and her opera debut in Basel in 1957. Caballé subsequently sang in operas throughout Europe. But it was the immediate success of her performance in the title role of the American Opera Society's production of Donizetti's *Lucrezia Borgia* in New York in 1965 that established her international reputation as a prima donna.

Her dramatic power, entrancing voice, clear tone, and outstanding ability to hit the high notes have enabled her to sing a wide variety of roles in the operas of Puccini, Rossini, Wagner, and Strauss. She has also sung contemporary opera, and teamed up with Freddie Mercury, of the rock band Queen, to perform a duet that was used as the anthem of the 1992 Barcelona Olympics. One of the leading 20th-century exponents of Zarzuela (a type of Spanish operetta), she celebrated the 30th anniversary of her American debut by singing Zarzuela and opera arias at a special concert at the Carnegie Hall in New York. She has sung in all the major opera houses of the world and has made many recordings of her work.

Caballero, Fernán (1796–1877)
Swiss-born Spanish writer

A somewhat florid writer, Caballero was for many years regarded as Spain's most important novelist.

Her real name was Cecilia Böhl von Faber. She was born in Morges, Switzerland, the daughter of a German Hispanic scholar and merchant. After the family moved to Spain in 1813, Caballero was married and widowed three times. In order to help support herself and her last husband, who died young, she turned to writing colourful and romantic novels about rural life in her native region of Andalusia.

Her first and most famous novel, *La gaviota*, was initially published in serial form in 1849; as a book, it was published in English as *The Seagull* (1867). Relating the story of a peasant girl who becomes an opera singer, it is regarded as being responsible for the rebirth of Spanish fiction, leading to the Spanish realist school of writing. She published various other novels, including *Clemencia* (1852), and *La familia de Alvareda* (1856), published in English as *Cottage and Castle in Spain* (1861), and several collections of Spanish folk tales. However, the unstructured form of her writing and its romantic nature do not have the same appeal to modern readers as they did to her contemporaries.

Cabrini, Saint Frances Xavier (1850–1917) *Italian-born American nun*

Frances Cabrini was the first American citizen to be made a saint (in 1946) for her charity work among Italian immigrant communities in the United States, South America, and Europe.

The youngest of 13 children, Maria Francesca Cabrini was born at Sant'-Angelo (near Lodi), Italy. After studying at a school run by the Daughters of the Sacred Heart, she became a teacher, having been denied admission to the order on account of the after-effects of the smallpox she had contracted caring for sick children. In

1874, guided by her priest, she started work in a small orphanage. After having finally taken her religious vows in 1877, she ran the institution for the next three years until Bishop Gelmini of Lodi was forced to close it because of the financial incompetence of its benefactress. On the advice of the bishop, Frances gathered seven nuns together and founded the Missionary Sisters of the Sacred Heart. She became the superior general of the order and drew up its rules and constitution, which were later approved by the pope.

Mother Cabrini, as she was now called, had originally planned to do missionary work in China. On the advice of Pope Leo XIII she decided instead to concentrate on helping the poor and neglected Italian immigrant communities in the Americas. She arrived with six sisters in New York in March 1889 and proceeded to set up 67 hospitals, schools, and orphanages (with 1,500 sisters) across the United States and in France, Britain, and South America. This "saint of the immigrants," as she is called, died in Chicago. November 13 is her feast day.

Calamity Jane (1852–1903) *American frontierswoman*

Calamity Jane became a legend in her lifetime, famed for her skill with a gun and on horseback in the Wild West.

Born in Princeton, in Missouri, Martha Jane Cannary moved with her family to Montana in 1865. Her parents soon died and Jane, who dressed and acted as if she was a frontiersman, worked as a muleskinner in Wyoming and accompanied a geological expedition into the Black Hills of Dakota. In 1876 she attached herself to General George Crook's campaign force against the Sioux Indians, but was forced out when it was discovered that she was a woman.

Jane met the U.S. marshal James B. (Wild Bill) Hickok when he was in Deadwood, South Dakota, for a few months in 1876 during the gold rush. There is no evidence that they were ever lovers, married, or had a child together, as Jane later claimed. Hickok

was killed during his short stay in Deadwood. Jane remained there and acquired a heroic reputation for nursing the victims of a smallpox epidemic. She may have acquired the name "Calamity" as a result of this episode. She is also said to have threatened "calamity" to any man who tried to marry her; in spite of this, she eventually married Clinton Burke, a cab driver in El Paso, Texas, in 1891. The marriage soon failed and Calamity Jane spent the rest of her working life with travelling Wild West shows. She gained an increasing reputation for drunkenness and rowdy behaviour and was fired from her last show, the Pan-American Exposition in Buffalo, New York, in 1901. After drifting for a few years, during which she peddled a cheap leaflet describing her life, she died of pneumonia in Terry, South Dakota. In compliance with her wishes she was buried next to Wild Bill Hickok in the Deadwood cemetery.

Calderón de la Barca, Fanny (1804–1882) *Scottish-born American writer*

Fanny Calderón de la Barca wrote about her experiences as a diplomat's wife in Mexico and Spain.

Born Frances Erskine Inglis in Edinburgh, she moved with her family to France and then to the United States, where they settled in Boston. An intelligent and charming young woman, she became friendly with the poet Henry Wadsworth Longfellow and the historian William H. Prescott. She married the Spanish diplomat Don Angel Calderón de la Barca in 1838 and two years later went with him to Mexico, where she wrote *Life in Mexico* (1843) about her experiences. Prescott admitted that he found it very useful when he came to write his well-known book about the Spanish conquest of Mexico.

When her husband was later minister of foreign affairs in the Spanish government in Madrid, Fanny wrote the book *Attaché in Madrid – Sketches of the Court of Isabella II*, giving her views on Spanish politics. After her husband died in 1861 she became the private tutor to the daughter of Isabella, who had by then lost her throne. When the Bourbons were restored to power, King Alfonzo XII gave Fanny Calderón de la Barca the title of marchioness. She died in Spain.

Caldwell, Sarah (1924–   ) *American opera director and conductor*

> If you approach an opera as though it were something that always went a certain way, that's what you get. I approach an opera as though I didn't know it.
>
> —Quoted by Jane Scovell Appleton in "Sarah Caldwell: The Flamboyant of the Opera," *Ms*, May 1975

Sarah Caldwell was the first woman to conduct New York's Metropolitan Opera.

She was born in Maryville, Missouri, and studied at the New England Conservatory in Boston and at the Berkshire Music Center at Tanglewood, Massachusetts. She showed early talent as a string player and conductor and staged her first opera, Vaughan Williams's *Riders to the Sea*, in 1947. Heavily influenced by Boris Goldsworthy at the New England Opera Theater, who produced affordable but technically advanced operas, Caldwell founded in 1957 the group which later became the Opera Company of Boston. The company specialized in contemporary music and introduced American audiences to the works of such composers as Rameau, Nono, Schuller, and Sessions. Her international reputation enabled her to attract famous singers, including Marilyn HORNE, Beverley SILLS, Nicolai Gedda, and Placido Domingo, to appear in the operas she produced and conducted.

In the 1960s and 1970s Caldwell toured the world with her productions. In 1975 she conducted the New York Philharmonic Orchestra at the Celebration of Woman Composers Concert and in 1976 she became the first woman to conduct the Metropolitan Opera, in a performance of Verdi's *La Traviata*. She became artistic director of the New Opera company of Israel in 1983.

Callas, Maria (1923–1977) *American-born Greek opera singer*

> Her magnetic stage personality and her passionate and conscientious artistry have made her the outstanding diva of our time.
>
> —Felix Aprahamian, *1000 Makers of the 20th Century*

Maria Callas was one of the greatest opera singers of the post-World War II era, known especially for her dramatic performances and her extensive range as a coloratura soprano.

She was born Cecilia Sophia Anna Maria Kalogeropoulos in New York City, of Greek parents. At the age of 14 she went with her mother to live in Greece, where she studied at the Athens Conservatory. In 1947 she gave her first major performance in the title role of Ponchielli's opera *La Gioconda* in Verona. This was followed by performances at the opera houses in Rome, Naples, and Buenos Aires, in 1949. In that year she married the Italian industrialist Giovanni Battista Meneghini, who became her manager. Callas made her international reputation with major performances in Verdi's *I Vespri Siciliani* (*The Sicilian Vespers*) at La Scala, Milan, in 1951, and in Bellini's *Norma* at Covent Garden in 1952, at the Chicago Opera in 1954, and at the Metropolitan Opera, New York, in 1956.

Callas went on to make numerous international appearances and was acclaimed for her dramatic skill and range in most of the exacting soprano roles. This made up for the fact that she was not a perfect vocalist. However, her professional successes were accompanied by disputes with her later managers over contracts and a turbulent private life. She separated from her first husband in 1959 and had a much publicized relationship with the Greek shipping magnate Aristotle Onassis. She retired from the stage in 1965, having appeared in some 40 roles and recorded 20 operas. She returned in the early 1970s to give a successful series of master classes in New York and to undertake extensive recital tours. She died in Paris.

Calvé, Emma (1858–1942) *French opera singer*

Calvé was one of the best-known opera singers of the late 19th century.

Emma Calvé was born in Decazeville, southern France, and studied at the Convent of the Sacred Heart in Montpellier. After singing training with Jules Puget in Paris, she made her operatic debut in Gounod's *Faust* in Brussels, in 1882. From 1885 to 1887 she appeared at the Opéra Comique in Paris and at La Scala, Milan, subsequently creating the role of Suzel in Mascagni's opera *L'Amico Fritz* in Rome in 1891. She went on to play Santuzza in Mascagni's *Cavalleria rusticana* at Covent Garden, London, in 1892 and at the Metropolitan Opera, New York, the following year. The next year she created the role of Anita in Massenet's *La Navarraise* at Covent Garden and in 1895 played the title role in his *Sappho* in Paris.

With her clear sensuous voice and lively personality, Calvé was best known for her performances in the title role of Bizet's *Carmen*, which she first sang at the Metropolitan Opera in 1893. She retired from the operatic stage in 1910 but continued to give concert performances. Her autobiography, *My Life* , was widely read. She died in Millau, France.

Camargo, Marie (Anne de Cupis de) (1710–1770) *French ballet dancer*

Marie Camargo was responsible for many technical and stylistic changes in ballet.

She was born in Brussels and made her debut, at the age of 16, in Jean Balon's ballet *Les Caractères de la danse* at the Paris Opéra. This success was followed by performances in more than 78 ballets and operas. Agile and fast, she perfected the jumping steps (the entrechat and the cabriole), which had previously been performed mainly by male dancers. She was also responsible for establishing the ballet dancer's standard leg position as standing out 90 degrees from the hip. She is credited with the shortening of the ballet skirt to its present length to enable more complex steps to be carried out and seen by the audience. She was the first to wear close-fitting underwear beneath her ballet skirt and to remove the heels from her ballet shoes. A shrewd businesswoman, she allowed her name to be used to advertise shoes and wigs.

The Camargo Society was set up in London in 1930 to revive interest in ballet. It succeeded in helping to establish the Vic-Wells Ballet (now the Royal Ballet), before disbanding in 1936.

Cameron, Julia Margaret (1815–1879) *British photographer*

Julia Cameron was one of the best British portrait photographers of the 19th century. Her subjects included such eminent figures as Alfred, Lord Tennyson and Charles Darwin.

Born and brought up in Calcutta, the third of seven daughters of Sir James Pattle of the Bengal Civil Service, she married Charles Hay Cameron, a lawyer, in 1838. As a young woman she became well known in Calcutta for her entertaining conversation and charity work. In 1848 she and her husband moved to London so that their children could go to English schools. They had many friends who were artists and writers and in 1860 they moved to Freshwater in the Isle of Wight, becoming neighbours of Lord Tennyson.

Julia did not take up photography until she was 48, when she was given her first camera by her son. She soon developed what began as a hobby into a serious art form. Having mastered the wet, or collodion, photographic process, she produced strikingly unconventional portraits in which the heads of her subjects almost filled the photographic plate. Although harshly lighted and often slightly out of focus, they were very distinctive. Julia took photographs not only of her famous friends and visitors, but also of posed groups and highly romanticized studies. Her photographic illustrations for Tennyson's *Idylls of the King* were published alongside the poem in 1875. Although she never worked as a professional photographer, she exhibited her work in London and received many photographic prizes, both in Europe and the United States. In 1875 she and her husband returned to India, where she died.

Campbell, Mrs. Patrick (1865–1940)
British actress

> Do you know why God withheld the
> sense of humour from women? That
> we may love you instead of laughing
> at you.
>
> —Comment addressed to a male
> admirer

Mrs. Patrick Campbell's great beauty
and wit made her one of the outstanding stage actresses of her generation.
Her friendship with George Bernard
Shaw is documented in some of her
published correspondence.

She was born Beatrice Stella Tanner
in London, the daughter of an English
father and an Italian mother, from
whom she inherited her dark good
looks. She studied in London and
Paris before running away at 19 to
marry Patrick Campbell, a London
stockbroker (he died in 1900). She
made her stage debut in 1888 in Liverpool, but it was her outstanding performance as Paula in Pinero's play *The
Second Mrs. Tanqueray* in 1893 that
made her famous. She then played
many leading roles, including Agnes in
Pinero's *The Notorious Mrs. Ebbsmith*,
Magda in Suderman's *Heimat*, and
several roles in Shakespeare and Ibsen.

Mrs. Campbell had a sharp wit and
often quarrelled with her managers
and her fellow actors. George Bernard
Shaw created the role of Eliza Doolittle for her in his play *Pygmalion* in
1914. Although Shaw was in love with
her, he never really forgave her for
walking out of rehearsals to go off on
honeymoon with her second husband
George Cornwallis-West. He never offered her any more parts in his plays,
but continued to write to her, modelling some of the characters in his
Heartbreak House (1917) and *The
Apple Cart* (1922) on her. This was revealed when she published her honest
and self-critical autobiography *My
Life and Some Letters* in 1922. She
continued to appear in revivals of *Pygmalion* and *The Second Mrs. Tanqueray* well into old age. She even
made a few films, including *Riptide*
(1933), but these did not do full justice
to her. She died in Pau, France.

Campion, Jane (1954–) *New Zealand film director*

Jane Campion is one of the most original new film directors to have emerged
in the 1990s.

She was born in Wellington, New
Zealand, into a theatrical family – her
mother is the actress Edith Campion
and her father a theatre director. After
studying at Victoria University, Melbourne, and at the Chelsea School of
Arts, London, Campion enrolled at
the Australian Film, Television and
Radio School in Sydney. She made her
debut with her student project *Peel*
(1981–82), which won a prize for the
best short film at the Cannes Film Festival in 1986. Her reputation was further enhanced by two more shorts
(*A Girl's Story* and *Passionless Moments* – both 1984) and the TV film
Two Friends (1986). Her next movie,
Sweetie (1989), which she cowrote, is a
black comedy about a schizophrenic
who wrecks a family. This film caused
considerable controversy when shown
at the Cannes Film Festival. It was followed by *An Angel at My Table* (1990),
about the New Zealand writer Janet
FRAME, which won awards for Best
Woman Director and Best Film at the
Venice Film Festival.

Jane Campion firmly established her
international reputation with *The
Piano* (1993), which won seven awards
at the Venice Film Festival and shared
the Cannes Palme d'Or. Campion was
the first woman director, and *The
Piano* the first Australian film, to win
this prestigious award. The film also
won three Academy Awards, including
one for Campion's screenplay.

Campion's most recent film is *The
Portrait of a Lady* (1997), based on the
novel by Henry James.

Cannon, Annie Jump (1863–1941)
American astronomer

One of the most distinguished astronomers of her generation, Annie
Cannon is noted for her work on stellar classification.

She was born in Dover, Delaware,
the daughter of a wealthy shipbuilder
who later became a state senator. She
studied at Wellesley and Radcliffe colleges and in 1896 joined the famous

group of women astronomers at Harvard College Observatory, who were working on a major programme of stellar classification under the direction of Edward Pickering. After examining astronomical photographs, Annie Cannon proved that most stars belong to only a few species. On the basis of this observation she developed the widely used Harvard system of spectral classification. Using this system she classified 225,300 stars listed in the nine-volume *Henry Draper Catalogue* (1924) and over 150,000 more stars in the *Henry Draper Extension*, the *Yale Zone Catalogue*, and the *Cape Zone Catalogue*.

Annie Jump became Curator of Astronomical Photographs at Harvard in 1911 and was appointed William Cranch Bond Astronomer in 1938. She was the first woman to receive an honorary doctorate from Oxford, and one of the few women to be elected to the American Philosophical Society. She was awarded the Henry Draper Gold Medal of the National Academy of Sciences in 1931 and the Ellen Richards Research Prize the next year. She continued to work until a few weeks before her death in Cambridge, Massachusetts. She was included in the National Women's Hall of Fame in 1994.

See also FLEMING, WILLIAMINA PATON; LEAVITT, HENRIETTA; MAURY, ANTONIA.

Caraway, Hattie (Ophelia) Wyatt
(1878–1950) *American politician*

Hattie Wyatt Caraway was the first woman to be elected to the U.S. Senate.

She was born near Bakerville, Tennessee, and married Senator Thaddeus Horatius Caraway from Arkansas. When he died in 1931 before his term had expired, the governor of Arkansas appointed Caraway to the vacant Senate seat. When she retained the seat in 1932, she became the first woman to be elected to the U.S. Senate. Twice reelected, she served until 1945 and was the first woman to preside over a session of the Senate.

She was an independently minded Democrat who supported prohibition,

much of the New Deal legislation, antilobbying bills, and equal rights for women. In 1943 she sponsored a forerunner of the Equal Rights Amendment. She was appointed to the Federal Employees Compensation Commission in 1945, five years before her death in Falls Church, Virginia.

See also FELTON, REBECCA ANN.

Carlota (1840–1927) *Wife of Emperor Maximilian of Mexico*

Carlota, who was the last empress of Mexico, had a tragic life.

She was born near Brussels, the daughter of King Leopold I of the Belgians. She was 17 when she married Archduke Maximilian of Austria, the brother of Emperor Francis Joseph I of Austria. They were appointed regents in Milan, which was then under Austrian control. After the Austrians were forced to leave by the Italians and the French in 1859, Carlota and Maximilian retired to Trieste, which was still under Austrian rule. Carlota, an ambitious and restless young woman, was delighted when the French emperor, Napoleon III, offered to make Maximilian emperor of Mexico.

When Carlota and Maximilian arrived in Mexico in May 1864, they were welcomed by the conservative pro-church party but not by the legal president, Benito Juarez. He and his supporters forcefully resisted the installation of the emperor and the empress, who were backed by French soldiers. During this period of active resistance, Carlota interested herself in Mexican history and myths, adopted the grandson of the ex-emperor of Mexico, Agustin Iturbide, did charity work among Mexican women, and rebuilt the historic Chapultepec Castle.

When Juarez's forces showed signs of defeating the French army, Napoleon III decided to withdraw his troops, thus threatening Maximilian's continued rule in Mexico. Carlota visited Europe in August 1866 to seek support for her husband, but neither Napoleon nor the pope would promise any further help. Carlota had a mental breakdown during her audience with the pope, and never recovered. She did not return to Mexico, where her husband was overthrown and executed in 1867. She was never told of her husband's fate during the remaining 60 years of her life, spent in seclusion near Brussels.

Carlyle, Jane (Baillie Welsh)
(1801–1866) *British literary figure*

The wife of the historian and critic Thomas Carlyle, Jane Welsh Carlyle was at the centre of artistic and intellectual life in mid 19th-century Britain.

She was born in Haddington, East Lothian, the only daughter of Dr. John Welsh, a strict disciplinarian who gave her a good education in Greek and Latin. She was a brilliant student. When she was 18 her father died of typhus, leaving her a considerable sum of money as well as land in Scotland. After a long courtship, despite the opposition of her mother, she married Thomas Carlyle in 1826. At first they lived on a farm at Craigenputtock, Dumfriesshire, where Thomas wrote *Sartor Resartus* which was not published until 1833. Because Jane felt isolated and lonely in rural Scotland, the Carlyles moved to London, settling in a house in Cheyne Row, Chelsea, in 1834. Here Jane had to endure poverty and Thomas's irritability and depressions until the success of his book *The History of the French Revolution* (1837) helped to ease the financial situation and, to some extent, enhanced the author's self-esteem. A woman of great emotional warmth, firm views, and often caustic wit, Jane gathered around her in Chelsea a circle of literary, artistic, and political friends including Charles Dickens, Guiseppe Mazzini, and John Ruskin. Although Jane was a talented writer, she refused to publish, despite Thomas's encouragement.

Jane and Thomas Carlyle had a difficult relationship apparently made worse by their sexual problems, said to arise from his impotence. They spent much time apart during their marriage; Thomas travelled widely while Jane stayed with friends. In the early 1860s her health collapsed as a result of being knocked down by a cab, and she died at the age of 65. Thomas was devastated and retired from public life. He wrote a sad memoir of her in *Reminiscences* (1881) and edited the *Letters and Memorials of Jane Welsh Carlyle*, which were published after his death in 1883. This volume revealed her as one of the most talented letter writers of her generation.

Caroline of Ansbach (1683–1737)
Wife of King George II of Great Britain and Ireland

> Through force of circumstances her proceedings were often devious, but in a certain robust integrity she never failed.
>
> —Peter Quennell, *Caroline of England* (1939)

Caroline exercised more power over British affairs than any previous monarch's wife.

The daughter of the margrave of Brandenburg-Ansbach in Germany, she married George Augustus, Prince of Hanover, in 1705 and went to England with him in 1714 when his father ascended the British throne as George I. When the king returned to Hanover the next year to attend to urgent matters, George Augustus took over temporarily as Defender of the Realm. For the first time he and Caroline were able to exert power and, after the king's return, they used their positions as the Prince and Princess of Wales to become active in politics. Caroline was ambitious for herself and her husband; being very sociable, she established a rival court to the king's at Leicester House in London. She entertained lavishly and gathered around her and the Prince the famous politicians, writers, musicians, and religious leaders of the age.

After her husband became King George II in 1727, Caroline exercised considerable political influence. She persuaded him to appoint Sir Robert Walpole as prime minister, with whom she established a strong working relationship. Together they eliminated rivals and influenced the king on important issues. She acted as regent during George II's frequent absences in Hanover and refused to allow her son, Frederick Louis, whom she hated, to share power. She was respected for her political ability, her intelligence, and her attractive personality. George II was devastated by her death.

Caroline of Brunswick (1768–1821)
Wife of King George IV of Great Britain and Ireland

> Fate wrote her a most tremendous tragedy and she played it in tights.
>
> —Max Beerbohm, *King George the Fourth*

Caroline of Brunswick's outrageous behaviour as the wife of the Prince Regent (later King George IV), and his vindictive reaction, brought the monarchy into disrepute at the beginning of the 19th century.

Caroline, who was born at Wolfenbuttel-Brunswick in Germany, married her first cousin George, Prince of Wales, the eldest son of George III, in 1795. The marriage was not a success since the prince was not attracted to Caroline. She bore him a daughter but the child was soon taken away from her and she was forced to live apart from her husband. There was much public sympathy for Caroline, who became a popular figure with the British people. Reports that she had committed adultery were investigated in 1806 and proved to be false. But she was reprimanded for her unconventional behaviour. When her husband became regent in 1811, Caroline was banned from the royal court and prevented from seeing her daughter regularly. This weakened her position to such an extent that she decided to go overseas.

From 1814 she travelled in Europe, the Mediterranean, and the Near East, escorted by the courtier Bartolomeo Pergami. Her indiscreet behaviour with him was secretly investigated by her husband, who collected evidence for a divorce. When George III died in 1820 and the Prince Regent became King George IV, Caroline wanted to return to England to become queen. She refused to accept a bribe of £50,000 a year for life if she surrendered the title and stayed in exile. On her return, George IV failed to persuade parliament to take away her title and grant him a divorce. But he did succeed in preventing her from attend-

ing his coronation in July 1821. Caroline, devastated by this prohibition, died the following month.

Caron, Leslie (1931–   ) *French ballet dancer and actress*

Leslie Caron made her name as a dancer in Hollywood musicals of the 1950s and went on to play straight dramatic roles in films.

She was born in Paris, the daughter of Claude Caron (a French chemist) and the American ballet dancer Margaret Petit. Leslie Caron studied at the National Conservatory of Dance in Paris and made her professional debut with the Champs-Elysées Ballet in 1949 in David Lichine's *La Rencontre*. Performing in other ballets with this company, she was seen by the actor-dancer Gene Kelly, who chose her to star opposite him in the movie *An American in Paris* (1951). The success of this film, and her spectacular dancing in the final ballet sequence, launched her career as the young innocent lead in 1950s musicals. These included *Glory Alley* (1952); *Daddy Long-Legs* (1955), in which she danced opposite Fred Astaire; and the title roles in *Lili* (1953), *Gaby* (1956), and *Gigi* (1958), appearing in the latter with the 70-year-old Maurice Chevalier.

In the 1960s Leslie Caron gave up musicals to concentrate on straight acting, appearing in many American, British, French, and Italian films, including *The L-Shaped Room* (1963), *Is Paris Burning?* (1966), and *Valentino* (1971). She has also performed in plays in London and Paris. In 1985 she returned to her first love and danced in the revue *On Your Toes*, with which she toured widely in the United States.

Leslie Caron has been married three times and has two children by her second marriage (1956–65) to the theatre director Sir Peter Hall.

Carpenter, Mary (1807–1877) *British philanthropist*

Mary Carpenter's philanthropic work among poor women and children in Britain, Europe, and North America was distinguished by its realism, tolerance, patience, and good humour.

She was born in Exeter, Devon, the

daughter of Lant Carpenter, a well-known Unitarian minister and educationalist. After receiving a solid education at her father's school in Bristol, she opened, with her mother, a girls' school in that city in 1829. Inspired by the American philanthropist Joseph Tuckerman, Mary Carpenter began her charitable work among poor children: in 1835 she founded the Working and Visiting Society and in 1846 opened a "ragged school" for slum children.

Carpenter became interested in the causes of child criminality, publishing her findings in *Reformatory Schools for the Children of the Perishing and Dangerous Classes, and for Juvenile Offenders* (1851). She warned that if the children of the deserving poor were not helped by society, they would become criminals. She used her own money to establish a reformatory school for boys in Bristol in 1852 and called for juvenile offenders to be treated less harshly than adults in her study *Juvenile Delinquents, their Condition and Treatment* (1853). Her ideas influenced the British parliament, which passed the Juvenile Offenders Act in 1854. She immediately opened a reformatory school for girls in Bristol and later set up an industrial school and a working men's club.

She continued to advise on the rehabilitation of juvenile offenders in Britain, Germany, and the United States and also lobbied for women to be allowed to study for university degrees, especially in medicine.

Mary Carpenter extended her ideas on education to Indian women, having visited India four times between 1866 and 1876. However, her attempts to set up a teachers' training college and a school for poor girls failed because of cultural differences.

Carr, Emily (1871–1945) *Canadian artist and writer*

Emily Carr is noted for her paintings of Native Americans and the forests of British Columbia; she is often regarded as a Canadian cultural icon.

She was born in Victoria, British Columbia. Although she suffered from ill health all her life, this did not prevent her from studying art in San Francisco, London, and Paris. In the late 1890s she began her visits to Native American camps in British Columbia, sketching the inhabitants and the surrounding forests. However, discouraged by lack of recognition for her work, she stopped painting for a number of years.

Public interest in Carr's work began to develop in the late 1920s, encouraging her to join the Canadian School of Painters in 1933.

Carr's paintings are primitive in style, having been influenced by the cubist and impressionist schools. Her style is best shown in *Cape Mudge: An Indian Family with Totem Pole* (1912) and *Woods and Blue Sky* (1932), which can be seen in the Beaverbrook Art Gallery, Fredericton, New Brunswick; and *Kispiax Village* (1929), displayed at the Art Gallery of Toronto.

After 1940 Carr was forced by ill health to give up painting, deciding instead to take up writing. Her first book, *Klee Wyck* (1941), was a collection of short stories about Indian life; it won the Governor-General's Award. This was followed by *The Book of Small* (1942), about her childhood, and *The House of All Sorts* (1944), about a boarding house. It was not until after her death that Carr's later works were published. They included her autobiographical volumes *Growing Pains* (1946), *The Heart of a Peacock* (1953), and *Pause: a Sketch Book* (1953) as well as a selection from her journals, *Hundreds and Thousands* (1966).

Carreño, Maria Teresa (1853–1917)
Venezuelan pianist and composer

The outstanding woman pianist of her day, Teresa Carreño was described as the "Valkyrie of the piano" because of the dramatic intensity of her interpretations and her versatile technique.

She was born in Caracas, Venezuela, where she was taught the piano by her father and Julius Hoheni. She gave her first recital in New York City when she was eight years old, after which she became a pupil of the American composer and pianist L. M. Gottschalk. In

1863 she played the piano for President Lincoln at the White House.

Carreño later studied with the pianists George Mathias and Anton Rubinstein in Paris; after making her Berlin debut in 1893, she became famous throughout Europe. Her repertoire included Beethoven's *Emperor Concerto* and Tchaikovsky's first piano concerto, which she played with great power; she was one of the first pianists to include Grieg's piano concerto in her performances.

Carreño was married four times, her musical tastes changing with her husbands. Her first marriage, to the violinist Emile Sauret, inspired her to compose a string quartet. Her second marriage, to the opera singer Giovanni Tagliapietra, led to her involvement in opera as a manager, performer, and conductor. Her third marriage, to the pianist and composer Eugène d'Albert, resulted in a greater subtlety in her playing as well as a number of compositions for the piano. Carreño's last marriage was to her second husband's brother. She died in New York.

Carriera, Rosalba (1675–1757) *Italian painter*

Rosalba Carriera was the most distinguished painter of portraits and miniatures in Venice in the early 1700s.

She was born in Venice, the eldest daughter of a poor public official. Rosalba helped her mother, a lacemaker, by drawing patterns, but after the fashion for lace declined she turned to painting miniatures on snuffboxes. She was one of the first artists to paint on ivory and to use pastels for portraits. Her talent was soon widely recognized in Italy; as a result she was elected to the prestigious San Luca Academy in Rome. Her delicate use of colour, her precision, and her ability to paint her sitters in a flattering light meant that she was soon in great demand from the kings and queens of Europe.

Rosalba was invited to Paris in 1720 to paint the young King Louis XV, subsequently being elected to the Royal Academy of Painting. In 1730 she visited Vienna, where she taught the empress of Austria to paint. After her travels Rosalba returned to Venice to live with her mother and sister. When her sister died in 1738, she became depressed and worked less and less. She was completely blind for the last seven years of her life.

Carrington, Dora (1893–1932) *British painter*

Carrington (as she was always known) was deeply involved with the Bloomsbury Group of writers and artists, especially the biographer Lytton Strachey.

Raised in a conventional British middle-class family, in 1910 she was allowed to attend the Slade School of Art in London, where she studied for three years, being taught by the painter Wilson Steer. Carrington became friendly with the painters Augustus John and C. R. Nevinson; it was from Nevinson's family that she learned about women's emancipation. As a result she refused to marry an ardent suitor, Mark Gertler, in case it compromised her artistic independence. Although she continued to see him, she became involved with Lytton Strachey in 1915 and, through him, with the Bloomsbury Group. Two years later she became Strachey's housekeeper at Tidmarsh Mill, near Pangbourne in Berkshire, where she embarked on a rigorous programme of self-education. She still painted but did not think her work good enough to exhibit. During this period her painting was influenced by such post-impressionists as Cézanne and Matisse.

In 1921 Carrington married Ralph Partridge, a friend of her brother. Together they lived in a bizarre ménage with the homosexual Strachey in his new house at Ham Spray in Sussex. She worked mostly on crafts, but her output declined because of the complications of her personal life. When Strachey, was dying of cancer, Carrington tried unsuccessfully to commit suicide. After his death, however, she succeeded in taking her own life. Most of her work is still in private hands, but examples of her painting can be seen in the Slade School and in the National Portrait Gallery of Scotland. In 1995 Emma THOMPSON took the title role in the film biography *Carrington*.

Carson, Rachel (Louise) (1907–1964)
American biologist

> Over increasingly large areas of the
> United States, spring now comes
> unheralded by the return of the
> birds, and the early mornings are
> strangely silent where once they
> were filled with the beauty of bird
> song.
>
> —*Silent Spring* (1962)

Rachel Carson was the author of several influential books about the environment, notably *Silent Spring*, which examined the possible dangers of the widespread use of modern artificial pesticides on food chains.

She was born in Springdale, Pennsylvania, where she developed a great love of the outdoors from an early age. After graduating in 1929 from the Pennsylvania College for Women, she obtained an MA in biology from Johns Hopkins University in 1932 and taught at the University of Maryland (1931–36). She later carried out postgraduate research into offshore life at the Marine Biological Laboratory at Woods Hole, Massachusetts. She worked as a marine biologist with the U.S. Bureau of Fisheries from 1936 to 1949 and in 1947 became the editor-in-chief of all the publications of the U.S. Fish and Wildlife Service.

Although Rachel Carson was a recognized authority in her field, her first book, *Under the Sea* (1941), did not attract much public notice. It was only with her second book, *The Sea Around Us* (1951), in which she warned of the dangers of polluting the sea, that she established a wider reputation. This was followed by *The Edge of the Sea* (1955).

Carson's last book, *Silent Spring* (1962), initiated considerable debate on the use of pesticides, resulting in more research into their effects; this in turn led to U.S. government controls on their use. Her books contributed to the growing awareness in the United States in the 1970s and 1980s of the dangers of environmental pollution.

Carter, Angela (1940–1992) *British writer*

By the time of her early death Angela Carter had established herself as one of the most individual voices in British contemporary fiction.

Born Angela Olive Stalker in Eastbourne, she grew up in London. When she was 18, her father, a Scottish journalist, arranged for her to become an apprentice journalist on *The Croydon Advertiser*. Two years later she left the paper to marry Paul Carter. She then studied English literature at Bristol University, after which she began to write fiction. Her early books *Shadow Dance* (1965), *The Magic Toyshop* (1967), *Heroes and Villains* (1969), *Love* (1971), and *The Infernal Desire Machine of Dr Hoffman* (1972) are characterized by an imaginative blend of fantasy, humour, and symbolism.

Following her divorce in 1971, Angela Carter went to live in Japan for two years. After her return to Britain her writing became more concerned with socialist and feminist issues, apparent in *The Passion of New Eve* (1978), *Fireworks* (1979), *The Bloody Chamber* (1979), and *The Sadeian Woman* (1979). Angela Carter was a strong critic of contemporary society; volumes of her selected journalism have been published as *Nothing Sacred* (1983) and *Shaking a Leg* (1995). This was followed by the novels *Nights at the Circus* (1984) and *Wise Children* (1991) and the collection of short stories *Black Venus* (1985). She wrote the screenplay for the movie *The Company of Wolves* (1984), which was based on one of her short stories, as well as plays for radio. She also published poetry, children's stories, and translations of fairy tales. In 1987 her book *The Magic Toyshop* was made into a film.

Carter taught creative writing at universities in Britain, the United States, and Australia, but her home was in London, where she had a son in 1984. Academic and popular interest in her work has continued to grow rapidly since her death of cancer at the age of 52.

Carter, Elizabeth (1717–1806) *British poet and classical scholar*

A highly respected personality, Elizabeth Carter was a member of the famous "Bluestockings," a group of

18th-century British women intellectuals.

She was born in Deal, Kent, the daughter of a clergyman who taught her Greek, Latin, and Hebrew; she later studied Arabic, Portuguese, history, and astronomy. Elizabeth Carter never married, devoting herself instead to looking after her father's family by his second marriage. In 1734 she began publishing poetry in *The Gentleman's Magazine* under the name "Eliza." After the publication of her *Poems upon Particular Occasions* (1738) she met the writer and critic Dr. Samuel Johnson, who honoured her by inviting her to write two essays for his magazine *The Rambler*. She later published another poetry collection, *Poems on Several Occasions* (1762).

Elizabeth Carter is best remembered for her translation of the work of the Greek philosopher Epictetus in 1758. She also belonged to the group of women intellectuals, led by Elizabeth MONTAGU, who were known as the "Bluestockings" because of the colour of their legwear. The word "bluestocking" has persisted in the language to denote any intellectually inclined woman.

Carter's memoirs and correspondence were published after her death.

Carter, Mrs. Leslie (1862–1937)
American actress

One of the greatest dramatic actresses of her era, Mrs. Leslie Carter had a strong stage presence, often being favourably compared to Sarah BERNHARDT.

Born Caroline Louise Dudley, in Lexington, Kentucky, she spent her early years in Cleveland, Ohio, where her father was a dry goods merchant. When she was eight years old, her father died and she moved with her brother and mother to Dayton, where she studied at the Cooper Seminary. With her bright red hair, flashing green eyes, slender figure, and lively personality she attracted many suitors. She married the wealthy Chicago industrialist Leslie Carter in 1880 and moved with him to his native city. They divorced in 1889, however, after which Mrs. Leslie Carter, as she liked to be called, embarked on a theatrical career under the management of David Belasco. She made her stage debut in 1890 in *The Ugly Duckling* (1890). Her first success was in *The Heart of Maryland* (1895); this was followed by leading roles in *Zaza* (1898), *Du Barry* (1901), and *Adrea* (1905).

Belasco exploited what he called "the magnetism of her highly keyed, temperamental nature" to present Mrs. Carter in grand dramatic roles at a time when musicals, farce, and melodrama dominated the American theatre.

Her partnership with Belasco ended in 1906 when she married the actor William Louis Payne. Belasco never forgave her for deserting him and never spoke to her again. Although she appeared under other management in *Kassa* (1909), *The Second Mrs. Tanqueray* (1913), and in Somerset Maugham's play *The Circle* (1921), her performances lacked the vitality she had displayed under Belasco's management. She died in Santa Monica, California.

Cartland, Dame Barbara (1901–)
British writer

> I don't believe in equal opportunity. I think it's terribly tiresome. The whole thing is absolutely terrible now because we've got vast unemployment. It's still a stigma for a man to be unemployed, and to be kept by a woman. It's not a stigma for a woman to be kept by a man.
>
> —Quoted by Naim Attalah in *Women* (1987)

Barbara Cartland is a writer of popular romantic novels whose enormous output has brought her fame and fortune.

The daughter of Major Bertram Cartland, she published her first novel, *Jigsaw* (1923), at the age of 22. Since then she has published over 400 books, many of them bestsellers. Although specializing in romantic novels, she has also published biographies of such subjects as ELIZABETH, empress of Austria, Empress JOSÉPHINE, and DIANE DE POITIERS. Her five volumes of autobiography include *The Isthmus Years* (1943), *The Years of Opportunity*

(1947), *I Search for Rainbows* (1967), *We Danced All Night* (1971), and *I Seek the Miraculous* (1978). In 1983 she broke a world record by writing 26 books in a single year.

Dame Barbara believes in the importance of health food in maintaining health and beauty in old age and has written several books on the subject. In 1964 she founded the British National Association of Health, of which she is the president. She has also been closely involved with charities, particularly the St. John Ambulance Brigade, and was made a DBE in 1991. Twice married, she became the step-grandmother of DIANA, PRINCESS OF WALES.

Casarès, Maria (1922–1996) *Spanish actress*

Casarès, who worked mainly in France, is considered the finest tragic actress to have appeared in French plays and films from World War II to the present.

The daughter of Santiago Casarès Quiroga, a member of the Republican government in Spain, she was born in La Coruña, a port in the rugged northwest of the country. In 1936 she fled to France with her family, after the Republicans had been defeated by Franco in the Spanish Civil War. Although the family had little money and were forced to stay in cheap hotels, Maria learned French and on her 20th birthday appeared in her first play, J. M. Synge's *Deirdre of the Sorrows*, which was an instant success.

Her incredible eyes, which could express a whole range of emotions from anger to love, her deep expressive voice, and her noble presence made her a natural choice for the great female dramatic roles, attracting such major playwrights as Albert Camus, with whom she had a long and close relationship. She was in constant demand, appearing not only in French classics, such as Racine's *Phèdre*, but in modern plays by Bertolt Brecht, Jean-Paul Sartre, and Jean Genet. Although she preferred the theatre, Casarès also appeared in classic films such as Marcel Carné's *Les Enfants du paradis* (1945) and Jean Cocteau's *Or-phée* (1949) and *Le Testament d'Or-phée* (1959).

Maria Casarès married another actor, "Dade" Schlesser, in 1978. He shared her philosophical attitude to life, which was fully revealed in 1980 in her autobiography *Résidente Privilégiée* (Privileged Resident – the words on her French identity card). She remained a Spanish citizen and, after the death of Franco in 1975, returned to Spain, where she staged a play to honour her country. She continued to appear in plays in France until a few months before her death.

Cassatt, Mary (1844–1926) *American painter*

> I am independent. I can live alone and I love to work. Sometimes it made him [Degas] furious that he could not find a chink in my armor, and there would be months when we just could not see each other, and then something I painted would bring us together again.

> —Quoted by Louisine W. Havemeyer
> in *Sixteen to Sixty, Memoirs
> of a Collector*

Cassatt is regarded as the first American impressionist painter.

Born in Allegheny City, Pennsylvania, she was inspired to become a painter after visiting European art galleries with her family during a five-year residence in Paris, which began when she was six years old. From 1861 to 1865 Cassatt attended the Pennsylvania Academy of Fine Arts but, as the course was too theoretical, left to study abroad. After receiving practical instruction in painting in Paris, Rome, Spain, and Belgium, she began, in 1872, to exhibit her work annually in Paris. Edgar Degas was so impressed with Cassatt's *Portrait of Ida*, shown in 1877, that he invited her to exhibit with the impressionist painters, which she started to do from 1879. Cassatt and her family then moved to Paris, where she specialized in painting scenes from domestic life, often using her sister and nephews and nieces as models.

Cassatt and Degas became great friends during this period: they had considerable influence on each other's work, and Cassatt produced some of her best impressionist paintings, including *The Cup of Tea* (1879) and *Woman and Child Driving* (1880).

Cassatt's later work shows the influence of Japanese art, which developed after she visited the Japanese Exhibition in Paris in 1890; her style of painting and etching became more formal and clearer, as seen in her painting *The Bath* (1891) and in the many colour prints she produced at this time. She also designed a wall painting for the Woman's Building at the Columbia Exposition in Chicago in 1891–92.

When her mother died in 1895, Cassatt returned on a visit to the United States, where she discovered that exhibitions of her early work had created an interest in impressionist art. Cassatt continued to paint until 1912, when she was forced to stop after developing cataracts in both eyes.

Castle, Barbara, Baroness (1910–)
British Labour politician

An ardent and vociferous defender of socialism, Barbara Castle spent 34 years in the House of Commons, during which she progressed from the back benches to the cabinet and back again, before moving to the European Parliament in 1979 and the House of Lords in 1990.

Born Barbara Anne Betts in Chesterfield, Derbyshire, she was educated at Bradford Girls' Grammar School. After graduating from St. Hugh's College, Oxford, she became involved in local government as a borough councillor and was employed at the ministry of food during World War II. She subsequently worked as a journalist and married Ted Castle, who later became Lord Castle of Islington. Having entered the House of Commons as Labour MP for Blackburn in 1945, she soon became known for her outspoken support of socialist causes. She served as chairman of the Labour Party from 1958 to 1959.

After the Labour Party's election victory in 1964, Castle joined the cabinet of Harold Wilson, first as minister of overseas development (1964–65) and then as minister of transport (1965–68). In the latter post she was

responsible for the introduction of the breath test for drunk drivers. As the first secretary of state for employment and productivity (1968–70), she courted controversy with her proposals for trade-union reform set out in the White Paper "In Place of Strife." With hindsight, the rejection of these proposals is often held to have sealed the fate of Labour and the trade unions in the late 1970s and 1980s.

Castle remained in the shadow cabinet during the Conservative government of the early 1970s and when Labour regained power in 1974 she became secretary of state for social services. However, when James Callaghan an inveterate opponent, replaced Wilson as prime minister in 1976, Castle was banished to the back benches, and in 1979 she left Westminster to become a Member of the European Parliament. There she led the British Labour Group and served as vice-chairman of the international socialist group (1979–86).

Castle's writings have often proved as lively and controversial as her speeches and policies. They include *The Castle Diaries* (1980; 1984), a study of the suffragettes Christabel and Sylvia PANKHURST published in 1987, and a volume of memoirs, *Fighting All the Way* (1993). In 1990 Castle was granted a life peerage as Baroness Castle of Blackburn. In recent years she has campaigned energetically for the rights of old-age pensioners.

Castro, Rosalía de (1837–1885)
Spanish poet and novelist

Writing in the Galician dialect, Rosalía de Castro was one of the greatest Spanish poets of the 19th century.

She was born in Santiago de Compostela and raised in Padrón, La Coruña province, in the Galicia region of Spain. She began writing poetry at the age of 11. Her earliest works, such as *La flor* (1857; The Flower), are in Spanish. In 1858 she married the historian Manuel Murguía, who was a great champion of the revival of Galician culture. In support of her husband Rosalía de Castro's later poetry is in Galician, being based on Galician folk poetry but with a new form and metre.

The best examples are in *Cantares gallegos* (1863; Galician Songs) and *Follas novas* (1880; New Leaves), which have considerably influenced later Spanish writers, including Federico García Lorca.

Rosalía de Castro also wrote novels in Spanish, including *La hija del mar* (1859; The Daughter of the Sea) and *Ruinas* (1867; Ruins), which were widely read at the time.

Although Galician is fast disappearing as a living language in Spain, Rosalía de Castro's reputation as a great poet seems secure.

Cather, Willa (1873–1947) *American writer*

> The disappearance of the old frontier left Miss Cather with a heritage of the virtues in which she had been bred but with the necessity of finding a new object for them. Looking for the new frontier she found it in the mind.

> —Lionel Trilling, quoted by Malcolm Cowley in *After the Genteel Tradition*

Willa Cather is known for her novels about frontierswomen in the old American West.

She was born on a farm in Back Creek Valley, near Winchester, Virginia. In 1883 she moved with her family to Red Cloud, Nebraska, spending her formative years among immigrant homesteaders, which greatly influenced her subsequent writing. She studied at home, at the local high school, and in Lincoln, where she attended the University of Nebraska and supported herself by writing drama criticism for the *Nebraska State Journal*. After graduating from college in 1895, she moved to Pittsburgh, Pennsylvania, becoming a journalist on *The Home Monthly* and then on *The Daily Leader*. However, in order to have more time for her own writing, she gave up journalism to became a teacher in Pittsburgh high schools. Her first book, *April Twilight* (1903), a collection of poems, was followed by *The Troll Garden* (1905), a collection of short stories. One story, "Paul's Case," caught the eye of the publisher and editor S. S. McClure, who offered her an editorial post on his magazine

in New York. As a result, she worked on *McClure's Magazine* for six years, eventually becoming a highly successful managing editor.

Willa Cather left journalism again in 1912 to concentrate on her fictional writing. Drawing on her own early experiences, she wrote a great series of novels about young pioneer women in Nebraska. *O Pioneers!* (1913) was followed by *The Song of the Lark* (1915), *My Antonia* (1918), *One of Ours* (1922), which won the Pulitzer Prize in 1923, and *A Lost Lady* (1923). Her subsequent fame and the changes this brought to her life led to problems; the disillusionment she felt at this time is reflected in her novel *The Professor's House* (1925). Cather's later novels, especially the bestselling *Death Comes for the Archbishop* (1927), mirror her growing interest in the American Southwest, where her brother lived.

Willa Cather always preferred the company of women. She lived for 15 years with her future biographer, Edith Lewis, in Greenwich Village, New York, where she died.

Catherine I (1684–1727) *Empress of Russia*

Catherine was empress of Russia from 1725 to 1727, following the death of her husband, Tsar Peter (I) the Great.

She was born Marta Skavronskya in Jacobstadt, Lithuania (now Jēkabpils, in Latvia), the daughter of a Catholic peasant. She first worked as a servant to a Lutheran pastor, receiving a basic education from him, before marrying a Swedish army officer. He deserted her when the Russians captured Lithuania from the Swedes. She then became the mistress of a Russian general, Boris Sheremetev, and subsequently of the tsar's chief minister, Prince Alexander Menshikov.

Still ascending the social ladder, she became the mistress of Peter I in 1705, converting to the Russian Orthodox religion and changing her name to Catherine. She was the tsar's closest companion and bore him 11 children, though most of them died in infancy. In 1712 Peter married her and officially recognized their children as his own, making them eligible to succeed to the throne. In many ways Catherine dominated her husband – she was the only person in his entourage who could calm his great rages. Such was her influence over him that he nominated her as his successor in 1724 and crowned her as his empress. When he died the next year, Prince Menshikov and the palace guards ensured that she, rather than other claimants, succeeded to the throne.

Although Catherine was now the reigning empress, her inexperience led her to rely strongly on the advice of her ministers in the Supreme Privy Council. However, she continued her husband's reforms and did what she could to help the peasants. She reigned for two years, being succeeded by her husband's grandson Peter II. Her children ELIZABETH and Peter III later ruled in Russia.

Catherine II (1729–1796) *Empress of Russia*

> If Fate had given me in youth a husband whom I could have loved, I should have remained always true to him. The trouble is that my heart would not willingly remain one hour without love.
>
> —Letter to Prince Potemkin, 1774

Known as Catherine the Great, Catherine II was a forceful ruler who had a major impact on both Russia and the rest of Europe in the late 18th century.

She was born Princess Sophia Augusta Frederika of Anhalt-Zerbst in the German city of Stettin (now Szczeczin, in Poland). At the age of 15 she visited Russia, where she converted from Lutheranism to Russian Orthodoxy, was rechristened Catherine, and married the 16-year-old Grand Duke Peter, who was the nephew and heir of Empress ELIZA-BETH of Russia. The marriage was a disaster, and Catherine loathed her son and only child, the future Tsar Paul I, who was born in 1754. But Catherine was ambitious, energetic, and a clever political operator. She established a good relationship with the Empress Elizabeth and made many friends at court. After her husband succeeded to the throne as Peter III, he

became unpopular, largely because of his contempt for Russia and its people; Catherine was able to have him deposed with the help of the palace guards in June 1762. She then became ruler and consolidated her power; her husband was murdered in prison later that year, possibly at Catherine's instigation.

Catherine had many influential ministers, lovers, and favourites during her reign but she always retained ultimate control. Influenced by the French thinkers Voltaire and Montesquieu, she regarded herself as an enlightened ruler. Her famous Instruction of 1767 was intended to reform the legal code, provincial and town government, and education. When it failed to achieve these ends, the aristocrats, on whom Catherine relied to help govern, had their powers over local affairs and the serfs on their estates increased by means of the Charter of the Nobility of 1785. Under her enlightened patronage, St. Petersburg became a great cultural centre, but she also introduced the first formal censorship in Russia.

Catherine pursued an aggressive foreign policy with the aim of expanding Russian territory. Between 1772 and 1795 she divided up Poland between Russia, Austria, and Prussia. She fought two wars against Turkey, annexing the Crimea in 1783 and other parts of the Black Sea region in 1792 and 1794. Although she secured the right for Russian ships to pass through the Turkish Straits into the Mediterranean, she was never able to realize her dreams of seizing Constantinople or the Balkans. By the time of her death in St. Petersburg, Russia had been accepted as a leading European power. This was her greatest achievement.

Catherine de' Médicis (1519–1589) *Regent of France*

> If things were even worse than they are after all this war they might have laid the blame upon the rule of a woman; but if such persons are honest they should blame only the rule of men who desire to play the part of kings. In future, if I am not any more hampered, I hope to show

that women have a more sincere determination to preserve the country than those who have plunged it into the miserable condition to which it has been brought.

—Letter to the Ambassador of Spain, 1570

As wife of King Henry II, Italian-born Catherine de' Médicis was the mother of three kings of France. Acting as either regent or chief adviser to her sons, she exerted great influence during France's religious wars in the late 1500s.

She was born Caterina de' Medici, in Florence, the daughter of Lorenzo de' Medici, Duke of Urbino. At the age of 14 she was married to the Duke of Orléans, who became King Henry II in 1547, and subsequently bore him ten children, seven of whom lived. However, Catherine played no part in governing France at this time, being overshadowed by DIANE DE POITIERS, the king's mistress, who had a greater influence over him.

This situation changed following Henry II's death in 1559; for the next 30 years Catherine served France as regent or adviser to her incapable sons, King Francis II (reigned 1559–60), King Charles IX (reigned 1560–74), and King Henry III (reigned 1574–89). Her overriding aim was to ensure that her dynasty held on to the throne of France during a time of civil war between the Catholics and the Protestants (Huguenots).

Catholic herself, Catherine nevertheless tried at first to reconcile the two sides; however, in 1567, after accepting that a reconciliation was not possible, she sought to suppress the Huguenots by force. When this failed, she returned to a policy of reconciliation and in 1570 granted them religious rights under the Peace of St. Germain. This agreement did not prevent her from instigating a massacre of the Huguenots on St. Bartholomew's Day, August 24, 1572, creating a new wave of persecutions of Protestants in France.

In her later years Catherine continued to negotiate between the leader of the Huguenots, Henry of Navarre (who had married her daughter MAR-GUERITE DE VALOIS), and the Catholic League, who sought to dominate her son Henry III . Although she did not prevent the religious wars again breaking out, she did manage to keep her family on the French throne.

Catherine was also a great patron of the arts; among other projects she commissioned the building of the Tuileries Palace in Paris.

Catherine de' Ricci, Saint
(1522–1590) *Italian mystic*

Catherine de' Ricci was a stigmatic (i.e., she bore the marks of the crucifixion of Jesus Christ on her hands and feet). By means of personal contact and letters she had a great influence over many people.

Born into a noble family in Florence, she changed her name from Alessandra to Catherine when she became a nun with the Dominican Order in 1535. She lived in their convent at Prato, near Florence, for the whole of her adult life, being appointed the prioress there in 1552 and remaining in this office until her death.

Catherine experienced ecstasies and other mystical phenomena. Her spiritual beliefs were greatly influenced by the religious teacher Savonarola, who lived in Florence. She was canonized in 1746; her feast day is February 13.

Catherine of Alexandria, Saint
(died *c.* 305) *Christian martyr*

St. Catherine of Alexandria, whose life and career may very well be entirely legendary, gave her name to the Catherine wheel firework.

According to the legend, she was born into a noble or royal Christian family in Alexandria. After being baptized, she had a vision that she had married Jesus Christ. At the age of 18 Catherine denounced the Roman Emperor Maxentius for his persecution of Christians (Egypt was then part of the Roman Empire). In an attempt to silence her Maxentius demanded that she debate the issue with 50 pagan philosophers. He was astonished and angry when Catherine converted not only them, but also the empress and some of his guards to Christianity. In retaliation he ordered that Catherine should be tied to a spiked wheel (later called a "Catherine wheel"). Although starved and tortured on the wheel, she survived this ordeal – only to be beheaded on the orders of the emperor (or possibly his son).

Catherine's body was supposedly taken to Mount Sinai, where her shrine can be seen in St. Catherine's monastery. Her feast day, November 25, was dropped from the liturgical calendar in 1969 because of doubts that she ever existed.

Catherine of Aragon (1485–1536)
First wife of King Henry VIII of England

The break-up of Catherine's marriage to Henry VIII triggered the events that led England to sever connections with Rome and eventually to become a Protestant country.

The daughter of Ferdinand II of Aragon and ISABELLA I of Castile, Catherine was born at Alcalá de Henares, Spain. She went to England in 1501 to marry Arthur, Prince of Wales, the eldest son and heir of King Henry VII. When Arthur died the following year without the marriage ever having been consummated, it was arranged that she should marry Arthur's younger brother Henry. As a result of arguments over the dowry and dynastic politics this did not happen until after Henry VIII became king in 1509. Their marriage was happy for a time: they were both patrons of the arts, and Catherine was an efficient ruler while Henry was away fighting the French between 1511 and 1514. She bore him six children between 1510 and 1518, but only a daughter survived infancy – later to become Queen MARY I.

By the 1520s it was clear that Catherine could have no more children. Henry's desire for a male heir and his love for Anne BOLEYN led him in 1527 to seek an annulment of his marriage to Catherine. Pope Clement VII delayed a decision for seven years because he could not afford to lose the political support of Catherine's nephew, the Holy Roman Emperor Charles V. Despite strong opposition from the pope, Henry secretly married Anne Boleyn in 1533 and had his mar-

riage to Catherine annulled by the new Archbishop of Canterbury, Thomas Cranmer. When, in 1534, the pope pronounced that Catherine's marriage was still valid, Henry formally severed his link with Rome and began his Reformation of the church and state.

Catherine was separated from her daughter Mary, whom she never saw again, and was forced to retire from public life. She refused to take the title of Princess Dowager. Nor would she recognize the Act of Succession, which declared that Mary was illegitimate, or the Act of Supremacy, which declared the king rather than the pope to be the head of the church. She died in poverty, shortly before the execution of Anne Boleyn.

See also ANNE OF CLEVES; HOWARD, CATHERINE; PARR, CATHERINE; SEYMOUR, JANE.

Catherine of Bologna, Saint
(1413–1463) *Italian mystic*

St. Catherine of Bologna was a nun who had mystical experiences, including visions and revelations.

She was born in Bologna, a member of the aristocratic Virgi family. After studying in Ferrara, in 1432 she entered the newly built convent of the Poor Clares in that city, where she served as mistress of the novice nuns for many years. In 1456 she moved back to Bologna to become an abbess.

Catherine wrote devotional works and hymns, as well as Italian and Latin prose and verse. *Le sette arme* (Seven Spiritual Weapons) is her most famous work. She died in Bologna; her feast day is March 9. There are paintings and miniatures of her in several Italian museums.

Catherine of Braganza (1638–1705)
Wife of King Charles II of Britain

Catherine of Braganza was born at Villa Viçosa, Alentejo, Portugal, the daughter of the Duke of Braganza (who later became King John IV of Portugal). She was raised a strict Catholic. In 1661 it was arranged by treaty that she should marry King Charles II, reinforcing a series of alliances between England and Portugal that stretched back for several centuries. Catherine's dowry included the port of Tangier in Morocco, Bombay in India, and Portuguese territories in the Far East, as well as a large sum in gold.

Catherine arrived in England in 1662. She loved Charles and was deeply upset to discover that he had a mistress, Barbara Villiers, the Duchess of Castlemaine, by whom he already had several children. She was forced, much against her will, to receive them at court. Catherine grew to tolerate her husband's mistresses and his illegitimate children, but her life was not made any easier by the fact that she was unable to have children herself. Catherine's childlessness also endangered her position as queen, since there were some members of parliament who, after Charles's brother became a Roman Catholic, wanted the king to marry again and produce a Protestant heir. Charles successfully resisted this pressure, but Catherine was forced to live apart from him.

Catherine was grief-stricken by Charles's death in 1685 and retired from public life. In 1692 she returned to Portugal, where she helped to renew the old alliance with England by promoting a commercial treaty (1703). In the year before her death Catherine governed Portugal as regent during the illness of her brother, King Pedro II .

Catherine of Genoa, Saint
(1447–1510) *Italian mystic*

St. Catherine of Genoa was noted for her care of the poor and sick.

She was born in Genoa, into the important and aristocratic Fieschi family. At the age of 16 she was married to another aristocrat, the wealthy Giuliano Adorno. It was an unhappy marriage since Adorno was unfaithful, bad-tempered, spendthrift, and pleasure-loving. Dissatisfied with her life, Catherine underwent a spiritual conversion in 1473. She became an ascetic and a mystic, profoundly influencing her husband, who – following his bankruptcy – became a Franciscan monk. They devoted themselves to looking after the poor and the sick in the Pammatone Hospital in Genoa. Catherine was the administrator of the

hospital from 1490 to 1496 and nearly died of the plague.

Catherine's mystical experiences and beliefs are recorded in her *Dialogues on the Soul and the Body* and *The Treatise on Purgatory*. These are regarded as spiritual classics. She died in Genoa and was canonized in 1737. Her feast day is September 15.

Catherine of Siena, Saint
(1347–1380) *Italian mystic*

Along with St. Francis of Assisi, St. Catherine of Siena is one of the principal patron saints of Italy.

She was born in Siena, the 23rd child of Giacomo and Lapa Benincasa. It is said that she had her first vision at the age of seven, which led her to vow her virginity to Jesus Christ. Although attractive and lively, she spent much time in penitential prayer. When her mother encouraged her to take better care of her appearance in order to increase her chances of marriage, Catherine responded by cutting off her hair.

In 1365 Catherine entered the Third Order of St. Dominic, where she lived in seclusion for three years, praying, fasting, and mortifying her flesh. After she had a vision of her mystical marriage to Christ, who instructed her to undertake charity work, she devoted the rest of her life to helping the poor and the sick.

Catherine continued to have visions and even experienced the pain (if not the marks) of the nails driven into Christ's hands and feet at his Crucifixion. Her great sanctity and work among the poor and the sick led to her acquiring the reputation of a miracle worker. She gathered around her a band of followers, both secular and religious, and was consulted by political leaders on the great issues of the day.

Catherine of Siena became involved in public affairs in 1375, when she attempted to broker a peace between the rebel city state of Florence and the pope's government in Rome. Shortly afterwards she was successful in persuading Pope Gregory XI to move the papal seat in Avignon, France, back to Rome. When he died, and the election of Pope Urban VI led to a great split in the Western Church, Catherine moved to Rome and urged the rebel churchmen and kings to return to his obedience. The task soon proved too much for her, and she died of a stroke.

Catherine of Siena wrote devotional works, poems, and letters. Her *Dialogue*, containing her beliefs, is considered to be a spiritual classic. She was canonized in 1461 and named patron saint of Italy in 1939. Her feast day is April 30.

Catherine of Sweden, Saint (*c.* 1331–1381) *Swedish nun*

The daughter of St. BRIDGET OF SWEDEN, St. Catherine was the first abbess of a new order of nuns founded in her mother's name in Sweden.

Born in Ulfasa, she married a Swedish aristocrat in 1343, but the marriage was never consummated. After her husband's death in 1351 Catherine became her mother's closest companion in Rome, sharing her ascetic life and accompanying her on pilgrimages within Italy and to the Holy Land. When her mother died, she returned with the body to Sweden in 1374 and became the first abbess of the Brigittine convent at Vadstena. Between 1375 and 1380 she successfully lobbied the Pope to have her mother canonized and the Brigittine Order recognized.

Catherine died in Vadstena. Although she has never been formally canonized, the Brigittines regard her as a saint, celebrating her feast on March 24.

Catherine of Valois (1401–1437) *Wife of King Henry V of England*

Through her second marriage Catherine of Valois was the grandmother of King Henry VII , the first of the Tudor monarchs of England.

She was born in Paris, the youngest daughter of King Charles VI of France and ISABELLA OF BAVARIA. After a difficult courtship, during which war broke out between England and France over the terms of the dowry, Catherine married Henry V at Troyes, France, in 1420. As a result of the marriage Catherine's brother was disinherited, and Henry V became the "adopted heir" to the throne of France.

Catherine was crowned queen in 1421 and soon gave birth to a son, the future King Henry VI . Henry V died in France in 1422. Catherine was passed over as regent, while her son was too young to rule, in favour of his uncles. In 1428 the British parliament passed a law forbidding Catherine to remarry without the consent of the king and his advisers, in case her new husband had too much influence over her son. Not prepared to wait until her son was old enough to give his permission, Catherine secretly married Owen Tudor, a Welsh squire, by whom she had four children. The eldest son from this marriage was the father of King Henry VII. Catherine died at the age of 36 at Bermondsey Abbey, near London.

Catt, Carrie (Lane Chapman) (1859–1947) *American suffrage leader*

> The sacrifice of suffering, of doubt, of obloquy, which has been endured by the pioneers in the woman movement will never be fully known or understood.
>
> —Speech, "For the Sake of Liberty," February 9–14, 1900

Carrie Catt played a major role in securing the right to vote for women in the United States.

She was born Carrie Lane in Ripon, Wisconsin. After graduating from Iowa State College in 1880, she became a high school principal and one of the first female school superintendents. She married Leo Chapman, a local newspaper editor, in 1885, but he died the following year. Carrie then became actively involved in the campaign to give women the vote. Before remarrying in 1890, she secured a legal contract from her new husband, George Catt, that she should be able to devote four months each year to the cause of women's suffrage.

An excellent administrator, Carrie Catt was chairwoman of the National American Woman Suffrage Association (NAWSA) from 1895 to 1900 and then president until 1905, when she resigned because of her husband's ill health. After his death she became head of the suffrage movement in New York State before resuming the presidency of NAWSA in 1915. She reorganized the movement and drew up the "Winning Plan," lobbying ceaselessly to change opinion at both the local and national levels and in the main political parties in favour of women's suffrage. Against considerable opposition the 19th Amendment to the Constitution, extending the vote to women, was passed by the Congress in June 1920.

Carrie Catt continued to campaign for women's rights. She was the founder-president of the International Woman Suffrage Alliance from 1902 to 1923 and helped set up the League of Women Voters in 1919. In her later years she became involved with the peace movement, especially the Committee for the Cause and Cure of War. Her writings include *Woman Suffrage and Politics: The Inner Story of the Suffrage Movement* (1923) and *Why Wars Must Cease* (1935). She died in New Rochelle, New York State.

See also ANTHONY, SUSAN B(ROWNELL); MOTT, LUCRETIA COFFIN; STANTON, ELIZABETH CADY; STONE, LUCY BLACKWELL.

Cavell, Edith (1865–1915) *British nurse*

> I realize that patriotism is not enough. I must have no hatred or bitterness towards anyone.
>
> —Her last words before being shot, October 12, 1915

Edith Cavell was a heroine of World War I who was shot by the Germans for helping Allied soldiers escape from German-occupied Belgium.

The daughter of a clergyman, she was born in Swardeston, Norfolk. After working in Belgium as a governess, she trained as a nurse at the London Hospital. She returned to Belgium in 1907 to become head of that country's first training school for nurses in Brussels. By the time World War I broke out in 1914 she had modernized nursing in Belgium.

When the Germans invaded Belgium in 1914, the training school for nurses in Brussels became a Red Cross hospital for wounded soldiers regardless of their nationality. The German military authorities soon found out that Edith Cavell was hiding fugitive Allied soldiers in the hospital, preparatory to their being smuggled across the border into neutral Holland. She helped about 200 soldiers to escape in this way before being arrested, along with 34 others, on August 5, 1915.

She was kept in a prison cell on her own for nine weeks, during which time she was tricked by the Germans into making a confession. She was then tried and sentenced to death, along with four others. Edith Cavell refused to defend herself and agreed that her sentence was a just one. Despite a last-minute appeal from the neutral American representative in Brussels for a pardon, Edith Cavell and her Belgian accomplice, Philippe Baucq, were executed by firing squad at dawn on October 12, 1915.

The execution of Edith Cavell caused outrage in Allied countries, which regarded her as a martyr. With hindsight it is clear that the Germans were legally, if not morally and politically, correct in executing her. By following her conscience she had broken the law governing the behaviour of civilians and medical personnel in an occupied country.

Cavendish, Margaret, Duchess of Newcastle (1624–1674) *English writer*

> For though it be the part of every good wife to desire children to keep alive the memory of their husband's name and family by posterity, yet a woman has no such reason to desire children for her own sake. For first her name is lost…in marrying, for she quits her own and is named as her husband; also,…neither name nor estate goes to her family according to the laws and customs of this country.
>
> —*CCXI Sociable Letters* (1664)

Margaret Cavendish is best known for writing one of the earliest autobiographies in the English language.

She was born at St. John's, near Colchester, Essex, the youngest of eight children of Sir Thomas Lucas, a wealthy landowner. After studying at home, and despite her great shyness, Margaret became maid of honour to Queen HENRIETTA MARIA. She accompanied the queen on her dramatic flight to Paris in 1644 to escape the English Civil War.

In 1645 Margaret met and married the royalist William Cavendish, later Duke of Newcastle, and they spent the next 15 years living in exile in Europe. Margaret could not have children and had no interest in domesticity.

A compulsive writer since childhood, she decided to earn a living from her writing after an unsuccessful visit to England to collect revenue from her husband's confiscated estates. Her first publications were *Poems and Fancies* and *Philosophical Fancies* (both 1653). She established her reputation with *Playes* (1662) and *CCXI Sociable Letters* (1664). Her *Orations of Divers Persons* (1662) called for much greater equality and freedom for women.

Margaret Cavendish regarded writing as the only escape for a woman in a male-dominated world. Although her works were ridiculed by contemporaries as futile and dull, later critics have admired her courage and the descriptive power of her writing. Her autobiography (1655) and her biography (1667) of her husband are widely regarded as valuable accounts of life among the aristocracy during and after the Civil War. She died in London. Through her analysis of what it meant to be a woman and a writer in the 17th century, Margaret Cavendish has an important place in the history of feminism.

Cecilia, Saint (2nd or 3rd century) *Christian martyr*

St. Cecilia is the patron saint of music.

According to unreliable historical sources, Cecilia was born into an aristocratic Roman family. A Christian from childhood, she vowed to remain celibate. When forced to marry the pagan aristocrat Valerianus, she convinced him to respect her chastity and converted him and his brother Tiburtius to Christianity. As a reward they were granted a vision of an angel. Valerianus and Tiburtius were eventually put to death for their faith. When Cecilia was caught burying them, she too was condemned to death. After an attempt to suffocate her in her bath

failed, she was ordered to be decapitated, living for three more days after being mortally wounded by the axe.

Although St. Cecilia has been venerated from the 6th century, this devotion increased considerably after Pope Paschal I transferred her body from the cemetery of St. Praetextatus to the Church of St. Cecilia in the Trastevere section of Rome in 821. St. Cecilia has been the patron saint of musicians since the 1500s; she is often depicted in paintings and sculptures playing a small organ or other musical instrument. Her feast day is November 22.

Cenci, Beatrice (1577–1599) *Italian noblewoman*

The tragic central figure in the murder of her brutal father, Beatrice Cenci was later immortalized in prose, poetry, and painting.

She was born in Rome, the daughter of the cruel and tyrannical aristocrat Francesco Cenci. After one of his frequent quarrels with his family, Cenci imprisoned Beatrice and her stepmother, Lucrezia, in the remote castle of Petrella, situated between Rome and Naples. Beatrice was cruelly treated there but failed in her attempts to escape. However, she fell in love with her jailer, Olimpio Calvetti, and they plotted with Lucrezia and two of her brothers to kill Francesco.

The murder of Francesco took place on September 9, 1598, and the Cenci family was soon arrested. Under torture they confessed to the crime, being subsequently tried and convicted by the papal court. Despite a plea for clemency, Pope Clement VIII condemned the Cenci to death and confiscated their property: Beatrice and Lucrezia were decapitated, and one of her brothers was tortured to death.

Beatrice's tragic life has been the subject of novels, plays, and poetry, notably Percy Bysshe Shelley's verse drama *The Cenci*. She is also the subject of a painting by the Italian artist Guido Reni.

Centlivre, Susanna (1667–1723) *British playwright*

> Nothing melts a woman's heart like gold.
>
> —*The Basset-Table* (1705)

Susanna Centlivre's plays, particularly her comedies, were extremely popular in Britain during the first half of the 18th century.

It is not clear whether she was born in Holbeach, Lincolnshire, or in Co. Tyrone, Ireland. Her wealthy father, named Freeman, owned land in both places. Susanna was strikingly beautiful and gifted in languages, having been educated by a French tutor. After leaving home at an early age, she had an affair with a student at Cambridge University, disguising herself as his valet since no females were allowed to reside in college. She later left for London, where she was married and widowed twice – both her husbands were killed in duels. Susanna then became an actress, touring England and often appearing in her own plays.

Her first play, in which she played the heroine, was the tragedy *The Perjured Husband* (1700). Her other plays included the comedies *The Gamester* (1705), *Love at a Venture* (1706), *The Platonick Lady* (1706), and *The Busy Body* (1709). Her output was not affected by her marriage in 1706 to Joseph Centlivre, a cook in the household of Queen ANNE. She went on to produce a total of 19 plays.

Mrs. Centlivre was a great defender of the Protestant succession and the Hanoverian dynasty in Britain; the poems and plays that she wrote during the period 1712–17 reflected her politics. She was attacked for this by Alexander Pope, who called her "the cook's wife in Buckingham Court."

In her best plays, such as *The Wonder! A Woman Keeps a Secret* (1714) and *A Bold Stroke for a Wife* (1718), Susanna created female characters of moral integrity. Her plays continued to be performed in London for many years after her death.

Cerrito, Fanny (1817–1909) *Italian ballet dancer*

One of the most talented ballerinas of her generation, Fanny Cerrito was also one of the few woman choreographers of the 19th century. Her dancing was distinguished by its energy, suppleness, and grace.

Born in Naples, she studied ballet at La Scala, Milan, before making her debut at the age of 15 in Naples. She then toured Italy and Austria and had seasons at La Scala (1838–39) and at Her Majesty's Theatre in London, (1840–46). She was particularly popular with British audiences, performing in a series of ballets including *Alma* (1842), in which she choreographed a *pas de trois*, and *Ondine*, which was created for her by the choreographer Jules Perrot in 1845 and provided Cerrito with her greatest role. In 1843 she danced the *pas de deux* from this ballet with Fanny ELSSLER at the Royal Command Performance in front of Queen VICTORIA. It was so successful that in 1845 Perrot staged his *pas de quatre*, in which Cerrito danced with three other great ballerinas: Marie TAGLIONI, Carlotta GRISI, and Lucile GRAHN.

Fanny Cerrito married her dancing partner, the choreographer Arthur Saint-Léon, in 1845; two years later she made her debut at the Paris Opéra in his *La Fille de marbre*. They separated in 1851, and she became the mistress of the Marques de Bedmar. She continued to dance at the Paris Opéra, appearing in Mazilier's *Orfa* (1852) and her own ballet *Gemma* (1854). She danced for two seasons in Russia (1855–57), during which she performed at the coronation of Tsar Alexander II. Cerrito retired in 1857, living for the rest of her life in Paris.

Chadwick, Florence (1918–1995) *American swimmer*

Florence Chadwick, who achieved fame by becoming, in 1951, the first woman to swim the English Channel both ways, broke many long-distance swimming records.

Born in San Diego, California, she began long-distance swimming as a child; at the age of ten she became the first child to swim the San Diego Bay Channel. Although she never competed in the Olympics, Chadwick continued to pursue her interest in long-distance swimming after studying law at college. She was determined to break Gertrude EDERLE's 24-year women's record for swimming the

English Channel. Unusually resistant to cold, she achieved this on August 8, 1950, by swimming from Cap Gris-Nez to Dover in 13 hours 20 minutes. The next year she set an even more impressive record by becoming the first woman to accomplish the difficult crossing, against the tides and in the fog, from England to France. In 1952 Chadwick became the first woman to swim the 21 miles from Catalina Island to the Californian coast, which she achieved in a record-breaking time of 13 hours 47 minutes.

Chadwick swam the English Channel from England to France twice more – in 1953 and 1955. In 1953 she also swam the Straits of Gibraltar and the Dardanelles, and made a return trip across the Bosporus.

Florence Chadwick became a stockbroker but continued to swim herself and to train others. She died in San Diego. The fact that many of her records have since been broken is at least partly due to the aid that modern long-distance swimmers receive from radar to keep them on the correct course.

Chaminade, Cécile Louise Stéphanie (1857–1944) *French composer and pianist*

Best known for her light piano pieces and songs, Cécile Chaminade was also a popular concert pianist, frequently performing her own works.

Born in Paris, she studied musical composition with Benjamin Godard. She began composing church music at the age of eight and soon attracted the attention of the composer Georges Bizet. At the age of 18 she gave her first piano recital, going on to give many recitals of her own work.

In addition to over 200 charming pieces for the piano, Chaminade composed more ambitious works, including the ballet symphony *Callirhoë* (1888); *Les Amazones* (1888), for chorus and orchestra; a *concertstück* (c. 1896) for piano and orchestra; and a flute concertino (1902). She also wrote such songs as "Madrigal", "Chanson slave", "Ritournelle", "Fleur de matin", and "Sans amour".

After her debut in London in 1892

Chaminade went on to give many other performances in England, where she was in great demand. In 1908 she made a successful tour of the United States. She also recorded several of her compositions, notably the *Scarf Dance* from *Callirhoë*.

Chamorro, Violetta Barrios de (c. 1929–) *Nicaraguan politician*

The first woman president of a Central American country, Violetta Chamorro brought an end to the long-running civil war in Nicaragua.

Born Violetta Barrios Torres in Rivas, Nicaragua, she was educated in the United States. On her return to Nicaragua she met and (in 1950) married Pedro Joaquin Chamorro Cardenal, editor of the *La Prenza* newspaper (which was owned by his family) and a leading conservative politician. As a vociferous opponent of the ruling Somoza regime he was frequently imprisoned or exiled. His murder by unknown gunmen in 1978 sparked off the Sandinista revolution and the overthrow of the Somoza regime in 1979. Violetta Chamorro became a symbol of the resistance to Somoza.

Although she supported the Sandinista revolution and served in the revolutionary government, Chamorro soon resigned when it began to pursue left-wing policies. She returned to *La Prenza* and became a leader of the moderate opposition to the Sandinistas. Her paper was banned in 1986 but was allowed to resume publication the following year. Selected as the presidential candidate for the National Opposition Union (a coalition of parties), in 1990 she defeated the Sandinista leader Daniel Ortega in free elections to become president of Nicaragua.

In office Violetta Chamorro tried to pursue a policy of national reconciliation. She ended the civil war, restricted the powers of the president, and revived the economy. Chamorro resigned the presidency in 1996.

Champmeslé, Marie (1642–1698) *French actress*

Marie Champmeslé, also known as La Champmeslé, was the leading tragic actress of her generation in France.

Marie Desmares was born into a distinguished family in Rouen and began acting in local theatres; after the death of her first husband, a merchant, she married the actor Charles Chevillet Champmeslé in 1666. They moved to Paris, where Marie upstaged her husband as an actor and was soon in great demand by the leading theatrical companies. Her appearance in Racine's *Andromaque* at the Hôtel de Bourgogne in 1670 so impressed the playwright that he wrote the title role of *Bérénice* for her. She went on to perform major roles in his dramas *Bajazet* (1672), *Ighigénie* (1674), and *Phèdre* (1677). Critics at the time attributed the success of Racine's plays to La Champmeslé's interpretation. She became his mistress, but they separated in 1679.

In 1680 Marie and Charles Champmeslé joined the new Comédie-Française company, with Marie starring in its inaugural performance of *Phèdre*. She remained with that company for the rest of her career, appearing on stage until illness forced her retirement.

The most popular actress of her day in France, La Champmeslé pioneered the chanting delivery that is so characteristic of classical French theatre.

Chanel, Coco (1883–1971) *French fashion designer*

> Fashion is architecture: it is a matter of proportions.
>
> —*Coco Chanel, Her Life, Her Secrets*

Coco Chanel pioneered the simple, low-waisted style of dress that dominated women's fashion in the 1920s. She also launched the famous Chanel range of perfumes.

She was born Gabrielle Bonheur Chanel into a poor rural family in Saumur, Maine-et-Loire. Orphaned at an early age, she and her sister moved to Deauville, where they worked in a dressmaker's shop. In 1913 Chanel opened her own shop in Deauville. After World War I she moved to Paris, where she opened a fashion house in the Rue Cambon.

Her loose-fitting, casual, but elegant clothes, in great contrast to the traditional stiff corseted style, appealed to the new liberated women of the 1920s. She was particularly famous for her "little black dress," made of jersey wool (an unfashionable material associated with maids' uniforms) and adorned with lavish costume jewellery. At the height of her career Coco Chanel was the wealthiest fashion designer in France, owning factories that manufactured textiles, jewellery, and perfume: her most famous fragrance, Chanel No. 5, was introduced in 1922. A prominent figure in fashionable society, she was a close friend of the Duke of Westminster. Although she became engaged to one of her directors, Paul Iribe, they never married.

By the late 1930s Chanel's clothes were no longer popular: she had to close down her fashion house, leaving only the perfumery business in operation. However, after World War II her distaste for contemporary fashion designs led Chanel to reopen her fashion house. Her new line of clothes, especially the Chanel suit with its boxy jacket, appealed to the women of the 1950s and 1960s; in the United States the new "Chanel look" came to symbolize high style and was copied by American manufacturers.

Coco Chanel remained active in fashion design right up until her death in Paris. Both her perfumery and her clothing businesses have continued to enjoy success.

Channing, Carol (1921–) *American actress*

Carol Channing is remembered for her exuberant singing roles in various musical comedies on stage and screen.

She was born in Seattle, Washington, the daughter of a Christian Science lecturer. After several years playing supporting roles in the theatre and appearing in comedy revues in nightclubs, she achieved stardom as Lorelei Lee in Anita LOOS's *Gentlemen Prefer Blondes* (1949) on Broadway, singing the hit song of the show, "Diamonds Are a Girl's Best Friend." Channing's interpretation of this role – characterized by big-eyed exuberance – was in marked contrast to the kittenish coyness Marilyn MONROE brought to the part in the film version (1953).

Carol Channing went on to appear in more stage musicals, including *Wonderful Town* (1953), *Show Girl* (1961), and – most notably – *Hello Dolly!* (1963); her performance as the brassy ambitious Dolly Levi in this play earned her a Tony Award and the New York Drama Critics Award for Best Actress. She also appeared in the screen musicals *The First Travelling Saleslady* (1956) and *Thoroughly Modern Millie* (1967), for which she received the Golden Globe Award for Best Supporting Actress. Returning to Broadway to star in *Jerry's Girls* (1984–85) and *Legends* (1986), she subsequently toured in the United States with *Carol's Broadway Revue* and *Hello Dolly!* (1994).

Chantal, Saint Jane Frances de
(1572–1641) *French nun*

St. Jane Frances de Chantal was a cofounder of the Visitation Order of nuns in France in the early 1600s.

She was born Jane Frances Frémiot in Dijon, the daughter of a lawyer. In 1592 she married Christophe de Rabutin, Baron de Chantal. They had four children, whom Jane Frances had to raise herself after her husband was killed in a hunting accident in 1601. Having ensured that her son and eldest daughter were provided for, in 1610 Jane Frances took her two youngest daughters and her spiritual adviser, St. Francis of Sales, to Annecy, in eastern France. Here, together with St. Francis, she set up the Visitation Order of nuns and became a nun herself.

On the instructions of the Archbishop of Lyon the Visitandines, or Salesian Sisters, were initially an order dedicated to religious contemplation. Later they became involved in nursing the sick and the poor, and finally the order set up boarding schools for upper-class girls. These were popular and led to a rapid expansion of the number of religious houses in the order.

At the time of St. Jane's death 86 houses of the Visitation Order were in existence. Her sanctity was widely recognized in her lifetime. She was canonized in 1767, and her feast day is August 21.

Charles, Dame (Mary) Eugenia
(1919–) *Dominican politician*

Dame Eugenia Charles was the first woman to become prime minister of a Caribbean country. Known as the "Iron Lady of the Caribbean," she was in office for 15 years and has been compared to Margaret THATCHER. She was made a DBE in 1991.

Born in Pointe Michel, Dominica, she went to London to study law, qualifying as a barrister in 1947. She returned to the Caribbean to practise law in Barbados and the Windward and Leeward Islands. Embarking on her political career in 1963, two years later she became cofounder and first leader of the moderate Dominica Freedom Party. In 1975 she was elected as a member of Parliament and became leader of the opposition to the government.

Eugenia Charles won the 1980 election and became prime minister, minister of foreign affairs, and minister of finance and development. In office she exposed corruption in government and the armed forces, surviving a number of emergencies and a coup attempt in 1981. She was criticized for being too dependent on U.S. aid and for encouraging President Reagan to invade Grenada in 1983 to depose the left-wing regime in that country.

Her party won subsequent elections in 1985 and 1990 but was defeated in the 1995 election by the United Workers' Party, after which she resigned the party leadership.

Charlotte (1896–1985) *Grand Duchess of Luxembourg*

Charlotte was a popular sovereign of Luxembourg during a period of great change in this small state.

The second daughter of Grand Duke William IV of Luxembourg, Charlotte Aldegonde Elise Marie Wilhelmine succeeded her sister Marie-Adelaide as grand duchess in January 1919. Marie-Adelaide had abdicated because of her pro-German reputation during World War I. On her accession Charlotte immediately sought the approval of the people of Luxembourg by calling on them to decide between her continued reign and a republic. In a referendum held in September 1919 three quarters of the electorate voted for her to stay as grand duchess. The same year she married Prince Felix of Bourbon-Parma, with whom she had six children.

After Luxembourg was overrun by the German army in May 1940, Charlotte fled with her government to Montreal. She remained there for the rest of World War II, making regular radio broadcasts to her occupied country that gave great hope to her people. After the war ended, she returned to Luxembourg and ruled until 1964, although she had given many of her responsibilities to her eldest son, Jean, three years earlier.

During her reign Charlotte presided over great changes in Luxembourg. After both world wars the constitution was rewritten. Universal suffrage was granted and the twice-violated disarmed neutrality clause was abolished. Social security schemes were introduced and labour laws were passed. After World War II Luxembourg was fully integrated into western Europe. It joined the Benelux Economic Union, NATO, and the European Economic Community now the (European Union).

As a result of her patriotism and democratic instincts Charlotte came to symbolize Luxembourg's evolution into a prosperous, democratic state.

Charrière, Isabelle Agnès Elisabeth de (1740–1805) *Dutch-born Swiss writer*

Isabelle de Charrière was an 18th-century intellectual who wrote commentaries on contemporary society.

She was born at Zuylen, Utrecht, the daughter of Baron van Tuyll van Serooskerken van Zuylen. Attractive and intelligent, she had many suitors, including James Boswell (the friend and biographer of Dr. Samuel Johnson). However, she married her brother's tutor in 1766, moving with him to Colombier, near Neuchâtel, Switzerland. Bored and unhappy with her married life there, she began an intense intellectual friendship with the writer Benjamin Constant.

She described her married life in several mainly autobiographical novels, the most impressive of which is *Caliste* (1787). She also wrote studies on aristocratic privilege, poverty, and morality, as well as comedies and a tragedy, using various pen names, including "Zélide," "Belle de Zuylen," and "Abbé de la Tour." She died in Colombier.

Chase, Edna Woolman (1877–1957) *American fashion editor*

Edna Woolman Chase's initiative, determination, and commitment to an elite style helped to improve the international reputation of American fashion.

She was born in Asbury Park, New Jersey, the only child of Franklyn and Laura Woolman. Her parents having divorced when she was a child, she was raised by her Quaker grandparents and educated by tutors and in private schools. When she was 18, she went to work in the circulation department of the society weekly magazine *Vogue*. By the time Condé Nast took over the magazine in 1909, Chase had become a fashion reporter. Nast, soon aware of her potential, promoted her to managing editor in 1911 and then to editor-in-chief three years later.

After the French fashion houses in Paris were forced to close because of World War I, Chase urged fashion designers in New York to present their own creations. To help them she organized the first fashion show to be held in the United States. After the war she was also in charge of the British and French editions of *Vogue*, making use of her detailed knowledge of the European fashion industry to transform the American fashion scene. Among other moves, she started the policy of crediting New York (and later Dallas and San Francisco) shops that sold the European fashions shown in *Vogue*.

Edna Woolman Chase had a deep knowledge of both the fashion and publishing worlds, enabling her to forge a link between them. She never doubted the importance of fashion in society and sought to refine its tastes.

Eager to promote the most contemporary fashions in art, writing, design, and photography, she was also a shrewd businesswoman, who recognized that fashion was an attractive career for a woman because it was so well paid. By the time of her retirement in 1952 she was a wealthy woman.

She was married twice and had a daughter (Ilka) by her first marriage to Francis Dane Chase. Ilka, an actress and writer, helped her mother to write her autobiography, *Always in Vogue*.

Chase, Lucia (1897–1986) *American ballet dancer*

Acclaimed for her dramatic performances, Lucia Chase was a founder member of the American Ballet Theater.

She was born in Waterbury, Connecticut, and studied at St. Margaret's School there. She later graduated from Bryn Mawr College, Massachusetts, and attended the Theater Guild School in New York City. Her early career on the stage was interrupted by her marriage in 1926, to the businessman Thomas Ewing. After his death in 1933 she returned to the stage, studying ballet with the ex-Bolshoi Ballet master Mikhail Mordkin. Having subsequently joined his ballet company, she danced leading roles in the ballets *Giselle* and *La Fille mal gardée* with them.

In 1940 Chase became a founder member and financial backer of the Ballet Theater (later the American Ballet Theater), remaining a codirector with Oliver Smith until 1980 and their principal dancer until 1960. Her dramatic interpretations of such ballets as Anthony Tudor's *Pillar of Fire* and *Dark Elegies* were widely acclaimed. Her performances in the classical ballets *Les Sylphides*, *Petrouchka*, and *Pas de quatre* and the modern ballets *Bluebeard*, *Judgment of Paris*, and *Tally-Ho* were also well received. She continued to dance into her seventies, even though she was officially retired, appearing as the mother of Lizzie BORDEN in Agnes DE MILLE's ballet *Fall River Legend*.

Lucia Chase received the New York Handel Medallion in 1975 and the U.S. Medal of Freedom in 1980 for her lifetime's achievements.

Châtelet, Emilie, Marquise du (1706–1749) *French scientist and translator*

The Marquise du Châtelet's most important work was her translation of Sir Isaac Newton's *Principia Mathematica* into French.

She was born Gabrielle Emilie le Tonnelier de Breteuil in Paris. Her father taught her Latin and Italian. After her marriage to the Marquis du Châtelet-Lomont in 1725, she made a study of the physical sciences and mathematics as her husband had become a soldier and spent much time away from home. Madame du Châtelet also led a lively social life in Paris, becoming the mistress of Voltaire, whom she met in 1733. She spoke in his defence when he angered the government by publishing his *Lettres philosophiques* in 1734.

With Voltaire she retired to her husband's estate at Cirey, which soon became a centre of scientific and literary activity. They set up a laboratory and conducted experiments to analyse the nature of fire, heat, and light. The marquise believed that heat and light were connected in that they both represented types of motion. She wrote a *Dissertation on the Nature and Propagation of Fire* (1744), which was published by the Academy of Sciences in Paris. Before her death in childbirth she translated Newton's *Principia Mathematica* into French. This was published in 1759.

Cher (1946–) *American pop singer and actress*

After performing as a pop singer with her husband as "Sonny and Cher" in the 1960s, Cher went on to develop a successful solo career as an actress and singer.

Cher was born Cherilyn Sarkisian in El Centro, California, the daughter of John and Georgia (Holt) Sarkisian: her father is of Armenian origin, while her mother is of Cherokee descent. After joining a backing group as a vocalist, her career in pop music took off when she married Salvatore "Sonny" Bono in 1964 and performed with her husband on the ABC television show *Shindig*. They had their first major hit with the song "I Got You Babe" the next year. As representatives of the counterculture movement they became extremely popular in the mid 1960s, although later they began to lose ground. From 1971 to 1974 they appeared together on CBS television in *The Sonny and Cher Comedy Hour*. However, they divorced in 1975, and Cher married the rock musician Gregg Allman, from whom she is also now divorced. Cher has a daughter, Chastity, from her first marriage and a son, Elijah Blue, from her second marriage.

From 1975 Cher embarked on a successful solo career in television, the theatre, films, and pop music. She appeared in Robert Altman's Broadway production of *Come Back to the Five and Dime, Jimmy Dean, Jimmy Dean* (1981) as well as in the film version (1982). Nominated for an Academy Award for Best Supporting Actress in *Silkwood* (1983), she won a Best Actress Award at Cannes for *Mask* (1985) and an Oscar for Best Actress in *Moon- struck* (1987). Her other movies include *The Witches of Eastwick* (1987), *Mermaids* (1990), and *The Player* (1992).

Chevreuse, Duchesse de (1600–1679) *French noblewoman*

The Duchesse de Chevreuse was a tireless political intriguer at the court of King Louis XIII of France.

She was born Marie de Rohan, the daughter of the Duc de Montbazon. After a neglected and troubled childhood, at the age of 17 she married Charles d'Albert, who later became the Duc de Luynes. The early death of her husband and her subsequent eccentric behaviour led to her expulsion from the court of Louis XIII. She was only able to return to court after her marriage to Claude de Lorraine, the Duc de Chevreuse.

A beautiful woman with more charm than scruples, she was soon having an affair with the English ambassador to France, Lord Holland. Together they managed to arrange for Holland's friend, the Duke of Buckingham, to have an affair with ANNE OF AUSTRIA, the queen of France, much to the outrage of Louis XIII. Marie also convinced the queen that if King Louis died early, she should marry his dashing brother Gaston d'Orléans. A great conspiracy ensued, and Marie was forced to flee to England in 1627. An extremely resourceful intriguer, she managed to return to France the next year but again was exiled in 1634 after she was discovered giving French state secrets to Spain.

Madame de Chevreuse's remarkable career of treason and intrigue continued with conspiracies against the king's first minister, Cardinal Richelieu, and his successor, Cardinal Mazarin. However, her political influence declined as she grew older and less beautiful; she eventually died at Gagny, near Paris.

Chiang, Mayling Soong (1900–) *Chinese political figure*

Mayling Soong Chiang is the widow of Chiang Kai-shek, president of Nationalist China (1928-49) and subsequently of the Nationalist government in exile in Taiwan.

She was born in Shanghai, China, the youngest daughter of Charles Soong, an American-educated businessman. Mayling studied at Wellesley College in the United States, graduating in 1917. Her family were all deeply involved in politics in China: her brother T. V. Soong became prime minister, her sister Ai-ling married H. H. Kung, who also served as prime minister, and her sister Ch'ing-ling married the Chinese revolutionary leader Sun Yat-sen (see SUN CH'ING-LING). Mayling also became involved in revolutionary politics.

She met the future Generalissimo Chiang Kai-shek when he was serving as a young officer in Sun Yat-sen's army. They married in 1927, and Chiang converted to Christianity. Although Mayling held few official posts, as an adviser to her husband she had a considerable influence on Chinese politics in the late 1920s and 1930s. When Chiang was captured by the forces of his rival, Chang Hsüeh-liang, she negotiated his release.

Madame Chiang Kai-shek was the first woman to be decorated by the Chinese government and became the director-general of the New Life Movement. She was a spokesperson for the Nationalist Chinese government on her many trips abroad, both before and after the Nationalists' flight to Taiwan following the Communist victory on the Chinese mainland in 1949. Since her husband died in 1975, she has lived mainly in the United States.

She has written a number of books, including *This Is Our China* (1940), *China Shall Rise Again* (1941), and *The Sure Victory* (1955).

Chicago, Judy (1939–) *American artist*

Judy Chicago is a leading feminist artist, whose work is exhibited in many of the major art collections in the United States.

Born Judy Cohen in Chicago, Illinois, she later adopted the name of her home town. While studying (1960–64) at the University of California, Los Angeles, she married Jerry Gerowitz in 1961. After he died, two years later, she taught external courses for her university until 1969. Her subsequent marriage to Lloyd Hamrol occurred at about the time of her involvement with the feminist art movement. She co-founded the Feminist Studio Workshop at the California Institute of Arts in order to provide women with a sympathetic environment in which to practise their art. The encouragement of women artists has been one of the abiding themes of her work, which included helping to establish the Women's Building as a successor to Feminist Studio Workshop.

Judy Chicago's works, such as *Menstruation Bathroom* (1971), attack traditional conceptions of female sexuality, causing some shock to members of the public. Her best-known work is *The Dinner Party*, a multimedia creation that occupied her for five years (from 1974); it was hugely popular when it was shown in Los Angeles, Chicago, and New York City. *The Dinner Party* takes the form of a triangular table, with embroidered runners and ceramic plates, individually set for 39 women representing different aspects of women's history. The table is set on a floor on which the names of 999 famous women are written. This work, which has yet to find a permanent home, is described in *The Dinner Party: Embroidering Our Heritage* (1979) and *The Dinner Party: A Symbol of Our Heritage* (1979).

Judy Chicago's work can be seen in the Los Angeles County Museum, the San Francisco Museum of Modern Art, the Oakland Museum of Art, and the Pennsylvania Academy of Fine Arts. She has also made films, including *Womanhouse* (1972), and written her autobiography, *Through the Flower: My Struggle as a Woman Artist* (1975).

Child, Julia (1912–) *American cookery expert*

Julia Child is well known through her cookery books and television programmes.

She was born Julia McWilliams in Pasadena, California, and graduated from Smith College in 1934. After working as a clerk in New York, she joined the Office of Strategic Services (OSS), the forerunner of the CIA, in 1941. She was sent to Ceylon (now Sri Lanka) where she met Paul Child, who also worked for the OSS. After World War II she went to California, where she attended the Beverly Hills Cookery School. In 1946 she married Child, who had joined the Foreign Service, which required the couple to move to Washington, D.C. He was subsequently posted to Paris, where they remained until 1954.

Living in Paris gave Julia an opportunity to study cooking at the Cordon Bleu School; eventually, with Simone Beck and Louise Bertholle, she set up L'Ecole des Trois Gourmandes. Julia continued to be associated with the school during the following years when her husband was posted to Marseilles, Bonn, and Oslo. She also collaborated with her two friends on the bestselling book *Mastering the Art of French Cooking* (Vol. 1, 1961; Vol. 2, 1970).

Julia returned to the United States in 1961 and settled in Massachusetts. The success of her book led to her being invited to host the programme *French Chef* on television, which was a great hit and ran from 1963 to 1973. She later hosted *Julia Child and Company* (1978–79), which was devoted to American cooking. She continued to produce cookery books, including *From Julia Child's Kitchen* (1975), *Julia Child and Company* (1978), a revised edition of *Mastering the Art of French Cooking* (1983), and *The Way to Cook* (1989). She has also produced videos, including the series *Cooking with Master Chefs* (1993). In 1982 she helped set up the American Institute for Food and Wine.

Child has received many awards, including the Peabody Award in 1964, the French Order of Merit for Agriculture in 1967, and the National Order of Merit in 1974.

Child, Lydia Maria (1802–1880)
American writer

> The more women become rational companions, partners in business and in thoughts, as well as in affection and amusement, the more highly will men appreciate *home* – that blessed work, which opens to the human heart the most perfect glimpse of Heaven, and helps to carry it thither, as on an angel's wings.
>
> —*Letters from New York*, Vol. I, January 1843

Lydia Maria Child campaigned for social and political reform in the United States.

Born Lydia Maria Francis in Medford, Massachusetts, she attended local schools before becoming a teacher. After moving to Maine to live with her brother, she wrote a number of historical novels. *Habonok* (1824) is about the conflict between the Puritan settlers and the Native Americans in Massachusetts. *Rebels* (1825) is a romance set during the American War of Independence, while *Philothea* (1836) is set in Ancient Greece.

In 1828 Lydia married the Boston lawyer and reformer David Lee Child. Together they became very influential supporters of the antislavery movement. Mrs. Child herself published a number of antislavery tracts, most notably *An Appeal in Favor of the Class of Americans Called Africans* (1833). She also wrote pamphlets, including *Anti-Slavery Catechism* (1836), and coedited with her husband the *Anti-Slavery Standard* (1840–44). In addition to her antislavery work she published a number of books on women's issues, including the *Frugal Housewife* (1829), the magazine *Juvenile Monthly* (1826–34), and *The History of the Condition of Women in Various Ages and Nations* (1835). She also wrote a number of biographies and the vivid *Letters from New York* (1843).

In the 1850s Mrs. Child became interested in religion, demonstrating her versatility by writing *A Progress of Religious Ideas* (1855). She stirred up considerable controversy when she volunteered to nurse the militant abolitionist John Brown, who was in prison at the time. She sold over 300,000 copies of her published *Correspondence between Lydia Maria Child and Governor Wise and Mrs. Mason of Virginia* (1860). After the abolition of slavery she took up the cause of Native Americans, writing the pamphlet *An Appeal for the Indians*. Her final book was *Aspirations of the World* (1878).

Chin Kieu (1948–   ) *South Korean violinist*

Chin Kieu is noted especially for her warm and expressive interpretations of the works of Elgar and Walton.

She was born in Seoul, South Korea, and studied music from an early age. She played in public for the first time when she was nine years old. Three years later she moved to New York where she studied under Ivan Galamian at the Juilliard School of Music, making her debut with the New York Philharmonic Orchestra in 1967. The next year she won the Leventritt Competition. She made her European debut in London in 1970 and has since performed with famous orchestras and conductors around the world. She appeared at the Salzburg Festival in 1973, the Vienna Festival in 1981 and

1984, the Edinburgh Festival in 1981, and at the 80th birthday concert of Sir William Walton in London in 1982.

Chin Kieu has made exceptional recordings of the concertos of the British composers Sir William Walton and Sir Edward Elgar. She married Geoffrey Leggett in 1984 and has two sons. Both her sister and brother are distinguished musicians.

Chisholm, Caroline (1808–1877)
British-born Australian social worker

Caroline Chisholm played an important pioneering role in social reform in Australia in the mid 19th century.

She was born Caroline Jones near Northampton, the daughter of a wealthy farmer. Raised as an evangelical Christian, she made it a condition of her marriage to Captain Archibald Chisholm in 1830 that she should be able to continue her charity work. Two years later they moved to Madras, India, where Chisholm was an officer in the army of the East India Company. While in India Caroline converted to Roman Catholicism, the religion of her husband. Concerned by the conditions of the families of soldiers in the Madras barracks, she set up the Female School of Industry for the Daughters of European Soldiers.

In 1838 the Chisholms moved to Australia and settled in Windsor, New South Wales. Captain Chisholm returned to duty in India in 1840, but Caroline remained in Australia, where she decided to help the poor immigrant women who were arriving in Sydney. She took some into her own home and pressurized the governor of New South Wales to supply a building for her Female Immigrants' Home. Having provided them with temporary shelter, she set about finding them jobs. Her labour registry set up for this purpose made no charge to its clients; it was so successful that she extended it to all unemployed people (she found jobs for 1,400 women and 600 men in the first year of her agency). Altogether Mrs. Chisholm cared for a total of 11,000 women and children in the 1840s, and by arranging for them to move out into country areas, she helped to lessen the problem of overcrowding in Sydney.

Having completed his tour of duty in India, Captain Chisholm joined Caroline in Australia in 1845. The following year they returned to Britain to lead a successful campaign to convince the British government of the need to correct the imbalance of the sexes in Australia. It was agreed that the families of British convicts who had been transported to Australia and served their sentences should be loaned the money to travel to Australia, which they could pay back later. The Chisholms set up the Family Colonization Loan Society in 1852, which proved to be a great success following the discovery of gold in Australia. By now Caroline was becoming widely known for her work: Charles Dickens wrote of her in *Household Works* (1851–52). Such was her fame that when she and her husband returned to Australia in 1854 with little money, public and private funds were raised to set them up in business.

Caroline continued her social work, campaigning for land reform, giving public lectures, and running a girls' school. She and her husband returned to Britain in 1866 and lived in considerable poverty for the rest of their lives in Liverpool and London, supported only by a small civil pension. In her later years Caroline became a supporter of the women's suffrage movement.

Chopin, Kate (1850–1904) *American short-story writer and novelist*

Kate Chopin was born Katherine O'Flaherty in St. Louis, Missouri, the youngest child of a wealthy Irish immigrant and his French-Creole wife. Her father was killed in a train accident when she was only four years old, leaving her to be brought up by her mother, grandmother, and great-grandmother. The latter was especially influential, since she believed that Kate and her brothers and sisters should become strong and self-sufficient. Kate received a good education at the Academy of the Sacred Heart in St. Louis; she learned to speak French and German, read widely in European literature, and became an accomplished pianist.

In 1870 Kate married Oscar Chopin and moved to New Orleans, where her husband was a cotton merchant. There they led a gracious life, spending their summers in the fashionable Louisiana Gulf coast resort of Grand Isle. The Chopins had six children before Oscar's business failed in 1880; after this they ran a general store among the Cajun community in Nachitoches Parish, central Louisiana. When Oscar died two years later, Kate and her children returned to live with her mother in St. Louis. After her mother's death in 1885 Kate started writing to support her family.

Drawing on her experiences of Creole and Cajun societies, she wrote sophisticated and realistic short stories, such as the collections *Bayou Folk* (1894) and *A Night in Acadie* (1897); she also wrote novels, including *At Fault* (1890) and *The Awakening* (1899), which were set in Louisiana. *The Awakening*, about the sexual awakening of a young wife and her subsequent suicide, gave rise to considerable criticism, after which Kate wrote little. She died in St. Louis.

Christie, Dame Agatha (1890–1976)
British writer

> She is a comely, ample woman with no outward traces of brilliance.
>
> —Sir Henry Channon, Diary, February 14, 1944

Agatha Christie was one of the most celebrated writers of detective stories, many of which have been made into films, TV series, and plays.

The daughter of a wealthy American expatriate, Frederick Miller, she was born in Torquay, Devon, and educated privately before going to Paris to study the piano and singing. In 1914 Agatha married Archibald (Archie) Christie, a pilot in the British Royal Flying Corps; during World War I she served as a nurse in the Red Cross hospital in Torquay. With her husband, now a colonel, Agatha had a daughter, Rosalind, but Christie's heavy drinking and many affairs destroyed their marriage. In 1926 Mrs. Christie had a much publicized breakdown during which she disappeared – to be found in a health resort apparently suffering from amnesia. The Christies divorced two years later.

Agatha Christie began writing after World War I. Her first detective novel, *The Mysterious Affair at Styles* (1920), introduced the eccentric Belgian detective Hercule Poirot; it was a great success. She achieved fame in 1926, the year of her disappearance, with *The Murder of Roger Ackroyd*. *Murder at the Vicarage* (1930) featured the detective Miss Jane Marple, a seemingly innocuous but extremely shrewd old lady living quietly in an English village. The same year Agatha married the archaeologist Sir Max Mallowan, often traveling with him on his excavations in Iraq, Syria, and Egypt. During World War II she worked in a hospital in London.

Agatha Christie wrote about 60 detective novels, 19 collections of short mystery stories, and 14 "whodunnit" plays. Translated into many languages, they have been made into films and produced on stage. Her play *The Mousetrap* opened in London in 1952 and enjoyed the longest continuous run of any play in the London theatre (still running in 1998). Her plots follow the classic formula for detective novels, her settings are evocative of a past age, and she maintains the suspense to the very last moment, when the villains are revealed through the superior detecting skills of her principal characters. She also wrote poetry, nonfiction, and (under the name Mary Westmacott) romantic novels. She was made a DBE in 1971.

Christie, Julie (1940–) *British actress*

A classic English beauty, Julie Christie made her name as a film actress in the mid 1960s and went on to star in both British and US films throughout the 1970s. In more recent years she has turned her attention to political and social issues.

Julie Frances Christie was born in Assam, India, the daughter of a British tea planter, and educated in Europe. She trained for the stage at the Central School of Speech and Drama in London, making her debut at an Essex repertory theatre in 1957. In 1961 she made her first appearance on British television in the serial *A For Andromeda*, which led to a small part in the film *Crooks Anonymous* (1962). Her first major role on the big screen came with John Schlesinger's *Billy Liar* (1963), in which she played Billy's understanding girlfriend.

Two very different films of 1965 established Christie as a star. One was Schlesinger's *Darling*, in which her performance as an amoral young woman earned her Oscar and British Film Academy awards as Best Actress; the other was the David Lean epic *Doctor Zhivago*, based on the novel by Pasternak, in which she costarred with Omar Sharif. Christie went on to play leading roles in two more screen adaptations of literary classics, *Far from the Madding Crowd* (1967) and *The Go-Between* (1971), before appearing with her lover Warren Beatty in the Hollywood films *McCabe and Mrs Miller* (1971), *Shampoo* (1975), and *Heaven Can Wait* (1978).

In the 1980s Christie became involved in various political and social campaigns, narrating the anti-factory-farming film *The Animals' Film* (1981) and presenting a documentary on Cambodia for Oxfam (1988). She continued to act on the big screen, notably in the Merchant-Ivory production *Heat and Dust* (1982), in which she played an Englishwoman retracing the footsteps of her great aunt in India, and *Fools of Fortune* (1990). In 1995 she returned to the West End stage in a revival of Pinter's *Old Times*, and the following year she was seen in both the fantasy adventure *Dragonheart* and Kenneth Branagh's *Hamlet*, in which she played Gertrude. Her performance in the drama *Afterglow* (1997) was hailed as a major comeback, earning her an Academy Award nomination as Best Actress.

Christina (1626–1689) *Queen of Sweden*

Queen Christina is remembered as a great patron of the arts.

She was born in Stockholm, the daughter of King Gustav II Adolph and Maria Eleanora of Brandenburg. Following her father's death in 1632, and owing to her mother's inability to rule, she was nominated to succeed him. Since she was only six years of age at the time, Sweden was governed in her name by the wise chancellor Count Axel Oxenstierna. Christina was educated in statecraft and languages so that in 1644, when she was 18 years old, she was ready to be proclaimed queen.

In keeping with her character Christina pursued independent policies both at home and abroad. In particular she helped to bring about an end to the Thirty Years' War, which had devastated much of central Europe and in which Sweden had been involved.

After the war many Swedish aristocrats, who did not have to pay taxes, became sufficiently wealthy to build themselves large palaces. This was resented by the clergy, merchants, traders, and farmers, who all had to pay heavy taxes. They therefore appealed to Christina to reform the tax system and take back some of the land she had given to her favourite aristocrats on her accession. Apparently sympathetic to this request, she used the threat of reform to persuade the aristocracy to accept her cousin Charles Gustav as her successor to the throne. She did not, however, actually carry out the reforms.

Although Christina had faithfully executed her duties as queen and had enjoyed her authority, she was bored by the day-to-day business of governing. Philosophy and science were more to her taste, which prompted her to attract to her court some of the great thinkers of the time, including Grotius and Descartes. During her reign the first Swedish newspaper was established, and she encouraged the pursuit of science and literature. She had no desire to marry and produce an heir, preferring – under the influence of Descartes and the Jesuits – to become a Roman Catholic. This meant that she could no longer be the queen of Sweden – a strictly Lutheran country. She therefore abdicated in 1654, converted to Roman Catholicism, and moved to Rome, where she lived under the protection of the pope. In Rome she continued to act as a patron of the arts and established a library and an art gallery. She died in Rome, where she was buried in St. Peter's Basilica.

Christine de Pisan (c. 1364–c. 1431) *Italian-born French writer*

> If it were customary to send little girls to school and to teach them the same subjects as are taught to boys, they would learn just as fully and would understand the subtleties of all arts and sciences. Indeed, maybe they would understand them better...for just as women's bodies are softer than men's, so their understanding is sharper.
> —*Le Livre de la cité des dames* (1405)

Christine de Pisan was one of the earliest professional woman writers.

She was born in Venice, the daughter of an Italian doctor and astrologer who worked in France at the court of King Charles V. Christine grew up at court; in 1378 she married the French knight Etienne du Castel, who became a court secretary. They had three children together before his death in 1390.

Christine then took the unusual step for a woman of turning to writing to support her children, producing a number of impressive works of poetry and prose. These include *Le Livre des faites et bonnes moeurs du Sage Roy Charles* (1405; The Deeds and Good Morals of Wise King Charles), a biography of Charles V. She is best known for starting a debate in the 15th century over the role of women in society; by rejecting the idea of inequality and listing female virtues, she introduced the novel concept of feminism. Indeed, some of her books have been so highly regarded in this context that they have been republished in English in this century; *Livres des trois vertus* (1402; published in English as *The Book of the Three Virtues*, 1985) and *Le Livre de la cité des dames* (1405; published in English as *The Book of the City of Ladies*, 1985) fall into this category. *La Vision* (1405), published in English as *Christine's Vision* (1993), is autobiographical.

Christine spent her final years in a nunnery. Her last work was a poem celebrating JOAN OF ARC and her early victories over the English.

Churchill, Caryl (1938–) *British dramatist*

Churchill's witty and inventive plays are informed by her radical feminist politics but generally avoid overt didacticism. Although a number of her plays were created for touring fringe groups, notably the Joint Stock Company, she has also enjoyed commercial success at the Royal Court Theatre, London, and in New York.

Born in London, Caryl Churchill emigrated to Canada with her family in the late 1940s and went to school in Montreal. At the age of 18 she returned to Britain to study at Lady Margaret Hall, Oxford, where her first two stage plays were produced. In the 1960s she wrote a number of plays for radio, including *The Ants* (1962), *Lovesick* (1966) and *Identical Twins* (1968). Her association with the Royal Court Theatre began in the early 1970s with *Owners* (1972), a satire on capitalism. This was followed by such plays as *Light Shining in Buckinghamshire* (1976), a partly improvised Joint Stock production set in the 17th century; *Cloud Nine* (1979), a sex comedy that also explores issues of imperialism; *Fen* (1983), which examines issues of land ownership in a small farming community; and *Serious Money* (1987), an award-winning satirical view of the London Stock Exchange after the "Big Bang" of 1986. Ironically, this play became a huge success owing largely to its popularity with the City audiences it sought to satirize. *Top Girls* (1982) featured a cast of female historical characters, while *Softcops* (1984) redressed the balance with an all-male cast.

Churchill has also written for television, notably *Turkish Delight* (1973), *The Legion Hall Bombing* (1978), and *Crimes* (1981). Her plays of the 1990s include *Mad Forest* (1990), set in Romania, *Lives of the Great Poisoners* (1991), and *The Skriker* (1994), a supernatural tale that incorporated mime, dance, and the music of composer Judith WEIR. She is married to the left-wing barrister David Harter and has three sons.

Çiller, Tansu (1946–   ) *Turkish politician and economist*

In 1993 Tansu Çiller became the first woman prime minister of Turkey.

She was born in Istanbul, the daughter of Muazzer Çiller. After studying and teaching economics at universities in the United States, she returned to Turkey to become professor of economics at Bosporus University, in 1983. Her publications include *Import Substitution and Protectionism in Turkish Industry* (1974) and *The Cost Increasing Effects of State Economic Enterprises in Economy* (1988). She married in 1963, persuading her husband to adopt her surname.

A member of the conservative True Path Party from 1990, she became the minister of state for economics after her party came to power in 1991. In 1993 she was elected leader of the party and became the premier of Turkey, the first woman to rule its 65 million Muslims. She was immediately faced with an upsurge in violence from the Kurdish separatist movement in southeast Turkey. Her response was to order a military clampdown on this area and the withdrawal of plans for greater autonomy for the Kurds. Turkey was heavily criticized by the international community for these abuses of human rights. Çiller had also to deal with a serious financial situation resulting in the collapse of the Turkish currency and stockmarket and a sharp rise in inflation. Her proposed economic reforms, especially privatization, were strongly opposed by some elements within her coalition. However, she managed to hold her government together and sold off more than 100 state enterprises. She also secured the approval of the Turkish legislature for several democratization measures in order to persuade the European Parliament to ratify an agreement for a customs union between Turkey and the European Union.

Tansu Çiller resigned as premier in December 1995, after an election in which the religious Islamic Welfare Party won the most votes but did not have enough seats to form a government. Consequently a new coalition government was formed between the Motherland Party, whose leader became prime minister, and Çiller's True Path Party. However, after the Motherland Party approved a parliamentary inquiry into corruption charges against Çiller, relating to privatization bids, the coalition broke up.

In a surprise move in June 1996 Çiller entered into a coalition with the Welfare Party, which she had previously denounced as a threat to Turkey's secular form of government and its ties with the West. Analysts suspect that she did this to thwart the investigation of corruption charges against her; indeed, she was cleared of these in November 1996. As deputy premier and foreign minister in the new coalition she defended Turkish rights in the Aegean and Cyprus against the Greeks. Çiller lost office in June 1997, when the coalition collapsed in disarray.

Cixous, Hélène (1937–   ) *French feminist, literary theorist, and writer.*

A prolific and versatile author, Hélène Cixous emerged as one of the leading exponents of feminist post-structuralism in the later 1970s. Her work explores the complex relationships between language, psychology, and the physical life of the body.

Cixous was born in Oran, Algeria, the daughter of a French doctor and a German midwife. As a Jew of mixed nationality brought up in a colonial society, she became conscious of issues of race, imperialism, and personal identity from an early age. After graduating from an Algerian lycée in 1955, Cixous moved to France and married; for the next decade she taught at provincial lycées while also pursuing her studies in English literature.

A turning point in Cixous's life came in 1964–65, when she left her husband and took their two children to Paris, where she became an assistant lecturer at the Sorbonne. After a year at the University of Nanterre, where she participated in the student uprising of May 1968, she was appointed professor of literature at the University of Vincennes, Paris, a position she still holds. During her first year at Vincennes, Cixous founded the critical review *Poétique* and made her name with the psychological novel *Dedans*, which won the Prix Médicis in 1969.

At this time Cixous established several pioneering courses in which Marxist, feminist, and psychoanalytical approaches to literature were explored. In 1974 she founded the Paris Centre for Research in Women's Studies, one of the first institutions of its kind. Her reputation as an original feminist thinker was secured by *Le Jeune Née* (*The Newly Born Woman*: 1975), a book written in collaboration with the psychoanalyst Catherine Clément. In this densely written work, Cixous gave a radical feminist twist to ideas about sexuality, language, and consciousness adapted from the psychoanalytical theory of Jacques Lacan. She also began to outline the theory of *écriture féminine* ("feminine writing") for which she is now best known. Cixous claims to identify a distinctively female type of creativity – sexual, anarchic, and spontaneous – that overflows the rigid categories of "masculine" logic and morality. These ideas were developed in two volumes of essays that made a wide impact when translated into English – *Le Rire de la Méduse* (*The Laugh of the Medusa*: 1976) and *Le Sexe ou la tête?* (*Castration or Decapitation?*: 1976).

Cixous's theoretical writings are notable for their use of literary techniques more often associated with fiction or poetry. Her own works of fiction include the novels *Angst* (1977) and *Vive l'Orange* (1979). Cixous has also enjoyed success in the theatre, her best-known play being *Portrait de Dora* (1976), which re-examines Freud's famous case history of a female "hysteric" from a feminist viewpoint. Several of her plays have been produced by Ariane MNOUCHKINE's Théâtre du Soleil, notably her *Histoire...de Norodom Sihanouk* (1985), an epic work about modern Cambodia. Cixous continues to write and teach, keeping up a steady stream of essays, books, articles, and lectures.

Claflin, Tennessee (1846–1923)
American feminist

Claflin, Victoria Woodhull (1838–1927) *American feminist, adventurer, and socialist*

Victoria and Tennessee Claflin were two of the most colourful and persuasive figures in the women's movement in the United States and Britain in the late 19th century.

They were born in Homer, Ohio, the daughters of Buck and Roxanna Claflin. Forced to leave Homer after Buck was suspected of setting fire to his place of work, the family became a travelling medicine and fortune-telling show, moving from place to place in Ohio. Encouraged by their mother, an ardent spiritualist, Victoria and Tennessee became clairvoyants, holding seances for money. After Victoria's brief marriage at the age of 15 to the alcoholic Dr. Canning Woodhull, by whom she had a son and a daughter, she rejoined the family show, which by then was touring the Midwest. In 1866 she married Colonel James Blood, with whom she and her sister moved to New York City, where Tennessee married John Bartels. There the sisters persuaded the millionaire Cornelius Vanderbilt that they could contact his recently deceased wife; in return he set them up as stockbrokers – the first professional women on Wall Street.

Although the sisters were now successful Wall Street brokers, Victoria also became involved with Pantarchy, a somewhat zany socialist movement that advocated communal love, with children and property shared. This led Victoria and Tennessee to set up *Woodhull and Claflin's Weekly* in 1870, which campaigned for equal rights for women, legalized prostitution, and a single standard of morality. In 1871 Victoria made the startling claim before the judiciary committee of the House of Representatives that women already had the right to vote in the United States. The next year, failing to be elected the leader of the National Woman Suffrage Association, she formed the Equal Rights Party, which nominated her for the U.S. presidency. That same year she and her sister published in their journal the first English translation of Karl Marx's *Communist Manifesto*. They also accused the well-known preacher Henry Ward Beecher of having an affair with the wife of their suffragist friend Theodore Tilton. Arrested on a charge of issuing an obscene publication, the sisters were imprisoned but subsequently acquitted and released.

Victoria divorced Colonel Blood in 1876 and the following year left for Britain, where in 1881 she married the landowner John Biddulph Martin. In England she became a society hostess and was actively involved with the British suffragist movement. She also became interested in eugenics, publishing the journal *The Humanitarian* from 1892 to 1910. Her other publications include *Stirpiculture, or the Scientific Propagation of the Human Race* (1888) and *Humanitarian Money* (1892). Her third husband died in 1897, and she settled on her country estate near Tewkesbury, Gloucestershire, where she died.

Tennessee, who had divorced John Bartels by then, accompanied Victoria to England. She also did well there, marrying a wealthy art collector, Francis Cook. When he was made a baronet in 1886, Tennessee, now Lady Cook, also became a society hostess and an outspoken advocate of women's rights. She was the author of *Constitutional Equality, A Right of Women* (1871).

Clairon, Mademoiselle (1723–1803) *French actress*

Mademoiselle Clairon was the leading French tragic actress of her day; she is particularly remembered for the natural style of acting that she introduced.

Born Claire Josèphe Hippolyte de La Tude in Condé-sur-l'Escaut, France, she was the illegitimate daughter of a poor seamstress. At the age of 12 she joined the Comédie Italienne. Her powerful singing voice enabled her to join the Paris Opéra in 1734, but she later transferred to the Comédie-Française, where she made her successful debut in Racine's *Phèdre*. Using the stage name Mademoiselle

Clairon, she went on to play many tragic roles, becoming the leading tragic actress of her day. Responsible for introducing historical costume to plays to give them greater authenticity, she also abandoned the characteristically formal declamatory style of acting, introducing a freer, more natural manner of speech.

Mlle. Clairon left the Comédie-Française in 1765 after she and others refused to perform with an actor they believed would bring the company into disrepute. She then abandoned the professional theatre and went to live with Voltaire, acting in his private theatre at Ferney and at the royal court. In 1773 she accepted an invitation to live at the court of the margrave of Ansbach in Germany, where she wrote *Mémoires et réflexions sur l'art dramatique* (1799).

After the margrave's death Mlle. Clairon returned to Paris, living off the proceeds of her book. As a result of the French Revolution she lost her state pension and died in poverty.

See also DUMESNIL, MARIE-FRANÇOIS.

Clare, Saint (1194–1253) *Italian nun*

St. Clare established the religious order known as the Poor Clares.

She was born in Assisi, the daughter of Count Favorino Scifi. Having turned down two offers of marriage, at the age of 18 she became a follower of St. Francis of Assisi, being much impressed by his spirituality. With her sister St. AGNES she obtained St. Francis's support for the establishment of a second order of Franciscans, known as the Poor Ladies of San Damiano (the Poor Clares). Her mother, the Blessed Ortolano, and her sister Beatrice later joined them.

Dedicated to the Franciscan ideal of poverty and contemplative prayer, the Poor Clares order was unique among the women's religious orders of that time for the austerity of its way of life. As abbess of the order's first convent at San Damiano from 1215, Clare devoted the later part of her life, when she was confined to her bed by illness, to seeking papal approval for her "Primitive Rule" for the running of the order. This Rule, based on the Franciscan rule of 1223, received the pope's approval just two days before she died.

Renowned in her lifetime for wisdom and spirituality, Clare acted as an adviser to many church leaders. She was canonized in 1255; her feast day is August 12. Her bones were transferred to the church of St. Clare in Assisi after it was built in 1260. In 1958 she was designated by Pope Pius XII to be the patron saint of television. This was due to her claim to have seen and heard a service in the church of St. Francis in Assisi from her convent cell at San Damiano.

Clarke, Martha (1944–) *American dancer and choreographer*

Martha Clarke was born in Baltimore, Maryland. Her dance studies began when she was a child, and she went on to train with Anna Sokolow, Charles Weidman, Alvin Ailey, and José Limón at the American Dance Festival in Connecticut; she later studied under Louis Horst at the Juilliard School of Music in New York City. She danced in *Suite for a Summer Day* (1962) for Horst's concert group and in *Session for Six*, *Lyric Suite*, *Time + 7*, and *Dreams* for Sokolow's company.

Martha Clarke then took a break from performing to visit Europe. On her return she moved to Hanover, New Hampshire, and in 1973 became one of the first female members of Pilobolus, a semicollective dance-theatre acrobatic troupe. In addition to her dramatic solos, she created duets with the dancer Robert Morgan Barnett and performed in many of the troupe's larger productions, including *Two Bits* (1973, co-choreographed with Alison Chase), *Aubade* (1973, with Barnett), *Terra Cotta* (1974, with Barnett), and *Monkshood* (1974), *Ciona* (1975), *Untitled* (1975), *Vagabond* (1975), *Grey Room* (1977), *Wakefield* (1977), *Nachturn* (1979), and *Fallen Angel* (1979), all choreographed by Pilobolus.

In 1979, after Pilobolus had become world-famous, Clarke and Barnett formed the Crowsnest company with the French choreographer Felix Blaska. This company's productions include *La Marquese de Solana* (1979), *Haiku* (1979), *The Garden of Villandry* (1980), *The Garden of Earthly Delights* (1984), *Vienna: Lusthaus* (1986), *The Hunger Artist* (1987), and *Miracolo d'Amore* (1988). Clarke has continued to create solos for Crowsnest and to choreograph dances with her colleagues Barnett and Blaska.

Clarke, Shirley (1925–1997) *American film-maker*

Shirley Clarke was one of the leading film-makers in New York in the 1950s and the 1960s; her films provide some of the best examples of American independent movie-making.

Born Shirley Brimberg in New York she studied at Stephens College, Johns Hopkins University, Bennington College, and the University of North Carolina. Her first career – as a dancer – began in the late 1940s within the avant-garde dance community centred on New York's Young Men's–Young Women's Hebrew Association's performance stage and Hanya HOLM's choreography classes. At the same time she was also studying film-making at the City College of New York; her first dance film, based on Daniel Nagrin's *Dance in the Sun*, appeared in 1954. The same year she made the non-dance film *Paris Parks* before continuing with her exploration of the possibilities for filming formal dance choreography in *Bullfight* (1955) and *A Moment in Love* (1957).

Clarke was one of a circle of avant-garde film-makers based in Greenwich Village and became heavily involved with the promotion and distribution of independent films in the 1950s and 1960s. She made one of the best and most widely viewed examples of abstract expressionist cinema in *Bridges-Go-Round* (1959), which was followed by three documentary films in the cinéma vérité style – *The Connection* (1962), *The Cool World* (1963), and *Portrait of Jason* (1967). These movies formed the basis of the New York independent feature film movement. Clarke's films had a moderate commercial success in the United States but were greeted with great critical acclaim in Europe, where she won many prizes for her work.

In the 1960s Clarke lectured on independent film at colleges and museums in the United States and Europe. After 1969 she turned to video as a new medium, a subject on which she gave a series of workshops. In 1975 she was appointed professor of film at the University of California, Los Angeles; her subsequent video works include *24 Frames per Second* (1977), *Mysterum* (1979), *Tongues* (1983), and *Ornette, Made in America* (1986).

Cleopatra (69–30 BC) *Egyptian queen*

> You know how much I was with your [adoptive] father [i.e. Julius Caesar], and you are aware that it was he who placed the crown of Egypt upon my head.
>
> —Plea to Octavian, 30 BC

Cleopatra is remembered as the beautiful and ruthless queen of Egypt who, by seducing both Julius Caesar and Mark Antony, nearly succeeded in her aim of ruling the ancient world.

She was born in Alexandria, and became the last of the Ptolemaic dynasty from Greece to rule Egypt. This dynasty lasted from 323 BC until the Romans took over in 31 BC. On the death of her father in 51 BC Cleopatra married, and shared the throne of Egypt with, her brother Ptolemy XIII Philopater. However, she then engaged in a struggle with her brother for control of Egypt, which she only won after obtaining the support of Julius Caesar, who was in Egypt to settle the succession and secure Egypt's wealth for the Roman Empire. He defeated and killed Ptolemy at the battle of Alexandria in 47 BC, and Cleopatra became the effective ruler of Egypt.

In accordance with tradition, Cleopatra then married her youngest brother, Ptolemy XIV, who became cosovereign with her. However, she consolidated her position with Caesar in 46 BC by bearing him a son, named Caesarion (later Ptolemy XV). Following Caesar to Rome, she was received there with all honours, although he outraged Roman society by dedicating a golden statue to her in the temple of Venus Genetrix. Cleopatra lived on

Caesar's property near the River Tiber for a year before his murder in 44 BC, after which she returned to Egypt. Back in Alexandria she had her brother murdered and placed her son Ptolemy XV with her on the throne.

After the battle of Philippi in 42 BC Mark Antony (who ruled the Roman empire with Octavian and Lepidus) called Cleopatra and other Eastern rulers to Tarsus in Cilicia (now in Turkey) to pay him homage before his attack on Persia. Cleopatra, hoping for another opportunity to increase her power, went to Tarsus expressly to seduce Mark Antony. Their love affair has been dramatized in Shakespeare's play *Antony and Cleopatra*. Unable to resist her, Mark Antony granted her every request. These included the dropping of a conspiracy charge against her and the murder of her younger sister Arsinoë. Mark Antony then spent the winter of 41–40 BC with his new mistress in Alexandria, where she bore him two children, the twins Alexander Helios and Cleopatra Selene.

Mark Antony then left Alexandria for Rome; here, following the death of his first wife Fulvia, he married Octavian's sister, OCTAVIA MINOR. This marriage did not last long, however, and in 37 BC Mark Antony married Cleopatra at Antioch, recognized their children, and granted her considerable territories that he had conquered in the East. Another son, Ptolemy Philadelphus, was born in 36 BC. Now securely established as Mark Antony's partner, Cleopatra financed his disastrous campaign against the Parthians, outraging Rome by staging a lavish triumph in Alexandria, which declared her, Mark Antony, and her children to be the rulers of the Egyptian and Roman empires.

Octavian, who was enraged by Mark Antony's treatment of his sister, declared war on Cleopatra in 32 BC, defeating her and Mark Antony at the battle of Actium the next year. She and Mark Antony fled to Egypt, where they were pursued by Octavian; attempts to negotiate with Octavian failed. Mark Antony, now a broken man, committed suicide after he had been wrongly informed, at Cleopatra's instigation, that she had taken her own life. After Cleopatra tried and failed once more in negotiations with Octavian to protect her rights and those of her children, she too committed suicide. She is said to have done so by allowing herself to be bitten by a poisonous snake. Her son Ptolemy XV was put to death by Octavian, and Egypt became a province of the Roman empire.

Cleopatra has fascinated writers and scholars for two thousand years. Reviled in ancient times because she was regarded as a threat to Rome, she has been admired in modern times as a determined queen, who used both her intelligence and her beauty in pursuit of her political ambitions.

Cline, Patsy (1932–1963) *American singer*

Patsy Cline has been called the "Queen of Country Music." Although her career was tragically cut short when she was killed in a plane crash near Camden, Tennessee, she continues to be a great influence on country music, her records outselling those of many contemporary artists.

She was born Virginia Patterson Hensley in Gore, near Winchester, Virginia. She taught herself to tap dance at the age of four and learned to play the piano by ear by the age of eight. Still a child, she began her career as a singer in churches and at benefits. After listening to radio broadcasts from the Grand Ole Opry in Nashville, Tennessee, she became a fan of country music. She moved to Winchester with her family, but after her parents split up, she had to leave school to work in a drug store. Singing whenever she could with bands playing in Winchester, she was persuaded by the famous Opry artist Wally Fowler to go to Nashville in 1948 to audition for the Grand Ole Opry. Although the audition was a success, she had to leave Nashville because she had little money, before her appearance at the Grand Ole Opry could be arranged.

Cline had no choice but to return to the drug store in Winchester, but she continued to sing locally. However, her style, a mixture of pure country and pop, was too good to be limited to local entertainments. In 1952 she met Bill Peer, who quickly recognized her potential and set about developing her career. Billing her as Patsy Hensley (Patsy Cline after she married Gerald Cline in 1953), he secured a recording contract for her with Four-Star Records. She recorded a number of songs with them, including "Walking after Midnight." This song became a hit after she sang it on Arthur Godfrey's *Talent Scouts* television show and at the Grand Ole Opry in early 1957. She recorded a couple of follow-up songs but temporarily retired from country music after she divorced her first husband; in September 1957 she married Charlie Dick, with whom she had two children.

Cline returned to music in 1960 when, after moving to Nashville, she became a member of the Grand Ole Opry and started recording songs under a new contract with Decca Records. She had a string of hits in the next three years, including "I Fall to Pieces," "Sweet Dreams," "Crazy," "She's Got You," "Faded Love," "Leavin' on Your Mind," "South of the Border," and "You Made Me Love You." These are regarded as some of the greatest country-music songs ever recorded.

Clinton, Hillary Rodham (1947–) *American lawyer*

The wife of U.S. President Bill Clinton, Hillary Clinton is a distinguished lawyer and journalist in her own right.

Hillary Rodham was born in Chicago, Illinois, the daughter of Hugh and Dorothy Rodham. She was educated at Wellesley College, Massachusetts, and Yale University, after which she joined the Rose Law Firm, of which she is now senior partner. She was appointed lecturer in law at Arkansas University, Little Rock, in 1979. From 1987 to 1991 she was chair of the Committee on Women in the Profession for the American Bar Association.

Hillary married Bill Clinton in 1975, becoming First Lady when he became president of the United States in 1993. Determined to take an active rather than a merely decorative role, she was appointed head of the president's Task Force on National Health Reform in 1993 but failed to steer any of its proposals into law. As First Lady, she has often provoked extreme reactions, being generally admired by feminists and career women but much disliked by right-wing conservatives. Her role in the "Whitewater affair," an alleged scandal concerning the financial and legal affairs of the Clintons during the 1980s, came under fierce scrutiny in the mid 1990s but no evidence of misconduct has emerged. In early 1998 she powerfully defended her husband in the media when allegations that he had had a sexual relationship with a young White House trainee threatened to destroy his presidency.

Mrs. Clinton has won many awards and distinctions for her work as a lawyer, including being voted One of the Most Influential Lawyers in America by the *National Law Journal* and winning the Outstanding Lawyer-Citizen Award of the Arkansas Bar Association.

Clive, Kitty (1711–1785) *British actress*

Kitty Clive was well known for the comic roles she played at the Drury Lane Theatre in London.

She was probably born in London, the daughter of William Raftor, an Irish lawyer. In 1728 she made her first appearance at the Drury Lane Theatre, then run by Colley Cibber, playing small parts. Her natural talent for comic roles and her strong singing voice made her sufficiently popular to be given leading roles. She appeared as Phillida in Cibber's ballad opera *Damon and Phillida* in 1729, but her first major success came as Nell in Charles Coffey's farce opera *The Devil to Pay* (1731). She went on to play most of the great British comic roles of her time.

Noted for her sharp wit and unstable temperament, Clive had many disputes with her fellow actors and managers. However, she remained closely involved with David Garrick's company from 1747 until her retirement in 1769. She was particularly good in farce, playing vulgar middle-class housewives and tomboys; she even wrote four farces and a burlesque herself. Like most comedians, she always wanted to play tragedy, though it is doubtful whether she would have been suited to it. Much to her annoyance, she was prevented from doing so by Garrick.

Her first marriage, to the lawyer George Clive in 1733, lasted only two years, but they remained friends after separating. After the failure of her marriage, she remained single, although she was greatly admired by the composer Handel and the writers Oliver Goldsmith, Dr. Samuel Johnson, and Horace Walpole. The latter gave her a cottage on his estate at Strawberry Hill, Twickenham, near London, after ill health forced her into retirement in 1769. For the last 15 years of her life she held a fashionable salon there, known as the "Clive-Den."

Close, Glenn (1947–) *American actress*

Glenn Close has established a reputation for being able to play a wide range of roles in the theatre and in films.

She was born in Greenwich, Connecticut, the daughter of William and Bettine Close. When she was seven years old, her mother and father, who was a surgeon, joined the Moral Rearmament movement. The family then moved to Zaïre in Africa (now the Democratic Republic of Congo), but Glenn was sent to a boarding school in Switzerland. Having wanted to act since childhood, she joined the Fingernails repertory group after returning to the United States. She also sang with various touring folk bands, including Up the People; in 1969 she married the guitarist Cabot Wade, but they divorced three years later.

By this time Glenn was studying anthropology and acting at William and Mary College, Virginia. She graduated in 1974, the year she made her debut on Broadway in *Love for Love*. She appeared in a number of other plays in New York City before achieving a considerable success in the musical *Barnum* (1980). She received an Obie Award from the Village Voice for *The Singular Life of Albert Nobbs* (1982) and Tony Awards for *The Real Thing* (1984–85) and *Sunset Boulevard* (1994–95).

Glenn Close made her debut on television with *Orphan Train* (1979) and was nominated for an Emmy Award and a Golden Globe Award for *Something about Amelia* (1984). She was also nominated for an Academy Award for her film debut in *The World According to Garp* (1982). She continued to play virtuous parts in such films as *The Big Chill* (1983) and *The Natural* (1984). In 1984 she married James Marias, a venture capitalist, but the marriage failed after three years. It was in 1987 that her screen image underwent a radical change with her portrayal of a vengeful murderous woman in *Fatal Attraction* (1987), for which she was nominated for Academy and Golden Globe Awards. She has built on this success with *Dangerous Liaisons* (1988), *Reversal of Fortune* (1990), *Hamlet* (1990), and *101 Dalmations* (1996).

Glenn Close continues to be in great demand both as a stage and a screen actress. She lives in upstate New York with her eight-year-old daughter Annie and Steve Beers, a carpenter who works on stage sets.

Clotilda, Saint (*c.* 475–545) *Wife of the Frankish King Clovis I*

Clotilda played an important role in the conversion of King Clovis to Christianity, an event regarded as a landmark in Christian history.

She was probably born in Lyon, France, the daughter of King Chilperic of Burgundy. In 492 she married Clovis I; although he was then a pagan, she was determined to convert him to Christianity. She persuaded him to allow their first two children to be baptized. On Christmas Day 496, following his victory over the Alemmani near Cologne, Clovis and 2,000 of his soldiers became Christians in order to secure the allegiance of the conquered Alemmani people to his kingdom.

After King Clovis died in 511, Clotilda's three sons became involved in a long and bloody power struggle for control of the Frankish kingdom. Saddened by the deaths of one of her sons and two of her adopted grandsons, Clotilda retired to Tours in France, having failed to bring about a peaceful agreement to the succession. In Tours she did good works, founded various religious institutions, and lived a pious life. She died in Tours, and her remains were eventually transferred to the Church of St. Leu in Paris in 1793. Her feast day is celebrated on June 3.

Clough, Anne Jemima (1820–1892) *British educationalist*

Anne Jemima Clough led a successful campaign to enable women to attend British universities.

She was born in Liverpool, the daughter of a cotton trader, and moved with her family to Charleston, South Carolina, in 1822. The family returned to Liverpool in 1836. When her father died ten years later, Anne became close to her brother, the poet Arthur Clough, who encouraged her desire to teach. After running a small school for poor children in Liverpool and gaining some teaching experience at various schools in London, she moved with her mother to Ambleside in the Lake District, where she set up a school for the children of friends.

Ill health and several deaths in the family forced Clough to give up the Ambleside school. After a short break her interest in education was revived by Barbara Bodichon, who wanted to found a college for the higher education of women. In 1866 Anne set up a branch of the Schoolmistresses' Association in Liverpool and helped to organize a series of lectures for townswomen in the north of England. In 1867 she became secretary of the North of England Council for Promoting the Higher Education of Women, which campaigned for women to be allowed to take university-level examinations.

In 1869 Cambridge University agreed to a higher local examination for women. Anne Clough was appointed to be head of Merton Hall, Cambridge, a residence for women attending the course of lectures that led to the examination. By 1875 a new residence, Newnham Hall, had been built; four years later it became Newnham College, with a full staff of lecturers. Anne Clough became the first principal of the college, a post in which she remained until her death.

After her appointment to Newnham College, Clough continued to be involved in the fight for equality of opportunity for women in higher education. The eventual opening up of all degree courses at Cambridge and other British universities to women was very much her achievement.

Cobbe, Frances Power (1822–1904)
Anglo-Irish essayist, travel writer, and social reformer

Frances Power Cobbe wrote widely on moral and religious questions, as well as campaigning actively for women's rights and the welfare of the disadvantaged.

She was born in Newbridge, near Dublin, the daughter of a wealthy Protestant landowner. Apart from two years at an exclusive girls' school in Brighton, which she despised, Frances was educated entirely at home. During her twenties she followed an ambitious course of private study that included Greek, geometry, and German philosophy. Although she would remain a strong theist, the strict evangelical creed of her parents was soon broadened by her scientific and philosophical interests. Her first book, *Essays on the Theory of Intuitive Morals*, was published anonymously in 1855.

A year later Frances's father died, leaving her with a comfortable private income for life. Now in her mid thirties, she embarked on a lengthy expedition to Italy, Greece, and the Holy Land. Italy remained her great love and she would return several times, writing numerous articles about its life and culture for the British press. Her travel writings were later collected in such volumes as *Italics* (1864) and *Cities of the Past* (1865). It was during her first visit to italy that she met and was influenced by the Unitarian

thinker Theodore Parker, whose radical theological writings she later edited for publication.

After returning to England in 1858, Frances Power Cobbe became increasingly involved in philanthropic work. At first she worked with Mary CARPENTER at her schools for pauper children in Bristol, but on discovering that this was not her forte she diversified into campaigns for workhouse reform and for better treatment of the insane and the terminally ill. From the 1860s onward she kept up a stream of cogent witty articles arguing for the admission of women to higher education and for married women's property rights: she also became one of the first prominent advocates for women's suffrage. Her views are summarized in her book *The Duties of Women* (1888), which argues for the full emancipation of women so that they can contribute fully to the great philanthropic and social movements of the age. She also continued to write on more abstract moral and religious questions, such as those raised by Darwinism and other scientific advances. Her later years were preoccupied with a passionate campaign against vivisection, which she abhorred. She published her autobiography in 1904, the year of her death.

Cochran, Jacqueline (1910–1980)
American aviator

During her career Jacqueline Cochrane set more speed, distance, and altitude records than any other aviator.

She was born in Pensacola, Florida. Orphaned at an early age, she was brought up by a poor family in Columbus, Georgia, leaving school when she was eight years old in order to work in a cotton mill. At the age of 14 she started work in a beauty salon; having learned the trade, she moved to New York to work in the cosmetics industry.

In 1932, at the suggestion of the flyer, banker, and industrialist Floyd Odlum (whom she married in 1936), Jacqueline Cochran took time off work to learn to fly. After quickly qualifying for her pilot's licence, in 1934 she sought to promote her new cosmetics business by attempting to set a new altitude record. Her failure to do so prompted her instead to concentrate on breaking speed records. In 1935 she became the first woman to fly in the Bendix Transcontinental Air Race, which she won in 1938 in a record time of 10 hours and 28 minutes. In the same year she set another record by crossing North America in 10 hours, 12 minutes, and 55 seconds. She was named as the world's outstanding woman pilot by the International League of Aviators in 1937, when she set a new 1,000-kilometre record, and again in 1938–39.

During World War II Cochran became a captain in the British Air Transport Auxiliary, being in charge of a group of women pilots who ferried planes from the aircraft factories to airfields in Britain and abroad. Following the entry of the United States into the war in 1941, Jacqueline Cochran trained women to fly transport planes in the United States in order to free men to fly combat aircraft. In 1943 she became the director of the Women's Airforce Service Pilots (WASPS) in the U.S. Air Force. From 1948 to 1970 she served in the Air Force Reserve, retiring with the rank of colonel.

In 1953 Cochran set new speed records over 15 kilometres (675.471 miles per hour), 100 kilometres (652.552 mph), and 500 kilometres (590.321 mph). The same year she became the first woman to fly faster than the speed of sound. She went on to become the first woman to land and take off from an aircraft carrier, and in 1961 she broke her own 100- and 500-kilometre records. Three years later she became the first and only woman to have flown at twice the speed of sound.

After 1970 Cochran concentrated on her cosmetics business, being twice named as businesswoman of the year. She was also active in politics, securing veterans' benefits for the WASPS in 1977. She wrote about her experiences in *Stars at Noon* (1954).

Colbert, Claudette (1903–1996)
French-born American actress

Specializing in sophisticated roles in light comedies, Claudette Colbert had a long and successful career in both the theatre and films.

Born Lily Claudette Chauchoin in Paris, she moved with her family to New York City in 1910. After attending Washington Irving High School, she studied briefly at the Art Students League. Her acting career started when she met the playwright Anne Morrison, who asked her to play a bit part in *The Wild Westcotts* (1923). She changed her name to Colbert and appeared on Broadway in *The Marionette Man* (1924), *A Kiss in a Taxi* (1925–26), and *The Barker* (1927). Her success in the latter play led to her film debut in *For the Love of Mike* (1927). This was followed by her first talkie, *A Hole in the Wall* (1928), which resulted in a long-term contract with Paramount Pictures.

Colbert's first big hit came as the vamp Poppaea in Cecil B. DeMille's *The Sign of the Cross* (1932). She went on to play the title role in his *Cleopatra* (1934) and might have become typecast as a seductress had she not appeared in Frank Capra's comedy *It Happened One Night* (1934). The intelligence, wit, and glamour she showed in that film won her an Academy Award for Best Actress.

Claudette Colbert is particularly remembered for the series of screwball comedies that she made in the 1930s and 1940s, including *Midnight* (1939) and *Palm Beach Story* (1942), in which she displayed an expert comic timing. However, she was a versatile actress, receiving Academy Award nominations for her more serious roles as the psychiatrist in *Private Worlds* (1935) and as the wartime wife in *Since You Went Away* (1944).

A shrewd businesswoman, Colbert left Paramount in 1945 and became a freelance actress, continuing to make movies until her retirement from films in 1960. However, her enduring popularity was evidenced in her successful return to the stage, playing in *The Marriage-Go-Round* (1958), *The Irregular Verb to Love* (1963), *The Kingfisher* (1978), and *Aren't We All* (1984–85). She also appeared on television in *Three Came Home* (1986) and *The Two Mrs. Grenvilles* (1987).

Colbert became an officer of the French Legion of Honour in 1988; the following year she received a Life Achievement Award at the Kennedy Center in Washington, D.C.

Colet, Louise (1810–1876) *French writer*

A prize-winning poet, Louise Colet was also noted for her passionate love affairs with several important French literary figures.

Born Louise Revoil in Aix-en-Provence, she moved to Paris in 1835 after she married Hippolyte Colet, a professor of music at the Conservatory there. The following year she published her first volume of poetry, *Les Fleurs du Midi* (1836). This was followed by *Poésies* (1844), *Chant des armes* (1846), *Ce qui est dans le coeur des femmes* (1852), and *Le Poème de la femme* (1856). Although contemporary opinion was divided over the merits of her poetry, she won the poetry prize of the Académie Française four times.

Beautiful and passionate, Madame Colet could be violent and vindictive in her behaviour towards others. After she separated from her husband, she had stormy love affairs with the writers Gustave Flaubert and Alfred de Musset. Later she wrote a scandalous account of her liaison with Flaubert in her novel *Lui* (1851). She went on to write more poetry as well as novels, plays, and other literary works. She died in Paris.

Colette (1873–1954) *French writer*

> Life as a child and then as a girl had taught her patience, hope, silence; and given her a prisoner's proficiency in handling these virtues as weapons.
>
> —*Chéri* (1920)

Colette is regarded as one of the great French writers of the earlier 20th century. Her novels are remarkable for their intense descriptions of nature, the pleasure and pain of love, and the mundane activities of daily life.

She was born Sidonie Gabrielle Claudine Colette in St.-Sauveur-en-Puisaye, Burgundy, the daughter of a tax collector. However, her one-legged father was a shadowy figure in her childhood; she was brought up and educated by her down-to-earth mother, "Sido." At the age of 20 she married the novelist and music critic Henry Gauthier-Villars and moved with him to Paris.

Discovering that she had a talent for writing, Gauthier-Villars encouraged Colette to produce her first four novels, which were published under his pen name, "Willy." Beginning with *Claudine à l'école* (1900; published in English as *Claudine at School*, 1930), the "Claudine" novels – a fictionalized, somewhat scandalous account of Colette's early life – were a great success.

Colette left Willy in 1904 and began writing her own stories. Drawing heavily on her rural upbringing, she based many of her strong female characters on her mother. This can be seen in many of her works, including *Dialogues des Bêtes* (1904; Animal Talks), *Sido* (1929), and *Le Fanal bleu* (1949; published in English as *The Blue Lantern*, 1963). After divorcing Willy in 1906, Colette became a vaudeville dancer and actress, describing this way of life in *La Vagabonde* (1911; published in English as *The Vagabond*, 1954).

In 1912, the year her mother died, Colette married the newspaper editor and diplomat Henry de Jouvenel, by whom she had a child. She turned their country house into a hospital for wounded soldiers during World War I, for which she was made a chevalier of the Legion of Honour in 1920. During this period she also wrote for the newspapers and ran a beauty salon. She continued to write novels, the best of which include *Chéri* (1920; published in English in 1929), *Le Blé en herbe* (1923; published in English as *The Ripening*, 1932), *La Fin de Chéri* (1926; published in English as *The Last of Chéri*, 1932), and *La Naissance du jour* (1928; published in English as *A Lesson in Love*, 1932).

In 1925 Colette left Henry de Jouvenel; after their divorce ten years later, she married her lover Maurice Goudekot. Although she suffered from arthritis in the last 20 years of her life,

Colette continued to write. Her later novels include *Gigi* (1945; published in English in 1952).

Colette became a member of the Royal Belgian Academy in 1935; nine years later she was the first woman to be admitted to the Goncourt Academy. She became a grand officer of the Legion of Honour in 1953, the year before her death. She received a state funeral, which was attended by thousands of mourners.

Collett, Camilla (1813–1895) *Norwegian writer*

A passionate believer in women's rights, Camilla Collett was the author of the first novel in Norwegian literature to deal with the position of women in society.

The daughter of a minister, she was born Camilla Wergeland in Kristiansand, Norway, and educated at home and in private schools. Growing up in a cultured household – her brother was the poet Henrik Wergeland – Camilla developed a great interest in literature and women's rights. At the age of 17 she fell in love with her brother's great literary rival, the conservative poet J. S. Welhaven. Their love affair ended in 1836, and five years later Camilla married Peter Jonas Collett, a professor of law and a literary critic. He encouraged her to start writing.

In 1855, after her husband, her brother, and her parents had died, Camilla published her most famous work, *Amtmandens døttre* (The Sheriff's Daughter). It was the first Norwegian novel to look at life realistically, attacking the subordinate role of women in society, in marriage, and in the home and calling for social reform. Although heavily criticized at the time, the novel had a great influence on other Norwegian writers, especially Henrik Ibsen, Bjørnstjerne Bjørnson, Jonas Lie, and Alexander Kielland.

The hostile reception given to her novel only increased Camilla's feminism, although in her autobiographical book *I de Lange naetter* (1862; In the Long Nights) she dealt with her childhood and youth in a less controversial manner. Her other works, which include short stories and the volumes of essays *Fra de Stummes Leir* (1877; From the Camp of the Silent) and *Mod Strommen* (1879; Against the Stream), were concerned with the emancipation of women. She died in Kristiana (now Oslo).

Collier, Constance (1878–1955) *British actress*

Constance Collier was a popular actress of both stage and screen in the early part of the 20th century.

She was born Laura Constance Hardie in Windsor, Berkshire. The daughter of professional actors, she appeared on stage for the first time at the age of four. In 1893 she joined the Gaiety Girls, a dancing troupe based in London's Gaiety Theatre. Although beautiful, she was so tall that she towered above the rest of the cast and dominated the stage. This might have limited her range of parts had she not met the actor-manager Sir Herbert Beerbohm Tree, who was himself very tall. As a member of his company at His Majesty's Theatre, London, from 1901 to 1908, she played many important Shakespearean parts: her Cleopatra was described by the critics as "superb and terrible." She was also impressive as Nancy in Comyns Carr's dramatization of *Oliver Twist*.

Constance Collier first toured the United States in 1908 and returned many times to play Shakespearean and other roles. In addition to acting, she produced a number of plays. These included *Camille*, *Peter Ibbetson*, and *Hay Fever*. She later wrote the libretto for the Deems Taylor opera (1931) that was based on *Peter Ibbetson*.

Collier's screen career started with her appearance in D. W. Griffith's *Intolerance* (1916) and continued until the 1950s. In 1933 she went to live in Hollywood, where she worked with Ivor Novello on two of his plays. She made her last appearance on the New York stage in *Aries Is Rising* (1939). She died in New York City.

Constance Collier published her memoirs, *Harlequinade: the Story of My Life*, in 1929.

Collins, Jackie (1937–) *British novelist*

> The author of *Hollywood Wives* and
> eight other novels is to writing what
> her big sister Joan is to acting.
>
> —Campbell Geeson

The younger sister of actress Joan
COLLINS, Jackie Collins is the author
of a series of bestselling novels based
on the lives of the rich and famous in
Hollywood.

She was born in London, the daughter of Joseph William and Elsa Collins.
Expelled from school at the age of 15,
she went off to Hollywood with the intention of becoming a film actress but
turned instead to writing about Hollywood. She had an instant success with
her first novel, *The World Is Full of
Married Men* (1968), which was later
made into a film. Her novels *The Stud*
(1969) and *The Bitch* (1979) were also
made into movies, starring Jackie's sister Joan.

Jackie's other novels include *The
Hollywood Zoo* (1975), *The World Is
Full of Divorced Women* (1975), *Lovers
and Gamblers* (1977), *Chances* (1981),
Hollywood Wives (1983), *Lucky* (1985),
Hollywood Husbands (1986), *Lady
Boss* (1990), and *Hollywood Kids*
(1994). *Chances* and *Lucky* have been
dramatized for television. She has sold
over 170 million copies of her books
around the world and is one of the
highest-earning British women writers.

Jackie Collins's novels have been
criticized as tasteless and exaggerated.
Usually featuring rich, ambitious people competing for power and money,
they are spiced with sex, drugs, and violence. However, some critics regard
her novels as the most enjoyable of
their kind and have interpreted them
as devastating satires of the often
empty lives of the rich and famous.

Collins, Joan (1933–) *British actress*

> The world cannot do without
> women, which is why there's resent-
> ment from men. They realise the fu-
> ture lies with us.
>
> —*The Independent*, April 13, 1991.
> Claiming that men are no longer nec-
> essary because women can be impreg-
> nated by sperm stored in a bank

After an early, unremarkable career as

a film actress, Joan Collins was successfully relaunched as a powerful sex
symbol in her forties with her appearance in the TV soap opera *Dynasty*.
She now enjoys the status of an international celebrity.

Born in London, she studied acting
at the Royal Academy of Dramatic
Art in London, making her stage
debut at the Arts Theatre in Ibsen's *A
Doll's House* in 1946. She launched her
screen career with *Lady Godiva Rides
Again* (1951), going on to appear in
over 50 films, including *Our Girl Friday* (1954), *Land of the Pharaohs*
(1955), *Island in the Sun* (1957), and
Road to Hong Kong (1962). By the late
1970s her career appeared to be declining, but her starring roles in *The Stud*
(1979) and *The Bitch* (1980), both
based on novels written by her sister
Jackie COLLINS, gave her a new image
as a mature, powerful, glamorous
woman that she went on to exploit in
her second career as a television actress.

She enjoyed her greatest success in
the ABC series *Dynasty* (1981–89), in
which she portrayed the glamorous vil-
lainess Alexis Carrington Colby to
such good effect that she became
identified with the role long after the
series finished. This performance won
her several awards, including the
Golden Globe Award in 1982 for the
best television actress in a drama series. Since then Collins has appeared
in a succession of series, mini-series,
specials, pilots, and films on television.
She also starred in a stage production
of Noël Coward's *Private Lives*, which
toured U.S. cities in 1991–92.

Joan Collins has been married four
times. She has two children from her
second marriage, to the actor and director Anthony Newley, and one child
from her third marriage, to the film
producer Ronald S. Kass. She has
published a number of books, including *The Joan Collins Beauty Book*
(1980), the biography *Katy: A Fight
for Life* (1982), two volumes of memoirs *Past Imperfect: An Autobiography*
(1978) and *Second Act* (1996), and the
novels *Prime Time* (1988) and *Love
and Desire and Hate* (1991).

Colonna, Vittoria (1492–1547) *Italian poet*

Vittoria Colonna is best remembered for her long platonic relationship with Michelangelo.

She was born at Marino, near Rome, into an aristocratic Roman family: her father was Fabrizio Colonna, who later became grand constable to King Ferdinand II of Naples. In 1509 Vittoria made an arranged marriage to Fernando Francisco de Avalos, Marquess of Pescara, a Spanish-Neapolitan soldier who fought for the Holy Roman Emperor. He achieved renown by capturing King Francis I of France at the battle of Pavia in 1525 but was killed in action later that year.

After her husband's death, Vittoria wrote over 100 poems in his memory and that of her father. They reflected her grief and her search for spiritual consolation. She befriended many of the leading writers of the day, including Pietro Bembo, Baldassare Castiglione, and Torquato Tasso, and religious reformers, such as Alfonso de Valdès and Bernardino Ochino. In 1538 she moved to Rome and met Michelangelo. During their long, platonic relationship (he was a homosexual) they exchanged sonnets and letters. Her highly spiritual verse, published as *Rime spirituali* (1538), shows the influence of Petrarch and itself influenced later Italian poets.

Vittoria spent the last seven years of her life in convents, first at Orvieto, then at Viterbo, and finally at St. Anna di Funari, in Rome.

Compton-Burnett, Dame Ivy (1884–1969) *British novelist*

> Life makes great demands on people's characters, and gives them great opportunities to serve their own ends by the sacrifice of other people.
>
> —Quoted by Elizabeth Sprigge in *The Life of Ivy Compton-Burnett* (1973)

Ivy Compton-Burnett's distinguished novels analysed Edwardian upper middle-class life through the skilful use of dialogue. In recognition of her contribution to British writing she was made a DBE in 1970.

She was born in Pinner, near London, the eldest of seven children of a doctor by his second wife; he had five children from his first marriage. Ivy was educated at home by a private tutor and at day and boarding schools before studying for a classics degree at the Royal Holloway College, London. After graduating in 1906, she was forced by her tyrannical mother (widowed since 1901) to return home and tutor her younger brothers and sisters. Her first novel, *Dolores* (1911), was written during this period. Following her mother's death in 1911, Ivy became head of the household, but her authoritarian attitude alienated her younger sisters, who left home. She was also dogged by tragedy; two of her favourite brothers died (one of pneumonia, in 1905; the other killed in 1916 during World War I), and her two youngest sisters committed suicide. After the family finally broke up, Ivy lived with her great friend, the antiques expert Margaret Jourdain, from 1919 until Jourdain's death in 1951.

Ivy Compton-Burnett's family life, with its tensions and violence, provided her with much material for her novels, which shared the theme of destructive relationships between members of late Victorian and Edwardian middle-class households over several generations. Her distinctive style relies on highly dramatic dialogue to convey an understanding of her characters. She wrote 20 novels, including *Pastors and Masters* (1925), *Brothers and Sisters* (1929), *Men and Wives* (1931), *A House and Its Head* (1935), *Daughters and Sons* (1937), *Parents and Children* (1941), *Elders and Betters* (1944), *Two Worlds and Their Ways* (1949), *Mother and Son* (1955), which won the James Tait Black Memorial Prize, *A Father and His Fate* (1957), *The Mighty and Their Fall* (1961), *A Heritage and Its History* (1959), and *A God and His Gifts* (1963). Many of her novels have been dramatized.

Connolly, Maureen (1934–1969) *American tennis player*

In her short career Maureen Connolly, nicknamed "Little Mo" because of her small size, proved herself to be one of

America's great woman tennis players. Her many achievements included the Grand Slam of four major singles titles in 1953.

The daughter of an officer in the U.S. Navy, she was born in San Diego, California. Beginning her tennis career as ball girl to the professional Wilbur Fulsom, she was coached by Eleanor "Teach" Tennant. In 1951, at the age of only 16, she caused a sensation by beating Shirley Fry to become women's singles champion at the U.S. Open Tournament at Forest Hills, New York. She won the U.S. Open again in 1952 and 1953 and held the Wimbledon women's singles title from 1952 to 1954 and the French title in 1953 and 1954. In 1953 Little Mo became the first woman to achieve the Grand Slam by taking the Australian, French, British, and U.S. titles. As a member of the winning U.S. Wightman Cup team from 1951 to 1954, she never lost any of her matches.

Little Mo bludgeoned her opponents into submission with long, powerful drives to the baseline of the court. She was ruthless in her approach and became totally involved in the game she was playing. After winning the U.S. Open for the first time in 1951, she lost only four matches in her subsequent career. Her Wimbledon finals against Doris Hart in 1953 and Louise BROUGH in 1954 are regarded as classic tennis matches.

Connolly's career was cut short in 1954 by a horse-riding accident in which she broke her leg. Retiring from tournament play, she married the Olympic horseman Norman Brinker, with whom she had two children, and worked as a tennis coach until forced to stop because of cancer. She died in Dallas, Texas, aged only 34.

Her autobiography, *Forehand Drive*, was published in 1957.

Cooper, Dame Gladys (1888–1971)
British actress

An outstanding and versatile actress whose career spanned 66 years on stage and screen, Gladys Cooper was noted for her beauty, talent, and a total commitment to her profession.

Gladys Constance Cooper was born in Lewisham, London, the daughter of a journalist. A beautiful child, she became a photographic model at the age of six. Later her picture appeared on more than 400 postcards, and she became a "pin-up" for British troops during World War I. Without any stage training she secured a job in 1905 with Seymour Hicks's touring show *Bluebell in Fairyland*; two years later she became a Gaiety Girl.

In 1911 Cooper made her first appearance as a "straight" actress in Oscar Wilde's *The Importance of Being Earnest*. This was followed by *Milestones* (1912) and her first film, *The Eleventh Commandment* (1913). Returning to the theatre, she played the lead in Sardou's *Diplomacy* (1913). From 1917 until 1933 she helped manage the Playhouse Theatre in London, proving to be a shrewd businesswoman.

A beautiful and gifted actress, Cooper gave a fine performance in Pinero's *The Second Mrs. Tanqueray* (1922) and made a successful debut on Broadway in Keith Winter's *The Shining Hour* (1934). She moved to Hollywood in 1940 and made over 30 movies, including *Rebecca* (1940), *That Hamilton Woman* (1941), *Now Voyager* (1942), *The Song of Bernadette* (1943), *Madame Bovary* (1949), and *My Fair Lady* (1964). In many of these films she portrayed dignified aristocrats.

Cooper continued to act into her old age, celebrating her 80th birthday on stage in Ira Wallach's *Out of the Question* (1968). Her last stage appearance, in Enid BAGNOLD's *The Chalk Garden* (1971), took place shortly before her death in London.

Gladys Cooper was married three times; her third husband was the actor Philip Merivale. For her services to the theatre she was made a DBE in 1967.

Corbin, Margaret (1751–c. 1800)
American military heroine

A soldier during America's Revolutionary War, Margaret Corbin was the first woman to be awarded a disability pension.

She was born Margaret Cochran in what is now Franklin County, Pennsylvania, the daughter of Robert Cochran, a Scots-Irish pioneer. Orphaned at the age of five when her father was killed and her mother kidnapped by Native Americans, she was raised with her brother by a maternal uncle. In about 1772 Margaret married John Corbin. Following the outbreak of the Revolutionary War, Corbin enrolled as a private in the first company of the Pennsylvania Artillery Regiment. As was customary at the time, Margaret accompanied the regiment as a general helper. She was with her husband on November 16, 1776, when he defended his artillery position on a ridge near Fort Washington on Manhattan Island, New York, against an attack by the British army. When Corbin was killed in the assault, Margaret took up his post, defending it until she was shot in the arm and captured. She was later freed by the British and allowed to go back to Pennsylvania.

In 1779, in recognition of her bravery and the loss of the use of one arm, Congress voted Margaret Corbin a pension for life and an annual clothing allowance. In order to receive these she enrolled in the Invalid Regiment, which was garrisoned at West Point, New York State, from 1778 until it was disbanded at the end of the Revolutionary War in 1783.

It is not clear what happened to Margaret Corbin after she left West Point. Some accounts say that she went to live in Westmoreland County, Pennsylvania, until her death and that she is buried in the graveyard at Congruity. In other accounts she has been identified with a "Captain Molly," living first near West Point (1785–89) and then at Highland Falls, New York, until her death.

In 1926, to celebrate the 150th anniversary of American independence, the Daughters of the American Revolution in New York had the remains of "Captain Molly" reburied at West Point and erected a monument to her. It has since been proved that these were not the remains of Margaret Corbin but those of another Revolutionary War heroine, Mary Ludwig Hays McCauley (known as "Molly Pitcher").

Corday, Charlotte (1768–1793)
French aristocrat

Charlotte Corday is remembered as the assassin who killed the revolutionary leader Jean Paul Marat in his bath.

Marie Anne Charlotte Corday d'Armont was born at Saint-Saturin, near Sées, Normandy, into a poor but aristocratic family; she was descended from the great French playwright Pierre Corneille. After attending a convent school, Charlotte lived a sheltered life with her aunt in Caen, Normandy. Although herself a royalist, she sympathized with the Girondins, moderate republicans who had been banned from Paris by the more radical Jacobins.

When the exiled Girondins moved to Caen, Charlotte took up their cause and went to Paris to assassinate an important Jacobin leader, Jean Paul Marat, who published the influential newspaper *L'Ami du peuple*. On July 13 she bought a butcher's knife and went to Marat's home in the Rue des Cordeliers, posing as a Jacobin sympathizer who wanted to betray the Girondin leaders. Refused entry at first, she tried again later in the day and was able to see Marat, who was in his bath, where he spent much time because of a painful skin condition. When Charlotte revealed the names of the Girondins in Normandy, Marat noted them and said that they would be guillotined. Charlotte then stabbed him to death. She was immediately arrested, convicted by the Revolutionary Tribunal, and guillotined on July 17, 1793.

Expecting to die, Charlotte had pinned her baptismal certificate to her dress in order that her name should be known, as well as a note explaining her motives: she saw herself as a martyr and a saviour of France, like JOAN OF ARC. However, her deed did not help the Girondins: the Jacobins went on to be even more repressive.

Corelli, Marie (1855–1924) *British novelist*

I'm not saying anything against her morals, but judging from her style

she ought to be here.
—Oscar Wilde, remark to the librarian in Reading jail

Marie Corelli was the author of romantic novels that proved very popular in the early part of the 20th century.

She was born Mary Mackay in London, the daughter of the Scottish songwriter, journalist, and poet Charles Mackay and Ellen Mills, a widow who became his second wife. After attending a convent school for a short period, Mary was educated by governesses at home. An accomplished pianist, she adopted the name Marie Corelli and an assumed Italian parentage in order to further her concert career. However, in 1885 she had a psychic experience, which she wrote about in her first novel, *A Romance of Two Worlds* (1886).

The success of this book encouraged Marie to become a professional writer. Subsequent novels with a psychic theme were also well received, but it was with *Barrabas* (1893), in which she gave a popular account of Christ's crucifixion, that Corelli established her reputation. Her next novel, *The Sorrows of Satan* (1895), another melodramatic treatment of a religious theme, sold more copies when it was first published than any previous British novel. The next year Marie Corelli reached the peak of her popularity with *The Murder of Delicia* (1896). Her many admirers included Mark Twain, the Prince of Wales, and the prime minister William Gladstone.

After 1900 Corelli's popularity declined, and she was criticized for her sentimentality and bad taste. She was so sensitive to criticism that she refused to let reviewers have advance copies of her books. Convinced of her own genius, she continued to write novels, including *The Master Christian* (1900), *God's Good Man* (1904), *The Devil's Motor* (1910), *Eyes of the Sea* (1917), and *The Secret Power* (1921).

From 1901 until her death Marie Corelli lived in Stratford-upon-Avon, in the house that is supposed to have belonged to Shakespeare's daughter. Her writing had made her a wealthy woman. However, although generous to the local people, she was opposed to the modernization of the town and was always in dispute with her neighbours and the town council.

Cori, Gerty Theresa Radnitz (1896–1957) *Czech-born American biochemist*

Gerty Radnitz Cori was one of the very few women to win a Nobel Prize and the first woman doctor of medicine to do so.

Gerty Radnitz was born in Prague and graduated from the Medical School there in 1920, the year in which she married her lifelong collaborator Carl Cori. She moved with him to the United States, taking a post in 1922 at the New York State Institute for the Study of Malignant Diseases in Buffalo. In 1931 she went with her husband to the Washington University Medical School, where she became professor of biochemistry in 1947.

In 1947 the Coris and Bernardo Houssay shared the Nobel Prize for physiology or medicine for their discovery of how glycogen (a carbohydrate stored in the liver and muscles) is broken down into glucose when the body requires energy for cell processes and how it is resynthesized in the body. They pinpointed the crucial role of phosphate in this process.

Corinna (*c.* 500 BC) *Greek poet*

Corinna was the author of lyric poetry on mythological themes.

Living in Tanagra, near Thebes, in Boeotia, she was one of the few Greek poets who used the Boeotian dialect. She drew on Boeotian legends for her narratives, which are written in a timelessly simple style. Corinna is known to have written about 50 books of poetry (epigrams and odes), but only fragments from two of her longer pieces have survived. The first describes the mountain gods Helicon and Cithaeron engaging in a singing contest. The second is concerned with the marriages of Asopus's daughters. They are written in five- or six-line stanzas with short lines.

Traditionally Corinna has been associated with the famous poet Pindar, whom she is said to have beaten five times in poetry competitions in about

500 BC. But recent discoveries of fragments of papyri cast doubt on this dating; indeed it is even possible that she lived as late as 200 BC.

Cornelia (2nd century BC) *Roman matron*

Cornelia was the mother of the great Roman reformers Tiberius and Gaius Gracchus. She was regarded as the ideal Roman matron, highly cultured and giving great care to the education of her children.

The daughter of Publius Cornelius Scipio Africanus Major, who had won the Second Punic War for Rome against Carthage (218–211 BC), she married Tiberius Sempronius Gracchus. They had 12 children, but only three survived: Tiberius and Gaius Gracchus and a daughter, Sempronia, who married Scipio Aemilianus .

After her husband died in 154 BC, Cornelia did not marry again; she even turned down an offer of marriage from King Ptolemy VIII of Egypt. Instead she concentrated on the education of her sons, in whom she instilled a sense of civic duty. They were later killed trying to reform the Roman state. After the murder of her son Gaius in 121 BC Cornelia retired to Misenum (now Miseno in Italy).

While some later historians have blamed Cornelia for encouraging her sons' radical ideas, in other accounts it would seem that on the contrary, she tried to restrain them.

Cornell, Katharine (1893–1974) *American actress*

Noted for her strong voice and expressive acting style, Katharine Cornell was often called the "first lady of the American theatre."

She was born in Berlin, the daughter of a doctor from Buffalo, New York State, who was studying surgery in Germany. When they returned to Buffalo, her father left medicine and managed a theatre. Having started acting when she was in school, Katharine joined the Washington Square Players in 1916, remaining with the company for two years. She toured with the Jessie BONSTELLE Stock Company in 1919 before going to London, to play the part of Jo in Louisa ALCOTT's *Lit-*

tle Women. She appeared on Broadway in *Nice People* in 1921, the year she married the director Guthrie McClintic. In the same year she achieved stardom in *A Bill of Divorcement.*

After this success Cornell starred in Pinero's *The Enchanted Cottage* (1923), G. B. Shaw's *Candida* (1924), Maugham's *The Letter* (1927), and Besier's *The Barretts of Wimpole Street* (1931, 1945), in which she played Elizabeth Barrett BROWNING, the role for which she is best remembered. She also took starring parts in Howard's *Alien Corn* (1934), Shakespeare's *Romeo and Juliet* (1934), Anderson's *The Wingless Victory* (1936), Chekhov's *Three Sisters* (1942), and Kitty's *Dear Liar* (1960).

From 1931 Cornell managed most of her productions, which her husband directed. After McClintic's death in 1961, Cornell retired from the stage. She wrote two volumes of autobiography: *I Wanted to Be an Actress* (1939) and *, Curtain Going Up* (1943).

Cornford, Frances (Crofts) (1886–1960) *British poet*

Frances Crofts Cornford was the granddaughter of Charles Darwin and a great grandniece of William Wordsworth.

She was born in Cambridge, the only child of Francis Darwin and Ellen Wordsworth. After being educated at home, she married Francis Macdonald Cornford, professor of ancient philosophy at Cambridge, in 1908. Their home became a haven for writers and artists, including Rupert Brooke and Christopher Hassall. Hassall encouraged Frances's interest in poetry, her first volume, *Poems*, being published in 1910. This was followed by *Spring Morning* (1915), *Different Days* (1928), *Mountains and Molehills* (1935), *Poems from the Russian* (1943), and *Collected Poems* (1954).

Cornford's poetry was traditional in style and drew much of its content from local Cambridge life. She was uninfluenced by such modern poets as T. S. Eliot. and Ezra Pound. She died in Cambridge.

Cornwell, Patricia (1956–) *American writer*

Patricia Cornwell is regarded as one of the best authors of crime novels of the 1990s.

She was born Patricia Daniels in Miami, Florida, the daughter of a lawyer. She studied at Davidson College, North Carolina; after graduating in 1979 she married her professor, Charles Cornwell. From 1979 to 1981 she worked as a police reporter on *The Charlotte Observer*, winning the North Carolina Press Association Award in 1980 for a series of articles on prostitution. It was with great reluctance that she gave up her career to accompany her husband to Richmond, Virginia, where he had decided to train to become a minister of religion.

Patricia Cornwell began her literary career in 1983 with a biography of Ruth Graham, the wife of the evangelist Billy Graham, who encouraged her to draw on her experience as a reporter to write a crime novel. In order to learn the latest developments in forensic science, she approached Dr. Marcella Fiero at the Virginia Morgue, for whom she wrote a number of technical reports.

In 1990 Cornwell published her first novel, *Postmortem*, featuring her female detective, the medical examiner Dr. Kay Scarpetta. The critical success of this book encouraged her to follow it up with more Scarpetta mysteries, including *Body of Evidence* (1991), *All That Remains* (1992), *Cruel and Unusual* (1993), *The Body Farm* (1994), *From Potter's Field* (1995), *Cause of Death* (1996), *Hornet's Nest* (1997), and *Unnatural Exposure* (1997). All these novels are well plotted and tautly written, providing the reader with continued suspense and authentic (often gruesome) details of the work of a medical examiner.

Court, Margaret Smith (1942–)
Australian tennis player

Margaret Smith Court has won a total of 66 major tennis championships, more than any other woman player in the history of the game. Her height (5 feet 8½ inches), mobility around the tennis court, and powerful serve, volley, and ground strokes made her the dominant player on the women's tennis circuit in the 1960s and early 1970s.

She was born Margaret Smith in Albury, New South Wales, Australia, and won the Australian women's singles title six times in succession between 1960 and 1966. She won the Wimbledon singles in 1963, 1965, and 1970; the U.S. Open singles in 1962, 1965, 1969, 1970, and 1973; and the French singles in 1962, 1969, and 1970. In 1970 she became only the second woman, after Maureen CONNOLLY in 1953, to win the Grand Slam of the Australian, French, British, and American tennis singlesj163. She is also the only player to have achieved the Grand Slam in doubles, winning all four major championships with Ken Fletcher in 1963.

She married a fellow Australian, Barry Court, in 1967 and has published two volumes of autobiography, *The Margaret Smith Story* (1964) and *Court on Court* (1974). She became a member of the International Tennis Hall of Fame in 1979.

Cowl, Jane (1884–1950) *American actress and playwright*

Jane Cowl had a long and very successful career in the American theatre. An actress of great versatility who was able to play both comic and tragic roles, she had an impressive stage presence and was called the "most beautiful woman on the American stage."

Also known as Jane Cowles, she was born Grace Bailey in Boston, Massachusetts. After studying at Columbia University in New York City, she made her stage debut under the management of David Belasco in *Sweet Kitty Bellairs* (1903). In 1906 she married the *New York Times* theatre critic Adolph Klauber, who was involved with many of her later productions. Her first leading role was in Belasco's production of Ditrichstein's *Is Marriage a Failure?* (1909), for which she received considerable critical acclaim. After leaving Belasco's company, she appeared in *The Upstart* (1910) and *The Gamblers* (1911) before achieving stardom in *Within the Law* (1912).

Jane Cowl went on to star in films, including Samuel Goldwyn's *The*

Spreading Dawn (1917). In the theatre she appeared in *Lilac Time* (1917), *Daybreak* (1917), *Information Please* (1918), and the smash hit *Smilin' Through* (1919–22), which she wrote with Jane Murfin using their pen name "Alan Langdon Martin." Cowl played an unforgettable Juliet in 1923 and appeared in Noël Coward's *Easy Virtue* in 1925–26. This was followed by her appearance in Sherwood's *The Road to Rome* (1927) and *The Jealous Moon* (1928), which she cowrote with Theodore Charles.

Cowl continued to appear in plays of her choice in the 1930s; her last success on Broadway was in Van Druten's *Old Acquaintance* (1940–41). After World War II she went to Hollywood and played some minor film roles; the last of these was in *Payment on Demand* (1951). She died of cancer in Santa Monica, California.

Crabtree, Lotta (1847–1924) *American actress*

Lotta Crabtree was a popular variety-hall star in both the United States and Britain in the late 19th century.

Born Charlotte Mignon Crabtree in New York City, she moved with her family to California in 1851 to dig for gold. Because her father failed to find any, her mother had to run a boarding house. It was there that Lotta met Lola MONTEZ, who taught her how to sing and dance. Encouraged by her mother, Lotta toured the mining camps singing ballads, dancing jigs, and playing the banjo. A great favourite with the miners, she was soon appearing in variety halls in San Francisco.

In 1864 her family returned to the East, where Lotta began appearing in variety acts in Chicago, Boston, and New York City. Her first great success was with John Brougham's *Little Nell and the Marchioness* (1867). For the next 20 years she was a highly popular figure on the variety circuit, touring the country with her own company. Her later successes include *Zip*, *Musette*, *The Little Detective*, *Nitouche*, and *Pawn Ticket*.

Lotta Crabtree was a curious mixture of the outrageous and the inno-

cent. She retained her youthful looks well into middle age, and her infectious high spirits endeared her to audiences in both the United States and Britain. She was one of the great entertainers of her time.

She retired in 1891, after an accident on stage, to her mother's country estate in New Jersey, her mother having acquired a large fortune by speculating in real estate. Lotta never married; when she died she left the bulk of her $4-million fortune to needy causes.

Craik, Dinah Maria (1826–1887) *British writer*

> Oh my son's my son till he gets him a wife, But my daughter's my daughter all her life.
>
> —"Young and Old" (*c.* 1887)

The author of novels, short stories, and poetry, Dinah Craik is best known for her novel *John Halifax, Gentleman*.

Born Dinah Maria Mulock in Stoke-on-Trent, Staffordshire, she was the daughter of a minister. She studied at local schools, continuing her education in London after the family moved there in 1846. Three years later she returned to Staffordshire with her mother to escape from her unstable father. Dinah's mother died in 1850, leaving her and her younger brother Benjamin with barely enough money to live on. She therefore turned to writing as a source of income. Her first novel, *The Ogilvies*, had been published in 1849; this was followed by *Olive* (1850), *The Head of the Family* (1851), and her most famous work, *John Halifax, Gentleman* (1857). This book, which celebrated the Victorian ideals of prudence, courtesy, and self-discipline, was later made into a film.

In 1859 Dinah and her brother moved to Hampstead in north London, where she became well known in literary circles. Benjamin died in 1863, after which Dinah sold their house in Hampstead. She married the publisher George Lillie Craik in 1865, and they moved to Bromley, Kent, where they built a house. Although they did not have any children, they adopted a girl in 1872. Dinah Craik continued to write, producing biographies, travel books, essays, and the children's story

The Lame Prince (1874), in addition to plays, poetry, and novels. The latter included *A Life for a Life* (1859), *Christian's Mistake* (1865), and *Young Mrs. Jardine* (1879). Her *Collected Poems* were published in 1881, and her short stories were collected in *Avilion* (1853).

A shrewd businesswoman, Mrs. Craik was earning large sums from her books towards the end of her life. When in 1864 she was granted a state pension, she generously gave it to needy writers. She died in Shortlands, Kent.

Crawford, Cheryl (1902–1986) *American theatre director*

As a director, producer, and actress, Cheryl Crawford had an important influence on the development of American theatre in the 1930s and 1940s.

She was born in Akron, Ohio, and began to study acting when she was at school and at Smith College. After her graduation in 1925 she joined the Theater Guild in New York as an assistant stage manager, later becoming the casting director. However, she left in 1930 to form the Group Theater with Harold Clurman and Lee Strasberg, whom she called "the Old Testament prophets." The Group Theater was renowned for developing the naturalistic techniques of Stanislavsky and the Moscow Art Theatre into the so-called "method", which has had a huge influence on American acting.

Cheryl Crawford left the Group Theater in 1937 to become an independent producer. In 1941 her revival of Gershwin's *Porgy and Bess* turned out to be an enormous success. Having helped Eva LE GALLIENNE and Margaret WEBSTER set up the short-lived American Repertory Company in 1945, she teamed up with Robert Lewis and Elia Kazan to establish the Actors' Studio in 1947.

At the same time, she continued to produce a number of successful plays and musicals, including Lerner and Loewe's *Brigadoon* (1947) and four plays by Tennessee Williams: *The Rose Tattoo* (1951), which won a Tony Award, *Camino Real* (1953), *Sweet Bird of Youth* (1959), and *Period of Adjustment* (1960). She also produced the revivals of O'Casey's *The Shadow of a Gunman* (1958) and Brecht's *Mother Courage* (1963), as well as Barbra STREISAND's *Yentl* (1975).

Crawford,   Isabella   Valancy (1850–1887) *Irish-born Canadian poet*

> I was born in front of a camera and really don't know anything else.
> —*Variety* magazine, April, 1973

Isabella Valancy Crawford was the first important female Canadian poet.

She was born in Dublin, the daughter of a physician. When she was eight years old, she emigrated with her family to Canada. They lived near the Kawartha Lakes in Ontario, an area of great natural beauty. Isabella received a good education at home in Greek and Latin as well as French and Italian literature. After her father died, she and her mother moved to Toronto, where they lived over a grocery shop. Isabella earned a meagre living writing stories for local newspapers and American magazines. Her writing reflected her appreciation of the natural beauties of the Canadian landscape and her search for perfect love – in this she was considerably influenced by the English Romantic and Victorian writers.

She published only one collection of her poetry during her short lifetime, *Old Spookses's Pass, Malcom's Katie, and Other Poems* (1884). These lyrical poems are full of vivid imagery. They only came to be truly appreciated after her death, when John W. Garwin edited and published her *Collected Poems* (1905).

Crawford, Joan (1908–1977) *American actress*

> The consummate movie star, she dressed the part, played it off screen and on, and adored every moment of it.
> —Joseph L. Mankiewicz

Joan Crawford became a Hollywood movie queen and one of the all-time greats of the cinema.

Born Lucille LeSueur in San Antonio, Texas, she worked in a variety of jobs before entering show business. After winning a dance contest, she danced professionally under her stepfather's name, "Billie Cassin," in nightclubs in Detroit and Chicago. By 1924 she was dancing in Broadway musicals, where she was spotted by MGM. Equipped with her new stage name, "Joan Crawford," which was chosen in a film-magazine contest, she made her screen debut as a dance-mad flapper in *Pretty Ladies* (1925). This was followed by *The Taxi Dancer* (1927), *Our Dancing Daughters* (1928), and her first talkies – *Untamed* (1929), *Dance, Fools, Dance* (1931), and *Dancing Lady* (1933).

In the 1930s Joan Crawford began to be given more serious roles in films, playing either sophisticated society women or poor girls who made good. Her career took a dive in 1938, when she was declared to be "box office poison," but she made a comeback as a dramatic actress in *The Women* (1939), *Susan and the God* (1940), *Strange Cargo* (1940), and *The Woman's Face* (1941).

Crawford's performance in *Mildred Pierce* (1945) won her the Academy Award for Best Actress in 1946 and had a major influence on her career. She went on to appear in a number of high-quality films, including *Possessed* (1947), for which she was nominated for an Academy Award, *Humoresque* (1947), *Sudden Fear* (1952), and *The Story of Esther Costello* (1957). At the end of her career she was starring in melodramas, including *Whatever Happened to Baby Jane?* (1962), with Bette DAVIS, and *The Caretakers* (1963).

Joan Crawford was married four times – to the actors Douglas Fairbanks Jr. (1929–33), Franchot Tone (1935–39), and Philip Terry (1942–46). Her fourth husband was Alfred Steele, the ex-chairman of Pepsi Cola. After his death in 1959 she joined the board of directors and helped the company with its publicity. She also adopted four children. After Crawford's death her adopted daughter Christina wrote *Mommie Dearest* (1978), which revealed how Joan Crawford had maltreated her children, presenting another side to her carefully crafted image as a screen idol.

Crawford Seeger, Ruth (1901–1953) *American composer and musicologist*

During her distinguished career Ruth Crawford Seeger composed a small number of highly regarded chamber pieces, made valuable collections of American folk music, and became an influential teacher.

Born Ruth Crawford in Liverpool, Ohio, she studied music at the School of Musical Art in Jacksonville, Florida, at the American Conservatory in Chicago, and with the well-known musicologist Charles Seeger (her future husband) in New York. She became the first American woman composer to win a Guggenheim Fellowship, which enabled her to spend 1932 in Paris and Berlin. Her music, far in advance of its time, was influenced by such contemporary composers as Alban Berg and Bela Bartok, but her string quartet (1931) foreshadowed the work of later composers, notably Gyorgy Ligeti and Witold Lutoslawski. Her other important works include a violin sonata (1926), *Suite for Wind Quintet* (1952), and *Three Songs* (1933). The latter work represented the United States at the 1933 festival of the International Society for Contemporary Music in Amsterdam.

Crawford Seeger was particularly interested in American folk music and supplied the accompaniments for Carl Sandburg's collection *The American Songbag* (1927). In 1935 she moved to Washington, D.C., and began work on transcribing and arranging the hundreds of recorded folksongs in the Library of Congress, many of which were published by John and Alan Lomax in their collection *Our Singing Country* (1941). Ruth Crawford Seeger was also involved in music teaching and published several collections, including *American Folk Songs for Children* (1948). Three of her children – Mike, Peggy, and Pete – became folk singers.

Crespin, Régine (1927–   ) *French singer*

Singing mainly soprano roles, Régine Crespin was one of the greatest French opera singers of the mid 20th century.

Born in Marseilles, she studied in Nîmes and at the Paris Conservatory, where she won song and opera prizes. She made her debut as Elsa in Wagner's *Lohengrin* at Mulhouse, France, in 1950, appearing soon afterwards in the same role at the Paris Opéra. The power and range of her voice enabled her to sing the leading soprano roles in a wide variety of operas; during the next seven years she sang the title role in Puccini's *Tosca*, Desdemona in Verdi's *Otello*, and Amelia in his *The Masked Ball*, as well as the Marschallin in Strauss's *Der Rosenkavalier*. In 1958 she appeared at Bayreuth, as Kundry in Wagner's *Parsifal*.

This marked the start of her international career, after which she went on to play the other great roles in the operas of Wagner and Verdi in Europe and North and South America. She made her debut at the Metropolitan Opera, New York, in 1962 as the Marschallin. She also played the Second Prioress in the Paris premiere of Poulenc's *The Carmelites* (1957) and the leading role in Fauré's *Penelope*, as well as a number of Berlioz and Offenbach roles.

Also an accomplished recitalist, Crespin sang Schumann and Wolf with great insight. Her international career was interrupted by a personal crisis in the late 1960s and early 1970s about which she has written in her autobiography *La Vie et l'amour d'une femme* (1982). When she began to sing again, she had to rework her voice before she could resume her career, this time as a mezzo-soprano.

Croly, Jane (1829–1901) *British-born American journalist and feminist*

Jane Croly campaigned vigorously in the late 19th century for the right of women to have the same employment opportunities as men.

She was born Jane Cunningham in Market Harborough, Leicestershire, the fourth child of Joseph and Jane Cunningham. Her father's unpopular Unitarian views led him to take his family to the United States in 1841. They settled first at Poughkeepsie, New York State, and then at nearby Wappinger's Falls. Jane was educated at home and then for a time kept house for her brother, who was a Congrega-

tionalist minister. Following her father's death in 1854, she was forced to work for a living, moving to New York City to embark on her career in journalism.

She began writing a women's column for *The Sunday Times and Noah's Weekly Messenger*; in 1857 she became the first woman to have her column syndicated to other papers – in New Orleans, Richmond, Baltimore, and Louisville. Writing for other New York papers, including *The Herald*, she used the pen name "Jennie June." In 1857 she married David Goodman Croly, a journalist on *The New York Herald*. After a brief and unsuccessful period running their own paper in Rockford, Illinois, the Crolys moved back to New York in 1860 and started work for *The World*. Jane Croly ran the women's department of the paper from 1862 to 1872, at the same time beginning her long association with the popular women's magazines published by William and Ellen Demorest.

Jane Croly had five children, four of whom survived to adulthood. Dividing her time between her home and her office, she proved that a mother and wife could compete successfully with men in a professional job. She believed that financial independence and economic equality for women were more important than the right to vote. Her beliefs and the ability to express them in journalistic terms made her one of the early advocates of feminism. She was heavily involved in the women's club movement (founding Sorosis, the General Federation of Women's Clubs, and the Women's Press Club) in the United States, which encouraged women to unite for their own improvement. In 1898 she published a *History of the Women's Club Movement in America*. She died in New York.

Cross, Joan (1900–95) *British opera singer*

Singing soprano roles, Joan Cross was one of the leading British opera singers of the mid 20th century.

Born in London, she studied music there with Gustav Holst, who was then music master at St. Paul's Girls' School, and at Trinity College of

Music. In 1924 she joined the opera chorus at the Old Vic theatre and was soon singing such roles as the First Lady in Mozart's *The Magic Flute*. She made her debut at Covent Garden as Mimi in Puccini's *La Bohème* in 1931 and from then until 1946 she was the principal soprano at the Sadler's Wells Opera Company. She sang the parts of Kupava in the British premiere of Rimsky-Korsakov's *The Snow Maiden* (1933) and Militrisa in his *The Tale of Tsar Saltan* (1933).

Joan Cross directed the Sadler's Wells Opera Company from 1943 until 1945. When the theatre was reopened after World War II, she sang the part of Ellen Orford in the British premiere of Benjamin Britten's *Peter Grimes*. Working closely with Britten in the English Opera Group, she created the roles of the Female Chorus in his *Rape of Lucretia* at Glyndebourne in 1946, Queen Elizabeth I in *Gloriana* at Covent Garden in 1953, and Mrs. Grose in *The Turn of the Screw* in Venice in 1954.

Cross began producing opera after World War II, including *Der Rosenkavalier* at Covent Garden in 1946 and *La Traviata* at Sadler's Wells in 1950. In 1948 she helped set up the opera school that later became the National School of Opera, of which she was a director until 1964.

Crothers, Rachel (1878–1958) *American playwright*

Rachel Crothers's popular plays gave a more accurate picture of the position of women in American society than the work of any other playwright of the time.

She was born in Bloomington, Illinois, and studied at the Illinois State Normal School (which became Illinois State University). Graduating in 1892, she went on to study drama in Boston, Massachusetts, and New York.

Her career as a playwright started in 1906 with the success of her first play, *The Three of Us*. She wrote and produced more than 25 plays in the next 30 years, including *A Man's World* (1909), *Young Wisdom* (1914), *Nice People* (1921), *Expressing Willie* (1924), *As Husbands Go* (1931), *When*

Ladies Meet (1932), and *Susan and the God* (1937). With their simple plots, expert dialogue, and happy endings, her plays were immensely popular, combining moral instruction with humour. Rachel Crothers had more critical successes in the theatre than any other American woman playwright. She died in Danbury, Connecticut.

Cullberg, Birgit (1908–) *Swedish choreographer and dancer*

Birgit Cullberg's ballets, strongly influenced by modern dance, are distinguished by their dramatic quality. She is regarded as one of the most important figures in the contemporary Swedish dance movement.

Born in Nyköping, Sweden, she was educated at Stockholm University before going to England to study dance with Kurt Joos at Dartington Hall and then to the United States to train under Martha GRAHAM. Returning to Sweden, she founded her own dance company in 1939 and married Anders Ek, whom she later divorced, in 1942.

In 1946 Cullberg cofounded the Svenska Dansteater, an avant-garde touring company. Her reputation as a choreographer was established in 1950 with her adaptation of Strindberg's *Miss Julie*, which combined modern and classical dance techniques. From 1952 to 1957 she was choreographer to the Royal Swedish Ballet, after which she went on to become guest choreographer to the New York City Ballet and the American Ballet Theater.

Birgit Cullberg returned to Sweden in 1967, since when she has worked mainly with her own company, the Cullberg Ballet, of which she is the director. She has also been involved in politics, especially the peace movement.

In addition to *Miss Julie*, Cullberg's works include *Medea* (1950), *The Moon Reindeer* (1957), the award-winning TV ballet *The Evil Queen* (1961), *Romeo and Juliet* (1969), the award-winning *Red Wine in Green Glasses* (1971), *Revolt* (1973), and *War Dances* (1979).

Cunard, Nancy (Clara) (1896–1965) *British writer, publisher, and campaigner*

A prominent figure in avant-garde literary circles during the 1920s, Nancy Cunard is now remembered more for her colourful personality than for her writings. She was a leading supporter of anti-Fascist causes and black civil rights.

Nancy Cunard was born into a wealthy Anglo-American family. Her father, Sir Bache Cunard, was the grandson of Samuel Cunard, the founder of the famous transatlantic steamship company, while her American-born mother, Lady Maud (known as 'Emerald'), was a conspicuous figure in London society. However, after an early and disastrously brief marriage to a Guards officer, Nancy rejected her parents' world and chose to move in Bohemian circles in London and Paris. By the age of 21 she had already published a number of poems in Edith SITWELL's magazine *Wheels*, and during the 1920s several collections of her self-consciously "modern" verse appeared. Although her poetry is no longer read, she made a more lasting contribution to 20th-century literature as a publisher. In 1928 she acquired a newspaper printing machine and started the Hours Press, which went on to publish significant work by Ezra Pound, Louis Aragon, Samuel Beckett, and other figures of the literary avant-garde.

In 1930 Nancy scandalized London society and incurred the particular wrath of her mother by cohabiting with Henry Crowder, a black jazz musician. The couple were obliged to flee to the continent, where Nancy brought further notoriety on herself by publishing *Black Man and White Ladyship* (1931), a highly personalized attack on her mother's life and values. In 1932 she organized a mixed-race ball to raise funds for eight black American youths condemned to death for an alleged assault on two white women. With Crowder, she edited *Negro* (1934), an influential anthology of black art and literature that also made an eloquent plea for civil rights. Following the outbreak of the Spanish Civil War in 1936, she joined the International Brigade as a reporter and published anti-Fascist articles in British newspapers.

In the decades after World War II Nancy Cunard suffered persistent problems with both her physical and her mental health. Nevertheless, she continued to campaign for a variety of personal causes, including political prisoners in Franco's Spain and Venetian gondoliers, whom she considered to be badly exploited. She died in France. A larger-than-life character, Nancy Cunard appears in numerous memoirs of the 1920s and 1930s and (lightly disguised) in several novels of the era.

Cunningham, Imogen (1883–1976)
American photographer

In a career that spanned 75 years Imogen Cunningham drew on a wide range of subjects for her photographs, including people, landscapes, cityscapes, and, especially, plants and flowers. Her work reflected the major advances in art photography that took place in the 20th century.

Cunningham was born in Portland, Oregon. Educated in Seattle state schools, she studied chemistry at the University of Washington. Having started to take photographs in 1901, she worked for eight years in the Seattle studio of Edward S. Curtis, who was acclaimed for his photographs of Native Americans. In 1909 Cunningham received a scholarship to study photographic chemistry at the Technical High School in Dresden, Germany. Returning to the United States in 1910, she opened a portrait studio in Seattle. Five years later she married the etcher Roi Partridge; she shocked the Seattle community by exhibiting a series of slightly out-of-focus pictures of him in the nude on Mount Rainier. The couple moved in 1917 to San Francisco and in 1920 to Oakland, where Partridge taught at Mills College.

In the 1920s Cunningham abandoned the Romantic style of photography that had previously influenced her work. Her images became less ornamental and more sharply defined. *Magnolia Blossom* (1925) was the first and most famous in her series of close-ups of plant forms exhibited at the 1929 "Film and Photo" exhibition in Stuttgart, Germany. In this new approach to her work she was influenced by the photographer Edward Weston.

By 1932 Cunningham had become a cofounder with Weston and other photographers of Group f/64 (f/64 is the aperture setting on a camera lens that produces the most sharply defined image). The group was dedicated to producing clarity of definition and simplicity of form in their photographs. Cunningham was also an accomplished portraitist; her subjects included Martha GRAHAM, Spencer Tracy, Cary Grant, and the photographer Alfred Stieglitz.

Cunningham divorced Roi Partridge in 1934. In 1947 she moved back to San Francisco, where she remained active as a photographer until a week before her death.

Imogen Cunningham received a number of honours and awards over the years, including a Guggenheim Fellowship (1970) and a Summa Laude Dignatus Award from the University of Washington (1974). On her 90th birthday in 1973 the Metropolitan Museum of Art in New York exhibited 64 of her prints. Her work was shown in museums throughout the United States, including the International Museum of Photography (1961), the San Francisco Museum of Modern Art (1951, 1964), and the Oakland Art Museum (1957).

Curie, Marie (Skłodowska) (1867–1934) *Polish-French chemist*

> In this shed with an asphalt floor, whose glass roof offered us only incomplete protection against the rain, which was like a greenhouse in summer and which an iron stove barely heated in winter, we passed the best and happiest years of our existence, consecrating our entire days to the work...I remember the delight we experienced when we happened to enter our domain at night and saw on all sides the palely luminescent silhouettes of the products of our work.
>
> —In the Preface to Pierre Curie's *Collected Works*

Marie Curie was a brilliant physicist who discovered radium and polonium and helped to elucidate the nature of radioactivity. She was the first woman to win a Nobel Prize and the first person to win a second Nobel Prize.

Marie Skłodowska was born in Warsaw, where her father was a physics teacher and her mother the principal of a girls' school. She acquired from her father an interest in science, although to aid the family finances she was forced, in 1885, to become a governess. Because there was no way in which a girl could receive any form of higher scientific education in Poland in the 1880s, in 1891 she followed her elder sister to Paris. Living in poverty and working hard, she graduated in physics from the Sorbonne in 1893, taking first place. She received a scholarship from Poland, which enabled her to spend a year studying mathematics; this time she graduated in second place.

In 1894 she met Pierre Curie, whom she married the following year. He was a physicist of some distinction who had already made several important discoveries and was working as chief of the laboratory of the School of Industrial Physics and Chemistry. Marie was at this time looking for a topic for research for a higher degree. Her husband was in full sympathy with her desire to continue with research, by no means a common attitude in late 19th-century France. She was also fortunate in her timing and choice of topic – the study of radioactivity. In 1896 Henri Becquerel had discovered radioactivity in uranium. Marie Curie had reason to believe that there might be a new element in the samples of uranium ore (pitchblende) that Becquerel had handled, but first she needed a place to work and a supply of the ore. It was agreed that she could work in her husband's laboratory. Her first task was to see if substances other than uranium were radioactive. Her method was to place the substance on one of the plates of Pierre's sensitive electrometer to see if it produced an electric current between the plates. In a short time Marie Curie found that thorium is also radioactive.

Her next discovery was in many

ways the most fundamental. She tried to see whether different compounds of uranium or thorium would have differing amounts of radioactivity. Her conclusion was that it made no difference what she mixed the uranium with, whether it was wet or dry, in powder form or solution; the only factor that counted was the amount of uranium present. This meant that radioactivity must be a property of the uranium itself and not of its interaction with something else. Radioactivity had to be an atomic property; it would soon be recognized as an effect of the nucleus.

One further advance was made by Marie Curie in 1898; she found that two uranium minerals, pitchblende and chalcolite, were more active than uranium itself. She drew the correct conclusion from this, namely, that they must contain new radioactive elements. She immediately began the search for them. By the end of the year she had demonstrated the existence of two new elements, radium and polonium, both of which were highly radioactive. No precautions were taken at this time against the levels of radiation, as their harmful effects were not recognized. (Indeed, her notebooks of this period are still too dangerous to handle.)

Her next aim was to produce some pure radium. The difficulty here was that radium is present in pitchblende in such small quantities that vast amounts of the ore were needed. The Curies managed to acquire, quite cheaply, several tons of pitchblende from the Bohemian mines – thanks to the intercession of the Austrian government. As there was too much material for her small laboratory, she was offered the use of an old dissecting room in the yard of the school. It was freezing in winter and unbearably hot in summer – Wilhelm Ostwald later described it as a cross between a stable and a potato cellar. The work was heavy and monotonous. The limitations of her equipment meant that she could only deal with batches of 20 kilograms at a time, which had to be carefully dissolved, filtered, and crystallized. This procedure went on

month after month, in all kinds of weather. By early 1902 she had obtained one tenth of a gram of radium chloride. She took this to Eugène Demarçay, who had first identified the new elements spectroscopically. He now had enough to determine its atomic weight, which he calculated as 225.93.

Although Marie Curie was no great theorist, she was an industrious experimentalist. Her thesis, presented in 1903, made her the first woman to be awarded an advanced scientific research degree in France. In the same year she was awarded the Nobel Prize for physics jointly with her husband and Henri Becquerel for their work on radioactivity.

In 1904, when her husband was given a chair at the Sorbonne, Marie Curie was offered a part-time post as a physics teacher at a girls' Normal School at Sèvres. It is also about this time that she first appears to have suffered from radiation sickness. Given all these distractions it is not surprising that for a few years after the completion of her thesis she had little time for research.

In 1906 Pierre Curie died in a tragic accident. The Sorbonne elected Marie to her husband's chair, and the rest of her life was largely spent in organizing the research of others and attempting to raise funds. She made two long trips to the United States in 1921 and 1929. On her first trip she had been asked what she would most like to have. A gram of radium of her own was her reply, and she returned from the United States with a gram, valued at $100,000. She also received $50,000 from the Carnegie Institution. In 1912 the Sorbonne founded the Curie Laboratory for the study of radioactivity. It was opened in 1914, but its real work could only begin after the war, during which Marie Curie spent most of her time training radiologists. Later her laboratory, with its gram of radium, was to become one of the great research centres of the world.

Her position in France was somewhat unusual. As a foreigner and a woman, France was never quite sure how to treat her. She was clearly very distinguished for in 1911 she was awarded her second Nobel Prize, this time in chemistry for her discovery of radium and polonium. Her eminence was recognized by the creation of the Curie Laboratory, yet at almost the same time she found herself rejected by the Académie des Sciences. She allowed her name to go forward in 1910 as the first serious female contender but was defeated. There is no doubt that this offended her. She refused to allow her name to be submitted for election again and for ten years refused to allow her work to be published in the proceedings of the Académie.

The following year, 1911, she became the centre of a major scandal. The physicist Paul Langevin, a former pupil of her husband, was accused of having an affair with her. Langevin had left his wife and four children, but although he was close to Madame Curie, it is by no means clear that there were grounds for the accusations. Some of her letters to Langevin were stolen and published in the popular press, and doubts were raised about Pierre Curie's death. Most of the attacks seem to have emanated from Gustave Téry, editor of *L'Oeuvre* and a former classmate of Langevin. Langevin retaliated by challenging Téry to a duel. Langevin faced Téry late in 1911 at 25 yards with a loaded pistol in his hand. Both refused to fire, and shortly afterwards the scandal died down.

Marie Curie's major published work was the massive two-volume *Treatise on Radioactivity* (1910). She died of leukaemia, probably caused by her persistent exposure to radioactivity. The Curies' daughter Irène JOLIOT-CURIE and her husband Frédéric continued the pioneering work on radioactivity for which they also received the Nobel Prize for chemistry.

Curtin, Phyllis (1922–) *American opera singer and music teacher*

Renowned for her acting and musicianship, Phyllis Curtin did much to promote the performance of contemporary American music around the world.

She was born Phyllis Smith in Clarksburg, West Virginia. After graduating from Wellesley College in 1943, she sang at the Tanglewood Music Center in Lenox, Massachusetts, and with the New England Opera Company. She first appeared with the New York City Opera in 1953 and made her debut at the Metropolitan Opera in 1961, singing the role of Fiordiligi in Mozart's *Così fan tutte*.

Curtin remained closely associated with the New York City Opera, for which she sang virtually all of Mozart's heroines, as well as Strauss's Salome and Verdi's Violetta (in *La Traviata*) and Mistress Ford (in *Falstaff*). She won international recognition for her performances in modern American operas, notably Carlisle Floyd's *Susannah*, in which she sang the title role for the opera's first performance in 1955. She also sang the first performances of Floyd's operas *Wuthering Heights* (1958; at the Santa Fe Opera) and *The Passion of Jonathan Wade* (1962; at the New York City Opera), as well as the American premieres of William Walton's *Troilus and Cressida* and Darius Milhaud's *Medea*. In 1958 Curtin made her European debut at the Brussels World Fair, in Floyd's *Susannah*.

Curtin retired from major stage work in 1984. She was a professor at Yale University's School of Music from 1979 to 1983, when she took up a similar post at Boston University's School of the Arts. She was also a noted teacher of master classes in the United States, Canada, Moscow, and Beijing, as well as being an artist in residence at Tanglewood from 1965.

Cushman, Charlotte (Saunders) (1816–1876) *American actress*

Noted for her powerful stage presence, Charlotte Cushman was America's first great native-born actress.

She was born in Boston into a distinguished family. However, the death of her father left the family in financial difficulties, and Charlotte was obliged to earn her own living. Intending to become an opera singer, she studied singing, making her stage debut at the age of 19 in Mozart's *The Marriage of*

Figaro. Deciding instead to switch to straight acting, in 1837 she became a member of the Park Company in New York. Moving to Philadelphia, she was stage manager of the Walnut Street Theater from 1842 to 1844.

Some of her best-known roles from the 1830s and 1840s were Meg Merrilees in *Guy Mannering* (1837), Nancy in *Oliver Twist* (1839), and Lady Macbeth (1843–44). In 1845 she went to England, where she starred in various London productions until her return to the United States in 1849.

After her official retirement in 1852, she lived in England and Rome. In 1870 she returned to the United States, where she gave a few stage performances and occasionally travelled to England to perform there too. She died of cancer.

With her deep voice and tall physique, Charlotte Cushman was ideally suited to powerful, dramatic roles, often taking male parts (such as Romeo and Hamlet). Although she suffered bouts of physical illness and depression, she continued to tour Europe and the United States, becoming a highly respected actress. In addition to her stage work, she gave encouragement to many actors, sculptors, artists, and musicians.

D

Dahl-Wolfe, Louise (1895–1989)
American fashion photographer

Dahl-Wolfe's pictures for *Harper's Bazaar* helped to change the image of American women from the "glamour girl" of the 1930s to the strong, relaxed, and approachable woman of the 1940s and 1950s. One of the first fashion photographers to use colour, Dahl-Wolfe was highly regarded for her attention to the composition and lighting of her pictures.

Louise Emma Augusta Dahl was born in Alameda, California, the youngest of three girls in an upper-middle-class family. She studied design and painting at the San Francisco Institute of Art from 1914 to 1917 and took night classes there from 1921 to 1922, while working as an electric-sign designer. Mainly self-taught in photography, she was influenced at this time by the work of the photographer Anne Brigman. After further studies in design, decoration, and architecture at Columbia University in New York City she travelled with the photographer and journalist Consuela Kanaga to Europe in 1927.

In Tunisia she met the artist Meyer ("Mike") Wolfe, whom she married in 1928 in New York. From 1932 to 1933 they lived in Gatlinburg, Tennessee, where Dahl-Wolfe photographed the people living in the area. Her first published photograph, *Tennessee Mountain Woman*, appeared in *Vanity Fair* magazine in 1933 and was included in the first exhibition of photography at the Museum of Modern Art in New York in 1937.

From 1933 to 1960 Dahl-Wolfe had her own studio in New York, working as a freelance advertising and fashion photographer. She also worked as a staff fashion photographer for *Harper's Bazaar* (1936–58). During this period Dahl-Wolfe began to produce the pictures that became her trademark. She used art history as a source for her photography, often posing her models in relation to artworks of various styles and periods. She also photographed celebrities, artists, and public figures, including COLETTE, Cecil Beaton, John F. Kennedy, and Paul Robeson.

Dahl-Wolfe received the Art Directors Club of New York Medal in 1939. Her work is housed in several important collections, including the Metropolitan Museum of Art and the Fashion Institute of Technology in New York and the Museum of Contemporary Photography in Chicago.

Damer, Anne Seymour (1748–1828)
British sculptor

The daughter of Field Marshal Henry Seymour Conway and granddaughter of the Duke of Argyll, she showed an early talent for art and literature. During her childhood she became a favorite of the writer Horace Walpole, who remained an enthusiastic admirer of her work throughout his life. She studied sculpture under Giuseppe Ceracchi and John Bacon.

In 1767 she married John Damer, who committed suicide in 1776 after squandering his fortune and falling heavily into debt. Anne subsequently embarked on a career as a professional sculptor, producing busts of many famous people. Her subjects included George III; the politician Charles James Fox, for whom she canvassed in 1780; Napoleon, whose wife JOSÉPHINE was an acquaintance of hers; and the actress Sarah SIDDONS. She also sculpted two stone heads representing the Thames and Isis rivers for the bridge at Henley-on-Thames in Oxfordshire in 1785. Opinions vary as to the quality of her work: Walpole claimed that she "has excelled the moderns in the similitude of her busts," while the painter Farington considered the sculptures "not very good likenesses but they might be known."

After the death of Walpole in 1797 Damer inherited Strawberry Hill, a former cottage that he had rebuilt over a period of 24 years in the style of a Gothic castle. She lived there until 1811, becoming friendly with the writers Mary and Agnes Berry. In her will Damer requested that her working tools and apron, and the ashes of a favourite dog, be placed in her coffin and buried with her.

d'Angeville, Henriette (1795–1871)
French mountaineer

> My heart beat furiously, my breathing was impeded, and deep sighs burst from my breast.
>
> —On first seeing the peak of Mont Blanc

Henriette d'Angeville was one of the first women to climb Mont Blanc. In 1809 a young peasant girl called Maria Paradis was literally dragged to the top by her guides, but in September 1838 Henriette d'Angeville made the ascent through her own efforts. One of her guides remarked, "She goes as well as we do and fears nothing." She had planned the expedition with great care and attention to detail, and her climbing costume combined practicality with eccentricity: under her dress she wore a pair of brightly chequered knickerbockers. On reaching the summit her guides hoisted her up onto their shoulders with the words, "Now, Mademoiselle, you shall go one higher than Mont Blanc." She drank a toast in champagne to the newborn Count de Paris, heir to the French throne, and sent off a carrier pigeon bearing news of her achievement.

During the next 25 years d'Angeville made more than 20 more ascents in the Alps; in 1864 she reached the summit of the Oldenhorn in a crinoline. In the year of her death the British mountaineer Lucy Walker became the first woman to climb the Matterhorn.

Danilova, Alexandra (1904–1997)
Russian ballet dancer and teacher

Danilova was one of the most popular ballerinas of her day. During her 25 years as a teacher at the School of American Ballet in New York (1964–89) she was a source of inspiration to many young dancers.

Alexandra Danilova was born in Peterhof and trained at the Imperial Ballet School in St. Petersburg. She left Russia in 1924 to tour with a small company led by George Balanchine and never returned to her native country. In 1925 she joined Sergei Diaghilev's Ballets Russes company in Paris, where she remained until the death of Diaghilev in 1929, dancing major roles in the new ballets *Le Pas d'acier* and *Apollon Musagète*.

Danilova became prima ballerina with the Ballets Russes de Monte Carlo in 1938. Noted for her interpretation of classical roles, she also gave outstanding performances in the ballets of Léonide Massine, including *Le Beau Danube*, *Gaîeté parisienne*, and *La Boutique fantasque*. In collaboration with Balanchine she choreographed such ballets as *Raymonda* (1946), in which she danced the leading role.

With her own company, Great Moments of Ballet, founded in 1954, Danilova toured North and South America, South Africa, and Japan for three years before retiring in 1957. She spent the rest of her career as a choreographer and teacher, staging ballets for the Metropolitan Opera (1959–61); La Scala, Milan (1961); the New York City Ballet (1974); and the Tokyo Ballet (1981). In 1977 she played an ageing dancer in the film *The Turning Point*.

Danilova was twice married but, in her own words, "sacrificed marriage, children and country to be a ballerina." She received a number of awards, including the Capezio Award (1958), the Dance Magazine Award (1984), and the Kennedy Center Award (1989). Her memoirs were published in 1986.

d'Aragona, Tullia (1508–1556) *Italian poet*

Tullia d'Aragona was born in Rome, possibly the illegitimate daughter of Luigi, Cardinal of Aragon. Little is known about her early life. She moved to Florence and became noted for her salon, a meeting place for some of the most brilliant and accomplished literary figures of the day. She had a succession of famous lovers, including the historian Jacopo Nardi and the poet Girolamo Muziano.

Her published works included the collection of poems, *Rime*, and an essay about love, *Dialogo dell'infinità d'amore* (Dialogue on the Infinity of Love), both of which appeared in 1547. She also wrote a narrative poem, *Meschino altramente detto il Guerrino* (Meschino, otherwise known as Guerrino), which was published in 1560, after her death.

Darling, Grace (Horsley) (1815–1842) *British heroine*

Grace Darling is remembered for her part in rescuing several survivors from a shipwrecked steamer, for which she was awarded a medal for bravery.

Born in Northumberland, she was the daughter of William Darling, the lighthouse keeper on one of the Farne Islands off the northeast coast of England. On September 7, 1838, the steamer *Forfarshire* was wrecked in seas too treacherous to attempt a rescue by the mainland lifeboat. Grace spotted a number of people clinging to the wreck and insisted on going out in a small boat with her father to rescue the survivors. This heroic deed earned her considerable fame and fortune, and several offers of marriage, but she chose to remain on the island. She died of tuberculosis at the age of 26.

Dashkova, Yekaterina Romanovna (1743–1810) *Russian aristocrat and patron of the arts*

A member of the noble Vorontsov family, she was born near St. Petersburg. In 1759 she married Prince Michael Dashkov, who died three years later. Dashkova played a major role in the successful plot to depose Emperor Peter III and put his wife, CATHERINE II, on the Russian throne.

After Catherine came to power in 1762, Dashkova hoped to be given an influential place in the court or government, but her requests were denied. During the next 20 years she travelled widely in Europe, making the acquaintance of Voltaire and Diderot and taking an active interest in the development of the arts. She had her two sons educated in England and lived for a time in Edinburgh. On Dashkova's return to Russia in 1782, Catherine appointed her director of the St. Petersburg Academy of Arts and Sciences. As the first president of the Russian Academy, she planned the academy's dictionary of the Russian language and wrote some of the entries herself.

When Paul I succeeded Catherine in 1796, he exiled Dashkova for the part she had played in deposing his father, Peter III. After Paul died in 1801, she returned to her estate near Moscow to write her memoirs, which were first published in England 30 years after her death.

David, Elizabeth (1913–1992) *British cookery writer*

Elizabeth David's enthusiasm for European food and culture, communicated through her cookery books and magazine columns, made a major impact on the eating habits of people in Britain after World War II.

She was born in Sussex, the daughter of Rupert Sackville Gwynne, a member of Parliament. At the age of 16 she went to live in France, staying with a French family and subsequently studying French literature and history at the Sorbonne. It was during this period that she developed her passion for French food, which was quite different from anything she had ever tasted before. Further travels in Europe and elsewhere introduced her to the culinary delights of the Mediterranean region, Italy, Greece, and Egypt.

On her return to England in 1947, three years after her marriage to Lieutenant-Colonel Ivan David, she found British cooking plain and unappetizing. Although food was still rationed in the early years after World War II, and "exotic" ingredients, such as olive oil and Parmesan cheese, were difficult or impossible to obtain, she taught herself to cook some of her favourite

European dishes and wrote her first book, *Mediterranean Food* (1950). This was followed by such titles as *French Country Cooking* (1951), *Italian Food* (1954), *Summer Cooking* (1955), and *French Provincial Cooking* (1960). David's recipes caught the imagination of the British people as the long years of rationing came to an end, making her books highly successful. She also wrote columns in newspapers and magazines, such as *Vogue*, the *Sunday Times*, and the *Spectator*. In the 1970s she turned her attention to traditional British cookery, publishing *Spices, Salts and Aromatics in the English Kitchen* (1970) and *English Bread and Yeast Cookery* (1977).

David received a number of honours during her lifetime, including the Order of the British Empire (1976), Chevalier du Mérite Agricole of France (1977), and Commander of the Order of the British Empire (1986). In 1984 she published *An Omelette and a Glass of Wine*, a collection of essays and autobiographical writings.

Davies, (Sarah) Emily (1830–1921)
British educationalist and suffragist

> We are told we ought to ask for £30,000 at least...not a large sum, considering that there is but one college of this sort...But considering how few people really wish women to be educated, it is a good deal.
>
> —Letter to Barbara Bodichon, regarding the foundation of Girton College, January 1867

The founder of Girton College, Cambridge, and an ardent suffragist, Emily Davies was nevertheless strongly opposed to the militant tactics of Emmeline PANKHURST and her associates.

Sarah Emily Davies was born in Southampton, the daughter of an Evangelical clergyman. She attended only a local school and therefore did not herself have a very high standard of education. In 1840 she moved with her family to Gateshead, in the north of England.

As a young woman she became interested in women's rights, making friends with a number of activists in this field, including Millicent FAWCETT, Elizabeth Garrett ANDERSON, and Barbara Bodichon. After visiting London, she set up in Gateshead a Northumberland and Durham branch of the Society for the Employment of Women.

After the death of her father in 1861 she moved permanently to London, later joining Dorothea BEALE and Frances BUSS in their campaign to allow women to take university examinations. In 1866 she founded the London Schoolmistresses Association, serving as its secretary until 1888. In 1869 Davies founded a college for women students at Hitchen, halfway between London and Cambridge, to enable students to take Cambridge exams, by arrangement with the examiners. Four years after its rather shaky start with five students it moved to Cambridge, becoming Girton College in 1874. In 1884 the university opened all examinations to women but did not grant them full degrees until after World War II. At the age of 89 Emily Davies made her last public appearance at the golden jubilee celebrations of Girton College.

A difficult and austere woman, Miss Davies was also an ardent suffragist. Having joined the Executive Committee of the London Society for Women's Suffrage in 1890, in 1906 she led a deputation to Parliament to demand the vote for women. She was, however, shocked by the tactics of Emmeline Pankhurst and her followers.

Emily Davies's books include *The Higher Education of Women* (1866) and *Thoughts on Some Questions Relating to Women 1860–1908* (1910).

Davis, Angela (1944–) *American philosopher and political activist*

Angela Yvonne Davis was born in Birmingham, Alabama. She studied at Brandeis University, Massachusetts, and at the Sorbonne in Paris, where her contact with radical Algerian students developed her interest in the civil rights movement. On returning to the United States she became involved with a number of protest groups, including the Student Nonviolent Coordinating Committee and the Black Panthers.

Davis completed her studies under the radical political philosopher Herbert Marcuse at the University of California, Los Angeles, in 1968. In the same year, after the death of Martin Luther King, she joined the Communist Party, becoming known as an active campaigner for the support and release of African-American political prisoners. However, in 1970 a judge was taken hostage and shot by African-American activists using guns registered in Davis's name. She was arrested and charged with conspiracy, kidnapping, and murder but finally acquitted of all charges after a long trial that received international publicity.

Davis combined her political activities with an academic career, teaching at the University of California, Santa Cruz, and San Francisco University. Her many publications include *If They Came in the Morning: Voices of Resistance* (1971) and *Women, Race and Class* (1980).

Davis, Bette (1908–1989) *American actress*

> She would probably have burned as a witch if she had lived two or three hundred years ago.
>
> —E. Arnot Robertson

A leading performer in films for more than 50 years, noted for her clipped speech and larger-than-life manner, Bette Davis was the first woman to receive the Life Achievement Award of the American Film Institute (1977).

Ruth Elizabeth Davis was born in Lowell, Massachusetts, and adopted the name Bette as a young girl. She began her acting career playing small parts in provincial companies and subsequently on Broadway, but her ambition was to work in films. Hired by Universal Studios in 1930, she made her screen debut with Humphrey Bogart in a forgettable film called *Bad Sister* (1931). Her first important picture, *The Man Who Played God* (1932), marked the beginning of a long and stormy association with the Warner Brothers studio. Although she fought against the restrictions of the studio system, Davis did some of her best work for Warner. She became known for her portrayals of such taut but unlikable characters as Mildred in *Of Human Bondage* (1934), a performance

that earned her an Academy Award nomination and made her a star. She went on to win Academy Awards for *Dangerous* (1935) and *Jezebel* (1938).

There followed a number of outstanding films, including *The Private Lives of Elizabeth and Essex* (1939); *The Little Foxes* (1941); *Now, Voyager* (1942); and *All About Eve* (1950), which critics consider her best movie. After a series of less successful performances in the 1950s she switched to character roles and began to appear in psychological thrillers, such as *Whatever Happened to Baby Jane?* (1962). During the next 20 years she frequently appeared in television movies. Her last film for the cinema was *The Whales of August* (1987).

Davis published three autobiographies: *The Lonely Life* (1962), in which she described the struggle of her professional and personal life; *Mother Goddam* (1975); and *This 'N That* (1987). She died in Neuilly-sur-Seine, France.

Davison, Emily (1872–1913) *British suffragette martyr*

> Deeds, not words
>
> —Inscription on Emily Davison's grave

A militant activist in the "Votes for Women" campaign, she is remembered for the manner of her death, after falling under the hoofs of the king's horse at the Epsom Derby.

Emily Wilding Davison was born in Blackheath, London. After studying at the universities of London and Oxford and graduating with a first-class honours degree in English language and literature, she worked as a teacher. Her involvement with the women's suffrage movement began in 1906, when she joined the Women's Social and Political Union (WSPU), founded three years earlier by Emmeline and Christabel PANKHURST. Davison soon became known as one of the WSPU's most militant campaigners and was frequently imprisoned for her activities, which included throwing stones in Manchester (1909), breaking a window of the House of Commons (1910), setting fire to Westminster pillar boxes (1911), and attacking a Baptist minister, whom she had mistaken for Lloyd George, at Aberdeen (1912). During her spells in prison Davison continued to register her grievances, often by going on hunger strike. Prevented by force-feeding from becoming a martyr to her cause, she threw herself downstairs in a suicide attempt at Holloway jail in 1911.

In June 1913 Davison made her last and most highly publicized protest, at Epsom racecourse during the Derby. Draped in a WSPU banner, she rushed onto the track and tried to seize the reins of King George V's horse as it thundered past. She was trampled underfoot and rushed to hospital, where she died of her injuries four days later. It is not clear whether or not she intended her death. At the funeral, her family and friends were joined by crowds of supporters from women's suffrage groups all over the country, as well as representatives of the major trade unions and other organizations.

Day, Doris (1924–) *American film actress*

Day's sunny, vivacious personality and healthy "girl-next-door" image made her popular with audiences everywhere.

Doris Day was born Doris von Kappelhoff in Cincinnati, Ohio. She began her career as a singer on local radio, moving on to sing with big bands on national broadcasts such as *Saturday Night Hit Parade* in the 1940s. Her first marriage, to Al Jorden in 1941, ended in divorce two years later. A second unhappy marriage, to George Weilder, lasted just three years, from 1946 to 1949.

In 1948 Day made her film debut in the musical *Romance on the High Seas*, playing a role that had been originally intended for Judy GARLAND. This was followed by a series of other musicals, including *April in Paris* (1952), *Calamity Jane* (1954) and *The Pajama Game* (1957). Day was soon able to demand large fees for her work. She partnered Rock Hudson and other screen idols in romantic comedies, such as *Pillow Talk* (1959), *Lover Come Back* (1961), *Send Me No Flowers* (1964), and *Do Not Disturb* (1964).

In 1968 she made her last film, *With Six You Get Egg Roll*, and transferred her success to the small screen with *The Doris Day Show* (1968–73) and other television appearances.

Day's third husband, producer Marty Melcher, became her business manager in the 1950s. After his death in 1968 she found out that he had lost most of her money by a combination of fraud and incompetence; the shock of this discovery caused her to have a nervous breakdown. Other details of her personal life, which was much less carefree than that of the characters she portrayed, were revealed in her autobiography, *Doris Day: Her Own Story* (1976).

Deborah (1209–1169 BC) *Old Testament prophetess and leader of Israel*

Deborah was a member of the Israelite tribe of Ephraim. She was one of the "judges," men and women chosen by God to lead the Israelites and settle their disputes. Her story is told in chapters 4 and 5 of the Old Testament book of Judges. The "Song of Deborah" in chapter 5, possibly written by Deborah herself, is one of the oldest poems in the Bible.

At that time the Israelites were threatened by the Canaanites under the command of Sisera. Deborah sent for Barak, son of Abinoam, and told him to lead an army of 10,000 Israelites to Mount Tabor, prophesying the defeat of Sisera and the Canaanites. Barak was not convinced and insisted that she go with him, although this would mean handing over the honour of the victory to a woman. Informed of the Israelites' movements, Sisera gathered his soldiers and chariots in the nearby valley of the Kishon River, thinking that they would have plenty of space to manoeuvre there. However, a violent thunderstorm swelled the river, sweeping away Sisera's army and throwing his battle plans into confusion. The Israelites won an easy victory, and Sisera fled. He took refuge with Heber the Kenite, who was not at war with the Canaanites, but was killed by JAEL, Heber's wife.

Decker, Mary (1958–) *American athlete*

Decker broke a series of world records for middle-distance running. Her first marriage, to U.S. marathon runner Ron Tabb, ended in divorce; since her second marriage, to British discus thrower Richard Slaney in 1985, she has been known as Mary Decker Slaney.

Mary Teresa Decker was born in Bunnvale, near Flemington, New Jersey, and grew up in Garden Grove, California. At the age of 11 she entered and won her first race, a cross-country run sponsored by the local parks department. Two years later she ran a mile in 4 minutes 55 seconds, and at the age of 14 she set the world outdoor record at 1,000 metres. This was followed in 1974 by indoor records at 880 and 1,000 yards. Despite frequent leg injuries and a number of operations, she became the dominant female runner, noted for her loping stride and powerful kick.

Between 1980 and 1986 Decker held numerous U.S. and world records in indoor and outdoor events ranging from 800 metres to 2 miles. However, her dreams of Olympic success were never fulfilled. The U.S. boycott of the 1980 Olympics in Moscow prevented her from competing that year, and in the 1984 Olympics she collided with Zola BUDD and failed to complete the 3,000-metre run.

Deland, Margaret Wade (1857–1945) *American novelist*

Born Margaretta Wade Campbell in Allegheny, Pennsylvania, she later recreated her home town as "Old Chester" in a series of realistic novels and short stories.

Deland's first work was *The Old Garden* (1886), a book of poems. She began the "Old Chester" series with her first novel, *John Ward, Preacher* (1888), which shocked her contemporaries by its unconventional views of religion and social questions. Subsequent books in the series, such as *Old Chester Tales* (1899) and *Around Old Chester* (1924), brought her great popularity for their nostalgic view of small-town life. Her other works include *The Iron Woman* (1911), *The Rising Tide* (1916), and the autobiography

If This Be I (As I Suppose It Be) (1935). She died in Boston.

Delaney, Shelagh (1939–   ) *British playwright*

> Women never have young minds. They are born three thousand years old.
> —*A Taste of Honey* (1958)

Born in Salford, Lancashire, Delaney left school at the age of 16 and was only 18 years old when her first and most famous play, *A Taste of Honey*, had its premiere in London in 1958. It was produced in New York in 1960 and received the New York Drama Critics' award for the best foreign play of the season; in 1961 it was made into a film. A realistic and sympathetic portrayal of the life of the working class in industrial northern England, it told the story of a white girl made pregnant by her black boyfriend. Critics labelled Delaney an "Angry Young Woman," linking her with the rebellious "Angry Young Men" of the late 1950s.

Delaney's subsequent plays, such as *The Lion in Love* (1960), were less successful, and much of her best work was written for the cinema. She wrote the screenplays for the films *Charlie Bubbles* (1968), starring Albert Finney, and *Dance With a Stranger* (1985), a film about Ruth Ellis, the last woman to be executed in England.

Delaunay, Sonia (1885–1979) *Ukraine-born French artist*

In collaboration with her second husband, Robert Delaunay, Sonia Delaunay developed the abstract technique known as orphism. She was also noted for her textile designs.

The daughter of a factory owner, Sonia Stern was born in Ukraine and raised by her uncle in St. Petersburg. Abandoning an early ambition to be a mathematician, she studied art in Karlsruhe (1903–04), and in Paris (1905), where she made the acquaintance of Picasso and Braque. A brief marriage of convenience with the art critic Wilhelm Uhde ended in 1910, when she married Robert Delaunay. She worked closely with her husband for some 30 years on abstract paintings, designs for Diaghilev's Ballets

Russes company, murals for the Paris Exposition of 1937, and a variety of other projects. She also decorated pottery, illustrated books, and designed dresses. Her textile designs of the 1920s enjoyed a revival in the 1970s.

After her husband's death in 1941 Delaunay worked independently. A solo exhibition of her paintings and designs in 1953 led to worldwide interest in her art, and in 1964 she became the first living female artist to have her works exhibited at the Louvre.

Deledda, Grazia (1871–1936) *Italian novelist*

Widely regarded as Italy's greatest woman novelist, Deledda wrote moving and dramatic works about life in her native Sardinia, for which she received the Nobel Prize for literature in 1926.

Grazia Deledda was born in Nuoro, Sardinia. Largely self-educated, she began writing short stories and articles for Sardinian and Roman journals before she was 18. After her marriage in 1897 she moved to Rome but continued to write about Sardinia and the simple, primitive, yet intense life of its peasants. Among her most famous early works are *Il vecchio della montagna* (1900; The Old Man of the Mountain), *Elias Portolu* (1903), and *Cenere* (1904), which was published in English as *Ashes* (1910).

Despite their regional setting, Deledda's novels appeal to readers all over the world owing to the author's keen psychological insight and sensitive characterizations, especially of women. In her later novels, including *La madre* (1920), published in English as *The Mother* (1928), she placed less emphasis on local detail and more on the religious and emotional elements that contribute to the dramatic effect of her stories. The autobiographical novel *Cosima* (1937) was published after her death.

de los Angeles, Victoria (1923–) *Spanish singer*

Renowned as an operatic soprano, de los Angeles later became a leading concert singer, noted especially for her interpretations of Spanish songs.

She was born Victoria Gómez Cima, into a musical family in Barcelona. A group of wealthy amateur musicians paid for her education at Barcelona's Conservatorio de Liceo, sparing her the necessity of touring with popular operetta companies, as most Spanish singers had to.

She made her operatic debut in Barcelona in 1945. Her American debut came five years later at New York's Carnegie Hall, and in 1951 she sang the role of Marguerite in Gounod's *Faust* at the Metropolitan Opera. Known for her musical and dramatic versatility, she performed at opera houses all over the world in a wide range of roles, including Desdemona in Verdi's *Otello*, Mélisande in Debussy's *Pélleas et Mélisande*, Mimi in Puccini's *La Bohème*, and the title role in Massenet's *Manon*. By 1970 she had more or less retired from the operatic stage, but she continued to make recordings and give recitals of Spanish songs.

Demessieux, Jeanne-Marie-Madeleine (1921–1968) *French organist and composer*

Born in Montpellier, southern France, Demessieux showed an early talent for music, becoming a church organist at the age of 12. She went on to win a number of music prizes at the Paris Conservatory (1937–40), where she studied under the organist Marcel Dupré. After her first public recital in 1946 at the Salle Pleyel, Paris, she gave concerts all over Europe and the United States; at a recital in London in 1947 she improvised an organ symphony in four movements. In 1952 she was appointed organ professor at the Liège Conservatory.

Demessieux was the first female guest organist at both Westminster Cathedral and Westminster Abbey; in 1967 she took part in the inauguration ceremony at Liverpool's Metropolitan Cathedral. Her compositions, most of which were written for the organ, include *Etudes* (1946), *Sept Méditations sur le Saint Esprit* (1947; Seven Meditations on the Holy Spirit), *Te Deum* (1965), and *Répons pour le temps de Pâques* (1968; Responses for Eastertide).

De Mille, Agnes (1909–1993) *American choreographer*

De Mille is best remembered for her work in musical comedy, notably *Oklahoma!* (1943), *Carousel* (1945), *Brigadoon* (1947), *Gentlemen Prefer Blondes* (1949), and *Paint Your Wagon* (1951). In all of these musicals she created dance routines that played an important part in the development of the characters and the plot rather than merely providing an entertaining interlude to the main action.

Agnes George De Mille was born in New York City, the daughter of playwright William Churchill De Mille and niece of the film director Cecil B. De Mille. At an early age she made up her mind to become a dancer, beginning her ballet training. However, she stopped this training for a time to concentrate on her academic studies, enabling her to graduate in English from the University of California at Los Angeles. After her first solo performance as a dancer in 1928 she spent the next 12 years touring the United States and Europe, dancing with the Ballet Rambert in London in the premiere of Anthony Tudor's *Dark Elegies* (1937).

From the 1940s De Mille devoted most of her time to choreography, working with the Ballet Theater (later the American Ballet Theater) in New York. She was invited to Broadway to choreograph *Oklahoma!*, which was a great success. A string of other hit musicals followed, but De Mille did not neglect her work with the Ballet Theater. In 1948 she created *Fall River Legend*, a ballet based on the true story of the accused murderess Lizzie BORDEN. Her last ballet, *The Other*, was staged in 1992, the year before her death.

De Mille received numerous awards for her work, including two Tony Awards in 1947 and 1982, the Kennedy Center Career Achievement Award (1980), and the National Medal of the Arts (1986). Noted for her wit and eloquence, she was frequently invited to give lectures, and she also wrote a number of books, such as *The Book of Dance* (1963) and *American Dances* (1980).

Dench, Dame Judi (1934–) *British actress*

Well known to British theatre audiences as a stage actress of great versatility, Judi Dench has also appeared frequently on television in roles that range from the classics to situation comedy.

Judith Olivia Dench was born in York, where her father was a doctor. Encouraged by her brother, the actor Jeffrey Dench, she studied acting at the Central School of Speech Training and Dramatic Art. She followed her first professional job as the Virgin Mary in *A Mystery Cycle* with the role of Ophelia for the Old Vic Company in 1957. Her performance was highly praised by the critics, and she became a member of the Old Vic Company; by the time she was 26 she had played leading roles in numerous other Shakespearean productions, including *Measure for Measure*, *A Midsummer Night's Dream*, *Twelfth Night*, *Henry V*, *Romeo and Juliet*, and *The Merry Wives of Windsor*. She subsequently joined the Royal Shakespeare Company, playing such roles as Anya in *The Cherry Orchard*, Isabella in *Measure for Measure*, and Titania in *A Midsummer Night's Dream*.

Throughout the 1960s Dench delighted critics and audiences alike in a wide range of classical and contemporary roles, from one of Chekhov's *Three Sisters* to the leading part of Sally Bowles in the London production of the Broadway musical *Cabaret*. In 1970 she met the actor Michael Williams, whom she married the following year. In the early 1980s they costarred in the television sitcom *A Fine Romance*.

Although she has worked with many other companies, Dench regards the Royal Shakespeare Company as her home base: "It's a family feeling where you can let your defences down." She played two of her favourite roles there in the late 1970s: Beatrice in Shakespeare's *Much Ado About Nothing*, and Juno in Sean O'Casey's *Juno and the Paycock*. For the latter performance she was honoured with a Best Actress award from the Variety Club. Andrew Lloyd Webber cast Dench as Grizabella, the Glamour Cat, in the original London production of his long-running musical *Cats* (1981), but she broke her ankle just before the opening night and was unable to perform. In 1997 she gave a highly praised performance as the ageing actress in David Hare's *Amy's View*.

Dench has appeared in only a handful of films, mostly in the 1980s and 1990s; these include *A Room with a View* (1985), *Henry V* (1989), and *Mrs Brown* (1997), in which she starred as Queen VICTORIA and earned an Oscar nomination as Best Actress. Since 1995 she has played the intelligence chief 'M' in the James Bond series of films. She has received numerous awards during the course of her career; in 1970 she was honoured with the Order of the British Empire, and in 1988 she was created Dame of the British Empire.

Deneuve, Catherine (1943–)
French actress

Once called "the most beautiful woman in the world" by *Look* magazine, Catherine Deneuve is well known in Europe not only as a sex symbol of the 1960s and 1970s but also as a serious actress.

She was born Catherine Dorléac in Paris; Deneuve was her mother's maiden name. Although both her parents were actors, she rarely went to the theatre as a child and did not plan on an acting career, intending instead to become an interior designer.

In 1960, having already made two films at the age of 13, she appeared with her sister Françoise Dorléac in the film *Les Portes Claquent (The Doors Slam)*. She was seen by French director Roger Vadim, famous for discovering Brigitte BARDOT, and he cast her in *Le Vice et la virtu* in 1961. Her success in this, her first major role, led to her playing the heroine in *The Umbrellas of Cherbourg* (1963). Deneuve won the Golden Palm award at the Cannes Film Festival for her performance and came to the attention of international audiences. At around the same time she gave birth to Vadim's child; she subsequently married and divorced the British photographer David Bailey and had a second child with the Italian actor Marcello Mastroianni in 1972.

Deneuve's next important film role was in a very different type of picture, Roman Polanski's *Repulsion* (1965), in which she played a murderous woman driven insane by a fear of intimacy. In 1967 she teamed up with her sister for the last time in *The Young Girls of Rochefort*. Françoise Dorléac died in a road accident soon after finishing the film. In the same year Deneuve played what is probably her best-known film role, in Luis Buñuel's *Belle de Jour*. For her extraordinary performance as a frustrated housewife, she won the Golden Lion award at the Venice Film Festival.

By 1980 Deneuve had matured as an actress and was acclaimed worldwide, having appeared in a number of American films, such as *Mayerling* (1968) and *Hustle* (1975). It was then that François Truffaut cast her in *The Last Métro* as an actress who becomes romantically involved with her leading man while she is hiding her Jewish husband from the Nazis. During the 1980s Deneuve continued to grow as an actress, while losing none of her beauty. In 1985 she was selected by the French Ministry of Culture to replace Brigitte Bardot as the new model for Marianne, a symbol of the French republic. In 1992 she was nominated for an Oscar in the award-winning *Indochine*.

Deng Yingchao (1904–1992) *Chinese politician*

Deng Yingchao was born in Guangshan county, Henan, China. As a student in 1919 she was involved in the May 4 movement, a protest against the increased Japanese influence and control in China following World War I. In the same year she joined the Awakening Society, a student movement led by Zhou Enlai, who was later to become her husband and China's premier.

Deng joined the Communist Party in 1924 and married Zhou in 1925. For several years they lived and worked underground in Shanghai and elsewhere, constantly fleeing from the Nationalists, whose mission was to stamp out the Communist movement. In 1934 they took part in the Long March, a 6,000-mile journey across China made by 100,000 supporters of Mao Zedong, of whom only 40–50 were women. Deng was one of the 8,000 Communists who survived the march, although she contracted tuberculosis along the way.

The Communists finally came to power in 1949, and Zhou was made prime minister, a post he held until his death in 1976. Deng was already a member of the Communist Party Central Committee, well loved by the nation; after Zhou died, she moved into the political spotlight. She was given a place on the Communist Party's Political Bureau in 1978, and from 1983 to 1988 she was head of the Chinese People's Political Consultative Conference. Ever loyal to the ideals of communism, she took a hard line against the prodemocracy demonstrations in Tiananmen Square, Beijing, in 1989. Throughout her long life Deng was also active in the women's movement, from her early involvement in the campaign against the binding of young girls' feet to her later work in the promotion of women's rights in general.

Desai, Anita (1937–) *Indian writer*
Desai's novels and short stories are vivid portrayals of life in India, often centring on the conflicts faced by middle-class women in traditional Indian society. Her skill in conjuring up the atmosphere and landscape of the country has earned her great critical acclaim and worldwide popularity.

Anita Mazumdar was born in Mussoorie, Uttar Pradesh. Her father was Bengali and her mother was German. She graduated from Delhi University in 1957 and married Ashvin Desai, a businessman, the following year. While their children were young, she began to write, producing such novels as *The Peacock* (1963) and *Voices in the City* (1968). *Fire on the Mountain* (1977) was an international success, while both *Clear Light of Day* (1980) and *In Custody* (1984) were nominated for the prestigious Booker Prize.

Desai's short stories include the collection *Games at Twilight* (1978), about the tensions of family life. She has also written children's books, notably *The Village by the Sea* (1982), set in a small fishing village near Bombay, which won the Guardian Prize for Children's Fiction. Among her more recent works are *Baumgartner's Bombay* (1988) and *Journey to Ithaca* (1995).

Desbordes-Valmore,   Marceline (1786–1859) *French poet*
Desbordes-Valmore's poetry, admired by such writers as Sainte-Beuve, Baudelaire, and Dumas *père*, is marked by sincerity and simplicity. Its musical quality greatly influenced Paul Verlaine, who acknowledged this in his biographical studies of poets, *Poètes maudits*.

Marceline Félicité Josèphe Desbordes was born in Douai. She had an unhappy, impoverished childhood and attempted to earn a living in the theatre, but ill health forced her to abandon the stage and concentrate on writing. Having married Valmore, an undistinguished actor, in 1817, she had to do hack work for Paris publishers to support him and their three children. Her volumes of verse include *Elégies et romances* (1819; Elegies and Love Songs), *Les pleurs* (1833; The Tears), *Pauvres fleurs* (1839; Poor Flowers), and *Bouquets et prières* (1843; Bouquets and Prayers). She also wrote a short novel, *Domenica*, published after her death.

Deshoulières,   Antoinette (1638–1694) *French poet and literary hostess*
Antoinette du Ligier de La Garde was born in Paris. In 1651 she married Seigneur Deshoulières, who was in the service of the Prince of Condé during the war of the Fronde. She followed her husband to Rocroi, near Brussels, and was rescued by him after she had been imprisoned by Spanish authorities. They returned to Paris in 1655 and separated four years later.

Influenced by the poetry and philosophy of the French scientist and philosopher Pierre Gassendi, she soon became a celebrated writer, sometimes called the "tenth Muse." She was the hostess of a literary salon that became a meeting place for all the famous literary figures of the period. Voltaire praised her poetry, which included idylls, odes, elegies, and madrigals, but her collected works were not published until after her death. She died in poverty in Paris.

Désirée (1777–1860) *Wife of King Charles XIV of Sweden*

Désirée Clary was born in Marseille, France, the daughter of François Clary, a wealthy merchant. She met Napoleon Bonaparte and became his fiancée after her sister Julie married Napoleon's brother Joseph in 1794. Napoleon was then a young and ambitious army officer, but Désirée had second thoughts about the marriage, and her father strongly opposed it, maintaining that "One Bonaparte in the family is enough."

Napoleon's attention subsequently turned to JOSÉPHINE de Beauharnais, whom he married in 1796, but he retained his interest in Désirée and tried to arrange an advantageous marriage for her. In 1798 she married Jean Bernadotte, one of France's leading generals, who received further promotions through his wife's connections with Napoleon.

In 1810 Bernadotte was elected crown prince of Sweden, with Napoleon's support, taking the throne as King Charles XIV in 1818. Désirée became his queen but did not join him in Sweden until 1823 and played only a minor role in Swedish affairs. Her son, whose godfather was Napoleon, became King Oscar I of Sweden in 1844. Désirée died in Stockholm.

Despard, Charlotte (1844–1939) *British social reformer*

Despard was an active campaigner on a number of social and political issues, notably women's suffrage and the Irish Republican movement. One of her last public appearances was at an anti-Nazi demonstration in Hyde Park, at the age of 91.

She was born Charlotte French, the daughter of a naval commander and the eldest sister of John French, who was to become the first Earl of Ypres and Lord Lieutenant of Ireland. As children they were devoted to each other, particularly after the early death of their father, but the divergence of their political opinions was to cause a rift between them in later life. In 1862 Charlotte made her home in London, and at the age of 26 she married Maximilian Despard. During their 20 years of childless marriage, Charlotte travelled with her husband and wrote novels, including *Chaste as Ice, Pure as Snow* (1874). Widowed in 1890, she dedicated herself to work with the poor in Nine Elms, London, where she opened a child welfare centre, one of the first in the country, and ran a working men's club.

During the following years Despard gave voice to her long-held feelings of revolt against the social order through her involvement with the Independent Labour Party and the PANKHURSTS' Women's Social and Political Union. She left the latter organization in 1907 to found the women's Freedom League, which campaigned not only for female suffrage but also on a broader range of left-wing issues. For Despard and her followers, equality of the sexes was just the first step on the road to socialist democracy.

Despard's main concern in her later years was Irish Home Rule, and she settled in Dublin after World War I. Her support for the rebel group Sinn Féin was an embarrassment to her brother during his term of office as Lord Lieutenant of Ireland (1918–21). After travelling in Soviet Russia in 1930, she returned to Ireland to found the Irish Workers' College in Dublin, with the aim of educating workers in the politics of socialism. She died bankrupt, having poured all her personal wealth into her cherished causes.

d'Este, Isabella (1474–1539) *Italian patron of the arts*

Isabella d'Este was born into a noble family, a powerful dynasty of northern Italy. The daughter of Ercole I d'Este, Duke of Ferrara, Isabella received a thorough education from private tutors in philosophy, languages, literature, and music. At the age of 16 she married the soldier and scholar Francesco II Gonzaga, Marquis of Mantua, and their court became a centre of Renaissance arts, culture, and scholarship.

Isabella's preference was for the fine arts, particularly painting; she had her portrait painted by Titian and Leonardo da Vinci, whom she counted among her personal friends. Baldassare Castiglione and Ludovico Ariosto were among the literary figures who benefited from her support and patronage. She was also fond of music, having a taste for lavish and flamboyant entertainments. During the Renaissance it became fashionable to have dwarfs at court; Isabella had part of her palace designed for them, remembering two of her favourites in her will.

While her husband was away on military campaigns, Isabella used her diplomatic skills and family connections to protect the interests of Mantua, preserving its independence. After her husband's death in 1519 she effectively ruled the city as adviser to her son, Federico II Gonzaga, who later became Duke of Mantua.

Destinn, Emmy (1878–1930) *Czech opera singer*

Emmy Destinn was noted for the range and control of her rich soprano voice. Born Ema Kittlová in Prague, she studied singing under Marie Loewe-Destinn, whose name she adopted. Destinn made her debut as Santuzza in Mascagni's *Cavalleria rusticana* in Berlin in 1898, and she remained associated with the Royal Opera House there for ten years. She also sang in London, where her performance in the role of Cio-Cio San in Puccini's *Madame Butterfly* was a great success in 1905.

Praised for her acting skill, as well as for the beauty of her voice, Destinn was chosen by Richard Strauss to play the title role in his *Salome* at its premiere in Berlin in 1906 and again in Paris in 1907. Following her New York debut in *Aïda* in 1908, Destinn sang for eight years with the Metropolitan Opera. In 1910 she played the role of Minnie in the premiere of Puccini's *Girl of the Golden West*. She retired in 1921 and died at Ceské Budějovice, Czechoslovakia.

de Valois, Dame Ninette (1898–   ) *Irish-born British choreographer and dancer*

As founder of the Royal Ballet, de Valois was a leader in the renewal of British ballet in the 20th century. She was created DBE in 1951.

Ninette de Valois was born Edris Stannus at Blessington, County Wicklow, Ireland. After training with teachers such as Enrico Cecchetti and making her debut in London, she became a soloist in Diaghilev's Ballets Russes company in 1923. There she danced lead roles in such ballets as Nijinksy's *L'Après-midi d'un faune* (1924), and Massine's *Le Tricorne* (1925). She left the company in 1925 to found, in London, the Academy of Choreographic Art, where students performed her works, as well as other ballets and dances. When theatre director Lilian BAYLIS reopened the Sadler's Wells Theatre in London in 1931, she invited de Valois to organize a ballet company there. This company became the Sadler's Wells Ballet, and in 1946 it moved to Covent Garden as the Royal Ballet. In 1931 de Valois also founded the Sadler's Wells Ballet School, which later became the Royal Ballet School.

De Valois's choreographed ballets, now rarely performed, were the backbone of the early Sadler's Wells repertoire. They include *Job* (1931), *The Rake's Progress* (1935), *Checkmate* (1937), and *The Prospect Before Us* (1940). She also choreographed for opera and commercial theatre, including Dublin's Abbey Theatre and the Festival Theatre in Cambridge. Her work was not confined to Britain and Ireland: she founded the Turkish School of Ballet in Ankara in 1948 and the Turkish State Ballet in 1956 and also helped ballet companies in Canada and Iran. In the later part of her career she returned to the Royal Ballet School to teach.

De Valois, who was named a Chevalier of the Legion of Honour in France in 1950, received many other honours, including the Albert Medal of the Royal Society of Arts (1964), the Erasmus Prize (1974), the Critics' Circle Award (1989), and the Order of Merit

(1992). In 1993 the Royal Festival Hall held a tribute to de Valois in honour of her 95th birthday. She wrote a number of books, such as *Invitation to the Ballet* (1937), *Come Dance with Me* (1957), and *Step by Step* (1977).

Devers, Gail (1966–) *American athlete*

Devers achieved fame by winning two gold medals in the 1992 Olympic Games at Barcelona, less than 18 months after treatment for a thyroid condition had left her feet so swollen and bleeding that she could barely walk

Yolanda Gail Devers was born in Seattle, Washington. She began running at high school; in 1984 she came second in the 100 metres in the national junior championships. In 1985 she moved on to the University of California at Los Angeles, competing in the 100-metre and 200-metre sprints and the 100-metre hurdles at the National Collegiate Athletic Association (NCAA) championships. Three years later, after winning the 100-metre sprint at the NCAA championships, she focused her attention on training for the 100-metre hurdles at the Olympic Games. She set a U.S. record of 12.61 seconds for that event in May 1988, going on to take second place in the Olympic trials.

It was around this time that Devers began to suffer from a variety of symptoms, including severe headaches, fainting, breathing difficulty, and muscle injury. She was eventually diagnosed as suffering from Graves's disease, a condition in which the thyroid gland becomes enlarged and can become cancerous. Since the normal treatment for this disease involves a type of drug that Olympic athletes are not allowed to take, Devers opted instead for radiation treatment. This made her feet swell and bleed; by March 1991 it seemed likely that she would have to have both feet amputated. However, her condition began to improve when the dosage of radiation was reduced. Later that year Devers was not only competing again, but winning: she came first in the 100-metre hurdles in the Athletics Con-

gress Championship and second in the World Championships at Tokyo in August 1991.

In 1992 Devers announced, "There is no hurdle too high I can't conquer." She went on to win Olympic golds at Barcelona in the 100-metre dash and the sprint relay; she would have taken a third gold medal in the 100-metre hurdles if she had not tripped at the last hurdle.

Devi, Kanan (1916–1992) *Indian film actress, director, and producer*

As well as being an actress of great charm and skill, Devi had a beautiful singing voice, which made her known as "the nightingale of Indian cinema." Many of the songs she made famous in her films of the 1940s and 1950s are still popular in India. For some, however, her most important achievement was establishing the respectability of acting as a profession for Indian women.

Kananbala Devi was born into a poor family in Bengal. She began her career as a film actress at the age of ten in the silent movie *Joydeb* (1926; *Hail to the Gods*). In 1936, having established her reputation in talking pictures, she joined the New Theatres studio in Calcutta. Her success in such films as *Vidyapati* (*The Learned Man*), *Mukt* (*Liberation*), *Lagan* (*Devotion*), and *Street Singer* brought her offers from Bombay, the centre of India's cinema industry, but she turned them down.

Instead, she retired from acting in the 1950s and set up her own production company, Srimati, or Lady Pictures. The film *Ananya* (*Injustice*) was the first of 12 box-office successes directed by Devi with the assistance of her husband, who had given up his naval career to join Srimati. His naval training was later put to good use, enabling him to defuse the bombs thrown into the garden of the couple's house during an armed uprising in Bengal in the 1970s.

Devi withdrew from the cinema industry in the late 1960s, disillusioned by the way it had changed: actors had begun to behave like spoilt children, and technological wizardry had become more important than acting ability. In 1968 she was awarded the Padma Shree, one of the highest honours an Indian civilian can receive. This was followed in 1976 by the Dadasaheb Phalke Prize for her contribution to Indian cinema over four decades. Devi never forgot the poverty of her early childhood, devoting the later years of her life to charitable work.

Diana, Princess of Wales (1961–1997) *Former wife of Charles, Prince of Wales*

Diana Frances Spencer was born in Sandringham, Norfolk, the daughter of the 8th Earl Spencer. She was educated in England and at a finishing school in Switzerland. In 1979 she began working at the Young England Kindergarten School in Pimlico, London. During this time she renewed her acquaintance with Prince Charles, and soon became the focus of media attention as a possible future queen. The couple announced their engagement on February 24, 1981, marrying five months later, on July 29. The following year Diana gave birth to their first son, Prince William.

The marriage of Charles and Diana was already under strain when their second son, Prince Henry, was born in 1984. For a while the couple maintained a public image of unity, but it soon became apparent that all was not well. The pressure of being constantly in the media spotlight (Diana was described as the most photographed woman in the world), combined with her unhappy domestic life, caused Diana to develop the eating disorder bulimia nervosa. These problems, aggravated by her husband's continuing relationship with his former friend Camilla Parker-Bowles, were revealed in Andrew Morton's book *Diana: Her True Story* (1992). The sensation that followed the publication of this book, and its serialization in a national newspaper, led to an announcement that the couple would separate. In a television interview in 1995, which attracted worldwide audiences, Diana admitted her own adultery with an army officer and complained of her treatment by the royal family. The interview received a mixed reception; while some observers felt that Diana had been unfairly treated, others thought that she was seriously disturbed. The marriage was finally dissolved in 1996.

During and after her marriage Diana strove to develop a caring image, particularly in her work with children and the sick. She won the hearts of people throughout the world, particularly for her concern for the care of AIDS victims and leprosy sufferers, making a point of showing that she was not afraid to make physical contact with people suffering from these diseases. Diana also served as patron of numerous charities.

In 1997 she focused public attention on the dangers of landmines during visits to Angola and Bosnia. Her courageous efforts to publicize the deaths and loss of limbs caused by undefused landmines was criticized by some members of the Conservative government as an intrusion into politics but she responded that her interest was purely humanitarian.

On August 31, 1997, Diana died following a car crash in Paris, with Dodi Fayed, her constant companion of recent months. This untimely death shocked the world and gave rise to unprecedented scenes of public mourning in Britain. Her funeral at Westminster Abbey was watched by over a million people in London and an estimated 2.5 billion on worldwide television.

Diane de France (1538–1619) *French noblewoman*

She was the illegitimate daughter of Henry II of France by a Piedmontese woman, Filippa Duci. Legitimated in 1547, Diane was married in 1553 to Orazio Farnese, son of the Duke of Parma. Farnese was killed the same year at the Battle of Hesdin, and in 1559 Diane was married to Marshal François de Montmorency.

During the French Wars of Religion (1562–98) François was a leader of the Politiques, a group that tried to find a middle course between the Catholic and Protestant parties. After her husband's death in 1579 Diane continued to work for the same goal and played a significant role in reconciling Henry III with the future Henry IV, a Protestant. A cultured and intelligent woman, she was an influential figure at the French court during the reigns of both kings. In 1582 Henry III made her Duchesse d'Angoulême. After his assassination, she had the bodies of Henry III and his mother, CATHERINE DE' MÉDICIS, brought to St. Denis for burial. She died in Paris.

Diane de Poitiers (1499–1566)
French noblewoman

A woman of legendary beauty, Diane de Poitiers was the mistress of Henry II of France and had considerable influence at his court. She was brought up in the court of ANNE OF FRANCE (also known as Anne of Beaujeu), Louis XI's daughter. Diane's marriage in 1515 to Louis de Brézé, grand seneschal of Normandy, brought her within influential circles and helped save her father when he was accused of treason against Francis I .

Soon after her husband's death in 1531, Diane became the mistress of the future Henry II, who was 20 years younger than her. During Henry's reign (1547–59) she allied herself, through the marriages of her daughter and granddaughter, with the two major factions at court, the Guise and the Montmorency families. She was made Duchess de Valentinois and played an important part in persuading Henry to accept the Treaty of Cateau-Cambrésis (1559), which ended the long war between France and Spain. With the wealth that she accumulated from the royal treasury she had the châteaus of Chenonceaux and Anet rebuilt.

After Henry's death in 1559 Diane's influence with the major factions protected her position at court. Henry's widow, CATHERINE DE' MÉDICIS, who had lived in obscurity throughout her husband's reign, forced Diane to give up the château of Chenonceaux, but she was allowed to retire to Anet, where she lived until her death.

Dick, Gladys Henry (1881–1963)
American physician

She worked in collaboration with her husband, George Dick, and together they made important discoveries regarding the cause of scarlet fever.

Gladys Rowena Henry was born in Pawnee City, Nebraska. Despite her parents' opposition, she studied medicine at Johns Hopkins University and received her MD in 1907. She met the American physician George Frederick Dick, whom she married in 1914, at the University of Chicago. For the rest of her career she worked with him at the McCormick Institute of Infectious Diseases in Chicago.

In 1923 George and Gladys Dick inoculated volunteers with bacteria taken from the blood of a scarlet fever victim and produced the disease in some of the volunteers, demonstrating that such bacteria cause scarlet fever. They also developed the Dick test, a skin test that shows whether or not a person is susceptible to scarlet fever.

Gladys Dick retired in 1953 and died in Menlo Park, California, in 1963. Her husband died four years later.

Dickens, Monica (1915–1992) *British novelist*

Much of her writing is semiautobiographical, drawing on her varied experience of the world of work and of life in general. Her "official" autobiography, *An Open Book*, was published in 1978.

Born in London, Monica Enid Dickens was the great-granddaughter of the novelist Charles Dickens. A rebellious child, she was expelled from St. Paul's Girls' School, allegedly for throwing her school uniform into the River Thames because it did not flatter her plump figure. After being presented at court as a debutante, she went "below stairs" to work as a cook and maid in private households of the upper middle classes. Her experiences at this time provided material for her first novel, *One Pair of Hands* (1939), which became a bestseller. It was followed by *One Pair of Feet* (1942), based on her wartime training as a nurse, and the hospital love story *Thursday Afternoon* (1942). After World War II she took a job as junior reporter at the office of a local newspaper, graphically re-created in her novel *My Turn to Make the Tea* (1951).

After marrying Roy Stratton, an American naval commander, Dickens went to live in Massachusetts, where she continued to write novels, stories, and a regular column for the magazine *Woman's Own*. She also gave lectures, about herself and her famous great-grandfather. Her writing became more serious in tone with *Kate and Emma* (1964), a study of child abuse based on first-hand observation of the work of the NSPCC. She subsequently became involved with the Samaritans – the subject of her novel *The Listeners* (1970) – and helped to found the first American branch of the organization in 1974. Her first book for children, *The House at World's End* (1970), was followed by the "Follyfoot" series of horse stories, tales inspired by her childhood passion for animals.

After the death of her husband in 1985, Dickens returned to Britain and settled in Berkshire. *Dear Doctor Lily* (1988), her first major work for nearly a decade, drew on 20 years of her life on both sides of the Atlantic. She went on to write four more novels; the last of these, *One of the Family*, was published posthumously in 1993.

Dickinson, Emily (1830–1886) *American poet*

> Success is counted sweetest
> By those who ne'er succeed.
>
> —"Success Is Counted Sweetest"

Now recognized as one of the greatest poets of 19th-century America (along with Ralph Waldo Emerson and Walt Whitman), Emily Dickinson lived a secluded life, becoming known as "the nun of Amherst."

Born in Amherst, Massachusetts, Emily Elizabeth Dickinson was the daughter of Edward Dickinson, an autocratic lawyer who dominated the lives of his children. She was educated at Amherst Academy and at nearby Mount Holyoke College, then called Mount Holyoke Female Seminary. When Dickinson was growing up, Amherst was a remote country town with only one church, the Congregational. Edward Dickinson, one of the wealthiest and most respected citizens of the town, was a leader of the church and a zealous defender of its orthodoxy. He saw to it that his family attended Sunday meeting, but he was unable to protect them completely from the transcendental doctrines put forward by Ralph Waldo Emerson. Emily received a book of Emerson's poems for Christmas in 1850 and was deeply influenced by his ideas, which reassured her that her religious doubts were not unreasonable. For the rest of her life she bought, read, and reread all of Emerson's books, which inspired many of her poems.

Dickinson wrote nearly 1,800 poems, several hundred of which are among the finest ever written by any American poet. The earliest surviving example was embroidered on a sampler when she was 15. She gave only 24 of her poems titles, and few were printed during her lifetime. Her most creative period, from 1858 to 1862, ended with an emotional crisis, after which she composed less often. Some of her greatest poems, however, were written in later life; for example, "A Route of Evanescence", "How Brittle Are the Piers", and "The Road Was Lit with Moon and Star". Apart from a small number of love poems, which have caused much speculation about her innermost feelings, Dickinson's main subject was the self and its ultimate destiny.

After her death, and against her dying wishes, Dickinson's poems were published by her sister Lavinia with the help of a friend and neighbour, Mabel Loomis Todd, and the clergyman Thomas Wentworth Higginson, with whom Emily had corresponded for 20 years. A complete three-volume edition of the poems as the poet had written them was published in 1955.

Didion, Joan (1934–) *American writer*

Joan Didion's novels examine the tensions of modern American life in a simple but distinctive style that has won her international acclaim.

Born in Sacramento, California, she studied at the University of California at Berkeley (1952–56). She was associate features editor at *Vogue* from 1956 to 1963, subsequently contributing to numerous other magazines and newspapers, including *Esquire*, the *Saturday Evening Post*, and the *National Review*. Some of her columns have been published in book form in the collections *Slouching Towards Bethlehem* (1968) and *The White Album* (1979). In more recent years she has commented on contemporary issues, such as the Reagan administration (1981–89) and the trial of O. J. Simpson in 1995.

The central figure of Didion's novels is usually a woman who is drawn into a chaotic situation that inevitably leads to despair or self-destruction. Her novels include *Run River* (1963), *A Book of Common Prayer* (1977), probably her best-known work; *Democracy* (1984), about the long extramarital affair of the wife of an ambitious politician; and *The Last Thing He Wanted* (1997), set in the Caribbean in 1984.

Didion has also worked on the screenplays for a number of films in collaboration with her husband John Gregory Dunne. These include *Play It as It Lays* (1972), based on her own novel of the same name; the 1976 version of *A Star Is Born;* and *True Confessions* (1981).

Dietrich, Marlene (1901–1992) *German-born American film actress and singer*

> If she had nothing but her voice, she could break your heart with it. But she also had that beautiful body and the timeless loveliness of her face.
>
> —Ernest Hemingway

The mysterious, sensual image Dietrich created for the film *The Blue Angel* (1930) remained her trademark throughout her long and successful career.

She was born Marie Magdalene Dietrich in a small village outside Berlin. Her father died when she was six years old, and after her mother's remarriage she adopted her stepfather's surname, von Losch, for a time. Having decided to become an actress, she supported herself while looking for work by posing as a photographic model. The legs that were to become world-famous on the big screen were first put on public display in advertisements for stockings and garters.

She played minor roles on the stage and in films from 1923 to 1929 but attracted little attention until the director Josef von Sternberg cast her as Lola Lola, a nightclub entertainer, in the German film *The Blue Angel* (1930). Her performance in this picture brought her worldwide fame. Von Sternberg took Dietrich to Hollywood, where they made many more films together, among them *Morocco* (1930), *Shanghai Express* (1932), *Blond Venus* (1932), and *The Scarlet Empress* (1934). Dietrich's later pictures included *Destry Rides Again* (1939), *A Foreign Affair* (1948), *Witness for the Prosecution* (1957), and *Judgment at Nuremberg* (1961).

Dietrich became an American citizen in 1937. Noted for her throaty voice and blasé singing style, she made many recordings and toured extensively as a solo entertainer, taking her one-woman show to nightclubs and concert halls all over the world until the mid 1970s. She never divorced the Czech film-maker she married in 1924, although she had many lovers, including von Sternberg and Ernest Hemingway. She spent her last years in lonely retirement in Paris.

Digby, Jane (1807–1881) *British adventurer*

Jane Digby was born in Norfolk, the daughter of an admiral. Her first marriage, to the politician Lord Ellenborough, was arranged before her 17th birthday and ended in divorce. She subsequently had three more husbands and numerous lovers, including the Austrian statesman Felix Schwarzenberg, King Ludwig of Bavaria, and King Otho of Athens.

By the time she reached middle age, Digby had matured into a cultivated and well-travelled woman, speaking several foreign languages and interested in fine arts and archaeology. In 1853 she went to Syria, where she met Sheikh Abdul Medjuel El Mezrab, who was to become her fourth and last husband. They spent nearly 30 years together, living in Damascus for six months of each year and spending the rest of their time as Bedouin nomads, moving from place to place with their sheep and horses. Jane was admired and respected among the members of the tribe for her courage, independence, and spirit of adventure. Although she wore the traditional Arab woman's robe and yashmak, she was still prepared to lead her husband's horsemen into battle at times of intertribal warfare. She died during an outbreak of cholera and dysentery in Damascus, with her husband at her side.

Dinesen, Isak (1885–1962) *Danish author*

Dinesen, also known by her married name Karen Blixen, wrote highly polished short stories, many of which have a supernatural background. In the film *Out of Africa* (1985), based on her autobiographical book of the same name, she was portrayed by the actress Meryl STREEP.

Karen Christence Dinesen was born into an aristocratic family at Rungsted, Denmark. In 1914 she married her cousin, Bror Blixen-Finecke, a Swedish baron, and went to live on a coffee plantation in Kenya. The marriage ended in divorce in 1922. When a depression in coffee prices in 1931 caused the bankruptcy of her plantation, she returned to Denmark and lived there until her death.

Karen Blixen's first stories appeared in Danish journals under the name "Osceola," but she used "Isak Dinesen" for most of her books, written in both English and Danish. *Seven Gothic Tales* (1934) gained her an international reputation, but *Out of Africa* (1937), an account of her years in Kenya, is generally regarded as her best work. This was followed by various collections of stories, including *Winter's Tales* (1942), *Last Tales* (1957), and *Anecdotes of Destiny* (1958). Under the name "Pierre Andrézel" she published *The Angelic Avengers* (1947), a novel set in England in 1841 but inspired by the Nazi occupation of Denmark during World War II.

Ding Ling (1904–1986) *Chinese author and feminist*

Ding Ling (or Ting Ling) was born into a family of landowners in Hunan province. Her father died when she was three, and her mother, contrary to tradition, became a teacher. Ding Ling went to Peking University, where she became involved in left-wing activities and campaigned against female inequality.

As a Communist activist in Shanghai in the 1930s she was jailed by the Nationalists but escaped to the Red Army headquarters in Yenan, disguised as a soldier. In an essay written in 1942 she courageously attacked male chauvinism within the Communist Party. After the Communist victory in 1949 she held numerous official posts in the literary world. Despite her reputation as "the woman warrior of New China," her spirit and outspokenness led to her downfall. Her works were banned, she was sent to labour reform in northern Manchuria, and finally she was imprisoned, spending five years in solitary confinement. In 1977 she returned to favour and was given a prominent position in the Writers' Union. She died in Beijing.

In an early short story, *Miss Sophie's Diary* (1928), Ding Ling shocked Chinese literary circles by revealing the sexual desires of the principal female character. In her novels of the 1930s she explored the conflict of love and revolution among urban radicals. She wrote less convincingly on peasant themes until her personal experience with land reform inspired *The Sun Shines over the Saggan River* (1948). Her best-known novel, it is a realistic depiction of the peasants' struggle against the richer farmers.

Dix, Dorothea (1802–1887) *American social reformer*

> In a world where there is so much to be done, I felt strongly impressed that there must be something for me to do.
>
> —Quoted by Lydia Maria Child (ed.) in *Letters from New York*, Vol. II

Dix is remembered for her efforts to secure better conditions and more humane treatment for prisoners and the mentally ill.

Dorothea Lynde Dix was born in Hampden, Maine. In 1816, at just 14 years of age, she began to teach school in Worcester, Massachusetts. Five years later she opened a school for young ladies in Boston, where she taught until 1835. During this period she also wrote many children's books and school textbooks.

In 1841 Dix began to teach a Sunday school class in the House of Correction at East Cambridge, Massachusetts. Horrified by the conditions there and especially by the fact that the mentally ill were imprisoned with convicted criminals and treated in the same way, she began a systematic survey of Massachusetts prisons, poorhouses, and asylums for the insane. Her shocking conclusions, delivered in 1843 in a "Memorial to the Legislature of Massachusetts," resulted in major improvements to the state lunacy asylum at Worcester. She then continued her campaign nationwide, eventually visiting every state east of the Rockies.

In 1848 Dix went to Washington, D.C., to promote a bill that would set aside public land for the support of the mentally ill. Such a bill was approved by Congress but was vetoed by President Franklin Pierce in 1854. Dix was heartbroken but continued her crusade until the Civil War broke out in 1861. She was appointed Superintendent of Women Nurses in the Union Army, the highest office held by a woman during the war. In 1865 she returned to her reform work.

Dix was directly responsible for the founding or enlarging of 32 mental hospitals in the United States, Canada, Britain, Europe, and Japan, and her work inspired the foundation or improvement of many others. In 1881 she retired to live at the New Jersey State Hospital in Trenton, the first mental hospital built as a result of her efforts.

Dix, Dorothy (1861–1951) *American newspaper columnist*

> The reason that husbands and wives do not understand each other is because they belong to different sexes.
>
> —Newspaper article

Dix was the first woman to write a regular column giving advice on readers' problems, especially those concerning personal relationships.

She was born Elizabeth Meriwether Gilmer in Woodstock, Tennessee. To support herself and her incurably ill husband, she became a writer for the women's page of the *New Orleans Picayune* in 1896. This was where she began writing her advice column, called "Dorothy Dix Talks." She continued her column after joining the staff of the *New York Journal* in 1901.

The column eventually appeared in almost 300 newspapers, and its practical, down-to-earth advice kept pace with the changing attitudes of the times. Dix's books include *How to Hold a Husband* (1939). She died in New Orleans, Louisiana.

Dodge, Grace Hoadley (1856–1914) *American philanthropist*

Grace Hoadley Dodge, who did much to promote women's education and the welfare of working women in the United States, was born in New York City into a business family; her great-grandfather was the merchant and pacifist David Low Dodge.

She was educated at home until the age of 16, when she went to school in Connecticut for two years. After teaching in Sunday schools and other establishments, she joined her parents in their humanitarian work for the New York State Charities Aid Association, devoting the rest of her life to voluntary service and social causes.

During the last two decades of the 19th century Dodge was involved in the development of the Industrial Education Association from the Kitchen Garden Association, which she had helped to found in 1880. She also funded, in 1887, the New York College for the Training of Teachers, which subsequently became Teachers College of Columbia University. In 1881 she began a discussion group for young factory workers, which eventually developed into a national organization, the Association of Working Girls' Societies.

Dodge's strong religious convictions led to her involvement with such groups as the Young Women's Christian Association; she served as president of the National Board of this organization from 1906 until her death. In 1907 she was instrumental in founding the New York Travelers' Aid Society, for the protection of women immigrants. In her will Dodge bequeathed more than $1.5 million to the charities and other causes she had supported during her life.

Domitilia, Saint Flavia (1st century AD) *Roman noblewoman*

Domitilia became a Christian in the latter part of the 1st century. Few details of her life are known with certainty. She was closely related to the Roman emperor Vespasian and his two sons: Titus, who succeeded him as emperor (79–81), and Domitian. Her husband, the Roman consul Flavius Clemens, died as a Christian martyr during Domitian's reign (81–96).

After the death of her husband Domitilia became a Christian and a church benefactor. According to one account she was banished to one of the Pontine Islands off the coast of Italy near Naples. In another account she and two foster sisters, Euphrosyne and Theodora, were put to death for their Christianity at the seaport of Terracina, north of Naples. A cemetery on the Ardeatine Way, still used by Christians in the 4th century, was named for St. Domitilla (as her name is often spelt). Her feast day, May 12, is shared with St. Achilleus and St. Nereus, who were martyred during Nero's reign (54–68).

Doolittle, Hilda (1886–1961) *American poet*

She was a member of the imagist movement of poets, who used precise images instead of abstract symbols in their verse. All of her work appeared under her pen name "H. D."

Hilda Doolittle was born in Bethlehem, Pennsylvania. When she was eight years old, her father, the astronomer Charles Leander Doolittle, moved the family to the outskirts of Philadelphia, where he was director of the Flower Observatory. H. D. entered Bryn Mawr College, Pensylvania, in 1904 but left in 1906 because of ill health. In 1911 she went to Europe, where she became involved with the imagist group led by Ezra Pound. She spent most of the rest of her life abroad, mainly in Great Britain and Switzerland. In 1913 she married Richard Aldington, a British poet and novelist who was also a member of the imagist group. They were later divorced. She died in Zurich, Switzerland.

H. D.'s first poems were printed in the magazine *Poetry* in 1913. Her work next appeared in *Des imagistes* (1914), an anthology published by Ezra Pound. *Collected Poems* (1925), probably her most widely read work, was still characterized by the concise observation of detail associated with imagist verse, but in *Red Roses for Bronze* (1931) she began to move towards the mystical and religious themes of her later work. After *The Walls Do Not Fall* (1944) H. D.'s verse tended to concentrate on classical mythology – sometimes, as in *Helen in Egypt* (1961), her last work, seeing all myths as one. She also wrote prose works, including the novels *Hedylus* (1928) and *Palimpsest* (1936) as well as her autobiographical *Tribute to Freud* (1956).

Douglas, Mary (1921–   ) *British social anthropologist*

In her work Mary Douglas has explored the systems of categorization used in various traditional societies.

Born to English parents in Italy, Margaret Mary Tew was educated at convent school and at St. Anne's College, Oxford, where she gained a BSc. In 1946 she returned to Oxford to train as an anthropologist under Sir Edward Evans-Pritchard, who had established a new school of social anthropology there. With funding from the school, she carried out field work among the Lele tribe of the Belgian Congo (now the Democratic Republic of Congo) in 1949–50, returning in 1953 and 1987. Her studies of this preliterate culture provided the material for her first book, *The Lele of the Casai* (1963).

In 1951 Mary married James Douglas and was appointed to a lectureship at University College, London.

She would remain at the college for over 25 years, becoming professor of social anthropology there in 1970. Since 1977 she has pursued a distinguished academic career in the United States, chiefly at Northwestern University, where she was appointed Avalon Foundation professor of the humanities in 1980 (emeritus professor since 1985).

Mary Douglas established her reputation with several works exploring the ways in which the categories of purity and uncleanness function in tribal societies. Her analysis of the Old Testament dietary laws in *Purity and Danger* (1966) was particularly influential. An important later book was *The World of Goods* (1979), which examined patterns of consumption in 'primitive' cultures. In the 1980s and 1990s her main focus has been the ideas of risk and moral responsibility that are acknowledged in traditional societies, a theme explored in *Risk and Culture* (1982), *Risk Acceptability* (1986), and *Risk and Blame* (1992). Her other publications include *Natural Symbols* (1970), *Cultural Bias* (1978), *How Institutions Think* (1986), and *In the Wilderness* (1993). Mary Douglas was appointed CBE in 1992.

Drabble, Margaret (1939–   ) *British novelist*

Margaret Drabble was born in Sheffield, the daughter of a lawyer and the younger sister of the writer A. S. BYATT. She was educated at The Mount School, York, where her mother was a teacher, then studied English at Newnham College, Cambridge. After her marriage to the actor Clive Swift in 1960 she worked briefly in the theatre, playing minor roles with the Royal Shakespeare Company at Stratford-upon-Avon.

Drabble's first novel, *The Summer Birdcage*, was published in 1963. It was followed by a story with a theatrical setting, *The Garrick Year* (1964); *The Millstone* (1966), which won the Llewellyn Rhys Memorial Prize; *Jerusalem the Golden* (1968); *The Waterfall* (1969), about an adulterous love affair; and *The Needle's Eye* (1972). The central characters of these

early novels are often educated middle-class women facing the conflicting demands of motherhood and intellectual fulfilment. As she was bringing up three young children herself at this time, Drabble often drew on her own experiences in her writing.

Divorced in 1975, Drabble later married the biographer Michael Holroyd. She continued writing novels, including *The Ice Age* (1977), *The Middle Ground* (1980), the trilogy *The Radiant Way* (1987), *A Natural Curiosity* (1989), and *The Gates of Ivory* (1991), and *The Witch of Exmoor* (1996). In 1979 she took on the editorship of a new edition of *The Oxford Companion to English Literature*. In the first version, published in 1985, Drabble modestly left her own life and work out of the text; this omission was put right in the revised edition of 1995. She has also written biographies of the novelists Arnold Bennett (1974) and Angus Wilson (1995) and a study of the interaction of literature and landscape, *A Writer's Britain* (1979).

Draper, Ruth (1884–1956) *American writer and performer of monologues*

She was born into an intellectual family in New York City, the granddaughter of Charles A. Dana, editor of the *New York Sun*. A talented child, she began reciting monologues at private functions in the early 1890s. In 1915 she made her debut as an actress in the play *A Lady's Name* in New York, and the following year she began performing her unique one-woman show. She entertained American troops in France in 1918 and made a triumphant London debut in 1920. She gave a command performance for the British royal family in 1926 and during her career performed on every continent.

In her 37 monologues, which she wrote herself, Miss Draper portrayed 58 different roles using simple props, such as a hat or a fan. Her most famous stage pieces include "The Italian Lesson," "At an English House Party," and "Three Generations." In 1951 she was honoured with a doctorate from Edinburgh University, and an honorary CBE.

Dressler, Marie (1869–1934) *Canadian-born American actress*

Dressler's expressive face and robust sense of the ridiculous made her a comedy favourite on stage and screen, but she was also an accomplished straight actress.

Born Leila Marie Koerber in Cobourg, Ontario, she took the name Marie Dressler at the beginning of her American stage career in 1883. After touring with a light opera company, she made her Broadway debut in *Robber on the Rhine* in 1892. She appeared in music halls with Lillian RUSSELL and other stars at the turn of the century, and she introduced and made famous the song "Heaven Will Protect the Working Girl."

Dressler was an instant success in her first film, *Tillie's Punctured Romance* (1914), but her screen career declined for a time after her involvement in an actors' strike in 1917. She regained stardom in such films as *The Divine Lady* (1929), *Anna Christie* (1930), and *Min and Bill* (1931), for which she won an Academy Award as Best Actress. Her last successes were *Tugboat Annie* (1933) and *Dinner at Eight* (1933). She wrote two volumes of autobiography, *The Life Story of an Ugly Duckling* (1924) and *My Own Story* (1934).

Drew, Dame Jane (1911–1996) *British architect*

Examples of Drew's work, which ranges from single buildings to whole towns, can be seen in Britain, Africa, India, Sri Lanka, and Kuwait. She was honoured with the title of DBE in 1996.

Jane Beverly Drew was born in Thornton Heath, south of London. After studying at the Architectural School in London (1929–34), she married the architect James Alliston and worked with him for a time. During World War II she ran her own architectural practice, becoming town-planning adviser to the West African colonies, where she was noted for her sensitive approach to the social and economic problems of the people. In 1945 Drew went into partnership with her second husband, Edwin Maxwell Fry, and others. They took on major projects in London, Africa, and India, where they designed buildings for the new capital city of the Punjab, Chandigarh. Their work in Nigeria includes Ibadan University College (1953–59) and the Olympic Stadium and Swimming Pool at Kaduna (1965).

Back in Britain, Drew became involved in the development of the Open University at Milton Keynes new town. Having helped to convince the government of the need for such an institution, she began designing the buildings of the Open University in the late 1960s, working on the project until its completion in 1977. She retired the following year.

Among Drew's many other architectural accomplishments are the Wesley Girls' School, Ghana (1946), the Hospital Building at the Kuwait Oil Company (1949–51), and the Festival of Britain Harbour Restaurant in London (1951). She also lectured at the Massachusetts Institute of Technology, Harvard University, and the University of Utah. In collaboration with her husband she wrote a number of books, including *Tropical Architecture in the Humid Zone* (1956), and edited *The Architects' Yearbook* (1946–62).

Drexel, Katharine (1858–1955) *American philanthropist*

She was born in Philadelphia, the daughter of Francis Anthony Drexel, an international banker. After her father's death in 1885 she decided to devote most of her inheritance, and the rest of her life, to the education of Native Americans and African Americans. She became a nun, joining the Sisters of Mercy in 1889, and – under the guidance of Bishop James O'Connor of Omaha and Archbishop Patrick Ryan of Philadelphia – she founded the Sisters of the Blessed Sacrament for Indians and Colored People in 1891.

Drexel established and maintained schools and convents throughout the United States, and in 1915 she founded Xavier University in New Orleans, Louisiana. At the time of her death her order of nuns numbered over 500 sisters with 63 schools. She had donated more than $20 million to helping African Americans and Native Americans take their place as citizens of the United States. In 1988 she was beatified, the first step towards being declared a saint.

Droste-Hülshoff, Annette Elisabeth von (1797–1848) *German writer*

Droste-Hülshoff is considered to be Germany's finest woman poet; her realistic short novels are regarded as forerunners of the 19th-century short story.

She was born at the Hülshoff mansion near Münster, the daughter of a noble Catholic family of Westphalia. After her father's death in 1826 she moved with her mother to Rüschhaus, a small estate near Hülshoff. Her first book of poems appeared in 1838. In 1841 she spent a year at the castle of her brother-in-law, Baron von Lassberg, in Meersburg near Lake Constance. There she became infatuated with the writer Levin Schücking, who was 17 years younger than her. Although he rejected her and married another woman in 1843, he later wrote a biography of the poet, *Annette von Droste* (1962). The success of a second volume of verse, published in 1844, enabled Droste-Hülshoff to buy a small cottage near Meersburg, where she spent her last years in poor health.

As a writer of epic ballads, notably *Das Hospiz auf dem Grossen Sankt Bernard* (1838; The Hospice on the Great Saint Bernard), Droste-Hülshoff followed in the Romantic tradition of Lord Byron and Sir Walter Scott. However, in her nature poems she avoided sentimentality and relied instead on earthy words or scientific description. Her most personal poetry is contained in *Das geistliche Jahr* (The Spiritual Year), a cycle of intense devotional poems expressing her early doubts about religion. Written mostly between 1818 and 1820, they were completed in 1839 but not published until 1851, three years after her death.

Of Droste-Hülshoff's prose works *Die Judenbuche* (1841; The Jews' Beech Tree) is the most famous. It is a realistic tale of guilt and retribution, set in Westphalia, telling how the murderer

of a Jewish tradesman is finally punished as a result of divine justice. A landmark in the history of the novella, it combines mystery, symbolism, realism, and regionalism.

du Barry, Countess (1743–1793) *Mistress of King Louis XV of France*

She was born Marie Jeanne Bécu, the illegitimate child of a dressmaker, in Vaucouleurs in northern France. After a convent education she worked briefly as an apprentice milliner and shop assistant under the name of Jeanne Vaubernier. At the age of 17 she became the mistress of Jean du Barry, who earned his living by providing beautiful women for young nobles. He brought Jeanne to Louis XV's attention and obtained for her the social credentials necessary to be presented at court as Louis's official mistress. She required legitimate birth and a noble husband, so du Barry obligingly invented a deceased father for Jeanne and married her to his brother Guillaume, Count du Barry, in 1768.

During her six years as royal mistress Madame du Barry took little part in politics, being more interested in the arts. She was banished to the abbey at Pont-aux-Dames after Louis XV's death in 1774, but two years later was allowed to live in the palace at Louveciennes. There she formed a close relationship with an old friend, the Duke de Brissac, which lasted from 1781 until his murder by a mob during the French Revolution, in September 1792. His head was cut off and thrown through the open window of Madame du Barry's salon, landing horrifyingly at her feet.

After her lover's death du Barry took refuge in England. While in London she contributed large sums of money for the relief of refugees from revolutionary France and for the royalist cause. On her return to France in March 1793 she found herself outlawed. A warrant for her arrest was signed by the Committee of Public Safety; she was then brought before the Revolutionary Tribunal, sentenced to death, and executed by guillotine in Paris.

du Deffand, Marquise (1697–1780)
French intellectual

Highly intelligent and witty, Madame du Deffand was noted for her Paris salon and for her correspondence with the writers Voltaire and Horace Walpole, the politician Jean-François Hénault, and other notables.

Marie Anne de Vichy-Chamrond was born into a noble family at the Château de Chamrond in Burgundy. Educated at a fashionable convent, she later (1719) married the Marquis du Deffand. After their separation in 1722 she led a brilliant and uninhibited life typical of the period.

When she became blind in 1753, Madame du Deffand employed as her companion Mademoiselle de Lespinasse, but in 1764, after a spectacular quarrel, du Lespinasse left her to set up a rival salon. At the age of 69 Madame du Deffand experienced the first passion of her life – for the British writer Horace Walpole, who was 20 years younger than her. Their peculiar bittersweet relationship lasted until her death; she left Walpole all her papers, which have been published in various editions.

Madame du Deffand's most famous remark, made in a letter to the French philosopher Jean d'Alembert in 1763, concerns the legend of St. Denis, who is said to have walked for six miles after his execution with his head in his hands. "The distance is irrelevant," wrote Madame du Deffand, "it is only the first step that counts."

Duff-Gordon, Lady Lucy (1821–69)
British travel writer and translator

Lucy Duff-Gordon is remembered for her travel letters from Egypt and South Africa and her translations of scholarly German works.

The only child of John Austin, a prominent legal authority, Lucy grew up in a highly intellectual milieu (John Stuart Mill was amongst the regular visitors to her childhood home). She was educated by private tutors and spent a number of years in Germany, where her father was pursuing his research. In 1840 she married Sir Alexander Cornewall Duff-Gordon, a wealthy baronet. For the next 20 years their London home would be a meeting-place for literary and other celebrities, including Dickens, Thackeray, and Tennyson, all of whom became good friends. Visitors from abroad included the German poet Heinrich Heine.

Lucy had shown an early talent for translation, publishing a rendering of Barthold Niebuhr's *Ancient Greek Mythology* (1839) while still in her teens. One of the first British intellectuals to show an awareness of the major developments in historical writing taking place in Germany, she published a series of translations in the 1840s and 1850s, including scholarly works by Ranke and Moltke. In 1850 she was active in establishing a library for working men in Weybridge, Surrey.

Following the collapse of her health in 1860, Lucy Duff-Gordon undertook the journey to South Africa that inspired her first original writing. The long descriptive letters that she sent to her mother were published as *Letters from the Cape* in 1862–63. Needing a warm climate, she settled in Egypt from 1862, where she became a celebrated character, known to the locals as "Sitt el kebeer" – "the Great Lady." Her *Letters from Egypt* appeared in 1863 and the posthumous *Last Letters from Egypt* in 1875.

du Maurier, Dame Daphne (1907–1989) *British novelist*

Daphne du Maurier is best known for her popular suspense fiction, such as *Rebecca* (1938), *My Cousin Rachel* (1951), *The Birds* (1952), and *Don't Look Now* (1970), all of which were made into films.

She was born in London, the daughter of the actor-manager Sir Gerald du Maurier and granddaughter of the writer George du Maurier. Her first novel, *The Loving Spirit* (1931), was set in Cornwall, as was much of her later work. In 1932 she married Frederick Browning, later Sir Frederick; the couple had three children.

The success of *Rebecca* in 1938 suddenly made du Maurier one of the most popular writers of her time. It was subsequently translated into 20 different languages. Her other novels include *Jamaica Inn* (1936), *Frenchman's Creek* (1941), *The Scapegoat* (1957), and *Flight of the Falcon* (1965). She also wrote plays; several collections of short stories; *Gerald: A Portrait* (1934), a biography of her father; *The du Mauriers* (1937), a family history; and her autobiography, *Growing Pains* (1977). Du Maurier was made a Dame Commander of the British Empire in 1969. She died in Par, Cornwall.

Dumesnil, Marie-Françoise (1713–1803) *French actress*

Marie-Françoise Marchand Dumesnil was born into a poor family in Paris. In 1737 she joined the Comédie-Française, making her debut in Jean Racine's tragedy *Iphigénie*. She soon established a reputation as one of the finest actresses of her time, performing with great passion in such plays as Racine's *Phèdre* and *Athalie* and Corneille's *Rodogune*. Voltaire was particularly impressed by her performance in the first production of his play *Mérope (1743)*.

Unlike her contemporary Mademoiselle CLAIRON, who was known for the historical accuracy of her costumes, Dumesnil preferred to dazzle her audience with rich, lavish gowns and jewellery. The rivalry between the two actresses began in 1743, when Clairon joined the Comédie-Française and took over Dumesnil's role in *Phèdre*, and continued long after Dumesnil's retirement in 1775. Clairon attacked Dumesnil's acting technique in her *Mémoires et réflexions sur l'art dramatique*, published in 1799; Dumesnil responded with dignity in her own memoirs the following year.

Duncan, Isadora (1878–1927) *American dancer*

> I have discovered the dance. I have discovered the art which has been lost for two thousand years.
>
> —*My Life* (1927)

One of the first performers of what came to be called "modern dance," she did more than any other person to bring about the revolution in dance during the early years of the 20th century. At a time when ballet had become routine and mechanical, her free movements showed that dance could be the natural expression of the human body and emotions. Her unorthodox lifestyle presented a constant challenge to the Victorian morals of society. She had tempestuous love affairs with the stage designer Gordon Craig and the millionaire Paris Singer, having a son by one and a daughter by the other.

Dora Angela Duncan was born in San Francisco, into a family with Scottish and Irish roots. At an early age she began to dance in the unconventional way for which she later became famous. By the age of six she was teaching neighbourhood children; she remained an inspiring teacher for the rest of her life. After a brief stint in the theatre and unsuccessful recitals in Chicago and New York City Duncan went to London. A set of figurines in the British Museum inspired her to adopt the Greek chiton – a loose tunic – as the freest, most expressive dance costume. Dancing barefoot, she gave her first successful performances in Budapest (1903), Berlin (1904), London (1908), and New York (1908).

Duncan's early work, of which *Primavera* is a typical example, was primarily lyrical. However, after her two children were accidentally drowned in 1913, she frequently turned to tragic and heroic themes, principally to the music of such composers as Beethoven and Wagner. In 1921 she was invited to establish a school of dance in the Soviet Union similar to those she had already established in Germany and France. She stayed for several years in Russia, where her work had a profound effect on the choreographer Michel Fokine. In 1922 she married the Russian poet Sergei Esenin, but the marriage was not a success. The couple separated soon afterwards, and Esenin committed suicide in 1925.

Duncan returned to France, where she gave her last performance in Paris in July 1927. She died at Nice, accidentally strangled when a scarf that she was wearing became tangled in the wheels of her car. A film of her life, *Isadora*, was made in 1969, starring Vanessa REDGRAVE.

Dunham, Katherine (1910–)
American dancer, choreographer, and teacher

An anthropologist as well as an artist, Dunham used her expert knowledge of the cultural heritages of Afro-Caribbean, Afro-Brazilian, and other peoples as the basis for her dance techniques and choreography.

Dunham was born in Joliet, Illinois, and earned a BA and an MA in anthropology at the University of Chicago. In 1931, while she was still a student, she formed a small dance group with other African-American artists, calling it Ballet Nègre. Encouraged by the choreographer Ruth Page, the group performed at the Chicago Civic Opera and in concerts. A Rosenwald fellowship enabled Dunham to make the first of several trips to the West Indies to study native dances and folklore. From this material she developed a repertoire of dances; in 1940 she and her company made their New York debut in a series of concerts that established her as a major figure in the world of dance. The company subsequently toured throughout the United States, Mexico, and Europe. Dunham also appeared as dancer and actress in Broadway musicals, such as *Cabin in the Sky* (1940) and *Carib Song* (1945); in films, including *Carnival of Rhythm* (1941) and *Star-Spangled Rhythm* (1942); and in her own revues.

In the 1940s and 1950s Dunham opened her own dance school in New York (its students included Eartha KITT, Marlon Brando, and James Dean), as well as schools in Chicago, Stockholm, Paris, and, in 1961, Port-au-Prince, Haiti (where she had a home from 1949). In 1963 she choreographed dances for the Metropolitan Opera production of *Aïda*. She served as an adviser to the First World Festival on Negro Art (1966), sponsored by the U.S. State Department, and was artistic and technical adviser to the president of Senegal in West Africa (1966–67). From 1968 she was a professor at Southern Illinois University in Edwardsville; she also taught at the Katherine Dunham Center for the Arts and Humanities in East St. Louis, Illinois.

Dunham published many short stories (some under the pen name Kaye Dunn), articles, and books, which included *Journey to Accompong* (1946), *Touch of Innocence* (1959), *Island Possessed* (1969), and *Kassamance: A Fantasy* (1974). She also wrote television scripts, which were produced in Australia, Britain, Italy, and Mexico. Among her many honours and citations were a Dance Magazine Award (1968), American Dance Guild Award (1975), Black Merit Academic Award (1983), Professional Achievement Award of the University of Chicago (1986), National Arts Medal (1989), and Capezio Dance Award (1991).

Dunham's tireless campaigning against racism led to the formulation of laws against segregation in Brazil and elsewhere, and her support of important causes lasted for well over half a century. In 1992 she staged a 47-day hunger strike in support of Jean-Bertrand Aristide, the deposed president of Haiti – a protest that focused international attention on the plight of the Haitian people.

du Pré, Jacqueline (1945–1987)
British cellist

> Jacqueline was born to play the cello. She thoroughly understands its genius, and so instinctive is her reaction to the music that one feels the subtlest ideas of the composer to be embraced.
>
> —Percy Cater, reviewing du Pré's debut, *Daily Mail*, 1961

Jacqueline du Pré was born in Oxford and began cello lessons when she was five years old. She eventually studied with the great cellists Paul Tortelier (in France), Mstislav Rostropovich (in Russia), and Pablo Casals (in Switzerland). As a student at the Guildhall School in London, du Pré won every possible prize for her playing. She began her professional career at the age of 16 with a concert at Wigmore Hall, London, in 1961.

Throughout the 1960s and early 1970s du Pré won widespread critical acclaim whenever she performed. Her interpretation of Elgar's cello concerto was particularly famous, and the work became associated with her. Music critics remarked on her "large, burnished tone, flawless technique, and passionate romantic spirit." In 1967 she converted to Judaism in order to marry the pianist and conductor Daniel Barenboim; the couple gave many performances and made a number of recordings together.

In 1973 it was discovered that du Pré was suffering from the crippling disease multiple sclerosis, or MS, and her performing career came to an end. However, she continued to work as a teacher and gave master classes on television. In 1976 she was honoured with the OBE. Her story formed the basis of the play *Duet for One* (1981), which in 1986 was turned into a film starring Julie ANDREWS as the cellist.

Duras, Marguerite (1914–1996)
French novelist and screenwriter

Marguerite Duras is associated with the "New Wave," a movement in French filmmaking that had a great influence on the development of European cinema in the 1960s.

Born Marguerite Donnadieu at Gia Dinh, Indochina (now Vietnam), she studied law at the Sorbonne and worked at the ministry of colonies from 1935 to 1941. During World War II she was involved in the Resistance, and at the end of the war she joined the Communist Party.

In 1942 she married the political philosopher Dionys Mascolo and settled down to writing. Several of her books have been translated into English, including *Sea Wall* (1950; translated in 1952), set in Indochina; *Sailor from Gibraltar* (1952; translated in 1967), a psychological romantic novel; *Little Horses of Tarquinia* (1953; translated in 1960), which explores the obstacles encountered in human relationships; and *India Song* (1973; translated in 1976). *L'Amant* (1984; published in English as *The Lover*, 1985) won the Prix Goncourt, France's most prestigious annual literary award.

In 1955 Duras began writing for the theatre, and in 1959 she produced the screenplay for the film *Hiroshima, mon amour*. The success of this film, in which past and present are merged in the emotions of the characters, encouraged her to continue writing for the cinema, often adapting her own novels for the screen. In 1966 she began directing films, including *Destroy She Said* (1969) and *Agatha* (1981). These experimental, atmospheric pictures, often produced on a low budget, brought her international acclaim.

Duse, Eleonora (1859–1924) *Italian actress*

> I did not use paint. I made myself up morally.
> —Article in *Le Gaulois*, July 27, 1922

With her rival Sarah BERNHARDT, Duse ruled the stage in the late 19th and early 20th centuries. The two actresses had contrasting styles: "the divine Sarah" was flamboyant, always playing herself no matter what the role, while "the Duse" tried to understand the psychological motives of the women she played, adapting her face, walk, voice, and gestures to each new character. As Duse observed, she did not "act" her roles, she "lived" them. Her underplayed technique is partly responsible for the modern American style of acting.

Duse was born in Vigevano into a theatrical family and began acting when she was just four years old. She first caught the attention of the public when she played Shakespeare's Juliet in Verona at the age of 14. In 1878 she went to Naples, where she won critical acclaim for her interpretations of Ophelia, Electra in Alfieri's *Oreste*, and the title role in Zola's *Thérèse Raquin*.

After seeing Bernhardt perform in 1882, Duse was encouraged to abandon the traditional roles that had begun to bore her for more demanding parts in new French plays, particularly by Alexandre Dumas the Younger. She formed her own troupe, which toured throughout Europe and the United States after 1890. Duse was idolized everywhere for her stirring performances in such plays as Dumas's *La Dame aux camélias*, Sardou's *Fédora*, Pinero's *The Second Mrs. Tanqueray*, and Ibsen's *The Doll's House* and *Hedda Gabler*.

Duse married the actor Teobaldo Cecchi and gave birth to his daughter in 1882. In 1897 she fell in love with the tempestuous poet Gabriele D'Annunzio, who wrote showy parts for her in such plays as *Francesca da Rimini* (1902). D'Annunzio wrote a fictional account of their affair in his novel *Il fuoco* (1900; published in English as *The Flame of Life*). Plagued by illness, Duse retired in 1909, but lack of money frequently forced her to return to the stage. Her last New York appearance, in 1923, was in her favourite Ibsen play, *The Lady from the Sea*. She died in Pittsburgh, Pennsylvania, while on tour.

Dutt, Toru (1856–1877) *Indian poet and novelist*

Dutt was one of the first Indian women to write poetry in English.

Born in Calcutta, she received her early education (in English) from her father, the poet Govind Chunder Dutt; both her parents were Christian converts. Between 1869 and 1873 she studied in France and England, becoming fluent in French. On her return to India she published her translations of French poetry, *A Sheaf Gleaned in Fields* (1875), and some English poems. She also began learning Sanskrit in order to translate from that language into English. Dutt died of tuberculosis in Calcutta at the age of 21.

Her best work is considered to be *Ancient Ballads and Legends of Hindustan*, published in 1882. Although Dutt's verse has certain defects, her narrative passages and descriptions of nature often equal the best in Western Romantic poetry. She also wrote two novels, which were published after her death: *Bianca; or the Young Spanish Maiden* (1878) and *Le Journal de Mlle. D'Arvers* (1879), which was written in French.

Dworkin, Andrea (1946–) *American feminist writer*

> In every century, there are a handful of writers who help the human race to evolve. Andrea is one of them.
>
> —Gloria Steinem, quoted on the dust jacket of Dworkin's novel *Mercy* (1990)

Born in Camden, New Jersey, Andrea Dworkin was educated at Bennington College, Vermont. Before joining the women's movement and starting to write on feminist issues, she had a variety of jobs, including those of waitress, receptionist, and factory worker.

In her writings Dworkin presents a darkly pessimistic view of modern society, in which men are constantly presented with images of women that lead to hatred and ultimately to violent crime, such as rape and wife-battering. Among her early works are *Woman Hating* (1974); *Out Blood: Prophecies and Discourses on Sexual Politics* (1976), a collection of essays; and *The New Woman's Broken Heart* (1980), a book of short stories.

Dworkin joined the feminist writer Catherine MacKinnon in a campaign against pornography, which they regarded as one of the major causes of sexism and a violation of equal rights. They eventually took their battle to the courts, hoping to have all forms of pornography made illegal, but lost their case. Dworkin set out her feelings on this issue in *Take Back the Night: Women on Pornography* (1980) and *Pornography: Men Possessing Women* (1980). Her more recent works include *Letters from a War Zone 1976–1987* (1989) and the novels *Ice and Fire* (1986) and *Mercy* (1990).

Dyer, Mary (died 1660) *English-born American Quaker martyr*

In 1635 Mary Dyer travelled with her husband, William, from their home in southwest England to Boston, Massachusetts. There she came to share the unorthodox religious views of Anne HUTCHINSON, who stressed faith in God rather than obedience to moral, church, or state laws – a doctrine known as antinomianism. Like Hutchinson, Mary Dyer and her husband were expelled from the Massachusetts Bay colony and moved in 1638 to Rhode Island, where William Dyer became one of the founders and leading citizens of Portsmouth. The Dyers travelled to England in 1650, and while there Mary became a Quaker. She returned to New England in 1657 and along with other members of the

Society of Friends began to travel through the area as a missionary.

In 1657 and 1658 harsh anti-Quaker laws were passed in Massachusetts. These included the death penalty for those who returned to the colony after banishment. Dyer began to visit imprisoned Quakers there, until she herself was imprisoned. She was released and banished, but returned in 1659 and was sentenced to death, together with William Robinson and Marmaduke Stevenson. Dyer was reprieved and banished again, but she refused to remain in Rhode Island, determined to obtain the repeal of "unrighteous laws of banishment on pain of death" in Massachusetts.

Dyer was finally hanged in Boston on June 1, 1660. "She hangs there as a flag," said a bystander as her lifeless body hung from the gallows. After her martyrdom there was only one other execution of a Quaker in Boston.

E

Eames, Ray (*c.* 1916–1988) *American designer and architect*

> She is equally responsible with me for everything that goes on here.
>
> —Charles Eames, speaking of their California studio (*c.* 1964)

In partnership with her husband, Charles, Ray Eames designed a wide array of products, ranging from toys to buildings. The couple are best known, however, for their comfortable and elegant furniture, made of plywood and other modern materials, produced in the 1940s.

Born Ray Kaiser, in Sacramento, California, she had already trained under the painter Hans Hoffman when she met her future husband in 1940. At that time Charles Eames was attempting to establish himself as an architect. While working at the Cranbrook Academy of Art, in Bloomfield Hills, Michigan, they met the Finnish architect Eero Saarinen. Charles had developed an interest in modernism during a trip to Europe, and he, Saarinen, and Ray began to experiment with modernistic furniture design using new materials, such as plywood.

In 1941 Charles and Ray married and moved to California, where they experimented with ways of bending and shaping plywood. By designing furniture and other items, as well as making documentary films for MGM, they began to build a thriving business. Their wood-shaping experiments paid off with a series of moulded plywood chairs in 1945–46. In general, their designs featured contrasting combinations of modern materials, including plywood, foam, polyester, and metal.

After their first few successful years in business Charles and Ray decided to design a modern, prefabricated house for themselves. Constructed at Santa Monica, it demonstrated their design ideals. The business continued to flourish, with designs including a fibreglass armchair (1950–53) and a famous "Lounge Chair" (1956), upholstered in black leather. Over the next few years the Eameses produced metal-framed furniture with leather upholstery, which was destined to start a fashion.

In 1960 they won a $20,000 Kaufmann International Design Award, and their wide-ranging partnership continued until Charles's death in 1978.

Earhart, Amelia (1897–*c.* 1937) *American aviator*

> Of course I realized there was a measure of danger. Obviously I faced the possibility of not returning when I first considered going.
>
> —*20 Hours : 40 Minutes – Our Flight in the Friendship* (1928)

A champion of women's role in aviation, Amelia Earhart made history in 1932 by becoming the first woman to fly across the Atlantic as a solo pilot.

Born in Atchison, Kansas, Earhart studied at Ogontz School in Rydal, Pennsylvania, and Columbia University. She served as a nurse with the Canadian Red Cross during World War I and after the war took up social work in Boston. Her enthusiasm for aviation began as a hobby in California, where she learned to fly; while working in Boston she was chosen to accompany Wilmer Stultz on a flight from Newfoundland to Wales. When their airplane, "Friendship," landed at Burry Port on June 18, 1928, she became the first woman passenger to complete a transatlantic flight. Thereafter Earhart made a career of flying;

she married the publisher George Palmer Putnam in 1931 and wrote three books about her flights. Her historic transatlantic solo flight started on May 20, 1932, when she took off in a single-engined Lockheed Vega aircraft from Newfoundland, landing in Londonderry, Northern Ireland, 13¼ hours later. Subsequent long-distance flights included the first solo flight from Hawaii to California, in 1935.

Earhart's career came to a mysterious and untimely end during an attempt to fly around the world, starting from Miami, Florida, in June 1937. In the last stage of the flight, after taking off on July 1, 1937, from New Guinea, the plane vanished before reaching its destination of Howland Island in the Pacific. Despite an extensive search, neither Earhart nor her navigator, Frederick J. Noonan, were ever found. Reports by U.S. Army veterans and inhabitants of Saipan hinted that the pair had been imprisoned there and perhaps killed by the Japanese, who were administering the island at that time, but the mystery was never solved.

Earhart's autobiography, entitled *Last Flight*, was edited by her husband after her death and published in 1938.

Eberhardt, Isabelle (1877–1904)
Swiss-born Russian writer and traveller

Isabelle Eberhardt's adventures and exploits provide a remarkable illustration of female independence in the days before equal opportunities.

Eberhardt's mother, Nathalie de Moender, was married to a Russian general but had eloped to Geneva with her children's tutor, Alexander Trophimowsky. There she gave birth to their illegitimate daughter, Isabelle. Perhaps as a result of her unconventional upbringing and her father's insistence on treating her as a boy, as a teenager Eberhardt suffered serious psychological illness, which led to dependence on drugs and alcohol. Nevertheless, she learned to speak six languages and to write in three of them – Russian, French, and Arabic.

In 1897 Eberhardt and her mother moved to Algeria, where they embraced Islam. Here, Isabelle, using a pen name, wrote a number of articles in French for publication in Paris. She was also deeply fascinated by the Sahara, which she frequently visited in Arab disguise, returning with lurid accounts of what she had seen.

Though she remained on friendly terms with the Arabs, Eberhardt also carried out duties for the French colonial government. In 1901 an attempt was made on her life, and she was forced to leave Algeria. However, she later returned after having married an Arab, Slimène Ehnni. In 1904 she became ill while reporting on a military campaign in Morocco; before she had fully recovered she was drowned in a flood, aged only 27.

Eberhardt's works include *Dans l'ombre chaude de l'islam* (1906; In the Warm Shade of Islam) and *Notes de route; Maroc, Algérie, Tunisie* (1908).

Eddy, Mary Baker (1821–1910)
American religious leader

> What I am remains to be proved by the good I do.
>
> —Writing in 1903

The founder of the Church of Christ, Scientist, Mary Baker Eddy is now recognized as a pioneer of modern spiritual healing, although her religious views were controversial in her own day. She urged that the New Testament saying "By their fruits shall ye know them" (Matthew 7:20) be used as a yardstick for her own life and work.

Mary Morse Baker, the daughter of a farmer, was born at Bow, near Concord, New Hampshire. Ill health hindered her education, but she was encouraged and helped by her talented elder brother. Her parents' Christian views influenced her own, but although deeply religious, she was independent and soon rejected her father's strict Calvinism, which taught that only a few "chosen" people may enter heaven.

In 1843 she married George Washington Glover, but he died only a year later. Over the next few years her spinal illness became worse, and she had to entrust her child's upbringing to others. In 1853 she married Daniel Patterson, an itinerant dentist, but the marriage proved unsuccessful.

205 **EDGEWORTH**

During her years of illness Eddy lost faith in traditional medicine and turned to homeopathy, hydropathy, and other alternative techniques. Her illness was temporarily healed in the early 1860s by a healer named Phineas P. Quimby, without the use of medication. Gradually she came to the conclusion that all disease was mental rather than physical.

Throughout her life Eddy turned to the Bible for comfort, guidance, and inspiration. In 1866 she was badly injured by a fall but found herself suddenly restored to health while reading about one of Jesus's healings in the Bible (Matthew 9:1–8). This experience was the start of the Christian Science movement, and she devoted the next three years to studying the Scriptures in an effort to understand spiritual healing. She set out her resultant philosophy of Christian Science in her book *Science and Health with Key to the Scriptures* (1875), in which she claimed that spirit alone is real, and in 1879 she set up the Church of Christ, Scientist.

Having divorced Patterson in 1873, she married one of her followers, Asa Gilbert Eddy, in 1877 and spent the rest of her long life studying, writing, healing, and teaching. She repeatedly revised *Science and Health*, which, with the Bible, became the basic scripture of Christian Science. Eddy also wrote a number of other books, among them *Unity of Good* (1891), her autobiography *Retrospection and Introspection* (1891), and *Manual of the Mother Church, the First Church of Christ, Scientist, in Boston, Massachusetts* (1895). One of her last acts, when she was 87, was to found the international daily newspaper *The Christian Science Monitor* in 1908. She died in Chestnut Hill, Massachusetts, leaving behind her a church with nearly 100,000 members.

Ederle, Gertrude Caroline

(1906–) *American swimmer*

In 1926 Trudy Ederle became the first woman to swim the English Channel.

Born in New York, the daughter of a West-Side butcher, Ederle learned to swim at Highlands, New Jersey. Between 1921 and 1925 she held 29 amateur national and world records for swimming, and in 1922 she broke seven world records in one afternoon at Brighton Beach, New York State. She was also a member of the U.S. 400-metre freestyle relay team that took the a gold medal in the 1924 Olympics.

On August 6, 1926, Trudy Ederle swam the English Channel from Cape Gris-Nez, France, to Kingsdown, England. Taking only 14 hours and 31 minutes to complete the 35 miles, she broke the existing men's record. Her achievements were rewarded with many honours, including the Helms Foundation Hall of Fame award in 1953.

See also CHADWICK, FLORENCE.

Edgeworth, Maria (1767–1849)
Anglo-Irish writer

> Those who fall cannot be destitute; and those who rise cannot be ridiculous or contemptible, if they have been prepared for their fortune by proper education.
> —*Madame De Fleury* (1805)

Maria Edgeworth is best known for her novels of Irish social life, which during her lifetime were widely read throughout Europe and the United States. Her Irish stories provided a model for the "regional novel" and greatly influenced such writers as Sir Walter Scott.

Born in Blackbourton, Oxfordshire, Maria Edgeworth was one of 22 children. Her long and happy life was dominated by her admiration for her father, Richard Lovell Edgeworth, and by her close family ties. From the age of 15 she lived in Ireland at the family estate at Edgeworthstown, county Longford, where she acted as her father's steward. Her tales began as "wee, wee stories" to entertain her brothers and sisters, but they also reflect the belief in moral and social improvement through education that she shared with her father. Her books *The Parent's Assistant* (1796–1800), *Early Lessons* (1801–1825), *Moral Tales for Young People* (1801), and *Popular Tales* (1804) all have a moral emphasis, as do the lively and sympathetic children's stories *Simple Susan* and *Lazy Laurence*.

Most of Edgeworth's books follow a pattern in which her characters are either good or bad; the good are suitably rewarded and the bad receive their just desserts. However, her most highly regarded adult novel, *Castle Rackrent* (1800), is more complex. Generally regarded as the first distinctively "Irish novel," it traces the gradual ruin of an Irish family over several generations, as seen through the eyes of an old retainer. Her well-observed portraits of fashionable society in *Tales of Fashionable Life* (1809 and 1812) and the brilliantly sketched characters of Lady Delacour in *Belinda* (1801) and Lady Davenant in *Helen* (1830) show her talent for characterization at its best.

Eleanor of Aquitaine (c. 1122–1204)
Wife of King Louis VII of France and later of King Henry II of England

As Duchess of Aquitaine, Countess of Poitiers, queen of France, and later queen of England, Eleanor played a key role in the 12th-century struggles between France and England.

Eleanor's grandfather, William IX, Duke of Aquitaine, was the earliest known troubadour, and she grew up in the atmosphere of poetry, literature, and music that was part of the 12th-century Renaissance in France. As the sole heir of her father, Duke William X, she became Duchess of Aquitaine on his death and shortly afterwards was married to her relative Louis, who was crowned King Louis VII of France in 1137. Eleanor had two daughters by Louis and in 1147 accompanied him on the Second Crusade. On this trip differences arose between them, and their marriage was annulled in 1152 on grounds of blood relationship.

Eleanor then married Henry Plantagenet, Count of Anjou and Duke of Normandy, who became King Henry II of England in 1154. In adding her duchy to her husband's lands, she helped to create the Angevin empire, which stretched from the Scottish border to the Pyrenees. Though she was more than 10 years older than Henry, their marriage was reasonably happy for 15 years, and Eleanor produced

five sons – William, Henry, Richard, Geoffrey, and John – and three daughters – Matilda, Eleanor, and Joan. By the time of John's birth in 1167, however, Henry had begun to tire of her and had found an exciting young mistress, Rosamond Clifford.

As his estranged wife Eleanor posed a powerful threat to Henry. It was perhaps at her instigation – and certainly with her help – that in 1173 her two eldest living sons, Henry and Richard, attempted to seize their father's French lands while encouraging the English barons to rise against him. Having suppressed this rebellion, Henry captured Eleanor and had her imprisoned in England. She did not enjoy complete freedom again until Richard succeeded his father in 1189.

Throughout her life Eleanor remained Duchess of Aquitaine and Countess of Poitiers, taking great interest in the government of these lands. A shrewd politician, she acted as a regent for her son Richard I while he was away on the Third Crusade and arranged his ransom in 1193. Returning to her foreign domains, she continued to take a keen interest in English politics. Though stunned by her beloved Richard's death in 1199, she smoothed John's path to the throne. The following year she travelled to Spain to arrange a marriage between her granddaughter Blanche and the future Louis VIII of France.

According to legend, Eleanor was a patron of the "courtly love" culture then flourishing in France, particularly at her court at Poitiers. She was not only the most cultured woman of her day but also one of the most beautiful. The troubadour Bernard de Ventadour was among the writers who dedicated compositions to her.

Eleanor was buried close to Henry II and Richard I in the abbey of Fontevrault, where she had often stayed and which she had generously endowed.

Eleanor of Castile (c. 1244–1290)
Devoted wife of King Edward I of England

The daughter of Ferdinand III of Castile and Joan of Ponthieu, Eleanor was married to Edward, the eldest son of Henry III of England, in Spain, in October 1254, soon after Edward had been made Duke of Aquitaine. They returned to England in 1255; but in 1264–65, at the height of the Barons' War against Henry III, Eleanor took refuge in France. She went with her husband on his pilgrimage to the Holy Land in 1270, and while they were away Henry III died. Edward and Eleanor were crowned in 1274. In 1278 Eleanor inherited the French provinces of Ponthieu and Montreuil from her mother.

Eleanor produced seven daughters and four sons and managed her finances shrewdly. After her death at Harby in Lincolnshire, Edward built 12 memorial crosses to mark the places at which her body had rested on its way to her funeral in Westminster Abbey in London. The last of these crosses gave its name to the London railway terminus, Charing Cross.

Eleanor of Provence (1223–1291)
Unpopular wife of King Henry III of England

The daughter of Raymond Berenger IV, Count of Provence, Eleanor married Henry on January 14, 1236. The couple were crowned six days later. Eleanor was unpopular in England because she was arrogant and persuaded her husband to place her foreign relatives in prominent government positions. The financial favours granted to them were a serious drain on the country and worsened the already bad relations between Henry and his barons.

In 1253–54 Eleanor acted as co-regent with the king's brother, the Earl of Cornwall, while Henry was away in Gascony. After Henry's death and the accession of her son as King Edward I in 1272 Eleanor became a nun at Amesbury Abbey, where she died.

Elion, Gertrude Belle (1918–)
American pharmacologist

For her work in developing effective drugs to treat leukaemia, malaria, herpes, and several other major diseases, Gertrude Elion was awarded a share of the Nobel Prize for physiology or medicine in 1988.

Elion was educated at Hunter College, New York City, and at New York University. In 1944, after various teaching and research jobs, she joined the Burroughs Wellcome Laboratories, where she worked closely with George H. Hitchings for the next 40 years.

Their research focused on the study of individual cancer cells, bacteria, and viruses, comparing their behaviour with that of normal cells. This enabled them to develop drugs that were able to attack the DNA of the cancer cells and microbes, and therefore inhibit their reproduction, without causing damage to normal cells. Their work greatly influenced the modern treatment of leukaemia as well as of herpes, malaria, urinary-tract infections, and diseases caused by antibodies. Elion and Hitchings were awarded the Nobel Prize for this work jointly with the Scottish pharmacologist James Black.

Elion has won many other awards and honours. Since 1983 she has held the title of Scientist Emeritus at Burroughs Wellcome, where her work on viruses in the 1970s became a springboard for the development of anti-AIDS drugs.

Eliot, George (1819–1880) *British novelist*

> The years seem to rush by now, and I think of death as a fast approaching end of a journey – double and treble reason for loving as well as working while it is day.
>
> —Letter to Miss Sarah Hennell, November 22, 1861

The place of George Eliot (the pen name of Mary Ann Evans) in the first rank of English writers rests on her profound understanding of human experience (both moral and emotional), her fine characterization, and her richly detailed representations of English provincial and rural society. She also drew attention to the conflicts encountered by intelligent women in the days before equal opportunities.

Mary Ann Evans – generally called Marian – was born in Chilvers Coton, Warwickshire. Her father, Robert Evans, was a craftsman who rose to be a land agent. His deep sense of duty and responsibility had a huge influence on Marian and inspired her characters Adam Bede and Caleb Garth. Marian was sent to schools in neighbouring towns, soon demonstrating her intelligence and studiousness. She left school at 16 and on her mother's death the following year kept house for her father, continuing her studies of languages and music at home. Her Christian faith changed from extreme piety to doubt after she moved with her father in 1841 to Coventry, where she made a number of new intellectual friends. However, distressed by the pain she was causing her father, she later resumed churchgoing.

Marian's new friends in Coventry included such intellectuals as Harriet MARTINEAU and Robert Owen. Here also she undertook the difficult task of translating the controversial German work *Das Leben Jesu, kritisch bearbeitet* (The Life of Jesus, Critically Treated) into English. "It makes her ill," a friend wrote, "dissecting the beautiful story of the Crucifixion."

Robert Evans died in May 1849. Friends took Marian on a European tour, and on her return she moved to London, where she assisted the publisher John Chapman in editing *The Westminster Review*, a philosophical journal. Though not a pretty woman, she had a powerful personality, and while she was lodging at Chapman's house, both his wife and mistress became jealous. She returned in distress to Coventry, but her talents were needed, and she was soon called back – as assistant editor in charge of book reviews. Her position brought her into contact with leading intellectuals and writers. Through her friend the philosopher Herbert Spencer she met the journalist and critic George Henry Lewes, with whom she went to live in July 1854. Lewes's wife had been unfaithful, but he could not divorce her because he had not openly condemned her at the time. However, for Marian her own union with Lewes was a true marriage, and it proved an ideal one.

Lewes encouraged Marian to try writing fiction. The three stories *Scenes of Clerical Life* appeared in 1858. Marian's next book and first novel, *Adam Bede* (1859), established her as the foremost woman novelist of the day. It was followed by *The Mill on the Floss* (1860), *Silas Marner* (1861), the historical novel *Romola* (1863), *Felix Holt, the Radical* (1866), *Middlemarch* (1871–72), and *Daniel Deronda* (1876).

The early works up to 1861 were written more quickly and spontaneously than her later novels, which reveal her as a modern author in the same class as Flaubert, Turgenev, and Tolstoy. The early works, which in her lifetime were generally considered her best, have a warmth and charm lacking in the later, more ambitious, books. These are the qualities that make *Adam Bede* and the moral fable *Silas Marner* so memorable. Both works describe a traditional England in which religious faith was simple and secure. In *The Mill on the Floss* Eliot paints her own portrait as Maggie Tulliver, the first of a series of characters modelled on her own search for a moral code.

George Eliot's *Middlemarch* is usually seen as her masterpiece and ranks with the greatest English novels. Its interlinked plots trace the fortunes of characters living in a country town (modelled on Coventry) in the months before the Reform Bill of 1832. The novel contains possibly her finest characterizations: the "spiritual grandeur" of Dorothea Brooke, the sterile scholarship of her husband Casaubon, and the frustrated ambitions of the doctor, Lydgate.

Lewes died in November 1878. Six months later Eliot married a family friend, John Walter Cross, who was more than 20 years her junior. After a marriage of less than two years she died in London.

Elizabeth (1437–1492) *Wife of King Edward IV of England*

A tough ambitious woman, Elizabeth lived through a turbulent period in English royal history.

The daughter of Sir Richard Woodville, Elizabeth was eager to promote the interests of her family. Already a widow with two children, she secretly married Edward IV on May 1, 1464, provoking the resentment of Richard, Earl of Warwick, and the powerful Nevilles. This was probably the reason for the murder of her father and brother in 1469.

When Edward IV died in 1483, his brother the Duke of Gloucester seized the throne as Richard III . Soon afterwards Elizabeth's sons, the boy King Edward V and his brother Richard, were murdered in the Tower of London, and Elizabeth's marriage was pronounced invalid. Then in 1485 Henry Tudor killed Richard III, made Elizabeth Queen Dowager, and (in 1486) married her daughter. Elizabeth retired to Bermondsey Abbey, near London, where she died.

Elizabeth (1596–1662) *Wife of King Frederick I of Bohemia*

> By virtue first, then choice, a Queen,
> Tell me, if she were not designed
> The eclipse and glory of her kind.
>
> —Sir Henry Wotton, "Elizabeth of Bohemia" (early 17th century)

Elizabeth was known as the "Winter Queen" because of her husband's brief and troubled reign in Bohemia in the winter of 1619–20, but her beauty, charm, and wit also won her the nickname "Queen of Hearts."

Elizabeth Stuart, the daughter of the future James I of England and his wife ANNE OF DENMARK, was born at Falkland Castle, Scotland, and brought up as a rigorous Protestant and royalist. She was married in 1613 to the Calvinist Elector Frederick V, who ruled over the Rhine region of the Holy Roman Empire.

In 1619, at the outbreak of the Thirty Years' War, Frederick was offered – and accepted – the Bohemian crown, becoming King Frederick I. This decision turned out to be misguided. Elizabeth, who in intelligence and determination was clearly superior to her indecisive husband, willingly shared his destiny in the tragic years that followed. After the Protestant defeat at the Battle of the White Mountain in 1620 they were forced into exile from Bohemia, finding refuge in the Netherlands in 1621. Frederick died in 1632.

Although her son became Elector Charles Louis after the Peace of Westphalia in 1648, he would not allow Elizabeth to join him in Heidelberg. The following year her brother Charles I of Britain was dethroned and executed. In 1660 the Stuart Restoration enabled her to return to England, together with her son Rupert, who had been a leading royalist commander during the Civil War. She died in London. Through her daughter SOPHIA, electress of Hanover, Elizabeth was the grandmother of the first Hanoverian king of Great Britain and Ireland, George I.

Elizabeth (1709–1762) *Empress of Russia*

Elizabeth was untrained to govern, but her ardent patriotism and hatred of war enabled her to overcome many difficulties. She was noted for her kindness, beauty, and patronage of the arts.

Also known as Elizabeth Petrovna, she was the daughter of Peter the Great and CATHERINE I, born three years before their marriage. Though she was recognized at once by her father and later legitimated, her strong claim to the throne was passed over consistently in the succession of rulers after her mother's death in 1727. She accepted this quietly until November 1740, when ANNA LEOPOLDOVNA, whose infant son had just become Emperor Ivan VI , seized the regency and threatened to banish Elizabeth to a convent. The court was divided into political factions; and when Sweden declared war in July 1741, the French ambassador and others persuaded Elizabeth to take action. With the help of the devoted Guards regiments she seized the throne in a bloodless coup. The war with Sweden was ended in 1743, with Russia slightly extending its territory in southern Finland.

Although she changed the political system by replacing the cabinet council with the senate, as established by her father, Elizabeth was more interested in cultural life than politics. She founded both the University of Moscow and the Academy of Arts at St. Petersburg. Elizabeth also ended capital punishment for political offences and tried to humanize the other sentences.

Elizabeth's health was declining when the Seven Years' War started in 1756, but she honoured her Austro-Russian alliance of 1746 and sent troops in to rout the Prussians. If Elizabeth's death had not caused Russia to withdraw from the war, Frederick the Great of Prussia would have been destroyed.

Elizabeth (1837–1898) *Wife of Francis Joseph I, emperor of Austria and king of Hungary*

Her striking beauty, lively spirit, and accomplished horsemanship made Elizabeth a fitting empress and queen.

The second daughter of Duke Maximilian Joseph and Ludovica of Bavaria, she married her cousin Francis Joseph I of the House of Habsburg (reigned 1848–1916) in 1854. Having been brought up in the unrestrained rural atmosphere of the family castle of Possenhofen, she found it difficult to adapt to the Viennese court and her domineering mother-in-law, the Archduchess Sophia. After the birth of the crown prince Rudolf in 1858, she became estranged from her husband, but they were reconciled during the disastrous war with Prussia and Italy in 1866. At this time Elizabeth helped bring about better relations between the Austrian and Hungarian halves of the empire. Her ability to speak Magyar fluently endeared her to the Hungarians.

In general Elizabeth played little part in public affairs, hated publicity, and quietly interested herself in literature. The suicide of her son in 1889 was a terrible shock. She herself met a violent death – as she stepped aboard a steamer at Geneva she was brutally stabbed by Luigi Luccheni, an Italian anarchist.

Elizabeth (1843–1916) *Wife of King Carol I of Romania*

Elizabeth is remembered as the author of much poetry and prose written under the pen name Carmen Sylva. The daughter of Prince Hermann of Wied and Princess Marie of Nassau, she was born in Neuwied Castle in the

Prussian Rhineland. In 1869 she married Prince Carol of Romania, who later became King Carol I. Their only child, a daughter, died at the age of four; as a result the grief-stricken Elizabeth was moved to establish many hospitals and orphanages and embark upon her literary activities.

Under the pen name Carmen Sylva Elizabeth wrote poems, novels, short stories, fairy tales, and plays and translated Romanian poems and legends into German. Her best prose included, in German, *Märchen einer Königin* (1901; translated as *A Real Queen's Fairy Book*, 1909) and, in French, *Pensées d'une reine* (1888; translated as *Thoughts of a Queen*, 1890).

Elizabeth and her lady-in-waiting Mite Kremnitz wrote several novels together under the pen names Dito and Idem. Elizabeth also published her memoirs, *From Memory's Shrine*, in 1911. She died in Bucharest.

Elizabeth I (1533–1603) *Queen of England and Ireland*

> I know I have the body of a weak and feeble woman, but I have the heart and stomach of a king.
>
> —Speaking to her army at Tilbury on the approach of the Spanish Armada, 1588

The reign of Elizabeth I, known as "Good Queen Bess," was a golden age for culture, commerce, and English naval supremacy. Elizabeth guided her country through the second phase of the Reformation, settling it upon a moderate Anglican foundation. A worldly Renaissance woman, she was in touch with every side of the nation's activity, from politics, finance, and religion to exploration, literature, and the arts. Her long reign provided stability, in which the country's life flourished as never before.

Daughter of King Henry VIII and his second wife, Anne BOLEYN, Elizabeth was born at Greenwich Palace. A clever child, she was carefully educated by Cambridge tutors of moderate Protestant inclinations. Brilliant at languages, she became a good classical scholar and wrote and spoke French and Italian fluently. As queen, this talent enabled her to conduct negotiations personally with foreign envoys. She was striking in appearance, with the red hair of the Welsh Tudors, high cheekbones, and a hooked nose. Like her grandfather Henry VII she was wary, shrewd, calculating though not ungenerous, and at heart humane. Distinctly autocratic, she had a genius for rule and used her femininity to manipulate men for political advantage.

During the reign of her half-brother Edward VI the handsome Thomas Seymour made unwanted advances towards her. This may have reinforced a fear of sexual intimacy aroused by the earlier execution for adultery of her mother and of her cousin and stepmother Catherine HOWARD. She was in grave danger during the reign of MARY I, her Catholic half-sister. Implicated in Protestant unrest, Elizabeth was sent to the Tower, very nearly executed, and later banished from court. This experience determined Elizabeth, when queen, never to recognize an heir who might become a focus for opposition. When she did succeed Mary in 1558, she set about reversing the disasters of her half-sister's reign – her bankrupt treasury, her persecution of Protestants, and her defeat in war.

Protestantism was re-established in 1559 as the national faith, and the Queen spent the rest of her life maintaining and enforcing it in the form of the Church of England. At the same time, she was hostile to Puritan Protestants, who wished to do away with ceremony. At the other extreme Roman Catholics posed a threat to the Anglican faith, but the Acts of Unity and Supremacy of 1559 established a tolerant attitude that lasted until 1570.

Elizabeth's minister Sir William Cecil (later Lord Burghley) dominated her early reign. He put pressure on her to stamp out French dominance in Scotland. This was achieved by the Treaty of Edinburgh (1560), when MARY, QUEEN OF SCOTS, renounced her claim to Elizabeth's throne. However, an attempt to regain Calais (lost by Mary I) ended in failure.

Home affairs were stable for the first decade of Elizabeth's rule. The religious settlement gained strength, and sound policies led to an economic recovery. The expansion of industry and trade, the development of natural resources, and the increase in population, notably that of London, were all features of the new prosperity. Resulting from the strong partnership between Elizabeth and Burghley, these achievements laid the foundation of the Elizabethan Age.

In 1569 a Catholic rebellion in the disadvantaged north of England challenged Elizabeth's rule and was harshly suppressed. After the pope excommunicated Elizabeth in 1570, her regime became less tolerant towards Roman Catholics, and from the 1580s persecutions increased. The Anglican Church was now firmly identified with English patriotism.

Elizabeth had done nothing yet to settle the question of the succession, and it was becoming clear that she did not intend to risk marriage. The Catholic Mary, Queen of Scots, after making a tragic mess of her rule in Scotland, had taken refuge in England in 1568. Many of Elizabeth's courtiers, both Anglican and Roman Catholic, wanted to marry Mary off to Elizabeth's Anglican cousin the Duke of Norfolk, thus tying her firmly to the English alliance. The intrigue was partly motivated by hostility to Cecil and jealousy of his influence with the queen. Robert Dudley, Earl of Leicester, whom Elizabeth loved, was one of those opposed to Cecil, but the queen did not allow her emotions to override her political judgment. She gave Cecil her support against the majority of the nobles in council – a move popular with her people. When Norfolk continued his design to marry Mary and then became involved in a conspiracy with the papal agent, Roberto di Ridolfi, he was found guilty of treason and executed in 1572, leaving Cecil in an even stronger position. Cecil's remarkable partnership with Elizabeth lasted for 40 years until his death in 1598, when he was succeeded by his son, Robert. The administration of both resulted in farsighted and consistent government that procured permanent benefits for the country. Mary continued to be a threat, and after being the focus of several plots against Elizabeth, she was executed in 1587.

In the years 1569–72 there was a showdown with Spain, which ended the old Anglo-Spanish alliance. The break was over the Low Countries, where Philip II of Spain was using savage measures to suppress a revolt against his rule. Meanwhile, Spain had overthrown Sir John Hawkins's persistent attempts to share in its Caribbean trade, maintaining its monopoly of the New World and the Pacific. When Spanish ships carrying the pay for Philip's troops in the Netherlands took refuge at Plymouth, Elizabeth chose to avenge Hawkins's losses and had the ships seized. This put an end to Spanish repression of the Dutch but further soured relations with Spain.

Elizabeth had both a geographical and a financial interest in the search for a northern passage to the Far East around Russia or North America, which dominated the 1570s. The voyages to the northeast opened up Russia's first direct contact with western Europe, resulting in diplomatic exchanges with Ivan the Terrible. Elizabeth also backed Martin Frobisher's voyages to find a northwest passage around Canada and – against Cecil's wishes – personally supported Francis Drake's voyage (1577–80) around the world. In the 1580s she backed Walter Raleigh's efforts to colonize Virginia with English settlers. The name Virginia was a direct mark of homage to Elizabeth, who was known as the "Virgin Queen."

The maritime and colonial conflict with Spain moved into open war after 1585 when, by the Treaty of Greenwich, Elizabeth pledged England to support the Dutch struggle for independence. She disliked the necessity and hated war, but was determined to suppress Spanish aggression. At this time the navy reached a fighting strength and efficiency not rivalled again until the rule of Oliver Cromwell, and it astonished Europe by defeating the great Spanish Armada in 1588. At the height of the invasion threat, Elizabeth appeared before the army at Tilbury, riding on a white horse and wearing a white plume, to make her famous speech. The long war reached a second peak in 1596 with the capture of Cádiz by Robert Devereux, Earl of Essex, Elizabeth's last favourite and Leicester's stepson. She intended him to take Leicester's place in the state, but his failed attempt to crush resistance in Ireland, his intrigues to further the accession of James of Scotland to her throne, and finally his open rebellion in 1601 resulted in her decision to have him executed. The strain of this event sapped her will to live. She had had similar difficulty over Norfolk's execution and that of Mary, Queen of Scots – forced upon her by Cecil, and her whole council – which had given her a temporary breakdown. She died at Richmond. With the possible exception of CATHERINE II (the Great) of Russia, Elizabeth I may be regarded as the greatest woman ruler in history.

Elizabeth II (1926–   ) *Queen of the United Kingdom*

> My whole life, whether it be long or short, shall be devoted to your service and the service of our great imperial family.
>
> —Radio broadcast, 1947

Elizabeth II has set out to continue and strengthen the reputation for royal dignity and sense of responsibility established so successfully by her father. She has continued his efforts to adapt Victorian ideas of monarchy to fit the expectations of modern times.

Princess Elizabeth Alexandra Mary, the elder daughter of Albert, Duke of York (later George VI) and his wife Elizabeth (now ELIZABETH, THE QUEEN MOTHER), was born in London. With little prospect of ever becoming queen, she was educated by private tutors, with her sister, Princess MARGARET, and developed a liking for history, languages, and music. Her life changed dramatically, however, when her uncle, Edward VIII, abdicated the throne in order to marry the American divorcée Wallis Simpson; Elizabeth's parents then became king and queen. However, the two princesses were too young to participate in public duties in the early years of their parents' reign. During World War II they lived at

Windsor Castle, but Elizabeth was already taking an interest in national affairs. Her broadcasts, made in the early years of the war, revealed her to be a serious and responsible person. She appeared in public on formal royal business for the first time in 1944 and later endeared herself to the public by insisting on joining the Auxiliary Territorial Service as a driver. After the war her position as heir to the throne involved her in ever increasing royal duties. In July 1947 Elizabeth was betrothed to Lt. Philip Mountbatten, a distant cousin; they were married in Westminster Abbey the following November. Philip, now His Royal Highness the Duke of Edinburgh, was good-looking and popular. It was clear that the reputation of the monarchy, restored beyond question by her parents after the abdication crisis, would be maintained by Elizabeth and her husband. The couple's first two children, Charles, and ANNE, THE PRINCESS ROYAL, were born in 1948 and 1950, respectively; they were followed by Andrew (born 1960) and Edward (born 1964).

Princess Elizabeth was on tour in Kenya when George VI died in February 1952, making her queen. Her coronation took place at Westminster Abbey on June 2, 1953. Her first major tour was of New Zealand and Australia in 1953, and since then she and Prince Philip have been more active than any previous royal couple in representing British interests and prestige not only within the Commonwealth but throughout the world.

The Queen has shown herself well aware of the problems surrounding a hereditary monarch and has revealed her public personality with taste and shrewdness. In 1970 the televizing of aspects of the royal family's domestic life marked the beginning of increased publicity over the private lives of the "royals" and showed the extent to which the Queen and Prince Philip were aware of the changing expectations of their subjects. The Queen is known to take a serious and informed interest in government business, conscious of her modern role as a symbol of British ambitions abroad. As Head of the Commonwealth, she attends Commonwealth conferences and serves as a symbol of unity and continuity in this loose confederation of countries.

Despite occasional reservations about her alleged aloofness, the Queen has retained a high degree of popularity – a phone-in poll in early 1997 suggested that around two thirds of the British public are still very much in favour of the monarchy. Taking into account the embarrassment caused by the highly publicized marital problems of the Queen's three eldest children, this response may be seen as a tribute to Elizabeth herself. During the 1990s she has agreed to various reforms designed to allay potential criticism of the monarchy as remote and outmoded – a process that has been accelerated in the wake of the extraordinary public response to the death of DIANA, PRINCESS OF WALES.

Elizabeth, the Queen Mother
(1900–   ) *Wife of King George VI of the United Kingdom*

> I'm glad we've been bombed. I can now look the East End in the face.
>
> —Remark after the bombing of Buckingham Palace (1940) during World War II

Succeeding unexpectedly to the throne after the crisis arising from Edward VIII's abdication, Elizabeth and her husband won the hearts of the public by steadfastly refusing to be evacuated from London and by their visits to bombed cities during World War II.

Elizabeth Angela Marguerite Bowes-Lyon was born in Hertfordshire, the youngest daughter of the 14th Earl of Strathmore. She spent her early life at the family home at Glamis in Scotland and was relatively unknown to the public when she married the Duke of York, the second son of George V, in 1923. Their daughters Elizabeth and Margaret were born in 1926 and 1930, respectively.

The abdication of Edward VIII in 1936 and their consequent accession to the throne brought an abrupt change to their lives, which they accepted with great determination. After the death of George VI in 1952 and her daughter's accession as ELIZABETH II, the Queen Mother devoted herself to ceremonial and charitable work with enormous popular success.

Elizabeth Farnese (1692–1766) *Wife of King Philip V of Spain*

Known as Isabella after she became queen of Spain, Elizabeth proved an intelligent and strong-willed woman. She was extremely influential during her husband's reign, particularly in foreign policy.

The daughter of Edward III, Duke of Parma, Elizabeth was born in Parma, Italy. After marrying the widowed Philip V in 1715, she dismissed the Princesse des URSINS, the dominant political figure in Philip's early reign, and established a close relationship with the king. She set out to revive Spanish power in the Mediterranean so that her sons Philip and Charles (later Charles III of Spain) might secure Italian thrones.

As Philip's adviser on foreign policy, Elizabeth persuaded him to distance himself from France, but an attempt in 1717–20 to regain Sardinia and Sicily from France was unsuccessful. She gave support to the Duke of Ripperda, who arranged the Austro-Spanish treaty of 1725. Friendly relations with the Austrians enabled her son Charles to succeed to the duchy of Parma in 1731. In the War of Polish Succession (1733–35), Naples and Sicily returned to Spanish rule. Her son Philip was then made Duke of Parma, while Charles became king of Naples and Sicily.

Elizabeth was a sensitive and cultured woman. On her husband's death in 1746 she retired to the royal palace at San Ildefonso, though she acted briefly as regent in 1759 while Charles was on his way back from Italy to succeed her stepson, Ferdinand VI .

Elizabeth of Hungary, Saint (1207–1231) *Hungarian princess*

Renowned for her efforts to relieve the suffering of the needy, Elizabeth is recognized as the patron saint of Catholic charities, of the third Franciscan order, of nurses, and of bakers.

Elizabeth was born in Hungary in 1207, the daughter of King Andrew II.

Aged only 14, she formed a marriage alliance with Louis IV of Thuringia, with whom she was lucky enough to fall in love. They had three children, but after six years of marriage Louis died while on a Crusade.

Inspired by the ideals of St. Francis of Assisi, Elizabeth selflessly served the war-impoverished Thuringians. Forced into exile after her husband's death by his family, she put her children in the care of relatives and joined the Third Order of St. Francis, donating her dowry to build a hospital for the poor at Marburg, Germany. She led a life of holiness and self-sacrifice until her early death at Marburg.

Within four years Elizabeth was canonized by Pope Gregory IX, and her shrine became a centre for pilgrimages. Renaissance painters often depicted her holding roses in her cloak, reflecting the legend that when she met her husband on one of her missions, the loaves of bread she was carrying became roses.

Elssler, Fanny (1810–1884) *Austrian ballet dancer*

Because of her earthy, sensuous style of dancing, which was often described as "pagan" in contrast to the delicate "Christian" style of her rival, Marie TAGLIONI, Essler attracted many fans. She was famous for adapting folk dances to ballet.

Franziska Elssler was born near Vienna, the daughter of a manservant to the composer Haydn. Though poor, she studied ballet with Jean Aumer at the Kärntnertor Theater, Vienna, and at the age of nine entered the ballet troupe of the Vienna Hoftheater, where the ballet master was Filippo Taglioni, Marie's father. She gave her first solo performance there in 1822.

Leaving Austria for Italy at only 14, she had an affair with the prince of Salerno. She danced with great success in many of Europe's cultural centers. In Paris she studied intensively with Auguste Vestris before her Paris Opéra debut in 1834. She was so wildly popular that, according to legend, fans dined on a pair of her dancing slippers. Later visits to the United States and Russia also brought wild acclaim. Her most famous appearances were in Jean Coralli's *Le Diable boiteux* (1836), Joseph Mazilier's *La Gypsy* (1839), and *Giselle*. Though never married, she had two children and amassed a fortune before retiring in 1851.

Emecheta, Buchi (1944–   ) *Nigerian writer and lecturer*

Her novels, which are often based on personal experience, examine the position of black African women, both as immigrants to Britain and within the culture of their homeland: they also explore wider themes of tyranny and oppression in human relationships.

Florence Onye Buchi Emecheta was born near Lagos, Nigeria, the daughter of a railway porter. By the age of 20 she was married with four young children. She moved to Britain with her husband and studied at the University of London in the early 1970s, graduating with an honours degree in sociology. Her first novel, *In the Ditch* (1972), is based on a series of articles written for the *New Statesman* magazine about her experiences as an immigrant. A sequel, *Second-Class Citizen*, followed in 1974, and the two novels were later published in one volume as *Adah's Story* (1983).

In *The Bride Price* (1976), *The Slave Girl* (1977), and *The Joys of Motherhood* (1979), Emecheta turned her attention to the problems faced by women in Nigerian society. She returned to her native country in 1980 as a visiting professor at the University of Calabar. Her own experiences at that time, and the experiences of her friends and relatives during the Nigerian civil wars, provided material for two novels published in 1982, *Double Yoke* and *Destination Biafra*. *Gwendolen* (1989) explores the isolation felt by young immigrants in an alien culture and also deals with the difficult subject of child abuse.

Emecheta's other works include television plays, such as *A Kind of Marriage* (1976); books for children, notably *Nowhere to Play* (1980) and *The Moonlight Bride* (1981); and an autobiography, *Head Above Water* (1986). She has lectured at universities across the United States, including Yale (1982), and also at the University of London.

Emma (*c.* 988–1052) *Wife of King Aethelred II and later of King Canute II of England*

The daughter of Richard I, Duke of Normandy, Emma was to become an influential figure in English politics. In 1002 she married Aethelred (II) "the Unready," by whom she had a son, later King Edward the Confessor. Aethelred was overthrown in 1013 by Sweyn Forkbeard, and after his death in 1017 Emma married the new king, Canute, Sweyn's son. The marriage was intended to bar her Anglo-Saxon family from the throne and subsequently favoured her children by Canute – a son, Hardecanute, and a daughter, Gunhild, who married the future Holy Roman Emperor Henry III.

On Canute's death in 1035 Emma strongly supported the claim of Hardecanute, but in 1037 his illegitimate half-brother, Harold Harefoot, became king and forced Emma into exile. When Hardecanute succeeded Harold in 1040, Emma gained great influence. After his death in 1042 she favoured the claim of King Magnus of Norway over that of her own son Edward. On becoming king, Edward allowed her to fade into obscurity, and she died at Winchester.

See also AELGIFU.

Ender, Kornelia (1958–   ) *German swimmer*

> Kornelia Ender was the heroine of the swimming pool. She won four gold medals and one silver and in one evening gained two of her titles in the space of half an hour.
>
> —Christopher Brasher, reporting on the Montreal Olympics (1976)

Considered by many to be the greatest woman swimmer ever, Kornelia Ender became in 1976 the first woman to win four gold medals at the same Olympic Games.

Kornelia Ender was born in Plauen, then in the German Democratic Republic (East Germany). At the early age of 13 she won three silver medals at the Munich Olympics; at 14 she was the fastest female short-distance swimmer in the world, with a time of 58.25 seconds for 100 metres. Between 1973 and 1975 she won a long list of international titles – more than any other woman had achieved.

In the 1976 Olympics at Montreal the rigorous training of East German women swimmers paid off: they took 11 gold medals, of which Ender won four. She equalled her own earlier record of 55.65 seconds in the 100-metre freestyle, broke the record for the 200-metre freestyle, and won golds for the 100-metre butterfly and the medley relay. Her team also came second in the freestyle relay, gaining Ender a silver medal. Her total of four gold and four silver Olympic medals now equalled the earlier achievement of Dawn FRASER.

After her triumph at the 1976 Olympics, Ender married her teammate Roland Mathes, a fellow swimmer with eight Olympic medals to his name. Her second husband, Steffen Grummt, was another top-class athlete.

Epinay, Louise-Florence d' (1726–1783) *French literary patron and writer*

Madame d'Epinay's fame sprang from her close friendships with the writers Rousseau, Diderot, and Grimm, though she was also an author in her own right.

The child of a noble family, Louise-Florence d'Esclavelles was born in Valenciennes, France. After being educated in a convent, she married a cousin, Denis d'Epinay, in 1745. Her husband was a philanderer, and she soon took lovers herself, notably the critic Friedrich Melchior von Grimm. Rousseau spent much time on her estate, where he wrote *La Nouvelle Héloïse*, but he became alienated from his hostess, Grimm, Diderot, and others who championed the power of reason and attacked religion.

Madame d'Epinay's own writings included articles, novels, and a fictional autobiography, *Mémoires de Mme. de Montbrillant* (published posthumously in 1818), in which many of her famous friends appear under thinly veiled pen names.

Esquivel, Laura (*c.* 1951–) *Mexican writer*

> A wondrous, romantic tale, fuelled by mystery and superstition, as well as by the recipes that introduce each chapter.
>
> —Karen Stabiner, describing *Like Water for Chocolate* in the *Los Angeles Times Book Review*, 1992

Laura Esquivel's fame rests on the popularity of the film *Like Water for Chocolate* (1992), based on her novel of the same name.

The daughter of a telegraph operator, Laura Esquivel was born and educated in Mexico. During her subsequent career as a teacher (which lasted eight years), she wrote and directed children's theatre. However, her marriage to the Mexican director Alfonso Arau opened up opportunities for screenwriting. Her first venture in this medium was *Chido One* (1985).

Since childhood Esquivel had been fascinated by food and cookery; in her novel *Como agua para chocolate* (1989; published in English as *Like Water for Chocolate*, 1992) she explores the symbolism of cooking. The book's title refers to the heroine's simmering emotions – at boiling point, like the water used to make hot chocolate. The principal character, struggling with the fact that the man she loves is going to marry her sister, pours her emotions into the cake she bakes for the wedding, which takes on both a symbolic and a real importance. A movie based on the novel, directed by Arau with a screenplay by Esquivel, was released in 1992 and was a universal success. The novel has since appeared in numerous translations.

Esquivel has since written further screenplays – for the children's film *Little Ocean Star* (1994) and for *Regina*, a feminist interpretation of the life of Jesus Christ.

Estrées, Gabrielle d' (1573–1599) *Mistress of King Henry IV of France*

Gabrielle was the daughter of Antoine d'Estrées, Marquis de Coeuvres. In 1590 Henry met and fell passionately in love with Gabrielle, who became his mistress in 1591. Her formal marriage (1592) to Nicolas d'Amerval was annulled in 1594. Henry showered Gabrielle with honours, making her the Marquise de Monceaux (1595), Duchess de Beaufort (1597), and Duchess d'Etamps (1598). She bore Henry three children: César, Duke de Vendôme, first of the Vendôme branch of the Bourbons; Catherine Henriette, Duchess d'Elbeuf; and Alexandre, grand prior of France. Henry was planning to divorce MARGUERITE DE VALOIS and marry Gabrielle when she died suddenly.

Eudocia (*c.* 401–*c.* 460) *Wife of Byzantine Emperor Theodosius II*

Athenian by birth and highly educated, Athenaïs (as she was known before she became empress) was the daughter of Leontius, a pagan philosopher. She went to Constantinople (Byzantium) to seek legal redress against her brothers over the inheritance of her father's property and there met PULCHERIA, the eldest sister of the young Emperor Theodosius II. Impressed by her elegance, beauty, and education, Pulcheria arranged for Athenaïs to marry her brother in 421. She embraced Christianity and took the name of Eudocia.

Eudocia was a cultured woman and poet, whose works include *The Victory of the Troops of Theodosius over the Persians* (421–22). As empress, she was noted for her pious works and her pilgrimage to Jerusalem in 438. She wielded great influence over her weak husband, but her enemies succeeded in persuading him that she had been unfaithful.

With his consent she left Constantinople in 443 and went to Jerusalem, where she spent the rest of her life building churches, monasteries, and hospices. She died in about 460 and was buried in Jerusalem. Her daughter, Licinia Eudoxia, married Emperor Valentinian III.

Eudocia Macrembolitissa (1021–1096) *Wife of two successive Byzantine emperors*

Famed for her wisdom, Eudocia played a prominent role in the administration of the empire of her first husband, Constantine X Ducas, who became emperor in 1059. When Constantine died in 1067, Eudocia acted as regent for their children. Her second husband became emperor in 1068 as Romanus IV Diogenes. After Romanus's defeat and capture by the Seljuk Turks at Manzikert in 1071, Eudocia again took over the government. After Romanus made an unsuccessful attempt to regain his throne and was succeeded by her son Michael , she retired to a nunnery.

Eudoxia (died 404) *Wife of Byzantine emperor Arcadius*

Eudoxia is best known for expelling the patriarch of Constantinople, St. John Chrysostom, who was an uncompromising critic of the extravagant behaviour of her court.

The daughter of Bauto, a Frankish soldier who had risen to be a military leader under the Roman emperor Valentinian II, Eudoxia had been given a Roman education but was brought up in Constantinople. Her marriage to Emperor Arcadius in 395 had been arranged by the corrupt Eutropius, but it was her beauty that had attracted the young emperor. A forceful Christian woman, Eudoxia dominated her weak husband. Their son became Emperor Theodosius II.

Eudoxia (1669–1731) *First wife of Peter the Great of Russia*

Yevdokia Fyodorovna Lopukhina, a member of the Russian nobility, married Peter in 1689 when he was only 17; a year later she gave birth to a son, Alexis. Although beautiful, she was not too intelligent, and Peter soon tired of her. When she refused him a divorce in 1698, he sent her to a nunnery. She managed to escape and joined forces with Alexis in an attempt to overthrow Peter. After the plot failed in 1718, Eudoxia confessed and was imprisoned; the other plotters, including Alexis, were tortured and executed. Eudoxia was released from prison in 1727 when her grandson, Peter II of Russia, ascended the throne. She died in Moscow.

See also CATHERINE I.

Eugénie (1826–1920) *Wife of Emperor Napoleon III of France*

Eugénie was infamous for meddling in

foreign policy, with disastrous results. She was also known for her contribution to European fashion.

Eugénie de Montijo, Comtesse de Teba, whose father had fought for the French in the Peninsular War, was born in Granada, Spain, and educated in Paris. Although a spirited and beautiful woman, Eugénie was entirely unprepared for the supreme role she unexpectedly came to play in 1853 after her marriage to Emperor Napoleon III.

She threw herself into charities but was unable to become a convincing patroness of learning or of the arts. Instead, she became known for the elegance and taste of her gowns and hats, setting the fashions for her generation and earning the nickname "Queen Crinoline." Status and power brought her little happiness, and the imperial couple soon grew apart. The birth of her son, Prince Louis Napoléon, in 1856 nearly cost the empress her life and became the excuse for denying the emperor further sexual relations. She complained bitterly when he was later unfaithful and began to speak out on policy whenever she disagreed with her husband. By supporting the papacy she managed to ensure that the pope's influence was preserved during Italian unification, but her high-handedness also had a tendency to mislead foreign diplomats, who sometimes thought she spoke for the emperor. She was at heart partly responsible for France's intervention in Mexico in the 1860s and for its declaration of war on Prussia in 1870.

After France's defeat in 1870 the emperor abdicated, and he and Eugénie escaped to Kent, England, where the emperor died in 1873. The cruelest blow came in 1879 when Louis Napoléon was killed in the Zulu War. Two years later, Eugénie moved to Hampshire, where she began to construct a tomb for her husband and son. France's recovery of Alsace-Lorraine in 1918 gave her, she said, her first joy since 1870. She died in Madrid.

Eulalia, Saint (*c.* 292–*c.* 304) *Spanish virgin martyr*

Legend relates that Eulalia, from Mérida in Spain, was martyred in 304 during the persecution of Christians under Emperor Diocletian. At 12 she confronted the Roman judge Dacian in Mérida and reproached him for the persecutions. When she refused to make a sacrifice to the pagan gods, Dacian had her tortured to death. She became the patron saint of Mérida, where her feast day is December 10. Her name and legend were also transferred to Barcelona, where she is commemorated on February 12.

Evans, Dame Edith (1888–1976) *British actress*

> She had a faculty for endowing a stage character...with such life that no other actress who subsequently attempted the part could escape unfavourable comparison.
>
> W. A. Darlington in the
> *Daily Telegraph* (1976)

Evans is best known for her comic roles, on both stage and screen, and for her performances of Shakespeare.

Edith Mary Evans was born in London, where she attended St. Michael's school and at 15 was apprenticed to a hat maker. She took up amateur dramatics for fun, but while performing with the Streatham Shakespeare Players, she was noticed by the producer William Poel. He cast her as Cressida in Shakespeare's *Troilus and Cressida* in 1912, and Evans, encouraged by her success, became a professional actress against her family's wishes.

In 1917 Evans was already working with the legendary actress-manager Ellen TERRY, and by the early 1920s she was hardly ever out of work. The critics loved her, but the public was barely aware of her because as a character actress she played such a variety of roles. In 1924 she gave an outstanding performance as Millamant in Congreve's *The Way of the World*. Joining the Old Vic Company in 1926, she played Portia in *The Merchant of Venice*, Katharina in *The Taming of the Shrew*, and other leading Shakespearean roles. Later she won many awards for her roles in Restoration comedies and plays by Shaw; perhaps her best-known part was as Lady

Bracknell in Oscar Wilde's *The Importance of Being Earnest*.

Evans was created a Dame Commander of the British Empire in 1946, and by the 1950s she was an institution of the British stage. She played a long run as Mrs. Lancaster in *Waters of the Moon* and appeared as the Countess in *The Dark Is Light Enough*, written for her by Christopher Fry.

Television and film began to take up more of her time than theatre. Her films include *The Queen of Spades* (1948), *The Importance of Being Earnest* (1951), *The Nun's Story* (1959), *Tom Jones* (1963), and *The Whisperers* (1967), for which she won three Best Actress awards. In 1964 Evans was directed by Noël Coward in his play *Hay Fever*, and took the role of Mrs. Forest in *The Chinese Prime Minister* – her last stage appearance in a play. At the age of 85 she performed in a one-woman show entitled *Edith Evans...and Friends*, playing a variety of characters. As always, she was a hit.

Evans, Janet (1971–) *American swimmer*

Janet Evans has drastically reduced the world-record times for long-distance swimming events. Her records for the 400-metre, 800-metre, and 1,500-metre events remained unbroken in the late 1990s.

Evans was born in Fullerton, California. She broke her first three world records (for the 400 metres, 800 metres, and 1,500 metres) in 1987 and over the next two years continued to whittle down her times. At the 1988 Olympics in Seoul she won gold medals for the 400-metre and 800-metre freestyle and for the 400-metre individual medley. Her time for the 400-metre freestyle – 4 minutes 3.85 seconds – set a new world record; the same year she set records of 8 minutes 17.12 seconds for the 800 metres and 15 minutes 52.10 seconds for the 1,500 metres (not an Olympic event). Evans bettered her own 800-metre record at the Pan-Pacific Championships in

1989, when she swam the distance in a time of 8 minutes 16.22 seconds.

Over the next few years Evans continued to win titles in these three events – at the Goodwill Games, the World Championships, and the Pan-Pacific championships. She also studied at Stanford University for two years but dropped out to prepare for the 1992 Olympics. Despite winning the 800 metres and coming in second in the 400 metres at Barcelona, she did not better any of her records, nor has she done so since. Janet Evans has also won numerous U.S. titles.

Exter, Alexandra (1882–1949)
Ukrainian painter and designer

Significant in her own right as an avant-garde painter and theatrical designer, Exter also provides an important link between Russian and western European art.

Alexandra Exter was born at Belestok, Ukraine, and studied art in nearby Kiev until about 1906. In 1908 she visited Paris for the first time and during repeated visits to western Europe was influenced by the cubist painters Picasso and Braque as well as by the futurists. Many of their innovations she took back to Russia and Ukraine.

Exter exhibited in Kiev and various Russian cities over the next few years before moving to St. Petersburg in 1912. Continuing to make visits to the West, she developed a bold and colourful abstract style, which led to her first experiments with stage design in 1916. In 1918 she began to teach in Kiev and at her own studio in Odessa, training such designers and painters as Pavel Tchelitchew. Here, with her pupils, she also produced vast designs for "agit" (propaganda) steam boats.

After 1920, when she married the actor George Nekrassov, Exter became increasingly interested in stage and costume design; in 1924 she extended her activities to films. That same year she emigrated to France. In later life Exter added decorative arts design to her already broad repertoire.

F

Faithfull, Emily (1835–1895) *British publisher and feminist*

Emily Faithfull made a major contribution to raising the employment prospects and thereby the social status of women.

She was born in Headley, Surrey, the youngest daughter of the rector. After attending school in London, she remained in the city to work with a group of feminists based at Langham Place, headquarters of a new periodical, *The English Woman's Journal*, which provided a platform for the major feminist writings of the time. The Langham Place offices also served as the administrative centre of the Society for Promoting the Employment of Women, which Emily Faithfull helped to found in 1859.

After training as a typesetter, Faithfull founded the Victoria Press in 1860; two years later Queen VICTORIA named her Printer and Publisher-in-Ordinary to the Queen. In 1863 Faithfull started *The Victoria Magazine*, which advocated the right of women to have well-paid jobs; by 1880 it had run to 35 volumes. She also founded, in 1865, a weekly journal called *Women and Work*, as well as encouraging women to voice their opinions at her Victorian Discussion Society.

Emily Faithfull was the first woman to join the Women's Trade Union League. A founder of the Women's Printing Society, she established the *West London Express*, using women compositors only, in 1877. This was so successful that she had to expand the original workforce of 19 and introduce modern steam machinery. During the 1870s she worked for the *Ladies Pictorial* and also founded the International Musical, Dramatic and Literary Association to help protect copyright.

Faithfull described her three lecture tours to America, made in 1872, 1877, and 1882, in *Three Visits to America* (1884). She was also the author of two novels: *Change Upon Change; A Love Story* (1868) and *A Reed Shaken With the Wind; A Love Story* (1873).

Faithfull, Marianne (1946–) *British singer, songwriter, and actress*

Having attracted enormous media attention in the 1960s as Mick Jagger's girlfriend, Marianne Faithfull later recorded a series of powerful albums featuring largely her own songs.

Born in London, the daughter of a university lecturer and an Austrian baroness, Faithfull was educated at St. Joseph's Convent School in Reading, Berkshire. At the age of 18 she married a London art dealer, who introduced her to Mick Jagger. Her association with the Rolling Stones led to a hit single with the Jagger–Richards song "As Tears Go By" in 1966. "Come and Stay with Me," "This Little Bird," and "Summer Nights" appeared in the following year. In 1967 Mick Jagger and the Rolling Stones were arrested on drug charges; Faithfull, by then Jagger's girlfriend, became headline news. At this time her own singing career petered out, and she turned to acting, appearing in the French film *The Girl on the Motorcycle* (1968) and in a live production of *Three Sisters*. In 1970 she played Ophelia in a film version of *Hamlet*. In the same year her relationship with Jagger came to an end, and she made an unsuccessful attempt to cure herself of her drug habit. For several years she disappeared from the media spotlight and lived in near destitution.

In 1977 Faithfull came back with a new album, the critically acclaimed *Broken English*, for Island Records.

Dangerous Acquaintances came out in 1981, followed by *Strange Weather* in 1987. In the mid 1990s she published her autobiography, *Faithfull* (1994), and found further critical praise with her performances of cabaret songs by Brecht and Weill.

Faludi, Susan (1959–) *American journalist*

> A superb crusading journalist, attacking injustice with a rare passion.
>
> —Carol Pogash, describing Faludi in *Working Woman* (1992)

A distinguished journalist known for her defence of civil liberties and human rights, Faludi is famous for her feminist book *Backlash: The Undeclared War Against American Women* (1991).

Susan Faludi was born in New York City, the daughter of a photographer; her mother was an editor. While studying at Harvard University, where she gained her BA degree, Faludi exposed an incident of sexual harassment that resulted in the suspension of one of the professors.

Having already edited newspapers at high school and college, Faludi embarked on a career as a journalist. Between 1981 and 1989 she worked on the *New York Times* as a copy clerk and then on the *Miami Herald*, the *Atlanta Constitution*, and the *Mercury News* as a reporter. In 1990 she took up a post as a reporter on the *Wall Street Journal*. Her articles brought to light such issues as the effect of budget cuts on the poor and the injustice of "ageism." In 1991 Faludi won a Pulitzer Prize for her article in the *Wall Street Journal* examining the social impact of a buyout of the Safeway store chain.

Faludi's reputation rests to a large extent on her meticulous research and the use of evidence to support her arguments. This is one of the great strengths of *Backlash*, her first book, which earned her the National Book Critics Circle Award. In it she argued that there has been a backlash against feminism in the United States, leaving women facing challenges as great as ever. In this context, she has consistently exposed propaganda designed to discredit feminists, college-educated single career women, and working mothers. However, Faludi has denied suggesting that there is a male conspiracy against women.

Farmer, Frances (1913–1970) *American actress*

> Frances Farmer had a warrior quality which never permitted her to give in or compromise herself...She had to take everything head on.
>
> —Jessica Lange

Although intelligent, beautiful, and talented, Frances Farmer is one of Hollywood's tragic figures. After gaining a reputation for being difficult to work with, she became increasingly unpopular, succumbing to alcohol abuse and mental illness.

Frances Farmer was born in Seattle, Washington, the daughter of a lawyer. After doing well at high school, she went on to study at the University of Washington. While there she won a trip to the Soviet Union as the prize for an essay competition held by a radical magazine.

In 1934 Farmer married the first of her three husbands, the actor Lief Erickson. Two years later she made her debut in Hollywood with four movies, including *Come and Get It*, directed by Howard Hawks and William Wyler. Regarded as her best film, it is the tale of a businessman who renounces his sweetheart (played by Farmer) for his ambitions and later finds himself competing with his son for the affections of her daughter (also played by Farmer). While Hawks was very impressed with Farmer, Wyler is quoted as saying, "The nicest thing that I can say about Frances Farmer is that she is unbearable."

The following year Farmer joined the Group Theater in New York, appearing in *Golden Boy* and a number of other productions on Broadway. She also made other Hollywood films, such as *The Toast of New York* (1937) and *Ride a Crooked Mile* (1938), but regarded much of this work with contempt. Unwilling to conform, she became increasingly unpopular in Hollywood. She appeared in four more films released in 1941–42, but emotional pressures had driven her to alcoholism, and in 1942 she was forced to retire. Her marriage broke down, and she spent the next seven years in a mental hospital.

Farmer recovered sufficiently in the 1950s to appear in two television movies, *Reunion* (1951) and *The Party Crashers* (1958), but never consolidated her early promise. Her autobiography was published in 1972, two years after her death from cancer. The tragic story of her early career was retold in three movies made during the 1980s, most notably in *Frances* (1981), starring Jessica LANGE.

Farrar, Geraldine (1882–1967) *American opera singer*

Famous for her expressive soprano voice and commanding stage presence, Geraldine Farrar was also an intelligent actress of striking beauty.

Born in Melrose, Massachusetts, she studied in Boston and Paris before going on to Berlin to train under Lilli LEHMANN. Miss Farrar made her professional debut in Berlin in 1901 when she appeared in *Faust*, after which she soon became a favourite star. In 1906 she made her American debut as Juliet in a production of Gounod's *Roméo et Juliette*, staged at the Metropolitan Opera House, New York.

Farrar remained with the Metropolitan Opera until her retirement from the operatic stage in 1922. During this period she starred in a number of world premieres, including Giordano's *Madame Sans-Gêne*, Humperdinck's *Königskinder*, and Puccini's *Suor Angelica*. Her most memorable performances were considered to be those she gave in the title roles of *Madame Butterfly*, *Carmen*, *Tosca*, and *Zazà*.

Although she had problems with her voice from 1915, Farrar made successful recordings throughout her operatic career and, following her retirement from opera, appeared on the concert platform until 1932. She also acted in several silent films between 1916 and 1923.

Farrar published her autobiography, *The Story of an American Singer*, in 1916; it was later revised as *Such Sweet Compulsion* (1938). She died in Ridgefield, Connecticut.

Farrell, Eileen (1920–   ) *American singer*

Eileen Farrell achieved fame as a dramatic soprano on the concert platform, the operatic stage, and the radio. She had a great gift for controlling her powerful voice, whose richness brought her a variety of awards and academic honours.

Born in Willimantic, Connecticut, she was taught first by her mother, who had enjoyed a successful career in both vaudeville and church music. She continued her musical studies with Merle Alcock and Eleanor McLellan; in 1941 her radio career began when she imitated the voice of opera singer Rosa Ponselle for a CBS broadcast. This experience stood her in good stead when much later she was chosen to supply the singing voice of the Australian soprano Marjorie Lawrence (acted by Eleanor Parker) in the film *Interrupted Melody*.

From 1941 until 1956 Farrell devoted herself to concerts, recitals, and singing on the radio. In 1956 she first appeared in opera, making her debut as Santuzza in *Cavalleria rusticana* in Tampa, Florida. In the same year she played Leonora in *Il Trovatore* in San Francisco, to which she returned two years later singing the title role in Cherubini's *Medea*. She went on to perform with the San Francisco Opera Company and the Chicago Lyric Opera before making her New York debut in 1960 at the Metropolitan Opera House, as Gluck's Alcestis. Although her concert performances as both Brünnhilde and Isolde with the New York Philharmonic Orchestra under Leonard Bernstein gave full scope to the dramatic qualities of her voice, she never sang these Wagnerian roles on stage.

Farrell's performances of Bach with the Bach Aria Society, New York, were as highly praised as her blues singing at the 1959 Spoleto Festival. From 1977 until 1980 she held the post of Distinguished Professor of Music at the Indiana School of Music, Bloomington. Afterwards she occupied the same post at the University of Maine, Orono.

Farrow, Mia (1945–   ) *American actress*

Daughter of the actress Maureen O'Sullivan and the film director John Farrow, Maria de Lourdes Villiers Farrow was born in Los Angeles. She went to convent schools in London and Madrid but contracted polio when she was nine. This childhood sickness probably contributed to her distinctive fragile looks. Farrow began to act in repertory theatre when she was 17, playing off-Broadway in 1963 and making her film debut a year later. A wide audience followed her character in the TV series *Peyton Place*, but it was her role in Roman Polanski's *Rosemary's Baby* (1968), that made her a star. Her performance earned her the French César Award for Best Actress, the David Donatello Award (Italy), and the Rio de Janeiro Film Festival Award. During the 1970s she appeared in *The Great Gatsby* (1974) with Robert Redford and in Agatha CHRISTIE's *Death on the Nile* (1978).

In 1982 Farrow appeared in *A Midsummer Night's Sex Comedy* with Woody Allen. This was the start of a long personal and working relationship in which Farrow starred in Allen's films *Zelig* (1983), *Broadway Danny Rose* (1984), *The Purple Rose of Cairo* (1985), *Hannah and her Sisters* (1986), *September* (1988), *Shadows and Fog* (1992), and *Husbands and Wives* (1992). Their relationship ended in a bitter and public court battle for custody of their son, Satchel (Sean), from which Farrow emerged victorious. Allen subsequently married her adopted daughter Soon-Yi. In 1994 she starred in the Irish comedy *Widow's Peak*, playing a role which her mother had acted ten years before.

Farrow's two marriages (1966–68, 1970–79), to Frank Sinatra and André Previn, ended in divorce; she has three sons by Previn, a son by Allen, and has adopted seven other children. Her memoir *What Falls Away* was published in 1997.

Fatimah (*c.* 605–*c.* 632) *Daughter of the Prophet Mohammed*

The youngest daughter of Mohammed, the Prophet of Islam, and his first wife, KHADIJAH, Fatimah was the founder of the Fatimid dynasty of Muslim rulers.

Born in Mecca, she grew up in a household that also included Ali Ibn Abi Talib, her father's cousin and devoted disciple, who was to become Fatimah's husband. When Mohammed suffered persecution, Fatimah went with him from Mecca to Medina, where they arrived in 622. Soon after this Fatimah married. A devoted mother, she gave birth to five children of whom Hasan (born *c.* 625) and Husayn (born *c.* 626) proved the most successful, being later venerated by the Shiite branch of Muslims.

Living near her father in Medina, Fatimah was able to be of support to him; Mohammed, in his turn, helped to bring about a reconciliation between Fatimah and her husband, who was known for his harshness and infidelity. It was Fatimah who nursed the Prophet during his final illness. Mohammed died in 632 and was succeeded by 'Abu Bakr, father of A'ISHA. A quarrel then developed between Fatimah and 'Abu Bakr, who refused to acknowledge her claim to part of Mohammed's property. Fatimah outlived her father by only a few months.

Described as the ideal wife "with blistered hands from grinding corn," Fatimah came to be revered by both Shiite and Sunni Muslims. According to Sunni tradition, Mohammed spoke of her as *sayyida*, or "supreme lady," of the universe. Fatimah produced a line of descendants, the Fatimids, who ruled North Africa and Egypt between 909 and 1171. Gradually she acquired cosmic significance, occupying a position in Shiite legend comparable to that of the Virgin Mary in Roman Catholicism.

Fauset, Jessie Redmon (*c.* 1882–1961) *American writer*

Jessie Redmon Fauset made her name with four major novels that deal perceptively with middle-class African-Americans' experiences of racial prejudice. The first of these, *There is Confusion*, appeared in 1924; it was followed by *Plum Bun* (1929), *The Chinaberry Tree* (1931), and *Comedy: American Style* (1933). The message of each novel is that African-American women should remain true to their roots instead of trying to imitate whites.

Born in Philadelphia, Pennsylvania, Fauset grew up in a poor African-American family but succeeded in graduating from Cornell University in 1905. Her education continued at the University of Pennsylvania, where she gained her MA degree, and at the Sorbonne in Paris. She taught French and Latin at a high school in Washington, D.C., before moving on to New York. There she co-edited the magazine *Crisis* with the black writer and activist William Dubois. Later she taught at the Tuskegee Institute, Alabama, and at the Hampton Institute.

As well as her novels, Fauset also wrote poetry; some of her verses are included in *Caroling Dusk* (1927), an anthology of African-American poetry. Fauset was the first African-American woman to be elected a member of the honorary literary society Phi Beta Kappa. She died in Philadelphia.

Fawcett, Dame Millicent (1847–1929) *British campaigner for women's rights*

> We want the electoral franchise...
> because we want women to have the ennobling influence of national responsibility brought into their lives.
>
> —Speech given in Manchester, February 13, 1899

For more than 50 years Millicent Fawcett was a leading figure in the women's suffrage movement in Britain. She was also a champion of higher education for women.

She was born Millicent Garrett in Aldeburgh, Suffolk, where her father was a merchant. Her sister, the pioneering physician Elizabeth Garrett ANDERSON, and her friend Emily DAVIES, founder of Girton College, Cambridge, inspired her lifelong commitment to the women's movement. In 1867 she married Henry Fawcett, professor of economics at Cambridge University and reformist member of

Parliament. As he was blind, Millicent acted as secretary to her husband. Within a year of her marriage Fawcett had a daughter, Philippa, and gave her first speech on women's suffrage. She served on the women's suffrage committee from 1867 besides working for the Married Women's Property Act, which – passed in 1893 – gave women some control over their property and earnings after marriage.

Fawcett's house in Cambridge became the base for a women's lecture scheme that developed into Newnham College, the second women's college of Cambridge University, in 1871. After her husband's death in 1884 Fawcett committed herself even more fully to the suffrage movement, cofounding a new suffrage society in 1886. In 1897 she was elected president of the National Union of Women's Suffrage Societies, a post she held until 1919.

As a speaker against home rule for Ireland and the leader of a women's commission to investigate the concentration camps set up in South Africa during the Boer War, Fawcett gained national recognition as a figure of political importance. After the Boer War she spoke out against the PANKHURSTS' militant approach to women's suffrage. When World War I broke out in 1914 she opposed the pacifists among her fellow suffragists, encouraging women to participate in the war effort. She was thus able to press her case for the enfranchisement of women more strongly. Her efforts were rewarded in 1918, with the passing of an act of Parliament granting the vote to all women over 30 years of age.

Millicent Fawcett's publications include a *Life of Queen Victoria* (1895), *Women's Suffrage* (1912), *Women's Victory and After* (1918), and a biography of the British social reformer Josephine BUTLER (1927). She was made a DBE in 1925.

Feinstein, Dianne (1933–) *American politician*

> For women to be effective in political life they've got to have an area of expertise in which they can speak with authority.
>
> —Interview for the *New York Times*, 1971

Labelled "Mrs. Clean" in the 1970s for her moral and ecological views, Feinstein regarded solving the problems in the cities as the way to nationwide reform. Mayor of San Francisco from 1978 to 1988, she became a Democratic senator from California in 1993.

Born Dianne Goldman in San Francisco, the daughter of a Jewish doctor and his Catholic wife, Dianne attended a convent school but was encouraged to understand and respect both the Catholic and the Jewish faiths. After gaining a degree in history and political science at Stanford University (1955), she began postgraduate studies in criminal justice, afterwards serving on the California Industrial Welfare Commission (1956–57). In 1962 Dianne married Bertram Feinstein, with whom she had a daughter.

During the 1960s Feinstein gained further experience of the criminal justice system, serving on several committees, and in 1970 she became Supervisor of the City and County of San Francisco. In 1978 Feinstein was elected mayor of San Francisco following the assassination of Mayor Mascone. The same year Feinstein's husband died; in 1980 she was married to Richard C. Blum.

In public office Feinstein adopted a liberal approach, for example, with regard to the homosexual issue, which she handled sympathetically but without giving in to pressure from extremists. After her ten years as mayor Feinstein committed herself to the Democrat cause nationally. She was elected to the Senate in 1993. In October 1994 her popularity rose with the passing of a bill to protect six million acres of desert in southern California.

Fell, Dame Honor Bridget (1900– 1986) *British cell biologist*

Honor Fell made significant progress in studying the biochemistry of vitamins and hormones.

Born in Filey, Yorkshire, Fell was educated at Edinburgh University, from which she received her PhD degree in 1924. In 1929, at the age of only 29, Honor Fell became director of Strangeways Laboratory in Cambridge, working there until 1970 and developing it as a centre for the study of cell biology. By removing the limb bones from mouse foetuses and culturing them in a suitable substance supplied with nutrients, Fell was able to show that excess amounts of vitamin A had the effect of dissolving the material between the individual cells of the limb bones. This reaction showed that cultures of bones or other organs could be used for biochemical studies of vitamins and hormones, which could be applied to a wide range of physiological problems.

In addition to her directorship at Cambridge, from 1941 until 1967 Fell served as Foulerton Research Fellow of the Royal Society, London, where she was appointed Royal Society Research Professor in 1963. In 1952 Fell was elected a Fellow of the Royal Society; 11 years later she was made a DBE. In 1965 she was awarded a prize by the Science Academy of the Institut de France.

Officially in retirement from 1970, Dame Honor continued to work at Cambridge, investigating the origin and development of arthritis using tissues from adult animals.

Felton, Rebecca Ann (1835–1930) *American political activist, writer, and lecturer*

Rebecca Felton was the first woman to sit in the U.S. Senate.

Born Rebecca Latimer near Decatur, Georgia, she attended the Madison Female College, at Madison, Georgia, where she graduated first in her class in 1852. The following year Latimer married a local physician, William Harrell Felton, who was already active in Democratic politics. By writing his speeches, planning his campaign tactics, and eventually helping him to draft legislation, Mrs. Felton gave her husband full support in his career as a U.S. Congressman. Together the Feltons promoted penal reform, temperance, and women's rights. Mrs. Felton used her column in the *Atlanta Journal* to express her strong views. In 1893 she served on the board of lady managers of the Chicago Exposition. A year later she became head of the women's executive board of the

Cotton States and International Exposition in Atlanta. In 1904 she became a member of the agricultural board at the Louisiana Purchase Exposition in St. Louis.

In a symbolic gesture, Governor Thomas W. Hardwick of Georgia appointed Mrs. Felton to the U.S. Senate seat vacated by the death of Senator Thomas E. Watson in 1922. Like him she strongly disliked the policies of former President Woodrow Wilson. After just two days (November 21–22) Mrs. Felton was replaced by Walter F. George, the duly elected senator.

Mrs. Felton's writings include *My Memoirs of Georgia Politics* (1911).

See also CARAWAY, HATTIE WYATT.

Fenton, Lavinia (1708–1760) *British actress*

Lavinia Fenton achieved fame by creating the role of Polly Peachum in John Gay's play *The Beggar's Opera*, which opened in London in 1728.

Fenton's father was probably a naval officer called Beswick, to whom her mother was not married; she therefore took the surname of her mother's husband. Lavinia began her working life as a street singer near her mother's coffeehouse in London's Charing Cross. Her acting debut as Monimia in Thomas Otway's *The Orphan; or, The Unhappy Marriage*, staged in 1726, brought her instant success. As a result she joined the company of players under the management of John Rich at Lincoln's Inn Fields Theatre, London. It was there that her performance as Polly created such a sensation. A famous painting by William Hogarth shows her in the part.

In 1729, at the peak of her career, Lavinia ran off with Charles Paulet, 3rd Duke of Bolton, remaining his mistress until they were married 23 years later after the death of his first wife. Lavinia, Duchess of Bolton, died in Greenwich.

Ferber, Edna (1887–1968) *American writer*

> A woman can look both moral and exciting – if she also looks as if it were quite a struggle.
>
> —*Reader's Digest*, December 1954

Edna Ferber was a prolific and much admired author of novels and short stories. Her novel *Show Boat* inspired the well-known musical of the same name.

Born in Kalamazoo, Michigan, Ferber spent her childhood in Appleton, Wisconsin. Here she became a reporter on a local newspaper before moving to work on a better paper in Chicago. However, finding the life of a reporter too demanding for her poor health, she turned to writing fiction.

Her first novel, *Dawn O'Hara* (1911), tells the story of a girl who succeeds in making a living as a writer. Such was the popularity of Ferber's character Emma McChesney, a travelling saleswoman of ladies' underskirts, that she was featured in more than 30 short stories. Published in 1924, *So Big*, a novel in which a woman overcomes the contempt of her local Illinois community to succeed as a farmer, won the Pulitzer Prize in 1925.

Each of Ferber's novels demonstrates her gift for accurate observation of people and places, which owed much to her early experience as a newspaper reporter. *Cimarron* (1930) depicts the Oklahoma land rush of 1889, while *American Beauty* (1931) describes life in Connecticut. *Saratoga Trunk* (1941) is set in New York State, *Great Son* (1945) in Seattle, Washington. In 1952 Ferber published *Giant*, in which she satirized modern Texan manners. *Ice Palace* (1958) vividly describes Alaska. Many of these novels were made into films.

Ferber also established a reputation as a successful playwright. She collaborated with George S. Kaufman on *Minick* (1924), *The Royal Family* (1927), *Dinner at Eight* (1932), and *Stage Door* (1936). Her life story was told in *A Peculiar Treasure* (1939) and *A Kind of Magic* (1963). She died in New York City.

Ferraro, Geraldine (Anne) (1935–) *American Democratic politician*

In 1984 Geraldine Ferraro became the first woman to be nominated for the vice-presidency by a major political party.

The daughter of Italian Roman Catholic immigrants, Geraldine Ferraro was born in Newburgh, New York. Her father died when she was eight, after which the family moved to New York City. Ferraro was educated at Marymount Manhattan College, from which she graduated in 1956. In 1960 she gained a law degree from Fordham University and qualified at New York University Law School. The same year Ferraro married John Zaccaro, a wealthy real estate developer, but retained her maiden name in her professional life. In 1961 she became a lawyer in New York, practising successfully until 1974. During this time she gave birth to two sons and a daughter.

From 1974 Ferraro served as assistant district attorney for Queens County, prosecuting crimes against such vulnerable groups as the elderly, women, and children. In 1978 the congressman of her district retired, and Ferraro was elected as his successor. Liked and respected in the House of Representatives, Ferraro established herself as strongly liberal. She opposed both the funding of right-wing guerrillas fighting in Nicaragua and much of President Ronald Reagan's economic policy. She was re-elected in 1980 and 1982.

When running for president in 1984, Walter Mondale chose Ferraro as his running-mate. The campaign ran into trouble, however, when allegations of tax fraud were made against her husband and her son was accused of being involved with illegal drugs. Ferraro herself was asked if she had violated the Ethics in Government Act. These difficulties probably contributed in 1992 to her narrow defeat in the primary election for the New York Democratic Senate nomination. In 1994 President Clinton appointed Ferraro U.S. ambassador to the United Nations Human Rights Commission in Geneva.

Ferraro's publications include her memoirs – *Ferraro, My Story* (1985) – and *Changing History: Women, Power and Politics* (1993). In 1994 she was inducted into the U.S. National Women's Hall of Fame.

Ferrier, Kathleen (1912–1953)
British singer

Kathleen Ferrier is remembered for the richness of her remarkably distinctive contralto voice, recordings of which, nearly 50 years after her death, are still frequently played. She had only ten years as a celebrated and much-loved singer before her early death from leukaemia.

Born in Higher Walton, Lancashire, she showed musical talent from an early age. Although she had won prizes as a pianist, Ferrier's first job was as a telephone operator. It was not until 1940, when she won a singing competition, that she decided to train as a singer in London on the advice of the conductor Sir Malcolm Sargent.

Having made her name as a soloist in a performance of Handel's *Messiah* in Westminster Abbey in 1943, Ferrier came to the notice of Benjamin Britten. In 1946 she sang the lead in his opera *The Rape of Lucretia* at its opening performance at Glyndebourne. A year later Ferrier sang the role of Orpheus in Gluck's opera *Orpheus and Eurydice*. Her reputation and popularity grew as she toured both Europe and the United States. Memorable performances of Mahler's *Das Lied von der Erde*, conducted by Bruno Walter at the 1947 Edinburgh Festival, and of Elgar's *The Dream of Gerontius*, conducted by Sir John Barbirolli, established Ferrier as an inspired interpreter of these composers. She was equally well known for singing English folk songs. Both Britten and Arthur Bliss composed works for her.

Scheduled to star in four performances of Gluck's *Orpheus* at Covent Garden in 1953, Ferrier was overcome by her illness. Having struggled through the first two performances in great pain, she was taken from the opera house on a stretcher. Eight months later she died in London. In the same year the Royal Philharmonic Society had awarded her their gold medal and she had been made a CBE. Kathleen Ferrier's early marriage to a man from her home town was unable to survive her meteoric rise to fame.

Ferrier, Susan (Edmonstone)(1782–1854) *Scottish novelist*

> But who can count the beatings of the lonely heart?
>
> —*The Inheritance* (1824)

Susan Edmonstone Ferrier made her name as a popular novelist with three books satirizing upper-class Edinburgh society.

Born in Edinburgh, she was the youngest of ten children of a lawyer who became chief clerk to the Court of Sessions. After the death of her mother in 1797 the 15-year-old Susan took over the management of the family home and the care of her father. She was encouraged to become a writer by Sir Walter Scott and the Duke of Argyll, who were friends of her father. With the assistance of the Duke's niece Charlotte Clavering Ferrier wrote her first novel, *Marriage*, in 1810. Published anonymously in 1818, *Marriage* was an immediate success, combining sardonic wit with a close observation of social detail. Ferrier's other two novels, *The Inheritance* (1824) and *Destiny* (1831), also enjoyed considerable popularity for their lively depictions of Scottish society.

After her conversion to evangelical Christianity Ferrier abandoned fiction writing, although she did subsequently publish short memoirs, an account of a visit to Sir Walter Scott, and a selection of letters (1898). As a member of the Free Church she concentrated on charity work, campaigning for temperance and the abolition of slavery. Shy by nature, as she grew older, her failing eyesight made her increasingly withdrawn. She died in Edinburgh.

Feuillière, Edwige (1910–) *French actress*

Regarded as the "First Lady" of French cinema in the 1930s and 1940s, Edwige Feuillière also enjoyed a successful career on the stage.

Born Caroline Cunati in Vérsoul, she studied in Dijon and Paris, making her debut in Paris, under the stage name Cora Lynn, as a light comedy actress. In 1929 she married the actor Pierre Feuillière, from whom she was subsequently divorced, although she retained his name in her subsequent career. In 1931 she became a member of the Comédie-Française, remaining with this company for two years during which she starred as Suzanne in Beaumarchais's *The Marriage of Figaro*. A limited repertoire, however, encouraged her to move from the theatre to films. One of her early screen successes was *Topaze* (1933).

By 1937 Feuillière had returned to the theatre, making her name as a leading tragic actress in Becque's *La Parisienne* and Dumas's *La Dame aux camélias*. She also appeared memorably in Giraudoux's *Sodom et Gomorrhe* (1943), Molière's *Amphitryon* (1947), and Claudel's *Partage de midi* (1948; *Break of Noon*). Cocteau's *L'Aigle à deux têtes* (*The Eagle with Two Heads*) was written especially for her; she took the part of the queen both on stage (1946) and in the later film version (1948).

Feuillière toured widely, appearing with her own company in London in the 1950s and 1960s. A charismatic personality and a beautiful voice contributed to her popularity and success. Her later films include *Le Blé en Herbe* (1954; *The Game of Love*) and *Cher menteur* (1980; *Dear Liar*).

Feuillière was made a Commander of the Legion of Honour and in 1984 she received the César Award of the French Academy.

Field, Sally (1946–) *American actress*

A talented film actress, Sally Field has been rewarded with two Oscars: one for her performance in *Norma Rae* (1979), the second for *Places in the Heart* (1984).

Born in Pasadena, California, Field was the stepdaughter of Tarzan star Jock Mahoney (1919–89). After studying at the Actors Studio, New York, she found her first success in the television situation comedy *The Flying Nun* (1966–70). Subsequently she established herself in the miniseries *Sybil* (1976), for which she won an Emmy Award for her role as a young woman with multiple personalities.

Field's first film was *The Way West* (1967). This was followed by *Smokey and the Bandit* (1977), *The End* (1978),

Hooper (1978), *Back Roads* (1981), *Absence of Malice* (1981), *Murphy's Romance* (1985), and *Punchline* (1987). In several of these films she costarred with Burt Reynolds, with whom she was romantically linked. In 1988 she formed her own production company, which made *Steel Magnolias* (1989), in which Field played the mother of the dying Julia ROBERTS. More recently she has starred with Robin Williams in the highly successful *Mrs. Doubtfire* (1993) and with Tom Hanks in *Forrest Gump* (1994).

Fielding, Sarah (1710–1768) *British writer and translator*

Sarah Fielding was one of the first British authors to write for children.

Born in East Stour, Dorset, she was a sister of the novelist Henry Fielding. Her first and most popular book was a romance called *The Adventures of David Simple in Search of a Faithful Friend* (1744); it tells the story of four young people rejected by their families and by society at large. The author sympathizes deeply with the difficulties of her heroines as they struggle to win independence and social status. In 1747 Fielding published a sequel, *Familiar Letters Between the Principal Characters in David Simple*. Henry Fielding contributed prefaces to each of these books to prevent suspicion that he had been responsible for any of the writing.

A friend of Samuel Richardson, Sarah Fielding wrote the first study of his book *Clarissa* in 1749. In the same year she published one of the very first works for children: *The Governess, or the Little Female Academy*. Her other works include *The Cry: A Dramatic Fable* (1754), written in collaboration with Jean Collier; *The History of Ophelia* (1785); and a translation of Xenophon's *Memorabilia and Apologia* (1762). Sarah Fielding died in Bath, Somerset.

Fields, Dame Gracie (1898–1979) *British singer and comedienne*

> Gracie...had absolutely no conceit. She never behaved in any way at all like a famous person.
>
> —Lillian Aza, quoted by David Shipman (ed.) in *Movie Talk* (1988)

Known for her strong Lancashire wit, Gracie Fields made her name as a singer with both comic songs, such as "The Biggest Aspidistra in the World," and sad ballads, most notably "Sally."

Born Grace Stansfield in Rochdale, Lancashire, she was a natural performer, first appearing on the stage at the age of seven. Gracie Fields rapidly made her mark in pantomime and revue before becoming one of the most popular vaudeville actresses; she was known to her devoted audience as "Our Gracie."

From 1915 to 1925 Fields toured England in revues produced by comedian Archie Pitt, whom she married in 1923. In 1928 she made the first of her nine Royal Command Performances. During the 1930s her popularity grew still further when she starred in a series of British film comedies. These included *Sally in Our Alley* (1931), *This Week of Grace* (1933), *Sing as We Go* (1934), *Queen of Hearts* (1936), and *Keep Smiling* (1938). Paradoxically, all these films, which did so much to relieve the burden of the Depression in the 1930s, made their star the world's highest paid actress.

In 1940 Fields divorced Archie Pitt and married the actor-director Monty Banks. By birth an Italian, he was not allowed to live in Britain after Italy entered World War II. The couple therefore left Britain for Hollywood, where Fields made more films, including *Holy Matrimony* (1943) and *Molly and Me* (1945). This move to the United States during the war cost Fields her popularity with the British working people, which she had worked so hard to earn. Although she returned to Britain in 1941, she continued to face rejection, with considerable sadness.

After the death of Banks in 1950 Fields moved to the Italian island of Capri, where she married an Italian electrician, Boris Alperovici, with whom she opened a restaurant much frequented by British tourists.

In 1978 she returned to her native Rochdale to open a theatre named after her. Always a favourite of the royal family, she was made a DBE in the same year. Her memoirs, *Sing as We Go*, were published in 1960.

Figner, Vera (1852–1942) *Russian revolutionary activist*

Leader of a populist revolutionary movement, Vera Figner spent 20 years in solitary confinement after her arrest in 1883.

The eldest of six children of a wealthy nobleman, she was born in the Kazan province of Russia and enjoyed a happy childhood. She was educated at home by governesses before attending the Rodionovsky Institute in Kazan. In 1870 she married the lawyer Aleksei Filippov. Two years later the couple went with Figner's sister Lidiya to Zurich, where both women joined a radical discussion group. Vera went on to attend medical school in Bern with her husband. About to finish her course, she heard that many of her friends had been arrested and that she was urgently needed in Russia.

After returning to Moscow, Figner obtained a licence to work as a paramedic. In 1879 she joined the terrorist branch of Narodnaya Volya (The People's Will) and became its agent in Odessa. There she wrote propaganda, established links with the army and navy, and in 1879 laid plans to blow up the tsar's train. Following the assassination of the tsar in 1881, Figner was made acting leader of the movement.

In 1883 Figner was arrested and a year later condemned to death. She spent the following year in the Peter-Paul Prison in St. Petersburg before being moved to the appalling Schlisselburg island fortress in the River Neva. She spent the next 20 years in solitary confinement during which she wrote her memoirs, *Kogda chasy zhizni ostanovalis* (When the Clock of Life Stopped), which were not published until 1921. In 1904 Figner was released into exile in Archangel in Siberia, and after the 1905 Revolution, she moved to Switzerland. She returned to Russia in 1914.

Following the 1917 Revolution, Figner was elected chairman of the Amnesty Committee, assisting a large number of freed political prisoners. In the Soviet Union she was regarded as a great heroine. Her collected works appeared in seven volumes in the period 1929–32. She published her *Memoirs of a Revolutionist* in 1927.

Finnbogadóttir, Vigdís (1930–) *Icelandic politician and teacher*

As the president of Iceland (1980–96) Vigdís Finnbogadóttir was the first woman in the world to serve as an elected head of state.

Born in Reykjavik, the daughter of a wealthy engineer, she was educated at the University of Iceland before going to France to study at the University of Grenoble and the Sorbonne in Paris, where she specialized in drama. She returned to Iceland in 1953 to work for the National Theatre, while continuing to study at the University of Iceland.

From 1962 until 1972 Finnbogadóttir taught French in a senior school in Reykjavik and French drama and theatre history at the university; she also presented arts programmes on television. During her summer vacations she was a cultural hostess for the Icelandic Tourist Board. While working as a translator, she produced an Icelandic version of Feydeau's farce *A Flea in Her Ear*, which brought her instant success and launched a career that culminated in 1972 with her appointment as a director of the Reykjavik Theatre Company. From 1976 she was a member of the Advisory Committee on Cultural Affairs in Nordic Countries, becoming its chairwoman in 1978.

In 1980 Finnbogadóttir was persuaded to run for the nonpolitical office of president of Iceland. Winning a little over a third of the total vote, she narrowly defeated her three male rivals to become the world's first democratically elected woman head of state. Reelected unopposed in 1984 and 1988, she began her fourth four-year term in office in 1992. She retired in 1996, having greatly raised the profile of the presidency during her tenure of the post.

"President Vigdis" married in 1954 and divorced in 1963. In 1972 she was among the very few single people in Iceland to be allowed to adopt a child: in her case, a daughter.

Firestone, Shulamith (1945–)
Canadian feminist campaigner

Shulamith Firestone was one of the first organizers of the U.S. Women's Liberation Movement that erupted in the late 1960s.

She was born into a prosperous Jewish family in Ottawa and studied at the Art Institute of Chicago, where she became active in the Civil Rights and anti-Vietnam agitation of the mid-1960s. However, like some other radical women at that time, she came to feel that the male "revolutionaries" of the counterculture had little understanding of the wrongs suffered by women and no particular desire to right them. This conviction led her to found the New York organization Radical Women, which has some claim to be the first modern feminist collective. In 1969 she formed the women's organization RedStockings, which published a journal of the same name: by combining "consciousness raising" sessions, which encouraged women to see their problems in political terms, with marches and other forms of public action, the group became the model for hundreds of similar organizations in North America and Europe. Firestone's chief publication was *The Dialectic of Sex: the Case for Feminist Revolution* (1970), a radical and provocative analysis of gender and class in modern society. She remained active in feminist campaigns during the 1970s but has subsequently taken a much lower profile.

First, Ruth (1925–1982) *South African writer and political activist*

One of the earliest white members of the African National Congress and a friend of such African leaders as Nelson Mandela and Walter Sisulu, Ruth First campaigned tirelessly for the abolition of apartheid.

Ruth First's parents were Jewish immigrants from the Baltic who were members of the International Socialist League. Ruth joined the Communist Party while she was still a student at Witwatersrand University and at the age of 21 was actively campaigning on behalf of black workers in the miners' strike of 1946.

In 1949 she married the lawyer Joe Slovo, who was also deeply involved in radical politics. Ruth at this time was secretary of the Communist Party Central Offices in Johannesburg and editor of the journals *Guardian* and *New Age*, which were later banned.

In 1956 Ruth and Joe Slovo were tried and acquitted at the infamous Treason Trials. In 1963 Ruth's book *South West Africa*, criticizing South Africa's involvement in what is now Namibia, was published. This led to her arrest and solitary confinement for six months. On being released, she left South Africa, recording the details of her imprisonment in *117 Days* (1965). After a short stay in Kenya the Slovos decided to move to England, where Ruth became a research fellow (1972) at Manchester University. From 1973 to 1979 she taught sociology at the University of Durham.

In 1979 the Slovos returned to Africa, where Ruth joined the Centre of African Studies in Mozambique as a teacher. She remained there until her death, which was caused by a letter bomb.

First's later books include *The South African Connection: Western Involvement in Apartheid* (1972), *Libya, the Elusive Revolution* (1974), and *Olive Schreiner* (1981). Her book *Black Gold; The Mozambique Miner* was published in 1983 after her death. *Every Secret Thing: My Family, My Country* (1997) is an attempt by First's daughter, the writer Gillian Slovo, to investigate her parents' controversial lives.

Fisher, Dorothy Canfield (1879–1958) *American writer*

Dorothy Canfield Fisher achieved fame both as an author and an educationalist. She published her fiction under her maiden name, Dorothy Canfield, but for her nonfiction she used her married name, Fisher.

The daughter of James Hulme Canfield, a professor of economics, and his artist wife Flavia, she was born Dorothea Frances Canfield in Lawrence, Kansas. She was educated first in Lawrence and later in Nebraska.

In 1894 Canfield and her lifelong

friend Willa CATHER cowrote a ghost story entitled *The Fear That Walks by Noonday*, which was published in the University of Nebraska Yearbook. Graduating from Ohio State University in 1899, Canfield then went to France to work at the Sorbonne, Paris, before returning to the United States to study at Columbia University for her PhD, which she completed in 1904. For a while Canfield worked as a secretary at the Horace Mann School in New York. However, after marrying John R. Fisher in 1907, she went to live on a farm in Arlington, Vermont, which had housed generations of her family and which became her base.

In the year of her marriage Canfield published her first novel, *Gunhild*; this was followed by *Squirrel Cage* (1912) and *The Bent Twig* (1915). *Hillsboro People*, also published in 1915, is a series of imaginative sketches of Vermont characters. *Understood Betsy* (1917), a novel for children, achieved great popularity.

Living in France with her family from 1916 until 1919, while World War I raged, she started a braille press and a home for orphan refugees. Supporting her husband and two children from the proceeds of her novels, she was well qualified to write about the subject of role reversal, which she did in *The Home-Maker* (1924). Never turning her back on controversial subjects, she always wrote with compassion and common sense. She published 11 volumes of short stories, a play, poetry, children's books, and a number of translations from the Italian.

Fisher's nonfiction includes *American Portraits* (1946) and *Our Independence* (1950). Always interested in education, in 1911 she had visited Maria MONTESSORI's school in Italy. When she returned home, she described the Montessori Method in *The Montessori Mother* (1912). She died in Arlington, Vermont.

Fiske, Minnie Maddern (1865–1932) *American actress and theatrical director*

Both as actress and director Minnie Fiske did much to popularize the plays of Henrik Ibsen in the United States.

Born Marie Augusta Davey in New Orleans, the daughter of a theatrical agent, she made her stage debut at the age of only three. By the age of 15 she was playing adult parts, using her mother's maiden name, Maddern. After marrying the critic and writer Harrison Grey Fiske in 1889, she felt obliged to retire from the stage. However, three years later she made a comeback in her husband's play *Hester Crewe*. Subsequent performances included Ibsen's *The Doll's House* and an adaptation of Thomas Hardy's *Tess of the D'Urbevilles*, which established her as a star.

In partnership with her husband Mrs. Fiske managed the Manhattan Theater in New York from 1901 until 1907, achieving recognition for such Ibsen productions as *Hedda Gabler* and *Rosmersholm*, which helped to establish the dramatist's work in the United States. As well as acting in these plays, Mrs. Fiske also directed them and gave much of her time to developing the potential of aspiring playwrights.

In 1908 Mrs. Fiske took the lead in Edward Sheldon's *Salvation Nell*, starring in his *High Road* four years later. On tour during the 1920s she won acclaim for her performance as Mrs. Malaprop in Sheridan's comedy *The Rivals*. Away from the theatre she campaigned for human rights and a number of other humanitarian causes. She died in Hollis, New York State.

Fitton, Mary (*c.* 1578–c. 1647) *Maid of honour at the court of Queen Elizabeth I of England*

Mary Fitton has been identified, on very flimsy evidence, as the "dark lady" mentioned in Shakespeare's sonnets.

Born at Gawsworth, Cheshire, Mary Fitton was the fourth child and second daughter of Sir Edward Fitton and his wife Alice. In 1595 she became a maid of honour at the court of Queen Elizabeth I. Not a great deal is known of her activities at the royal court, although it is recorded that in 1600 the Queen attended the marriage celebrations of another maid of honour, at which Mary Fitton led the dances. In the same year the poet William Herbert, Earl of Pembroke, became her lover. When meeting him at secret assignations, it is said that she frequently disguised herself as a man. In 1601 Pembroke was banished from court and imprisoned briefly in the Fleet Prison, London, for fathering her illegitimate son, who lived a very short life. On his release Pembroke refused to marry Mary, but in 1607 she did marry Sir William Polwhele, who was probably her second husband.

Interest in Mary Fitton centres on her hypothetical association with William Shakespeare. Was she the "dark lady" of the sonnets? And did the printer's dedication of the sonnets to "Mr. W. H.," believed to be the young man mentioned in the poems, refer to William Herbert? Some romantically inclined authors have suggested a love triangle between Herbert, Fitton, and Shakespeare, chronicled in the somewhat mysterious sonnets. There is, however, no evidence to support this theory; in addition, a portrait, believed to be of Mary Fitton, disqualifies her on the grounds that she had fair hair.

Fitzgerald, Ella (1918–1996) *American jazz singer*

Ella Fitzgerald was widely known as the "First Lady of Song."

Born in Newport News, Virginia, Ella Jane Fitzgerald was raised in Yonkers, New York. When her mother died in 1932, Fitzgerald escaped from both her stepfather and an orphanage to which the Board of Education had sent her. For two years she survived on the Harlem streets, scratching a living by singing and dancing for money. At the age of 16 she entered the Amateur Night talent contest at the well-known Apollo Theater. There she was spotted by the drummer Chick Webb, who employed her with his band for the next five years. Collaborating with Van Alexander, she produced her first hit, "A-Tisket, A-Tasket," in 1938, using her own tune. This song featured in her repertoire for many years afterwards. When Webb died in 1939, she ran the band herself until 1942.

With the ending of the big-band era, Fitzgerald worked independently as a cabaret artiste and concentrated on her unique style of scat-singing, featured so effectively in the song "Lady be Good". Using this technique she treated her voice as an instrument capable of high-speed jazz improvisation. It brought her 12 Grammys, as well as many other musical awards. Equally popular were her renderings of ballads, especially "My Heart Belongs to Daddy."

In 1956 Fitzgerald embarked on her most ambitious recording project, which lasted 11 years. Beginning with the songs of Cole Porter, she produced a series of albums devoted to the works of individual composers, including Rodgers and Hart, Duke Ellington, Irving Berlin, George and Ira Gershwin, Jerome Kern, and Johnny Mercer. The 19 volumes of these "Song Books" contain almost 250 songs. Fitzgerald continuously extended her repertoire to include songs from television shows as well as some of her own compositions.

In 1941 Fitzgerald married Bernie Kornegay, whom she divorced two years later, and from 1949 until 1953 she was married to Ray Brown of the Oscar Peterson Trio, by whom she had a son.

Fitzgerald, Penelope (1916–) *British novelist and writer*

Penelope Fitzgerald is known for her elegantly written novels, including the Booker Prize-winning *Offshore* (1979), and her biographical studies of 19th- and early 20th-century figures from the world of art and literature.

She was born Penelope Mary Knox in Lincoln. Her father was the essayist and humorist E. V. A. Knox, who later became editor of *Punch* (1932–49), while her uncles included the religious writer Mgr Ronald Knox. In 1939 she graduated from Somerville College, Oxford, with a first-class honours degree in English; she later worked in journalism and as an English tutor in London. She married Desmond Fitzgerald in 1941.

Fitzgerald was in her late fifties when her first work was published, a biography of the painter Edward Burne-Jones (1975). In 1977 she published *The Knox Brothers*, a biography of her father and his brothers, and her first novel, *The Golden Child*. This was followed by *The Bookshop* (1978), a keenly observed study of the tensions and rivalries within a small community, and *Offshore* (1979), which won the Booker Prize. The latter, a tale of life on a Thames houseboat, was based on personal experience: Fitzgerald and her family had once lived on a river barge.

Fitzgerald's subsequent novels include *Human Voices* (1980), a satire set at the wartime BBC, and *At Freddie's* (1982), about a London stage school. *Innocence* (1986) and *The Beginnings of Spring* (1988) are set in Florence and Moscow respectively, while the love story *The Gate of Angels* (1990) is a convincing re-creation of life in Edwardian Cambridge. She has also continued to write nonfiction, winning the Rose Mary Crawshaw Prize for the biography *Charlotte Mew and Her Friends* (1984). Her more recent work includes *The Blue Flower* (1995).

Fitzgerald, Zelda (1900–1948) *American painter and novelist*

Zelda Fitzgerald achieved greater fame as the wife of writer F. Scott Fitzgerald than through her own work.

Born Zelda Sayre in Montgomery, Alabama, she was the sixth child of a Supreme Court judge. After being educated mainly at home, she became a typical Southern belle. In 1918 she met her future husband and became engaged to him; although she broke off the engagement, they eventually married in 1920. At this time F. Scott Fitzgerald's first novel, the semiautobiographical *This Side of Paradise*, was accepted for publication and became an instant success. The following year Zelda gave birth to a daughter, Frances Scott (Scottie).

To escape media attention, in 1924 the Fitzgeralds moved to the south of France. Here Zelda Fitzgerald tried to write about the struggle of modern women for independence, although she had to contend with her husband's increasing addiction to alcohol. Finding the writing more and more difficult, Zelda thought of becoming a ballerina, practising her dancing night and day. However, when an opportunity came for her to join the San Carlo Opera Ballet in Naples, she turned it down.

During the winter of 1928–29 Zelda Fitzgerald wrote a series of six sketches. Five of these were published in *College Humor* jointly with her husband; the sixth, which appeared in *The Saturday Evening Post*, omitted her name entirely. In 1930 Zelda suffered the first of several severe mental breakdowns. She nevertheless went on writing her novel *Save Me the Waltz*, which was published in October 1932. In 1933 her paintings were shown in New York.

Over the next few years Zelda became increasingly eclipsed by her husband's growing success. As a result of her worsening mental state she was eventually admitted to the Highland Hospital, Asheville, Alabama, where she remained until March 1940. The following December Scott, who was by that time living with another woman, died suddenly of a heart attack. Zelda herself went on working intermittently at a novel, *Caesar's Things*, which was never finished. She died tragically in a hospital fire along with nine other women.

Fitzherbert, Maria (1756–1837) *Secret wife of King George IV of Britain*

Born Maria Anne Smythe in Brambridge, Hampshire, she was the youngest daughter of a Roman Catholic, Walter Smythe. As a child she visited Paris, where she dined with Louis XV. Her spontaneous laughter as the king pulled a chicken to pieces with his fingers is said to have brought her a gift of sugar plums.

In 1775 Maria married Edward Weld of Lulworth, in Dorset, but was widowed within three months. Three years later, in 1778, she married Thomas Fitzherbert of Swynnerton, Staffordshire, but was again widowed in 1781. With a comfortable income Mrs. Fitzherbert now moved to Richmond, outside London, where she rapidly attracted a select crowd of admirers. Here she first met the Prince of

Wales (later King George IV) in 1785, who found her combination of beauty and intelligence irresistible.

On December 21, 1785, in Mrs. Fitzherbert's drawing room, a Church of England clergyman pronounced the prince and Mrs. Fitzherbert "man and wife." Although the Act of Settlement (1689) would have obliged the prince to forfeit his right of succession to the throne if he married a Roman Catholic, and the Royal Marriage Act (1772) forbade the prince to marry without the consent of the king (George III), Mrs. Fitzherbert was for a time treated by the Prince of Wales and the entire court as if she were legally his wife. However, when seriously challenged by the king, the prince weakly denied that there had been a marriage with Mrs. Fitzherbert. Moreover, he agreed to marry CAROLINE OF BRUNSWICK, the ceremony taking place in 1795. During her separation from the prince following his marriage to Caroline, Mrs. Fitzherbert turned to her confessor for advice. He assured her, on papal authority, that she could resume her relationship with the prince without sinning. She gave a magnificent breakfast party to celebrate.

However, the prince fell under the influence of Mrs. Fitzherbert's enemies, and eventually, at a dinner given for King Louis XVIII of France, she received the unforgivable insult of being told she had no fixed place at dinner. She took the opportunity to sever all ties with the prince and withdrew from the court in about 1808.

The Prince of Wales succeeded to the throne as George IV in 1820. During his final illness ten years later it was Mrs. Fitzherbert for whom King George asked; he is also said to have died wearing her portrait around his neck. She outlived him by seven years, dying in Brighton.

Flagstad, Kirsten (1895–1962) *Norwegian opera singer*

Kirsten Flagstad achieved a worldwide reputation for her singing of soprano roles in Wagner's operas. Remarkably, international fame came only in her forties, although she went on recording well into her sixties.

Born in Hamar, Norway, she had learned the part of Elsa in Wagner's *Löhengrin* by the age of ten. She studied singing in both Stockholm and Oslo, where she made her debut in 1913 singing the role of Nuri in Eugen d'Albert's *Tiefland* at the National Theatre. For the next 20 years her career was restricted to Scandinavia, where she attracted scant critical attention but took the opportunity to master a wide operatic repertoire.

In 1933 Flagstad was invited to perform at the Bayreuth Festival. As a result of her success there she was contracted to sing at the Metropolitan Opera, New York, where in 1935 she sang Sieglinde in *The Valkyrie*, appearing only four days later as Isolde in *Tristan and Isolde*. Her performance as Brünnhilde in *The Valkyrie* in the same season established her as a star. Equal acclaim greeted her in Vienna and at Covent Garden, London.

In 1941 during the Nazi occupation of Norway Flagstad returned home to a life of semiretirement. While she had been in America, her second husband, Henry Johansen, had joined the Norwegian Nazi Party. Although she persuaded him to resign his membership and agreed to sing only in such neutral countries as Switzerland, doubts remained regarding Flagstad's own politics. After World War II she returned to America, where she was greeted with fierce protests. However, Flagstad's strength of character enabled her to re-establish her reputation, and she sang two further seasons with the Metropolitan Opera in 1950 and 1952, making her final appearance there in Glück's *Alceste*.

In 1953 Flagstad gave her final operatic performance as Dido in Purcell's *Dido and Aeneas*. From 1958 until 1960, having retired from the stage, she was the director of the Norwegian State Opera. She died in Oslo.

Flanagan, Hallie (1890–1969) *American theatre historian and administrator*

Hallie Flanagan made her name as the successful director of many theatrical enterprises. As director of the Federal Theater Project of the Work Projects

Administration (1935–39), she was described by President Franklin D. Roosevelt as "the third most powerful woman in America after my wife and Frances PERKINS."

Born Hallie Ferguson in South Dakota, she was educated at Grinnell College, Iowa, and went on to study at Workshop 47 with George Pierce Baker. In 1927 she was given a Guggenheim Award, which enabled her to travel to Europe to further her studies. As a result of this experience, in 1928 she published *Shifting Scenes of the Modern European Theater*.

When Flanagan returned to America she launched and directed an experimental theatre programme at Vassar College, New York State. This proved extremely popular. Recognizing her talent, in 1935 Harry Hopkins, administrator of President Roosevelt's New Deal relief programmes, asked Flanagan to direct a theatre programme intended to provide employment for unemployed actors, directors, and other theatrical workers. Until 1939 she devoted her energies to balancing the demands of art with those of practical human needs. Her work in the Federal Theater Project led to the staging of more than 1,000 productions, notably the Living Newspapers – documentary productions dealing with matters of topical interest (such as unemployment and current affairs). It also resulted in the establishment of African-American companies and children's theatres. Flanagan's book *Arena* (1940) chronicles these turbulent years.

When political and bureaucratic opposition finally undermined her efforts, Hallie Flanagan went back to Vassar, where in 1931 she had cowritten and directed *Can You Hear Their Voices?* She recorded her work there in her book *Dynamo* (1943). In 1942 she moved to Smith College, Northampton, Massachusetts, where she became dean. Sadly, in 1946 illness forced her resignation, although she managed to serve as professor of drama until her retirement in 1955.

She was married twice – to John M. Flanagan and, after his death, to Philip H. Davis.

Fleming, Peggy (1948–) *American skater*

> Peggy lands softly, and everything she does is connected. It's pure ballerina.
>
> —Gabriele Seyfert, runner up to Fleming in the Winter Olympics, 1968

Three times world champion and Olympic gold medallist in 1968, Peggy Fleming is remembered for her graceful, effortless style. Her hallmark was a series of moves known as the "spreadeagle, double axel, spreadeagle," which involved taking off from an outspread posture into an extremely difficult jump and landing in the same posture.

Born in San Jose, California, Peggy Fleming was the second of four sisters. Starting to skate at the age of nine, two years later she was entering competitions. In 1960, aged 12, she won the Pacific Coast junior figure skating championship; after further wins over the next three years she became U.S. women's champion. The slight 15-year-old was selected to compete in the 1964 Winter Olympics, where she performed creditably.

Having gained a bronze at the world championships in 1965, she won the gold easily in 1966, although the event was overshadowed by the death of her father only hours later. Fleming repeated her world championship success in 1967 and 1968 and also gained four more U.S. titles in the period 1965–68.

In 1968 Fleming won a gold medal at the Grenoble Winter Olympics, despite a fall in the first 30 seconds and several other errors. After her Olympic win Fleming retired from amateur skating and signed a long-term professional contract, making popular appearances on television. She continued to appear on television as a commentator and later became a representative of UNICEF. She married Gregory Jenkins.

Fleming,   Williamina   Paton (1857–1911) *Scottish-born American astronomer*

> Sparkling and friendly though she was, her reputation as a strict disci-

plinarian lived after her, and as late as the 1930s elderly ladies who had worked with her in their youth still regarded her with awe.

—Dorrit Hofleit, *Notable American Women* (1971)

Williamina Fleming spent her working life at the Harvard College Observatory, where she played an important part in developing the Harvard Classification System of stars.

Williamina Paton, as she was born, came from Dundee in Scotland; the daughter of a craftsman, she worked for several years as a school teacher. In 1877 she married James Fleming, with whom she emigrated to Boston, Massachusetts, in the following year. After her marriage broke up she was forced to support her young son and began working for Edward Pickering, director of the Harvard College Observatory, as a maid. Quickly recognizing her intelligence, Pickering offered her temporary employment as his assistant in 1879. She was given a permanent post in 1881. She remained at the observatory for the rest of her life, serving as the curator of astronomical photographs from 1899 until her death.

Mrs. Fleming worked with Pickering on the classification of stars according to their spectral types; she was thus involved in the introduction of the original 17 classes arranged alphabetically from A to Q in terms of the intensity of the hydrogen lines in their emission spectrums. This system was later modified and improved by her colleagues Annie CANNON and Antonia MAURY.

Fleming was largely responsible for the classification of over 10,000 stars, published in 1890 in the *Draper Catalogue of Stellar Spectra*. In the course of her work she discovered 10 novae and over 200 variable stars; she estimated that by 1910 she had examined nearly 200,000 photographic plates.

See also LEAVITT, HENRIETTA SWAN

Flynn, Elizabeth Gurley (1890–1964)
American political radical and labour organizer

A popular saying in Alderson [prison] went as follows: "They

work us like a horse, feed us like a bird, treat us like a child, dress us like a man – and then expect us to act like a lady."

—*The Alderson Story*

A committed communist, Elizabeth Gurley Flynn was imprisoned during the McCarthy era in America and given a state funeral in Moscow's Red Square some ten years later.

Born in Concord, New Hampshire, she was the daughter of a socialist engineer and his Irish nationalist wife. The family moved to the South Bronx, where Flynn was educated. She regularly attended socialist meetings, making friends with several leading anarchists. On leaving school she became a member of the International Workers of the World (IWW).

In 1908 Flynn married a miner, John Jones; they had a daughter a year later and a son in 1910. (The marriage ended in divorce in 1920.) In 1912 Flynn became involved in organizing strikes, especially of textile workers, at Lawrence, Massachusetts, and in Paterson, New Jersey. In this work she became involved, both personally and professionally, with the Italian anarchist Caro Tresca, with whom she had an affair that lasted until 1925.

During World War I Flynn's pacifist sympathies led to charges of spying being made against her and her fellow IWW leaders, but these were finally dropped. Determined to protect immigrants under threat of deportation, in 1920 she became one of the founders of the American Civil Liberties Union, from which she was expelled 20 years later because of her communist associations.

In 1936, after ten years of semiretirement brought about by severe heart disease, Flynn became a full member of the Communist Party. Women's issues formed the major subjects of her column in the *Daily Worker*. In 1942 she ran for Congress on these same issues.

Having organized the defence of fellow radicals suffering persecution at the start of the Cold War, in 1951 Flynn was charged under the Smith Act with attempting to overthrow the American government. This led to a sentence of three years' imprisonment. After her release she was elected chairman of the national committee of the Communist Party in 1961. Following her death in Moscow, during a visit to the Soviet Union, she received a state funeral in Red Square. Her publications include *Women in the War* (1942), *Women's Place in the Fight for a Better World* (1947), and an autobiography, *I Speak My Piece* (1955).

Fonda, Jane (1937–) *American actress*

> I am not a do-gooder. I am a revolutionary. A revolutionary woman.
> —*Los Angeles Weekly*, November 28, 1980

Best known as a film star, Jane Fonda has also worked as a political activist and since the 1980s has made a name for herself as a fitness expert.

The daughter of actor Henry Fonda, Jane was born in New York City, spending her childhood in California and New England. After attending Vassar College, New York State, she went to Paris to study art. On returning to the United States, she modelled for *Vogue* and joined the Actors' Studio, where she was taught "Method" acting by Lee Strasberg.

Fonda made her acting debut on Broadway in 1960 in *Tall Story*. In 1964 she interrupted an increasingly successful career in American films to return to France, where she succeeded Brigitte BARDOT as Roger Vadim's wife. She allowed him to cast her as a "sex-kitten" in such films as *La Ronde* (1964; *Circle of Love*) and *Barbarella* (1968). In 1965 she appeared in the American comedy western *Cat Ballou*, following this with *Barefoot in the Park* (1967) and a highly acclaimed performance as a marathon dancer in *They Shoot Horses, Don't They?* (1969). Fonda's portrayal of a call girl in *Klute* (1971) won her an Oscar as Best Actress.

Rejecting the roles in which her father and husband had cast her, Fonda discovered a political voice in the late 1960s. In 1972 she appealed to American pilots on Hanoi radio to cease their bombing raids, which brought her official censure from the U.S. State Department. With Donald Sutherland she formed the Anti-War Troupe, which toured military camps in Vietnam; *Free the Army* (1972) and *Introduction to the Enemy* (1974) are filmed records of this tour. Fonda's opposition to the Vietnam War was given further expression in *Coming Home* (1973), for which she was awarded her second Oscar as Best Actress. Fonda's emerging feminism features in *A Doll's House* (1973), *Julia* (1977), and *9 to 5* (1980), while her political views influenced the nuclear-disaster movie *The China Syndrome* (1979).

Fonda's later films include *Agnes of God* (1985), *The Morning After* (1986), *Old Gringo* (1989), and *Stanley and Iris* (1990). She costarred with her father and with Katharine HEPBURN in *On Golden Pond* (1981). In 1984 she won an Emmy Award for her performance in the television movie *The Dollmaker*.

In 1973 Fonda married the political activist Tom Hayden, with whom she toured the United States lecturing on political theory. During the 1980s Fonda produced a series of books and videos on health and fitness for women of all ages. Her third husband is Ted Turner, the multimillionaire media tycoon. Now retired from acting, she lives in Atlanta, Georgia.

Fontana, Lavinia (1552–1614) *Italian artist*

By the age of 18 Lavinia Fontana had made a name for herself as a painter of portraits and religious subjects. Later in her life she moved to Rome from her native Bologna to become a painter at the papal court.

Born in Bologna, the daughter of the well-known Bolognese painter Prospero Fontana, Lavinia showed an early talent for painting, which her father was happy to encourage. Painting in his studio under his supervision, she soon established a reputation of her own as a portraitist.

Fontana's husband Gian Paolo Zappi, an artist from Lucca, whom she married in 1577, became a member of the household. The couple had 11 children, only three of whom outlived their mother. The scope of Fontana's work can be seen by comparing her

Portrait of a Noblewoman (1580) with *Noli me tangere* (1581), a deeply religious work. She spent the 1590s concentrating on religious themes and painting a series of impressive altarpieces, including the *Holy Family with the Sleeping Christ* for the Escorial palace.

At the invitation of Pope Clement VIII, on the death of her father in 1600 she moved to Rome as an official painter to the papal court. Once there, she was offered a number of commissions producing several important altarpieces. Her fortunes and status rose as her workshops in Rome and Bologna continued to produce works of excellence. Fontana served as a role model for many younger women artists.

Fontanne, Lynn (1887–1983) *British-born American actress*

Lynn Fontanne and her husband Alfred Lunt (collectively known as the Lunts) became the most famous and admired couple in the American theatre.

Lille Louise Fontanne was born in Woodford, Essex, and made her stage debut in 1904 in the chorus of *Cinderella*, a Christmas pantomime presented at London's Drury Lane Theatre. Fontanne emigrated to the United States in 1916, her first Broadway success occurring in *Dulcy* in 1921. The Lunts were married a year later, making their debut as a couple in 1924 in *The Guardsman*.

Excelling in high comedy, the pair struck an original note with their sophisticated conversational technique and sharp wit. They scored particular success in George Bernard Shaw's plays. During World War II they worked in Britain, entertaining troops. In a performance of *There Shall Be No Night* in 1943 at London's Aldwych Theatre, a nearby bomb practically blew them off the stage. They insisted that the play should continue, however, to the great delight of the audience.

The Lunts also appeared on television in *The Great Sebastians* (1957), winning an Emmy for *The Magnificent Yankee* (1965). Lynn Fontanne died in Genesee Depot, Wisconsin, six years after her husband.

Fonteyn, Dame Margot (1919–1991) *British ballet dancer*

Margot Fonteyn is recognized as one of the 20th century's greatest ballerinas, achieving worldwide popularity during her ten-year partnership with Rudolf Nureyev (1962–72). She was also one of the earliest prima ballerinas to have learned her art in Britain.

Born Margaret (Peggy) Hookham in Reigate, Surrey, she was the daughter of a mining engineer. She spent much of her early life in China, where she studied dance with George Goncharov in Shanghai. On returning to London, she joined the Vic-Wells Ballet School, which became the Sadler's Wells Ballet and subsequently the Royal Ballet. Here she was taught by Ninette DE VALOIS, who noticed her exceptional talent.

Fonteyn made her debut as a snowflake in *The Nutcracker* in 1934. By 1935, when Alicia MARKOVA left the company, Fonteyn took over many of her leading roles. In that year she danced Young Treginnis in de Valois's *The Haunted Ballroom* and also took the role of Odette in *Swan Lake*. Two years later she starred as Princess Aurora in *The Sleeping Beauty*.

While Fonteyn established an international reputation as a great interpreter of classical roles, she also appeared successfully in ballets choreographed for her by Sir Frederick Ashton, in particular *Symphonic Variations* (1946), *Daphnis and Chloë* (1951), and *Ondine* (1958).

In 1954 Fonteyn was appointed president of the Royal Academy of Dancing and five years later became guest artist to the Royal Ballet, which might have given the impression that she was reducing her commitments as a ballerina. However, the arrival of Rudolf Nureyev from the Leningrad Kirov Ballet in 1962 took her to still greater peaks. She partnered him in many great productions at the Royal Ballet over the next ten years. At the age of 62 she danced at La Scala, Milan, as Lady Capulet in Nureyev's *Romeo and Juliet*.

Not only was Fonteyn an outstanding dancer, but her winning personality made her the ideal presenter in 1980 of a British television series *The Magic of Dance*. In 1955 she became the wife of Panamanian politician Dr. Roberto Arias and was created a DBE. Her book *Pavlova Impressions* was published in 1984. She died in Panama City.

Fossey, Dian (1932–1985) *American zoologist*

Dian Fossey became famous for her work on the behaviour of the mountain gorillas in Rwanda and Zaïre (now the Democratic Republic of Congo) in Africa.

Born in San Francisco, Fossey both trained and practised as an occupational therapist. However, a long-cherished dream of visiting Africa came true in 1963, when she embarked on a seven-week safari to the Olduvai Gorge in Tanzania. There she met the pioneering palaeontologists Louis and Mary LEAKEY, who persuaded her to return to Africa three years later. Jane GOODALL, an expert on chimpanzees, encouraged her to establish a work station in the Virunga mountains. Fossey set up the Karisoke Research Centre in Rwanda, where for 18 years she worked in conditions of growing isolation.

Fossey grew more and more concerned with conservation and published her views in 1983 in *Gorillas in the Mist*. In 1988 this was made into a film with Sigourney WEAVER playing the role of Fossey.

In 1985 Fossey's mutilated body was found near the centre, hacked to death by machete. It was suspected that poachers, whose devastating attacks on the gorillas she had tried to stop, were responsible for her murder, although this was never proved.

Foster, Hannah Webster (1758–1840) *American writer*

Hannah Webster Foster made her name both as a novelist and as a contributor to a number of journals. Her best-selling novel *The Coquette* (1797) has recently found a new readership and an academic interest.

Born in Salisbury, Massachusetts, she was the daughter of a merchant, Grant Webster. Although uncertainty surrounds her childhood and education, it is clear from her published work that she was well read. In 1785 she became the wife of the Reverend John Foster, minister of the First Church of Brighton, Massachusetts, and devoted herself to enriching the literary and social lives of the members of her husband's parish. Mrs. Foster was the mother of six children. Following her husband's death, she moved to Montreal to be near two daughters who, like her, earned their living by writing.

Foster wrote exclusively for magazines and newspapers until 1797, when she published anonymously *The Coquette: or the History of Eliza Wharton*, subtitled *Founded on Fact*. For this, her most memorable book, she drew largely on the life of a distant cousin of her husband. Clearly influenced by Samuel Richardson's novel *Clarissa*, Foster chose to allow her characters to express their points of view in an exchange of letters. The central characters are strongly drawn: Eliza, daughter of a clergyman, longs for riches and adventure, while Major Sandford, revelling in rakish behaviour, sets out to win her. Eventually both characters are punished for their unconventional conduct; the author takes every opportunity to point out their faults and the consequences of these. During its first 40 years this novel was reprinted 13 times. But it was not until 1866 that it was published under Foster's name.

In 1798 Foster published *The Boarding School; or Lessons of a Preceptress to Her Pupils*. Far less popular than *The Coquette*, it urged girls to conform to the domestic norms and stay married to dull husbands. After *The Boarding School* Foster published only one brief newspaper article. She died in Montreal.

Foster, Jodie (1962–) *American film actress and director*

> You have to make love to 30 million spectators – and be slightly aloof.
>
> —On movie acting, *International Herald Tribune*, August 26, 1983

A sophisticated child star, Foster has developed into an Oscar-winning leading lady.

Born Alicia Christian Foster in Los Angeles, she spent most of her childhood acting, appearing in numerous TV productions. She made her film debut aged ten in Disney's *Napoleon and Samantha* (1972). After a number of other parts in family movies Foster starred in Martin Scorsese's *Alice Doesn't Live Here Anymore* (1975) as a hard-drinking street urchin; a year later she portrayed a child prostitute in Scorsese's *Taxi Driver* and took the part of the provocative Tallulah in *Bugsy Malone*. She gave a chilling performance as a young murderer in *The Little Girl Who Lives Down the Lane* (1977). Despite the pressures of film work, Foster succeeded in completing a BA degree in literature at Yale University.

Foster made her name as an adult star playing a rape victim in *Accused* (1988), winning an Oscar as Best Actress for her performance. Her part in *The Silence of the Lambs* (1991) brought her a second Oscar. In the same year Foster tried her hand successfully at directing with *Little Man Tate*; she has since directed *Home for the Holidays* (1996). Her other films of the 1990s include *Nell* (1995), which brought her a further Oscar nomination, and the science-fiction drama *Contact* (1997). Foster is well known for shunning publicity. In 1998 she announced her first pregnancy but refused to disclose "the father or the method."

Fox, Margaret (1833–1893) *American spiritualist*

Through their well-publicized seances, Margaret Fox and her sister Kate established a cult from which modern spiritualism dates.

Margaret Fox was born in Ontario, Canada, but in 1847 her family moved to a farm near Hydesville, New York State. Within a year rumours that strange sounds were coming from the house spread through the neighbourhood. Margaret and her younger sister Katherine (Kate) did nothing to discourage the popular view that spirits

were responsible. Leah Fish, their elder sister, capitalized on the situation by organizing public demonstrations of her sisters' powers. Returning with Leah to her home in Rochester, Margaret and Kate became famous for their "Rochester rappings," coded rapping sounds that were said to enable "actual communication" to be made with the spirits.

In 1850 the sisters moved to New York City, where they held many seances. They managed to convince Horace Greeley of their authenticity, and he wrote praising them in his *New York Tribune*. In the 1870s they visited England, where spiritualism had also grown popular.

In 1872 Kate married H. D. Jencken. In 1888 Margaret, a Roman Catholic convert, announced that she and her sister were hoaxers. However, her followers refused to accept her "confession," which she was persuaded to withdraw. Thereafter she continued to make a living from her "skill." She died in Brooklyn, New York.

Frame, Janet (Paterson) (1924–) *New Zealand writer*

Janet Frame is regarded as New Zealand's greatest contemporary novelist and short-story writer.

Born in Oamaru near Dunedin, New Zealand, the daughter of a railroad worker, Frame trained and worked for a short time as a teacher (1943–45). Her early life was overshadowed by the death by drowning of two of her sisters and her brother's frequent disabling attacks of epilepsy. This undoubtedly contributed to a mental breakdown that forced her to spend the years 1947–54 in various psychiatric hospitals. During this time she published her first collection of short stories, *The Lagoon* (1951), which won a national literary award.

After leaving the hospital, she spent a year (1954–55) at the home of the New Zealand writer Frank Sargeson, where she wrote her first novel, *Owls Do Cry*, which was published in 1957. In 1956, funded by a state grant, she left New Zealand, spending the next seven years writing more novels and short-story collections in Spain and

England. Since 1963, apart from working visits to the United States, she has remained in New Zealand.

In all her books Frame draws on the experiences of her early life to explore the relationship between language and truth and the nature of reality. Her other novels include *The Edge of the Alphabet* (1961), *Scented Gardens for the Blind* (1963), *The Adaptable Man* (1965), *A State of Siege* (1966), *Intensive Care* (1970), *Living in the Manioto* (1979), and *The Carpathians* (1988). Frame has also published more volumes of short stories, including *The Reservoir and Other Stories* (1966) and *You Are Now Entering the Human Heart* (1983). *The Pocket Mirror* (1967) is a collection of her early verse.

Frame has written three volumes of autobiography: *To the Island* (1983), *An Angel at My Table* (1984), and *The Envoy from Mirror City* (1985). These were made into an award-winning film, *An Angel at My Table* (1990), directed by Jane CAMPION.

Francesca da Rimini (died *c.* 1283) *Italian noblewoman*

The tragic love story of Francesca da Rimini has been an inspiration for generations of writers and artists, from Dante to the Pre-Raphaelites and Rachmaninov.

Born Francesca da Polenta, the daughter of Guido da Polenta, Lord of Ravenna, she had an arranged marriage to Gianciotto Malatesta (known as "the Lame"), the son of Malatesta, Lord of Rimini. According to some accounts she believed that she was to marry Paolo (known as "the Fair"), the handsome brother of her deformed husband. In other accounts Francesca was already in love with Paolo before her betrothal. Whatever the truth may be, Gianciotto discovered that she was having an affair with his brother and murdered both of them.

Dante introduced the tragic couple in Canto V of his *Inferno*, where he himself meets them; as a Christian, he recognizes their sinfulness, rejecting their excuse that they entered into their adulterous relationship after reading about the love of Lancelot for Guinevere in Arthurian legend. Dante

uses their fate to expose the dangers of medieval love poetry in the light of Christian teaching.

Their relationship has also inspired plays by Silvio Pellico and Gabriele D'Annunzio, operas by Hermann Gotz and Rachmaninov, a symphonic poem by Tchaikovsky, and paintings by Ingres and Dante Gabriel Rossetti.

Frank, Anne (1929–1945) *German Jewish diarist*

> Her diary endures, full-blooded, unselfpitying, a perpetual reminder that the enormity of the Nazi crime amounted not to the abstraction of "genocide" but the murder of six million individuals.
>
> —Simon Schama, *1000 Makers of the 20th Century*

The victim of German concentration camps, Anne Frank is famous for the diary in which, as a young girl, she recorded two years spent in Amsterdam in hiding from the Germans during World War II.

Born in Frankfurt-am-Main, Germany, she fled with her family to Amsterdam in the Netherlands when Hitler came to power in 1933. Anne's father Otto, a German businessman, expected to find safety from the Nazis in Holland. However, after Holland had been overrun by the Germans, the family was threatened with deportation. On July 9, 1941, they went into hiding with four fellow Jews in the back room of Otto Frank's business premises. Gentile friends secretly brought them food. However, Dutch informers betrayed their hiding place to the Gestapo, who arrested them on August 4, 1944.

The family was sent to the concentration camp at Auschwitz in Poland, where Anne's mother died in 1945. Anne and her sister were sent on to Bergen-Belsen, where they caught typhus and died. When Auschwitz was liberated by the Russians, Otto Frank was found alive, although sick in the hospital. Friends later restored to him his daughter's diary, found in the family's hiding place. It appeared in print in 1947 entitled *Het Achterhuis* (The Diary of a Young Girl). With remarkable insight for one so young, Anne relates the day-to-day events of her confined existence during the years 1941–44. In a world mutilated by German brutality the diary is notable for expressing Anne's continued faith in the goodness of mankind.

In the postwar years Anne Frank's diary has been seen as a symbol of Jewish suffering in the Holocaust and as a monument to the courage of a teenager who was deprived of her right to a normal childhood and eventually of her life. It has been translated into more than 30 languages. A recent unexpurgated edition in English (1995) reveals both Anne's capacity to criticize the adults around her and her awakening sexuality.

The premises on the Prinsengracht Canal in Amsterdam in which the family hid have been opened as a museum; Anne Frank's name has been used throughout Europe for schools and other institutions as a reminder of those terrible years.

Frankenthaler, Helen (1928–)
American painter

Helen Frankenthaler's brilliantly coloured works are fine examples of the style known as action painting, in which paint is poured or splashed onto the canvas to form large abstract designs. She pioneered a new method of achieving this.

The youngest of three daughters, she was born in New York City. Her parents encouraged her to exploit her artistic talents to the full, but sadly her father, a judge in the New York Supreme Court, died when she was only 11.

In 1945 Frankenthaler went to Bennington College, Vermont, to study art with Paul Feeley. A year later she attended the Arts Students League in New York; she subsequently worked under Hans Hoffman. Frankenthaler married the painter Robert Motherwell in 1958 and became stepmother to his daughters. The couple divorced in 1971.

Frankenthaler's work was first shown in 1951. Although early in her career she had absorbed contemporary techniques, such as cubism, her painting *Mountains and Sea* (1952) estab-

lished her individual style. To achieve her most distinctive effect – a sense of transparency usually associated with watercolours – she diluted oil paint to the consistency of watercolour and, working on the floor, poured it onto unprimed canvas, a technique in which she was influenced by Jackson Pollock (see KRASNER, LEE). While the images created were largely unplanned, Frankenthaler could also exert a measure of control over some forms.

She achieved critical recognition in 1959 when she won first prize at the Paris Biennale. A year later she had a major solo exhibition in New York, and in 1966 she was one of four painters chosen to represent the United States at the Venice Biennale. Her work was also selected for exhibition at the Montreal Exposition (1967).

During the 1970s Frankenthaler experimented with a variety of media, including acrylics, while exerting increasing control in her painting. Visits to the West Coast had prompted her to use larger canvases and rollers to apply thicker paint.

In 1985 a major retrospective exhibition of Frankenthaler's work was mounted at the Guggenheim Museum in New York.

Franklin, Aretha (1942–) *American singer*

Known as "Queen of Soul," Aretha Franklin was among the first performers of soul music to be regarded as a star by white audiences. She is also well known as a gospel and blues singer and composer.

Born in Memphis, Tennessee, Aretha Franklin moved with her family to Detroit in 1944. The church in which her father was preacher drew many famous singers, while the family home was the meeting place for such people as Mahalia JACKSON, James Cleveland, B. B. King, and Dinah Washington, who became a source of encouragement and inspiration for the young Aretha.

After cutting her first disc when she was only 12, Aretha Franklin decided to make singing her career when she graduated from high school. Initially she appeared on the circuits she knew best, singing gospel to African-American congregations. In 1967 Franklin became more widely popular when she released a spate of hits such as "I Never Loved a Man," "Baby, I Love You," and "Respect." The last was taken up as the signature tune of the civil rights movement.

Franklin has won numerous awards, including many Grammys, the American Music Award (1984), and the Rhythm and Blues Foundation Lifetime Achievement Award (1992). In 1987 she was inducted into the Rock 'n' Roll Hall of Fame.

Franklin, Rosalind (Elsie) (1920–1958) *British scientist*

Rosalind Franklin made a major contribution to the discovery of the molecular structure of DNA (deoxyribonucleic acid), the organic compound that determines the genetic make-up of all living things.

London-born, Franklin studied natural sciences at Newnham College, Cambridge, being awarded her BA degree in 1941. She was first employed by the British Coal Utilisation Research Association, where she helped to discover and describe the processes by which coal absorbs other materials. In 1947 she went to Paris to work in the field of x-rays with Jacques Méring at the Laboratoire Centrale des Services Chimiques de L'Etat. This research led Franklin to extend her inquiries into how and why the formation of graphite in heated carbons brought about changes in their structure. Her work was of great importance for atomic technology.

At the age of 31 Franklin took up a post at the Biophysical Laboratory at King's College, London, where she used her knowledge gained in the field of x-rays to work on DNA. Her x-ray photographs of DNA clearly showed that the molecule had a spiral shape. This was of great assistance to James Watson and Francis Crick, who went on to show that the DNA molecule has the form of a double helix, i.e., a structure like a spiral staircase.

In 1953 Franklin moved to Birkbeck College, London, to work in its Crystallography Laboratory. Here she turned her attention to considering the molecular structure of the tobacco mosaic virus. Together with colleagues Franklin was able to prove that the RNA (ribonucleic acid) in the virus was a single-stranded helix, different from the double helix found in the DNA of some other viruses and the higher living organisms.

Franklin died of cancer at the early age of 37. During her short working life she published more than 40 papers.

Fraser, Dawn (1937–) *Australian swimmer*

> It would take a book – and she has written one – to do justice to Dawn Fraser, the queen of swimming.
> —Sports writer and journalist Pat Besford, 1976

In the 1964 Olympics Dawn Fraser became the first swimmer to win three successive gold medals for the same event (the 100-metre freestyle). During her ten-year career she set 27 world records and was the first woman to swim 100 metres in under a minute.

Born into a large family in Balmain, Sydney, Fraser showed an early talent for swimming. She won the first of her numerous Australian titles in 1955. In 1956, aged only 19, Fraser became a national heroine when she won two gold medals at the Melbourne Olympics, for the 100-metre freestyle and the freestyle relay. At Rome in 1960 she again won a gold for the 100-metre freestyle, repeating the feat in 1964 in Tokyo, despite the fact that she had only just recovered from a car crash in which her mother was killed. In each of her successive wins of the 100-metre freestyle she also set a new world record, cutting her time to 59.5 seconds in 1964.

By now Fraser had won four gold and four silver Olympic medals, a record for a female swimmer that was only equalled by Kornelia ENDER in 1976. However, immediately after her Olympic success in 1964 her career was interrupted. At the Tokyo Olympics she had unwisely appeared at a parade against the rules and had also been involved in a prank to capture the flag of a competing nation. As a result she was banned from competition for ten years, bringing an abrupt end to her string of successes.

At around this time Fraser married Gary Ware; the couple had a daughter, but the marriage did not last. In addition to her other swimming titles she had won eight Commonwealth Games medals and was awarded the MBE in 1967. The film *Dawn!*, telling her life story, was released in 1979.

Fredegund (died 597) *Wife of the Frankish King Chilperic*

Notorious for her ruthlessness and cruelty, Fredegund was queen by marriage of Neustria, a Frankish kingdom corresponding to present-day northern France.

Fredegund, or Frédégonde, became the mistress of Chilperic while she was a palace servant. In about 568 she persuaded Chilperic to murder his wife Queen Galswitha so that she could become queen. Galswitha's sister BRUN-HILDE was the wife of Chilperic's half-brother, King Sigebert I of Austrasia, a Frankish kingdom corresponding to present-day northeastern France and west Germany; Galswitha's murder caused a family feud that lasted over 40 years.

During this war Fredegund had Sigebert assassinated in 575. In 584 Chilperic was assassinated in mysterious circumstances. For the rest of her life Fredegund engaged in political intrigue and acts of sadistic brutality, some committed to secure the throne of Neustria for her son Chlotaire II. She finally defeated her old enemy Brunhilde in 597 but died herself only months later.

Frederick, Pauline (*c.* 1920–) *American newscaster*

Pauline Frederick made her name as a pioneering woman broadcaster of "hard news."

Born in Galitzin, Pennsylvania, she was educated at George Washington University, where she took an MA degree in international law. On graduating she began to develop a career in freelance journalism, gaining experience of both writing and broadcasting. In 1945 she travelled to China. On her return a year later she took up a post

as news commentator for ABC, where she stayed until 1953. Besides broadcasting breakfast-time news, her job, unique for a woman, included preparing material for the televised evening news.

In 1948 Frederick became the first woman to take responsibility for the coverage of a national political convention. Two years later, as the Korean War began, it was she who covered the crucial meetings of the United Nations Security Council. Continuing her role as commentator on political crises, in 1950 Frederick was employed by NBC to cover United Nations business. For the next 24 years she covered all the major international crises – Suez, Hungary, the Congo, Cuba, Cyprus, Vietnam, and the Middle East.

In 1976 Frederick undertook the major responsibility of umpiring the televised debate between Jimmy Carter and Gerald Ford during the presidential election campaign. She went on to work for National Public Radio as a senior international affairs analyst. Frederick's innovative work has brought her many well-deserved prizes.

Freeman, Mary E. Wilkins (1852–1930) *American writer*

Best known for her short stories and novels, Mary Wilkins Freeman had a gift for vivid and detailed description of the landscape and characters of New England. She is regarded as one of the finest short-story writers of the 19th century.

Born Mary Eleanor Wilkins in Randolph, Massachusetts, she moved with her family to Brattleboro, Vermont, in 1867. After studying at Mount Holyoke Female Seminary (1870–71), Massachusetts, she returned home and continued to educate herself through reading. It was at this time that she began writing for children. When her parents died in 1883, she went to live with friends in Randolph, where she published her first story for adults in a Boston newspaper.

Wilkins soon became a popular contributor to *Harper's Magazine*. Her stories appeared in book form in *A*

Humble Romance (1887) and *A New England Nun* (1891). They are marked by the author's insight into the people and Puritan culture of New England: despite their obvious talents, many of her characters fail to realize their potential because poverty or social convention restricts their development. As a novelist Wilkins was less successful in developing plot and motive. Among her novels are *Jane Field* (1893), *Pembroke* (1894), *Jerome* (1897), and *The Heart's Highway* (1900); *Pembroke* is generally regarded as the best of these. She also wrote a play, *Giles Corey, Yeoman* (1893), about the Salem witch trials.

In 1902 Mary Wilkins married Dr. Charles M. Freeman and moved to Metuchen, New Jersey. Subsequently she published further collections of stories, including *The Wind in the Rose Bush* (1903) and *Edgewater People* (1918).

Fremstad, Olive (1871–1951) *Swedish-born American opera singer*

Described as an interpreter of genius in the great operatic soprano roles that spanned her singing career, Anna Olivia Fremstad was born illegitimate in Stockholm. At the age of ten she was taken to the United States and adopted by an American couple with Swedish roots living in Minnesota. She began her musical education by studying the piano in Minneapolis and singing in New York before travelling to Berlin in 1893 to spend two years studying under Lilli LEHMANN.

On May 21, 1895, Fremstad made her stage debut playing Azucena in Verdi's *Il Trovatore* with the Cologne Opera, with which she worked for the next three years. In 1898 she went to study in Italy, returning to Germany in 1900 to become a member of the Munich Opera. During her three years with this company she sang a wide repertoire, her Carmen drawing great acclaim. In 1902 she scored a similar success in England singing in Wagner's operas at London's Covent Garden, where she also sang in Dame Ethel SMYTH's *Der Wald*.

Fremstad made her debut at the Metropolitan Opera House, New York, on November 25, 1903, singing Sieglinde in Wagner's *The Valkyrie*. She appeared regularly at the Metropolitan for the next 11 seasons, during which both Toscanini and Mahler conducted her in Wagnerian roles. She was the first person to sing the title roles of Strauss's *Salome* and Gluck's *Armida* in the United States. Despite her success with audiences, a dispute with the manager of the Metropolitan forced her resignation from the company in April 1914. She then moved to the Chicago Opera, with which she appeared for the last time singing the role of Tosca in Minneapolis in 1918.

Of the few recordings she made, only "O don fatale" from Verdi's *Don Carlos* does justice to her vocal range. The American writer Willa CATHER based the heroine of her novel *The Song of the Lark* (1915) on Olive Fremstad.

French, Marilyn (1929–) *American novelist, feminist, and literary critic*

Marilyn French is best-known for her hugely successful novel *The Women's Room* (1977) and for a number of nonfiction works in which she angrily attacks the male-dominated ethos of U.S. society.

Marilyn Hazz was born into a poor family of Polish extraction living in New York. Although she showed considerable academic promise, she left college in 1950 to marry Robert M. French. After some dozen years as a suburban wife and mother, she resumed her education in the early 1960s, firstly at Hofstra College and then at Harvard University, where she earned her doctorate with a thesis on James Joyce. During this period she was divorced from her husband and came under the influence of the burgeoning U.S. feminist movement. Having previously lectured at various East Coast colleges, she was appointed a fellow of Harvard in 1976.

Marilyn French achieved celebrity with her first work of fiction, *The Women's Room*, which became a bestseller in America and Europe. The novel describes the crippling sense of frustration felt by a suburban housewife, and her long difficult journey to independence and fulfilment. As one of the first novels to combine a radical feminist analysis within the conventions of middlebrow fiction, the book struck a chord with women from a wide range of backgrounds and has been credited with changing lives.

Having become a full-time writer, Marilyn French published a second novel, *The Bleeding Heart*, in 1981: the book examines the difficulties of marriage in a culture that is presented as being obsessed with power and success at the expense of feeling. The same view of modern U.S. society as innately patriarchal and hostile to women is central to her major works of nonfiction *Beyond Power: On Women, Men, and Morals* (1985) and *The War against Women* (1992). French's other publications include the novels *Her Mother's Daughter* (1987) and *Our Father* (1994) and the critical work *Shakespeare's Division of Experience* (1981).

Freud, Anna (1895–1982) *Austrian-born British child psychoanalyst*

Anna Freud, the youngest daughter of Sigmund Freud, is well known for her pioneering work as a child psychoanalyst.

Born in Vienna, she left school early and after teaching at a primary school in Vienna worked with her father as his secretary and pupil. In 1922 she became a practising analyst, and from 1925 until 1928 she was chairman of the Vienna Psychoanalytical Society.

In 1936 Anna Freud published *Das Ich und die Abwehrmechanismen* (published in English as *The Ego and the Mechanisms of Defence* in 1937), which had a profound effect on others working in her field. She suggested that, as children, human beings learn to protect themselves through not giving in to impulses, which they learn could expose them to risky situations. Other learned defence behaviours include living vicariously through others, turning aggressive feelings inwards to the point of self-harm, identifying with an overpowering enemy, and separating intellect from feeling. Anna Freud did much to establish the language of the psychology of adolescence.

A devoted daughter, with the Nazi threat to Jews growing, in 1938 Anna Freud accompanied her father to London, where other members of her family were already living. During the years of World War II she organized a residential nursery for homeless children. At this time she collaborated with the American Dorothy Burlingham in writing *Young Children in Wartime* (1942), *Infants without Families* (1943), and *War and Children* (1943).

In 1949 Anna Freud founded the Hampstead Child-Therapy Clinic, which she directed for 30 years from 1952. She believed that children use play to adjust to the outside world and thought that analysis should provide an aid to education. Perhaps the most effective summary of her ideas is contained in *Normality and Pathology in Childhood* (1968).

Frideswide, Saint (died *c.* 735) *English abbess*

St. Frideswide is the patron saint of the city and university of Oxford.

The first account of St. Frideswide dates from the 12th century. This suggests that she was a Christian Saxon noblewoman who escaped from her home in Oxford and went into hiding in nearby woods for three years to avoid an arranged marriage to a royal suitor. Apparently her would-be husband pursued her to the city gates of Oxford, where he was suddenly struck blind by lightning from a storm. Frideswide was so grateful that in 703 she founded a convent at Oxford, where she lived peacefully, eventually becoming its abbess. From 1004 a shrine to her stood in the church of St. Frideswide's Priory, built on the site of her religious house. The site is now occupied by Christ Church Cathedral.

Frideswide was made into a saint in 1481; her feast day is celebrated on October 19. It is not known why this saint, renamed Frévisse, had a devoted following at the village of Bomy in the centre of Artois, France.

Friedan, Betty (1921–) *American feminist and writer*

> Over and over women heard in
> voices of tradition...that they could
> desire no greater destiny than to

glory in their own femininity...to pity the neurotic, unfeminine, unhappy women who want to be poets or physicians or presidents.

—*The Feminine Mystique* (1963)

Betty Friedan achieved fame as the author of the bestselling *The Feminine Mystique* (1963), which explored the social pressures that led American women to confine themselves to unfulfilling homemaking roles in the 1950s. In 1966 she established the National Organization for Women (NOW), of which she became the first president.

Born Betty Naomi Goldstein in Peoria, Illinois, she was educated at Smith College, where in 1942 she received a degree in psychology. She spent a year as a graduate student at the University of California, Berkeley, before moving to New York. After working in several different jobs, she married Carl Friedan, a theatrical producer, in 1947. For the next ten years she undertook the role of wife and mother while working freelance as a journalist for such magazines as *Harper's* and *Good Housekeeping*.

In 1957 Friedan sent a questionnaire to her contemporaries from Smith, asking if they were content with their lives since leaving college. She found that only a tiny minority felt fulfilled. Having extended her research through further questionnaires, interviews, and discussions with "experts," she published her results in *The Feminine Mystique*. She argued that women were deceived into believing that happiness could be found through devotion to home and family, whereas the actual experience of most women was a feeling of frustration and loss of self-esteem.

Friedan elaborated her views and added to the ensuing debate by lecturing and broadcasting. In 1966 she founded NOW, a civil-rights group whose chief aim was to obtain equal rights and job opportunities for women. In her capacity as NOW's president Friedan ran campaigns to end advertising that reinforced conventional perceptions of women, to increase the number of women in government, to legalize abortion, and to extend childcare. For many years NOW remained the most effective organization representing women's interests.

Although she gave up the presidency of NOW in 1970, Friedan continued with her feminist work: she was a prime mover behind the Women's Strike for Equality of August 26, 1970, the 50th anniversary of women's suffrage in the United States. She worked tirelessly for ratification of the Equal Rights Amendment to the U.S. Constitution while continuing to develop her career as an author and journalist. Her other books include the autobiographical *It Changed My Life* (1976), *The Second Stage* (1982), and *The Fountain of Life* (1993).

Frink, Dame Elisabeth (1930–1993)
British sculptor

Elisabeth Frink is regarded as one of Britain's most distinguished sculptors.

Born in Thurlow, Suffolk, she studied at the Guildford School of Art (1947–49) before continuing her training at the Chelsea School of Art (1949–53), where Bernard Meadows, one of Henry Moore's assistants, was an important influence. She later taught at Chelsea (1953–60) and at St. Martin's School of Art (1955–57). From 1967 to 1972 Frink lived in the Camargue region of southern France, which is famous for its horses; this reinforced her lifetime's love of these animals and inspired some of her best work.

Frink began her career sculpting birds and warriors, rapidly achieving a distinctive style characterized by a roughly textured exterior. She held her first solo exhibition aged only 21. Two years later she won a prize in an international competition with her *Monument to the Unknown Political Prisoner*.

Frink's sculptures typically feature horses and riders, or other figures in movement, as well as male heads – often of soldiers or victims of suffering. She worked using plaster-soaked cloths applied to a wire framework. This allowed her to quickly build up a figure, which was finished with a coat of bronze. Her mature sculptures are smooth-surfaced. Frink also expressed her talent in drawings and lithographs.

Examples of Frink's sculptures can be seen in numerous art collections in Britain, Europe, and the United States, including the Tate Gallery, London, and the Museum of Modern Art, New York. She was regularly commissioned to provide public works worldwide; examples of these are the lectern in Coventry Cathedral; the Kennedy Memorial, Dallas, Texas; and the altar cross in Liverpool (Catholic) Cathedral. In 1982 Frink was made a DBE. Three years later London's Royal Academy mounted a major exhibition of her work.

Frith, Mary (c. 1584–1659) *English criminal*

Known as "Moll Cutpurse," she became notorious as a pickpocket, highwaywoman, forger, and receiver of stolen goods; she dressed in men's clothing and was accompanied by a vicious dog.

The daughter of a shoemaker in the City of London, she started work as a domestic servant, doing housework and looking after children, but had "a natural abhorrence to the tending of children." Turning to a life of crime, she began dressing as a man in order to be more readily accepted as a member of the criminal fraternity. Audacious and intelligent, she eventually came to rule London's underworld.

Moll was a friend of the highwaymen Captain James Hind and Richard Hannam. She was herself sent to Newgate prison for armed robbery but was released by paying £2,000 to her victim, the parliamentary general Lord Fairfax (a confirmed Royalist, she allegedly declared that she would only rob the king's enemies). There is an account of her doing public penance at Paul's Cross for her offences and apparently showing remorse, but it was discovered that she was drunk at the time, having consumed three quarts of sack. She died in London, a wealthy woman.

Known for her high spirits and admired for her daring deeds, Moll became a folk heroine. Thomas Middleton and Thomas Dekker made her the heroine (somewhat reformed) of their comedy *The Roaring Girle* (1611), and Nathan Field put her in his play *Amends for Ladies* (1618).

Fry, Elizabeth (1780–1845) *British prison reformer*

> Were ladies to make a practice of visiting them [i.e., hospitals, lunatic asylums, and workhouses], a most important check would be obtained on a variety of abuses, which are far too apt to creep into the management of these establishments.
>
> —*Observations on the Visiting, Superintendance and Government of Female Prisoners* (1827)

Elizabeth Fry is remembered for her work in reforming British prisons in the 19th century and improving the lives of prisoners, especially women and their children.

Born Elizabeth Gurney in Norwich, she was the third daughter of John Gurney, a rich wool merchant and banker. The family were Quakers. When she was 17, inspired by the preaching of the American Quaker William Savery, she began to teach poor children from her village. In 1800 she married Joseph Fry, another Quaker banker. Together they raised 11 children, but this did not prevent Elizabeth from continuing her charitable work of nursing, teaching, and healthcare. She also began to speak at Quaker meetings.

In 1813 Fry went with a friend to visit the women prisoners in Newgate prison, London, where she found 300 women in apalling conditions – fighting, swearing, and screaming. Picking up a child, she spoke to the women so movingly that they listened in silence. She told them of ways in which their lives and those of their children could be improved. Establishing the Association for the Improvement of Female Prisoners in Newgate in 1817, she started a prison school and helped the women make clothes to sell.

Those in authority, including members of Parliament, began to respect Fry's humanitarian attitudes, which she knew brought out the best in prisoners. Despite difficulties caused by her husband's bankruptcy in 1828, she visited prisons in France, Germany, Denmark, and the Low Countries in the 1830s, urging the authorities to undertake reforms. She made a last, exhausting visit to France in 1843.

Fry also campaigned to improve the conditions under which convicts were transported to Australia. Her prison work continued until her death at Ramsgate.

Fuller, Loie (1862–1928) *American dancer and choreographer*

Loie Fuller became famous for her pioneering work in creating new forms of dance.

She was born Marie Louise Fuller on a farm near Chicago. Her career began when she was three years old; for the next 24 years she danced and acted a variety of roles in vaudeville and circus acts. She was particularly well known for her comic impersonations of pert maidservants.

In 1891 Fuller invented her exotic "skirt dance," which involved the play of different coloured lights on yards of whirling silk. The dance won her instant fame; she performed it all over the United States and in Europe. In 1892 she danced at the Folies Bergères in Paris, where her sophisticated and imaginative techniques caught the attention of avant-garde audiences: such artists as Toulouse-Lautrec and Rodin based work on her.

Loie Fuller drew inspiration from the natural world in choreographing her dances, which included *Butterfly* (1892) and *Clouds* (1893). Later she created scenic ballets, such as *Bottom of the Sea* (1906) and *Ballet of Light* (1908). By 1921 she was working in the open air, utilizing the effects of the elements. Her resourceful imagination and natural curiosity drove her to explore the technology of the effects she was engaged in creating. Inspired by the physicist Marie CURIE, she choreographed a *Radium Dance*.

As well as achieving great success in the theatre, Fuller founded a school of dance in 1908. She also pursued an active interest in business, theatrical management, and politics.

Fuller, Margaret (1810–1850) *American writer, critic, and feminist*

> As men become aware that few have had a fair chance, they are inclined to say that no women have had a fair chance.
> —*Women in the Nineteenth Century* (1845)

A respected literary critic and a pioneer advocate of women's rights, Margaret Fuller was also America's first professional newspaperwoman and the first woman foreign correspondent and war correspondent. Her intellectualism was a major stimulus to other writers and thinkers.

She was born Sarah Margaret Fuller in Cambridgeport, Massachusetts. A child prodigy, she was subjected by her father to vigorous intellectual training: she began to study Latin at six and by the age of ten was a proficient classicist. The rigours of such an intensive education left Margaret suffering permanent health problems. In 1836 she spent a year teaching at the experimental Temple School in Boston. Later she opened her own experimental school, the Greene School (1837–1839), in Providence, Rhode Island.

In about 1835 Margaret became friendly with Ralph Waldo Emerson, which led to her involvement in the activities of the American transcendentalists. From 1840 to 1842 she edited the transcendentalist journal *Dial*. About this time she developed what she called "conversations," discussions by women about cultural and controversial topics of the day. Ideas brought out in her discussion groups foreshadowed the American feminist movement. These conversations eventually resulted in her book *Woman in the Nineteenth Century* (1845), an early plea for women's rights.

In 1844 Margaret Fuller joined the staff of Horace Greeley's *New York Tribune* as a book reviewer. She soon became known as one of the keenest literary critics of her day, not hesitating, for example, to challenge Longfellow's high standing as a poet.

As correspondent for the *Tribune*, Fuller toured Europe in 1846, interviewing, among others, Thomas Carlyle in England, George SAND in Paris, and Giuseppe Mazzini in Rome. Mazzini aroused her interest in the republican movement in Italy, and in 1847 she returned to Rome as a supporter of the revolution against the papal government of the central Italian states. She later secretly married one of the revolutionaries, Giovanni Angelo, Marquis Ossoli, and took part with him in the unsuccessful defence of Rome against the French in 1849. In 1850 Marquis and Marchioness Ossoli and their two-year-old son Angelo embarked for America. They perished in a shipwreck off Fire Island, New York State.

Margaret Fuller's unpublished history of the Roman Republic, which she thought her masterpiece, was lost with the family. Her major writings were collected by her brother Arthur into the two volumes *At Home and Abroad* (1856) and *Life Without and Life Within* (1858).

G

Gabor, Zsa Zsa (1918–) *Hungarian-born American actress*

> The Gabor sisters are three of the world's true celebrities...they are famous for being famous.
>
> —Elsa Maxwell, 1952

Zsa Zsa Gabor, like her sisters Eva and Magda, was well known in the United States long before she made a film. Her fame rests on her striking looks, her numerous marriages, and her appearances in gossip columns and on TV talk shows.

Born Sari Gabor in Budapest, she made her stage debut at the age of 15 in Vienna and was named Miss Hungary 1936. In 1941 she joined her actress sister Eva in the United States and began cultivating her image as a star. Her film career did not begin until the 1950s, her first major film being John Huston's *Moulin Rouge* (1953), a biopic of the artist Toulouse-Lautrec, in which she played the role of the dancer Jane Avril. However, with the exception of a minor part in Orson Welles's *Touch of Evil* (1958), she was to make only B-pictures, such as *The Girl in the Kremlin* (1957), in which she appeared shaven headed; and *Queen of Outer Space* (1958), in which she played a scientist wearing a ball gown and jewels.

Although Gabor continued to appear in films and on stage throughout the 1960s and 1970s, she was now world famous simply for her numerous marriages and affairs. She had married, among others, the actor George Sanders, the hotelier Conrad Hilton, and Jack Ryan, inventor of the Barbie doll. She had also been romantically linked with countless other men, including, it is rumoured, Richard Burton, President John F. Kennedy, and Rafael Trujillo, dictator of the Dominican Republic. This last liaison caused her to be described in Congress as "the most expensive courtesan since Madame de Pompadour," as Trujillo had given her furs and a Mercedes-Benz just as the United States had loaned his country $1.3 million. Consequently she was much in demand on talk shows, during which she offered her caustic and humorous views on men, women, and diamonds. She also wrote *Zsa Zsa's Complete Guide to Men* (1969) and *How to Get a Man, How to Keep a Man, and How to Get Rid of a Man* (1971).

Zsa Zsa's most recent marriage was to German aristocrat Frederick von Anhalt, but it was a brush with the law that brought her headlines in 1990. Having been stopped by a traffic policeman, she slapped him for being "disrespectful" and spent three days in jail.

Galla Placidia (*c.* 390–450) *Roman noblewoman*

Half-sister of the Western Roman Emperor Honorius, Galla Placidia ruled the Empire for a decade after his death.

The daughter of Emperor Theodosius the Great, she grew up in Ravenna, where the Roman imperial residence had moved in response to the threat from the Visigoths. When the Visigoths sacked Rome in 410, Galla Placidia was captured by the chieftain Alaric; after his death she married his brother Ataulf. When Ataulf was murdered in 416, she was ransomed to the Roman general Constantius, whom she later married (unwillingly it is said). Galla Placidia received the title Augusta in 421 when her husband was named co-emperor by Honorius. On Constantius's death in 421 Honorius banished her to the court of her nephew Theodosius II, the Eastern Roman Emperor, in Constantinople.

In 425 Galla Placidia returned from exile as regent for Valentinian III, her six-year-old son and Honorius's successor as the Western Emperor. She ruled the Western Empire from Ravenna, where, as a generous patron of the arts, she commissioned several famous churches, including her Mausoleum, which is still well preserved. Although in around 433 she was displaced as Valentinian's chief adviser by Flavius Aëtius, Galla Placidia retained the title Augusta and probably continued to exert some influence until her death in Rome.

Galli-Curci, Amelita (1889–1963)
Italian opera singer

Amelita Galli-Curci was born in Milan and received her musical education at the Conservatory there. Although she was a prize-winning piano student, she decided instead to become a singer, teaching herself the high florid style of soprano singing known as coloratura. After making her opera debut at Trani, southern Italy, in 1907 as Gilda in Verdi's *Rigoletto*, in 1909 she performed in Bizet's *Don Procopio* in Rome. Tours of Egypt, Russia, and South America followed, but she was still almost unknown in the United States when she made her American debut in Chicago in 1916, again as Gilda. She joined the Chicago Opera Association and made her New York debut to great acclaim in the title role of Meyerbeer's *Dinorah* in 1918.

Galli-Curci first appeared with the Metropolitan Opera Company of New York in 1920, as Violetta in Verdi's *La Traviata*. She then remained at the Metropolitan until 1930, when she was forced to retire from singing because a goitre was affecting her throat.

The beauty of Galli-Curci's singing, her fluency, and the warmth of her voice so impressed audiences and critics that flaws in her technique were forgiven. She built up a repertoire of nearly 30 roles. Among these were Juliette in Gounod's *Romeo and Juliet*, Cio-Cio-San in Puccini's *Madame Butterfly*, Lucia in Donizetti's *Lucia di Lammermoor*, the title role in Delibes's *Lakmé*, and Elvira in Bellini's *I Puritani*. Following a throat operation, Galli-Curci returned to the stage in Puccini's *La Bohème* in 1936, but this was her last performance. In 1940 she retired to California, where she remained until her death.

Gandhi, Indira (1917–1984) *Indian stateswoman*

> I don't mind if my life goes in the service of the nation. If I die today, every drop of my blood will invigorate the nation.
>
> —Said the night before her assassination on October 31,1984

Beginning her political career in the struggle for independence from Britain, Indira Gandhi came to dominate Indian politics in her last two decades. Except for a 22-month interval in the late 1970s, she was prime minister from 1966 until her assassination in 1984.

Born Indira Priyadarshini Nehru in Allahabad, she was the only child of Jawaharlal Nehru, who became India's first prime minister in 1946. Following a childhood she described as "an abnormal one, full of loneliness and insecurity," and schooling in India and Switzerland, she entered Somerville College, Oxford, in 1938 but returned to India in 1941 without taking a degree.

In London Indira had become reacquainted with Feroze Gandhi. She had known Gandhi, a journalist from Allahabad who was unrelated to Mahatma Gandhi, in her childhood. In March 1942 they married, despite opposition because she was a Hindu and he a Parsi. Six months later they were arrested for their support of the nationalist movement. On their release in 1943 they returned to Allahabad, where they were to live until 1946 and where their two sons, Rajiv and Sanjay, were born.

In 1955 Mrs. Gandhi joined the working committee of the ruling Congress Party. Following Nehru's death in 1964, she joined the cabinet of Lal Bahadur Shastri as minister of information. In 1966, after the sudden death of Shastri, Congress Party leaders made her prime minister, in the belief that they would be able to control her. However, she successfully organized her own supporters, who were opposed to the conservative wing of the party, and won decisive election victories in 1971 and 1972.

After her strong stand during the crisis with Pakistan in 1971, which resulted in the creation of the new state of Bangladesh (formerly East Pakistan), Mrs. Gandhi seemed unassailable, but India began to experience economic and law-and-order problems. In 1975, accused of corruption, she imposed a state of emergency and postponed elections, which she later (1977) lost. However, subsequent corruption charges and imprisonment did not stop Mrs. Gandhi and her wing of the party, renamed Congress (I), from winning a landslide victory in the election of January 1980.

Among developing and nonaligned nations Mrs. Gandhi had considerable influence and respect, but she lost Western support over her refusal to denounce the Soviet invasion of Afghanistan: she also failed to deal effectively with growing religious violence within India. In 1980 her younger son and political heir-apparent, Sanjay, was killed in an aeroplane crash. Thereafter she turned for assistance to her elder son, Rajiv Gandhi, who became her eventual successor.

On October 31, 1984, Mrs. Gandhi was assassinated in New Delhi by two Sikh members of her special security force. This murder was apparently in retaliation for the army's 1984 raid on the Golden Temple at Amritsar, the holiest Sikh shrine and headquarters of extremists demanding greater autonomy for the Punjab.

Garbo, Greta (1905–1990) *Swedish-born American film actress*

> What, when drunk, one sees in other women, one sees in Garbo sober.
>
> —Kenneth Tynan, *The Sunday Times*, August 25, 1963

Garbo's combination of talent with beauty and an air of mystery made her one of the legends of cinema.

Born Greta Lovisa Gustafsson in Stockholm, her childhood was overshadowed by poverty and unemployment. She began work at the age of 14 in a hairdresser's, then became a salesgirl in a department store, where she was chosen to appear in one of its publicity films. After appearances in similar films she won a scholarship to the Royal Theatre Dramatic School in Stockholm. While there she was chosen by the director Mauritz Stiller to play the second lead in *The Story of Gösta Berling* (1924) under the name Greta Garbo. The film, which was well received by European critics, launched Garbo as a promising young film actress. When Stiller secured a contract with Louis B. Mayer later that year, he insisted on bringing Garbo, whom he continued to coach and manage, with him to Hollywood.

Garbo's magnetic screen presence in the silent movie *The Torrent* (1926) ensured her instant stardom. She went on to appear in *Love* (1927) and *Flesh and the Devil* (1927), costarring in both movies with the popular leading man John Gilbert, whose name was linked romantically with hers. The resulting publicity, and her taciturn manner offscreen (she was dubbed the "Swedish Sphinx"), sowed the seeds of her legend.

In *Anna Christie* (1930), advertised with the slogan "Garbo talks!", her distinctive low voice was heard for the first time. This was followed by her greatest successes: *Grand Hotel* (1932), *Queen Christina* (1933), *Anna Karenina* (1935), and *Camille* (1936). Although Garbo displayed an unexpected comic talent in Ernst Lubitsch's *Ninotchka* (1939), she was becoming increasingly reclusive. Following unfavourable reviews of another comedy, *Two-Faced Woman* (1941), she retired, refusing all offers of new films.

Echoing the much-quoted line from *Grand Hotel* with which she is so often identified – "I want to be alone" – Garbo spent the rest of her long life in seclusion. In 1955 she was honoured with a special Academy Award for "a series of luminous and unforgettable performances," but she did not attend the ceremony.

Gardner, Ava (1922–1990) *American film actress*

A Hollywood leading lady for over two decades, Ava Gardner came to personify the screen *femme fatale* in the late 1940s and early 1950s, being voted the world's most beautiful woman.

She was born Lucy Johnson in Grabton, North Carolina, into a poor farming family. When she was 18, her brother-in-law sent a portfolio of his pictures of her to MGM studios, which gave her a screen test. The green-eyed brunette evidently impressed Louis B. Mayer, who was reported to have said of her, "She can't talk. She can't act. She's terrific!" Given a seven-year contract, she was taught acting and received elocution lessons to remove her Southern accent.

After five years of obscurity playing small parts in minor movies, Gardner rose to stardom as a ravishing seductress in *The Killers* (1946), thereby establishing her position as a leading screen *femme fatale*. She brought a combination of sensuality and cynicism to a succession of films with some of the foremost leading men of the time, most notably *One Touch of Venus* (1948), *The Snows of Kilimanjaro* (1952) with Gregory Peck, *Mogambo* (1953) with Clark Gable, for which she won an Academy Award nomination, *The Barefoot Contessa* (1954) with Humphrey Bogart, and *The Sun Also Rises* (1957). She also appeared in the successful musical *Show Boat* (1951). Her brief, well-publicized marriages to Mickey Rooney (1942–43), bandleader Artie Shaw (1945–46), and Frank Sinatra (1951–57) reinforced her screen image.

During the 1950s Gardner's relations with MGM soured, and eventually, with some difficulty, she left to become an independent actress. During this period she made such films as *On the Beach* (1959), *Night of the Iguana* (1964) with Richard Burton, *Mayerling* (1969), and *The Cassandra Crossing* (1977), before eventually retiring from film work in 1981.

Garland, Judy (1922–1969) *American singer and film actress*

> Such a tragedy. Too much work, too much pressure, the wrong kind of people as husbands.

> —Bing Crosby, speaking of Garland, 1976

A Hollywood legend, Judy Garland achieved the status of superstar before dependence on drugs and alcohol prematurely ended her life.

She was born Frances Gumm, in Grand Rapids, Michigan, the daughter of vaudeville players. Having made her debut at the age of three, she went on to tour the United States as part of the Gumm Sisters act. In 1931 the sisters changed their name to Garland, with Frances becoming Judy. Signed by MGM at the age of 13, Judy made her movie debut in the short *Every Sunday* (1936). In 1937 she drew critical acclaim for her performance in *Broadway Melody of 1938* and began her partnership with child star Mickey Rooney in *Thoroughbreds Don't Cry*.

Her portrayal of Dorothy in *The Wizard of Oz* (1938) made her an international star. Her rendering in that film of "Over the Rainbow," the song with which she became identified, helped Garland to win a special Academy Award for her "outstanding performance as a screen juvenile." Several successful musicals followed, including *For Me and My Gal* (1942) and *Meet Me in St. Louis* (1944); among the songs she made memorable were "You Made Me Love You," "For Me and My Gal," "I Got Rhythm," "Embraceable You," "Look for the Silver Lining," and "Meet Me Tonight in Dreamland."

By the 1950s Garland's life and career were being affected by psychological problems, weight gain, dependence on drugs, and the failure of marriages to composer-conductor David Rose and director Vincente Minnelli. Her dismissal by MGM in 1951 led her to attempt suicide. However, she recovered to give a superb performance in *A Star Is Born* (1954), receiving an Oscar nomination for Best Actress.

Garland's third husband, the producer Sidney Luft, helped her to revive her career with sell-out appearances in London and New York, culminating in her Carnegie Hall concert of 1961; but during the 1960s she made only four films. Although her dramatic performances in *Judgment at Nuremburg*

(1961) and *A Child Is Waiting* (1963) were acclaimed, her career was in decline.

Garland married Mark Herron in 1965 and Mickey Deans in 1968. She attempted a cabaret season in London that year but was booed. The following year she died there from an overdose of sleeping pills. Garland had three children, including the singer and actress Liza MINNELLI.

Garnett, Constance (1861–1946)
British translator of Russian literature

Constance Garnett's fine translations made the work of Tolstoy, Chekhov, Dostoevsky, and other great Russian writers accessible to the English-speaking world. Written in a clear direct style and with, it has been said, "a scrupulous literary conscience," they exerted a great influence on English literature and thought.

Born Constance Black in Brighton, where her father was a coroner, she was the sister of the radical social campaigner and novelist Clementina Black. Educated first at home and then at Brighton High School, Constance won a scholarship to Newnham College, Cambridge, at the age of 17 and in 1883 gained a first-class honours degree in classics.

After three years as a private teacher she was appointed librarian at the People's Palace, a technical college in London's East End. In 1889 she married Edward Garnett, a publisher's reader who was to become an influential critic. Garnett had many friends among the Russian exiles in London; it was in this period that Constance learned Russian and joined the socialist Fabian Society. After the birth of her only child, the future novelist David Garnett, in 1892 Constance visited Russia, taking with her money for famine relief and political papers for her friend the Russian revolutionary Sergei Stepniak; she also visited the novelist Tolstoy. On her return to Britain in 1893 she began, with Stepniak's encouragement, to translate the classics of Russian literature.

Between 1894 and 1928 Constance Garnett produced the editions of Tolstoy, Chekhov, Dostoevsky, Turgenev, and Gogol that remained the standard versions for half a century. She brought to her work great concentration, a respect for both languages, and a love of 19th-century Russia and its people. Although her eyesight, which was never good, deteriorated in later life, she continued to translate, dictating after hearing the Russian read aloud.

Gaskell, Elizabeth Cleghorn (1810–1865) *British novelist and biographer*

The kind of patriotism which consists of hating all other nations.
—*Sylvia's Lovers* (1863)

Although the sympathetic rendering of life at different levels of society in her novels brought her popularity and acclaim, Mrs. Gaskell is now best remembered for her biography of Charlotte BRONTË.

Born Elizabeth Stevenson in London, she was raised by her aunt in the northern town of Knutsford, which was to be the model for her small-town saga *Cranford* (1853). In 1832 she married William Gaskell, a Unitarian minister in Manchester. She saw herself first as a wife and mother and second as a writer, a duality that profoundly influenced her work. Her first novel, *Mary Barton* (1848), begun as therapy after the death of a baby son, was inspired by the plight of northern mill workers in the "hungry forties." The book brought her into contact with Charles Dickens, and she began writing for his magazine *Household Words*.

Mrs. Gaskell was an innovator among English novelists. *Mary Barton* and *North and South* (1855) put the industrial north on the literary map, while *Ruth* (1853) tackled the problems of the unmarried mother, a subject considered shocking at that time. Her best later novels were *Cousin Phillis* and *Sylvia's Lovers* (both 1863), and particularly *Wives and Daughters* (unfinished at her death and published in 1866). All these books combine psychological depth with social content, anticipating the modern "psychological novel."

Mrs. Gaskell brought her novelist's ability to evoke a place and a way of life, and her keen eye for the detail of daily affairs, to *The Life of Charlotte Brontë* (1857). These qualities, and her obvious empathy with a fellow woman novelist, made it a classic biography.

Geller, Margaret Joan (1947–)
American astronomer

Margaret Geller has worked on a major survey of galaxies with the aim of mapping all the galaxies in a large region of the sky.

The daughter of a crystallographer from Ithaca, New York State, Geller was encouraged as a small child to study science and mathematics. She was educated at the University of California, Berkeley, and at Princeton where she obtained her PhD in 1975. After a period in England at the Institute of Astronomy, Cambridge, Geller moved in 1980 to Harvard, where she was appointed professor of astronomy in 1988. She is also a staff member of the Smithsonian Astrophysical Observatory.

In the early 1980s Geller, in collaboration with John Huchra, began carrying out for the Center for Astrophysics (CfA) a survey of some 15,000 galaxies by examining and comparing their red shifts (changes in their emission spectrums indicating the speed of recession from our galaxy). The purpose of this work was to map all galaxies above a certain brightness, out to a distance of about 650 million light years, in a particular sector of the heavens. Geller was are aware that to some observers the sky lacked the uniformity predicted by the big-bang theory (the theory that all the matter and energy in the universe originated in one enormous explosion). In 1981, for example, a gap of 100 million light years had been discovered in the constellation Bootes. She considered the possibility that this was a local phenomenon, and that the predicted uniformity would become more apparent on further investigations on a much larger scale.

But when the distribution of galaxies was plotted it was found that they had neither a uniform spread, nor a random scattering, but large-scale clusters grouped into enormous structures. The largest of these, named the "Great Wall," stretches for more than 500 million light years. It was difficult to see how anything as massive could have been formed within the context of current cosmological theory; when Geller reported the initial results of the CfA survey in 1989, she noted, "Something fundamental is missing in our models."

Gellhorn, Martha (Ellis) (1908–98)
American writer and journalist

As both a distinguished foreign correspondent and a writer of fiction, Gellhorn took as her main theme the realities of war and human suffering.

Martha Gellhorn was born in St. Louis, Missouri, the daughter of a gynaecologist. She attended the prestigious Bryn Mawr College, but left abruptly in order to pursue her literary ambitions in Paris. In the 1930s she joined *Collier's Weekly* as a foreign correspondent and went to Spain to cover the Spanish Civil War. Having remained in Europe, she witnessed the German invasion of Finland at the outbreak of World War II. In 1940 Gellhorn married the novelist Ernest Hemingway, who was also a war correspondent in Europe. They both covered the events of World War II, but their stormy marriage ended in divorce in 1945.

Gellhorn continued to report on wars and revolutions as they broke out in various parts of the world; her experiences of the 1940s and 1950s were gathered in her first nonfiction book, *The Face of War* (1959). In 1966 she reported on the conflict in Vietnam, and a year later she provided first-hand descriptions of the fighting in the Middle East. From 1983 to 1985 she covered the conflict and suffering in Central America. Her last years were spent mainly in Britain.

During her time as a journalist, Gellhorn also found time to write fiction. In 1934 she published her first novel, *What Mad Pursuit. A Stricken Field* (1940) soon followed, and in 1948 she published two books, *Lianao* and *The Wine of Astonishment*. Her sympathy for the world's oppressed is more apparent in her shorter works, and she became renowned for her collections of short stories, which include

The Trouble I've Seen (1936), *The Hon-
eyed Peace* (1953), *Two by Two* (1958),
and *The Weather in Africa* (1978).

Genée, Dame Adeline (1878–1970)
Danish-born British dancer

Born Anita Jensen in Århus, she became interested in dance at an early
age, encouraged by her uncle Alexandre Genée and his Hungarian wife
Antonia Zimmerman. Dancers themselves, they became her adoptive parents when she was eight. She named
herself Adeline after the famous opera
singer Adelina PATTI.

Trained in the classical French style,
Adeline made her debut in Christiania
(now Oslo) at the age of ten, later joining her uncle's touring company and
performing in Berlin and Munich. In
1896 she first performed the role with
which she became identified, that of
Swanhilda in *Coppélia*.

Genée rose to fame as one of the
most popular stars of the Edwardian
stage in England. Given a six-week
contract by London's Empire Theatre
in 1897, she remained as their prima
ballerina for the next ten years. She
performed a mixture of classical solo
pieces and lighter more accessible
work, to which she lent a personal
charm and humour that attracted large
audiences at a time when classical ballet was becoming less popular. She
also worked extensively in America
after making her debut there in 1907,
playing a total of five seasons between
1909 and 1917, mainly in revues.

In 1910 Genée married Frank Isitt,
a businessman. After the outbreak of
World War I in 1914 she performed
less and less, finally retiring from regular stage work in 1917. Her last public
performance was in *The Love Song*, for
charity, in 1932–33.

Genée became the first president of
the Association of Operatic Dancing
(later the Royal Academy of Dancing)
in 1920, retiring in 1954. She was created a DBE in 1950.

Geneviève, Saint (*c.* 422–*c.* 500)
French nun

St. Geneviève, whose feast day is January 3, is the patron saint of Paris. According to legend she saved the city
when it was threatened by the Huns.

Geneviève was probably born at
Nanterre, outside Paris. Having decided at the age of seven to devote herself to a religious life, she became a
nun at 15. Her prophecies about the
dangers she saw facing Paris angered
the citizens; but when Attila threatened the city in 451, Geneviève reportedly persuaded the citizens to stand
firm. Attila soon abandoned his siege
of Paris to attack Orléans, over 70
miles away, where he was defeated.

Geneviève later led an expedition to
secure food for the Parisians when the
Salian Franks besieged the city. This
impressed the Frankish King Childeric
and his successor Clovis; her influence
with them secured the release of many
Parisian prisoners.

Geneviève was buried in Paris in the
Church of the Holy Apostles Peter and
Paul, which she had persuaded Clovis
to build on the burial site of Saint
Denis, the patron saint of France. It
later became known as the Church of
St. Geneviève. Repeated claims of her
miraculous protection of Paris, especially from the plague in 1129, contributed to her legend in the Middle
Ages. During the French Revolution
most of her relics were destroyed,
those surviving being moved to the
Church of Saint-Étienne-du-Mont. The
church is still visited by pilgrims
today.

Genlis, Comtesse de (1746–1830)
French writer

The Comtesse de Genlis was born
Stéphanie Félicité Ducrest de Saint-
Aubin, near Autun, in eastern France.
She married the Comte de Genlis in
1762, becoming lady-in-waiting to the
Duchess of Chartres in 1770. She later
became the mistress of the duchess's
husband, the future Duc d'Orléans.
Madame de Genlis tutored their children, including the future King Louis
Philippe, for whom she wrote *Théâtre
d'éducation*, a four-volume set of short
plays. She also wrote other educational works, including *Adèle et Théo-
dore* (1782), and in *Deux réputations*
(1784) she attacked the growing tendency towards intellectual atheism.

After both her husband and the Duc
d'Orléans were executed in 1793, dur-

ing the French Revolution, the Comtesse left France to live in England and Switzerland.

During her exile Madame de Genlis wrote *Précis de la conduite de Mme. de Genlis dupuis la Révolution* (1796; Summary of the Conduct of Mme. de Genlis since the Revolution). She hoped that this would convince the Republicans, who did not trust her, that she was not hostile to them. Accordingly she was allowed to return to France in 1802.

Now living in Paris, Madame de Genlis became one of Napoleon's favourite novelists. In 1812 he made her Inspector of Primary Schools in Paris. She went on to write nearly a hundred novels, the best known of which is Napoleon's favourite, *Mlle. de Clermont* (1802). Many of these books were historical novels in praise of the pre-Revolutionary regime. Her ten volumes of *Mémoires* (1825) give a somewhat scandalous account of her times.

Gentileschi, Artemisia (*c.* 1597–*c.* 1652) *Italian painter*

> I have the greatest sympathy for your lordship, because the name of a woman makes one doubtful until one has seen the work.
>
> —Letter to Don Antonio Ruffo, a patron, January 30, 1649

Artemisia Gentileschi was one of the most prominent followers of Caravaggio, the Baroque painter noted for his striking realism and his innovations in the use of chiaroscuco (light and shade).

Born in Rome, she was taught by her father, the painter Orazio Gentileschi, who was himself a disciple of Caravaggio, and Agostino Tassi, the landscape painter. In her teens Artemisia suffered unfavourable publicity following a long court case brought by her father against Tassi, who stood accused of raping her. This episode encouraged her independence of spirit and may, it has been suggested, have influenced her choice of subjects.

Artemisia's style was at first indistinguishable from her father's, but after moving from Rome to Florence, she developed her own approach. It was here that she produced her most famous work, *Judith and Holofernes*, which now hangs in the Uffizi, Florence. Inspired by the story in the Apocrypha of the Jewish heroine JUDITH, who slew the invading general Holofernes, the painting depicts his decapitation graphically and vividly. While her father had abandoned Caravaggio's extreme contrasts of light and shade and softened his colours, Artemisia intensified both to powerful effect. Around this time she also produced *Judith and Her Maidservant* and was commissioned by Michelangelo to work on the ceiling of Casa Buonarroti. At the age of 23 she was admitted to the Florentine Accademia del Disegno.

Between 1620 and 1626 Artemisia worked in Rome, mainly on portraits (often of historical figures, such as CLEOPATRA), narrative works, and vibrant female nudes. She then moved to Naples. In 1638 she joined her father in England, where he had become court painter to King Charles I . Here she was in great demand as a portrait painter; among the many works she produced in England is a self-portrait now displayed in Hampton Court Palace. Artemisia returned to Naples in 1639, more famous than her father. Despite her renown she is thought to have died in poverty.

Germain, Sophie (1776–1831) *French mathematician*

Sophie Germain was born in Paris, where she grew up during the French Revolution and the Reign of Terror. Until the age of 18 she educated herself, despite the objections of her parents, who cut off the heat and light to her room. However, she was so fascinated by mathematics that even this did not discourage her; finally her parents gave in and allowed her to pursue her studies. She obtained lecture notes from the new Ecole Polytechnique, to which women were not admitted, and began to correspond with prominent mathematicians, claiming to be a male student named Le Blanc. The eminent mathematician Joseph-Louis Lagrange was so impressed by one of her papers that he became her personal tutor.

Germain became interested in what are now known as "Chladni figures," the patterns formed by sand sprinkled on a vibrating plate. She entered a competition held by the Académie Française to provide a mathematical explanation for these figures, which she won at her third attempt in 1816. She was then admitted to the Institut de France. Germain published her results in 1921 as *Recherches sur la théorie des surfaces élastiques*.

During her career Germain made significant advances in acoustics and, in particular, number theory as well as elasticity. She worked on the famously unsolved problem of Fermat's "last theorem," which states that the equation $x^n + y^y = z^n$ has no solution if n is a whole number greater than 2, giving a broader proof than had been available.

Germain corresponded with many eminent mathematicians, including Adrien-Marie Legendre and Carl Friedrich Gauss, who did not suspect she was a woman for some years. Gauss recommended her for an honorary doctorate from the University of Göttingen, but she died from cancer before it could be awarded. Her work on elasticity was later utilized in the design of the Eiffel Tower, although her name is not among the 72 names inscribed there.

Gertrude of Helfta, Saint (1256–c. 1302) *German mystic*

St. Gertrude of Helfta, who is sometimes called St. Gertrude the Great, was probably born near Eisleben, Saxony. From the age of five she lived at the Benedictine convent of Helfta where she studied under St. Mechtild, who taught her such secular subjects as Latin and philosophy.

It was not until she had her first mystical experience at the age of 25 that Gertrude decided to become a nun. The revelations and the visions of Christ that she experienced are described in *Revelationes divinae pietatis* (Revelations of Divine Love), which has become a classic of mystical theology. The work, which is written in good Latin, is in five volumes, but only volume two was completely written by Gertrude. The two other works that have been attributed to her are *Exercitia spiritualia* (Spiritual Exercises), a book of seven meditations, and *Preces Gertrudianae* (Prayers of Gertrude), which, although it bears her name, is not authentic.

The main theme of Gertrude's work is the humanity of Christ. Together with St. Mechtild she laid the foundation for the cult of the Adoration of the Sacred Heart, in which Christ's heart, often bleeding, is used as a symbol of his love and sacrifice. St. Gertrude's feast day is observed on November 16.

Gibson, Althea (1927–) *American tennis player*

Althea Gibson was the first African American to win a major U.S. or British title. Tall, elegant, and quick, she was noted for her powerful serve and volley.

Born in Silver City, South Carolina, Gibson grew up in Harlem, New York. She started playing lawn tennis seriously at the age of 13 with the ambition of becoming "the best woman tennis player who ever lived." After leaving school, she worked in a factory until support from a prominent Southern African-American family enabled her to continue her studies, improve her game, and take a degree in physical education.

In 1950 Gibson became the first African-American player to compete in the American Lawn Tennis Association championships at Forest Hills, during which she nearly beat the reigning Wimbledon champion, Louise BROUGH. The next year she was the first black player at the British championships. Her game, based on speed, strength, and aggression, improved, and in 1956 she took the French and Italian Open championships and shared the French and British doubles, the latter being the first major Wimbledon title for a black player. In 1957–58 she was the top-ranked U.S. woman player, dominating women's tennis. She won the Italian Open (1957), the British and U.S. singles (1957–58), and again shared the Wimbledon doubles (1957–58).

Gibson turned professional in 1958, playing tennis and golf, and performed occasionally as a nightclub singer and movie actress. She won the U.S. professional singles title in 1960. After retiring as a player, she served as New Jersey's commissioner of athletics from 1975 until 1985 and in 1980 was among the first six athletes to be elected to the Women's Sports Hall of Fame. In 1991 she became the first woman to receive the National Collegiate Athletic Association's top honour, the Theodore Roosevelt Award.

Gilman, Charlotte Perkins (Stetson) (1860–1935) *American reformer and writer*

> Where young boys plan for what they will achieve and attain, young girls plan for whom they will achieve and attain.
>
> —*Women and Economics* (1898)

An economist, Charlotte Perkins Gilman was mainly identified with the labour and women's rights movements.

Born Charlotte Perkins in Hartford, Connecticut, she had an unhappy childhood, during which her father deserted the family and her mother withheld affection. Largely self-educated, Charlotte was well read in anthropology, sociology, and economics. At the age of 18 she went to the Rhode Island School of Design, later becoming a teacher and commercial artist.

In 1884 Charlotte married the artist Charles W. Stetson but separated from him four years later, after suffering severe depression following the birth of their daughter. She moved to California, where she lectured on women's issues and labor and social policy and began to write. Divorced from Stetson in 1894, she married George H. Gilman, a New York lawyer, in 1900.

Mrs. Gilman attacked social wrongs in her writings and also on the lecture circuit. Her most influential work, *Women and Economics* (1898), written after three years of political activity and travel, advocated organized economic independence for women. *The Yellow Wall Paper* (1899), a short story in which a woman goes slowly insane, is considered her best piece of fiction. She also published, singlehandedly, a journal of reform, *The Forerunner* (1909–16). She became increasingly convinced of the need for women to assert what she saw as their peaceful, co-operative nature to counterbalance male destructiveness. She explored these ideas in *Man-Made World* (1911) and *His Religion and Hers* (1923).

Diagnosed as suffering from cancer in 1932, Mrs. Gilman committed suicide in Pasadena, California, when the disease could no longer be controlled. Her autobiography was published later that year.

Gimbutas, Marija (1921–1994) *Lithuanian-born American archaeologist, anthropologist, and writer*

Marija Gimbutas is noted for her review of European prehistory from a feminist perspective. The name "archaeomythology" has been given to her unique approach to archaeology.

She was born Marija Alseika in Vilnius, Lithuania, the daughter of two physicians. While attending the University of Vilnius (1938–42), she married Jungis Gimbutas (in 1941); the couple were to have three children. After further studies at the universities of Vienna (1944) and Tübingen (1945–46), Gimbutas moved to the United States, where she became a research fellow at Harvard in 1950 and took U.S. citizenship in 1955.

Gimbutas's studies of prehistoric cultures took her back to Europe for extensive travels; her results were published in such books as *Gods and Goddesses of Old Europe, 7000–3500 BC* (1974). Gimbutas believed that the ancient societies she studied had been matriarchial and therefore harmonious.

In the early 1960s Gimbutas was lecturing at Harvard. In 1964 she became professor of Indo-European archaeology at the University of California, Los Angeles, remaining there until her retirement in 1989.

Ginsburg, Ruth Bader (1933–) *American judge*

In 1993 Ruth Bader Ginsburg became only the second female, and the second Jewish person, to be appointed a

Supreme Court judge in the United States. She has spent much of her career working to end discrimination against women.

Born and brought up in Brooklyn, New York, Ruth Bader attended Cornell University, where she met her future husband, Martin Ginsburg. Two years after graduating, and by now married and a mother, she entered Harvard and then Columbia law schools. Although graduating first in her class, Ginsburg found it difficult to obtain work in a male-dominated profession. In 1959 she took up a clerkship with the U.S. District Court of Appeals in New York, later teaching at Rutgers University Law School in Newark, New Jersey, before becoming the first tenured woman professor at Columbia in 1972.

Ginsburg attracted public attention during the 1970s as both her teaching and the cases she argued in the courts highlighted the extent of discrimination against women. Described as the "legal architect of the modern women's movement," she argued six cases on women's rights in the U.S. Supreme Court between 1973 and 1976, winning five of them. However, her belief that the law should not favour either sex over the other and, in particular, her reservations about some high-profile cases have brought criticism from women's groups.

In 1980 Ginsburg became a circuit judge in the U.S. Court of Appeals for the District of Columbia, where she became known for her academic rigour and her evenhanded approach. Ginsburg was nominated by President Clinton to the U.S. Supreme Court in 1993, becoming only the second woman to be appointed to this post, after Sandra Day o'CONNOR in 1981.

Ginzburg, Natalia Levi (1916–1991)
Italian writer

The author of novels, short stories, plays, and essays, Natalia Ginzburg was one of the major Italian writers of the post-World War II period.

She was born Natalia Levi into an intellectual Jewish family in Palermo, Sicily. In 1919 her father took up a professorship in Turin, where their house later became a centre of antifascist activity. In 1938 Natalia married the socialist publisher Leone Ginzburg, who was imprisoned for his antifascist work in 1942. Forced to leave Turin, Natalia moved to a small town in the Abruzzi, where she began writing. Her husband died in prison in 1944.

Natalia's first short stories, published in the Florentine magazine *Solaria*, and her first short novel *La strada che va in città* (1942), appeared under the pen name Alessandra Tornimparte. The novel, published in English as *The Road to the City* (1945), tells the story of a country girl who, attracted by the excitement of city life, is seduced and enters into a loveless marriage. This theme of women's marital unhappiness, explored in a simple style but with deep psychological insight, is a recurring one throughout her work. Her novels of the 1950s and 1960s concern the problems faced by younger Italians during the fascist period. They include *Tutti i nostri ieri* (1952), published in English as *A Light for Fools*; and *Lessico famigliare* (1963; *Family Sayings*), which won the Strega Prize. Her later novels, such as *Famiglia* (1977; *Family*), explore the break-up of the family in modern society, and especially the way in which this has affected women.

Ginzburg also wrote several dramas on similar themes, including *L'inserzione* (1968; *The Advertisement*); a collection of critical essays entitled *Mai devi domandarmi* (1970; *Never Must You Ask Me*); and *La famiglia Manzoni* (1983; *The Manzoni Family*), a biography of the novelist and poet Alessandro Manzoni.

Gipps, Ruth (1921–) *British composer and conductor*

Ruth Gipps began studying music at the age of four, as a pupil at her mother's School of Music in Bexhill, Sussex. Her first piece of music was published when she was eight. She later studied at the Royal College of Music, London, where Ralph Vaughan Williams taught her composition, gaining her diploma in 1936. In 1942 her symphonic poem *Knight in Armour* was conducted by Sir Henry Wood on the last night of the Proms in London. She was awarded a doctorate in music from Durham University in 1948.

In her early career Gipps worked mainly as a concert pianist and an orchestral oboist, only later taking up conducting, a field in which very few women were then active. Choirmaster of the City of Birmingham Choir from 1948 to 1950, she became musical director of the London Repertoire Orchestra in 1955. In 1959 she toured the United States on an award from the English-Speaking Union Ford Foundation; two years later she became director of the Chanticleer Orchestra, which she founded herself.

As a composer Gipps has experimented with a variety of forms. Between 1942 and 1980 she composed five symphonies, concertos for violin, piano, and horn, chamber music, choral pieces, and a ballet, *The Sea Nymph*. In 1967 she became chair of the Composers' Guild of Great Britain and was appointed a professor at the Royal College of Music. She was honoured with the OBE in 1981.

Gish, Dorothy (1898–1968) *American actress*

Gish, Lillian (1896–1993) *American actress*

Stars of the silent screen, Lillian and Dorothy Gish went on to enjoy long and distinguished careers both in films and on the stage. Lillian Gish's career in theatre, films, and television lasted for over 85 years – proof, as the film critic Kevin Brownlow put it, that "the entire history of the feature film is contained within a lifetime."

Born Lillian and Dorothy de Guiche in Ohio, they began their careers as child actresses: deserted by their father, they were taken to New York by their mother, where all three performed in touring theatre companies. In 1912 the sisters began their famous association with the director D. W. Griffith, to whom they were introduced by their friend Mary PICKFORD; they made their screen debut in *An Unseen Enemy* (1912). After making several one-reel films with Griffith for the Biograph Company, Lillian and

Dorothy went with him to Hollywood in 1913. Two years later they both featured in Griffith's Civil War epic *The Birth of a Nation* (1915), a film simultaneously acclaimed as the first great work of art in the cinema and condemned for its racism. The sisters went on to appear together in Griffith's *Hearts of the World* (1918), *Broken Blossoms* (1919), and *Orphans of the Storm* (1922), while Lillian appeared without Dorothy in *Intolerance* (1916). Lillian also advised Griffith on set design and the financial aspects of filmmaking; she herself directed a film, *Remodeling Her Husband* (1920), in which her sister starred.

After leaving Griffith in the 1920s the sisters rarely worked together, although they remained close. Lillian began working for MGM in 1925, insisting on the right to approve both directors and scripts. Although the light-hearted mood of the 1920s did not suit her – she excelled in ethereal waiflike roles – she made a number of successful films, including King Vidor's *La Bohème* (1926), *The Scarlet Letter* (1926), and the prairie tragedy *The Wind* (1928). Unable to make a successful transition to sound pictures, she returned to the stage in the mid 1930s, scoring notable successes in *Camille* (1936) and as Ophelia in John Gielgud's *Hamlet* (1936). Although she concentrated mainly on stage and television work from then on, Lillian's later film appearances were well received by critics, if not always commercially successful. They include the western *Duel in the Sun* (1947), for which she was nominated for an Academy Award; Charles Laughton's masterpiece *Night of the Hunter* (1955), with Robert Mitchum; Robert Altman's *A Wedding* (1978); and Lindsay Anderson's *The Whales of August* (1987), with Bette DAVIS. Lillian Gish received a Special Academy Award for "her superlative artistry" in 1970 and a Life Achievement Award from the American Film Institute in 1984.

Dorothy Gish, like her sister, played innocent young girls in her early career but soon developed a more down-to-earth image, later becoming equally adept as a comedian. She made a few films in Britain in the late 1920s, including *Madame Pompadour* (1927), the first film made at Elstree Studios. However, after appearing in three sound films, Dorothy concentrated on stage work from 1928 to 1944. She acted mainly in light comedies, her greatest successes being *Life with Father* and *The Magnificent Yankee*. Her last screen appearance was in *The Cardinal* (1963). She died in Rapallo, Italy.

Glanville-Hicks, Peggy (1912–1990)
Australian-born American composer

Peggy Glanville-Hicks's work, as a composer, music critic, and organizer of concerts, was of great importance in promoting new music after World War II.

Born in Melbourne, she began her musical studies at the Conservatorium there in 1927, before moving to Europe in 1931. Studying under Ralph Vaughan Williams and Malcolm Sargent at the Royal College of Music in London, she won a scholarship to continue her studies in Vienna and in Paris (where she was taught by Nadia BOULANGER). In 1938 she married the composer Stanley Bate, with whom she later formed the ballet company Les Trois Arts. The same year her *Choral Suite* was conducted by Sir Adrian Boult in London; it was the first Australian work to be performed at a festival of the International Society for Contemporary Music.

Based in the United States from 1942 to 1959 (she became a U.S. citizen in 1948), Glanville-Hicks divided her energies between promoting contemporary music and composing her own work. With Carlton Sprague-Smith she cofounded the International Music Fund, to re-establish new music in Europe after World War II, and became a director of the New York Composers' Forum, organizing concerts at such venues as the Metropolitan Museum and Central Park. From 1948 to 1958 she was an influential music critic in the pages of the *New York Herald Tribune*. In 1955 she assisted Yehudi Menuhin in promoting concerts of Indian music.

Glanville-Hicks's own music is wide-ranging in style and form. Her opera *The Transposed Heads* (1953), based on Thomas Mann's short novel, incorporates oriental elements, while both *Nausicaa* (1961), a collaboration with Robert Graves, and *Sappho* (1965), based on the work of Lawrence Durrell, draw on the Greek folk forms that Glanville-Hicks had discovered after moving to Athens in 1959. She also wrote ballet music, most notably *The Masque of the Wild Man* (1958); pieces for the harp and percussion; film scores; orchestral works; and songs. In 1967 Glanville-Hicks underwent surgery in New York to remove a brain tumour. Although she recovered, she composed little afterwards, concentrating instead on her work as Director of Asian Studies at the Australian Music Centre in Sydney.

Glasgow, Ellen (1874–1945) *American novelist*

Ellen Glasgow is remembered for her novels dealing with the social history and manners of Virginia and the myths and hypocrisies of a changing Southern culture. She received a Pulitzer Prize for her last novel, *In This Our Life* (1941), about the decay of an aristocratic family.

Ellen Anderson Gholson Glasgow was born in Richmond, Virginia, into an affluent and socially prominent family. Privately educated because of ill health, which persisted all her life, she took a degree in politics at the University of Virginia despite her failing hearing, which she eventually lost. Apart from visits to Europe, where she met Henry James and other writers and was encouraged in her literary ambitions, Ellen Glasgow spent all her life in Richmond.

Ellen Glasgow's first novel, *The Descendant*, was published in 1897; it was followed by *Phases of an Inferior Planet* (1898). Set in New York City, both novels established the tone of her subsequent work with their intention to shock. *The Voice of the People* (1900) was the first of a series of five novels dealing with the conflict of the social classes in Virginia; in *Virginia* (1913), considered by some to be the best novel in this series, Glasgow gives a portrait of a young woman growing up in a mindless, dying society. With *Barren Ground* (1925), the story of a woman's struggle with the land, she began a period of major writing that included *The Romantic Comedians* (1926), *They Stooped to Folly* (1929), and *The Sheltered Life* (1932), a trilogy of ironic novels of manners set in a thinly disguised Richmond. She became a member of the American Academy of Arts and Letters in 1938.

Although Glasgow lived an apparently conventional life in Richmond until her death, this contrasted sharply with the tone of her work, which demanded a radical change in women's position in Southern society. *The Woman Within*, her intellectual and spiritual biography, was published posthumously in 1954.

Glaspell, Susan (1882–1948) *American novelist and playwright*

Glaspell's fiction describes a troubled and disordered present in which her characters must seek the virtues and strengths of the past. Her plays – more experimental and contemporary – represent her major achievement.

Susan Glaspell was born in Davenport, Iowa, and educated at Drake University, Des Moines. She worked on a Des Moines newspaper for two years before starting to write novels and short stories, some of which are collected in *Lifted Masks* (1912). Her novel *The Visioning* (1911) was influenced by the socialist ideas of the writer George Cram Cook, whom she married in 1913. Two years later she helped him and others, including Eugene O'Neill, to found the Provincetown Players in Massachusetts, a group that became a showcase for her plays. In the early 1920s she accompanied Cook to Greece, where he died in 1924. Her biography of Cook, *The Road to the Temple*, was published in 1926.

Glaspell's plays include the one-act *Suppressed Desires*, a satire on psychoanalysis written with Cook for the Provincetown Players' opening season in 1915, and such full-length works as *Bernice* (1920) and *The Verge* (1921),

which, with *Inheritors* (1921), was produced by the Providence troupe in Greenwich Village, New York, after their successful move there. *Alison's House* (1930), which concerns the continuing influence of a great woman poet (supposedly Emily DICKINSON) on her family 18 years after her death, won Glaspell a Pulitzer Prize.

After the failure of *The Comic Artist*, cowritten with her second husband, Norman Matson, Glaspell retired from the theatre and returned to writing novels. Among these are *Norma Ashe* (1942) and *Judd Rankin's Daughter* (1945).

Glendinning, Victoria (1937–) *British writer and journalist*

Glendinning is best known for her works of literary biography, most of which concern 20th-century women writers.

Born Victoria Seebohn, she was educated at Millfield School in Somerset before attending Somerville College, Oxford, where she graduated in modern languages, and Southampton University, where she studied social administration. While still at university she married Professor Nigel Glendinning, in 1958. The marriage was dissolved in 1981 and a year later she married the Irish novelist Terence de Vere White (who died in 1994).

During her first marriage she worked variously as a teacher (1960–69), a journalist, and a part-time social worker (1970–73), while also bringing up four sons. After several years as an editorial assistant on the *Times Literary Supplement* she became a full-time writer in 1978.

Most of Glendinning's works are biographical. They include *Elizabeth Bowen: Portrait of a Writer* (1977), *Edith Sitwell: A Unicorn among Lions* (1981), *Vita: a biography of V. Sackville-West* (1983), *Rebecca West: a life* (1987), and *Trollope* (1992), which won the 1992 Whitbread biography award. She was head of the Booker Prize panel in 1992. Her novels include *The Grown-Ups* (1989) and *Electricity* (1995). She has also edited, with her son Matthew Glendinning, *Sons and Mothers* (1996).

Gluck, Alma (1884–1938) *Romanian-born American singer*

Alma Gluck's brilliant soprano voice, charm, and beauty made her a popular favourite among opera lovers and concert-goers in the early years of the 20th century.

Born Reba Fiersohn in Iasi, Romania, she emigrated to the United States with her parents in 1890. She worked as a typist in New York until her marriage to Bernard Gluck in 1906, after which she began to study singing. She made her debut at the Metropolitan Opera House in 1909 as Sophie in Massenet's *Werther*.

Although her opera career lasted only three years, Gluck built her repertoire up to more than 20 roles. Most notable among these were Gilda in Verdi's *Rigoletto* and Eurydice in Gluck's *Orpheus and Eurydice*. However, feeling that her talents were better suited to the concert stage, she began a concert career in 1913. Later, with the advent of sound recording, she became one of the first successful recording artists. Alma Gluck had two children – the music writer Marcia Davenport by her first husband and the actor Efrem Zimbalist, Jr. by her second husband, the violinist Efrem Zimbalist, whom she married in 1914.

Glyn, Elinor (1864–1943) *British writer*

> Would you like to sin
> With Elinor Glyn
> On a tiger skin?
> Or would you prefer
> To err
> With her
> On some other fur?
>
> —Anonymous, after 1907

A popular writer of action-filled romantic novels, Elinor Glyn is perhaps best known as the author of *It*, for which she also wrote the screenplay. Filmed in 1927, *It* immortalized its star, Clara BOW, who became world-famous as "the 'It' Girl."

She was born Elinor Sutherland on Jersey, the daughter of a Scottish civil engineer who died when she was a baby. Her childhood was spent in Canada with her mother and her aristocratic French grandmother, whose background in royal circles was a strong influence. Her mother later remarried and the family returned to Jersey. Rebelling against her overbearing stepfather and a series of governesses, Elinor spent much time on her own, reading and exercising her imagination. She grew up to be a striking beauty; but although surrounded by male admirers, she did not marry until she was 28, when she accepted an offer of marriage from the landowner Clayton Glyn.

Glyn's first novel was *The Visits of Elizabeth* (1900), a well-observed portrait of English country-house society; however, her first major success, *Three Weeks* (1907), was very different. A romantic flight of fantasy, relating the story of an affair between a young Englishman and an older eastern European queen, it was regarded in its day as scandalous. After 1908 her husband's debts forced Glyn to write for a living. *His Hour* (1910) was inspired by a winter she spent at the Russian court in St. Petersburg, and the novels that followed, such as *Halcyon* (1912), *The Man and His Master* (1915), and *The Career of Catherine Brown* (1917), reflected her private fantasies with their aristocratic heroines and dashing heroes, based on such real-life figures as Lord Curzon. These novels were hugely popular, despite their improbable plots and grammatical flaws.

In 1920 Glyn became a Hollywood scriptwriter, adapting *Three Weeks* and *It*, which was a great success, for the screen. After a short spell in film production she returned to Britain in 1929. Her later novels include *Did She?* (1934) and *The Third Eye* (1940). *The Philosophy of Love* (1923) and her autobiography *Romantic Adventures* (1926) express her personal views on life and love.

Godden, Rumer (1907–) *British writer*

The author of novels, plays, and poetry for adults as well as children's stories, Margaret Rumer Godden was born in Eastbourne, Sussex. During her infancy her family moved to India, where she spent her childhood. She was sent to high school in England but eventually returned to India, married, and began raising a family. She also opened a children's dancing school and published her first novel, *Chinese Puzzle*, in 1936. Her first book for children was *The Doll's House* (1947).

Godden's first major success was *Black Narcissus* (1938), which, like much of her fiction, deals with the lives of foreigners in exotic lands, such as India. It tells the story of a group of nuns struggling to found a mission in the Himalayas. Among her many other novels, several of which have been filmed, are *The Greengage Summer* (1958), *The Battle of the Villa Fiorita* (1963), *In This House of Brede* (1969), *The Peacock Spring* (1975), and *Coromandel Sea Change* (1990).

Godden's many books for children blend fantasy and reality and present a unique child's-eye view of the adult world. They include *Impunity Jane* (1954), *Miss Happiness and Miss Flower* (1961), *The Rocking Horse Secret* (1977), *Fu-Dog* (1989), and *Great Grandfather's House* (1992).

Godden's biographies *Hans Christian Andersen* (1955) and *Gulbadan, Portrait of a Rose Princess at the Mughal Court* (1981) are considered classics. She has also written an autobiography, *A Time to Dance, No Time to Weep* (1987). Her other nonfiction includes *Bengal Journey* (1945); *Two under the Indian Sun* (1966), a memoir co-written with her sister Jan Godden; *Butterfly Lions* (1977); and *A House with Four Rooms: A Memoir* (1989).

Godden, who now lives in Scotland, was made an OBE in 1993.

Godiva (died *c*. 1086) *English countess*

Godiva, more properly Godgifu (meaning "gift of God"), is renowned for the legend of her naked ride through the marketplace at Coventry. However, there is no factual basis for this ride and no contemporary evidence that she ever visited Coventry.

She first appears in English sources about 1028, when, ill and apparently near death, she donated an estate to the abbey of Ely, Cambridgeshire. She subsequently recovered and married Leofric, the Earl of Mercia, with whom she founded a monastery at Coventry. The chronicler Florence of Worcester (died 1118) mentions the couple but says nothing about the famous ride.

The earliest account of Godiva's ride comes from the chronicler Roger of Wendover (died 1236), who relates in his *Chronica* for 1057 that the countess appealed to her husband to lift the heavy burden of taxes he had imposed on Coventry. Wearied by her pleas, Leofric agreed to do so on condition that she ride nude through the town. Having let down her hair so that only her beautiful legs showed, Godiva mounted a horse and made the journey. In his *Polychronicon* the 14th-century chronicler Ranulf Higden states that Leofric subsequently lifted all the taxes on Coventry except the tax on horses. An inquiry made during the reign of King Edward I (1272–1307) showed that no tolls were paid there, except for those on horses.

Later accounts dating from the 17th century embellish the legend by suggesting that Godiva had ordered everyone to remain indoors with windows shut and assert that she was seen by the tailor Peeping Tom, who was then struck blind or dead. A Godiva Procession has been held since 1673 as part of the Coventry Fair, which takes place every seven or eight years.

Goldberg, Whoopi (1949–　) *American actress*

Perhaps the most prominent African-American actress in films today, Whoopi Goldberg became an international star in Steven Spielberg's *The Color Purple* in 1985.

Born Caryn Johnson in New York City, she made her stage debut at the age of eight at the Hudson Guild Theater, going on to work with Helena Rubinstein's Children's Theater. In 1974 she moved to San Diego, where she cofounded the city's Repertory Theater, and then to San Francisco. In the late 1970s she abandoned serious dramatic work and developed her talents for satirical comedy and impersonation, changing her name both to promote her new image and to protect her privacy. Her act *Whoopi Goldberg* was a Broadway hit from 1984 to 1985.

Her major film debut came with the adaptation of Alice WALKER's novel *The Color Purple*, in which her portrayal of a Southern black woman's struggle in the late 19th century won her an Oscar nomination for Best Actress and an award from the National Association for the Advancement of Colored Peoples. The films that followed were, with the exception of the drama *Clara's Heart* (1987), undistinguished comedies. Goldberg turned to television, appearing in the series *Moonlighting* (1985–86), for which she won an Emmy nomination, and *Bagdad Café*.

Goldberg's career revived in 1990 when she began appearing in TV's *Star Trek: The Next Generation*. The same year she won an Oscar for Best Supporting Actress in *Ghost*, in which she portrayed a fake medium who suddenly finds she has real powers. *Sister Act* (1992), in which she played a singer who hides in a convent to escape the Mafia, was a huge success, although its more inferior sequel was not. Goldberg's recent movies include Robert Altman's *The Player* (1992), *Corrina, Corrina* (1993), and *The Associate* (1997). She also had her own TV show in 1992–93 and, with comedians Billy Crystal and Robin Williams, organized cable TV's *Comic Relief* for the homeless in the United States.

Goldman, Emma (1869–1940)
Lithuanian-born American anarchist and writer

> As to the great mass of working girls and women, how much independence is gained if the narrowness and lack of freedom of the home is exchanged for the narrowness and lack of freedom of the factory, sweatshop, department store, or office?
>
> —"The Tragedy of Women's Emancipation," *Anarchism and Other Essays* (1911)

Emma Goldman, popularly known as "Red Emma," saw private property, the Church, and the state as the greatest evils of the world, believing instead in "perfect, unrestrained freedom for everyone." Her writings include *Anarchism and Other Essays* (1911), *The*

Significance of Modern Drama (1914), and *My Disillusionment in Russia* (1923).

She was born in Kaunas, Lithuania, but moved during her childhood to St. Petersburg. While working for a glove manufacturer, she absorbed some of the prevailing revolutionary ideas. In 1885 Emma and her half-sister Helena emigrated to the United States, settling in Rochester, New York. She obtained work in a textile plant there and married Jacob Kerchner, a fellow worker, whom she later divorced on the grounds of his impotence. In 1889 she moved to New York and, angered by the unjust execution of anarchist labour leaders convicted of a bomb-throwing incident in Chicago's Haymarket Square (1886), became an anarchist. She became close to the anarchist Alexander Berkman, whom she helped with his plan to assassinate Henry Frick, the steel magnate whose plant was the centre of the Pittsburgh steel strike (1892); the plot failed, and Berkman was sentenced to 22 years' imprisonment (he was released in 1906).

Emma developed into an effective labour agitator and in 1893 was jailed for one year for inciting workers to riot. After her release she went to Vienna to receive training as a midwife and nurse. On her return to the United States in 1896, she began working as a nurse in the urban slums but became increasingly known for her lecture tours, speaking not only on political matters but also on the drama of Strindberg and Ibsen. In 1901 she was accused (without proof) of complicity in the assassination of President McKinley and was jailed for two weeks.

Goldman published the anarchist magazine *Mother Earth* with Berkman from 1906 to 1917. During this period most of her time was spent writing, travelling, and lecturing. She was now arguing for dramatic social changes, particularly in the position of women in relation to marriage, children, and sexual fulfilment. In 1916 she spent two weeks in jail for distributing information on birth control, and the following year she and Berkman were sentenced to two years in a federal penitentiary for opposing the draft for World War I. Shortly after their release they were deported to Russia.

Disillusioned with the Bolshevik regime, Goldman and Berkman fled Russia in 1921 and finally settled in France, where in 1931 Goldman wrote *Living My Life*. In 1934 she was permitted to re-enter the United States for 90 days on a lecture tour. With Berkman now dead, she went to Barcelona in 1936 to aid Spanish anarchists against Franco. Goldman died of a stroke in Toronto, Canada, and is buried beside the Haymarket anarchists in Chicago.

Goncharova, Natalia Sergeyevna
(1881–1962)   *Russian-born   French painter*

Natalia Goncharova not only initiated the "rayonnist" art movement, which depicted subjects in a semi-abstract style characterized by slanting lines, but also became an influential and successful set designer, most notably for Sergei Diaghilev's Ballets Russes company.

She was born in Ladyzhino, in the Tula province of western Russia. In 1898, after a period as a science student, she began studying sculpture at the Moscow Academy of Art. Turning to painting in 1904, she was attracted on the one hand by the colours and forms of primitive Russian folk art and on the other by the two-dimensional representation of solid forms of the cubist painters and the bright aggressive colours of the fauvists. With Mikhail Larionov, the painter with whom she spent most of her life and finally married on her 74th birthday, she founded the rayonnist movement. Goncharova and Larionov displayed their work in all the major post-impressionist and futurist exhibitions in Europe between 1909 and 1915.

Goncharova mounted her own exhibitions in Moscow and Petrograd (now St. Petersburg), where her primitive forms and striking colours surprised the public. In 1914 she began designing for the stage, being acclaimed particularly for her set and costume designs for Moscow's Kamerny The-

atre. She and Larionov went to Geneva in 1915 to design the set for Rimsky-Korsakov's ballet *Le Coq d'or* (*The Golden Cockerel*), after which they toured Europe with Diaghilev's Ballets Russes before settling in Paris. Apart from brief returns to Russia to collaborate with fellow painter and set designer Alexandra EXTER on a magazine, Goncharova remained in France, becoming a French citizen in 1938. Her most successful work was for the Diaghilev productions of Stravinsky's ballets *Les Noces* (1923) and *The Firebird* (1926). She continued both to paint and to design theatre sets until the end of her life.

Gonne, Maud (1866–1953) *Irish nationalist and actress*

Maud Gonne is remembered both as a beauty who inspired many famous love poems by William Butler Yeats and as an Irish nationalist who helped found the republican movement Sinn Féin .

She was born in Aldershot, Surrey; her father was Anglo-Irish, and her English mother died when Maud was very young. Educated in France, at the age of 16 she went to Dublin, where her father was assistant adjutant general. With the encouragement of the French journalist Lucien Millevoye, with whom she later had two children, Gonne dedicated her life to the cause of Irish independence. She engaged in constant political agitation against the British, protesting in favour of evicted tenants and political prisoners, lecturing abroad to raise funds, and founding the women's group Inghinidhe Na Eireann (Daughters of Ireland) in 1900. In 1903 she married Major John MacBride, who had fought against the British in South Africa. After MacBride's execution for his part in the Easter Rising of 1916, Gonne became a relief worker during the "The Troubles." She continued to demand total independence long after the 1921 treaty that established the Irish Free State. She helped to found the Republican Women's Prisoners' Defence League and was imprisoned several times herself.

After some brief experience in acting, Gonne had joined Yeats's Young

Irish Theatre movement in the early 1890s and became a lifelong friend and source of inspiration to him. He remarked of her beauty, "It belonged to famous pictures, to poetry, to some legendary past." The heroine of his play *The Countess Cathleen* (1892) was modelled on her, and in 1902 she took the title role in his *Cathleen Ni Houlihan* in Dublin. But despite Yeats's persistence, she refused his many offers of marriage.

Maud Gonne's autobiography, *A Servant of the Queen*, was published in 1938, and another book, *Scattering Branches*, in 1940. Her son Sean MacBride was Irish foreign minister from 1948 to 1951; he was awarded the Nobel Peace Prize in 1974.

Goodall, Jane (1934–　) *British zoologist*

Jane Goodall gained fame for her research on chimpanzees in the wild, having conducted the longest continuous field study of wild animals in their natural environment.

Goodall was born in London and trained as a secretary. Although she had no university degree or formal training in ethology, she had always been a keen amateur naturalist. With the encouragement and help of the Kenyan anthropologist Louis S. B. Leakey, she began to study chimpanzees in 1960 at the Gombe Stream Reserve in Tanzania, on the shores of Lake Tanganyika. She was awarded a doctorate from Cambridge University in 1965 after submitting a thesis on chimpanzee behaviour and has been the scientific director of Gombe Wildlife Research Institute since 1967. Goodall has served as a visiting lecturer at many universities around the world and founded the Committee for Conservation and Care of Chimpanzees in 1986.

Through close, long-term, daily observation of a group of chimpanzees at Gombe, Goodall was able to win their trust and began to note individual differences among them. She was the first scientist to report that chimpanzees were not entirely vegetarian, as had first been thought, but would hunt, kill, and eat small game, with adults sharing their kills. Goodall also noticed that the chimpanzees would manipulate plant stems to collect termites and use rocks as weapons against predators. This meant that they used tools, something previously regarded as a strictly human activity.

Goodall's books about her discoveries include *My Friends the Wild Chimpanzees* (1967), *In the Shadow of Man* (1971), *The Chimpanzees of Gombe: Patterns of Behavior* (1986), *Through a Window: My Thirty Years with the Chimpanzees of Gombe* (1990), and *The Chimpanzee: The Living Link between "Man" and "Beast"* (1992). She has received several awards for her research and for conservation, including the Albert Schweitzer Award (1987).

See also FOSSEY, DIAN.

Goolagong, Evonne (1951–　) *Australian tennis player*

> Evonne...took both King and Court at Wimbledon, without leaving them one single set, with an ease that was almost infuriating in view of her radiant smiles.
>
> —Former tennis player and sports writer Gianni Clerici, 1974

Twice winner of the women's singles title at Wimbledon, Evonne Goolagong was a graceful player with a likable on-court personality. As an exceptional volleyer, she was also remarkably successful in doubles.

One of eight children of an agricultural worker, Evonne Goolagong was born in Barellan in rural New South Wales, of part-Aboriginal stock. Her talent for tennis was discovered by Vic Edwards, a travelling coach, who took charge of her training and education in Sydney. When Evonne was 16, Edwards predicted that she would win Wimbledon by 1974. In fact, after becoming Australian junior champion in 1970, she won the Wimbledon women's singles in 1971, beating Billie Jean KING in the semi-final and Margaret COURT in the final. The same year she also won the French Open and two doubles titles.

Goolagong ranked among the top women players throughout the next decade, winning the Australian Open four times (1974–76, 1978) as well as two other singles titles and a number of doubles titles.

Although she and her doubles partner Peggy Michel took the women's doubles at Wimbledon in 1974, Goolagong did not win the singles again during this period, despite being a finalist three times.

In 1975 Goolagong married a Briton, Roger Cawley, thereafter playing under the name Evonne Cawley; she gave birth to a daughter, Kelly, in 1976. Her career continued unabated: in 1980 she again became Wimbledon singles champion, the first mother to do so since 1914.

Gordimer, Nadine (1923–) *South African writer*

Considered one of the foremost novelists writing in English today, Nadine Gordimer was awarded the Nobel Prize for literature in 1991. Her work, which also includes many essays and hundreds of short stories, centres mainly on the destructive effects of the former system of apartheid in South Africa.

Gordimer was born in the small gold-mining town of Springs, Transvaal, and began writing at the age of nine, publishing her first story when she was 15. Although her schooling had been limited, she attended the University of Witwatersrand for a year, which opened up the cultural life of Johannesburg to her. Her early stories, later collected in *Face to Face* (1949), were published in such American magazines as *The New Yorker*. She became more widely known with *The Soft Voice of the Serpent and Other Stories* (1952) and an acclaimed autobiographical first novel, *The Lying Days* (1953). The novel describes a white girl's growing awareness of the racism and lack of intellectual stimulation in her provincial home town. Of her teenage years in Springs Gordimer said: "My particular solitude as an intellectual by inclination was so complete I did not even know I was one." Racism and white liberals' inadequate responses to it are recurring themes of her early novels, such as *A World of Strangers* (1958), *Occasion for Loving*

(1963), *The Late Bourgeois World* (1966), and *A Guest of Honour* (1970).

In 1974 Gordimer jointly won the Booker Prize for *The Conservationist*, the story of how a wealthy Afrikaner's complacency is shaken by the presence of a dead man abandoned beside a river. The three novels that followed were more overtly political. *Burger's Daughter* (1979), in which the heroine, the daughter of communists, reluctantly faces up to her duty to fight oppression, was banned in South Africa. *July's People* (1981) depicts a black-majority takeover as experienced by a white South African woman, while *A Sport of Nature* (1987) is an epic tale of African politics revolving around the white wife of a black revolutionary.

Gordimer's post-apartheid novels *None to Accompany Me* (1994) and *The House Gun* (1997) focus on the lives of white liberals in the transitional time between the release of Nelson Mandela and South Africa's first multiracial elections.

Gordon, Ruth (1896–1985) *American actress and scriptwriter*

Ruth Gordon's career as a stage and film actress and Hollywood scriptwriter lasted for 70 years.

She was born in Wollaston, Massachusetts, moving as a teenager to New York City in order to study acting. Despite being told that she did not have any talent, she made her Broadway debut in 1915 as Nibs in *Peter Pan* (with Maude ADAMS), after which she was seldom absent from the stage. She made her London debut as Mrs. Pinchwife in Wycherley's *The Country Wife* at the Old Vic in 1936. This was followed by Owen Davis's *Ethan Frome* (1936), Ibsen's *A Doll's House* (1937), and Chekhov's *Three Sisters* (1942); but her greatest success was as Mrs. Levi in Thornton Wilder's *The Matchmaker* (1954).

Ruth Gordon is now best remembered for her unusually long film career, which began in the silent era with a bit part in *Camille* (1915). She combined her theatre work with small film parts until, after costarring with Greta GARBO in *Two-Faced Women* (1941), she turned to scriptwriting. Making her TV debut in 1963 in Edward Albee's *The American Dream*, she returned to the big screen two years later as Natalie Wood's mother in *Inside Daisy Clover*. In 1969 she won the Academy Award for Best Supporting Actress for her role as a witch in Roman Polanski's *Rosemary's Baby* (1968), starring Mia FARROW. Probably the outstanding performance of her later years was in the film *Harold and Maude* (1971), as an 80-year old woman who marries a teenager. Gordon continued to appear in films, including the Clint Eastwood comedies *Every Which Way But Loose* (1978) and *Any Which Way You Can* (1980), until her death at the age of 89.

Gordon wrote several plays, including *Over Twenty-One* (1944), and the autobiographical piece *The Actress*, which she adapted for the screen. She also collaborated with her husband, Garson Kanin, on several screenplays, including *A Double Life* (1947) and the Katharine HEPBURN and Spencer Tracy comedies *Adam's Rib* (1949) and *Pat and Mike* (1952).

Gore-Booth, Eva (Selina) (1870–1926) *Irish poet and social campaigner*

As well as producing several volumes of lyrical verse, Eva Gore-Booth campaigned energetically for the rights and welfare of working women.

Eva was born at Lissadell House in County Sligo, the daughter of a wealthy Protestant landowner. Her elder sister Constance later became famous as the militant Irish nationalist Countess MARKIEWICZ. As young women both sisters were noted beauties; their friends and admirers included W. B. Yeats, who later wrote several poems about them.

Although the two sisters had already founded a suffrage society in Sligo, the real turning-point in Eva's life occurred in 1896 while she was on holiday in Italy. There she met Esther Roper, the secretary of NESWS (North of England Society for Woman's Suffrage). She returned with Roper to Manchester, and eventually ran NESWS in the belief that she, and the Society, had a duty to help the much exploited women working in the textile mills of Lancashire.

In the following years, although suffering from tuberculosis, she founded and became joint secretary of the Salford Women's Trade Union Council, edited *The Women's Labour News*, and served on Manchester's Education Committee. She and Roper founded one of the first women's trade unions, the Manchester Barmaid's Association (established because a new Licensing Act threatened to put many of the barmaids out of work). As well as continuing their social work and supporting the Women's Right to Work campaign, the two women played a leading part in the general election in Wigan in 1906. Because of Gore-Booth's failing health, she and Roper moved to London in 1913. Following the outbreak of World War I in 1914, both women declared themselves pacifists and laboured hard for the pacifist cause. They continued to campaign for rights for women, but were more concerned with rights in the workplace than with the right to vote.

Gore-Booth's poetry, most of which dealt romantically with Irish themes, was published in several volumes during the first quarter of the century. In 1929 Esther Roper collected her friend's work in *The Collected Poems of Eva Gore-Booth*. Probably the best-known of these poems is "The Waves of Breffny," a romantic description of the Irish landscape.

Goudge, Elizabeth (1900–1984) *British novelist*

Elizabeth Goudge was a best-selling novelist in both Britain and the United States, whose work was admired for its portrayal of England and its people and for a strong sense of the continuity of life. She was also a successful author of children's books and religious works.

She was born at Wells, Somerset, the daughter of Dr. Henry Leighton Goudge, an Anglican priest and Regius Professor of Divinity at Oxford. Elizabeth was educated at boarding school and at Reading University, after which she taught art and design. Her play *The Brontës of Haworth*

(1932) succeeded in London, but after the failure of a second play, a publisher suggested that she turn to novels. Her first was *Island Magic* (1934), about Guernsey, where her mother's family lived.

Goudge's first major success in both Britain and the United States was *Green Dolphin Country* (1944), a historical novel set in 19th-century New Zealand and in the Channel Islands, which won a Literary Guild Award and was filmed in 1947. Other major novels include *Gentian Hill* (1949) and *The Child from the Sea* (1970), which told the story of King Charles II's supposed secret wife, Lucy WALTER. Goudge also wrote a family trilogy, comprising *The Bird in the Tree* (1940), *The Herb of Grace* (1948), and *The Heart of the Family* (1953). Her books for children include *Smoky-House* (1940), a story of smugglers; *The Little White Horse* (1946), which won a Carnegie Medal in 1947; and *Linnets and Valerians* (1964).

From 1950 most of Goudge's books were religious, including a biography of Christ entitled *For God So Loved the World* (1951), *St. Francis of Assisi* (1959), and three anthologies of spiritually comforting verse, the last of which was *A Book of Faith* (1976). Her autobiography, *The Joy of the Snow*, appeared in 1974.

Grable, Betty (1916–1973) *American actress*

> Her work symbolized that era of gaudy Technicolored escapism for which many craved in World War II.
>
> —Tom Vallance

Betty Grable, whose legs were famously insured with Lloyd's for $1 million, was the star of a series of screen musicals in the 1940s. She was the U.S. armed forces' most popular pin-up girl during World War II.

The daughter of a stockbroker, she was born in St. Louis, Missouri. Encouraged by her mother, who was determined that her daughter should become a star, Betty moved to Hollywood in 1928, having begun to sing, dance, and play piano at the age of five. Her part in the movie *Let's Go Places* (1930) was arranged by her mother, but Betty's studio contract was cancelled when it was discovered that she was only 13. Nevertheless, she was hired by Samuel Goldwyn in 1930 as one of his chorus line, the "Goldwyn Girls." Her major film debut came in the musical *The Gay Divorcee* (1934), but her career failed to take off. Signed up and then dropped by several studios during the 1930s, she sang with Ted Fiorita's band and, after her marriage to Jackie Coogan in 1937, worked with him in vaudeville. The couple divorced in 1941.

Grable's big break finally came when she replaced Alice Fay in *Down Argentine Way* (1940). A string of box-office hits followed, including *Song of the Islands* (1942), *Coney Island* (1943), *Pin-Up Girl* (1944), *Diamond Horseshoe* (1945), and *Mother Wore Tights* (1947). Well aware of her limited talents ("I'm no actress, and I know it"), Grable nevertheless became the idol of servicemen: the famous pictures of her in a bathing suit that emphasized her shapely legs appeared on aeroplanes and in barrack-rooms everywhere. Her "girl-next-door" appeal also brought her a large following among young women, who identified with an ordinary woman leading an extraordinary life in her films.

In the 1950s Grable's career faltered, due partly to arguments with her studio and partly to the advent of younger stars, such as Marilyn MONROE, with whom she appeared in her last film, *How to Marry a Millionaire* (1953). But in 1965, after a period of semi-retirement, she divorced musician Harry James, her husband of 22 years, and returned to the stage, scoring a major success in *Hello, Dolly!* (1965–67). At the time of her death she was preparing for a revival of *No, No, Nanette* in Australia.

Graf, Steffi (1969–) *German tennis player*

Seven times winner of the women's singles title at Wimbledon, Steffi Graf was ranked the world's No. 1 woman tennis player until 1997. By the age of 22 she had won 500 professional matches, the youngest player to do so.

Born in Bruehl, she was coached by her father, Peter, and later trained by Pavel Slozil. At the age of 13 she became the youngest player ever to receive a ranking from the World Tennis Association. In 1984 she won an Olympic demonstration event and reached the last 16 at Wimbledon. Her first major title came in 1986, when she won the German Open. The following year she took the French Open and reached the semi-finals at Wimbledon and the U.S. Open. In 1988, in addition to winning the gold medal at the Seoul Olympics, Graf won the Grand Slam of four major titles – the U.S., Australian, French, and British. But for her defeat by Arantxa Sanchez Vicario in the French Open, she would have repeated this impressive feat in 1989.

Graf remained at the very top of her sport until the late 1990s, taking the Australian title in 1990, the Wimbledon title in 1991–93 and 1995, and the U.S. Open in 1994 and 1995. She has also won many doubles competitions with her partner Gabriela SABATINI. 1996 brought victory over Arantxa Sanchez Vicario in the French Open and at Wimbledon and over Monica SELES in the U.S. Open; it also became the year in which media publicity focused on her father's problems with the German tax authorities. Hampered by injury, she was displaced as the world's No. 1 by the Swiss player Martina Hingis in April 1997.

Graham, Katharine Meyer

(1917–) *American newspaper owner*

As owner of the Washington Post Company, which publishes the *Washington Post* and other newspapers, Katharine Graham was described in the 1970s as "the most powerful woman in America."

The daughter of publisher Eugene Meyer, Katharine Meyer was born in New York City and educated at Vassar College and the University of Chicago. She began her career in journalism as a reporter for the *San Francisco News* in 1938, moving the following year to the *Washington Post*, for which she worked sporadically while her husband Philip Graham, whom she had

married in 1940, was on war service. On his return Philip Graham became assistant publisher of the *Post*; in 1948 the Grahams bought the paper from Eugene Meyer for the token sum of $1. With Philip as president, they formed the Washington Post Company, acquiring *Newsweek* in 1961 and expanding the circulation of their papers significantly.

Katharine became president of the company in 1963, after her husband committed suicide. Although grief-stricken, she developed an aggressive approach, expanding into radio, TV, and paper mills. In the early 1970s her newspapers were at the forefront of campaigning journalism in the United States, exposing irregular activities in the military by publishing the "Pentagon Papers" in 1971. After winning a legal battle to publish this material, the *Washington Post* brought to light and documented the Watergate scandal (1972–74), which led to the resignation of President Richard Nixon in 1974.

In the 1980s, having been succeeded as publisher of the *Post* by her son Donald, Katharine turned her attention to international affairs. She served on a number of national and international committees dealing with development issues, most notably the Brandt Commission (1982). Retaining a role in the Washington Post Company, she was chair of the company from 1991 to 1993, when she became chair of its executive committee. She is also a fellow of the American Academy of Arts and Sciences. Her autobiography, *Personal History*, was published in 1997.

Graham, Martha (1894–1991) *American dancer and choreographer*

Opposed to traditional ballet with its graceful movements, Martha Graham exerted a major influence on the evolution of modern dance by inventing intense, angular movements that seemed to give overt form to the emotions.

Born in Allegheny, Pennsylvania, but raised in California, Martha Graham studied ethnic, primitive, and new creative dance forms at the Denishawn school in Hollywood (see ST. DENIS,

RUTH) and later in New York. From 1923 to 1925 she danced in the Greenwich Village Follies in New York City. Discontented with both the Denishawn emphasis on the exotic and the commercial dance performed in New York, she joined the staff of the Eastman School of Music in Rochester, New York State, in 1925. There she began to experiment with the movement potential of the body and its power "to give substance to things felt." Influenced by Oriental dance and the freely invented movements of Isadora DUNCAN, she began to develop her own unique dancing style. She later formed her own school and company in New York City.

Graham's first independent New York recital, at the 48th Street Theater in 1926, astonished and shocked the public. Examples of her austere early works were *Revolt* (1927), *Heretic* (1929), *Lamentation* (1930), and the masterly *Primitive Mysteries* (1931). Her *American Provincials* (1934), *Frontier* (1935), and *American Document* (1938) dealt with themes from American history.

After 1938 Graham's productions became increasingly elaborate. *Letter to the World* (1940) was based on the inner life of Emily DICKINSON, and *Deaths and Entrances* (1943) was inspired by the "doom-eager" BRONTË sisters. Many of her important works had their roots in Greek drama and myth, including *Cave of the Heart* (1946), *Night Journey* (1947), *Clytemnestra* (1958) – the first full-length work in modern dance – and *Phaedra* (1962). Other works, on a variety of themes, included the joyful *Appalachian Spring* (1944), *Judith* (1950) and *Embattled Garden* (1958), both on religious themes, and *Cortege of Eagles* (1967), *Acts of Light* (1981), and *Rites of Spring* (1984).

Graham retired from the stage in 1969 but continued teaching and directing her company, touring worldwide. She also commissioned scores from such composers as Paul Hindemith, Aaron Copland, William Schuman, Gian Carlo Menotti, and Norman Dello Joio. Among her many honours were the Aspen Award (1965) and the Presidential Medal of Freedom (1976).

Grahn, Lucile (1819–1907) *Danish ballet dancer*

Known as the "Taglioni of the North," Lucile Grahn was one of the greatest exponents of the 19th-century Romantic style in ballet. Although Maria TAGLIONI was seen as the embodiment of this style, and was the first to dance on *pointes*, Grahn was much admired for her lightness and her ability to pirouette.

Born in Copenhagen, Grahn revealed her ambition to be a ballerina at the age of four, making her official debut aged seven as Cupid. After studying dance, she worked in the Royal Danish Ballet, where the choreographer Auguste Bournonville was a strong influence. She created the role of Astrid in his *Valdemar* (1835) and was the first to dance his *La Sylphide* (1836) at the Royal Theatre in Copenhagen. Her reputation in Denmark was secured with her performance in *Don Quixote* (1837). However, although still under contract to the Royal Theatre, continuing quarrels with Bournonville led her to apply for leave to study in Paris.

In 1839 Grahn began a three-year period with the Paris Opéra. This was followed by visits to St. Petersburg and London, where in 1845 she performed in the famous production of Jules Perot's *Pas de quatre* with Taglioni, Carlotta GRISI, and Fanny CERRITO. After her marriage to the Austrian singer Friedrich Young in 1856, Grahn retired from the stage and became ballet mistress at the Leipzig State Theatre (1869–75). In Munich she choreographed opera ballets for Richard Wagner; most notably the Bacchanale for his *Tannhäuser*. On her death she left her fortune to the people of Munich, where a street was named after her.

Grasso, Ella (1919–1981) *American politician*

Ella Grasso was the first woman to be elected as a U.S. state governor in her own right, without succeeding her husband.

She was born Ella Tambussi in Windsor Locks, Connecticut, and was educated at Mount Holyoke College, Massachusetts, where she taught economics and sociology briefly before serving as assistant state director of research for the War Manpower Commission (1943–46). In 1942 she married the teacher Thomas Grasso. By 1953 she had become a member of the Connecticut Legislature, and from 1958 to 1970 she served as state secretary for Connecticut, where she turned her office into an open "people's lobby."

A Democratic national committeewoman from 1956 to 1958, Grasso was active on state and national platform committees, collaborating on the minority report opposing U.S. policy in Vietnam that was presented at the 1968 Democratic Party Convention in Chicago. She was elected to the U.S. House of Representatives in 1969 and served in the 92nd and 93rd Congresses from 1970 to 1974. In 1974 she campaigned successfully for the governorship of Connecticut, which was in financial trouble.

By introducing harsh cuts in public spending, Grasso was able to balance the state budget, but at the cost of her popularity. This was restored in 1978 when, after the state was subject to a major blizzard, she organized a huge emergency relief programme. In the election that year she won a landslide victory, taking over three quarters of the towns in Connecticut. After being diagnosed as having ovarian cancer, she ran the state government from her hospital bed for two weeks before resigning on December 31, 1980. She died just over a month later in Hartford, Connecticut.

Grau, Shirley Ann (1929–) American novelist

Shirley Ann Grau is a Pulitzer Prize-winning author of novels and short stories about the U.S. South. Although she has been described as a regional writer, her books describe the universal experience of coping with racism.

She was born in New Orleans and attended the Booth School in Montgomery, Alabama, where many of her stories are set. After taking a BA degree at Tulane University, Louisiana, in 1950, she spent a further year there doing research in English literature. She taught creative writing at the University of New Orleans in 1966–67.

Grau's stories were first published in 1954 in such magazines as *Holiday*, *The New Yorker*, *Mademoiselle*, and the *Saturday Evening Post*. Her first book was *The Black Prince* (1955), a collection of short stories that had generally favourable reviews. However, real critical acclaim came with the publication of her first novel, *The Blue Sky* (1958), which was praised for its realistic description and lyrical quality. It was followed by *The House on Coliseum Street* (1961) and *The Keepers of the House* (1964), which won her a Pulitzer Prize. Other works include *The Condor Passes* (1971), *Evidence of Love* (1977), *Nine Women* (1986), and, more recently, *Roadwalkers* (1994), a novel about an African-American mother and daughter hailed for its "vigorous prose" and bold story line.

Green, Anna Katherine (1846–1935) American novelist

Anna Katherine Green was possibly the first, and certainly one of the most prolific, American writers of detective fiction.

Born in Brooklyn, New York, Green graduated from Ripley Female College in Poultney, Vermont, in 1866. She originally wrote poetry, which – although well received at the time – is not read today. However, she discovered her real talent when her first mystery, *The Leavenworth Case* (1878), became a best-seller. A combination of melodrama and skilful plotting, the novel lent itself well to dramatization on stage and screen. As her father had been a successful defence lawyer, she had a considerable knowledge of the law, which she used to great effect.

Green featured her detective Ebenezer Gryce in several novels and also wrote books with female detectives, including *The Golden Slipper and Other Problems for Violet Strange* (1915). Among Green's more than 40 other books are *The Doctor, His Wife, and the Clock* (1895), *The Filigree Ball* (1903), and *The House of the Whispering Pines* (1910), as well as two volumes of poetry and a verse drama written in the 1880s.

Green, Hetty (1835–1916) *American financier*

Known as the "Witch of Wall Street," Hetty Green was believed to be the richest American woman of her time.

She was born Henrietta Howland Robinson in New Bedford, Massachusetts, the sole heiress to the Howland and Robinson millions acquired in whaling and trade with China. Educated privately, she spent her youth with a wealthy aunt. After her mother's death in 1860, Hetty accompanied her father to New York City; on his death five years later she inherited a fortune of around $10 million. Hetty had always been interested in business and finance, having been accustomed in her youth to reading the financial pages to her grandfather, whose sight was poor. In 1867 she married businessman Edward Henry Green, and the couple agreed to pursue independent financial activities.

Mrs. Green, whose business was based mainly on lending money, became a Wall Street operator and New York Stock Exchange member. A shrewd and successful trader, she acquired immense tracts of real estate, engineered at least one upward movement in railway stock prices, and profited hugely from the 1907 money shortage, which she had foreseen and prepared for by selling large blocks of her holdings.

As Mrs. Green lived modestly in a Hoboken apartment, wore old clothes, and withdrew from public view in her later years, she gained a reputation in the press as a miser and an eccentric. It was said that her son had his leg amputated because she took him to a free clinic rather than pay a doctor to attend to him promptly. She was also known for her sharp sense of humour: when asked why she had obtained a revolver permit, she replied that it was to defend herself against lawyers. At her death her fortune of more than $100 million was divided between her son and a daughter.

Greenaway, Kate (1846–1901) *British illustrator*

Kate Greenaway was a pioneer in modern children's book illustration, creating in her work charming costumes that had a lasting influence on children's fashions.

The daughter of John Greenaway, a wood engraver and draftsman whose love of art inspired her own work, Catherine Greenaway was born in Hoxton, London, and grew up in the northern English village of Rolleston. She studied in London at the South Kensington art school and at the Slade. Her artistic influences were Japanese prints, the Pre-Raphaelites, the British artists John Leech and George Boughton, and most importantly, the critic John Ruskin, who later taught her and publicly acclaimed her work.

Greenaway's first success came with the publication of a collection of valentines, *The Quiver of Love* (1875). Having established a style influenced by her rural upbringing and her interest in earlier English dress, she began submitting her portrayals of children's life to magazines. The turning point in her career was the publication of the children's album *Under the Window* (1879), for which she furnished both colour woodcuts and verses. It sold 150,000 copies, including French and German editions.

By 1890 sales of her books had exceeded 700,000 copies, and her style had spawned many imitators. Books in which she illustrated her own verse include *A Day in a Child's Life* (1881), *The Language of Flowers* (1884), and *The Marigold Garden* (1885). Her drawings were also much in demand by other authors of books for children; she illustrated Robert Browning's *The Pied Piper of Hamelin* (1889) among other works. Her annual *Almanack* was published from 1883 through 1895 and again in 1897.

Greer, Germaine (1939–) *Australian writer and feminist*

Mother is the dead heart of the family, spending father's earnings on consumer goods to enhance the environment in which he eats, sleeps and watches television.

—*The Female Eunuch* (1970)

Germaine Greer, whose bestseller *The Female Eunuch* (1970) made her an international celebrity, was the public face of feminism in the 1970s.

She was born near Melbourne. After a convent education she attended the University of Melbourne, where she gained a BA in 1959, and the University of Sydney, from which she obtained her master's degree in 1961. In 1964 she travelled to England on a scholarship to study English literature at Cambridge University, earning a PhD in 1967. From 1967 to 1973 she lectured at the University of Warwick, and from 1980 to 1983 she was professor of modern letters at the University of Tulsa.

·In *The Female Eunuch* Greer rejected the stereotype of feminity that had "castrated" women, i.e., conditioned them to believe that to be passive and dependent is natural. She urged women to fight against this attitude by exploring their sexuality and creative potential. The success of the book led to international renown, and Greer became a television personality and a successful journalist, writing for *Spare Rib*, *Esquire*, and *The Sunday Times*, among other publications. Her debate in 1971 with Norman Mailer on the subject of women's liberation caused much controversy. In *The Obstacle Race* (1979) Greer turned her attention to the obstacles to women's achievement in the art world.

In 1984 Greer once again caused a storm with *Sex and Destiny: The Politics of Human Fertility*, in which she apparently reversed many of her earlier ideas. She stressed the importance of motherhood to women, attacked the developed world's attempts at population control as hostile to children, and opposed sexual permissiveness. Greer turned to more personal themes in the critically acclaimed *Daddy: We Hardly Knew You* (1989), which describes her odyssey in search of her father's hidden life. More recently she has put forward a view of ageing as a kind of female liberation in *The Change:*

Women, Ageing, and the Menopause (1991).

Among her other works are *Shakespeare* (1981), *The Madwoman's Underclothes: Essays and Occasional Writing 1968–85* (1986), and, reflecting her interest in re-establishing early women writers, *The Uncollected Verse of Aphra Behn* (1989). In 1998 she signed a contract worth a reputed half a million pounds to write *The Whole Woman*, a sequel to *The Female Eunuch* attacking many of the trends in contemporary feminist thought.

Gregory, Cynthia (1946–) *American ballet dancer*

Cynthia Gregory was noted for her technical perfection and lyrical grace in both classical and modern ballets.

Born in Los Angeles, California, she began taking ballet lessons at the age of five. She performed with Eva Lorraine's California Children's Ballet Company for four years before taking classes with several noted dance instructors, including Michel Panaieff, Robert Rosselat, and Jacques d'Amboise, who recommended her to the San Francisco Ballet. Awarded the Ford Foundation Scholarship to work with that company in 1961, she was promoted to soloist dancer within a few months. In 1965 Gregory moved to New York to join the American Ballet Theater (ABT); she was promoted to principal dancer in 1967. Her repertory included the leads in *Swan Lake*, *Les Sylphides*, *Coppélia*, *Carmen*, and *Miss Julie*. She also danced in such modern works as Alvin Ailey's *The River* (1971) as well as the title roles in Rudolf Nureyev's revival of *Raymonda* (1975) and Mikhail Baryshnikov's production of *Cinderella* (1984). In 1984 she danced in Twyla THARP's *Bach Partita*. The following year ABT celebrated her 20th anniversary with the company, presenting excerpts from ballets in which she had had leading roles. In 1990 Gregory danced with Fernando Bujones in celebration of ABT's 50th birthday; in 1993 she chaired the panel of judges of the New York International Ballet Competition.

Gregory was a permanent guest artist with the Cleveland/San Jose Ballet from 1986 and a guest dancer with many international companies, including the Zurich, Vienna State Opera, Stuttgart, and San Francisco ballets, and the National Ballet of Cuba. She also toured on her own and with Bujones, dancing in South America, Australia, and Taiwan. She made her acting debut in a television serial in 1981.

Gregory's awards include a *Dance Magazine* Award (1975), the Harkness Ballet Foundation's First Annual Dance Award (1978), the Dance Educators of America Achievement Award (1983, 1987), and a Citation of Merit from the International Arts Club (1991). She is the author of *Ballet Is the Best Exercise* (1986).

Gregory, Isabella Augusta, Lady

(1852–1932) *Irish playwright and theatre director*

> The Abbey was the centre of her life, and because of her, and her partnership with Yeats, it survived.
>
> —Ulick O'Connor, *Celtic Dawn*

A founder director of Dublin's Abbey Theatre, Lady Gregory also made notable contributions to the early 20th-century Irish literary revival with her translations of Irish legends and her comedies based on folklore.

Born Isabella Augusta Persse at Roxborough, County Galway, she married Sir William Gregory, a retired governor of Ceylon (now Sri Lanka), in 1880. Her literary career did not begin until after his death in 1892. In 1898 she met the poet W. B. Yeats, becoming his lifelong friend and patron. With Yeats and Edward Martyn she cofounded in 1899 the Irish Literary Theatre (later to become the Abbey Theatre), and her home, Coole Park, became the centre of the "Irish Renaissance." In 1904 Lady Gregory became codirector, with Yeats and the dramatist J. M. Synge, of the newly opened Abbey Theatre, the building of which was financed by Annie HORNIMAN. As the theatre's most active director, she fought the battles over the production of such controversial plays as Synge's

The Playboy of the Western World and O'Casey's *The Plough and the Stars*.

Lady Gregory translated a number of the Old Irish sagas into a lyrical but somewhat mannered version of Irish peasant dialect known to its detractors as "Kiltartanese" (from the village of Kiltartan near Coole Park). These were published as *Cuchulain of Muirthemne* (1902) and *Gods and Fighting Men* (1904). As a dramatist she has been unfairly overshadowed by others in the revival. She was influenced by the French classical theatre, particularly by Molière, although her characters are Irish peasants in comic plays about Irish rural life.

Her most frequently performed works are one-act comedies, such as *The Rising of the Moon* and *The Workhouse Ward*, and tragedies, including *The Gaol Gate*. However, her heroic three-act dramas *The White Cockade* (1905) and *Grania* (1911), based on Irish history and legend, show her ability to handle a more extended form of play. Her dedication to restoring Irish culture and political independence is reflected in all her writings, including her memoirs, political, pamphlets, dramas, and children's books. In 1914 she published *Our Irish Theatre: A Chapter of Autobiography*.

Grenfell, Joyce (1910–79) *British entertainer*

Joyce Grenfell is remembered for her comic monologues – mainly gently satirical character studies of society women, working girls, middle-class housewives, and middle-aged spinsters – which she delivered live on stage in the 1940s and 1950s and also on radio and television. One of her best-loved impersonations was that of the warm-hearted and hopelessly optimistic nursery-school teacher, whose most famous line, "George – don't do that," became a catchphrase.

Born Joyce Irene Phipps in London, she was a niece of Nancy ASTOR and a frequent guest at Cliveden, the Astors' stately home in Buckinghamshire. She married Reginald Grenfell in 1929. In her early career she worked as a journalist, writing radio reviews for the *Observer*. Her first comic monologues were broadcast on radio in the 1930s, and in 1939 she made her stage debut in the *Little Revue*. In the early 1940s she appeared in a number of other stage revues, before setting off on a tour of military hospitals to entertain the wounded in the latter part of World War II.

Grenfell gradually built up her act, increasing her repertoire of characters and incorporating songs, which she wrote in collaboration with the composer Richard Addinsell. In 1955 she performed in the United States for the first time, where her one-woman show, *Joyce Grenfell Requests the Pleasure*, was a great success. She also appeared in a number of films – notably *The Happiest Days of Your Life* (1949), *Laughter in Paradise* (1951), and the *St. Trinians* films of the 1950s – in which she excelled in the roles of gauche or gawky females filled with good-humoured enthusiasm.

On British television, Grenfell was a regular panellist on the celebrity quiz show *Face the Music* in the 1960s and 1970s. After her retirement from the stage in 1973 she produced a number of books, including two volumes of autobiography: *Joyce Grenfell Requests the Pleasure* (1976) and *In Pleasant Places* (1979).

Grey, Dame Beryl (1927–) *British ballet dancer*

A former prima ballerina of the Sadler's Wells Ballet, Beryl Grey toured widely throughout her career. She was the first Western ballet dancer to perform with both the Bolshoi Ballet and the Chinese Ballet.

Grey's real name was Beryl Groom. Born and educated in London, she studied ballet under Madeline Sharp before winning a scholarship to the Sadler's Wells Ballet School at the age of nine. In 1941 she appeared with the Sadler's Wells Ballet in several productions, including *Swan Lake* and *Comus*, in which she danced her first solo role. The following year, aged only 15, she became the company's prima ballerina.

Grey remained with Sadler's Wells until 1957, dancing in many traditional ballets (at 16 she was the

youngest ever Giselle) and modern works, such as Frederick Ashton's *The Quest* (1943) and Ninette DE VALOIS's *Checkmate* (playing the Black Queen). In 1950 she married Dr. Sven Svenson, with whom she had a son.

After 1957 Grey worked as a freelance ballerina and performed in many venues throughout the world. In 1957–58 she appeared with the Bolshoi Ballet in Moscow and several other cities; in 1964 she danced in Beijing and Shanghai with the Chinese Ballet.

Grey retired as a dancer in 1966 but continued working as a producer and director. She was artistic director of the London Festival Ballet from 1968 to 1979 and has served on the councils of many arts organizations. Among the numerous honours that she has received is that of DBE in 1988. She has also published three books about ballet.

Grey, Lady Jane (1537–1554) *Queen of England for nine days*

As the granddaughter of King Henry VIII's elder sister Mary, Lady Jane Grey had a claim to the English throne. Married against her will in 1553 to Lord Guildford Dudley, son of the Duke of Northumberland, she was used as a pawn by Northumberland, who was King Edward VI's regent, in his determined effort to retain his power after the king's death.

Jane was born at Bradgate, Leicestershire, the eldest daughter of Henry Grey, later Duke of Suffolk. Raised as a Protestant, she was skilled in Hebrew, Greek, Latin, French, and Italian and corresponded with eminent Protestant theologians on the Continent. After plans to marry Jane to Edward VI had failed, her father arranged her marriage to Lord Guildford Dudley. During Edward's last illness Northumberland had him sign a "device" excluding Henry VIII's daughters, the future queens MARY I and ELIZABETH I, from the throne in favour of Jane. On July 10, 1553, four days after Edward's death, Jane was proclaimed queen.

Her reign lasted only until July 19. The country supported the Catholic Mary's claim, and Northumberland's forces were dispersed by troops loyal to Mary. Lady Jane's life was initially spared, but her father's participation in Wyatt's Rebellion (1554), a revolt against Mary's proposed marriage to Philip II of Spain, convinced Mary that she did not need another focus of Protestant opposition and a further rival to the throne. Jane and her husband were executed on Tower Hill on February 12, 1554.

Grigson, (Heather Mabel) Jane
(1928–90) *British writer on food and cookery*

Grigson is admired both for her simple wholesome recipes and for the appealing style of her writing.

After graduating from Newnham College, Cambridge, in 1953, Jane McIntire worked as an editorial assistant for two years before taking a job as an Italian translator. She went to live in Wiltshire with her husband, the poet Geoffrey Grigson, and together they made many visits to France. The end of her translator's job in 1967 coincided with the publication of her first cookery book, *Charcuterie and French Pork Cookery*. She continued to produce more books after becoming cookery correspondent for the *Observer Magazine*, including the cookery classics *English Food* (1974), *Jane Grigson's Vegetable Book* (1978), and *Jane Grigson's Fruit Book* (1982). Her daughter, Sophie Grigson, also writes and broadcasts on cookery.

Grimké, Angelina Emily
(1805–1879) *American abolitionist and feminist*

Grimké, Sarah Moore (1792–1873)
American abolitionist and feminist

Staunch advocates of the abolition of slavery, the Grimké sisters combined their antislavery campaign with a crusade for women's rights.

Sarah and Angelina Grimké were born into an aristocratic family in Charleston, South Carolina. Despite (or perhaps because of) the fact that their father, a judge, himself owned slaves, the sisters grew up with a deep conviction of the injustice of slavery. Becoming Quakers in their twenties, they moved to Philadelphia and be-

came actively involved in the abolitionist movement.

Inspired by the work of the abolitionist leader William Lloyd Garrison, in 1836 Angelina wrote the pamphlet *An Appeal to the Christian Women of the South*, urging Southern women to express their opposition to slavery. The same year her sister made a similar appeal in her *Epistle to the Clergy of the Southern States*. These pamphlets aroused the disapproval of South Carolina officials, who threatened the sisters with imprisonment should they ever return to their home state. Despite this, Sarah and Angelina freed the slaves whom they had inherited as part of their father's estate before moving to New York in 1836.

Joining the American Anti-Slavery Society, they became the society's first women lecturers. At first they confined their talks to small gatherings of women but later defied convention by addressing large mixed audiences in church halls around New England. This provoked the condemnation of the General Association of Congregational Ministers of Massachusetts, who denounced women preachers and reformers in a pastoral letter. Sarah responded by publishing *Letters on the Equality of the Sexes* and *The Condition of Women* (both 1838), and the sisters thereafter broadened their campaign to press for women's rights.

After Angelina's marriage in 1838 to the abolitionist Theodore Dwight Weld, Sarah joined their household – first in New Jersey, where Weld set up some liberal schools, and then in Massachusetts. Sarah and Angelina continued to campaign together for the emancipation of slaves and women; their most influential joint publication was *American Slavery as It Is: Testimony of a Thousand Witnesses* (1838).

Grimshaw, Beatrice (*c.* 1871–1953)
Irish traveller and writer

An intrepid traveller in the South Seas, Grimshaw wrote at least 33 travel books and adventure stories based on her experiences.

Born in Cloona, County Antrim, Grimshaw was educated in Belfast,

Caen (France), and London. She soon proved her stamina by becoming a record-breaking cyclist, covering a greater distance in 24 hours than any woman previously. After establishing herself as a writer and journalist, she began travelling as a correspondent for shipping companies. She went to Tahiti in 1906 and afterwards travelled widely in the South Pacific, writing articles for the *Daily Graphic* and *National Geographic* magazines.

Settling for a time in Papua New Guinea, Grimshaw grew tobacco and explored the dangerous Sepik and Fly rivers. Among her other adventures in the South Seas, she prospected for diamonds and went diving in the Torres Strait. Her many writings include *In the Strange South Seas* and *From Fiji to the Cannibal Islands* (both 1907), *The New New Guinea* (1910), and the novels *The Red Gods Call* (1910) and *The Victorian Family Robinson* (1934). Continuing to write, Grimshaw retired to Australia in 1939. She died in Bathurst, New South Wales.

Grisi, Carlotta (*c.* 1819–1899) *Italian ballet dancer*

One of the foremost ballerinas of the Romantic era, Grisi is best known for having created the title role of *Giselle* at the Paris Opéra Ballet in 1841.

A cousin of the singers Giuditta and Giulia GRISI, she was born in Visinada in Italy (now in Croatia) and first appeared on stage at about the age of eight. After training at La Scala ballet school in Milan, she joined La Scala ballet company. In 1833–34 she met the choreographer Jules Perrot in Naples. They became lovers and began to tour and work together, later marrying. She eventually left Perrot for her dancing partner, Lucien Petipa.

Having appeared in Vienna, London, and Paris, Grisi joined the Paris Opéra Ballet. Perrot, collaborating with Jean Coralli, choreographed all her solos for the title role of *Giselle*; the premiere of the ballet in 1841 was a sensational success. The writer Théophile Gautier, who had supplied the scenario for *Giselle* by adapting an old legend, fell in love with Grisi and remained her lifelong friend.

After *Giselle* Grisi danced the title roles in the first performances of *La Péri* (1843) and Perrot's *Esmeralda* (1844). In 1845, with Marie TAGLIONI, Lucile GRAHN, and Fanny CERRITO, she danced one of the four solos in the premiere of Perrot's *Pas de quatre* in London. Since all four women were celebrated ballerinas, a dispute arose over precedence; eventually they agreed to appear in ascending order of age. Grisi also created the title roles of *Paquita* (1846) and *Griseldis* (1848). In 1850 she danced in Russia. Soon afterwards she retired and went to live in Geneva.

Grisi, Giulia (1811–1869) *Italian opera singer*

> A brilliant voice…always true and strong,…nobility of carriage, grace and truth of gesture…
>
> —Description of Grisi in *Journal des débats* (1832)

With a consistent vocal quality over two octaves, Giulia Grisi was one of the finest operatic sopranos of the 19th century.

Born in Milan, a cousin of the ballerina Carlotta GRISI, Giulia took her first musical instruction from her elder sister Giuditta Grisi (1805–40), a mezzo-soprano. Their aunt was also a singer, and an uncle was among Giulia's other teachers. At the age of 16 Giulia made her operatic debut in Bologna, in Rossini's *Zelmira*. In 1828–29 she performed in Florence, Pisa, and Milan (at La Scala).

Bellini wrote the roles of Juliet for her and Romeo for Giuditta Grisi in his opera *The Capulets and the Montagues*; the sisters sang opposite each other to great acclaim at the first performance of the opera in 1830. The following year Bellini wrote the part of Adalgisa for Giulia in *Norma*. Giulia continued singing in Italy until 1832, when she fled to escape her rigid contract with La Scala.

The same year (1832) Grisi was invited to join the Italian Opera in Paris, where she appeared in Rossini's *Semiramide*; she remained with the company for the next 17 years, singing at the Italian Theatre in Paris every winter. During this period she became famous for many roles, including Desdemona in Rossini's *Otello*, Elvira in Bellini's *The Puritans*, and Norina in Donizetti's *Don Pasquale*. From 1832 she also sang in London every summer (except 1842) for 27 years.

In 1839 Grisi sang opposite the Italian tenor Giovanni Mario in the London premiere of Donizetti's *Lucretia Borgia*. This marked the start of a successful partnership that lasted until Grisi's retirement from the operatic stage in 1861. During this time Grisi and Mario toured together, singing in St. Petersburg (1849), New York (1854), and Madrid (1859). Although lifelong friends, they never married, as Grisi was unable to obtain a divorce from her husband, Gérard de Melcy, whom she had married in 1836.

After Grisi retired from opera, she continued to make concert appearances for several years.

Gruberová, Edita (1946–) *Slovakian opera singer*

A leading exponent of the flamboyant style of soprano singing known as coloratura, Gruberová is famed for her performances of technically demanding roles, including the Queen of the Night in Mozart's *The Magic Flute* and Zerbinetta in Strauss's *Ariadne on Naxos*.

Born in Bratislava, Czechoslovakia, Gruberová studied music with Maria Medvecká in Prague and with Ruthilde Boesch in Vienna. She gave her first operatic performance in Bratislava in 1968, as Rosina in Rossini's *The Barber of Seville*. Her first appearance with the Vienna State Opera, which she joined officially two years later, was as the Queen of the Night in 1970. She sang the same role when she made her debuts at Glyndebourne (1973), the Salzburg Festival (1974), and the Metropolitan Opera, New York (1977). Her first performance at London's Covent Garden (1984) was as Juliet in Bellini's *The Capulets and Montagues*.

Gruberová's other major roles include Gilda in Verdi's *Rigoletto*, Violetta in his *La Traviata*, Lucia in Donizetti's *Lucia di Lammermoor*, and Manon in Massenet's opera of that name. She has sung in many cities in Europe and elsewhere, including Milan (at La Scala), Munich, Hamburg, Frankfurt, Zurich, Barcelona, and Chicago, while also appearing at Bayreuth and other festivals. Gruberová has made recordings of a number of the roles in her repertoire and has appeared in a video of *Rigoletto* opposite Luciano Pavarotti.

Guggenheim, Peggy (1898–1979)
American art collector and patron

> The day Hitler walked into Norway
> I walked into Léger's studio and
> bought a wonderful 1919 painting
> from him for one thousand dollars.
> —*Confessions of an Art Addict* (1960)

Peggy Guggenheim was one of the principal collectors and patrons of 20th-century art. Rich and beautiful, she led a colourful life, which she recounted in two autobiographies.

The second of three sisters, Peggy (whose real name was Marguerite) was born in New York City into the wealthy Jewish Guggenheim family: her uncle, Solomon, was the founder of the Guggenheim Museum in New York. Peggy's father fostered her interest in culture during annual trips to Europe, leaving her $450,000 on his death in the *Titanic* disaster in 1912.

Educated by tutors at home, Peggy later attended the Jacobi School in New York. Shortly after World War I she went to Paris and adopted a Bohemian lifestyle, marrying the artist Laurence Vail in 1922. They had two children but were divorced in 1930. Guggenheim subsequently had a number of lovers, including Samuel Beckett and the artist Yves Tanguy.

In 1938, assisted by the artist Marcel Duchamp, Peggy Guggenheim opened the Guggenheim Jeune gallery in London, mounting exhibitions of work by contemporary artists and buying one picture from each collection herself. The gallery was closed the same year. Advised by the art expert Herbert Read, Guggenheim now began to acquire works of art in France, despite the outbreak of World War II, and had them shipped to the United States. She herself followed in 1941, the year she married the artist Max Ernst.

Ernst and the poet André Breton helped Guggenheim to expand her collection, and in 1942 she opened a gallery in New York called Art of This Century. This contained works by, among others, Picasso, Braque, Chagall, Klee, Kandinsky, Dalí, and Miró. Guggenheim showed works by the abstract expressionists, who were just emerging, and gave crucial patronage to Jackson Pollock.

In 1946 she divorced Ernst and settled in Venice, living in a palazzo on the Grand Canal in which she established a permanent exhibition of her works of art. Guggenheim wrote two books, *Out of this Century* (1946) and *Confessions of an Art Addict* (1960). Her collection, worth $30 million on her death, was left to the Guggenheim Museum and to the Guggenheim Collection at her palazzo in Venice.

Guilbert, Yvette (1868–1944) *French singer*

The subject of several paintings and caricatures by Toulouse-Lautrec, in which she is depicted wearing a yellow dress and long black gloves, Yvette Guilbert was best known for the air of innocence with which she sang extremely risqué songs.

Born Emma Laure Esther Guilbert in Paris, she was barely making a living as a seamstress before she made her theatrical debut at Les Bouffes du Nord in 1890. She became a popular comic singer in the leading cafés and theatres of Paris, also touring England, Germany, and the United States, where in 1920 she opened a school of acting in New York.

At first Guilbert sang ballads of Paris's Latin Quarter, the area on the south bank of the Seine that was a centre for students and artists. Later her repertoire consisted of historical songs and ballads, some of which were written for her by Aristide Bruant, which she sang in costume and in a dramatic style.

Yvette Guilbert was the author of *L'Arte de chanter une chanson* (1918; How to Sing a Song), the first textbook on the subject. She also wrote two novels (both published in 1920) and an autobiography, *La Chanson de ma vie* (1929).

Gunnell, Sally (1966–) *British athlete*

Sally Gunnell was the British heroine of the 1992 Olympics, winning a gold medal in the 400-metre hurdles. She became world champion and world record holder for the same event in 1993.

Born and educated in Chigwell, Essex, Sally Jane Janet Gunnell was the best junior long-jumper in England at the age of 13. A tall athlete, she began an impressive series of international wins in track events with a gold medal for the 100-metre hurdles in the 1986 Commonwealth Games.

Specializing in the 400-metre hurdles and the 4×400-metre relay, she won two golds in the 1990 Commonwealth Games and a silver (for the hurdles) in the 1991 world championships. At the 1992 Olympic Games in Barcelona, as captain of the British women's team, Gunnell won the gold medal for the hurdles and a bronze for the relay. Her marriage to the athlete Jonathan Bigg took place the same year.

Gunnell's successes continued in 1993, when she became world champion and world record holder in the 400-metre hurdles (with a time of 52.74 seconds) and won a bronze medal for the 4×400-metre relay in the world championships. She was rewarded by being appointed an MBE. In 1993–94 she became European Cup champion, Commonwealth champion, and World Cup champion in the hurdles.

The 1996 Olympics brought disappointment, however. A recurrent leg injury destroyed Gunnell's hopes of carrying off a medal for her country. She is the author of a book, *Running Tall* (1994), about her career.

Guyon, Jeanne-Marie (1648–1717) *French mystic and writer*

> My prison walls cannot control
> The flight, the freedom of the soul.
>
> —"A Prisoner's Song" (*c.* 1695–1702)

Although a deeply spiritual woman, Madame Guyon held religious views too unconventional to go unchallenged. Her numerous writings include religious treatises advocating the form of passive mysticism known as quietism.

The daughter of a nobleman, Jeanne-Marie Bouvier de la Motte was born in Montargis, near Orléans. Convent-educated, she wanted to become a nun but at the age of 16 was persuaded by her parents to marry the 38-year-old Jacques Guyon du Chesnoy. She bore him five children before his death 12 years later.

While staying in Geneva, the young widow met François Lacombe, a friar who introduced her to quietism. This form of mysticism promoted passive contemplation, the surrender of the individual will, and an indifference to both life and death. In 1681, feeling herself called to the spiritual life (and having provided for her children), Madame Guyon began to travel through Europe with Father Lacombe, preaching quietism. She wrote her first books during this tour, but her ideas were controversial, and on her return to Paris in 1686 she was arrested and imprisoned for a time.

After her release Madame Guyon was introduced into court circles by Madame de MAINTENON. She became friendly with Abbé François Fénelon, who later became Archbishop of Cambrai, but the association brought them both into conflict with leading churchmen, notably Bishop Bossuet. In 1695 the Commission of Issy denounced quietism, and Guyon's books *The Short and Very Easy Method of Prayer* (1688) and *The Song of Songs Interpreted According to the Mystic Sense* (1685) were condemned. Madame Guyon spent the next seven years in and out of prison, finally (in 1702) being released and exiled to Blois, where she died 15 years later.

Gwyn, Nell (1650–1687) *English actress and mistress of King Charles II*

> Shall the dog lie where the deer once couched?
>
> —Refusing a lover after the death of Charles II

Described by Samuel Pepys as "Pretty, witty Nell," Nell Gwyn was the only one of the king's mistresses to be popular with the people.

Born Eleanor Gwyn (or Gwynne) in Hereford, she worked as an orange seller at the Theatre Royal in Drury Lane, London. After becoming the mistress of Charles Hart, an actor, she made her first stage appearance around 1664. She acted in many of John Dryden's plays, notably *The Indian Emperor* (1667), and was the leading comedian of the King's Company until 1669, playing such roles as Lady Wealthy in *The English Monsieur*. She was an excellent singer, dancer, and reciter of saucy verses, excelling in pert sprightly roles. She became the mistress of Charles Sackville, 6th Earl of Dorset, in about 1667, and of King Charles II a year or so afterwards.

Admitted to the inner circles of the court, she began a famous rivalry with another of Charles's mistresses, Louise de Kérouaille, Duchess of Portsmouth. Nell bore Charles two sons: Charles Beauclerk (1670–1726), whom the king created Baron Heddington, Earl of Burford, and 1st Duke of St. Albans; and James (1671–80), Lord Beauclerk. She is said to have helped to establish the Chelsea Royal Hospital for old soldiers. Her portrait was painted by the court painter, Sir Peter Lely.

Faithful to Charles, she retained his affection until his death in 1685. His last request of his brother James II – "Let not poor Nelly starve" – resulted in a pension that assured her comfort until her death.

H

Hadid, Zaha (1950–) *Iraqi architect*

> The idea of tradition, through time, becomes manifest in different ways.
> —Quoted in *The Times*, September 1994

Zaha Hadid, who was born in Baghdad, studied at the Architectural Association in London from 1972 to 1977, after which she started her own architectural practice. In 1988 she held an exhibition at the Museum of Modern Art, New York.

Hadid's designs, with their geometric shapes and sharp lines, show the influence of the Russian constructivist movement of the early 20th century. Examples of her work can be seen in Europe, Japan, and Hong Kong. They are typified by one of the Pavilions at the Groningen Museum in the Netherlands.

In Britain her design for the Vitra Fire Station was nominated for the BBC design awards in 1994. In the same year she was the controversial winner of a competition to design the Cardiff Bay Opera House in Wales.

Hagen, Uta (1919–) *German-born American actress*

Hagen made her Broadway debut in a 1938 production of Chekhov's *The Seagull*, which starred Alfred Lunt and Lynn FONTANNE. From 1938 to 1948 she was married to the actor José Ferrer, with whom she appeared in several plays, including Maxwell Anderson's *Key Largo* (1939) and a notable 1943 production of *Othello*, starring Paul Robeson. In 1947 she and Herbert Berghof, who was to become her second husband, founded the Herbert Berghof Studio, at which she continued to teach into the 1990s.

Hagen's other starring roles included Blanche in Tennessee Williams's *A Streetcar Named Desire* (1948), Martha in Edward Albee's *Who's Afraid of Virginia Woolf?* (1962), and Ranevskaya in Chekhov's *The Cherry Orchard* (1968). She also appeared in several films, notably *The Boys from Brazil* (1978) and *Reversal of Fortune* (1990).

Hagen also published two books on acting – *Respect for Acting* (1973), written with Haskel Frankel, and *Challenge for the Actor* (1991) – as well as her memoirs, *Sources* (1983).

Hahn, Emily (1905–1997) *American writer*

Emily Hahn was the author of over 50 books covering a wide range of subjects. Best known for her perceptive books about China, including the authorized biographies *The Soong Sisters* (1941: see CHIANG, MAYLING SOONG; SUN CH'ING-LING) and *Chiang Kai-shek* (1955), she also wrote popular biographies of Fanny BURNEY, Aphra BEHN, and Frieda LAWRENCE. In addition she was a prolific contributor to *The New Yorker* magazine from 1929 until her death.

Born in St. Louis, she studied mining engineering at the University of Wisconsin and worked as an oil geologist after graduating in 1926. In 1928 Hahn moved to New York, where she taught geology at Hunter College and started writing her *New Yorker* articles.

Two years later she left the United States for Africa. Her experiences in the Belgian Congo (now the Democratic Republic of Congo), where she worked for the Red Cross among the pygmies, provided material for her travel book *Congo Solo: Misadventures Two Degrees North* (1933).

In 1935 Hahn went to Shanghai, where she worked as a school teacher and wrote for magazines. During this time she met Zhou Enlai and other Chinese revolutionary leaders. She later moved to Hong Kong, where, during World War II, she met Charles Boxer, a British Intelligence officer and later professor of Portuguese at London University, whom she married in 1945.

Hahn wrote many travel volumes, including *China to Me* (1944, reprinted 1987), *England to Me* (1949), and *Africa to Me* (1964). Her works on women's issues include *Love Conquers Nothing: A New Look at Old Romance* (1952), *Once Upon a Pedestal: An Informal History of Women's Lib* (1974), and *Eve and the Apes* (1988).

Hale, Clara (1905–1992) *American social activist*

Clara Hale, or "Mother" Hale as she came to be called, was the founder of Hale House in Harlem, New York, a home for the abandoned children and orphans of drug addicts. In 1985 she was awarded the Medal of Freedom by President Ronald Reagan, who called her an "American hero."

Born Clara McBride in Philadelphia, she was widowed while still in her twenties. To support her family she became a licensed foster parent, raising over the next 30 years a total of some 40 foster children.

In 1969, when Clara Hale had already retired from this work, her daughter Lorraine brought her a two-month-old infant to care for. She had just rescued the child from an addict mother living on the streets on the understanding that the child would be cared for while the mother received treatment for her addiction. Within two months Hale was caring for 22 babies, many of whom were still suffering from the addictions inherited from their mothers. In the early 1970s the project received government funding, and in 1975 a large brownstone building was purchased and became Hale House.

With the help of staff and volunteers, Mother Hale nursed about 1,000 addicted babies at Hale House. In 1989 the government funding stopped, but the project has since been maintained by private donations and has expanded to offer housing and education for mothers who complete their detoxification treatment and a home for mothers and babies with AIDS.

Hall, (Marguerite) Radclyffe (1880–1943) *British writer and poet*

> You're neither unnatural, nor abominable, nor mad; you're as much part of what people call nature as anyone else; only you're unexplained as yet – you've not got your niche in creation.
> —*The Well of Loneliness* (1928)

Radclyffe Hall is best known for her novel *The Well of Loneliness*, in which she dealt frankly with lesbianism – a taboo subject at that time, since it was regarded as an unnatural aberration. Publication of this book led to an obscenity trial in which the court found it an obscene libel and ordered its suppression.

Born in Bournemouth, and educated at King's College, London, and in Germany, Radclyffe Hall inherited considerable wealth from her grandfather at the age of 21. This enabled her to live an independent life, in which she elected to become a writer. Her first volume of poems, *Twixt Earth and Stars*, was published in 1906. There followed more poetry, eight novels, and a number of short stories. She was awarded two literary prizes for her novel *Adam's Breed* (1926), an account of the religious aspirations of an illiterate waiter.

The Well of Loneliness, published two years later, was a frankly autobiographical attempt to court public sympathy for the "congenital invert." It carried a sympathetic prefatory note by Havelock Ellis, the eminent pioneer of sexology. Moreover, at the subsequent obscenity trial such respected writers as E. M. Forster and Virginia WOOLF were prepared to give evidence as to its literary merit, but the judge saw fit to disallow their evidence. In the United States the courts were more tolerant, and the charge of obscenity was thrown out. When the book was finally allowed to be published in Britain it had a considerable effect on the attitude of the public to homosexuality in general, which eventually led to a change in the law.

From 1907 Radclyffe Hall lived with the former society beauty Mrs. Mabel Batten and through her met Una, Lady Troubridge. After Mrs. Batten's death in 1916, Lady Troubridge became Radclyffe Hall's lover and lifelong companion. They lived in London, Sussex, and Paris, where they socialized with other well-known lesbians. Radclyffe Hall was an active member of the Council of the Society for Psychical Research and a fellow of the Zoological Society.

Her later novels, because they contained no controversial subjects, attracted less attention.

Hallowes, Odette (1912–1995)
French Resistance heroine

> I am a very ordinary woman to whom a chance has been given to see human beings at their best and at their worst...I completely believe in the potential nobility of the human spirit.
> —Quoted by Mrs. Stella McGurk in a letter to *The Times*, March 22, 1995

"Odette," as she was universally known, operated as a British agent in France during World War II until her capture and merciless torture by the Germans.

Born Odette Marie Celine Brailly in Amiens, and educated at a convent in that city, she came to Britain in 1932, a year after marrying the Englishman Roy Sanson. During World War II she was recruited by the British Special Operations Executive to work in France with the French Resistance, joining the British officer Captain Peter Churchill's network "Spindle" as a courier in 1942.

The following year the group moved to Annecy, where they were infiltrated by the Germans. Both Odette and Peter Churchill were captured by the Gestapo. By claiming that they were married, and that Churchill was a nephew of Winston Churchill, they escaped execution. Odette was taken to Paris, where – imprisoned and tortured by the Germans – she behaved with immense courage by not betraying any of her colleagues. In 1943 she and Churchill were sent to Ravensbrück concentration camp, where they remained until the end of the war.

Odette married Peter Churchill in 1947, after the death of her first husband. In 1956 their marriage was dissolved, and Odette married Geoffrey Hallowes, a wine importer. She received the George Cross, Britain's highest award for civilian bravery, in 1946 and was appointed to the French Legion of Honour in 1950. The film *Odette* (1950), starring Anna NEAGLE, portrays her heroic wartime deeds.

Hamilton, Alice (1869–1970) *American physician*

Known for her pioneering work in the study of industrial diseases and industrial hygiene, Alice Hamilton, who was born in New York City, received her MD from the University of Michigan in 1893. She continued her medical studies at Johns Hopkins University and in Germany. From 1897 to 1905 she was a professor at the Northwestern University Medical School for Women.

During the 1910s and early 1920s Dr. Hamilton studied industrial diseases, first for Illinois and later for the federal government. During World War I she investigated the high-explosives industry, discovering that many of the deaths that were supposedly caused by heart failure were actually the result of nitrous fume poisoning. Her findings contributed to the adoption of corrective practices in industrial hygiene and to the passage of workmen's compensation laws. In the case of the viscose rayon industry it was shown that the carbon disulphide used caused mental disease, paralysis, and blindness.

From 1919 until 1935, when she retired, Dr. Hamilton was assistant professor of industrial medicine at Harvard Medical School. The first woman professor at Harvard, she was, however, unable to use the Harvard Club, a male-only preserve. She published some of her findings on women working in dangerous industries in a Department of Labor bulletin entitled *Women Workers and Industrial Poisons*. Among her other publications was the classic textbook *Industrial Toxicology* (1934).

Hamilton, Emma, Lady (*c.* 1765–1815) *British adventuress*

Famous as the beautiful and vivacious mistress of Horatio Nelson, Lady Hamilton was born Emma Lyon in Cheshire, the daughter of a village blacksmith. Little is known of her early life, except that she is thought to have worked as a nursemaid, barmaid, and a shop assistant before becoming, briefly, the mistress of Sir Henry Fetherstonehaugh in 1780.

From 1781 to 1786 Emma was the mistress of Charles Greville and lived quietly in London, where she often posed for the artist George Romney. When Greville tired of her, he sent her to his uncle, Sir William Hamilton, the British ambassador to the court of Naples, on condition that Hamilton settle all his debts. Emma soon became Hamilton's mistress and, in 1791, his wife. Lady Hamilton became a favourite at the Neapolitan court and a close friend of Queen Maria Carolina. As the wife of the British ambassador she had considerable political influence, which she made use of for the benefit of the British government.

Lady Hamilton first met Nelson in Naples, probably in 1793, but they did not become lovers until 1798. After his success at the Battle of the Nile the Hamiltons joined Nelson in his triumphal tour of England in 1800. The three lived together until Sir William's death in 1803.

Having given birth to Nelson's daughter, Horatia, in 1801, Emma continued to live with him until his death at the Battle of Trafalgar in 1805. Although she was left fortunes by both men, her gambling and extravagant lifestyle led her heavily into debt. After fruitless attempts to obtain pensions from the governments of both Britain and Naples she was imprisoned for debt in 1812. In 1813 she escaped to France, where she died, penniless, two years later.

Hammond, Dame Joan (1912–1996) *New Zealand singer*

Joan Hammond was famous for her expressive soprano voice which she used to great effect, notably in Puccini roles and choral works.

She was born in Christchurch, New Zealand, and grew up in Sydney, where she studied the violin at Sydney Conservatory. An active sportswoman, she became a junior golfing champion. After an injury to her arm she gave up the violin and began to train as a singer. The Sydney golfing fraternity sponsored her further voice studies in Vienna in 1936.

Hammond's career as a singer blossomed in 1938, when she appeared as Nedda in Leoncavallo's opera *I Pagliacci*, making her London debut in a recital that same year. World War II prevented her from taking up contracts with the Vienna State Opera (1939) and La Scala, Milan (1940). Instead she served as an ambulance driver in wartime England, entertained the troops, and sang occasionally with the Carl Rosa Touring Company. She did, however, make a number of recordings in 1941, notably the aria "O My Beloved Father", from Puccini's opera *Gianni Schicchi*, which sold more than a million copies.

After the war Hammond sang with the Vienna State Opera, making her London debut at Covent Garden in 1948, appearing in New York in 1949, and playing Tatyana in Tchaikovsky's *Eugene Onegin* (in Russian) in Moscow in 1957. Her operatic career was brought to a premature end in 1964 by a heart condition, after which she retired to Australia. She was made a DBE in 1974. In 1970 she published her autobiography, *A Voice, a Life*.

Handel-Mazzetti, Enrica von (1871–1955) *Austrian writer*

Baroness von Handel-Mazzetti is known for her historical novels, written under the pen name Marien Kind.

Born in Vienna, she was a descendant of Roman Catholic German and Protestant Hungarian nobility. Her early novels, such as *Meinrad Helmpergers denkwürdiges Jahr* (1900; Meinrad Helmperger's Memorable Year), *Jesse und Maria* (1906), and *Die arme Margaret* (1910; Poor Margaret), draw on the theme of religious conflict between Catholics and Protestants in the

17th and early 18th centuries. *Karl Ludwig Sand* (1924–26), a trilogy, centres on the life of a German student executed for the murder of a dramatist.

Her other novels include *Stefana Schwertner* (3 vols., 1912–14), *Der deutsche Held* (1920; The German Hero), *Frau Maria* (3 vols., 1929–31), and *Graf Reichard* (3 vols., 1938–39). She also wrote poetry, plays, and short stories.

Hansberry, Lorraine (1930–1965)
American playwright

Lorraine Hansberry is best known for her *Raisin in the Sun*, the first play by an African-American woman to be produced on Broadway. It won the New York Drama Critics' Circle Award as the best play of the 1959 season. The critical acclaim for this play, which concerns the attempt by a black family in Chicago to move out of the ghetto into a white neighbourhood, had a major effect on the rise to prominence of African-American actors, writers, and producers in the U.S. theatre.

Lorraine Hansberry was born in Chicago; her father was a real estate broker and banker who won a lawsuit against restrictive covenants. She studied drama and stage design at the University of Wisconsin before moving to New York. In 1953 she married Robert Nemiroff, a songwriter, music publisher, and theatrical director. Her second play, *The Sign in Sidney Brustein's Window* (1964), concerns anti-Semitism and local politics; her husband was involved in its production at the time of her death from cancer.

Although Hansberry never took an active role in politics, she wrote *The Movement: Documentary of a Struggle for Equality* in 1964. *To Be Young, Gifted and Black*, autobiographical selections from her writings adapted for the stage by Nemiroff, was produced in 1969 and published in 1970.

Han Suyin (1917–) *Chinese-born British writer and doctor*

Han Suyin is best-known for her novel *A Many Splendoured Thing* (1952), which is set in Hong Kong. With autobiographical overtones, it explores the ideological situation in the former colony through the love affair of a Chinese girl and a British reporter. In 1955 it was made into a successful film.

Born Elizabeth Zhou (Chow) in Beijing, the daughter of a Belgian mother and a Chinese engineer, Han Suyin was educated there and at Yenching, Brussels, and the Royal Free Hospital in London, where she studied medicine. She returned to China and in 1938 married General P. Tang, who was killed in the civil war in 1947. After a spell working at Queen Mary Hospital in Hong Kong, she went to Singapore where in 1952 she married L. Comber, a British police officer. For the next few years she combined a private practice with work at an anti-tuberculosis clinic. She was divorced in 1958, and in the same year was appointed to Nanyang University, where she lectured for two years in contemporary Asian literature. She was married for a third time in 1971, to Vincent Ruthnaswamy, and now lives in Switzerland.

Han Suyin wrote three more novels in the 1950s: *Destination Chungking* (1953), *And the Rain my Drink* (1954), and *The Mountain is Young* (1958); *Four Faces* appeared in 1963. Her next three books, *The Crippled Tree* (1965), *A Mortal Flower* (1966), and *Birdless Summer* (1968), made up an historical trilogy. Contemporary Chinese history is the subject of *The Morning Deluge* (1972), *The Wind in the Tower* (1976), and *Eldest Son: Zhou Enlai and the Making of Modern China (1898–1976)* (1994).

Hard, Darlene Ruth (1936–) *American tennis player*

The number one amateur player from 1960 until 1963, Hard ranked among the top 10 American women players for 10 successive years.

Born in Los Angeles, Darlene Hard first achieved national ranking in 1954, when she was placed seventh. She led the United States team to victories over Britain in four Wightman Cup matches (1957, 1959, 1962, 1963) and to victory in the international Federation Cup competition in 1963. She became a professional instructor in 1964.

Darlene Hard's most important titles included the U.S. singles (1960 and 1961) and U.S. doubles (1958–62), the Wimbledon doubles (1957, 1959, 1960, 1963) and mixed doubles (1957 and 1959), and the French singles (1960) and French doubles (1955, 1957, and 1960).

Harlow, Jean (1911–1937) *American film actress*

> She didn't want to be famous. She wanted to be happy.
>
> —Clark Gable

Nicknamed the "Blonde Bombshell," Jean Harlow, with her platinum-blonde hair and beautiful figure, became the first sex symbol of the talkies. She described herself as "the worst actress in Hollywood," although she was regarded as an accomplished comedian and a sympathetic actress.

Born Harlean Carpenter in Kansas City, Missouri, she was the daughter of an affluent dentist. At the age of 16 she eloped with a millionaire's son, with whom she moved to Hollywood, taking small parts in such films as *Love Parade* (1929) and Laurel and Hardy's *Double Whoopee* (1929). Her marriage broke up shortly before her appearance in Howard Hughes's World War I film *Hell's Angels* (1930). This was the start of her career as a star; in 1931 she took leading roles in the early gangster film *Public Enemy* and Frank Capra's romantic comedy *Platinum Blonde*.

In 1932 Harlow joined MGM and appeared as a blonde temptress in *Red Dust* with Clark Gable. The same year she married Hollywood director Paul Bern but was almost immediately involved in an affair with Gable. Two months later Bern committed suicide. This caused a huge scandal in Hollywood, especially as Bern was rumoured to have taken his life as a result of impotence. Harlow's third marriage, to lighting director Harold Rosson in 1933, lasted only a year. Among the films she made in 1933 was the comedy *Bombshell*, often regarded as her most successful movie. In 1934 she formed a close friendship with William Powell, her costar in the film *Reckless* (1935), in which she played the part of a woman who has to come to terms with her husband's suicide.

In 1937, while making *Saratoga* with Clark Gable, Harlow died of kidney failure, largely because her mother, a Christian Scientist, refused to allow her to have treatment. In 1965 two films were made about her life, both called *Harlow*: one starred Carroll Baker, the other, a made-for-TV movie, starred Carol Lynley.

Harris, Julie (1925–) *American actress*

Best known for her sensitive portrayals of complex characters on stage, screen, and television, Julie Harris was born in Grosse Pointe Park, Michigan, and studied drama in New York City and at the Yale University School of Drama. After making her Broadway debut in 1945, she trained at the Actors Studio (1946–49). In this period she appeared with the Old Vic Company in Britain and the American Repertory Company, winning acclaim for her roles in *Henry IV, Part II* and Sophocles's *Oedipus*. In 1950 she achieved stardom as the 12-year-old tomboy, Frankie, in Carson MC-CULLERS's *The Member of the Wedding*, even though she was then 25. Her performance in the same role in the film version (1953) earned her an Academy Award nomination.

Julie Harris received Tony Awards as Best Actress for her portrayal of Sally Bowles in *I Am a Camera* (1951); for *The Lark* (1955), in which she portrayed JOAN OF ARC; for *Forty Carats* (1968); and for *The Last of Mrs. Lincoln* (1972). She also had a distinguished television career, winning Emmy Awards for *The Little Moon of Alban* (1958) and *Victoria Regina* (1961). She played Juliet in a 1960 Stratford, Ontario, production of *Romeo and Juliet* and Ophelia in Joseph Papp's New York production of *Hamlet* (1964).

Harris's portrayal of Emily DICKIN-SON on Broadway in the one-woman show *The Belle of Amherst* (1976) earned her a fifth Tony Award. The performance also was taped for television. Her other films include *East of Eden* (1955), *The Hiding Place* (1975),

Gorillas in the Mist (1988), and *The Dark Half* (1993). She also appeared on the television series *Knots Landing* (1979–87).

Harrison, Jane Ellen (1850–1928)
British classical scholar

A woman of great intelligence and learning, she helped to broaden the scope of classical studies by including archaeological, anthropological, and philosophical material.

Jane Ellen Harrison was born in Yorkshire, the daughter of a timber merchant. She was educated at home until the age of 15, when she exchanged the strict regime of her governesses for that of Cheltenham Ladies' College. It was her family's churchgoing that first brought her into contact with classical languages, through Latin prayers and the original Greek of the Gospels. She also learned German and Hebrew at an early age.

In 1874 Harrison won a scholarship to Newnham College, Cambridge, where she studied classics, graduating five years later with the highest marks ever awarded to a female student. She subsequently moved to London, where she broadened her mind with studies in archaeology, literature, and art and gave lectures at the British Museum. Her early publications included *Myths of the Odyssey in Art and Literature* (1882) and *Introductory Studies in Greek Art* (1885). From 1889 to 1896 she was vice-president of the Hellenic Society.

By this time Harrison found herself increasingly drawn away from the study of art towards that of religion, and in 1903 she produced her most famous work, *Prolegomena to the Study of Greek Religion*. By this time she had returned to Newnham as a research fellow and lecturer in classical archaeology. The *Prolegomena* was generally very well received, and it was followed by *Themis, a Study of the Social Origins of Greek Religion* (1912), *Ancient Art and Ritual* (1913), and *Epilegomena to the Study of Greek Religion* (1921).

Harrison also produced a number of works in collaboration with other scholars, notably a series of translations from Russian with Hope Mirrlees.

Hathaway, Anne (*c.* 1556–1623) *Wife of William Shakespeare*

Born at Shottery, near Stratford-on-Avon, Warwickshire, Anne Hathaway married the great dramatist and poet William Shakespeare (1564–1616) in 1582. They had three children; Susanna was born in 1583 and the twins Hamnet and Judith in 1585. Hamnet died in 1596. Although not much is known about her life, her cottage, near Stratford, can still be seen.

Hatshepsut (*c.* 1540 BC–1469 BC) *Queen of Egypt*

> Now my heart turns to and fro,
> In thinking what will the people say,
> They who shall see my monument in
> after years,
> And shall speak of what I have done.
> —Inscription on her obelisk

One of the first great women recorded in history, Hatshepsut, the daughter of Thutmose I, reigned with her husband and half-brother Thutmose II from 1496 until his death in 1490. At this point her stepson and nephew Thutmose III should have succeeded to the throne. However, Hatshepsut, acting as regent, proclaimed herself ruler with the full power and titles of pharaoh in 1489. From then on she was pictured with the attributes of a male ruler, signified by her wearing the kingly false beard.

Hatshepsut's 20-year reign was a period of peace and prosperity for Egypt, although she is thought to have been involved in some military campaigns in Nubia at the start of her reign. She sent a trading expedition to Punt (an ancient country on the Somali coast of northeastern Africa), which was recorded in detail on the walls of her great mortuary temple at Deir el-Bahri, near Thebes; it brought back exotic cargoes of spices, ebony, and ivory. She erected two obelisks at Karnak and opened the turquoise mines at the Wadi Maghareh.

After Hatshepsut's death in 1469 Thutmose III reasserted his right to the throne and attempted to obliterate her memory by defacing her monuments. Her tomb in the Valley of the Kings was left unfinished.

Hawkes, Jacquetta (1910–1996) *British archaeologist*

Jacquetta Hawkes's numerous books on British archaeology did much to popularize the subject.

The daughter of the Nobel prizewinning biochemist Sir Frederick Hopkins, she was born and educated in Cambridge, becoming the first woman to study archaeology and anthropology to degree level at the university there. Her first serious excavation took place in the early 1930s; she married the archaeologist Christopher Hawkes in 1933. *The Archaeology of Jersey* appeared in 1939 and *Prehistoric Britain*, written with her husband, appeared in 1944. *Early Britain* followed in 1945.

In the years after World War II Jacquetta Hawkes worked with the Post-War Reconstruction Secretariat and then joined the Ministry of Education. She was also secretary of the UK Commission for UNESCO from 1943 to 1949, serving on the Commission's Central Committee from 1966 to 1979.

In 1953 the British playwright and novelist J. B. Priestley (1894–1984) became her second husband; together they wrote such works as *Journey Down the Rainbow* (1955), a critique of modern American life in letter form.

Hawkes's other interests included the British Film Institute, of which she was a governor from 1950 to 1957, and the Campaign for Nuclear Disarmament, which she cofounded in 1957. In the 1970s she was editor of the *Atlas of Ancient Archaeology* (1974) and the *Atlas of Early Man* (1976). She also wrote on Egyptian topics, producing a biography of the archaeologist Sir Mortimer Wheeler in 1982. Her new *Shell Guide to British Archaeology* appeared in 1986. She also wrote plays and a book of poetry, *Symbols and Speculations* (1948).

Hawn, Goldie (1945–) *American actress*

> The brightest dumb blonde since Queen Boadicea sliced Roman kneecaps.
>
> —Victor Davis

Goldie Hawn became famous on the television show *Rowan and Martin's Laugh-In* (1968–73) as the pretty, giggling, dumb blonde.

Born in Washington D.C., the daughter of a Jewish musician, she dropped out of drama school to become a go-go dancer. Her first major film role, as the mistress of an apprehensive dentist (played by Walter Matthau) in *Cactus Flower* (1969), won her an Oscar as Best Supporting Actress. She gained much popularity during the 1970s in comedy roles, including the Boulting brothers film *There's a Girl in My Soup* (1970), with Peter Sellers, and *Foul Play* (1978).

In 1980 Hawn established herself as a huge star with the title role in *Private Benjamin*, of which she was also the executive producer. Her subsequent films of the 1980s, for example *Protocol* (1984) and *Overboard* (1987), were less successful, but she has returned to the top with her more recent comedies, including *Bird on a Wire* (1990) with Mel Gibson, *House-Sitter* (1992) with Steve Martin, and *First Wives Club* (1996) with Diane KEATON and Bette MIDLER. She is married to the actor Kurt Russell.

Hayden, Melissa (1928–) *Canadian ballet dancer*

As a prima ballerina Hayden combined a brilliant dancing technique with great dramatic ability.

Born Mildred Herman in Toronto, she studied there at the Boris Volkoff Ballet School before going in 1945 to New York. Here she attended the School of American Ballet and the Vilzak-Scholler School, dancing with the Radio City Music Hall corps de ballet. The same year she joined the Ballet Theater (now American Ballet Theater) and within a year became a soloist. She toured South America with the Ballet Alicia Alonso in 1949.

From 1950 Hayden danced with the New York City Ballet (NYCB), except for a two-year period (1953–55) when she returned to Ballet Theater. She danced major roles in George Balanchine's *Agon* (1957), *Stars and Stripes* (1958), *A Midsummer Night's Dream* (1962), and *Cortège Hongrois*, which he created especially for her during her final season (1973) as a farewell tribute. Other major roles she danced at NYCB include Clorinda in *The Duel*, Young Girl in *The Still Point*, Profane Love in *Illuminations*, and the title roles in *Firebird* and *Medea*.

Hayden was also a frequent guest star with the National Ballet of Canada, the Royal Ballet (London), the Chicago Opera Ballet, the San Francisco Ballet, and the Boston Ballet. She also danced on television and in films, including Charlie Chaplin's *Limelight* (1952). She was an artist-in-residence at Skidmore College in 1973, founding her own dance school, of which she became the director, in Saratoga, New York State, a year later. From 1976 to 1977 she was the artistic director of Pacific Northwest Dance, Seattle, and in 1983 became a faculty member in the dance department at the North Carolina School of the Arts. She also staged Balanchine ballets for companies, including a work for the Ballet de San Juan (1982) and *Allegro Brillante* for the Ohio Ballet (1983).

Hayden received many awards in recognition of her work: a Dance Magazine Award in 1961, an honorary doctorate from Skidmore College in 1970, and the Handel Medallion from the City of New York in 1973. She was the author of *Melissa Hayden: Off Stage and On* (1963), *Dancer to Dancer* (1981), and *The Nutcracker Ballet* (1992).

Hayes, Helen (1900–1993) *American actress*

> An actress's life is so transitory – suddenly you're a building.
>
> —Said at the ceremony renaming New York's Fulton Theater in her honour, November 1955

Helen Hayes was regarded as the "First Lady" of the American theatre. Despite her diminutive size (she was only five feet tall), she had a regal stage presence that she used to good effect in the title roles of Maxwell Anderson's *Mary of Scotland* (1933) and Laurence Houseman's *Victoria Regina* (1935), two of her most memorable performances.

Born Helen Hayes Brown in Washington, D.C., she made her professional debut at the age of five, and appeared thereafter in a wide range of comedies, including *What Every Woman Knows* (1926). In 1928 she married the playwright and journalist Charles MacArthur, making her film debut in his tearjerker *The Sin of Madelon Claudet* (1931), for which she won an Academy Award for Best Actress. Her other notable films of this period include *Arrowsmith* (1931) and *A Farewell to Arms* (1932).

After her stage successes of the 1930s she starred as Viola in *Twelfth Night* (1940), as Harriet Beecher STOWE in *Harriet* (1944), and in Thornton Wilder's *The Skin of Our Teeth* (1955), Tennessee Williams's *The Glass Menagerie* (1956), Anouilh's *Time Remembered* (1957), and O'Neill's *Long Day's Journey into Night* (1971). In 1964 she founded the Helen Hayes Repertory Company, which presented Shakespeare readings.

She did, however, return to the screen, notably as the Dowager Empress in *Anastasia* (1956) and as an eccentric stowaway in *Airport* (1970), for which she won an Oscar for Best Supporting Actress. She also appeared as Miss Marple, the prim but perceptive amateur detective, in several television versions of Agatha CHRISTIE's murder mysteries.

During a career that spanned more than 80 years Helen Hayes received many honours, including Oscars, Tony and Emmy Awards, the 1981 Lifetime Achievement Award from the Kennedy Center for the Performing Arts, and the 1981 Presidential Medal of Freedom. In 1955 New York's Fulton Theater was renamed in her honour. When this theatre was demolished in 1982, Broadway's Little Theater was renamed after her. She wrote two novels as well as three volumes of autobiography: *A Gift of Joy* (1965), *On Reflection* (1968), and *My Life in Three Acts* (1990).

Haywood, Eliza (*c.* 1693–1756) *British novelist and playwright*

Born Eliza Fowler, the daughter of a London merchant, she married Valentine Haywood in 1717 but was soon abandoned by him. Subsequently she supported herself and her two children by acting and writing. Her novels – she wrote nearly 40 between 1719 and 1730 – were often based on society scandals. Two of them, *Memoirs of a Certain Island Adjacent to Utopia* (1725) and *The Court of Carmania* (1727), contained such thinly disguised libellous portraits of her contemporaries that she was denounced by both Alexander Pope, in his poem *The Dunciad*, and by Jonathan Swift.

Haywood's later novels, notably *The History of Miss Betty Thoughtless* (1751) and *The History of Jemmy and Jenny Jessamy* (1753), were popular and widely read. She also wrote poetry and pieces for periodicals, such as *The Tea Table*. Between 1744 and 1746 she published the monthly periodical *The Female Spectator*, the first women's periodical to be edited by a woman.

Hayworth, Rita (1918–1987) *American film actress*

> Every man I've known has fallen in love with Gilda and wakened with me.
>
> —On the effect of her starring role in *Gilda* (1946)

A cousin of Ginger ROGERS, Rita Hayworth was the personification of glamour and beauty in the 1940s and 1950s.

Born Margarita Carmen Cansino in Brooklyn, New York, the daughter of a Spanish dancer and a Ziegfeld girl, she began dancing in her father's nightclub at the age of 13, progressing to small dancing parts in B-movies. In 1937 she married a promoter, Edward Judson, who changed her name, dyed her hair red, and used his influence to win her a contract with Columbia Pictures. She had starring roles in *Blood and Sand* (1941) and *Gilda* (1946), her best-known film, danced with Fred Astaire in *You'll Never Get Rich* (1941) and *You Were Never Lovelier* (1942), and starred with Gene Kelly in *Cover Girl* (1944), Columbia's first Technicolor musical.

In 1943 Hayworth married Orson Welles, who directed her and starred with her in *The Lady from Shanghai* (1948). In 1949, as her career began to decline, she married the "playboy prince" Aly Khan, a marriage condemned by the Vatican. Her later roles were unspectacular, except for her performance as a faded beauty in *Separate Tables* (1958), a role for which she was cast by her fifth husband, the producer James Hill. This was her last major role. She suffered alcoholic breakdowns and by 1982 was diagnosed as having Alzheimer's disease. Her life story was made into a television film, *The Love Goddess*, in 1983.

Head, Bessie (1937–1986) *South African-born Botswanian novelist*

Born in Pietermaritzburg, the daughter of a white mother and a black father, Bessie Head became one of southern Africa's most famous writers.

Brought up in a foster home, she became a teacher and married at a young age. In her early twenties she left her husband, fleeing to Botswana, where she worked as an agricultural labourer, to escape apartheid in South Africa. Her first novel, *When Rain Clouds Gather* (1968), tells this story.

Bessie Head's later novels, *Maru* (1971), *A Question of Power* (1974), and *A Bewitched Crossroad* (1984), deal with different aspects of the same theme of cultural surrender. *The Collector of Treasures* (1977) is a collection of short stories based on native folk tales. In 1981 she published a history of the village community in which she lived, *Serowe: Village of the Rain Wind*.

Head, Edith (1907–1981) *American costume designer*

Edith Head's costume designs for Hollywood films earned her eight Academy Awards – more than any individual except Walt Disney has ever won.

Born in Los Angeles, Edith Head was educated there at the University of California and at Stanford University, Palo Alto. She taught modern languages and art before joining Paramount as a costume designer, working on cowboy films, musicals, comedies, and classical dramas. She became their chief designer in 1938, the first woman to hold such a post.

Among her first successes were her

designs for Mae WEST's outfits in *She Done Him Wrong* (1933). Her first Academy Award was for her designs for *The Heiress* (1949). She continued to receive awards for her designs over the next quarter of a century: *All About Eve* (1950), *Samson and Delilah* (1950), *A Place in the Sun* (1951), *Roman Holiday* (1954), *The Facts of Life* (1960), and *The Sting* (1973) were all Academy Award winners.

In 1967 Head moved from Paramount to Universal Studios. By this time she was universally regarded as Hollywood's leading costume designer.

Hearst, Patricia (1954–) *American heiress*

Granddaughter of William Randolph Hearst, the flamboyant newspaper proprietor whose career inspired Orson Welles's film *Citizen Kane* (1941), Patty Hearst achieved notoriety after being kidnapped by terrorists belonging to the Symbionese Liberation Army (SLA).

The kidnap occurred in February 1974, while Patty was sitting in her flat with her boyfriend. After several weeks of captivity, during which she had apparently been brainwashed, she issued tape-recorded statements ridiculing American capitalism, of which her grandfather was the supreme example. She also participated in two bank robberies with members of the SLA, one of which was recorded on closed-circuit television.

Patty Hearst's ordeal with the SLA ended in September 1975, when she and a companion were captured in San Francisco by FBI agents. She was put on trial and convicted in March 1976 for bank robbery and the use of firearms. Sentenced to seven years' imprisonment, she spent three years behind bars before receiving a pardon from President Carter in February 1979. In 1982 she published a book about her ordeal, *Every Secret Thing*.

Heck, Barbara Ruckle (1734–1804) *Organizer of American Methodism*

Barbara Ruckle Heck, often known as the "Mother of American Methodism," was born in Ballingrane, County Limerick, Ireland, where she converted to Methodism at the age of 18. She and her husband, Paul Heck, were second-generation German refugees; in 1760 they emigrated to New York City with her cousin Philip Embury and his wife Margaret. In Ireland Embury, a carpenter, had been appointed as a preacher by John Wesley.

In 1766 Barbara Heck was so distressed by the way her companions' lives seemed to have strayed from what she regarded as a spiritual path that when she found them playing cards, she threw the cards into a fire. She then demanded that Embury should preach to her and their fellow immigrants to stop their decline into godlessness. Embury, inspired by her zeal, led a return to Methodism. In 1768 he helped to found a Wesleyan chapel at John Street in New York, thought to be the first such chapel in the colonies.

Following the guidance of John Wesley, the Hecks were Loyalists during the American Revolution. Consequently they were forced to move to Canada, first to Sorel near Montreal, then to Augusta, Ontario, where they remained until Barbara's death.

Heilbron, Dame Rose (1914–) *British lawyer and judge*

She was the first woman to serve as recorder in the crown court and only the second (after Elizabeth Lane) to be appointed a High Court judge. In 1974 she was created a DBE.

Rose Heilbron was educated at Belvedere School in Liverpool and graduated from Liverpool University in 1935 with a first-class honours degree. The following year she won a scholarship to Gray's Inn and embarked on a successful legal career, rising from barrister (1939) to King's Counsel (1949; Queen's Counsel from 1952). In 1956 she was appointed recorder of Burnley, the first female holder of such a post, and in 1974 she became a High Court judge in the family division, presiding over the northern circuit from 1979 to 1982. In 1975 she chaired the Home Secretary's Advisory Group on Rape.

Heilbron retired in 1988, after a career spanning over 50 years. She married Dr. Nathaniel Burstein in 1945;

their daughter Hilary followed in her mother's footsteps by becoming a barrister in 1971.

Helena, Saint (*c.* 255–330) *Mother of Emperor Constantine the Great*

According to tradition, Helena was born at Drepanon in Bithynia, an ancient region of Asia Minor south of the Black Sea, which became an important province of Rome in the 1st century BC. The daughter of an innkeeper, she was chosen as the concubine of Constantius Chlorus, who abandoned her for political reasons when he became Roman emperor. However, their son Constantine, at the beginning of his reign (306), gave her the title of Augusta, Dowager Empress, and under his influence she became a Christian in 312.

The 4th-century historian Eusebius of Caesarea writes that Helena made a pilgrimage to the Holy Land in 324 and arranged for the building of two basilicas: one at Bethlehem and the other on the Mount of Olives in Jerusalem. According to tradition, in Jerusalem she found the Holy Cross (the cross used to crucify Christ), the Holy Sepulchre (the tomb of Christ), and the nails that fastened Christ's body to the cross. No contemporary sources, however, mention these discoveries, the earliest reference being made by St. Ambrose in 395 in his funeral oration for Emperor Theodosius.

Helena died in Nicomedia, northwest Asia Minor. She was first buried in Rome, then transferred to Constantinople, and finally, in the 9th century, reburied in the Abbey of Hautvilliers in the archdiocese of Reims in France. Her feast is kept on August 18 in the Roman Catholic Church; her emblem is the cross.

Hellman, Lillian (1905–1984) *American playwright*

> I cannot and will not cut my conscience to fit this year's fashions, even though I long ago came to the conclusion that I was not a political person and could have no comfortable place in any political group.
>
> —Letter to the House Committee on Un-American Activities, *The Nation*, May 31, 1952

Widely regarded as the most accomplished woman playwright of her time, Lillian Hellman was born into a Jewish family in New Orleans and was educated in New York City, where she studied intermittently at Columbia and New York universities. From 1925 to 1928 she worked on the *New York Herald Tribune* as a reviewer and for MGM in Hollywood as a reader of plays (1927–30) and of scripts (1930–32). In 1925 she married the playwright Arthur Kober, but the marriage did not last. Subsequently she lived, until his death in 1966, with the detective writer Dashiell Hammett, who encouraged her to write.

She made a successful debut in the theatre with *The Children's Hour* (1934), about the havoc wrought by a child's malicious accusations of lesbianism among the staff of a girls' school. The play ran for 86 weeks on Broadway, but because of its subject matter was banned from several other cities. Her most celebrated achievement is her portrait of the rapacious Hubbard clan of the American South, chronicled in *The Little Foxes* (1939) and *Another Part of the Forest* (1946).

Hellman took up public themes – labour agitation, fascism, appeasement, and isolationism – in many of her plays, including the antifascist *Watch on the Rhine* (1941), which won the Critics' Circle Award, and *The Searching Wind* (1944). She visited Spain during the Civil War (1936–39) and travelled to Russia in 1944. During the era of the McCarthy witch-hunts both she and Hammett were called before the Un-American Activities Committee, but she refused to divulge any names, although she herself no longer had any communist sympathies. Her later plays include *The Autumn Garden* (1951), a study of the illusions of middle age, and *Toys in the Attic* (1960), an exposé of family love.

Lillian Hellman adapted most of her plays for the screen, notably *The Little Foxes* (1941) and *Another Part of the Forest* (1948). In 1955 she translated and adapted Anouilh's play about JOAN OF ARC, *The Lark*, for the stage and wrote much of the libretto for Leonard Bernstein's operetta *Candide*

(1956) with the poet Richard Wilbur and Dorothy PARKER. Her four volumes of memoirs are *An Unfinished Woman* (1969), *Pentimento: A Book of Portraits* (1973), *Scoundrel Time* (1976), and *Maybe* (1980). Parts of the first two volumes form the basis for the film *Julia* (1977), in which the character based on Hellman is played by Jane FONDA.

Héloïse (*c.* 1100–1164) *French abbess*

> I need not say more about the basic impossibility of combining matrimony and scholarship but think of the details...you are immersed in your theological or philosophical ideas, and at that moment the infants begin to squall...can your attention remain uninterrupted?
>
> —Words attributed to Héloïse by Peter Abelard in *Historia Calamitatum Abaelardi*

Héloïse is known for her love for her husband, Peter Abelard (1079–1142), the theologian and philosopher. Their correspondence, which was first published in Latin in 1616, tells of their passion for each other and its tragic consequences.

Héloïse was the brilliant niece of Canon Fulbert of Notre Dame, Paris. Because of her remarkable intelligence he arranged for her education under the guidance of Abelard at a time when it was very unusual for women to be educated. Abelard and Héloïse fell passionately in love, and as a result Héloïse gave birth to a son, Astralabe. Despite a secret marriage Fulbert was enraged by their deception, and they were forced to flee to Brittany. Héloïse found safety from his vindictive wrath by entering a convent at Argenteuil, but Abelard was less fortunate – Fulbert exacted his revenge by hiring thugs to castrate him (1118). Abelard, destroyed by shame, became a monk at the Abbey of St. Denis, persuading his wife to become a nun at Argenteuil, although she protested that her love for him was undiminished and far exceeded her love for God. In the end they both settled for the religious life. Abelard founded a Benedictine convent, the Paraclete, of which Héloïse became the abbess. He went on to become a famous theologian and philosopher.

By chance, 12 years later his account of their tragedy, *Historia Calamitatum Abaelardi*, was brought to her. In their ensuing correspondence Héloïse at first talked of her undying love for him, while he tried to turn her thoughts towards God. The later letters deal with monastic discipline. Admired for their style and erudition, the letters show both writers' interest in matters of faith and morality.

Under Héloïse's guidance the Paraclete convent became one of the most distinguished in France; she herself was known for her wisdom and learning.

Hemans, Felicia Dorothea (1793–1835) *British poet*

Felicia Hemans's poems, describing incidents of history and legend and portraying strong affection for country, home, family, and religion in a lyrical style, were very popular in her day. She was also admired by contemporary poets, including Wordsworth, Shelley, and Byron; Wordsworth described her as "that holy Spirit, sweet as the spring" in his *Extempore Effusion*. Although she is now seldom read, her poem "Casabianca," better known by its famous first line, "The boy stood on the burning deck," is often remembered.

Born Felicia Dorothea Browne in Liverpool, she began to write poetry as a child, publishing three volumes of poems between 1808 and 1812. In 1812 she married Captain Alfred Hemans. Six years later, shortly after the birth of the youngest of their five sons, Hemans travelled to Rome for his health but decided not to return to his family.

Mrs. Hemans was now obliged to make use of her writing to support her family, producing a large number of books of verse on a wide range of topics and in a wide range of styles. Among these are *The Siege of Valencia* (1823), *The Forest Sanctuary* (1825), *Records of Women* (1828), and *Songs of the Affections* (1830). She also wrote magazine stories and a play, *The Vespers of Palermo* (1823), which was promoted by her friend Sir Walter Scott.

In 1831 Felicia Hemans went to live with her brother in Dublin, where she died.

Henie, Sonja (1912–1969) *Norwegian-born American ice skater*

Best known for transforming figure skating with her balletic style, Sonja Henie also became a Hollywood film star.

Born in Oslo, and trained as a ballet dancer, Henie became a Norwegian champion skater at the age of ten. She won the women's world figure-skating title ten times between 1927 and 1936, winning the Olympic championship in 1928, 1932, and 1936. In 1932 and 1936 she took the Grand Slam, i.e., the Olympic, World, and European titles. In 1936 she turned professional and starred in touring ice-skating revues.

Between 1937 and 1945 Henie made ten films in Hollywood, including *One in a Million*, *Thin Ice*, and *My Lucky Star*. In 1941 she took American citizenship (her first two husbands were American), and in 1951 she began producing her own ice shows. She married the Norwegian shipowner Niels Onstad in 1956. Together they built up a large collection of impressionist and postimpressionist art, founding the Sonja Henie-Niels Onstad Art Centre in Oslo in 1968. Henie died of leukaemia in Oslo.

Henrietta Anne, Duchesse d'Orléans (1644–1670) *English princess*

The youngest daughter of King Charles I and HENRIETTA MARIA, Henrietta was the favourite sister of King Charles II and sister-in-law of King Louis XIV of France.

Born at Exeter, Devon, she was taken to France in 1646 to join her mother in exile during the English Civil War, which ended in the execution of her father. The restoration of Charles II in 1660 made possible her marriage in 1661 to Philippe, Duc d'Orléans, known as "Monsieur," the homosexual brother of Louis XIV of France.

Installed at the French court with the title of "Madame," Henrietta reacted to her husband's lack of interest by having affairs with the Comte de Guiche and with the king himself. In 1670 she travelled to England and played an important part in the negotiations between Louis XIV and Charles II regarding the Secret Treaty of Dover, which allied France and England against the Dutch. She died at St.-Cloud on June 30, 1670, immediately after returning to France. There was speculation that she had been poisoned, although peritonitis is a more likely explanation for her death at the early age of 26. Her two daughters were Marie-Louise, who married King Charles II of Spain, and Anne-Marie, who became queen of Sardinia.

Henrietta Maria (1609–1669) *Wife of King Charles I of England*

Henrietta Maria was born in Paris, the youngest child of King Henry IV of France and MARIE DE MÉDICIS. She was married by proxy to Charles on May 1, 1625, when she was 15 and he was 24. Her Roman Catholicism and preference for French favourites at court made her extremely unpopular in England. She supported Charles during the Civil War, raising funds for him in the Netherlands in 1642; this, combined with her unpopularity, helped to undermine the king's position and contributed to his downfall and execution in 1649.

Henrietta Maria had fled to France in 1644. She visited England at the Restoration in 1660 and again in 1662 but returned to France in 1665, dying four years later at Colombes, near Paris. She was the mother of two kings of England, Charles II and James II, and of HENRIETTA ANNE, who became the wife of Philippe, Duc d'Orléans, brother of Louis XIV of France.

Hepburn, Audrey (1929–1993) *Belgian-born American actress*

Audrey Hepburn was internationally famous for her elegance and beauty as well as for her elfin charm; her most memorable roles include the call girl Holly Golightly in *Breakfast at Tiffany's* (1961) and Eliza Doolittle in *My Fair Lady* (1964). In 1988 she became a goodwill ambassador for UNICEF, travelling extensively in the Third World, in recognition of which she was awarded the Jean Hersholt Humanitarian Award after her death.

Born Edda Van Heemstra Hepburn-Ruston in Brussels, the daughter of an Anglo-Irish banker and a Dutch baroness, she grew up mostly in London. She spent part of her childhood trapped (while on vacation) in Nazi-occupied Holland, where she carried messages for the Resistance. After the war she returned to London, winning a scholarship to the Ballet Rambert School.

In 1951 Hepburn was discovered by the French novelist COLETTE, who insisted that she star in the Broadway production of her book *Gigi*. The enthusiastic reviews led to a starring role in the Hollywood film *Roman Holiday*, with Gregory Peck, for which she won an Academy Award. In 1953 Hepburn married Mel Ferrer, winning a Tony Award in 1954 for her performance opposite her husband in a Broadway production of *Ondine*. She also appeared with Ferrer in the film *War and Peace* (1956), playing the part of Natasha. Subsequent films included *Funny Face* (1957), *The Nun's Story* (1959), *Two for the Road* (1966), and the thriller *Wait until Dark* (1967), which earned her an Oscar nomination.

Having divorced Ferrer in 1968, Hepburn married an Italian psychiatrist, Andrea Dotti, the following year and retired from the screen for eight years. She returned in *Robin and Marian* (1976) and appeared in the all-star thriller *Bloodline* in 1979. Her last major appearance, in the comedy *They All Laughed* (1980), was followed by a cameo role in *Always* (1989). She died of cancer in Tolochenaz, Switzerland.

Hepburn, Katharine (1907–)
American actress

> I find a woman's point of view much
> grander and finer than a man's.
>
> —*Newsweek*, November 10, 1969

Katharine Hepburn was the winner of four Academy Awards as Best Actress (the last when she was 74) and also received eight nominations. She was best known for her portrayals of assertive women of means – a role that she played out in real life as well.

Born into a privileged New England family in Hartford, Connecticut, she attended Bryn Mawr College before making her Broadway debut in 1928. Her later work included *The Philadelphia Story* (1939), *As You Like It* (1950), *The Millionairess* (1952), and the musicals *Coco* (1969) and *The West Side Waltz* (1981). In 1957 she appeared in *Much Ado about Nothing* and *The Merchant of Venice* at the American Shakespeare Festival in Stratford, Connecticut.

Hepburn made her film debut in George Cukor's *A Bill of Divorcement* (1932) and won instant critical acclaim, although not popularity – she was known as "Katharine of Arrogance" at RKO studios. The following year she received the first of her Oscars – for *Morning Glory* (1933). Her other notable films of this period were *Little Women* (1933), *Alice Adams* (1935), and the comedy *Bringing Up Baby* (1938) with Cary Grant.

In 1942 she costarred in the first of ten comedies – *Woman of the Year* – with Spencer Tracy, who was to become her friend and secret lover for 27 years. Their other films together include the comedies *Adam's Rib* (1949), *Pat and Mike* (1952), and *Desk Set* (1957) as well as *Guess Who's Coming to Dinner* (1967), for which Hepburn won her second Oscar. It is said that when shooting began on *Woman of the Year*, Hepburn remarked to Spencer Tracy "I'm rather tall for you, Mr. Tracy," to which he replied "Don't worry, I'll soon cut you down to size."

Later successes included *The African Queen* (1951) with Humphrey Bogart, *Suddenly Last Summer* (1959), and two more films in which she gave Oscar-winning performances: *The Lion in Winter* (1968; shared with Barbra STREISAND) and *On Golden Pond* (1981), in which she costarred with Henry Fonda.

On television Hepburn gave memorable performances in *The Glass Menagerie* (1973), *The Corn Is Green* (1979), *Mrs. Delafield Wants to Marry* (1986), and *The Man Upstairs* (1992). Her last appearance was in cable television's *One Christmas* (1994). Hepburn wrote two books, *The Making of "The African Queen"* (1987) and the autobiographical *Me: The Stories of My Life* (1991).

Hepworth, Dame Barbara (1903–1975) *British sculptor*

> However abstract, Hepworth's sculptures nearly always suggest a human presence or a relationship of one person to another.
>
> —Richard Calvocoressi, in *Makers of Modern Culture* (ed. Justin Wintle)

One of the foremost abstract sculptors of her time, Hepworth – together with artist Ben Nicholson and sculptor Henry Moore – led the abstract movement in Britain in the 1930s.

Born in Wakefield, Yorkshire, Barbara Hepworth trained at the Leeds School of Art before going on to attend the Royal College of Art in London (1921–24). She then studied in Rome and Florence for two years. She and her first husband, the sculptor John Skeaping, both became members of a radical artists' group, the Seven and Five Society. They had a son together before their marriage ended in divorce in 1931.

By this time Hepworth's work was receiving some critical acclaim. From 1931, when she met Ben Nicholson (whom she later married), her sculptures became increasingly abstract. For example, in this period she produced her pieces "Pierced Form" and "Reclining Figure" (both 1932). In 1933 she became a member of the Abstraction-Création association and the British Unit One group. Her work, now mostly in wood, became larger and more complex. With Nicholson she moved to St. Ives in Cornwall in 1939, a notable piece of this period being "Wave" (1943–44).

After her marriage to Ben Nicholson had ended in 1951, Hepworth began to work in bronze and stone, producing large pieces to be set in landscape – sometimes using organic shapes, sometimes geometric shapes. Examples of the latter include "Single Form" (1964) for the UN building, New York City, and the bronze "Four Square (Walk Through)" (1966). One of her last works was the nine-piece group "Family of Man" (1972). She died in a fire in her studio in St. Ives.

Barbara Hepworth was awarded the Grand Prix at the São Paulo Biennale in 1959 and was made a DBE in 1965.

Herodias (died *c.* 40 AD) *Wife of Herod Antipas, ruler of Galilee*

According to the Gospels of Matthew (14:1–12) and Mark (6:17–28) Herodias arranged the execution of St. John the Baptist.

Herodias was the mother of SALOME by her first husband, Herod Philip (half-brother of Herod Antipas). John the Baptist incurred Herodias's displeasure when he censured her marriage to Antipas as incestuous and therefore unlawful.

Determined to exact her revenge, Herodias persuaded Salome to ask for the head of John the Baptist on a platter when Antipas offered to grant Salome any wish for having pleased him with her dancing at his birthday celebration. Antipas was obliged to comply.

Eventually Herodias's ambitions for her husband led to his ruin. She persuaded Antipas to seek a royal title, which displeased the Roman emperor Caligula, who banished him.

Herschel, Caroline Lucretia (1750–1848) *German-born British astronomer*

Sister of the astronomer Sir William Herschel, whom she assisted in his work, Caroline Herschel was also recognized as a noted astronomer in her own right.

Born in Hanover, Caroline Herschel followed her brother William to England in 1772, where she embarked on a successful career as a soprano soloist in performances conducted by her brother. When in 1782 he became totally absorbed in astronomy, she followed his example – in fact they worked together on observational astronomy for the next 50 years. They began by building small telescopes to sell in order to finance their own larger instruments. Having discovered the planet Georgium Sidus, now known as Uranus, William was appointed Astronomer Royal in 1787; Caroline was nominated as his assistant. Between 1786 and 1797 she discovered eight comets and 14 nebulae: her Index to

Flamsteed's Observations of the Fixed Stars and a list of errors and corrections were published by the Royal Society in 1798.

After her brother's death in 1822 Caroline returned to Hanover and worked on the reorganization of his catalogue of nebulae. For this *Reduction and Arrangement in the Form of a Catalogue in Zones of all the Star Clusters and Nebulae Observed by Sir William Herschel* she was awarded the Gold Medal of the Royal Astronomical Society in 1828. In 1835 both she and the mathematician Mary SOMERVILLE were elected honorary members of the Royal Astronomical Society – the first women to receive this honour. Caroline also became a member of the Royal Irish Academy in 1838.

On her 96th birthday Caroline received a gold medal from the king of Prussia, and about a year later, shortly before she died, she received a copy of *Cape Observations* by her nephew Sir John Herschel from Cape Town, where he was continuing the work begun by his father and his aunt.

Hess, Dame Myra (1890–1965)
British pianist

Known especially for her piano transcription of the chorale from Bach's cantata no. 147 under the title "Jesu, Joy of Man's Desiring," Myra Hess also received acclaim for her lunchtime concerts in the National Gallery, London, during World War II.

Myra Hess was born in London, where at the age of 12 she won a scholarship to study at the Royal Academy of Music under Tobias Matthay. She made her debut in 1907 playing Beethoven's fourth piano concerto with Sir Thomas Beecham conducting; this performance enjoyed great success. Thereafter she toured Britain, Europe, and North America to equal acclaim. She also played chamber music and formed a piano duo with her cousin Irene Scharrer.

Known for her brilliant technique, Hess was also much admired for her sensitive interpretations of Mozart, Schumann, and Bach as well as Beethoven. She received honorary doctorates from Cambridge, London,

and several other universities. In 1941 she was made a DBE for her unfailing appearances at the National Gallery lunchtime concerts during the war, in spite of the frequent air raids taking place at that time.

Hesse, Eva (1936–1970) *German-born American sculptor*

Hesse's brilliantly original sculptures brought her international attention in the 1960s.

Eva Hesse emigrated with her Jewish family from Hamburg to the United States in 1939. The family settled in New York, where Eva studied at the Pratt Institute from 1952 to 1953 and at the Cooper Union from 1954 until 1957.

Eva married Tom Doyle in 1962 and the couple lived for some time in Germany. After returning to the United States, she travelled to Mexico and taught at the New York School of Visual Art. Her strange sculptures, created from a variety of unusual materials, including rubber, plastic, and string, were widely exhibited during the 1960s and 1970s.

Highsmith, Patricia (1921–1995)
American crime writer

Patricia Highsmith is best known for her psychological thrillers featuring the gentleman murderer Tom Ripley, who first appeared in her third novel, *The Talented Mr. Ripley* (1955); for this book she was awarded the Edgar Allen Poe Scroll by the Mystery Writers of America.

She was born in Fort Worth, Texas, and educated at Columbia University. Her first novel, *Strangers on a Train* (1950), was made into a successful film thriller by Alfred Hitchcock in 1951. In 1963 she moved to Europe, where she had a cult following, settling in Italy, France, and finally Switzerland, where she lived alone with her cats.

Highsmith's later novels featuring Tom Ripley include *Ripley under Ground* (1971), *Ripley's Game* (1974), and *Ripley under Water* (1991). Among her other books are *The Price of Salt* (1952), which she wrote under the pen name Claire Morgan, and *The Animal Lover's Book of Beastly Murders* (1975), about animals killing humans.

She also wrote several volumes of short stories.

Hilda, Saint (614–680) *English abbess*

Hilda was baptized with her kinsman King Edwin of Northumbria by Paulinus, the first Archbishop of York, in 627. She studied monasticism under Bishop Aidan, a famous Celtic monk, and in 649 became abbess of Hartlepool Abbey in northeast England, a double monastery of monks and nuns. In 657 Hilda founded a double monastery herself at Whitby, Yorkshire, on land donated by King Oswiu, Edwin's successor, where she ruled wisely for 22 years.

Five of her monks became bishops, one of whom was St. Wilfrid of York. She also encouraged the monk Caedmon, England's first Christian poet, in his literary efforts. Her monastery became an important centre of learning and was host in 664 to the famous Synod of Whitby, which rejected Celtic ecclesiastical customs in favour of the Roman reforms of Theodore of Tarsus. Hilda herself had favoured the Celtic position. She died at Whitby. Her feast day is November 17.

Hildegard, Saint (1098–1179) *German mystic and scholar*

Abbess of the Benedictine convent of Bingen, west Germany, Hildegard was known as the "Sybil of the Rhine" because of her great learning and spiritual powers. Although never officially canonized, she has been commonly regarded as a saint since the 15th century.

Born into a noble family in the Rhineland of Germany, Hildegard was entrusted at the age of eight to the care of the Blessed Jutta's community, which was attached to the abbey of St. Disibod in Diessenberg. In 1136 she succeeded Jutta as prioress and after 1147 moved her community to Bingen, where she became abbess. She also founded several other convents.

Hildegard claimed that from infancy God had given her visions in which her soul beheld the "shade of living light," a reflection of things past, present, and future. Twenty-six of her visions were collected in the *Scivias* (1141–52; "Scivias" is an abbreviated form of *Eciens vias Domini*, the one who knows the ways of the Lord). Considering her gift of visions not only a personal revelation but a vocation to reform the world, she travelled widely, giving spiritual advice to laymen as well as to church dignitaries and emperors. Her correspondents included four popes, two emperors, King Henry II of England, and St. Bernard of Clairvaux. She was a pioneer in science and left several works on medicine and natural history, including the *Liber subtilitatum* (Book of Subtleties), *De simplicines medicae* (On Healing Herbs), and the *Liber divinorum operum* (1163–74; Book of Divine Works).

Hildegard was also an accomplished artist and musician: she wrote what is thought to be the earliest surviving Mass music composed by a woman. Much of this only became widely known in the 1980s and 1990s, when recordings of her work attracted considerable popularity. Her feast is kept in Germany on September 17.

Hill, Octavia (1838–1912) *British social reformer*

Octavia Hill founded many organizations and programmes for dealing with the problems of the urban poor. She also campaigned for the preservation of open spaces, becoming in 1895 one of the cofounders, with Sir Robert Hunter and Canon Hardwicke Rawnsley, of the National Trust.

Born in Wisbech, Cambridgeshire, she was influenced by the sanitary reform work of her grandfather Thomas Southwood Smith and by the Christian Socialism of Frederick Maurice. In 1856 Miss Hill became secretary of the women's classes at Maurice's Working Men's College and in 1869 founded the Charity Organization Society with him. The work of this organization spread to Europe and the United States. She helped orginate the case-study approach in social work by looking at the individual's problems in the context of his or her environment.

Aided by the art critic and writer John Ruskin, Miss Hill purchased three houses in a London slum in 1865 and set up an experiment in housing management that stressed joint responsibility of tenant and manager. Her work expanded until ultimately she was managing some 6,000 dwellings. The Society of Women Housing Managers grew out of this. From 1905 to 1908 she served with Beatrice WEBB on the Poor Law Commission. Her books included *Homes of the London Poor* (1875) and *Our Common Land* (1878).

Hiller, Dame Wendy (1912–)
British actress

Wendy Hiller's successful career on stage and screen spanned over 55 years.

Born in Bramhall, Cheshire, Wendy Hiller made her London debut in Ronald Gow's adaptation of *Love on the Dole* in 1935 after working with the Manchester Repertory Theatre for five years. Her performance was such a success in both London and (a year later) in New York that George Bernard Shaw asked her to play the title role in his *St. Joan* and Eliza Doolittle in his *Pygmalion* at the Malvern Festival in 1936. Her Eliza Doolittle reached a wider public when she went on to play the role in the 1938 film version starring Leslie Howard as Professor Higgins. This remarkably successful British film, in which Howard and Hiller gave memorable performances highly regarded by Shaw himself, was withdrawn in 1964 when the musical version *My Fair Lady* was released.

In 1937 Hiller married the dramatist Ronald Gow and gave an acclaimed performance in his adaptation of Thomas Hardy's *Tess of the D'Urbervilles*. Throughout the 1940s Hiller performed on both the London and New York stages; a notable New York performance was the title role of *The Heiress*, an adaptation of Henry James's *Washington Square*. Hiller's film successes of this period include an adaptation of another Shaw play, *Major Barbara*, and *I Know Where I'm Going* (1945). Later stage performances include the roles of Isobel in the New York City production of Robert Bolt's *Flowering Cherry* (1959) and Miss Tina in Henry James's *The Aspern Papers* (1962). In London she

played Gunhild Borkman in Ibsen's *John Gabriel Borkman* (1975–76) and Lady Bracknell in Wilde's *The Importance of Being Earnest* (1987).

Wendy Hiller's later films include *Separate Tables* (1958), for which she received an Academy Award, and *A Man for All Seasons* (1966). She continued to work on radio and television into the 1990s. In 1975 she was created a DBE.

Hippius, Zinaida Nikolayevna (1867–1945) *Russian writer*

Hippius is best known for her symbolist poetry and for literary criticism written under the pen name Anton Krainy.

Born in Belev, Tula, in west central Russia, she married the poet Dmitry Merezhkovsky in 1889. Together they maintained a salon for writers, intellectuals, and philosophers in St. Petersburg. She was also instrumental in founding a philosophical journal in 1903. Although Hippius and Merezhkovsky originally sympathized with the revolutionary movement, they were bitterly opposed to the Bolshevik Revolution of 1917. Their anti-Soviet views were so strong that they emigrated to Paris, in about 1919, where they became highly influential in émigré circles.

In addition to her poetry and literary criticism Hippius also wrote plays, stories, novelettes, and a superb volume of memoirs, *Zhivye litsa* (1925; Living Faces). Her finest poems were published as *Sobraniye stikhov* (1904–1910; Collected Poems) and *Siyaniya* (1938; Radiances).

Hite, Shere D. (1943–) *American writer, feminist, and sex researcher*

Hite's bestselling books about male and female sexuality in America caused a sensation when they were first published in the late 1970s and 1980s.

Born in St. Joseph, Missouri, Shere Hite was brought up by her grandparents. She worked as a model after studying history at Florida and Columbia Universities. Her first prominent role in the burgeoning feminist movement was as director (1972–78) of the National Organization for Women (NOW) in New York City. She also lectured for various women's groups and at several universities, and became a consultant editor on journals concerning sex education and sexuality.

From 1970 onwards Hite researched sexuality by means of detailed and explicit questionnaires. In 1974 she published *Sexual Honesty: By Women For Women*. Her second book on the subject, *The Hite Report: A Nationwide Study of Female Sexuality* (1976), sold two million copies. The book overturned many traditional assumptions about female sexuality, most notably with its emphasis on clitoral orgasm and its assertion that for many women penetrative intercourse was by no means the central sex act. Five years later she published *The Hite Report on Male Sexuality*, followed in 1987 by *The Hite Report on Women*. Her feminist views are seen at their most radical in *The Hite Report on the Family: Growing Up Under Patriarchy* (1994). This book received such a hostile reception from U.S. critics that Hite decided to leave America for Europe. Hite's critics allege that her statistics and sampling methods are flawed; yet it is indisputable that she has changed our ideas about sex by using genuine information provided by real people.

Hobby, Oveta Culp (1905–1995) *American newspaper publisher and public official*

In 1953 Oveta Hobby became only the second woman to hold a post in the U.S. cabinet.

Born Oveta Culp in Killeen, Texas, she studied at Mary Hardin Baylor College and the University of Texas law school. After graduating, she became the first woman to sit in the Texas House of Representatives, serving from 1926 until 1931. In 1931 she married William Pettus Hobby, owner of the *Houston Post*, and joined that newspaper as research editor, becoming executive vice-president and editor in 1938.

During World War II Hobby was chief of the women's interest section of the War Department Bureau of Public Relations, and in 1942 she was appointed the first director of the newly created Women's Auxiliary Army Corps (later the Women's Army Corps). She served as a colonel until 1945, becoming the first woman to earn the Distinguished Service Medal.

In 1953 Hobby was appointed to the newly established cabinet post of secretary of health, education, and welfare by President Eisenhower. After resigning in 1955, she returned to the *Houston Post* as editor and president, becoming in 1965 chair of the board, a position she held until she sold the newspaper in 1983. One of the country's wealthiest women, she died in Houston.

Höch, Hannah (1889–1978) *German artist*

A member of the short-lived Berlin dada movement, Hannah Höch created a remarkable series of photomontages during the years of the Weimar Republic (1918–33). Her work, and that of such fellow dadaists as John Heartfield, George Grosz, and Raoul Hausmann, helped to promote the medium of photomontage as a major art form, still practised by many artists at the end of the 20th century.

Born Joanne Höch in Gotha, the eldest of five children, she was taken out of school at the age of 15 to care for her younger sister, Marianne. With her parents' support, in 1912 she went to Berlin to study at the School of Applied Arts in Berlin-Charlottenburg for two years, later enrolling under Emil Orlik at the State Museum of Applied Arts in Berlin. To support herself while studying, Höch took part-time work at Berlin's major newspaper and magazine publisher, Ullstein Verlag. From 1916 to 1926 she worked as a pattern designer in the handicrafts department, which produced brochures on knitting, crocheting, and embroidery and a two-page spread on women's handicrafts for the fashionable women's magazine *Die Dame*. Many of Höch's subsequent photomontages contained images taken from Ullstein press periodicals.

In 1915 Höch met the Viennese artist Raoul Hausmann, with whom she began an affair that lasted until 1922. The two made their first photomontages in 1918. Through Hausmann,

Höch became acquainted with the experimental artists of the avant-garde Berlin dada movement and took part in all of their major exhibitions, including the First International Dada-Messe ("Dada Fair") in 1920. Produced at a time of great change and growth in the mass media, Höch's work was less overtly political than that of her fellow dadaists; she also showed drawings and paintings in exhibitions rather than through the mass distribution channels they favoured.

During the mid 1920s Höch became a key figure in the constructivist movement in abstract art, which included László Moholy-Nagy, Theo van Doesburg, and Kurt Schwitters, who became her close friend. From 1926 to 1929 she lived in Holland, exhibiting at the acclaimed "Film and Photo" exhibition in Stuttgart in 1929, before returning to Berlin in 1930. In 1938 Höch married the businessman and pianist Kurt Matthies (they divorced in 1944). Although her work found less interest, she continued to exhibit in museums and galleries internationally until her death in West Berlin.

Hodgkin, Dorothy Crowfoot (1910–1994) *British chemist and crystallographer*

Known for her work on the use of x-ray diffraction to determine the structure of molecules, Dorothy Hodgkin helped to determine the structure of penicillin in the 1940s and of vitamin B_{12} in the early 1950s. She was awarded the Nobel Prize for Chemistry in 1964, the third woman (and the first British woman) to receive this honour. She was admitted to the Order of Merit in 1965, the first woman to be so honoured since Florence NIGHTINGALE.

Born in Cairo, where her father was in the Egyptian ministry of education, Dorothy Crowfoot was educated at Oxford University (1928–31). Having moved to Cambridge to study for her doctorate, she began her work in x-ray crystallography under the Irish crystallographer John Bernal. She returned to Oxford to join the faculty in 1934. In 1937 she married the African-

ist Thomas Hodgkin; the couple went on to have three children.

Hodgkin's detailed x-ray analysis of cholesterol was a milestone in the field of crystallography at a time when such work was slow and tedious. From 1948 to 1956 she was occupied in determining the structure of vitamin B_{12}, vital in controlling pernicious anaemia; it was for this work that she received the Nobel Prize. She then turned to analysing the complex three-dimensional structure of insulin using sophisticated computers, which were by then available (even so, it took nearly 35 years to finally accomplish this task). She also carried out research on other compounds, including vitamin D.

Dorothy Hodgkin was elected to the Royal Society in 1947 and received their Royal and Copley Medals. In 1957 she was a founder of the Pugwash Conference on Science and World Affairs. From 1960 to 1977 she was the first Wolfson Research Professor of the Royal Society. Other honours awarded her included membership in the Russian Academy of Science (1976) and the Dimitriou Award (1984). She was also Chancellor of Bristol University from 1970 to 1988.

Hoffman, Malvina (1887–1966) *American sculptor*

Malvina Hoffman is known principally for her 101 bronze figures of ethnic types, commissioned in 1929 for the Hall of Man in the Museum of Natural History, Chicago.

The daughter of the composer and pianist Richard Hoffman, she was born in New York City. In 1919 she travelled to Europe to train with the sculptor Auguste Rodin, who sent her to study in the local medical school so that she would have a detailed grasp of human anatomy. She created sculptures of her friends in the artistic circles in which she moved in the years before World War I; notable among these are her likenesses of Anna PAVLOVA and the pianist Ignace Paderewski.

In 1930 Hoffman started work on her commission for the Chicago museum, which she completed in 1933.

Her book *Heads and Tails* (1936) tells the fascinating story of her worldwide travels with her husband, the musician Samuel Grimson, researching ethnic types. She also published a book on sculptural techniques, *Sculpture Inside and Out*, in 1937. She continued to work into her old age.

Hogg-Priestly, Helen Battles Sawyer (1905–1993) *American-born Canadian astronomer*

Helen Hogg-Priestly was an internationally recognized expert on variable stars within globular star clusters, devoting her career to cataloguing them in the *International Astronomical Almanac*.

Born in Lowell, Massachusetts, she graduated from Mount Holyoke College, Massachusetts, in 1926 and became interested in star clusters while doing research for her doctorate at Radcliffe College. In 1935 she and her first husband, Frank Hogg, became affiliated with the University of Toronto. A year later she became a lecturer and research assistant, spending much of her time at the David Dunlop Observatory, Ontario. In 1950 she was awarded the Annie J. Cannon Prize of the American Astronomical Society for her work. In 1957 she became a professor of astronomy, being named professor emeritus on her retirement from the post in 1976. On the death of her husband in 1951 she took over the writing of his popular weekly newspaper column on astronomy in the *Toronto Daily Star*, keeping it going for a further 30 years. In 1985 she married Francis E. L. Priestly, who died in 1988.

In 1967 Hogg-Priestly received the Rittenhouse Silver Medal and in 1976 was made a Companion of the Order of Canada. In 1984 Asteroid 2917, which had been discovered in 1980, was renamed Asteroid Sawyer Hogg after her. She was the author of many scholarly works, including *The Stars Belong to Everyone* (1976).

Holiday, Billie (1915–1959) *American jazz singer*

Billie Holiday is considered one of the greatest jazz singers of all time. Her inimitable phrasing – singing slightly behind the beat – gave her songs an air of wistfulness that was purely instinctive, for she had no training or technical knowledge.

Born Eleanora Fagan in Philadelphia, she was raised in Baltimore and New York City, calling herself "Billie" after the film star Billie Dove and "Holiday" after her father, Clarence Holiday, a top jazz guitarist. She first heard jazz recordings of Louis Armstrong and Bessie SMITH when she was working in a brothel. Having escaped from there, she worked as a singer in various Harlem nightclubs until she was discovered by the legendary record producer John Hammond, who introduced her in 1933 to Benny Goodman, with whose band she made her first recordings.

Between 1935 and 1942 Holiday made over 100 records with various small jazz groups, mostly featuring the pianist Teddy Wilson. She also sang with the Count Basie Orchestra (1937) and Artie Shaw's band (1938), and made recordings with the saxophonist Lester Young. By the end of the 1930s she had become a big star, and she turned to solo cabaret work from 1940. In the 1940s she appeared in several films, including *New Orleans* (1947) with Louis Armstrong. In 1946 she gave her first solo concert in New York's Town Hall.

In spite of her success as a singer, Holiday's personal life was unhappy. Her early poverty and exposure to racial discrimination were followed by a brief marriage to the trumpeter Joe Guy. By 1947 she was hopelessly addicted to heroin, which led to periods in hospital and spells of imprisonment on narcotics charges. Nevertheless, she appeared on television in *The Sound of Jazz* (1957) and toured Europe in the 1950s; her ghosted autobiography, *Lady Sings the Blues* (1956), was also the title of a biographical film (1973) starring Diana ROSS.

Eventually Holiday succumbed to her addiction; she was admitted to hospital in New York and arrested on her deathbed for the possession of narcotics – a charge widely believed to be false.

Holland, Agnieszka (1948–) *Polish film director and screenwriter*

A leading figure in the Polish "New Wave" movement during the 1970s, Agnieszka Holland, who is of Polish Jewish descent, graduated from the Prague Film School in 1971. She then worked as an assistant director on Krystof Zanussi's *Illumination* (1973), making her debut as director of a feature film the following year with *Evening at Abdan's*.

From 1972 to 1981 Holland was a member of a film production group in Warsaw led by the director Andrzej Wajda. During this time she worked with Wajda on several of his films. She became widely known when her own film, *Provincial Actors* (1979), tied for the International Critics' Prize at Cannes in 1980; it was followed by *The Fever* (1980) and *The Lonely Woman* (1981). *The Story of a Bomb* (1981), about Polish resistance to imperial Russia, was banned under the martial law imposed in December 1981; thereupon Holland left Poland for Paris to escape repression. She then directed documentaries for French television and worked with Wajda on his historical drama *Danton* (1982). Her *Angry Harvest* (1985), based on the events leading up to the murder of the Polish dissident priest Father Jerzy Popieluszko, was made in Germany.

Holland returned to Poland after the political reforms of 1989. Her later films include *Europa, Europa* (1991), about a Jewish boy who pretends throughout the war to be a Hitler Youth, and *Oliver, Oliver* (1993); both these films were based on true stories. Her delightful version of Frances Hodgson BURNETT's children's classic *The Secret Garden* (1993) was highly acclaimed in the West, but *Total Eclipse* (1996), about the French poets Verlaine and Rimbaud, received poor reviews.

Holm, Hanya (1893–1992) *German-born American dancer and choreographer*

A pioneer of modern dance, Hanya Holm is best known for the dances she created for Broadway musicals, including *Kiss Me, Kate* (1948), which won the New York Drama Critics Award for choreography, *My Fair Lady* (1956), and *Camelot* (1960).

Born Johanna Eckert in Worms, Germany, she studied dance with the Swiss composer Emile Jacques-Dalcroze. From 1921 she danced with Mary Wigman's company and taught at the Wigman Institute in Dresden. In 1931 she was sent by Wigman to open a branch of her school in New York, but after five years Holm abandoned Wigman's angular emotional style. She then gave the school her own name, developing a dance technique that gave more emphasis to speed, precision, and rhythm. She also taught at the Bennington College Summer School of Dance in Vermont from 1934 to 1939. In 1941 she established the Colorado College Summer Dance School, which she directed until 1983.

Holm's masterpiece *Trend* (1937) was an avant-garde dance visualization of Edgard Varèse's work *Ionization*, for which the stage was extended over the orchestra pit, enabling the dancers to form floor patterns visible from above. Her *Metropolitan Daily* (1938) is thought to have been the first modern dance work to be televised.

In 1948 Holm created a number of dances for the Broadway show *Ballet Ballads*, the success of which led to her later highly popular Broadway work. She also choreographed for opera and the screen. When she took out a copyright on her dances for *Kiss Me, Kate* in 1952, she became the first choreographer to copyright a dance routine.

Holtby, Winifred (1898–1935) *British writer and feminist*

A vigorous campaigner for feminist, pacifist, and egalitarian causes, she was also known as a novelist, especially for her last and most popular work, *South Riding*, published posthumously in 1936. In the last years of her short life she suffered from a progressive kidney disease, which ultimately caused her death.

Born into an old Yorkshire farming family, Winifred Holtby was educated at Queen Margaret's School, Scarborough, and Somerville College, Oxford. Her university studies were interrupted by a period of service in the Women's Army Auxiliary Corps in France (1918–19), but she subsequently returned to Oxford and graduated two years later with an honours degree in modern history. She made her home in London, working as a freelance journalist and lecturing on international political and social problems, with particular emphasis on feminist issues.

In the mid 1920s Holtby travelled in Europe and South Africa, where she was struck by the oppression and injustice suffered by the black workforce. On her return to Britain she became a director of the left-wing periodical *Time and Tide* and used this new position to further her campaigns for world peace and equal rights for all.

Holtby's first novel was *Anderby Wold* (1923), set in her native Yorkshire on an East Riding farm where progressive methods have begun to clash with time-honoured tradition. It was followed by *The Crowded Street* (1924), *The Land of Green Ginger* (1927), *Poor Caroline* (1931), and *Mandoa, Mandoa!* (1933), set in northeast Africa. Her last novel, *South Riding* (1936), is the work for which she is now remembered: an intimate portrait of a Yorkshire community, it won the James Tait Black Memorial Prize. She also wrote short stories, notably the collection *Truth is Not Sober* (1934); several plays; and a critical study of Virginia WOOLF. Her close friendship with the writer Vera BRITTAIN is recorded in the latter's *Testament of Friendship* (1940) and in *Selected Letters of Winifred Holtby and Vera Brittain 1920–1935* (1960).

Hopper, Grace Murray (1906–1992) *American computer scientist and naval officer*

Internationally known for her pioneering work in developing computer technology, Grace Hopper played an important role in the development of COBOL (common business-oriented language).

Born Grace Murray in New York City, she graduated in mathematics and physics from Vassar College, Poughkeepsie, in 1928. In 1930 she married Vincent Hopper; although they were divorced 15 years later, she retained her married name. In 1936 she went on to Yale University, where she was awarded a PhD. After returning to Vassar to teach mathematics, Hopper joined the U.S. Naval Reserve as a lieutenant in 1943.

A year later she was assigned to the Bureau of Ordnance's Computation Project at Harvard, where she worked on Mark I, the first large-scale automatic calculator – forerunner of the electronic computer. Remaining in the Naval Reserve, Hopper continued to work as a research fellow at Harvard; during this period she coined the word "bug" for an inexplicable computer failure. (In the first instance, it is said, she was referring to a moth that had accidentally invaded Mark I's circuits.)

In 1949 Hopper joined Eckert-Mauchly Computer Corporation as a senior mathematician. There she designed a new program for converting instructions into machine-readable codes. She stayed with the company through two takeovers, in 1957 being part of the team that developed the first English-language data-processing compiler, called Flow-matic. This provided a basis for the programming language COBOL. In 1962 she was elected a fellow of the Institute of Electrical and Electronic Engineers. She retired as a commander in the Naval Reserve in 1966 but was recalled to active duty a year later to help standardize the Navy's computer languages. When she finally retired with the rank of rear admiral in 1986, at the age of 80, she was the oldest officer in active service. She then joined the Digital Equipment Corporation as a senior consultant.

In 1969 Hopper became the Data Processing Management Association's first computer science Man of the Year. In 1991 President George Bush awarded her the National Medal of Technology. She was inducted into the National Women's Hall of Fame in 1994.

Hopper, Hedda (1885–1966) *American actress and gossip columnist*

Noted for her biting wit and flamboyant hats, Hedda Hopper wrote a Hollywood gossip column that was credited, during its 28-year run, with being able to create or destroy a star.

Born Elda Furry in Hollidaysburg, Pennsylvania, she studied piano and singing in Pittsburgh before making her stage debut in 1907. She was working as a Broadway chorus girl in 1913 when she married the actor DeWolf Hopper. She then moved to Hollywood and had a successful career, appearing in such silent films as *Wings* (1927) and *The Last of Mrs. Cheyney* (1929).

In 1936 Hedda Hopper began to host a radio chat show; two years later she embarked on a second, extremely successful career as a gossip columnist. With its scandal and chit-chat about the Hollywood stars challenging that of the veteran Hollywood gossip Louella PARSONS, Hopper's column was syndicated to 3,000 daily and 2,000 weekly newspapers. Hedda Hopper supported many right-wing causes and was known for her lifelong personal vendettas against, among others, Constance Bennett and Elsa Maxwell. Her Beverly Hills mansion was known as "the house that fear built." Hopper also published two best-selling autobiographical books, *Under My Hat* (1952) and *The Whole Truth and Nothing But* (1963).

Horne, Lena (Calhoun) (1917–) *American singer and actress*

Lena Horne enjoyed a long and successful career in the theatre and as a nightclub and cabaret singer. Her glamour, powerful voice, and sensual presence have made her an immensely popular entertainer.

Born and educated in Brooklyn, New York, Lena Horne, encouraged by her mother, made her debut at the age of 16 in the chorus line at Harlem's legendary Cotton Club. In 1934 she made her Broadway debut in *Dance with Your Gods*, but she gradually changed from dancing to singing with a band. In 1942, while singing in a Hollywood nightclub, she won a contract with MGM, the first black artist to be given a long-term film contract. She appeared in the musicals *Cabin in the Sky*, with Ethel WATERS, and *Stormy Weather* (both 1943) and made guest appearances in several other musicals.

Influenced by her grandmother, an active campaigner for both women's rights and black rights from the 1890s to the 1930s, Horne fought against racism throughout her career. During the McCarthy era she was accused of communism, along with her friend the African-American actor and civil rights activist Paul Robeson, but was never officially charged. In the late 1950s she left Hollywood, subsequently making only three more films.

During the 1980s Horne's one-woman Broadway show was the longest running one-person show in Broadway history. She has also written two volumes of memoirs, *In Person* (1951) and *Lena* (1965).

Horne, Marilyn (1934–) *American opera singer*

Known for the range of her voice, Marilyn Horne excelled in singing both mezzo-soprano and soprano roles.

Born in Bradford, Pennsylvania, and brought up there and in California, she attended the University of Southern California on a singing scholarship. It was there that she met her future husband, the conductor Henry Lewis. She was still a student when her singing voice was used on the soundtrack of the film *Carmen Jones* (1955), starring Dorothy Dandridge. She made her debut as Háta in Smetana's *The Bartered Bride* in Los Angeles in 1954.

From 1956 to 1959 Horne sang in Europe, appearing as Marie in Alban Berg's *Wozzeck* in San Francisco in 1960 (a role she repeated at Covent Garden in London in 1964). She and Joan SUTHERLAND made their New York City debuts together in February 1961 in the American Opera Society's concert version of Bellini's *Beatrice di Tenda*. Horne made her Metropolitan Opera debut in 1970, as Adalgisa in a production of Bellini's *Norma*, with Joan Sutherland in the title role; she later gave highly successful performances at the "Met" in *Carmen*, *The*

Barber of Seville, and *The Italian Girl in Algiers*. She also helped to revive interest in the operas of Rossini, Bellini, and Donizetti. Her autobiography *Marilyn Horne, My Life*, which she wrote with Jane Scovell, appeared in 1983.

Horney, Karen (1885–1952) *German-born American psychoanalyst*

> It seems to me impossible to judge to how great a degree the unconscious motives for the flight from womanhood are reinforced by the actual social subordination of women.
> —"The Flight from Womanhood,"
> *Feminine Psychology* (1926)

Strongly critical of classical Freudian theory, Karen Horney developed a new and controversial approach to psychoanalysis.

Born Karen Danielssen in Hamburg, she studied medicine, despite the disapproval of her father, at Freiburg and Göttingen universities, completing her medical training in Berlin with a thesis on traumatic psychosis. In 1909 she married Oscar Horney, a fellow student, with whom she had three daughters. She studied psychoanalysis with Karl Abraham, a friend and follower of Freud, subsequently practising and teaching in Berlin. At this time she began to challenge Freud's view of human nature and focused on feminine psychology. Separated from her husband in 1926, in 1932 she moved to the United States, becoming a U.S. citizen in 1938.

Horney became a mainstay of the neo-Freudians; in 1937 she wrote *The Neurotic Personality of Our Time*, in which she attacked Freudian antifeminism. *New Ways in Psychoanalysis* (1939) was a far-reaching reinterpretation of Freudian concepts. While she recognized the importance of early childhood experiences in determining neurotic conflicts, she contended that the analyst must also be aware of current fears and impulses. She also stressed the necessity of understanding the environmental context in which neurotic conflicts are expressed. Her view of human beings allowed much more scope for development and ratio-

nal adaptation than Freudian determinism permitted. These controversial views led to her expulsion from the New York Psychoanalytic Society in 1941, but the same year she founded the Association for the Advancement of Psychoanalysis and the American Institute of Psychoanalysis.

Karen Horney was the editor of the *American Journal of Psychoanalysis*. Her own publications include *Our Human Conflicts* (1945) and *Neurosis and Human Growth* (1950). Before her death from abdominal cancer, she learned that the Karen Horney Clinic was to be opened in New York.

Horniman, Annie (1860–1937) *British theatre manager and patron*

A supporter of the Irish theatre movement and the founder of repertory theatre in England, Annie Horniman, a flamboyant monocled character, had been passionate about the stage since her teenage years.

She was born in Forest Hill, London, the daughter of a wealthy tea merchant who, as a Quaker, disapproved strongly of the theatre. She studied at the Slade School of Art in London. While travelling abroad during her vacations she saw the plays of Ibsen performed in Germany, which inspired her to use her family money to sponsor the theatre.

Having met the Irish poet and playwright W. B. Yeats, in 1903 she decided to move to Ireland, where she took over an old Dublin theatre and financed its rebuilding as the Abbey Theatre, which opened the following year. Here she financed the first staging of Yeats's *The Land of Heart's Desire* and with J. M. Synge and Lady GRE-GORY was instrumental in bringing about a renaissance of the Irish theatre. She acted as unpaid secretary to Yeats until 1907, when she quarrelled with him and returned to Manchester.

In Manchester Horniman bought and reconstructed the Gaiety Theatre, where she ran her own repertory company until 1917. Here she staged plays by George Bernard Shaw, who held her in very high esteem. At the Gaiety she also put on performances of the classics as well as plays by such local writers as Harold Brighouse and Allan Monkhouse, who were integral to what became known as the "Manchester School." Although the venture failed financially in 1917 and the theatre was sold in 1921, the idea of repertory theatre was copied in many other British cities. Sybil THORNDIKE and her husband, the director Lewis Casson, were among the members of Annie Horniman's company who went on to highly acclaimed careers in the theatre. On her retirement Horniman donated her library of plays to the British Drama League.

Hosmer, Harriet Goodhue (1830–1908) *American sculptor*

Born in Watertown, Massachusetts, Harriet Hosmer studied clay modelling in Boston and anatomy at the medical school of St. Louis University. In 1852 she moved to Rome, where she studied with the British sculptor John Gibson, remaining there working on commissions for many years before returning to the United States.

Hosmer became the most successful sculptor of her day. One of her first commissions was a statue of the tragic Beatrice CENCI, made in 1857 for the Mercantile Library of St. Louis, Missouri. More light-hearted subjects include "Will-o'-the-Wisp," "Sleeping Faun," and "Puck." The purchase of "Puck" by the Prince of Wales (later King Edward VII) made it so popular that it was reproduced 30 times. A bronze cast of a statue she made of the American artist Thomas Hart Benton stands in Lafayette Park, St. Louis. "Zenobia," her best-known work, is in the Metropolitan Museum of Art, New York.

Hosmer exhibited in London in 1862 and in the United States two years later. She spent much of her time in England and was a friend of the poet Elizabeth Barrett BROWNING. Finally returning to the United States in 1900, Hosmer produced a statue of Queen ISABELLA I of Spain, who had supported Christopher Columbus's voyages to the New World. This was commissioned by the city of San Francisco and unveiled in 1894.

Harriet Hosmer was also known as an intrepid climber – Mount Hosmer in Missouri is named after her.

Houston, Whitney (1963–   ) *American pop and soul singer*

A remarkably successful singer with a worldwide reputation, Whitney Houston has won five Grammy Awards, several American Music Awards, and the "best-selling pop artist of the year trophy" at the Monte Carlo Music Awards festival. She has recently embarked on a parallel career as a movie actress.

She was born in Newark, New Jersey, the daughter of Cissy Houston (one of Aretha FRANKLIN's backing singers) and a cousin of the soul singer Dionne WARWICK. Her career began with gospel singing and a partnership with her mother. While still at high school she was a backing singer for, among others, Chaka Khan, supplementing her income with modelling for fashion magazines.

At the age of 19 she was brought to the attention of Clive Davis, the head of Arista Records, who in 1985 encouraged her to move into pop and enabled her to release her debut album, *Whitney Houston*. This album yielded three number-one hit singles and also attracted a following with its love ballads. In 1988 Houston's "Where Do Broken Hearts Go" became her seventh American number one, breaking the record held by the Beatles. Her first three albums sold more than 40 million copies.

In 1992 Houston recorded the Dolly PARTON song "I Will Always Love You" – another record-breaking number that topped the charts for 14 consecutive weeks. This song also featured in her film debut, *The Bodyguard* (1992), with Kevin Costner, which was an enormous box-office success. Despite poor critical reviews, the film's soundtrack sold 28 million copies. That same year she married the hip-hop singer Bobby Brown, with whom she had a daughter the following year. Houston subsequently appeared in the film *Waiting to Exhale* (1995) and also took the title role in *The Preacher's Wife* (1996), directed by Penny MARSHALL.

Howard, Catherine (*c.* 1520–1542)
Fifth wife of King Henry VIII of England

Catherine's brief reign as queen of England (1540–42) ended with her execution for treason on grounds of unchastity and adultery.

Born into an aristocratic Roman Catholic family, Catherine was the daughter of Lord Edmund Howard and granddaughter of Thomas Howard, 2nd Duke of Norfolk. She was married to Henry VIII in 1540, immediately after his divorce from ANNE OF CLEVES. Catherine had attracted Henry's attention towards the end of 1539; the match had been encouraged by Henry's more conservative advisers, notably Catherine's uncle Thomas Howard, 3rd Duke of Norfolk, who was eager to discredit the king's chief minister, Thomas Cromwell, who had arranged the king's unfortunate marriage to the Protestant Anne of Cleves.

The wedding of Henry and Catherine took place on July 28, the day on which Thomas Cromwell was executed. However, the marriage did not go well; Henry, now 49, was grossly overweight and unwell, while Catherine was young and beautiful. In November 1541 a clandestine meeting with her former music teacher Henry Mannock came to light, and a further liaison with her cousin Thomas Culpepper, whom she had also known before her marriage, was suspected. Archbishop Thomas Cranmer, a zealous Protestant, charged Catherine with unchastity before marriage and adultery after it. Both charges were probably true, and both men were executed. Catherine was subsequently charged with high treason by parliament and beheaded in February 1542.

See also CATHERINE OF ARAGON; BOLEYN, ANNE; SEYMOUR, JANE; PARR, CATHERINE.

Howe, Julia Ward (1819–1910) *American reformer and writer*

> Mine eyes have seen the glory of the
> coming of the Lord:
> He is trampling out the vintage where
> the grapes of wrath are stored.
> —"Battle Hymn of the Republic"

> She could always discover sunlight
> behind the shadows and the clouds;
> evil to her was but the promise of
> good, and good the promise of
> something better.
> —Ellen M. Mitchell, *Julia Ward
> Howe*

Julia Ward Howe is best known for writing the text of "The Battle Hymn of the Republic," which she wrote after visiting the Federal army at the Potomac in 1862. Her aim was to provide more dignified words to the anti-slavery tune "John Brown's body lies a' mouldering in the grave." Her new version was first published in *The Atlantic Monthly* in 1862. In 1908 she became the first woman to be elected to the American Academy of Arts and Letters.

Born in New York City into a wealthy family, she married Samuel Gridley Howe, a reformer and teacher of the blind, in 1843 and thereafter lived chiefly in Boston. They had six children.

Both Mrs. Howe and her husband were leading abolitionists; she helped him edit the *Commonwealth*, an important abolitionist periodical. She also worked for many other public causes, principally related to women's rights, and was president of such organizations as the New England Woman Suffrage Association and of the American branch of the Woman's International Peace Association. In addition to her women's rights work Mrs. Howe lectured extensively and wrote several works of social criticism, including *Is Polite Society Polite?* (1895).

Mrs. Howe published three books of verse, among them *Passion Flowers* (1854) and *Words for the Hour* (1857); two travel sketches, including *A Trip to Cuba* (1860); a biography, *Margaret Fuller* (1883); and several other works. She was also the editor of the *Woman's Journal* from 1870 to 1890. Although her works are no longer widely read, they provide an interesting historical view of American social and political idealism in the latter half of the 19th century. She died in Newport, Rhode Island.

Hrosvitha (*c.* 935–*c.* 972) *German nun and writer*

> To think that you, who have been nurtured in the most profound philosophical studies and have attained knowledge in perfection, should have deigned to approve the humble work of an obscure woman!
>
> —*The Play of Roswitha*, "Epistle of the Same to Certain Learned Patrons of This Book" (*c.* 960)

Hrosvitha was the author of the first known plays by a woman writer.

Hrosvitha (also spelt Roswita or Hroswitha) was born into a noble Saxon family in Gandersheim, near Göttingen, and became the canoness of a Benedictine nunnery. She wrote six plays in Latin – *Gallicanus, Dulcitius, Callimachus, Abraham, Pafnutius,* and *Sapientia*. These plays, written in the style of the Roman comic dramatist Terence but with Christian rather than pagan themes, seem to have been produced for the education of Hrosvitha's fellow nuns rather than for performance. The manuscripts were discovered by Conrad Celtis in around 1500.

Hrosvitha also wrote narrative poems, legends of the saints, a life of the Virgin Mary (see MARY THE VIRGIN, SAINT) and a chronicle of the life of the Holy Roman Emperor Otto I (the Great) in verse.

Huch, Ricarda (1864–1947) *German novelist and poet*

Known and greatly respected as a leader of the intellectuals in the German women's movement of her day, Ricarda Huch was described by the writer Thomas Mann as "*Deutschlands erste Frau*" (the First Lady of Germany). In 1931 she became the first woman to be admitted to the Prussian Academy of Literature but resigned in 1933 in protest at the Academy's expulsion of Jewish writers.

Born in Braunschweig, Germany, into a wealthy Protestant family, she was the sister of the novelist Rudolph Huch. She received a PhD degree from the University of Zurich in 1892, remaining in that city as a teacher in a girls' school. In the 1890s she began to publish poems, later collected in *Gesammelte Gedichte* (1929; Collected Poems) and *Herbstfeuer* (1944; Autumn Fire).

Huch is best known for her historical novels, which include *Erinnerungen von Ludolf Ursleu dem Jüngeren* (1893; published in English as *Recollections of Ludolf Ursleu the Younger*, 1913–1915); *Aus der Triumphgasse* (1901; Triumph Alley); and *Vita somnium breve* (1902; reissued as *Michael Unger*, 1946). Her scholarly works include several volumes on German Romanticism, including *Die Blütezeit, Ausbreitung und Verfall der Romantik* (1899–1902; The Blossoming, Spread and Decline of Romanticism), as well as studies in German and Italian history, notably *Der Grosse Krieg in Deutschland* (1912–14; The Great War in Germany), about the Thirty Years' War, and *Die Geschichten von Garibaldi* (1906; The History of Garibaldi).

After two unhappy marriages Huch lived in Munich from 1910, during World War II moving to Jena, where she lived alone and in poverty. In 1947 she was elected president of the first Congress of German Writers in Berlin but died soon afterwards.

Humphrey, Doris (1895–1958) *American dancer and choreographer*

One of the great pioneers of American modern dance, Doris Humphrey worked with the Denishawn Company, run by Ruth ST. DENIS and Ted Shawn, from 1917 to 1927; she also experimented with choreography while working there. After leaving Denishawn, Humphrey and her partner Charles Weidman established their own company to experiment with abstract and unaccompanied dance (*Water Study*, 1928), with natural sounds (*The Life of the Bee*, 1929), and with simple folk music (*The Shakers*, 1931).

Her first extended work, a trilogy (*Theatre Piece, With My Red Fires,* and *New Dance*) presented in 1936, began her lifelong exploration of the art of dance as an affirmation of human dignity. This theme was reiterated movingly in *Inquest* (1944).

Forced to retire as a performer because of arthritis, Humphrey became in 1945 the artistic director of the José

Limón Company. Among the powerful works she created for the company were *Lament for Ignacio Sanchez Mejias* (1947), *Day on Earth* (1947), *Ritmo Jondo* (1953), and *Ruins and Visions* (1954).

Humphrey also founded the Juilliard Dance Theater (1955) and taught choreography at the Bennington and Connecticut College summer schools of dance. Her authoritative *Art of Making Dances* was published in 1959. She died in New York City.

Huntingdon, Selina Hastings, Countess of (1707–1791) *British Methodist leader*

The Countess of Huntingdon played an important role in the evangelical revival in England during the 18th century.

Born Selina Shirley, the daughter of the 2nd Earl Ferrers, she married the Earl of Huntingdon in 1728 and was converted to Methodism some ten years later by her sister-in-law, Lady Margaret Hastings. After her husband's death in 1746 Selina devoted herself to social and religious causes, using the considerable fortune she had inherited to support the work of George Whitefield (one of the founders of Methodism) in North America. Using her right as a peeress, she made him her chaplain in 1748. Other evangelical clergymen were appointed and supported in this way. She eventually assumed leadership of Whitefield's followers, a Calvinist Methodist sect that became known as "The Countess of Huntingdon's Connexion."

In 1768 Selina Huntingdon established Trevecca House in South Wales for training evangelical clergymen, after she had learned that theological students at Oxford who were suspected of Methodism were expelled. (The college was moved in 1792 to Cheshunt, Hertfordshire, and in 1904 to Cambridge.) She also built chapels in such fashionable towns as Brighton and Bath to enable the aristocracy to be introduced to Methodism.

In 1779 her method of supporting Methodist ministers was disallowed by the Consistory Court in London; in order to save her chapels she registered them as dissenting places of worship under the Toleration Act of 1689. She died in London; in her will she left her 64 chapels to four people.

Huppert, Isabelle (1955–) *French actress*

One of France's finest actresses, Isabelle Huppert is known for her portrayal of characters whose outward innocence disguises an inner evil. She has described her method of acting: "I start by thinking about what might have happened to the character before the story began, and this preparation helps you to work on what's underneath, the unseen part which has to be very much built into your mind."

Isabelle Huppert was born in Paris and attended a course of Russian studies at the university there before enrolling at the National Conservatory of Dramatic Art. She was inspired to study acting after playing small roles in television films while she was a student at the university. Her screen debut came in 1971 with a small part in *Faustine et le bel été*.

Huppert first came to critical notice in 1974 in Bertrand Blier's *Les Valseuses* (*Going Places*), but it was her interpretation of the role of Pomme in *La Dentellière* (*The Lacemaker*) that made her an international star in 1977, earning her a British Academy Award as Most Promising Newcomer for her performance. The following year she played the title role of a teenage murderer in Claude Chabrol's *Violette Nozière*, which earned her the Best Actress Award at the Cannes Film Festival.

She made her Hollywood debut in Michael Cimino's epic Western *Heaven's Gate* (1980), one of the film industry's biggest flops. After this she decided to return to France, where she has starred in such films as Bertrand Tavernier's *Coup de torchon* (1981; *Clean Slate*), Blier's *My Best Friend's Girl* (1982), and Chabrol's *Madame Bovary* (1991). In 1994 she starred in the U.S. film *Amateur*.

Hurston, Zora Neale (c. 1901–1960) *American novelist and folklorist*

One of the most influential African-American writers, and one of the first to assimilate the folk tradition of the rural South into her writing, Zora Hurston was a forerunner of such writers as Toni MORRISON and Alice WALKER.

Zora Neale Hurston was born in Eatonville, Florida, a town founded by African Americans. When she was nine, her mother died and her father, a Baptist minister, remarried. Taking casual jobs at first, at the age of 14 she joined a theatre troupe and travelled to Baltimore, where she graduated from Morgan Academy in 1918, subsequently studying at Howard University (1919–1924). Her first published story, "John Redding Goes to Sea," appeared in 1921. Following the success of "Spunk" (1925), she moved to New York, where she enrolled at Barnard College to study anthropology, graduating in 1928.

Quickly recognized as a major figure in the "Harlem Renaissance," Hurston drew some criticism for her lack of interest in exploring black issues in the context of a white society. She collaborated with Langston Hughes on a play, *Mule Bone* (1930), but the two fell out over the authorship, and the play was not produced during her lifetime.

From 1928 to 1932, financed by a Rosenwald grant, Hurston researched Southern folklore. Material she gathered in Louisiana was used in *Mules and Men* (1935), which deals with voodoo practices. From 1936 to 1938 she held a Guggenheim fellowship to do similar research in Haiti and Jamaica, which resulted in *Tell My Horse* (1938). Her remarkable novels are *Jonah's Gourd Vine* (1934), *Their Eyes Were Watching God* (1937), *Moses, Man of the Mountain* (1939), and *Seraph on the Suwanee* (1948). *Dirt Tracks in the Road* (1942) is loosely based on her early years.

During the 1950s Hurston withdrew from public life. Her belief in the preservation of a separate black culture meant that she refused to accept integration as a condition of black advancement and led her to oppose the Supreme Court's ruling on desegregation in schools, which aroused much hostility. Increasingly ill in her last years, she died in poverty in Fort Pierce, Florida. She was inducted into the National Women's Hall of Fame in 1994.

Huston, Angelica (1951–) *American film actress and director*

A tall imposing character actress, Angelica Huston is the daughter of the Hollywood director John Huston and granddaughter of the actor Walter Huston.

Born in Los Angeles, California, she grew up on her father's estate in County Galway, Ireland, and was educated in London. She made her film debut at the age of 16 in her father's *A Walk with Love and Death* (1969), but both she and the film were so ruthlessly panned by the critics that she decided to give up acting and became a model.

Returning to films some five years later, she appeared in *The Last Tycoon* (1976), *Frances* (1982), and *Prizzi's Honour* (1985), for which she received an Academy Award for Best Supporting Actress. Her later films include the well-received *Crimes and Misdemeanours* (1989); she was nominated for Best Actress Oscars for her roles in both *Enemies, a Love Story* (1989) and *The Grifters* (1990). *The Addams Family* appeared in 1991, and *The Perez Family* in 1995.

In 1996 Huston made her debut as a director with *Bastard out of Carolina*, based on Dorothy Allison's novel, and followed this with *Terrible Beauty*, about the Irish revolutionary Maude GONNE.

Hutchinson, Anne (1591–1643) *English-born American religious leader*

The daughter of a clergyman with Puritan leanings, Anne Marbury was born in Alford, Lincolnshire. She married William Hutchinson, a merchant, in 1612 and subsequently bore 15 children. In 1634 she emigrated with her family to Massachusetts Bay, where she joined the congregation of John Cotton and soon developed a reputation for having unorthodox opinions.

Becoming the leader of a small group that met weekly for religious discussion, Anne Hutchinson challenged the most basic conviction of the

Puritan commonwealth, namely, that God's will can be discovered only through the Bible. She denounced the Massachusetts clergy, except Cotton and her brother-in-law John Wheelwright, for being "under the covenant of works" (that is, enslaved by doctrine), rather than liberated through Christ.

By 1637 Massachusetts was divided into two hostile camps. Governor John Winthrop and the majority of the clergymen regarded Hutchinson's followers as a threat to the colony. She was therefore brought before the General Court for trial. The record indicates that the verdict was rigged before the trial had even begun. It also reveals Hutchinson to have been a brilliant woman, well able to hold her own against the leaders of New England. However, her case was finally destroyed by her own testimony, in which she sought to justify herself by describing divine revelations.

She was finally excommunicated and banished in 1637. The following year she moved to Rhode Island with some friends, including Mary DYER, setting up a democratic settlement on land acquired from the Narragansett tribe. After the death of her husband, Hutchinson moved to Long Island and then to Pelham Bay, where she and all but one of her household were massacred by Native Americans. She was inducted into the U.S. National Women's Hall of Fame in 1994.

Hyman, Libbie Henrietta (1888–1969) *American zoologist*

Hyman's six-volume work *The Invertebrates* (1940–68), representing years of patient scholarship, has been widely used as a standard textbook by students of zoology.

Born in Des Moines, Iowa, Libbie Hyman studied zoology at the University of Chicago (1906–10), remaining there as a research assistant until 1931. Finding no satisfactory textbooks to work with, she decided to write her own – *A Laboratory Manual for Elementary Zoology* (1919) and *A Laboratory Manual for Comparative Vertebrate Anatomy* (1929) are still in use (in later editions). Their success made her financially independent.

After travelling in Europe, she left Chicago and moved to New York City, living close to the American Museum of Natural History, where she carried out research on invertebrates. In 1937 she became a research associate of the museum, thereafter devoting the rest of her life to research that culminated in her classic *The Invertebrates*.

Hypatia (*c.* 370–415) *Greek philosopher*

The daughter of Theon, a celebrated Alexandrian mathematician, Hypatia was renowned for her beauty, modesty, learning, and eloquence among both the pagan and Christian communities of Alexandria. She studied under Plutarch the Younger and taught in Alexandria, becoming the most important figure in the city's Neoplatonic school.

She collaborated with her father in his writings and wrote commentaries on mathematics and astronomy herself, although none of these survives intact. Much of our knowledge of Hypatia comes from letters from one of her pupils, Synesius of Cyrene, asking her for scientific advice. From these letters it appears that she invented, among other things, an astrolabe for measuring the altitude of the stars and a hydroscope for measuring the specific gravity of liquids.

She was said to have supported Orestes, the pagan governor of Egypt, in his political opposition to St. Cyril, the Patriarch of Alexandria. Scandalous stories about her friendship with Orestes were circulated, which – combined with disapproval of her non-Christian beliefs – eventually caused her tragic death. A Christian mob, incited by fanatical clergy under the leadership of Cyril, dragged Hypatia from her carriage and carried her into the Church of the Caesareum, tore her limb from limb, and burnt her broken body in the street. She is the heroine of Charles Kingsley's historical novel *Hypatia* (1853).

I

Ibarbourou, Juana de (1895–1979)
Uruguayan poet and short-story writer

Known as a "wife-and-mother" poet and affectionately nicknamed "Juana of America," Juana de Ibarbourou gained a reputation as an erotic author, although she herself rejected this view of her work.

Juana (or Juanita) Fernández Morales was born in Melo, near the Uruguay–Brazil border, and educated at a convent school. At the age of 18 she fell in love with a young soldier, whom she married and with whom she moved to Montevideo.

Ibarbourou's love poems are inspired by her feelings for her husband and expressed in simple language. Love and nature are related to her own sensual experience through such symbols as water, fire, fruit, and flowers. In her early collections *Las lenguas de diamante* (1919; Tongues of Diamond) and *Raíz salvaje* (1922; Savage Root) she reveals an unashamed awareness of her own femininity. By 1929 she was popular enough to be named "Juana of America" at a public ceremony, although her next book (1930) attracted little attention.

Juana's mature work was less exuberant than her early writings, reflecting her frequent bouts of depression. *Perdita* (1950; Lost) expresses her bewilderment, while her prose works show an increasing preoccupation with religion. In 1950 she was elected president of the Uruguayan Society of Authors. She continued to write poetry, though none of this late work achieved the popularity of her early collections.

Ibárruri Gómez, Dolores (1895–1989) *Spanish political figure*

> It is better to die on your feet than to live on your knees.

> —Radio broadcast during the Spanish Civil War, July 19, 1936

Ibárruri is best known for her powerful and emotional antifascist speeches made during the Spanish Civil War.

Born into a poor mining family in the Basque region of Spain, Dolores was one of 11 children. Because her family was unable to pay for her to train as a teacher, she became a seamstress and housekeeper. This menial work made her increasingly aware of the inequality and unfairness of society, encouraging her to drift away from Roman Catholicism towards socialism. She joined the Spanish Socialist Party in 1917. Her articles in a paper for miners appeared under the pen name "La Pasionaria" ("The Passion Flower"). Her husband, Julian Ruiz, with whom she had six children, shared her left-wing beliefs.

Ibárruri became a founder member of the Spanish Communist Party in 1921, and in 1934 she founded the Antifascist Women's League. Elected to the Spanish parliament in 1936, she became a fierce opponent of Franco's fascism during the Spanish Civil War (1936–39). Her extremely emotive speeches were an important inspiration for the Communist side; but when Franco triumphed (in 1939), Ibárruri was forced to flee to the Soviet Union, where she remained for 38 years. While in exile she acted as secretary-general and then president of the Spanish Communist Party. Returning to Spain in 1977, she again entered parliament, at the age of 81. Her autobiography, *El único camino* (1962), appeared in English as *They Shall Not Pass* (1966), her most famous slogan.

Inchbald, Elizabeth (1753–1821)
British actress and writer

Elizabeth Inchbald is remembered as one of the very few successful women playwrights of her time, as well as being a witty and beautiful actress.

Born Elizabeth Simpson in Stanningfield, Suffolk, she ran away from home at the age of 18 to become an actress, despite suffering from a speech impediment. In 1772 she married the actor and painter Joseph Inchbald, with whom she frequently appeared in provincial theatres. After her husband's death in 1779 she received many offers of marriage, all of which she rejected.

Mrs. Inchbald, a popular figure on the London stage, was a close friend and admirer of the legendary actress Sarah SIDDONS. She retired from acting in 1789, after which she wrote a number of comedies and farces, some of which were adaptations of French plays. The successful publication of *A Simple Story* (1791), regarded as a forerunner of Charlotte BRONTË's *Jane Eyre*, was followed by a second less noteworthy, novel, *Nature and Art* (1798). Mrs. Inchbald died in London.

Ingelow, Jean (1820–1897) *British writer*

Jean Ingelow is known chiefly for her poetry, which reveals an intimate knowledge of nature as well as a meditative religious quality.

She was born in Boston, Lincolnshire, later moving to London to begin her career as a writer. Her 25 volumes of verse were influenced by Wordsworth and Tennyson. The most popular volume, *Poems* (1863), was received enthusiastically and includes her most celebrated poems, "Divided" and "The High Tide on the Coast of Lincolnshire, 1571."

Jean Ingelow also wrote children's stories, usually under the pen name "Orris." The most popular of these was *Mopsa the Fairy* (1869). Her novels, such as *Off the Skelligs* (1872), were once popular but are now hardly ever read. Ingelow died in London.

Irene (c. 752–803) *Byzantine empress*

Irene was ruler of the Byzantine empire from 797 to 802, the first woman to rule the empire as a sovereign in her own right. To emphasize this she insisted on being called "Basileus" ("King").

Irene was born in Athens. An orphan with no dowry, she attracted Leo, the son of Emperor Constantine V, by her beauty and talents, marrying him in 769. The couple became emperor and empress in 775; on Leo's death in 780 Irene ruled jointly with her ten-year-old son Constantine VI. However, she was ambitious to gain total control of the empire. In adulthood her son turned out to be a poor and unpopular ruler, enabling her in 797 to have him deposed and blinded, along with her husband's five brothers. She then governed as sole ruler from 797 to 802.

Irene's most significant achievement was to resolve the dispute over the use of icons in the Orthodox Church. She decreed at the Council of Nicaea in 787 that the persecution of those who believed in honouring icons should be brought to an end. The restoration of icons and the many tax exemptions that Irene granted to monasteries made her popular with the Church. However, threats to the empire from the Arabs and Bulgars resulted in costly payments of "tribute" money, while Charlemagne's coronation as the Western emperor in 800 undermined her power. In 802 Irene was deposed and banished to Lesbos, where she died.

Irigaray, Luce (c. 1930–) *French feminist, philosopher, and psychoanalyst*

Irigaray is known for her radical criticism of Western intellectual culture from a feminist perspective.

Born in Belgium, Irigaray came to France in the 1960s and took a succession of degrees in psychology, psychoanalysis, linguistics, and philosophy. From 1970 until 1974 she taught at the university of Vincennes. At this time her main preoccupation was a reexamination of the works of Freud, in association with Jacques Lacan's Freudian School in Paris, studying the links between language and psychology.

Her work, which is distinguished by its scope and depth, includes *Speculum de l'autre femme* (1974; published in English as *Speculum of the Other Woman*, 1985) and *Ce Sexe qui n'en est pas un* (1977; published in English as *This Sex Which Is Not One*, 1985), in which she explores the interdependence of psychoanalysis, philosophy, and male dominance in Western culture. In *Speculum of the Other Woman* Irigaray attacks the exclusively "male" orientation of Freud and the rigid "male" thought patterns that she saw in her colleague Jacques Lacan's radical revisions of Freud. Irigaray was consequently forced to leave Lacan's Freudian School as well as her teaching position at Vincennes.

By the late 1980s she had established an international reputation as a rigorous and creative thinker of considerable importance. Her articles "For Centuries We've Been Living in the Mother-Son Relation" (1983), "Is the Subject of Science Sexed?" (1985), and "I, You, We: Towards a Culture of Difference" (1992) show the breadth of her knowledge and understanding. After leaving Vincennes, she became a private psychotherapist and has since taught at a number of prestigious institutions worldwide.

Irigaray is aware of the paradox of combining feminism with the study of the male-oriented philosopher Freud. She recognizes the tendency of Western culture to promote male references as "natural"; while challenging this attitude, she has not tried to overthrow it too abruptly. Her strategy is to work within this male-dominated culture and "infect" it with feminist ideas. Some feminists disagree with this sophisticated strategy. For example, the Americans Mary Daly and Ann Rosalind Jones have proposed making a "cleaner" break. However, Irigaray's coupling of psychoanalysis and feminist theory has certainly opened new avenues of thought for intellectuals in the late 20th century.

Isabella (1292–1358) *Wife of King Edward II of England*

Isabella is infamous for overthrowing her husband and plotting his murder with her lover, Roger Mortimer.

Isabella was the daughter of King Philip IV of France and his wife Jeanne of Navarre. She was betrothed to Edward in 1303 as part of a peace treaty between France and England; they were married in 1308, shortly after Edward became king.

Edward and Isabella started quarrelling almost immediately, though during a civil war in 1312 between Edward and the barons Isabella tried to promote peace. The first of their four children, the future King Edward III, was born in 1312. Their marriage held together tolerably well for the next ten years, but problems arose as a result of Edward's friendship with Hugh Despenser, whom Isabella detested. Isabella then began to enter into intrigues with her husband's opponents. As a result, in 1324 her properties were seized, and her allowance was reduced. From then on her activities were closely watched.

In 1325 Isabella was sent to France to end a disastrous war with her brother, King Charles IV. While there she arranged for Prince Edward to do homage to Charles and refused to return home. In September 1326 she organized an invasion of England under the leadership of her lover, Roger Mortimer, an exiled English baron. Edward II, who was deserted by almost everybody, had to abdicate in favour of his young son in January 1327. This left Isabella and Mortimer free to rule as regents. Later that year they had Edward murdered while he was imprisoned in Berkeley Castle, Gloucestershire.

The dictatorship of Isabella and Mortimer (October 1326 to October 1330) aroused hatred and unrest. Their rule ended when Edward III, fearing for his life, seized the pair and condemned Mortimer to a traitor's death. Isabella wisely withdrew to retirement in Norfolk, where she died.

Isabella I (1451–1504) *Queen of Castile*

By marrying Ferdinand of Aragon, Isabella united the two important kingdoms of Aragon and Castile, thus forming the basis of modern Spain. The couple ruled jointly during a dramatic age that witnessed the discovery of America by Europeans and the horrors of the Inquisition.

Isabella was born at Madrigal, Castile, the daughter of John II of Castile and Isabella of Portugal. When her half-brother Henry IV died in 1474, she contested the throne of Castile with JUANA LA BELTRANEJA, whom Henry had claimed as his daughter and heir. Isabella's victory was due in part to the generalship of Ferdinand of Aragon, whom she had married in 1469. As a result of their marriage alliance Ferdinand and Isabella became joint rulers of the whole of Spain.

Isabella's chief aim as ruler was to increase royal power at the expense of the nobles. To this end she took over their lands and created a permanent army. Perhaps her most controversial act was to re-establish the Inquisition, which condemned and persecuted non-Catholics with terrible brutality. This led to over 170,000 Jews being expelled from Spain – an enormous loss to the cultural and economic wellbeing of the country. Isabella's devout Roman Catholicism also led her to play a personal role in the campaign against the Muslims of Granada, resulting in their defeat in 1492. In this same year Isabella, after some misgivings, decided to extend her patronage to the Italian navigator Christopher Columbus. This turned out to have been considerably wiser than her religious policy. He returned having discovered the New World, which was attached thereafter to the crown of Castile.

Isabella's last years were troubled by the deaths of three of her five children and the madness of her daughter Juana (see JOANNA THE MAD). Isabella died at Medina del Campo. In her will she praised the Inquisition's fight against heresy but pleaded for just treatment of the Native Americans.

Isabella II (1830–1904) *Queen of Spain*

Queen from the age of three, Isabella was unable to maintain a stable government. Her personal popularity was offset by her scandalous lifestyle, and she was eventually forced into exile.

Isabella was born in Madrid, the daughter of Ferdinand VII and Maria Christina of Naples. When she became queen, her mother ruled as regent until she was 13. At the age of 16 she married her cousin, Francisco of Assisi. She subsequently caused considerable scandal by her sexual intrigues and allowed herself to fall under the influence of such religious fanatics as Sister Patrocinio, a nun, and Father Antonio Claret, a Catalan evangelist. Political instability plagued her entire reign, during which Spain was ruled by 60 different governments.

Isabella survived assassination attempts in 1847 and 1852, but she was finally dethroned in 1868. She was exiled to Paris and in 1870 abdicated in favor of her son, Alfonso XII. She died in Paris.

Isabella of Bavaria (1371–1435) *Wife of King Charles VI of France*

The daughter of Duke Stephan III of Bavaria, Isabella (also known as Isabeau or Elisabeth de Bavière) was married to Charles VI in 1385. As a result of the king's madness she played a large part in ruling the country from 1393.

Although at first an ally of the Duke of Burgundy, who had arranged her marriage, she soon learnt to use the differences between the Burgundians and their enemies, the Armagnacs, for her own financial advantage. Making use of political crisis in 1409, she managed to dispense with controls over her spending and had her supporters placed in all administrative posts. In 1415, although government finances were in total confusion, she demanded an annual income of 150,000 gold francs.

Isabella was banished to Tours by the Armagnacs in 1417, but she escaped and joined John the Fearless of Burgundy to fight her own son, Charles. In 1420 she signed the Treaty of Troyes, which disinherited Charles in favour of Henry V of England, who married her daughter CATHERINE OF VALOIS. However, in 1422 both Henry V and her husband died and she lost her remaining power and influence. She died in Paris and was buried without honours at St.-Denis.

Isabel of Angoulême (c. 1187–1246)
Second wife of King John of England

Isabel was the daughter of the Count of Angoulême. King John divorced his first wife and married her in 1200, when she was 12 or 13 years old, despite her previous engagement to Hugh of Lusignan, Count of la Marche. The marriage involved John in a war with Hugh and, as a result, with King Louis VIII of France, leading to the loss of John's French lands. Isabel was the mother of Henry III of England, who succeeded King John.

After John's death in 1216 Isabel returned to France; in 1220 she married Hugh of Lusignan's son Hugh, to whom her own daughter had been engaged. However, the couple grew apart, and in 1243 Isabel retired to a convent at Fontevraud, France, where she died.

J

Jackson, Glenda (1936–) *British actress and politician*

> I work to live and I have a strong Puritan ethic. To work at my best I have to be interested, and what interests me more than anything are the difficulties the work presents. Even if I am working in rubbish, the strictures I place on myself make the acting difficult.
>
> —Describing her approach to work

After a glowing career as an actress on stage, in films, and on television, Glenda Jackson has also been successful in the very different field of politics.

Jackson was born in Birkenhead, Cheshire, into a working-class family. After leaving school, she worked for a while in a shop, but through an amateur theatre group she soon developed her interest in acting. In 1954 she won a scholarship to study at the Royal Academy of Dramatic Arts (RADA) in London. Having graduated with honours, she worked for several years as an actress and stage manager with English and Scottish repertory companies. In 1963 she joined the Royal Shakespeare Company, appearing as Charlotte CORDAY in its London production of *Marat/Sade* in 1965 and then in the Broadway production and the film. Her stage successes over the next two decades included *Hedda Gabler* (1975), *Antony and Cleopatra* (1978), *The House of Bernarda Alba* (1986), *Mother Courage* (1990), and *Mourning Becomes Electra* (1991).

She appeared in many films, including *Sunday, Bloody Sunday* (1971), *The Return of the Soldier* (1982), *Turtle Diary* (1985), and *The Rainbow* (1989). She won Academy Awards for Best Actress in 1971 for *Women in Love* and in 1974 for *A Touch of Class*. She also won an award in 1972 for her portrayal of ELIZABETH I in the popular BBC television series *Elizabeth R*.

Glenda Jackson has been a socialist and a member of the Labour Party since the age of 16. In 1992 she retired from acting after being elected MP for the constituency of Hampstead and Highgate (in London). In 1997 she became a member of the new Labour government when she was appointed a junior minister responsible for transport in London. A strong character, she is known for her wit, energy, and commitment to hard work.

Jackson, Mahalia (1911–1972) *American singer*

Jackson was noted for her expressive contralto voice and for her moving interpretations of gospel songs. Known as the "Queen of the Gospel Song," she helped popularize this form of music amongst both black and white Americans.

Jackson was born in New Orleans, Louisiana. As a child she sang in the choir of the Baptist church at which her father preached. She found inspiration in both the Holiness Church and in the blues music of Bessie SMITH and others, but was very devout and would never perform in nightclubs. At 16 she went to Chicago, where she led a quartet of singers that performed in churches. Gradually attracting wide attention, she made her first recording in 1934, and by the mid 1940s she was a popular recording star. A million copies of her record "Move On Up a Little Higher" (1947) were sold. In 1950 she gave her first, highly successful concert at Carnegie Hall in New York. She sang at civil rights rallies in the 1960s and gave a moving rendering of "Precious Lord, Take My Hand" at Martin Luther King's funeral. Mahalia Jackson died in Evergreen Park, Illinois.

Jacobi, Mary Putnam (1842–1906)
British-born American physician

A brilliant physician, Mary Jacobi was a pioneer of medical education for women and a campaigner for social reform.

Born Mary Corinna Putnam in London, the daughter of the publisher George Putnam, she spent most of her life in New York City, to which her family emigrated in 1847. Graduating from the New York School of Pharmacy in 1863, she spent a year at the Women's Medical College of Pennsylvania and worked in a Boston hospital before studying (1868–71) at the Ecole de Médecine in Paris.

After receiving her MD degree, she took a teaching post at the Women's Medical College of the New York Infirmary (a position that she retained until 1896). While there, as a result of her firsthand experience of the inferior training and professional status afforded to women in medicine, in 1872 she founded the Association for the Advancement of the Medical Education of Women. This organization persuaded Cornell University to admit women students to medical courses.

In 1873 she married Dr. Abraham Jacobi, a pioneer of pediatric medicine, with whom she collaborated in offering medical treatment to the poor, campaigning for reforms in working conditions, and advocating women's suffrage. In 1880, in recognition of her outstanding ability and commitment, Mary Jacobi became the first woman to win election to the New York Academy of Medicine. In spite of her busy life in clinical medicine, she found time to write medical textbooks and articles, particularly on women's complaints. Her nonmedical books include *Common Sense Applied to Woman Suffrage* (1894).

Jacobs, Helen Hull (1908–1997)
American tennis player

Jacobs ranks among the great women players in tennis history. She set a record in taking the U.S. singles title four years in succession (1932–35) and was elected to the Tennis Hall of Fame in 1962.

Helen Jacobs was born in Globe, Arizona, and studied at the University of California. She was national junior tennis champion in 1924 and 1925. Her tennis career took off when she won the singles crown at Forest Hills, New York State, in 1932; she retained this title for the next three years. Jacobs also won the U.S. outdoor doubles title in 1932, 1934, and 1935 and the mixed doubles crown in 1934. At Wimbledon, she won the singles title in 1936 and was a finalist six times in total.

During World War II Jacobs served in the Naval Reserve; she re-enlisted in the Navy in 1949, achieving the rank of commander in 1953. A prolific writer, she was the author of several books on tennis and volumes of autobiography, as well as many magazine articles.

Jacqueline of Bavaria (1401–1436)
Countess of Holland, Zeeland, and Hainault

In addition to the provinces she ruled by right of inheritance, Jacqueline (or Jacoba) of Bavaria also gained and lost territories and political leverage by means of her four marriages. At various times she was Duchess of Brabant, Duchess of Bavaria, and Countess of Ostrevant, Bohemia. Her life illustrates the interweaving of dynastic interests and princely politics in the 15th century.

Born at Le Quesnoy, Flanders, Jacqueline was the only child of William, Count of Holland, Zeeland, and Hainault, and of his wife Margaret, daughter of Philip the Bold of Burgundy. Her arranged marriage at the age of 14 to John of Touraine, the third son of King Charles VI of France, was part of a complicated scheme to link Burgundy with the French crown. However, her husband died in 1417, the same year that Jacqueline succeeded to her father's estates. Her uncle John the Fearless, Duke of Burgundy, then arranged her second marriage to her cousin John IV of Brabant. This attempt to join Hainault and Holland to Brabant was complicated when another of Jacqueline's uncles, John of Bavaria, disputed her possession of Hainault. In 1419 John the Fearless brought about a compromise, and Jacqueline's husband surrendered Holland and Zeeland to John of Bavaria.

Angrily renouncing her husband and her marriage, Jacqueline escaped to England, where in 1422 she married the anti-Burgundian Humphrey, Duke of Gloucester. With him she soon invaded her former possessions, but Humphrey's action almost caused a break in the important alliance between Burgundy and the English. The Duke of Burgundy, Philip the Good, persuaded the pope to annul the troublesome marriage, and in 1425 Humphrey abandoned Jacqueline. In 1428 she was forced to surrender the administration of her territories to Duke Philip; she also promised never to remarry without Philip's permission.

However, in 1432 she did marry again, this time to the Dutchman Francis of Borselen, and tried to start a rebellion against Burgundy in Holland. Defeated once more, she had to abdicate in Philip's favour. In spite of being married four times, she died without heirs at Teilingen.

Jael (12th century BC) *Old Testament heroine*

Jael, an Israelite woman who was married to Heber the Kenite, killed the Canaanite commander Sisera. Her story is told in the Old Testament book of Judges (4:15–22).

After the Israelites, led by DEBORAH and Barak, had massacred the army of the Canaanites, the Canaanite leader Sisera fled on foot, finally seeking asylum in the tent of Heber and Jael. When Sisera asked for water, Jael "gave him milk and butter in a lordly dish," lulling him into such a sense of security that he fell asleep. Jael, in spite of the neutrality of the Kenites, then drove a tent peg through the temple of the sleeping Canaanite, impaling him to the ground. This act of Jael's brought peace to the Israelites from the Canaanites for 40 years.

Jakubowska, Wanda (1907–) *Polish film director*

Jakubowska is best known for her 1948 film *The Last Stop*, which is based on her experiences in Nazi concentration camps during World War II. She has also been extremely influential in the development of the postwar Polish cinema.

Born in Warsaw, Jakubowska attended Warsaw University, where she studied art history, before gaining recognition for her documentary films in the 1930s. Her internment in the German concentration camps at Auschwitz and Ravensbrück during World War II inspired her film *The Last Stop* (1948), which stunned audiences by depicting the horrors of concentration-camp life with a bleak realism that owed much to her skill as a documentary maker. Having helped to establish the avant-garde Society of the Devotees of the Artistic Film (START) in 1929–30, she went on to become its artistic director in 1955. Her involvement with START and the style of her subsequent films, which include *Soldier of Victory* (1953), *It Happened Yesterday* (1960), *The Hot Line* (1965), and *Colours of Love* (1987), have had a huge impact on the Polish film industry.

James, P(hylis) D(orothy), Baroness (1920–) *British detective novelist*

Celebrated as one of the "queens of crime," P. D. James is renowned for her classic detective novels, which draw on her experiences as a nurse and a member of the police department's forensic science unit.

Born in Oxford, the daughter of a government tax official, James worked in the theatre before joining the Red Cross as a nurse in World War II. She served as a hospital administrator from 1949 until 1968, when she joined the Home Office to work with the forensic science service of the police department. In 1972 James was transferred to the criminal policy department, where she remained until becoming a fulltime writer in 1979.

In her early work James exploits her specialist knowledge, often locating her murder scenes in hospital environments. Her first novel, *Cover Her Face*

(1962), introduced her poetry-writing detective Adam Dalgleish, who features in many of her subsequent works. Love and jealousy, leading to murderous consequences, dominate *Unnatural Causes* (1967), *Shroud for a Nightingale* (1971), and *Death of an Expert Witness* (1976); a feminist note is introduced by the woman private investigator Cordelia Gray in *An Unsuitable Job for a Woman* (1972) and *The Skull Beneath the Skin* (1982).

James's reputation was secured by the international success of *A Taste for Death* (1986). Her subsequent works include the futuristic novel *The Children of Men* (1992), *Original Sin* (1994), and *A Certain Justice* (1997). Many of James's novels have been adapted for film and television. She was awarded the Crime Writers Association Cartier Diamond Dagger in 1987 and was made a baroness in 1991.

Jamison, Judith (1943–) *American dancer and choreographer*

Judith Jamison is a leading soloist who has been celebrated for her compelling stage presence and style.

Born in Philadelphia, Jamison attended classes in music and dancing at the Judimar School. She subsequently made her debut in the American Ballet Theater's 1964 production of *The Four Marys*. From there she moved to Alvin Ailey's American Dance Theater in New York, where she took many solo roles, some of which were choreographed especially for her. In 1972 she was appointed to the Board of the National Endowment for the Arts.

Having toured extensively at home and in Europe, Jamison left the American Dance Theater in 1980 to become a soloist and choreographer for several other dance companies (including the New York based Maurice Hines Dance School); in 1981 she starred in the Broadway musical *Sophisticated Ladies*. Returning in 1990 to the American Dance Theater, she became its artistic director.

Jekyll, Gertrude (1843–1932) *British garden designer, horticulturist, and writer*

Gertrude Jekyll created natural gardens for country houses, drawing inspiration from both the French impressionist painters and from traditional cottage gardens. Her example helped make gardening an acceptable profession for women.

Gertrude Jekyll was born in London and attended the South Kensington School of Art, later establishing a studio in her parents' home. She became skilled at painting, embroidery, wood carving, and metalwork, but she also contributed articles to *The Garden*, a periodical founded by her friend William Robinson. In 1883 she began to create a garden on a plot of land beside her mother's house at Munstead Heath in Surrey.

Jekyll suffered from severe nearsightedness, and around 1890 she had to give up studio work. Instead, she devoted herself to gardening, collaborating with the young architect Edwin Lutyens, whom she met in 1889. She taught him how to link a house to its natural setting by means of a garden and introduced such features as clipped yew trees, pools, steps, and pergolas. Their most notable gardens were at Deanery Garden, Sonning, Berkshire; Marsh Court, Stockbridge, Hampshire; Folly Farm, Sulhampstead, Berkshire; and Hestercombe House, Somerset.

From 1910 Jekyll worked alone, but after World War I she and Lutyens collaborated again on the design of war cemeteries. Jekyll designed three gardens in the United States, one of which survives at the Glebe House in Woodbury, Connecticut (1927).

Gertrude Jekyll saw gardening as a creative relationship with nature. Combining an artist's sense of colour with a practical knowledge of plants, she designed wide herbaceous borders that reflected the changing seasons. Sometimes these borders were colour-co-ordinated, perhaps in silver and white, for example. She phased out the use of bedding plants, preferring traditional cottage garden flowers, such as honeysuckle and pinks. A regular contributor to *Country Life* magazine, she also wrote many books, of which the most popular were *Wood and Garden* (1899) and *Colour in the Flower Garden* (1908).

Jemison, Mae Carol (1956–)
American physician and astronaut

Mae Jemison became the first African-American woman astronaut on September 12, 1992, when the space shuttle *Endeavor* was successfully launched.

Jemison studied chemical engineering at Stanford and then medicine at Cornell, where she gained her MD in 1981. After serving her internship in Los Angeles, she joined the Peace Corps and worked as area medical officer for Liberia and Sierra Leone (1983–85).

Returning to the United States in 1985, Jemison applied to join NASA as an astronaut. However, following the 1986 *Challenger* disaster, NASA had stopped recruiting at all levels, and it was not until 1987 that Jemison was accepted into the programme. She was assigned in 1989 to Mission STS-47 Spacelab J, a joint U.S.-Japanese project during which it was proposed to study space sickness and the effects of weightlessness on the development of several species of animal.

After her successful flight in the *Endeavor*, Jemison left NASA in 1993 to accept a position on the faculty at Dartmouth College, New Hampshire.

Jennings, Elizabeth (Joan) (1926–) *British poet*

Writing verse that is mostly traditional in form, Elizabeth Jennings has explored personal issues, such as isolation and mental illness, from a spiritual angle that reflects her Roman Catholic faith.

Jennings was born into a Roman Catholic family in Boston, Lincolnshire. Her family later moved to Oxford, where she attended Oxford High School and then St. Anne's College. After a number of years working in the Oxford city library, she was employed as a reader by a London publisher (1958–60).

Her first volume of verse, called simply *Poems* (1953), won an Arts Council Prize, and her collection *A Way of Looking* (1955) received the Somerset Maugham Award.

About 1960 Jennings suffered a mental collapse and attempted suicide. Although she gradually recovered in hospital, the traumatic experience profoundly influenced her poetry. She reflected on her own suffering and that of her fellow patients in *Recoveries* (1964) and *The Mind Has Mountains* (1966), which also won her another award.

Jennings's poems are notable for their discipline and clarity. Although her themes are personal, her work is marked by restraint, formality, and reserve – qualities she retains even when writing of her own mental illness. Her volumes include *Lucidities* (1970), *Hurt* (1970), *Consequently I Rejoice* (1977), *Moments of Grace: New Poems* (1979), and *Tributes* (1989). Volumes of *Collected Poems* appeared in 1967 and 1986, and *Selected Poems* in 1979. Jennings also published a translation of Michelangelo's sonnets (1961) and a book on Robert Frost (1964). In 1992 she was made a CBE.

Jeritza, Maria (1887–1982) *Czech singer*

Beautiful and glamorous, Jeritza enjoyed a glowing career as an operatic soprano and was especially famed for her appearances in Vienna and New York.

Born Maria Jedlitzka in Brün, Austria (now Brno in the Czech Republic), Maria Jeritza studied singing in Brün and Prague. She gave her first operatic performance in 1910 in Olmütz (now Olomou). This was followed the next year by her first performance in Vienna. After this she became a great Viennese favourite in operas by Puccini, Massenet, Wagner, and Richard Strauss, creating the title role of Strauss's *Ariadne auf Naxos* in 1912.

Jeritza first appeared at the Metropolitan Opera, New York, in 1921 as Marietta in Eric Korngold's *Die tote Stadt*; she returned to the "Met" every season for the next 12 years, succeeding Geraldine FARRAR as the star of the company. Her most popular role was Tosca in Puccini's opera. After World War II she made only occasional appearances, chiefly in Vienna and New York. Her autobiographical *Sunlight and Song* was published in 1924. She died in Orange, New Jersey.

Jex-Blake, Sophia Louisa (1840–1912) *British physician*

Sophia Jex-Blake was one of the first women to become a practising physician in Britain. A pioneer of medical education for women, she successfully campaigned for legislation to allow women to become medically qualified and to practise as physicians.

Born in Hastings, Sussex, Jex-Blake was privately educated before studying at Queen's College for Women, London, where she subsequently taught mathematics (1859–61). After holding a further teaching post in Germany, she went to the United States to observe American teaching methods. While working as a volunteer in a Boston hospital, she was inspired to become a physician.

Jex-Blake was accepted as a student at the Women's Medical College of New York Infirmary, but after returning to Britain she had to overcome great opposition before she could qualify as a doctor. In 1869 she and several other women gained admittance to the Edinburgh Medical School, but they were forced to leave in 1873 when the institution refused to allow them to graduate. Undeterred, Jex-Blake opened the London School of Medicine for Women in 1874, channelling her energies into campaigning for parliamentary legislation to permit women to qualify as doctors. She finally achieved success in 1876; after graduating with an MD from the University of Bern the following year, Jex-Blake was licensed to practise as a doctor by the King's and Queen's College of Physicians. Returning to Edinburgh, she opened a dispensary and a medical school for women. In 1894 she finally persuaded the Edinburgh Medical School to accept women students.

Jezebel (died *c.* 843 BC) *Queen of Israel*

Jezebel, the archetype of a wicked woman, was notorious for her vicious scheming and defiance of the prophets as recorded in the Old Testament (Kings I and II).

The daughter of the Phoenician priest-king Ethbaal, ruler of the cities of Tyre and Sidon (in modern Lebanon), Jezebel married King Ahab of Israel. Fierce and domineering, she persuaded Ahab to introduce the Phoenician nature gods Baal-Melkast and Ashtaroth, discouraged the worship of the Israelite god Jehovah, and had many of Jehovah's prophets killed.

The most notorious of her many despotic deeds was the seizure of a vineyard coveted by her husband. When the owner, Naboth, refused to give up his vineyard, Jezebel unjustly accused him of blasphemy and had him stoned to death.

Enraged by Jezebel's defiance of Jehovah and her treatment of Naboth, Elijah, one of Jehovah's prophets, confronted Ahab with the predictions that he and his heirs would perish and that Jezebel's body would be devoured by dogs.

In about 853 BC, as had been foretold, Ahab died in battle. Jezebel retained influence during the reign of their son until he was overthrown by Jehu, a military commander chosen by Elijah's successor, Elisha. Jezebel, who taunted Jehu after he had defeated her son, was thrown to the ground from a window, and her body driven over by Jehu in his chariot. When she came to be buried, it was discovered that most of her corpse had been eaten by dogs.

Jhabvala, Ruth Prawer (1927–) *German-born Anglo-Indian writer*

> India...is not a place that one can pick up and put down again as if nothing had happened. In a way it's not so much a country as an experience, and whether it turns out to be a good or a bad one depends, I suppose, on oneself.
>
> —*The Travellers* (1973)

Jhabvala's novels, short stories, and screenplays explore the clash between Indian and Western cultures.

Born in Germany, the daughter of a Polish Jewish lawyer, Jhabvala came to England in 1939 when her parents fled Nazi persecution. On graduating from the University of London, where she studied English literature, she married a visiting Indian architect in 1951 and moved with him to India, where she spent the next 24 years.

Her first novel, *To Whom She Will*,

appeared in 1955 and introduced the theme that dominates her work: the conflict between Western attitudes and Indian urban life, which is often seen from the perspective of an outsider looking in. The outsider is both fascinated and repelled, while at the same time having his or her prejudices challenged. *Esmond in India* (1958) and *A Backward Place* (1963) were followed by *Heat and Dust* (1975), which won the Booker Prize.

Jhabvala moved to New York City in 1975; her novel *In Search of Love and Beauty* (1983) finds a parallel to her Indian experiences in the exile of Europeans in America.

Her many screenplays in association with the film-makers James Ivory and Ismail Merchant include the acclaimed *Shakespeare Wallah* (1965), the story of an English theatre company touring in India; adaptations of the E. M. Forster novels *A Room with a View* (1986) and *Howards End* (1992), both of which won Academy Awards for Best Adapted Screenplay; and *Jefferson in Paris* (1995). Her screenplay for *The Remains of the Day* (1993) also received an Oscar nomination. Her collections of short stories include *An Experience of India* (1971) and *Out of India* (1986). She was made a CBE in 1998.

Jiang Qing (1914–1991) *Chinese politician*

The wife of the Chinese Communist leader Chairman Mao Zedong (Mao Tse-tung), Jiang Qing (Chiang Ch'ing) was one of the leaders of the Chinese Cultural Revolution (1966–69) and became notorious as the ruthless head of the "Gang of Four" radical politicians.

The daughter of a carpenter, she was born in Shandong (Shantung) province, and took drama classes before studying literature at Qingdao University. She then worked as a film and stage actress in Shanghai. When the Japanese attacked China in 1937, Jiang Qing fled to Yan'an, the headquarters of the Chinese Communist Party (CCP). While there she studied Marxist-Leninist political theory, underwent some military training, and

met Mao, 20 years her senior, whose third wife she became in 1939.

From 1950 to 1954 Jiang Qing was attached to the ministry of culture, but it was not until the 1960s that she became prominent with a campaign to purge bourgeois values from art and literature and replace them with proletarian and revolutionary themes. With the advent of the Cultural Revolution in 1966 she became cultural adviser to the People's Liberation Army. Claiming to speak for Mao, she mercilessly used her position to inspire a general terror throughout China and to pursue personal vendettas. In 1969 she was promoted to the Politburo of the CCP.

When Mao died in late September 1976, Jiang Qing, as leader of the "Gang of Four," attempted to seize absolute power but was ousted after only ten days. She was arrested and detained until finally tried in 1980–81 for subversion of the government and the torture and wrongful imprisonment of many innocent people. The trial, which was televised, caused a national sensation and proved dramatic: Jiang Qing claimed that she had acted only at Mao's behest and remained defiant to the last, even daring her accusers to execute her. The death sentence was duly passed but suspended for two years; it was commuted to life imprisonment in 1983. In June 1991 the Chinese government released a report stating that Jiang Qing, who had been released to undergo medical treatment in May 1984, had committed suicide.

Jingo (*c.* 170–*c.* 269) *Semi-legendary empress of Japan*

Jingo (or Jingu Kogo) is mentioned in early Japanese chronicles and, perhaps more reliably, in Chinese and Korean records, though it is uncertain whether she really existed. Magical stories were told about her conquest of Korea.

According to 8th-century Japanese accounts, Jingo was married to Emperor Chuai (reigned 192–200). She was dowager empress from 200, later acting as regent for her son Ojin until her death. It is also recorded that she personally led a conquest of Korea in 200. She supposedly used two magic jewels to control the tides during the expedition. Another story tells how Ojin remained in her womb for three years while she completed the campaign.

Early Chinese records tell a different story. A Japanese country called Yamatai was ruled by an unmarried queen, Pimiku, who sent an embassy and tribute to the Chinese king of Wei in 238. It is possible that Pimiku and Jingo are the same person and that Yamatai is Yamato, the area around Nara where the Japanese state took shape. At that time the ruling house of Yamato was seeking Chinese recognition that it was supreme in Japan.

Korean histories confirm that the Japanese had invaded Korea by the 4th century. It is possible that Jingo lived as late as this – the order of events in Japanese history has not been recorded with great accuracy – but if this is the case, she cannot have been the same person as Pimiku.

Joan, Pope (9th century) *Legendary pope*

Joan was reputed to have been pontiff (855–58) between the tenures of Leo IV and Benedict III, although the validity of the story has long been discounted.

Said to have been born in Germany to English parents, Joan took a Benedictine monk as her lover and, disguising herself as a man, followed him to Athens. There she became a notable scholar who, on her return to Rome, worked as a papal notary or clerk. Her election to the papal throne is said to have followed her appointment as a cardinal by Leo IV.

Joan was alleged to have given birth during a papal procession. Various versions of the story follow this unlikely confinement: in one version she was taken from Rome and stoned to death; in another she was said to have died during the birth and been buried where she lay.

The story of Pope Joan was largely propagated by the writings of two 13th-century Dominican scholars, the Frenchman Stephen of Bourbon and the Polish Martin of Troppau. Perpetuated by gossip, the tale proved irresistible and made its way into literature and the chronicles. It was largely accepted as fact until being finally discredited in the 17th century. Subsequent research has proved that only a few weeks elapsed between the pontificates of Leo IV and Benedict III.

Joanna I (1326–1382) *Queen of Naples and Countess of Provence*

Joanna's life was largely determined by dynastic rivalry over her throne of Naples.

Joanna (or Giovanna) succeeded to the throne of Naples in 1343 on the death of her Angevin (Norman) grandfather, King Robert. Her marriage alliance with her second cousin, Andrew of Hungary, resulted in tensions between the Hungarians and Angevins at court. When Andrew was murdered in 1345, Joanna was accused of being involved. She therefore fled abroad when Andrew's brother, King Louis of Hungary, invaded Naples in 1348 and took refuge in Avignon, Provence, where the papal court was based at that time. As Countess of Provence she sold Avignon to the pope, who in return declared her innocent of her husband's murder, enabling her to return to Naples the same year. She and her second husband, Louis of Taranto (also a cousin), were crowned in 1352. After Louis's death Joanna married James III of Majorca; when he died, she was married a fourth time, to Otto of Brunswick. She remained childless.

In 1378 Joanna gave her support to the breakaway Pope Clement VII at Avignon against Pope Urban VI in Rome. In retaliation Urban offered the throne of Naples, which he had the right to bestow, to another of Joanna's cousins, Charles of Durazzo. Charles seized Naples in 1381 and had Joanna imprisoned in Lucania, where she was put to death the following year.

Joanna the Mad (1479–1555) *Queen of Castile and Aragon*

The sensitive Joanna, whose name in Spanish is Juana la Loca, played little part in government, leaving the control of her kingdom to her male relatives. Her mental instability was heightened by her husband's unfaithfulness and made still worse by his sudden death.

Born in Toledo, Spain, Joanna (or Juana) was the third child of Ferdinand of Aragon and ISABELLA I of Castile. In 1496 she married Philip of Burgundy, son of Emperor Maximilian I, and lived with him in the Habsburg Netherlands for several years. They had two sons, the future emperors Charles V and Ferdinand I, and four daughters.

Joanna's husband, who was known as "Philip the Handsome," took no trouble to conceal his love affairs with other women. This caused Joanna great distress and contributed to the periods of insanity that she began to suffer after 1502. She had become heiress to the Castilian throne in 1500 after the unexpected deaths of her older brother and sister, but there was some concern that she was unfit to govern. She did become queen of Castile when her mother died in 1504, but Philip was determined to rule on her behalf. Her father, who had acted as regent until she reached Spain from the Netherlands, had to step aside, leaving the government to Philip.

Philip's sudden death in 1506 caused Joanna to become permanently unbalanced; at first she refused to leave Philip's embalmed body. From 1509 her father took over the regency again, and Joanna was settled at Tordesillas, where she lived, in total neglect of her person, mourning her dead husband.

Ferdinand had designated Joanna as heiress to Aragon, but in 1517 her son Charles assumed the title of king of Castile and Aragon, with Joanna's permission. In theory mother and son ruled jointly, but Charles wielded all the power. In 1520 a group of rebels tried to use Joanna against her unpopular son, but while expressing sympathy for them, she refused to sign any documents. She died much later at Tordesillas.

Joan of Arc, Saint (c. 1412–1431)
French military leader

I was in my thirteenth year when God sent a voice to guide me. At first I was very much frightened. The voice came toward the hour of noon, in summer, in my father's garden.

—Spoken at her trial, 1431

In the latter part of the Hundred Years' War Joan claimed that she had been divinely chosen to drive the English army out of France. The surprising success of her military exploits gave the war-weary French people hope. Joan, sometimes referred to as the "Maid of Orléans," became a popular heroine and the symbol of French national unity.

Joan was born in the village of Domrémy, Lorraine, the daughter of a peasant farmer. Raised as a devout Christian under her mother's guidance, Joan was deeply religious; at the age of 13 she began to hear voices and see visions of St. Michael, St. Margaret, and St. Catherine. Her voices told her to free the city of Orléans from the English, who were besieging it, and to take the dauphin to Reims where he would be crowned king of France.

Determined to accomplish her mission, Joan persuaded Robert de Baudricourt, captain of the nearby town of Vaucouleurs, to equip her with men's clothing, arms, and a mounted escort. In 1429 she travelled to see the dauphin at Chinon in the Loire Valley. At first sceptical, Charles had her questioned by a group of distinguished theologians, who were able to confirm that she was not a heretic. Thus reassured, he gave her a squire, a page, heralds, and a confessor, sending her with a small force to Orléans, where she joined the army resisting the English siege. Clothed in white armour, under a banner showing Christ in Judgment, in May 1429 she led a series of assaults against the English so successfully that they finally gave up the siege and retreated. The news of the liberation of Orléans and Joan's part in it spread quickly across France.

The next step in Joan's plan was to bring about the coronation of the dauphin, the only surviving son of the late King Charles VI, in spite of the fact that he had been disinherited in the Anglo-French Treaty of Troyes in 1420. Her motive in having the dauphin crowned was to restore a sense of French national unity. Although the road to Reims, where the coronation was to take place, was obstructed by several English-occupied towns, with the help of the Duke of Alençon Joan quickly recaptured them, enabling the dauphin to be crowned in the cathedral as Charles VII in July 1429, with Joan in attendance.

Paris, meanwhile, was occupied by the Duke of Burgundy, an ally of the English. Charles's councillors advised him to try to resolve this situation by diplomatic means. However, Joan and the other military leaders were eager to press their advantage and take the city by force. After a period of indecision Charles reluctantly accompanied them, but Joan's attempt to storm the city walls failed. The dejected king moved back to the Loire Valley, disbanding his large "army of the coronation."

In April 1430, after six months of inactivity, Joan slipped away from the king and with a small band of soldiers proceeded around Paris to Compiègne, which was under siege by the Burgundians. After her attempt to free the town had failed, she was captured and imprisoned.

Despite all that Joan had done for Charles, the king made no attempt to communicate with her captors or to negotiate her ransom. The English, whom she had humiliated at Orléans, were determined to exact their revenge on her. Their supporter Pierre Cauchon, Bishop of Beauvais, persuaded the Burgundians to hand her over for 10,000 francs. The English-controlled University of Paris, which had influence over theological matters, insisted that she be tried by Cauchon and the Inquisitor of France for her many "crimes." In November 1430 Joan was taken to Rouen, where her trial lasted from January to May 1431.

Although witchcraft was one of the original charges against Joan, the main charge at her trial was for heresy. The trial was conducted under the harsh procedures of the Inquisition, with several apparent injustices. The Inquisitor's representative was rarely present, and Cauchon, who had failed to provide Joan with a lawyer, was left as the presiding judge. She was also detained in a civil prison instead of an ecclesiastical prison. It was, in fact, a political trial disguised as an ecclesiastical process. The main issues were Joan's refusal to submit to the authority of the Church in the interpretation of her voices and her habit of wearing men's clothes. Submission to the Church's authority would have meant conceding that she had been deceived by her voices and that her mission was false. She answered the charges against her cautiously and with courage. Eventually she was taken to the cemetery of St. Ouen to see where she would be burnt if she did not submit. After her request to be judged by the pope had been refused, in despair she renounced her "crimes and errors"; she was sentenced to life imprisonment. However, a few days later she dressed again in men's clothes and restated her belief in her voices. On May 30, 1431, she was taken to the market place at Rouen and, before a large crowd, was burnt to death at the stake.

Towards the end of the war, after the French had recovered Rouen, efforts were made to establish the truth about Joan. Finally, in 1455, Pope Callixtus III initiated a formal retrial, known as the Trial of Rehabilitation, which in 1456 declared the earlier trial invalid. Thus Joan was vindicated 25 years after her death. She was beatified in 1909 and canonized in 1920. Her feast day is on the anniversary of her death.

Joan's military career lasted only a year. During this brief period she took part in ten or more military actions, including three at Orléans, and was twice wounded. She stated at her trial that she had never killed anyone, but she never shrank from danger, usually leading an attack in full view of the enemy. It is said that she was a charismatic leader who conducted herself as if she had been an experienced military tactician. Her routing of the English at Orléans was an important strategic victory in the Hundred Years' War, blocking the English advance south of the Loire. The further military victories and the coronation itself both demoralized the English and encouraged the French. As a result of her remarkable life and death Joan has remained for over 500 years a great symbol of French courage, virtue, and patriotism.

Joan of Navarre (*c.* 1370–1437) *Second wife of King Henry IV of England*

As the wife first of the Duke of Brittany and then of the king of England, Joan was unavoidably drawn into the political rivalries between the two territories.

The second daughter of King Charles II of Navarre, Joan was married for the first time in 1386, to John IV, Duke of Britanny. By the time she was 29 she had produced eight children. When John died in 1399, she became regent for her eldest son, John V.

In 1403 Joan married King Henry IV of England by proxy. This formal alliance did not result in any children. When Henry died in 1413, she remained on friendly terms with her stepson Henry V, but in a few years the rivalry with Brittany, ruled by her son, made her position awkward. In 1419 she was accused of witchcraft and was imprisoned until 1422. She died at Havering-atte-Bowe, Essex; her tomb and effigy are in Canterbury Cathedral, beside the tomb of Henry IV.

John, Gwen (1876–1939) *British artist*

Gwen John, the elder sister of the artist Augustus John, is noted for her restrained portraits and watercolours.

Born in Haverfordwest in Pembrokeshire, Gwen John moved with her family to nearby Tenby following the early death of her mother. She studied at the Slade School, London (1895–98), and at Whistler's Académie Carmen in Paris (1898–1900) before showing her paintings with the New English Art Club (1900–11). In 1900 she exhibited jointly with her brother at the Carfax Gallery, a display that emphasized their contrasting styles: his bright and ebullient work of an extrovert; hers more subdued in mood and colour, reflecting her shy reclusiveness.

In 1904 Gwen returned to Paris, where two years later she worked as a model for the sculptor Auguste Rodin, with whom she had a disappointing personal relationship. She had a similar relationship with the poet Rainer Maria Rilke before converting to Roman Catholicism in 1913 and moving to Meudon. Here she spent a considerable amount of her time in a Dominican convent painting portraits of the nuns, and became increasingly withdrawn from society. Her reclusiveness in these later years was reflected in the austerity of her work. She died on a visit to Dieppe after collapsing and being taken to the local hospital.

Johnson, Amy (1903–1941) *British aviator*

> Had I been a man I might have explored the Poles or climbed Mount Everest, but as it was my spirit found outlet in the air.
>
> —Quoted by Margot Asquith (ed.) in *Myself When Young* (1938)

Amy Johnson was a pioneer of women's aviation who made several long-distance record attempts. She was also the first woman to gain a British ground engineer's licence.

Born in Hull, Johnson studied economics at the University of Sheffield before working as a secretary in London. This enabled her to earn sufficient money to learn to fly; in 1928 she passed the tests for her private pilot's licence. Only two years later she made an attempt on the record for a solo flight from London to Darwin, Australia, piloting a biplane that she herself had modified. The flight took 17 days, three days in excess of the existing record, but it won her a rapturous welcome in Darwin and worldwide publicity and admiration.

In 1931 she flew across Siberia to Tokyo, and in the following year set a new record of four days and ten hours for a solo flight from London to Cape Town. The previous record for this journey was held by the Scottish pilot Jim Mollison, whom she married that same year. With her husband she flew from London to India and across the Atlantic from England to the United States, trips that Johnson had previously made alone. They also made a new record-breaking flight to Cape

Town together. The marriage, however, could not withstand the publicity, and they were divorced in 1938.

In the early years of World War II Johnson flew for the Air Transport Auxiliary as a ferry pilot. In January 1941 she disappeared in her plane over the Thames Estuary; neither her body nor her plane was ever found.

Johnson, Dame Celia (1908–1982)
British actress

Celia Johnson was a versatile actress who worked in both the theatre and films, playing a wide variety of roles. Perhaps she is best remembered for the restrained passion she brought to her role as a middle-class English housewife in David Lean's film *Brief Encounter*.

Born in Richmond, Surrey, Johnson attended St. Paul's Girls' School in London before studying at the Royal Academy of Dramatic Art in London. She made her debut on the British stage in *A Hundred Years Old* in 1929; her first appearance in New York was as Ophelia in *Hamlet*, in 1931. On the London stage she won critical acclaim for her portrayals of Elizabeth Bennet in an adaptation of Jane AUSTEN's *Pride and Prejudice* and of Mrs. de Winter in Daphne DU MAURIER's *Rebecca*, before turning to the cinema.

Johnson made her film debut in Noël Coward's 1942 production *In Which We Serve*, subsequently appearing in Dodie SMITH's *Dear Octopus* (1943). She then starred with Trevor Howard in *Brief Encounter* (1945), one of the classics of the British cinema, for which she was nominated for an Oscar for Best Actress. Her last film was *The Prime of Miss Jean Brodie* (1969), for which she won the British Film Academy Award as Best Supporting Actress.

Meanwhile, Johnson's stage career flourished. She appeared in plays ranging from modern comedies, such as Alan Ayckborn's *Relatively Speaking* (1967), to serious dramas by Shaw, Ibsen, and Chekhov. She again appeared in *Hamlet* in London, this time as Gertrude, in 1971.

She married the author Peter Flem-

ing in 1935 and was made a DBE in 1958.

Johnson, Pamela Hansford (1912–1981) *British novelist, playwright, and critic*

Johnson's work, which has been described as "quintessentially British," ranged from social realism and light satire to experimental drama and literary criticism.

Born in London, the daughter of parents involved in the theatre, Johnson worked first as a bank clerk and then as a book reviewer. Her first novel, *This Bed Thy Centre* (1935), set in working-class south London, was sufficiently successful for her to decide to make a career of writing.

Johnson is best known for her satire of the literary world in her trilogy featuring the comic character Dorothy Merlin: *The Unspeakable Skipton* (1959), *Night and Silence, Who is Here* (1962), and *Cork Street, Next to the Hatters* (1965). Among her later novels is *The Honours Board* (1970), which focuses on the relationships between teachers at an English public school.

Her other works include a critical study of the British novelist Ivy COMPTON-BURNETT (1953), the experimental radio play *Six Proust Reconstructions* (1958), and *On Iniquity* (1967), an analysis of contemporary society written after the trial of the infamous "Moors Murderers" (whose crimes involved the kidnapping and torturing of children), at which she was a reporter.

Although briefly engaged to the poet Dylan Thomas, Johnson married her first husband, Gordon Stewart, in 1936. In 1950 she married the novelist C. P. Snow (Baron Snow), with whom she collaborated on several projects.

Johnson, Virginia E(shelman) (1925–) *American sociologist*

Virginia Johnson and William H. Masters (1915–) are known for their pioneering studies of human sexual behaviour.

Virginia Johnson was born in Springfield, Missouri. Having studied psychology and sociology, in 1957 she joined a research programme led by Masters at the Washington University

School of Medicine in St. Louis. With the co-operation of hundreds of men and women volunteers, they used scientific equipment to study the changes that occur in the body during sexual activity. In 1964, when Masters established the Reproductive Biology Research Foundation (now called the Masters and Johnson Institute), Johnson became a research associate and later codirector. The results of their project were published in *Human Sexual Response* (1966).

In 1970, having counselled hundreds of couples with sexual problems, Masters and Johnson published *Human Sexual Inadequacy*; the following year they themselves were married. They later wrote *The Pleasure Bond – A New Look at Sexuality and Commitment* (1975), *Homosexuality in Perspective* (1979), and *Heterosexual Behaviour in the Age of Aids* (1988). Their own marriage broke up in 1993.

Joliot-Curie, Irène (1897–1956)
French nuclear physicist

In 1935 Irène Joliot-Curie and her husband Frédéric (1900–58) shared the Nobel Prize for Chemistry for their discovery of artificial radioactivity.

Born in Paris, Irène was the daughter of Marie CURIE. She was educated by her mother but was also influenced by the socialist ideas of her grandfather. During World War I she worked as a radiographer, becoming in 1918 her mother's assistant at the Radium Institute in Paris. In 1925 Frédéric Joliot, an engineer, also became an assistant there. The following year Irène and Frédéric were married, both thereafter using the surname Joliot-Curie.

In 1934 the Joliot-Curies discovered that radioactive isotopes, with half-lives of about three minutes, could be created in aluminum irradiated by a strong radium source. After announcing this discovery of artificial radioactivity, they gave chemical proofs of the atomic transmutations. They were both also interested in politics, and in 1936 Irène was appointed an undersecretary of state in the Popular Front Government.

In the late 1930s the couple both contributed greatly to the progress of nuclear physics. Irène's work on the results of bombarding uranium with neutrons led directly to the discovery of nuclear fission by Otto Hahn in 1938.

In 1946 Irène succeeded her mother as director of the Radium Institute. She and her husband were also organizers of the French atomic energy commission, on which they served as commissioners. However, in 1950 they were both removed because of their Communist affiliations. Irène Joliot-Curie died in Paris of leukaemia, caused by her years of work with radioactive materials. She was succeeded as director of the Radium Institute by her husband.

Jong, Erica (1942–) *American writer*

> Gossip is the opiate of the oppressed.
>
> —*Fear of Flying* (1973)

Erica Jong's novels and poems have enjoyed widespread popularity. She is perhaps best known for her novel *Fear of Flying* (1973).

Born Erica Mann in New York City, she graduated from Manhattan's High School of Music and Art and from Barnard College. She then took an MA at Columbia University in 1965. With her second husband, the child psychiatrist Allan Jong, she lived from 1966 to 1969 in West Germany, where Jong was serving in the U.S. Army.

After her return to the United States Erica began to publish poetry in magazines; in 1971 her first volume of poetry, *Fruits and Vegetables* was published. Later books of verse include *Half-Lives* (1973), *Loveroot* (1975), *At the Edge of the Body* (1979), *Ordinary Miracles* (1983), and *Becoming Light: Poems New and Selected* (1992). Some of her poetry is a frank celebration of her sexuality; other poems reflect her experience with psychoanalysis.

Her first novel, *Fear of Flying*, had a mixed critical reception but was an immediate popular sensation, both for its humour and for its sexual content. Its sequel, *How to Save Your Own Life* (1977), enjoyed a more moderate success. This book was published in the year that she married her third husband, the writer Jonathan Fast.

Retaining her former surname, Jong next wrote a feminist parody of the bawdy 18th-century novel, which she called *Fanny: Being the True History of the Adventures of Fanny Hackabout-Jones* (1980). This was followed by *Serenissima: A Novel of Venice* (1987), in which her heroine travels back in time to carry on a love affair with Shakespeare. Jong's most recent books include the novels *Any Woman's Blues* (1990) and *Of Blessed Memory* (1997) and an autobiography, *Fear of Fifty: A Midlife Memoir* (1994).

Joplin, Janis (1943–1970) *American rock singer*

> Don't compromise yourself. You are all you've got.
>
> —Quoted in *Reader's Digest*, April 1973

Joplin's passionate blues-influenced singing, hedonistic lifestyle, and early death have made her a popular icon of the late 1960s.

Born in Port Arthur, Texas, where she spent her formative years, Joplin sang in a minor country-and-western band in the early 1960s. Shortly after registering at a university in 1962, she abandoned her studies and fronted the band Big Brother and the Holding Company. In 1967 her explosive performance at the Monterey Festival brought her wide media coverage; the following year the band's album *Cheap Thrills* sold over a million copies.

She then parted from Big Brother and the Holding Company to embark on a solo career. Unfortunately this career was cut short by her addiction to both alcohol and drugs. In 1970, shortly after recording an album (released as *Pearl* in 1971) with a new group, the Full Tilt Boogie Band, she died of a (probably accidental) heroin overdose. Her songs, which included "Ball and Chain," "Me and Bobby McGee," and "Get It While You Can," remained popular; her *Greatest Hits* was released in 1972, after her death. Joplin's sadly short life was the subject of a TV documentary, *Janis*

(1974), and inspired the film *The Rose* (1979).

Jordan, Dorothy (1762–1816) *Irish-born British actress*

Dorothy Jordan is remembered for her rambunctious tomboy roles in stage comedy and farce – and for her scandalous lifestyle.

Born near Waterford into a theatrical family (her mother was an actress and her father a stagehand), she made her acting debut in 1777 in Shakespeare's *As You Like It*. Taking the stage name "Miss Francis" (her mother's professional name was "Mrs. Francis"), in 1779 she appeared in Henry Fielding's farce *The Virgin Unmasked* at the Crow Street Theatre, Dublin. Subsequently she spent six years performing with the Tate Wilkinson company in northern England, before making her London debut in David Garrick's play *The Country Girl* at Drury Lane in 1785. Her success led to comic parts in plays by Shakespeare, Congreve, and Sheridan (such as that of Viola in *Twelfth Night*), which required her to dress in men's clothes. These tomboy roles, which she played with great gusto, became her trademark.

Jordan's off-stage life proved little less dramatic than her stage roles. Having changed her name to "Mrs. Jordan" when she was pregnant with the first of her 15 illegitimate children, she became the mistress of the Duke of Clarence (later King William IV), who fathered ten of her offspring. Parliamentary disapproval of the future monarch's liaison with Mrs. Jordan contributed to their amicable separation in 1811, under the terms of which Jordan received a generous pension; their eldest child was made Earl of Munster when Clarence became king in 1830.

Jordan retired from the stage in 1814 and the following year went to live in France, later dying in poverty at Saint-Cloud.

Joseph, Helen (1905–1992) *British-born South African political activist*

Helen Joseph, a white South African, campaigned tirelessly for social equality and the dismantling of apartheid, despite government attempts to suppress her.

Born in England, Joseph graduated from the University of London in 1927 and emigrated to South Africa in 1931. After World War II, during which she served as an intelligence officer providing information about South Africa, Joseph trained as a social worker. Working in one of the racially segregated townships around Cape Town, she witnessed the poverty created by so-called "separate development."

Joseph devoted the rest of her life to the anti-apartheid cause. In 1955 she helped to establish the Congress of Democrats, the white subsidiary of the African National Congress (ANC), and she became secretary of the Federation of South African Women. Joseph was charged with treason in 1957; although acquitted in 1961, she was placed under house arrest from the following year until cancer forced her hospitalization in 1971. Banned (i.e., restricted in her movements and meetings with other people) throughout this period, in 1964 she was also officially registered as a communist, which restricted her access to the media. She was again banned in the period 1980–82. In 1983 she became a patron of the United Democratic Front (UDF), an international anti-apartheid organization linked to the ANC.

Eighteen months before Joseph's death in Johannesburg on Christmas Day 1992, the last of the apartheid laws was repealed; shortly after her death a new constitution was passed, giving all South Africans the right to vote. Joseph's contribution to the successful struggle against apartheid is described in her books, which include *If This Be Treason* (1963) and *Side by Side* (1986).

Joséphine (1763–1814) *First wife of Napoleon Bonaparte*

As empress of France Joséphine led a glittering lifestyle and was a leader of fashion. However, she failed to bear Napoleon a son, prompting him to divorce her in 1809.

Born at Trois-Ilets on the Caribbean island of Martinique and christened Marie Josèphe Rose, the future empress was the daughter of Joseph Tascher de La Pagerie, a sugar planter. At 16 she was sent to France to marry Vicomte Alexandre de Beauharnais, an army officer who was also originally from Martinique. Her education had been limited, but she had acquired a reputation for her graceful carriage and coquetry.

Despite the birth of two children, Eugène in 1781 and Hortense de BEAUHARNAIS in 1783, the marriage soured almost at once. A moody bookish young man, Alexandre tried to impose his interest in philosophy on Joséphine. She was uninterested, and also resented the fact that he was often away from home. Their marriage foundered when Alexandre sailed to Martinique with his mistress and cast a slur on Joséphine's reputation. She managed to vindicate herself, winning in 1785 a legal separation, financial support, and custody of Hortense.

Joséphine spent the next three years in Paris, developing the taste for fashion and sophistication that would later be her hallmark. In 1788 she visited Martinique again but returned in 1790 to a very different Paris. There was a growing hatred of the aristocracy, and although she pretended to have republican sympathies, she was arrested and imprisoned in 1794. With the overthrow of Robespierre the same year her friend Tallien obtained her release; her husband had been guillotined two weeks earlier.

Joséphine's charms were her only resource. She acquired an influential lover and used his connections to retrieve some of Alexandre's property. She soon became a hostess in the corrupt society that emerged in Paris after the Terror. However, her appetite for clothing, jewellery, and fine furnishings far exceeded her income. Her decision to marry the promising young general Napoleon Bonaparte in 1796 was probably a bid to gain financial security. Two days later he left to command the French army in Italy.

Joséphine was unprepared for and unresponsive to Napoleon's passionate love letters from Italy. She delayed joining him and began an affair with

Hippolyte Charles, a smart and witty captain. When news of the affair reached Napoleon during his Egyptian campaign (1798–99), he vowed to divorce Joséphine upon his return. Frightened and penitent, Joséphine persuaded him to change his mind and began to take her marriage seriously. She felt threatened by the hostility of the Bonapartes and was painfully conscious that she had failed to bear Napoleon a child. To enhance her status she persuaded Pope Pius VII to force Napoleon to renew his marriage to her at a religious ceremony on the eve of his coronation in 1804.

Having secured her status as empress, Joséphine was now in a much stronger position. Her tact and her knowledge of the social graces and etiquette of the old aristocracy greatly helped Napoleon in his effort to create a dignified imperial court out of his motley retinue of politicians and warriors. Nevertheless, after he had proved that he was capable of fathering a child by making one of his mistresses pregnant, he decided to divorce Joséphine. The couple announced the dissolution of their civil marriage in 1809. The Catholic marriage was then declared null for contrived reasons.

Joséphine retired to her estate of Malmaison and was granted a large allowance. She continued to spend money on extravagant parties, paid for by Napoleon. He visited her occasionally and, in his letters, tried in vain to curb her spending habits. After Napoleon's abdication Emperor Alexander I of Russia, one of his conquerors, came to offer her protection, but she died at Malmaison within a few weeks.

See also MARIE LOUISE.

Joyce, Eileen (1912–1991) Australian pianist

Eileen Joyce was a virtuoso performer on the piano and harpsichord, who played with top orchestras around the world.

The daughter of an itinerant labourer, Joyce was born in a tent in Zeehan, Tasmania. She was educated in Perth, Western Australia, until the age of 15, when her musical talent was spotted by the composer and pianist Percy Grainger. He sent her to study at the Leipzig Conservatory in Germany, where she became a pupil of the eminent pianists Artur Schnabel and Robert Teichmüller.

She then settled in London and studied under Tobias Matthay at the Royal College of Music, benefitting from the sophisticated system of piano teaching that he was then developing. Impressed by Joyce's talent, the conductor Sir Henry Wood invited her to make her London debut at one of his BBC Promenade Concerts. This performance displayed her obvious technical brilliance and won her many admirers.

During World War II Joyce played with the London Philharmonic Orchestra, giving many concerts of the large number of popular piano concertos in her extensive repertoire. After the war she extended this repertoire to include works by 20th-century composers. She also recorded soundtracks for films, most notably the Rachmaninov second piano concerto used in *Brief Encounter* (1945), and took a part in *Wherever She Goes*, a film telling the story of her childhood.

Juana Inés de la Cruz (1651–1695) *Mexican poet, scholar, and nun*

Sister Juana is considered the greatest lyric poet of the colonial period in Mexico. She was also an early feminist and is reputed to have amassed the largest library in Latin America.

Born Juana de Asbaje y Ramírez in San Miguel de Nepantla, she was brought up by her mother's parents, learning to read when she was three. She became known for her intelligence and learning and at the age of 14 was invited to become a lady-in-waiting at the viceroy's court in Mexico City. Here she was popular because of her charm, beauty, and poetic talents. She longed to attend the university but was not allowed to do so, although the professors were astonished at her knowledge.

In 1669 Juana entered a convent, where she assembled a large library and devoted herself to further study and to writing poetry, plays, and prose. Her sonnets and love lyrics are among the finest in the Spanish language. Her five plays include two comedies and three religious allegories, or *autos sacramentales*. In *The Divine Narcissus* she brought together Christian, Greek, and Aztec religion and mythology. Three volumes of Sister Juana's poetry, prose, and plays were published by her admirers in Spain.

In 1690 Sister Juana became involved in a controversy. She had written a letter to the bishop of Puebla, challenging his views on women's education, and he had published it under the false name "Sister Filotea," criticizing her for neglecting her religious duties. Sister Juana responded in an autobiographical essay, *Reply to Sister Filotea de la Cruz* (1691), addressed to the bishop. In this remarkable work she defended women's right to be educated and denounced the repression of women by men and the Inquisition. However, she sold her library of 4,000 books, gave the money to the poor, and devoted her last years to a spiritual life. She died of the plague while nursing her sister nuns during an epidemic in Mexico City.

Juana la Beltraneja (1462–1530)
Heiress to the throne of Castile

Juana's claim to the Castilian throne was based on the assumption that she was the daughter of King Henry IV of Castile. She came to be called Juana la Beltraneja when rumours spread that her father was really the royal favourite Beltrán de la Cueva.

Juana was born in Madrid, the daughter of Juana of Portugal and, it was assumed, of her husband Henry IV. She became Henry's heiress, but the Castilian nobility later claimed that she was illegitimate. Although the accusation was never proved, the king's changeable attitude toward her claim to the throne did little for the child's good name. In 1464 he gave in to the nobles and made his half-brother Alfonso his heir, promising to marry Alfonso to Juana. In 1465 he changed his mind again, provoking a civil war. After Alfonso's death in 1468 Henry recognized his half-sister

Isabella as heiress, but in 1470, after she had married Ferdinand of Aragon, he declared that Juana was his true daughter and the rightful heiress to the throne.

When Henry died in 1474, Isabella became Queen ISABELLA I, even though Alfonso V of Portugal took Juana's side and offered to marry her. Juana later chose to enter a convent rather than marry Juan, the son of Ferdinand and Isabella. She died in Lisbon.

Judith (6th century BC) *Old Testament heroine*

> Give me a beguiling tongue
> to wound and kill
> those who have formed such cruel
> designs
> against your covenant.
>
> —Judith, 9:13

Judith, whose name means "Jewess," saved the Israelites from destruction by deceiving and killing the Assyrian general Holofernes. Her story is told in the apocryphal Old Testament book named after her, and she is the subject of a famous painting by Artemisia GENTILESCHI.

When the Israelites refused to pay homage to the Assyrian King Nebuchadnezzar, he sent an army under his general Holofernes to enforce his demands. The Assyrian army besieged the town of Bethulia, which protected the route to Jerusalem – the fate of the Jewish nation thus hung in the balance.

Judith, a pious widow, left Bethulia as if in flight, making use of her beauty to infiltrate the Assyrian camp. Invited to a feast in Holofernes's tent, she waited until he fell into a drunken stupor before cutting off his head with his own sword, taking the severed head back with her to Bethulia.

Inspired by Judith's bravery and the knowledge that the Assyrian forces were now leaderless, the Bethulians routed the confused Assyrian force, thus raising the siege and safeguarding Jerusalem.

Juliana (1909–) *Queen of the Netherlands*

A very popular queen, Juliana was

known during her reign for her independent and informal style.

Juliana Louise Emma Marie Wilhelmina was born in The Hague, the only child of Queen WILHELMINA and Prince Henry of Mecklenburg-Schwerin. She was privately tutored in a class with several other girls and later studied law at the University of Leiden.

Her interest in the welfare of the Dutch people was evident in the 1930s when she formed the National Crisis Committee to provide relief from the economic depression. Juliana married Prince Bernhard of Lippe-Biesterfeld in 1937; their four daughters are BEATRIX (born 1938), Irene (born 1939), Margriet (born 1943), and Maria Christina (born 1947).

In World War II, just before the Germans occupied the Netherlands in 1940, Juliana and the four princesses escaped to Britain and then to Canada, where they spent most of the war years. Returning after the war, Juliana became queen in 1948 when Wilhelmina's poor health led to her abdicate. After a long and successful reign Juliana herself abdicated in 1980, on her 71st birthday. She was succeeded by her daughter Beatrix.

Julian of Norwich (c. 1342–after 1416) English mystic

> And then our good Lord opened my ghostly eye, and shewed me my soul in the midst of my heart. I saw the soul so large as it were an endless world.
>
> —*Revelations of Divine Love*

Julian's *Revelations of Divine Love* is regarded as one of the most important accounts of medieval religious experience.

Little is known of the life of Julian (or Juliana); she was probably born in Norwich and educated by nuns. Having prayed for an illness in the belief that "pain...maketh us to know our self, and to ask mercy" (*Revelations*), Julian became seriously ill in May 1373. During this illness she experienced 16 visions of Christ's Passion, the Virgin Mary, and the Holy Trinity.

These experiences persuaded her to become a recluse, living in a cell at the Church of St. Julian in Norwich, where she spent some 20 years in contemplation of her visions before writing her *Revelations of Divine Love.* This work combines vivid descriptions of her experiences with subtle theological discussion. Her writing is enlivened by the use of vivid, but everyday, images; for example, she compares a hazel nut lying in the palm of her hand to the world resting in the hand of God.

Although never officially canonized, Julian's unofficial feast day is celebrated on May 13.

Julia the Elder (39 BC–14 AD) *Roman princess*

An important member of the Augustan imperial dynasty, Julia later became infamous through scandal and died a tragic death.

Julia was the daughter of the Emperor Augustus by his wife Scribonia. Raised in the home of Augustus and his third wife, LIVIA, she learned the accomplishments of a princess. In 25 BC she married Marcellus, the emperor's nephew and heir, but he died in 23. In 21 Julia married Marcus Agrippa, by whom she had five children: Gaius, Lucius, Julia the Younger, AGRIPPINA THE ELDER, and Agrippa Postumus. Only a year after Agrippa's death in 12 BC she was married a third time – to Tiberius, the future emperor. This marriage was not a success, the couple leading separate lives.

Julia began to acquire a bad reputation, and when Tiberius retired to Rhodes in 6 BC, her behaviour became openly scandalous. In 2 BC Augustus accused her of having had affairs with several Roman senators; she was banished to the island of Pandateria and then, in 4 AD, to Rhegium. Tiberius was responsible for ordering her death by starvation ten years later.

Jung Chang (1952–) *Chinese linguist and writer*

Jung Chang has been highly praised for her *Wild Swans* (1991), an epic saga of the lives of three women – Jung Chang herself, her mother, and her grandmother – in modern China. At one level it is a deeply moving personal and family history; at another it has been described as "an unforgettable portrait of the brain-death of a nation." The book has become a best-seller in the Western world.

Jung Chang was born in Yibin, Sichuan province, in the People's Republic of China. At the age of 14 she became, briefly, a Red Guard. She subsequently worked as a "barefoot doctor," electrician, and steelworker before being accepted as a student of English at Sichuan University, where she became an assistant lecturer after graduating.

In 1978 Jung Chang left China for Britain, obtaining a scholarship to York University. There she became the first person from the People's Republic to be awarded a doctorate in Britain, receiving a PhD in linguistics in 1982. Jung Chang is now married to an Englishman, lives in London, and teaches at the School of Oriental and African Studies, which is part of London University.

K

Kael, Pauline (1919–) *American film critic*

> Wasn't there perhaps one little Von Trapp who didn't want to sing his head off, or who screamed that he wouldn't act out little glockenspiel routines for Papa's party guests?
>
> —In a controversial review of *The Sound of Music* (1966)

Kael's outspoken, perceptive, and witty reviews have been enormously influential, not only on the public but also on America's film-making establishment.

Pauline Kael was born in Petaluma, California, one of five children. Her father, a Polish Jew, ran a farm in Sonoma County, where the family lived until the Great Depression drove them to San Francisco. After leaving high school, Pauline studied philosophy at the University of California, Berkeley. Her reputation for outspoken witticisms began with her review (1953) of Charlie Chaplin's *Limelight*, which she famously called "Slimelight." There followed reviews in various journals and a number of radio broadcasts. Kael also became the manager of a cinema, for which she wrote film notes.

In 1965 a collection of Kael's reviews was published as *I Lost It at the Movies*. Described as "sane" and "salty," these writings ridiculed pretentious art films. Settling in New York, Kael freelanced on several journals, though she was fired from *McCall's* for her comments on *The Sound of Music*. In 1968 her second collection of reviews, *Kiss Kiss, Bang Bang*, was published. The same year she joined *The New Yorker*, to which she contributed regularly for 23 years except for a short spell working at Paramount Studios.

Further review collections were published as *Going Steady* (1970), *Deeper into Movies* (1973), *When the Lights Go Down* (1980), *State of the Art* (1985), and *Movie Love* (1991). Perhaps Kael's most famous review was "Raising Kane," in which she reassessed the 1941 movie *Citizen Kane*, giving Orson Welles's cowriter Herman J. Mankiewicz credit for more input than Welles himself.

Married and divorced several times, Kael has one daughter. She lectured at various colleges and universities before retiring in 1991.

Kahlo, Frida (1907–1954) *Mexican painter*

Kahlo's very personal paintings were influenced both by Mexican folk art and by the surrealist movement.

Born Magdalena Carmen Frida Kahlo y Calderón in Coyoacán, Mexico City, Kahlo had a Mexican mother and a German-born Jewish father. She was educated at the national preparatory school and originally intended to study medicine. However, she was severely injured in a bus accident in 1925, leading to long spells in hospital and further operations at various times throughout her life. She began to paint while recovering from one of these operations. The accident and its result provided a powerful fund of images for her work. Many of her colourful stylized paintings are self-portraits, and her own experiences are clearly expressed in such works as *Henry Ford Hospital* (1932).

Since the age of 13 Kahlo had been infatuated with the Mexican mural painter Diego Rivera, and in 1929 they married. Their difficult and intense relationship was another recurrent theme in Kahlo's art. As a result of their left-wing politics the couple were virtually forced to move to the United States in the early 1930s, returning to Mexico late in 1933.

Kahlo was strongly attached to her family home in Coyoacán, where she assembled a notable collection of folk art. In 1938 she met André Breton, founder of the surrealist movement, in the United States. He and Marcel Duchamp helped arrange for major exhibitions of her work to be held in Paris and the United States. Her picture *What the Water Gave Me* (1938), perhaps her most abstract painting, particularly fascinated Breton. Its fantastic elements are drawn directly from her personal experience, and this autobiographical quality is evident again in such works as *The Broken Column* (1944).

In the early 1940s Kahlo taught at La Esmeralda school of the arts in Mexico City, where she established a loyal following. She did not have a major exhibition in Mexico until 1953. After her death in Coyoacán, Rivera donated her house to the Mexican people as a museum. Her work was declared to be of national importance in 1985.

Karan, Donna (1948–) *American fashion designer*

Taking her own clothing needs as a starting point, Karan designed clothes that successfully met the demands of modern working women.

Born Donna Faske in Forest Hills, Queens, New York, Donna was a child of the fashion business: her father was a tailor, her mother was in clothing sales, and her stepfather also worked in the industry. After studying at Parsons School of Design in New York, she became an assistant to the sportswear designer Anne Klein. She became Donna Karan on her first marriage, to Mark Karan. When Klein died in 1974, the 26-year-old Karan (who had had a baby daughter a week before) became chief designer at the Klein company. Working with Louis Dell'Olio, she built up the business very successfully.

In 1984 Karan's own business, Donna Karan Co., was established. Like Klein, Karan specialized in comfortable and interchangeable separates – skirts, trousers, jackets, tops. This approach appealed to women who valued her keen sense of style but who also wanted practical clothes. She claimed that the jacket should be the basic building block of a contemporary woman's wardrobe. Worn in different combinations, it could serve for home, work, and leisure. She even avoided the word "fashion" and designed clothes with reference to herself rather than to models. Her subsidiary label DKNY celebrated New York City with a less expensive version of the same idea – clothing that was smart and stylish enough for urban life while remaining practical and casual. She was also known for her large bold accessories.

In the 1990s Karan expanded into menswear (inspired by Stephan Weiss, her second husband and business partner) and fragrance. She received numerous Coty and Council of Fashion Designers of America awards in the 1970s, 1980s, and 1990s, but the surest sign of her clothing's success is its enormous popular appeal.

Karle, Isabella Helen (1921–) *American crystallographer*

Isabella Karle was one of the first scientists to make successful use of x-ray crystallography – a technique in which the structures of crystals are worked out by observing how they diffract x-rays directed at them.

Born Isabella Lugoski in Detroit, Michigan, she was the daughter of Polish immigrants; her father was a house painter and her mother a seamstress. Isabella first heard Engish spoken when she began school. Later, while studying at the University of Michigan, she met the physicist Jerome Karle. They married in 1942, and in 1943 Isabella was awarded her PhD. Her husband's studies were devoted to x-ray crystallography, for which he would later win the Nobel Prize for chemistry (1985). The technique was also to be of great importance for Isabella's work. Jerome and Isabella worked together during World War II on the nuclear Manhattan Project in Chicago and afterwards moved to the

Naval Research Laboratory in Washington, D.C.

Isabella Karle has made a number of major contributions to the development of x-ray crystallography and has written over 200 papers on the subject. In the 1950s Jerome Karle and Herb Hauptman developed new techniques for interpreting the way x-rays were affected by crystals; Isabella Karle revealed the potential of these methods by using them successfully in her research. In her first major success in 1969 she established the structure of venom extracted from South American frogs. This was followed in 1975 with the structure of the large valinomycin molecule, a protein that carries potassium through biological membranes. In 1979 she worked out the structure of another protein, antamanide, and more recently she has determined the structure of the natural drug enkephalin.

Kartini, Raden Adjeng (1879–1904)
Javanese princess and writer

Remembered in Java on Kartini Day (her birthday, April 21), Kartini did much for the cause of women's education and freedom in Indonesia.

Born in Majong, central Java, Kartini was the daughter of the regent of Djapara. As her father worked for the Dutch colonial government, she was allowed to attend a Dutch school, where she became aware that opportunities available to Western women were denied to her Indonesian countrywomen.

During her teens Kartini was forced by tradition to give up school and live a secluded life, but she wrote letters to Dutch friends and to political figures, lamenting the status of women in Indonesia. Her most notable correspondent was the education minister, J. H. Abendanon.

In 1903 Kartini married the regent of Rembang, who sympathized with her aim of setting up a girls' school. Tragically, she died the following year after giving birth to a son. However, in 1911 Abendanon had her letters published in a volume entitled *Door duisternis tot licht* (Through Darkness into Light). This stimulated support for her

ideas in the Netherlands. The Kartini Foundation was set up, and the first girls' school was established in Java in 1916.

Käsebier, Gertrude (1852–1934)
American photographer

Käsebier was a pioneer of pictorialism, a turn-of-the-century school of American photography characterized by pastoral themes and soft-focus effects.

She was born Gertrude Stanton in Des Moines, Iowa, and lived in a log cabin near a Colorado mining settlement until her family moved to Brooklyn, New York, in 1864. After two years at a girls' seminary in Bethlehem, Pennsylvania, Gertrude returned to New York City. There she met Eduard Käsebier, whom she married in 1874.

Gertrude Käsebier was in her late thirties, her three children nearly grown, when her artistic flair first found expression. In 1888 she began to study painting at the Pratt Institute in New York; however, she soon turned to photography. In 1893 she made the first of several trips to Europe to study at the Académie Julian in Paris and to travel. In the French countryside surrounding Crécy-en-Brie she took her first serious photographs. On returning to the United States Käsebier became apprenticed to a portrait photographer; in 1897 she opened her own portrait studio in New York.

She took numerous photographs of New York socialites as well as her fellow photographers Alfred Stieglitz and Adolph de Meyer. She also contributed to a number of magazines. In 1898 Käsebier began a series of intuitive romantic images of motherhood, accompanied by carefully chosen titles. In *The Heritage of Motherhood* (1900) a woman sits alone in a barren rocky landscape, isolated yet strong, in a world that both idealized and constricted the role of women.

Käsebier was a pictorialist: she eliminated unwanted detail and created impressionistic images that resembled paintings. Through the organization known as the Photo-Secession, of which she was a founding member, Stieglitz promoted her work by publishing images in *Camera Notes* (1902) and *Camera Work* (1903). He also exhibited her photographs at the New York Camera Club (1899) and the Little Galleries of the Photo-Secession (1906). During this period Käsebier associated and exhibited with several other pictorial photographers, including Alvin Langdon Coburn and Clarence H. White. With White she formed the Pictorial Photographers of America in 1916.

Pictorialism had gone out of fashion by 1910, but Käsebier was faithful to it until the end of her career, when her eyesight began to fail. She closed her studio around 1925. In 1929 the Brooklyn Academy of Arts and Science held a retrospective exhibition of 35 of her photographs. She died in New York City.

Kassia (about 840) *Byzantine poet*

> You meet your friend, your face
> brightens – you have struck gold.
>
> —Translation by Patrick Diehl
> (1978)

An original Christian writer of deep emotion, Kassia is the only Byzantine woman poet whose work has survived.

Of noble birth, Kassia avoided being chosen as the bride of Emperor Theophilus by retorting angrily when the emperor quoted an insulting saying about women. A deeply spiritual woman, she founded a convent and spent her days writing poems and hymns. Her "Mary Magdalene," which is still used by the Greek Orthodox Church in Holy Week, is a passionate speech of penitence as if spoken to Christ by MARY MAGDALENE.

Kauffmann, Angelica (1741–1807) *Swiss painter*

> While she was standing between her
> two beaux, and finding an arm of
> each most lovingly embracing her
> waist, she contrived, whilst her arms
> were folded...to squeeze the hand of
> both.
>
> —J. T. Smith, on Kauffmann's
> coquetry in his biography of the
> sculptor Joseph Nollekens (1828)

As well as painting portraits, Angelica Kauffmann, who worked in Rome and London, tackled complex historical and mythological themes usually reserved for men.

Maria Anna Catharina Angelica Kauffmann was born in Chur, Switzerland, the daughter of the painter Johann Joseph Kauffmann. As a child she was a talented musician and painter. She received her first artistic commission (to paint the portrait of a bishop) at the age of 11. In 1754 and again in 1762–65 she visited Italy; during the second visit, while staying in Rome, she completed a famous portrait of the neoclassical art historian and archaeologist J. J. Winckelmann. In Rome she was also influenced by the neoclassical painter Anton Raphael Mengs and was elected a member of the Accademia di San Luca.

Kauffmann moved to England in 1766 with Lady Wentworth, wife of the British ambassador to Italy and quickly establised herself in London as a portraitist and painter of large-scale historical and mythological scenes, such as *The Interview of Hector and Andromache* (1769). In 1767 she was secretly married to a man masquerading as the Count van Horn, who turned out to be the count's estranged servant. This caused a scandal when the real count returned to England.

Kauffmann was a founder member of the Royal Academy of Art (1768), the first president of which, Sir Joshua Reynolds, was one of her admirers. She was also friendly with other notable painters of the day, including Nathaniel Dance and her countryman Henry Fuseli. In the 1770s she decorated neoclassical buildings designed by the Adam brothers. After her husband died in 1781, she married the Venetian painter Antonio Zucchi and returned to Rome, where she spent the rest of her life, prominent in artistic and social circles.

Kaye, M(ary) M(argaret) (1909–) *British writer and illustrator*

M. M. Kaye's fiction draws on her experiences in India in the days of the British Empire and on her extensive travels. She is probably best known for her historical epic *The Far Pavilions* (1978).

Mary Margaret Kaye was born in

Simla, India, the daughter of Sir Cecil and Lady Kaye. She married Major-General Godfrey Hamilton, with whom she travelled widely; they had two daughters.

Kaye's first story appeared in 1940. In the 1950s she published a number of exotic detective novels, such as *Death Walks in Kashmir* (1953). Her major achievement, however, is *The Far Pavilions*, a saga set in 19th-century India dealing with "sahibs, murder, power and romance." She spent 14 years writing it, while at the same time struggling against cancer.

Writing as Mollie Kaye, she is also the author of several children's books, including *The Ordinary Princess* (1980). Kaye illustrated some of her own works, and her autobiography, *The Sun in the Morning*, appeared in 1990.

Kaye, Nora (1920–1987) *American ballet dancer*

> I never take anything for granted. I question each tradition, each interpretation, each movement…This urge to question and to discover is, I think, the trademark of American ballet.
>
> —Writing in *Theater Arts* (1950)

An important figure in 20th-century ballet, Kaye is best known for her portrayal of inner conflict as Hagar in Antony Tudor's *Pillar of Fire* (1942).

Born Nora Koreff to Russian parents in New York, she later changed her name to Kaye because it sounded more American. Having started dancing at the age of four, she attended the Metropolitan Opera ballet school from the age of ten, joining the ballet company at 15. She worked for a time with George Balanchine's company and studied with Michel Fokine before becoming a founder member of the American Ballet Theater in 1940.

Kaye spent most of her career with the American Ballet Theater, becoming the company's prima ballerina after her 1942 appearance in *Pillar of Fire*. As many as 24 ballets were created for her. Famed for her dramatic performances, she was equally effective in both contemporary works, for example Tudor's *Lilac Garden* and

Agnes DE MILLE's *Fall River Legend*, and the traditional ballets *Giselle* and *Swan Lake*. Working for the New York City Ballet in 1951–53, Kaye gave an "inhuman" rendering of a female insect in Jerome Robbins's *The Cage*.

After retiring as a performer in 1961, Kaye worked as a producer with her third husband, the director-choreographer Herbert Ross. Between 1977 and 1983 she was an artistic director for the American Ballet Theater.

Keaton, Diane (1946–) *American actress*

> She brings nicely scrambled wit…to even the lowliest undertakings.
>
> —Jay Cocks in *Time*, 1976

Keaton developed her charming "nice-girl" image through appearances in Woody Allen's comedies but has also shown her talent independently as a more serious actress.

Born Diane Hall in Los Angeles, Keaton later adopted her mother's maiden name to distinguish herself from another actress. As a child she loved to perform and sing – at Santa Ana High School, California, she won a "Miss Personality" contest and was in musical productions. After attending colleges in California, Diane joined the Neighborhood Playhouse in New York. In 1968 she was appointed understudy to the female lead in the Broadway musical *Hair* and was promoted to the actual part a few months later. Keaton paradoxically attracted attention as the only member of the cast not to strip.

In 1971 Keaton appeared in the Broadway production of Woody Allen's *Play It Again, Sam*. This marked the start of a personal and working relationship with Allen that shaped her career in the 1970s. As well as performing in the film version of *Play It Again, Sam* (1972), she appeared with Allen in *Sleeper* (1973) and *Love and Death* (1975). After a couple of films in which she attempted to escape her on-screen pairing with Allen, Keaton won an Oscar for her performance in the title role of his *Annie Hall* (1977). This tender comedy was partly a portrait of their real-life relationship. Like the couple in the film, Keaton and Allen then split up, though they remained friends and would work together again. The same year Keaton appeared in the thriller *Looking for Mr. Goodbar*, which revealed her dramatic range more fully.

Keaton's other films include all three parts of *The Godfather* (1972, 1974, 1990), the comedy *Baby Boom* (1987), in which she played a New York career woman who finds herself ostracized after inheriting a baby, Allen's *Manhattan Murder Mystery* (1993), and the highly successful *First Wives Club* (1996). In 1997 she earned an Oscar nomination as Best Actress for her performance in *Marvin's Room*. Keaton also directed films in the late 1980s and 1990s.

Keeler, Christine (1942–) *British model and call girl*

Christine Keeler became infamous for her affair with the British secretary of state for war John Profumo while carrying on a relationship with a Soviet agent. Bound up as it was with espionage and political intrigue, the scandalous "Profumo affair" resulted in a major political crisis.

Keeler, a stunningly beautiful 18-year-old call girl, began to move in influential circles as a result of her involvement with an osteopath, Stephen Ward, whom she had met while working at a cabaret in London. Ward was noted for introducing beautiful and available young women to his wealthy patients.

When John Profumo first saw Keeler in 1961, she was bathing naked in a swimming pool at Cliveden, then the home of the British politician Lord Astor. The couple soon began an affair. However, Ward had already encouraged Keeler in a liaison with Evgeni Ivanov, an official at the Soviet Embassy in London, so that he could supply MI5, the British counterintelligence agency, with information about Ivanov's activities. Keeler's affair with Profumo lasted only a few weeks, and he was unlikely to have told her any official secrets; however, after she leaked the story to the press in 1962,

he faced accusations that his behaviour had posed a threat to national security. In March 1963 he lied to the House of Commons about his involvement with her, but the police were now investigating Ward in connection with offences of living on immoral earnings, and the truth of the affair came out. Profumo was forced to resign in June.

Ward committed suicide in August 1963. In December of that year Keeler was tried for lying under oath in another court case, found guilty, and sentenced to nine months in prison. A film about her life story, shot in Denmark, was released the same month. Another film about the affair, *Scandal*, came out in 1989.

Keene, Laura (*c.* 1826–1873) *British-born American actress and theatre manager*

> She had...the rare power of varying her manner, assuming the rustic walk of a milkmaid or the dignified grace of a queen.
>
> —Joseph Jefferson, quoted by John Creahan, 1897

Laura Keene was one of the first woman theatre managers in the United States. Her long-running production of Tom Taylor's *Our American Cousin* helped to establish New York as the principal American theatrical centre.

Originally called Mary Moss, Foss, or Lee (there is some doubt about her real name), she was born in London and made her first appearance on stage as Shakespeare's Juliet in 1851 (at the Richmond Theatre, Surrey). Trained by an aunt, Mrs. Yates, and by Madame VESTRIS, Keene travelled to New York in 1852 and appeared in a play called *The Will*. After moving on to Baltimore and travelling to California and Australia, she returned in 1855 to New York, where she founded a playhouse that later became the Olympic Theater.

Keene's first production, in 1856, was Shakespeare's *As You Like It*, in which she herself took the role of Rosalind. However, she specialized mainly in contemporary drama, using a resident company. The famous American actors Joseph Jefferson and E. A.

Sothern both made their reputations in *Our American Cousin*, which ran from 1858. At the start of the Civil War Keene put on popular musical shows and melodramas but gave this up in 1862 to go on tour. Her reputation never recovered after President Lincoln was assassinated in 1865 during one of her company's performances of *Our American Cousin* in Washington.

Keller, Helen (1880–1968) *American writer and social worker*

> She likes stories that make her cry – I think we all do, it's so nice to feel sad when you have nothing particular to be sad about.
>
> —Annie Sullivan, in a letter of December 12, 1887

Though unable to see or hear, Helen Keller refused to be discouraged by her disabilities and inspired millions with her achievements.

Helen Adams Keller was born in Tuscumbia, Alabama, the daughter of a newspaper editor. At 19 months she suffered an attack of scarlet fever from which she was left deaf and blind; she was also unable to speak. When she was six, her parents appealed for help to Boston's Perkins Institute for the Blind, which sent them one of their graduates, the 20-year-old Annie Sullivan (see MACY, ANNE MANSFIELD SULLIVAN). This girl, who had herself been blind but had partially recovered, was an inspiration to Helen, quickly teaching her the names of objects by an alphabet based on the sense of touch. Annie also introduced Helen to sign language, taught her to read by the Braille system, and taught her to write using a special typewriter. In 1890 Helen learned to speak by feeling the vibrations of the larynx and mimicking them. By working on her voice, she achieved a strangely pitched but comprehensible tone.

From 1896 until 1900 Helen attended school in Boston with the help of Annie, who accompanied her to all classes and repeated the lectures and discussions by touch. After private tutoring she passed the entrance examinations for Radcliffe College, which she entered in 1900, again faithfully supported and helped by Annie. Helen's textbooks were printed in Braille, and she sat her examinations with her own typewriter. With Annie's help she also wrote her autobiography, *The Story of My Life* (1902). When Helen graduated with honours in 1904, she was disappointed that Annie's role had not been acknowledged. Helen's remarkable intelligence and perseverance enabled her to learn French and German as well as philosophy.

In 1905 Annie married John Macy, after he agreed that Helen should come first in their lives. Under Macy's influence Helen became a militant socialist and suffragist. After Macy left them in 1914, Polly Thompson, a young Scotswoman, moved in with Helen and Annie as their secretary-housekeeper. Finding it difficult to manage financially, Helen accepted one of Andrew Carnegie's lifetime pensions but also undertook many lecture tours, wrote several books, made a film based on her life, and even appeared on the vaudeville circuit to raise the public's awareness of the problems of deaf-blind people. In 1924 she began a campaign to raise funds for the newly formed American Foundation for the Blind; through her tours and lectures she and Annie raised an amazing $2 million for the charity. In 1927 she published *My Religion*, relating her conversion to the Swedenborgian philosophy; three years later *Midstream*, the second volume of her autobiography, appeared.

Annie's blindness recurred again in the 1930s, and in 1936 she died. Though devastated by this loss, Helen, with Polly's help, overcame her grief by her remarkable determination. The two women moved to a house in Connecticut built for them by the American Foundation. Helen became a fierce antifascist before World War II, supported American involvement in the war, and visited military hospitals, providing inspiration to the wounded. After the war she and Polly travelled the world to help the blind overseas. In 1960 Polly died, and a year later Helen had a stroke. She lived another seven years and died, aged 88, in Westport, Connecticut. Her burial urn was placed next to those of Annie and

Polly in the National Cathedral in Washington, D.C.

Kelly, Grace (1929–1982) *American actress and wife of Prince Rainier III of Monaco*

> A Dresden doll with a kind of platinum beneath the delicate porcelain.
> —Maurice Chevalier, describing Kelly

Grace Kelly had already earned a considerable reputation as a film actress before marrying Prince Rainier and becoming Princess Grace of Monaco.

A niece of the playwright George Kelly, Grace was born in Philadelphia, the daughter of a rich businessman. She was educated privately, later studying at the American Academy of Dramatic Arts in New York City, from which she graduated in 1949. Her first professional appearance on stage was at the Bucks County Playhouse in a revival of George Kelly's *The Torchbearers* in 1949. The same year she made her Broadway debut in Strindberg's *The Father*.

Grace Kelly's first film, *Fourteen Hours* (1951), was a documentary drama made in New York. A year later the Hollywood Western *High Noon* (1952) brought her a seven-year contract with MGM, although her most important films, *Dial M for Murder*, *Rear Window*, and *The Country Girl* (all 1954) were made at other studios. For her performance in *The Country Girl* she won an Academy Award as Best Actress. Her MGM films include *The Swan* (1956) and *High Society* (1956), a musical remake of *The Philadelphia Story*.

In 1956 Grace Kelly gave up her film career to marry Prince Rainier of Monaco. The fairy-tale romance combined with her beauty and elegance captured the public imagination. However, Grace's life ended in sudden tragedy in 1982 when her car plunged off a road in southern France. She died in Monaco from her injuries, leaving three children.

Kelly, Petra (1947–1992) *German politician*

A civil-rights campaigner and antinuclear protester, Kelly put environ-

mental issues on the political agenda through her work with the Green Party, which she cofounded.

Born Petra Lehmann in Bavaria, Kelly took her surname from her Irish stepfather, with whom she and her stepmother emigrated to the United States in 1960. They settled in Georgia, and in 1966–70 Petra studied for a degree in international relations at the American University, Washington, D.C. As a student she joined protests against the Vietnam War and nuclear arms.

After moving to Amsterdam to take an MA degree, Kelly became an employee of the EEC, developing her interest in environmental, educational, and health issues. In 1972 she joined the German Social Democratic Party, but in 1979 differences of opinion led Kelly and several friends to leave and found the Green Party. The publicity that the Greens gave to environmental issues, notably the setting up of U.S. nuclear missiles in West Germany, had a huge impact on public opinion. In the 1983 elections the Greens won 5.6% of the vote – a large figure for a special-interest party. Because of the proportional representation system, the Green Party gained 27 seats in parliament, one of which was taken by Kelly, their principal spokesperson.

Kelly's political career flourished throughout the 1980s, but in the 1990 election, after the unification of East and West Germany, her party lost support, and she fell out of favour with her colleagues. In 1992 she and her long-standing companion Gert Bastian were found dead. Bastian, it seemed, had shot Kelly and then himself.

Kemble, Frances (1809–1893) *British actress and writer*

> Maids must be wives and mothers,
>   to fulfill
> The entire and holiest end of
>   woman's being.
> —"Woman's Heart" (1839)

Although she viewed herself as a writer, Frances Kemble became an actress through necessity. She turned out to be one of the great talents of her age.

Frances Anne (usually known as

Fanny) Kemble could hardly have avoided going on the stage, since her mother was an actress and playwright, her father, Charles Kemble, was an actor and the manager of the Covent Garden theatre, and his sister was the great actress Sarah SIDDONS. Fanny was more interested in writing, but in 1829 she reluctantly agreed to appear at Covent Garden as Juliet to help save the theatre from bankruptcy. The public loved her, and she restored the fortunes of Covent Garden with further appearances in Shakespearean and other roles.

In 1832–34 Fanny went on tour with her father to the United States. While there she married Pierce Mease Butler, an upper-class Philadelphian, and retired from the stage. To Fanny's horror her husband turned out to be a slave owner. After visiting his plantation in 1838, she wrote about the conditions there in *Journal of a Residence on a Georgian Plantation*, but her husband's opposition prevented its publication until 1863.

Fanny had given birth to two daughters, but her marriage was unhappy, and after years of separation she obtained a divorce in 1850. Dividing her time between Europe and the United States, she gave public readings of Shakespeare from 1848 to 1868. Her writings, which became more prolific in later life, include three volumes of poetry and one of plays, her life story in three instalments (1878, 1882, and 1890), and a novel, *Far Away and Long Ago* (1889).

Kempe, Margery (1372–*c.* 1438) *English mystic and autobiographer*

> Thou shalt have more merit in Heaven for one year of thinking in thy mind than for a hundred years of praying with thy mouth.
>
> —*The Book of Margery Kempe* (*c.* 1431–36)

Outspoken, uninhibited, and illiterate, Margery Kempe was an unlikely person to have produced the first autobiography in English. Dictated to scribes by the author, it tells of her mystical experiences and remarkable series of pilgrimages.

She was born Margery Burnham in King's Lynn, Norfolk, the daughter of a merchant who later became the town mayor. Margery married a merchant named John Kempe. After giving birth to her first child, she suffered a psychological illness but was cured following a vision of Christ. Margery vowed to devote her life to God and began to go on pilgrimages. With a tendency to indulge in "boisterous crying" when she had visions, she also believed in mortification (the self-infliction of pain or denial of pleasure for spiritual benefit) and was apt to criticize and scold fellow pilgrims.

After giving birth to a total of 14 children, Margery took a vow of celibacy with her husband in 1413. In 1413–15 she made her longest pilgrimage, to the Holy Land, returning via Rome. Soon afterwards, in 1417, she visited the shrine of St. James of Compostela in Spain. She then spent several years nursing her husband and recovering from an illness. When John died, Margery undertook a journey to Germany with her daughter-in-law, followed by a further series of trips to English pilgrimage sites. In about 1431 she started dictating her life story, which is known as *The Book of Margery Kempe*.

Kendal, Felicity (1946–   ) *British actress*

Although primarily a theatrical actress, Felicity Kendal is best known for costarring in the classic sitcom *The Good Life*. A combination of mischievous sex appeal and apparent vulnerability accounts for her personal charm.

The daughter of two Shakespearean actors, Felicity Kendal was born in Olton, Warwickshire, but spent the first 19 years of her life in India, where she attended six convent schools. She made her first appearance on stage at the age of nine months. At the age of nine she appeared as Puck in *A Midsummer Night's Dream*; she later played many of Shakespeare's heroines, including Viola, Jessica, and Ophelia in India and Juliet back in Britain.

Kendal's first marriage (later dissolved) was to the actor Drewe Henley. They had a son, Charley, who outdid his mother by first appearing on stage aged six weeks. Kendal performed in a wide variety of stage plays in the 1970s, 1980s, and 1990s, ranging from Shakespeare to Alan Ayckbourn's *The Norman Conquests* (1974). She has also appeared in a number of Tom Stoppard's plays, including *Hapgood* (1988), *Arcadia* (1993), and *Indian Ink* (1995); her involvement with Stoppard led to the break-up of his marriage to the TV doctor Miriam STOPPARD in the 1990s.

She had already appeared in several television programmes before filming four series of *The Good Life* in 1975–78. She and Richard Briers played a couple who had "downshifted" from a conventional suburban lifestyle to a self-sufficient one, turning their back garden into a farm.

In 1983 Kendal married Michael Rudman, shortly after converting to Judaism. She gave birth to a second son, Jacob, but this marriage was also dissolved, in 1994. In addition to her continued stage career, Kendal made further appearances in television productions.

Kendrick, Pearl (1890–1980) *American microbiologist*

Pearl Kendrick is best remembered for her discovery of a vaccine against whooping cough, formerly the most lethal childhood disease in the West.

Kendrick was born in Wheaton, Illinois. She graduated with a science degree from Syracuse University in 1914 and afterwards (1914–19) worked as a science teacher and high school principal in New York State. After a brief spell as a laboratory assistant in New York, she went to Michigan and in 1926 was appointed by the Michigan Department of Health as associate director of the Western Michigan Branch Laboratory in Grand Rapids. She later became public health officer for Michigan.

In 1932 Kendrick obtained a doctorate from John Hopkins University. Following this she and Dr. Grace Elderling spent several years studying pertussis (whooping cough), visiting sick children to take specimens. In 1939 Kendrick developed a vaccine against pertussis, which she later incorporated into a single shot for diphtheria, pertussis, and tetanus (DPT), which is now in general use.

In the 1940s Pearl Kendrick held a number of advisory roles relating to public health issues, notably with the World Health Organization in 1949–50. From 1951 she lectured at the University of Michigan. She became a member of several professional organizations and published papers in scientific journals. Pearl Kendrick died in Grand Rapids.

Kennedy, Helena (Ann), Baroness (1950–) *Scottish barrister, writer, and broadcaster*

As both a practising lawyer and a writer-broadcaster, Helena Kennedy has shown a particular concern for issues of civil liberties, especially as they affect women.

Born into a working-class family in Glasgow, Helena Kennedy was aware from an early age of injustices in the workplace and decided to be a lawyer while still at school. From 1968 Kennedy studied law in London and, after qualifying, set up a practice with others who shared her left-wing views. She has represented a wide variety of clients, including an anarchist, one of the Guildford Four (wrongly accused of an IRA bombing), and the child murderess Myra Hindley, earning a reputation for her legal acumen and persuasive manner in court. She came to the attention of the general public in 1987 when she presented a BBC television documentary series about the law, *The Heart of the Matter*. The hard-hitting television drama series *Blind Justice* (1988) was based on some of her cases. In 1990 she co-produced Channel 4's *Women Behind Bars*. Her view that women have historically been the victims of injustice is represented by the title of her 1992 book *Eve was Framed*. She was made a QC in 1991 and served as a member of the Bar Council from 1990 until 1993. Three years later she accepted the chancellorship of Oxford Brookes University. Following Labour's victory in the 1997 general election she was created a working peer.

She has a son by her former partner Iain Mitchell, with whom she lived from 1978 to 1984, and a son and a daughter from her marriage to Iain Hutchinson in 1986.

Kenny, Elizabeth (1886–1952) *Australian nurse*

> Panic plays no part in the training of a nurse.
>
> —*And They Shall Walk* (with Martha Ostenso)

Elizabeth Kenny is widely known for her method of treating patients suffering from poliomyelitis.

Kenny was born in Warialda, New South Wales. When she began to work in the Australian bush with patients paralysed by polio, she was not familiar with the generally accepted treatment, which was to immobilize limbs with casts and splints. The method she devised relied instead on the stimulation of paralysed muscles, which proved very effective in dealing with early stages of the illness. Her work was interrupted during World War I, when she served as an army nurse, but she returned to nursing polio victims after the war. In spite of opposition from sceptical doctors, the Queensland government gave her funding to set up a clinic in Townsville in 1933.

In 1940 Sister Kenny made a trip to the United States. The National Foundation for Infantile Paralysis and the University of Minnesota gave her an opportunity to lecture and to demonstrate her methods at the Minneapolis General Hospital. The American Medical Association approved her methods, and in 1942 the Sister Kenny Institute was set up in Minneapolis to train nurses and physiotherapists. Clinics in other places followed. Elizabeth Kenny died in Toowoomba, Queensland.

Kent, Joan of (1328–1385) *English princess*

Described by the 14th-century chronicler Jean Froissart as "the most beautiful of all the kingdom of England," Joan, who was known as the Fair Maid of Kent, was the wife of Edward, the Black Prince, eldest son of King Edward III of England.

She was the daughter of Edmund of Woodstock, Earl of Kent, youngest son of King Edward I of England. Joan's first husband was Sir Thomas Holland, who assumed the title of Earl of Kent in her right in 1360, a few months before his death. In 1361 Joan married Edward, Prince of Wales (the Black Prince). A warrior hero who supposedly wore black armour, Edward died in France before becoming king, but the couple's son succeeded his grandfather as King Richard II.

Kenyon, Dame Kathleen (1906–1978) *British archaeologist*

> The worst possible thing to do is to clear along the face of a wall, as its relation to the layers is thus destroyed. It is necessary to cut a section at right angles to each wall, in order to decide which layers are earlier...
>
> —Article published in 1939

Kenyon is principally noted for her excavations at Jericho, which revealed the oldest known city in the world. She also carried out significant excavations at Jerusalem and at several sites in Britain and wrote many books on archaeology.

Kathleen Kenyon was born in London, the eldest daughter of Sir Frederick George Kenyon, director of the British Museum, and his wife Amy. Kathleen was educated at St. Paul's School for Girls, London, and at Somerville College, Oxford. In 1929 she joined Gertrude Caton-Thompson on a project to excavate the site of Great Zimbabwe in Africa. Returning to England, she worked on the Roman site at St. Albans, Hertfordshire (1930–35). During this period she also joined a dig at Samaria, Palestine. In the late 1930s and again after World War II she led several archaeological projects in Britain and one at Sabratha, North Africa (1948–51). She also held senior posts at the University of London Institute of Archaeology (1935–46) and at other learned institutions.

Kenyon's most important work took place in the 1950s. Appointed director of the British School of Archaeology in Jerusalem, she led excavations at

Jericho (1952–58), discovering and dating many layers of deposits, down to a neolithic site dating to *c.* 8000 BC. These discoveries were recorded in her *Digging up Jericho* (1957). Kenyon also undertook excavations in Jerusalem in the 1960s, later writing the book *Digging up Jerusalem* (1974).

Kathleen Kenyon had lectured for many years in Britain, and also at the Archaeological Institute of America (1959), when she was appointed principal of St. Hugh's College, Oxford, in 1962. She held this post until 1973, the year she was made a DBE. She died five years later at Wrexham, Wales.

Kerr, Deborah (1921–) *British actress*

> She is an actress of unusual charm, a charm that is both physical and intellectual.
>
> —From a review of *Colonel Blimp* (1943), in *New Movies* magazine

The star of many films in both Britain and Hollywood, Deborah Kerr was six times nominated for an Oscar for Best Actress. Perhaps because of her refined Scottish beauty, with red-gold hair and blue-green eyes, she tended to be typecast in graceful ladylike roles.

Deborah Jane Kerr-Trimmer was born in Helensburgh, Scotland. After her father's death she moved with her mother and brother to England and later went to school in Bristol. There she also attended a dance studio run by her aunt and became good enough to win a scholarship to the Sadler's Wells Ballet School. However, after a year she left to pursue her interest in drama.

Having played a few small parts on stage and one on screen, Kerr was given her first significant film role as a Salvation Army officer in *Major Barbara* in 1940. This was followed by parts in other British films, notably *The Life and Death of Colonel Blimp* (1943), Alexander Korda's *Perfect Strangers* (1945), and *Black Narcissus* (1946), in which she played a nun. During this period she met and (in 1945) married Anthony Bartley, by whom she was to have two daughters.

Black Narcissus won Kerr a contract with MGM to costar with Clark Gable in *The Hucksters* (1947). Although a success, she seemed unable to break her typecast "ladylike" mould in the films that followed. The only exception was her performance as a lustful wife in *From Here to Eternity* (1953). This and her roles in *Edward, My Son* (1949), *The King and I* (1956), *Heaven Knows, Mr. Allison* (1957), *Separate Tables* (1958), and *The Sundowners* (1960) won her Oscar nominations.

Having divorced her first husband in 1959, Kerr married Pieter Viertel in 1960. Her career continued with such films as *The Night of the Iguana* (1964), but in 1969 she retreated to Switzerland, where she lived in semiretirement. In the 1980s she appeared on television in *A Woman of Substance* (1984) and in several more films, including *The Assam Garden* (1985). Deborah Kerr was clearly moved when she received an honorary award at the Oscar ceremony in 1994: she was made a CBE in 1998.

Key, Ellen (1849–1926) *Swedish writer, feminist, and pacifist*

> Woman, however, as the bearer and guardian of the new lives, has everywhere greater respect for life than man, who for centuries, as hunter and warrior, learned that the taking of lives may be not only allowed, but honourable.
>
> —*Renaissance of Motherhood* (1914)

Ellen Key idealised the role of women as mothers of children, bearing and educating the next generation, and as "mothers of society," protectors of life and promoters of peace.

Born in Sundsholm, in southeast Sweden, Key was the daughter of a wealthy landowner. She was taught at home and afterwards became a teacher. In 1868 her father became a liberal member of Parliament and moved his family to Stockholm. As his assistant Ellen learned much about politics.

While working as a school teacher in Stockholm (1880–99), Key began lecturing on social issues at the Workers' Institute in 1883. She showed herself to be a creative thinker in the many essays she published from 1884 to 1899. From the late 1890s she emerged as a significant formulator of public opinion. Her most famous book, *Barnets århundrade* (1900; published in English as *The Century of the Child*, 1909) was followed by other influential works. In 1903 Key embarked on a six-year lecture tour of Europe.

Key argued that women had great potential as advocates of peace. As a liberal pacifist she believed that patriotism should involve not territorial ambition but love for one's culture and people.

Key was criticized for some of her liberal views; for example, she placed a higher value on love than on the institution of marriage. Yet she also stressed the importance of fidelity, self-discipline, and duty. Believing motherhood to be of prime importance for society, she argued that women should stay at home to bring up their children. Women without children, however, should enter the political arena in the role of peacemakers and peacekeepers.

Key promoted the neutrality of Sweden during World War I. Having settled permanently in Sweden in 1910, she continued to write. She died at Alvastra.

Khadijah (*c.* 564–619) *First wife of the Prophet Mohammed*

A wealthy Arabian widow some 15 years older than Mohammed at the time of their marriage, Khadijah supported him after he became Prophet, and he was faithful to her until her death.

Khadijah had been married twice before and had two families. She was wise in her handling of the money she inherited from her second husband and at first appointed Mohammed as her agent. After marrying, they built a strong relationship; Khadijah bore six or more children, only one of whom, FATIMAH, survived them both.

See also A'ISHA.

Khan, Ra'ana Liaquat Ali (1905–1990) *Pakistani politician and diplomat*

> She had little time for the mullahs unless they respected women's rights.
>
> —Ahmed Rashid, *The Independent*, 1990

Ra'ana Liaquat Ali Khan helped to found the modern state of Pakistan, of which her husband was the first prime minister. She did much to alleviate suffering and founded a number of welfare organizations.

The daughter of a government official, Ra'ana Pant was born in Almora in the United Provinces of India (now in Uttar Pradesh) and educated in Naini Tal and Lucknow. In 1929 she gained an MA in economics and sociology at Lucknow University for a thesis on women's labour in agriculture. After training as a teacher, she became professor of economics at a girls' college in Delhi.

In 1933 Ra'ana married Liaquat Ali Khan, a member of the United Provinces Legislative Council; the marriage produced two sons. Ra'ana and her husband worked together for the cause of an independent state for Indian Muslims.

In 1947 India was partitioned, with the creation of the independent Muslim state of Pakistan, of which Liaquat Ali Khan became prime minister. Within days Pakistan was swamped with Muslim refugees from India and racked with famine and disease. Begum Ra'ana stepped in to ease the crisis, helping the hungry and homeless and calling on Muslim women to nurse the sick. She founded the Pakistan Cottage Industries (1948), the All Pakistan Women's Association (1949), the Women's National Guard (1949), and other organizations.

In 1951 tragedy struck when Ali Khan was brutally assassinated. However, Ra'ana's own political career was still at its height. In 1952 she became a delegate to the United Nations, and between 1954 and 1966 she was the first Muslim woman to serve as a foreign ambassador – first to the Netherlands, then to Italy, and finally to Tunisia. From 1973 to 1976 she was governor of Sind province. She received the United Nations Human Rights Award in 1979.

A consistent defender of women's rights, Begum Ra'ana opposed oppressive Islamic legislation in the 1980s. She died in Karachi.

Kimura, Doreen (*c.* 1935–) *Canadian psychologist*

Doreen Kimura's experimental work has shown that the two halves of the brain specialize in different types of thought process. She has also examined differences between male and female aptitudes and how body asymmetry is linked to certain skills.

Kimura was born at Winnipeg, Manitoba, and educated at McGill University, Montreal, where she received her PhD in 1961. After working briefly at the University of California, Los Angeles, and at McMaster University, Hamilton, she moved to the University of Western Ontario, London, and was later appointed professor of psychology in 1974.

Kimura's early work was concerned with possible differences in function between the left and right sides of the brain. She found that people could more easily remember numbers when they were played into the right ear (connected with the left side of the brain) and melodies when they were played into the left ear (linked to the right side of the brain). She eventually concluded that the left part of the brain processes words and numbers, while the right side handles such concepts as music and spatial relationships.

In the 1970s Kimura extended her work to studying differences between the sexes. She found women to be better at arithmetic and the use of language. Men seemed to perform better at certain spatial tasks and at mathematical reasoning. Kimura thought the answer might lie in the level of sex hormones in each case. She found that the women's spatial skills increased when they had low levels of the hormone oestrogen and that the men's weaker skills improved when testosterone levels were low.

More recently Kimura has begun to study body asymmetry. She has found that men tend to be larger on the right side and women larger on the left. Much to her surprise, Kimura found that these body differences might have a link with intellectual skills. Thus right-larger individuals, whether male or female, are likely to be better at handling mathematical problems.

King, Billie Jean (1943–) *American tennis player*

> I've always wanted to equalize things for us…Women can be great athletes.
>
> —Interview, September 1973

Billie Jean King won numerous championships and fought for greater equality in the prize money awarded to women and men. Despite a series of knee and heel operations, she was considered the leading woman player of her generation.

She was born Billie Jean Moffit in Long Beach, California. After winning her first tournament at the age of 13, she was given coaching by the former American champion Alice MARBLE. At 17 she won the Wimbledon women's doubles title with Karen Hantz. Between 1961 and 1979 she won a record 20 Wimbledon titles: six singles, ten doubles, and four mixed doubles. She also won four U.S. singles titles (1967, 1971, 1972, 1974), the Australian Open (1968), and the French Open (1972).

In 1965 Billie Jean had married Larry King while they were students at Los Angeles State College. Between 1965 and 1973 she was ranked first in the United States seven times and first in the world four times. In 1971 she became the first woman athlete to earn more than $100,000 in a single year. In acknowledgment of her successes Billie Jean was voted female Athlete of the Year in 1967 and again in 1973. She did a great deal to raise the profile of women's tennis in 1973 when she defeated 55-year-old ex-champion Bobby Riggs in a "Battle of the Sexes," after he had claimed that men's competition was far superior to women's.

King, Coretta Scott (1927–) *American civil-rights activist*

Though she was trained as a singer, Coretta Scott's life changed when she married Martin Luther King, Jr. Actively supporting his causes both before and after his assassination, she also used her talent for singing to promote the civil-rights movement at concerts across the United States.

Coretta Scott was born in Heiberger, Alabama. She took a degree in music and education at Antioch College in Ohio and continued her studies at the New England Conservatory of Music in Boston, Massachusetts. While in Boston she met the Atlanta minister Martin Luther King, Jr., who was doing graduate work in philosophy at the university. They were married in 1953. The following year, after receiving her degree in music, she and her husband returned to the South.

Throughout the years of Martin Luther King's tireless work in the civil-rights movement, Coretta accompanied him on marches and speaking tours, while managing her family of four children. After his assassination she continued his work with the Southern Christian Leadership Conference and was the president of the Martin Luther King, Jr. Memorial Center in Atlanta.

Kingsley, Mary (1862–1900) *British explorer and writer*

Mary Kingsley's two expeditions to West Africa were packed with adventures and discoveries.

A niece of the writer Charles Kingsley, Mary Henrietta Kingsley was born in London and had almost no formal education. She was expected to look after her mother and brother while her father, the traveller George Kingsley, pursued his research, but she made good use of his library. When she was 20, the family moved to Cambridge, where Mary's brother was to study. In 1892 both her parents died, and the following year Mary set out for West Africa.

On this trip Kingsley learned to navigate a ship, got to know the traders and did some trading herself, and worked on some aspects of the research that her father had left unfinished. She learnt about the lives of native Africans, having little sympathy for missionaries and colonists who interfered with African traditions.

After returning to England in 1894, Kingsley set out for West Africa again the same year, this time to explore and to study the cannibal tribes. Still dressed as a Victorian lady, she travelled in a canoe up the Ogowé River, where she collected specimens of formerly unknown fish. In the uncharted territories upstream she encountered the cannibal Fan tribes, whom she described as "uncommon fine" people. She pressed on through forests and swamps (once emerging from the water with a collar of leeches) toward the Rembwé River, eventually reaching Libreville (the capital of Gabon). Before going home, she climbed Mount Cameroon (13,760 feet).

Mary Kingsley returned to England in 1895 and quickly became famous for her adventures, which she recounted in lectures and described in her vivid books *Travels in West Africa* (1897) and *West African Studies* (1899). In 1897 she protested against the "hut tax" imposed on West Africa. She died of typhoid fever while nursing victims of the Boer War in South Africa.

Kirch, Maria Margarethe (1670–1720) *German astronomer*

Maria Kirch devoted her life to astronomy. In addition to discovering a new comet, she published correct astronomical predictions.

Born in Panitzsch, near Leipzig, Maria Margarethe Winkelmann was the daughter of a Protestant minister. She developed an early passion for astronomy, inspired by the self-taught "peasant" astronomer Christoph Arnold of Sommerfeld. At the age of 22 she married the respected astronomer Gottfried Kirch, undeterred by the fact that he was an impoverished widower 31 years older than herself. Sharing his fascination for astronomical calculations, she helped him produce celestial calendars and ephemerides (annual predictions of the positions of the planets). Having discovered a comet in 1702, in 1709 she published a prediction of the 1712 conjunction of the Sun, Saturn, and Venus.

After Gottfried's death in 1710, Maria continued her work alone. Despite having little belief in astrology, she responded to popular demand in her pamphlet (1712) on the conjunction of Jupiter and Saturn, expected in

1713, by including an astrological interpretation of the event. The same year she went to Berlin to work at the private observatory of her husband's friend Baron von Krosigk, but he died two years later, and she moved to Danzig. Declining an invitation to Russia from Peter the Great, in 1716 she moved back to Berlin, where her son Christfried had been appointed director of the city observatory. Kirch remained there until her death, continuing to make astronomical calculations.

Kirkpatrick, Jeane (1926–) *American scholar and diplomat*

Jeane Kirkpatrick became known internationally when she was appointed U.S. ambassador to the United Nations by President Ronald Reagan.

Jeane Duane Jordan was born in Duncan, Oklahoma. She graduated from Barnard College in New York City and obtained an MA degree from Columbia University in 1950. In 1955 she married her fellow academic Evron Kirkpatrick, who later became executive director of the American Political Science Association. After bringing up their three sons, Jeane Kirkpatrick returned to Columbia University, where she was awarded a PhD in 1968. She taught political science at Georgetown University from 1967 to 1981 and was active in Democratic party politics. In 1972 she helped to set up an organized campaign to counter the influence in the party of the left-wing Senator George McGovern and his supporters.

In the later 1970s Kirkpatrick (now a university professor) voiced strong opposition to the foreign policy of the Carter administration, believing that it underestimated the dangers of communist dictatorships while harshly condemning right-wing regimes that supported American interests. The next president, Ronald Reagan, aware of these views, offered her the post of U.S. ambassador to the United Nations, in which she served from 1981 until 1985. During this period she caused repeated controversy but successfully raised the level of American influence at the United Nations. Soon after resigning, Kirkpatrick became a member of the Republican Party.

Kitt, Eartha (1928–) *American singer and actress*

Admired for her feline grace and unmistakable throaty voice, Eartha Kitt achieved worldwide renown as a cabaret singer, performing such famous songs as "Just an Old-Fashioned Girl."

Eartha Mae Kitt was born in the town of North, South Carolina. Her father, who was a farmer, had had a good crop for the first time in years and decided to name his daughter after the earth. Soon afterwards he disappeared and Eartha's mother struggled to manage the farm and bring up her two daughters. At the age of eight Eartha was invited to Harlem, New York, to live with an aunt.

After singing in a Methodist Church choir and attending the New York School of the Performing Arts, at 16 Eartha was auditioned by Katherine DUNHAM, who offered her a place in her dance troupe. As a singer and dancer in the Bal Nègre company, she toured the United States, Latin America, and Europe. She stayed on in Paris, where she made popular appearances at Carroll's nightclub. In 1951 Orson Welles invited her to play Helen of Troy in *Faust*. She learned the part in two days and was praised for her performance.

On returning to New York, Kitt performed in Manhattan nightclubs, singing "C'est si bon" and other songs. In 1952 she achieved success on Broadway in *New Faces*, making the film version in 1954. In 1953–54 she had a number of hit singles, including "I Want to Be Evil," "Santa Baby," and "Somebody Stole de Wedding Bell."

Eartha Kitt married in 1960 and had a daughter, though she was later divorced. In addition to further appearances on stage, in cabaret, and on television, she acted in a number of films, including *St. Louis Blues* and *The Mark of the Hawk* (both 1957). Her stage shows included *Jolly's Progress* (1959), *The Owl and the Pussycat* (1965–66), and *Timbuktu!* (1978).

Kitzinger, Sheila (Helen Elizabeth)
(1929–   ) *British writer on pregnancy, childbirth, and the care of babies*

Sheila Kitzinger is widely known as an advocate of so-called natural childbirth – i.e. childbirth in which the expectant mother is given special breathing and relaxation exercises rather than anaesthetic.

Sheila Webster was born in Somerset and educated in Taunton at Bishop Fox Girls' School, before attending Ruskin and St. Hugh's Colleges, Oxford, where she studied social anthropology. In 1951 she went to the department of anthropology at the University of Edinburgh to carry out research into British race relations. After marrying the economist Uwe Kitzinger in 1952, she left Edinburgh and worked with the Open University. She became a member of the Advisory Board of the National Childbirth Trust in 1958 and is now also a consultant to the International Childbirth Educational Association of the USA. She has five daughters.

Kitzinger has written extensively about childbirth and childcare in a series of books beginning with *The Experience of Childbirth* (1962). Her 1980 book *Pregnancy and Childbirth* sold more than a million copies, establishing her as a prominent advocate of natural childbirth. Later publications include *Birth Over Thirty* (1982), *Giving Birth: How it Really Feels* (1987), *The Crying Baby* (1989), *Homebirth* (1991), *The Year After Childbirth* (1994), and *Becoming a Grandmother* (1997). Other books elaborate on her view that problems in childbirth can be reduced through education and the use of relaxation techniques, notably *Education and Counselling for Childbirth* (1977) and *The Good Birth Guide* (1979).

Klein, Melanie (1882–1960) *Austrian-born British psychoanalyst*

Melanie Klein revolutionized child psychoanalysis by using play techniques to tap into children's unconscious minds. She also added to the understanding of serious mental illnesses in adulthood.

Born in Vienna of Jewish parents, Melanie Reizes gave up plans for a medical career when she married a cousin, Stephan Klein, in 1903 (the couple were divorced in 1923). In 1912, after the birth of her three children, Melanie decided to train as a psychoanalyst. Studying in Budapest with Sándor Ferenczi, she became a devotee of Freud, who had claimed that adult anxieties, fantasies, and sexual feelings originate in childhood. After further studies in Berlin with Karl Abraham she joined the Berlin Psychoanalytical Society and became interested in child psychology. She remained in Berlin until 1926, when she went to London and joined the British Psychoanalytical Society.

By giving her child subjects toys to play with and noting their spontaneous actions and conversations, Klein identified in very young children such emotions as anxiety, envy, aggression, and sadism. She published her findings in *The Psychoanalysis of Children* (1932). Her conclusions shocked the public, and her technique of giving the children no guidance was also controversial. However, it is now recognized that Klein's ideas are quite logical in suggesting that adult emotions are already present in early childhood; they also show that a better understanding of child psychology enables later problems to be prevented.

Klein's studies on children led her to undertake work on adult paranoid schizophrenia and depression. By the time of her death in London she had written a second book, *The Narrative of a Child Analysis*, which was published in 1961.

Klumpke, Dorothea (1861–1942) *American astronomer*

Dorothea Klumpke was the first woman to be awarded a doctorate by the Paris Observatory and the first woman member to be elected to the Astronomical Society of France.

She was born in San Francisco, but after her parents' separation she and her three sisters went to live in Switzerland with their mother. The family later moved to Paris so that Dorothea's sister Augusta could further her medical studies. All the girls were talented: Julia flourished as a violinist and Anna as a painter, while Dorothea studied at the Paris Observatory and received her doctorate in mathematics.

Her thesis, on the rings of Saturn, continued the work of Sonya KO-VALEVSKY. Dorothea also worked on the spectra of stars and studied meteorites. Remaining at the Observatory, she later headed a team working on a catalogue of stars that was being produced for the International Astronomical Congress.

Knight, Dame Laura (1877–1970) *British painter*

Dame Laura Knight is best remembered for her paintings of circus and gypsy life, fairgrounds, and ballets. Her realistic style made her painting accessible to the general public in her lifetime, but later caused her work to go out of fashion.

Born Laura Johnson in Derbyshire, she was raised with two elder sisters by her mother and grandmother in Nottingham. Laura's mother taught at the Nottingham School of Art, which Laura joined at the age of 13; it was there that she met the painter Harold Knight, her future husband. After their mother died, Laura and her sister Nellie lived for a while in a cave under Nottingham Castle. In 1894 Laura began to visit Staithes on the Yorkshire coast, and after their marriage (1903) she and Harold settled at nearby Roxby before moving to Newlyn, a fishing village in Cornwall.

The Knights joined the artistic circle known as the "Newlyn School." Laura concentrated on painting children and female nudes – her *Daughters of the Sun* was exhibited at London's Royal Academy of Arts in 1910. During World War I Laura served as a war artist. Based in London from 1918, she painted ballet subjects with the co-operation of Diaghilev and Anna PAVLOVA.

In the 1920s and 1930s Laura Knight was elected to a number of artistic institutions, becoming an associate of the Royal Academy in 1927 and a full member in 1936. In 1929 she was made a DBE.

In the late 1920s and early 1930s Knight travelled around many parts of the world painting gypsies and circuses. During World War II she was again an official war artist; later she recorded the Nuremberg trials of war criminals. She wrote two autobiographies (1936 and 1965).

Koch, Marita (1957–) *German athlete*

One of the best ever all-around sprinters, Marita Koch won numerous gold medals at major championships and set 16 world records.

She was born in Wismar, then in the German Democratic Republic (East Germany). Having competed for the GDR at the Montreal Olympics in 1976, Koch combined her athletics career with a long-term medical course, begun in 1977. By 1978 she had broken the world records for 200 metres and 400 metres, later setting three more records for 200 metres and six more for 400 metres. Her other five world records were in relay events.

In the 400 metres Koch was three times European champion (between 1978 and 1986) and Olympic gold medalist at Moscow in 1980. Until 1986 she was defeated only twice in this event. At the 1983 World Championships Koch won gold medals in the 200 metres and two relays as well as a silver in the 100 metres In indoor competition Koch won titles for 200 metres and 400 metres and set the fastest-ever time (7.04 seconds) for 60 metres.

The GDR team did not compete in the 1984 Olympics. However, Koch set her fourth 200-metre record (of 21.71 seconds) that year, following it up in 1985 with a triumphant performance at the World Cup in Canberra, Australia. After winning the 200 metres decisively, she helped her team to victory in the 4 × 400-metre relay with a record-breaking time and then won the 400 metres with her seventh record (of 47.60 seconds).

After competing in 1986, Koch decided to retire, having suffered from an Achilles tendon injury. She married her coach, Wolfgang Meier, giving birth to their daughter, Ulrika, in 1990.

Kollontai, Aleksandra Mikhailovna (1872–1952) *Russian revolutionary, feminist, and diplomat*

Kollontai saw feminism as a central issue in the revolutionary movement, as it is women who often suffer most in oppressive or unjust societies.

Aleksandra Mikhailovna Domontovich was born into a wealthy aristocratic family in St. Petersburg and married an army officer, Vladimir Mikhailovich Kollontai. She joined the revolutionary movement in the 1890s and promoted its aims as a writer and agitator. Leaving Russia for western Europe in 1908 to escape arrest, she concentrated on women's issues, attacking "bourgeois" feminists for failing to accept that the workers' revolution must necessarily also demand the liberation of women. She joined the Bolsheviks in 1915.

After the 1917 October Revolution Kollontai worked in various high posts, promoting the interests of women through proposed changes to the marriage laws, maternity and child care, and better legal rights. However, she fell from favour within the party owing to her views on workers' democracy and her passion for women's issues. She was sent on diplomatic assignments to Norway (1923–30), Mexico (1926), and Sweden (1930–45) as a way of forcing her out of domestic politics. In 1944 she played a vital role in negotiating the armistice to end the war between the Soviet Union and Finland. Surviving the ravages of Stalinist persecution, she held the honorary rank of ambassador extraordinary until her death in Moscow.

Kollwitz, Käthe (1867–1945) *German artist*

Kollwitz's powerful graphic works handle themes of death, social oppression, and war. She has been seen as the last great German expressionist.

She was born Käthe Schmidt into a wealthy liberal family in Königsberg, East Prussia. Käthe studied painting in Berlin and Munich (1884–89) but soon began to concentrate on printmaking in the form of etchings, lithographs, and woodcuts. In 1891 she married Dr. Karl Kollwitz, who ran a clinic in one of the poorer sections of Berlin.

Käthe Kollwitz's most important early works were two series of etchings. The first, *Weavers' Rebellion* (c. 1894–98), was inspired by Gerhard Hauptmann's political drama *The Weavers* (1892), describing an unsuccessful revolt of Silesian weavers. This and another series of etchings, entitled *The Peasants' War* (1902–08), brought her fame. After 1910 Kollwitz also took up sculpture.

Early in World War I Kollwitz's youngest son was killed in battle. This tragedy profoundly affected her life and to some extent accounted for her preoccupation with death. For years she worked on a granite monument to her son depicting his grieving parents, which was installed as a war memorial at Diksmuide, Flanders, in 1932.

During the Weimar Republic Kollwitz became the first woman member of the Prussian Academy of Fine Arts, heading the graphic arts section from 1928. She resigned in 1933 as a protest against Hitler's regime, under which she was soon forbidden to exhibit her work. During the period 1934–36 she produced a series of lithographs on the theme of death, including *Death Seizing a Woman* (1934), a copy of which is in the Fogg Art Museum, Cambridge, Massachusetts. Her sadness was further intensified when her husband died in 1940 and a grandson was killed two years later in World War II. In addition to this, her studio was bombed in 1943, and much of her work was destroyed. Kollwitz died shortly before the end of the war, in Moritzburg, near Dresden.

Korbut, Olga (1955–) *Soviet gymnast*

> If there had not been [such] a thing as gymnastics I would have had to invent it.
>
> —Comment in 1972

At the age of 17 the five-foot Olga Korbut amazed the world with her skill, grace, and agility at the 1972 Olympic Games.

Born in Grodno in Belarus, Olga

Valentinovna Korbut was the fastest runner in her class at school, despite being the shortest child. Taking up gymnastics at the age of ten, she impressed her tutors Elena Volchetskaya and Ronald Knysh and made rapid progress. She went on to gain high placings in several national and international competitions.

In 1972 Korbut was selected to join the Soviet team at the Olympic Games in Munich. Her routine on the uneven bars, which included a back somersault, was the most daring ever seen, earning Korbut a silver medal (a fall during this difficult routine denied her the highest award). On the beam, however, where she performed a back flip, and in the floor routine she was awarded golds, and she took a third gold medal for being a member of the winning team.

After further wins in European and world events, Korbut again competed at the Olympics in 1976, taking a silver for her beam routine. The following year she retired and married the rock musician Leonid Bortkevich, giving birth to a son in 1979. After teaching in the Soviet Union, she emigrated to the United States in 1991 and continued to teach in Atlanta.

Kovalevsky, Sonya Vasilievna (1850–1891) *Russian mathematician*

> While Saturn's rings still shine,
> While mortals breathe,
> The world will ever remember your name.
>
> —Fritz Leffler, obituary poem on Kovalevsky (1891)

Kovalevsky is best known for her work on partial differential equations in which she extended some earlier results of the French mathematician Baron Cauchy, formulating the Cauchy–Kovalevsky theorem. She also won the Borodin Prize of the French Académie des Sciences in 1888 for her memoir *On the Rotation of a Solid Body about a Fixed Point*.

The daughter of a wealthy general, she was born in Moscow and brought up on a large country estate under the instruction of an English governess. One of the children's rooms in the family home had temporarily been papered with some mathematical lecture notes, and it was from studying these as a child that Sonya gained a grounding in mathematics and a desire to pursue the subject.

In 1867 the family moved to St. Petersburg, and Sonya managed to receive some formal teaching at the Naval Academy. To further her opportunities for education she entered into a marriage of convenience with the young scientist Vladimir Kovalevsky in 1868; the following year she went with him to Heidelberg, where she studied at the university. However, women were not allowed to attend public lectures, and in 1871 the couple moved to Berlin, where Sonya received private classes from Karl Weierstrass. He was so impressed with her work that he persuaded the Göttingen authorities to award her a doctorate in 1874 for a thesis on partial differential equations. Despite this, there was no hope of a woman finding a job as a professional mathematician.

In 1878 the Kovalevskys returned to Russia and made some unwise investments in property. With mounting debts, Vladimir committed suicide in 1883. By this time Weierstrass had arranged for Sonya to be appointed to a lectureship in mathematics at the University of Stockholm. She took up the post in 1884 and five years later became a professor. She died suddenly from pneumonia, in the prime of her career.

Krasner, Lee (1908–1984) *American painter*

> Painting is not to be confused with illustration.
>
> —Interview for *Arts Magazine*, 1967

An important painter in the style known as abstract expressionism, or action painting, Krasner did not achieve full recognition until after the death of her more famous husband, Jackson Pollock.

Born in Brooklyn, New York, of Jewish parentage, Lee Krasner decided on art as a career at the age of 13. She was educated in New York City, studying life drawing at Cooper Union (from 1926) and the Art Students League. In 1929 she joined the National Academy of Design. An exhibition containing works by Matisse, Mondrian, and Picasso deeply impressed her at this time. While waitressing in Greenwich Village to help fund her studies, Krasner met modernist artists, and despite taking a teaching course in 1933, she decided to pursue her earlier ambition. From 1934 to 1943 she was sponsored by a government scheme, painting large-scale murals. She studied with Hans Hofmann in 1937–40. Then, in 1942 she met Pollock. "Bowled over" by his work, she married him in 1945.

The marriage posed a threat to Krasner's career. Pollock overshadowed her with his fame and also needed support because of his alcoholism; nevertheless, Krasner continued painting in the bedroom of their Long Island farmhouse while Pollock used the barn. She produced a series of detailed "Little Images," including *Shell Flower* (1947). They were described by a critic as "calligraphy of the soul." Krasner's first show took place in 1951. For her second in 1955 she tore up some earlier canvases and used them in collages.

Following Pollock's death in a car crash in 1956, Krasner's work became somewhat sombre, though critics noted references to the rhythms and forms of nature. From the late 1950s her reputation grew steadily. She showed works nearly every year, regularly holding solo exhibitions until her death.

Kristeva, Julia (1941–) *Bulgarian-born French philosopher, psychoanalyst, and writer*

Kristeva's theoretical writings explore the philosophy of language, literature, and culture from a modern feminist perspective. Influenced by Sigmund Freud and Jacques Lacan, she has linked psychoanalysis to both philosophy and sociology.

Born in Slivno, Bulgaria, where she initially studied linguistics, Kristeva moved in 1966 to Paris, where she attended the Collège de France. She also became a research assistant to Claude Lévi-Strauss, professor of linguistics at the University of Paris and the founder of modern structuralism. During the late 1960s she wrote her first articles and was an editor of the journal *Tel Quel*.

After the 1968 student revolts in Paris, Kristeva's interests shifted from the study of language and symbols to psychoanalysis, especially in relation to femininity and motherhood. In 1974 her doctoral dissertation, published in 1984 as *Revolution in Poetic Language*, earned her the position of professor of linguistics at the University of Paris. Kristeva's experiences as a practising psychoanalyst and as a mother led to several important books, including *Polylogue* (partially translated as *Desire in Language*, 1982), *Pouvoirs de l'horreur* (1980; published in English as *Powers of Horror*, 1982), and *Histoires d'amour* (1983; published in English as *Tales of Love*, 1987). These works reflect her concern with the effect on everyday life of love and desire. Kristeva's first novel, *Les Samouraïs* (1990; published in English as *The Samurai*, 1992) is a thinly veiled autobiographical account.

Kristeva's complex theory of *sémanalyse* ("semanalysis") suggests that humans are subject to two different but interlocking psychological systems, the "semiotic" and the "symbolic." By the semiotic she means the basic impulses of our presocial prelinguistic existence, which are usually restrained. On the other hand, the symbolic is the objective order of language, law, morality, and meaning. Kristeva accounts for their dynamic interrelation through her concept of the "chora," a place where the body forms – and is formed by – language.

Krupskaya, Nadezhda Konstantinovna (1869–1939) *Soviet educationalist*

Already a revolutionary in her own right, Krupskaya became the wife of the Soviet leader V. I. Lenin and his closest companion. An important figure in Soviet education, she helped shape the early Soviet school curriculum.

Krupskaya was born in St. Petersburg, the daughter of a minor noble who had an unsuccessful career as an army officer. Having grown up resenting the injustices of Tsarist Russia, she attended courses for women at the university, which enabled her to teach at evening classes for workers. At this time she also became an active revolutionary. In 1894 she met Lenin at a Marxist study group. After both had been arrested, she married him in exile in 1898.

Krupskaya travelled constantly with Lenin and served as his personal secretary, friend, editor, and (occasionally) nurse. Her own interests in education continued, and after the October Revolution in 1917 she joined the board of the government department responsible for education. She soon became a familiar national figure as she travelled throughout the country, campaigning against illiteracy.

Krupskaya's philosophy of education and morality was inspired by the views of Leo Tolstoy, Jean-Jacques Rousseau, and Karl Marx. She believed in combining learning and labour; she also had great respect for the "natural goodness" of ordinary people, while condemning vulgarity and coarseness. Krupskaya had no time for those people who placed their own interests above those of society.

After Lenin's illness in 1922, her values quickly brought her into conflict with Stalin. This situation continued after Lenin's death in 1924, as Krupskaya tried vainly to preserve what she felt were the moral values of communism. She managed to survive Stalin's hostility and later died in Moscow.

Kumaratunge, Chandrika Bandaranaike (1945–) *Sri Lankan politician*

A highly cultured woman, Kumaratunge has had the courage to follow both her parents in the immensely difficult task of leading war-torn Sri Lanka. She was elected president of Sri Lanka in 1994.

She was born Chandrika Bandaranaike in Colombo, Ceylon (which became the republic of Sri Lanka in 1972), and educated at a convent there. Her father, Solomon Bandaranaike, was the founder of the Sri Lankan Freedom Party (SLFP); he was prime minister of Ceylon from 1956 until his assassination three years later, when Chandrika was 14. Her mother, Sirimavo BANDARANAIKE, succeeded him as prime minister (1960–65, 1970–77, 1994–). Meanwhile, Chandrika had been studying politics at the University of Paris. In 1974 she joined the executive committee of the SLFP Women's League and continued to rise within the party. From 1977 to 1985 she was chairwoman and managing director of a Sri Lankan daily newspaper, the *Dinakara Sinhala*.

In 1978 Chandrika married the actor and politician Vijaya Kumaratunge; they had two children. In 1984 she and her husband founded the Sri Lanka Mahajana Party, which shared aims with the SLFP. While he was engaged in establishing the interparty People's Alliance (PA), Vijaya was assassinated in 1988.

Kumaratunge continued with the political struggle; by 1994 she was president of the PA and her mother's deputy as leader of the SLFP. When the PA was elected to office in August, Kumaratunge became the prime minister of a new government, committed to eliminating poverty and ending the civil war between the Sinhalese and Tamil communities that has plagued the country since the late 1970s. In November 1994 Kumaratunge was elected Sri Lanka's first woman president, and her mother replaced her as prime minister. In late 1995 government forces temporarily subdued the Tamil rebels, but the civil war continued.

Kurz, Selma (1874/75–1933) *Austrian soprano*

Selma Kurz was famed for her wide vocal range and brilliant technique. Particularly admired by the composer Gustav Mahler, her voice was reputedly so agile that she could sustain a trill for 20 seconds.

Kurz was born into a Jewish family in Bielitz, Lower Silesia (now Biala-Bielsko, Poland). She gained her first singing experience in a synagogue choir. Sponsored by a patron, she went to study in Vienna and then in Paris with Mathilde Marchesi. Her operatic debut was with the Hamburg Opera in 1895, when she played the title role in Ambroise Thomas's *Mignon*. After three years with the Frankfurt Opera she was invited by Mahler to join the Vienna Royal Opera. In the role of Mignon once again, she made her first appearance with them in 1899.

Kurz continued with the Vienna Royal Opera until about 1927, gaining a dazzling reputation throughout Europe and beyond. Her many important roles included Tosca, Gilda in *Rigoletto*, Violetta in *La Traviata*, the Queen of the Night in *The Magic Flute*, and Oscar in *The Masked Ball*. She also made numerous recordings.

In 1910 Kurz married Josef Halban. The couple had two children, one of whom, Desi, became a singer herself. Kurz's only concert appearances in the United States took place in 1921, just after she had suffered a heart attack. On her death in 1933 she was honoured with a state funeral.

Kuzwayo, Ellen (1914–) *South African social campaigner and writer*

Ellen Kuzwayo has often been called "the Mother of Soweto" for her comprehensive social work on behalf of blacks and coloureds in the South African townships.

Born in Thaba Patchoa in what was then the Orange Free State, Kuzwayo became known as a leading speaker for the Black Consciousness movement, which urged a return to traditional African values. Her book *Call Me Woman* (1985) was both an autobiography and a celebration of community: it became the first work by a black South African to be awarded the Central News Agency (CNA) Prize. It recounts her life's work and suffering, including the time in 1977 when, aged 63, she was detained without trial for her resistance to the apartheid regime. She later made use of the oral tradition of her people in *Sit Down and Listen*

(1990), a volume of short stories about life in the townships. Two films made use of her help: *Awake from Mourning* (1981) and *Tsiamelo: A Place of Goodness* (1984), which describes how her extended family was forcibly removed from their home in the country.

Kyo, Machiko (1924–) *Japanese actress*

The first Japanese actress to become known in the West, Machiko Kyo also created some of the most memorable female characters in Japanese cinema. In over 80 films her roles have ranged from the tragic to the comic.

Born Motoko Yano in Osaka, she began her career aged 12, as a dancer with the Shockiko Girls' Opera, later appearing with the Tokyo Nippon Gekijo, another all-female company. Because of the trim and glamorous figure she had developed as a dancer, Kyo was noticed by the Daiei film studio, which signed her up as an actress.

It was clear from Kyo's first film, *Final Laugh* (1949), that her provocative style was unique on the Japanese screen. Before her time Japanese film actresses had never been open about their bodies. Because of her looks she tended always to be limited to a similar type of role. However, in Akira Kurosawa's *Rashomon* she managed to extend her range, and the success of this film in the West brought her international attention. She went on to star in other Japanese films, including *Gate of Hell* (1953), *Street of Shame* (1956), and *Odd Obsession* (1959).

Kyo's first American film, *Teahouse of the August Moon* (1956), was also her first comedy. Her success in it led MGM to seek more comic roles for her. Kyo continued to extend her acting range in such films as *The Face of Another* (1966), *The Family* (1974), *Yoba, Tora's Pure Love* (1976), and *Kesho* (1985).

L

Labille-Guiard, Adelaide (1749–1803) *French artist*

Adelaide Labille-Guiard was a leading portrait painter of the late 18th century, producing pictures of the royal family and the aristocracy before the French Revolution and of members of the new republican government afterwards.

The daughter of a merchant, Adelaide Labille studied with François Elie Vincent, a painter of miniatures, before her marriage to Louis Guiard in 1769. She subsequently learned the art of pastel drawing from Quentin de la Tour and oil painting from François André Vincent, the son of her first teacher. An exhibition of her work at the Salon de la Correspondence, Paris, in 1782 included a portrait of François André Vincent, who eventually became her second husband.

In 1783 she was accepted into the Academy, a body of distinguished French artists – mostly male. To earn her place she had been asked to produce a series of pastel portraits of other members of the Academy, the most famous of these pictures being her *Portrait of the Sculptor Pajou*. There were only three other women in the Academy, and Labille-Guiard campaigned throughout her career for better recognition of female artists. Many women learned to paint at her studio, and after the French Revolution she tried to obtain government funding for female art education.

Her other famous paintings include a self-portrait, exhibited at the Academy in 1785, and *The Chevalier Receiving the Order of St. Louis*, which was destroyed during the French Revolution.

La Fayette, Madame de (1634–1693) *French novelist*

> Most mothers think that to keep young people away from lovemaking it is enough never to speak of it in their presence.
> —*The Princess of Cleves* (1679)

Remembered chiefly as the author of *The Princess of Cleves*, first published anonymously in 1678, Madame de La Fayette introduced serious historical fiction to French literature.

Marie Madeleine Pioche de la Vergne was born into the lesser nobility in Paris. She married François Motier, Comte de La Fayette, in 1655 and lived for a few years on his estate in the Auvergne before returning to Paris alone. It was said that the couple had separated after the birth of their second son, but this report was not substantiated, and the count often visited his wife in Paris.

Madame de La Fayette's famous salon in Paris brought together some of the most notable figures in French literary society, including Jean de Segrais, Jean de La Fontaine, Madame de SÉVIGNÉ, and the celebrated author François de La Rochefoucauld, a close friend. She began writing herself at this time, publishing much of her early work anonymously, such as the short story *La Princesse de Montpensier* (1662), about a loveless marriage. The same theme was taken up in her most famous novel, *La Princesse de Clèves*, published in English as *The Princess of Cleves* (1679). One of the chief landmarks in the history of French fiction, it is distinguished by sharp psychological insight and contains a notable portrait of La Rochefoucauld.

One of the first writers to break away from the romantic absurdities of contemporary French historical fiction, Madame de La Fayette also wrote the novel *Zaïde* (1670; published in English as *Zayde: A Spanish History*, 1678), *Histoire de Madame Henriette d'Angleterre* (1720), *La Comtesse de Tende* (1724), and *Memoires de la cour de France* (1731; Memoirs of the French Court). She is said to have spent her later years in retirement, although her *Lettres inédites*, published in 1880, suggest that she remained active in the French court up to her death.

Lagerlöf, Selma (Ottiliana Louisa)
(1858–1940) *Swedish novelist*

> Does it always end so with a
> woman? When they build their
> palaces they are never finished.
> Women can do nothing that has
> permanence.
> —*The Miracles of Antichrist* (1899)

Lagerlöf's imaginative and lyrical prose contributed to the literary revival in Sweden in the 1890s. She was the first Swede to receive the Nobel Prize for literature (1909) and the first woman to be elected to the Swedish Academy (1914).

She was born on her family's estate, Mårbacka, in the province of Värmland. The legends, folktales, and sagas she heard in her childhood days at Mårbacka strongly influenced her writings. A central theme in many of her novels was the threat to provincial aristocratic culture from the new industrialism.

Lagerlöf was an inspired storyteller and also made important stylistic innovations. Her most famous work, which reflects deep involvement in religious and ethical questions, is *Gösta Berlings saga* (1891; published in English as *The Story of Gösta Berling*, 1898), about a defrocked priest who is spiritually regenerated after a life of debauchery. The best of her later works include *Antikrists mirackler* (1897; published in English as *The Miracles of Antichrist*, 1899), which depicts modern socialism in a small Sicilian community; *Jerusalem* (2 vols., 1901–02; published in English in 1915 and 1918); *Nils Holgerssons underbara resa* (2 vols., 1906–07; published in English as *The Wonderful Adventures of Nils*, 1907), a children's story about a boy who flies across the country in

the form of a goose; and a family trilogy set in Värmland *Löwensköldska ringen* (1925; translated into English as *The Ring of the Lowenskolds*, 1931), *Charlotte Löwensköld* (1925), and *Anna Svärd* (1928). With her Nobel Prize money Lagerlöf bought back the family home at Mårbacka, which her father had been forced to sell in the 1880s, and lived there until her death.

Laine, Dame Cleo (1927–) *British jazz singer and actress*

One of the most versatile and dazzling jazz singers of our time, Cleo Laine is also an accomplished actress who has appeared on stage in plays and musicals.

She was born Clementina Dinah Campbell in Southall, Middlesex. Her father was Jamaican, and her mother was British. Despite the family's poverty, the young Clementina took singing, dancing, and piano lessons, which were to provide a good foundation for her future career, along with the songs her father sang and her brother's collection of jazz records. At the age of three she began performing at parties, and while still at school she decided to pursue a career on the stage.

To help support the family, Clementina left school at 14 and worked in several jobs before becoming a singer with the Johnny Dankworth Seven, one of Britain's leading jazz groups, and changing her name to Cleo Laine. In 1956 and 1957 she won first place in the "girl singer" category of the readers' poll in the music magazine *Melody Maker*. During that time Laine began recording with the Dankworth group, which had expanded into a big band. By 1958 critics were calling her "easily the best jazz singer in Europe today."

Laine and Dankworth were married in 1958, and the same year she won great acclaim for her performance in the play *Flesh to a Tiger*. The following year she made her London debut in the musical *Valmouth* (1959). Because there were not many roles for black women at that time, Laine did not return to the West End until 1962, when she appeared in both *A Time to Laugh* and *Cindy-Ella*. In 1971 London audiences saw her in a spectacular revival of the classic American musical *Show Boat*. Laine stopped the show nightly with her singing of Jerome Kern's song "Bill." In the United States she played the role of Princess Puffer in the 1986 musical version of Charles Dickens's unfinished novel *The Mystery of Edwin Drood*, first in Central Park, and then on Broadway for a year.

Between stage plays Laine continued to work as a singer. She made her U.S. concert debut in 1972, causing *The New York Times* critic John S. Wilson to write: "The British, who have been dropping one rock group after another on us for years, have meanwhile been hoarding what must be one of their national treasures." After appearing at New York's Carnegie Hall in a sell-out concert in 1973, Laine returned to North America regularly each year for a tour. The recording of a tenth-anniversary concert at Carnegie Hall won her the first Grammy Award to be given to a British vocalist.

Back in Britain her marriage and musical partnership with Johnny Dankworth have stood the test of time, with Dankworth composing and arranging many of Laine's songs. Each year the couple hold a festival and workshop for young musicians near their home in Buckinghamshire. For her services to jazz, Laine was appointed a DBE in 1997.

Lamb, Lady Caroline (1785–1828)
British novelist

> Mad, bad, and dangerous to know.
> —On Lord Byron

> Avoid her.
> —Lord Byron, on Lady Caroline
> Lamb

Lady Caroline Lamb is remembered more for her tempestuous affair with the poet Lord Byron, and her mental decline when the relationship ended, than for her writings.

She was born Lady Caroline Ponsonby in Roehampton, the only daughter of the third Earl of Bessborough, and educated in Italy until the age of nine. In 1805 she married William Lamb, who, as the second Viscount Melbourne, later became Queen Victoria's first prime minister.

In the spring of 1812 Lady Caroline became disastrously infatuated with Lord Byron, with whom she conducted an affair in a blaze of publicity. Byron broke off the relationship several months later, and Lady Caroline avenged herself by publishing the novel *Glenarvon*, based on her version of the affair. The book was anonymous, but everyone knew who had written it and what it was about. Her other publications were *A New Canto* (1819), a book of verse in feeble imitation of Byron's *Don Juan*; and two more novels, *Graham Hamilton* (1822) and *Ada Reis* (1823).

Lady Caroline, always highly strung, was already having marital problems when she met Byron. After the affair ended, her behaviour became even more eccentric, both in private and in public, threatening her husband's political career. As a result the couple went through a series of estrangements and reconciliations that culminated in their formal separation in 1825. The previous year Lady Caroline had fainted, in true Byronic fashion, on accidentally meeting the poet's funeral procession; she was said never to have regained her reason. The story of her life was retold by Robert Bolt in the film *Lady Caroline Lamb* (1972), starring Bolt's wife Sarah Miles in the title role.

Landowska, Wanda (1877–1959)
Polish harpsichordist and teacher

Wanda Landowska was largely responsible for a revival of interest in the harpsichord. She became the 20th century's greatest player and supporter of the instrument.

Born in Warsaw, Landowska began playing the piano at the age of four and later studied at the Warsaw Conservatory and privately in Berlin. At 23 she moved to Paris and began to travel widely through Europe as a pianist, touring Russia in 1909. She eventually became a French citizen.

Already something of an authority on early music, Landowska became professor of the harpsichord at the Berlin High School for Music in 1912. After World War I she established a school for the study of early music in

St.-Leu-la-Forêt, near Paris, which attracted students from all over the world. In 1927 a concert hall was built there, in which she presented concerts of early music. She also assembled a large collection of harpsichords. Landowska performed frequently in Paris, both as a pianist and harpsichordist, and in 1923 she appeared in the United States as a soloist with the Philadelphia Orchestra. She commissioned the Spanish composer Manuel de Falla to write a concerto for harpsichord, the solo part of which she played in its first performance in Barcelona in 1926. François Poulenc's *Concert champêtre* (1928) for harpsichord and small orchestra was also written for Landowska.

In 1940 she moved to the United States, where she became known for her harpsichord recitals and recordings, particularly of the music of Johann Sebastian Bach. After settling in Connecticut, Landowska devoted herself mainly to teaching and writing. A collection of her articles was published after her death under the title *Landowska on Music*.

lang, k d (1962–   ) *Canadian popular singer and songwriter*

After making her name in traditional country music, lang went on to develop her career in other directions. A lesbian herself, she has a particularly enthusiastic following amongst gay women.

Kathryn Dawn Lang was born in Consort, Alberta. She learned to play the piano and guitar as a child, and developed an interest in country music. After studying at drama college in Vancouver, she began her career as a performance artist. In 1983 she recorded her first album, *A Truly Western Experience*, with a group she named "the reclines" in honour of the country singer Patsy CLINE, who had died in a plane crash 20 years earlier.

Shadowland (1988), an album in a more traditional country-and-western style, brought lang to the attention of a wider audience. In the same year she took part in the Amnesty International tour with Sting, Bruce Springsteen, and others. lang's subsequent albums include *Absolute Torch and Twang* (1989), the highly successful *Ingenue* (1992), *All You Can Eat* (1995), and *Drag* (1997). She also wrote the soundtrack for the film *Even Cowgirls Get the Blues*. Her singles include "Friday Dance Promenade," "Crying" (with Roy Orbison), "Constant Craving," and "If I Were You," and she has won three Grammy Awards. In 1992 she made her acting debut as the star of the film *Salmonberries*.

Lange, Dorothea (1895–1965) *American photographer*

One of the first photojournalists, Dorothea Lange is best known for her pictures of migratory farm people during the Depression of the 1930s.

She was born Dorothy Nutzhorn in Hoboken, New Jersey, and attended a teacher-training school in New York before studying with photographer Clarence White at Columbia University. In 1916 she opened a photography studio in San Francisco and became a society photographer.

During the Depression she switched her attention from the affluent to the miseries of the down-and-out, taking pictures of homeless men wandering the city streets and people standing in food queues. Later she worked as a photographer for the Farm Security Administration, recording the migration of "Okies" and other farm workers from the Oklahoma Dust Bowl. Her photographs, which appeared in newspapers and magazines, helped the campaign for government relief programmes for migrant workers. In collaboration with her husband, the economist Paul Taylor, Lange produced *An American Exodus: A Record of Human Erosion* in 1939. Her most famous portrait, *Migrant Mother*, hangs in the Library of Congress and was chosen by experts in 1960 as one of the 50 best photographs of the first half of the 20th century.

During World War II Lange photographed Japanese Americans who had been moved to relocation centres from their homes on the West Coast. After the war she took photographs for *Life* magazine, including studies of Mormon towns and of life in Ireland.

She also worked as a freelance photo-journalist in Asia, Egypt, and South America. Shortly after her death from cancer an exhibition of her work opened at New York's Museum of Modern Art.

Lange, Jessica (1949–) *American actress*

> She is like a delicate fawn, but crossed with a Buick.
>
> —Jack Nicholson, describing Lange

In the 1980s and 1990s Lange established a reputation as a screen actress of great versatility, winning Academy Awards for her performances in *Tootsie* (1982) and *Blue Sky* (1994).

Jessica Lange was born in Cloquet, Minnesota, and studied at the University of Minnesota. In 1970 she married the Spanish photographer Paco Grande and travelled around the United States and Europe with him. She danced in the chorus at the Opéra Comique in Paris and did modelling work in New York before becoming an actress. Her first appearance on the big screen, in the remake of *King Kong* (1976), was not a great success, but she gradually built up her reputation with such pictures as *The Postman Always Rings Twice* (1981), *Frances* (1982), and *Tootsie* (1982). The last of these earned her an Academy Award as Best Supporting Actress (to Dustin Hoffman in drag).

In *Crimes of the Heart* (1986) Lange co-starred with Diane KEATON and Sissy Spacek as three eccentric sisters reunited at their old Carolina home, and in *Music Box* (1989) she played a lawyer defending her father on a charge of war crimes. In the early 1990s she played opposite Robert De Niro in two films, *Cape Fear* (1991) and *Night and the City* (1992). Having been nominated for a number of Best Actress Oscars, she finally won this award for her performance in *Blue Sky* (1994).

It was not until 1992 that Lange made her professional stage debut in New York, as Blanche Dubois in Tennessee Williams's play *A Streetcar Named Desire*. She later played the same role in a television version, and in 1996 she took the part of Blanche in a new production of the play in London's West End. The actor and dramatist Sam Shephard, her costar in *Frances* and *Crimes of the Heart*, has been her partner since 1982 and is the father of two of her children. She also has a daughter by the dancer Mikhail Baryshnikov.

Langtry, Lillie (1852–1929) *British actress*

> The sentimentalist ages far more quickly than the person who loves his work and enjoys new challenges.
>
> —Quoted in *New York Sun*, 1906

Remembered as much for her beauty and extravagance as for her acting career, Langtry was known as "the Jersey Lily." Her many admirers included the Prince of Wales, later King Edward VII , whose daughter she bore.

Born Emilie Charlotte Le Breton on the island of Jersey, she was the only girl in a family of six boys, which soon made her into a tomboy. The daughter of the dean of Jersey, she was educated at home by a series of tutors. By the time she was 15, she was already both very beautiful and very aware of it.

In 1874 a yacht owned by Edward Langtry came into the harbour at Jersey; Lillie fell in love with it and its owner, to whom she was soon married. The couple moved to London, where Langtry became the latest "professional beauty" – one of a number of married ladies who dressed well and were often photographed. When she and her husband separated in 1881, Langtry had to earn a living to support herself and her daughter. Deciding to become an actress, she made her professional debut as Kate Hardcastle in *She Stoops to Conquer* at the Theatre Royal in London's Haymarket. She surprised critics with her acting ability and caused a sensation as the first lady of society to go on the stage.

Langtry subsequently went on tour in Britain, the United States, and South Africa and became the first woman to endorse a commercial product. She was famous in New York City even before she arrived there in 1883 to make her debut in the play *An Unequal Match*. Her performance was not well received by the critics; however, when she later returned to New York, she appeared to great acclaim in the play *The Highest Bidder*. After appearing in several more plays on both sides of the Atlantic, Langtry attempted the classics, portraying Lady Macbeth and Shakespeare's Cleopatra. The *Daily Telegraph* in London called her "the finest Cleopatra of our time."

Langtry's success on the stage enabled her to amass a fortune; in 1898 her wealth was estimated at more than $2 million. Widowed in 1897, she married Hugo (later Sir Hugo) de Bathe in 1899, becoming a successful owner of racehorses. Her acting career continued into the 20th century, and in 1913 she made her first film, *His Neighbor's Wife*. In 1917 she wrote her autobiography. At the end of World War I Langtry retired to Monaco. There she lived in splendour and became an amateur gardener, winning several prizes for her efforts.

Lansbury, Angela (1925–) *British-born American actress*

In her early films Lansbury was usually cast in supporting roles (she was nominated for three Academy Awards as Best Supporting Actress), often as the spiteful rival of the more glamorous female lead. In the 1980s she became a familiar face on British and American television in the crime series *Murder, She Wrote*.

Angela Brigid Lansbury was born in London, the daughter of an actress, and was educated at a stage school in Kensington. During World War II she was evacuated to the United States, where she continued her drama studies. After moving to Hollywood, she made a number of films for MGM, including *Gaslight* (1944), *National Velvet* (1944), *The Picture of Dorian Gray* (1945), *The Three Musketeers* (1948), and *Samson and Delilah* (1949). In the 1950s she was seen in such pictures as *The Court Jester* (1955), *The Long Hot Summer* (1958), and *The Reluctant Debutante* (1958). Often cast as a domineering older woman, she received an Oscar nomination in *The Manchurian Candidate* (1963) for her performance as the mother of a killer played by Laurence Harvey, who was just three

years younger than Lansbury in real life. Her other films include *Moll Flanders* (1965), *Bedknobs and Broomsticks* (1972), *Death on the Nile* (1978), and *The Company of Wolves* (1985). In 1992 she provided the voice for Mrs. Potts, a singing teapot, in Disney's *Beauty and the Beast*.

Lansbury has also won acclaim for her performances on stage and television. Having made her Broadway debut in *Hotel Paradiso* (1957), she went on to become a star of such musicals as *Anyone Can Whistle* (1964), *Mame* (1966–68), *Gypsy* (1973–74), and *Sweeney Todd* (1979). In 1975 she returned to London to play Gertrude in *Hamlet* at the National Theatre. Her most memorable television role – though some critics thought it a waste of her talent – was as Jessica Fletcher in the television crime series *Murder, She Wrote* (from 1984), which won four Golden Globe Awards. In 1991 Lansbury received the BAFTA Silver Mask for Lifetime Achievement.

Lansing, Sherry (1944–) *American film executive*

Hard-working and ambitious, Sherry Lansing quickly rose through the cinema industry to become the first female head of a major Hollywood studio as president of feature films at 20th Century-Fox.

Sherry Lee Lansing was born in Chicago, the daughter of a Jewish refugee from Nazi Germany. A gifted child, she was educated at the University of Chicago Laboratory High School and Northwestern University, where she studied theatre. She graduated in 1966 and moved to Los Angeles, where she worked as a teacher for three years. In 1969 she became a model and appeared in a number of television commercials. After playing minor roles in such films as *Loving* and *Rio Lobo* (both 1970), she decided that she wanted to make her career in the cinema industry – but on the other side of the camera. She took a couple of film courses and worked as a script reader before joining MGM as executive story editor in 1975. Her career progressed rapidly, and in 1977 she became a vice president at Columbia, where she took charge of the production of such films as *The China Syndrome* and *Kramer vs. Kramer*.

In 1980 she was appointed president of feature films at 20th Century-Fox, a post she held for three years before leaving to form her own production company, Jaffe-Lansing, with fellow producer Stanley R. Jaffe. They had a string of successes, including *Fatal Attraction* (1987) and *The Accused* (1989), in which Jodie FOSTER gave an Oscar-winning performance as a rape victim. In 1992 Lansing became chair of Paramount Pictures, where she produced such films as *Indecent Proposal* (1993) and *Forrest Gump* (1994).

La Roche, Sophie von (1731–1807) *German writer*

Sophie von La Roche was the author of what is said to be the first German novel written by a woman.

She was born Sophie Gutermann in Kaufbeuren, Bavaria, the daughter of a doctor. In 1754 she married Georg von La Roche; when their daughters went away to boarding school in 1766, Sophie relieved her boredom by writing her first novel. Her cousin and childhood sweetheart, the writer Christoph M. Wieland, helped her to find a publisher, who produced it in German as *Geschichte des Fräuleins von Sternheim* in 1771; it was published in English as *The History of Lady Sophia Sternheim* in 1776. This novel takes the form of a series of letters, similar to those of the British writer Samuel Richardson's *Clarissa*, on which it is modelled. A sentimental work in which passion takes its proper place beside morality and virtue, it also reveals La Roche's concern with social problems, economics, and women's education. The novel was widely popular.

While the family lived near Koblenz, the writer Goethe was a frequent visitor to La Roche's literary salon. He was attracted briefly to her younger daughter, Maximiliane, who later married Pietro Brentano. The writers Clemens Brentano and Elisabeth (Bettina) von ARNIM, important figures in the Romantic movement, were the grandchildren of Sophie von La Roche.

Larrocha, Alicia de (1923–   ) *Spanish pianist*

One of the world's great concert pianists, de Larrocha was particularly famous for her dazzling interpretations of the music of Spanish composers such as Enrique Granados and Manuel de Falla. Critics praised her flawless technique; she was greeted with great enthusiasm wherever she played.

Alicia de Larrocha y de la Calle was born in Barcelona. Her mother and aunt were both pianists. Although marriage had ended her mother's career, her aunt had become a teacher at the Academia Marshall in Barcelona. Before she was four, Larrocha's talent at the piano came to the attention of Frank Marshall, the founder of the school, who took charge of her instruction. She made her first public appearance at the age of five and had already given many successful concerts in Barcelona when she was invited to play with the Madrid Symphony Orchestra. She was then only 12 years old. Between 1940 and 1947 Larrocha gave concerts throughout Spain with many different orchestras. In 1947 she began to tour the rest of Europe, performing in Paris, London, Edinburgh, Geneva, and elsewhere.

In 1954 Larrocha made her U.S. debut with the Los Angeles Philharmonic. The following year she played at the Town Hall in New York before returning to Europe. Back in Barcelona she taught at the Academia Marshall with her husband, the pianist Juan Torra, and became director of the school in 1959.

Larrocha returned to New York in 1965 to play with the New York Philharmonic and a year later made her Carnegie Hall debut playing Manuel de Falla's *Nights in the Gardens of Spain*. She won Grammy Awards in the United States in 1974 and 1975, and *Musical America* magazine named her "Musician of the Year" in 1978.

Lauder, Estée (1908–   ) *American businesswoman*

The cosmetics company that Estée

Lauder founded with her husband in 1946 became a billion-dollar enterprise. In 1970 she was named one of the Top Ten Outstanding Women in Business by *Harper's Bazaar*.

She was born Estée Mentzer in New York City, the daughter of poor Jewish immigrants from Hungary. Having made a humble start in the cosmetics industry, selling a face cream produced by her uncle, she gradually worked her way up to developing her own products. In 1946, with her husband Joe Lauder, she founded the cosmetics company Estée Lauder Inc. Working to a modest budget, they advertised their goods by giving away free samples to the public. Their first major success came in the 1950s with a scented bath oil called "Youth Dew." In the 1960s they introduced the Aramis range of products for men and the Clinique range of hypoallergenic fragrance-free cosmetics. Their son Leonard joined the company in 1958, becoming vice president in 1962, president in 1972, and chief executive officer in 1982.

Lauder's fortune has enabled her to maintain a lavish lifestyle – in 1996 she was listed as the fifth best-paid female executive in the United States – and she has also contributed to a variety of causes, including the restoration of the Palace of Versailles in France. In 1985 she published her autobiography *Estée: A Success Story*. The many honours she has received in her later life include the Athena Award (1985) and the Golda Meir 90th Anniversary Tribute Award (1988).

Laurencin, Marie (1885–1956) *French painter, designer, and illustrator*

> Why should I paint dead fish, onions, and beer glasses? Girls are so much prettier.
>
> —Quoted in *Time*, June 18, 1956

Marie Laurencin is best known for her portraits of elegant women.

She was born in Paris, where she studied briefly but was otherwise self-taught. In the first decade of the 20th century she became part of a Bohemian group that included Picasso, Braque, and Henri Rousseau as well as the poet Guillaume Apollinaire, who became her lover in 1908. She depicted some of them, as well as herself, in *L'Assemblée*, a group portrait painted around 1909 and one of her most ambitious works. Having married the German artist Otto von Waerjen in 1914, Laurencin was forced to flee with him to Spain when World War I broke out. She continued to correspond with Apollinaire, but did not return to Paris until after his death.

Although Apollinaire included Laurencin in his *Cubist Painters* (1913), her art had little connection with that style. After World War I her work became increasingly decorative, commonly depicting pretty young women in delicate pastel colours. Examples include *In the Park* and *The Rehearsal*. She also designed sets for Sergei Diaghilev's Ballets Russes and for the Comédie Française, illustrated books, and produced designs for wallpaper, textiles, and fashions. A collection of her poetry was published in 1926.

La Vallière, Louise, Duchesse de (1644–1710) *French aristocrat*

The mistress of King Louis XIV of France, Madame de La Vallière was the mother of four of his children, although only two of them survived to adulthood.

Louise Françoise de la Baume le Blanc was born in Tours, the daughter of an army officer, and grew up at the court of the Duc d'Orléans. In 1661 she became maid of honour to HENRIETTA ANNE of England, who was married to Louis XIV's brother. The king was attracted to Henrietta but could not openly show his affection, so he pretended to court her maid instead. He soon lost interest in his sister-in-law, and La Vallière became his mistress.

When the relationship became known, La Vallière's jealous rivals at court began to conspire against her. But this simply strengthened her position in Louis's affections: he made her the centre of attention at court and threw parties in her honour at the Palace of Versailles. She bore him four children, two of whom died in infancy. The surviving daughter and son were later legitimized.

In 1667 the king took a new mistress, the Marquise de MONTESPAN. He gave La Vallière the title of duchess and the estate of Vaujours in Lorraine, but refused to let her leave court; when she tried to escape in 1671, she was forced to return. It was not until 1674 that La Vallière was allowed to retire to a Carmelite convent in Paris, where she remained until her death. There she wrote *Réflexions sur la miséricorde de Dieu par une dame pénitente* (1680; Reflections on the Mercy of God by a Penitent Lady), and she demonstrated her repentance of her past sins by living a life of extreme austerity.

Lavin, Mary (1912–1996) *American-born Irish writer*

Lavin is remembered for her short stories about everyday life in provincial Ireland, with all its faults and virtues. Highly observant, she drew her inspiration from those around her – family, friends, and even passers-by. She was honoured with many awards, including the Katherine Mansfield Prize and two Guggenheim fellowships, and was president of the Irish Academy of Letters from 1971 to 1973.

Born in East Walpole, Massachusetts, Lavin moved to Ireland with her parents at the age of nine. The family settled in Dublin, and Mary was educated at Loreto College, a convent school, before studying literature at University College, Dublin. Her first short story, "Miss Holland," was written while she was studying for a PhD and published in the *Dublin Magazine*. It brought her support and sponsorship from the writer Lord Dunsany, who read the story and recognized her talent.

In 1942 Lavin married William Walsh, a lawyer, and moved to a farm in County Meath. The success of her first collection of stories, *Tales from Bective Bridge* (1942), which won the James Tait Black Memorial Prize, encouraged her to continue writing. During the next 40 years she published many more collections, including *A Single Lady* (1956), *In the Middle of the Fields* (1967), *A Memory and Other Stories* (1972), *The Shrine and Other Stories* (1977), and *A Family Likeness* (1985). In the early part of her career she also wrote two novels, *The House in Clewe Street* (1945) and *Mary O'Grady* (1950).

Lavin was twice married and widowed. After the death of her first husband in 1954 she moved back to Dublin with her three daughters. Their house became a lively and friendly meeting place for contemporary Irish writers, including Sean O'Faolain. In 1969 Lavin married Michael MacDonald Scott, a former Roman Catholic priest, who died in 1990.

Lavoisier, Marie (Anne Pierrette) (1758–1836) *French chemist*

Marie Lavoisier's first husband was Antoine Lavoisier, known as the father of modern chemistry; the couple worked together in their Paris laboratory for 23 years.

She was born Marie Paulze, the daughter of a farmer-general – a member of a private group that had bought the right to collect taxes. In 1771, at the age of 14, she married Antoine Lavoisier, who was himself a farmer-general as well as being a chemist. Marie studied under the great painter Jacques Louis David and learned Latin and English. Her skills as a draughtswoman are evident in the 13 pages of illustration that accompany her husband's *Traité élémentaire de chimie* (1789; Elementary Treatise on Chemistry) and are signed "Paulze Lavoisier sculpsit" ("engraved by Paulze Lavoisier"). Marie Lavoisier also translated a number of important chemical texts, such as Richard Kirwan's *Essay on Phlogiston* (1784).

It is indisputable that Marie and Antoine Lavoisier worked together in the Paris laboratory – there is a celebrated painting by David from about 1788 showing them doing so. It is unclear, however, what contribution Marie made to Antoine's work on combustion and respiration. In 1794, during the French Revolution, both her husband and her father were guillotined as tax farmers. Marie Lavoisier's last service to her husband was to collect and publish his *Mémoires de chimie* (1803; Memoirs of Chemistry) in two volumes.

Soon afterwards Marie met the physicist Sir Benjamin Thompson, Count Rumford. Following their marriage in 1805, she began to refer to herself as Madame Lavoisier de Rumford. The relationship was not a happy one – Rumford is said to have remarked that Lavoisier was lucky to have been guillotined – and they separated in 1809. For the next 25 years Marie Lavoisier's home remained a meeting place for famous scientists of the day.

Lawrence, Frieda (1879–1956) German-born literary figure

The wife of the writer D. H. Lawrence, Frieda Lawrence had a profound influence on her husband's work: many of his most memorable female characters – including Ursula in *The Rainbow* and Constance in *Lady Chatterley's Lover* – were partly based on her.

Frieda Emma Johanna Maria von Richthofen was born in Metz, which was then part of Germany. Her father was Baron Friedrich von Richthofen, a former army officer who had been appointed civil governor of the city. The World War I German air ace Baron von Richthofen, known as the Red Baron, was a cousin. At the age of 19 she married her first husband, Professor Ernest Weekley, and they settled in Nottingham, where she bore him three children. In April 1912 her life changed dramatically when she met D. H. Lawrence, who was then one of her husband's students. They fell in love and left for Germany together the following month. Two years later they were married.

At first they lived a life of great hardship, travelling from place to place in Europe. Despite her aristocratic background, Frieda was content with this existence: she had a naturally happy temperament and a great capacity for enjoying the simple things in life. Lawrence was also attracted by her great beauty and her impulsive disregard for conventional behaviour. In many ways her character was the complete opposite of his, and their personalities often clashed, but they had only one short spell of estrangement during their relationship.

In the early 1920s their travels took

them further afield, to Ceylon (now Sri Lanka), Australia, and New Mexico, where Frieda settled after Lawrence's death in 1930. She published a volume of recollections, *Not I, but the Wind*, in 1936. Four years before her death Frieda married Angelo Ravagli, an artist. She died in New Mexico on her 77th birthday.

Lawrence, Gertrude (1898–1952) British actress and singer

Although she was not a great singer or dancer and was sometimes criticized for overacting, Gertrude Lawrence was a star performer on Broadway and in London's West End. From the 1920s until her death the leading writers of plays and musicals, including George Gershwin, produced works for her.

She was born Gertrude Alexandra Dagmar Klason in London. Her father, who took the professional name of Arthur Lawrence, was a mildly successful singer who became a heavy drinker. Soon after Gertrude's birth he ran away from home, leaving Gertrude to be brought up by her mother in poverty. She began dancing as a child to earn money and subsequently attended the Italia Conti stage school.

As she grew up, Lawrence met other performers, including the young Noël Coward and Beatrice LILLIE. Soon Lawrence was appearing in a series of musical shows produced by André Charlot. Having found fame in London, she travelled with one of the shows to New York's Broadway, where she also became a star.

In 1930 Noël Coward wrote the comedy *Private Lives* as a vehicle for Lawrence and himself – a show that solidly established Lawrence as a great comic actress. It was followed by *Tonight at 8:30* (1936), a group of nine one-act plays by Coward, which established Lawrence and Coward as a team in the public mind. Strangely, although they remained lifelong friends, they never performed together again. Coward stayed in London, while Lawrence met and married American theatre owner and manager Richard Aldrich. She continued her career on Broadway, starring in a wide range of shows, such as the thoughtful drama *Susan and God* (1937), the original and influential musical *Lady in the Dark* (1944), and a revival (1945) of Shaw's classic *Pygmalion*.

In 1949 Lawrence found a book called *Anna and the King of Siam*, which she decided would make a perfect musical. She persuaded the American team Richard Rodgers and Oscar Hammerstein to write it for her. The result was *The King and I*, which introduced such memorable songs as "Hello Young Lovers," "Getting to Know You," and "Shall We Dance." It opened on Broadway in 1951, with Lawrence in the role of Anna, and was her greatest success. Sadly, it was also her last. Lawrence's life story was retold in the film *Star!* (1969) with Julie ANDREWS in the title role.

Lazarus, Emma (1849–1887) *American poet*

> Give me your tired, your poor,
> Your huddled masses yearning to
>   breathe free,
> The wretched refuse of your teem-
>   ing shore,
> Send these, the homeless, tempest-
>   tost, to me,
> I lift my lamp beside the golden
>   door!
> —"The New Colossus" (1883)

Emma Lazarus is remembered for the sonnet "The New Colossus," in which she paid tribute to the Statue of Liberty as a beacon of freedom and compassion. The poem has been a source of hope and inspiration to countless immigrants entering the United States. The full text is engraved on a bronze plaque inside the pedestal of the Statue of Liberty in New York harbour.

The daughter of German-Jewish immigrants, Emma Lazarus was born in New York City, where she began writing poetry at an early age. Her collections include *Poems and Translations* (1866), *Admetus and Other Poems* (1871), and *Songs of a Semite* (1882). The last of these contains *The Dance to Death*, a poetic drama about medieval Jewish life. She also translated into English the *Poems and Ballads of Heinrich Heine* (1881).

Leakey, Mary (1913–1996) *British archaeologist and palaeontologist*

In 1976 Mary Leakey discovered footprints in volcanic ash in Tanzania, proving that the ancestors of the modern human race were already walking upright some 3.75 million years ago.

She was born Mary Douglas Nicol in London, the daughter of the landscape painter Erskine Nicol. She travelled widely in her youth but had little formal education. Her interest in archaeology and her skill in drawing brought her into contact with the world of palaeontology (the study of fossilized animals and plants). She met the anthropologist and archaeologist Louis Leakey in the early 1930s and married him in 1936. During the next 36 years Mary worked with her husband on his East African field trips, collaborating with him as excavator, author, and palaeontologist. From 1960 she was director of research of the important Olduvai Gorge excavations. The second of their three sons, Richard Leakey, followed his parents into palaeontology.

Many of the more dramatic discoveries associated with the Leakeys were in fact made by Mary rather than her better-known husband. It was Mary Leakey who discovered the skull of *Proconsul africanus*, the first fossil ape skull ever to be found, in Kenya in 1947. It was also Mary who found the 1.75 million-year-old skull of *Zinjanthropus boisei*, claimed by the Leakeys to be the true ancestor of man, in the Olduvai Gorge, Tanzania, in 1959.

After Louis's death in 1972 Mary continued working in northern Tanzania, in the Laetoli beds near Lake Eyasi. It was there in 1976, in rock much older than the lowest Olduvai levels, that she made what she described as "the most remarkable find" of her whole career. Preserved in the volcanic ash she found trails of footprints resembling those that would have been left by people walking side by side, or even arm in arm. These provided clear evidence that man's ancestors had already adopted an upright posture a million years earlier than the experts had thought. An account of her researches was included in her autobiography *Disclosing the Past* (1984).

Leavitt, Henrietta Swan (1868–1921) *American astronomer*

> Her most important work required greater understanding and even more meticulous care...even though it lacked the glamour and popular appeal of the newly opened field of stellar spectroscopy.
>
> —Dorrit Hoffleit, *Notable American Women* (1971)

Leavitt is best known for her studies of a class of stars known as Cepheid variables, highly luminous supergiant stars in which the brightness varies regularly. In these stars she demonstrated a relationship between brightness and the period of variation of the brightness.

The daughter of a Congregational minister, Henrietta Leavitt was born in Lancaster, Massachusetts. Her interest in astronomy was aroused while she was at Radcliffe College (then the Society for the Collegiate Instruction of Women), from which she graduated in 1892; in 1895 she became a volunteer research assistant at the Harvard College Observatory. She accepted a permanent post there in 1902 and soon became head of the department of photographic photometry. Like her colleague Annie Jump CANNON she was extremely deaf.

Leavitt's work involved the measurement of the brightness of stars as recorded on a photographic plate. This is known as the photographic magnitude, as opposed to the visual magnitude, which is the brightness as seen by the eye. The accurate measurement of visual magnitudes had been part of the programme of the Harvard College Observatory since the 1870s. In 1907 the director of the observatory, Edward Pickering, announced plans to use the photographic magnitudes of a group of stars near the north celestial pole as standards of reference for other stars. Leavitt was selected to measure these magnitudes, known as the "north polar sequence," and the results were published in 1917 in the *Annals of Harvard College Observatory*.

Leavitt also worked on other variable stars – stars whose brightness varies over a period of time – and she discovered roughly one half of those known in her time. She is best known, however, for her studies of the Cepheid variables. The variation in brightness of these stars is extremely regular, and in 1908 Leavitt noted that the brighter Cepheids had the longer periods of variation. By 1912 she was able to show a fixed mathematical relationship between the brightness and the period of variation. This apparently simple discovery led to an invaluable means of determining very great distances. Previously only distances out to a hundred light-years could be estimated, but an extension of Leavitt's work enabled astronomers to calculate distances of galaxies up to ten million light-years away.

See also FLEMING, WILLIAMINA PATON; MAURY, ANTONIA.

Lecouvreur, Adrienne (1692–1730) *French actress*

> This incomparable actress, who almost invented the art of speaking to the heart.
>
> —Voltaire, describing Lecouvreur

Adrienne Lecouvreur was known for her natural style of acting, which came as a welcome change from the overdramatic performance of other actors of the day, and for her insistence on historical accuracy in the design of costumes.

She was born near Epernay in northeastern France, the daughter of a hatmaker. Having made her stage debut in an amateur production of Corneille's play *Polyeucte* at the age of 14, she joined the Comédie-Française in 1717. Her first professional performance was in the title role of Crebillon's *Electre*. Lecouvreur acted in both tragedies and comedies, but she was particularly acclaimed for her tragic acting. Voltaire was among her admirers, and she performed in a number of his plays. Maurice de Saxe, a French soldier who later became marshal of France, was her lover for several years. In 1848 Eugène Scribe and Ernest Legouvé gave a rather sensational account of her life in their play *Adrienne Lecouvreur*.

Lecouvreur's immense popularity made other actresses jealous, and some people said that her sudden death was due to poisoning by a rival. Because acting was then considered a disreputable profession, and she had not had time to renounce it before dying, she was refused a Christian burial. Voltaire was outraged that one of the greatest actresses of the time should have to be buried secretly at night, in a corner of a Paris street, and he wrote a poem condemning the hypocritical attitude of the Church.

Lee, Ann (1736–1784) *British mystic*

Ann Lee was the founder of the United Society of Believers in Christ's Second Appearing, known popularly as the Shakers.

According to tradition she was born Ann Lees in Manchester. Uneducated, she worked in a factory and as a cook. In 1758 she joined the "Shaking Quakers," a branch of the Quaker movement headed by Jane and James Wardley.

In 1762 Ann married Abraham Stanley, by whom she had four children in a few years. All the births were difficult, and all the children died in infancy. Ann regarded this calamity as divine retribution for succumbing to her sexual desire; this led her to the conclusion that celibacy should be a Shaker principle.

Meanwhile the Wardleys had become convinced that Christ's second coming would be in the form of a woman. When Ann was released from prison, to which she had been sent for preaching blasphemy in the street, she was greeted by her associates as "Mother Ann" or "Ann of the Word," the fulfilment of the Wardleys' conviction and their new leader.

In 1774 Ann Lee went to America with her husband, her brother, and a few followers and founded the first Shaker settlement in Watervliet, near Albany, New York State. She was twice imprisoned during the American Revolution on a charge of treason and for refusing to take an oath of allegiance. Although communal living was not part of the early Shaker doctrine, Ann's group was forced into it for security and survival. Between 1781 and 1783 Ann toured New England as a missionary, performing alleged miracles of healing. She often met with hostility and mob violence, but she converted Baptist Joseph Meachem, who later led the development of her movement.

Lee, Gypsy Rose (1914–1970) *American entertainer*

> God is love, but get it in writing.
>
> —Attributed remark

Gypsy Rose Lee made her name as a striptease artist, developing a style of dancing and singing that was both suggestive and sophisticated. She was the first entertainer of this type to achieve stardom.

Born Rose Louise Hovick in Seattle, Washington, she began performing in vaudeville with her mother and sister at the age of six. In the 1930s she turned to the type of sex-and-comedy entertainment known as burlesque and found fame at Minsky's Theater in New York. She moved on to the Ziegfeld Follies in 1936 but retired from striptease the following year.

After a number of film appearances, she returned to the stage for shows such as *Gypsy Rose Lee and Her American Beauties* (1949) and *A Curious Evening with Gypsy Rose Lee* (1958). She also performed in *Auntie Mame* (1960) and *The Threepenny Opera* (1961). Her last film was the undistinguished comedy *The Trouble with Angels* (1966).

Lee also wrote a number of mystery stories, including the thriller *The G-String Murders* and a play, *The Naked Genius* (1943). Her autobiography, *Gypsy* (1957), was made into a musical in 1959 and filmed in 1962 with Natalie Wood in the title role. The National Legion of Decency rated the film as "objectionable," but some members of the audience found it disappointingly inoffensive.

Lee, Jennie (1904–1988) *British politician*

At the age of 24 Jennie Lee became the youngest member of the House of

Commons and in 1964 she was appointed Britain's first minister of arts. She was married to the socialist statesman Aneurin Bevan, who is remembered for the introduction of the National Health Service.

A miner's daughter, Jennie Lee was born in Lochgelly, Fife. She studied at the University of Edinburgh, graduating in education (1926) and law (1927), then taught for two years. Her interest in socialist politics began while she was a student; during the General Strike of 1926 she worked at the strike headquarters in Edinburgh. In 1929 she stood as the Labour candidate for North Lanark and was elected to Parliament. Two years later she lost her seat in the House of Commons but remained actively involved with the Labour Party, giving lectures all over Europe, the United States, and the Soviet Union and publishing such books as *Tomorrow Is a New Day* (1939) and *Russia Our Ally* (1941).

In 1934 Lee married Aneurin (known as Nye) Bevan, and she was content to let her career take second place to his until his death in 1960. She became an MP again in 1945, after wartime work at the Ministry of Aircraft Production, and held a number of ministerial positions in the second half of the 1960s before retiring in 1970, when she was created Baroness Lee of Asheridge. While minister of arts she played an important role in the establishment of the Open University, which provides degree courses for people of all ages and educational backgrounds. In 1980 she published a collection of personal and political memoirs, *My Life with Nye*.

LeFanu, Nicola (1947–) *British composer*

In compositions such as *The Old Woman of Beare* (1981), which was inspired by a medieval Irish poem, LeFanu combines theatrical effect with lyricism.

Nicola Frances LeFanu was born in Wickham Bishops, Essex. Her mother was the composer Dame Elizabeth MA-CONCHY. LeFanu was educated at St Mary's School, Calne, Wiltshire, then at the University of Oxford and the Royal College of Music in London. In 1973 she was awarded a fellowship to Harvard and Brandeis universities, where she studied composition with Earl Kim and Seymour Shifrin. In 1977 she became a lecturer at King's College, London, and in 1993 she was appointed professor of musical composition there. She left the following year to become professor and head of the department of music at the University of York. Her husband is the Australian-born composer David Lumsdaine.

Much of LeFanu's early music drew on Celtic themes (her mother was of Irish parentage). She made her name with pieces such as *Antiworld* and *The Last Laugh* (both 1972), dramatic works for the concert stage that combine music, singing, dancing, and acting. She also wrote chamber music, notably the oboe quartet *Variations* (1968) and the cello octet *Deva* (1979); orchestral pieces, such as *The Hidden Landscape* (1973) and *Columbia Falls* (1975); and the operas *Dawnpath* (1977) and *The Story of Mary O'Neill* (1986). The last of these, commissioned by the BBC, featured electronically produced music. Her more recent works include the operas *Blood Wedding* (1992) and *The Wildman* (1995).

Le Gallienne, Eva (1899–1991) *British actress, director, and producer*

Eva Le Gallienne believed that classic drama should be made available to the public in theatres in the same way that books were accessible to everyone in libraries. She pursued this ideal by founding and directing the short-lived Civil Repertory Company in New York.

She was born into an intellectual family in London: her father was a poet, and her mother was a journalist. They surrounded Le Gallienne with literature from an early age and sent her to France to be educated. She returned to London at the age of 14 with a strong desire to act and was accepted into the Royal Academy of Dramatic Art (RADA). In 1914 she appeared on stage for the first time.

The following year Le Gallienne moved to New York, where she immediately found employment in minor roles in forgotten plays of the day. It was not until 1921, when she played the leading role of Julie in the Broadway production of Ferenc Molnár's masterpiece *Liliom*, that Le Gallienne captivated New York audiences. Her performance as the battered but noble wife paved the way for the rest of her successful career.

Other important roles followed, and in 1926 Le Gallienne fulfilled her dream of running her own theatre. She founded, organized, and directed the Civic Repertory Company, whose aim was to offer classic theatre at bargain prices. From 1926 until the theatre was forced out of business by the Depression of the 1930s, Le Gallienne directed and appeared in dozens of classic plays, ranging from Chekhov's *Three Sisters* and Ibsen's *Hedda Gabler* to Shakespeare's *Romeo and Juliet*; she also presented there her own adaptation of Lewis Carroll's *Alice in Wonderland*.

Throughout the rest of her long career Le Gallienne was always hopeful that she would be able to reopen her company. In 1946, together with producer Cheryl CRAWFORD and director Margaret WEBSTER, she founded the American Repertory Company, but it closed the following year. The failure did nothing to decrease Le Gallienne's appetite for work; she appeared on the New York stage throughout the 1940s, 1950s, and 1960s and directed productions all over the United States. She rounded off her stage career in the mid 1970s with a highly acclaimed performance as the head of a theatrical clan in *The Royal Family*, a revival of the 1927 play by George S. Kaufman and Edna FERBER about the Barrymore family.

Lehmann, Inge (1888–1993) *Danish seismologist*

It was Inge Lehmann who, in 1936, first put forward the view that the Earth's core consisted of two parts – an inner and an outer core. For many years it had been thought that the Earth consisted merely of a core, mantle, and crust.

Born in Copenhagen, Inge Lehmann studied at the university there and at Newnham College, Cambridge; she received her PhD from Copenhagen University in 1928. She then became head of the Danish Geodetic Institute, where she undertook research into earthquakes. Lehmann found that the velocity of the primary waves of an earthquake increased quite sharply within the core. She reasoned from this that there is an outer core and an inner core separated by a discontinuity about 700 miles (1,200 km) from the centre of the Earth.

Lehmann continued working at the Geodetic Institute until her retirement in 1953.

Lehmann, Lilli (1848–1929) *German opera singer*

Lilli Lehmann was one of the greatest and most versatile operatic sopranos in the second half of the 19th century. She was particularly famous for her performances in the operas of Wagner and Mozart.

She was born in Würzburg and grew up in Prague, where she was taught singing by her mother, Marie Löw, a former leading soprano. Lehmann made her debut in Prague in 1865 as the First Boy in Mozart's *The Magic Flute*. After engagements in Danzig and Leipzig she became a soprano at the Berlin Opera in 1870. In 1876 she took part in the first Bayreuth Festival as Woglinde (a Rhinemaiden), Helmwige (a Valkyrie), and the Woodbird, in the first performance of Wagner's complete *Ring* cycle. She made her London debut in 1880 as Violetta in Verdi's *La Traviata*.

Lehmann gradually developed into a dramatic soprano, becoming famous for her interpretations of such Wagnerian roles as Isolde and Brünnhilde. She was the first to sing these roles in the United States. Her repertory consisted of 170 roles in over 100 operas, which she sang in German, French, and Italian.

From 1901 until 1910 Lehmann helped to organize, and performed at, the Salzburg Festival. She retired from opera in 1910 but continued to give recitals, finally leaving the concert stage in 1922. A superb teacher, she numbered among her pupils Geraldine FARRAR and Olive FREMSTAD.

Lehmann, Lotte (1888–1976) *German-born American opera singer*

One of the greatest singers of the German repertory, Lotte Lehmann gave memorable performances in the operas of Richard Strauss, notably in the role of the Marschallin in his *Der Rosenkavalier*.

Lehmann was born in Perleberg in Germany. After studying in Berlin, she made her debut in Hamburg in 1909 as the Third Boy in Mozart's *The Magic Flute*. In 1914 she joined the Vienna Opera, where she sang in the premieres of a number of Strauss's operas, the second version of *Ariadne auf Naxos* (1916), *Die Frau ohne Schatten* (1919), and *Arabella* (1933). She also performed regularly at Covent Garden, London, from 1924 to 1935, and made her U.S. debut in Chicago in 1930 as Sieglinde in Wagner's *The Valkyries*. Lotte Lehmann's other Wagnerian roles included Eva in *Die Meistersinger von Nürnberg* and Elsa in *Lohengrin*, and she was also famous for her interpretation of Leonore in Beethoven's *Fidelio*.

After Austria was annexed by Germany in 1938, Lehmann moved to the United States, where she sang at the Metropolitan Opera, New York, until 1945. She was a superb singer of lieder, giving frequent recitals until 1951. After her retirement from the stage she taught master classes in Santa Barbara, California, and in London.

Lehmann, Rosamond (Nina) (1901–1990) *British writer*

Rosamond Lehmann's novels are marked by their perceptive characterization of women and portrayal of women's emotions.

She was born in Bourne End, Buckinghamshire, into a distinguished family. Her father was the humorist and MP Rudolph Chambers Lehmann, and her great-uncle was the painter Henri Lehmann; her brother John Lehmann became an essayist and poet, and her sister Beatrix Lehmann became an actress and writer. Educated at Girton College, Cambridge, Rosamond published her first novel, *Dusty Answer*, in 1927 after her early marriage to Leslie Runciman had ended. Like several of her later works it dealt with the passions of a young society woman; it was highly successful.

Lehmann's work is marked by stylistic elegance, psychological perception, and sensitivity in her portrayal of the lives and characters of young women and adolescent girls. Perhaps her best-known novel is *The Ballad and the Source* (1944), in which the history of three generations of a family is seen from the viewpoint of a 14-year-old girl. She published a sequel, *A Sea-Grape Tree*, in 1976. Her other works, written after her second marriage, include the novels *A Note in Music* (1930), which dealt with the controversial issue of homosexuality; *Invitation to the Waltz* (1932) and its sequel *The Weather in the Streets* (1936); and *The Echoing Grove* (1953). *The Gypsy's Baby* (1946) is a collection of short stories, many of which were originally published during World War II in her brother's journal *New Writing*.

When her daughter Sally died from polio in 1958, Lehmann took an interest in spiritualism, believing that contact could be made between the living and the dead. She published a memoir with mystical overtones, *The Swan in the Evening: Fragments of an Inner Life*, in 1967 and later became president of the College of Psychic Studies.

Leibovitz, Annie (1950–) *American photographer*

Leibovitz specializes in celebrity portraits of the stars of stage and screen, especially the icons of popular culture, photographed with a unique blend of spontaneity and careful composition. Her subjects are portrayed as real people – often in a different light from their public image.

Leibovitz travelled widely during her childhood, living in Connecticut, Texas, Alaska, the Philippines, and elsewhere. Her mother was an enthusiastic taker of family snapshots, and Annie bought her first camera to record a family holiday in Japan in 1968. She developed her interest in photography as an art form while studying painting at the San Francisco

Art Institute and took her first "celebrity portrait," a sneak picture of the poet Allen Ginsberg, in 1970. She sent the photo to the magazine *Rolling Stone* and was immediately commissioned to photograph the rock musician John Lennon in New York. (Ironically, it was Leibovitz who later took the famous portrait of Lennon with his wife Yoko ONO just hours before his murder in 1980.)

Leibovitz's early sessions with Lennon encouraged her to develop a more collaborative method of working with her subjects. She went on to photograph other rock musicians and politicians for *Rolling Stone*, first in black and white and later in colour. One of the most demanding commissions of this period was an intimate photographic record of a concert tour by the Rolling Stones in 1975, which involved her spending every waking hour with the band, her camera constantly in her hand.

In 1983 Leibovitz became chief photographer for the magazine *Vanity Fair*, an appointment that brought her a wider range of assignments and made her a household name in the United States. In 1987 the American Society of Magazine Photographers honoured her with the Innovation in Photography Award. A collection of photographs from the first two decades of her career went on display at the Smithsonian National Portrait Gallery, Washington, D.C., in 1991 and was subsequently exhibited around the world.

Leigh, Vivien (1913–1967) *British actress*

> In Britain, an attractive woman is somehow suspect. If there is talent as well it is overshadowed. Beauty and brains just can't be entertained; someone has been too extravagant.
>
> —Quoted by Gwen Robyns in
> *Light of a Star* (1967)

Her most memorable successes were in the cinema, as Scarlett O'Hara in *Gone With the Wind* (1939) and as Blanche DuBois in *A Streetcar Named Desire*.

She was born Vivian Mary Hartley in Darjeeling, India. Educated in England, France, Italy, and Bavaria, she studied acting at the Royal Academy of Dramatic Art (RADA) and made her debut in the film *Things Are Looking Up* in 1934. She went on to play a further 18 film parts, winning Academy Awards as Best Actress for *Gone With the Wind* (1939) and *A Streetcar Named Desire* (1951). As a stage actress she made her name in the comedy *The Mask of Virtue* (1935), and her subsequent work in the theatre surpassed her film performances.

From 1940 to 1961 Vivien Leigh was the wife of Laurence Olivier; they performed together on stage in Britain and the United States for almost 20 years. Their partnership was particularly successful in the plays of Shakespeare, notably *Romeo and Juliet*, *Antony and Cleopatra*, *Macbeth*, and *Titus Andronicus*, but Leigh also excelled in more modern stage roles. In the 1940s she toured North Africa, Australia, and New Zealand.

The nervous problems that finally brought Leigh's marriage and career to an end began in the 1950s. Her last film role was in *Ship of Fools* (1965), and she made her last stage appearance the following year in Chekhov's *Ivanov* in New York. She died of tuberculosis.

Lenclos, Ninon de (1620–1705)
French society woman

Madame de Lenclos's numerous affairs with some of the most illustrious and wealthy men in France ensured that she died a rich woman.

She was born Anne de Lenclos (or Lanclos) in Paris, the daughter of a member of the lower nobility. Her lovers included Louis II de Condé, the Huguenot leader Gaspard de Coligny, the Marquis de Sévigné and his son Charles de Sévigné, and the Marquis de Villarceaux. ANNE OF AUSTRIA disapproved of Lenclos's lack of religious respect and had her sent to a convent in 1656. After her release Lenclos defended her behaviour and beliefs in *La Coquette vengée* (1659; The Flirt Avenged).

In her early fifties Lenclos settled into a more respectable way of life. Renowned for her wit, taste, and style, she gave fashionable receptions that attracted many notable artists and writers, such as Molière, Racine, and the very young Voltaire. Her powerful friends included Mme. de MAINTENON and Queen CHRISTINA of Sweden.

Lenglen, Suzanne (1899–1938)
French tennis player

Suzanne Lenglen is considered to be one of the game's greatest woman players. Supremely graceful, she lost only one match between 1919 and 1926. She also set a fashion for a shorter style of tennis dress.

Born in Compiègne in northern France, she showed considerable talent for the game of tennis at an early age. Trained by her father, she won the world hard court (clay) championship in Paris in 1914 at the age of 15. Quick and accurate, she seldom gave opponents a chance, rarely losing a set. She won the Wimbledon singles title a record five straight times (1919–23) and again in 1925, and the French singles every year from 1920 to 1926 except 1924, when she missed the championship through illness.

In doubles she won the Wimbledon title six times (1919–23 and 1925) and the French title twice (1925–26). In 1926 she became the first tennis player to sign a contract and undertake a professional tour. She retired the following year and opened the Lenglen School of Tennis in Paris. After her early death from pernicious anaemia she was awarded the Cross of the Legion of Honour.

Lennox, Annie (1954–) *Scottish rock singer and songwriter*

> Most really inspired music has a kind of friction about it. There's an element of danger, of roughness and crudeness that goes along with something very melodic. But underlying all that, you have to have a fantastic rhythm.
>
> —Describing her philosophy of music

Annie Lennox made her name as one half of Eurythmics, a duo that was classified as synth-pop (a high-tech version of disco) but transcended this category with the quality of their melodies. She launched her solo career in the early 1990s.

She was born an only child in Aberdeen. Her father, a railway worker, played the bagpipes. Having grown up listening to Scottish folk music, Annie showed an early talent that enabled her to move to London to study flute, piano, and harpsichord at the Royal Academy of Music. Realizing that she didn't fit in with her classmates, and afraid that she would end up playing the flute in an orchestra, Lennox left the Royal Academy in 1975 and gave up classical music. She took up singing, supporting herself with waitress jobs, and in 1976 she met rock guitarist Dave Stewart. They fell in love and helped form a band called the Tourists, which released three moderately successful albums before breaking up in 1980.

Although no longer lovers, Lennox and Stewart had similar musical tastes, which encouraged them to form a duo. They chose the name Eurythmics, to combine the ideas of "Europe" and "rhythm." Their first album, *In the Garden* (1982), was a failure, but the pair were not discouraged. With lyrics mostly by Lennox and music mostly by Stewart, *Sweet Dreams Are Made of This* (1983) became their breakthrough album. Its title song soared to number one worldwide in the summer of 1983, with the album selling more than a million copies. Their next album, *Touch* (1984), did the same, and two of the songs – "Here Comes the Rain Again" and "Who's That Girl?" – became hit singles.

Lennox's androgynous look attracted as much media attention as the music. Lennox has explained, "I wanted to present myself as a woman that was not of the girlish, girly ilk...I wanted to reinvent myself, so it was natural for me to wear more mannish clothes because it gave me more power." The music videos that Lennox made show her posing almost like a robot.

In 1985 Lennox and Stewart recorded *Be Yourself Tonight*, bringing in outside musicians to create a new sound; Lennox also sang a duet with Aretha FRANKLIN. During that same period Lennox had a small part in the film *Revolution* (1985), starring Al Pacino.

Eurythmics finally broke up, and in the early 1990s Lennox released two highly successful solo albums, *Diva* (1992) and *Medusa* (1995).

Lennox, Charlotte (Ramsay)
(1720–1804) *British writer*

Charlotte Lennox is remembered for her sentimental novels, which were popular with women.

She was born in New York colony, the daughter of the governor, Colonel James Ramsay. At the age of 15 Charlotte was sent to England to live with an aunt, whom she found to be insane. Her father died soon after, and she was forced to support herself. After failing as an actress, she turned to writing and was befriended by Samuel Johnson and Samuel Richardson. In 1747 she married Alexander Lennox, a customs employee.

Mrs. Lennox's popularity was based on her sentimental novels, such as *The Life of Harriet Stuart* (1750) and *The History of Henrietta* (1758). Her best work, however, is a satire, *The Female Quixote; or The Adventures of Arabella* (1752). In the early 1750s she published *Shakespeare Illustrated*, a collection of the stories and historical accounts on which Shakespeare's plays are based. This work, in three volumes, also contains critical notes that, in the words of *The Gentleman's Magazine* (1804), "intended to prove that Shakespeare has generally spoilt every story on which his plays are founded, by torturing them into low contrivances, absurd intrigues, and improbable incidents."

Mrs. Lennox also dramatized several of her novels and wrote poetry. Her comedy *The Sisters* (1769), based on her novel *The History of Henrietta*, was condemned by critics on its opening night.

Lenya, Lotte (1898–1981) *Austrian singer and actress*

> To come out onstage and know instantly whether you have your audience in your hands. That happens to me all the time.
>
> —Describing her love of the stage

Lotte Lenya is recognized as the greatest interpreter of the music of her husband, composer Kurt Weill; she made her name in the 1928 premiere of his work *The Threepenny Opera*.

She was born Karoline Wilhelmine Blamauer in Hitzing, Vienna, to poor parents. Her father, an abusive alcoholic, forced her to leave home at the age of 11. In 1914 she went to Switzerland to study ballet and drama. After World War I Berlin became the European capital of the arts; Lenya therefore moved to Berlin to pursue her career on the stage in 1920.

In 1924 Lenya was introduced to a young composer named Kurt Weill, who went on to collaborate with the playwright Bertold Brecht on a number of successful operas. Two years later Lenya and Weill were married. Lenya acted and sang in several Weill–Brecht productions, and all three achieved fame with the 1928 production of *The Threepenny Opera*. Playing the important role of Jenny made Lenya a star; in 1931 she appeared in the film version of the play. Lenya also appeared in 1931 in Weill and Brecht's opera *The Rise and Fall of the City of Mahagonny*.

When the Nazis came to power in Germany in the early 1930s, Lenya and Weill, who was Jewish, fled to Paris and then finally settled in the United States in 1936. After appearing in Max Reinhard's production of *The Eternal Road* (1937) and Weill's musical about the sculptor Cellini, *The Firebrand of Florence* (1945), Lenya deserted the stage. It was not until her husband's sudden death in 1950 that she resumed her career and devoted herself to preserving his musical legacy. She appeared in her original role in the wildly successful off-Broadway production of *The Threepenny Opera* in 1954, made several historic recordings of Weill's work, and sang his songs at Carnegie Hall in 1965.

Lenya occasionally appeared in the works of other composers, the most notable example being the 1966 Broadway production of the musical *Cabaret*, in which she played the role of the landlady. For that performance she was nominated for a Tony Award.

During that same period Lenya appeared in a number of films, such as the James Bond thriller *From Russia with Love* (1963) and *The Roman Spring of Mrs. Stone* (1961), for which she was nominated for an Academy Award. However, her most cherished activity was giving life to the works of her late husband, Kurt Weill.

Lessing, Doris (1919–) *British writer*

> What's terrible is to pretend that the second-rate is first-rate. To pretend that you don't need love when you do; or you like your work when you know quite well you're capable of better.
>
> —*The Golden Notebook* (1962)

Lessing is widely regarded as one of the most distinguished writers of fiction of the late 20th century. Among her themes are the individual's exercise of freedom within society, the power relations between men and women, and the shaping force of political ideologies.

She was born Doris May Tayler in Kermanshah, Persia (now Iran), the daughter of a bank official. In 1924 her family moved to Southern Rhodesia (now Zimbabwe), where they owned a farm. She attended a convent school and Girls' High School in Salisbury (now Harare) but left at the age of 15. In her twenties she was twice married – her second husband was Gottfried Lessing – but neither marriage was a success. In 1949 she moved to England with the youngest of her three children.

Lessing's first book, the novel *The Grass Is Singing* (1950), was set in Africa and written while she was still living there. The five-novel series *Children of Violence* (1952–69), following the life of Martha Quest from her Rhodesian childhood to the year 2000, examines the politics of race and war. Her most famous work, *The Golden Notebook* (1962), was seen as a landmark in women's writing and led Lessing to be identified as a feminist writer, a label that tends to obscure her broader interest in personal freedom.

Her other novels include *Briefing for a Descent into Hell* (1971), an explo-

ration of the theories of the British psychiatrist R. D. Laing; the five-novel *Canopus in Argos: Archives* series (1979–83), in which she uses science fiction to present an apocalyptic view of humanity; the prize-winning *The Good Terrorist* (1985); *The Fifth Child* (1988), about the nature of evil; and *Love Again* (1996).

Among Lessing's volumes of short stories are *This Was the Old Chief's Country* (1951), *African Stories* (1964), *The Temptation of Jack Orkney and Other Stories* (1972), and *The Real Thing: Stories and Sketches* (1993). Lessing has also written poetry and plays. Her nonfiction writing includes the idiosyncratic *Particularly Cats* (1967; reissued with an additional chapter in 1991), *A Small Personal Voice: Essays, Reviews, Interviews* (1975), *African Laughter: Four Visits to Zimbabwe* (1992), and two volumes of memoirs, *Under My Skin* (1994) and *Walking in the Shade* (1997).

Levertov, Denise (1923–1997) *British-born American poet and essayist*

Levertov's verse covers a wide range of themes, from personal concerns to social and political issues.

She was born in Ilford, Essex, and educated at home by her parents. Her mother was Welsh, and her father, a Russian Jew, later became a clergyman in the Church of England. Levertov moved to the United States in 1948 after her marriage to the American writer Mitchell Goodman; she became a U.S. citizen in 1955. She taught at several colleges, notably Tufts University and Stanford University; she was also poetry editor of the *Nation* (1961–62) and *Mother Jones* (1976–78).

The poetry in her first book, *The Double Image* (1946), was written in a formal style, while later volumes were acclaimed for their free-verse rhythms, lyrical language, and unique personal vision. Levertov's intense pacifism is seen in virtually all of her work. Collections of her verse include *Collected Earlier Poems, 1940–1960* (1979); *Poems, 1960–1967* (1983); and *Poems, 1968–1972* (1987). The last of these contains such poems as "Relearning the Alphabet," "To Stay Alive," and "Footprints." Her essays were published in *The Poet in the World* (1959) and *Light Up the Cave* (1981).

Levi-Montalcini, Rita (1909–   ) *Italian cell biologist*

Levi-Montalcini is known for her studies of the development of embryological tissue and for her discovery of what is now known as nerve growth factor. She was a joint winner of the Nobel Prize for physiology or medicine in 1986.

Rita Levi-Montalcini was born in Turin and educated at the university there, graduating from medical school just before the outbreak of World War II. Because she was Jewish, Levi-Montalcini found that posts in Italy's academic establishments were closed to her during this period of increasing anti-Semitism. Undaunted, she converted her bedroom into a makeshift laboratory and proceeded with her studies of the development of chick embryos. She was joined by her former professor, Giuseppe Levi, a Jew who had also been forced out of his job by the Fascists. Between 1941 and 1943 Levi-Montalcini lived first in a country cottage in the Piedmont region, then in hiding in Florence. After the Allied liberation of Italy in 1944 she worked as a doctor among refugees in Florence, and in 1945 she returned to the University of Turin.

Two years later she moved to the United States, where she continued her work on chick embryos under professor Viktor Hamburger at the Washington University, St. Louis. By the early 1950s she had demonstrated that the number of nerve cells produced in these embryos could be influenced by an agent (later termed nerve growth factor) obtained from mouse tumour cells grown in the laboratory. In 1952 she was joined by an American biochemist, Stanley Cohen, who collaborated with her in this work.

Levi-Montalcini was appointed associate professor at St. Louis in 1956 and later became professor (1958–77). She was also director of the Institute of Cell Biology of the Italian National Research Council in Rome from 1969 until her retirement in 1978.

The early studies of Levi-Montalcini represent a key advance in the understanding of embryological tissue development. Indeed, in the 1980s it was established that the nerve growth factor she discovered influences the growth of nerves in the brain and spinal cord. The value of her work earned her the 1986 Nobel Prize for physiology or medicine, which she shared with Stanley Cohen.

Lewis, Edmonia (1845–after 1909) *American sculptor*

Edmonia Lewis's work is noted for its strikingly emotional portrayal of women, slaves, and Native Americans, reflecting her concern for equality and civil rights. She also sculpted busts of such famous people as Henry Wadsworth Longfellow and Abraham Lincoln.

Mary Edmonia Lewis was born in Greenbush, New York State, the daughter of an African-American father and a Native-American mother. Her parents died when she was young, and she was brought up by her mother's people, the Chippewa. At the age of 17, in her third and final year at school, she was accused of poisoning two of her fellow students, who were white. Having been acquitted of this charge, she moved to Boston and trained as a sculptor with Edward Augustus Brackett.

The sale of some of her early work, notably a bust of the African-American Civil War officer Colonel Robert Shaw, enabled her to travel in 1867 to Rome, where she met the American sculptors Harriet HOSMER and Anne WHITNEY. She worked there for several years, creating sculptures and paintings such as *Forever Free* and *Hiawatha's Wedding*. One of her best-known works, *Hagar in the Wilderness*, was produced in 1868. In the 1870s she returned to the United States and exhibited her sculptures in San Francisco and at the Centennial Exposition (1876) in Philadelphia. Her last major work was *The Death of Cleopatra*, a graphic study of the dying queen just moments after the fatal snakebite. Lewis subsequently retired to Rome, having converted to Catholicism; the exact date of her death is unknown.

Leyster, Judith (1609–1660) *Dutch painter*

One of the few female painters of Holland's golden age, Judith Leyster was the only woman member of the painters' guild known to have had her own workshop.

Leyster was probably born in Haarlem, the daughter of a brewer. Few details of her early life are known, but she is said to have shown exceptional artistic talent at an early age. She may have trained with the Haarlem painter Frans Pieter de Grevver, for it is in connection with his family that she was mentioned in 1628 as one who painted "with a good keen sense." Her earliest known signed and dated works indicate that she was soon greatly influenced by the work of another Haarlem master, Frans Hals. Leyster was accepted into the Haarlem painters' guild in 1633. After her marriage in 1636 to the painter Jan Miense Molenaer she moved to Amsterdam.

Leyster specialized in genre painting – the depiction of domestic scenes from everyday life. She gave little attention to her interior settings, frequently creating a sense of intimacy with dramatic lighting effects from a single candle or oil lamp. Only about 20 paintings have been confirmed as Leyster's work, many of them signed with her monogram – an intertwined "J" and "L" with a star (her family name means "leading star"). They include *The Jolly Toper*, *The Flute Player*, *The Proposition*, and a self-portrait painted around 1635.

Following her death most of Leyster's work was wrongly attributed to other artists, mainly Frans Hals. Leyster was finally recognized in 1893, when Cornelis Hofstede de Groot published an article about her. A century later, in 1993, the first exhibition of her work was shown in her native city and in Worcester, Massachusetts.

Lidman, Sara (1923–) *Swedish writer*

Sara Lidman is regarded as one of the most original writers in Sweden today. She has been particularly praised for a series of novels about life in the far north of her native land.

Sara Adela Lidman was born in Missenträsk, Västerbotten, in the north of Sweden. Forced by illness to abandon her studies at Uppsala University, she began writing instead. Her first four novels, *The Tar Still* (1953), *Cloudberry Land* (1955), *The Rainbird* (1958), and *Carry Mistletoe* (1960), were set in the sparsely populated region where she grew up. They describe the harsh life of a struggling community and reflect some of the political and social concerns that were to become more evident in her later work.

In the 1960s Lidman travelled in South Africa, Kenya, and Vietnam, and used some of these experiences in her subsequent writings. Based on interviews and conversations with local people, they include *Conversations in Hanoi* (1965) and *Mine* (1968). She returned to fiction writing with *Thy Servant Heareth* (1977), about the arrival of the railroad in northern Sweden. This was the first of a series of acclaimed novels, which include *Child of Wrath* (1979), *The Wonderful Man* (1983), and *The Iron Crown* (1985), that trace the history of her native region back to the time of the earliest settlers. Lidman has also written nonfiction and plays.

Liliuokalani, Lydia Kamekeha (1838–1917) *Queen of Hawaii*

The last monarch of Hawaii, Queen Liliuokalani was also a gifted poet, composer, and songwriter, her best-known song being "Aloha Oe" ("Farewell to Thee").

Born in Honolulu, she became queen of the islands on January 29, 1891, following the death of her brother, King Kalakaua. Her husband John O. Dominis, a governor of Oahu, died in the same year. Queen Liliuokalani's brief (four-year) reign was marked by political turmoil in a period of economic depression and increasing U.S. influence. She tried to change the reform constitution of 1887 and return to autocratic government, but she was overthrown by resident Americans in January 1893.

Although the U.S. President Grover Cleveland supported her cause, the dethroned queen was finally forced to abandon her protests. In January 1895, detained in the royal palace, she formally abdicated and swore allegiance to the Republic of Hawaii. The United States annexed the islands in 1898, and Liliuokalani was eventually granted a small pension by the Hawaii territorial legislature.

Lillie, Beatrice (1894–1989) *Canadian-born British singer and comedian*

Widely considered to be one of the funniest female performers of her time, Bea Lillie could make audiences roar with laughter merely by raising an eyebrow, twitching her nose, or giving an icy smile.

Born in Toronto, she made her first stage appearance in a Canadian music hall in 1914. Later that year she moved to England and settled in London, making her British debut in the revue *Not Likely!* (1914). In 1920 she married Robert Peel, who succeeded to a baronetcy in 1925, bringing Lillie the title of Lady Peel. Their son was killed during World War II.

Lillie, who was equally effective in the theatre and in cabaret, usually played in revues. Often she appeared under the management of the impresario André Charlot, sometimes with the actress and singer Gertrude LAW-RENCE. Like Lawrence, she gave notable performances in the plays of Noël Coward, and it was Bea Lillie who made famous Coward's song "Mad Dogs and Englishmen."

Lillie's stage appearances included *Charlot's Revue of 1924*, in which she made her Broadway debut, *This Year of Grace* (1928), *At Home Abroad* (1935), *The Seven Lively Arts* (1944), *Inside U.S.A.* (1948), *An Evening with Beatrice Lillie* (1952), and *Auntie Mame* (1958). During World War II she toured the Mediterranean, North Africa, and the Middle East, entertaining the troops. She last appeared on stage in 1964 in the New York production of *High Spirits*, a musical based on Coward's famous comedy *Blithe Spirit*. Her autobiography, *Every Other Inch a Lady*, was published in 1972.

Lin, Maya (1954–   ) *American sculptor and architect*

Maya Lin made her name with a prizewinning memorial to the American military personnel killed in the Vietnam War, a V-shaped wall of black granite engraved with nearly 60,000 names. This was erected and dedicated in Washington, D.C., in 1982 and became a popular tourist attraction. She has said, "Sculpture to me is like poetry, and architecture is like prose."

Maya Lin was born in Athens, Ohio, the daughter of Chinese immigrants – a poet and a ceramic artist who had moved to the United States in the 1940s. As a high-school student she developed an interest in existentialist ideas about death, which inspired some of her subsequent work in memorial sculpture. Her proposal for the Vietnam Veterans Memorial was produced in 1981 as a competition entry during her architecture studies at Yale University. Lin's sculpture won the competition and brought her great acclaim, despite a protest by certain Vietnam veterans who wanted a more traditional statue to be erected at the memorial site.

After further studies at Harvard and Yale, interrupted by a short period of employment with a firm of architects in Boston, Lin set up her own studio in New York. Although she continued to accept commissions for memorials and similar pieces – notably the Civil Rights Memorial (1989) in Montgomery, Alabama, and the Women's Table at Yale (1993) – she demonstrated her versatility with a wide range of other sculptures and architectural designs. These included two projects in New York: a loft renovation at the Museum of African Art (1993) and a large clock called "Eclipsed Time" for Penn Station (1994). Modelled on the movement of Sun, Earth, and Moon that produces an eclipse, the clock is an oval of illuminated translucent glass on which the time is indicated by a moving metal disc that casts a shadow over the numerals.

Lincoln, Mary Todd (1818–1882)
Wife of President Abraham Lincoln

Mary Todd was born in Lexington, Kentucky, into a well-to-do and socially prominent family and received a good education. In 1839 she went to Springfield, Illinois, to live with her sister. There she met Abraham Lincoln, nine years her senior, a lawyer and state legislator. After a long courtship marked by a broken engagement, they were married on November 4, 1842. Of their four sons only the oldest, Robert Todd Lincoln, survived to adulthood.

The course of the marriage was not always smooth. Lincoln was reserved, introspective, and deficient in social graces, whereas his wife was vivacious, self-centred, and ambitious. Nevertheless Mary Lincoln took pride in her husband's progress in law and politics, realizing her highest ambition when he was elected 16th president of the United States in 1860. Life in the White House, however, was not what she had expected; she made many enemies with her sharp tongue and by meddling in matters not her concern.

Mary Lincoln was with the president at Ford's Theater on April 15, 1865, the night he was shot. After his death her mental health began to decline. For three years she lived in Chicago, then she went to Europe. In 1871, shortly after her return to the United States, her youngest son, Thomas (Tad), died at the age of 18. His death came as a shattering blow to his mother, who had already lost two of her sons.

In 1875 Mary Lincoln began to show signs of acute mental abnormality. Fearing that she would squander all her money and perhaps even commit suicide, her son Robert Todd Lincoln brought insanity proceedings against her. A jury found her insane, and she spent four months in a private sanatorium before being released into the care of her sister in Springfield. The following year another jury declared her sane.

During the next four years Mrs. Lincoln lived in Europe, mainly in Pau, France. Her health was poor, and despite her comfortable income she complained incessantly of poverty. In 1880 she returned to the United States to live with her sister. She died in Springfield two years later, a tragic figure who had descended from the heights of First Lady to the depths of despair.

Lind, Jenny (1820–1887) *Swedish singer*

Her singing, remarkable for its purity, range, agility, and breath control, earned Jenny Lind the nickname the "Swedish nightingale."

Johanna Maria Lind was born in Stockholm, where she studied singing and made her operatic debut in 1838. In 1841 she went to Paris and studied with Manuel Garcia. There she met Giacomo Meyerbeer, who greatly admired her voice and recommended her to the Berlin Opera. She made her Berlin debut in 1844 in the title role of Bellini's *Norma*. She then embarked on a series of enormously successful appearances throughout Europe, making her London debut at Her Majesty's Theatre in 1847 as Alice in Meyerbeer's *Robert le Diable*. For the next three years she appeared regularly in London, where she sang the role of Amalia in the first performance of Verdi's *I Masnadieri*.

In 1849 Lind withdrew from opera but continued to sing in concerts. She went to the United States in 1850 and made extensive concert tours under the management of P. T. Barnum. She married Otto Goldschmidt, her accompanist, in Boston in 1852 and settled in England with him in 1856. Together they founded the Bach Choir in London. After retiring from the concert stage in 1883, Lind taught at the Royal College of Music, London, for several years.

Littlewood, Joan (1914–) *British stage director*

Littlewood's fresh original approach, using experimental techniques such as improvisation and audience participation, influenced the work of theatre directors throughout Europe and elsewhere. She is best remembered for the satirical musical drama *Oh, What a Lovely War!* (1963).

Joan Maud Littlewood was born in

London and studied at the Royal Academy of Dramatic Art (RADA). In 1935 she founded an amateur theatre company, the Theatre Union, in Manchester. The company became known for its successful productions of experimental plays, but it was forced to disband at the outbreak of World War II in 1939. It was re-formed as the Theatre Workshop in Manchester after the end of the war and moved to the Theatre Royal, Stratford, London, in 1953.

Littlewood's productions reflected the left-wing ideals of the company, both in the reworking of established plays, such as Shakespeare's *Richard II* (1955), and in the introduction of new plays by working-class writers, such as Brendan Behan's *The Quare Fellow* (1956) and Shelagh DELANEY's *A Taste of Honey* (1958). When the Theatre Workshop's more successful productions, including the musical *Fings Ain't Wot They Used T'Be* (1959), began to transfer to the West End, Littlewood felt that the company's ideals had been compromised. She left in 1961 but returned two years later to produce *Oh, What a Lovely War!*, a musical satire about World War I.

In 1962 Littlewood directed the film *Sparrows Can't Sing*, based on a play by Stephen Lewis that the Theatre Workshop had staged two years earlier. The film is a lively comedy set in London's East End, starring a host of British character actors such as Barbara Windsor and Roy Kinnear. In the mid 1960s she worked abroad for a time, in Tunisia and Calcutta, before returning to the Theatre Workshop for such productions as *So You Want to Be in Pictures?* (1973). She moved to France in 1975, after which she worked only occasionally in Britain. In 1994 she published her autobiography, *Joan's Book*, and in 1995 the Directors' Guild honoured her with their Lifetime's Achievement Award.

Lively, Penelope (1933–) *British writer*

Having established her reputation as a writer of children's books, Lively made a successful move to adult novels in the late 1970s and was awarded the Booker Prize for *Moon Tiger* in 1987. Her interest in history – and in the links between past and present time – is reflected in much of her work.

She was born Penelope Margaret Greer in Cairo, and studied history at Oxford University. In 1957 she married Jack Lively, a teacher of politics at the university. She began writing for children with such stories as *The Whispering Knights* (1971); *The Ghost of Thomas Kempe* (1973), about a 17th-century sorcerer who haunts a 20th-century family; *Going Back* (1975); and *A Stitch in Time* (1976), which explores the relationship between two girls who lived in the same place a hundred years apart. Her first novel for adults, *The Road to Lichfield*, appeared in 1977. It was followed by *Treasures of Time* (1979), about a famous archaeologist; *Judgement Day* (1980); and *Perfect Happiness* (1983), about a widow who makes a new life for herself.

Lively's greatest success of the 1980s was *Moon Tiger* (1987), which won the Booker McConnell Prize for Fiction. Its heroine, a dying historian, recalls her life from the 1920s to the 1970s, notably a love affair in Egypt during World War II. More recent novels include *City of the Mind* (1991), which examines the changing face of London; *Cleopatra's Sister* (1993), set in the fictitious African state of Callimbia; and *Heat Wave* (1996). Although she is best known as a novelist, Lively has also written short stories, notably the collection *Pack of Cards* (1986), and scripts for radio and television. Among her nonfiction works are *The Presence of the Past: An Introduction to Landscape History* (1976) and an autobiographical volume, *Oleander, Jacaranda* (1994).

Livia (58 BC–29 AD) *Wife of the Roman Emperor Augustus*

In her lifetime Livia was honoured throughout the empire and even hailed as a living goddess by some of the Greek cities.

Livia Drusilla was born into a distinguished Roman family and married her cousin Tiberius Claudius Nero.

Their first son, the future Emperor Tiberius, was born in 42 BC. Livia's husband took part in the Perusine War against Octavian (later Augustus) in 41 and afterwards fled with her to Sicily and Greece. When they returned to Rome in 39, Octavian fell in love with Livia, and her husband willingly divorced her. The marriage took place on January 17, 38 BC, around the time that Livia gave birth to her former husband's second son, Nero Claudius Drusus.

In spite of the inevitable gossip, Livia proved the ideal wife for Octavian, who became Rome's first emperor and took the title Augustus (meaning sacred) in 27 BC. Beautiful and intelligent, she ruled his household in the simple way that he desired; she retained his affection until his death in 14 AD. Her influence on him was said to be considerable, but she exercised it discreetly. The marriage proved childless, and it was alleged that she had a hand in the deaths of Augustus's heirs, ensuring the succession of her own son Tiberius. These rumours were probably untrue. In his will Augustus adopted Livia into the Julian family and renamed her Julia Augusta.

In the early years of Tiberius's reign Livia remained influential, but the relationship between mother and son became strained. She left a vast fortune, but her will was not executed until the reign of Emperor Caligula, her great-grandson.

Lloyd, Chris Evert (1954–) *American tennis player*

A right-hander with a strong two-handed backhand, she was noted for her coolness under stress and was ranked among the top three women players of her generation.

Born Christine Marie Evert in Fort Lauderdale, Florida, she began playing tennis at the age of six. In 1972, after losing to Billie Jean KING in the semifinals of the U.S. Open, she turned professional. She won her first major singles titles, the French Open and Wimbledon, in 1974. A consistent performer, she took four more French Open titles (1975, 1979, 1980, 1983)

and won the Wimbledon title again in 1976 and 1981. She dominated the U.S. Open with six victories in eight years (1975–78, 1980, 1982). Her first Australian title, in 1982, gave her a chance at the "Grand Slam" of four major titles that year, but she was eliminated at Wimbledon. Virtually unbeatable on clay courts, she won her thousandth singles match in 1984.

Chris Evert was married to the British tennis player John Lloyd from 1979 to 1987; together they wrote *Lloyd on Lloyd* (1985). She retired from the professional tennis circut in 1989.

Lloyd, Marie (1870–1922) *British vaudeville singer*

One of the most famous names in music-hall, Marie Lloyd built up an international reputation with such songs as "Oh! Mr. Porter," "My Old Man Said Follow the Van," and "A Little of What You Fancy Does You Good," delivered with a mixture of wit and coarse vitality.

She was born Matilda Alice Victoria Wood in London, the daughter of a waiter. At the age of 15 she gave her first public performance, under the stage name Bella Delmere, at the Royal Eagle Music Hall. As Marie Lloyd she sang at the Middlesex Music Hall, where her rendition of "The Boy I Love Sits Up in the Gallery" was a great success. This led to a year's contract at the Oxford Music Hall, also in London, after which she spent three years in pantomime at Drury Lane.

In 1894 Lloyd returned to music hall and spent the rest of her career there. During the next 25 years she toured the halls of Britain and similar establishments in the United States, South Africa, and Australia, becoming one of the most popular female performers of her time. Her act was witty, often verging on the improper, but she never descended to explicit vulgarity, relying instead on winks and gestures to suggest her double meanings.

After a brief period of semiretirement she returned to the stage for a 50th-birthday celebration in 1920. Old-style music-hall shows were enjoying a revival at that time, and Lloyd made many more appearances during the last two years of her life. At her final performance, just a few days before her death, she sang one of her most famous songs, "I'm One of the Ruins that Cromwell Knocked About a Bit."

Lockwood, Belva Ann (1830–1917)
American lawyer

> I have been told that there is no precedent for admitting a woman to practise in the Supreme Court of the United States. The glory of each generation is to make its own precedents. As there was none for Eve in the Garden of Eden, so there need be none for her daughters on entering the colleges, the church, or the courts.
>
> —Quoted by Mary Virginia Fox in *Lady for the Defence* (1917)

An active campaigner for women's rights and votes for women, Lockwood became in 1879 the first woman to practise before the Supreme Court in the United States.

Belva Ann Bennett was born in Royalton, New York State. After teaching in Royalton for four years, she married a local man who was killed in an accident in 1853. She subsequently studied at Genesee College in Lima, New York; after graduating in 1857, she taught at Lockport and was principal of McNall Seminary in Oswego. In 1868 she married a dentist, Dr. Ezekiel Lockwood.

In 1873 Belva took a law degree at the National University, Washington, D.C., and began practising in the district court of the District of Columbia. There was still much discrimination against women, especially married women, in the legal profession: Lockwood had been refused admission to law courses at three universities, including Harvard. When she applied in 1875 to practise in the court of claims, and in 1876 to practise before the bar of the Virginia supreme court, she was denied on grounds that included her sex and marital status.

After campaigning successfully for a change in the law, in 1879 Lockwood was admitted to practise before the Supreme Court. She obtained legisla-

tion that gave women in the District of Columbia equal property rights and equal guardianship of their children; she was also attorney for the eastern and emigrant Cherokee Indians when the Cherokee Nation brought claims against the United States. In 1884 she ran for the U.S. presidency as a member of the National Equal Rights Party. She was also active in the cause of international peace, belonging to the Universal Peace Union and serving on the nominating committee for the Nobel Peace Prize.

Lockwood, Margaret (1916–1990)
British actress

Lockwood gave some of her best performances as wicked women. She adopted her trade mark – a beauty spot on her left cheekbone – in the 1944 film *A Place of One's Own*.

Margaret Mary Lockwood was born in Karachi, India (now in Pakistan), where her father worked as railway company administrator. In 1920 the family moved to London. Margaret was a timid child who took refuge from her domineering mother in daydreams of stardom. She studied dancing at the Italia Conti School in London and made her first stage appearance as a fairy in *A Midsummer Night's Dream*. In 1931 she had a walk-on part in Noël Coward's *Cavalcade*, and two years later began training at the Royal Academy of Dramatic Art (RADA).

Lockwood's first film appearance, in *Lorna Doone* (1934), was followed by a number of other minor roles. International stardom came four years later, with *Bank Holiday* and *The Lady Vanishes*. She then went to Hollywood but did not stay long; after *Rulers of the Sea* (1939) she returned to Britain, where she spent the rest of her career.

In *The Man in Grey* (1943), a costume melodrama, Lockwood played a scheming woman who murders her best friend after stealing her husband. This was the first of many similar roles, culminating in her highly successful portrayal of an aristocratic highwaywoman in *The Wicked Lady* (1945) and a serial poisoner in *Bedelia* (1946). Lockwood subsequently told her studio that she was "sick of sinning," but her popularity with the public waned as her parts became less villainous. Undeterred, she turned her attention to the theatre and television, appearing in Agatha Christie's *Spider's Web* (1954–56) and a revival of Oscar Wilde's *An Ideal Husband* (1965).

In 1937 Lockwood had married Rupert Leon, a man whom her mother disliked so intensely that Margaret kept the marriage a secret for six months. However, when the couple divorced in 1950, Mrs. Lockwood supported her son-in-law in his attempt to gain custody of their daughter, Julia. Margaret won the battle, but she never forgave her mother for this betrayal. Julia Lockwood went on to become a successful actress, appearing with her mother in a British television series, *The Flying Swan* (1965). In the early 1970s Margaret Lockwood starred in *Justice*, another popular television series, this time with the actor John Stone, who had been her lover for many years.

Lockwood's last film role was as the wicked stepmother in *The Slipper and the Rose* (1976), a musical version of the story of Cinderella. In 1981, after receiving a CBE, she retired, spending the remainder of her life as a recluse.

Lollobrigida, Gina (1927–) *Italian actress*

Primarily known for her beauty, Lollobrigida performed in many Italian, French, and American films of the 1950s and 1960s. She was frequently cast in earthy roles as a sexual temptress; her arch-rival Sophia LOREN once remarked, "She is good as a peasant but incapable of playing a lady."

Gina Lollobrigida was born in Subiaco into a middle-class family. As a child she was given private lessons in singing, dancing, drawing, and languages, skills that were to come in handy when her family was forced to move to Rome during World War II. Lollobrigida helped to make money by singing, making sketches of American soldiers, and posing for Italian comic strips. After the war she won a scholarship to Rome's Academy of Fine Arts, where she studied sculpture and painting.

In 1947 film director Mario Cosa spotted the beautiful Lollobrigida on the street and offered her a job as a film actress. After a number of minor roles she had her first important part in *Miss Italy* (1949). The role was appropriate, for two years earlier she had been named "Miss Rome" and was the runner-up for "Miss Italy."

Lollobrigida continued to make Italian and French films throughout the 1950s; the French film *Fanfan the Tulip* (1953) brought her widespread attention in the United States. Her first American film was *Beat the Devil* (1954), with Humphrey Bogart. She subsequently went back and forth between Europe and the United States, appearing in such films as *Trapeze* (1955), *Solomon and Sheba* (1959), *Come September* (1963), and *Buona Sera, Mrs. Campbell* (1968). In Europe in the late 1950s Lollobrigida was voted most popular star for three years in a row. Her U.S. career declined at the end of the 1960s, but she continued to act in Italy and coproduced a number of films there.

Lombard, Carole (1908–1942) *American actress*

The wacky heroine of numerous film comedies of the 1930s, Carole Lombard was briefly married to the actor Clark Gable before her tragic death in an air crash.

Born Jane Alice Peters in Fort Wayne, Indiana, she is said to have taken her screen name from the Carroll Lombardi Pharmacy in New York City. At the age of 12 she was offered her first film role, as a tomboy in *A Perfect Crime* (1921). Having enjoyed this experience, she opted for a career in the cinema on leaving school four years later. An attractive blonde, she had no difficulty finding work, especially in the short comedy films made by Mack Sennett in the late 1920s. She joined Paramount in 1930 and appeared in more than 20 pictures over the next four years.

Twentieth Century (1934) was the first of several highly successful screwball comedies in which Lombard combined sophisticated glamour with zany humour. It was followed by *My Man Godfrey* (1936), *Nothing Sacred* (1937), *Mr. and Mrs. Smith* (1941), and *To Be or Not To Be* (1942). The range of her dramatic talent was demonstrated by more serious roles in such films as *Vigil in the Night* and *They Knew What They Wanted* (both 1940).

In 1939 Lombard married the actor Clark Gable, star of *Gone With the Wind*. Just three years later she was tragically killed, together with her mother and 20 other people, when the aircraft in which they were travelling from Las Vegas to Los Angeles crashed in Nevada. In 1976 an unmemorable film was made of the couple's short-lived romance, starring James Brolin and Jill Clayburgh in the title roles.

Longueville, Duchesse de (1619–1679) *French noblewoman*

A celebrated beauty, Madame de Longueville is remembered for her intrigues against the monarchy.

The daughter of Henri II de Bourbon, Prince de Condé, and Charlotte de Montmorency, Anne Geneviève de Bourbon-Condé was born at Vincennes, where her father was imprisoned for opposition to the crown. At the age of 23 she married the Duc de Longueville, a 47-year-old widower.

Subsequently she became the mistress of the French writer La Rochefoucauld, author of the celebrated *Maximes*. Through him she became involved in political intrigue, initially in the Fronde, a movement of rebellion against Cardinal Mazarin, the first minister. In 1649, during the first war of the Fronde, she gave birth to La Rochefoucauld's son at the Paris Hôtel de Ville. Her husband and her brothers Louis II, Prince de Condé, and Armand, Prince de Conti, were arrested in 1650 in the second war of the Fronde. Mme. de Longueville escaped to raise forces against the crown and subsequently helped to defend Bordeaux against the royal army in 1652 and 1653. She was forced to remain in exile until 1659, when her brother Louis, known as the Great Condé, made peace with the government.

In later life Mme. de Longueville became increasingly pious and used her influence at court to protect the Jansenists, a puritanical Roman Catholic group opposed by the king. She died in retirement at the Carmelite convent in Paris where she had been educated as a girl.

Lonsdale, Dame Kathleen (1903–1971) *British crystallographer*

Kathleen Lonsdale was one of the early pioneers of x-ray crystallography, a technique in which x-rays are used to determine the structure of crystals and molecules.

The daughter of a postman, she was born Kathleen Yardley at Newbridge, County Kildare, and moved to England with her family in 1908. She went on to study physics at Bedford College, London, graduating in 1922, and spent most of the following 20 years based at the Royal Institution on the research team of William Henry Bragg. In 1946 she moved to University College, London, where she served as professor of chemistry and head of the department of crystallography from 1948 until her retirement in 1968.

At the Royal Institution Lonsdale was a member of the team headed by Bragg, which included such scholars as William Astbury, John Bernal, Dorothy HODGKIN, and John Robertson. It was from this group that most of the concepts and techniques of x-ray crystallography emerged in the 1920s and 1930s. Lonsdale herself was responsible for one of the first demonstrations of the power of the new techniques when, in 1929, she published details of the six-sided ring structure of benzene. This was followed in 1931 by the equally significant structure of the more difficult hexachlorobenzene.

Lonsdale's other work on crystals included research on the structure of synthetic diamonds and, in the 1960s, that of bladder stones. She edited the first three volumes of the *International Tables for X-ray Crystallography* (1952, 1959, 1962) and also produced a survey of the subject in her *Crystals and X-rays* (1948).

As a Quaker and a convinced pacifist Lonsdale refused to register in 1939 for government service or civil defence – despite the fact that as a mother of three young children she would have been exempted from any such service. Fined for this in 1943, she refused to pay and served a month in Holloway Prison instead.

When, 285 years after its foundation, the Royal Society finally decided to admit women to its fellowship, Lonsdale was the first to be elected (1945) and she became the society's vice president in 1960. She was appointed a DBE in 1956 and also became, in 1968, the first woman to serve as president of the British Association for the Advancement of Science.

Loos, Anita (1893–1981) *American writer*

> I'm furious about the Women's Liberationists. They keep getting up on soapboxes and proclaiming that women are brighter than men.
> That's true, but it should be kept very quiet or it ruins the whole racket.
> —Quoted in *The Observer*, "Sayings of the Year," December 30, 1973

Loos is best known for her novel *Gentlemen Prefer Blondes* (1925), a satirical view of a "dumb" blonde out to catch a rich husband. It was made into a play in 1926, a hit musical in 1949, and a film, starring Jane RUSSELL and Marilyn MONROE, in 1953.

She was born in Sisson, California, the daughter of Richard Beers Loos, a humorist and theatrical producer. She began acting in her father's company at the age of five and writing for his paper at the age of ten. By 1912 she was writing film scripts for the pioneer director D. W. Griffith, and in 1919 she married the director John Emerson, with whom she collaborated in some of her work.

With the introduction of talking pictures she progressed from writing subtitles for silent films to producing screenplays for such movies as *San Francisco* (1936) and *Susan and God* (1940). She also dramatized the French writer COLETTE's novels *Gigi* and *Chéri* and produced two volumes of memoirs, *A Girl Like I* (1966) and *Kiss Hollywood Goodbye* (1974).

Lopez, Nancy (1957–) *American golfer*

Nancy Lopez's powerful drives, superior putting, and consistent play brought her immediate recognition as a professional. In 1978, her first full season with the Ladies Professional Golf Association (LPGA), she dazzled the sports world by winning nine tournaments, including a record five in a row. She became the first player to be honoured as both Rookie of the Year and Player of the Year.

Of Mexican descent, Nancy Marie Lopez was born in Torrance, California, and raised in Roswell, New Mexico. Taught golf by her father, she won her first tournament in 1966 and by the age of 12 had won the first of three state women's tournaments. She attended the University of Tulsa, where she won the intercollegiate title in 1976. She dropped out after her second year of college to turn professional.

Lopez maintained her dominant position in women's golf throughout the 1980s, and by the early 1990s she had won more than $3 million. In 1980 she became the first woman to enter the All-American Collegiate Golf Hall of Fame. LPGA player of the year in 1978, 1979, 1985, and 1988, she entered the Professional Golfing Association Hall of Fame in 1989.

Lorde, Audre Geraldine (1934– 1992) *American poet, writer, and feminist*

Audre Lorde was an African-American feminist poet, who was proud to be a lesbian as well as the mother of two children.

Lorde was born the daughter of Grenadian parents in New York City and educated at the National University of Mexico, Hunter College, New York, and Columbia University. She became professor of English at Hunter College in 1980. Her first publication was the poetry collection *The First Cities* (1968), in which she examined issues of sex and race, often by exploring her own childhood memories. Subsequent volumes of poetry, including the highly praised *From a Land Where Other People Live* (1973), *Chosen Poems: Old and New* (1982), and *Our*

Dead Behind Us (1986), confront similar themes. After she contracted cancer in the late 1970s she wrote about her struggle with the disease in *The Cancer Journals* (1980) and *Burst of Light* (1988), a volume of essays.

Lorde's other works include the "biomythography" *Zami: A New Spelling of My Name*, a partly fictionalized memoir in which she describes the pressures of growing up as a black lesbian in the 1950s and 1960s, and *Sister Outsider* (1984), a collection of essays and speeches.

Loren, Sophia (1934–) *Italian actress*

> It is always the woman who must keep the thread straight, to save the marriage. Women choose for the family – though sometimes they must sacrifice themselves.
>
> —Quoted in *The Sunday Telegraph*, September 2, 1984

An international film star of great beauty, Loren is also an actress who can handle many different kinds of roles. In 1991 she won a special Oscar for her contribution to the art of film.

Born Sofia Scicolone in Rome, she was educated in Pozzuoli, a small town near Naples. Her family was very poor, and she enrolled in the local teachers' institute at the age of 12, hoping to earn her living in education. At that time, she recalls, she was not attractive: "I was tall, thin, ugly and dark...All eyes. No flesh on my bones." However, during the next few years her body blossomed, and after winning second place in a beauty contest, she moved to Rome with the intention of becoming a film star. Her break came in 1950 when she met film producer Carlo Ponti, who would later become her husband.

Ponti sent her for acting lessons and gave her her first starring role. In the next three years Loren made more than 20 films, often working on three different movies at the same time. She became famous all over Europe, and in 1955 she made her first U.S. film, *The Pride and the Passion*, with Cary Grant and Frank Sinatra. This was followed by a string of other films, including *The Black Orchid*, for which she was given the Best Actress award at the Venice Film Festival in 1958.

In 1961 Loren won an Academy Award for Best Actress for her brilliant performance in the Italian-made film *Two Women.* Throughout the 1960s and 1970s she continued to act in such films as *It Started in Naples* (1960), *The Millionairess* (1960), *Lady L* (1965), *A Countess from Hong Kong* (1967), *La Mortadella* (1971), and *Man of La Mancha* (1973). *Yesterday, Today, and Tomorrow* (1963), which won an Oscar for Best Foreign Film, and *Marriage Italian Style* (1964) were among a number of films in which she costarred with Italian actor Marcello Mastroianni.

In 1980 Loren became one of the small number of film stars who have played themselves in a screen version of their own life story. The film, *Sophia Loren: Her Own Story*, was based on her autobiography published in 1979. Her most recent appearances have been in the TV film *The Fortunate Pilgrim* (1988) and *Ready to Wear* (1994). She has been a naturalized French citizen since the mid 1960s.

Loroupe, Tegla (1973–) *Kenyan athlete*

In 1994 Tegla Loroupe became the first Kenyan woman to win the New York City Marathon.

Tegla Loroupe was born into a poor family of the Bokot tribe in Kapenguria, a small town in Kenya's Rift Valley. As a child she developed her athletic skills by running to school – to avoid being punished for lateness – and in rounding up the cattle on her parents' farm. In 1994 she entered the New York City Marathon for the first time and won, completing the course of 26 miles and 385 yards in just two hours, 27 minutes, and 37 seconds. A small frail-looking figure, not quite five feet tall and weighing only 78 pounds (35 kg), she became a role model for fellow Kenyan women, who were not generally encouraged to take part in sporting or other activities outside the home.

Less than two weeks before the following year's marathon Loroupe received the tragic news that her elder sister, Albina, had died. Knowing that her sister would not have wanted her to withdraw from the race, Loroupe successfully defended her title on November 12, 1995, drawing ahead of her closest rival in the 18th mile. She dedicated the event to Albina, inspired by her dying wishes: "My mother told me that right before Albina died, she asked her to tell me that she'll keep her fingers crossed for me and to have courage." In November 1996 she lost her title, finishing in seventh place.

Lowell, Amy (1874–1925) *American poet and critic*

Amy Lowell was a strong force in introducing new poetry – particularly imagism – to the United States. According to her definition, imagism required "simplicity and directness of speech; subtlety and beauty of rhythms; individualistic freedom of idea; clearness and vividness of presentation; and concentration." Fat and far from handsome, she is said to have covered all the mirrors in the family home of Sevenels, where she spent most of her life. She also had many eccentricities, such as smoking large black cigars. All of this, combined with her successful public readings and her social prominence, made her extremely newsworthy. However, her work is now little read.

Born in Brookline, Massachusetts, into a wealthy and distinguished New England family that included the poet James Russell Lowell, she grew up in an intensely intellectual atmosphere. Inspired by a performance by the actress Eleonora DUSE in 1902, Amy Lowell began to write poetry. Her first book, *A Dome of Many-Colored Glass* (1912), was fairly conventional, but in 1913 she fell under the influence of Ezra Pound and his new school of imagism. From this time on she devoted her life to writing and publicizing the new poetry.

Lowell's first book to contain imagist poetry was *Sword Blades and Poppy Seeds* (1914). It was followed by *Men, Women, and Ghosts* (1916), which includes her celebrated poem "Patterns," dramatizing the frustrating restrictions that senseless tradition puts on

life and art. Later collections of verse included *Can Grande's Castle* (1918), *Legends* (1921), and *What's O'Clock* (1925), for which she was awarded a Pulitzer Prize. Lowell experimented with many forms, including Chinese and Japanese, but her most successful poems centre on American themes.

Her critical studies were also well received. In *Six French Poets* (1915) she translated and discussed the work of her French contemporaries, while in *Tendencies in Modern American Poetry* (1917) she publicized the imagist cause and the work of her fellow American poets. Her other works include *A Critical Fable* (1922), which was modelled on James Russell Lowell's *A Fable for Critics*, and a biography of John Keats (1925).

Lowndes, Marie Adelaide Belloc (1868–1947) *French-born British writer*

Best known for her novel *The Lodger* (1913), Marie Lowndes was the great-granddaughter of the chemist Joseph Priestley and the sister of author Hilaire Belloc. Her father was a member of the French bar, and Marie remained fiercely proud of her French background and very close to her French relatives throughout her life. In 1896 she married Frederic Sawrey Lowndes, the editor of *The Times*.

She published her first story, *Pastel*, when she was 16. Her early novels, notably *Barbara Rebell* (1905), were well received by the critics, who were rather disappointed by *The Lodger*, originally published in instalments. However, this fictionalized story about Jack the Ripper eventually sold more than a million copies and was filmed four times, first by Alfred Hitchcock in 1926.

The success of *The Lodger* inspired Lowndes to write several more psychological mystery stories exploring the mind and motives of criminals. Her other books include the novels *What Timmy Did* (1921), *The Story of Ivy* (1928), and *The Christine Diamond* (1940); *What of the Night?* (1943), a collection of short stories set in wartime Britain; and three volumes of reminiscences about her childhood in

France and her involvement in literary and political life in Britain.

Loy, Myrna (1905–1993) *American actress*

Loy partnered the actor William Powell in 13 films, notably *The Thin Man* (1934) and its five sequels; in these films they played a high-living husband-and-wife team of private detectives whose witty affectionate banter won the hearts of the public. Voted the Queen of Hollywood in 1937, she was never nominated for an Academy Award during her long career but received an honorary Oscar in 1991.

Born Katerina Myrna Adele Williams in Montana, she moved to Los Angeles with her family in 1919. Her first job in show business, as a chorus girl, led to minor parts in numerous silent films of the late 1920s, including the original version of *Ben Hur* (1926). Rudolph Valentino suggested that she change her name from Williams to the more exotic-sounding Loy: "I didn't intend to keep it very long. But then I signed a contract and I was stuck with it." She also found herself stuck with exotic roles; despite her red hair and freckles, she was frequently cast as an Oriental temptress.

By the end of 1933 Loy had appeared in over 40 talking pictures, including *The Jazz Singer* (1927), *A Connecticut Yankee* (1931), *Love Me Tonight* (1932), and *The Mask of Fu Manchu* (1932). It was not until 1934, however, that she was officially given star billing by MGM. In that year she costarred with Clark Gable and William Powell in *Manhattan Melodrama*, directed by W. S. Van Dyke, who saw the potential of Loy and Powell as a comic team. Later the same year he cast them as the newly married sleuths Nick and Norah Charles in *The Thin Man*, an inexpensive film based on the novel by Dashiell Hammett. It was an enormous success and spawned five sequels, ending with *The Song of the Thin Man* (1946).

During World War II Loy worked for the Red Cross, and in the later 1940s she became involved with the United Nations, serving as a U.S. representative and film adviser to UNESCO. After appearing as the perfect wife in *The Best Years of Our Lives* (1946), she tried to change her screen image but began to be offered less desirable roles, such as that of an alcoholic mother in *From the Terrace* (1960). She subsequently turned to the stage, making her Broadway debut in 1968, and in the 1970s and early 1980s she appeared in a number of TV films, notably *Summer Solstice* (1981) with Henry Fonda.

Luce, Clare Boothe (1903–1987) *American playwright, journalist, and political figure*

> The American Republic is now almost 200 years old, and in the eyes of the law women are still not equal with men. The special legislation which will remedy that situation is the Equal Rights Amendment. Its language is short and simple: *Equality of rights under the law shall not be abridged in the United States or by any state on account of sex.*
>
> —Quoted in *Bulletin of the Baldwin School*, Pennsylvania, September 1974

Known for her sharp wit, Clare Boothe Luce had little time for men who considered themselves intellectually superior to women. When a male member of Congress patronizingly remarked that she had the best mind of any woman in the House of Representatives, she retorted, "The mind knows no sex."

Born Clare Boothe in New York City, she married her first husband, George Tuttle Brokaw, a wealthy New Yorker, in 1923. After her divorce in 1928 she entered magazine publishing; she became associate editor of *Vogue* in 1930 and served as managing editor of *Vanity Fair* in 1933. In 1935 she married the millionaire publisher Henry R. Luce.

Luce's career as an author began with the novel *Stuffed Shirts* (1931), which ridiculed New York society. Her best-known play, *The Women* (1936), is an unromantic picture of life among wealthy wives and divorcées. Later plays include *Kiss the Boys Goodbye* (1938) and *Margin for Error* (1939).

During World War II she worked as a war correspondent, reporting directly from Indochina and other fronts. Her only child, Ann Clare Brokaw, died in a car accident in 1944; Luce subsequently became a Roman Catholic.

Her political career began in the 1940s, when she served as a Republican congresswoman from Connecticut (1943–47) and played an important part in the 1944 presidential campaign. In 1953 President Dwight D. Eisenhower gave her the important diplomatic post of ambassador to Italy, where she remained for four years. She received many honours during her lifetime, including the Hammerskjold Medal (1966) and the Medal of Freedom (1983).

Lucy, Saint (4th century) *Christian martyr*

Considered the patron saint of the eyes, Lucy is frequently represented with a dish containing her eyes, which were supposedly plucked out during her martyrdom.

No details of Lucy's life have survived; she is said to have been born into a wealthy Sicilian family, but there is no historical evidence for this. A legendary account dating from the 5th or 6th century relates that St. AGATHA appeared to her in a vision and encouraged her to remain steadfast in her virginity. Another legend says that she was betrayed to the Roman authorities by a man she had rejected; condemned to life in a brothel, she was miraculously saved from this punishment. She is also alleged to have survived a sentence of death by burning, eventually being killed by the sword during the Roman Emperor Diocletian's persecution of the Christians.

A Greek inscription found at Syracuse, in Sicily, shows that she was venerated there in the 5th century; her name was introduced into the list of declared saints of the Roman Catholic Church in the 6th century. Her feast day is December 13.

Lumley, Joanna (1946–   ) *British actress*

For much of her career – until her award-winning performance in the TV comedy series *Absolutely Fabulous* – Lumley portrayed elegant, sophisticated women, chiefly on television but also in the theatre and cinema.

Born in Srinagar, Kashmir, India, she moved with her army family to Malaya (now part of Malaysia) in 1951 and was subsequently educated at schools in Kent and Sussex. After working for three years as a model in the 1960s, she made her first television appearance in a bread commercial. She gradually broke into the world of acting with small parts in TV soap operas and situation comedies, such as *Coronation Street* and *Steptoe and Son*. With her upper-class accent and modelling background she found herself typecast in the roles of glamorous secretary or girlfriend, but as a single mother – her son Jamie was born in 1967 – she could not afford to be too choosy about her work.

Lumley's first major part on British television was as Purdey, assistant to secret service agent Patrick MacNee in *The New Avengers* (1976–78). This was followed by a similar role as the time-traveller Sapphire in *Sapphire and Steel* (1979–82), with David McCallum. Her genuine talent for comedy was revealed in the cult series *Absolutely Fabulous* (1992–95), in which she played the champagne-swilling, sex-mad fashion editor Patsy Stone. Costarring in the show with its creator, Jennifer SAUNDERS, she carried off a BAFTA award for her performance.

Lumley has also worked as a stage actress, notably in the plays of Noël Coward and Somerset Maugham, and has appeared in such films as *Trail of the Pink Panther* (1982) and *Shirley Valentine* (1989). Her publications include *Stare Back and Smile* (1989), memoirs of her early life and career, and *Girl Friday* (1994), an account of a survival challenge for a television documentary that involved her spending nine days alone on an uninhabited island off the coast of Madagascar.

Lupescu, Magda (*c.* 1900–1977) *Romanian adventuress*

Madame Lupescu was the mistress of

King Carol II of Romania and later became his wife.

She was born in Iaşi, Romania, the daughter of a Jewish father and a Roman Catholic mother. Her father is said to have changed his surname from Wolff to pursue his career as a chemist, because there were restrictions on the numbers of Jews allowed to join such professions. Already married and divorced in the mid 1920s, Lupescu became the mistress of Crown Prince Carol, son of King Ferdinand I of Romania. Carol was married at the time to Princess Helen, mother of his son Michael. The ensuing scandal forced Carol to give up his claim to the throne in 1925, and when Ferdinand died two years later, it was Prince Michael who became king of Romania.

Carol returned from exile in 1930 and was allowed to reclaim his crown in return for a promise that Lupescu would remain abroad. However, once King Carol's position was secure, Lupescu came to live at the royal palace in Romania. Her strong influence over the king, combined with her Jewish background (at a time of growing anti-Semitism), made her unpopular with Romanian society. Carol established a personal dictatorship in 1938, but his mishandling of foreign policy at the beginning of World War II forced him to abdicate and flee with Lupescu.

The couple were chased across Spain to Portugal, from whence they travelled to Cuba, Mexico, and Brazil. They are said to have arrived at the Copacabana Palace Hotel in Rio de Janeiro with over 100 pieces of luggage, six dogs, and two gold crowns studded with precious stones. In 1947 they were married in Brazil, and Carol gave his new wife the title of Princess Elena. They subsequently took up residence in Portugal at Estoril, where a second, more formal ceremony of marriage was performed in 1949. Carol died four years later.

Lupino, Ida (1918–1995) *British-born American actress, director, and screenwriter*

Lupino made her name as a screen actress, often portraying tough underworld characters, and went on to become one of Hollywood's first female film directors.

She was born in London into a theatrical family. In 1931, at the age of 13, she began training at the Royal Academy of Dramatic Art (RADA), and the following year she was given a leading role in the film *Her First Affaire* (1932). After moving to Hollywood, she played a prostitute in *The Light That Failed* (1939), a murderous adultress in *They Drive by Night* (1940), a gangster's moll in *High Sierra* (1941), and a homicidal housekeeper in *Ladies in Retirement* (1941). Her performance as an ambitious schemer in *The Hard Way* (1942) earned her a New York Film Critics' Award.

In 1949 Lupino set up a production company called Film Makers with her second husband, Collier Young. There she wrote screenplays tackling such controversial issues as rape, bigamy, unmarried mothers, and career women. After taking over the direction of their first production, *Not Wanted* (1949), when the original director had a heart attack, Lupino subsequently produced and directed all the company's films, notably *The Bigamist* and *The Hitchhiker* (both 1953).

In the 1950s she joined Charles Boyer, David Niven, and Dick Powell in *Four Star Playhouse*, a series of television dramas. She also starred in the television situation comedy *Mr. Adams and Eve* (1957–58) with her third husband, Howard Duff; directed episodes of action series such as *The Untouchables* and *The Fugitive*; and appeared in a number of TV movies of the 1970s. In 1972 she returned to the big screen to play Steve McQueen's mother in *Junior Bonner*, a Western directed by Sam Peckinpah.

Lurie, Alison (1926–) *American writer*

Lurie's novels and other works are well-observed, often satirical commentaries on modern society, especially marital relationships in the professional middle classes. *Foreign Affairs* (1984), about a group of Americans in London, won the Pulitzer Prize for fiction in 1985.

Born in Chicago, Alison Lurie studied at Radcliffe College, Massachusetts. She began teaching in the English department at Cornell University in 1968 and became professor of English there in 1979. Many of her works are set in the academic world, with a recurring cast of characters whose ordered lives are suddenly thrown into confusion by unexpected events or chance encounters. Her early novels include *Love and Friendship* (1962), *The Nowhere City* (1965), and *Imaginary Friends* (1967), about two sociologists who join a religious sect. *Real People* (1970) centres on a successful woman novelist, *The War Between the Tates* (1974) deals with student politics and the Vietnam War, and *Only Children* (1979) is set during the Depression.

Lurie has produced a number of works of nonfiction, including *The Language of Clothes* (1981) and *Don't Tell the Grown-ups: Subversive Children's Literature* (1990). She has also written children's books of her own, such as *The Heavenly Zoo: Legends and Tales of the Stars* (1980) and *Fabulous Beasts* (1981). Among her more recent works are the novel *The Truth about Lorin Jones* (1988) and a collection of short stories, *Women and Ghosts* (1994).

Lutyens, Elisabeth (1906–1983) *British composer*

Lutyens was amongst the pioneers in British music of the 12-tone technique of composition. In 1969 she was made a CBE.

The daughter of the architect Edwin Lutyens, Agnes Elizabeth Lutyens was born in London and studied at the Ecole Normale in Paris. One of her early compositions, based on a poem by Keats, had its first performance while she was a student at the Royal College of Music, London, and her ballet *The Birthday of the Infanta* (1932) brought her into the public eye. In 1939 she composed her Chamber Concerto No. 1, using the 12-tone technique. This method of composition, pioneered by the Austrian Arnold Schoenberg and his followers, was still regarded as experimental in

Britain at that time, and it was many years before Lutyens was accepted as a major composer.

She wrote prolifically throughout her career, producing both the words and music for such stage works as *Infidelio* (1954) and *Isis and Osiris* (1970). Among her orchestral and instrumental works are *Concertante* (1950), *Nocturnes* (1955), *Symphonies* (1961), *The Winter of the World* (1974), and *Tides* (1978). Her vast output of choral and vocal music includes settings of English, French, Italian, Japanese, and African poetry and a motet (1952) based on a passage from Wittgenstein's *Tractatus Logico-Philosophicus*. She also wrote film scores and music for radio and theatre plays. Her autobiography, *A Goldfish Bowl*, appeared in 1972.

Luxemburg, Rosa (1871–1919) *Polish-born German revolutionary*

> Shamed, dishonoured, wading in blood and dripping with filth, thus capitalist society stands.
>
> —*The Crisis in the German Social Democracy* (1919)

Rosa Luxemburg's political theories were extremely influential; she was one of the founders of the German Communist Party.

She was born in Zamość, into a family of Jewish merchants. While attending schools in Warsaw, she became active in revolutionary clubs. Fearing arrest, she went to Switzerland in 1889, continuing her education in Zurich. There she studied political economy and wrote her doctoral dissertation *The Industrial Development of Poland*.

Although she kept in contact with Polish socialists, she moved to Germany in May 1898 to work in the Social Democratic Party (SPD) and established her reputation as a brilliant political writer with the booklet *Social Reform or Revolution?* (1899). During Russia's 1905 revolution she went to Warsaw and was imprisoned for a short time. She returned to Berlin and became a teacher in the SPD school (1907–14), where she set out her interpretation of Marxism in *The Ac-*

cumulation of Capital (1913), published in English in 1951.

During World War I Luxemburg joined Karl Liebknecht in organizing the Spartacus League, out of which grew the German Communist Party. She was in prison during most of the war, but her writings, such as *The Crisis in the German Social Democracy* and the *Spartacus Letters*, continued to appear. Released in 1918, she reluctantly supported an unsuccessful uprising, known as the Spartacist Revolt, against the government. Although she was very critical of the Russian Bolsheviks' dictatorship, her ultimate aim in Berlin was a new government based on workers' councils something like those introduced during the Russian Revolution.

Luxemburg's studies of capitalism modified Marx's ideas by considering the new role of imperialism. In *The Accumulation of Capital* she argued that capitalism would survive until it dominated the whole world through imperialist expansion. Her theory stressed the potential revolutionary energy of the common people. Rejecting Lenin's Russian party structure, she favoured instead an organization with internal democracy and mass participation. Luxemburg's considerable influence was due as much to her life of courageous action as to her theory. Although crippled from childhood and plagued with poor health, she never shunned work or danger. Her murder in Berlin by soldiers who were later acquitted of the crime made her a martyr and enhanced her reputation among radicals.

Lympany, Dame Moura (1916–) *British pianist*

Moura Lympany made many recordings, especially of the works of Rachmaninov, and gave concert performances all over the world.

Born Mary Johnstone in Saltash, Cornwall, she showed exceptional talent on the piano at an early age and gave her first concerto performance at the age of 12. After studying at the Royal College of Music, London, and at Liège in Belgium, she embarked on a successful career as an international concert pianist. By her mid twenties she had won many prizes, and in the postwar period she became the first Western pianist to perform in the Soviet Union. Although she had a wide and varied repertoire, the works of 20th-century British composers, including Frederick Delius, John Ireland, and Alan Rawsthorne, were her speciality.

Lympany was twice married and divorced, and her only son died tragically young. After many years away from the concert stage she made a triumphant return and continued to perform in her seventies and eighties. She received many awards in the latter part of her career, including the Medal of Cultural Merit from Portugal and the Charles Heidsieck Prize from the Royal Philharmonic Society (both 1989). In 1992 she was honoured with the award of a DBE.

Lynn, Dame Vera (1917–) *British singer*

With her good looks, winning smile, and such patriotic songs as "The White Cliffs of Dover" and "We'll Meet Again," Vera Lynn became known as the "Forces' Sweetheart" during World War II.

Born Vera Margaret Welch in East Ham, London, she started singing in public at the age of seven, became a dancer four years later, and made her first broadcast, with bandleader Joe Loss, in 1935. She subsequently sang with the Charlie Kunz band and the Ambrose Orchestra before going solo in 1940. During World War II she became a household name with her radio show *Sincerely Yours* (1941–47), and in 1944 she went to Burma to entertain the troops.

In the 1950s Lynn performed all over the world, sang on radio and television, and had a number of hit records, notably "Auf Wiederseh'n," which reached the top of the charts in the United States in 1952 and eventually sold more than 12 million copies. She also made many albums: her *Twenty Family Favourites* returned to the British top 30 in June 1984, the 40th anniversary of the D-Day landings. In 1975 she published her autobiography, *Vocal Refrain*, and was made a DBE. Her many other honours include the Freedom of the City of London (1978), the Burma Star Medal and War Medal (1985), and the European Woman of Achievement Award (1994).

Lytton, Lady Constance (1869–1923) *British suffragette*

Arrested and imprisoned on a number of occasions, Lady Constance was shocked to discover that suffragettes of her aristocratic background were treated quite differently from their "sisters" in the lower classes, and she set out to bring this inequality to public notice.

Constance Georgina Lytton was born in Vienna, the daughter of a diplomat who later became Earl of Lytton. She spent much of her early life in the foreign places to which her father was posted, including Paris (1873), Lisbon (1874), and India (1876–80), and was educated by governesses in her various homes.

Lytton became involved with the women's suffrage movement in her late thirties, and was first arrested for joining a protest demonstration in February 1909. Having been sentenced to four weeks in Holloway, she was confined to the prison hospital with an alleged heart condition, but soon suspected that she was being given preferential treatment because of her social rank. She registered her protest by threatening to carve the slogan "Votes for Women" across her body but got no further than the first letter, scratched with a hairpin over her heart. Her treatment in Newcastle prison following a second arrest in October of the same year confirmed her suspicions: after a 56-hour hunger strike she was not forcibly fed, like other suffragettes, but examined by a heart specialist and allowed to go free.

The following year, at a protest demonstration in Liverpool, Lytton disguised herself as a working-class woman and gave the false name of Jane Warton when she was arrested. This time she suffered the same treatment as the other suffragettes in prison, and was force-fed without any prior attempt to determine whether or not her heart could stand the strain. On her release she was too weak to publicize the point that she had now proved, but her brother did so on her behalf in a letter to *The Times*. He called for a public inquiry into the matter, but the Home Office refused.

Lady Constance never fully recovered from the harsh punishment she had received in the persona of Jane Warton; she suffered a stroke in 1912 and remained an invalid for the rest of her life. However, this did not prevent her from continuing her campaign, speaking at public meetings, organizing petitions, and telling her story in the book *Prisons and Prisoners: Some Personal Experiences by Constance Lytton and 'Jane Warton, Spinster'* (1914).

M

Macaulay, Catherine (1731–1791)
British historian

One of the earliest woman historians to write a history of England, Catherine Macaulay also wrote many pamphlets in support of political liberty and equal opportunities for boys and girls in education.

Born Catherine Sawbridge in Kent, she was educated in the classics at home by her father. In 1760 she married George Macaulay, an obstetrician. In 1763 the first book of her eight-volume *History of England* was published. Praised by some for its scope, it was condemned by others for its lack of objectivity. She associated with the intellectuals of her day, including Dr. Samuel Johnson. In 1766 her husband died, and in 1774 Catherine moved to Bath. During this period she visited Paris, where she was regarded as a leading British historian. At the age of 47 she somewhat shocked her friends by marrying William Graham, a man less than half her age. With him she moved to Berkshire, where she completed her history, which covered the period from the reign of James I to the accession of George I (1603–1714).

In 1785 Catherine and her husband travelled to the United States, where they were guests of the future American president, George Washington. This friendship resulted from her support for the colonists in the American Revolution.

Macaulay, Dame Rose (1881–1958)
British writer

Rose Macaulay was a leading literary figure in the years between the two world wars. Her novels had a wide readership, richly deserved for their urbanity and skill.

Emilie Rose Macaulay was born in Rugby, Warwickshire, and spent eight years of her childhood in Italy. After studying history at the University of Oxford, she lived mainly in London but spent time living and travelling on the Continent. She published her first novel, *Abbots Verney*, in 1906, but first attracted attention with the witty and clever *Potterism* (1920), a satirical attack on middle-class pretensions and false values. *Dangerous Ages* (1921), which won the Prix Femina Vie Heureuse, presents the problems that beset four generations of women, while *Told by an Idiot* (1923) ridicules the foolishness of a typical English family. Macaulay also wrote critical works, including *Some Religious Elements in English Literature* (1931), a biography of Milton (1934), and *The Writings of E. M. Forster* (1938).

During World War II Macaulay worked as an ambulance driver in London, and it was some time before she returned to writing novels: *The World My Wilderness* appeared in 1950. Her last and best-known novel was *The Towers of Trebizond* (1956). Awarded the James Tait Black Memorial Prize, it wittily combines religion, travel, love, adventure, comedy, and tragedy.

Macaulay also wrote three volumes of verse and several travel books, including *They Went to Portugal* (1946), as well as several volumes of essays and articles for various periodicals. She received the title of DBE in 1958.

Three volumes of her letters were published after her death, notably *Letters to a Friend* (1961), her correspondence with an Anglican priest, Father Hamilton Johnson, in which she records her love for, and 20-year-long secret affair with, a married ex-priest,

Gerald Donovan, who died in 1942. Although Rose Macaulay never married, this relationship was central to her life and considerably influenced her later work. *Letters to a Friend* also describes her return to the Anglican Church after the death of her lover.

MacDonald, Flora (1722–1790) *Scottish Jacobite heroine*

Flora MacDonald is renowned as the woman who helped Prince Charles Edward Stuart, the "Young Pretender," to escape from Scotland after the battle of Culloden in 1746.

Born in Milton, on South Uist in the Outer Hebrides, she was the daughter of a farmer, Ranald MacDonald, but was brought up and educated by Lady Margaret and Sir Alexander Macdonald.

In June 1746, while visiting the neighbouring island of Benbecula, she met Charles Edward Stuart, who was at that time a fugitive after the defeat of the Jacobites at Culloden Moor. She agreed to help the prince escape to the island of Skye and included him, disguised as a maidservant, in her party. From Skye he was able to escape to exile in Europe. When her role in the prince's escape was discovered, she was imprisoned in the Tower of London, although she was released under the Indemnity Act of 1747.

In 1750 Flora married Allan Macdonald of Kingsburgh, and in 1774 they emigrated to North America, settling in Fayetteville, North Carolina. Her husband, who served in the British Army, was taken prisoner in the American Revolution. Flora returned alone to Scotland but was later rejoined by her husband. They had seven children. She died in Kingsburgh, Scotland.

MacInnes, Helen (1907–1985) *Scottish-born American writer*

The author of novels of adventure and espionage, Helen MacInnes wrote a number of highly intelligent and fast-moving bestsellers.

Helen Clark MacInnes was born in Glasgow and graduated from the university there. In 1932 she married Gilbert Highet, with whom she moved to New York City in 1937; she became a U.S. citizen in 1951.

Above Suspicion (1941), MacInnes's successful first novel, was quickly followed by *Assignment in Brittany* (1942), *While Still We Live* (1944), and *Horizon* (1945), all of which are set in Europe during World War II. Most of her later novels, including *The Venetian Affair* (1963), *The Salzburg Connection* (1968), *Prelude to Terror* (1978), and *Ride a Pale Horse* (1984), are tales of espionage, conspiracy, and political intrigue set during the Cold War. Skilfully constructed, MacInnes's novels are compelling because of their intelligent characters, realistic descriptions, and clever plots combining pace and suspense.

MacLaine, Shirley (1934–) *American actress, dancer, and writer*

Shirley MacLaine, a star of both stage and screen, is also known as a strong feminist and political activist.

She was born Shirley MacLean Beaty in Richmond, Virginia, the older sister of the actor Warren Beatty. After studying at the Washington School of Ballet, she appeared in the chorus line of *Oklahoma* in 1950 and *Me and Juliet* in 1952. It was while she was in the chorus of *The Pajama Game* that she was by chance a last-minute replacement for the female lead and was spotted by the film producer Hal Wallis. She made her film debut in Alfred Hitchcock's *The Trouble with Harry* (1955), but her early reputation was based on the comic skill she demonstrated in *Around the World in 80 Days* (1956).

Proving to be an actress of great versatility, she excelled in both comic and dramatic roles, appearing in such farces as *Ask Any Girl* (1959), for which she won a BAFTA award. In *Some Came Running* (1958) she played a downtrodden floozy, while in *The Apartment* (1960) she portrayed a naive lift operator with a troubled love life. She was a high-kicking dancer in *Can-Can* (1960) and a Parisian prostitute in *Irma La Douce* (1963), which bought her an Oscar nomination. In 1968 she starred in the acclaimed musical *Sweet Charity*.

In the early 1970s MacLaine concentrated on her club act, returning to the big screen in the ballet film *The Turning Point* (1977). *Terms of Endearment* (1983) brought her an Academy Award as Best Actress for her performance as the domineering mother of Debra Winger. Other noteworthy films include *Madame Sousatzka* (1988), for which she won the Golden Globe Award as Best Actress; *Steel Magnolias* (1989); *Postcards from the Edge* (1990); *Used People* (1992); and *Guarding Tess* (1994).

MacLaine returned to the stage in 1984 with the song-and-dance revue *Shirley MacLaine on Broadway*. In 1990 she toured the United States in the stage musical *Out There Tonight*. She has also appeared frequently in television specials, winning an Emmy Award in 1980 for *Shirley MacLaine… Every Little Movement*.

Apart from acting, Shirley MacLaine became known for her feminist and liberal views and for her belief in cosmic and spiritualistic phenomena. In 1975, after a visit to China, she produced a much-acclaimed but somewhat controversial documentary film, *The Other Half of the Sky: A China Memoir*. Her books recounting supernatural experiences include *You Can Get There from Here* (1975); *Out on a Limb* (1983), which was made into a television movie in 1987; and *Going Within: A Guide for Inner Transformation* (1989). She also wrote *My Lucky Stars: A Hollywood Memoir* (1995).

Maconchy, Dame Elizabeth
(1907–1994) *British composer*

Dame Elizabeth Maconchy is chiefly known for her chamber music, notably her 12 string quartets, which are much influenced by the work of Béla Bartók.

Elizabeth Maconchy was born in Broxbourne, Hertfordshire, to Irish parents. After studying in London, where she was a pupil of Charles Wood and Vaughan Williams at the Royal College of Music, she went for a short while to Prague to study with Karel Jirák; here her first large-scale composition, the Piano Concertino (1928), was performed in 1930. After this her work gradually became known in Britain and Europe; it was included in the festivals of the International So-

ciety for Contemporary Music held in Prague (1935), Paris (1937), and Copenhagen (1947). She succeeded Benjamin Britten as president of the Society for the Promotion of New Music. In 1959 she became the first woman to chair the Composers' Guild of Great Britain.

In 1957 Maconchy composed her first opera, *The Sofa*, which has a libretto by Ursula Vaughan Williams. She also composed stage works for children, for which she herself wrote the librettos. Her other works include *Siren's Song* (1974), the cantata *Héloïse and Abelard* (1979), settings of the poems of Gerard Manley Hopkins and Anacreon, *Romanza* (1980), for viola and ensemble, and *Life Story* (1985), for string orchestra. In 1930 she married the writer William LeFanu. Their daughter is the composer Nicola LEFANU.

Maconchy was awarded the Cobbett medal for chamber music in 1960 and was made a DBE in 1977.

Macy, Anne Mansfield Sullivan
(1866–1936) *American teacher*

Anne Macy is known as the teacher and lifelong companion of the blind and deaf Helen KELLER, who attributed much of her success in overcoming her handicaps to her teacher and friend.

Anne Sullivan was born in Feeding Hills, Massachusetts. As her eyesight had been seriously weakened by an infection during childhood, she went in 1880 to the Perkins Institute for the Blind, near Boston, where she learned the manual alphabet; in 1886 she graduated from the institute with a brilliant record.

In the meantime, Sullivan's eyesight had been restored through a series of operations, and in 1887 she became the teacher of the blind and deaf Helen Keller, then seven years old. She taught Keller the manual alphabet and the Braille system and assisted her education at the Perkins Institute (1889–93), the Cambridge (Massachusetts) School for Young Ladies (1896–1900), and Radcliffe College (1900–04), communicating the content of class lectures to her pupil by spelling them into her hand. She later accompanied Keller on numerous travels and lecture tours on behalf of the American Foundation for the Blind, for which they together raised $2 million.

In 1905 Sullivan married John Albert Macy, a literary critic who had helped Helen Keller with her autobiography. The marriage was not happy, and the couple separated in 1913. Anne Macy continued her remarkable relationship with Keller, even though her own eyesight had deteriorated to near blindness by 1935. She died in Forest Hills, New York.

In 1955 Keller published a tribute to her teacher. William Gibson's play about Macy, *The Miracle Worker*, was originally made for television but came to Broadway in 1959; it was made into a feature film in 1962 starring Anne BANCROFT in the title role.

Madison, Dolley (1768–1849) *Wife of President James Madison*

As First Lady, Mrs. Madison became the centre of Washington society during her husband's presidency. She also acted as First Lady for the previous president, the widowed Thomas Jefferson.

Born Dolley Payne into a Quaker family in Guildford county, North Carolina, she was brought up in Virginia. In 1783 her parents moved to Philadelphia, where in 1790 she married a Quaker lawyer, John Todd, Jr., who died along with one of their children in the yellow-fever epidemic of 1793. In 1794 Dolley married Congressman James Madison, 17 years her senior. When Madison became Secretary of State in 1801, she served as "unofficial First Lady" during the rather spartan presidency of Thomas Jefferson, a widower.

During her husband's presidency (1809–17) she became the unquestioned centre of Washington society, best known for her lavish Wednesday evening receptions, at which politicians, diplomats, and selected members of the general public gathered. The atmosphere of friendliness at these gatherings helped to soothe some of the tensions between Federalists and Republicans at a time of intense party rivalries. Her correspondence indicates, moreover, that not only was she an effective counterbalance to her husband's rather colourless public personality, but her influence on Madison's political decisions was not insignificant.

The Madisons retired to their plantation in Virginia in 1817 and continued to entertain lavishly and support the profligate habits of Dolley's son John Payne Todd. After her husband's death in 1836 Mrs. Madison returned to Washington and again became a leading political hostess. She made her last public appearance at a ball for President Polk in 1848.

Madonna (1958–) *American singer and actress*

Madonna has probably sold more records throughout the world than any other female entertainer. She exploited her looks, her dancing, and her voice to become the ultimate sex symbol of the 1980s. Her success in the much coveted role of Eva PERÓN in the film *Evita* has done nothing to diminish her reputation.

Born Madonna Louise Veronica Ciccone into an Italian family in Rochester, Michigan, she studied performing arts at the University of Michigan before going on to the Alvin Ailey Studios in New York City to study dance. In 1979 she performed as a dancer in Paris, and also played with rock bands in New York. Her first big hit in the United States, "Holiday," came in 1983 – the year she released her first album.

Madonna achieved international stardom in 1985 with her best-selling album *Like a Virgin*, which contained five hit singles. That year she also had her first screen success with her performance in *Desperately Seeking Susan*. Her albums continued to be hugely successful, notably *True Blue* (1986), which was at the top of the album charts in 28 countries, and *Like a Prayer* (1989). Her films of the period, however, including *Who's That Girl* (1987) and *Dick Tracy* (1990), were not as well received. By the late 1990s Madonna had enjoyed 11 U.S. number one hit singles and a series of success-ful albums, including *Erotica* (1992), *Bedtime Stories* (1994), and the sound-track to *Evita* (1996). Her other films include the documentary *In Bed with Madonna* (1991), *Body of Evidence* (1992), *Dangerous Games* (1993), and *Four Rooms* (1995).

Highly influential as a role model and a fashion icon, Madonna has not hesitated to enhance her career by shameless self-promotion as well as by modelling of designer clothes. Her controversial book *Sex* was published with much media attention in 1993.

Madonna was married to the Ameri-can actor Sean Penn from 1985 until 1989. Her daughter, Lourdes Maria Ciccone Leon, born in 1996, is the child of her former personal fitness trainer, Carlos Leon. On her most re-cent album, the highly praised *Ray of Light* (1998), she presents a more ma-ture and spiritual image.

Magnani, Anna (1908–1973) *Italian actress*

Anna Magnani, who specialized in playing passionate sensual women of great inner strength, was the star of many Italian and American films from the 1940s to the 1960s.

She was born in Alexandria, Egypt, and raised in the slums of Rome by her grandparents. She studied at the Academy of Dramatic Art in Rome, supporting herself by working as a nightclub singer and performing in vaudeville.

Married to the director Goffredo Alessandrini in 1935, she appeared in Italian motion pictures and on the stage from the early 1930s; however, it was not until she appeared in Vittorio De Sica's *Teresa Venerdi* (1941) that her career began to take off. In 1946 she starred as a passionate, defiant, and pregnant woman in Roberto Ros-sellini's film *Rome: Open City* and was named Best Foreign Actress by the U.S. National Board of Review for her performance. The following year she starred in *Love*, for which she was awarded the Italian Silver Ribbon and named Best International Actress at the Venice Film Festival. Among her other important films are Luchino Vis-

conti's *Bellissima* (1951) and Jean Renoir's *The Golden Coach* (1953), both comedies; her performance in the latter was a parody of the type of role that had made her famous.

Tennessee Williams wrote his play *The Rose Tattoo* with Magnani in mind, but she was reluctant to play it on the stage because she felt her Eng-lish was inadequate. She agreed, how-ever, to do the film version in 1955; in this, her first American film, she won the 1956 Academy Award for Best Ac-tress for her interpretation of the hero-ine.

Magnani's other films include *The Fugitive Kind* (1960), with Marlon Brando; Pier Paolo Pasolini's *Mamma Roma* (1962); and *The Secret of Santa Vittoria* (1969), with Anthony Quinn. In her last years she was frequently seen on Italian television. She died in Rome.

Maillart, Ella (1903–1997) *Swiss sportswoman, adventuress, and writer*

> Nobody can go? I shall go.
>
> —Youthful challenge often repeated
> by Ella Maillart

During her long life Ella Maillart pro-gressed from Olympic sportswoman – through French teacher in Wales, ac-tress in Berlin, and sculptor's model wherever she could find employment – to intrepid traveller who made her last journey across Chinese-occupied Tibet at the age of 83.

Born in Geneva, Ella Maillart was the daughter of a prosperous furrier and a Danish athlete who inspired in her daughter a love of challenging sports. Ella Maillart founded Switzer-land's first women's hockey team, was a member of the Swiss sailing team in the 1924 Olympics, and skied for her country from 1931 to 1934.

After visiting Moscow in the 1930s to study film production, she joined a group of Russians who were crossing the Caucasus Mountains on foot. This produced material for her book *Among Young Russians: From Moscow to the Caucasus* (1932).

Her most gruelling journey was a 3,500-mile trek from Beijing to Kashmir through Turkestan in 1935, accompanied by Peter Fleming, the younger brother of the writer Ian Fleming (creator of James Bond). Fleming, who was then a correspondent for *The Times*, wrote his version of the expedition in *News from Tartary*, in which he honestly admitted that "It was she not I, who did the dirty work." Maillart's account, published as *Forbidden Journey* (1937), records the Bronze Age conditions they survived, noting that before washing one of Fleming's shirts in icy and dirty water, she had to remove 174 nits from the seams.

Maillart's next book, *The Cruel Way: Two Women and a Ford in Afghanistan* (1947), described a fraught journey across Afghanistan with a morphine-addicted fellow traveller. During World War II she spent most of her time living in ashrams under the guidance of various gurus.

After the war Maillart returned to Switzerland, settling in a chalet in the commune of Chandolin, where she died at the age of 94. However, during her time there she skied until she was 77, led parties of tourists to far-off lands well into her eighties, and undertook a journey across Tibet. At the age of 91 she made her last journey to Goa, to further her interest in Indian culture.

Maintenon, Marquise de (1635–1719) *Mistress and second wife of King Louis XIV of France*

> There is little point in girls of common extraction learning to read as well as young ladies or being taught as fine a pronunciation…etc. It is the same with writing. All they need is enough to keep their accounts and memoranda; you don't need to teach them fine handwriting or talk to them of style: a little spelling will do. Arithmetic is different. They need it.
>
> —*Lettres sur l'éducation des filles* (1713)

Madame de Maintenon combined three strands in her long life – mistress and later secret wife of Louis XIV, progressive educationalist, and woman of deep religious conviction.

She was born Françoise d'Aubigné in Poitou, France, a granddaughter of the Huguenot soldier-poet Agrippa d'Aubigné. Françoise spent her childhood in poverty and obscurity in Martinique. Brought up a Protestant by her Aunt Villette, she converted to Roman Catholicism after her return to France in 1647, when she was living with another aunt, Madame de Neuillant. In 1652 she married an elderly poet, Paul Scarron, and became the hostess of a noted Paris salon frequented by literary figures. Widowed and left penniless in 1660, she retreated to a convent and lived on a pension from the dowager queen, ANNE OF AUSTRIA.

Introduced to Louis XIV by her friend Madame de MONTESPAN, who was his mistress, Françoise became the governess of his illegitimate children. In 1674 she was able to buy the Château de Maintenon, and a year later was made a marquise. Her popularity with the king grew as Madame de Montespan fell from favour, and in about 1680 Madame de Maintenon became Louis's mistress. When Queen Marie-Thérèse died in 1683, Louis secretly married Madame de Maintenon.

Although she promoted a more austere and moral climate at court, her influence over Louis's policies was minimal. She was, however, particularly interested in education, and in 1686 she founded a school at the convent of St. Cyr, which offered education and moral instruction to girls of the nobility who, like herself, had been left without fortunes. The school was admired throughout Europe as a progressive institution in which many young women flourished. Maintenon invited the dramatist Racine in 1689 to write a sacred drama for the school: he produced *Esther* and *Athalie* (1691). However, as she became increasingly devout, the school became more religious, and by 1692 it had become a regular convent of the Ursuline order of nuns.

When the king died in 1715, Maintenon entered St. Cyr and lived in religious retirement. Her letters, which cover the years between 1655 and her death, reveal her character and educational ideals.

Makarova, Natalia (1940–   ) *Russian ballet dancer and actress*

A star of the Kirov Ballet in Leningrad, Makarova defected to the West, becoming equally acclaimed in America and Europe.

Born in Leningrad (now St. Petersburg), Natalia Makarova graduated from the Kaganova Ballet School and in 1959 from the Leningrad Choreographic School. She joined the Kirov Ballet company in Leningrad and became one of its most gifted ballerinas, dancing important roles in *Les Sylphides* and *Cinderella* and touring Europe with the company (1961). On this tour she danced *Giselle* in London, a triumph she repeated on the company's tour of the United States (1961 and 1964). In 1965 she received the gold medal at the Second International Ballet Competition in Varna, Bulgaria.

While on tour with the Kirov in London in 1970 Makarova decided to remain in the West. She joined the American Ballet Theater in 1972, appearing on television with the legendary dancer Rudolf Nureyev, but continued to dance in England and on the Continent as a guest artist with all the major European ballet companies. Her fragile beauty made her an ideal Giselle, and she scored critical and popular triumphs in Antony Tudor's *Romeo and Juliet*, *Jardin aux lilas*, and *Pillars of Fire*, as well as in such classical ballets as *Coppélia*, *Swan Lake*, and *Sleeping Beauty*. In 1974 she first staged *La Bayadère* for American Ballet Theater.

In 1980 she founded her own troupe, Makarova and Company, performing the lead roles in *Ondine*, *Vendetta*, and *Raymonda* in New York City. In 1983 Makarova made her musical-comedy debut in the revival of *On Your Toes* on Broadway, for which she won a Tony Award for Best Actress. Returning to England in 1984, she staged *Swan Lake* for the London Festival Ballet and conceived and presented the 1987 television series *Ballerina* for the BBC. In 1988 Makarova was a guest artist with the Kirov Ballet during its visit to London, appearing with the company for the first time in 18 years. She appeared again with the Kirov in 1989 in Leningrad, returning to Russia for the first time since her defection in 1970. In 1991 she made her dramatic debut in the play *Tovarich* in London, and in 1992 she appeared in *Two for the Seesaw* in Moscow.

Among her awards are the title of Honoured Artist of the Russian Federation (1970), the Pavlova Prize, Paris (1970), and the Laurence Olivier Award (1984). Her book *A Dance Autobiography* appeared in 1979.

Makeba, Miriam (1932–   ) *South African singer and political activist*

Miriam Makeba is often referred to as "Mother Africa" or the "Empress of African Song" for her part in bringing the rhythmic sounds of Africa to the West.

A member of the Xhosa people, Miriam Makeba was born in Prospect township outside Johannesburg. She began singing with her Methodist school choir, making her first solo performance in front of King George VI on his visit to South Africa. Working as a maid in Johannesburg, she sang with local bands at weddings and funerals before joining a group called the Black Mountain Brothers and touring with them around South Africa, Rhodesia, and the Congo (1954–57).

In 1959 Makeba appeared in the all black jazz opera *King Kong*, after which she married (as her third husband) a fellow star, the South African trumpeter Hugh Masekela. In 1959 the anti-apartheid film *Come Back, Africa*, in which she appeared, was shown at the Venice Film Festival; Makeba then left South Africa for London, where she met the black activist and entertainer Harry Belafonte. Impressed by her singing of African folk songs, he was instrumental in arranging for her to appear in New York clubs and *The Steve Allen Show* on television. In the 1960s she became one of the best-known singers in the United States, touring with Belafonte and making hit records, including the "Click Song" and "Wimeweh." In 1963 she attended conferences in Ethiopia and also testified before the UN Committee on Apartheid. In 1968 she married the American "black power" radical

Stokely Carmichael. Her association with the militant Black Panthers led to the cancellation of recording contracts and concerts in the United States.

Makeba then moved to Guinea in West Africa and combined her recording work with cultural and diplomatic missions, addressing the United Nations and performing at official African events. In 1986 she won the Dag Hammarskjöld Peace Prize. In 1987 she was special guest on the singer Paul Simon's *Graceland* tour, which brought her international recognition again. The following year she produced her first American album in 20 years, *Sangoma*, a collection of tribal songs. *Welela* followed in 1989. In 1990 Makeba visited Johannesburg for the first time in 31 years. 1991 saw the release of the pop/jazz/blues fusion album *Eyes on Tomorrow*. She still lives in Guinea and is now married to Bageot Bah.

Malina, Judith (1926–) *German-born American theatre director*

> The odyssey of the Living Theater... a company that has produced more guts, passion and controversy than any other in our time.
>
> —Jack Kroll, *Newsweek*

Judith Malina is best known as the co-founder (with Julian Beck) of the Living Theater, an off-Broadway theatre group in New York City that inspired the radical theatre of the 1960s.

She was born in Kiel in Germany and studied at the Dramatic Workshop of the New School for Social Research, making her acting debut in New York in 1945. In 1948 she married Julian Beck, with whom she founded the Living Theater three years later. The group's aim was to produce little-known, new, or experimental plays by such writers as Gertrude STEIN, Luigi Pirandello, T. S. Eliot, Jean Cocteau, and August Strindberg, as well as the works of such unknown playwrights as Jack Gelber. In fact it was Gelber's study of drug addiction, *The Connection*, that became the company's first major success (in 1959).

In 1961 the company made its first tour of Europe with *The Connection*, as well as plays by Bertolt Brecht and William Carlos Williams. Hugely popular in Europe, where it won many awards, the company faced problems back in New York. Its 1963 production of Kenneth H. Brown's *The Brig*, a play about the dehumanizing effect of military discipline, so upset the authorities that they closed the theatre; Malina and Beck were briefly jailed for violations of the tax laws. In 1964 they brought *The Brig* to London, remaining in Europe and travelling between West Berlin, Brussels, and Rome until 1968. Adopting the ideas of the French actor and theatre director Antonin Artaud, the Living Theater moved towards deliberately confronting its audiences in such works as *Paradise Now* (1968), a "spiritual and political voyage for actors and spectators."

After touring the United States in 1968, the Becks decided to abandon middle-class audiences and bring their productions to working people. They travelled around Europe, worked in Brazil (1970–71) and Pittsburgh, and returned to Europe before settling in New York in 1984. After Julian's death in 1985, Judith continued to direct the company with Hanon Reznikov.

Mallet-Joris, Françoise (1930–) *Belgian-born French novelist*

An important figure in modern French writing, Françoise Mallet-Joris has tackled such varied topics as lesbianism and Roman Catholicism.

Born Françoise Lilar in Antwerp, the daughter of a Belgian cabinet minister and the dramatist Suzanne Lilar, she was educated in Philadelphia and at the Sorbonne in Paris. In 1947 her volume of poetry *Sunday Poems* appeared. Her first novel, *Le Rempart de Béguines* (1950), which was published in English as *The Illusionist* in 1952, describes a lesbian love affair between a young woman and her father's mistress; it became both a scandal and a bestseller. *Les Mesonges* (1956; published in English as *House of Lies*, 1957) followed; *L'Empire Celeste* (1958; published in English as *Café Celeste*, 1959), in which she describes the clientele of a Montmartre café, won the prestigious Prix Femina. The autobiographical *Lettre à moi-même* (1963; published in English as *A Letter to Myself*, 1964) relates the circumstances of her conversion to Roman Catholicism.

Mallet-Joris's later publications, *Allegra* (1976) and *The Wink of an Angel* (1983), show her increasing preoccupation with spiritual matters. For many years she worked in publishing and also wrote songs, children's books, and biographies. She is on the panel for the Prix Femina and in 1973 was elected president of the Académie Goncourt.

Mandela, Winnie (1934–   ) *South African politician*

Although once highly regarded for her courageous support of her imprisoned husband Nelson Mandela, Winnie Mandela forfeited public esteem by being implicated in criminal violence.

Descended from a tribal chief, Winnie Mandela was born Nomzamo Winifred Madikizela in Bizana, Transkei, the daughter of a history teacher at a missionary school. In 1953 she moved to Johannesburg to study paediatric social work, becoming South Africa's first black social worker. In 1956 she met Nelson Mandela, the future president of South Africa, and began working with him for the African National Congress (ANC), of which he became the effective leader. A black nationalist organization, the ANC was dedicated to the abolition of apartheid. Winnie and Nelson were married in 1958.

The ANC was banned in 1960, and Nelson Mandela was imprisoned from 1962 until 1990. During his long incarceration Winnie was imprisoned (1969–70) and forced into internal exile (1977–85), during which time she was constantly harassed by the police. Nevertheless she continued her social and educational work and campaigned ceaselessly against apartheid and for the release of her husband. In 1985 she returned to the black township of Soweto, where she became involved in militant politics; she was seriously criticized for the first time for her support of "necklacing" – a horrific way of burning suspected government collab-

orators to death – as a legitimate measure in the political struggle. During 1988–89 leading anti-apartheid activists turned against her when she and her bodyguards, known as the Mandela United Football Team, were implicated in the kidnapping and beating to death of a 14-year-old black youth, Stompie Seipei. However, on Nelson Mandela's release from jail in 1990, she was temporarily restored to favour and shared in his political activities and goodwill missions abroad.

At Stompie's murder trial in May 1991 Winnie Mandela's chief bodyguard was convicted of the murder. She was convicted only of the kidnapping and sentenced to six years in prison, a sentence later commuted to a fine of some £9,000. In 1992 she and Nelson separated following reports of an affair between Winnie and a younger man, as well as allegations of her mismanagement of the funds under her control. At this time she also resigned all her posts in the ANC. However, in 1993 she made a political comeback with her election to the presidency of the ANC Women's League. In 1994 she won a seat in parliament in South Africa's first multiracial elections, becoming deputy minister of arts, culture, science, and technology in Nelson Mandela's government. The following year she was removed from this post after she strongly condemned government policies. She remains an MP and was re-elected president of the Women's League in 1997.

In September 1997 allegations put before South Africa's Truth and Reconciliation Committee, which was set up to investigate crimes committed during the apartheid era, linked Winnie Mandela to eight murders and various other violent crimes. Since her divorce from Nelson Mandela in 1996 Winnie has adopted the surname Madikizela-Mandela.

Mandelstam, Nadezhda (1899–1980) *Russian writer and critic*

As the wife of the persecuted poet Osip Mandelstam, Nadezhda spent many years in internal exile. After his death she devoted herself to preserving her husband's memory.

Born Nadezhda Khazina in Saratov, Russia, she studied art in Kiev and later worked as a translator in the several European languages in which she was fluent. In 1920 she married the celebrated Russian poet Osip Mandelstam, who was arrested in 1934 for composing an unflattering portrait of Stalin. He and his wife were then exiled to Voronezh in Russia until 1937. Released briefly, they were harassed by the police and forced to move from place to place in a desperate attempt to find work and shelter. Mandelstam was rearrested in 1938 and sent to a labour camp near Vladivostok, where he died alone.

Nadezhda was then forced to survive by working in factories and teaching English. Her main preoccupation, however, was to collect her husband's poems, which had been banned, committing many of them to memory and smuggling as many as possible out of Russia. She also wrote two books, *Hope against Hope* (1971) and *Hope Abandoned* (1973), in which she described their lives and the fate of the Russian intelligensia under Stalin. The second volume also documents the time she spent after her husband's death as a semi-exile.

Manley, Mary de la Rivière
(?1663–1724) *English writer*

One of the first English women to make a living as a writer and journalist, she was also the first to be arrested for libel.

Mary de la Rivière Manley was the daughter of the Royalist Sir Roger Manley, future governor of Jersey. The place and date of her birth are disputed: she may have been born in 1663 or 1672, in Jersey or in Holland. After the death of her father in 1688 she married her cousin John Manley, who already had a wife and deserted Mary after the birth of their son. Mary subsequently became companion to the Duchess of Cleveland (1693–94) and began to write; her first two plays, *The Lost Lover* and *The Royal Mischief*, were produced in London in 1696. For six years she lived with John Tilley, warden of the Fleet Prison, and in 1705 she published her first novel, *The Secret History of Queen Zarah*.

Manley's fiction was based on current political gossip and scandal, spiced with romantic or erotic detail, and featured characters who were thinly disguised versions of real people. *The New Atalantis* (1709), an attack on the Whigs that led to her arrest for libel, was published with a key to assist the reader in identifying the public figures involved. She also produced Tory propaganda in the form of pamphlets, sometimes writing in collaboration with Jonathan Swift, whom she succeeded as editor of the journal *The Examiner* in 1711. Her other works include *Memoirs of Europe* (1710), the autobiographical *The Adventures of Rivella* (1714), the tragedies *Almyna* (1706) and *Lucius* (1707), and *The Power of Love* (1720).

Manning, Olivia (1908–1980) *British novelist*

Olivia Manning and her husband spent much of World War II abroad working for the British Council (an organization that promotes British developments in science, literature, and the arts). These experiences provided the background for the two trilogies of novels for which she is best known.

Born in Portsmouth, Hampshire, the daughter of a naval officer, Olivia Manning trained at art school and then took a variety of jobs in London before writing her first novel, *The Wind Changes*, which was published in 1937. In 1939 she married R. D. (Reggie) Smith, a British Council lecturer in Bucharest. Their experiences there provided the background for her Balkan Trilogy – *The Great Fortune* (1960), *The Spoilt City* (1962), and *Friends and Heroes* (1965) – which is set at the start of World War II.

In 1942 Olivia Manning and her husband were evacuated to Athens and then to Cairo, where she became press officer to the United States Embassy. After Cairo the couple moved to Jerusalem and then to Palestine, where Olivia worked for the British Council before returning to London in 1945. This period provided the setting for her Levant Trilogy – *The Danger Tree*

(1977), *The Battle Lost and Won* (1978), and *The Sum of Things* (1980). In 1988 the complete sequence of novels was made into a TV series, *Fortunes of War*, starring Kenneth Branagh and Emma THOMPSON.

Back in London Olivia Manning worked as a freelance journalist and book reviewer, as well as writing novels. Her other works include the novels *Artist among the Missing* (1949), *School for Love* (1951), and *The Play Room* (1969), the volume of short stories *Growing Up* (1948), and a collection of humorous sketches, *My Husband, Cartwright* (1956). She was made a CBE in 1976.

Mansfield, Katherine (1888–1923)
New Zealand short-story writer

Katherine Mansfield's highly acclaimed short stories have exerted a strong influence on modern fiction.

Born Katherine Mansfield Beauchamp in Wellington, New Zealand, she attended Queen's College, London, from 1903 to 1906. After spending a brief time in New Zealand, she returned to England in 1908 and married George Bowden, but the marriage did not last. She then spent an unhappy period in Germany, about which she wrote in her first collection of stories, *In a German Pension* (1911). After returning to London she wrote stories for *The New Age* and other periodicals and met the critic John Middleton Murry, with whom she lived and whom she finally married in 1918. She also had complex uneasy relationships with the writers D. H. Lawrence and Virginia WOOLF.

Mansfield's New Zealand childhood, and particularly the tragic death of her brother in World War I, had a profound influence on her life and art. This was reflected in *Prelude* (1918), which movingly portrays the exuberant children, repressed women, and rough men in a New Zealand family. Struggling against emotional turmoil and ill health, Mansfield moved to the south of France. Desperately seeking a cure for tuberculosis, she produced in the last years of her life some of her finest work, including *Bliss and Other Stories* (1920) and *The Garden Party*

and Other Stories (1922), which contains the comically poignant masterpiece "The Daughters of the Late Colonel," in which two women spend their lives terrorized by their father; and "The Garden Party," in which a young girl tells of her confrontation with death.

Strongly influenced by Chekhov, Mansfield learnt that plot is not as important as atmosphere and that a single moment of insight can provide the material for a story. Description, dialogue, and, above all, imagery are used to develop her themes.

Mansfield died suddenly at Fontainbleau, near Paris, where she was following a course of spiritual discipline. *The Dove's Nest*, published in 1923, after her death, contains her last stories, and *Something Childish* (1924) is a collection of earlier work. Her *Journals* (1927) and *Letters* (1928) were edited by Middleton Murry.

Manton, Sidnie Milana (1902–1979)
British zoologist

Sidnie Manton was an outstanding biologist who made significant contributions to animal taxonomy and physiology.

Manton was born in London and educated at Cambridge University. She was appointed university demonstrator in comparative anatomy (1927–35) at Cambridge and then director of studies in natural science at Girton College, Cambridge (1935–42). From 1943 until 1960 she was visiting lecturer, assistant lecturer, and reader in zoology at King's College, London. Until her retirement in 1967 she was research fellow of Queen Mary College, London. She was married in 1937 to John Harding, who became Keeper of Zoology at the British Museum (Natural History Section).

Manton's most significant work was on the structure, physiology (especially locomotion), and evolution of the arthropods. Her revision of the Arthropoda, indicating their different evolutionary lines, into the Chelicerata (spiders, scorpions, mites, ticks, etc.), the Crustacea (lobsters, crabs, etc.), and the Uniramia (insects, centipedes, and millipedes), plus the extinct Trilobita (trilobites), has now been accepted by most biologists. She was the author of *The Arthropoda: Habits, Functional Morphology and Evolution* (1977), as well as many papers on the coelenterates (jellyfish, sea anemones, etc.) and on arthropod evolution, locomotion, feeding mechanisms, etc. Manton was elected a fellow of the Royal Society in 1948 and received the Linnean Society's Gold Medal in 1963. In her retirement she bred new varieties of cats, having published *Colourpoint, Longhair and Himalayan Cats* in 1971.

Marble, Alice (1913–1990) *American tennis player*

Tall and lithe, Alice Marble revolutionized tennis by introducing the powerful serve and aggressive volley into the women's game, which she dominated from 1936 to 1940.

Born on a farm in Plumas County, California, she grew up in San Francisco. An all-round athlete, excelling at baseball and basketball, she turned to tennis at 15 and developed her strong masculine style of play. She took the California junior title at 17, the state women's championship at 19, and a year later was ranked third nationally, behind Helen WILLS and Helen JACOBS. In 1933 she collapsed during a tournament and became a semi-invalid suffering from bouts of anaemia and tuberculosis, which kept her out of competition for two years.

She returned to the game in 1936, when she won her first U.S. singles title; she took this title again in 1938, 1939, and 1940. In addition she won the singles championship at Wimbledon (1939), the U.S. doubles title (1937–40), and the British doubles title (1938–39). In 1940, after she turned professional, she played exhibition tennis. During World War II she served as a physical fitness adviser in the Hale America movement, designed to keep the country's women and young people fit.

After her retirement Marble became a sportswriter and designed women's tennis wear. Her autobiography, *The Road to Wimbledon*, appeared in 1946. A second autobiographical volume, *Courting Danger*, was published in 1991.

Marcos, Imelda (Romualdez) (1929–) *Philippine political leader*

Imelda Marcos, the First Lady of the Philippines during her husband's presidency, has had a remarkable career as, successively, the darling of impoverished Filipinos, an autocratic leader in her husband's administration, and an indicted embezzler.

Born in Tolosa, on the Philippine island of Leyte, into a lesser branch of the politically prominent Romualdez family, Imelda became a beauty queen and singer before marrying Congressman Ferdinand E. Marcos in 1954. Her plaintive songs helped him to campaign successfully for a Senate seat and, in 1965, for the presidency. Imelda Marcos became a powerful figure after the institution of martial law by her husband in 1972. She served as her husband's emissary in China, the Soviet Union, and Libya before becoming the first governor of metropolitan Manila, a post she held from 1975 until 1986. Named minister of human settlements in 1978, she was responsible for relocating people and industries to reduce the threat of urban revolt but was frequently criticized during this period for appointing relatives to lucrative governmental and industrial positions. Martial law came to an end in 1981, but Marcos continued his authoritarian rule.

Despite her image as patron of the poor, Imelda Marcos developed showcase projects in the capital, such as the Cultural Centre (1969) and, later, an adjacent complex including the Plaza Hotel, the Centre for International Trade Exhibits, and the Folk Arts Theatre. She built the National Arts Centre on the slopes of Mount Makiling and held international film festivals from 1981 to 1983.

In 1986, after an election that Ferdinand Marcos won by fraudulent practices, a popular uprising forced the Marcoses to flee to Hawaii. Evidence then began to emerge that during his years in office Marcos and his wife and close associates had embezzled billions of dollars from the Philippine economy. Ferdinand and Imelda Marcos were subsequently indicted by the U.S. government on racketeering charges. However, in 1990, after Ferdinand's death, Imelda was acquitted of all charges by a federal court. In 1991 she was allowed to return to the Philippines, where she stood unsuccessfully for the presidency in 1992. She was found guilty of corruption by a Philippine court in 1993. Since then she has worked tirelessly from her luxurious apartment to rehabilitate her husband's name and prove that his wealth was acquired from legitimate trade in precious metals before he entered politics. She herself claims that she was only motivated by a desire to help the poor of her country. Nevertheless, her fame rests largely on her immense wardrobe, her legendary number of pairs of shoes, and her misplaced sense of regal prerogative. She was elected to the Philippine congress in 1995.

See also AQUINO, CORAZON.

Margaret I (1353–1412) *Regent of Denmark, Norway, and Sweden*

Known as Scandinavia's greatest medieval ruler, Margaret was the daughter of King Valdemar IV Atterdag of Denmark and was married at the age of ten to King Haakon VI of Norway.

Growing up at the Norwegian court, she showed skill as a scholar and a stateswoman. On Valdemar's death in 1375 she had her five-year-old son, Olaf, elected king of Denmark over the competing claims of the house of Mecklenburg. Haakon VI died in 1380 and was succeeded in Norway by Olaf; the resulting dynastic union of Denmark and Norway was to last over 400 years.

Margaret was regent in both kingdoms. She asserted her son's hereditary claim to the Swedish throne, held by King Albert of the rival Mecklenburg house, but Olaf died in 1387. That same year she adopted her grandnephew, Eric of Pomerania, as her heir and continued to rule, being hailed as "sovereign master, lady, and guardian" in Denmark and, in 1388, as "mighty lady and master" in Norway.

In 1388 she supported a revolt of Swedish nobles against the unpopular King Albert, who was deposed in 1389, although his partisans long continued to hold out in Stockholm, Finland, and Gotland. Margaret was recognized as Sweden's "sovereign lady and rightful master" in 1389.

Eric was crowned monarch of the three kingdoms at Kalmar, Sweden, in 1397. Thus began the Kalmar Union, which lasted in principle until 1521. The aristocratic councils of the three kingdoms sought to preserve their internal independence, but Margaret strove consistently to centralize power by building up a strong treasury through taxation and establishing a network of provincial sheriffs who owed loyalty to the crown. She also dominated the appointment of bishops. Although Eric came of age in 1401, Margaret continued to rule until her death. While seeking to regain Schleswig from the Count of Holstein, she died of the plague in Flensburg, Schleswig.

Margaret, Maid of Norway (*c.* 1283–1290) *Queen of Scotland*

Declared queen of Scotland at the age of three, this unfortunate child lost her life at sea at the age of seven.

Margaret was the granddaughter of Alexander III, King of Scots; her mother was Alexander's daughter Margaret, who died in childbirth, and her father was Erik II, king of Norway. She succeeded to the throne of Scotland in 1286 on the death of her grandfather. Since she was only three years old, six guardians were appointed to govern the country in her name while she was still a child. She was betrothed to the infant Prince Edward of England (the future King Edward II) but died at sea while travelling from Norway to Scotland. On her death there were 13 contestants for the crown, and King Edward I of England declared himself overlord of Scotland. He eventually chose John Balliol to be King of Scots in 1292.

Margaret, Princess (1930–) *Sister of Queen Elizabeth II of the United Kingdom*

A haughty but witty woman, Princess Margaret has been a staunch supporter of the British monarchy.

Princess Margaret Rose was born at Glamis Castle, Angus, Scotland, the second daughter of the Duke of York (later King George VI). When her uncle King Edward VIII abdicated in 1936, Margaret's father became king, making her second in line to the throne (after her elder sister, Princess Elizabeth). She was the first member of the royal family in the direct line of succession to be born in Scotland for more than 300 years.

In 1955 Margaret abandoned her plan to marry Group Captain Peter Townsend, a divorced man, out of loyalty to her sister (who had become queen in 1952) and in response to establishment opposition. In 1960 she married Antony Armstrong-Jones, a photographer. Princess Margaret assumed the title of Countess of Snowdon the following year, when her husband was created Earl of Snowdon.

As a representative of the Queen, she made official tours of British East Africa in 1956, the West Indies in 1958, the United States in 1965, Canada in 1967, and Yugoslavia and Japan in 1969. She was divorced from her husband in 1978, the first member of the British royal family to be divorced since Henry VIII in the 16th century. Princess Margaret was given custody of their two children, David, Viscount Linley, and Lady Sarah Armstrong-Jones, and Lord Snowdon retained his title of earl. Viscount Linley married Serena Stanhope in 1993, and Lady Sarah married Daniel Chatto in 1994.

Princess Margaret is patron or president of many charities and organizations, including the National Society for the Prevention of Cruelty to Children, the Guides, and the Royal Ballet. Her official and charitable activities have been suspended since early 1998 when she suffered a mild stroke.

Margaret, Saint (c. 1045–1093) *Wife of King Malcolm III of Scotland*

Noted for her piety, Margaret, the patron saint of Scotland, reformed the Scottish Church, bringing it into line with the Roman reforms that governed the Church in England and on the Continent. She also brought Benedictine monks to Scotland.

Born in exile in Hungary, she was the granddaughter of Edmund Ironside, king of Wessex, and the elder sister of Edgar Aethling, the only English prince to survive the Norman Conquest. In 1067 she travelled with Edgar to Scotland, where they placed themselves under the protection of the king, Malcolm III Canmore, whom she married that same year.

Margaret was the mother of three Scottish kings: Edgar, Alexander I, and David I (who ruled from 1093 to 1153). Her daughter Matilda married King Henry I of England, uniting the Anglo-Saxon and Norman lines. Margaret died in Edinburgh and was canonized in 1251. Her feast day is November 16.

Margaret of Anjou (1430–1482) *Wife of King Henry VI of England*

Queen Margaret was a staunch defender of the house of Lancaster in the Wars of the Roses.

The daughter of René the Good of Anjou, king (in name only) of Naples, Margaret was married to Henry in 1445 in an attempt to bring about peace between England and France. The insanity of the king virtually made her regent, and the principal defender of the ruling house of Lancaster. When her position was contested by the Duke of York, a claimant of the throne by an older line (both the houses of York and Lancaster claimed royal right by descent from Edward III), the protracted Wars of the Roses began.

At first victorious, the Lancastrians suffered a crushing defeat at Towton in 1461, and Margaret and Henry were compelled to flee to Scotland. Edward IV, the son of the late Duke of York, was declared king. In a last attempt, Margaret, collecting her supporters, fought the battle of Tewkesbury (1471) and was totally defeated. She and her son were taken prisoner, and the latter, when led into the presence of the royal victor, was killed. Henry died soon after, possibly murdered, in the Tower of London.

Margaret remained in prison for almost five years before King Louis XI of France ransomed her in 1476 for 50,000 crowns. She died in poverty at Dampière, in Anjou.

Margaret of Austria (1480–1530)
Regent of the Netherlands

Margaret of Austria served as an able regent of the Netherlands during the infancy of the future Holy Roman Emperor Charles V.

She was born in Brussels, the daughter of the Habsburg Archduke Maximilian (later the Holy Roman Emperor Maximilian I) and Mary of Burgundy. In 1483 Margaret was betrothed to the heir to the French throne (later Charles VIII), who repudiated her in 1491. Six years later she married Prince John of Spain, who died after only a few months of marriage. In 1501 Margaret married Philibert II, Duke of Savoy, who died three years later.

Appointed regent of the Netherlands by her father in 1507, Margaret acted as guardian to her infant nephew Charles (the future Holy Roman Emperor Charles V), who had succeeded her brother Philip (I) the Handsome on his death the previous year. In 1515 Charles was declared to be of age to rule; he reappointed Margaret as regent four years later to enable him to secure the German throne and the imperial succession for himself. During this period of her rule Habsburg dominion was extended in the northeastern Netherlands. Margaret was Charles's representative at Cambrai in 1529, where she negotiated with Louise of Savoy, who spoke on behalf of her son Francis I of France. The settlement negotiated between them is known as the "Paix des Dames" ("Peace of the Ladies").

Margaret of Parma (1522–1586) *Regent of the Netherlands*

The Duchess of Parma was appointed regent of the Netherlands by her half-brother, Philip II of Spain. After being replaced by the Duke of Alba, she later returned to the Netherlands as head of the civil administration.

Margaret of Parma was the illegitimate daughter of the Holy Roman Emperor Charles V and Johanna van der Gheerst. At the age of 14 she was married to Alessandro de' Medici, Duke of Florence, who was murdered less than a year later. In 1538 she married Ottavio Farnese, Duke of Parma, and bore him a son, Alessandro Farnese (later Duke of Parma), in 1546.

In 1559 Margaret was appointed regent of the Netherlands by her half-brother, Philip II of Spain. She proved to be an able and masterful administrator who, as a staunch Catholic, suppressed an uprising by Calvinist extremists in 1567. Although peace was restored, Philip II sent the Duke of Alba to the Netherlands to replace Margaret, who resigned. Alba's stern anti-Protestant measures precipitated a revolt against Spanish rule.

Margaret returned to the Netherlands, however, when her son became governor in 1580, and was appointed head of the civil administration. She held this position until she retired to Italy in 1583.

Margaret Tudor (1489–1541) *Wife of King James IV of Scotland*

Margaret Tudor played a key role in uniting England and Scotland.

The elder daughter of King Henry VII of England and the sister of Henry VIII, Margaret Tudor was married to James IV of Scotland in 1503. This alliance was intended to guarantee peace between England and Scotland. However, the peace broke down following the death of Henry VII in 1509 and James was killed at Flodden in 1513, when he invaded England. Margaret then became regent for her infant son, James V.

In 1514 she married Archibald Douglas, Earl of Angus, and bore him a daughter who became the mother of Lord Darnley. Forced to surrender the regency to John Stewart, Duke of Albany, in 1515, Margaret fled to England but returned to Scotland the following year. She became estranged from Angus and sided with Albany, whom she married shortly after obtaining papal approval for an annulment in 1527. Margaret and Albany continued to advise the young King James V and played an active role in the political conflict between the pro-English and pro-French parties at the

Scottish court until 1534. Margaret died seven years later at Methven Castle in Perth.

In 1565 Darnley became the second husband of Margaret's granddaughter, MARY, QUEEN OF SCOTS, who a year later gave birth to their son, Margaret's great-grandson, James VI of Scotland. He assumed the throne of England as James I in 1603, uniting the thrones of England and Scotland.

Margrethe II (1940–) *Queen of Denmark*

Margrethe II became the first woman to rule Denmark in her own right when she succeeded her father, Frederick IX, in 1972. The Danish constitution had been altered in 1953 to allow the accession of a woman. (The first Margrethe, MARGARET I, had acted as regent of Denmark in the 14th century for her son Olaf.)

Margrethe was born in Copenhagen to King Frederick IX and Queen Ingrid. She studied constitutional law and philosophy at Copenhagen University; archaeology at Girton College, Cambridge; Danish affairs at Århus University; and sociology at the London School of Economics. Archaeology was an interest she shared with her maternal grandfather, King Gustav VI Adolf of Sweden, whom she accompanied on expeditions.

In 1967 Margrethe married a French diplomat, Count Henri de Laborde de Monpezat, who by royal decree became Prince Henrik. They have two sons, Prince Frederick, who was born in 1968, and Prince Joachim, born in 1969. Margrethe is an accomplished artist and has illustrated such books as *The Lord of the Rings* (1977–78), *Norse Legends* (1979), and *Bjarkemaar* (1982).

Marguerite de Valois (1553–1615) *Wife of King Henry IV of France*

Famous for her *Mémoires*, which appeared in 1628, Marguerite de Valois was also known as La Reine Margot or Margaret of France.

She was born in St. Germain-en-Laye, the daughter of King Henry II of France and CATHERINE DE' MÉDICIS. In 1572 she married Henry, king of Navarre, and intrigued against one of her brothers, King Henry III of France, while abetting the ambitions of another brother, François, in the Netherlands. Driven from court by Henry III in 1583, she was placed under house arrest at Usson, where she lived with a series of lovers. In 1589 her husband became Henry IV of France, but their marriage was dissolved in 1599 to enable him to marry MARIE DE MÉDICIS.

In 1605 Marguerite returned to Paris, where she built a palace and founded a convent. A woman of considerable intelligence, she left a collection of poems as well as her famous memoirs.

Marguerite of Navarre (1492–1549) *Wife of King Henry of Navarre*

> A father will have compassion on his son. A mother will never forget her child. A brother will cover the sin of his sister. But what husband ever forgave the faithlessness of his wife?
>
> —*The Mirror of the Sinning Soul* (1531)

> Though jealousy be produced by love, as ashes are by fire, yet jealousy extinguishes love as ashes smother the flame.
>
> —The *Heptameron*, "Novel XLVIII, the Fifth Day" (1558)

Marguerite of Navarre was a noted patron of Renaissance artists and a writer.

Also known as Marguerite (or Margaret) of Angoulême or of Orléans, she was born in Angoulême, France, the daughter of Charles d'Orléans, Count of Angoulême, and the learned Louise of Savoy. Her brother became King Francis I of France. Taught Hebrew, German, Latin, Italian, and Spanish by her mother, she also studied philosophy, history, and theology, making a great impression at the court of Louis XII, where she grew up.

In 1509 Marguerite was married to the Duke of Alençon, who died in 1525. Two years later she married Henry d'Albret, king of Navarre. Her court at Nérac was a centre for humanist and Protestant thinkers, to whom she gave refuge if they were suspected of heresy. She herself wrote religious verse, including *The Mirror of the Sinning Soul* (1531), which was condemned by the orthodox theologians at the Sorbonne. Her other works include *The Marguerites of the Marguerite of Princesses* (1547), a collection of songs, poems, and allegorical comedies. Her best-known work, the *Heptameron*, a collection of short tales, was published in 1558, after her death.

Her daughter, Jeanne d'Albret, became a Huguenot leader and the mother of King Henry IV of France.

Maria Theresa (1717–1780) *Archduchess of Austria and queen of Bohemia and Hungary*

A woman of great political ability and power, Maria Theresa brought stability to central Europe and did much to modernize Austria. It is also largely due to her that Vienna became an important European capital.

Maria Theresa was born in Vienna, the oldest daughter of Emperor Charles VI and Elizabeth-Christina of Brunswick-Wolfenbüttel. In 1713 her father, the last male of the old Habsburg line, passed a special act, the Pragmatic Sanction, to enable Maria Theresa, as a woman, to succeed to his Austrian territories. In 1736 she married Francis Stephen of Lorraine, who exchanged his claim to Lorraine for the grand duchy of Tuscany. Their marriage established the house of Habsburg-Lorraine.

In 1740 Charles VI died unexpectedly, and Maria Theresa was soon challenged in the War of the Austrian Succession by Frederick II of Prussia, who invaded Silesia, one of the richest and most populous of the Habsburg lands. In 1741 Charles Albert, Elector of Bavaria, joined forces with France and invaded her dominions. Later that year he occupied Prague, and the following year he was crowned Holy Roman Emperor, becoming Charles VII, but he died in 1745. Maria Theresa's husband succeeded him as Francis I. Her claim to the Austrian succession was recognized by the Treaty of Aix-la-Chapelle in 1748, but Silesia remained in Prussian hands.

Instigating reforms of government and society, Maria Theresa sought to modernize Austria with the help of a distinguished group of advisers. Friedrich Haugwitz, for example, supervised a major reform of the Austrian central government and virtually unified Austria and Bohemia, enabled Austria to maintain a large standing army, and guaranteed a steady flow of tax revenue. Gerhard van Swieten, a Dutch physician, helped to extend the work of reform to medicine, to education, and to cultural affairs. Under the influence of Wenzel von Kaunitz, her foreign affairs adviser, Maria Theresa was determined to regain Silesia, and the subsequent Seven Years' War (1756–63) found Austria allied with France and Russia against Prussia and Britain. Although Prussia was hard pressed, it retained Silesia, and Austria suffered a disastrous defeat.

In 1765 Francis I died and his eldest son, Joseph, became emperor and coregent with Maria Theresa. However, they had serious differences in outlook and in political style, Joseph finding his mother's reforms too moderate. Nonetheless, her policy of centralization encouraged the social, architectural, and cultural development of Vienna as a great European capital. Under pressure from Joseph and Kaunitz, Maria Theresa reluctantly agreed to participate in the First Partition of Poland (1772), by which Austria acquired Galicia. But her desire for peace ensured that Austria did not become involved in a full-scale conflict with Prussia in the War of the Bavarian Succession (1778–79). Despite ill health, she remained able and powerful until her death. During her 40-year reign she managed to preserve the integrity and unity of the Habsburg monarchy in central Europe and carried out a wise and moderate programme of reform that contributed to Austria's survival as a great power until World War I.

She and Francis had 16 children, several of whom played an important role in European history: Joseph, her immediate successor, became an enlightened ruler who instigated sweeping reforms, while Maria Antonia achieved lasting fame as France's MARIE ANTOINETTE.

Marie Antoinette (1755–1793) *Wife of King Louis XVI of France*

> Little did I dream that I should have lived to see disasters fallen upon her in a nation of gallant men, in a nation of men of honour and of cavaliers. I thought ten thousand swords must have leapt from their scabbards to avenge even a look that threatened her with insult. But the age of chivalry is gone.
>
> —Edmund Burke, *Reflections on the Revolution in France* (1790)

> Courage! I have shown it for years; think you I shall lose it at the moment when my sufferings are to end?
>
> —Remark on the way to the guillotine, October 16, 1793

Marie Antoinette's uncompromising rejection of any reforms that might diminish royal power was largely instrumental in the downfall of the monarchy in the French Revolution.

She was born Maria Antonia in Vienna, the eleventh daughter of Francis I and MARIA THERESA of Austria. Her marriage at the age of 15 to the heir apparent to the French throne (later Louis XVI) was arranged to bolster the Austro-French alliance. However, she was never popular in France, partly because of a traditional French dislike of Austria and partly because she was seen as a spoilt woman lacking any training for the demanding role of queen of France. Ignoring her husband, who was indifferent to her, and confining herself to a narrow circle of favourites, Marie Antoinette sought diversion in expensive entertainments and a luxurious lifestyle.

After the first of her children was born in 1778, she abandoned frivolity and began to perform her duties soberly. But her reputation was irreparably damaged in 1785–86 by the "Diamond Necklace Affair," after which it was widely but mistakenly believed that the queen had sold herself to Cardinal de Rohan for a piece of jewellery. By 1789 she was neither loved nor respected by the French people, and she was instrumental in Louis's decision not to implement the reforms demanded by the National Guard. After the march on Versailles in October 1789 and the removal of the royal family to the Tuileries, the king and queen ignored the advice of the constitutional monarchist Mirabeau to rally the provinces against Paris. Mirabeau died early in 1791. Later that year the royal family attempted to escape but was recognized at the village of Varennes and taken back to Paris virtually under arrest.

Marie Antoinette then encouraged Louis in his secret negotiations with the moderate leaders to accept the new constitution; at the same time, she urged her brother Leopold II of Austria to threaten the revolutionaries by assembling an alliance of European armies on the borders of France. When Louis did accept the new constitution, however, Marie Antoinette secretly disavowed it in her correspondence abroad. Her Austrian intrigues provoked the final storming of the Tuileries in 1792, during which she and Louis were captured and accused of treason. Louis was executed in January 1793, and Marie Antoinette was separated from her children, placed in solitary confinement, and tried as "the widow Capet" before the Revolutionary Tribunal. On October 16, 1793, she was executed on the guillotine.

Marie de France (12th century) *French poet*

Marie de France is often referred to as France's first woman poet, but little is known about her life.

She seems to have been born in France but to have spent much time in England at the court of King Henry II. It has been suggested that she was either a member of the French royal family or the illegitimate daughter of Geoffrey Plantagenet and, therefore, the half-sister of Henry II. There is no doubt, however, that Marie was a highly educated woman.

Her most important writings are her 12 *lais* (lays), short narrative poems based on traditional Celtic stories of love, adventure, and the supernatural. Dedicated to a "noble, brave, and courtly king," probably Henry II, they are written in rhyming couplets. *Le Lai de Lanval* is often considered her masterpiece. The influence of her use of the *lai* extended throughout medieval European literature.

An exception to the love theme is *The Purgatory of St. Patrick* (*c.* 1190), in which the saint visits Purgatory and returns to describe what he saw there. Marie also wrote verse fables, said to be based on a version of Aesop by King Alfred. They were published under the title *Isopet* in about 1180.

Marie de Médicis (1573–1642) *Wife of King Henry IV of France*

Marie de Médicis lived a full and politically active life. Instrumental in bringing Cardinal Richelieu to power in France, she subsequently plotted unsuccessfully to oust him.

Maria de' Medici (Marie de Médicis is the French form of her name) was born in Florence, the daughter of Francesco, Grand Duke of Tuscany. She married King Henry IV of France in 1600, and they had six children. Unhappy with his flagrant infidelities, Marie gathered around herself ultra-Catholic and pro-Spanish forces diametrically opposed to her husband's policies.

When Henry was assassinated in 1610, Marie assumed the regency for her nine-year-old son, Louis XIII. Politically inept, she was unable to control the nobility and bring them into line to support the monarchy. In April 1617 Louis XIII finally seized the reins of power and exiled Marie to Blois. She soon escaped and unsuccessfully raised arms against her son (1620). Marie's protégé, the future Cardinal Richelieu, interceded with Louis to allow her to return to the council in 1622, for which he was appointed cardinal (1622) and the king's chief minister (1624).

Marie had expected Richelieu to pursue her pro-Spanish policies, but instead the cardinal pursued an anti-Spanish policy in Italy, thwarted the powers of the nobility at home, and ruthlessly suppressed France's Huguenots. Marie, aided by her younger son, Gaston, Duc d'Orleans, Louis's wife, ANNE OF AUSTRIA, and the pro-Spanish party at court, plotted to oust him from power. In November 1630 Louis was forced to choose openly between his mother and his first minister. After first siding with his mother, he finally decided to support the cardinal.

Marie was imprisoned, but escaped to Brussels in 1631. Having spent some time in London (1638–41) she died at Cologne in Germany.

During her years of power she built the Luxembourg Palace in Paris, the galleries of which were decorated by Rubens.

Marie Louise (1791–1847) *Second wife of Napoleon Bonaparte*

Marie Louise was a considerable force in 19th-century European politics. She was married three times, first to Napoleon Bonaparte.

The daughter of Emperor Francis I of Austria, Marie Louise was chosen by Napoleon as his second wife in 1810, after the dissolution of his marriage to the empress JOSÉPHINE. Napoleon was anxious to produce an heir by this marriage and to establish a bond between his own upstart regime and the Habsburgs, one of Europe's oldest royal houses. The match, which the Austrian foreign minister Metternich helped to arrange, was originally political, but Napoleon developed a genuine affection for his bride. This deepened when she gave birth to an heir, who was proclaimed king of Rome on March 20, 1811.

When Napoleon abdicated in 1814, Marie Louise lacked the courage to join him in exile, instead returning to her father. In Vienna Metternich introduced her to the womanizer Count Adam von Neipperg, who quickly seduced her. Created Duchess of Parma, Piacenza, and Guastalla in 1816, she proved to be a relatively liberal ruler in conjunction with Neipperg, with whom she had two children. After Napoleon's death in 1821 she married Neipperg. After Neipperg died in 1829, the unpopular reactionary policies of her new secretary of state led to an uprising in 1831, which drove Marie Louise from Parma. Restored by the Austrians, she thereafter abandoned her liberal policies. In 1834 she was married to Count de Bombelles, who outlived her.

Markham, Beryl (1902–1986) *British-born Kenyan aviator, racehorse trainer, and writer*

Beryl Markham, a well-known beauty, trained six Kenya Derby winners, had a scandalous affair with the Duke of Gloucester, and flew the Atlantic solo in an action-packed life.

Born Beryl Clutterbuck in Melton Mowbray, Leicestershire, she grew up on a farm in Kenya, where her father trained and bred racehorses. Her mother and brother remained in England. Beryl learned to hunt with the African tribesmen and to speak Swahili, Nandi, and Masai while being apprenticed to her father as a horse trainer and breeder. Remaining alone in Kenya after her father lost his fortune in 1919 and went to Peru, she became the first woman in Africa to receive a racehorse trainer's licence.

In her late twenties Beryl Markham learned to fly, becoming a commercial pilot transporting mail, passengers, and supplies to various outposts of Africa. In 1936 she made a historic solo transatlantic flight from east to west, taking off from England and crash-landing in Nova Scotia, Canada, almost 21½ hours later. She was the first person to achieve this Atlantic crossing east to west.

Beryl Markham was married three times, first to the rugby player Jock Purves, in a marriage that lasted only two years. In 1929 she married Mansfield Markham, with whom she had a son. Markham threatened to sue the Duke of Gloucester, who became infatuated with his wife during a visit to Kenya in the 1930s. Markham accepted substantial damages, but the couple separated soon after and were divorced in 1942. After her successful transatlantic flight Beryl went to live in California, where she married the writer Raoul Schumacher, but this marriage also ended in divorce (in 1947). She then returned to Kenya to train horses. She died in Nairobi. Her autobiography, *West with the Night*, was published in 1942 and reissued in 1983 at a time of renewed interest in colonial Africa.

Markiewicz, Constance, Countess (1868–1927) *Irish nationalist politician*

Known as "Madame" and the "Red Countess," Constance Markiewicz was the first woman to be elected (1918) to the British parliament; however, as a Sinn Féin member for a Dublin constituency she did not take her seat. (See also ASTOR, NANCY, VISCOUNTESS.)

Born in London, the sister of the future trade unionist Eva GORE-BOOTH, Constance was educated at home on the family estate in County Sligo, until she was presented at court in London in 1887. A society beauty, she studied art at the Slade School in London in 1894 before travelling to Paris, where in 1899 she married the Polish painter Count Casimir Markiewicz.

In 1903, after travelling in Europe, Constance returned with her husband to Ireland and became involved in Irish cultural and political movements in Dublin, joining the Gaelic League, the Abbey Theatre, and Sinn Féin. In 1907 she helped cofound the United Arts Club; two years later she founded the youth movement, Na Fianna.

In 1913 Countess Markiewicz participated in the Dublin strike, and in the Easter Rising of 1916 she led 120 Republican soldiers, dressed in the green uniform of the Citizens' Army, for which she was imprisoned and sentenced to death. This sentence was subsequently commuted to life imprisonment, and she was held in Aylesbury Prison, Buckinghamshire, until the 1917 amnesty of Irish rebels. Although she was elected a member of Parliament while still in prison, she and other Republican MPs refused to take their seats in Westminster as a Nationalist protest.

In 1919 Constance became Minister for Labour in the Dáil Eireann, the outlawed Irish parliament. After the partition of Ireland and the creation of the Irish Free State in 1921, she continued to fight and raise funds for the Republicans, and was elected MP for Dublin South in 1923. Repeatedly imprisoned, she also went on hunger strike. In 1926 she joined De Valera's Fianna Fáil party; she was re-elected to the Dáil in 1927 but died later that year in Dublin.

Markova, Dame Alicia (1910–)
British ballet dancer

> Glorious bouquets and storms of applause...to hear in the applause that unmistakable note which breaks through good theatre manners and comes from the heart, is to feel that you have won through to life itself. Such pleasure does not vanish with the fall of the curtain, but becomes part of one's own life.
>
> *—Giselle and I* (1960)

One of the world's greatest ballet artists, Dame Alicia Markova has been feted as a prima ballerina with several internationally famous companies.

Alicia Markova was born Lilian Alicia Marks in London. Among her ballet teachers were Serafina Astafieva, Enrico Cecchetti, and Nikolai Legat. At the age of 14, nicknamed "the miniature Pavlova," she joined Sergei Diaghilev's Ballets Russes, dancing lead roles in such ballets as Massine's *La Boutique fantasque* and Balanchine's *Le Chant du rossignol*, which was created for her in 1925. After Diaghilev's death in 1929 she danced with the Blum Company, London, and then at the Metropolitan Opera House, New York, before joining, in 1931, the Vic-Wells (later Sadler's Wells) Ballet in London under the direction of Ninette DE VALOIS. She became prima ballerina there in 1933.

In 1935 Markova and the dancer Anton Dolin formed their own ballet company, which toured until 1938, the first such company to perform in large provincial towns. She then danced with the Ballet Russe de Monte Carlo from 1938 to 1941. In her career as a popular star with the American Ballet Theater (1941–45) Markova created the leads in Antony Tudor's *Romeo and Juliet* (1943) and Massine's *Aleko* and was highly successful in the ballets *Giselle*, *Firebird*, and *Swan Lake*; she was the first British dancer to take the lead in *Giselle* and the full-length *Swan Lake*.

Re-forming their company in the United States in 1945, Markova and Dolin toured Central America, among other places; the company became the London Festival Ballet in 1950. Markova was prima ballerina until 1952, after which she made guest appearances with many companies, including the Royal Winnipeg Ballet, Royal Danish Ballet, and Chicago Opera Ballet, until she retired from dancing in 1962.

Markova was made a DBE in 1963, the year she became ballet director of the Metropolitan Opera in New York. From 1970 she was professor of ballet and performing arts at the University of Cincinnati and from 1972 guest professor at the Royal Ballet School. She was named governor of the Royal Ballet in 1973 and president of the London Festival Ballet (later the English National Ballet) in 1986.

Markova received the Dance Magazine Award in 1957; the Queen Elizabeth II Award from the Royal Academy of Dancing, of which she was vice president from 1958, in 1963; and honorary doctorates from two British universities, Leicester (1966) and East Anglia (1982). Her autobiographical *Giselle and I* was published in 1960, and *Markova Remembers* in 1986.

Marlborough, Sarah Churchill, Duchess of (1660–1744) *English aristocrat*

A close friend of Queen ANNE, Sarah Jennings married John Churchill, an ancestor of Winston Churchill. After the War of the Spanish Succession Churchill became the Duke of Marlborough.

Sarah Jennings was born in Sandridge, in Hertfordshire. She was brought up in the household of the Duke of York (later King James II), where she became the confidante of his daughter, the future Queen Anne. In 1678 she married the duke's protégé, the distinguished soldier Colonel John Churchill. In 1688, following Sarah's advice, the Protestant Anne abandoned her Catholic father, James II, to retain her hopes of eventually becoming queen.

After Anne succeeded King William III in 1702, she bestowed important household offices and favours on

Sarah and made Churchill Duke of Marlborough for his generalship in the War of the Spanish Succession (1701–14). Relations between the two women cooled after 1705 because the duchess urged the Tory-minded queen to appoint Whig ministers, which she was compelled to do by the duke's friend, the powerful lord treasurer Sidney Godolphin. In 1710 Anne dismissed the Whig ministers, and the Tories came to power. In 1711 the Marlboroughs also lost their positions, and the duke was charged with embezzlement. They lived abroad until 1714.

After the duke's death in 1722 the duchess spent her last 20 years completing Blenheim Palace, which Anne had begun for him, while conducting endless quarrels and lawsuits with the architect Sir John Vanbrugh and her own family. She also arranged her own and her husband's papers for publication.

Marlowe, Julia (1866–1950) *British-born American actress*

Julia Marlowe and her husband E. H. Sothern appeared together to great acclaim in many Shakespearean productions in American theatres in the years preceding World War I.

Born Sarah Frances Frost at Caldbeck in the Lake District, she was taken to the United States in 1871. After appearing on stage as a child, she made her adult debut in New York City in Mrs. Lovell's *Ingomar* in 1887. She toured in Shakespearean repertoire for a number of years, though her greatest early successes were in such plays as Clyde Fitch's *Barbara Frietchie* (1899) and Paul Kester's *When Knighthood Was in Flower* (1900).

Marlowe made her first appearance with the actor E. H. Sothern in 1904 in *Romeo and Juliet*. They were married in 1911, continuing to act together, mainly in plays by Shakespeare and Sheridan, until her retirement in 1915. After retiring, she made a few appearances with Sothern on special occasions. She died in New York.

Marsden, Kate (1859–1931) *British traveller and nurse*

Kate Marsden was so moved by the plight of lepers that she undertook a marathon journey to leper colonies in Siberia.

Born in London, the daughter of a lawyer, Kate Marsden trained as a nurse before going in 1878 to Bulgaria to tend the casualties of the Russo-Turkish war. She then moved to New Zealand to care for her dying sister, remaining there to become superintendent of Wellington Hospital.

Deeply moved by the horrors of leprosy during her time in Bulgaria, she planned a journey to the leper colonies in Yakutsk, 2,000 miles across the wastes of Siberia. In order to accomplish this extraordinary mission she managed to engage the patronage of the Russian Tsarina Marya, wife of Tsar Alexander III, as well as that of the Princess of Wales (later Queen ALEXANDRA) and her mother-in-law, Queen VICTORIA. Marsden's account of the journey, *On Sledge and Horseback to Outcast Siberian Lepers*, was published in 1893. Although there was scepticism from some quarters that such a feat could be possible, there was widespread admiration for her bravery. To counter her critics, in 1921 she published *My Mission to Siberia: A Vindication*.

In 1892 Kate Marsden was elected to a fellowship of the Royal Geographical Society, one of the first women to receive this honour. During the last years of her life she lived as an invalid in England.

Marshall, Penny (1942–   ) *American film director and comedienne*

Born Penny Marscharelli in Brooklyn, New York, Penny Marshall grew up in a working-class neighbourhood in the Bronx and was given her show business break by her older brother, the film director Garry Marshall, in the TV comedy show *The Odd Couple* in 1971. In 1976 he created especially for her *Laverne and Shirley*, which ran until 1983.

Marshall made her debut as a director with the comedy *Jumpin' Jack Flash*, starring Whoopi GOLDBERG, in 1986. *Big* (1988), starring Tom Hanks as a 13-year-old boy whose wish to become an adult is granted, was a considerable box-office success and was later made into a Broadway musical. Her *Awakenings* (1990), a touching film set in a psychiatric hospital, starred Robin Williams, who earned an Oscar nomination for his role, and Robert de Niro. Marshall's later films include *A League of Their Own* (1992), about a women's baseball team, *Renaissance Man* (1994), and *The Preacher's Wife* (1996), starring Whitney HOUSTON.

Martineau, Harriet (1802–1876)
British writer and social reformer

> Is it to be understood that the principles of the Declaration of Independence bear no relation to half of the human race?
>
> —*Society in America* (1837)

> The sum and substance of female education in America, as in England, is training women to consider marriage as the sole object in life, and to pretend that they do not think so.
>
> —As above

Harriet Martineau lived an active intellectual life as a writer and political commentator, becoming a keen abolitionist after visiting the United States.

Born in Norwich, into a strict puritanical home, Harriet Martineau received a good education and became intensely religious in her late teens. The collapse of the family business in 1829 left her with no income. However, in 1831 she won three prizes in the *Unitarian Monthly Repository* for essays designed to convert Jews, Catholics, and Muslims. The prize money, supplemented by small loans, enabled her to devote all her time to writing stories for periodicals: these generally portrayed the sufferings of the poor and showed the need for social and economic reforms. The stories were collected as *Illustrations of Political Economy* (9 vols., 1832–34), *Poor Laws and Paupers Illustrated* (1834), and *Illustrations of Taxation* (1834). These works enabled her to acquire a wide circle of influential friends in London, among them Thomas Malthus and Thomas Carlyle.

In 1834–35 Martineau visited the United States, where she became an eager abolitionist. She published *Society in America* (1837) and *A Retrospect of Western Travel* (1838), both of which were successful in England but deeply resented in the United States for their criticism of American life and their abolitionist views. Becoming ill in 1839, she lived as an invalid at Tynemouth until 1844. During this time she wrote children's stories, collected in *The Playfellow* (1841), and two novels. Her recovery was, she believed, a result of hypnotic treatment. This caused her to write *Letters on Mesmerism* (1844) in support of the practice, which distressed many of her friends, particularly as she had now turned against formal religion and seemed to be attracted to a form of mystical thought.

In 1845 Martineau moved to the Lake District, where she became friends with Dorothy WORDSWORTH and her brother, William Wordsworth, and was inspired to write *Forest and Game-law Tales* (1845). A trip to Egypt and Palestine resulted in *Eastern Life, Past and Present* (1848). Other works to attract attention include *History of England During the Thirty Years' Peace* (1849), the strongly antitheological *Letters on the Laws of Man's Social Nature and Development* (1841), and *Philosophy of Comte, Freely Translated and Condensed* (1853). From 1852 to 1866 she contributed to the *London Daily News*, writing radical articles on a range of subjects from economics to the evils of prostitution. Becoming incurably ill in 1854, she wrote her courageous *Autobiography*, which was not published until a year after her death.

Marx, Eleanor (1855–1898) *British socialist*

The youngest of the three daughters of Karl Marx, Eleanor Marx grew up in a household that was a centre for revolutionary exiles. She became a strong and much respected speaker on socialist principles.

Jenny Julia Eleanor Marx was born in Soho, London, where she learned a great deal about revolutionary politics and became fluent in French and German. Her work as a teacher, translator, and typist gave her financial independence while she earned a name for herself writing and speaking on socialism. She also had unfulfilled theatrical aspirations, and her support for Ibsen's plays, some of which she translated, did much to popularize his work in London.

After her father's death in 1883 Eleanor edited the fourth volume of his *Das Kapital*. She strongly identified with the needs of the poor, demonstrating on "Bloody Sunday" in 1887 and supporting the strikes of 1889. As a protégée of Friedrich Engels, she edited his *Revolution and Counter-Revolution* (1896) after his death. She lived openly with Edward Aveling, a socialist, for 24 years, but their relationship brought her little happiness and she committed suicide at the age of 43.

Mary I (1516–1558) *Queen of England and Ireland*

> When I am dead and opened, you shall find "Calais" lying in my heart.
>
> —Quoted in Holinshed's *Chronicles*, Vol. III

Known as "Bloody Mary" for her persecution of Protestants, Mary I restored Roman Catholicism to England during her reign (1553–58).

Mary Tudor was born in Greenwich Palace, London, the daughter of King Henry VIII and CATHERINE OF ARAGON. From an early age she displayed the intense piety that was to be such a marked feature of her adult life. When Catherine failed to produce a son, Henry asked the pope to annul their marriage on the basis that he had married his brother's widow (which was against the law of the Church). However, the pope forbade an annulment on the grounds that Catherine's first marriage had never been consummated. Henry therefore had himself declared head of the Church of England, which thus became independent of papal authority, so that the marriage could be annulled.

After the end of her parents' marriage in 1533 and Henry's remarriage to Anne BOLEYN, Mary was consistently loyal to her mother, refusing to deny the authority of the pope. In September 1533, following the birth of her half-sister, the future Queen ELIZABETH I, Mary was disinherited, and her household was dissolved. In 1536 Anne Boleyn was executed, and a faction at court immediately began to campaign for Mary's reinstatement. The king, however, continued to insist that Mary should accept the repudiation of papal authority. Although she yielded later that year, she was not restored to the succession until 1544.

With her father's death and the accession of her young half-brother Edward VI in 1547 Mary again became heir to the throne. She found herself increasingly at odds with the Protestant policies pursued by the Privy Council, led by the Duke of Northumberland. When the king became ill in 1553, Northumberland persuaded him to name Lady Jane GREY, the great-granddaughter of Henry VII, as his successor in order to exclude the Catholic Mary. Edward died in July 1553, and Lady Jane Grey abdicated after nine days in the face of popular and aristocratic support for Mary, who became queen.

Mary's main aim was to restore Roman Catholicism as the state religion; she therefore repealed Edward's Protestant legislation and in 1554 reintroduced the heresy laws. Failing to appreciate the strength of English hostility to Catholic Spain, in 1554 Mary announced her proposed marriage to her cousin Philip II of Spain, provoking a rebellion led by Sir Thomas Wyatt, who wished to put the Protestant Princess Elizabeth on the throne. Mary quelled the rebellion and embarked on a policy of religious persecution in which over 300 Protestants were burned at the stake, including Bishops Hooper, Latimer, and Ridley, and Archbishop Cranmer. The marriage of Mary and Philip took place in July 1554, and Philip immediately played an important part in negotiating the settlement with the papacy, which was ratified by parliament in January 1555. Thereafter, however, he lost interest both in Mary and in England and left the country after the failure of her pregnancy.

Mary struggled with a heavy burden of debt, strong Protestant opposition, and the complex problems of re-establishing the Roman Catholic Church. Drawn into a futile and unpopular war with France on her husband's behalf, in 1558 she lost Calais, the last English possession on the Continent. She died childless after a series of phantom pregnancies, having failed to produce the longed-for Catholic heir to the English throne, and was succeeded by Elizabeth.

Mary II (1662–1694) *Queen of England, Scotland, and Ireland*

Mary II ruled jointly with her husband, William III, following the "Glorious Revolution" of 1688.

She was born in London, the eldest child of James, Duke of York (later King James II), and Anne Hyde, his first wife. Although her father was a Roman Catholic, Mary and her sister Anne (later Queen ANNE) were brought up as Protestants. In November 1677 Mary married her cousin the Protestant William of Orange and went to live with him in the Netherlands.

After her father became king of England, Scotland, and Ireland in 1685 and began a programme of pro-Catholic policies, Mary was placed in the difficult position of having to choose between supporting her Catholic father and allegiance to her Protestant husband. Taking the side of William against James, she supported his invasion of England with Dutch and English troops in 1688, when her father fled the country; these events later became known as the "Glorious Revolution."

In February of the next year Mary and her husband were proclaimed joint sovereigns, with William as sole administrator. They were crowned at Westminster Abbey on April 11, 1689. During William's military campaigns in Ireland (1690–91), where he finally defeated James, and on the Continent (1692–94) Mary acted ably and efficiently as regent. She was an intelligent and educated woman, popular in both England and Holland. She died childless, from smallpox, in London.

Mary, Queen of Scots (1542–1587) *Queen of Scotland*

Becoming queen of Scotland shortly after her birth, Mary later married the French dauphin and became queen of France when he took the throne. After returning to Scotland, she was forced to abdicate and fled to England, where she was executed by her cousin Queen ELIZABETH I.

Mary Stuart was born in Linlithgow, Scotland, the daughter of King James V of Scotland and his queen, the French noblewoman Mary of Guise. Through her father she was a granddaughter of MARGARET TUDOR, the elder sister of King Henry VIII of England, and therefore a claimant to the English throne. James V died a few days after her birth; and since his two legitimate sons had died the previous year, Mary succeeded to the throne of Scotland as an infant, and her mother became regent.

At the age of five Mary, a Roman Catholic, was sent to the court of King Henry II of France and CATHERINE DE' MÉDICIS, where she received an excellent education. In 1558 she married the dauphin, who later became Francis II. After Francis's death in 1560 Mary returned to Scotland (1561). Her own mother had died in June 1560, and Mary, while remaining a Catholic herself, accepted the Presbyterian Church led by John Knox.

In 1565 Mary married her cousin Lord Darnley, who was also a claimant to the English throne as a grandson of Margaret Tudor. The marriage was unpopular, and Mary, finding her husband lacking in intelligence and morality, quickly excluded him from any real authority. The following year, jealous of the influence he thought David Riccio, Mary's French secretary, had over her, Darnley was involved in Riccio's murder. That same year Mary gave birth to the future King James VI of Scotland (James I of England). In 1567 Darnley was murdered, almost certainly by James Hepburn, Earl of Bothwell, who was to become Mary's third husband. He abducted Mary (so she later alleged) and married her after rapidly divorcing his wife. Whether she had been his mistress before this and was party to the plot to murder Darnley remains unclear, resting on the much disputed evidence of the "casket letters." Conveniently "found" in a casket four months after the murder, these incriminating letters were alleged by Mary's enemies to have been written by her to Bothwell, but they may have been forgeries. Opinion turned against her, and the Scottish nobles rebelled. Mary and Bothwell were defeated in battle at Carberry Hill (1567), when she was deserted by her army; she was imprisoned at Lochleven Castle and forced to abdicate in favour of her son. Bothwell fled to Orkney and from there to Denmark, where he was imprisoned until his death.

Mary escaped in 1568 and fled to England, probably hoping to persuade her cousin Queen Elizabeth to support her reinstatement. However, as a claimant to the English throne and in Catholic eyes the rightful queen of England, Mary's presence was a source of great embarrassment to Elizabeth, and Mary was imprisoned. Since she was a focus for numerous plots against Elizabeth, many involving Spanish help, parliament pressed for Mary's execution. Until 1587 Elizabeth refused to agree to order her cousin's death. Eventually, as a consequence of Mary's proven involvement in Anthony Babington's plot against her life, Elizabeth reluctantly agreed to have her beheaded. Mary died at Fotheringhay Castle near Peterborough, at the age of 44. Her remains were moved to Westminster Abbey by her son.

Mary Magdalene, Saint (1st century) Follower of Jesus Christ

Mary Magdalene's background is obscure, but she appears in the New Testament as the first witness of Christ's Resurrection.

Her name recalls her town of origin, Magdala in Galilee (modern Migdal). The New Testament singles her out among those women who accompanied Jesus from Galilee (Mark 15:40; Matthew 27:55–56; Luke 8:2) as having witnessed his death, burial, and Resurrection. While all four Gospels record these events, two (Mark and John) add that she was the first to personally encounter the risen Jesus.

The reference to Jesus casting seven demons out of Mary Magdalene (Mark 16:9; Luke 8:2) has led some readers from earliest times to identify her with the sinful woman of Luke 7:36–50 who annointed Jesus's feet with her tears and dried them with her hair. (See also MARY OF BETHANY.)

Although in the Christian tradition Mary Magdalene is usually taken to have been a repentant prostitute, in some contexts she has been seen as the first apostle. Hippolytus of Rome (died 235) described her as the "apostle to the apostles" in his commentary on the Song of Songs. Legends are also found in the writings of the Gnostics, an early Christian sect, in which she plays a dominant part in post-Resurrection dialogues with Jesus and instructs the apostles. The Gnostic Gospel of Philip began a long history of speculation concerning the personal relationship of Mary Magdalene and Jesus.

Her feast day is July 22, and her emblem an ointment jar.

Mary of Bethany (1st century) New Testament character

Mary of Bethany and her sister Martha were visited by Jesus, who commended Mary's spirituality. According to St. John they were the sisters of Lazarus, whom Jesus had raised from the dead.

In the account given by St. Luke (10:38–42) Jesus received hospitality from the sisters when he visited Bethany, a village near Jerusalem. While Mary sat at Jesus's feet and listened to his teaching, Martha made herself busy with preparations for their meal. Eventually Martha complained to Jesus about having to do all the work by herself. In reply Jesus rebuked Martha for being "troubled about many things" while neglecting the "one thing...needful" that Mary had chosen – that is, for immersing herself in humdrum duties to the neglect of more spiritual concerns. Since the early days of the Christian Church the sisters have been interpreted as representing the active (Martha) and contemplative (Mary) sides of Christian life.

A number of further details about Mary appear in the Gospel of St. John. According to John, Martha and Mary were the sisters of Lazarus, the man whom Jesus raised from the dead (John 11:1–46). John also identifies Mary with the woman who anointed Jesus's feet with costly ointments and wiped them with her hair (John 12:1–9). When Judas Iscariot complained about this extravagance, remarking that the money could have been given to the poor, Jesus defended Mary with the comment, "the poor always ye have with you; but me ye have not always."

In St. Luke's Gospel (7:37–50) an unnamed "woman which was a sinner" also anoints Jesus's feet. Traditionally this woman has been identified with St. MARY MAGDALENE, leading some commentators to assume that the two Marys were the same person. The Gospels, however, give no real support for this view.

Mary of Modena (1658–1718) *Second wife of King James II of England, Scotland, and Ireland*

An accomplished linguist and musician, Mary of Modena became Duchess of York and subsequently queen of England, although James's marriage to an Italian Catholic was regarded with hostility by his people and parliament.

Born Marie Beatrice d'Este in Modena, Italy, Mary was a devout Catholic and had strong aspirations to become a nun. Only the intervention of the pope persuaded her that her betrothal to the Catholic heir presumptive to the throne of England, Scotland, and Ireland, James, Duke of York, was a vocation more worthy than confining herself to a convent.

Mary became James's second wife in 1673. After losing six infant children, she gave birth to their son James Edward Stuart in 1688, by which time James had become king. This posed the threat of a Roman Catholic succession, one of the factors that precipitated the "Glorious Revolution" of 1688 and James's removal from the throne. Mary (MARY II), James's daughter by his first wife, and her Protestant husband William of Orange were then invited to land an army in England with a view to taking the throne.

Mary of Modena fled to France with her son and husband. Her son, who became known as the "Old Pretender," was urged by his supporters to claim the throne as the rightful Stuart heir in the Jacobite Rebellion of 1715. After the failure of this rebellion the Old Pretender lived in permanent exile in Rome. Mary remained in St. Germain, Paris, for the rest of her life.

Mary of Teck (1867–1953) *Wife of King George V of the United Kingdom*

A popular queen, Mary was also a talented needlewoman with a strong interest in antique furniture and the arts.

Princess Victoria Mary Augusta (known as Princess May) was born in Kensington Palace, London, the daughter of Francis, Duke of Teck, and Princess Mary Adelaide, a granddaughter of George III. In 1891 she became engaged to Albert, Duke of Clarence, the eldest son of the Prince of Wales (later King Edward VII). This engagement was partly inspired by the Duke of Clarence's grandmother, Queen VICTORIA, who saw Princess May as a suitable future queen. However, six weeks after their betrothal the Duke of Clarence died of pneumonia.

Queen Victoria, still bent on seeing her protégée become queen, then encouraged George, Duke of York, the second son of the Prince of Wales, to propose marriage to Princess May. Accordingly they were married in 1893. When her husband became king in 1910 as George V, May became queen of England and empress of India.

Queen Mary was an austere and regal figure, especially in her later years, when she always appeared in public wearing a toque (a tall, round, brimless hat). She was, however, regarded with affection by the British people. She made known her strong disapproval of Mrs. Wallis Simpson (the future Duchess of WINDSOR), the unacceptable consort of her eldest son, who became King Edward VIII on the death of George V in 1936. After the abdication of Edward, Queen Mary provided considerable support for her shy second son and his family, when he inherited the throne as George VI. In the early years of his reign she did much to encourage public support for the monarchy.

Queen Mary outlived George VI by over a year. She saw the beginning of the reign of her granddaughter ELIZABETH II, but died in Marlborough House, London, three months before Elizabeth's coronation.

Mary the Virgin, Saint (late 1st century BC–early 1st century AD) *Mother of Jesus Christ*

Known to Christians as the Virgin Mary, St. Mary is particularly venerated by Roman Catholics and Eastern Orthodox Christians.

Very little is known of the life of Mary; the fullest accounts of her occur in the New Testament Gospels of Luke and Matthew. The Gospel of St. John records that she was present at the Crucifixion, and according to the Acts of the Apostles (1:14) she was in Jerusalem during the growth of the early Christian Church.

The Gospel of St. Luke (1:26–38) describes the Annunciation (the announcement by the Archangel Gabriel that Mary was to conceive the Son of God by the Holy Spirit), Mary's subsequent marriage to Joseph, and her meeting with her cousin Elizabeth when Elizabeth hails her as the mother of the Messiah, prompting Mary's song of praise (the Magnificat). Although Mary is believed by Christians to have been a virgin at the time of the birth of Jesus, Matthew claims (1:16–20) that Joseph, rather than Mary, provides Jesus with the lineage from King David, which St. Paul asserts in Romans (1:3).

The Roman Catholic Church believes that Mary herself was conceived free from original sin. This is known as the doctrine of the Immaculate Conception. The feast of the Conception of the Blessed Virgin Mary has been celebrated by Roman Catholics (on December 8) since 1471. It has, however, been a controversial issue in Christian theology, becoming a dogma of the Roman Catholic Church only in 1854.

The belief that Mary was taken up bodily into heaven, known as the Bodily Assumption, was declared a doctrine of the Roman Catholic Church in 1950 by Pope Pius XII. Four years later this pope announced that Mary should be regarded as the Queen of Heaven.

Since the Reformation Protestants have tended to play down the role of Mary in Christianity. This is not intended as a criticism of Mary herself but as a reaction to what Protestants consider the exaggerated veneration of Mary by Catholics, which has been interpreted as diminishing the role of Jesus as the only saviour. The Eastern Orthodox Churches have also treated Mary as a focus of piety in their liturgy, venerating her as *Theotokos* (the Mother of God).

Masina, Giulietta (1920–1994) *Italian actress*

Giulietta Masina was the wife and inspiration of the leading Italian filmmaker Federico Fellini, who dedicated most of his work to her. She appeared in many of his films.

The daughter of a schoolteacher, Giulia Anna Masina was born near Bologna in Italy. While studying at the University of Rome, she worked as an actress in the Ateneo Theatre Group and on the radio in the series *Cico and Pallina*, written by Federico Fellini. Masina made her professional stage debut in 1939. In 1943 she married Fellini, who went on to become a highly acclaimed film director during the 1950s.

Masina first attracted attention when she won the Italian Critics' Award for her performance in Alberto Lattuada's *Senza Pietà* (1948; *Without Pity*). Her first major screen role was in Fellini's *La Strada* (1954); three years later she won the Best Actress Award at the Cannes Film Festival for her portrayal of the naive prostitute in Fellini's *Le notti di Cabiria* (*The*

Nights of Cabiria). She was also acclaimed in Fellini's *Il bidone* (1955; *The Swindle*), *Giulietta degli spiriti* (1965; *Juliet of the Spirits*), and *Ginger e Fred* (1985; *Ginger and Fred*). Masina died of cancer less than five months after her husband's death.

Mata Hari (1876–1917) *Dutch dancer and spy*

Mata Hari has come to personify the seductive female spy.

The daughter of a businessman, she was born Margaretha Geertruida Zelle at Leeuwarden and educated in a convent school. At the age of 18 she married Campbell MacLeod, a 40-year-old Scot who was a commissioned officer in the Dutch Colonial Army. After three years in Amsterdam, during which she bore two children, she accompanied her husband to Java in 1897.

On the couple's return to the Netherlands, Margaretha divorced her husband. In 1903 she went to Paris and established herself as a dancer with a repertoire of sultry and erotic dances, which she claimed had symbolic religious significance. Known first as "Lady MacLeod" and then as "Mata Hari" (a Malay name meaning "Eye of the Dawn"), she became famous in most of the major cities of Europe, taking several government officials and military men as her lovers.

In 1907 she allegedly joined the German secret service. During World War I she travelled between The Hague and Paris, passing on secret information acquired from the high-ranking allied officers who were among her admirers. She herself claimed to be a double agent, simultaneously working as a spy for the French in Belgium. However, the French, growing increasingly suspicious of her continued meetings with German officials and military officers, arrested her on February 13, 1917. She was tried in a military court and sentenced to death by firing squad. Mata Hari was executed in Vincennes, France, on October 15, 1917, but her guilt has remained a matter of controversy.

Matilda (1102–1167) *Wife of the Holy Roman Emperor Henry V*

Matilda was an unsuccessful claimant to the English throne, but her son by her second husband, Geoffrey, Count of Anjou, became King Henry II, England's first Plantagenet monarch.

Also known as Maud, Matilda was born in London, the daughter of King Henry I of England. Her marriage in 1114 to Emperor Henry V of Germany and the Holy Roman Empire was arranged by her father. She was widowed in 1125, and German leadership passed by election to Lothair II. However, Matilda was recognized by the English barons as heiress to the English crown in 1126 after the death of Henry's son William. Two years later she married Geoffrey Martel, Count of Anjou, who was nicknamed "Plantagenet" because of the sprig of broom (*plante genêt*) he wore on his helmet.

On her father's death in 1135 Matilda's claim to the English succession was contested by Stephen of Blois, who seized the throne with the support of the barons and the Church. In 1139 Matilda invaded England and established a stronghold in the southwest during a period of inconclusive civil war. In February 1141 she captured Stephen at Lincoln, but this period of ascendancy ended when her forces were routed and her brother and ally Robert was captured at Winchester in September; in November Matilda released Stephen in exchange for her brother. Never popular in England, Matilda finally returned to Normandy in 1148. In 1152, however, the Treaty of Wallingford recognized her son Henry as Stephen's heir. He became King Henry II, the first Plantagenet king of England.

Matilda of Tuscany (1046–1115) *Countess of Tuscany*

One of the most powerful rulers of medieval Italy, Matilda was a strong supporter of the papacy.

Also known as Matilda of Canossa, she was born in Lucca, Tuscany, the daughter of Boniface II of Canossa. On his death in 1052 she inherited a large part of northern Italy. Intelligent and well educated, she was married first to her stepbrother Godfrey the Hunchback, Duke of Lorraine, who died in 1076. At the age of 43 she married the 17-year-old Duke of Bavaria, but they separated six years later.

Matilda controlled Tuscany, part of Umbria, and Emilia-Romagna, making her the ruler of much of northern and central Italy. A strong supporter of Pope Gregory VII, she engaged in a long-running feud with Henry IV, the Holy Roman Emperor, and helped to finance the pope's troops in their fight against him. When Henry's son Conrad attempted to seize power from his father, Matilda supported Conrad. However, she eventually made peace with the new emperor, Henry V.

Matilda died at the Benedictine monastery of Polirone, near Mantua. By willing her lands to both the papacy and Henry V, her legacy caused confusion and further bloodshed.

Matthews, Jessie (1907–1981)
British actress, singer, and dancer

Jessie Matthews, a star of musicals in the 1920s, became widely known after World War II as Mrs. Dale in the popular radio serial *Mrs. Dale's Diary*.

Born in London's Soho, the daughter of a street trader, Jessie Matthews was one of 11 children. She made her stage debut at the age of ten, becoming a chorus-line dancer as a teenager. In the 1920s she rose to stardom in such musical revues as C. B. Cochran's *One Damn Thing after Another* (1927) and Noël Coward's *This Year of Grace* (1928). In 1930 she reached perhaps the height of her fame in *Evergreen*, playing opposite Sonnie Hale, who became her second husband.

During the 1930s Matthews moved into films, making the movie version of *Evergreen*, with its famous ceiling dance and song, "Over My Shoulder," in 1934. In all she made 17 films, of which ten were musicals. Choosing to remain in Britain rather than promote her career in Hollywood, she became best known after World War II for her role as Mrs. Dale in the long-running radio serial *Mrs. Dale's Diary*. She also directed a short film, *Victory Wedding*, in 1944.

Problems originating in Matthews's difficult childhood took their inevitable toll on her later life. All three of her marriages ended in divorce, and she had a number of nervous breakdowns during her career.

Matute (Ausejo), Ana Maria (1926–) *Spanish novelist*

Widely regarded as one of Spain's leading 20th-century writers, Ana Matute now has an international reputation.

Ana Maria Matute Ausejo was born in Barcelona. She grew up during the period of the Spanish Civil War (1936–39), which led to the 30-year dictatorship of General Franco. Her best-known novel, *Los hijos muertos* (1959; *The Lost Children*, 1965), gives a personal and moving account of the problems of growing up during a civil war. Written so as not to appear critical of the regime, it managed to escape censorship.

Matute's subsequent novels continued to explore the themes of war and childhood suffering. They include *Los soldados Lloran de noche* (1964; Soldiers of the Night) and *La torre vigia* (1971; The Watchtower). She has also written a number of stories for children and has been a visiting lecturer at several American universities.

Maury, Antonia Caetana (de Paiva Pereira) (1866–1952) *American astronomer*

> In my opinion the separation by Antonia C. Maury of the c- and ac-stars is the most important advancement in stellar classification since the trials by [Herman Karl] Vogel and Pietro Angelo [Secchi].
>
> —Ejnar Hertzsprung, letter to William Henry Pickering, July 22, 1908

Antonia Maury was a highly regarded Harvard astronomer whose innovations in the classification of stars have proved to be of permanent significance.

Born into a family of distinguished scientists in Cold Spring-on-Hudson, New York State, Antonia Maury was the granddaughter of John William Draper, who pioneered the application of photography to astronomy; the niece of Henry Draper, the astronomer after whom the Harvard star catalogue is named; a cousin of the oceanographer Matthew Maury; and the daughter of a clergyman who was also a well-known naturalist. Her sister Carlotta became a palaeontologist, and she herself was also an ornithologist.

Educated at Vassar College, New York State, Maury graduated in 1887 and became an assistant to Edward Pickering at Harvard College Observatory in 1889. She worked there with other women astronomers, including Annie CANNON and Henrietta LEAVITT, until her retirement in 1935, apart from a period (1899–1908) lecturing at various eastern colleges.

Maury worked on the classification of stars for the Harvard catalogue, introducing the labels "a," "b," "c," "ab," and "ac" to denote their brightness. Her classifications, which included those of 681 bright northern stars, were published in the Harvard *Annals* in 1896. The astronomer Ejnar Hertzsprung saw the significance of her classification system and used it in his work on giant stars in 1905. Maury also worked on binary stars, notably Beta Lyrae, making important discoveries in her investigations.

During her retirement Maury continued her studies. She also served for several years as curator of the Draper Park Museum at Hastings-on-Hudson, New York.

Mayer, Maria Goeppert (1906–1972) *German-born American physicist*
Maria Goeppert Mayer won a share of the 1963 Nobel Prize for physics for her work on the structure of the nucleus of atoms.

Maria Goeppert was born at Kattowitz in Germany (now Katowice in Poland). She studied at the University of Göttingen, where she obtained her PhD in 1930 and met her husband, the physical chemist Joseph Mayer. Emigrating to America in 1931, she was employed at Johns Hopkins University, Baltimore (1931–39), Columbia University, New York (1939–46), and the Argonne National Laboratory (1946–60). In 1960 she became professor of physics at the University of California, La Jolla, San Diego.

In 1963 Mayer shared the Nobel Prize for physics with Hans Jensen and Eugene P. Wigner for their work on nuclear shell theory. This is the theory that the particles in the nucleus of an atom (protons and neutrons) are arranged in a series of different layers (shells). Scientists already knew that the electrons orbiting the nucleus were arranged in different shells. Mayer and her colleagues thought a similar theory applied to the nuclear particles could help explain why some nuclei were particularly stable. Mayer argued that the so-called "magic numbers" – 2, 8, 20, 50, 82, and 126 – of either protons or neutrons in particularly stable nuclei could be explained in this way. She concluded that the magic numbers were the numbers of particles needed to fill up certain shells. Full shells were more stable than half-empty ones. The stable nuclei of helium (with 2 protons and 2 neutrons), oxygen (8 of each), calcium (20 of each), and tin (50 protons) all fit neatly into this pattern.

McAliskey, Bernadette (1947–)
Northern Irish politician

> The war is over and the good guys lost.
>
> —Remark on the day that the IRA ceasefire was announced in August 1994

An openly declared sympathizer of IRA terrorism in Northern Ireland, as Bernadette Devlin she became in 1969 the youngest-ever British MP.

Born into a poor Catholic family, Bernadette Devlin was raised in Dungannon, County Tyrone. Educated at St. Patrick's Girls' Academy, Dungannon, and Queen's University, Belfast, she was still a student when she ran as an Independent Unity candidate for Mid-Ulster. Elected at the age of 21, she broke the record set in 1781 by William Pitt the Younger when he became the youngest-ever MP at the age of 22. After her election victory she published an autobiography, *The Price of My Soul* (1969).

Devlin was a key figure in Irish politics during the 1970s, and as a result of her aggressive stance at the head of a Catholic riot she was arrested and spent nine months in prison. Following the birth of her illegitimate daughter in 1971, Devlin lost Catholic support. In 1973 she married Michael McAliskey, changing her name to his, but did not run in the 1974 general election. In 1975 she cofounded the Irish Republican Socialist Party and was elected chair of the Independent Socialist Party. Four years later she was unsuccessful in her attempt to win a seat in the European parliament. In 1981 McAliskey supported the IRA prisoners who went on hunger strike, and she and her husband survived an assassination attempt in which they were both shot and wounded.

In 1997 McAliskey's pregnant daughter, Roisin McAliskey, was held in prison in the UK, awaiting extradition to Germany on charges of attempted murder and possessing explosives arising from an IRA mortar attack on a British army base. Bernadette McAliskey's support for her daughter (who was finally released in 1998 on medical grounds) was widely publicized, as was her continuing opposition to the IRA ceasefire.

McBride, Patricia (1942–) *American ballet dancer*

A dancer of enormous versatility and wide repertoire, Patricia McBride has danced many roles created for her by George Balanchine at the New York City Ballet.

Patricia McBride was born in Teaneck, New Jersey. She won a scholarship to the School of American Ballet, the New York City Ballet's official school, at the age of 14 and made her professional debut at 15 with André Eglevsky's Petit Ballet Company in *Come Play with Me*. In 1959 she joined the New York City Ballet (NYCB), and by 1961 she had become one of its principal dancers.

Known for her dazzling technique and her portrayal of character parts, McBride has performed all the classical roles as well as modern works by the NYCB's founding choreographer, George Balanchine. The 22 roles that Balanchine created for her include *Harlequinade* (1965), *Jewels* (1967), and lead parts in *Who Cares?* (1970). McBride also danced in Jerome Robbins's *Dances at a Gathering* and *Dyb-*

buk Variations (1974). She often made guest appearances on television and at dance concerts and festivals.

In 1973 McBride married a fellow NYCB dancer, Jean-Pierre Bonnefoux, who later became head of dance at Indiana University. After a 30-year career McBride retired in 1989 with a spectacular gala tribute staged in her honour by the NYCB. She herself danced 12 items on the programme and was showered with 13,000 roses during the final standing ovation.

McCarthy, Mary (Therese) (1912–1989) *American writer*

> An interviewer asked me what book I thought best represented the modern American woman. All I could think of to answer was: *Madame Bovary*.
>
> —*On the Contrary* (1961)

Mary McCarthy was known for her biting literary and dramatic criticism and her witty novels, with their incisive social commentary. Her writings reflect her hatred of hypocrisy and her commitment to left-wing causes.

Born in Seattle, Washington, McCarthy was orphaned at the age of six and raised by a variety of relatives. She recounted this ordeal in *Memories of a Catholic Girlhood* (1957), which has become known as a landmark in autobiographical writing. (A second autobiographical volume, *How I Grew*, about her school years, appeared in 1987.) After graduating from Vassar College, New York State, in 1933, she reviewed books and became an intellectual Trotskyite.

McCarthy's attacks in *The Nation* on the low standards of contemporary critics and her acid theatrical reviews for *The Partisan Review* gained her a reputation for severity. Some of her essays are collected in *On the Contrary* (1961), *Mary McCarthy's Theater Chronicles, 1937–62* (1963), and *The Writing on the Wall* (1970). *The Mask of State* (1974) assembles her reportage on Watergate, and *The Seventeenth Degree* (1974) collects her anti-Vietnam War pamphlets. She also wrote on art in *Venice Observed* (1956) and *The Stones of Florence* (1959).

Encouraged to write fiction by the

critic Edmund Wilson, who became her second husband in 1938, McCarthy published such novels as *The Company She Keeps* (1942), *The Oasis* (1949), *The Groves of Academe* (1952), and *A Charmed Life* (1955). In 1963 she achieved notoriety with the publication of *The Group*, her bestselling sexually explicit novel about eight Vassar graduates. It was made into a film in 1966. Her later works include *Birds of America* (1971) and *Cannibals and Missionaries* (1979). She also wrote short stories.

Mary McCarthy was awarded the Edward MacDowell Medal and the National Medal for Literature in 1984. At the time of her death she was involved in a long-running literary feud with the writer Lillian HELLMAN. When McCarthy alleged that "everything she writes is a lie, including 'and' and 'the,'" Hellman filed a libel suit but died before the case could come to trial.

McClintock, Barbara (1902–1992)
American geneticist

At the age of 81 Barbara McClintock received the 1983 Nobel Prize for physiology or medicine for her discovery of so-called "jumping genes," i.e., genes that can move from one spot to another on the chromosomes of a plant and thereby change the future generations of the plant.

The daughter of a physician, McClintock was born in Hartford, Connecticut, and educated at Cornell's College of Agriculture, where she received her PhD in 1927 for work in botany. Remaining at Cornell, McClintock conducted research into chromosomes. Thomas Hunt Morgan and other geneticists, working mainly with *Drosophila* fruit flies, had already established that gene action was connected with the chromosomes. *Drosophila* chromosomes, however, were too small to reveal much detail. McClintock therefore chose to work with a variety of corn in which the chromosomes were much more visible. Using new staining techniques, she identified and numbered the ten corn chromosomes. In a series of papers (1929–31) McClintock demonstrated the existence of "linkage groups" in corn. A linkage group is a group of genes that tend to be inherited together because they are sited near each other on a chromosome. McClintock was able to identify the changes in a chromosome that were responsible for a change in the physical characteristics of the corn plants. This was a landmark discovery, as others had suspected this but had been unable to prove it.

In 1936 McClintock was offered a post as assistant professor in the new genetics department at the University of Missouri. She remained there until 1941. In 1944 she was elected to the U.S. National Academy of Sciences, becoming only the third woman to be so honoured. McClintock then joined the Carnegie Institute's Cold Spring Harbor Laboratory, New York, where she remained until her death.

In the 1940s at Cold Spring Harbor McClintock began working on what she later called "jumping genes." By breeding corn plants, she studied a group of genes responsible for changes in pigmentation in the plants. After several years' careful breeding, McClintock proposed that in addition to the normal genes responsible for pigmentation there were two other genes involved, which she called "controlling elements." One controlling element was found fairly close to the pigmentation gene and operated as a switch, turning the gene on and off. The second element appeared to be located further away on the same chromosome and was a "rate gene," controlling the rate at which the pigment gene was switched on and off. McClintock discovered that the controlling elements could move along the chromosome to a different site and could even move to different chromosomes where they would control different genes. McClintock gave a full description of this process of "transposition," as it became known, in 1951, in her paper *Chromosome Organization and Genic Expression*. Her work was largely ignored until 1960, when controlling elements were identified in bacteria.

McColgan, Liz (1964–) *Scottish middle- and long-distance runner*

Liz McColgan is noted for her perse-vering attitude towards running, despite injuries to her knee. In 1991 she was World Champion in the 10,000 metres.

Born Elizabeth Lynch in Dundee, she went to the United States to study at the University of Alabama and then returned to Scotland. She won a gold medal in the 10,000 metres in the 1986 Commonwealth Games, which were held that year in Edinburgh. In 1987 she married the steeplechaser Peter McColgan. The following year she won a silver medal at the Seoul Olympics. After giving birth to her daughter, McColgan returned to running in 1991, when she retained her Commonwealth title in Auckland, New Zealand, and won the New York marathon in just 2 hours, 27 minutes, the fastest time for a female marathon runner. Later that year she won the 10,000 metres at the World Championships in Tokyo. The following year, however, contrary to expectation, she did not take the gold at the Barcelona Olympics for that event.

In 1993 she was advised to give up running following two knee operations, but she carried on, resuming her training programme in Florida under the guidance of her husband. In 1995 she returned to racing, coming fifth in the London marathon and fourth in the 10,000 metres in the European Cup. The following year she competed in the 10,000 metres at the Atlanta Olympics but failed to win a medal; she also participated – unsuccessfully – in her seventh marathon.

McColgan has also been involved in working with young people in athletics and has been the Athletics Development Officer of Dundee District Council since 1987. She was made an MBE in 1992.

McCullers, Carson (1917–1967)
American writer

Carson McCullers is remembered for her haunting stories of love and loneliness in the Deep South.

Born Lula Carson Smith in Columbus, Georgia, in her mid teens she had rheumatic fever, the first of many serious illnesses that were to plague her life. From the age of 13 she wanted to be a concert pianist, and in 1934 she went to New York, financed by the sale of family jewels, intending to study music at the Juilliard School. However, she immediately lost all her money on the subway and abandoned music for writing, having already written several plays as an adolescent. She therefore studied creative writing at an evening class while working to earn a living during the day. In 1937 she married James Reeves McCullers, forming a tumultuous relationship that was overshadowed by his alcoholism and her recurrent illnesses and marked by divorce, remarriage, redivorce, and his suicide in 1953.

McCullers's first novel, *The Heart Is a Lonely Hunter* (1940; filmed 1968), centres on a deaf-mute whom four characters believe to understand their secret aspirations. The book brought McCullers critical acclaim and introduced the theme of intense thwarted relationships between isolated suffering individuals that dominates her subsequent fiction. *Reflections in a Golden Eye* (1941; filmed 1967) deals with frustrated and perverted sexuality on a military base in the U.S. South. In 1942 she obtained a Guggenheim Fellowship and spent time at the Yaddo Artist Colony in Saratoga, New York State. *The Member of the Wedding*, which delineates the painful maturing of an adolescent who must learn to accept her brother's forthcoming marriage and her own approaching womanhood, was published in 1946.

After receiving a second Guggenheim Fellowship, McCullers and her husband (whom she had remarried the previous year) visited Paris, but returned when she had a stroke, which was followed by a long illness and a suicide attempt. Nevertheless, in 1950 she successfully dramatized *The Member of the Wedding*, which was made into a film in 1952. In 1951 she published a collection of short stories, *The Ballad of the Sad Café*; the title story, which tells of a masculine woman in love with a dwarf who victimizes her, was successfully dramatized by Edward Albee. The same year McCullers visited England, where she stayed with the writer Elizabeth BOWEN and became close friends with Edith SITWELL.

Although McCullers kept working, illness took its toll. Her later works were less successful, although the novel *Clock without Hands* (1961), an ironic examination of the effects of racism in the South, and the play *The Square Root of Wonderful* (1958), based on her own marriage, are noteworthy. She died after being in a coma for 47 days following a stroke.

McKenna, Siobhán (1922–1986) *Irish actress*

Siobhán McKenna is best known for her interpretations of the great Irish heroines in the plays of Sean O'Casey and J. M. Synge, which she performed many times in London, New York, and Dublin.

Siobhán McKenna was born in Belfast. While still at school she translated plays into Irish Gaelic for the Gaelic Repertory Theatre in Galway; she also appeared in many of these plays. After graduating from the National University in Galway in 1943, she joined the prestigious Abbey Players in Dublin for three years. In 1947 she made her London debut in Paul Carroll's *The White Steed*. Alternating between London's West End and Dublin theatres, she appeared in plays by Shaw, Chekhov, and Brecht, receiving the London *Evening Standard* award for Best Actress for her performance in the title role of Shaw's *Saint Joan* in 1954.

In 1955 McKenna made her Broadway debut in *The Chalk Garden*. She was also highly acclaimed in the film version of Synge's *The Playboy of the Western World* (1962) and in her one-woman show *Here Are Ladies* (1975), incorporating extracts from works by James Joyce and Samuel Beckett.

McKenna, Virginia (1931–) *British actress*

Virginia McKenna had a distinguished career as an actress before her portrayal of Joy ADAMSON in *Born Free* – but it is for her performance in this film that she is best known.

Born in London, Virginia McKenna graduated from the Central School of Speech Training and Dramatic Art

there. She began her career in repertory theatre in Dundee in 1950, first appearing in London a year later in *A Penny for a Song*. In 1952 she made her screen debut in Pinero's *The Second Mrs. Tanqueray* and appeared in *Father's Doing Fine* later that same year. She continued her stage work, however, playing the Shakespearean roles of Perdita in *The Winter's Tale* (1951) and Rosalind in *As You Like It* (1954), as well as the part of Sister Jeanne in the Royal Shakespeare Company's production of John Whiting's *The Devils* in 1961. Notable among her films of this period are *A Town Like Alice* (1956), *Carve Her Name with Pride* (1958), and *The Wreck of the Mary Deare* (1959).

McKenna's first marriage, to the actor Denholm Elliott, ended in 1956, and a year later she married Bill Travers, her costar in *Born Free* (1966). In this, her best-known film, McKenna played the conservationist Joy Adamson, who established a close relationship with a lioness, Elsa. McKenna and Travers also appeared together in other films, including *Ring of Bright Water* (1969). McKenna's later stage roles included parts in the musicals *A Little Night Music* (1976), *The King and I* (1979), and *Winnie* (1988).

Since retiring from stage and film work, McKenna has devoted her energies to various animal welfare causes with her husband. Among these is the Born Free Foundation, which they established to ensure that the former island home of Gavin Maxwell, author of *Ring of Bright Water*, remains a wildlife sanctuary for otters.

McPherson, Aimée Semple (1890–1944) *Canadian-born American evangelist*

Aimée Semple McPherson's theatrical style, reputation as a faith healer, and masterly public relations strategy brought her the fame and wealth she appeared to crave.

Born Aimée Elizabeth Kennedy near Ingersoll, Ontario, she was an active member of the Salvation Army. Aimée left high school early and in 1908 married a travelling Pentecostal evangelist, Robert Semple. In 1910 they went as missionaries to Hong Kong, where Robert died of typhoid fever. Joining her mother in New York City, with her daughter Roberta, Aimée continued her revival work. In February 1912 she married Harold McPherson, a grocery salesman. Their son Rolf later became Aimée's successor.

In 1918 Aimée moved to Los Angeles with her mother and children and from there went on extensive revival tours throughout the United States, Canada, and Australia. She was divorced from McPherson in 1921. Meanwhile, her "Foursquare Gospel" movement was attracting both audiences and donations, and her Angelus Temple, with seating for over 5,000, was opened in Los Angeles in 1923. Later that year a Bible school – the Lighthouse of International Foursquare Evangelism – also opened. A radio broadcasting station was installed in the temple in 1924. The International Church of the Foursquare Gospel, in which faith healing played an important part, was incorporated in 1927.

In May 1926 Aimée disappeared while swimming in the Pacific near Venice, California, and was presumed drowned. However, she reappeared about a month later in a small town on the Arizona-Mexico border, claiming to have been kidnapped and held for ransom. A grand jury investigation of the incident led to a charge of perjury, but the case was dismissed. There were allegations that she had spent part of the time in Carmel, California, with Kenneth Ormiston, her radio station operator. This bizarre episode led to division within the Foursquare Gospel leadership, but a majority remained loyal to Aimée, and the movement continued to grow despite financial difficulties during the 1930s.

Aimée's third marriage, to David Hutton in 1931, also ended in divorce (1934). In the next few years she was involved in litigation against her mother and daughter over control of the Angelus Temple. She therefore spent less time preaching, concentrating instead on her writing and her teaching in the Bible school. She also oversaw the churches of the Foursquare Gospel that had sprung up in several countries. Her death from an overdose of sedatives was ruled accidental.

Her books include *This Is That* (1919; revised edition, 1923), *In the Service of the King* (1927), and the compilation *The Story of My Life* (1951), published after her death.

Mead, Margaret (1901–1978) *American anthropologist*

> It is of very doubtful value to enlist the gifts of women if bringing women into fields that have been defined as male frightens the men, unsexes the women, muffles and distorts the contribution women can make.
>
> —*Male and Female* (1948)

> We are living beyond our means. As a people we have developed a lifestyle that is draining the earth of its priceless and irreplaceable resources without regard for the future of our children and people all around the world.
>
> —"The Energy Crises—Why Our World Will Never Again Be the Same," *Redbook*, April 1974

Margaret Mead is best known for her studies of child-rearing and the family amongst peoples of different South Pacific societies. Her liberal views, coupled with active participation in public affairs, made her a controversial scientific figure.

Born in Philadelphia, Pennsylvania, the daughter of two teachers, Margaret Mead was chiefly educated at home by her grandmother, who was also a teacher. After graduating from Barnard College in 1923, she entered graduate school to study under Franz Boas at Columbia University, where she was especially influenced by the anthropologist Ruth BENEDICT. Mead was awarded her MA in 1924 and her doctorate in 1929. Known as a tireless field investigator, she undertook her first field trip (to Samoa) in 1925. Later field researches were carried out in collaboration with students and other colleagues, including the New Zealand psychologist Reo Fortune (her second husband) and the British biologist Gregory Bateson (her third husband), who had developed anthropological interests. On these expeditions she studied the Manus people of the Admiralty Islands; the Arapesh, Mundugumor, Tchambuli, and Iatmul of New Guinea; and the Balinese. Characteristically she investigated change through repeated visits to a society; for example, she made seven trips to Manus Island over a period of 47 years.

Mead soon became known for her publications on temperamental differences between the sexes in different societies: *Coming of Age in Samoa* (1928), *Growing Up in New Guinea* (1930), and *Sex and Temperament in Three Primitive Societies* (1935). The results of pioneering research in Bali, in which she applied photographic techniques to the study of personality, were published (with Bateson) in *Balinese Character* (1942).

From 1940 Mead became involved in action programmes in diet, mental health, and technological change. She also undertook studies of contemporary national character, published in *And Keep Your Powder Dry* (1942; revised edition, 1965) and *Soviet Attitudes towards Authority* (1951), parallel to those of Ruth Benedict and Geoffrey Gorer.

Following Ruth Benedict's death in 1948, Mead became director of the Columbia University Research in Contemporary Cultures; in 1954 she became an adjunct professor at Columbia. After a lifelong association with the American Museum of Natural History she became, in 1965, its Curator Emeritus of Ethnology but did relatively little formal teaching. Her major influence was through writing, lecturing, and in later years also through television. She expressed candid views on almost every national and global issue of her time, becoming particularly concerned with the rift between the generations in the 1960s, which she addressed in *Culture and Commitment* (1970). She received many awards and was president of the American Association for the Advancement of Science in 1976. Among her last books were *A Way of Seeing* (1970), *Blackberry Winter: My Earlier Years*

(1972), and *Letters from the Field, 1925–1975* (1977).

Since her death, Mead's reputation has been seriously damaged by accusations that much of her anthropological work was based on faulty or insufficient research.

Meinhof, Ulrike Marie (1934–1976)
German political activist

The cofounder of the Baader-Meinhof Gang, Ulrike Meinhof misguidedly believed that violence and terrorism were the only ways of bringing about political change.

Born in Oldenburg, Ulrike Meinhof was the daughter of the assistant director of the State Museum. She was educated at the high school in Hesse and at the universities in Marburg and Münster, where she became involved in the antinuclear movement. She edited a student paper, *Das Argument*, going on to become a respected journalist and editor of the left-wing paper *Konkret* in 1959. In 1961 Meinhof married the Communist activist Klaus Rainer Röhl. Their twin daughters were born the following year, but the couple divorced in 1968.

Meinhof's politics became more extreme after she interviewed the arsonist Andreas Baader in prison. It now seemed to her that violence was the only means of changing society. In May 1970 she helped to free Baader from prison, and after a brief stay in Jordan they returned to Germany to form the underground guerrilla organization known as the Baader-Meinhof Gang, or Red Army Faction. This brutal organization conducted bank robberies and perpetrated senseless acts of violence, planting bombs aimed at destroying large industrial groups as well as the U.S. Army bases in West Germany.

Ulrike Meinhof was arrested in 1972 for her part in freeing Baader and was sentenced in 1974 (with Baader and two other members of the Gang) to eight years' imprisonment. She committed suicide in Stammheim high security prison. Baader and the other two also committed suicide in prison some 18 months later. By 1984 most of the rest of the gang had been arrested.

Meir, Golda (1898–1978) *Israeli stateswoman*

> I can honestly say that I was never affected by the question of the success of an undertaking. If I felt it was the right thing to do, I was for it regardless of the possible outcome.
>
> —Quoted by Masie Syrkin in *Golda Meir: Woman with a Cause*

> Pessimism is a luxury that a Jew can never allow himself.
>
> —"Sayings of the Year," *The Observer*, December 29, 1974

Israel's first woman premier (1969–74), Golda Meir proved to be a resolute, indefatigable, and tough-minded national leader.

Born Goldie Mabovitch in Kiev in Ukraine, she was eight when she and her family emigrated to Milwaukee, Wisconsin, where she trained as a teacher. By the time she married Morris Myerson, a sign painter, in 1917, she was deeply involved in the Zionist movement. In 1921 the Myersons emigrated to Palestine, living on a kibbutz for two years before moving to Jerusalem.

Goldie Myerson began her political career in 1928 as secretary of the Women's Labour Council, a branch of Histradut, the labour federation that served as a shadow government before independence; in 1934 she became a member of Histradut's executive committee. She was then elected as a delegate to the World Zionist Congress and became a leading figure in the movement to establish a Jewish state in Palestine, helping both before and after independence to raise money for Israel in the United States.

Goldie Myerson was one of the 25 signatories of Israel's declaration of independence on May 14, 1948, and in that year was appointed Israel's first envoy to the Soviet Union. In 1949 she entered the Knesset (Israeli parliament), serving as minister of labour (1949–56) and as minister for foreign affairs (1956–65). From 1953 to 1966 she chaired the Israeli delegation to the United Nations. Widowed in 1956, she took the Hebrew form of her name, Golda Meir.

Meir was named general secretary of the dominant Mapai (Labour) Party in 1966, and when Levi Eshkol, the premier, died in office in 1969, she was chosen as interim premier. After winning an election later that year, she remained in office. Her greatest crisis came when Egypt and Syria attacked and almost overwhelmed Israel in the Yom Kippur War of October 1973. Committed to bringing peace to the Middle East, she resigned in June 1974 in the wake of the war.

Meir published her autobiography, *My Life*, in 1975 and resumed an active role in the Mapai Party in 1976. She died in Jerusalem after a 12-year struggle against leukaemia.

Meitner, Lise (1878–1968) *Austrian-born Swedish physicist*

Lise Meitner and her nephew Otto Frisch provided the explanation for the fission of uranium, on which nuclear energy is based.

The daughter of a lawyer, Meitner was born in Vienna and entered the university there in 1901. She studied science under Ludwig Boltzmann and obtained her doctorate in 1906. From Vienna she went to Berlin to attend lectures by Max Planck on theoretical physics. Here she began to study the new phenomenon of radioactivity in collaboration with Otto Hahn, beginning a partnership that was to last 30 years.

In Berlin Meitner met with prejudice against women in academic life. Banned from entering laboratories in which males were working, she was forced to work in an old carpentry shop. At the outbreak of World War I in 1914 she became a nurse in the Austrian army, continuing to work with Hahn during periods of leave. In 1918 they announced the discovery of the radioactive element protactinium.

After the war Meitner returned to Berlin as head of the department of radiation physics at the Kaiser Wilhelm Institute. There she investigated the relationship between the gamma and beta rays emitted by radioactive material. In 1935 she worked with Hahn on the transformation of uranium nuclei when bombarded by neutrons.

Confusing results had been obtained earlier by Enrico Fermi.

By this time Meitner was beginning to fear a different sort of prejudice. Following Hitler's annexation of Austria in 1938, she was no longer safe from persecution and, like many Jewish scientists, left Germany. With the help of Dutch colleagues she found refuge in Sweden, obtaining a post at the Nobel Institute in Stockholm. Hahn, with Fritz Strassman, continued the uranium work and in 1939 published results showing that nuclei much lighter than those of uranium were present. Shortly afterwards Lise Meitner and Otto Frisch published an explanation, interpreting these results as fission of the uranium nuclei. The nucleus of uranium absorbs a neutron, and the resulting unstable nucleus then breaks into two fragments of roughly equal size. In this induced fission two or three neutrons are ejected. For this discovery Meitner later received a share in the 1966 Enrico Fermi Prize of the Atomic Energy Commission.

Lise Meitner became a Swedish citizen in 1949 and continued work on nuclear physics. In 1960 she retired to Cambridge, England.

Melba, Dame Nellie (1861–1931)
Australian singer

> Music is not written in red, white, and blue. It is written in the heart's blood of the composer.
>
> —*Melodies and Memories* (1925)

> She retained a keen sense of her own fiscal value. When she was invited to dinner by a rich hostess who suggested that after the meal she might "sing a little song" Melba declined. It was no trouble, she agreed, to sing a little song. But it was even less arduous to sign a little cheque.
>
> —Joseph Wechsberg, *Red Plush and Black Velvet* (1962)

Dame Nellie Melba achieved worldwide fame for the great purity of her soprano voice. The great French chef Auguste Escoffier named his ice-cream and peach dish *pêche Melba* after her. Melba toast is also named after her, apparently because while staying at the Savoy Hotel in London, she particularly enjoyed a piece of toast that a waiter had accidentally burnt.

Born Helen Porter Mitchell near Melbourne, in Australia, she did not study singing until after her marriage in 1882 to Charles Nesbitt Armstrong, although she was an accomplished pianist and organist. In 1886 she went to Europe, making her operatic debut in Brussels as Gilda in Verdi's *Rigoletto* in 1887. It was then that she took the name Melba, from Melbourne.

In 1889, singing the title role of Donizetti's *Lucia di Lammermoor* at Covent Garden in London, she was recognized as the leading female vocalist of her generation, in succession to Adelina PATTI. After appearances in Italy, France, and Russia she made her New York debut at the Metropolitan Opera as Lucia in 1893 and sang with the company until 1911. She toured the United States during 1897 and 1898.

In her later years Melba excelled in such roles as Violetta in Verdi's *La Traviata* and Mimi in Puccini's *La Bohème*. Created a DBE in 1918, Melba was associated with Covent Garden until her retirement in 1926. She then returned to Australia and became president of the Melbourne Conservatory. She published the autobiographical *Melodies and Memories* in 1925.

Mercouri, Melina (*c.* 1925–1994)
Greek actress and politician

> When you are born and they tell you "What a pity that you are so clever, so intelligent, so beautiful but you are not a man," you are ashamed of your condition as a woman. I wanted to act like a man because the man was the master.
>
> —Quoted in *Ms.*, October 1973

Melina Mercouri made many well-known films before becoming a Greek member of parliament and minister of culture.

Born Maria Amalia Mercouri in Athens into a politically prominent family, she attended the National Theatre Academy against her parents' wishes and appeared on stage in Athens and Paris. She made her film debut in Michael Cacoyannis's *Stella* in 1955. In 1956 she met the expatriate

American film director Jules Dassin (who became her second husband in 1966), and she starred in many of his productions, notably *He Who Must Die* (1957), *Never on Sunday* (1960), for which she won a Best Actress award at Cannes and an Oscar nomination, *Phaedra* (1961), the heist movie *Topkapi* (1964), and as a latter-day Medea in *A Dream of Passion* (1978). In 1967 she made her debut on Broadway in *Illya Darling*, a musical version of *Never on Sunday*, but it was not a great success.

Mercouri lived in exile in Paris and the United States during the 1967–74 rule of the Greek military junta. Her autobiography, *I Was Born Greek*, was published in 1971, the title a gesture of protest at the revoking of her Greek citizenship by the military regime. On its demise she returned home, and in 1977 she became a socialist member of parliament. As culture minister (1981–89; 1993–94) she pressed (unsuccessfully) for the repatriation of the Elgin marbles, sculptures that had been removed from the Parthenon in Athens and placed in the British Museum in the early 19th century.

Merman, Ethel (1909–1984) *American musical-comedy singer and actress*

One of the greatest stars of Broadway, Ethel Merman was noted for her powerful penetrating singing voice and her unrestrained style.

Born Ethel Zimmerman in Astoria, Long Island, New York, she shortened her surname to Merman in 1929 and worked in vaudeville, joining the team of Clayton, Jackson, and Durante (she later appeared in several Broadway shows with Jimmy Durante). In 1930 George Gershwin cast her in *Girl Crazy*, a new show starring Ginger ROGERS, in which Merman's singing of "I Got Rhythm" made her a star overnight. In George White's 1932 musical *Scandals* she popularized the song "Life Is Just a Bowl of Cherries." After a short stint in Hollywood Merman returned to Broadway to star in one of her biggest hits, Cole Porter's *Anything Goes* (1934), in which she sang "Anything Goes," "You're the Top," and "I Get a Kick Out of You."

Her subsequent Broadway shows included *Red, Hot and Blue* (1936), *Du Barry Was a Lady* (1939), *Panama Hattie* (1940), *Something for the Boys* (1943), and the Irving Berlin hits *Annie Get Your Gun* (1946) and *Call Me Madam* (1950). In 1959 she received the New York Drama Critics Award for her performance as the stage mother in *Gypsy*. In 1970 she took over the lead in *Hello, Dolly!*

Merman made many films, notably the screen versions of *Anything Goes* (1936) and *Call Me Madam* (1953). Her other films include *There's No Business Like Show Business* (1954) and *It's a Mad, Mad, Mad, Mad World* (1963). She was married and divorced four times.

Messalina, Valeria (*c.* 18–48) *Roman noblewoman*

The third wife of Emperor Claudius, Valeria Messalina was notorious for her sexual excesses and violent intrigues.

She married Claudius, her second cousin, a year or two before his accession in 41 and was the mother of two of his children, Brittanicus and OC-TAVIA (who became the wife of Emperor Nero). At court she was said to have harassed rivals, collected bribes, and even promoted executions. The gentle Claudius was quite unaware of such scandals, even removing from office, at her urging, those senators who were hostile to her. She held a public wedding ceremony with Gaius Silius, in mockery or defiance of Claudius, perhaps as prelude to a coup against the emperor. Claudius, however, was warned of the plot by his freedman Narcissus and ordered Messalina's execution in 48.

Meynell, Alice (1847–1922) *British poet and essayist*

Alice Meynell's poetry, journalism, and essays made her one of the best-known woman writers of the 19th century. She was also an active suffragist.

Born Alice Christiana Gertrude Thompson in Barnes, London, she spent much of her childhood in Italy, where she was educated by her father. Her mother was a concert pianist, and her sister became the famous military painter Elizabeth BUTLER. In about 1872 she converted to Roman Catholicism. Her first book of poems, *Preludes*, was published in 1875 and was highly praised by the writers John Ruskin and George ELIOT.

In 1877 she married Wilfrid Meynell, a journalist, with whom she had eight children. Together the Meynells edited several magazines, notably the Catholic *Weekly Register* (1881–95) and the monthly *Merry England* (1883–95). Mrs. Meynell also wrote for these publications and for other periodicals, including the *Pall Mall Gazette*, to which she contributed a weekly column in 1894, becoming its art critic from 1902 until 1905. At this time she was also actively involved in the suffragist movement and held a salon for such writers as George Moore, Coventry Patmore, and Alfred, Lord Tennyson.

Alice Meynell's prose writings were published in various essay collections, among them *The Rhythm of Life* (1893), *The Colour of Life* (1896), *The Children* (1897), and *Second Person Singular* (1921). She also published biographies of the painter Holman Hunt (1893) and Ruskin (1900). Her delicate and gentle poetry, which in some ways resembles that of both Elizabeth Barrett BROWNING and Christina ROSSETTI, appeared in volumes published in 1893, 1896, 1902, and 1917.

Michel, Louise (1830–1905) *French socialist, writer, and anarchist*

A tireless revolutionary throughout her life, who served several terms of imprisonment, Louise Michel became a member of the socialist Fabian Society during her time in London during the 1890s.

The illegitimate daughter of a landowner and a servant girl, Louise Michel was born at Vroncourt, near Domrémy. Raised by her grandfather, she was well educated and wrote poetry, later becoming a teacher. However, in 1852 she lost her job because of her outspoken criticisms of the political regime under Napoleon III. In 1856 she joined secret republican clubs while teaching in Paris. Around this time she also wrote several novels, including *Les Microbes humains* (The Human Microbes), on themes of social protest.

During the Franco-Prussian War (1870–71) Michel became an increasingly militant republican. After France was defeated in the war, a conservative government was established at Versailles. Michel joined the revolutionary Commune of Paris (1871) in opposition to this government: she oversaw social and educational policies as well as fighting at the barricades. Imprisoned at Versailles for preaching revolution through violence, she was tried and sentenced to life imprisonment in the penal colony on the French Pacific island of New Caledonia. She remained there until the amnesty of 1881, studying, teaching, and writing poetry.

On her return to France Michel immediately became politically active again, speaking at meetings throughout the country until her arrest in 1882. The following year she was sentenced to six years' imprisonment for inciting a mob to break into a bakery during a food riot. On her release in 1889 she resumed her political work, leading strikes in the Vienne district in 1890. Again arrested, Michel fled to London, knowing the authorities planned to have her certified insane. While living in East Dulwich, south London, she worked tirelessly to raise funds for European revolutionary groups. She returned to France in 1896, continuing her work and lecturing on the new developments in Russia until her death.

Midler, Bette (1945–) *American actress and comedienne*

Witty and ebullient, Bette Midler has had a successful career on stage, screen, and TV as well as being a noted recording artist and cabaret star.

Born in Honolulu, Hawaii, Bette Midler made her screen debut as an extra in *Hawaii* (1965). She then moved to New York, where she appeared in the stage shows *Fiddler on the Roof* (1966–69), *Salvation* (1970), and *Tommy* (1971; with the Seattle Opera Company). In 1972 she embarked on a successful career as a cabaret performer, becoming noted for her brash, satirical, witty, and often coarse style. She became nationally known after television appearances and such albums as *The Divine Miss M* (1973), for which she won a Grammy Award, and *Songs for the New Depression* (1975). Her later albums include *Broken Blossoms* (1979), *Midler Madness* (1980), and *Some People's Lives* (1990).

Resuming her film work, Midler gave an impressive performance in *The Rose* (1979), a story about a self-destructive rock star (based on Janis JOPLIN), for which she received an Oscar nomination. In 1985 she married an Argentinian commodity dealer, Martin von Haselberg. Her later movies include *Down and Out in Beverly Hills* (1986), *Ruthless People* (1986), *Outrageous Fortune* (1987), *Beaches* (1988), and *For the Boys* (1991), for which she received a second Oscar nomination. In 1996 Midler appeared with Diane KEATON and Goldie HAWN in the comedy *First Wives Club*.

Midori (1971–   ) *Japanese violinist*

A musician of exceptional talent, Midori acquired a worldwide reputation while still in her twenties.

Born Gota Mi Dori in Osaka, Japan, Midori showed great talent as a child violinist. Her mother, Setsu Goto, also a violinist, began teaching her daughter to play when she was very young. At the age of ten Midori moved to America to study, first with Dorothy DeLay at the Aspen Music School and then at the Juilliard School in New York.

Midori's talents so impressed the Indian conductor Zubin Mehta that he made her a soloist with the New York Philharmonic Orchestra on a tour of Asia, including Hong Kong, Korea, Thailand, and her native Japan. After returning to the United States, she played with the Boston Symphony, the Chicago Symphony, the Berlin Philharmonic, and the London Symphony orchestras under such conductors as Leonard Bernstein and André Previn.

Following numerous television appearances, Midori took part in the television show *Christmas at the White House* in 1983. In 1990, at the age of 19, she made her solo recital debut at Carnegie Hall, New York.

Milanov, Zinka (1906–1989) *Yugoslav opera singer*

A soprano of great power, Zinka Milanov was well known in the opera houses of Europe before becoming the leading dramatic soprano at the Metropolitan Opera in New York.

Born in Zagreb, Croatia, Zinka Milanov began to study singing at the Zagreb Academy of Music when she was 14 and made her first concert appearance a year later. After graduating from the academy, she made her operatic debut in 1927 in Ljubljana as Leonora in Verdi's *Il Trovatore*, after which she was a leading singer at the Zagreb opera until 1935. Later she sang in various opera houses in central Europe, notably the German Theatre in Prague, and in 1937, at the invitation of the conductor Arturo Toscanini, she performed the soprano part of Verdi's *Requiem* at the Salzburg Festival in Austria.

Later that year she made her debut at the Metropolitan Opera in New York, again singing the role of Leonora in *Il Trovatore*. Until her retirement in 1966 Milanov was the Metropolitan's leading dramatic soprano, specializing in the Italian repertoire, particularly Verdi's operas. The role that she most frequently performed was Aida.

Millay, Edna St. Vincent (1892–1950) *American poet*

> My candle burns at both ends;
> It will not last the night;
> But, ah, my foes, and, oh, my
>   friends—
> It gives a lovely light!
>   —"First Fig," *A Few Figs from
>   Thistles* (1920)

Described as "the foremost woman poet of America" during the 1920s and early 1930s, Edna St. Vincent Millay had been relegated to the status of minor poet by the 1970s because her style seemed old-fashioned and her viewpoint sentimental. Nevertheless, because of her early stance as an "emancipated woman," she has remained a heroine of the women's movement.

Born in Rockland, Maine, Millay spent her childhood years in various New England towns and was educated at Columbia University and then Vassar College. Her mother nurtured and supported her daughter's literary talent, and in 1912, while still a student, Millay's poem "Renascence" was published in *The Lyric Year*, an annual anthology of prizewinning verse. In 1917, after graduating, she moved to New York City, living an unconventional life in Greenwich Village. Her first volume of poetry, *Renascence and Other Poems*, appeared that year. Her second volume of poems, *A Few Figs from Thistles*, was published in 1920. These poems epitomized the spirit of the "flaming youth" of the 1920s with their demands for free love, equality, and freedom from conventional taboos.

In 1923 Millay married Eugen Jan Boissevan, a Dutch-born New York importer. Two years later the couple bought a farm at Austerlitz in upstate New York, where they spent the rest of their lives. Edna St. Vincent Millay was a prolific writer, producing 15 volumes of verse, notably *The Harp-Weaver and Other Poems*, for which she won the Pulitzer Prize for Poetry in 1923. She wrote five verse plays, three of them in one year (1921), and the libretto for Deems Taylor's opera *The King's Henchman* (1927). She also published several translations, including (with George Dillon) Baudelaire's *Flowers of Evil*.

She also produced essays and dialogues, some under the pen name Nancy Boyd, and short stories. Millay was a fine writer with a genuine sense of human compassion. However, her use of traditional poetic forms, including the sonnet sequence, seemed outmoded when her contemporaries were experimenting with free verse. She was elected to the National Institute of Arts and Letters in 1929 and the American Academy of Arts and Letters in 1940. A final volume of poems, *Mine the Harvest*, was published in 1954, after her death.

Miller, Lee (1907–1977) *American photographer*

Remembered for her evocative photographs of the liberation of Paris and of the concentration camps at Buchenwald and Dachau in 1945, Lee Miller was also widely known for her fashion photography.

Born in Poughkeepsie, New York State, she was taught the basics of photography by her father before travelling to Paris to study in 1925. She returned briefly to the United States (1927–29) to work at the Arts Students League in New York before going back to Paris as a student of the photographer and painter Man Ray. Miller remained in Paris until 1932, subsequently returning to New York to open her own photography studio, which she ran for a year.

In 1934 Miller married an Egyptian businessman, Aziz Eloui Bey, and lived in Egypt and Europe until she separated from him in 1939. She then moved to Britain with the painter Roland Penrose, whom she married in 1947, the year that their son Anthony was born.

In 1940 Miller became a photographer in London for *Vogue* magazine. She also took many photographs of wartime scenes; her book with E. Carter, *Grim Glory: Pictures of Britain under Fire*, appeared in 1941. From 1942 to 1945 she worked as the official war correspondent for the U.S. Forces and was assigned to cover the liberation of Paris and the terrible scenes created by German depravity at the concentration camps of Buchenwald and Dachau. After the war she returned to *Vogue* in London as a journalist and photographer, a position she held until 1954.

Retrospective exhibitions of Miller's work were held in New York (1985), London (1986), and San Francisco (1987). Her son's biography of her, *The Lives of Lee Miller*, appeared in 1985.

Millett, Kate (1934–) *American feminist writer and sculptor*

> Many women do not recognize themselves as discriminated against; no better proof could be found of the totality of their conditioning.
>
> —*Sexual Politics* (1970)

The care of children, even from the period when their cognitive powers first emerge, is infinitely better left to the best-trained practitioners of both sexes who have chosen it as a vocation, rather than to harried and all too frequently unhappy persons with little time or taste for the work of educating minds however young or beloved.

—As above

Kate Millett's *Sexual Politics* has been an extremely important book for women all over the world.

Katharine Murray Millett was born in St. Paul, Minnesota. After graduating from the University of Minnesota in 1956, she went on to earn an honours degree from Oxford University in 1958. Returning to the United States, she worked as a sculptor in Greenwich Village, New York, before moving to Japan, where she lived from 1961 to 1963 and held her first one-woman show. There she met the sculptor Fumio Yashima, who returned to New York with her. They were married in 1963.

Millett then taught English at Barnard College and became involved in the developing women's movement, becoming one of the early committee members of the National Organization for Women (NOW) in 1966. Her first book, *Sexual Politics* (1970), was conceived as a thesis for her PhD (which she obtained at Columbia in 1970). An attack on the patriarchal nature of society as the root cause of female oppression, her book was a rallying point for the feminist movement. In 1971 she made a film about women, *Three Lives*, and subsequently wrote *The Prostitution Papers* (1973). Her autobiography, *Flying*, appeared in 1974, and in 1977 she published *Sita*, the painful account of her doomed love affair with another woman.

Throughout the 1970s Millett was actively involved in feminist politics, particularly in demonstrations for the proposed Equal Rights Amendment to the U.S. Constitution. In 1979 she visited Iran to campaign for women's rights but was expelled by the new Islamic regime of Ayatollah Khomeini; her account of this experience, *Going to Iran*, was published in 1981. Millett also continued to work as a sculptor, mounting several solo exhibitions of her work in New York and Los Angeles, but found herself under increasing mental strain. *The Loony Bin Trip* (1990) is the harrowing story of her mental breakdown, hospitalization, and recovery. Her *The Politics of Cruelty* was published in 1994.

Minnelli, Liza (1946–) *American singer and film actress*

An Oscar-winning actress with a powerful singing voice and an explosive personality, Liza Minnelli is still best known for her performance in the film *Cabaret* (1972).

The daughter of actress and singer Judy GARLAND and her third husband, the film director Vincente Minnelli, Liza Minnelli was born in California. She appeared on screen for the first time at the age of two, when she joined her mother in *In the Good Old Summertime* (1949). In 1953 she danced on the New York stage while her mother sang. Ten years later Minnelli made her acting debut off-Broadway in *Best Foot Forward*. In 1965 she became the youngest-ever winner of a Tony Award for her performance in *Flora, the Red Menace*. By this time she had already made professional recordings and started a career in cabaret.

In 1968 Minnelli made her screen debut in *Charlie Bubbles*, going on the following year to star in *The Sterile Cuckoo*, for which she received an Oscar nomination. Her greatest international success came with *Cabaret* (1972), in which she played Sally Bowles, an American nightclub singer in 1930s Berlin (her first screen singing role). Based loosely on Christopher Isherwood's book *Goodbye to Berlin* (1929), the film won eight Oscar awards, including one for Minnelli as Best Actress. Her later films, notably *A Matter of Time* (1976), *New York, New York* (1981), and *Stepping Out* (1991) never quite matched the success of *Cabaret*, although *Arthur* (1981) and its sequel *Arthur II: On the Rocks* (1988) achieved considerable popularity. In 1978 Minnelli had returned to Broadway and won another Tony

Award in *The Act*. She made a television film, *A Time to Live*, in 1985.

Minnelli's private life has been almost as traumatic as her mother's – after being divorced three times, she underwent a cure for drug and drink problems at the Betty Ford Clinic. In 1987 she returned to the stage with enormously popular concert performances in New York's Carnegie Hall and in London.

Mirren, Helen (1946–) *British actress*

An actress of considerable versatility, with many successes on stage and screen, Helen Mirren is perhaps best known to the general public for her role as a detective in the TV series *Prime Suspect*.

Born in Southend-on-Sea to a Russian-born father and a Scottish mother, Helen Mirren (whose surname was Mironoff until she was ten) made her debut with the National Youth Theatre as Cleopatra when she was 18. However, instead of concentrating on an acting career, she trained as a teacher before joining the Royal Shakespeare Company in 1968. She spent most of the next 15 years with the company, playing such Shakespearean roles as Ophelia (1970), Lady Macbeth (1974), and Cressida. She also played contemporary parts, including roles in David Hare's *Teeth 'n' Smiles* (1975) and Ben Travers's *The Bed before Yesterday*, and spent a year touring Africa and North America with Peter Brook's experimental theatre troupe.

Mirren's screen career began in 1968 with Brook's *A Midsummer Night's Dream*. Her later films include *The Long Good Friday* (1980), *Excalibur* (1981), *Cal* (1984) – for which she won the Best Actress Award at the Cannes Film Festival – *The Mosquito Coast* (1986), *The Cook, The Thief, His Wife, and Her Lover* (1989), and *Some Mother's Son* (1997). Her highly acclaimed performance as the queen in *The Madness of King George* (1994) won her an Oscar nomination.

In the 1990s Mirren's fame has rested mainly on her starring role in the British television series *Prime Suspect*, in which she played Detective Chief Inspector Jane Tennison. The series won an Emmy Award and has been a success with both critics and audiences on both sides of the Atlantic. In 1994 Mirren returned to the London stage in a highly acclaimed production of Turgenev's *A Month in the Country*.

Mistinguett (1875–1956) *French music-hall performer*

Mistinguett's name is synonymous with Parisian music hall, especially the Moulin Rouge and the Folies-Bergère, where she appeared with Maurice Chevalier.

Born Jeanne-Marie Bourgeois in Enghien-les-Bains, she made her Paris debut at the Casino de Paris as a singer under the name Mistinguett in 1890. She appeared in light comedy and musical plays and was for a time part-owner of the Moulin Rouge cabaret, where she gave many performances.

Mistinguett became really popular around 1910 when she was partnered by Maurice Chevalier in sparkling revues at the Folies-Bergère. Her spectacularly lavish costumes and massive hats were her hallmark; she was also said to have had the most beautiful legs in the world (they were insured for 1,000,000 francs). In 1917 she performed in her own *Revue Mistinguett*.

As an actress Mistinguett specialized in portraying working-class Parisian women; she was also acknowledged as an original comedienne, giving her best performance in Sardou's *Madame Sans-Gêne* in 1921. Most of her career was spent in Paris, but she visited the United States in 1911 and 1951 and appeared in London in 1947. She retired in 1951. She published two volumes of memoirs: *Mistinguett and Her Confessions* (1938) and *Mistinguett, Queen of the Paris Night* (1954).

Mistral, Gabriela (1889–1957) *Chilean poet and diplomat*

Awarded the Nobel Prize for literature in 1945, Gabriela Mistral also became a symbol of the nationalist aspirations of her country.

Born Lucila Godoy de Alcayaga in Vicuña, northern Chile, the daughter of a schoolteacher, she herself taught for many years in rural schools. In 1912 she became the head of the Los Andes School in Punta Arenas in southern Chile. The grief she felt following the suicide of her fiancé in 1909 was expressed in the poetry she started to write at this time. In 1914 she received a prize for her poems *Sonetos de la muerte* (Sonnets of Death). Her second collection of poems, *Desolaçíon* (Desolation), which deals with themes of suffering, nature, and religious experience, was published in 1922. In that year she was sent by the Chilean government to Mexico to study aspects of the educational system. Returning in 1924, she was honoured for her "outstanding cultural work." The same year *Ternura*, a collection of songs for children, appeared.

In 1925 Mistral became a diplomat, representing Chile at the League of Nations. A year later she was appointed chair of the Institute of International Intellectual Co-operation in Paris, a post she held until 1939. In 1934 she also became Chilean consul in Madrid. Mistral was later made an honorary consul by the Chilean government with the option to open a consulate wherever she chose to settle. She held posts in Lisbon, Nice, Rio de Janeiro, and Los Angeles. In 1944 Mistral was diagnosed as having diabetes and moved to the United States for the sake of her health. She then served as a delegate to the United Nations.

Mistral's other writings include two more collections of poems, *Tala* (1938) and *Lagar* (1954), and novels on Chilean life.

Mitchell, Joni (1943–) *Canadian singer and songwriter*

> I've looked at life from both sides
> now
> From up and down, and still
> somehow
> It's life's illusions I recall
> I really don't know life at all.
>
> —"Both Sides Now" (1969)

Joni Mitchell is noted for her haunting voice and thoughtful introspective lyrics.

Born Roberta Joan Anderson, the daughter of a grocer, in McCleod, Alberta, Joni Mitchell was educated in Saskatoon, Saskatchewan. As a nine-year-old child she had polio but subsequently recovered from paralysis. Intending to become a commercial artist, she studied at Alberta College of Art in Calgary. However, having taught herself to play the guitar and the ukelele, she began to play and sing in coffee houses in Toronto in 1964, moving a year later to Detroit with her husband Chuck Mitchell. Soon separated from him, she became successful as a songwriter as well as a performer and moved on to New York City.

1967 saw the release of her albums *Songs to a Seagull* and *Clouds*. She then moved to California, where she became involved with the singer Graham Nash and made a series of reflective albums, including *Ladies of the Canyon* (1970), *Blue* (1971), *Court and Spark* (1974), and *The Hissing of Summer Lawns* (1975). In the late 1970s her style became more jazz-influenced, notably on the album *Mingus* (1979). Her more recent albums include *Dog Eat Dog* (1986), *Night Ride Home* (1991), and *Turbulent Indigo* (1994).

Joni Mitchell now lives on an estate 100 miles north of Vancouver. In 1997 she was reunited with the daughter she had by a boyfriend in 1965 and subsequently gave up for adoption.

Mitchell, Juliet (1934–) *New Zealand-born British feminist*

Mitchell has used psychoanalytical ideas to re-examine the patriarchal values of society.

Born in New Zealand, Mitchell moved with her family to Britain in 1944. She was educated at King Alfred School, Hampstead, London, and St. Anne's College, Oxford, where she graduated in English. After postgraduate studies in Oxford, in 1962 she became a lecturer at the University of Leeds for a year before taking up a similar appointment at the University of Reading (1965–70).

Since 1971 she has been a freelance broadcaster and writer about her adopted subject, psychoanalysis. Her early books *Women: the Longest Revolution* (1966), and *Women's Estate* (1972) interpreted the women's movement in orthodox Marxist terms. However, in *Psychoanalysis and Feminism* (1974) she expressed dissatisfaction with the role of women as defined in traditional socialist theory. With Ann OAKLEY she co-edited the essay collections *The Rights and Wrongs of Women* (1976), *What is Feminism?* (1986), and *Who's Afraid of Feminism?* (1998). She has sat on the editorial boards of several left-wing publications, notably *New Left Review* and *Social Praxis*.

Mitchell, Margaret (1900–1949)
American novelist

> Now he disliked talking business with her as much as he had enjoyed it before they were married. Now he saw that she understood entirely too well and he felt the usual masculine indignation at the duplicity of women. Added to it was the usual masculine disillusionment in discovering that a woman has a brain.
>
> —*Gone with the Wind* (1936)

Margaret Mitchell became internationally famous as the author of *Gone with the Wind*, one of the most successful bestsellers ever written.

She was born in Atlanta, Georgia, the daughter of the president of the Atlanta Historical Society, and was raised in a family deeply concerned with local history. Margaret attended Smith College in 1918, but after her mother's death the following year she returned to Atlanta to keep house for her father and brother.

After her marriage to John Marsh in 1925 she began to collect together the stories of the Civil War and Reconstruction that she had heard in her childhood, transforming them into a colourful historical novel of more than 1,000 pages. It tells the story of Scarlett O'Hara, an egotistical Southern belle, which revolves around her romantic involvements and her attempts to restore Tara, the family plantation badly damaged during the Civil War. This work, finally published in 1936 as *Gone with the Wind*, was her only book.

Winner of the Pulitzer Prize and the U.S. National Book Award, *Gone with the Wind* made publishing history, setting a sales record of 50,000 copies in one day and 1.5 million copies in its first year of publication. It was translated into some 30 languages and was the longest novel ever transcribed into Braille. The film based on the book, released in 1939 and starring Vivien LEIGH and Clark Gable, is probably the most popular motion picture ever made.

Margaret Mitchell died at the age of 49 in Atlanta after being hit by a car.

Mitchell, Maria (1818–1889)
American astronomer

> For women there are, undoubtedly, great difficulties in the path, but so much the more to overcome. First, no woman should say, "I am but a woman!" But a woman! What more can you ask to be?
>
> —Address to students, 1874

The first woman astronomer in the United States and the first woman to be elected to the American Academy of Arts and Sciences, Maria Mitchell is remembered for her discovery in 1847 of a new comet, for which she was awarded a gold medal by the king of Denmark.

She was born in Nantucket, Massachusetts, the daughter of William Mitchell, who started life as a cooper and became a school teacher and amateur astronomer of some distinction. Maria's brother, Henry Mitchell, became the leading American hydrographer. She herself was mainly educated by her father, whom she helped in the checking of chronometers for the local whaling fleet and in determining the longitude of Nantucket during the 1831 eclipse. From 1824 to 1842 she worked as librarian at the Nantucket Athenum, and in 1849 she became the first woman to be employed full time by the U.S. Nautical Almanac, with whom she computed the ephemerides of Venus (tables giving the future position of the planet). In 1865 she was appointed professor of astronomy and director of the observatory at the newly founded Vassar College in New York State.

Maria Mitchell was clearly fortunate to come from a highly talented family. She was also helped by coming from Nantucket, an area where women were expected to demonstrate an unusual degree of independence while the local men were absent on their long whaling voyages. It was also an area in which it was common for the average person to possess a familiarity with mathematics, astronomy, and navigation.

Mitchison, Naomi (1897–) *British writer*

A prolific writer and wide-ranging traveller, Naomi Mitchison wrote over 80 novels as well as travel books and three volumes of autobiography.

Born in Edinburgh, the daughter of the eminent scientist John Scott Haldane and the suffragist Kathleen Taylor, Naomi grew up in Oxford and studied science at the college that is now St. Anne's. She worked as a Voluntary Aid Detachment (VAD) nurse in London before marrying (in 1916) the barrister G. R. Mitchison, who later became a Labour MP and was created a baron in 1964. She herself was involved in politics, running as a Labour candidate in 1935, and also worked as a pacifist and in the women's movement, becoming an early campaigner for birth control.

Her first novel, *The Conquered*, was published in 1923. It was the first of a series of historical tales and romances set in pre-Christian times, including *When the Bough Breaks* (1924), *Cloud Cuckoo Land* (1925), *Black Sparta* (1928), *The Corn King and the Spring Queen* (1931), *The Swan's Road* (1954), and *Cleopatra's People* (1972). Her most controversial novel, *We Have Been Warned* (1935), with its explicit scenes of seduction, rape, and abortion, was censored.

In 1937 the Mitchisons moved to Argyll, where Naomi became involved in Scottish public affairs; in 1945 she became a member of the Argyll County Council, a position she held for the next 20 years. She was on the Highland Panel (1947–65) and the Highlands and Islands Advisory Council (1966–75). She also travelled extensively and in 1963 was made the Tribal Adviser and Mother to the Bakgatla of Botswana. After returning to Scotland, she continued to write, her later publications including the science fict

ion novel *Memoirs of a Spacewoman* (1962); the autobiographical volumes *Small Talk* (1973), *All Change Here* (1975), and *You May Well Ask* (1979); the travel book *Mucking Around* (1981); and her wartime diaries, published as *Among You Taking Notes* (1985).

Mitford, Jessica (Lucy) (1917–1996) *British-born American journalist and writer*

The younger sister of the novelist Nancy MITFORD, Jessica Mitford was noted for her books on controversial social and political issues.

The sixth of the seven children (six daughters and one son) of the eccentric 2nd Baron Redesdale, she was born in London and privately educated. Her only brother, Tom, was killed on active service in World War II in 1945. Two of her sisters, Unity and Diana, and her parents were fascist sympathizers. In 1937 she made headlines by eloping to Spain with Esmond Romilly, a nephew of Winston Churchill, who had joined the International Brigade to fight General Franco. They moved to the United States in 1939, but after joining the Canadian Air Force, Romilly was killed in action in World War II in 1941.

With her second husband, the lawyer Robert Treuhaft, whom she married in 1943, Mitford became involved with the American Communist Party, suffering considerable harassment during the McCarthy era. During the 1950s she was also secretary of the local Civil Rights Congress in Oakland, California.

In 1960 Mitford published an autobiography of her early life, *Daughters and Rebels*; a second volume of memoirs, *A Fine Old Conflict*, about her political activities, appeared in 1977. Her first investigative book, *The American Way of Death* (1963), was sharply critical of the American funeral industry. In *The Trial of Dr. Spock* (1969) she examined the 1968 conspiracy trial of the famous paediatrician. Another book, *Kind and Unusual Punishment: The Prison Business* (1973), attacked the U.S. penal system, and *The Ameri-*

can Way of Birth (1992) casts a critical eye on obstetrics.

Her other books include *Poison Penmanship: The Gentle Art of Muckraking* (1979), *Faces of Philip: A Memoir of Philip Toynbee* (1984), and *Grace Had an English Heart: The Story of Grace Darling, Heroine and Victorian Superstar* (1988). At the time of her death she was working on a new edition of *The American Way of Death*. She had been an American citizen since 1944.

Mitford, Mary Russell (1787–1855)
British writer

Mary Russell Mitford was best known for her sketches of English country life, but she also wrote several plays, one of which was performed at London's Drury Lane Theatre.

She was born in Alresford, Essex, the daughter of a country doctor, and was largely self-educated. As a child she won £20,000 in a lottery, which her father lavished on building a house in Reading. His extravagances forced the family to move to a labourer's cottage, and Mary turned to writing to support the family.

Her *Miscellaneous Poems* appeared in 1820, after which she wrote a series of sketches of English rural life for *Lady's Magazine*, which were widely popular. Collected as *Our Village*, the essays went through several editions between 1824 and 1832.

Notable among her other works are *Rienzi*, a tragedy, performed at Drury Lane in 1828; two earlier tragedies, *Julian* (1823) and *Foscari* (1826); and the novels *Belford Regis* (1835) and *Atherton* (1854). A memoir, *Recollections of a Literary Life*, appeared in 1852.

Mitford, Nancy (1904–1973) *British novelist*

> English women are elegant until they are ten years old, and perfect on grand occasions.
>
> —Quoted by L. and M. Cowan in *The Wit of Women* (1973)

The eldest of six daughters of the eccentric 2nd Baron Redesdale, Nancy Mitford was best known for her witty satirical novels about English upper-class society.

A sister of the writer Jessica MITFORD, she was born in London and educated privately. In 1928 she started writing articles for magazines; her first novel, *Highland Fling*, was published in 1931. Nancy married Peter Rennell Rodd, the son of Lord Kendell, in 1933 (they were divorced in 1958). During World War II she opened her house to many of the Free French led by General de Gaulle, whom she greatly admired. After the war she settled in France.

Her novels, the best known of which are *The Pursuit of Love* (1945), *Love in a Cold Climate* (1949), *The Blessing* (1959), and *Don't Tell Alfred* (1960), were based on her own past and feature a cast of eccentrics whose views and antics reveal the social foibles of the English aristocracy. Her admiration of French culture led to such biographical studies as *Madame de Pompadour* (1954), *Voltaire in Love* (1957), and *The Sun King* (1966).

Nancy Mitford is also remembered as co-editor, with A. S. C. Ross, of a volume of essays, *Noblesse Oblige: An Inquiry into the Identifiable Characteristics of the English Aristocracy* (1956), in which she popularized the terms "U" (upper class) and "non-U" to describe social characteristics, particularly in speech. She had previously defined the differences between "U" and "non-U" in her essay "The English Aristocracy," published in *Encounter* magazine. A clever venture into social semantics, *Noblesse Oblige* also contributed notably to comic literature.

Mnouchkine, Ariane (1938–)
French theatre director

Ariane Mnouchkine is best known as the founder in 1964 of the collective Théâtre du Soleil in Paris with 40 amateur student actors; she remains one of Europe's leading directors.

Born in Boulogne-sur-Seine, the daughter of a film producer, she first became involved in theatre while at Oxford University. On her return to Paris she founded a student theatre group, the Association Théâtrale des Étudiants, putting on plays and organizing workshops.

In 1961 she directed a production of *Ghengis Khan* among Roman ruins. After travelling in Cambodia and Japan, she founded her Théâtre du Soleil, in which all members of the company collaborate in the productions. The early productions of this group, including Maxim Gorky's *Les Petits Bourgeois*, were influenced by Stanislavsky's theories of naturalistic acting. Their first major success came in 1967 with their production of Arnold Wesker's *The Kitchen*. Influenced by theatrical traditions as diverse as that of the Chinese, the Italian commedia dell'arte, and the Greek classical theatre, their successes included *Clowns* (1968) and *1789*, an epic of the French Revolution that was first produced, to great acclaim, in 1970.

The same year the French government gave the company a disused munitions warehouse as a permanent base. Later productions include *L'Age d'or* (1975), *Mephisto* (1979), and Hélène CIXOUS's *L'Indiade*, a political drama about the independence and partition of India. In 1983 the company produced *The King of Cambodia*, a play about Prince Sihanouk, also by Hélène Cixous.

The Théâtre du Soleil, in spite of its success, is still run on egalitarian lines, with Mnouchkine often found selling programmes or collecting tickets at the door.

Model, Lisette (1901–1983) *Austrian-born American photographer and teacher*

Best known for her photographs of people, in which her subjects often almost fill the frame, Lisette Model left an indelible mark on the history of photography.

She was born Elise Amelie Felicie Stern in Vienna, the daughter of a Jewish doctor and musician, who changed the family name to Seybert in 1902 in response to a growing climate of anti-Semitism in Austria. Showing a considerable talent for music, in 1918 Model began formal piano lessons with Edward Steuermann and then studied (1920–24) under Arnold Schoenberg.

After her father's death in 1924 the family moved to France, where Lisette studied singing in Paris. Introduced to photography in 1933 by her sister Olga, she began photographing members of the bourgeoisie on vacation on the Promenade des Anglais in Nice the following summer. Framed at eye level and closely cropped in the darkroom, Model's pictures were published in the French magazine *Regards* in 1935 and under the title "Why France Fell" in the American newspaper *PM* in 1941.

In 1935 she met the artist Evsei (Evsa) Konstantinovich Model in Nice, and they married in Paris in 1937 before emigrating the following year to the United States to escape the political situation in Europe. Model concentrated on photographing street life, focusing throughout the 1950s on people, nightclubs, jazz musicians, and the curious reflections cast from the streets onto shop windows. The *PM* portfolio caught the attention of the art director Alexey Brodovitch, who hired her as a photographer for *Harper's Bazaar* (1941–55).

Model turned to teaching in 1949, first at the California School of Fine Arts in San Francisco and then at the New School for Social Research in New York (1951–82), which awarded her an honorary doctorate in the fine arts in 1981. Notable among her students was Diane ARBUS, later an acclaimed photographer herself. Model was awarded a Guggenheim Fellowship in 1965 and participated in numerous solo and group exhibitions in the United States and abroad, including Leading Photographers, a travelling exhibition series organized by the Museum of Modern Art in New York, which toured from 1949 to 1954.

Retrospective exhibitions of Model's work were held at the New Orleans Museum of Art in 1981 and at the National Gallery of Canada in Ottawa in 1990. She continued lecturing and taking photographs until almost the end of her life.

Modersohn-Becker, Paula (1876–1907) *German painter*

Considered a forerunner of expressionism, Modersohn-Becker created figure paintings that – since her death

– have been recognized as some of the most powerful in the 20th century, although they were considered shocking during her lifetime.

Born in Dresden, Paula Becker trained in London and (from 1896 to 1898) at the School for Women Artists in Berlin. In 1897 she visited the artists' colony at Worpswede, near Bremen, settling there the following year and becoming a pupil of the painter Mackensen. Her first exhibition, which was held in 1899, was not well received; she subsequently moved to Paris, spending some time at the Académie Colarossi and the Ecole des Beaux Arts.

In 1901 she returned to Germany and married Otto Modersohn. Between 1903 and 1907 she returned to Paris four times and was influenced by the group of artists, including Matisse and Derain, known as Les Fauves, whose work she saw exhibited in 1905. She was also influenced by Gauguin and Van Gogh, whose emphasis on line and strong use of colour she introduced into German painting. Her studies of country women and children, notably *Old Peasant Woman* (1904), reveal these influences.

Modersohn-Becker's work includes landscapes, still-life studies, and portraits, such as that of her close friend Rainer Maria Rilke (1906), who became her biographer, as well as several self-portraits. In 1907 her husband persuaded her to return to Worpswede, where she gave birth to their daughter. However, Modersohn-Becker died of a heart attack within a month.

Modjeska, Helena (1844–1909) *Polish-born American actress*

Renowned as one of the finest tragediennes of the 19th century, Helena Modjeska rivalled Sarah BERNHARDT and Eleanora DUSE.

The daughter of a musician, Helena Opid was born in Cracow. She ran away from home in 1860 to form a theatre company with her actor husband Gustave Modjeska. After leaving him, she joined a Warsaw theatre company and in 1868 married a Polish aristocrat, Charles Chlapowski. Until 1876, when she and her husband emigrated to the United States, she was the most admired actress in Poland, known for her portrayal of both classical and Shakespearean roles as well as more modern characters.

Having learned English, Modjeska toured the United States with great success and revisited Poland for a year in 1878. She also performed in London (1880–82 and 1890), starring in such plays as Friedrich Schiller's *Maria Stuart* and Shakespeare's *Romeo and Juliet*, and was highly acclaimed as Ophelia and as Lady Macbeth. After visiting Poland again in 1903, she retired from the stage, giving a final farewell performance in New York at the Metropolitan Opera House in 1905. Her autobiographical *Memories and Impressions* was published in 1910, after her death.

Modotti, Tina (1896–1942) *Italian-born Mexican photographer and revolutionary*

Tina Modotti is best known for her photographic portraits of Mexican peasants and her still lifes and plant studies. Her vision contributed significantly to the burgeoning Mexican cultural renaissance of the 1920s. She is also renowned for her dedication to her revolutionary ideals.

Born Assunta Adelaide Luigia Modotti in Udine, Italy, Tina Modotti was educated in Italian and Austrian schools until 1908, when she went to work in a silk factory in Udine to help support her family. In 1913 she emigrated to San Francisco, working first as a seamstress and then as a model and freelance dressmaker. In 1917 she married an American painter-poet of French-Canadian origin, Robaix ("Robo") de l'Abrie Richey. The couple moved to Los Angeles in 1918 and lived a bohemian life with artists, poets, and dancers. Modotti acted in several silent films in 1920 and 1921, including *The Tiger's Coat* (1920).

In 1920 Modotti met Edward Weston, a friend of her husband, and almost immediately they began an intense relationship of mutual influence. After the death of her husband from smallpox in 1922 Modotti encouraged Weston to move to Mexico with her, as she had become interested in Mexico's artistic and cultural activity. In 1923 they took up residence in Mexico City. Modotti, deeply influenced by Weston's purity of vision and further inspired by the political and cultural upheavals of the day, began to produce her best work, including *Roses, Mexico* (1925), a bold study of four densely packed roses (which achieved renown in 1991 when a print was sold at a then-record auction price of $165,000). In Mexico Modotti and Weston developed strong ties with the country's most illustrious artists and writers, among them Diego Rivera and José Clemente Orozco.

After Weston moved back to California in 1926, Modotti remained in Mexico City, joining the Communist Party in 1927. At this time she was photographing murals and editing the magazine *Mexican Folkways*. She also began an affair with the Cuban revolutionary Julio Antonio Mella in 1928, but following his assassination in 1929, Modotti was tried for complicity in his murder. Although she was found innocent, her radical politics led to her deportation in 1930, and she lived for a while in Berlin, publishing some of her photographs in *Arbeiter Illustrierte Zeitung*, before moving to the Soviet Union in 1931. There she abandoned photography for politics, carrying out communist missions in fascist Europe and working for the Communist Party in the early years of Stalinism. In 1935 she went to Spain, where she worked for the organization Red Aid during the Spanish Civil War. In 1939 she returned to Mexico under a false passport, living more or less in isolation until her death from a heart attack.

Monk, Meredith (1942–) *American choreographer and composer*

Meredith Monk's innovative works combine music, movement, words, and objects, often in unconventional locations. She formed her own company, The House, in 1968.

Monk was born in Lima, Peru, the daughter of a professional singer. While continuing to study music and beginning to compose, she studied modern dance with Bessie Schönberg at Sarah Lawrence College, graduating in 1964. Briefly working with the experimental Judson Dance Theater, she soon established an individual approach to creative work. In 1966 she presented her *16 Millimeter Earrings*, adding film to the music and movement media she was already using. Monk then added elements from the environment to her components: *Vessel* (1971), for example, began in her own home and concluded in an empty car park.

Quarry (1985) explored the effects of World War II on a child, while *Atlas* (1992) was based on the life of British explorer Alexandra Daniels. *American Archaeology No. 1: Roosevelt Island*, a multimedia, site-specific piece for the island in the middle of Manhattan's East River, had its premiere in 1994. The first act was presented in a park in late afternoon; the second was performed in and around an abandoned hospital after dark. The idyllic setting of the first act contrasted with the bleak vision of the second, recalling the island's history as a repository for the insane and the destitute. A peacefully lighted hilltop was a sign of hope at the end.

For all her works Monk composed the music as well as the dances, often requiring the company members (herself included) to sing as well as to dance and act.

Monroe, Harriet (1860–1936) *American poet and editor*

Harriet Monroe is best known as the founder and editor of *Poetry*, the most important American magazine devoted to verse, which first appeared in Chicago in October 1912. In it she published poems by many of the leading experimenters of the 1910s and 1920s – Wallace Stevens, Ezra Pound, T. S. Eliot, Carl Sandburg, Vachel Lindsay, Elinor WYLIE, and Hart Crane among them. The magazine continues to appear.

She was born in Chicago, Illinois, and educated at a private school in Georgetown, D.C. Having something of a reputation in Chicago as a poet, she was selected to write the Columbian Ode for the city's world's fair in

1893. In 1896 she published a biography of the architect John Wellborn Root, her brother-in-law, and in 1903 she issued five verse plays under the title *The Passing Show*.

Her own poetry – collected in the volumes *Valeria and Other Poems* (1892), *You and I* (1914), and *Chosen Poems* (1935) – is generally undistinguished. However, her autobiography, *A Poet's Life: Seventy Years in a Changing World* (1937), is a fascinating chronicle of the literary revolution of the early 20th century, particularly its development in Chicago. She died in Arequipa, Peru.

Monroe, Marilyn (1926–1962) *American film star*

> I have too many fantasies to be a housewife…I guess I *am* a fantasy.
>
> —Quoted by Gloria Steinem in "Marilyn: The Woman Who Died Too Soon," *The First Ms. Reader* (ed. by Francine Klagsbrun)

> The times being what they were, if she hadn't existed we would have had to invent her, and we did, in a way. She was the fifties' fiction, the lie that a woman has no sexual needs, that she is there to cater to, or enhance, a man's needs.
>
> —Molly Haskell, *From Reverence to Rape*

Marilyn Monroe's blonde sexiness, girlish voice, and apparent vulnerability brought her worldwide adulation. However, the pressures of Hollywood proved too much, and her life ended tragically in suicide. What remains is a legend.

Born Norma Jean Baker, the illegitimate daughter of Gladys Baker, a film-negative cutter who was in and out of mental hospitals during Marilyn's childhood, she spent most of her early years in foster homes and orphanages. At the age of 14 she married Jim Dougherty. She found work as a photographic model, and by 1946 she was quite successful, appearing in national magazines. That same year she was divorced and began to find bit parts in films, taking acting lessons in 1948 before signing with Columbia Pictures.

In the film world she was first ridiculed as a "dumb blonde" but was soon transformed into a "sex goddess." She made movies for several years but did not really claim the public's attention until she appeared in the Bette DAVIS vehicle *All About Eve* (1950). During the next four years she made over 20 films, the best being *Don't Bother to Knock* (1952), *Niagara* (1952), *How to Marry a Millionaire* (1953), and *Gentlemen Prefer Blondes* (1953). In 1954 she married the baseball star Joe diMaggio but divorced him nine months later. She was already having anxiety problems at the studios, being constantly late and highly nervous. Ambitious to be a serious actress, she studied with Lee Strasberg at the Actors' Studio in New York City in 1955, after making *The Seven Year Itch*. Two of her most popular and successful films followed: *Bus Stop* (1956) and *The Prince and the Showgirl* (1957), in which she appeared with Laurence Olivier.

In 1956 she was converted to Judaism before marrying the playwright Arthur Miller. In *Some Like It Hot* (1959) she displayed a genuine flair for comedy. Monroe's last film, *The Misfits*, written for her by her husband, was released in 1961. During the filming she was depressed and suffering from exhaustion, taking both pills and alcohol to keep going. She divorced Miller just before the film opened. Suspended by her studio for chronic absences and lateness, she died from an overdose of sleeping tablets in Los Angeles on August 5, 1962, just as she was trying to start work again on *Something's Got to Give*.

Her life and death have been the subject of endless speculation and countless books.

Montagu, Elizabeth (1720–1800) *British writer and intellectual*

> Wit in women is apt to have bad consequences; like a sword without a scabbard, it wounds the wearer and provokes assailants. I am sorry to say the generality of women who have excelled in wit have failed in chastity.
>
> —Quoted by Angeline Goreau in *Reconstructing Aphra* (1750)

The original "bluestocking," Elizabeth

Montagu was so called because she allowed the wearing of blue stockings, rather than formal black silk stockings, at her literary gatherings.

Born Elizabeth Robinson, the daughter of a country gentleman in York, she was brought up by her grandmother. After a thorough education she married Edward Montagu, the grandson of the 1st Earl of Sandwich, in 1742. After the death of their son in 1744 she devoted herself to the literary salons that she hosted at her London houses in Mayfair's Hill Street and later in Portman Square. She became a much-loved patron of young writers and artists; Samuel Johnson is known to have thought highly of her conversational skills.

With the exception of three dialogues that the poet Lord Lyttelton allowed her to add to his *Dialogues of the Dead* (1760), her only published work was the anonymous *Essay on the Writings and Genius of Shakespeare* (1769), in which she ably defends Shakespeare against the criticism of Voltaire. Her private letters more fully illustrate the literary fashions of the times.

After the death of her husband in 1776 Elizabeth Montagu became sufficiently rich to employ the leading architects and painters of her time, including Robert Adam, Capability Brown, and Angelica KAUFFMANN, on the decoration of her town and country houses.

See also CARTER, ELIZABETH; MORE, HANNAH.

Montagu, Lady Mary Wortley
(1689–1762) *English writer and feminist*

> A woman, till five-and-thirty, is only looked upon as a raw girl, and can possibly make no noise in the world till about forty. I don't known what your ladyship may think of this matter; but 'tis a considerable comfort to me, to know there is upon earth such a paradise for old women.
>
> —Letter to Lady Rich, September 20, 1716

> To say truth, there is no part of the world where our sex is treated with so much contempt as in England...I think it the highest injustice our knowledge must rest concealed, and be as useless to the world as gold in the mine.
>
> —Letter, 1753

One of the most versatile women of her time, Lady Mary Wortley Montagu is remembered for her poetry, her essays, and her letters from Turkey, where her husband was British ambassador.

The daughter of Evelyn Pierrepont, Duke of Kingston, she was born in London. Her mother, Lady Mary Fielding, was a cousin of the novelist Henry Fielding. Mary was educated at home, acquiring a good knowledge of English and French literature and also writing verses and teaching herself Latin.

In 1712 she defied her father by eloping with Edward Wortley Montagu, a Whig MP. After her husband took up a treasury post in London in 1714, Lady Mary became well known in court and literary circles for her beauty and wit; she made many literary friends, including Alexander Pope and John Gay. In 1715, however, she contracted smallpox, which left her scarred.

From 1716 to 1718 her husband was ambassador to Turkey, and Lady Mary accompanied him to Constantinople. Having observed the Turkish practice of inoculation against smallpox, she allowed her son to be vaccinated – the first English person to be so treated – and went on to promote the practice in England. Her literary reputation is based largely on a brilliant series of letters, the 52 "Turkish embassy letters," she wrote on her return. Based on her diary and correspondence during her stay, they contain vivid descriptions of Turkish life and culture, including the sultan's harem. They were published in 1763, after her death.

Back in England Lady Mary established a literary salon. She quarrelled with Pope in 1723, and from 1728 he frequently attacked her in his satires. Her own verse responses to the writings of others included vigorous attacks on Pope and Swift. In 1735 she wrote a play, *Simplicity*, based on a comedy by Pierre de Marivaux, but this was not performed until 1967. Her *Nonsense of Common-Sense* essays, which appeared in 1737–38, deal with a variety of issues, including politics, feminism, and moral cynicism.

In 1736 Lady Mary became infatuated with the Italian writer Francesco Algorotti; she proposed that they live together in Italy, but when she went there in 1739, on the pretext of travelling for her health, he failed to join her. Nonetheless, she remained in Italy for more than 20 years except for a four-year stay in France (1742–46). Although she suffered from several periods of serious illness and the breakdown in 1756 of a ten-year relationship with the young Count Ugolino Palazzi, she did not return to England until after the death of her husband in 1761. Her letters from Italy to her daughter include charming details of her simple lifestyle there, as well as criticisms of the books she read.

Montespan, Marquise de (1641–1707) *French noblewoman*

Madame de Montespan, a charming and witty aristocrat, was the mistress of King Louis XIV from 1667 until 1680.

Born Françoise Athénaïs de Rochechouart-Mortemart in Tonnay-Charente, the daughter of the Duke de Mortemart, she married the Marquis de Montespan in 1663. The marriage was an unhappy one and the couple were constantly in debt. Beautiful, witty, and exceedingly ambitious, Madame de Montespan became lady-in-waiting to Queen Marie Thérèse in 1664. She plotted to win the king's attention by becoming an intimate of Louise de La Vallière, the king's mistress. By 1667 she had replaced La Vallière in the king's affections and became his mistress, although she was not legally separated from her husband until 1674.

The children she bore the king were legitimated by him. Her three sons became the Duc du Maine, the Comte de Vexin, and the Comte de Toulouse. Her youngest daughter, Françoise

Marie, Mademoiselle de Blois, later married Philippe II, Duc d'Orléans, who was regent during the minority of Louis XV.

At court Madame de Montespan encouraged such writers as Racine and De Boileau. However, she was not popular and in January 1680 she was implicated in what came to be known as the "Poisoning Scandal." There was evidence that she had attempted, by potions and "conjurations," to retain the king's love and had participated in Black Masses to bring about the king's death should he abandon her. The evidence was suppressed because of her position, but she lost the king's affection, which was then directed towards their children's governess, Madame de MAINTENON. Madame de Montespan retired from court in 1691 to the Paris Convent of St. Joseph.

Montessori, Maria (1870–1952) *Italian physician and educator*

> And if education is always to be conceived along the same antiquated lines of a mere transmission of knowledge, there is little to be hoped from it in the bettering of man's future. For what is the use of transmitting knowledge if the individual's total development lags behind?
>
> *—The Absorbent Mind* (1967)

> If help and salvation are to come, they can only come from the children, for the children are the makers of men.
>
> —As above

The originator of the method of education that bears her name, Maria Montessori was also the first woman to obtain a medical degree in Italy.

Maria Montessori was born in Chiaravelle, Ancona. After graduating in medicine from the University of Rome in 1896, she worked in the university's psychiatric clinic. There she became interested in the education of children with learning difficulties, and at a state school for such children she achieved remarkable results, using methods similar to those developed by the French physician and teacher Jean Itard and his student Edouard Séguin. Convinced that such methods would be even more effective with normal children, Montessori undertook further study and research. From 1904 to 1908 she was professor of anthropology at the University of Rome, while at the same time working as a government school inspector and a medical doctor. In 1907 she opened the first Montessori school in the slums of Rome, enrolling neglected children aged three to six. The mental and social development of the children in this school and others established under her direction amazed observers and soon attracted international attention.

In 1909 Montessori produced her book *Il metodo della pedagogia scientifica* (published in English as *The Montessori Method*, 1912), in which she gave a detailed account of her system. She stressed the need for each child to develop at his or her own pace, believing that voluntary learning and the development of the senses through the child's natural creative potential would increase the child's self-discipline and self-confidence.

During the 1920s and 1930s she travelled and conducted courses in many countries. Many of her ideas have been incorporated into nursery education in Europe and the United States, and there are Montessori kindergartens and schools around the world. She died at Noordwijk in the Netherlands.

Montez, Lola (1818–1861) *British dancer and adventuress*

Lola Montez was an indifferent dancer, but her beauty and charm won the affection of King Ludwig of Bavaria, whose policies she greatly influenced.

She was born Marie Dolores Eliza Rosanna Gilbert in Limerick, Ireland, the daughter of a British army officer who was stationed there. Marie was educated in Montrose, Scotland, and in Paris. Determined to become a "Spanish" dancer, she adopted the stage name Lola Montez. Her career proved to be only moderately successful, but her great beauty captivated audiences on the Continent, notably the elderly King Ludwig of Bavaria, whose mistress she became in 1847. Having been granted the title Countess of Landsfeld, she exerted great influence over the king's policies and so angered his subjects that she was obliged to flee in 1848.

Her many other amorous liaisons included romances with Franz Liszt and Alexandre Dumas the Elder. She continued to dance, performing in the United States and Australia, and was married three times (being widowed by one husband and divorcing two others) before settling in New York. There she spent the last two years of her life doing charitable works.

Montgomery, L(ucy) M(aud) (1874–1942) *Canadian novelist*

> One spring I was looking over my notebook of plots...I found a faded entry written many years before: "Elderly couple apply to orphan asylum for a boy. By mistake a girl is sent them." I thought this would do. The result was *Anne of Green Gables*.
>
> —Quoted in *Contemporary Authors*

L. M. Montgomery is best known as the author of the perennially popular girls' story *Anne of Green Gables* and its many sequels, which chronicle Anne's life from childhood to motherhood.

Lucy Maud Montgomery was born at Clifton, Prince Edward Island. Because her mother died when she was a baby, she was raised by her grandparents. After training as a schoolteacher at the Prince of Wales College, Charlottetown, she studied for a time at Dalhousie College, Halifax, Nova Scotia. She then returned home to care for her grandmother for 13 years. *Anne of Green Gables* appeared in 1908, followed by *Anne of Avonlea* (1909), *Anne of the Island* (1915), and *Anne's House of Dreams* (1917). Another sequel, *Rilla of Ingleside* (1921), provides a fascinating description of the impact of World War I on the island community.

In 1911 Montgomery married Ewan MacDonald, a Presbyterian minister, and moved to Leaskdale, Ontario. In *Magic for Marigold* (1921) she brilliantly describes the terrors and mysteries of early childhood. *Anne of Windy Poplars* appeared in 1936.

Montpensier, Duchesse de (1627–1693) *French princess*

The Duchesse de Montpensier, better known as Mademoiselle or La Grande Mademoiselle, spent much of her early life involved in political intrigue against her cousin King Louis XIV.

Anne Marie Louise d'Orléans was born in Paris, the daughter of Gaston, Duc d'Orléans (brother of King Louis XIII), and his wife, Marie de Bourbon, Duchesse de Montpensier in her own right. Through her mother, who died when Mademoiselle was a week old, she became the richest heiress in France.

Several royal suitors were considered for her, including Charles II of England, when he was still without a throne; her cousin, the future Louis XIV; and Ferdinand III, the Holy Roman Emperor. However, she and her father became involved in the Fronde (1650–53), a series of revolts led by some of France's leading princes, including the Prince de Condé, against the king and his minister Mazarin. In March 1652 Mademoiselle led an army that drove the king's forces from Orléans. In July she ordered the guns of the Bastille in Paris to be turned on the king's troops as they sought to destroy Condé's army at the Porte St. Antoine. When the king returned to Paris in October, however, she and her father went into exile. In 1657 she returned to court but was banished again in 1662 for refusing to marry Alfonso VI of Portugal.

In 1669 Mademoiselle fell in love with the future Duc de Lauzun, who was greatly beneath her in rank. In December 1670 the king agreed to their marriage but later refused and had Lauzun imprisoned for almost ten years. On his release Lauzun and Mademoiselle were secretly married in 1681 or 1682, but the marriage was unhappy, and they separated in 1684. She spent the rest of her life doing religious and charitable works and writing. As well as her memoirs, she wrote two short novels – *Vie de Mme. de Fouquerolles* (1653) and *La Princesse de Paphlagonie* (1659) – and a volume of literary portraits, including one of Louis XIV, which was published in 1659 under the name of her secretary, Jean Regnauld de Segrais.

Moore, Demi (1962–   ) *American actress*

A sex symbol of the 1990s, the beautiful, husky-voiced Demi Moore has had a highly publicized career in films.

Born Demi Guynes in New Mexico, she began a modelling career at the age of 15 in Los Angeles. This led to television work in a soap opera, followed by her film debut in *Blame It on Rio* in 1984. Her first starring role came the same year in *No Small Affair*. In 1985 she starred in *St. Elmo's Fire* with Rob Lowe, who was also her costar in *About Last Night…*(1986).

Moore's first major success came with *Ghost* (1990); in 1991 she coproduced the thriller *Mortal Thoughts* and appeared in the comedy *The Butcher's Wife*. She was highly acclaimed for her performance opposite Tom Cruise in the military courtroom drama *A Few Good Men* (1992), and in *Indecent Proposal* (1993) she played opposite Robert Redford as a woman offered $1M to have an adulterous affair. *Disclosure* (1995), a tale of sexual harassment, was followed by *Striptease* (1996), in which she played a stripper. Although both this film and *G.I. Jane* (1997), in which she played an army trainee, attracted huge prerelease publicity, their box-office performance was disappointing.

Moore received perhaps the greatest publicity of her career in 1991, when she appeared naked and heavily pregnant on the front cover of the magazine *Vanity Fair*. She is married to the actor Bruce Willis.

Moore, Marianne (Craig) (1887–1972) *American poet*

Known for its qualities of irony and sharply observed detail, Marianne Moore's innovative poetry shows the influence of imagism – a literary movement that stressed the importance of precise imagery. Embracing a wide variety of subject matter, ranging from animals to current affairs, it is also marked by unconventional forms of stanza and poetic metre.

Marianne Moore was born in Kirkwood, St. Louis, Missouri, and attended Bryn Mawr College, Pennsylvania, graduating in 1909. She taught at the Indian School in Carlisle from 1911 to 1915. In 1918 she moved to New York, living first in Manhattan and then in Brooklyn, where she spent most of her life and was a devoted fan of the Brooklyn Dodgers baseball team. She worked as a secretary until 1921 and as a librarian from 1921 to 1925.

In 1915 some of her poems were published by T. S. Eliot in *The Egoist*, a British periodical specializing in imagist verse, and in *Poetry*, a Chicago-based magazine that published avant-garde poets. *Poems*, her first volume, appeared in Britain in 1921; it was published in the United States in 1924 as *Observations*, winning the Dial Award. From 1925 to 1929 Moore was acting editor of *The Dial*, an influential literary magazine. In 1952, following the publication of her *Collected Poems* (1951), she won the Pulitzer Prize, the U.S. National Book Award, and the Bollingen Prize. In 1954 she published a verse translation of *The Fables of La Fontaine*. Later publications include *O To Be a Dragon* (1959), *The Arctic Fox* (1964), and *Tell Me, Tell Me* (1966).

Moore's work is admired by those who place a high value on poetic craftsmanship; T. S. Eliot praised her "swift dissolving image," and William Carlos Williams saw in her poetry "a swiftness impaling beauty."

Moore, Mary Tyler (1936–) *American actress*

Best known as a popular TV comedy actress, Mary Tyler Moore starred in her own highly successful TV show, *The Mary Tyler Moore Show*, from 1970 to 1977. She was admitted to America's TV Hall of Fame in 1985.

Mary Tyler Moore was born in Brooklyn, New York, and trained as a dancer. She first appeared on television in 1955, singing and dancing on Hotpoint appliances in a series of commercials. Small parts in various TV series followed, including one in *Richard Diamond, Private Eye*, which ran from 1957 to 1959. Her big-screen debut came in 1961 with *X-15*.

The same year she became the costar in the TV comedy series *The Dick Van Dyke Show*, for which she won Emmy Awards in 1964 and 1965. Her enormous popularity in this series, which ran until 1966, led to her playing the lead in a Broadway production of *Breakfast at Tiffanys* (1966). After some minor film roles she returned to television work in 1970 with her own show, for which she won Emmy Awards in 1973, 1974, and 1976 and the Series Actress of the Year in 1974.

In 1980 Moore received an Oscar nomination for her role in Robert Redford's *Ordinary People* in addition to a Special Tony Award for her performance on Broadway in *Whose Life Is It Anyway?* Sadly, however, in this same year Moore's 24-year-old son committed suicide. She went on to appear in such TV films as *Heartsounds* (1984), *Lincoln* (1988), *The Last Best Year* (1990), and – notably – *Stolen Babies* (1993), in which her portrayal of a child dealer earned her an Emmy Award for Outstanding Supporting Actress. She also appeared in the films *Six Weeks* (1982) and *Just Between Friends* (1986). The production company MTM Enterprises, which she formed with her second husband, Grant Tinker, in 1970, has been responsible for such TV shows as *Lou Grant* and *Hill Street Blues*.

Morante, Elsa (1912–1985) *Italian novelist, poet, and short-story writer*

One of Italy's most important writers of the 20th century, Elsa Morante won many prominent prizes for her novels. She was married (1941–62) to the Italian writer Alberto Moravia.

Elsa Morante was born and educated in Rome. Her first collection of short stories, *Il gioco segreto* (Secret Jest), was published in 1941. Her first novel, *Menzogna e sortilegio* (Lies and Riddles), appeared in 1948, winning the Viareggio Prize, and was published in English as *House of Liars* in 1951. It was followed by *L'isola di Arturo* (1957; *Arturo's Island*, 1959), a tale of childhood and the loss of innocence, which won her the prestigious Strega Prize.

Morante's major work, *La storia* (1974; *History*, 1977), is set in Italy during World War II and describes the fate of a family under fascist rule. Her last novel, *Aracoeli* (1982), deals with male homosexuality and also with the brain illness from which she herself was suffering at the end of her life.

Her collections of verse include *Alibi* (1958) and *Il mondo salvato dai ragazzini* (1968; The World Saved by Little Children). She also translated the work of Katherine MANSFIELD into Italian.

More, Hannah (1745–1833) *British writer and reformer*

> Books, the Mind's food, not exercise!
>
> —*The Bas Bleu* (1786)

> She was born with a birch-broom in her hand, and worst of all was a shameless flatterer and insatiable of flattery. Her acceptance of a pension in compensation for a husband is a vile blot, never to be expunged from her character.
>
> —Caroline Bowles, letter to Robert Southey, December 21, 1834

A member of the bluestocking circle of Elizabeth MONTAGU, Hannah More wrote a number of successful plays before devoting herself to poetry and religious writing.

One of five daughters of a schoolmaster, Hannah More was born in Stapleton, near Bristol. She was pupil and later a teacher at the family's school in Gloucestershire. For six years (1767–73) Hannah was engaged to a Mr. Turner. When he finally decided against their marriage, he made Hannah a lifetime annual allowance of £200 in recompense.

In 1773 Hannah More began writing plays, which brought her to the attention of the actor David Garrick. In 1774 she moved to London, where she became sufficiently successful for Garrick to introduce her to the important literary people of the day, including Samuel Johnson. She also became a friend of Elizabeth Montagu and the bluestockings. Her plays of this period include *The Inflexible Captive* (1774), *Percy* (1777), and *The Fatal Falsehood* (1779).

In the 1780s More's work gradually became more serious as she turned from the theatre to religious poetry in *Bas Bleu* (1786) and a long series of ethical and religious tracts that began with *Estimate of the Religion of the Fashionable World* (1790). Moral tracts for the poor followed with *Village Politics by Will Chip* (1793) and *Cheap Repository Tracts* (1795–98), which included the well-known "The Shepherd of Salisbury Plain" and sold over two million copies. The Religious Tract Society was formed as a result of this work. She also wrote on the education of girls in *Strictures on the Modern System of Female Education* (1799), but her conservative views were at odds with the radical approach of Mary WOLLSTONECRAFT, whose plea for equality of education she rejected.

Friends of the abolitionist William Wilberforce, Hannah More and her sister took up his suggestion to start a school in a mining district in Somerset. Hannah continued her writing while there, publishing a moralistic novel, *Coelebs in Search of a Wife*, in 1809, followed ten years later by *Moral Sketches*.

Moreau, Jeanne (1928–) *French actress and film director*

> I don't think success is harmful, as so many people say. Rather, I believe it indispensable to talent, if for nothing else than to increase the talent.
>
> —Quoted by Oriana Fallaci in *The Egotists* (1963)

> The love, suffering, and happiness I experience in life appear in my movies, become an integral part of them. When I see a film after I've made it, I see my own life before me.
>
> —Interview, 1963

Jeanne Moreau is one of France's most respected actresses; she has also made her name as a director.

Born in Paris, the daughter of an Englishwoman who moved to France to dance in the Folies-Bergère, Jeanne Moreau trained at the National Conservatory of Dramatic Art. Two years later, at the age of 20, she joined the Comédie-Française, where she was the youngest member of the company. In 1952, by now well trained in the strict tradition of French classical acting, she left the Comédie and performed for a season with the Théâtre National Populaire. Subsequently she appeared on the stage in such productions as Shaw's *Pygmalion*, Cocteau's *La Machine infernale*, and Tennessee Williams's *Cat on a Hot Tin Roof*.

Moreau made her film debut in 1949 in *Dernier Amour*, but it was not until 1958, when she starred in Louis Malle's *Les Amants*, that she became internationally known. Her sensual beauty, as well as her superb acting ability, attracted the attention of leading directors. Among her successes were Roger Vadim's *Les Liaisons dangeureuses* (1959), Peter Brook's *Moderato Cantabile* (1960) – for which she won the Best Actress Award at the Cannes Film Festival – Michelangelo Antonioni's *La Notte* (1961), and François Truffaut's *Jules et Jim* (1961), the story of a love triangle. Her performance in *Jules et Jim* has been considered the greatest of her career, and the film became an instant classic.

Other films include Orson Welles's *Chimes at Midnight* (1964), Luis Buñuel's *Diary of a Chambermaid* (1964), Truffaut's *The Bride Wore Black* (1967), Bertrand Blier's *Les Valseuses* (1974; *Going Places*), Rainer Werner Fassbinder's *Querelle* (1982), *La Femme Nikita* (1990), and *The Summer House* (1993).

In 1975 Moreau turned to directing and starred in her own first film, *Lumière*, the story of the friendship of four actresses. She also directed *L'Adolescente* (1978), about a young girl's coming-of-age, *Adieu, Bonjour* (1994), and *Solstice* (1997). In 1993 she costarred with Alec Guinness and Lauren BACALL in a British television film, *A Foreign Field*, about a group of people revisiting a World War II battlefield in Normandy. One of her most recent film roles is that of a writer in Ismail Merchant's *The Proprietor* (1997).

Jeanne Moreau was made an officer of the Legion of Honour in 1988.

Morisot, Berthe (1841–1895) *French painter*

Berthe Morisot was the first woman to join the impressionist group of painters. Her letters and journals are valuable source material for the history of impressionism.

She was born in Bourges, the great-granddaughter of the 18th-century painter Honoré Fragonard. Breaking away from her early classical training, she studied with Camille Corot from 1862 to 1868. In about 1869 she met Edouard Manet, who used her as a model for several of his works, and in 1874 she married his brother Eugène. She in turn influenced the style of Manet's painting, persuading him to adopt the lighter colours of the impressionists and to work outdoors.

Morisot exhibited with the impressionists but retained her own distinctive style, characterized by lightness and transparency, delicacy and subtlety. Her interiors as well as her open-air scenes are bathed in radiant light. She worked in both oil and watercolour, painting numerous landscapes and many portraits of women and children in the intimate atmosphere of family life. After about 1885 her work was influenced by Auguste Renoir.

Among her paintings are *The Cradle* (1873) and *Young Woman in Ball Dress* (1879–1880), both of which are in the Louvre in Paris. She also made etchings and lithographs. Her work was exhibited throughout the 1880s in Paris, London, Brussels, and Boston. She held a major solo exhibition in 1892, the year of her husband's death. Her letters to her sister reveal how difficult she found it to reconcile the roles of mother and artist.

Morrell, Lady Ottoline (1873–1938) *British literary patron and writer*

> I never heard her utter an unkind word – of how many clever women can we say the same?
>
> —Margot Asquith, obituary of Lady Ottoline Morrell, *The Times*, 1938

Lady Ottoline Morrell entertained all the leading political, literary, and artistic figures of her generation, first at her house in London and later at Garsington Manor, Oxfordshire. Visitors, several of whom were also her lovers, included the Liberal statesman H. H. Asquith, the philosopher Bertrand Russell, the painter Augustus

John, and the writers W. B. Yeats, D. H. Lawrence, Virginia WOOLF, and T. S. Eliot.

Born in London, Lady Ottoline was the daughter of Lieutenant-Colonel Arthur Bentinck, heir to the Duke of Portland. She was educated at home and for a short time at Somerville College, Oxford, where she studied politics and Roman history. In 1902 she married Philip Morrell, who became an MP in 1906, and in 1908 she began to give her "at-homes."

Lady Ottoline, who was six feet tall and somewhat ill at ease in company, was nevertheless known for her brilliant conversation and unorthodox views, as well as her exotic clothes. Despite her generous hospitality, Lady Ottoline's patronage was caricatured in both Aldous Huxley's *Crome Yellow* (1921) and D. H. Lawrence's *Women in Love* (1921), causing her considerable distress. In 1924 she returned to London to live. Her writings are collected in *Ottoline* (1963) and *Ottoline at Garsington: Memoirs 1915–18* (1974), both of which were edited by R. Gathorne-Hardy.

Morrison, Toni (1931–) *American writer and educator*

> I think women dwell quite a bit on the duress under which they work, on how hard it is just to do it at all. We are traditionally rather proud of ourselves for having slipped creative work in there between the domestic chores and obligations. I'm not sure we deserve such big A-pluses for all that.
>
> —Quoted in *Newsweek*, March 30, 1981

Toni Morrison was awarded the 1993 Nobel Prize for literature for her novels describing the African-American experience, which were praised for their "visionary force and poetic import."

She was born Chloe Anthony Wofford in Lorain, Ohio, of parents whose families had been sharecroppers in the South. Graduating from Howard University in 1953, she earned a master's degree in English from Cornell University two years later. She then worked as an editor for the publishers

Random House in New York and taught literature at several universities, notably Princeton. Her marriage to Harold Morrison, a Jamaican architect, ended in divorce.

As an editor and educator Morrison has sought to move the work of African-American writers from the sidelines to a central place in American culture. Her novels deal with the efforts of African Americans to survive the cultural, economic, and social tensions within their communities. Set in specific periods in American history, these novels include *The Bluest Eye* (1970) and *Sula* (1973), which deal with poor Black Southerners. The bestseller *Song of Solomon* (1977), which won the U.S. National Book Critics' Circle Award, tells of Northerners seeking their past. *Tar Baby* (1981) is set in the Caribbean. Her later novels include *Beloved* (1987), for which she received the Pulitzer Prize for fiction, *Jazz* (1992), and *Paradise* (1998).

Moses, Grandma (1860–1961) *American painter*

Grandma Moses has been described as an "authentic primitive" – that is, a painter whose talent developed in complete isolation from contemporary artistic trends. Despite her lack of technical training, she became renowned for her naive but highly individualistic paintings.

Born Anna Mary Robertson into a farming family in Greenwich, New York State, she was one of ten children. She became a "hired girl," and in 1887 married Thomas Salmon Moses, a farmhand. They rented a farm near Staunton, Virginia, and then moved in 1905 to Eagle Bridge, New York, where Grandma Moses spent the rest of her long life. Her husband died in 1927; of their ten children, five died in infancy.

At the age of 67, when she was no longer able to do farm work because her hands were crippled with arthritis, Grandma Moses began painting in oils. At first she copied picture postcards but then turned to painting original farm scenes and landscapes "so that people will see how we used to live." She worked from memory rather than from life; always a keen observer, she had an instinctive feeling for colour and composition.

Her paintings were discovered by a New York collector who was touring the area in 1938; he arranged for some to be shown in 1939 at the Museum of Modern Art in New York in an exhibition entitled Contemporary Unknown American Painters. In 1940 she had her first one-woman show in a New York gallery. She painted more than 1,000 pictures and exhibited in the United States, Canada, and Europe. She also received numerous awards.

Mott, Lucretia Coffin (1793–1880)
American abolitionist and feminist

> It is not Christianity, but priestcraft that has subjected woman as we find her. The Church and State have been united, and it is well for us to see it so.
> —Speech, Woman's Rights Convention, Philadelphia, 1854

> Let woman then go on – not asking as favour, but claiming as right, the removal of all the hindrances to her elevation in the scale of being – let her receive encouragement for the proper cultivation of all her powers, so that she may enter profitably into the active business of life.
> —"Discourse on Woman" (1850)

Lucretia Mott was one of America's most vociferous opponents of slavery and racial intolerance, as well as being a staunch fighter for equal rights for women.

Lucretia Coffin was born in Nantucket, Massachusetts. At the age of 13 she entered the Society of Friends school near Poughkeepsie, New York State, where she later taught. At the school she met James Mott, a student and teacher, whom she married in 1811. Towards the end of the decade she was made a Quaker minister. Throughout their lives both husband and wife were active in the same causes.

Lucretia Mott spoke around the country on reform subjects and attended the founding convention of the American Anti-Slavery Society in 1833. At the world antislavery convention in London in 1840 she and other women delegates were denied official recognition. Angered by this exclusion, Mott and Elizabeth Cady STANTON organized the 1848 convention in Seneca Falls, New York State, at which the U.S. women's rights movement was launched.

The most prominent woman abolitionist, she organized aid during the American Civil War (1861–65) and sheltered fugitive slaves, continuing to fight for racial equality after the end of the war and the abolition of slavery. Throughout the 1860s she also continued to fight for women's rights, presiding over the 1866 Equal Rights Convention.

See also ANTHONY, SUSAN B(ROWNELL); STONE, LUCY BLACKWELL.

Mowlam, Marjorie (Mo) (1949–)
British Labour politician

As minister for Northern Ireland (1997–) Mo Mowlam has won widespread admiration for her open and down-to-earth style.

Mowlam was born in Coventry and educated at a comprehensive school there. In 1971 she graduated in social anthropology from Durham University before going to do postgraduate studies at Iowa University, where she was awarded an MA and a PhD. She lectured for a year at Florida State University (1977–78) before moving to Newcastle-upon-Tyne University.

Mowlam stood successfully as a Labour MP for Redcar in 1987, and a year later became the party's assistant front-bench spokesperson on Northern Ireland. In 1989 she helped to coordinate Labour's campaign for the European parliament, and was appointed opposition spokesperson on City and corporate affairs (1989–92). During the 1990s she rose steadily through the party ranks, serving as shadow spokesperson on the Citizen's Charter (1992–93), national heritage (1993–94), and Northern Ireland (1994–97). Despite undergoing surgery for a brain tumour only months earlier, she was appointed minister for Northern Ireland after Labour's election victory in May 1997. In this role she has continued to support the troubled peace process as the best way forward for resolving the region's difficulties. Her tenure has seen the resumption of the IRA ceasefire (July 1997) and the beginning of substantive talks involving Sinn Féin and most of the Unionist parties (September 1997). In January 1998 she took the controversial step of meeting convicted Loyalist killers in the Maze prison in an attempt to avert a return to all-out sectarian violence.

Muir, Jean (1928–1995) *British fashion designer*

A champion of the classic "little black dress," Jean Muir was the designer specially favoured since the 1960s by middle-aged women seeking elegance.

Jean Muir was born in London to Scottish parents and educated at a boarding school in Bedford, where she taught herself to sew. She began her career as a salesgirl and sketcher at the London department store Liberty's in 1950, moving in 1956 to Jaeger as an apprentice designer of knitwear. In 1961 she started a new company called Jane & Jane, but left it in 1966 to establish a firm under her own name with her husband Harry Lenckert as codirector and financial manager.

Muir's designs for women's clothes, famous for their graceful lines, elegance, and perfect tailoring, have been popular since the 1960s. Her dresses, in particular, flatter most women, not exclusively those with slim figures. She won many honours, including the British Fashion Industry Award in 1984, the Chartered Society of Designers Medal in 1987, and the Australian Bicentennial Award in 1988. In 1984 she became a trustee of the Victoria and Albert Museum in London and was created a CBE.

Munro, Alice (1931–   ) *Canadian writer*

One of Canada's best writers of fiction, Alice Munro's short stories are noted for their intensity, poetic imagery, and economy of style.

Born Alice Anne Laidlaw in Wingham, Ontario, she began to write fiction at the age of 15. In 1949 she enrolled at the University of Western Ontario to study journalism. Her first published short story, "The Dimensions of a Shadow," appeared in a student publication, *Folio*, the following year. After college she married James Munro and moved to Vancouver, British Columbia, where she continued to write.

Her short stories from this period were published in the collection *Dance of the Happy Shades* in 1968. Immediately attracting critical acclaim, this collection won the Governor General's Literary Award in 1969. Two subsequent collections, *Who Do You Think You Are?* (1978) and *The Progress of Love* (1986), also won this award. Her second collection, *Lives of Girls and Women*, was published in 1971, winning the Canadian Booksellers Award. Returning to Ontario the same year, she became writer-in-residence at the University of Western Ontario in 1974 and published a further collection, *Something I've Been Meaning to Tell You*.

In 1976 Munro divorced her first husband and married Gerald Fremlin. The following year she received international recognition for her work, becoming the first Canadian to win the Canada-Australia Literary Prize. In 1978 *Who Do You Think You Are?* (published in the United States and Britain as *The Beggar Maid*) was a candidate for the Booker Prize. In 1982 *The Moons of Jupiter* appeared on *The New York Times* list of the best books published during that year, and in 1986 *The Progress of Love* was similarly listed. In 1990 *Friend of My Youth*, her seventh collection of short stories, was nominated for *The Irish Times* Aer Lingus Fiction Prize. *Open Secrets* was published in 1994.

Münter, Gabriele (1877–1962) *German expressionist painter*

Best known for her landscapes and interiors, in 1909 Gabriele Münter was a cofounder with Wassaly Kandinsky of the New Artists Association of Munich. Two years later they both exhibited at the first Blau Reiter (Blue Rider) show, organized by Kandinsky and other expressionist painters.

Born in Berlin, Gabriele Münter began studying art at the Düsseldorf

Ladies' Art School in 1897 but left to travel in the United States for three years before returning to Germany to work with Kandinsky at his Phalanx School in Munich. Travelling throughout Europe (1903–08) with Kandinsky, she exhibited with him in Paris, where Münter was influenced by the work of Paul Gauguin. She and Kandinsky then settled in Murnau in Bavaria, where they worked with two Russian artists, Von Werefkin and Jawlensky.

During World War I Münter and Kandinsky left Germany for Switzerland and then travelled to Sweden. In 1917 they split up, and Kandinsky returned to the Soviet Union, where he married. Münter's style subsequently changed: she abandoned the brilliant colours she had previously used for a more subdued style, painting mainly portraits of women.

Murasaki, Shikibu (c. 978–c. 1030)
Japanese novelist, diarist, and poet

Shikibu Murasaki is renowned as one of Japan's greatest prose writers.

Although it is not known where Murasaki was born, it has been discovered that her father was a government official and provincial governor who belonged to a minor branch of the powerful Fujiwara clan. In her childhood Murasaki learnt some Chinese by overhearing her brother's lessons. (It was considered unladylike in Japan at that time for women to be educated.) In about 998 she married her cousin Fujiwara no Nobutaka, living happily with him and having children until he died in 1001.

In 1004, when her father was posted to a distant province, Murasaki entered the service of the staid Empress Akiko, in which she remained until her death. By the time of her arrival at the royal palace Murasaki had begun writing her great six-part novel *The Tale of Genji*, parts of which were read at court long before its completion. Telling the story of the adventures and romances of a prince and his son, it is considered the greatest achievement of Japanese literature.

Murasaki's diary of court life (1007–10) reveals her as a sensitive, introspective woman whose kind and gentle nature was evident only to those who knew her well. She admits that at court she was considered a censorious prig. The diary contains fascinating thumbnail sketches of some of her famous contemporaries. She was also well regarded as a poet. Nothing is known about her later years, except that she was still in the empress's service in 1025.

Murdoch, Dame Iris (1919–   )
British writer and philosopher

> Writing is like getting married. One should never commit oneself until one is amazed at one's luck.
>
> —*The Black Prince* (1973)

> A tousled heel-less, ladder-stockinged little lady – crackling with intelligence, but nothing at all of a prig.
>
> —George Lyttleton, describing Murdoch in *The Lyttleton Hart-Davis Letters*

As a philosopher and novelist Dame Iris Murdoch has earned a worldwide reputation. In 1997 her husband made it known that she was suffering from Alzheimer's disease, a sad end to a brilliant intellectual career.

Jean Iris Murdoch was born in Dublin and educated at the Froebel Educational Institute in London and then at Badminton School, Bristol. She graduated from Somerville College, Oxford, in 1942 with first-class honours in classics, and from 1948 to 1963 she was a tutor in philosophy at St. Anne's College, Oxford. In 1956 she married the scholar and critic John Bayley.

Iris Murdoch's first published book was *Sartre, Romantic Rationalist* (1953), a portrait of the French philosopher. She then turned to writing novels that, despite their underlying philosophical themes, have attracted a wide readership. Her first novel, *Under the Net*, was published in 1954. Other early works are *The Flight from the Enchanter* (1956), *The Sandcastle* (1957), and *The Bell* (1958).

Murdoch began to acquire an international reputation with *A Severed Head* (1961), which she and J. B. Priestley dramatized in 1963. Later novels, many of them exploring themes of love and dominance, include *An Unofficial Rose* (1962); *The Unicorn* (1963); *The Italian Girl* (1964), which she and James Saunders dramatized in 1967; *The Red and the Green* (1965); *The Time of the Angels* (1966); *The Nice and the Good* (1968); *A Fairly Honourable Defeat* (1970); *The Black Prince* (1973); *A Word Child* (1975); *The Sea, The Sea* (1978), for which she won the Booker Prize; *Nuns and Soldiers* (1980); and *The Philosopher's Pupil* (1983).

Some critics see *The Good Apprentice* (1985) as marking a shift to a looser, more realistic, but still philosophical fictional style. It was followed by *The Book and the Brotherhood* (1987), *The Message to the Planet* (1989), *The Green Knight* (1993), and *Jackson's Dilemma* (1995).

Murdoch continued to write philosophical nonfiction works, including *The Sovereignty of Good* (1970) and *The Fire and the Sun* (1977), both strongly influenced by Plato, and *Metaphysics as a Guide to Morals* (1993). Her plays include *The Servants and the Snow* (1970), *The Three Arrows* (1972), *Art and Eros* (1980), and *The Black Prince* (1989).

In 1987 she was made a DBE.

Musgrave, Thea (1928–   ) *Scottish composer*

Thea Musgrave's music has been heard on radio and at international music festivals. Several of her operas have been performed at London's Covent Garden and in New York. She has also conducted leading orchestras.

Thea Musgrave was born in Edinburgh and studied at the university there between 1947 and 1950. She was also a pupil of Hans Gál, the Austrian-born composer who lived in Scotland, and subsequently studied with Nadia BOULANGER in Paris until 1954. During her student years she was awarded the Donald Francis Tovey Prize and the Lili Boulanger Memorial Prize. After teaching at London University (1958–65), she held a variety of lecturing posts at British and American universities, including a period as visiting professor at the University of Califor-

nia at Santa Barbara in 1970. In 1987 she became a lecturer at Queen's University, New York City. She has also served on the music panel of the Arts Council of Great Britain and the executive committee of the Composers' Guild.

Thea Musgrave's early works include the specially commissioned *Cantata for a Summer's Day* (1954), the ballet *A Tale of Thieves* (1953), and the chamber opera *The Abbot of Drimrock* (1955). She has also written full-scale operas, including *The Decision* (1964); *The Voice of Ariadne* (1973), commissioned for the 1974 Aldeburgh Festival; *Mary, Queen of Scots* (1976); *A Christmas Carol* (1979), for which she herself adapted Dickens's novel as the libretto; and *Harriet, the Woman Called Moses* (1985), based on the life of Harriet TUBMAN. She also wrote concertos for clarinet (1967), for horn (1971), and for viola (1973), as well as chamber music and such instrumental pieces as *Space Play* (1974), for wind quintet and string quartet. *Occurrence at Owl Creek Bridge* (1981) is a half-hour radio opera. In 1984 she collaborated with Richard Rodney Bennett on *Moving into Aquarius*, a piece written as a tribute to Michael Tippett on his 80th birthday. Her later orchestral works include *The Seasons* (1988) and *Rainbow* (1990).

Musgrave is married to Peter Mark, conductor and general director of the Virginia Opera Association. She herself has worked as a conductor with orchestras in Britain and the United States, giving premieres of several of her own works.

Mutter,   Anne-Sophie   (1963–   ) *German violinist*

> Ten years from now, thirty years from now, I want more or less to be doing the same thing. Just better.
>
> —Comment made during an interview

Anne-Sophie Mutter is a musician of quite outstanding talent, whose performances all over the world have dazzled both critics and the public.

She was born in Rheinfeld in West Germany and began to take violin lessons at the age of five. After studying the instrument for only one year, she won the first prize in Germany's Jugend Musiziert ("young musicians") competition in 1970, becoming at the age of six the youngest person ever to do so. The same year she also won a national prize for her piano playing. Having won the same prizes in 1974, she was asked not to compete for them again.

Anne-Sophie Mutter was educated at home by her mother and private tutors. After her violin tutor, Erna Honigberger, died in 1973, she went on to study with the Polish violinist Henryk Szeryng. At this time her father limited her public appearances to two a year. In 1976 when the conductor of the Berlin Philharmonic Orchestra, Herbert von Karajan, heard her play, he invited her to perform with him in Berlin. She so impressed him that the following year she performed Mozart's violin concerto in G major with him at the Salzburg Easter festival.

Since then Mutter has performed as a soloist with major orchestras in London, New York, and elsewhere – always receiving sensational reviews. She has also made many recordings, frequently needing to play the music only once for it to be perfect. She was appointed a guest teacher at the Royal Academy of Music in London in 1985.

Myrdal, Alva (1902–1986) *Swedish public official, sociologist, and writer*

Alva Myrdal's work for disarmament brought her the 1982 Nobel Peace Prize, which she shared with Alfonso García Robles of Mexico.

Born Alva Reimer in Uppsala, she studied at Stockholm, Uppsala, and Geneva universities. In 1924 she married the Swedish economist Gunnar Myrdal, who shared the 1974 Nobel Prize for economics with Friedrich von Hayek. Alva became head of the UN Department of Social Welfare in 1949 and director of UNESCO's Department of Social Sciences in 1950.

From 1955 to 1961 Alva Myrdal was the Swedish ambassador to India, Burma, and Ceylon (now Sri Lanka). In 1962 she was elected to the Riksdag (the Swedish parliament) and headed Sweden's delegation to the UN disarmament conference in Geneva. She became minister of disarmament and church affairs in 1966 and held both disarmament posts until 1973, playing an important part in the international peace movement.

Myrdal's *The Game of Disarmament: How the United States and Russia Run the Arms Race* was published in 1977. She was awarded the Albert Einstein Peace Prize in 1980 and a share of the Nobel Peace Prize in 1982.

N

Naidu, Sarojini (1879–1949) *Indian poet and political activist*

Highly respected for her poetry, Sarojini Naidu also had the distinction of being the first woman president of the Indian National Congress.

Born in Hyderabad, the eldest daughter of Aghorenath Chattopadhyay, founder of the local Nizam College, she entered Madras University at the age of 12, graduated from King's College, London, at 19, and studied briefly at Girton College, Cambridge. While in England she became involved in the women's suffrage movement. Returning home, she married out of her Brahman caste: her husband, M. G. Naidu, belonged to the socially inferior Ksatriya caste. The hostess of a brilliant Bombay literary salon, Naidu published her first volume of verse, *The Golden Threshold*, in 1905, the year in which she launched her public career by speaking at the All-India Social Conference in Calcutta. Raising the status of Indian women, notably by the abolition of purdah, then became her lifelong concern. In 1908 she organized emergency relief in flood-stricken Hyderabad. In 1913 Naidu published a second volume of verse in English, *The Bird of Time*; as a result she was elected to the Royal Society of Literature in 1914 and hailed as "the Nightingale of India."

Following the publication of *The Broken Wing* (1917), Naidu abandoned poetry to commit herself to Gandhi's campaign for Indian independence from British rule. In 1925 she became the first woman to serve as president of the Indian National Congress, the main political arm of the independence movement. Naidu lectured on behalf of Congress in North America (1928–29), was imprisoned for anti-British agitation (1930, 1932, 1942–43), took part in the inconclusive London Round Table Conference (1931), and served with a delegation to uphold the interests of Indians in South Africa (1932). At India's independence (1947) she became the first woman governor of an Indian state, Uttar Pradesh (then United Provinces), and died in office.

Nation, Carry (1846–1911) *American temperance campaigner*

> ...a bulldog running along at the feet of Jesus, barking at what He doesn't like.
>
> —Describing herself, quoted by Herbert Asbury in *Carry Nation*

Notorious for her militancy, Carry Nation helped to establish the climate of public opinion that made constitutional prohibition possible in 1920.

Carry Amelia Moore, born in Garrard County, Kentucky, acquired a lifelong hatred of alcohol following her disastrous marriage in 1867 to an alcoholic physician, Dr. Charles Gloyd, whom she left ten years later. She subsequently married David Nation, a lawyer and minister. While living in Kansas, a prohibition state, in the 1890s, she began what became a violent campaign of direct action against illegal saloons, wrecking bottles, barrels, and drinking premises, initially with iron bars and stones; from 1901 onwards she wielded a hatchet, which became the symbol of her crusade. David Nation divorced her that year for desertion. Undeterred, she extended her "hatchetations" from San Francisco to New York, broadening her targets to include smoking, corsets, short skirts, and foreign foods. Nearly six feet tall, weighing over 12 stone, and starkly dressed in black and white, she survived numerous physical attacks and was arrested over 30 times.

Carry Nation also lectured incessantly, selling souvenir hatchets to pay her fines and to fund a refuge in Kansas City for the wives of alcoholics. An active suffragist, she was disavowed by both official suffrage organizations and temperance movements, which found her fanaticism embarrassing and counterproductive. In response she compiled a rambling autobiography, *The Use and Need of the Life of Carry A. Nation* (1904), in self-justification. However, perhaps acknowledging her own instability, she retreated to a mountain farm in Arkansas in her last years. The Volstead Act, introducing nationwide prohibition of alcohol, passed into law nine years after her death in Leavenworth, Kansas.

Navratilova, Martina (1956–)
Czech-born American tennis player

Navratilova won the Wimbledon women's singles title a record nine times.

Born near Prague, she took up tennis at the age of five, winning the Czech singles title in 1972, 1973, and 1974. Angered by travel restrictions in communist Czechoslovakia, she defected to the United States in 1975. Turning professional shortly after her arrival in America, she entered into a career rivalry with the Wimbledon title-holder Chris Evert LLOYD, going on to win the Wimbledon singles a record nine times (1978–79, 1982–87, 1990), as well as the U.S. Open in 1983–84 and 1986–87. She also won over a hundred other tournament victories, including 54 Grand Slam events, of which 36 were doubles, a record equalled only by Margaret COURT. Beaten in the 1994 Wimbledon final, she announced her retirement from competitive singles the same year.

Navratilova became an American citizen in 1981, after immense media interest in her private life. This centred on her relationship with the writer Rita Mae Brown and her public defence of homosexuality. Her earnings from tennis, said to exceed $9 million,

also aroused media attention. Some of this money was used by Navratilova to establish a federation for the benefit of underprivileged children.

Her books include *Being Myself* (1985) and *Feet of Clay* (1996).

Nazimova, Alla (1879–1945) *Russian actress*

Alla Nazimova was particularly noted for her performances in the plays of Henrik Ibsen.

Born Alla Leventon in the Crimean port of Yalta in Russia, Nazimova studied music in St. Petersburg and Odessa before abandoning the violin to study drama in Moscow with Stanislavsky. She made her stage debut with the Paul Orleneff company in St. Petersburg (1904), later travelling with them to the United States. Her sensational impact in America led her to master English in six months in preparation for a starring role in *Hedda Gabler* (1906). This marked the start of a long career as an interpreter of the works of Ibsen, including *A Doll's House* (1907), *The Master Builder* (1907), and *Ghosts* (1935–36).

In 1910 New York's leading theatrical producers, the Shubert brothers, built and named the Nazimova (later 39th Street) Theater in her honour. As a star of the silent screen she appeared in *Camille* (1921), in a film version of *A Doll's House* (1922), and in her own interpretation of *Salome* (1923), inspired by Aubrey Beardsley's illustrations for this play by Oscar Wilde. A U.S. citizen from 1927, she returned to the stage to triumph in Chekhov's *The Cherry Orchard* (1928–29) and Eugene O'Neill's *Mourning Becomes Electra* (1931–32). She died in Hollywood.

Neagle, Dame Anna (1904–1986) *British actress*

> No star has ever been less theatrical than Anna Neagle. She gives the impression of being a genuine person.
>
> —Freddie Carpenter (director), quoted by Sheridan Morley in *The Great Stage Stars* (1986)

London-born Marjorie Robertson made her debut as a dancer in 1917, then worked as a chorus girl in musical revues. In 1930 she adopted her mother's distinctive maiden name to become Anna Neagle and made her first film. From 1931 her career developed under the guidance of director Herbert Wilcox, whom she married in 1943. Having played stage roles as different as Olivia in *Twelfth Night* (1934) and the title role in *Peter Pan* (1937), she attained star status with her performance as the Queen in Wilcox's film *Victoria, the Great* (1937). This film was remarkable for the skill with which Neagle changed from a vivacious teenager to a venerable monarch, winning her the Cup of Nations award in Vienna.

During World War II Anna Neagle travelled extensively to entertain Allied troops. After the war she portrayed the heroism of the French-born British agent Odette HALLOWES, who was captured and tortured by the Germans, in *Odette* (1950), while in *The Lady with the Lamp* (1951) she presented an idealized portrait of the life of Florence NIGHTINGALE. However, most of her films of the late 1940s and 1950s were frothy comedies and musicals, such as *Piccadilly Incident* (1946) and *Spring in Park Lane* (1948), in which she starred with Michael Wilding. Their success made her Britain's International Top Box-Office Actress every year from 1949 to 1952.

Retiring from the screen in 1958 after appearing in over 30 films, Anna Neagle overcame the problems of her husband's bankruptcy in 1961 and her own cancer shortly afterwards. Returning triumphantly to the stage, she enjoyed a six-year run in London, Australia, and New Zealand in *Charlie Girl* (1965–71), making over 2,000 appearances as Lady Hadwell; she then appeared in revivals of the musicals *No, No, Nanette* (1973) and *My Fair Lady* (1978–82). She was created a DBE in 1969.

Neal, Patricia (1926–) *American actress*

> She was a blonde, yet she had a dark look. Her voice was grownup, drawling but a little harsh – all beyond her years...But...she failed to establish herself as a major screen actress, perhaps by choice.

> —David Thomson, *A Biographical Dictionary of Film* (1994)

Patsy Louise Neal was born in Packard, Virginia, and studied drama at Northwestern University. Working first as a model, she made her stage debut at the age of 20. In the same year (1946) she won a Tony Award for her role in *Another Part of the Forest*. Following her screen debut in 1949, Neal made over a dozen, mostly uninspiring, films before marrying the writer Roald Dahl in 1953. After her marriage she was far more selective in the work she accepted, making a film every two or three years and winning an Oscar for her role as a long-suffering housekeeper in the contemporary Western *Hud* (1963).

Crippled by a series of severe strokes in the 1960s, she fought back to health, receiving the Heart of the Year Award from President Lyndon B. Johnson for her outstanding courage. She continued to make films and television appearances until 1989.

Divorced from Dahl in 1983, she published her autobiography, *As I Am*, in 1988. A film, *The Patricia Neal Story* (1981), which stars Glenda JACKSON and Dirk Bogarde, re-enacted the drama of her struggle to win back her faculties.

Necker, Suzanne (1739–1794) *Swiss-born French writer*

Famed for her literary salon, Suzanne Necker was also noted for her philanthropic activities.

Born in Crassier, the daughter of a Protestant minister, Suzanne Curchod was engaged as a young girl to the future historian Edward Gibbon, who had been sent to Switzerland by his father because of his conversion to Roman Catholicism. However, Gibbon's father also opposed the match, so instead Suzanne married the Swiss banker Jacques Necker. Madame Necker used her social skills as hostess of a sparkling literary salon to further her husband's political ambitions, and in 1771 he became director-general of the finances of France – effectively, prime minister.

Famed for her beauty, wit, and wisdom, Madame Necker was also an active philanthropist, founding a hospital (1776) in Paris, which later bore her name, and which remains a centre of paediatrics. Her husband's fall from power (1790) drove them into retirement, and she died in her native Switzerland.

Suzanne Necker's publications included an essay on divorce, *Réflexions sur le divorce* (1794), and five volumes of miscellaneous writings (1798–1802), published after her death. Her daughter, Anne Louise, later became the intellectually formidable Madame de STAËL.

Needham, Dorothy (Mary Moyle)
(1896–1987) *British biochemist*

London-born Dorothy Moyle studied at Girton College, Cambridge, before going on, in 1920, to do research in physiology at the university's Biochemical Laboratory, where she specialized in the biochemistry of muscle. Although she later did research and taught in the United States, France, Germany, and Belgium, Cambridge remained her base and the metabolism of muscle tissue the main focus of her work until her retirement in 1963. Her *Machina Carnis* (1971) is a definitive history of the subject.

In 1924 Dorothy married the scientist Joseph Needham, who became an authority on the history of science and technology in China. During World War II Dorothy Needham worked on secret assignments relating to chemical warfare and helped to organize cooperation between British and Chinese scientists. In 1948 she was honoured by being elected a Fellow of the Royal Society. As her husband had become a fellow in 1941, the couple were the first husband and wife team to have been elected fellows since Queen VICTORIA and Prince Albert.

Nefertiti (14th century BC) *Wife of King Amenhotep IV of Egypt*

Probably born in Mitanni, an empire based in what is now northern Iraq, Nefertiti became the chief wife of the intellectual Egyptian ruler Amenhotep IV (reigned about 1379–1362 BC). She bore him six daughters but no son. His reign was distinguished by a religious revolution, strongly supported by Ne-fertiti, that renounced the established pantheon of gods in favour of a single, supreme deity, Aton. Aton, represented by a sun disc, was revered as the source of life and the bounties of nature.

Inspired by his divine mission, Amenhotep changed his name to Akhenaton ("He Who Serves Aton") and abandoned the capital at Thebes for a new one, Akhetaton ("Place of Aton's Effective Power," now Tell-el-Amarna). While the lives of Akhenaton and Nefertiti were devoted to Aton, they continued themselves to be revered by the masses as deities, which they accepted as their due. The religious revolution was accompanied by a change in artistic style, which rejoiced in brightness and beauty. It is symbolized by the elegant painted limestone head of Nefertiti – celebrated in an Egyptian hymn as "youthful forever and ever" – found at Amarna in 1912 and now in the Egyptian Museum in Berlin. Nefertiti is also depicted in painted reliefs at the temple of Aton in Karnak and in tomb scenes at Amarna.

While the arts flourished, Egypt's foreign empire decayed as a result of the king's neglect; his reign passed through an obscure but definite crisis, possibly connected with the intervention of the king's forceful mother, Tiy. Thereafter Nefertiti was obliged to live in seclusion, deprived of her official title and ceremonial primacy. Smenkhkhare, the king's son-in-law, became his successor. However, after his short reign he was succeeded by another of Akhenaton's sons-in-law, Tutankhaton. This king, abandoning Amarna for Thebes, restored the old gods and assumed the style Tutankhamun, apparently with Nefertiti's approval.

Negri, Pola (1894–1987) *Polish actress*

> She had a blind and uncritical admiration of her own genius in the blaze of which her sense of humour evaporated like a dewdrop on a million-watt arc lamp.
>
> —Rodney Ackland, quoted by David Thomson in *A Biographical Dictionary of Film* (1994)

Born Barbara Appolonia Chalupiec in Junowa, Poland, she surrounded herself with mystery from her childhood, claiming that her father was a gypsy violinist who had died, no one knew how, in exile in Siberia. After working as a dancer in St. Petersburg, Negri spent the years between 1913 and 1917 making films in Warsaw. By 1920 she was in Germany, where she won acclaim by playing strong passionate women in Ernst Lubitsch's films *Carmen* (1918), *Madame du Barry* (1919), and *Medea* (1920).

In 1922 Negri became the first star of the Continental cinema to be invited to Hollywood, where her roles in the silent films *The Charmer* (1925) and *Loves of an Actress* (1928) drew almost as much public attention as her devotion to Rudolph Valentino. When he died suddenly, she was devastated, fainting at his funeral, a typically theatrical gesture much ridiculed by the American press.

Negri's heavy foreign accent denied her a Hollywood career in the talkies; however, she continued to enjoy success in German films in the 1930s. World War II drove her first to France and then to the United States, where she lived out her long retirement.

Nesbit, E(dith) (1858–1924) *British novelist*

> Nesbit, it seems, remained emotionally about twelve years old all her life. Perhaps this is why she found it so easy to speak as one intelligent child to another.
>
> —Alison Lurie, quoted by Jane M. Bingham (ed.) in *Writers for Children* (1988)

Edith Nesbit was the author of *The Railway Children* (1906) and a series of popular novels for children featuring the Bastable family.

Born in London, the daughter of an agricultural chemist who died when she was three years old, Edith Nesbit was educated abroad. A member of a cultured family, she was introduced by her sister to the writers Algernon Swinburne, Dante Gabriel Rossetti, and William Morris. As a girl she was a tomboy, more interested in playing pirates than dressing dolls. Because

she soon realized that most people did not live her comfortable sort of life, she became an early socialist. In 1880 she married Hubert Bland, with whom she was one of the founders in 1884 of the Fabian Society. This association, which included among its members George Bernard Shaw and Sidney and Beatrice WEBB, was to help establish the Labour Party and have a lasting influence on its policies.

With her husband Nesbit had two sons and two daughters, but he was frequently unfaithful to her; following the collapse of his business and health, Edith was forced to give up her hopes of becoming a poet in order to support her family by writing cheap fiction and sentimental verses under the name E. Nesbit. In the 1890s she began to tell the adventures of the six Bastable children, who were quite unlike the prissy boys and girls usually portrayed in books for young readers.

The Bastables got into frequent fights, used slang, and invariably defied grown-ups. Edith was obviously a Bastable herself – quick-tempered, generous, and happy to shock her neighbours by smoking and wearing outrageous clothes. The Bastables' adventures appeared in book form in *The Story of the Treasure Seekers* (1899) and two sequels. In *The Railway Children* (1906) a family whose father is wrongly imprisoned struggles to prove his innocence. As well as writing in an unfussy direct style without talking down to her readers, Nesbit also developed the use of fantasy in settings of everyday life. *The Story of the Amulet* (1906) is about time travel and *The Enchanted Castle* (1907) about ghosts.

Bland died in 1914; in 1917 Edith married an engineer, Terry Tucker. Her last book, *The Lark*, appeared in 1922.

Nevelson, Louise (1900–1988) *Russian-born American sculptor*

Louise Nevelson was most famous for her large abstract wooden sculptures, which she joined together to form sculptural walls.

Born in Kiev, then part of Russia, Louise Berliawsky emigrated with her family to the United States in 1905 and grew up in Rockland, Maine. After moving to New York City, she married businessman Charles Nevelson in 1920; thereafter she trained in drama before studying painting at the Art Students' League in 1928. Leaving her husband and child, Nevelson then studied with art theorist Hans Hofmann in Munich in 1932; she returned to New York that year to assist the Mexican master Diego Rivera with his murals at the Rockefeller Center. In the 1930s she began to produce her own figurative sculptures in terracotta, wood, bronze, and plaster; many were influenced by the pre-Columbian art of Central America.

By the 1950s Nevelson's work had become more abstract. Many of her works from this period used natural objects, broken furniture, bric-a-brac, and open wooden boxes arranged to make free-standing sculptural walls, often painted black, white, or gold. These "environmental sculptures," which she claimed were inspired by childhood memories of rows of bright jars stacked high on shelves in sweet shops, became her trademark. Their mystical titles – *Sky Columns Presence* (1959), *Silent Music II* (1964), *Homage to the World* (1966) – earned her the reputation of being one of the most spiritual practitioners of modern art.

From the 1960s onwards Nevelson employed light-reflecting industrial materials, such as aluminum, Plexiglass, lucite (*Transparent Sculpture VI*, 1967–68), and steel (*Transparent Horizon*, 1975). She also produced lithographs and collages, as well as celebrating her adopted country's 200th birthday with a white-painted wooden interior, *Bicentennial Dawn* (1976). In 1977 she designed the Chapel of the Good Shepherd for St. Peter's Lutheran Church in New York City (1977); when her sculpture group *Shadows and Flags* was installed on the Legion Memorial Square in the Wall Street area of New York in 1978, the square's name was changed to Louise Nevelson Plaza.

Honoured in 1967 by the Whitney Museum of American Art in New York with a major retrospective exhibition, Nevelson was a medallist of the American Institute of Architects in 1977 and elected to the American Academy of Arts and Letters in 1979. The Pompidou Centre in Paris honoured her with another major retrospective in 1988 but she died shortly before its opening. There are permanent collections of her work at the Whitney Museum, the Carnegie Institute in New York, and the Art Institute of Chicago.

Ngoyi, Lilian Masediba (1911–1980)
South African civil-rights activist

As president of the African National Congress Women's League, Lilian Ngoyi campaigned tirelessly for the abolition of apartheid.

Born near Pretoria, Lilian Ngoyi was condemned by family poverty to cut short her education and to work in a variety of menial jobs. Marriage brought three children and widowhood at the age of 40. Angered by the exploitation she had experienced as a worker in a clothing factory, Ngoyi joined the struggle against apartheid by campaigning against the Pass Laws, which severely restricted black people's freedom of movement. Joining the Women's League of the African National Congress, Ngoyi became a superb orator, enabling her to advance rapidly in the movement; she became president of the Women's League in 1953 and president of the Federation of South African Women in 1956.

Having been several times arrested and imprisoned for her political activities, she was finally charged with treason in 1956. The trial proceedings were dragged out for more than four years, throughout which she was imprisoned, enduring 71 days of solitary confinement. Despite her eventual acquittal Ngoyi was sentenced to five years' house arrest at her home in Orlando township, where she died almost 20 years later, a decade before the abolition of apartheid.

Nice, Margaret Morse (1883–1914)
American ornithologist

Nice's career demonstrated to countless others that a housewife without a doctorate, raising...children, could, by studying the birds in her own backyard, make "the outstanding contribution of the present quarter century to ornithological thinking in America."

—Kenneth C. Parkes, quoted by Barbara Sicheman and Carol Hurd Green in *Notable American Women* (1980)

Margaret Morse, daughter of a history professor at Amherst College, Massachusetts, began writing about birds at the age of 12; by her twenties she was a researcher in biology at Clark University in Worcester, Massachusetts, where she met and married medical student Leonard Blaine Nice in 1909. From then on she continued her studies, independently of any university, wherever her husband took a teaching post – in Oklahoma, Ohio, and Chicago.

In 1910, the year in which the first of their five daughters was born, Margaret Nice published her first learned paper, *The Food of the Bob-White*, in the *Journal of Economic Entomology*. It was the product of two years' patient research. As her family grew, she also took up the study of child psychology and between 1915 and 1933 published 18 articles based on her observations of her own children. In 1924 she published a comprehensive study of *The Birds of Oklahoma* and in 1939 produced a popular account of ornithology for amateurs, *The Watcher at the Nest*. Her most significant work was a long-term study of the song sparrow, based on observations made in her own back garden in Ohio. Tagging, naming, and numbering sparrows with lengths of coloured wool, Margaret Nice broke new ground by tracking the behaviour of individual birds rather than of whole flocks.

Meanwhile she maintained a prolific output of reviews and reports, producing over 250 articles in the course of her lifetime, despite having almost no secretarial backup and, apart from a few grants, relying on her husband to finance her work. In addition, her command of German and Dutch enabled her to forge new links between American and European ornithologists. In her later years she became an outspoken campaigner on conservation issues, especially on the excessive use of pesticides, which can endanger wildlife habitats.

Nightingale, Florence (1820–1910)
British health reformer

> She would speak to one and nod and smile to as many more; but she could not do it to all you know. We lay there by the hundreds; but we could kiss her shadow as it fell.
>
> —A wounded soldier in the Crimean War, quoted by Cecil Woodham-Smith in *Florence Nightingale* (1951)

The founder of the modern nursing profession, Florence Nightingale placed an even higher priority on the reform of army medical services. She was also regarded as a leading expert on hospital design and on public health policy in India, even though she had never been there.

Born in Florence, from which her first name was taken, she was the second daughter of wealthy parents who gave her an excellent education and were horrified when she tried to use it to follow a career. Florence found herself increasingly drawn towards nursing, a task that, in the England of her day, was undertaken largely by poor, uneducated women who could find no better employment. Florence's family was therefore appalled at the thought of her exposing herself to the company of such people, let alone to the risk of infection.

Florence, however, persisted and prepared herself as thoroughly as she could by studying parliamentary reports on public health and hospitals; she also attended a basic training course for nurses at the Institution of Protestant Deaconesses at Kaiserswerth in Germany. In 1853 Florence finally found a job as superintendent of the Institute for the Care of Sick Gentlewomen in London. Here her reforms of its organization soon improved its efficiency but left her yearning for a greater challenge than "this little molehill" could offer. In 1854 the outbreak of the Crimean War revealed disastrous incompetence in the British army's supply and medical services; wounded soldiers were ferried across the Black Sea to the base hospital at Scutari, near Istanbul, where they were virtually abandoned to die of neglect. At the request of her old friend Sidney Herbert, the secretary of war, Florence Nightingale was appointed to lead a relief mission of 38 nurses to Scutari, only to find that the army doctors were so hostile to her interference that they prevented her nurses from even entering the wards.

Within days of her arrival, however, hundreds of fresh casualties began arriving after the Battle of Inkerman. The Scutari hospital, infested with rats and lice, had insufficient food, water, bedding, clothing, bandages, and operating tables to cope with the influx. Florence, however, had £30,000, raised by *The Times*, which she used first to take over all the kitchens and ultimately both the Scutari base hospital and its forward counterpart in the Crimea. Wards were lime-washed, blocked drains cleared, and laundries established. The death rate among the wounded dropped from over 40% to just over 2%. The army doctors still loathed her for putting them to shame, but the soldiers and the British public adored her. Queen VICTORIA became a great admirer and a lifelong supporter of her reforms.

Returning home a national heroine, "The Lady with the Lamp," as she was dubbed, ducked the huge welcome prepared for her and began a campaign to improve health conditions in the army, which, even in peace time, had twice the death rate of civilian society. Apart from improvements in diet, barracks, and washing facilities, Florence's campaign led to the establishment of an Army Medical School (1857). In 1860 Florence Nightingale used the £45,000 subscribed by the British public to the Nightingale Fund in recognition of her work in the Crimea to establish the world's first modern training school for nurses. Set up at London's St. Thomas's Hospital, it had a curriculum personally devised by Florence Nightingale.

These achievements were made in spite of having no public position, making no public appearances, and for the last 40 years of her life scarcely leaving her room. Having contracted a severe fever in the Crimea, she lived as a semi-invalid, enthroned on a couch from which she received a constant stream of visitors and deputations. She also conducted a vast correspondence with influential individuals and institutions, inquiring, cajoling, and threatening in pursuit of her aims. By 1901 she was completely blind as well as housebound.

In 1907 King Edward VII made her the first woman to be invested with the Order of Merit, an honour he had personally created to recognize individuals who had made an outstanding contribution to national life. But by then Nightingale nurses had revolutionized hospital care throughout the English-speaking world. Her principal book, *Notes on Nursing* (1859), was in great demand throughout her lifetime.

Florence Nightingale declined a state funeral and a place in Westminster Abbey, choosing burial beside her parents in a country churchyard. Her tombstone was simply marked "F.N. Born 1820. Died 1910."

Nijinska, Bronislava (1891–1972)
Russian ballet dancer and choreographer

Born in Minsk, Belarus, the daughter of professional dancers and sister of the future ballet star and choreographer Vaslav Nijinsky (1890–1950), Nijinska, like her brother, trained at the Imperial Ballet School in St. Petersburg. Graduating in 1908, she became a soloist with the Maryinski company before joining Serge Diaghilev's Ballets Russes, with which she performed in Paris and London (1909–14). Returning to Russia during World War I, she started a ballet school in Kiev but went back to work for Diaghilev in 1921, following Leonide Massine as his principal choreographer.

In 1922 she choreographed Igor Stravinsky's *Le Renard*. Her own major creations were *Les Noces* (1923) and *Les Biches* (1924). Further spells of work in Buenos Aires and Paris, where she choreographed *La Valse* (1929) for Ida Rubinstein, were followed by a short-lived attempt to create her own ballet company (1932).

From 1935 onwards Nijinska devoted most of her time to choreography. Living mainly in the United States, she founded a ballet school in Los Angeles in 1938. In 1964 she staged triumphant revivals of *Les Noces* and *Les Biches* at London's Covent Garden.

Nilsson, Birgit (1918–) *Swedish opera singer*

Birgit Nilsson was one of the foremost Wagnerian sopranos of all time and a frequent performer at the Bayreuth Festival.

Marta Birgit Svensson grew up in rural Karup, where her contribution to the church choir and school concerts revealed a talent that was later developed by the Scottish tenor Joseph Hislop at the Stockholm Royal Academy of Music. Following her debut there in 1946, she achieved a major success in Verdi's *Lady Macbeth* with the Royal Opera. Engagements followed at Glyndebourne, the Vienna State Opera, and La Scala in Milan.

In 1948 she married Bertil Niklasson. Her exceptionally powerful voice and masterly interpretation of major Wagnerian roles, such as Isolde and Brünnhilde, made her almost an annual fixture at the Bayreuth Festival from 1953 until 1970. She also proved no less adept in roles created by Mozart, Richard Strauss, and Puccini. Birgit Nilsson made her American debut in 1956 in San Francisco and her New York debut with the Metropolitan Opera in 1959, appearing there continually until her retirement in 1982.

Nilsson's recordings include two complete versions of Wagner's *Ring* cycle. In 1969 the Austrian government acclaimed her lifetime's achievement with the honorary title of Kammersangerin (court singer), and in 1981 the Swedish government issued a postage stamp in her honour.

Nin, Anaïs (1903–1977) *French-born American writer*

Anaïs Nin is best known for the seven-volume *Journals*, which include frank accounts of her sex life.

The daughter of Spanish composer Joaquin Nin, Anaïs Nin was born in fashionable Neuilly, near Paris. Following her father's desertion of the family, she moved at the age of 11 with her Cuban mother to live in New York, where she began to write a diary, initially as a plea for her father's return. This was the origin of the multivolume diary covering the period from 1931 to 1974 and published as *Journals* (1966–83), which became her most celebrated work and a major source for her novels. Nin returned to France after completing her education and lived there until the outbreak of World War II, taking an active part in intellectual life and exploring such avant-garde movements as surrealism and psychoanalysis, which she studied under Otto Rank.

Her first published work was *D. H. Lawrence: An Unprofessional Study* (1932). This critical account of the British novelist (who had died in 1930) was admired by the Paris-based American writer Henry Miller, who became her lover and a lifelong friend. In 1936 Nin published her first novel, *The House of Incest*. After returning to New York City in 1939, she published at her own expense a series of novels and short stories: *Winter of Artifice* (1939), *Under a Glass Bell* (1944), *Ladders to Fire* (1946), *Children of the Albatross* (1947), *The Four-Chambered Heart* (1950), *A Spy in the House of Love* (1954), and *Solar Barque* (1958).

Although acclaimed by many leading writers, these works were largely ignored by critics and the general reading public. Recognition finally came to Nin in 1966 with the publication of the first volume of her diaries, covering the years 1931 to 1934, which reawakened interest in the interlinked five-novel sequence running from *Ladders to Fire* to *Solar Barque*. The diaries are remarkable for their frank account of the writer's sexual life and fantasies, as well as their depiction of the world of the artistic avant-garde. Praised for their lyrical style and psychological insight, they have also been dismissed as undisciplined and self-obsessed.

Nin's later works included *The Novel of the Future* (1968) and, published after her death, *Delta of Venus* (1977) and *Little Birds* (1979), erotic works written during the 1940s when she badly needed money.

Noddack, Ida (Eva Tacke) (1896–1979) *German chemist*

Ida Noddack is remembered for her discovery of the element rhenium but is perhaps more remarkable for her prediction of nuclear fission.

Ida Eva Tacke was born at Lackhausen in Germany and educated at the Technical University in Berlin, where she met her future husband, Walter Noddack, when they were both working in a testing laboratory. After their marriage they became lifelong partners in research. Their collaboration led to the discovery by means of x-ray spectroscopy of a new element, which they named rhenium, after the Rhine River, near which Ida had been born.

In 1934 Ida offered a new interpretation of the results of an experiment in which the physicist Enrico Fermi had bombarded uranium with slow neutrons in the hope of producing artificial elements. She wrote: "It is conceivable that in the bombardment of heavy nuclei with neutrons, these nuclei break up into several large fragments which are actually isotopes of known elements, not neighbours of the irradiated element." This hypothesis amounted to a description of what came to be known as nuclear fission. Although Ida Noddack forwarded a copy of her paper to Fermi, he ignored it. Her insight was finally confirmed in 1939 by the work of Lise MEITNER and Otto Frisch, who established nuclear fission as the basis of the atom bomb and of nuclear energy.

In the course of her long career Ida Noddack published over 100 learned papers, notably on the photochemical problems affecting the human eye.

Noether, Amalie (1882–1935) *German mathematician*

> In the judgment of the most competent living mathematicians, Fraulein Noether was the most significant mathematical genius thus far produced since the higher education of women began.
>
> —Albert Einstein, in his obituary of Noether in *The New York Times*

A mathematician of outstanding ability, Amalie Noether, always known as Emmy, delighted her students with her gift for clarifying complicated ideas. She also broke the traditional male monopoly of faculty status in German universities. Her departure to the United States in response to Nazi oppression of Jews deprived Göttingen University of one of its most able mathematicians.

Emmy Noether was the eldest daughter of Max Noether, professor of mathematics at the University of Erlangen. She initially intended to become a teacher of English and French. Because women at that time were barred from becoming official students at universities, she was only allowed to attend lectures (1900–02). Switching from languages to mathematics, she persisted in her studies and was eventually awarded a doctorate in mathematics in 1907. Despite this, as a woman she was still barred from joining the university faculty and forced to continue her research independently.

In 1915 she was invited by Professor David Hilbert to the University of Göttingen, where she gave lectures that had to be officially timetabled in Hilbert's name. Meanwhile she worked on the mathematical problems raised by Einstein's general theory of relativity. Emmy Noether was recognized as an "unofficial associate professor" in 1919 and accepted as a member of the Göttingen faculty in 1922, albeit without a salary; instead she received periodic grants in recognition of her teaching.

Throughout the 1920s she continued her research and established new fields of mathematical inquiry, such as the general theory of ideals and noncommutative algebras, in which the order of multiplying numbers affects the result. In the field of abstract algebras the concept known as "Noetherian rings" became an area of further exploration by later mathematicians. In 1933 the Nazi government banned Jews from teaching in universities, and Emmy Noether emigrated to the United States, accepting a professorial chair at Bryn Mawr College in Pennsylvania. She died two years later from complications following surgery, having published some 45 learned papers in the course of her career.

Noonuccal, Oodgeroo Moongalba
(1920–1993) *Australian writer and Aboriginal rights activist*

Oodgeroo Noonuccal is the tribal name adopted by Kath Walker in 1988; she became Australia's first published Aboriginal writer in 1964, using her birth name.

Brought up with the Noonuccal tribe on Stradbroke Island, Queensland, Kathleen Jean Walker worked as a domestic servant in her birthplace, Brisbane, from the age of 13 until she joined the Australian Women's Army Service during World War II. Largely self-educated, in 1964 she published her collection of poems *We Are Going. The Dawn Is at Hand* followed in 1966, and the two works, with additional material, were reissued in 1970 as *My People, a Kath Walker Collection*. A selection of Aboriginal stories, *Stradbroke Dreamtime*, appeared in 1972.

Thanks to a Fulbright Scholarship she was able to visit the United States and lecture on Aboriginal rights in 1978–79. In 1985 she published *Quandamooka, the Art of Kath Walker*. An active member of the Aboriginal Arts Board, she also ran a Centre for Aboriginal Culture on Stradbroke Island, for children of all races. The Australian composer Malcolm Williamson arranged some of her poems for choir and orchestra as *The Dawn Is at Hand*, which had its first performance in 1989.

Norman, Dorothy Stecker
(1905–) *American photographer, writer, and political activist*

Known for her writings on and devotion to the American photographer Alfred Stieglitz, Dorothy Norman was also praised for her own photographic nature studies, architectural views, and portraits of prominent cultural figures.

Born into a prosperous German-Jewish family in Philadelphia, Dorothy Stecker attended Smith College and the University of Pennsylvania, as well as studying art history at the Barnes Foundation in Merion, Pennsylvania. In 1925 she married businessman Edward Norman, moving with him to New York, where she involved herself in such campaigning organizations as the American Civil Liberties Union, the Urban League, and Margaret SANGER's Birth Control League.

In 1926 she met Alfred Stieglitz, founder of the Intimate Gallery on Park Avenue and a pioneer in the use of photography in support of social causes. Finding that his ideas exactly mirrored her own twin passions for the arts and activism, she became his devoted pupil, disciple, and lover, despite the 40-year gap in their ages and his marriage to Georgia O'KEEFFE. In 1932 they worked together to open An American Place, a gallery that provided the focus for their photographic work until his death in 1946. Editing *Twice a Year: A Book of Literature, the Arts and Civil Liberties* from 1938 to 1948 and writing a column three times a week for the *New York Post* from 1942 to 1949, Norman also became deeply involved in India's struggle for independence from British rule.

In 1973 she published the first full-length biography of Stieglitz and wrote *Encounters – A Memoir* (1987), in which she recorded her impressions of Theodore Dreiser, Lewis Mumford, and other members of Steiglitz's artistic and intellectual network. The International Center of Photography in New York City subsequently honoured her life's achievement as a photographer of portraits, architecture, and nature with a retrospective exhibition.

Norman, Jessye
(1945–) *American opera singer*

Jessye Norman is an immensely popular singer with an exceptionally broad repertoire.

Born in Augusta, Georgia, Jessye Norman won a scholarship to Howard University in Washington, D.C., before continuing her musical education at the Peabody Conservatory and the University of Michigan, where she received a master's degree in music (1968). Winning the Munich International Music Competition that year enabled her to launch her professional career; she made her operatic debut at the German Opera, Berlin, in 1969 as

Elisabeth in Wagner's *Tannhäuser*. In 1972 Jessye Norman made her debut at La Scala, Milan, in the title role of Verdi's *Aïda*, and at Covent Garden in London as Cassandre in *Les Troyens* by Berlioz. In the same year she finally made her American debut at a Hollywood Bowl concert, as well as scoring further triumphs at the Tanglewood Festival in Massachusetts and the Edinburgh Festival. Touring the world for the next decade, Norman developed an unusually versatile repertoire, ranging from Mozart and Mahler to Poulenc and Gershwin and from Negro spirituals to Schoenberg.

Her formidable physique, while adding to the depth and range of her voice and her commanding presence on stage, has precluded her from those classic opera roles by Mozart and Verdi that demand agility as well as dramatic power. Jessye Norman first appeared at the Metropolitan Opera in New York in September 1983, once again as Cassandre. A month later she took part in the gala staged to mark the centenary of the "Met." Her extraordinary popularity and critical standing have enabled her to attract audiences to unlikely successes, such as Schoenberg's *Erwartung*, the Metropolitan Opera's first one-character opera, as well as rarely performed works by Bartók and Janáček.

Jessye Norman has been showered with honours. On Bastille Day (July 14) 1989 she was invited to sing to a global audience in a TV broadcast organized to celebrate the bicentennial of the French Revolution. In 1990 she was named an Honorary Ambassador to the United Nations.

Normand, Mabel (1894–1930) *American actress*

Mabel Normand's career as a comedienne of silent movies and costar of Charlie Chaplin came to a premature end because of her association with two murders.

Born Mabel Fortescue in Boston, Massachusetts, she began her film career in 1911 after meeting producer-director Mack Sennett in New York and moving with his company to Hollywood in 1912. In 1914 she starred with Charlie Chaplin and Marie Dressler in *Tillie's Punctured Romance*, a classic of the silent screen. Typically playing comic tomboy roles, she became a regular in Sennett's Keystone Kops knockabout shorts, before progressing to become Chaplin's costar and occasional director. Her first solo feature, *Mickey* (1917), was a triumph.

Despite marriage to the popular actor-director Lew Cody, her career came to an end as a result of her entanglement in two major scandals. The first involved the murder of director William Desmond Taylor at his Hollywood home. The investigation led to allegations that she was involved with Taylor in drug abuse and orgies, although she was cleared of any part in the killing. Soon afterwards, however, Normand invited her chauffeur to a drinking party at the home of actress Edna Purviance, Chaplin's leading lady. The chauffeur shot another male guest. Normand never made another film and died of tuberculosis in Monrovia, California, aged 35.

North, Marianne (1830–1890) *British botanical painter*

North devoted her life to drawing and painting the flowers and trees of the world, and in the course of her travels she discovered a number of previously unclassified species. The North Gallery at Kew Gardens was opened in 1882 to display her work.

Marianne North was born in Hastings, Sussex, the daughter of Liberal MP Frederick North. Her father's family owned an estate in Norfolk, and Marianne spent part of her childhood there. Apart from a brief unhappy period at a school in Norwich, she had little formal education, but taught herself to paint and took a keen interest in the plants that grew at Kew and in the botanic gardens in Hastings. A tour of Europe with her parents in the late 1840s gave Marianne the opportunity to study and sketch the flowers that grew there, and a subsequent trip to Syria and Egypt introduced her to more exotic flora.

After the death of her parents, North embarked on an ambitious project to paint the plant life of the world in its natural surroundings. In the early 1870s she travelled to Jamaica, Canada, the United States, and Brazil, then moved on to Japan, Borneo, Java, and Singapore. In 1877–79 she toured the Indian subcontinent and explored the foothills of the Himalayas. On her return to England she offered her ever-increasing collection of drawings and paintings to Kew Gardens to be exhibited in a new gallery built at her own expense. There was considerable interest in her work among naturalists such as Charles Darwin, who encouraged her to continue her travels; between 1880 and 1885 she visited Australia, New Zealand, South Africa, and Chile.

Ill health finally obliged North to retire, and in 1886 she settled in a house in Gloucestershire. There she cultivated a beautiful garden, with plants from many regions. Her autobiography, *Recollections of a Happy Life*, was edited by her sister and published posthumously in 1892.

Norton, Caroline (1808–1877) *British writer and campaigner on women's issues*

Caroline Norton, as a result of her failed marriage to a litigious barrister, became involved in the reform of the legal status of women in 19th-century Britain.

Caroline Elizabeth Sarah Sheridan was born in London, the granddaughter of the dramatist and politician Richard Brinsley Sheridan. A precocious child, she had her first poetic work, *The Dandies' Rout*, published when she was only 13. In 1827 she made a disastrous marriage to the Honourable George Norton, a lawyer and wastrel; she bore him three sons in as many years, as well as publishing a successful book of verse, *The Sorrows of Rosalie* (1829), to supplement the family income.

Caroline left her husband in 1830, obtaining a legal separation from him in 1836. He responded by charging her friend, the prime minister Lord Melbourne, with having had "criminal conversation" (i.e., committed adultery) with Caroline. The motive may

have been political rather than personal because when the case came to court, the jury thought the prosecution evidence so feeble that they dismissed the charge without even leaving the courtroom. Defeated, Norton denied Caroline access to their sons. Caroline responded by suing him for custody. Melbourne, whatever his relationship with Caroline, was still prime minister and managed to persuade parliament to pass an Infant Custody Act, guaranteeing mothers at least limited access to their children.

Caroline continued to write poetry, publishing *The Dream* (1840) and *Aunt Carry's Ballads* (1847) as well as a novel, *Stuart of Dunleath* (1851). In 1855 she became entangled in another lawsuit with her estranged husband, who tried to claim that the income from her writings should be his. Caroline's well-argued pamphlet *English Laws for Women in the Nineteenth Century* helped promote the 1857 Marriage and Divorce Act, strengthening the rights of wives.

Caroline's most successful poetry, *The Lady of La Garaye* (1862), was followed by novels drawing on her own unhappy experiences, *Lost and Saved* (1863) and *Old Sir Douglas* (1867). George Norton's death (1875) enabled Caroline to enjoy just a few happy weeks as the wife of Sir William Stirling-Maxwell, whom she married in 1877. Norton's case against Lord Melbourne inspired the farcical breach of promise case of *Bardell vs Pickwick* in Dickens's *Pickwick Papers*, which was written soon afterwards. Caroline herself became the model for the central character in George Meredith's novel *Diana of the Crossways* (1885).

Novak, Kim (1933–) *American actress*

> The head of publicity of the Hollywood studio told me, "You're a piece of meat, that's all." When I made my first screen test the director explained to everyone, "Don't listen to her, just look."
>
> —Quoted by Derek Winnert in *The Virgin Encyclopaedia of the Movies* (1995)

Big, blonde, and beautiful, Kim Novak was never a natural in front of the camera; however, she occasionally rose above the stereotyped roles in which she was usually cast and by sheer determination broke out of the starlet mould for which the studio system originally destined her.

Born Marilyn Pauline Novak in Chicago, the daughter of Czech immigrants, she emerged from obscurity as "Miss Deepfreeze" in a series of refrigerator commercials. Spotted by Columbia studios, at the age of 20 she was launched as a sex symbol and potential successor to Rita HAYWORTH, a previous Columbia discovery who had become "difficult."

Novak showed that she could be more than a dumb blonde with her portrayal of the tortured girlfriend of a drug abuser (Frank Sinatra) in *The Man with the Golden Arm* (1955). She gave her finest screen performance in the dual role of Madeleine/Judy, the object of James Stewart's obsession in Hitchcock's masterly thriller *Vertigo* (1958). Hitchcock, however, thought her acting wooden and remained unimpressed. In Billy Wilder's *Kiss Me, Stupid* (1964) Novak showed unexpected skill in a comic role. However, a serious car accident and a weight problem denied her the opportunity to develop her career further. During the subsequent decades she made periodical comebacks in such films as *Just a Gigolo* (1979) and *Liebestraum* (1991).

Nüsslein-Volhard, Christiane
(1942–) *German biologist*

Christiane Nüsslein-Volhard shared the 1995 Nobel Prize for physiology or medicine with Edward Lewis and Eric Wieschaus for their work on the development of fruit flies. This work led subsequently to other biologists making important discoveries of the genes responsible for development, regeneration, and repair of tissues in higher animals.

Nüsslein-Volhard was educated at the University of Tübingen. After a spell at the European Molecular Biology Laboratory at Heidelberg, she moved in 1981 to the Max Planck Institute for Development, Tübingen, where she has served since 1990 as the director of the department of genetics.

From 1978 to 1981 Nüsslein-Volhard collaborated with Eric Wieschaus on identifying the genes responsible for the development of the fruit fly *Drosophila melanogaster*. After examining many thousands of specially bred mutant flies, they had managed by 1980 to identify the main development sequence in *Drosophila*.

Nüsslein-Volhard also succeeded in illuminating the general process of development. It had long been thought that differentiation in early embryos – head from tail, for example, or back from front – was caused by varying concentrations of substances along the axis of the egg. This theory of "morphological gradients," as it is known, has recently been supported by experimental work carried out by Nüsslein-Volhard and her Tübingen colleagues.

O

Oakley, Ann (1944–) *British writer and sociologist*

Ann Oakley is known both for her novels and for her feminist writings, which have influenced contemporary attitudes to such issues as housework and motherhood. In 1991 she became professor of sociology and social policy at the University of London.

She was born Ann Titmuss in London. Her mother was a former social worker, her father a social analyst involved in the foundation of the welfare state. After studying at Chiswick Polytechnic, Somerville College, Oxford, and London University, she married Robin Oakley and bore him three children. In ·1974 she became a research officer at Bedford College, London.

Oakley's writings are largely concerned with feminist issues, examining the position of women in modern society and the roles traditionally assigned to them. Her first book, *Sex, Gender and Society* (1972), was followed by two publications focusing on the role of women in the home, *Housewife* and *The Sociology of Housework* (both 1974). She collaborated with Juliet MITCHELL on the essay collections *The Rights and Wrongs of Women* (1976), *What is Feminism?* (1986), and *Who's Afraid of Feminism?* (1998). The birth of her children inspired two books on motherhood, *Becoming a Mother* (1979) and *Women Confined* (1980). Her other works include the autobiographical *Taking It Like a Woman* (1984), and the novels *The Men's Room* (1988), which was serialized on BBC television, *Scenes Originating in the Garden of Eden* (1993), and *A Proper Holiday* (1996). Her *Essays on Women, Medicine and Health* appeared in 1994.

Oakley, Annie (1860–1926) *American sharp-shooter*

> I can shoot as well as you...You take one shot while I hold the object for you, and then I take the next one, you acting as holder for me.
>
> —Addressing her husband, quoted by Courtney Ryley Cooper in *Annie Oakley: Woman at Arms*

Described by Chief Sitting Bull as "Little Sure-Shot," Annie Oakley became a legend in her own lifetime on account of her shooting skills.

Phoebe Anne Oakley Moses was born into a Quaker family in Patterson Township; Darke County, Ohio. As a child she showed such astonishing talent with a rifle that she helped to clear the mortgage on the family farm in just five years by shooting game. In a shooting match at Cincinnati she beat Frank E. Butler, a marksman who performed in vaudeville theatres, by a single point. Butler eventually married her and became her manager and assistant.

In 1885 Annie and Butler joined Buffalo Bill's celebrated Wild West Show, touring worldwide for 17 years. Annie Oakley's amazing stunts included shooting a cigarette from her husband's lips, hitting a dime tossed up 90 feet away from her, and cutting a playing card with a single shot – edge on. Her trick of shooting the pips out of a playing card thrown in the air led to a new phrase in American English – an "Annie Oakley" was the name given to a punched free ticket for a performance or other public occasion.

The 1946 Irving Berlin musical *Annie Get Your Gun* was based on her remarkable life; the film version of this musical appeared in 1950.

Oates, Joyce Carol (1938–) *American writer*

A prolific and versatile author, Oates has produced over 50 works, including novels, short stories, plays, essays, and poetry.

Joyce Carol Oates was born in Lockport, New York State. After her education at the universities of Syracuse and Wisconsin, she taught English at the universities of Detroit, Windsor, Ontario, and Princeton, where she was writer-in-residence (1978–81), while simultaneously pursuing her own literary career. Her works explore the theme of violence in American life in a wide range of genres, from neogothic fantasies to historical novels and naturalistic stories set in decaying inner-city ghettos.

Her first collection of short stories, *By the North Gate*, was published in 1963 and her first novel, *With Shuddering Fall*, in 1964. Her fourth novel, *them* (1969), won a U.S. National Book Award and was the final volume in a trilogy chronicling the lives of three American families from the Depression years to the race riots of the 1960s. *Son of the Morning* (1978) depicts the fanaticism of an evangelical preacher, while *Foxfire: Confessions of a Girl Gang* (1993) deals with teenage aggression. Her short stories, published in volumes such as *Last Days* (1984), *Raven's Wing* (1985), and *The Assignation* (1988), won her the prestigious O. Henry Award in 1970 and again in 1986. She edited the *Oxford Book of American Short Stories* in 1993. In 1987 she published *On Boxing*, a celebration of a sport that has long fascinated her. Joyce Carol Oates has also published thrillers under the pen name Rosamond Smith and edits the *Ontario Review* with her husband, Raymond J. Smith.

Oberon, Merle (1911–1979) *British film actress*

Dark-eyed, graceful, and hauntingly beautiful, Merle Oberon was one of the most captivating Hollywood stars of the 1930s and 1940s.

Estelle Merle Thompson was born in Bombay, the daughter of a British army officer and a Singhalese mother. To conceal her mixed-race background, she later manufactured a false biography, claiming to have been born in Tasmania of mixed Irish, French, and Dutch ancestry.

After moving to England in the early 1930s, she became a dance hostess (as "Queenie O'Brien") at London's fashionable Café de Paris and played bit parts (as "Estelle Thompson") on stage and in films. This led to her being discovered by the Hungarian-born producer Alexander Korda, the dominant force in British film-making in the 1930s. In 1933 Korda, who became the first of her four husbands, launched her to stardom by casting her as Anne BOLEYN in his hugely successful film *The Private Life of Henry VIII*. This appearance brought her to the attention of Sam Goldwyn, who took her to Hollywood. The following year she played opposite Douglas Fairbanks Snr in *The Private Life of Don Juan* and with Leslie Howard in the film version of Baroness ORCZY's *The Scarlet Pimpernel*.

A severe car crash in 1937 might have ended her career prematurely, but facial surgery saved her classic features and she went on to give her most notable performance, as Cathy in the 1939 Hollywood version of Emily BRONTË's *Wuthering Heights*. Thereafter she worked mainly in the United States. In 1945 she played George SAND in the Chopin biopic *A Song to Remember* and in 1954 Napoleon's JOSÉPHINE in *Desirée*. Her last screen appearance was in 1973.

O'Brien, Edna (1932–) *Irish writer*

> My aim is to write books that in some way celebrate life and do justice to my emotions.
> —Quoted in *Chambers Biographical Dictionary of Women*

Edna O'Brien is best known for a series of novels exploring the sexual lives of young Irishwomen in flight from a puritanical male-dominated culture.

Born at Tuamgraney, County Clare, in the rural west of Ireland, Edna O'Brien was educated at convent schools and trained as a pharmacist. In 1960 she found overnight celebrity with her first novel, *The Country Girls*, a semi-autobiographical account of two village innocents who escape to the intoxicating bright lights of Dublin. Their story was continued in *The Lonely Girl* (1962) and *Girls in Their Married Bliss* (1963), which moves the scene to London. Typically O'Brien's heroines experience solitude, frustration, and male treachery and respond with rebellion and self-destructive behaviour; although they enjoy intermittent good times, these seldom last long.

Long banned in her native country for the frankness of their descriptions of female sexuality, O'Brien's novels in their turn depict Ireland as puritanical, hypocritical, and violent. However, her work found an appreciative audience in Britain: in 1962 she received the Kingsley Amis First Novel Award for *The Country Girls* and in 1971 the *Yorkshire Post* Novel Award for *A Pagan Place* (1970). She has continued to produce novels and stories at a prodigious pace. *Johnny I Hardly Knew You* (1977), a tale of crime and passion, was written in just three weeks. She has also written plays, nonfiction, a children's book entitled *The Dazzle* (1981), and a volume of verse, *On the Bone* (1989). In 1965 *The Lonely Girl* was filmed as *The Girl with Green Eyes*, for which she wrote the screenplay. Her more recent novels include *House of Splendid Isolation* (1994) and *Down By the River* (1996), a grim tale of rape and infanticide in rural Ireland.

O'Connor, Flannery (1925–1962)
American writer

O'Connor's fiction is characterized by terse deceptively simple prose, a keen ear for Southern dialect, and violent, grotesque, and bizarre characters.

Born Mary Flannery O'Connor in Savannah, Georgia, she graduated from the Georgia State College for Women (1945) and earned a master's degree in creative writing from the University of Iowa (1947).

Brought up a Roman Catholic in a region dominated by fundamentalist Protestants, she attacked the shortcomings of traditional Southern culture in her first novel *Wise Blood*

(1952), a tragicomic story of religious extremism. In *A Good Man Is Hard to Find* (1955) she offered readers "nine stories about original sin." Her second and last novel, *The Violent Bear It Away* (1960), is another story of pride and fanaticism. A second volume of short stories, *Everything That Rises Must Converge*, appeared shortly after her early death from lupus, a debilitating disease of the skin and internal organs that reduced her to an invalid from the age of 25. Also published after her death were her essays on the craft of writing, *Mystery and Manners* (1969), and a selection of her letters, *The Habit of Being* (1979). The central theme of her writing is a traditionally Catholic concern with sin and the need for redemption.

O'Connor, Sandra Day (1930–)
American judge

Sandra Day O'Connor was the first woman to be appointed a justice of the U.S. Supreme Court.

Born in El Paso, Texas, Sandra Day took bachelor and law degrees from Stanford University before marrying (1952) her classmate John Jay O'Connor III and being admitted to the California Bar. After some years living in Germany, where she was employed as a civilian lawyer by the U.S. Army, she worked in legal practice in Arizona, then became a Republican activist, serving as the state's assistant attorney general (1965–68). From 1969 she was a state senator, becoming senate majority leader in 1973. In 1974 she left politics to become judge of the superior court of Phoenix and then in 1979 a judge of the court of appeals.

In July 1981 President Ronald Reagan, redeeming an electoral pledge, nominated her to become the first woman justice of the U.S. Supreme Court. Her appointment was unanimously confirmed by the Senate.

O'Connor, Sinead (1967–) *Irish singer and songwriter*

O'Connor is an intense and uncompromising performer whose voice has been described as ranging "from an ethereal whisper hanging over your shoulder to a torrid scream raging outside your window."

Dublin-born Sinead O'Connor suffered a deeply traumatic childhood. Following the break-up of her parents' marriage when she was eight, she lived with her mother, a fanatical Roman Catholic who subjected her to physical and sexual abuse. Having been expelled from a succession of Catholic schools and repeatedly arrested for shoplifting, she ended up in a reform school at 14. Here her musical talent came to the notice of a sympathetic teacher. O'Connor subsequently moved to Dublin where she begged, sang on street corners, and worked as a waitress to support her studies at the College of Music.

In 1985 she was heard by an English record producer who brought her to London to record her first album, *The Lion and the Cobra* (1987), a sometimes harrowing collection that won high praise from the critics. International stardom followed in 1990, when the ballad "Nothing Compares 2 U," topped the charts in 16 countries; a second album, *I Do Not Want What I Haven't Got*, also proved a massive success.

Despite these triumphs, O'Connor's career remained dogged by her outspoken (and sometimes outlandish) statements on political and religious matters. This trend culminated in autumn 1992, when an American audience responded to her previous action of ripping up a picture of the Pope on live television by booing her off stage at a high-profile New York concert. The following months were marked by withdrawal from public performance, near-breakdown, and an apparent suicide attempt.

In 1994 O'Connor returned with *Universal Mother*, a gentler collection dealing with themes of motherhood and women's spirituality. The same interests surface on the extended-play disc *Gospel Oak* (1997).

Octavia (c. 40–62) *First wife of the Roman emperor Nero*

The daughter of the emperor Claudius and his ruthless wife MESSALINA, Octavia was, through her mother's line, a granddaughter of OCTAVIA MINOR, the wife of Mark Antony.

At the age of 13 she was married to her cousin the future emperor Nero (reigned 54–68), who was himself only 16. Mentally unbalanced and unfaithful, he eventually divorced her in 62 to marry Poppaea Sabina.

Octavia was, however, so personally popular that Nero felt obliged to recall her to Rome, where her enthusiastic reception by the mob enraged Poppaea. Exiled to the island of Pandataria (now Ventotene) on a false charge of having been unfaithful to Nero, Octavia was murdered there by assassins sent by Nero. The dramatist Lucius Annaeus Seneca, Nero's tutor and adviser, is thought to be the author of a 1st-century tragedy based on Octavia's life, although it may have been written by Curiatius Maternus.

Octavia Minor (died 11 BC) *Roman aristocrat*

The beautiful and virtuous Octavia was the sister of Octavian, who eventually became the emperor Augustus, and the long-suffering wife of Mark Antony.

Octavia was initially married to Gaius Claudius Marcellus, who became consul in 50 BC. They had two daughters and a son. Although Octavia's ambitious granduncle Julius Caesar wanted to divorce her from Marcellus so that he could marry her to his ally Pompey (whose wife Julia, Caesar's daughter, had recently died), both Marcellus and Pompey objected to the proposed arrangement.

Following the death of Marcellus in 40, Octavia agreed to marry Mark Antony, and in 37 she was able to defuse a major political crisis arising from the rivalry between her brother and her husband.

Despite Octavia's fine qualities and great tact, however, Antony became hopelessly obsessed with the Egyptian queen, CLEOPATRA, leading to further friction with Octavian. Even though Octavia came to the East in 35 with troops and money to support his cause, he refused to see her, formally divorcing her in 32. This led to open war and to the suicides of Antony and Cleopatra following their military defeat by Octavian. Nevertheless, Octavia continued to care for Antony's children by both his first wife Fulvia and Cleopatra. Octavia's son by her first husband, Marcus Marcellus, was adopted by Octavian, now the emperor Augustus, as his heir. Marcus, however, died prematurely in 23, grievously mourned by Octavia, who withdrew from public life. Her two daughters by Antony became the grandmothers of the emperors Caligula and Nero. Augustus perpetuated Octavia's memory by building a ceremonial arch named in her honour, the Porticus Octaviae (Gate of Octavia).

O'Hair, Madalyn Murray (1919–)
American atheist campaigner

A colourful and controversial figure, Madalyn Murray O'Hair has acquired fresh notoriety since her unexplained disappearance in 1995.

Born in Pittsburgh, Pennsylvania, the daughter of a Presbyterian father and a Lutheran mother, Madalyn Mays served in World War II as a codebreaker with the Women's Army Corps and was decorated for service in Italy and Africa. After the war she graduated with a BA from Ashland College (1948) and LLB from South Texas College of Law (1953). Having failed in her ambition to become a lawyer, she became increasingly concerned to promote atheism and in 1963 brought a suit against the city of Baltimore to outlaw Bible reading and prayers in public schools. This eventually led the U.S. Supreme Court to ban such practices as unconstitutional.

O'Hair's subsequent efforts to obtain legal bans on the display of religious objects in public places, to end tax exemptions on buildings used for public worship, and to remove the words "In God We Trust" from U.S. currency have been denied by the Supreme Court. Following the breakup of her unconventional marriage to William J. Murray, she married Texas artist Richard Franklin O'Hair in 1965. In that same year she published *Why I Am an Atheist* and founded American Atheists, the world's largest atheist organization. Her other foundations include United World Atheists and the American Atheist Library and Archives.

Since August 1995 O'Hair has been at the centre of a mystery that remains unresolved. In that month O'Hair, her youngest son, and her granddaughter disappeared without trace from their Texas home. Although many of her associates believe that the family was murdered or abducted by religious extremists, the police have discounted such theories. The discovery that well over $600,000 is missing from an American Atheists bank account held in New Zealand has led others to believe that the trio is in hiding there. A third theory is that O'Hair, knowing that she was dying, arranged the disappearance to avoid any possibility of a Christian burial.

O'Hara, Maureen (1920–) *Irish-born American film actress*

> The essential O'Hara is a free spirit who refuses to behave like a lady.
>
> —Rodney Farnsworth, quoted in the *International Dictionary of Films and Filmmakers* (1997)

A red-haired green-eyed beauty, O'Hara became known as the "Queen of Technicolor" for her glamorous leading roles of the 1940s and 1950s.

Born Maureen Fitzsimons in Millwall, near Dublin, she made her radio debut at the age of 12 and received a thorough grounding in the performing arts at the Abbey Theatre School, Dublin, the Guildhall School of Music, London, and the London College of Music. Her screen debut came in 1938 and her first starring role the following year in Alfred Hitchcock's *Jamaica Inn*. Later that year she travelled to Hollywood to play the gipsy Esmeralda in the classic Charles Laughton version of *The Hunchback of Notre Dame*. She went on to make over 50 more American films, notably several with director John Ford and his favourite leading man, John Wayne; these include the Western *Rio Grande* (1950) and the romantic comedy *The Quiet Man* (1952). As a redhead, O'Hara was vulnerable to typecasting and frequently found herself playing the rebellious spitfire needing a strong man to tame her for her own good.

Maureen O'Hara's stunning good looks led film-makers and critics alike to underestimate her very real abilities as an actress. She had her revenge, after a 20-year layoff, playing a superb cameo role as the manipulative mother in *Only the Lonely* (1991).

O'Keeffe, Georgia (1887–1986)
American painter

> This woman who lives fearlessly, reasons logically, who is modest, unassertive and spiritually beautiful and who, because she dares paint as she feels, has become not only one of the most magical artists of our time but one of the most stimulatingly powerful.
> —Blanche Matthias, *Chicago Evening News*, 1926

Taking natural objects such as rocks, clouds, and flowers as her subjects, Georgia O'Keeffe reduced them to an almost abstract simplicity.

Born on a farm in rural Wisconsin, O'Keeffe studied for four years (1904–08) at the Art Institute of Chicago and the Art Students League in New York. In 1912 a summer painting course run by Arthur Dow introduced her to Asian art; from that year until 1918 she taught art in Texas. In 1916 photographer Alfred Stieglitz, the founder of the avant-garde 291 Gallery in New York, began to exhibit her work. She moved to New York in 1918, marrying Stieglitz in 1924 and becoming his model for an extensive series of portrait photographs. At this time O'Keeffe's painting focused on close-up views of flowers, such as *Black Iris* (1926) and *Black Flower and Blue Larkspur* (1929), both now in the Metropolitan Museum of Art, New York. New York City itself and the East River also supplied her with subject matter.

Her career took a new turn with her discovery of the bleak grandeur of the desert landscape of New Mexico in 1929. She moved there permanently after Stieglitz 's death in 1946. Typically her desert views included bold horizon lines, huge skies, and such motifs as rocks, flowers, and animal skulls and bones. A world tour by plane in 1959 opened another new dimension to her art as she began to paint skyscapes as seen from the viewpoint of an aeroplane. Space, simplicity, sensuousness, and an atmosphere of reverential stillness remained the abiding hallmarks of her highly individual work.

Georgia O'Keeffe was honoured by the award of the gold medal for painting of the National Institute of Arts and Letters (1970), the Presidential Medal of Freedom (1977), and the National Medal of Arts (1985).

See also NORMAN, DOROTHY STECKER.

Olga, Saint (*c.* 890–969) *Russian ruler*

The first Russian saint, Olga played a leading part in bringing Christianity to Russia.

Olga, a peasant by birth, married Igor, prince of Kiev, who met her while out hunting. Igor was assassinated in 945 during a revolt against the taxes raised to pay for his border wars. Olga then ruthlessly avenged his death, scalding the ringleaders to death and executing hundreds of others. She became Russia's first female ruler, acting as regent of Kiev until her son Svyatoslav was old enough to take the throne in 955.

Around 957 she was baptized in Constantinople, becoming the first member of the ruling house of Kiev to embrace Christianity and taking the name Helena. On returning to Russia, she campaigned on behalf of her new faith. After her death she was canonized by the Orthodox Church under her original name of Olga. Svyatoslav remained a pagan, but Olga's grandson St. Vladimir I renewed her efforts to spread Christianity in Russia.

Oliphant, Margaret (1828–1897)
British writer

Over the course of her career as a writer Margaret Oliphant was to produce some 120 books and almost as many short stories and articles.

Born in Wallyford, Scotland, Margaret Wilson married her cousin, the artist Francis Wilson Oliphant, in 1852. The couple moved to Italy, where Francis died in 1859, leaving Margaret with three children to support. She also took responsibility for supporting her brother's children, thereby condemning herself to a life of literary toil. She had already been publishing stories about Scottish life since 1849, chiefly for the Edinburgh-based *Blackwood's Magazine*. *Caleb Field*, a historical novel, had appeared in 1851, and a domestic romance, *The Athelings*, was published in 1857.

Oliphant's best-known works were four linked novels, the *Chronicles of Carlingford*, which detailed small-town life with humour and insight and were published anonymously between 1863 and 1866; in *Salem Chapel* she portrayed the struggle between a bright young minister and his narrow-minded congregation, while *Miss Marjoribanks* describes the attempts of a young lady to get on in local society. In 1868 her efforts were recognized by the award of a government pension of £100 a year. Later she experimented with tales of the supernatural in *Stories of the Seen and Unseen*. She also wrote a much-praised *Literary History of England 1790–1825* (1882) and biographies of the controversial preacher Edward Irving and of her traveller cousin Laurence Oliphant. Her last works were a history of Blackwood's, *Annals of a Publishing House*, and an autobiography that poignantly evokes the unremitting grind of constant composition. Both were published after her death.

Olsen, Tillie (1913–) *American writer and political activist*

Olsen's writings on poverty, gender, and class have inspired not only a generation of feminist scholars but also novelists such as Margaret ATWOOD and Maxine Hong Kingston.

Tillie Lerner was born in Omaha, Nebraska, the daughter of Russian refugees who had fled their homeland following the failure of the 1905 revolution. Her father, a labourer, had maintained his political commitments and was secretary of the Nebraska Socialist Party. Poverty obliged her to leave school in the eleventh grade and complete her education by reading in public libraries. At 17 she joined the Young Communist League, and in 1932 she was jailed for distributing political leaflets. Enforced leisure gave

her the time to write political poetry and begin a novel, *Yonnondio*, which takes its title from a Native American word meaning "lament for the lost." In 1936 she began to live with the printer and trade unionist Jack Olsen, whom she married in 1943, and with whom she had four daughters.

Olsen did not resume writing until the 1950s and published her first volume of short stories, *Tell Me a Riddle*, when she was nearly 50. The volume won an O. Henry Award, and her stories have since appeared in over 50 anthologies. Her novel, which took almost 40 years to complete, appeared finally in 1974 as *Yonnondio: From the Thirties*, in which a young woman tells the story of her family's catastrophic efforts to escape poverty by moving from the countryside to the big city. It was hailed as a crushing indictment of deprivation in American society. Tillie Olsen's autobiographical *Silences* appeared in 1965, and in 1984 she published her own anthology of women's writings, *Mother to Daughter, Daughter to Mother*.

Olympias (*c.* 375–316 BC) *Greek ruler*

The formidable mother of Alexander the Great, Olympias was effective ruler of Macedon from 319 to 316 BC.

Olympias, the daughter of Neoptolemus, king of Epirus, was originally named Myrtale. Trained as a priestess in the cults of Orpheus and Dionysius, she became the principal wife of Philip II, ruler of Macedon, in 357 BC. When he divorced her to marry Cleopatra, niece of Attalus, in 355, she returned briefly to Epirus as its ruler; however, following Philip's assassination in 356, she returned to Macedon, where she had Cleopatra and her daughter killed.

Although the regent Antipater prevented her from exercising much influence over her son, Alexander, after his early death in 323 and the death of Antipater in 319, she was able to seize Macedon and indulge in an orgy of vengeful murders. After killing Alexander's half-witted half-brother and successor Philip III Arrhidaeus, she installed Alexander's posthumously born child as a puppet king, Alexander IV. Years of patience and intrigue had finally brought her undisputed power, but it was not to last. In 316 she was cornered in Pydna by Antipater's son, Cassander, and condemned to death. Cassander's soldiers refused to execute the mother of the world-conquering Alexander, and it was left to the relatives of her victims to carry out the sentence.

Onassis, Jacqueline Kennedy
(1929–1994) *American First Lady and fashion leader*

> I do not think it is altogether inappropriate to introduce myself...I am the man who accompanied Jacqueline Kennedy to Paris.
>
> —President John F. Kennedy, remark made at a Paris press conference, 1963

As the wife and then the widow of President Kennedy, she earned wide admiration for her gracious and dignified manner.

Born Jacqueline Lee Bouvier in Southampton, New York State, she was educated at Vassar College, Poughkeepsie, the Sorbonne in Paris, and George Washington University. While working as a photojournalist for the *Washington Times-Herald* in 1952, she met Senator John F. Kennedy of Massachusetts and married him the following year. After Kennedy became president in 1961, she promoted cultural events, supervised the redecoration of the White House, became involved in conservation issues, and planned what was to become the John F. Kennedy Center for the Performing Arts. Her elegance and dress sense were widely imitated, and she became one of the world's most photographed women.

Devastated by her husband's assassination in Dallas, Texas, in November 1963, she retired to New York with her children Caroline and John. In 1968 she married the millionaire Greek shipowner Aristotle Onassis, who was over 20 years her senior. Although the marriage was not a success, they remained formally married until his death in 1975. Widowed for a second time, Mrs. Onassis devoted herself to a career in publishing, specializing in the arts, until her death from cancer in New York.

Ono, Yoko (1933–) *Japanese artist and activist*

The experimental artist Yoko Ono became better known as the wife of John Lennon of the Beatles.

Having moved to the United States after World War II, the Tokyo-born Ono married composer Toshi Ichiyanagi and became involved in avant-garde films, music, and art. After divorcing her first husband, she married Tony Cox and then, in London, left him to marry John Lennon in 1969. She was subsequently blamed by many fans for the break-up of the Beatles in 1970. Lennon and Ono were by this time involved in high-profile and often highly unconventional protests against the Vietnam War and nuclear weapons; their most celebrated demonstration involved staying in bed together for days while being filmed and interviewed. "Give Peace a Chance," which they recorded together as The Plastic Ono Band in 1969, became an unofficial anthem for peace protesters worldwide. Ono continued to collaborate with Lennon on most of his solo projects.

Following the birth of their son Sean in 1975, Lennon effectively gave up his musical career to become a househusband; he was murdered by a deranged fan in 1980. Ono's astute management of his estate has reportedly made her one of the world's richest women. Admirers of her book *Grapefruit* (1970) and album *Season of Glass* (1981) argue that her own creative talents are less negligible than her detractors have claimed.

Orczy, Baroness (1865–1947) *Hungarian-born British novelist*

Orczy is mainly remembered as the creator of the Scarlet Pimpernel, an aristocratic hero whose adventures have inspired several films and television series.

The daughter of composer-conductor Baron Felix Orczy, Emma ("Emmuska") Magdalena Rosalia Maria Josefa Barbara Orczy was educated in Brussels and Paris. From the age of 15 she lived in London, where she studied art before marrying an English artist, becoming Mrs. Montague Barstow. Writing under her own much more distinctive name, she achieved celebrity with *The Scarlet Pimpernel* (1905), an historical romance of the French Revolution. In it the foppish (but secretly heroic) English aristocrat Sir Percy Blakeney uses daring and disguise to outwit the cruel secret policeman Chauvelin and rescue French aristocrats from the guillotine, spiriting them away to safety in England. The novel was an adaptation of a stage play that she had written in collaboration with her husband; premiered in Nottingham in 1903, it triumphed on the London stage in the same year that it was published as a novel.

Although Baroness Orczy went on to produce sequels, such as *Elusive Pimpernel* (1908), as well as many other detective stories, historical adventures, and romances, none repeated the huge success of her first book. From 1920 onwards she lived in Monte Carlo. She published her autobiography, *Links in the Chain of Life*, in 1947.

Ouida (1839–1908) *British romantic novelist*

One of the most popular writers of her day, Ouida earned wealth, fame, and more than a little ridicule with her extravagant and unrealistic novels.

Marie Louise de la Ramée was born in Bury St. Edmunds, Suffolk, of a French father and English mother. Her pen name, "Ouida," was taken from her own childish attempts to say "Louise." Educated in Paris, she settled in London in 1857 and began her literary career by contributing stories to popular magazines. She later embarked on lengthy romantic novels notable for their exotic settings, improbable plots, cardboard characters, and often lurid titles, such as *Held in Bondage* (1863). Despite these shortcomings and her frequently laughable ignorance of the male world, which often figured prominently in her works, Ouida churned out a stream of bestsellers that won a large following on both sides of the Atlantic.

Queen VICTORIA was a devoted fan, and the writer Edward Bulwer-Lytton hailed her *Folle-Farine* (1871) as "a triumph of modern English fiction." As well as 45 novels she also wrote animal stories, tales for children, and occasional essays.

In a striking example of life imitating art, Ouida used her literary income to enable her to live in Italy as lavishly as a princess in one of her own novels. By the 1890s she had lost her popularity but not, unfortunately, her taste for luxury. Deep in debt, she forsook her beloved Florence for Lucca in 1894 and finally died, destitute, in Viareggio. Her children's classic *A Dog of Flanders* (1872) continued to appeal to later generations of readers, and her adventure *Under Two Flags* (1867) was filmed in 1916, 1922, and 1936. *Two Little Wooden Shoes* (1874) provided the basis for Mascagni's opera *Lodoletta* (1917).

Ouspenskaya, Maria (1876–1949) *Russian actress and drama teacher*

A striking character actress, Ouspenskaya became a Hollywood star at the age of 60. However, her main importance was as a teacher of the dramatic techniques of Konstantin Stanislavsky (1863–1938), which later formed the basis of "Method" acting.

Born in Tula, Russia, Maria Ouspenskaya was in her mid-thirties before she joined Stanislavsky's Moscow Art Theatre and toured with the company throughout Russia. In 1924 the company visited the United States, and Ouspenskaya decided to remain, making her New York debut that year in an off-Broadway play, *Paris Pigeons in the Saint*. Having worked in the experimental theatre of director Richard Boleslavsky, she began to play regular Broadway roles in the 1930s.

In 1936 she made her film debut, recreating her stage role of Baroness Von Obersdorf in an adaptation of Sinclair Lewis's *Dodsworth*. The performance won her an Academy Award nomination for Best Supporting Actress, as did her role in *Love Affair* (1939). Her best-known part was probably that of the gypsy fortune teller in *The Wolf Man* (1941). She continued to appear in films until the year of her death, in a house fire.

P

Page, Geraldine (1924–1987) *American actress and drama teacher*

> She believed that if she could rid her students of the burden of trying to act, they would do their best work.
>
> —Robert Knopf, quoted in the *International Directory of Theatre*

During her distinguished acting career Geraldine Page consistently gave preference to the stage over the screen and to challenging rather than high-profile roles.

Born in Kirksville, Missouri, Geraldine Page trained at the Goodman Theater Dramatic School in Chicago (1942–45) and later at the Herbert Berghof School and the American Theater Wing in New York. She made her New York debut in 1945, her television debut in 1946, and her movie debut in 1947. Page first achieved widespread acclaim in 1952, when she starred in Tennessee Williams's *Summer and Smoke*; seven years later she greatly enhanced her reputation in the same dramatist's *Sweet Bird of Youth*, in which she played opposite Paul Newman. Although she remained strongly identified with Williams's demanding female roles, Page also excelled in plays by such diverse contemporary dramatists as André Gide, Terence Rattigan, and Eugene O'Neill. A dedicated teacher of drama, she cofounded the Actors' Studio Theater with Newman and her second husband, the actor-director Rip Torn, in 1963; her other projects included the Sanctuary Theater, established in 1976 to employ actors between regular engagements.

Film versions of *Summer and Smoke* and *Sweet Bird of Youth* appeared in 1961 and 1962, respectively. Other films to star Page include *Toys in the Attic* (1963), Woody Allen's *Interiors* (1978), and *The Trip to Bountiful* (1985), for which she won the Academy Award for Best Actress at the age of 60. She also won Emmy Awards for her appearances in the television plays *A Christmas Journey* (1966) and *The Thanksgiving Visitor* (1968). Her numerous other honours included New York Critics' Circle Awards (1953, 1959), a Golden Globe Award (1962), a BAFTA Award (1979), and no less than eight Academy Award nominations. Despite this track record, as a member of the Mirror Repertory Company (from 1983) she could often be found playing supporting roles for as little as $15 per performance.

Paglia, Camille (1947–) *American writer and lecturer*

> There is no female Mozart because there is no female Jack the Ripper. Great art and great crime are similar deviations...Most women have too much empathy to want to be involved in anything like that.
>
> —Interview in *The Sunday Times*, June 7, 1992

A university teacher of English by profession, Paglia emerged in the 1980s as a controversialist by choice.

Born into an academic Italian-American family in Endicott, New York State, she developed precocious interests in art history and Hollywood films. Her quest for role models led her from Amelia EARHART to Elizabeth TAYLOR and Simone de BEAUVOIR before she found her ideals in MADONNA, Oscar Wilde, and the Marquis de Sade.

In 1968 Paglia graduated in English with the highest academic honours from the State University of New York at Bighamton; in 1974 she followed this with a PhD from Yale. Paglia's subsequent period of teaching at Bennington College, Vermont, was enlivened by periodic fist fights with her students. Lacking a single academic focus, she then took a series of short-term or part-time teaching jobs, ranging from Yale to night classes for factory workers. In 1984 she finally found a home in what was to become Philadelphia's University of the Arts.

After seven rejections and constant rewriting, the first volume of her *Sexual Personae: Art and Decadence from Nefertiti to Emily Dickinson* appeared in 1990. Identifying pornographic, voyeuristic, and sadistic elements in the art and literature of the West, from ancient Greece to the Romantics, it became a bestseller and made her famous. She went on, by means of numerous provocative interviews, to make herself notorious, attacking liberals and orthodox feminists alike and gleefully challenging fashionable orthodoxies with such statements as "Education is, by definition, repressive...There is nothing pleasant about learning to read or to think." Calling for a core curriculum based on the classics, she denounced such "nonsubjects" as women's studies and African-American studies. Although her pronouncements include many apparent paradoxes and contradictions, one consistent theme is her insistence that women, rather than men, are the more powerful sex. The more recent publications of this self-styled "bisexual antifeminist feminist" include *Sex, Art and American Culture* (1992) and *Vamps and Tramps* (1995).

Paige, Elaine (1948–) *British singer and actress*

A star of stage musicals in Britain and the United States, Elaine Paige has earned the nickname "Leather Lungs" because of her powerful voice.

Elaine Bickerstaff was born in Barnet, north London, and attended the Ada Foster Stage School, where she changed her surname to Paige. Her early career was built on appearances in such contemporary musicals as *Hair* (1968), *Jesus Christ Superstar* (1973), and *Grease* (1973). She then broadened her range by working at the main-

stream Chichester Festival Theatre and the avant-garde Theatre Royal, Stratford East, London. In 1978 she created the title role in the Tim Rice–Andrew Lloyd Webber musical *Evita*, based on the life of Eva PERÓN, and received the Society of West End Theatres Award for Best Actress in a Musical; only American union rules prevented her from repeating her triumph on Broadway. In 1981 she created the role of Grizabella in another Rice–Lloyd Webber musical, *Cats*. Rice also provided lyrics for the musical *Chess*, which brought Paige the Variety Club Award for Showbusiness Personality of the Year in 1986.

In 1990 Paige's long-term personal relationship with Tim Rice ended, and she threw herself into a round of recordings and appearances. Her starring role (1993–94) in a play based on the tragic life of Edith PIAF won her an award from the British Association of Songwriters, Composers, and Authors. The mid 1990s brought Paige a long-delayed triumph on the American stage when she starred in the Broadway production of Lloyd Webber's *Sunset Boulevard*.

Since 1981 Elaine Paige has recorded 14 solo albums (including eight consecutive gold albums in Britain) and a British number-one single, *I Know Him So Well* (with Barbara Dickson).

Paley, Grace Goodside (1922–) *American writer*

> That's what you listen for and what you expect when you are a kid: the next conversation will tell you what it's all about, if you only listen to it.
>
> —Describing her storytelling, *Caliban* (1988)

Paley's stories explore the quiet heroism of individuals and communities faced with the trials of daily life.

Grace Paley grew up in the Bronx, New York, surrounded by an extended Jewish family that kept up a tradition of storytelling in Russian, Yiddish, and English. The family was also highly politicized as a result of its members' experiences of persecution and exile.

While attending Hunter College and New York University, Paley strove to become a poet but was not to publish her first volume of verse, *Leaning Forward*, until she was in her sixties. Her first collection of short stories, *The Little Disturbances of Man* (1959), was based on her experiences in an army camp during World War II and displays her skill in capturing the varieties of urban speech and deploying them to comic effect. Further volumes of short stories included *Enormous Changes at the Last Minute* (1974), *Later the Same Day* (1985), and *Long Walks and Intimate Talks* (1991). Despite her relatively limited output, she has commanded increasing respect from critics and has a growing following among readers.

In 1970 the U.S. National Institute of Art and Letters gave Paley its award for short fiction, and in 1980 she was elected to the American Academy and Institute of Arts and Letters. A lifelong campaigner for feminism and world peace, she founded the Greenwich Village Peace Center in 1961 and organized protests against nuclear weapons and the Vietnam War.

Palmer, Lilli (1914–1986) *German actress*

An elegant beauty who usually played somewhat worldly characters, Palmer made her name in British films in the late 1930s.

She was born Lillie Marie Peiser in Posen, Germany (now Poznań in Poland). The daughter of a surgeon and an actress, she was determined to follow her mother's profession rather than become a doctor, as her father wished. With great determination she continued her studies in the mornings, training at stage school in the afternoons. After further training in Berlin she made her stage debut in 1932. She then appeared in musicals at the Darmstadt State Theatre until the Nazi government cancelled her contract because she was Jewish. Having fled to France in 1933, she eked out a living in cabaret before crossing to England a year later.

Palmer made her film debut in 1935 and progressed to starring roles over the next few years. In 1941 she starred in a stage production of *No Time for Comedy* with Rex Harrison, who became her husband in 1943. Throughout World War II she appeared successfully in British films, working with such leading directors as Carol Reed and Roy Boulting. After the war Palmer and Harrison moved to Hollywood to take up film offers. Her Broadway debut followed in 1949. Although she found acclaim playing opposite her husband in the stage comedy *Bell, Book, and Candle*, their marriage broke up soon after the play transferred to London in 1954. Her performance in *The Fourposter* won her the Best Actress Award at the 1952 Venice Film Festival.

Palmer later married the Argentine actor-writer Carlos Thompson and based herself in Zurich. During the 1960s and 1970s she worked throughout Europe, making films in French, German, Spanish, and Italian as well as such English-language movies as *The Boys from Brazil* (1978). A skilled painter and successful novelist, she published her bestselling autobiography, *Change Lobsters and Dance*, in 1975.

Pan Chao (*c.* 46–117) *Chinese scholar*

A co-author of the *History of the Former Han Dynasty*, which was started by her father, Pan Chao (or Ban Zhao) is remembered mainly for her influential *Lessons for Women*.

Born in Fufeng, Shensi province, Pan Chao was educated by her father, Pan Piao, who began the compilation of the *History of the Former Han Dynasty*. This became a model for subsequent dynastic histories. After the death of Pan Piao this project was carried on by Pan Chao's brother, Pan Ku. Pan Chao was married at 14 and had one son, Ts'ao Ch'eng, before her husband, Ts'ao Shih-shu, died. Pan Chao then moved to the home of her brother Pan Ku, who was living in the imperial capital, Loyang. Together they worked on the *History of the Former Han Dynasty*, which still remained incomplete at Pan Ku's death in 92.

Emperor Ho then ordered Pan Chao to complete the *History*, appointing her at the same time tutor to Empress Teng and her entourage. In this capacity Pan Chao taught classics, mathematics, history, and astronomy. Following Ho's death in 106, Teng assumed the regency on behalf of her son, ruling China in his name for the next 15 years. Pan Chao became Teng's trusted counsellor, and Pan Chao's son, Ts'ao Ch'eng, was raised to high rank at court. How much of the *History of the Former Han Dynasty* can be directly attributed to Pan Chao is uncertain, although she is usually credited with the technically demanding section on astronomy.

Although her collected writings filled 16 volumes, most perished long ago, leaving only four poems, some addresses to the throne, and a moral treatise, *Lessons for Women*. This put forward the conventional Confucian view that wives should subordinate themselves to their husbands, but it also emphasized the value of female education. For centuries Pan Chao's standing rested less on her achievements as a scholar than on this work and her own reputation as a virtuous widow, dedicated to the memory of her late husband.

Pandit, Vijaya Lakshmi (1900–1990)
Indian politician and diplomat

Mrs. Pandit was the first Indian woman to become a government minister and the first female president of the United Nations General Assembly. She was later Indian ambassador to a number of countries, including the United States.

Born Swarup Kumari Nehru, daughter of Motilal Nehru, an eminent lawyer, she was the sister of Jawaharlal Nehru, future leader of the struggle for independence and first prime minister of the Republic of India. Educated in India and Europe, she became politically active in 1920, helping to mobilize women in the nationalist cause. In 1921 she married Ranjit S. Pandit, a lawyer, and adopted the name Vijaya Lakshmi ("Victory and Prosperity").

Mrs. Pandit was imprisoned three times by the British colonial government for nationalist activities. She worked in local government in her native Allahabad before holding posts in the legislature and cabinet of the United Provinces (now Uttar Pradesh), serving as minister for local government and health (1937–39) – the first woman in India to be appointed a government minister.

From 1946 Mrs. Pandit was a leading international diplomat, heading India's delegation to the United Nations (1946–48 and 1952–53). She also served as India's ambassador to the Soviet Union (1947–49) and to the United States (1949–51). In 1953–54 she served as president of the UN General Assembly, the first woman and the first Asian to hold this position. From 1954 to 1961 she was India's high commissioner in the United Kingdom and simultaneously ambassador to Ireland.

Resuming her domestic political career in 1962, Mrs. Pandit was appointed governor of Maharashtra state (until 1964) and then became a member of the Indian parliament (1964–68). In 1977 she emerged from her retirement to give outspoken support to the Congress for Democracy, a party opposed to the dictatorial rule of her niece Indira GANDHI. In 1979 she published her memoirs, *The Scope of Happiness*.

Pankhurst, Dame Christabel (Harriette) (1880–1958) *British suffragette*

> Christabel cared less for the political vote itself than for the dignity of her sex...Militancy to her meant the putting off of the slave spirit.
>
> —Emmeline Pethwick-Lawrence,
> *My Part in a Changing World*

The eldest daughter of Emmeline PANKHURST, Christabel joined her mother as a militant activist in the fight for women's votes.

Born in Manchester, Christabel was the eldest daughter of the reforming lawyer Dr. Richard Pankhurst and Emmeline Pankhurst. As a child she dreamed of being a dancer. However, following her father's sudden death in 1898, she found herself serving as an assistant in the fancy goods shop her mother had opened to help support the family.

Deciding to follow her father in the legal profession, Christabel found that women were banned from training at the Inns of Court. Instead, she took a law degree at Manchester University, passing with first-class honours. In 1903 she joined her mother and her younger sister Sylvia PANKHURST in founding the Women's Social and Political Union (WSPU) to agitate for the vote for women. True to their slogan "Deeds Not Words," Christabel began their campaign of militancy in 1905 by interrupting a Liberal Party meeting. Her arrest and imprisonment attracted widespread publicity for the cause. A brilliant witty speaker with a beautiful voice, Christabel used her charm to win many recruits for the WSPU. Although she was capable of inspiring great devotion, she reserved her own emotions for causes rather than people. A formidable organizer and strategist, she took little part in demonstrations herself, being considered too valuable to the movement for her contribution to be interrupted by imprisonment.

From 1912 onwards, as the campaign reached its peak, Christabel directed it from exile in Paris, where she edited the WSPU's journal, *The Suffragette*. When World War I broke out, she – like her mother – suspended agitation to work for the war effort. When women's contribution to victory was acknowledged in 1918 by the award of the vote to women aged 30 or over, Christabel ran for Parliament as leader of the Women's Party she had founded, but was not elected.

Looking for another crusade, she became convinced of the imminence of Christ's second coming. From 1921 to 1932 she fervently preached this message throughout the United States, before returning to Europe; she was created a DBE in 1936 in recognition of her services to political life. She returned to the United States after the outbreak of World War II, dying in Los Angeles. Her history of the suffragette movement, *Unshackled: The Story of How We Won the Vote*, was published in 1959, after her death.

Pankhurst, Emmeline (1858–1928)
British suffragette

> The argument of the broken pane of glass is the most valuable argument in modern politics.

> —*Votes for Women*, February 23, 1912

> Women had always fought for men, and for their children. Now they were ready to fight for their own human rights.

> —*My Own Story* (1914)

Emmeline Pankhurst and her daughters Christabel PANKHURST and Sylvia PANKHURST were largely responsible for obtaining the right to vote for British women.

The daughter of liberal-minded parents, Emmeline Goulden was born in Manchester. In 1879 she married a lawyer, Dr. Richard Pankhurst, an MP and the author of *On the Subjection of Women*. It was Pankhurst who was to draft the first bill to propose giving women the vote, which was supported by his friend John Stuart Mill. Pankhurst also drafted the Married Women's Property Acts (1870, 1882), which secured some legal rights for women over their own assets and income after marriage. In 1885 the Pankhursts moved to London, where Richard Pankhurst attempted to build a practice as a lawyer. However, his radical views restricted his success, and Emmeline opened a fancy goods shop to supplement their income. In 1889 Emmeline began her own career as an activist by founding the Women's Franchise League, which in 1894 won the right for married women to vote in local, but not national, elections.

Dr. Pankhurst died in 1898, leaving Emmeline with four children to support. This she did by taking a job (in addition to running her shop) as a registrar of births and deaths, an occupation that increased her contact with working people and encouraged her sympathy for the plight of overburdened women. With the support of her daughters Christabel and Sylvia, in 1903 she formed the Women's Social and Political Union (WSPU) to agitate for female suffrage at the national level. Moving the WSPU headquarters to London in 1906, she decided to pursue a far more militant strategy than that adopted in the suffragist movement headed by Millicent FAWCETT.

Instead of contenting themselves with meetings and petitions, the Pankhursts' supporters organized dramatic demonstrations and perpetrated acts of civil disobedience ranging from window smashing and arson to chaining themselves to public buildings.

Repeatedly jailed for her offences, Emmeline kept the WSPU at the forefront of the battle for women's rights until the outbreak of World War I. She then suspended all agitation, asserting that at a time of national crisis women had "the right to serve." Putting her formidable propaganda machine at the service of the war effort, she eagerly recruited men for the armed forces and women for the support services and munitions factories. She herself visited the United States, Canada, and Russia to urge the industrial mobilization of their female populations.

In 1918 the female contribution to Britain's victory was acknowledged by the prime minister, Lloyd George, who granted women aged 30 and over the right to vote. In 1928 they were finally given the vote at the same age as men. Mrs. Pankhurst died three weeks after the passing of the Representation of the People Act, which gave men and women equal voting rights, knowing her life's goal had been achieved. Less than two years after her death a statue in her honour was erected in the shadow of the Houses of Parliament.

Pankhurst, (Estelle) Sylvia (1882–1960) *British political activist*

The second daughter of Emmeline PANKHURST, Sylvia, like her sister Christabel, became a militant activist for the right of women to vote. However, Sylvia later broke with her family, believing that there were other causes worth fighting for.

Born in Manchester, the daughter of Dr. Richard Pankhurst and Emmeline Pankhurst, leader of the suffragette movement, Sylvia won scholarships enabling her to study at the Manchester Municipal School of Art and the Royal College of Art in London. At the same time, she became involved with her mother and her sister Christabel in the militant struggle for female suffrage. Several times imprisoned, she also endured forcible feeding when she went on hunger strike. Between spells of imprisonment she used her artistic talents to design banners, posters, and even a tea service to promote the suffragette cause.

Sylvia eventually disagreed with her mother and sister over their political objectives. Living in London's East End, she became convinced that working-class women had other and more urgent needs than the vote – including better wages, housing, and medical care. Her mother and sister focused on the vote as their sole objective, assuming that other necessary reforms would follow from it and could be deferred until the major objective had been won. Emmeline and Christabel Pankhurst also believed that the suffragette movement would best achieve its aim by relying on an elite of educated dedicated militants, free from family ties. Sylvia, by contrast, believed that a movement for democracy should itself be democratic, involving women of all classes and drawing its strength from their ideas and enthusiasm, rather than from self-appointed leaders.

In 1913 Sylvia broke with the main suffragette movement. As a pacifist, she opposed participation in World War I as fervently as her mother and sister supported it. Activism, however, remained the moving force of her life, and she continued to agitate on behalf of socialism and pacifism. After a period of painting in the pottery district of Stoke-on-Trent, she eventually settled in Ethiopia, where she later campaigned against the Italian invasion of 1936. She died in Addis Ababa. Her published works include *The Suffragette Movement* (1931), *The Life of Emmeline Pankhurst* (1936), and *Ethiopia: A Cultural History* (1955).

Pardo Bazán, Emilia, Countess of (1852–1921) *Spanish writer and feminist*

Emilia Pardo Bazán was a writer of great power and originality who introduced Spanish readers to many of the concerns of writers from France and Russia.

Born into an aristocratic family in La Coruña, Galicia, she was inspired to write after moving to Madrid in 1868 with her husband, Señor de Quiroga. For most of her life she lived in Madrid, where she eventually established a famous literary salon. Her reputation as a writer was initially based on a controversial essay, "The Critical Issue" (1883); this essay introduced to Spain the literary preoccupations of France and Russia, especially the realism of Emile Zola, whose novels dealt vividly with contemporary social problems.

Her own most important novel, *The Manors of Ulloa* (1886), portrayed the decay of an aristocratic family in her native Galicia, which remained the setting for her best writing. For Emilia Pardo Bazán the physical beauty of the Galician landscape was in striking contrast to the moral decline of its inhabitants. The sequel, *Mother Nature* (1887), continued this theme. With *Sunstroke* (1889) and *The Blues* (1889) she progressed to a more modern interest in the psychological problems of perception and awareness.

Pardo Bazán's intellectual interests, ranging from Darwinism to feminism, were expressed in over 500 articles, reviews, poems, and short stories. She also ran a library for women and campaigned so outspokenly for their rights that her scandalized husband separated from her. In 1916 she was accorded the highly unusual honour for a woman of being appointed professor of literature at the Central University of Madrid.

Paretsky, Sara (1947–) *American crime writer*

> The response I get from women who read my books is a feeling of empowerment.
> —Interview in *USA Today*, July 25, 1991

A pioneer of contemporary crime fiction with a feminist angle, Paretsky has won a devoted readership in America and Europe.

Born in Ames, Iowa, Sara Paretsky earned both a PhD in history and a master's degree in business administration at the University of Chicago before embarking on a career marketing insurance. Having already published the crime novels *Indemnity Only* (1982), *Deadlock* (1984), and *Killing Orders* (1985), she left business in 1986 to devote herself to full-time writing. In the same year she founded Sisters in Crime to promote the work of female writers in the traditionally male field of the thriller. Within five years it had over 600 members. An active feminist, she also became director of the National Abortion Rights Action League of Illinois in 1987.

Paretsky's novels feature the private investigator V. I. (Victoria Iphigenia) Warshawski – "Vic" to her friends – who confronts a variety of bad-guys, from anti-abortion fanatics and corporate fraudsters to corrupt Chicago politicians and reactionary archbishops. By creating a resourceful karate-chopping private eye who is also both female and believable, Paretsky successfully broke a powerful literary taboo and inspired dozens of imitators. In 1987 she was recognized as one of *Ms.* magazine's Women of the Year, and a year later she received a Silver Dagger Award from the Crime Writers Association for *Blood Shot*, a characteristically topical mystery about the dumping of toxic waste. A feature film, *V. I. Warshawski*, based on the novels and starring Kathleen TURNER in the title role, appeared in 1991 but proved disappointing. A radio dramatization in Britain was, however, enthusiastically received.

Pargeter, Edith Mary (1913–1995) *British novelist and translator*

Pargeter is best known for a series of crime mysteries set in the Middle Ages and featuring the monk-detective Brother Cadfael, which she wrote under the pen name Ellis Peters.

Edith Pargeter was born in the small village of Horsehay, Shropshire. She did not go to college but worked instead as an assistant to a pharmacist from 1933, writing novels in her spare time. She joined the Women's Royal Naval Service in 1940 and was awarded the British Empire Medal for her wartime work. In 1951 she published *Fallen into the Pit*, the first of an extensive series of detective novels featuring Inspector Felse; the quality of this series was acknowledged in 1963 by the Mystery Writers of America's Edgar Allen Poe Award. In 1968 Pargeter's expert translations of Czech poetry and novels won her the gold medal of the Czechoslovak Society for International Relations.

In 1977 the true story of the transference of the relics of St. Winifred to Shrewsbury Abbey inspired *A Morbid Taste for Bones: A Medieval Whodunnit*, the first of Pargeter's books to be published under the name Ellis Peters. This novel featured her most successful fictional creation, Brother Cadfael, an ex-soldier turned monk who, as a herbalist, is an expert on both medicines and poisons. Successive Cadfael novels followed, leading to a BBC television series of adaptations. Set in the Anglo-Welsh border country, the stories unfold against the background of the civil wars that plagued the reign of King Stephen (1135–54).

Pargeter's expert knowledge of medieval life enabled her to evoke both the daily hardships of ordinary people and the complexities of courtly intrigue. As a writer she never allowed her mysteries to decline into mere puzzles but determined that they should remain true novels with well-rounded characters. In 1981 she received the Crime Writers Association Silver Dagger and in 1993 accepted its highest award, the Diamond Dagger. The Shrewsbury area has subsequently developed Cadfael tours, which attract thousands of devoted fans.

Parker, Bonnie (1911–1934) *American criminal*

> They're punks. They're giving bank robbing a bad name.
>
> —John Dillinger, describing Bonnie Parker and Clyde Barrow

As the female half of the notorious Bonnie and Clyde, Bonnie Parker was one of America's most wanted criminals of the mid 1930s.

Born in the small town of Rowena, Texas, Bonnie Parker was working as a waitress in Dallas when she met the ex-convict Clyde Barrow, a small-time thief from a similar background. Shortly after their meeting he was sentenced to two years' imprisonment for theft but escaped after 20 months, using a gun Parker smuggled into jail for him. She, meanwhile, had also been imprisoned briefly on suspicion of stealing a car.

Parker and Barrow then embarked on a spree of robbing banks, gas stations, and restaurants throughout the Mississippi Valley. They were aided at various times by Barrow's brother, Buck, and Buck's wife, Blanche, and by Ray Hamilton and W. D. Jones. Their raids and escapes soon became legendary. On one occasion they crashed through a garage door to escape arrest, and on another they successfully evaded a posse of 200 that had surrounded them. In the course of their crimes they killed six policemen and a similar number of civilians. However, since banks were objects of popular hatred in many rural areas during the Depression (because they were responsible for repossessing farms when tenants could not keep up mortgage payments), Barrow and his gang were widely seen as folk heroes.

Their legend was further enhanced by Parker's versified prediction of their bloody end in "The Story of Bonnie and Clyde" (otherwise known as "The Story of Suicide Sal"). They died in an ambush near Ruston, Louisiana, when the car in which they were sitting was riddled with bullets by six policemen armed with submachine guns.

The exploits of the Barrow gang inspired a mediocre 1958 film, *The Bonnie Parker Story*, and the far superior *Bonnie and Clyde* (1967), starring Warren Beatty and Faye Dunaway, which earned two Academy Awards and a further seven nominations.

Parker, Dorothy (1893–1967) *American writer and wit*

> Men seldom make passes
> At girls who wear glasses.
>
> —"News Item," *Enough Rope* (1926)

> She is a combination of Little Nell and Lady Macbeth.
>
> —Alexander Woollcott,
> *While Rome Burns* (1934)

Dorothy Parker was one of the sharpest wits of the Algonquin "Round Table," a celebrated group of writers who met for lunch at the Algonquin Hotel in New York. Her one-liners, mostly from the 1930s, still make people laugh.

Born Dorothy Rothschild in West End, New Jersey, the daughter of a clothing salesman, she lost her mother at the age of five and loathed her stepmother so much that she refused to speak to her. A basic education at Miss Dana's Academy was supplemented by her strong appetite for reading. At 11 Dorothy discovered the novels of Thackeray and decided that she was going to be a writer herself.

In 1916 she sold some poems to the editor of *Vogue* and was given a job writing picture captions and advertisements. The following year she was hired by a new publication, *Vanity Fair*, and married Edwin Pond Parker II. In 1919 she became *Vanity Fair's* drama critic, but her scathing reviews soon got her fired. She then wrote for the *Saturday Evening Post* and *The New Yorker*, contributing book and theatre reviews to the latter (1927–33) under the pen name "Constant Reader."

Parker at this stage in her career was one of a high-profile group of writers including Robert Benchley, Robert Sherwood, James Thurber, and H. L. Mencken. Known collectively as the "Round Table," they were renowned for the brilliance of their conversation, their sharp critical comments on the manners and morals of their day, and the amount of alcohol they consumed. Having divorced her first husband in 1928, Parker married Alan Campbell in 1933 and moved to Hollywood, where she collaborated with her husband and other writers on some 15 film screenplays, most notably *A Star Is Born* (1937), which received an Oscar nomination.

Despite her dislike of Hollywood, Parker remained there throughout a roller-coaster relationship with her second husband, which included divorce, remarriage, separation, and reconciliation. She returned to New York in 1963 but wrote little more. She died in her apartment, alone except for her pet poodle.

Dorothy Parker's publications included the volumes of verse *Enough Rope* (1926) and *Not So Deep as a Well* (1936) as well as short stories, such as "Big Blonde," which won an O. Henry Award as the best short story of the year in 1929. Most of her stories first appeared in *The New Yorker* in her Round Table years; they were published in book form as *After Such Pleasures* (1932) and *Here Lies* (1939).

Parks, Rosa (1913–) *American civil-rights campaigner*

> ...a person who wanted to be free and wanted others to be free.
> —Describing herself in *The Chicago Tribune*, April 3, 1988

On December 1, 1955, Rosa Parks violated the racial segregation laws of Montgomery, Alabama, by refusing to give up her seat on a bus to a white man. Her arrest for this offence sparked off a bus boycott lasting 382 days, which brought its organizer, Martin Luther King Jr., to national prominence and led the U.S. Supreme Court to declare segregated seating unconstitutional.

Rosa Louise (Lee) McCauley was born in Tuskegee, Alabama. In 1932 she married Raymond Parks, an African-American civil-rights activist. From 1943 to 1956 she served as a secretary for the Montgomery branch of the National Association for the Advancement of Colored People. The price of victory in the bus boycott and the subsequent legal test case was a high one for Rosa and her husband. She was imprisoned, both lost their jobs, Raymond had a nervous breakdown, and Rosa was hospitalized for ulcers arising from stress.

Moving to Detroit, Michigan, in 1957, she joined Martin Luther King Jr. and his Southern Christian Leadership Conference in working to achieve greater racial justice by nonviolent means. Until 1965, however, she continued to rely for her livelihood, as she always had, on her skills as a seamstress, surviving several years of personal and family hardship. In that year she joined the staff of Congressman John Conyers Jr., a Democrat from Michigan, serving in his office until 1988. In 1987 she founded an institute to provide leadership and career training for young African Americans.

Parr, Catherine (1512–1548) *Sixth and last wife of King Henry VIII of England*

A learned and pious woman, Catherine Parr was also a kind stepmother to Henry's children.

The daughter of Sir Thomas Parr, Master of the Household to Henry VIII, Catherine was married as a child to Edward Borough, who died in or before 1529. Next she was married to John Neville, Baron Latimer, who died in 1542. She then became engaged to Sir Thomas Seymour, brother of Jane SEYMOUR, Henry VIII's third wife, who died after giving birth to their son and heir, Prince Edward.

Catherine Parr came to the attention of the ageing and disillusioned monarch following the disgrace and execution of his fifth wife, Catherine HOWARD. Although Catherine Parr was by then in love with Sir Thomas Seymour, she had little option but to accept the king's proposal of marriage, the alternative being to jeopardize the fortunes of her family and possibly even their lives. She believed, moreover, that it was her duty to God to work for religious reform – she was deeply sympathetic to the cause of Protestantism. She therefore married Henry in 1543.

As queen, Catherine appears to have moderated Henry's savage outbursts against his political and religious opponents. Tortured by gout and other painful afflictions, he responded with occasional gratitude to her constant kindness. However, there were also times that he was so infuriated by her ability to argue obscure points of theology with him that he threatened to have her executed. Although keenly aware of the perils of court intrigue all around her, Catherine was probably mainly responsible for reconciling the king to his daughters, the future queens MARY I and ELIZABETH I, and to restoring the succession to them. As early as 1544 Catherine was sufficiently trusted, both for her character and her competence, to act as regent of the kingdom when Henry left England to supervise the siege of Boulogne. In 1547, within weeks of Henry VIII's death, Catherine was able to marry Sir Thomas Seymour. She died in childbirth the following year.

One of the reluctant queen's devotional works, *The Lamentation or Complaint of a Sinner*, was published after her death during the reign of Elizabeth I, which could not have been done without royal approval – clear proof of Elizabeth's respect and affection for a kind stepmother.

See also ANNE OF CLEVES; BOLEYN, ANNE; CATHERINE OF ARAGON.

Parsons, Louella (1881–1972) *American gossip columnist*

> The first person I ever cared deeply and sincerely about was – myself.
>
> —Quoted by George Eells in
> *Hedda and Louella*

As Hollywood's most influential gossip writer of the 1930s, Louella Parsons was credited with the power to make or break careers.

Louella Oettinger, from Freeport, Illinois, was born Jewish, raised as an Episcopalian, and became a fervent Roman Catholic. In 1905 she married John D. Parsons, whose child she subsequently bore. Although this deeply unhappy marriage ended in either divorce or desertion, Louella later maintained that her husband had been killed in World War I. She subsequently married a physician, Henry Watson Martin.

Having worked briefly as a teacher, Parsons became a reporter for the *Chicago Tribune* and in her spare time wrote hundreds of screenplays for silent films. In 1914 she began to write a syndicated movie column, the first woman to do so, and in 1919 she moved to New York City, becoming cinema editor of the *New York American* in 1923. From 1926 onwards she worked in Hollywood. Her daily syndicated gossip column, printed in 600 newspapers, focused on the lives and loves of screen stars. The 1930s saw her at the peak of her power. Vain and often vindictive, Louella Parsons inspired wariness rather than affection in the Hollywood community. Nevertheless, she could also be gracious and generous.

From 1934 to 1938 she also cohosted the radio show *Hollywood Hotel*, which presented dramas featuring film stars. By the early 1950s, with the large Hollywood studios in decline, her influence was on the wane. She finally retired in 1964, having published two volumes of autobiography, *The Gay Illiterate* (1944) and *Tell It to Louella* (1961).

See also HOPPER, HEDDA.

Parton, Dolly (1946–) *American singer, songwriter, and actress*

> I look like a woman, but I think like a man...If you're gonna be a success you've got to work, work, work.
> —Describing herself in *The Guardian*, January 24, 1997

Dolly Parton, the country girl who became an outstanding country singer, is as famous for her blonde wigs, full bosom, and colourful clothes as for her singing.

The fourth of 12 children, Dolly Rebecca Parton was born on her parents' farm in Locust Ridge, Tennessee. Poor but musical, the family made their own entertainment, drawing on local traditions of gospel music. Even before she had left high school, Dolly had appeared on television, made recordings, and begun to write songs in collaboration with her uncle, Bill Owens.

In 1964 Bill Phillips took her tune "Put It Off until Tomorrow" into the Country top ten. Having moved to Nashville, Tennessee, the capital of country music, she joined the Porter Wagoner TV show in 1967, leaving in 1974 when the international success of her song "Jolene" enabled her to form her own family-based band and launch a solo career. She had already been voted best female songwriter by *Billboard* magazine in 1971. A shrewd businesswoman with a keen sense of her own appeal – "I knew what I had to sell" – by 1976 she had replaced the family members of her band with topline professionals and was hosting her own TV music series. Performing in places as varied as the Grand Ole Opry and New York's Carnegie Hall, she extended her musical range into pop and rock and her performances to the cinema screen, starring with Jane FONDA and Lily Tomlin in the comedy *9 to 5* (1980).

Parton went on to develop her mischievous comic talent in such films as *The Best Little Whorehouse in Texas* (1982) and *Steel Magnolias* (1989). Besides her own hits, such as "My Tennessee Mountain Home," "Coat of Many Colors," and "Here You Come Again," she also wrote "I Will Always Love You" (1982), later a hit for Whitney HOUSTON. In 1985 she opened her own theme park, "Dollywood." She also has her own record company, Rising Tide, as well as television and film production companies.

Since 1966 Parton has been married to a builder, Carl Dean. Their relationship has remained closely private. Her autobiography, *Dolly: My Life and Other Unfinished Business*, was published in 1994.

Patti, Adelina (Juana Maria) (1843–1919) *British opera singer of Italian parentage*

A legendary soprano, Adelina Patti had a voice (even judged by recordings made in her sixties) of quite extraordinary purity.

Born in Madrid, the daughter of Italian opera singers, Adelina Patti was taken as a child to New York, where she appeared in concerts soon after their arrival. Adelina's sister Carlotta taught her piano, and she was initially trained as a singer by her halfbrother Ettore Barili. Adelina made her operatic debut in the title role of Donizetti's *Lucia di Lammermoor* in New York in 1859. Her London debut came in 1861, and her Paris debut the following year. In 1877 she finally appeared at La Scala, Milan, as Violetta in Verdi's *La Traviata*. However, Covent Garden, London, remained her main operatic home, and in 1898 she became a British citizen. She formally retired from the stage in 1895 but continued on the concert platform until her official farewell at the Royal Albert Hall in 1906.

In 1914, shortly after the outbreak of World War I, she came out of retirement at the age of 71 to sing again at the Royal Albert Hall to raise money for the Red Cross. She delighted the audience by singing for the last time "Home Sweet Home," which she had always included in her recitals. She died at Craig-y-Nos Castle, in south Wales, which is now devoted in part to her memory.

Although limited as an actress, Adelina Patti possessed a voice unrivalled in its purity, range, and control. In an age of rigid morals her personal life was a subject of controversy. From 1868 to 1885 she was married to the Marquis de Caux; from 1886 to 1898 to the French tenor Ernesto Nicolin; and from 1899 to Baron Rolf Cederstrom, a Swedish-born naturalized Briton.

Pauker, Ana (1893–1960) *Romanian Communist politician*

A turbulent revolutionary in her youth, Ana Pauker was a cofounder of the Communist Party in Romania. She served as Romania's minister of foreign affairs from 1947 to 1952 – the first woman in the world to hold such a position.

Born in a village in Moldavia, Ana Rabinsohn was the daughter of a rabbi. After completing her secondary education, she worked as a teacher and in 1915 joined the Social Democratic Party of Romania. In 1917–18 she took part in revolutionary movements inspired by the outbreak of revolution in Russia, and in 1920 she married a fellow activist, Marcel Pauker. The couple were among the founders of the Communist Party of Romania in 1921, and a year later Ana was elected to its central committee. Arrested in 1925, she escaped and fled to Moscow, where she enrolled in the International Leninist School (1928–31) and worked for the executive committee of the Communist International. In 1934 she returned to Romania during a railway workers' strike, hoping to promote industrial unrest. Although imprisoned again in 1936, she was later (1941) exchanged for two Romanian politicians captured by the Soviets during World War II. She then helped to organize a division of Romanian prisoners of war to serve in the Soviet army.

From 1945 to 1952 Pauker played a leading part in establishing Communist rule in postwar Romania, serving as secretary of the central committee of the Communist Party of Romania (1945–48) and minister of foreign affairs (1947–52). She also helped to organize the taking of farmland from private ownership and the creation of a state-controlled agricultural system. In 1952 a power struggle within the party led to her dismissal amid accusations of illegal financial dealings. However, she is thought to have wielded considerable power behind the scenes until her death.

Paul, Alice (1885–1977) *American social reformer*

Alice Paul was an aggressive member of the women's suffrage movement both in Britain and the United States. Although she was jailed for civil disobedience in both countries, she became a respected member of the establishment.

Born into a Quaker family in Moorestown, New Jersey, Alice Paul graduated from Swarthmore College in 1905 and continued her studies at the University of Pennsylvania, from which she received her PhD in 1912. During a period of graduate work in England (1907–10) she became a fervent participant in the militant suffragette movement led by Emmeline PANKHURST and was jailed three times for acts of civil disobedience. In 1912 she took the chair of the American Woman Suffrage Association, but the following year she resigned to become a founder member of the more aggressive Congressional Union for Woman Suffrage. In 1917 this organization merged with the National Woman's Party. Paul's agitational activities in the cause of women's suffrage brought her three further prison sentences in the United States.

After the 19th Amendment to the Constitution finally gave American women the right to vote, Alice Paul played a key role in promoting the first attempt to get an equal rights amendment through Congress (1923). She went on to enlist the support of the League of Nations for the cause of women's rights, and in 1938 she founded the World Party for Equal Rights for Women. She helped ensure that the preamble to the United Nations Charter included an affirmation of equal rights between men and women; she also ensured that the U.S. Civil Rights Act of 1964 did so.

Pavlova, Anna Pavlovna (1881–1931) *Russian ballet dancer*

Anna Pavlova was possibly the greatest, and almost certainly the most famous, prima ballerina in the history of ballet.

Pavlova was born in St. Petersburg. Despite an impoverished family background and childhood frailness, she was accepted to train with the Imperial Ballet School attached to the Maryinsky Theatre. Her main teacher was Marius Petipa, the French-born creator of the modern classical ballet in Russia. Pavlova made her debut at 17, and by 1906 she had become the Maryinsky's principal ballerina. In 1907 she made her first foreign tour, and in 1908, on her second, joined Sergei Diaghilev's revolutionary Ballets Russes company in Paris, dancing opposite the brilliant Vaslav Nijinsky. Despite great acclaim, Pavlova soon left the Ballets Russes for London. In 1910 she formed her own dance company and made her New York debut, going on to tour throughout North America.

London, however, was to remain her home, and in 1912 she purchased Ivy House in Hampstead, where she established her own school of dance. She made her last appearance in St. Petersburg in 1913 and spent the rest of her career almost constantly on tour, bringing ballet to millions for the first time through the drawing power of her legendary name. Her immense repertoire included over 20 ballets and some 80 shorter pieces. Her most famous role, *The Dying Swan*, was created specifically for her in 1905 by the master choreographer Michel Fokine. She did choreograph a ballet of her own, *Autumn Leaves*, but was otherwise content to perform the classics to perfection. She also included in her programmes dances from Poland, Russia, and Mexico and took a serious interest in the dances of India and Japan.

Pavlova married her manager, Victor Dandre, in 1914 but kept their relationship a closely guarded secret until the year of her death. Childless herself, she founded a home for Russian refugee orphans in Paris in 1920.

Peck, Annie Smith (1850–1935) *American mountaineer*

Having established her reputation as a Greek scholar, Annie Smith Peck became an early pioneer of mountaineering for women.

Annie Smith Peck was born in Providence, Rhode Island, and educated at the University of Michigan. After studying Greek in Athens, she became professor of classics at Smith College, Massachusetts.

Peck did not climb her first peak, Mount Shasta in the Cascades on the American–Canadian border, until she was 38. Her next ascents, at the age of 45, took place during a visit to the Alps and included the Matterhorn. In 1897, sponsored by the *New York World*, she climbed Popacatapetl and Orizaba in Mexico – the latter, at 5,669 metres (18,600 ft), the highest peak ever climbed by a woman at that time. By 1900 she was climbing in the Italian Dolomites and representing the United States at the International Congress of Alpinism in Paris. On her return she helped found the American Alpine Club in 1902.

In 1904 and 1906 she made repeated attempts to scale the as yet unclimbed Huascaran in Peru; in 1908 she claimed to have reached the summit of its lower North Peak. Two years later, at the age of 60, she attempted the volcano of Coropuna, also in Peru. A committed feminist, she hoisted a banner on the summit of Coropuna proclaiming "Votes for Women."

Peeters, Clara (1594–c. 1660) *Flemish artist*

Peeters is remembered for her meticulous still-life studies, many of which feature breakfast or banquet scenes.

Little is known for certain about the life of Clara Peeters except that in 1639 she married Henrik van Joossen in the same Antwerp church in which she had been baptized. She may have been working in Amsterdam in 1612 and in The Hague in 1617.

A pupil of Jan Brueghel, Peeters was one of the first painters to specialize in the still-life compositions that became a firm favourite with 17th-century artists and patrons. Some of her paintings are flower studies of a type that became – particularly popular at that time – partly because the people of the Low Countries were avid gardeners, partly because they enabled artists to show off their skill in handling complex shapes and a dazzling range of colours. Peeters's favourite subject, however, was food, which she depicted in works ranging from deceptively simple treatments of bread and cheese or fish to elaborate banquet scenes. These featured exotic fruits, lavish tableware, and the effects of light reflected from silver, jewels, and coins (an unusual motif that occurs in several of her works).

Thirty-two of her paintings are known to have survived, ranging in date from 1608 to 1657. They can be seen in the Rijksmuseum, Amsterdam; the Ashmolean Museum, Oxford; and the Prado, Madrid, as well as in various museums in the United States.

Pelletier, Madeleine (1874–1939)
French feminist and health worker

A physician by profession, Pelletier became one of France's most radical and outspoken campaigners for women's rights.

Born Anne Pelletier she was brought up in a rigidly respectable Parisian household and endured a wretched childhood. Despite leaving school at 12, she managed to qualify as a doctor and at 25 became the first woman appointed to the staff of a government welfare organization.

A respectable career was not, however, her goal. Having changed her first name to Madeleine, Pelletier took to wearing men's clothes and became a leading militant in the struggle to win for French women the right to vote; as editor of *La suffragiste*, she advocated the sort of violent tactics pioneered by the PANKHURSTS in England. In 1905 she became secretary of the Groupe de la Solidarité des Femmes (Women's Solidarity Group). She also involved herself in the work of the Socialist International but failed to persuade the communists to give their support to the cause of women's suffrage. Despite her radicalism, in 1906 she became the first woman qualified to work in mental hospitals. Four years later she ran as a Feminist Party candidate in elections for the French national assembly but attracted little support. In order to see conditions in communist Russia for herself, Pelletier travelled alone through Russia in 1922 amid the turmoil following the revolution.

As she grew older, Pelletier's views became even more radical, and she abandoned the communists for the anarchists, who had a more favourable attitude to female equality. She also campaigned in favour of birth control and abortion rights and openly performed abortions, although this was illegal in France at that time, until she was arrested in 1939. Sentenced to internment in a mental asylum, she died shortly afterwards.

Her publications include *Woman's Struggle for Her Rights* (1908), *The Sexual Emancipation of Woman* (1911), and *The Feminist Education of Girls* (1914).

Pérec, Marie-José (1968–) *French athlete*

A sprinter, Pérec has competed successfully in the 100 metres and 200 metres as well as scoring an unmatched series of triumphs in the 400 metres.

Born on the Caribbean island of Guadeloupe, an overseas department of France, Marie-José Pérec trained at the French National Institute of Sport and Physical Education while also studying to gain a professional qualification in electronics. At the age of 20 she set a national record in the 400 metres and made her Olympic debut in Seoul.

She has subsequently dominated the 400-metre event, winning gold medals at the 1991 World Championships in Japan, the 1992 Olympics in Barcelona, the 1994 European Championships in Helsinki, and the 1995 World Championships in Göteborg, Sweden.

In 1996 she took gold medals in both the 400 metres and the 200 metres at the Olympic Games in Atlanta, becoming the first athlete ever to accomplish this double.

Perey, Marguerite Catherine (1909–1975) *French nuclear chemist*

Marguerite Perey was an outstanding scientist, remembered for her identification of the element francium. She was honoured by many awards, including admission to France's Legion of Honour.

The daughter of an industrialist, Marguerite Perey was born at Villemomble and educated at the Faculté des Sciences de Paris. She began her career in 1929 as an assistant in the Radium Institute in Paris under Marie CURIE. In 1940 she moved to the University of Strasbourg and became professor of nuclear chemistry in 1949 and director of the Centre for Nuclear Research in 1958. In 1962 she was the first woman to be elected to the French Academy of Sciences.

By the 1930s chemists had discovered all the elements of the periodic table below uranium except for those with atomic numbers 43, 61, 85, and 87. Many false claims had been made for the discovery of element 87; however, in 1939 Perey found in the radioactive decay of actinium-227 the emission of alpha-particles as well as the expected beta-particles. Since an alpha-particle is basically a helium nucleus with an atomic mass of 4, this implied that Perey had discovered a nucleus with a mass number of $227 - 4 = 223$, which on further investigation turned out to be the relative atomic mass of the missing element with an atomic number of 87. She originally called it actinium K but in 1945 named it francium (after newly liberated France). Mme. Perey's death was hastened by prolonged exposure to radiation in the course of her scientific work.

Perkins, Frances Coralie (1880–1965) *American reformer*

Frances Perkins was an active worker in industrial health and safety issues, especially as they affected women and children. She was also the first woman to hold a cabinet post (as secretary of labour) in the U.S. government.

Born into a prosperous Boston family, Frances Perkins graduated from Mount Holyoke College in 1902. After a brief period as a teacher she joined the settlement-house movement in the slums of Chicago; she later worked with immigrant girls in Philadelphia. In 1910 she received a master's degree in social economics from Columbia University. Driven by a sense of public service, she disregarded her personal preference for a private life and became executive secretary of the Consumers' League of New York City and also of its Committee on Safety. Her experience in these posts made her an expert on health and safety issues.

In 1913 Perkins married Paul Caldwell Wilson but retained her maiden name for public purposes. Throughout the administrations of New York governors Alfred E. Smith and Franklin D. Roosevelt, Perkins played a leading part in efforts to reform labour conditions, campaigning especially for a 54-hour maximum working week for women. As state industrial commissioner during the worst years of the Depression (1929–33), she extended her expertise into the fields of unemployment insurance and unemployment statistics.

On becoming president of the United States, Franklin D. Roosevelt chose Perkins as his secretary of labour. She continued in office until 1945, just after Roosevelt's death. Her main achievements were the Social Security Act (1935), the Fair Labor Standards Act (1938), and the Wages and Hours Act (1938). She also supported the abolition of child labour and the establishment of the Civilian Conservation Corps. In 1946 she published a memoir of the president entitled *The Roosevelt I Knew*.

Perón, Eva (c.1919–1952) *Argentine actress and political leader*

The second wife of President Juan Perón, Eva Perón was known as "Evita" by the poor, who regarded her as their champion. She rose from humble origins to become a powerful political influence and – after her early death from cancer – a legendary figure.

Maria Eva Duarte was born into a poor family in Buenos Aires province. Details of her childhood are obscure, which is how she wanted it kept, but she moved to the capital in her teens and used her striking appearance to help her become an actress in films and on radio. Soon after the military seized power in 1943, Evita met one of the leaders of the coup, Juan Perón, whose mistress she became. Perón's bid for personal power in 1945 led to his imprisonment, but Evita rallied his supporters among the labour unions and the urban poor (*descamisados* – "shirtless ones"), forcing the government to release him.

On October 17 Perón and Evita, speaking from the balcony of the presidential palace, addressed an ecstatic crowd of 300,000. A few days later they were married. When he was elected president, she became – in effect if not in name – minister for health and labour issues. Purging the unions of anyone suspected of disloyalty to Perón, she also took over virtually every radio station in the country and closed down or banned over a hundred newspapers or magazines hostile to her husband's regime.

A gifted orator, she campaigned vigorously for women's rights, winning them the vote. To pass herself off as a good daughter of the Roman Catholic Church, she ensured that religious education was made compulsory in schools. When she was snubbed by the social elite, who ran the prestigious Charitable Welfare Society but considered her too lower-class to serve as its patroness, she suppressed it and replaced it with her own Maria Eva Duarte de Perón Social Welfare Foundation. Funded by a national lottery and donations from interests eager to cultivate her, the foundation became an immense instrument of personal power, channelling funds to schools, hospitals, retirement homes, and other pet projects sponsored by her.

By travelling widely through Argentina, Eva Perón kept in touch with the realities of the life of the poor from whose ranks she had risen. This not only gained her personal popularity but also enabled Perón to present himself as a leader who truly understood his people and their needs. Her bid for the vice presidency in 1951 was, however, blocked by the army. Shortly afterwards she died of cancer, aged only 33.

Her elaborate funeral was accompanied by extravagant gestures of public grief from her devoted followers, and her embalmed body subsequently became the focus of popular veneration before finally being laid to rest in her family plot. Despite her arrogance, ruthlessness, and greed, Evita successfully projected an image of herself as a self-sacrificing martyr, passionate only for the good of her people. Her extraordinary career inspired the hit musical *Evita*, by Tim Rice and Andrew Lloyd Webber, which was subsequently made into a film starring MADONNA.

See also PERÓN, ISABEL.

Perón, Isabel (1931–) *Argentine political leader*

The third wife of President Juan Perón, Isabel (or Isabelita) succeeded him as president after his death. However, unable to maintain a stable government, she was ousted by a military coup in 1976.

Born Maria Estela Martinez in La Rioja, Argentina, she trained to become a dancer. While touring Panama, she met the exiled former president of Argentina, Juan Perón, and became his secretary. In 1961 she became his third wife.

When Perón was invited to return to Argentina in 1973, Isabel accompanied him but initially took no part in politics until he chose her as his vice-presidential candidate in the second election of that year. The election posters depicted her with Perón and the shadowy presence of her predecessor, Perón's second wife, the enormously popular Eva PERÓN. Perón was duly elected president. When he died in 1974, Isabel, as vice president, succeeded him in office. However, she proved unequal to the pressures of a major political and economic crisis, and her incompetence provided an excuse for a military coup in 1976. Ousted from office, she was kept under arrest until 1981, when she was allowed to seek exile in Spain. Having renounced leadership of the Perónist movement in 1985, she was allowed to return to Argentina in 1988, provided she did not seek political office or make political statements.

Perovskaya, Sophie (1854–1881)
Russian revolutionary

An aristocrat, Perovskaya embarked on a revolutionary career that culminated in the assassination of Tsar Alexander II.

Perovskaya was the daughter of the governor-general of St. Petersburg. Ironically, given her later actions, she was born in domestic apartments in the buildings of the ministry of internal affairs – the government department responsible for law and order and internal state security. Following an attack on the tsar, her father was disgraced, and the family retired to live on their estates in the Crimea. Like many younger members of the aristocracy, Sophie was discontented with a life of idleness and concerned at the poverty of the Russian peasants, on whose labour the whole system of privilege depended.

Despite her father's objections, she left home and became involved in a network of like-minded young aristocrats who combined studying social conditions with building a revolutionary organization. In 1872–73 she worked as a nurse in rural areas. Arrested by the police in 1874, she was released for lack of firm evidence against her and joined a revolutionary group that called itself "Land and Liberty." When the group split over tactics in 1879, she went with the faction that favoured outright terrorism.

In February 1881 at the age of 27 Perovskaya organized the successful assassination of the tsar. She was arrested in March and publicly hanged in April, alongside four male conspirators. The effect of Perovskaya's action was counterproductive, at least in the short term. While Alexander II had been a cautious reformer, his successor, Alexander III, used the assassina-

tion to justify extreme measures of repression, violent persecution of Jews, and – thanks to Perovskaya's involvement – the banning of women from universities, to which they had only recently (1876) been granted admission.

Peters, Mary (1939–) *British athlete*

An all-round athlete, Peters specialized in the pentathlon, a combination two-day event involving shot put, 100-metre hurdles, high jump, long jump, and 200-metre sprint. She won an Olympic gold medal for this event in 1972.

Mary Elizabeth Peters was born in Halewood, Lancashire, but brought up in Northern Ireland, where she became a teacher of home economics. She represented Northern Ireland in the pentathlon at every Commonwealth Games from 1958 to 1974. At the 1970 Games she won the gold medal for both the pentathlon and the shot put.

Her eventual success at Olympic level was a reward for persistence. At the 1964 Tokyo Olympics she finished fourth, but an ankle injury pushed her back to ninth at the Mexico Olympics in 1968. In 1972 in Munich she needed to run a personal best in the 200 metres to win the gold. In achieving this, at the age of 33, she set a new world points record for the combined event. In the course of her career she also set British records for the 100-metre hurdles, the shot put (twice), and pentathlon (six times).

Since retiring from the track, Peters has developed a distinguished career as a sports administrator, managing the British women's athletics team at both the 1980 Moscow Olympics and the 1984 Los Angeles Olympics. She became president of the British Athletic Federation in 1996. An active campaigner on behalf of sports for the disabled, she was made a CBE in 1990. An athletics stadium in Belfast has been named in her honour.

Pethick-Lawrence, Emmeline
(1871–1954) *British social worker and suffragette*

Pethick-Lawrence was one of the leading voices in the British campaign for women's right to vote, which she later described as "the greatest bloodless revolution since history began."

Born Emmeline Pethick in Bristol, she was educated in England, France, and Germany. Her involvement with social work began at the West London Mission in 1890; there she met Mary Neal, with whom she founded the Esperance Club for working girls in 1895. She went on to create holiday hostels for the women and their children, and set up a co-operative dressmaking firm with working conditions that were ahead of their time, such as an eight-hour day, a minimum wage, and annual leave.

In 1901 she married Frederick Lawrence, a newspaper editor who later became Baron Pethick-Lawrence. Already active in the women's suffrage movement, she joined the Women's Social and Political Union (WSPU) in 1906 and became honorary treasurer. Her husband supported the suffragettes' cause, and together they edited the weekly newspaper *Votes for Women* from 1907 to 1914. Frederick also joined Emmeline in some of her protest demonstrations, which led to five spells in prison and a number of hunger strikes. In 1912 the Pethick-Lawrences left the WSPU, which had become too militant for their liking, and in 1914 they joined the United Suffragists. Emmeline subsequently became involved with the Women's International League for peace and attended the International Women's Congress in The Hague in 1915.

At the first opportunity, in 1918, Emmeline stood for parliament as a Labour candidate. Having failed to win her seat, she lent her support to Frederick in his political career and continued to campaign on pacifist and feminist issues. In 1938 she published her autobiography, *My Part in a Changing World*. She served as president of the Women's Freedom League for many years and was elected its President of Honour in 1953, the year before her death.

Pfeiffer, Michelle (1958–) *American actress*

She has never given a lazy performance...she has the double talent of always seeming in character and always herself.

—Alan Dale, *International Dictionary of Films and Filmmakers* (1997)

A noted beauty who became a sex symbol in the mid 1980s, Pfeiffer is also an accomplished actress of great versatility.

Born and raised in Santa Ana, California, Michelle Pfeiffer had a happy suburban childhood and graduated from high school with no particular ambitions. In 1977 she was working as a supermarket checkout girl. Two years later she entered (and won) the Miss Orange County beauty pageant, hoping the publicity would get her an introduction to a theatrical agent. It did. He arranged for her to have acting lessons and appear in television commercials, and by 1980 she had made her debut in both television and films.

Despite her relative lack of training, which she has always freely admitted, Pfeiffer's subsequent career has been meteoric. She first achieved major notices for her role as a drug-dependent gangster's wife in Brian De Palma's 1983 film *Scarface*. In 1987 she more than held her own with Susan SARANDON and CHER in *The Witches of Eastwick*. The following year she showed her versatility with appearances in the thriller *Tequila Sunrise*, the comedy *Married to the Mob*, and the costume drama *Dangerous Liaisons*, which brought her an Academy Award nomination for Best Supporting Actress. In 1989 she received a Best Actress nomination for her role as a sultry nightclub singer in *The Fabulous Baker Boys* and played in a stage version of Shakespeare's *Twelfth Night*.

Subsequent triumphs have included the spy drama *The Russia House* (1990), *Batman Returns* (1992), in which she played Catwoman, and *The Age of Innocence* (1993). Her most recent films are *Dangerous Minds* (1995), in which she played an inner-city teacher; *Up Close and Personal* (1996), a love story; and *One Fine Day* (1997), a comedy dealing with the problems facing a woman architect who is also a single parent.

Philippa of Hainault (c. 1314–1369)
Wife of King Edward III of England

A native of Hainault (now a province of Belgium), Philippa became one of the most popular English queens of the Middle Ages.

Philippa was the daughter of William the Good, Count of Hainault and Holland, and the granddaughter of King Philip III of France. At the age of 13 she married her second cousin, King Edward III, shortly after he came to the English throne in 1327. She was to bear him five daughters and seven sons.

Unlike previous foreign queens, Philippa did not come to the English court accompanied by large numbers of relatives expecting gifts, favours, and appointments, a circumstance that had invariably made for unpopularity. Although renowned for her gentleness and compassion, she nevertheless accompanied her warrior husband on his expeditions to Scotland (1333) and her native Flanders (1338–40). In 1347 Edward prepared to sack the French port of Calais when it finally surrendered to him after a long siege. Six civic leaders – the so-called "burghers of Calais" – offered to be hanged if the king would spare the city. Tradition holds that Philippa was so moved by their gallant gesture that she successfully pleaded with her husband to spare not only the city but the burghers as well.

Philippa was also the patroness of the chronicler Jean Froissart, who acted as her secretary. His account of the first half of the Hundred Years' War (1337–1453) remains a key primary source for historians. Queen's College at the University of Oxford was founded by Philippa's chaplain in 1341 and named in her honour.

Phryne (4th century BC) *Greek courtesan*

Born Mnesarete in Thespiae, Boeotia, she grew wealthy as a courtesan in Athens, even though her dark complexion earned her the nickname Phryne (Toad). As the mistress of the great sculptor Praxiteles, she may have been the model for his statue of Aphrodite, goddess of love, as well as for Apelles's painting *Aphrodite Rising from the Sea*. She was said to have been so rich that she offered to pay for the rebuilding of the walls of Thebes after its destruction – on condition that it bore the inscription "Destroyed by Alexander, rebuilt by Phryne." The offer was not taken up.

Accused of defiling sacred religious ceremonies – a capital offence – she was brought to trial. Her defence lawyer, Hyperides, who was also one of her many lovers, despaired of persuading the judge by the skill of his arguments alone. He therefore partially opened her robe to reveal her stunning figure. She was immediately acquitted and carried in triumph by her admirers to the Temple of Aphrodite.

Piaf, Edith (1915–1963) *French singer*

Edith Piaf came to represent Paris. When she died, the traffic in the city came to a standstill as the Parisians, to whom she meant so much, flocked onto the streets to catch a glimpse of her funeral procession.

She was born Edith Giovanna Gassion, the daughter of a Parisian café singer who abandoned her at birth, leaving Edith to be raised by her grandmother. Blinded after an attack of meningitis at three, she recovered her sight at seven. Her father, a circus acrobat, took her on tour and encouraged her to sing. This traumatic beginning to her life haunted Edith Piaf throughout her successful years but did nothing to extinguish her prodigious talent or her magnetic personality.

Performing her songs on street corners, she was heard by a nightclub owner, who gave her a cabaret job. At his suggestion she called herself Piaf – Parisian slang for a "little sparrow." Piaf's luck changed with her opening at the cabaret. Maurice Chevalier, who happened to be in the audience, was instantly enthralled by her songs. Through him she found her way into the mainstream Parisian theatre. She also appeared in films, but it is as a singer that she is known.

"La vie en rose", an evocative love song she wrote for herself, made Piaf an international star. During World War II she entertained French prisoners-of-war and secretly aided the Resistance by helping several to escape. After the war she toured widely but could never escape the legacy of the early years. Her insecurity was expressed by stormy personal relationships and illness made worse by drugs and drink. She could earn $1,000 for a single performance but gave to the needy as though she had no use for money herself.

With her throaty resonant voice, so at variance with her waiflike appearance, Piaf sang nostalgically of the tragedies of her own life. Her songs "Je m'enfou pas mal", "Mon Légionnaire", and "Non, je ne regrette rien", her theme song, reflected her personality. She also wrote two autobiographical volumes, *Au bal de la chance* (1958; The Dance of Luck) and *Ma Vie* (1964).

Piaf's funeral procession drew hundreds of thousands of mourners onto the streets of Paris. She is buried in Paris's Père Lachaise cemetery, alongside the greatest artists France has produced.

Pickford, Mary (1893–1979) *Canadian-born American actress*

A hugely successful star of the silent screen, Mary Pickford captivated audiences worldwide with her winsome little-girl persona; she also made a number of successful talkies.

Born Gladys Mary Smith in Toronto, she performed on stage from the age of five and made her Broadway debut in 1907. Her film career began in 1909, thanks to the pioneer director D. W. Griffith. In 1911 she married the actor Owen Moore.

Pickford's long blonde curls and winning manner soon made her a leading star, personifying sweetness and innocence in such silent films as *Tess of the Storm Country* (1914), *Rebecca of Sunnybrook Farm* (1917), *Pollyanna* (1920), and *Little Lord Fauntleroy* (1921), in which she played both the young lord and his mother. Her charm in these films earned her the nickname "the world's sweetheart."

A sharp sense of business made Pickford the moving spirit in bringing together Charlie Chaplin, Douglas Fairbanks Sr., and D. W. Griffith to establish United Artists (1919). This company enabled actors and film makers to bypass the commercial studios and make the films they thought were worthwhile. In the 1920s Mary Pickford was a superstar with a huge following. Having divorced her alcoholic first husband in 1919, she married Douglas Fairbanks in 1920, an event that attracted nationwide publicity. "Pickfair," their palatial home in Beverly Hills, became the social focus for Hollywood's film community.

Unlike many silent screen stars, Mary Pickford made a successful transition to sound, cut her curls, and won an Academy Award for her lead performance in *Coquette* (1932). Pickford retired from films in 1933, divorced Fairbanks in 1936, and in 1937 married the film actor Charles "Buddy" Rogers. In 1935 she published her autobiography, *My Rendezvous with Life*. Her status as Hollywood's first female screen idol was acknowledged by a special Academy Award in 1976. Although Pickford was one of the richest women in America, her last years were sad and reclusive; alone in Pickfair except for her staff, she sought escape in drink.

Piozzi, Hester Lynch (1741–1821) *British society hostess and writer*

As Hester Thrale, she became a close friend of Dr. Samuel Johnson. She later published anecdotes about him as well as their correspondence.

Born Hester Lynch Salusbury in Wales, she reluctantly married a prosperous London brewer, Henry Thrale, in 1763; two years later he became an MP. In 1764 Dr. Johnson, compiler of the first comprehensive dictionary of the English language, became a friend of the Thrales; he was a constant visitor to their home for the next 20 years. Mrs. Thrale delighted both Johnson and other distinguished guests with her excellent hospitality and witty conversation.

In 1780 Mrs. Thrale engaged an Italian musician, Gabriel Piozzi, as a music teacher for her daughter. Thrale died in 1781, and three years later Hester married Piozzi, much to the surprise and dislike of Johnson and other friends. The couple were, however, very happy and visited Italy together, where Mrs. Piozzi contributed to the *Florence Miscellany*, a collection of essays by a number of writers.

Johnson died in 1784, the year of Hester's marriage to Piozzi. In 1786 she published *Anecdotes on the late Samuel Johnson*, which gives a colourful and affectionate account of his eccentric personality but is also a defence of her own conduct. In 1788 she published a selection of their correspondence, *Letters To and From the Late Samuel Johnson*. Her later writings included light verse and accounts of her travels, as well as *British Synonymy* (1794), an early thesaurus.

Pitt-Rivers, Rosalind (1907–1990)
British scientist

A medical researcher, Pitt-Rivers made important studies of the thyroid gland (which regulates the body's growth and use of energy).

Rosalind Venetia Henley was born and educated in London, taking her undergraduate degree at Bedford College and her PhD at University College. From 1939 to 1942 she worked at University College Hospital before transferring to the National Institute for Medical Research, where she served as head of its chemistry division from 1969 to 1972. During her researches into the operation of the thyroid gland she discovered the hormone triiodothyronine, one of two hormones produced by the thyroid; she also co-wrote several standard texts on the thyroid and its functioning. She married George Pitt-Rivers in 1931 and was elected a Fellow of the Royal Society in 1954.

Pizzey, Erin (1939–) *British campaigner and writer*

Despite her later success as a novelist, Erin Pizzey is best known for her work with victims of domestic violence.

The daughter of a British diplomat, Erin Patricia Margaret Carney was born in China and grew up shuttling between her father's various overseas postings and a strict convent school in England. Failing to achieve any qualifications at school, she left home at 17 after the death of her mother. In 1961 she married the broadcaster Jack Pizzey.

During the 1960s Erin Pizzey worked as an adviser on welfare benefits in west London. This brought her into contact with deprived families whose economic difficulties were often made worse by domestic violence. At that time women trapped in such situations usually had to endure them simply for lack of alternative accommodation, even on a temporary basis. Pizzey therefore founded Britain's first refuge in which battered wives could live with their children, safe from violent partners, while they tried to build a new life for themselves. In 1971 she founded Chiswick Women's Aid to draw attention to the general problem of domestic violence against women. Further publicity came from the fact that her refuge was frequently prosecuted by the local authority for breaking the housing regulations against overcrowding.

In 1974 Pizzey's book *Scream Quietly or the Neighbours Will Hear* drew attention to the fact that abuse was as prevalent among middle-class families as among the deprived. In 1979 she became director of Chiswick Family Rescue, an organization that dealt with all sorts of domestic abuse. In the same year she divorced her husband to marry a psychologist, Jeffrey Shapiro, with whom she wrote *Prone to Violence* (1982).

During the 1980s Pizzey lived in Italy and wrote numerous popular novels, such as *The Watershed* (1983) and *First Lady* (1987). In 1983 she received the Nancy Astor Award for journalism, and in 1994 was awarded the San Valentino d'Oro prize for literature. In 1997, following the break-up of her second marriage, she returned to Britain, penniless and obliged to live on welfare benefits.

Plath, Sylvia (1932–1963) *American poet and novelist*

I am afraid of getting married.
Spare me from cooking three meals
a day – spare me from the relentless
cage of routine and rote.

—Letter to her mother, 1949

One of the outstanding poets of her generation, Sylvia Plath became a heroine to many feminist readers with her intense and harrowing work. She was married to Ted Hughes, the future poet laureate, who edited her Pulitzer Prize-winning *Collected Poems* after her suicide.

Born in Boston, Massachusetts, Sylvia Plath lost her professor father at the age of eight. Her mother became a college teacher to support the family. A gifted student who wrote poetry from early childhood, Sylvia attended the prestigious Smith College, Massachusetts, but while there she suffered severe depression and a nervous breakdown, which led to an unsuccessful attempt to take her own life. She recovered, however, graduating in 1955 and winning a Fulbright Scholarship, which enabled her to study at Newnham College at Cambridge University. At Cambridge she met the British poet Ted Hughes, whom she married in 1956.

In 1957 they went to the United States, where Sylvia spent a year teaching at Smith College, Massachusetts. After returning to England in 1959, the couple settled first in London, where Sylvia gave birth to their daughter, and then in rural Devon. In 1960 Plath's first volume of poetry, *A Winter Ship*, was published anonymously, and in the same year a second volume, *The Colossus*, appeared under her own name. Following the birth of her second child, she wrote a radio play, *Three Women*, set in a maternity home. In 1962 her marriage broke down, and a year later Plath committed suicide. Her last days and death are movingly described in *The Savage God* (1972), a book on suicide by the poet Al Alvarez.

Plath's only novel, *The Bell Jar* (1963), describes the mental and family pressures driving a woman to a crisis so profound that she attempts suicide. A largely autobiographical account of her collapse as a student, it was published shortly before her death under the pen name Victoria Lucas.

After her death the publication of further powerful poems under the titles *Ariel* (1965), *Crossing the Water* (1971), and *Winter Trees* (1972) gained Plath recognition as one of the most intense and original poetic voices of her generation. In 1981 Plath's ex-husband, Ted Hughes, edited her *Collected Poems*, which included many previously unpublished poems. In 1982 this volume was awarded the Pulitzer Prize for poetry. Plath's letters to her mother between 1950 and her death were published in 1975 as *Letters Home*. An unexpurgated edition of her journals appeared in 1998, the same year in which Hughes published his own account of their life together in his *Birthday Letters*.

Plisetskaya, Maya (1925–   ) *Russian ballet dancer and choreographer*

As prima ballerina with Moscow's famous Bolshoi Ballet, Plisetskaya danced in most of the leading classical roles during the 1960s and 1970s.

Born in Moscow, she studied at the Bolshoi Theatre Ballet School from the age of nine. She became a principal dancer with the Bolshoi Ballet as soon as she joined it in 1943 and prima ballerina on the retirement of Galina ULANOVA in 1962. In 1959 she toured America with the Bolshoi and subsequently made guest appearances in Paris, Marseilles, and Brussels.

Plisetskaya's first work as a choreographer was a ballet based on Tolstoy's *Anna Karenina* using music composed by her husband, the conductor Rodion Schedrin; it was staged in 1972 and filmed in 1974. Her works *The Seagull* (1980) and *Lady with a Lapdog* (1985) also used Schedrin's music. Plisetskaya served as guest director at the Rome Opera Ballet from 1984 to 1986 and with the Spanish National Ballet from 1987 to 1990. In 1988, aged 63, she danced in a celebration of her lifetime's achievement organized by admirers in Boston. She founded the Maya Plisetskaya International Ballet Competition in 1994.

Considered muscle-bound by her detractors, Plisetskaya was one of the first ballerinas to take the same classes as male dancers. Fans praised her combination of impeccable technique and dramatic power and consider her performances of *The Dying Swan* to have equalled those of the legendary Anna PAVLOVA.

Plowright, Joan (1929–) *British actress*

Joan Plowright has never seemed a star on stage but a most reliable member of a profession at work.

—Margery Morgan, *International Directory of Theatre*

The widow of Laurence Olivier, Joan Plowright is a versatile actress in her own right. Noted for the emotional directness of her performances, she has starred in classics by Shaw, Ibsen, and Shakespeare, as well as works by contemporary dramatists.

Joan Ann Plowright was born in Brigg, Lincolnshire. She trained at the Laban Art of Movement studio in Manchester (1949–50) and the Old Vic Theatre School in London (1950–52), having already made her stage debut in repertory. In 1952 she joined the prestigious Bristol Old Vic company and toured with them in South Africa. After performances at the Nottingham Playhouse and the avant-garde Royal Court Theatre in London, she made her Broadway debut in 1958.

In 1961 Plowright became the third wife of the actor-director Laurence Olivier. She joined the National Theatre company established by her husband for its first season in 1963 and remained its leading actress until 1974. Her many honours include a Tony Award (1960), awards from the *Evening Standard* newspaper (1963), the Variety Club (1977), and the Society of West End Theatres (1978), and two Golden Globes (1993).

Plowright has also appeared in many films, starting with *The Entertainer* (1960), in which she played opposite Olivier. Since turning 60 in 1989, she has made no fewer than 16 films, including *101 Dalmatians* (1996) and the Merchant–Ivory production *Surviving Picasso* (1997).

She was created a CBE in 1970 and is also on the Council of the Royal Academy of Dramatic Art (RADA).

Pocahontas (*c.*1596–1617) *Native-American heroine*

She next under God, was still the in-

strument to preserve this colony from death, famine and utter confusion.

—Captain John Smith, *The Generall Historie of Virginia: The Fourthe Book* (1624)

Considering how brief her life was, Pocahontas has gained an enduring place in American tradition as a symbol of trust and goodwill; she symbolizes the reconciliation and harmony that can exist between different races and cultures.

Born with the clan name Matoaka, Pocahontas was the daughter of Powhatan, paramount chief of a federation of Algonkian-speaking Native Americans who inhabited the Virginia tidewater. English colonists founded the settlement of Jamestown there in 1607. Although friction soon developed between the tribes and the colonists, Pocahontas innocently visited the colony, where – as a child – she was seen as no threat.

In December 1607 Powhatan's men captured one of the colony's military leaders, Captain John Smith, and took him to Werowocomoco, the chief's main residence and the birthplace of Pocahontas. Writing in his *Generall Historie of Virginia*, Smith recorded that it was Pocahontas who saved him from execution. While some historians have mistrusted Smith as a storyteller who usually portrayed himself as a hero, research has shown that for the most part his stories were true. Since being saved by a little girl scarcely shows him as a hero, there is little reason to disbelieve him in this case. On the other hand, since he had no knowledge of the Algonkian language, it is quite possible that Smith completely misunderstood what was said. Powhatan may simply have been forcing Smith into a ritual gesture of submission to show his own people that the newcomers were accepting him as their overlord.

Following Smith's safe return to Jamestown, a truce was arranged between the two sides. Pocahontas was allowed to continue to visit Jamestown, although armed clashes took place from time to time. In 1611 a new governor of the colony, Sir Thomas

Dale, went on the offensive, forcing Powhatan inland. In 1613 Pocahontas was captured by a trick. As Powhatan's favourite daughter, she was considered to be a valuable hostage in negotiations for the return of British prisoners. Taken to Jamestown and treated with courtesy, she was taught to speak English, baptized as a Christian in 1614, and given the name Rebecca. In that same year she married an English settler, John Rolfe, with the approval of both Dale and Powhatan. Another truce was agreed, which this time lasted until the chief's death in 1622. In 1615 Pocahontas gave birth to a son, Thomas.

Rolfe in the meantime had shown the colonists that by growing a new crop, tobacco, the settlement would at last have a profitable export to support it. In 1616 the Rolfe family returned to England, where Captain John Smith greeted Pocahontas most affectionately. Pocahontas was presented at the court of King James I, where her dignified manner made an excellent impression. The tavern near St. Paul's Cathedral where she stayed was renamed the "Belle Sauvage" in her honour. Governor Dale and the Virginia Company took advantage of this favorable publicity to raise more cash and colonists for Jamestown.

In March 1617, after a visit of seven months, the Rolfes prepared to return to Virginia. However, while they were waiting for a ship at Gravesend, Pocahontas became ill, probably with smallpox, and died. She was buried in the local church, St. George's, though the exact site of her grave has been lost. John Rolfe died in 1622, but Thomas, after being educated in England, returned to Jamestown; through him many proud Virginia families trace their descent from Pocahontas. The story of Pocahontas has provided the inspiration for many works of fiction, from *Captain Smith and Princess Pocahontas* (1805) to the Disney cartoon film *Pocahontas* (1995).

Pompadour, Marquise de (1721–1764) *Mistress of King Louis XV of France*

> Born sincere, she loved the King for himself; she had righteousness in

her soul and justice in her heart; all this is not to be met with every day.

> —Voltaire, describing Madame de Pompadour

Madame de Pompadour had a considerable influence on French politics as a result of her liaison with the king. She also worked closely with him in a number of architectural ventures.

Jeanne Antoinette Poisson was born in Paris, the daughter of a financial speculator, François Poisson, who was forced to flee France in disgrace when his daughter was only four. His friend Le Normant de Tournehem brought the girl up, gave her a first-class education, and married her to his nephew Charles Guillaume Le Normant d'Etioles.

By the time of her marriage at the age of 20 Jeanne was already the centre of an admiring circle of artists and intellectuals, including Voltaire. Eventually, this circle included King Louis XV. When the king's current mistress died suddenly in 1744, Madame d'Etioles was granted a legal separation from her husband, and Louis XV made her his new official mistress, granting her the title of Marquise de Pompadour.

Brilliant and beautiful, Madame de Pompadour gained great influence over the king and to some extent the policies of France. Historians have long blamed her for the shift in diplomatic alliances that led to the disastrous Seven Years' War (1756–63), as a result of which France lost Canada and other valuable territories. However, although for a while the king sought her approval for major official appointments, her direct responsibility for the choice of mediocre ministers has been exaggerated.

Her influence was far greater in matters of art than in politics. She shared the king's passion for building and worked enthusiastically with him to supervise the construction of extravagant palaces, such as the Petit Trianon at Versailles, the Château de Bellevue, and the great royal porcelain factory at Sèvres. The king did not, however, share her enthusiasm for the literary and intellectual circle known as Les Philosophes and their great project, an encyclopedia to summarize all useful knowledge. Perhaps his instincts were correct, for their sharp criticisms of the French monarchy contributed to its downfall a generation later.

Pons, Lily (1904–1976) *French-born American opera singer*

A dramatic soprano, Lily Pons was a great favourite at the Metropolitan Opera, New York, as well as at the opera houses of London, Paris, and South America.

Born Alice Joséphine Pons in Draguignan, near Cannes, she studied piano at the Paris Conservatory before singing in variety theatres while still in her teens.

She made her operatic debut in the title role of Delibes's *Lakmé* at Mulhouse, France, in 1928 and proved to be the first soprano in 50 years capable of reaching the high F that Delibes had written into a passage of the opera known as the "Bell Song." In 1931 Pons appeared at the Metropolitan Opera House in New York in the title role of Donizetti's *Lucia di Lammermoor* and was an instant success. She remained at the "Met" for some 30 years as principal soprano, specializing in French and Italian roles. In 1940 she became an American citizen.

Lily Pons also sang on radio and television and made a number of film appearances. During World War II she toured battlefields in North Africa and Asia to entertain Allied troops. A community in Maryland was named Lilypons in her honour. Her second husband was the distinguished conductor André Kostalenetz.

Popova, Lyubov Sergeevna (1889–1924) *Russian artist and designer*

A pioneer of abstract painting in the 1910s, Popova also designed innovative sets and costumes for the theatre.

The daughter of the wealthy owner of a linen factory, Popova moved to Moscow in 1906 and studied art privately before visiting Italy in 1910 and St. Petersburg in 1911. In 1912 she established her own studio in Moscow and travelled to Paris, where she was attracted to the newly emergent cubist movement. On returning to Russia, she came under the influence of Vladimir Tatlin, the founder of constructivism, a style of abstract geometrical painting. Popova, who began exhibiting her own canvases from 1914, made an important contribution to the constructivist movement through her use of colour and texture.

In 1916 Popova visited Samarkand in Uzbekistan, where she was greatly impressed by the remains of its Islamic architecture. After marrying the art historian Boris von Edding in 1918, she taught for two years at the Free Art Studios. The turmoil of postrevolutionary Russia gave scope and stimulus to her versatility and inspired her to create posters, book covers, costumes, and theatre designs. Popova's work was represented in the First Russian Art Exhibition held in Berlin (1922) and in the Art of Moscow Theatre 1918–1923 exhibition held in Moscow (1923). In 1924 she produced a range of textiles for the First State Textile Print Factory but died soon afterwards in an epidemic that swept Moscow; she was only 35.

Popova's work was exhibited after her death at the First Exhibition of Cinema Posters and the Paris International Exhibition of Decorative Arts in 1925.

Popp, Adelheid (1869–1939) *Austrian trade unionist*

Adelheid Popp led one of the earliest strikes by women. A socialist and feminist, she became a militant trade unionist in spite of much ridicule from her male colleagues. She was also an influential journalist and editor who ended her career as a government official.

Adelheid Dworak was born in Inzersdorf near Vienna. Her family was poor, and by the age of eight she was having to work to supplement the meagre family income. This led to periods of ill health and a fragmented formal education. However, the young Adelheid was an industrious reader, mainly of socialist literature, who managed to educate herself sufficiently to have become the editor of the Austrian Socialist Women's Association paper, *Arbeiterinnen Zeitung*, by the age of 23.

The following year (1893) she founded the discussion group Libertas, which encouraged women to discuss political issues and to learn to express themselves. In this same year she led 600 women working at a clothing factory near Vienna into one of the first all-women strikes in recorded history. In this brave gesture of feminist trade unionism she was bitterly opposed by her family and had to suffer the derision of the male members of the Austrian Trade Union Congress, who failed to back her.

In 1894 she married, adopting her husband's name of Popp. After this she remained leader of the Austrian Socialist Women's Association, concentrating their demands on women's suffrage, equal pay for women, divorce reform, and the provision of adequate nursery care to enable married women with families to earn an independent income.

In the early years of the 20th century she became a government official and made a valuable contribution to women's rights. Her volume of reminiscences was published in English as *Autobiography of a Working Woman* (1912). She died before the Nazi Party had completely destroyed the country she loved.

Popp, Lucia (1939–1993) *Czech-born Austrian opera singer*

A lyric soprano with a clear light tone, Popp was especially associated with the operas of Mozart and Richard Strauss; however, she also achieved distinction in works by Verdi, Puccini, and Mahler, among other composers.

Lucia Popp was born in Uhorska, Czechoslovakia, and studied music at the Bratislava Academy. In 1963 she made her professional debut in Bratislava, playing the Queen of the Night in Mozart's *The Magic Flute*. She joined the Vienna State Opera that same year, later becoming the company's principal soprano. In the mid 1960s she made her debuts at Covent Garden, London, and the Metropolitan Opera, New York. Clarity of voice and a slight physique gave her a youthful stage presence, tragically contra-

dicted by her early death from a brain tumour.

Porete, Marguerite (died 1310) *French mystic and religious writer*

Marguerite Porete is remembered as the author of *The Mirror of Simple Souls*, now regarded as one of the great religious works of the 13th century. However, at the time it was condemned by church authorities, and Marguerite was burnt at the stake as a heretic.

Little is known of her background, but she is thought to have been born into a socially prominent family in Valenciennes, northern France. From the quality of her writing she was obviously well educated and familiar with theology and the literature of the French court. However, she chose to forsake her family and join the Beguines, a loose-knit community of religious women who were dedicated to a life of poverty and abstinence but who – unlike nuns – did not live in a convent or follow a rule of life based on church teachings.

Marguerite began writing *The Mirror of Simple Souls* in 1285 and completed it ten years later. Combining poetic prose and dialogue, it stresses the essential identity of the soul with God and contains lyrical, somewhat erotic depictions of divine love. The book found a wide readership. However, because it implied that the sacraments and teachings of the Christian Church were unnecessary as a means of achieving salvation, it was condemned as heretical by the Bishop of Cambrai in about 1300, and all known copies were burnt. Nevertheless, Marguerite continued sending copies to prominent churchmen, although she was threatened with excommunication if she persisted in doing so.

Finally imprisoned, she refused to answer questions at her trial and was condemned to be burnt as a heretic.

Porter, Katherine Anne (1890–1980) *American fiction writer*

Katherine Anne Porter's high standing as a writer rests on her relatively small output of meticulously polished work, remarkable for the lucidity of its language, its descriptive power, and the complexity of its characterization.

Katherine Anne Maria Veronica Callista Russell Porter was born in Indian Creek, Texas, and educated at a convent and private schools in Texas and Louisiana. She did not go on to college. Married at 16 after running away from home, she was divorced at 19. She then worked as a journalist in Chicago and Denver, took on "hack writing of all kinds," and had a spell as an actress before moving first to Greenwich Village in New York and then to Mexico in 1920. Mexico provided the setting for her first published story, *Maria Concepción* (1922).

Her first collection of stories, *Flowering Judas*, appeared in 1930. This book won Porter a Guggenheim Fellowship, which enabled her to travel in Mexico and in Europe, where she married a French consular official. Returning to the United States in 1938, by which time she was once more divorced, Porter married a professor of English but within four years was divorced for a third time. *Pale Horse, Pale Rider*, a collection of three short novels for which Porter drew on her own experiences of Southern life, was published in 1939.

Nazism provided a central element in her third collection, *The Leaning Tower* (1944), and in *Ship of Fools* (1962), her only full-length novel, which took over 20 years to write. This book depicts the journey of a group of passengers, mostly German, sailing from Veracruz in Mexico to Bremerhaven in Germany on the eve of the Nazi takeover. It draws on her own experience of a similar 27-day voyage in 1931. Her last work, *The Never-Ending Wrong* (1977), dealt with the celebrated 1920s trial of the alleged anarchist murderers Nicola Sacco and Bartolomeo Vanzetti, in whose defence she had been involved. Their execution is now widely regarded as a major miscarriage of justice.

Porter's *Collected Short Stories* received the National Book Award and the Pulitzer Prize for fiction in 1965, the year in which *Ship of Fools* was adapted for the cinema.

Post, Emily (1873–1960) *American authority on etiquette*

The author of the immensely successful *Blue Book of Social Usage*, Emily Post won a place for herself in American social history.

Born Emily Price in Baltimore, Maryland, the daughter of a wealthy architect, she was educated privately. After travelling abroad, at the age of 20 she married a banker, Edwin Main Post, whom she later divorced. She then turned to writing fiction to contribute to the maintenance of her two sons.

At the suggestion of her publisher, Emily Post drew on her familiarity with polite circles to write a handbook, which was first called *Etiquette in Society, in Business, in Politics and at Home*. Later editions were titled *Etiquette: The Blue Book of Social Usage*. Unlike previous etiquette manuals, *The Blue Book* was readable and straightforward and did not assume that only the wealthy would wish to know how to behave correctly. In America's dynamic society there were many people whose commercial success required that they should be able to deal with social situations for which their upbringing had not prepared them. *The Blue Book* therefore became a bestseller, going through ten editions and 90 printings in its author's lifetime.

Emily Post's name and position as an arbiter of manners became known to millions of Americans not only through her book but also through her own radio programme and a syndicated column, which appeared in over 200 newspapers. Her other publications on etiquette included *How to Behave Though a Debutante* (1928) and *Children Are People* (1940). Emily Post, also an expert on domestic architecture and interior decor, published *The Personality of a House* in 1930. In 1946 she founded the Emily Post Institute for the Study of Gracious Living.

Potter, (Helen) Beatrix (1866–1943) *British writer and illustrator of children's books*

Beatrix Potter, the lonely London girl, grew up to become the author of a series of children's classics featuring animals that have been translated into many languages. In a later quite separate career she became a hill farmer, specializing in the breeding of Herdwick sheep.

Born in London, the daughter of a wealthy but rigidly respectable family, Beatrix Potter was educated at home with few opportunities to make friends of her own age. She grew up a lonely dreamy child who turned to her pets for company. With this background she became an expert on wildlife, studying the countryside on family holidays in Scotland and the Lake District and making meticulous drawings of specimens at the Natural History Museum in South Kensington, near her home. Despite her lack of formal scientific training, she wrote an expert paper on fungi and made many detailed studies of plants and animals based on her own dissections. However, the male-dominated learned institutions, such as the Royal Botanic Gardens at Kew and the Linnean Society, ignored her valuable work, which has only recently been recognized.

Foiled in her aspirations to become a biologist, Beatrix turned to writing. At the age of 27 she began to send illustrated stories in letter form to a sick child. These formed the basis of *The Tale of Peter Rabbit*, which was privately printed in 1900 and was followed by *The Tailor of Gloucester* in 1902. The London publisher Frederick Warne relaunched both books commercially in 1903, and a stream of new titles followed from then on, brilliantly illustrated with her own watercolour paintings. The stories of Squirrel Nutkin, Jeremy Fisher, Mrs. Tiggywinkle, and Benjamin Bunny were soon translated into other languages and have remained favourites with children since their first appearance.

Beatrix became engaged to Frederick Warne's son Norman, against the wishes of her parents, but he died before they could marry. However, she remained close friends of the Warne family, and when their publishing house was bought by Penguin Books in the 1980s, Beatrix Potter's copyrights

were their main interest. In 1913 at the age of 47 she finally married, becoming Mrs. Heelis, the wife of a country lawyer. She then gave up writing and became a successful sheep farmer in her beloved Lake District, making use of her fortune to buy up large tracts of land to preserve it from being built on. At her death she bequeathed her estate to the National Trust.

Beatrix Potter's home, Hill Top at Sawrey in the Lake District now receives thousands of visitors a year. The original illustrations for her books are preserved in London at the Tate Gallery.

Praed, Rosa (1851–1935) *Australian writer*

Although she wrote autobiographical works and plays, Rosa Praed is best known for her romantic novels set at the turn of the century, which she wrote under the name Mrs. Campbell Praed.

She was born Rosa Murray-Prior in southern Queensland, the daughter of a prominent livestock raiser who was also a public servant and politician. Her girlhood was spent in Brisbane and on remote farmsteads in the Australian outback, where she came into contact with Aborigines and learnt about their way of life. After her marriage to Arthur Campbell Praed she continued living on remote Queensland farmsteads. The hardships and other experiences of her childhood and early married life are reflected in her novels *An Australian Heroine* (1880) and *The Romance of a Station* (1886). They also provided material for two autobiographical books – *Australian Life: Black and White* (1885) and *My Australian Girlhood* (1902) – in which Praed wrote about Aborigines with perception.

In 1875 the Praeds left Australia for England and settled in London, where Rosa mixed in literary circles and became acquainted with prominent literary figures of the day, including Oscar Wilde – whom she portrayed in her novel *Affinities* (1885). Over the next 40 years Rosa produced as many novels, many of them set in Australia. The best known are *The Head Station*

(1885), *Outlaw and Lawmaker* (1893), *Nulma* (1897), *Fugitive Anne* (1903), and *Lady Bridget in the Never-Never Land* (1915). In *Policy and Passion* (1881) and *The Bond of Wedlock* (1887), which was dramatized as *Ariane* and performed in London in 1888, Praed explores the problems and disillusionment brought about by marriage, drawing on her own unhappy experiences.

After the final breakdown of her marriage and the deaths, in tragic circumstances, of her four children Rosa Praed sought comfort in spiritualism and the occult. She set up house with a medium, Nancy Haward, whom she believed to be the reincarnation of a Roman slave girl, and wrote several books on occult subjects.

Price, Leontyne (1927–) *American opera singer*

Leontyne Price, a lyric soprano, was the first African-American opera singer to perform on television and the first African-American prima donna. She was admired and loved by opera-goers worldwide.

Mary Violet Leontyne Price was born in Laurel, Mississippi, the daughter of a midwife. As a child she sang in her local church choir and in 1948 went on to study at the prestigious Juilliard School in New York. She first won acclaim as Bess in an international touring production of George Gershwin's *Porgy and Bess*. In 1955 she made her television debut in NBC's production of Verdi's *Tosca*, then undertook a major European tour to sing in Vienna (1959) and Milan (1960). Her debut at the Metropolitan Opera House, New York, came in 1961, when she sang the role of Leonora in Verdi's *Il Trovatore*. This performance immediately established her as a prima donna.

Although the natural bent of Price's talent inclined her towards the classic Verdi roles, her versatility also enabled her to perform Mozart, Tchaikovsky, and Puccini. When the new Metropolitan Opera House was opened in 1966, it was Leontyne Price who was chosen to create the role of Cleopatra in a new opera, *Antony and Cleopatra*, commissioned from Samuel Barber.

Leontyne Price retired from the operatic stage in 1985 but has continued to give concerts. In 1989 the National Academy of Recorded Arts and Sciences gave her a Lifetime Achievement Award.

Prichard, Katharine (Susannah) (1883–1969) *Australian communist and writer*

A founding member of the Australian Communist Party, Katharine Prichard wrote 12 novels as well as many short stories, poems, and plays, many of which were deeply influenced by her socialist beliefs.

Katharine Prichard was the daughter of Tom Prichard, editor of the *Fiji Times*, and she herself was born in Levuka, on Ovalau. After attending schools in Tasmania and Melbourne, she worked as a journalist for a Melbourne newspaper. In 1908 the paper sent her to London, which made such a deep impression on her that four years later she returned to the city to work as a journalist. In 1915, while still in London, she published her first novel, *The Pioneers*, which won a publisher's competition. This was made into a film in Australia the following year.

In 1916 Katharine Prichard returned to Australia; three years later she married the war hero Captain Hugo Throssell V.C. and settled in Perth, Western Australia.

It was not until 1920 that she allowed her deep socialist convictions to become public. In that year she helped to found the Australian Communist Party, and much of her subsequent work was an expression of her socialist beliefs. This was particularly true of *Black Opal* (1921), *Working Bullocks* (1926), and *Coonardoo: The Well in the Shadow* (1929) – generally regarded as her best works – and also of her trilogy set in the goldfields of Western Australia: *The Roaring Nineties* (1946), *Golden Miles* (1948), and *Winged Seeds* (1950). Her last novel, *Subtle Flame* (1967), dealt with some of the problems of being the editor of a newspaper.

Katharine Prichard's husband committed suicide in the early 1930s, which is said to have influenced the ending of her novel *Intimate Strangers* (1937). A story of marital breakdown and subsequent reconciliation for the cause of the socialist revolution, it was successfully dramatized for Australian television. Prichard's son, Ric Prichard Throssell, wrote a play, *For Valour* (1976), (based on his father) which explores the decline of a war hero after the war. He also wrote a biography of his mother, *Wild Weeds and Wind Flowers* (1975). This was published only 12 years after the publication of Katharine's own autobiography, *Child of the Hurricane*.

Primus, Pearl (1919–1994) *Trinidadian dancer, teacher, and choreographer*

Blending African and Caribbean sources with American traditions of blues, jazz, and jitterbug, Pearl Primus created new and vibrant forms of dance.

A star athlete at school, Pearl Primus originally planned to be a doctor. However, after passing her premedical examinations, she found that career closed to her by racial prejudice. In 1941 she won a scholarship with the New Dance Group, a New York dance school and performing company. She soon became a member of the school's faculty and began to choreograph her own works, notably *Strange Fruit*, depicting a woman's reaction to a lynching, and *The Negro Speaks of Rivers*, based on life along the Mississippi (both 1943). In 1944 she gave her first solo concert, in Manhattan, and headed her own company in the elaborate *African Ceremonial*. Before long she was performing in places ranging from Greenwich Village jazz clubs to Broadway theatres. Having toured with her own troupe in a revival of the musical *Show Boat*, she was awarded a Rosenwald Foundation scholarship, which enabled her to visit Africa for the first time in 1948.

While visiting her native Trinidad in 1953, Primus met dancer Percival Borde; following their marriage, they founded a dance school in New York City. From 1959 Primus directed a performing arts centre in Monrovia, Liberia, and travelled throughout Africa performing with her husband. After retiring from performance in 1980, she became director of the Black Studies School at the State University of New York. She was honoured with the National Medal of the Arts in 1991.

Pulcheria (399–453) *Byzantine aristocrat*

As the elder sister of one emperor and the wife of another, Pulcheria exercised a powerful influence over the Byzantine (eastern Roman) empire for nearly 40 years.

Pulcheria was the daughter of Flavius Arcadius, emperor of the eastern half of the Roman empire from 383 to 408, and of his wife EUDOXIA. At the age of 15 Pulcheria was installed as regent on behalf of her younger brother, Theodosius II (reigned 408–450). During this period (about two years) of direct rule by Pulcheria, who was a fervent Christian, life at the imperial court was conspicuously respectful of religion and morality.

Although Theodosius assumed his full powers in about 416, Pulcheria remained a major influence. In 421 she arranged his marriage to Athenaïs, who became a Christian and took the name EUDOCIA. However, Pulcheria and Eudocia quarrelled over their religious beliefs, and in 443 Eudocia retired from court to live in Jerusalem. For a while the grand chamberlain, Chrysaphius, became the emperor's most trusted counsellor, but he fell from favour shortly before Theodosius's death. Pulcheria was then able to intervene decisively to ensure that Marcian, an ex-soldier and elder statesman, was named as her brother's successor. She even agreed to marry Marcian – though purely as a formality – to ensure that the succession stayed within the Flavian line.

In 451 Pulcheria convened the historic Council of Chalcedon, an ecumenical church council that debated crucial points of theology; she was applauded by the bishops when she attended its opening. Pulcheria also used her personal fortune to build churches in the imperial capital, Constantinople, and left all that remained at her death to the poor.

Pye, Edith Mary (1876–1965) *British Quaker nurse, pacifist, and international relief worker*

After training as a midwife, Edith Pye joined the Society of Friends (the Quakers), for which she served as an international relief worker in the aftermath of both world wars. She also organized Quaker relief work in the Spanish Civil War.

Edith Pye was born in London, where she trained as a nurse and midwife before becoming Superintendent of District Nurses in London in 1907. This was an important post for someone who had just turned 30. The following year Pye became a member of the Society of Friends, and it was for her work as a Quaker that she became best known.

During World War I, with the help of her friend Hilda Clark (1881–1955), the daughter of the Quaker owner of the Clark's Shoe Factory, Pye went to France to organize a maternity hospital within the war zone. When the hospital found a permanent home in Châlons, Pye was appointed to the Legion of Honour. After the war Pye and Clark moved to Vienna to organize the relief work of the Society of Friends in that devastated city. They then moved on to the Ruhr Valley in Germany, where they helped to alleviate the misery of postwar refugees. At this time Pye was appointed vice-chairman of the German Emergency Committee.

In 1927 Pye found herself in China for the Women's International League for Peace and Freedom, on whose executive committee she served for many years. In the 1930s, during the Spanish Civil War, she was appointed by the Society of Friends to organize their relief work in Spain.

Back in Britain in the late 1930s, she tirelessly helped the Quakers work with Jewish and other refugees from Germany. During World War II she argued for a partial lifting of the Allied blockade to help the problem of starvation in Europe and became a leading member of the Famine Relief Committee. After the war she worked in France and Greece (1944–51), assisting in solving the enormous problems of displaced persons in postwar Europe.

Edith Pye won an international reputation as an inspiring personality, whose work for peace and the relief of the devastation wrought by war was unequalled.

Pym, Barbara (1913–1980) *British novelist*

Pym's novels are well-crafted comedies of English provincial life with a cast of vicars, spinsters, and academics. However, they often deal with darker themes, such as loneliness and unrequited love.

Barbara Mary Crampton was born in Shropshire, and educated at St. Hilda's College, Oxford. After graduating, she returned to her parents' home and stayed with them until World War II, during which she served with the Women's Royal Naval Service. From 1946 she worked in London as an editor at the International African Institute. During this period she shared a succession of homes with her sister, with whom she eventually retired to an Oxfordshire village – more or less as she had predicted in a short story she had written while still a student.

Pym's first novel, *Some Tame Gazelle*, is a love story set against the background of university life in Oxford; it was written soon after she graduated but did not find a publisher until 1950. Publication encouraged her to resume writing, and within a few years she produced *Excellent Women* (1952), *Less Than Angels* (1955), and *A Glass of Blessings* (1958). Typically, her novels feature educated but emotionally unfulfilled women whose lives are focused on such institutions as the church or the public library.

During the 1960s Pym's literary career came to a halt when an attempt to write under the pen name Tom Crampton led to consistent rejection of her manuscripts. However, interest in her work revived in 1977 when the poet Philip Larkin praised her as the most underrated novelist of the century in a survey for *The Times Literary Supplement*. Pym's later novels include *Quartet in Autumn* (1977) and *The Sweet Dove Died* (1978), which was based on her own passion for a younger man. Shortly before she died of cancer, she was elected a Fellow of the Royal Society of Literature. Four more of her novels were published in the years after her death.

Q

Qiu Jin (1875–1907) *Chinese revolutionary*

Qiu Jin (or Ch'iu Chin) was a feminist who chose JOAN OF ARC as her role model. She was involved with her cousin Hsü Hsi-Lin in planning an abortive uprising against the Manchu rulers, who captured and beheaded her.

The youngest daughter of a lawyer, Qiu Hin was well educated before her arranged marriage in 1893 to Wang T'ing-Chun, with whom she had two children. As a feminist she strongly opposed the binding of women's feet, a crippling procedure traditionally imposed on women for cosmetic reasons. She also founded a school for girls.

In 1904 she left her family to study in Tokyo, where she joined a radical student group committed to ousting the Manchu government. In 1906 she returned to China, achieving considerable public notice as an advocate of both feminist and anti-Manchu causes. At this time in her life she was appointed head of a college and founded a women's journal, whose main platform was the need to liberate women in order to enable China to be taken seriously by the West.

The following year she joined her cousin Hsü Hsi-Lin in planning an uprising in Hankou. However, their plans misfired, and they were both captured. Hsü was executed immediately, but Qiu Jin was tortured before being beheaded. Under torture she refused to confess to any crimes or to implicate any of her associates.

She is still regarded as a martyr of the early revolutionary movement that laid the foundations for modern China.

Quant, Mary (1934–) *British fashion designer*

Mary Quant was one of the prime movers who made London a centre of fashion in the 1960s. Both the boutique and the miniskirt were her creations.

Born in Blackheath, London, she attended nearby Goldsmith's College to study art. There she met Alexander Plunkett Greene, whom she married in 1957. In 1955 they joined photographer Archie McNair to open one of London's first boutiques – Bazaar – on the fashionable King's Road, Chelsea.

Rebelling against the dowdy middle-aged dress conventions followed by even such trendsetters as the young Princess MARGARET, Quant designed and made clothes that were cheap and cheerful, combining bright colours and novel materials, such as PVC, to produce a distinctive "mod" look. A decade later, when *Time* magazine proclaimed the existence of "Swinging London" as the world centre of music, fashion, and design, Quant's miniskirts, skinny-rib sweaters, and vinyl boots came to typify an era. She pioneered the concept of the boutique – a small shop with outrageous decor, extremely loud background music, and young staff – which was widely imitated.

In 1966 Quant was awarded the OBE, published her autobiography, *Quant by Quant*, and diversified into a range of cosmetics specifically aimed at the young. She was also honoured with a Design Council award in 1971 and was elected to the British Fashion Council Hall of Fame in 1990.

Quindlen, Anna (1953–) *American journalist*

As a columnist for *The New York Times* Anna Quindlen became known nationwide as the voice of the baby-boomer generation. Her approach to journalism can be summarized by her remark, "I think of a column as having a conversation but with a person that it just happens I can't see."

Born in Philadelphia, she graduated from Barnard College and was immediately hired by *The New York Post*. In 1977 she joined the staff of *The New York Times*, initially working as a city hall reporter. In 1981 she became the youngest ever journalist to take over the *About New York* column. In 1983 she received the Mike Berger award for Distinguished Reporting. Her *Life in the 30's* column, which ran from 1986 to 1989, echoed with wit and accuracy the concerns of people in their thirties and was syndicated in 60 newspapers.

Over 60 of her columns were republished in book form as *Living Out Loud* in 1988. A new column, *Public and Private*, also spawned a book of reprints, *Thinking Out Loud*, in 1993. Her writing was praised for its conversational directness, distinctive voice, and the comprehensiveness of its concerns, which ranged from such domestic topics as abortion and homelessness to international situations, such as the Gulf War.

In 1991 Quindlen published a novel, *Object Lessons*, which told the story of an Irish-Italian-American girl growing up on the fringes of New York City. That same year *Glamor* magazine hailed her as one of its ten Women of the Year. In 1992 she won a Pulitzer Prize for commentary, becoming only the third woman writer to be so honoured.

Quirot, Anna (1963–) *Cuban athlete*

Anna Quirot is one of the most successful of the dedicated Cuban competitors who have been carefully trained to bring credit to the regime of Fidel Castro.

A graduate of the state-sponsored Havana Institute of Physical Education, she won no fewer than eight medals at the Pan-American Games between 1979 and 1991. At the 1989 World Cup meeting she won the 400 metres and the 800 metres and was also a member of the winning 4×400-metre relay team. At the 1992 Olympics held in Barcelona she took the bronze in the 800 metres. Severe burns sustained in a household accident in 1993 prevented her from competing in track and field events for two years, but she resumed her career in 1995, winning the 800 metres in the World Athletics Championships at Gothenburg, Sweden.

R

Rachel (early 2nd millennium BC) *Old Testament character*

> Rachel was lovely in form, and beautiful. Jacob was in love with Rachel.
>
> —Genesis 29:18

Rachel was the second wife of the patriarch Jacob, whose 12 sons founded the 12 tribes of Israel. Her story is told in the book of Genesis (29–35).

Rachel lived at Haran in Paddan-Aram (now northern Syria). She was the younger daughter of Laban and looked after his sheep. Laban's sister Rebecca, who lived with her husband Isaac far away in the south, advised her son Jacob to journey north and find himself a bride from among Laban's family. When Jacob arrived, he fell in love with Rachel and agreed to work for Laban for seven years in return for her hand in marriage. The wedding day came, but Laban tricked Jacob into marrying Rachel's elder sister, Leah, in her place. (Traditionally the younger sister could not be given in marriage before the elder.) To win Rachel as his second wife, Jacob worked for another seven years.

Although Rachel was Jacob's favourite wife, she had difficulty conceiving children. Jacob already had ten sons and a daughter when she eventually gave birth to Joseph. After 20 years at Haran Jacob decided to return home. Before setting out, Rachel stole her family's idols and hid them in her camel's saddle. When Laban pursued Jacob's party and searched their tents, Rachel sat on the saddle and said she could not move because of her monthly period.

When the journey was nearly complete, Rachel gave birth to her second child. Aware that she was dying, she named him Ben-Oni ("Son of My Sorrow"), though he was later renamed Benjamin. Jacob raised a pillar to Rachel's memory at the spot where she died, just north of Bethlehem.

Rachel (1821–1858) *French actress*

Mademoiselle Rachel was the leading tragic actress of her day, best known for her performances in the title role of Racine's tragedy *Phèdre*.

Rachel was born Elisa Félix in Mumpf, Switzerland, the daughter of a poor Jewish family. By 1831 the family had settled in France, where Elisa and her sister sang in the streets and cafés, first in Lyon and then in Paris. Having begun to study drama, Elisa caught the attention of the actor Samson, who was impressed with her poise, especially in classical costume. She took the name Rachel to make her debut at the Comédie-Française in 1838, as Camille in Corneille's *Horace*.

Rachel played most of the major tragic roles in the French classical repertoire, *Phèdre* being her greatest triumph, and repeated her successes on world tours. She also acted in new plays: one, *Adrienne Lecouvreur* (1849), was written for her by Eugène Scribe and Ernest Legouvé. She was known for her clear speaking voice, restrained movements, and compelling on-stage personality, together with a strong will offstage. Rachel died in Le Cannet, France.

Radcliffe, Ann (1764–1823) *British novelist*

The work of Ann Radcliffe helped to create the fashion for Gothic novels – fantastic tales of terror and suspense featuring the supernatural and the macabre – in the 1790s.

Ann was the daughter of William Ward, a London merchant, and grew up among well-to-do relatives who introduced her to fashionable literary and intellectual circles. At the age of 23 she married William Radcliffe, an Oxford graduate who became an eminent journalist.

Ann Radcliffe's first novel, *The Castles of Athlin and Dunbayne* (1789), failed to arouse much enthusiasm, but her fortunes were soon to change. The four novels that appeared in the next few years – *A Sicilian Romance* (1790), *The Romance of the Forest* (1791), *The Mysteries of Udolpho* (1794), and *The Italian* (1797) – were all highly successful works in the Gothic tradition begun by Horace Walpole with *The Castle of Otranto* (1764). Radcliffe's brand of writing set the style of the Gothic romance, and her books are still regarded as among the most distinguished examples of this type of novel.

Radcliffe's stories were popular because of the sense of mystery and terror that they inspired. Although her complicated plots are unconvincing and her characters are generally one-dimensional, she made skilful use of poetic descriptions of landscape to enhance the romantic mystery-laden atmosphere of her tales. Her last work, the historical novel *Gaston de Blondeville*, was written in 1802 but did not appear until 1826, three years after her death in London.

Raine, Kathleen (Jessie) (1908–)
British poet and academic

> The ever-recurring forms of nature mirror eternal reality.
> —Introduction, *The Collected Poems of Kathleen Raine* (1956)

Kathleen Raine's poetry is firmly in the Romantic tradition and reflects her own philosophical and mystical beliefs. A biologist by training, she was inspired by the natural world in much of her poetry.

Though born in London, Raine spent the years of World War I as an evacuee in the north-east of England. Feeling she belonged in the remote hamlet where she lived with her grandmother and aunt, she later resented having to return to the London suburbs.

Raine's time studying natural sci-

ences at Girton College, Cambridge, was followed by two failed marriages – to Hugh Sykes Davies and Charles Madge, both writers. The marriage to Madge produced three children, and Raine was plagued with guilt after its failure. She turned to writing poetry. The first of her many collections, *Stone and Flower* (1943), shows a keen awareness of nature.

From 1955 to 1961 Raine was a research fellow at Girton. She became known for her writings on William Blake, one of her chief inspirations, and also produced several translations of French literature. Some of Raine's best mature poetry, including *The Hollow Hill* (1965), *The Lost Country* (1971), and *On a Deserted Shore* (1973), resulted from her frustrated love affair with the writer Gavin Maxwell, which she discusses in her collected autobiographies (1991). In 1981 Raine founded the journal *Temenos*, "devoted to the Arts of the Imagination."

Rainer, Yvonne (1934–) *American choreographer and dancer*

> *No* to spectacle, no to virtuosity, no to transformations and magic and make-believe.
> —On her style of choreography in the 1960s

Yvonne Rainer is best known for her experimental work with the Judson Dance Theater Company in the early 1960s.

Born in San Francisco, Rainer began her training as a dancer at the Martha Graham School, New York, in 1957. In 1960 she attended a summer school run by Anna Halprin in California and became interested in dance based on everyday activities. On returning to New York, she studied with Merce Cunningham.

In the early 1960s Rainer performed in several productions by James Warring, and in 1961 she choreographed her first pieces, *The Satie Spoons* and *The Bells*, for his workshops. Her attendance at Robert Dunn's experimental composition class (with Trisha BROWN and others) helped Rainer to form ideas that led to the foundation of the Judson Dance Theater in 1960.

The company's favoured techniques involved chance, repetition, and the performance of apparently ordinary tasks as part of a dance routine. As well as appearing in many of the company's productions, Rainer choreographed a large number of them, especially in the period 1960–64. Her finest achievement was probably *Trio A*, in which three dancers of either sex perform a carefully planned routine built up of such simple activities as walking and running.

In 1970 Rainer launched *Continuous Project – Altered Daily*, an experimental production choreographed as she went along. Since 1971 she has concentrated on a series of unusual productions combining live dancers with film. In 1984 she appeared in a video appropriately entitled *Beyond the Mainstream*.

Rainey, Ma (1886–1939) *American blues singer*

> She rolled out the blues in a deep,
> earthy, majestically pulsant voice,
> her only movement a slow rhythmic,
> almost hypnotic swaying.
>
> —John S. Wilson, *Show Business
> Illustrated* (1961)

Known as the "Mother of the Blues," she was an immensely popular blues singer who toured the Southern states and was noted for her wild diamond-studded appearance.

Born Gertrude Malissa Nix Pridgett in Columbus, Georgia, she first appeared on stage in her home town at the age of 12. When she first heard the blues in 1902, she became an instant convert and "sang them from then on." She married William ("Pa") Rainey in 1904, and together they toured with the Rabbit Foot Minstrels for many years. Ma Rainey was the main link between the blues as an authentic rural tradition and the more sophisticated interpretations of the genre by such later singers as Bessie *Smith*, whom she "discovered."

In 1923 Rainey made the first of over 100 recordings accompanied by Lovie Austin's Blues Serenaders. The records were enormously popular. Rainey continued to perform in "tent shows," often with her own band, the Georgia Jazz Band. She was said to be a very good employer, with a generous and warm-hearted personality. The public loved her and flocked to such touring shows as *Louisiana Blackbirds* (1927), which was seen by thousands. She retired in 1933 after her mother and sister died, remaining in Rome, Georgia, until her own death six years later.

Ramabai, Pandita (1858–1922) *Indian feminist and educator*

Pandita (a title meaning "female learned one") Ramabai was a powerful advocate of education for Indian women as well as change in their subservient status.

She was born Sarasvati Ramabai, into a family of Brahmins near the port of Mangalore in southern India. After being orphaned at the age of 16 she survived by teaching Sanskrit and reciting the Hindu scriptures (which earned her the title Pandita).

In 1881 she married a man of a lower caste, which exposed her to considerable public censure. Her feminist views had already aroused disapproval. Conservative elements in Indian society at that time regarded the education of women, especially in medicine, as deeply provocative. Her husband's death only two years after their marriage encouraged Ramabai to take her daughter to England to be educated. While they were in England, mother and daughter were baptized as Christians. In England Ramabai earned her living by teaching Sanskrit at Cheltenham Ladies College. In 1886 they departed for America, where Ramabai learnt fundraising techniques. She also lectured widely on the plight of Native-American women in the United States, and formed many societies pledged to collecting money for a home for widows in India.

In 1869 Ramabai returned to Bombay, where – with the money she had collected in the United States – she opened a boarding school for high-caste child widows, many of whom were aged between 9 and 12. Following the famine in 1896–97, she set up the Mukti Sadan (House of Salvation), an institute for women and children near Poona.

Sarasvati Ramabai wrote two books, *High Caste Hindu Women* (1887) and *Testimony* (1917). She also translated the Bible into Marathi.

Rambert, Dame Marie (1888–1982)
Polish-born British dancer

> I don't do cartwheels any more, but I still do a barre to keep supple.
>
> —Quoted in *Dance* magazine, February 1973

As not only a dancer but also a teacher and ballet-company director, Rambert was one of the most important figures in the history of British ballet.

Cyvia Rambam (later Miriam Ramberg and then Marie Rambert) was born in Warsaw, where she first began to study dance. She later studied in Geneva with Emile Jacques-Dalcroze, whose assistant she eventually became. Invited to join Diaghilev's Ballets Russes in Paris to assist with the choreography, she became a dancer with the company in 1913.

During World War I Rambert moved to London, where she danced, taught, and had the chance to study with the eminent teacher Enrico Cecchetti. In 1918 she married the playwright Ashley Dukes, who helped her open a ballet school in London two years later. Her ballet company, Ballet Club, was formed in 1930; five years later its name was changed to Ballet Rambert, and in 1966 it became the Modern Dance Company. In its early years the company performed only on Sundays, on the tiny stage of London's Mercury Theatre. Later, as a major ballet company, it toured the world.

Rambert had a keen eye for talented newcomers and gave them great encouragement and support. Among the great dancers and choreographers she helped to train were Dame Alicia MARKOVA, Sir Frederick Ashton, Hugh Laing, and Antony Tudor.

Marie Rambert was created a DBE in 1962. Her autobiography, *Quicksilver*, was published in 1972. She died in London.

Rambouillet, Marquise de (1588–1665) *French noblewoman*

The Marquise de Rambouillet is remembered for her fashionable salon, an important meeting place for intellectuals of the day. By bringing these people together she helped to shape language and manners in 17th-century Paris.

She was born Cathérine de Vivonne in Rome, the daughter of the French ambassador there and his Italian wife. At the age of 12 Cathérine was married to Charles d'Angennes, the Marquis de Rambouillet.

Disgusted by the vulgarity and ignorance she found at the court of King Henry IV in Paris, the marquise set herself the goal of improving society. She designed her town house, the Hôtel de Rambouillet, in an original style that would foster a sense of culture. There she received her guests, who included distinguished members of French society and leading artists, poets, playwrights, and other intellectuals. In this civilized company the art of polite conversation was cultivated, and social manners were refined. Corneille read his *Polyeucte* to the marquise's guests, and the churchman Bossuet is said to have preached his first sermon before them.

The influence of the marquise's salon declined in the late 1640s. Rival salons arose, and Molière poked fun at the exaggerated elegance of the language and manners at such establishments in his plays *Les Précieuses ridicules* (1659; *The Affected Young Ladies*) and *Les Femmes savantes* (1672; *The Blue-Stockings*). Nevertheless, the marquise continued to receive guests until her death.

Rame, Franca (1929–) *Italian actress, playwright, and theatre manager*

With her husband, Dario Fo, Franca Rame evolved a style of theatre that conveyed political comment through broad physical comedy. She is also a noted feminist and civil-rights campaigner.

Born into a family of professional travelling comedians, Franca Rame became familiar with stock performing techniques at an early age. It was while she was appearing at a theatre in Milan that she met Dario Fo, then an architecture student. The couple married in 1954 and soon afterwards went into partnership, writing, performing, and producing plays.

Although their work became increasingly political during the 1960s, Rame's experience of improvisational techniques gave their drama a spontaneous quality it never lost. In 1968 the couple established a new company, Nuova Scena, with a communist agenda. Two years later, however, they distanced themselves from the Communist Party and formed a new leftist theatre company called La Comune. In such plays as Fo's *Accidental Death of an Anarchist* (1970) Rame and Fo satirized capitalism and what they saw as oppressive institutions, notably the church and the traditional family. The proceeds of their productions went to assist the political causes they favoured.

In the 1970s Rame campaigned successfully for the cause of political prisoners in Italy. Then, from 1977, she began to concentrate on feminist issues. She travelled to many countries, giving over 1,000 performances of her collection of feminist monologues, published as *Tutto casa, letto e chiesa* (1978; All Home, Bed, and Church, also performed in English as *Female Parts*). Particularly well known among her works is *Rape* (1983), a harrowing monologue based on her own experience of a sexual assault (instigated, she believes, by her political opponents). In 1987 Rame and Fo wrote *The Open Couple*, a bitter comedy about the collapse of a modern marriage; they separated the following year, but have subsequently worked together on a number of projects. In 1997 they led a campaign against Rome's bid to host the Olympic Games in 2004.

Rand, Ayn (1905–1982) *Russian-born American novelist*

> I will never live for the sake of another man, nor ask any other man to live for mine.
>
> —*Atlas Shrugged* (1957)

Ayn Rand, who used her books to promote a creed of ruthless individualism, is best known for *The Fountainhead*, a lengthy biographical novel defending the independence of an architect.

She was born in St. Petersburg and graduated from the university there in 1924. Two years later she left the Soviet Union for the United States, where she worked at a variety of jobs, chiefly as a scriptwriter for Hollywood studios; in 1931 she became a U.S. citizen.

The idea central to Rand's work is that the strong flourish best in a totally free society in which they are allowed to further their own goals and ambitions. Her first novel, *We, the Living* (1936), concerns a group of young Russian individualists who are trapped and destroyed by the totalitarian Soviet regime. The hero of *Anthem* (1938), which is set in an imagined future, refuses to conform to a regulated society. However, it was *The Fountainhead* (1943), a novel about an individualistic architect (based apparently on Frank Lloyd Wright) that made Rand a celebrity. Her next novel, *Atlas Shrugged* (1957), is about a group of people who plan a new society based on an ideal of self-fulfilment. *For the New Intellectual* (1961) brings together the more philosophical passages from Rand's novels.

Rand also wrote *The Virtue of Selfishness* (1965), *Capitalism: The Unknown Ideal* (1966), *The Romantic Manifesto: A Philosophy of Literature* (1969), *The New Left: The Anti-Industrial Revolution* (1971), and *Philosophy: Who Needs It?* (1982). The monthly journal *The Objectivist*, which Rand helped edit, set out her theory of objectivism, which advocated "rational self-interest" and unregulated capitalism.

Rankin, Jeannette (1880–1973) *American legislator and suffragist*

> You can no more win a war than you can win an earthquake.
>
> —Quoted by Hannah Josephson in *Jeannette Rankin: First Lady in Congress* (1974)

Remembered as a feminist, pacifist, and reformer, Jeannette Rankin was also the first woman elected to the U.S. Congress.

Jeannette Rankin was born near Missoula, Montana, and graduated from the University of Montana in 1902. For several years she was a social worker in Seattle. She was also active in the women's suffrage movement, being a leading member of the National American Woman Suffrage Association.

At that time Montana was one of the few states in which women could vote. In 1916 Rankin stood as a Republican candidate for Montana and was elected to Congress. She continued to support women's issues and promote pacifism, voting against the declaration of war in 1917.

After spending much of the interwar period as a lobbyist and social worker, Rankin again represented Montana in the House of Representatives in 1941–43 but was unsuccessful in her bid for a seat in the Senate. In 1941 she was the only member of the House to vote against declaring war on Japan. Rankin continued to lecture and work for women's rights, peace, and disarmament; in 1968 she led 5,000 women in the Jeannette Rankin March on Capitol Hill, Washington, D.C., in a protest against the Vietnam War. She died in Carmel, California.

Rankin, Judy (1945–) *American golfer*

Judy Rankin was the first woman golfer to earn more than $100,000 in a season. Noted for her concentration and steady play, she was consistently placed high in the Women's Open and won numerous tournaments in the Ladies' Professional Golf Association (LPGA) tours.

Born Judy Torluemke in St. Louis, Missouri, she began playing golf at the age of six. At 14 she was the youngest person ever to win the Missouri Amateur Tournament. She repeated this success at 16 and turned professional at 17. In 1967, aged 22, she married Walter "Yippy" Rankin.

In 1976 Judy Rankin won six LPGA tournaments and earned the enormous sum of $150,734. She fared nearly as well in 1977, coming back with five wins and $122,890. In both these years she was not only named LPGA Player of the Year but also won the Vare Trophy for lowest scoring average.

Rantzen, Esther (1940–) *British television presenter*

For 21 years the presenter of the popular BBC consumer programme *That's Life*, Esther Rantzen is also noted for her charitable work.

Educated at the North London Collegiate School and Somerville College, Oxford, Esther Rantzen began her media career on BBC radio in 1963. Transferring to television two years later, she worked as a researcher and reporter before becoming producer and presenter of *That's Life* in 1973. The series, which focused on consumer issues and matters outrageous or simply bizarre, made Esther Rantzen a household name in Britain.

Rantzen married her BBC boss, Desmond Wilcox, in 1977 and had three children. Her interests later focused on family and social issues. In particular, she founded the charity Childline, which offers help by telephone to children in distress. Rantzen also became president of a charity combating postnatal depression. She has appeared in various TV shows in addition to *That's Life*, and since the programme ended in 1994, she has hosted a twice-weekly topical talk show, simply called *Esther*. In 1991 she was appointed an OBE.

Rathbone, Eleanor (Florence) (1872–1946) *British feminist, social reformer, and politician*

In the closing years of the 19th century Eleanor Rathbone was a leading speaker for the Women's Suffrage Society. A specialist on family economics, she wrote a number of books on the subject, which influenced the post-World War II legislation setting up Britain's welfare state. After becoming an MP in the 1930s, she championed the cause of Indian women. A passionate opponent of appeasement in the 1930s, she was greatly concerned for Jewish refugees from Nazi Germany during World War II.

Eleanor Rathbone was born into a large Quaker family in Liverpool. Although the family had a long-established merchant background, many of its members were well-known philanthropists. Eleanor's father was a Liberal MP, and therefore the family spent a considerable amount of time in London. After attending school in London, Eleanor went to Oxford University to study classics. She then returned to Liverpool, where she became an unpaid visitor for the Liverpool Central Relief Society. She was also an active member and speaker for the nonmilitant wing of the Women's Suffrage Society under Dame Millicent FAWCETT. In 1902 she met Elizabeth Macadam, who was running a women's settlement. The two women entered into a relationship that endured until Eleanor Rathbone's death.

Specializing in family economics, Rathbone wrote two influential books, *How the Casual Labourer Lives* (1909) and *The Condition of Widows under the Poor Law in Liverpool* (1913). In 1909 she was elected the first woman member of Liverpool City Council, as an independent. In the 1920s she was an unsuccessful parliamentary candidate for a Liverpool seat, but in the 1930s she was elected to Parliament. Deeply interested in the status of women in India, she wrote a book denouncing child marriage, *Child Marriage: The Minotaur* (1934). She also forcefully attacked the government's appeasement policy towards Mussolini and Hitler and advocated intervention in the Spanish Civil War. She expressed these views in her book *War Can Be Averted* (1937).

During World War II Eleanor Rathbone showed great concern for displaced persons in Europe, particularly for the Jewish refugees from German anti-Semitism. This concern led her to become an ardent Zionist but she died before witnessing the founding of the state of Israel.

Ratushinskaya, Irina (Borisovna)
(1954–) *Russian poet*

> It's nonsense to talk about limited human rights…It's like limited breath.
>
> —Interview, *The Spectator*, 1988

Although imprisoned by the Soviet authorities for her dissident activities, Irina Ratushinskaya continued writing in jail, producing poems and a memoir that have touched the emotions of many.

Born in Odessa of part-Polish ances-

try, Irina Ratushinskaya could read by the age of three and familiarized herself with the works of the great Russian authors as a young child. She wrote her first rhyming poem at the age of five. Her mature poetry, which reveals her Roman Catholic faith and her loathing for the oppressive Soviet regime, began to be secretly distributed while she was studying physics at Odessa University. Later, when working as a teacher in 1978, she was dismissed for opposing an anti-Semitic admissions policy.

In 1979 Ratushinskaya married Igor Gerashchenko, an engineer, and the couple settled in Kiev. He shared her views, and in 1981 both of them openly denounced the exiling of the physicist Andrei Sakharov, who had campaigned for human rights. After a brief period in prison the couple campaigned still more actively for human rights and distributed forbidden literature.

In 1982 Ratushinskaya was arrested, interrogated, and sentenced to seven years hard labour and a further five years in exile. Despite the brutal prison regime, she continued to write poems on slips of paper hidden in the gloves she had to stitch. After memorizing each one, she destroyed it. Other poems she scratched onto soap with charred matchsticks. Altogether she composed some 300 poems in prison.

The arrival of *glasnost* brought Ratushinskaya's release in 1986. She and her husband left for London and later moved on to the United States, where Ratushinskaya became the poet-in-residence at Northwestern University, Evanston, Illinois. The poems published in *No, I'm Not Afraid* (1986) and other collections and her prison memoir, *Grey Is the Colour of Hope* (1988), are deeply moving works that reveal both her literary talent and her courage. In 1992 she published a novel, *The Odessans*.

Ray, Dixy Lee (1914–1994) *American scientist and public official*

An outspoken character, Dixy Lee Ray supported the U.S. nuclear industry and was sceptical about the extremes of the environmental movement. She also promoted the idea of better science education for all.

Ray was born in Tacoma, Washington. As a child she was interested in the sea and marine life, which was later to become her area of expertise. She graduated from Mills College, California, in 1937, received a PhD in biology from Stanford University in 1945, and taught at the University of Washington. Her field of specialization was marine crustaceans. In 1963 she became director of the Pacific Science Center in Seattle, which involved her in activities to awaken public interest in science.

Having joined the U.S. Atomic Energy Commission (AEC) in 1972, Ray became its head a year later. Believing that nuclear energy would be needed to replace fossil fuels, she sought to expand nuclear plants while safeguarding the environment. In 1974, when the AEC ceased to exist, she was appointed assistant secretary of state for oceans and international environmental and scientific affairs, but she resigned after a dispute with Henry Kissinger. In 1976 Ray, running as a Democrat, was elected governor of Washington and served in that position until 1981, when her bid for reelection failed.

Together with Lou Guzzo, her policy adviser, Ray wrote two books, *Thrashing the Planet* (1990) and *Environmental Overkill* (1993).

Rayner, Claire (Berenice) (1931–)
British advice columnist, journalist, and novelist

Claire Rayner is widely known as an advice columnist, broadcaster, and speaker on many subjects. She has also written more than 75 books, which include both fiction and nonfiction.

Born into a Jewish family in London's East End, Claire was educated at the City of London School for Girls before training to be a nurse and midwife. In the 1950s and 1960s she worked as a nursing sister in several London teaching hospitals and married an actor, Desmond Rayner, in 1957. They have two sons and a daughter.

In 1966 Claire Rayner became the medical correspondent of the magazine *Woman's Own*, writing under the name "Ruth Martin" until 1975, after which she used her own name. She has also written many advice columns in tabloid newspapers and broadcast a series on the BBC, *Claire Rayner's Casebook*. As well as a wide variety of newspaper and magazine articles, she has written many nonfiction books on medical and associated subjects, such as *Key Facts of Practical Baby Care* (1967), *People in Love* (1968), *Family Feelings* (1977), *The Body Book* (1978), and *Safe Sex* (1987).

In addition to this prolific nonfiction output Claire Rayner has written over 30 novels, of which the 12-volume saga *The Performers* (1973–86) is perhaps the most widely read. As "Sheila Brandon" she has written seven hospital novels, including *Cottage Hospital* (1963) and *The Private Wing* (1971).

Using the name "Ann Lynton," this remarkably versatile writer has also contributed to many nursing journals and national newspapers.

Reagan, Nancy (1923–) *Wife of President Ronald Reagan*

> She's a warm and generous person…How do you describe someone that makes your life like coming into a warm room?
>
> —Ronald Reagan, describing Nancy, 1981

As First Lady Nancy Reagan attracted attention mainly for her style and her extravagance. However, her stated ambition was to help young people, notably in tackling alcohol and drug abuse.

Anne ("Nancy") Robbins was born in Manhattan, the daughter of an actress. Her father, a used-car salesman, deserted the family soon after her birth, and Nancy lived with her aunt in Bethesda, Maryland, while her mother earned a living on Broadway. After her mother's remarriage Nancy moved to Chicago, where she attended school and, prophetically, took the lead role in a play called *First Lady*. She later gained a BA in drama at Smith College, Massachusetts, and became a professional actress.

Having appeared in several stage

productions by the mid 1940s, Nancy signed a seven-year contract with the film studios MGM. She first met Ronald Reagan, at that time president of the Screen Actors Guild, when he helped her to prove that she had been wrongly listed as a communist supporter. They married in 1952.

After the birth of two children Nancy retired from acting, having appeared in 11 films, including one – *Hellcats of the Navy* (1957) – with her husband. The Reagans settled in California, where Ronald became governor in 1966. As his wife, Nancy became known both for her expensive tastes and for campaigning on behalf of American prisoners in Vietnam, the elderly, and disabled and disadvantaged children. This combination was also a feature of her life as First Lady (1981–89). While capable of spending over $200,000 on dinner plates, she was also interested in social issues and campaigned against drug abuse, using the slogan "Just Say No." In the later 1990s she has won widespread admiration for the way in which she has coped with her husband's development of Alzheimer's disease.

Récamier, Jeanne Françoise Julie Adelaide (1777–1849) *French society hostess*

> A countenance full of candour and at times mischief, which the expression of goodness rendered irresistibly attractive.
>
> —M. Livy (ed.), *Recollections and Correspondence Extracted from the Papers of Mme. Récamier* (1859)

Noted for her beauty and charm, Madame Récamier was a popular society hostess in late 18th- and early 19th-century Paris.

Born Jeanne Françoise Julie Adelaide Bernard in Lyon, she was the daughter of a financier who later took up an important public position in Paris. Young "Juliette" remained in Lyon, where she was educated at a convent. When she was 15, she joined her parents in Paris, where she married one of her many suitors – the 42-year-old banker Jacques Récamier.

Madame Récamier soon became famous for her salon, where eminent political and artistic figures used to meet. Among her admirers were Lucien Bonaparte, brother of Napoleon, and Count Bernadotte, the future king of Sweden. However, she seems to have remained faithful to her husband.

Madame Récamier's own sympathies were with the royalists, and she disliked the society Napoleon was creating. In 1805, as her husband began to lose money, she was exiled from Paris by Napoleon and took up residence in Geneva with her friend Madame de STAËL. While there she helped inspire her friend's novel *Corinne*. She is also thought to have had a love affair with Prince Auguste of Prussia but to have ended it when her husband reflected that, having shared his wealth, she was rejecting him in his poverty.

After moving on to Rome and then Naples, Madame Récamier returned to Paris on the restoration of the monarchy in 1815. Although she found it impossible to entertain as lavishly as before, in 1819 she took rooms in the Abbaye-aux-Bois and received guests there, including the writer Châteaubriand. After her husband's death in 1830 Châteaubriand became her closest friend until his death in 1848. She outlived him by only ten months.

Redgrave, Lynn (1943–) *British actress*

Lynn Redgrave rose to stardom as a result of her appearance in the film *Georgy Girl* (1966), for which she shared the Best Actress Award of the New York Film Critics.

The younger daughter of actors Sir Michael Redgrave and Rachel Kempson and the sister of Vanessa REDGRAVE, Lynn was born in London, where she studied at the Central School of Speech and Drama. She made her professional stage debut in London as Helena in *A Midsummer Night's Dream* (1962). After touring for a time with the Dundee Repertory Company, she appeared with the National Theatre Company in 1963–66. In 1974 she settled in the United States.

Lynn Redgrave's films include *Tom Jones* (1963), *Girl with Green Eyes* (1964), *Georgy Girl* (1966) – in which she gave a humorous and touching performance as an "ugly duckling" – *The Last of the Mobile Hotshots* (1970), Woody Allen's *Everything You Always Wanted to Know About Sex (but were Afraid to Ask)* (1972), and *The Happy Hooker* (1975), in which she played the title role of Xaviera Hollander.

On stage Redgrave appeared in *Black Comedy* (1967), *My Fat Friend* (1974), *The Two of Us* (1975), Shaw's *Mrs. Warren's Profession* (1976) and *Saint Joan* (1977), and *Aren't We All* (1985). She cohosted the American television talk show *Not for Women Only* and appeared in three American series, *Teachers Only*, *House Calls*, and the short-lived *Chicken Soup*, with comedian Jackie Mason. In 1990 Lynn and Vanessa Redgrave acted together in both a West End production of Chekhov's *Three Sisters* and a television remake of *Whatever Happened to Baby Jane?*

In 1993 Lynn Redgrave was nominated for a Tony Award for her one-woman show, *Shakespeare for My Father*, a homage to Sir Michael Redgrave. Her book *This Is Living: An Inspirational Guide to Freedom* was published in 1988.

Redgrave, Vanessa (1937–) *British actress*

Acclaimed as one of the leading actresses of our time, Vanessa Redgrave has also earned a reputation for her outspoken political views.

Vanessa Redgrave was born in London into a well-known acting family. Her father was the actor Sir Michael Redgrave, and her mother is the actress Rachel Kempson. Her paternal grandparents and a great-grandfather were also members of the acting profession. On the evening of her birth Laurence Olivier, who was appearing in *Hamlet* with her father, announced to the audience, "Tonight a lovely new actress has been born."

As a result of her parents' careers, Redgrave travelled a good deal as a child and had private lessons. From 1954 to 1957 she attended London's Central School of Speech and Drama, and she made her London stage debut

the day after her 21st birthday, appearing with her father in *A Touch of the Sun*. Over the next few years Redgrave played leading roles in several West End plays, including Ibsen's *The Lady from the Sea* (1960) and RSC productions of *As You Like It* and *The Taming of the Shrew* (1961). During this period Redgrave was arrested during a protest against nuclear weapons, though the event did not damage her career. Thereafter she continued to alternate acting with political activity, earning particular notoriety for her statements expressing sympathy for the IRA and Palestinian terrorism.

After marrying the director Tony Richardson and giving birth to their daughter Natasha (who also became an actress), Redgrave returned to the stage to great acclaim in Chekhov's *The Seagull* in 1964. International fame came in 1966 with the release of her first film *Morgan – A Suitable Case for Treatment*. American critics acclaimed her performance, and the film was a major success at the Cannes Film Festival, where Redgrave won the Best Actress Award.

Redgrave and Richardson had another daughter, Joely, also a future actress, but divorced in 1967. In 1969 Redgrave had a son by the actor Franco Nero. During the 1960s and 1970s she performed both on the stage and on screen, appearing in the films *A Man for All Seasons* (1966), *Camelot* (1967), *Isadora* (1968), *Murder on the Orient Express* (1974), and *Julia* (1977). For this last film, in which she starred with Jane FONDA, Redgrave won an Oscar for Best Supporting Actress.

In the 1980s Redgrave's films included *Playing for Time* (1980), which was made for television and earned her an Emmy Award; and *The Bostonians* (1984) and *Prick Up Your Ears* (1987), both of which brought her Academy Award nominations. On stage she appeared in both London and New York in Tennessee Williams's *Orpheus Descending* (1988–89). Highlights of the 1990s include a London production of *Three Sisters* and the TV movie *Whatever Happened to Baby Jane?* (both 1990, with her sister Lynn REDGRAVE);

and the films *Howards End* (1992) and *Mrs. Dalloway* (1998).

Rego, (Maria) Paula (Figueiroa) (1935–) *Portuguese-born British artist*

One of the most original figurative artists of her generation, Rego came to prominence with a series of exhibitions in the 1980s. Her work combines humour and fantasy with an element of the sinister and fearful.

Paula Rego was born into a prosperous cultured family in Portugal and educated at St. Julian's School, Carcavelos, and at the Slade School of Fine Arts, London. She was awarded the Gulbenkian Foundation Bursary in 1962–63 and held her first exhibitions in the mid 1960s. In 1959 she married the British artist Victor Willing, with whom she had two daughters and a son. From 1983 to 1990 she was a part-time lecturer at the Slade School, before becoming the first associate artist at the National Gallery in London.

Rego has held many solo shows, including exhibitions at Lisbon (1965, 1971, 1974 and 1978), Oporto (1977) and at various London galleries (1981, 1982, 1984, 1985, 1987 and 1991–96). She has also exhibited at Bristol (1983), Amsterdam (1983) and New York (1985). Her large triptych *Crivelli's Garden* (1992) hangs in the restaurant of the Sainsbury Wing of the National Gallery. More recently, her interest in the world of childhood and fairytale came to the fore in the exhibitions *Peter Pan* and *Nursery Rhymes*, both of which have also been published in book form. She is the subject of the substantial monograph *Paula Rego* (1992) by John McEwen.

Reid, Beryl (1920–1996) *British actress*

Originally a comedienne whose radio performances greatly appealed to the British public, Beryl Reid later became a respected character actress in mainstream theatre.

Born in Hereford and educated in the north of England, Reid gave her first stage performance at the age of 16. As a comedienne she appeared in revues, variety shows, and pantomimes before making her first film in 1940. In the 1950s and 1960s she entertained large radio audiences, most notably by conversations with her imaginary friend "Marlene." She also played many television roles.

In 1965 Reid was a great success in the title role of *The Killing of Sister George*, a play about an ageing lesbian actress that was later staged at the New York Belasco Theater and won her a Tony Award; she also starred in the film of this play. Her subsequent stage parts included Madame Arcati in Noël Coward's *Blithe Spirit* (1970) and the nurse in *Romeo and Juliet* (1974). Following up early film successes, such as *The Belles of St. Trinians* (1954), she continued to appear in occasional movies, including *Entertaining Mr. Sloane* (1969). Later stage successes included *Born in the Gardens* (1979–80) and the role of Mrs. Candour in Sheridan's *The School for Scandal* (1983).

Reid received the Best TV Actress Award from BAFTA for her role in *Smiley's People* (1982). In 1986 she was appointed an OBE.

Renault, Mary (1905–1983) *British-born South African novelist*

Renault is best known for her popular historical novels of the ancient world. She also attracted attention for her sympathetic attitude towards homosexuality.

Born Mary Challans in London, she studied at Oxford University. During World War II she served as a nurse; her experiences in this profession provided background material for several early novels, including *Promise of Love* (1939) and *Return to Night* (1947). After the war she moved to South Africa, where she began her series of novels set in ancient Greece.

Renault's historical books were carefully researched. She did not modernize her characters, nor did she impose modern standards or values on them. *The King Must Die* (1958) and *The Bull from the Sea* (1962) are set in the Minoan civilization and retell the story of Theseus. *The Last of the Wine* (1956) and *The Mask of Apollo* (1966) are set in the Greek world of Socrates and Plato. Her trilogy of stories comprising *Fire from Heaven* (1970), *The Persian Boy* (1977), and *Funeral Games* (1981) recounts the life and times of Alexander the Great.

In *The Charioteer* (1953), a novel set in World War II, Renault deals sympathetically with the dilemmas confronting gay men at a time when homosexual acts between males were still illegal.

Rendell, Ruth, Baroness (1930–)
British novelist

> Her writing style is muted, purposely so, and that makes the extraordinary situations all the more biting.
> —Newgate Callendar, *The New York Times Book Review*, 1980

Ruth Rendell is famous for her detective novels and psychological thrillers. Placing terrible events in apparently normal everyday settings, she shows an uncanny understanding of the dark side of human nature.

Born and educated in London, Ruth Barbara Grasemann gained her first writing experience on a local newspaper. In 1950 she married Donald Rendell. They had a son and divorced after 25 years of marriage, only to remarry two years later.

Rendell's first novel, *From Doon with Death* (1964), introduced the detective Reginald Wexford and his assistant Mike Burden, who feature in a whole series of detective stories, including *Wolf to the Slaughter* (1976), *Shake Hands for Ever* (1975), *An Unkindness of Ravens* (1985), and *Simisola* (1994). Praised for their clever plots and for keeping the reader in suspense, Rendell's books have been compared favourably with those of Agatha CHRISTIE. This is no compliment to Rendell, who openly admits a hatred for Christie's novels.

Rendell has also written short stories, such as *The New Girl Friend*, a grim tale that won her the Edgar Allan Poe Award in 1975. By this time she was turning her attention to psychological thrillers, such as *A Demon in My View* (1976), *A Judgement in Stone* (1977), and *Live Flesh* (1986). In these books the emphasis is not so much on crime detection as on the psychological processes that turn apparently normal people into violent criminals. These disturbing novels showed her literary skill in a new light, and in 1991 she won a Diamond Dagger from the Crime Writers' Association for a lifetime's achievement in crime writing.

Writing under the pen name Barbara Vine, she produced further books in the same sinister vein, including *A Dark-Adapted Eye* (1986), *A Fatal Inversion* (1987), *King Solomon's Carpet* (1991), and *The Brimstone Wedding* (1996). Many of her novels and stories have been televised.

Rendell was made a baroness in 1997.

Reno, Janet (1938–) *American lawyer and politician*

Appointed the first woman attorney general of the United States in 1993, Janet Reno brought to the role new ideas, liberal opinions, and a fresh response to the challenge of crime.

Reno was born in Miami. Her Danish father and her spirited, somewhat eccentric mother were both journalists. She attended Cornell University and Harvard Law School before becoming a lawyer in Florida in 1963. Over the next 15 years she worked for private firms and on the legislature of the state of Florida, which appointed her state attorney for Dade County in 1978.

During the 1980s Reno was faced with riots and escalating drug-related crime in Miami; in addition, she worked towards better legal protection for children. Her nomination for the post of attorney general came when both previous candidates stood down over the so-called "Nannygate" affair – both had employed illegal immigrants as nannies. Being unmarried and childless, Reno was seen as a safe candidate by President Clinton. However, she was also highly suitable on the grounds of her sound principles, well-tested legal skills, and reputation for defending civil rights.

The start of Reno's period in office was marred by a disaster in which 72 members of a religious cult based in Waco, Texas, died in a fire while under siege by the FBI. Although Reno incurred some criticism, she took full responsibility for the decisions made, thereby earning public respect. Her concerns in office have included more flexible sentencing of drug offenders, the strengthening of child pornography laws, and the reduction of televised violence.

Resnik, Regina (1922–) *American opera singer*

As well as performing widely in North and South America and Europe, Resnik has also been active as a director and producer.

Resnik was born in New York City. She graduated from Hunter College in 1942 and later that year made her debut as a soprano at the Brooklyn Academy of Music. In 1943 she sang with the Opera Nacional in Mexico City, appearing in the title role of *Fidelio*. She subsequently won a contract with the Metropolitan Opera in New York and made her debut there in 1944 as Leonora in *Il Trovatore*, replacing Zinka MILANOV at 24 hours' notice. In 1946 Resnik married the lawyer Harry W. Davis, with whom she later had a son.

Resnik continued singing at the Metropolitan Opera. By cultivating the deeper part of her voice, she began in 1955 to sing mezzo-soprano roles, including Carmen, Marina in Mussorgsky's *Boris Godunov*, Clytemnestra in Richard Strauss's *Elektra*, and Venus in Wagner's *Tannhäuser*.

Resnik made her Covent Garden debut as Carmen in 1957 and continued to sing there until 1972. She was active as an opera director and producer from 1971 and continued to sing at the Metropolitan Opera until 1974. In 1975 she was married a second time, to Arbit Blatas.

Rhodes, Zandra (1940–) *British fashion designer*

> Every woman has something wonderful about her, no matter what her size. I enjoy finding the key to each individual.
>
> —Remark made in the 1980s

Rhodes's highly imaginative and colourful fashion creations are designed to make the wearer both look and feel marvellous. They reflect not only her artistic skill but also the joy she takes in her work.

Born in London, Zandra Rhodes studied textile design at art college in Kent and then at the Royal College of Art, London (1961–64). After graduating, she founded a screen-printing studio with Alex MacIntyre, who was also her live-in partner for 12 years. Screen prints on such fabrics as chiffon and taffeta have always played a big part in her designs, and she claims to enjoy the printing stage best. In 1966 she founded a dressmaking business, and within two years her boutique in a fashionable part of London had attracted many young clients. Working freelance from 1968 onwards, she drew an increasingly large clientele.

In 1975 Rhodes founded Zandra Rhodes UK Ltd. and opened a chain of shops. Four years later she began selling ready-made clothes, at first in Australia. Although she had already won several awards, she failed to win the commission to make Princess DI-ANA's wedding dress in 1981; Rhodes has suggested the Queen may have been put off by her pink hair. In the 1980s and 1990s she exhibited widely in the United States and won an Emmy Award for her designs for the CBS TV show *Romeo and Juliet on Ice* (1984).

Promoting her designs as far afield as India, Japan, and China, Zandra Rhodes continues to enjoy worldwide success. Her work is represented in the costume collections of major museums and art galleries in Britain, the United States, and Canada, and in 1996 she founded the Zandra Rhodes Museum of Fashion and Textiles in London. She was appointed a CBE in 1997.

Rhys, Jean (1894–1979) *British novelist*

> If you want to write the truth you *must* write about yourself…I am the only real truth I know.
>
> —Interview, *The Guardian*, 1968

In her partially autobiographical novels Jean Rhys wrote about women who were losers. Tragic, isolated, frustrated, and exploited, they arouse pity, if not respect.

Born Gwen Rhys Williams on the Caribbean island of Dominica, at that time a British possession, Jean Rhys went to England at 16 to continue her education. She briefly studied drama in London and then worked as a chorus girl. After World War I she married a Dutch-French journalist who took her to Paris. They had two children, one of whom died young.

In Paris some of Rhys's writings were discovered by a friend and shown to the writer Ford Madox Ford, who encouraged her to publish. Her short-story collection *The Left Bank, and Other Stories* (1927) and the depressing novel *After Leaving Mr. Mackenzie* (1931) were soon followed by the breakdown of her marriage. She later remarried twice. Although she continued to write, her books did not sell well, and after the outbreak of World War II she sank into obscurity.

In 1958 the BBC broadcast a request for information about Rhys, since they wanted to dramatize her novel *Good Morning, Midnight* (1939). Rhys contacted them herself. Encouraged by this renewed interest, she wrote her most successful novel, *Wide Sargasso Sea* (1966), a tale based on the story of Mr. Rochester's first wife in Charlotte BRONTË's *Jane Eyre*. Rhys published two more volumes of short stories before her death.

Ricard, Marthe (1889–1982) *French feminist, spy, and social reformer*

A secret agent in World War I and a Resistance Worker in World War II, Marthe Ricard led an eventful and dangerous life. When she settled down with her third husband in Paris after the liberation, she became a city councillor devoted to the cause of cleaning up prostitution.

Marthe Betenfeld was born in a German-occupied village in east France in the aftermath of the Franco-Prussian War. Her first husband, Henri Richer, was killed in World War I in 1916. After this she became a French secret agent in northern Spain, where she seduced Baron von Krohn, the German military attaché in San Sebastián. From the baron she obtained highly secret information about the movement of German submarines, which she passed on to Paris. After the war she was awarded the Legion of Honour for this dangerous work.

Marthe's next marriage was to an Englishman, Thomas Crompton, with whom she lived in England. However, after his early death she returned to France shortly before World War II. There she worked, undercover again, as a member of the Resistance.

After her third marriage Marthe (now Madame Ricard) moved to Paris, where she was elected a city councillor. In this capacity the former secret-service agent mounted a campaign against the city's legalized brothels, in which young girls were forced to work as the sexual slaves of the hypocritical men who made use of them. Her campaign was successful, and in 1945 legal brothels in Paris were closed; a year later the necessary legislation had been enacted to make the ban on legal brothels nationwide.

Unfortunately, neither the problem nor the men who make use of the services of prostitutes went away. Prostitution was forced onto the streets, and exploitation of young girls, especially girls needing the money to finance their drug habits, fell into the hands of ruthless pimps, who were even less desirable than the keepers of legal brothels. In the 1970s, therefore, Ricard was forced to concede that some form of authorized prostitution might be better than the unrestricted trade on the streets.

Rich, Adrienne (1929–) *American feminist poet*

> Nothing less than the most radical imagination will carry us [women] beyond this place, beyond the mere struggle for survival.
>
> —*On Lies, Secrets and Silence* (1979)

A noted feminist and campaigner for lesbian and gay rights, Rich has written both personal and political poetry.

Adrienne Rich was born into a Jewish family in Baltimore, Maryland, where she went to school. Encouraged to read poetry by her father, she began to write within the academic male-dominated tradition that she later rejected. In the year she graduated from Radcliffe College, W. H. Auden selected her work to be published in the

Yale Younger Poets series, as *A Change of World* (1951). Although both this collection and her next volume, *The Diamond Cutters* (1955), were praised for their neatness and grace, Rich's marriage in 1953 brought about a change in her style. The drudgery of housework and looking after her three children provoked a more embittered free-verse form of expression in *Snapshots of a Daughter-in-Law* (1963) and *Necessities of Life* (1966).

In the 1960s Rich supported the student protests against the Vietnam War and in favour of African-American civil rights. In 1970 her husband died, and her subsequent collections *The Will to Change* (1971) and *Diving into the Wreck* (1973) marked the rise of her reputation as a feminist. Selected for the U.S. National Book Award in 1974, she accepted it not in her own right but on behalf of all women. Her prose work *Of Woman Born*, which expressed fiercely negative emotions about motherhood, appeared in the same year as a collection of lesbian love poems (1976). Later works, including *A Wild Patience Has Taken Me This Far* (1981) and *An Atlas of the Difficult World* (1991), continue to explore such issues as gender, class, and race. Rich has held many professorships and teaching posts, as well as receiving a number of awards and honorary degrees.

Richardson, Dorothy M. (1873–1957) *British novelist*

> They invent a legend to put the blame for the existence of humanity on women and, if she wants to stop it, they talk about the wonders of civilizations and the sacred responsibilities of motherhood. They can't have it both ways.
>
> —*Pilgrimage*, Vol. II (1938)

Richardson is best remembered for her multivolume novel *Pilgrimage* (1938). This provides an important early example of the use of the "stream-of-consciousness" technique, in which the novelist records thoughts and feelings as they pass through a character's mind.

Dorothy Miller Richardson was born in Abingdon, Berkshire. She led a sheltered life until she was 17, when her parents separated; thereafter she cared for her mother for several years. Moving to London, she worked mostly as a teacher and was drawn into feminist and socialist circles. Her love affair with the writer H. G. Wells was commemorated later in *Pilgrimage* (Wells is represented as Hypo Wilson). It was not until 1917, by which time she had already written two books on the Quakers, that Richardson married the artist and illustrator Alan Odle.

The first section of *Pilgrimage*, entitled *Pointed Roofs*, appeared in 1915. During the next 23 years Richardson devoted herself to completing the work. The other 11 sections are *Backwater* (1916), *Honeycomb* (1917), *The Tunnel* (1919), *Interim* (1919), *Deadlock* (1921), *Revolving Lights* (1923), *he Trap* (1925), *Oberland* (1927), *Dawn's Left Hand* (1931), *Clear Horizon* (1936), and *Dimple Hill* (1938). The entire work was published in four volumes in 1938. Complex and sensitive, it describes the inner feelings, thoughts, and attitudes of its heroine, Miriam Henderson. It is remarkable for its subtle exploration of the feminine consciousness at a time when women's role in society was being re-evaluated. Although *Pilgrimage* is not widely read today, it is an important landmark in the history of the modern English novel.

Richardson, Henry Handel (1870–1946) *Australian novelist*

Henry Handel Richardson was the pen name of Ethel Florence Lindesay Richardson, whose trilogy *The Fortunes of Richard Mahony* (1930) is one of the greatest works of fiction by an Australian.

Ethel Richardson was born in Melbourne and educated at the Presbyterian Ladies' College there. In 1888 she went to Leipzig, Germany, to study music and returned only once to Australia (in 1912). Literature interested her more than music, however, and after her marriage in 1895 to John G. Robertson, an English scholar of German, she devoted herself to writing. Following her husband's appointment as professor of German at the University of London, they settled in England.

Richardson's first novel was *Maurice Guest* (1908). Set in Leipzig, it tells the story of a young English music student whose career is destroyed by a tragic love affair. It was followed by *The Getting of Wisdom* (1910), which reflects Richardson's own experiences at school. Her famous trilogy, consisting of *Australia Felix* (1917), *The Way Home* (1925), and *Ultima Thule* (1929), was published in 1930 as *The Fortunes of Richard Mahony*. Based on her father's life, it chronicles the fortunes of an English doctor who emigrates to Australia during the 19th-century gold rush and attempts to assimilate himself into the culture there.

Richardson also wrote the novel *Young Cosima* (1939), about the intertwining lives of Cosima WAGNER, Hans von Bülow, and Richard Wagner, and produced several short stories and an unfinished autobiography, *Myself When Young* (1948).

Richardson, Miranda (1958–)
British actress

During the 1990s Miranda Richardson gave a series of award-winning film performances that are as diverse as they are accomplished. However, she is still best known in Britain for her comic performance as Queen ELIZABETH I in the BBC TV series *Blackadder*.

Richardson was born to middle-class parents in Lancashire. Since her only sister was eight years her senior, Miranda was often alone as a child: her early fascination with acting was fostered by appearances in school plays. After leaving school, Richardson studied for two years at the Bristol Old Vic School. In 1979 she became a member of the Library Theatre in Manchester, first as an assistant stage manager and then as an actress.

Richardson made her London stage debut in 1981 in the play *Moving*. Over the succeeding years she played many roles in repertory theatres all over England. Several small roles on television included a part in the miniseries *A Woman of Substance* (1984).

Wider fame came in 1985, when Richardson starred in the film *Dance with a Stranger* as Ruth Ellis, the nightclub hostess who in the 1950s shot her lover and became the last woman to be hanged in Britain. The critics hailed Richardson as a new find. In 1987 she took a role in Steven Spielberg's *Empire of the Sun*, but by the time the film was released, her part had been drastically edited, and it was five more years before she stepped back into the cinematic limelight. Meanwhile, her television career prospered following her *tour de force* as the capricious "Queenie" in *Blackadder II* (1985), with Rowan Atkinson.

In the early 1990s Richardson appeared in three films: *Enchanted April* (1991), *The Crying Game* (1992), and *Damage* (1992). She played a meek neglected wife in *Enchanted April*, an Irish terrorist in *The Crying Game*, and a woman nearly a generation older than herself in *Damage*. All three, very different, roles earned excellent reviews. Richardson won the BAFTA Award, was nominated for an Oscar for *Damage*, and was named Best Supporting Actress by the New York Film Critics' Circle for all three films. She has often specialized in playing brittle neurotic women: in 1994 she took the role of T. S. Eliot's unstable wife in the film *Tom and Viv*, while in 1997 she played the promiscuous self-destructive Pamela in the TV adaptation of *A Dance to the Music of Time*.

Ride, Sally (1951–) *American astronaut*

> She is flying with us because she is the very best person for the job. There is no man I would rather have in her place.
>
> —Robert Crippen, commander of NASA's seventh shuttle mission, 1983

In 1983 Sally Ride became the first American woman in space – a distinction she earned on account of her scientific record, good team work, and talent for calm problem solving.

Sally Ride was born in Encino, California, and attended high school in Los Angeles. A talented tennis player who rose to the rank of 18th nationally, she had difficulty deciding between tennis and science as a career. Having opted to study physics and English at Stanford, she went on to gain a doctorate in physics, during which time she did some research on xray astronomy. On completing her studies in 1978, she saw an advertisement for trainee astronauts with NASA and applied on impulse.

Ride was one of six women and 29 men chosen for the programme. In 1981 and 1982 she was "capsule communicator" for the second and third shuttle missions; her job was to give instructions from the ground to the crew of the shuttle. She also helped design a mechanical arm for repairing satellites. As one of the four scientists selected for the crew of the seventh mission in 1983, she had to test the arm in space. During the highly successful mission she also performed many experiments at zero gravity.

During her time with NASA Ride married a fellow astronaut, but the couple later divorced. She remained an astronaut until 1987, when she took up an academic post at Standford University, later moving to the University of California, San Diego, to become professor of physics in 1989.

Riding, Laura (1901–1991) *American poet, writer, and critic*

> Art, whose honesty must work through artifice, cannot avoid cheating truth.
>
> —Preface, *Selected Poems: In Five Sets* (1975)

Although recognized as a talented writer, Laura Riding was never popular with the public or with critics. Her poetry was difficult and eccentric, and much the same could be said of her personality.

Born Laura Reichenthal in New York, she was educated in Brooklyn and at Cornell University. Having decided that the way to the truth was through poetry, she began writing poems in which she used her own made-up words. In the early 1920s she married the lecturer Louis Gottschalk and became involved with the group of poets known as the Fugitives, although she later denied that they had

influenced her. The year after her marriage had broken down, her first poetry collection, *The Close Chaplet* (1926), appeared under the name Riding Gottschalk.

In 1926 Riding moved to London, where she became closely involved with the poet Robert Graves. Together they wrote *A Survey of Modernist Poetry* (1927), founded a publishing company, and – after Riding's complicated emotional life led to a spectacular suicide attempt – moved to the Spanish island of Majorca and founded a journal, *Epilogue*. Riding wrote novels and prose works as well as poetry during this period.

At the outbreak of the Spanish Civil War (1936) Riding and Graves left Majorca and in 1940 travelled to the United States. Their host, the critic Schuyler B. Jackson, divorced his wife and married Riding a year later. Having completely disowned Graves, Riding now rejected poetry, although she continued to write prose. She and her husband traded citrus fruit in Wabasso, Florida, while working on a book about language and meaning. Riding's publications after Jackson's death in 1968 included the philosophical work *The Telling* (1972).

Rie, Dame Lucie (1902–1995) *Austrian-born British potter*

Lucie Rie's pottery won admiration for its elegance and simplicity. Her work now fetches high prices.

Lucie Gomperz was born in Vienna. She developed her interest in ceramics at the Vienna School of Arts and Crafts before opening her own studio in 1927. By 1936 she had won two major awards for her textured earthenware pots.

With her husband, Hans Rie, Lucie moved to London after the Nazi takeover of her country in 1938. The marriage did not last, but Lucie Rie's reputation as a potter grew, and many other artists were influenced by her simple forms and subtle glazes.

After World War II, during which she made jewellery and buttons, Rie worked closely with the German-born potter Hans Coper until 1958. From 1960 she taught at the Camberwell

College of Art, London. She held major exhibitions in Europe and Japan and received several honours, including that of DBE in 1991.

Riefenstahl, Leni (1902–) *German film director, photographer, and actress*

> I am fascinated by what is beautiful, strong, healthy, by what is living.
>
> —Interview, *Cahiers du Cinéma*, 1965

Leni Riefenstahl is notorious for having made the Nazi propaganda movie *Triumph of the Will* (1935). An athletic blonde, she personified the Nazi ideal of German womanhood but denied having ever been a member of the party.

Helene ("Leni") Riefenstahl was born in Berlin. Her childhood love of fantasy led to an interest in art and dance, which she studied, later becoming a dancer. In the mid 1920s Arnold Franck invited her to star in a series of films about mountaineering, which became extremely popular. Riefenstahl's own first film, *The Blue Light* (1932), was in a similar vein.

By now famous, Riefenstahl caught the attention of Hitler. At his invitation she filmed the 1934 Nuremberg rally, producing a skilfully shot and emotive propaganda film, *Triumph of the Will*. Also in tune with Nazi thinking was *Olympia* (1938), Riefenstahl's artistic film of the 1936 Olympic Games. Despite some pressure from Goebbels, Hitler's head of propaganda, she included prominent footage of black athletes. Both films won awards, but Reifenstahl had made enemies, as she found out on a visit to Hollywood in 1938–39.

Riefenstahl resisted further propaganda commissions during World War II, but this did not save her from being imprisoned afterwards by the Allies. Although she was later allowed to resume her work, her reputation never recovered. In the 1950s and 1960s she visited Africa and photographed and filmed the Nuba tribe; she published the photographs, but the film *Nuba* (1977) was never released. In her old age Riefenstahl worked as a magazine photographer and published several books of photographs, including *My Africa* (1982).

Rigg, Dame Diana (1938–) *British actress*

> Diana Rigg is the best Cordelia I have ever seen; entirely believable.
>
> —R. B. Marriot, in a review of *King Lear*, 1962

Although she began her career on stage, Diana Rigg became an international star through her role as a glamorous superspy in the 1960s TV series *The Avengers*. Since then she has returned to the stage to give many distinguished performances.

Rigg was born in Doncaster, Yorkshire, but spent her early years in Jodhpur, where her father was manager of the Indian State Railway. She returned to England at the age of eight, where her teacher, noticing her love of poetry and her talent for speaking verse, encouraged Diana to become an actress.

After studying at the Royal Academy of Dramatic Art (RADA) in London, Rigg made her first appearance on the London stage in 1961 in Jean Giraudoux's *Ondine*. She then played many Shakespearean roles at Stratford-upon-Avon in the summer of 1962, including Cordelia in *King Lear*.

In 1964 Rigg made her New York debut with the Royal Shakespeare Company in *King Lear* and *The Comedy of Errors*. The following year she was acclaimed for her role as Emma Peale in the television series *The Avengers* and was nominated for an Emmy Award. In the wake of her new popularity Rigg appeared in several movies over the next few years, including *A Midsummer Night's Dream*, the Bond film *On Her Majesty's Secret Service* (1969), and *Julius Caesar*.

The 1970s brought Rigg back to the stage, with leading roles in *Abélard and Héloïse* (1970), and Tom Stoppard's *Jumpers* (1972) and *Night and Day* (1978). Never afraid to try anything new, Rigg performed in musical theatre in the title role of *Colette* (1982) and appeared in the film version of the musical *A Little Night Music* (1977). She also appeared on the London stage in *Follies* (1987). In 1992–94 she was acclaimed for her performance in the Greek tragedy *Medea*, winning a

Tony Award in 1994. In 1997 she won the *Evening Standard* Best Actress Award for her performances in Brecht's *Mother Courage* and Albee's *Who's Afraid of Virginia Woolf?* She was also nominated for an Emmy for her role as the sinister Mrs. Danvers in a TV production of Daphne DU MAURIER's *Rebecca*.

In addition to her acting work, Diana Rigg has been involved in fundraising activities in the cause of the arts in Britain. She was appointed DBE in 1994.

Riley, Bridget (1931–) *British painter*

> No painter, dead or alive, has ever made us more aware of our eyes than Bridget Riley.
>
> —Robert Melville, *New Statesman*, 1971

Bridget Riley has become one of the most famous women artists in history with her distinctive abstract paintings, which use repeated patterns to create an illusion of movement. Although her pictures are fascinating for their optical effects, they were created as a serious form of self-expression.

Born in London, Riley lived in Cornwall during World War II with her mother, sister, and aunt. She later attended boarding school and studied art at London's Goldsmith's College (1949–52) and Royal College of Art (1952–55). However, she was unable to find an artistic direction and left the Royal College early to nurse her sick father. Soon afterwards she herself suffered a mental and physical breakdown.

After a slow recovery Riley began to take jobs; one, as an art teacher, helped her develop her own ideas through the creative challenges she set the children. Then, in 1958 a failed love affair inspired her to start painting her intense black-and-white optical pictures. After gathering further ideas and inspiration travelling in Europe, Riley put on her first show in London in 1962.

In the mid 1960s she was associated with the fashion for "op art," a type of abstract painting that made calculated use of optical phenomena to achieve its effects. Although she participated in *The Responsive Eye*, an op-art show in New York (1965), she became disillusioned with the movement and disliked seeing her style exploited by popular culture and the fashion industry.

Nevertheless, Riley's work became highly fashionable and was snapped up at her shows. Although she remained deeply involved in the design of her pictures, she began to entrust their execution to assistants. In 1968 she exhibited her first colour compositions in Venice, where they won a major award. In the 1970s she toured and exhibited internationally. Her output of the 1980s included a highly praised series based on diagonals rather than uprights and horizontals.

Riley has taught at art colleges and served as a trustee of the National Gallery, London. Optical colour effects remain her distinctive expressive form in the 1990s, as in *Sapphire* (1995).

Roberts, Julia (1967–) *American film actress*

> When this movie is over are you going to take acting classes?
>
> —Director Herbert Ross to Roberts, during the filming of *Steel Magnolias* (1989)

Julia Roberts rose to stardom with the release of *Pretty Woman* (1990). Auburn-haired, long-legged, and generally appealing, she was the top female box-office draw of 1990 and 1991.

Born in Smyrna, Georgia, Roberts came from a family with theatrical connections. After high school, she went to New York and became a model and actress. Without ever taking serious acting classes, she soon landed a minor role in *Blood Red* (1986; released 1989), a film starring her brother Eric. After this Roberts appeared in three more movies (one for TV) before taking Meg RYAN's place as a dying girl in *Steel Magnolias* (1989). She won a Golden Globe Award and an Oscar nomination for her performance. The next year she made her name with *Pretty Woman*, in which she played a charming prostitute who spends a week as the escort of a millionaire, falls in love, and regains her identity and self-respect. The part brought her a second Oscar nomination.

Roberts was now an established star. During the early 1990s she made a succession of mainly successful films, became engaged to the actor Keifer Sutherland, and narrowly avoided marrying him in 1991. In 1993–95 she was briefly married to the singer Lyle Lovett. Roberts's more recent films include *Prêt à Porter* (1994), *Something to Talk About* (1996), and Woody Allen's musical *Everyone Says I Love You* (1997). Just as her star appeared to be fading she found renewed success with the hit comedy *My Best Friend's Wedding* in 1997.

Robins, Elizabeth (*c.* 1862–1952) *American actress, feminist, and writer*

Elizabeth Robins was the first actress to introduce the heroines of Henrik Ibsen to English-speaking audiences. She was also a suffragist and a writer.

Robins was born in Louisville, Kentucky, educated at Zanesville, Ohio, and gave up a medical course to go on the stage. She appeared with the Boston Museum Stock Company (1885) and travelled with the well-known actors Edwin Booth and Lawrence Barrett. Her marriage to George Richmond Parks soon ended in widowhood.

In 1889 Robins moved to London. After witnessing a production of Ibsen's *A Doll's House*, she became fascinated with his works. In 1891 she played Nora in *A Doll's House* and Hedda in the first English production of *Hedda Gabler*, having commissioned a translation of it. Robins then learnt Norwegian and translated *The Master Builder*, appearing as Hilda in her own production of the play (1893). Productions of four more Ibsen plays followed (1893–97). In addition to many other roles in London, Robins also took *Hedda Gabler* to the United States in 1898.

In 1902 Robins gave up acting and became prominent in several women's suffrage organizations in Britain and the United States. Not long before this she had begun writing under the pen name C. E. Raimond. Her play *Votes for Women!* was performed in London in 1907, and its companion novel, *The Convert*, appeared the same year. From 1908 Robins was president of the Women Writers' Suffrage League, which she cofounded.

Robins's other writings include the novels *Come and Find Me* (1908), based on a journey to Alaska to look for her brother, and *My Little Sister* (1913), a story of prostitution. Robins's experiences of performing Ibsen's dramas were recorded in *Ibsen and the Actress* (1928).

Robinson, Joan (1903–1983) *British economist*

> Like no other living economist, Robinson has been able to link theory with reality.
>
> —Edward Nell, 1975

Robinson helped to formulate the ideas of the economist John Maynard Keynes, making them both more accessible to the public and more applicable to society.

Born Joan Maurice in Camberley, Surrey, she was educated at St. Paul's Girls' School, London, and graduated in economics from Girton College, Cambridge, in 1925. The following year she married Austin Robinson. They had two daughters.

Joan Robinson became an assistant lecturer at Cambridge in 1931 and spent her entire career at the university, eventually becoming professor of economics (1965–71). In the 1930s she worked with Keynes on the development of his theories, which were to help lift the worldwide economic Depression. Her book *Introduction to the Theory of Employment* (1937) clarified Keynes's ideas for a wider readership.

As a Marxist Robinson believed that free-market capitalism is ultimately an unstable system. Like Keynes, she also held that prices cannot be expected to relate directly to the amount of money in the economy and that it is permissible for governments to overspend in order to create fuller employment. After World War II Robinson defended Keynes's ideas against those economists, especially in the United

States, whom she accused of distorting them to fit a capitalist agenda.

Robinson was a fellow of several Cambridge colleges and wrote numerous books on economics, including *The Accumulation of Capital* (1956) and *Economic Philosophy* (1962). Something of an eccentric, she slept in an unheated hut in the garden.

Robinson, Mary (1944–) *Irish lawyer and stateswoman*

> Instead of rocking the cradle [the women of Ireland] have rocked the system.
>
> —On her election as president of the Republic of Ireland, 1990

Mary Robinson became the first woman president of Ireland when she was narrowly elected, with the help of the women's vote, in 1990.

Mary Bourke was born into a Roman Catholic family in Ballina, County Mayo. However, she later broke the family mould by studying law at the traditionally Protestant Trinity College, Dublin, and by marrying a Protestant. After graduating with first-class law degrees from Trinity College and King's Inns, Dublin, she went on to gain a first-class LLM degree from Harvard Law School in 1968 and became an eminent lawyer.

In 1969 she was appointed as a law professor and lecturer at Trinity College, Dublin; a few months later she was elected to the Irish Senate. After marrying Nicholas Robinson in 1970, she combined a successful career with raising three children. She ran twice as a Labour Party candidate for the Dáil (parliament) but resigned from the party in 1985 over what she saw as the injustice of the Anglo-Irish Agreement toward Northern Ireland's Unionists.

When Robinson ran against Brian Lenihan for the post of president in 1990, she was thought to have little chance of winning. However, her agenda of liberal reform on such issues as contraception, divorce, and homosexuality found growing support, and the very close ballot came out in her favour. In office she modified the largely ceremonial role of president, using her charm and evident sincerity to influence both internal and international affairs. Her devotion to the cause of human rights prompted her to resign a few months before the end of her term in 1997 in order to take up a position as United Nations Commissioner on Human Rights.

Robson, Dame Flora (1901–1984) *British actress*

> If you are not moved by [Robson's] performance, then you are immovable and have no right to be on this earth.
>
> —St. John Ervine, reviewing James Bridie's *The Anatomist* (1931)

During a brilliant career in "character" roles ranging from Shakespeare to Eugene O'Neill, Dame Flora Robson proved that an actress lacking glamour can rise to the top. She was especially well known for playing Queen ELIZA-BETH I.

Flora Robson was born in Durham and grew up in north London. After training at the Royal Academy of Dramatic Arts (RADA), she performed in London and Oxford in 1921–23. A shortage of employment then forced her to work in a factory until a friend recommended her to the Cambridge Festival Theatre in 1929. After two years there she returned to London and impressed audiences with her versatility. Her parts included the bloodthirsty HERODIAS in *Salome*, a drunken prostitute in Bridie's *The Anatomist* (both 1931), the snobbish Gwendolen in *The Importance of Being Earnest*, and Lady Macbeth (both 1933).

Among Robson's early films was Alexander Korda's *Fire over England* (1937), in which she played Queen Elizabeth I. She built on her success in this role during her brief Hollywood career (1939–42), when she played Elizabeth to Errol Flynn's Essex in *The Sea Hawk* (1941). On the New York stage she played the title role of *Elizabeth the Queen* (1942).

The most famous of Robson's subsequent stage roles was perhaps that of Paulina in Shakespeare's *The Winter's Tale* (1951). Her many achievements were acknowledged when she was made a DBE in 1960. Robson retired in 1969, a year after giving an inspired comic rendering of Miss Prism in *The Importance of Being Earnest*.

Rochefort, Christiane (1917–)
French novelist

Christiane Rochefort burst onto the French fiction scene with her scandalous *Le Repos du guerrier* (1958; published in English as *Warrior's Rest*, 1959). This has been followed by a series of ironic novels that have established her as one of France's best contemporary fiction writers.

Christiane Rochefort was born in Paris, where she studied medicine and psychiatry at the Sorbonne. However, she did not qualify as a doctor and had many jobs, including teacher, journalist, office worker, and publicist before the publication in 1958 of her first novel, *Le Repos du guerrier*, which was an instant success. A frank account of a young girl's experiences as the mistress of a sadistic alcoholic, it was criticized for its eroticism. Nevertheless, it was made into a film in 1962 by Roger Vadim and won the Prix de la Nouvelle Vague.

Her reputation now established, Christiane Rochefort's next novel, *Les Petits Enfants du siècle* (1961; *Children of Heaven*, 1962), won the Prix Populiste. An amusing attack on the French social welfare system, it tells the story of a working-class family living in a Paris housing scheme.

Her other books include *Les Stances à Sophie* (1963; *Cats Don't Care for Money*, 1965), which Rochefort claims to be based on her four years of unhappy marriage; *Une Rose pour Morrison* (1966; *A Rose for Morrison*), which she dedicated to Bob Dylan; and *Les Enfants d'abord* (1976; *Children First*), an essay on young children.

She has also translated John Lennon's *In His Own Write*, published as *En flagrant délire*.

Roddick, Anita (1942–) *British businesswoman*

Anita Roddick is well-known as the founder of The Body Shop, a retail chain selling beauty products manufactured without cruelty to animals and with an emphasis on health and environmental awareness.

Born in West Sussex into an Italian immigrant family, Anita Perilli learned much from her parents' imaginative approach to running their restaurant business. After school and college she worked in journalism, teaching, and the women's-rights department of the United Nations. She also went on a study trip to Israel.

After marrying Gordon Roddick in 1970, Anita opened a guesthouse and then a restaurant with her husband. Neither was very successful, and Roddick, who now had two daughters, decided to try a new business to support the family. The first Body Shop, which opened in Brighton in 1976, aimed to supply simple natural cosmetics, free from animal testing and packaged in re-usable containers. The shop's success was boosted by a widely publicized complaint about its name from two local funeral parlours. Roddick opened further shops in Britain and Europe in the late 1970s, and in 1984 the company's shares were floated on the open market.

Now managing director of a hugely successful company, Roddick continues to promote ideas about the environment, animal rights, and civil liberties through the organization. In 1993 the company was accused of hypocrisy over these issues by a British TV channel, but Roddick brought a libel action against them and won. In 1994 she became chief executive of the company, which by then had over 800 shops worldwide.

Rodnina, Irina Konstantinovna (1949–) *Russian ice skater*

Irina Rodnina dominated pair skating in the 1970s with her partners Alexei Ulanov and Aleksandr Zaitsev. She won a total of 23 medals, including three Olympic golds and ten world titles, equalling Sonja HENIE's record.

Rodnina was born in Moscow, where she trained as a skater at the Central Institute of Physical Culture. Between 1969 and 1972, with Ulanov as her partner, she won three successive world championships and the Olympic gold medal (1972). At the Winter Olympics, however, their partnershp was undermined when Ulanov fell in love with Liudmila Smirnova of the rival Soviet partnership and decided to marry her. Afterwards, at the world championships, he dropped Rodnina on the ice during their routine and injured her.

Though distressed by these events, Rodnina was determined to continue skating, necessitating a major search in the Soviet Union to find her a new partner. Aleksandr Zaitsev turned out to be the perfect man for the job. He and Rodnina together won the 1973 European championship with maximum scores of 6 from all 12 judges. They completely outshone the new Ulanov–Smirnova partnership, and in 1975 they were married. Rodnina and Zaitsev went on to win every world championship in which they took part until 1981; the only break in their reign occurred in 1979, when Irina gave birth to their son. They also won the Olympic gold medals in 1976 and 1980.

Rodnina and her partners were noted for their athletic, complex, and technically near-perfect routines. She and Zaitsev were particularly known for their side-by-side double axels (rotating jumps).

Rogers, Ginger (1911–1995) *American actress and dancer*

Rogers made over 70 films and won an Oscar for one of them, *Kitty Foyle*, but is best known as Fred Astaire's dancing partner in ten film musicals of the 1930s.

She was born Virginia Katherine McMath in Independence, Missouri. Her mother was a screenwriter, which helped the young Virginia to break into show business in her teens, when she performed in vaudeville and with jazz bands as a dancer. She appeared on Broadway in 1929 in *Top Speed* and a year later in *Girl Crazy*. Her screen debut was in *Young Man of Manhattan* (1930), and she later featured in the musicals *42nd Street* (1932) and *Gold Diggers of 1933*.

Rogers and Astaire began their memorable partnership with a dance number in *Flying Down to Rio* (1933). They went on to star in *The Gay Divorcee* (1934), *Roberta* (1935), *Top Hat* (1935), *Follow the Fleet* (1936), *Swing Time* (1936), *Shall We Dance?* (1937), *Carefree* (1938), and *The Story of Vernon and Irene Castle* (1939). It was said that he gave her class and she gave him sex appeal. Certainly it was not just their immaculate footwork but also their great charisma and style that made them so popular. In 1949 they joined forces again for *The Barkleys of Broadway*.

During a lull in the fashion for musicals Rogers turned to straight acting, which she preferred. She appeared in *Stage Door* (1937) and won the Best Actress Academy Award in 1940 for *Kitty Foyle*. She also showed a flair for comedy in *Bachelor Mother* (1939) and *The Major and the Minor* (1942). Rogers appeared in another dozen or so films into the mid 1960s; on the Broadway stage she was seen in *Love and Let Love* (1951) and *Hello Dolly!* (1965). She made her London stage debut in *Mame* (1969) and was featured in the popular anthology films *That's Entertainment!* (1974), and *That's Dancing!* (1984).

Rogers was married five times. Her autobiography, *Ginger: My Story*, was published in 1991. She received the Kennedy Center award for lifetime achievement in 1992 and died three years later at her home in Rancho Mirage, California.

Roland (de la Platière), Marie-Jeanne (1754–1793) *French revolutionary patriot and writer*

> O, Liberty, what crimes are committed in thy name!
>
> —Last words

A courageous woman who believed in justice and political freedom, Madame Roland de la Platière fell foul of Robespierre, who sent her to the guillotine.

She was born Marie-Jeanne (Manon) Philipon in Paris. Her father, a jeweller, encouraged his gifted daughter in her education, enabling her to become exceptionally talented in music, painting, and literature. In 1780 she married Jean-Marie Roland de la Platière, a government inspector general who shared her enthusiasm for the philosophy of Jean Jacques Rousseau and the movement for political equality.

After the outbreak of the French

Revolution they moved to Paris, where in 1791 Madame Roland established a salon that attracted the most influential political personalities of the time, including leaders of the moderate Girondin wing of the revolutionary party. Through her connections she gained for her husband the post of minister of the interior in March 1792. Louis XVI removed him from office in July, but after the king was deposed the following month, Roland was reinstated. Although the Girondins and the more extreme revolutionaries led by Robespierre and Danton co-operated at first, they began to disagree over the fate of the monarchy and other issues. Robespierre denounced the Girondins in April 1793, and a few weeks later they were disbanded with the aid of the Parisian mob.

Accused of royalist sympathies, Madame Roland was arrested in June. During her imprisonment she wrote her eloquent memoirs, and in November, dressed in white, she appeared before a tribunal but was given no chance to speak in her own defence. She was condemned to the guillotine. When her husband – who had earlier escaped to Normandy – learnt of her death, he committed suicide.

Roosevelt, Eleanor (1884–1962)
American humanitarian

> No one can make you feel inferior without your consent.
>
> —*This Is My Story* (1937)

The wife of President Franklin D. Roosevelt, Eleanor Roosevelt was one of America's great reforming leaders. She was an important influence on national policy towards youth, African Americans, women, the poor, and the United Nations. As well as being one of the most active First Ladies, she was also an important public personality in her own right.

Anna Eleanor Roosevelt was born in New York. Her parents, Elliott and Anna Hall Roosevelt, were members of socially prominent families, and she was a niece of President Theodore Roosevelt. She had a very unhappy childhood. Her mother, widely known for her beauty, called Eleanor "Granny." Eleanor was very fond of her father, but he was banished from the family because of alcoholism. Her parents died when she was young, and she was raised strictly by her grandmother Hall. These experiences made her feel insecure and inadequate, leaving her with a longing for praise and affection.

After attending private classes, Eleanor was sent at the age of 15 to Allenswood, a finishing school in England. With the encouragement of the headmistress, Marie Souvestre, the shy girl emerged as a school leader. She returned to New York in 1902 to make her debut in society, but she soon became frustrated by its narrowness and took work with the city's poor at a settlement house. In March 1905 she married her distant cousin Franklin D. Roosevelt. She was given in marriage by President Theodore Roosevelt.

During the next 11 years Eleanor Roosevelt gave birth to six children, five of whom survived. Her somewhat domineering mother-in-law assisted in the children's upbringing. After her husband's election to the New York State Senate in 1910, Eleanor performed the social role expected of the wife of a public official. When her husband became assistant secretary of the navy during World War I, she became involved in war work with the Red Cross.

At the end of the war came a grave personal crisis when Eleanor discovered that her husband loved another woman. Despite a reconciliation, she decided to build a life of her own after their return to New York in 1921. She became active in the League of Women Voters, the Women's Trade Union League, and the women's division of the Democratic Party. Within a year Franklin Roosevelt was stricken with polio.

Eleanor Roosevelt was determined to keep alive her husband's interest in public affairs. Encouraged and trained by Louis Howe, Roosevelt's close adviser, she became her husband's political stand-in. By 1928, when Franklin Roosevelt was well enough to stand as a candidate for the post of governor of New York, Eleanor had become a public figure in her own right, having founded a project to help the unemployed in 1926 and become part owner of the Todhunter School in New York in 1927.

When her husband became president in 1933, Eleanor was afraid that the move to the White House would cut her off from her own activities. Determined to avoid this, she changed the traditional role of First Lady, holding weekly press conferences with women reporters, lecturing throughout the country, and running her own radio programme. Her newspaper column, *My Day*, was published daily for many years. Travelling widely, she served as her husband's eyes and ears and influenced his administration towards measures to aid the underprivileged and racial minorities.

In 1941 Eleanor Roosevelt ventured into public office herself, as codirector of the Office of Civilian Defense, though she later resigned when some of her appointments were criticized. During World War II she visited troops in England, the South Pacific, and the Caribbean, as well as on U.S. military bases.

After her husband died in April 1945, Eleanor Roosevelt gave a further 17 years' public service, perhaps the most significant of her career. In December 1945 she was appointed a member of the U.S. delegation to the United Nations by President Harry Truman. As chair of the Commission on Human Rights, she helped draft the UN Declaration of Human Rights. She resigned from the United Nations in 1952 but was reappointed by President John Kennedy in 1961. Eleanor Roosevelt remained active in Democratic Party politics; she was a strong supporter of Adlai Stevenson in the presidential campaigns of 1952 and 1956 and at the Democratic convention in 1960.

In her later years Eleanor Roosevelt maintained a home for her large family at Val-Kill, Hyde Park. She continued to receive and write numerous letters and led a busy social life. "I suppose I should slow down," she said on her 77th birthday. She died in November of the following year in New York and was buried in the rose garden at Hyde Park next to her husband. Her many books include *This Is My Story* (1937), *This I Remember* (1949), and *On My Own* (1958).

Rosenberg, Ethel (1915–1953) *American Communist and alleged spy*

Ethel Rosenberg and her husband Julius (1918–53) were at the centre of a communist spy case during the Cold War. They were both sent to the electric chair.

Born of Jewish parents and raised on the poor Lower East Side of New York, Ethel Greenglass married Julius Rosenberg in 1939. Both were committed communists, and during World War II it is known that Julius was recruited by the KGB officer Anatoli Yakovlev to carry out intelligence work. In 1944–46 Ethel's younger brother, David Greenglass, worked on the Los Alamos atomic bomb research project in New Mexico, and it seems that Ethel and Julius persuaded him to pass them sensitive information.

A mistake by Yakovlev in 1945 later provided the FBI with evidence of Greenglass's activities, leading to his arrest. In return for leniency Greenglass gave information that implicated his sister and her husband, who were arrested in 1950. Although the Rosenbergs could have saved their lives by making a similar deal, they maintained their complete innocence to the end. The true extent of their guilt and of the threat they posed was questioned at the time and has remained controversial. Some researchers think that Ethel may have been an innocent pawn manipulated by both her husband and the FBI. However, in the early 1950s the Cold War was at its height, and public feeling ran high. Greenglass got away with a 15-year prison sentence, but despite appeals for their lives from around the world, the Rosenbergs were sentenced to death in 1951 and executed two years later. They are the only Americans to have been executed for spying during peace time.

Rose of Lima, Saint (1586–1617) *Peruvian mystic*

St. Rose of Lima was the first native of the New World to be declared a saint by the Roman Catholic Church.

Born in Lima, Peru, Rose was the daughter of the Spaniard Caspar de Flores and his wife. Although baptized Isabel, she was called Rose because of her beauty. Taking St. CATHERINE OF SIENA as her model, she longed for the simple and godly life of a nun. However, her family had other plans for her. Having lost most of their money, they saw in their beautiful daughter an opportunity to increase the family fortunes by finding her a rich husband. Although they forbade Rose to become a nun, she nevertheless insisted on taking a vow of virginity and remained at home to support her family by gardening and sewing; according to tradition she rubbed lime on her hands to destroy their beauty.

Finally, at 20, she was allowed to become a member of the third order of Dominicans and withdrew to a hermitage in the garden, where she tended the poor and sick in a small infirmary. As a mystic, Rose experienced both spiritual joy and desolation. As well as coping with illness and ridicule, she was interrogated by the notorious Inquisition. She spent her last three years with friends in Lima, where she died after a long illness.

Rose was honoured by a public funeral and was canonized in 1671. Her feast day as patron saint of South America and the Philippines is the date of her death, August 23.

Ross, Diana (1944–) *American singer*

Described as a "total entertainer," Diana Ross brought together elements of traditional black rhythm-and-blues with popular white styles to become one of the most successful performers of the late 20th century.

Diana Ross was born and raised in a poor area of Detroit, sharing a single bedroom with her five brothers and sisters. As a girl, Diana learned to sing gospel music in a local church choir. After studying fashion in high school, she began singing with the Primettes, a group she had founded with her friends Mary Wilson and Florence Ballard.

Ambitious to promote the group, Ross contacted Berry Gordy, who had recently founded the Motown record label in Detroit. In the early 1960s Gordy began to employ the Primettes as backup singers and then launched them as a group in their own right, renamed the Supremes.

It was their tenth single that brought the Supremes widespread success in 1964. "Where Did Our Love Go?" sold two million copies and was followed by a succession of hit singles, including "Baby Love" (1964). The group's magic formula was the combination of Ross's delicate yearning vocals, a melodic musical style that appealed to both white and black audiences, and a sexy style of presentation.

In 1967 Ballard was replaced by Cindy Birdsong, and the group was renamed Diana Ross and the Supremes. After three more years Ross went solo and continued to enjoy success with further albums and singles, including "Ain't No Mountain High Enough" (1970). During the 1970s she became known for her elaborately choreographed stage shows and extravagant dresses. Having married Robert Silberstein in 1971, she had three daughters but was later divorced (1976). In 1972 she played Billie HOLIDAY in the film *Lady Sings the Blues*; she has also made two other movies, *Mahogany* (1975) and *The Wiz* (1978).

Ross's successes of the 1980s and 1990s included the albums *Chain Reaction* (1986) and *The Force behind the Power* (1991). In the mid 1980s she married the Norwegian Arne Naess, with whom she had two sons.

Rossetti, Christina Georgina (1830–1894) *British poet*

Christina Rossetti's poetry reflects her intense devotion to religion. She is best known for such early poems as "Goblin Market," but her work covers a wide range, from sonnets and ballads to nonsense verse.

Christina Rossetti was born in London, the youngest of a talented family. Her father, an emigrant from Italy, became a professor of Italian at London University. Her brothers Dante Gabriel and William Michael were members of the Pre-Raphaelite circle which enabled her to publish some of her early poems in the Pre-Raphaelite journal, *The Germ*, in 1850. Christina was a highly sensitive girl, often troubled by ill health. Educated at home, she wrote poetry from an early age. She later became engaged to the Pre-Raphaelite painter James Collinson but broke off the engagement after he joined the Roman Catholic Church in 1850, since she herself was a staunch Anglican. It is possible that she had also fallen in love with the poet and painter William Bell Scott, who was her brothers' friend.

Rossetti's early poetry is best represented by the collections *Goblin Market and Other Poems* (1862) and *The Prince's Progress and Other Poems* (1866), which combine moral allegory with sensual imagery. The increasing importance of religion in her life is evident in her later poetry. Her poems show a mastery of poetic form and emphasize values of patience and resignation.

In the 1860s Rossetti joined an Anglican association dedicated to helping unmarried girls who had lost their virginity and drifted into prostitution after being rejected by society. Unhelpfully called the Home for Fallen Women, it presumably filled a need for both the helped and the helpers.

In 1866 Rossetti turned down a second offer of marriage – from the scholar Charles Bagot Cayley – and continued to live a secluded life with her mother and sister. In 1871 she developed Graves's disease, a painful and disfiguring illness of the thyroid gland that led her to become still more reclusive. She died in London.

Rothschild, Miriam Louisa
(1908–) *British zoologist*

A widely respected entomologist, Miriam Rothschild has made over 300 contributions to scientific journals, catalogued the Rothschild Collection of Fleas, and written several books.

Born into the Rothschild banking family, she was the elder daughter of the Honourable N. C. Rothschild and a granddaughter of the 1st Baron Rothschild. In spite of her father, who did not approve of higher education for women, she studied at home to be-

come a world-class entomologist; she catalogued the Rothschild Collection of Fleas, housed in the British Museum (Natural History), in six illustrated volumes.

In 1943 Miriam married Captain George Lane, with whom she had four children before the marriage was dissolved in 1957.

Miriam Rothschild has received many honorary degrees, including a DSc from Oxford University, and has published many papers on insects. In 1977 she published a paper giving the first description of the flea's jumping mechanism and hosted the International Flea Conference at her Northamptonshire home. A trustee of the British Museum, she has written a number of books, including *The Butterfly Gardener* (1983), *Animals and Man* (1986), and a biography of her grandfather, *Dear Lord Rothschild* (1983).

Rowbotham, Sheila (1943–)
British feminist and social historian

She made her name in the 1970s with her often provocative writings on feminism and socialism. As a research fellow in the department of sociology at Manchester University in the 1990s, she turned her attention to economic and social issues affecting women and the nature of their work in the modern world.

Sheila Rowbotham was born in Leeds and studied at St. Hilda's College, Oxford. After teaching for a number of years in secondary schools and colleges, she turned to adult education with the Workers' Educational Association (WEA). An active socialist since her undergraduate days, she contributed to left-wing journals such as *Black Dwarf*. In the late 1960s she became involved with the emerging women's movement, setting out its principles in the pamphlet *Women's Liberation and the New Politics* (1970). She cowrote the controversial *Beyond the Fragments: Feminism and the Making of Socialism* (1979) with Lynne Segal and Hilary Wainwright.

Rowbotham's publications as a historian are chiefly concerned with the changing position of women in society. They include *Women, Resistance and*

Revolution (1972), *Hidden from History* (1973), *Women's Consciousness, Man's World* (1973), *Dutiful Daughters* (1977), and *Dreams and Dilemmas* (1983). Among her most recent works are two books produced in collaboration with Swasti Mitter: *Dignity and Daily Bread* (1994), a collection of case studies of women in low-paid casual work in Britain and the developing world, and *Women Encounter Technology: Changing Patterns of Employment in the Third World* (1995).

Roy, Gabrielle (1909–1983) *Canadian writer*

Gabrielle Roy produced at least two works that rank among the finest French-Canadian writing. Her novels and short stories are marked by their human insight and compassion.

She was born in St. Boniface, Manitoba, to French parents who had migrated west from Quebec. Gabrielle was educated at a convent, and after attending a teacher-training school in Winnipeg, she taught in rural Manitoba and in her hometown. In 1939 she settled in Montreal to become a writer; eight years later she married Marcel Carbotte.

Two of Roy's books are regarded as perhaps the best of all French-Canadian novels. These are *Bonheur d'occasion* (1945; *The Tin Flute*, 1947), which is a perceptive account of family life in a Montreal slum; and *Alexandre Chenevert, caissier* (1954; *The Cashier*, 1955), which sympathetically relates the gloomy life of a bank clerk whose terminal illness symbolizes the problems in society.

Roy wrote a number of other novels and short stories, including *La Petite Poule d'eau* (1950; *Where Nests the Water Hen*, 1951), which tenderly and humorously describes life in isolated rural Manitoba; and *Ces Enfants de ma vie* (1977; *Children of My Heart*, 1979). She died in Quebec.

Rubin, Vera Cooper (1928–) *American astronomer*

Vera Rubin's work is significant in revealing that a large proportion of the mass of the universe is composed of so-called "dark matter," i.e., matter that cannot be detected by its absorption or emission of light or other electromagnetic radiation.

Born in Philadelphia, Pennsylvania, Rubin was educated at Vassar College, at Cornell, and at Georgetown University, Washington, D.C., where she obtained her PhD in 1954. Since 1965 she has worked at the Carnegie Institution, Washington, D.C., while also being on the staff of the department of terrestrial magnetism.

Rubin's main work has been concerned with measurements of the rotation of galaxies, which has revealed one of the more persistent problems of modern astronomy. Concentrating on spiral galaxies, she has measured the speed of rotation of the arms of the galaxy as their distance from the centre increases. These speeds of rotation of the spiral arms are measured by determining their doppler shifts. Doppler shifts occur in the emission spectra of moving bodies; the light emitted from a body moving away from an observer will show a shift towards the red end of the spectrum, while a blue shift occurs when the body moves towards the observer. The degree of spectral shift is proportional to the speed of the source.

The initial assumption, based on Kepler's laws, was that rotational speed would decrease with distance from the centre of the galaxy. The rotational speed also depends on the mass of the galaxy. Rubin, however, found that the rotational speed of spiral galaxies either remains constant with increasing distance from the centre or rises slightly. The only possible conclusion, assuming the laws of motion to be correct, was that the figure taken for the mass was too low. But since all visible matter had been taken into account in assessing the mass of the galaxy, the missing mass must be present in the form of "dark matter." Rubin found similar results as she extended her survey. It seemed to her in 1983 that as much as 90% of the universe is not radiating sufficiently strongly on any wavelength to be detectable on Earth and therefore fell into this category known as dark matter.

Rubin's work has presented modern astronomy with two major problems.

First, to calculate the amount of dark matter in the universe and describe its distribution, and second, to identify the particles that make up the dark matter.

Earlier in her career, in collaboration with Kent Ford, Rubin made the extraordinary discovery that the Milky Way moves at a peculiar rate of 500 km per second quite independently of the expansion of the universe. When their results were published in 1975, they were met with considerable scepticism, and it was assumed they had miscalculated the distances of the measured galaxies. However, work by others in 1982 seems to have confirmed their measurements.

Rubinstein, Helena (1871–1965) *Polish-born American beauty expert and cosmetics manufacturer*

> There are no ugly women, only lazy ones.
>
> —*My Life for Beauty* (1965)

Rubinstein's multimillion-dollar cosmetics and beauty business demonstrates how even the most successful company starts with a simple idea and someone with the determination to carry it through.

The daughter of a Jewish merchant, Rubinstein was born in Kraków, Poland, attended Kraków University, and briefly studied medicine in Zurich. In 1902 she travelled to Australia to visit relatives in Melbourne and took with her a jar of facial cream mixed according to a family formula. Noticing that the climate had a drying effect on women's skin, she sent home for a large supply of the cream to sell in Australia. Before long she had made $100,000. She then left for Europe, where she studied with skin experts and opened her own beauty salons.

Helena Rubinstein's first salon was opened in London in 1908, and over the next two decades she expanded her operations to France, Italy, Austria, Canada, and the United States. She settled in New York City, where she earned an estimated fortune of $100 million.

Rubinstein was married for 25 years to an American, Edward Titus, and later to a Georgian nobleman, Artchil Gourielli-Tchkonka. She amassed a large collection of books on beauty and wrote several herself. The Helena Rubinstein Charitable Foundation endowed many art projects as well as institutions for the poor. Her autobiography, *My Life for Beauty*, was published in 1965, the year of her death.

Rukeyser, Muriel (1913–1980) *American writer*

Principally known as a poet, Muriel Rukeyser also wrote essays and plays and translated poetry. Much of her work deals with issues of social justice.

Born into an affluent Jewish family in New York, she graduated from the Fieldston School there and attended Vassar College in Poughkeepsie from 1930 to 1932. Soon after leaving Vassar, she began to take an active interest in social justice, being jailed in 1933 for associating with African Americans at the Scottsboro trials in Alabama.

When she was 21, Rukeyser's first volume of poetry, *Theory of Flight*, was published as the 1935 selection of the Yale Series of Younger Poets. It was widely praised for its keen observation, emotional intensity, and deep concern with social issues. The collection *U.S.I.* (1938), which deals with the oppression and illness suffered by miners in West Virginia, earned Rukeyser a place as one of the leading younger American poets. She went on to produce a number of other books of poetry, including *A Turning Wind* (1939), *The Soul and Body of John Brown* (1940), *Wake Island* (1942), *The Beast in View* (1944), *The Green Wave* (1948), *Orpheus* (1949), *Waterlily Fire* (1962), and *29 Poems* (1970).

Rukeyser's experience as a single mother and her opposition to American involvement in Vietnam came together in *Body of Waking* (1958) and *Breaking Out* (1973). In the 1960s she went to Hanoi to plead for the life of the poet Kim Chi-Ha, and in 1965 her only novel, *The Orgy*, was published. She also wrote biographies, film scenarios, plays, children's books, and translations.

Russell, Dora (1894–1986) *British feminist*

I shall certainly never quite recover from the feeling of disgrace I had in marrying.

—Letter, 1921

The second wife of the philosopher Bertrand Russell, Dora Russell was an influential feminist and peace campaigner.

Born and educated near London, Dora Black gained a first-class degree at Girton College, Cambridge. She became a fellow of the college in 1918. Dora shared the left-wing pacifist views of the much older Cambridge academic Bertrand Russell, with whom she began an affair in 1919. She followed him on a trip to the Soviet Union and in 1921 lived with him while he lectured in China, where she became pregnant. The couple married as soon as Russell's divorce from his first wife came through and together wrote *The Prospects of Industrial Civilization* (1923).

Frustrated at finding herself overshadowed by her famous husband, Dora Russell began to concentrate her intellectual efforts on women's rights. She campaigned for birth-control information to be made available to women, especially the working classes, and in 1924 cofounded the Workers' Birth Control Group. In her books *Hypatia, or, Women and Knowledge* (1925) and *The Right to Be Happy* (1927) she argued that women should be allowed sexual freedom. With her husband she founded an experimental school (1927–43), at which their two children were educated; she was also a cofounder of the National Council for Civil Liberties (1934). Although both Russells preached sexual freedom and Bertrand enjoyed numerous affairs, when Dora gave birth to two children by an American, Griffin Barry, the result was separation and divorce (1932–35). In 1940 Dora was married again, to Pat Grace, who died in 1949.

After World War II Dora Russell became active in the campaigns against the build-up and testing of nuclear weapons during the Cold War. She travelled widely with the "Women's Peace Caravan" and continued to be involved in antinuclear demonstrations until weeks before her death. Her autobiography, *The Tamarisk Tree*, was published in two volumes (1974, 1980).

Russell, Jane (1921–   ) *American film actress*

Flattery'll get you anywhere.

—Line spoken in *Gentlemen Prefer Blondes* (1953)

Russell, who appeared mainly in lightweight films, was best known for her buxom figure, which made her a World War II pin-up.

The daughter of a former actress, Russell was born in Bemidji, Minnesota. She worked as a receptionist and model before training as an actress and had failed two screen tests by the time her ample bust won her the female lead in Howard Hughes's Western *The Outlaw* (1941). Hughes designed a special bra to show off her natural endowments, and when the film was first shown in 1943, Russell's cleavage caused a scandal. *The Outlaw* lived up to its name by being banned until 1950. Meanwhile Russell became a leading sex symbol through the publicity stills.

Russell made up for her limited acting abilities with a robust sense of humour, which served her well in comedies such as *The Paleface* (1948; released 1952) in which she took the role of CALAMITY JANE, playing opposite Bob Hope as an incompetent dentist. In the mid 1950s she costarred with Marilyn MONROE in *Gentlemen Prefer Blondes* (1953) and with Jeanne Crain in its sequel *Gentlemen Marry Brunettes* (1955). She also appeared in 3-D in *The French Line* (1953). Russell's last film was *Darker than Amber* (1970); after this she appeared in TV bra commercials.

Russell, Lillian (1861–1922) *American singer and actress*

Lillian Russell became internationally famous under the nicknames "Airy-fairy Lillian" and "the American Beauty." In 1890 she made the first long-distance telephone call, singing down the line from New York City to President Cleveland in Washington, D.C. She was also known for her 40-

year relationship with the financier "Diamond Jim" Brady.

Russell's real name was Helen Louise Leonard. She was born in Clinton, Iowa, and moved with her family to Chicago when she was four. She had singing and violin lessons, later studying opera with Leopold Damrosch in New York City and making her debut in the chorus of Gilbert and Sullivan's *H.M.S. Pinafore* in New York in 1879. The following year she first appeared under the name Lillian Russell as "the English Ballad Singer" at Tony Pastor's theatre; she also toured California in *Babes in the Wood*.

Lillian Russell returned to New York to take her first starring role, in the comic opera *The Great Mogul; or, the Snake Charmer*, in October 1881. In 1883, while working as the leading lady of a small opera company, she eloped to London with the composer Edward Solomon. She married him in 1884 and starred in his operettas until she discovered that he was a bigamist. This marriage (the first of four) was annulled in 1892.

After appearing with the comedy duo Weber and Fields in the revues *Fiddle-dee-dee* (1900) and *Whoop-dee-doo* (1903), Russell played in *Lady Teazle* (1904), a musical version of Sheridan's *School for Scandal*. From then on she acted chiefly in straight plays, including *Barbara's Millions* (1906) and *Wildfire* (1908).

Because her theatrical career declined after 1912, Russell turned to giving lectures and to social work and politics; she also wrote beauty columns for two Chicago newspapers. She died in Pittsburgh, Pennsylvania.

Russell, Rosalind (1911–1976) *American actress*

Rosalind Russell was known for playing witty, sophisticated, wisecracking career women and for her part as Mame Dennis in the stage show and film *Auntie Mame*.

Born in Waterbury, Connecticut, she attended Marymount College in Tarrytown, New York state, for two years, then graduated from the American Academy of Dramatic Arts in New York City in 1929. Her first acting job was with a stock company in Saranac Lake, New York, in 1930. She played small parts on Broadway before going to Hollywood, where she made her film debut in the melodrama *Evelyn Prentice* (1934).

For 16 years she starred in Hollywood films, including *Craig's Wife* (1936), *The Women* (1939), *No Time for Comedy* (1940), and the classic *His Girl Friday* (1940), in which she played a fast-talking journalist. *The Women* had a cast of 135 women headed by Russell, who gave a lively and spirited comic performance. By contrast, in 1946 she played the nurse who developed new treatments for polio in *Sister Kenny* (1946).

In 1951 Russell returned to the stage, touring the United States in *Bell, Book and Candle*. In 1953 she starred on Broadway in *Wonderful Town* and received a Tony Award for her performance. She won widespread praise in 1956 for her portrayal of the title role of *Auntie Mame* and was nominated for the Best Actress Academy Award in the film version (1958).

Russell's later films include *Picnic* (1955), *A Majority of One* (1961), *Gypsy* (1962), *Five Finger Exercise* (1962), and *The Amazing Mrs. Pollifex* (1970). Suffering from crippling arthritis, she retired after appearing in the television film *The Crooked Hearts* (1972). She died in Beverly Hills, California.

Ruth (late 2nd millennium BC) *Old Testament character*

> Where you go I will go, and where you stay I will stay. Your people will be my people, and your God my God.
>
> —To Naomi, Ruth 1:16

Ruth's story, told in the biblical book named after her, is a tale of courage, persistence, and eventual success. Ruth rose from poverty to become the wife of a respected man and, traditionally, the great-grandmother of King David.

Ruth was born in the land of Moab and married Mahlon, an Israelite of a family that had emigrated from Bethlehem in neighbouring Judea. When Mahlon and his brother died some ten years later, their widowed mother, Naomi, was left with her two foreign daughters-in-law. She decided to return to Judea. However, Ruth, who loved Naomi, refused to let her go alone, and the two women went to Bethlehem together.

There they found themselves in a difficult position; Ruth was a foreigner, and while Naomi had land she lacked a husband to protect and support them. Naomi therefore encouraged Ruth to glean (i.e. to pick up leftovers from the harvest) on the land of a man named Boaz, who was a relative of Naomi's husband.

In this way Boaz learned that Ruth was supporting her mother-in-law and had left her native land in order to do so. Impressed by her loyalty, he instructed his workers to ensure that Ruth obtained an adequate share of the harvest. When Naomi heard of his, she told Ruth to perfume herself and go and lie at Boaz's feet during the night. Ruth did so, and this symbolic act of devotion impressed Boaz so much that he decided he would like to marry her. Accordingly, he persuaded Naomi's closest kinsman to give up his right to buy Naomi's land; Boaz then bought the land from Naomi and married Ruth. Tradition has it that their son, Obed, was the grandfather of King David.

Rutherford, Dame Margaret
(1892–1972) *British actress*

Although her dearest wish was to be a traditionally beautiful leading lady, Margaret Rutherford is remembered for her humorous performances as a solid, bulldog-faced, middle-aged English eccentric.

Rutherford was born in south London. Her mother died when she was only three, leaving her to be brought up by an aunt who was devoted to the theatre and encouraged her to act. At school Rutherford developed a great love for the arts and took private drama lessons. She also prepared to be a teacher. When her aunt died and left her a small amount of money, she felt secure enough to attempt a career on stage. After an introduction to the theatre manager Lilian BAYLIS she was ac-

cepted as a student at the Old Vic Theatre in 1925. She appeared in many small roles with that company and others over the next few years.

In 1933, at the age of 41, Rutherford made her first appearance in London's West End. She was finally noticed by audiences and critics six years later, when she played Miss Prism in Wilde's *The Importance of Being Earnest*. This performance was followed by a very different role as the brooding vengeful Mrs. Danvers in Daphne DU MAURIER's *Rebecca*. Returning to comedy, Rutherford then appeared as the eccentric medium, Madame Arcati, in Noël Coward's *Blithe Spirit*.

Rutherford claimed not to be funny, but her deliberate lack of humour often made her hilarious. Although she made several films, she preferred the stage, on which she continued to appear until the 1960s. She is most fondly remembered for the film versions of *The Importance of Being Earnest* (1952), *Blithe Spirit* (1945), and her Oscar-winning role in *The VIPs* (1963). She also starred in a number of films as Agatha CHRISTIE's eccentric sleuth Miss Marple. In these highly successful movies she appeared with her husband, Stringer Davis, whom she married in 1945. Rutherford was made a DBE in 1967.

Ruysch, Rachel (1664–1750) *Dutch painter*

Rachel Ruysch's painstaking paintings of flowers are still highly prized for their vivid colours and accurate representation of natural forms.

Rachel Ruysch was born in Haarlem in northern Holland, the daughter of a professor of anatomy who was also a talented painter. She studied with the well-known flower painter Willem von Aelst, who assisted in bringing out her own talent as a skilful painter of flowers.

In 1693 she married the painter Juriaen Poole, with whom she had ten children. This did not stop her from painting, however, and in 1708 the couple were appointed court painters to the elector palatine in Dusseldörf. Here they painted exclusively for the prince until his death in 1716, when they returned to Amsterdam.

Some 100 of Ruysch's paintings survive, commanding high prices. However, her style has been widely copied, and many flower paintings in ornate frames bearing the legend "Rachel Ruysch" were not created by her.

Ryan, Meg (1961–) *American film actress*

Blonde and petite, Ryan is best known for the scene in *When Harry Met Sally* (1989) in which she fakes sexual ecstasy in a busy restaurant.

Ryan was born in Fairfield, Connecticut, and studied at Bethel High School and New York University. To fund her journalism course she managed to win a part in the TV soap *As the World Turns*, which turned out to be a great success. She also appeared in TV commercials, and her mother (who was a casting agent) found her a minor movie role in 1981. Other parts followed, and it seemed she was meant to be an actress rather than a journalist.

Ironically, Ryan was cast as a journalist in the science-fiction film *Innerspace* (1987). Here, as in *D.O.A.* (1988), she played opposite Dennis Quaid, whom she married in 1991. After the birth of their son, Ryan achieved stardom with her performance in *When Harry Met Sally*, in which she played a young woman who believes it is possible to be "just good friends" with a man – and is proved wrong.

Ryan's fame was now assured. Most popular among her films of the next few years was *Sleepless in Seattle* (1993), a sentimental romance; again playing a journalist, Ryan falls in love with a widower in far-off Seattle after hearing him speak on a radio phone-in. Ryan tackled a difficult challenge in *When a Man Loves a Woman* (1994), in which she played an alcoholic wife and mother. *French Kiss* (1995), which she also coproduced, is a romantic comedy in which Ryan stars with Kevin Kline, while *Addicted to Love* (1997) is a black comedy that earned Ryan some of her best reviews.

Ryder, Winona (1971–) *American film actress*

> She is not only intelligent and serious, she's also blessed with the ability to be good-natured.
>
> —Michael Lehmann, *c*. 1989

Ryder is known for playing individual, sometimes eccentric, young women. In little over a decade she has appeared in an interesting range of films.

Winona Ryder (originally Horowitz) was named after her birthplace, Winona, Minnesota; her parents both worked in publishing and followed a somewhat unconventional lifestyle. Winona's several childhood homes included a hippie commune and a suburb of Petaluma, near San Francisco, where she spent her unhappy high-school days.

It was during her studies at the American Conservatory Theater, San Francisco, that Winona Ryder passed her first screen test, aged 15. Over the next few years her roles included a shy bespectacled country girl in *Square Dance* (1987), a girl with an awareness of the paranormal in *Beetlejuice* (1988), and the 13-year-old cousin and bride of Jerry Lee Lewis in *Great Balls of Fire!* (1989). In the black comedy *Heathers* (1989) she played the groupie, turned betrayer, of a trio of cliquey high-school bullies.

In 1990 Ryder appeared in the fantasy *Edward Scissorhands* and became the girlfriend of its star, Johnny Depp. At this time she was also committed to two other films, and the heavy schedule became too much. Ryder was forced to withdraw from one contract on grounds of ill health; however, success was in store. Her performance as an innocent unloved wife in *The Age of Innocence* (1993) won her a Golden Globe Award for Best Supporting Actress, and she received an Oscar nomination for her portrayal of the tomboy Jo March in *Little Women* (1994). More recently she has appeared with Daniel Day-Lewis in a film version of Miller's *The Crucible* (1996) and in the science-fiction shocker *Alien Resurrection* (1997).

S

Sabatini, Gabriela (1970–) *Argentinian tennis player*

Gabriela Sabatini is regarded as "the uncrowned Queen of Tennis" who never quite fulfilled her potential during her playing career.

She was born in Buenos Aires, Argentina, the daughter of Osvaldo and Beatriz Sabatini. Encouraged by her father, she started playing tennis at the age of six. Four years later she was ranked the number-one player in the under-12s group in Argentina. After being talent-spotted in a tournament in Buenos Aires, she moved to Key Biscayne to be coached by the former Chilean player Patricio Apey. She made headlines in the United States when she reached the final 16 in the U.S. Open in 1984.

Realizing her potential, Apey immediately signed up Sabatini with a firm of sports managers. Within months she was endorsing a line of tennis wear for the Sergio Tarchiani fashion house. This was the first of a long line of lucrative endorsements that have made her one of the richest women in tennis, with an annual income of about $8 million.

After turning professional in 1985, Sabatini came frustratingly close to winning all the major women's singles titles but never quite succeeded. She reached the semifinals of the French Open and won the Japan Open in 1985. The following year she was the runner-up at the French Open and reached the semifinals at Wimbledon. In 1987 she was the runner-up in the Italian Open and reached the semifinals of the French Open; with Steffi GRAF, she was also runner-up in the women's doubles at the French competition. That same year she won the Japan Open and the Volvo Classic Tournament in Brighton, England.

In order to improve her fitness Sabatini took on a new coach, Angel Gimenez. In 1988 she won the Italian Open and the Virginia Slims Championship in New York and was a finalist in the U.S. Open. She also won the Italian Open again in 1989 and reached the finals of the German Open. In 1990 she reached the peak of her career when she won the Virginia Slims Tournament in Florida. She then changed her coach again, hiring Carlos Kirmayr, to win the U.S. Open.

Gabriela Sabatini was a finalist at Wimbledon in 1991 and won the Italian Open in 1991 and 1992. Her career declined after this, and although she won the Virginia Slims Tournament in New York in 1994, she retired from professional tennis in 1997 to concentrate on her business interests.

Sabin, Florence Rena (1871–1953) *American medical researcher and public health worker*

Florence Sabin was the first woman to be made a full professor at Johns Hopkins University (1917) and the first to become a member of the U.S. National Academy of Sciences (1925). She is also remembered for her championship of the Sabin Health Bills, which gave Colorado one of the best public health programmes in the United States.

Sabin was born in Central City, Colorado. After studying music and attending Smith College, she worked as a teacher to raise money to put herself through medical school. She entered Johns Hopkins University in 1897; after receiving her medical degree in 1900, she joined the staff there. She won a $1,000 prize for her study of the lymphatic system of pigs and went on to give the Harvey Memorial Lecture on the subject in 1916. A year later she was made a full professor of histology at Johns Hopkins.

Her research there was devoted to the determination of the origins of the lymphatic system and of blood vessels and cells in the developing embryo. In 1925 she went to the Rockefeller Institute for Medical Research to investigate cellular mechanisms of bodily defence against infections, especially tuberculosis. She went on to become the head of the department of cellular studies there and became the president of the American Association of Anatomists. In 1929 she was received by President Herbert Hoover in the White House. After her retirement to Denver, Colorado, in 1938 she became active in promoting her Health Bills, which became state law in the early 1940s. Among other things, the new laws implemented TB screening, thereby halving the state's death rate from TB. She received 15 honorary degrees during her medical career.

Sablé, Marquise de (c. 1599–1678) French writer and literary hostess

> It is just as great a folly to listen to oneself speak when one is conversing with others as to talk to oneself.
> —*Maximes* (1678)

Madame de Sablé held a famous salon in Paris that attracted many prominent literary figures, notably the writer and moralist La Rochefoucauld. She has been given the credit for making the "maxim" into a new category of literary composition.

The daughter of Louis XIII's governor, the Marquis de Courtenvaux, she was born Madeleine de Souvré in Touraine. In 1514 she married the Marquis de Sablé, with whom she had four children. However, the marriage was unhappy; Madame de Sablé had to endure her husband's love affairs with other women until his death in 1540.

A woman of intelligence and beauty, Madame de Sablé frequented the famous salon of the Marquise de RAMBOUILLET at the Hôtel de Rambouillet, where she met many writers and intellectuals. She also became friendly with the mathematician and scientist Blaise Pascal.

In 1646, together with her friend the Comtesse de Maure, the Marquise de Sablé began to hold her own salon at her Paris home. Many learned and philosophical discussions took place there, and the philosopher Antoine Arnauld, La Rochefoucauld, and Madames de SÉVIGNÉ and de LA FAYETTE were frequent visitors. The discussions that took place at her salon helped La Rochefoucauld, who valued Madame de Sablé's judgment, to formulate his famous *Maximes* (1665), precise and highly literate analyses of human behaviour. Her own *Maximes* were published in 1678, shortly after her death. She also wrote a treatise on friendship, *Amité*. In her later years the Marquise de Sablé retired to the celebrated convent of Port Royal, where she died.

Sacagawea (c. 1784–1884) Native-American guide

A member of the Shoshone tribe, Sacagawea was the only woman to accompany the Lewis and Clark Expedition, which set out in 1804 to find a westward route across America. Her Minnetarre name was Tsa-ka-ka-wias, which means "Bird Woman," while her Shoshone name, Bo-i-naiv, means "Grass Maiden." Sacagawea is also sometimes spelled Sacajawea or Sahcargarweah.

Captured by the Minnetarre tribe as a child, Sacagawea was gambled away in 1804 to a French Canadian named Toussaint Charbonneau, whose wife she became. She was living in the Dakotas with her husband when Lewis and Clark reached there. Charbonneau and Sacagawea were engaged as guides and spent the winter at Fort Mandan, where Sacagawea's son, Baptiste, was born on February 11, 1805. Although she had not seen her country since she was a child, she was able to guide the expedition there and took them to meet her people, arriving on August 17, 1805. She was immediately recognized and managed to prevail over the determination of her brother, now a tribal leader, to destroy the whites for their goods. Apart from her brother, all her family was dead except the child of a dead sister, whom she immediately adopted. According to the custom of her people, she never admitted that the child was other than her own. Sacagawea then accompanied the party to the West Coast and returned with Captain Clark in 1806 by way of the Yellowstone, another region she knew well.

On their return to the Minnetarre country Charbonneau refused to accompany the explorers to civilization, and Sacagawea remained with him. She then disappeared from view until she was found, an old woman, in the Shoshone Agency in Wyoming, where she remained until her death.

Sachs, Nelly (1891–1970) *German-born Swedish poet*

> In spite of all the horrors of the past, I believe in you [the German people].
>
> —Accepting the 1965 Peace Prize of German Publishers

Nelly Sachs's powerful and moving poetry about the suffering of the Jewish people earned her the Nobel Prize for literature in 1966 (shared with the Israeli author Shmuel Yosef Agnon).

Leonie (Nelly) Sachs was born and raised in Berlin, the only daughter of a wealthy Jewish industrialist. Educated at home, she read widely and began writing poems and short plays as a young girl. Although some of her early verse appeared in newspapers, it was mainly conventional and attracted no critical notice. After reading the novel *Gösta Berling* by Selma LAGERLÖF, she began to correspond with the Swedish author, who helped Sachs and her mother escape from Nazi Germany to Sweden in 1940. The rest of the family died in concentration camps.

To support herself and her mother Sachs learned Swedish and earned a living by translating Swedish literary works into German. Gradually she developed the unrhymed strongly rhythmic style characteristic of her mature poetry. Her first collections, *In den Wohnungen des Todes* (1946; In the Dwellings of Death) and *Sternverdunkelung* (1949; Eclipse of a Star), dealt starkly with the agony of the death camps, while her later books, *Und niemand weiss weiter* (1957; And

No One Knows Any More) and *Flucht und Verwandlung* (1959; Escape and Metamorphosis), although still dealing with the persecution of the Jews, show the influence of the prophetic literature of the Cabbala. A selection of her work was translated into English and published as *O the Chimneys* in 1967.

Sackville-West, Vita (1892–1962) *British writer and gardener*

> Women, like men, ought to have their youth so glutted with freedom they hate the very idea of freedom.
>
> —Letter to Harold Nicolson, June 1, 1919

Vita Sackville-West is best known as a writer for her long poem *The Land* (1927), which won the Hawthornden Prize, and her novel *The Edwardians* (1930).

The daughter of the third Baron Sackville, Victoria Mary Sackville-West was born at Knole, the ancestral family home at Sevenoaks in Kent. She was educated at home. By the time she was 18, she had written eight novels and five plays. In 1913 she married Harold Nicolson, a journalist and diplomat, and they spent some years in Tehran, Persia (now Iran). This experience gave rise to her first book, *Poems of West and East* (1917), and the later prose work *Passenger to Teheran* (1926). She produced other works, but they were little appreciated outside her immediate circle of literary and artistic friends, the so-called "Bloomsbury Group," until *The Land* was published. A close friend and possibly the lover of Virginia WOOLF, she was the model for the androgynous hero/heroine of Woolf's novel *Orlando* (1928), which was dedicated to her. Sackville-West's witty novel about Knole, *The Edwardians*, was followed by *All Passion Spent* (1931), in which the heroine, in her desire to be an artist, fights against social convention.

Vita Sackville-West also wrote several nonfiction works, including *Knole and the Sackvilles* (1922), an account of her home and family; the biography *Joan of Arc* (1936); and *Pepita* (1937), a fictionalized biography of her maternal grandmother, who was a Spanish dancer. Together with her husband

Vita Sackville-West created a magnificent garden at Sissinghurst Castle, their home in Kent, which she wrote about in her poem *The Garden* (1946). During her later years she was the gardening correspondent on *The Observer*. Her last novel, *No Signposts in the Sea*, appeared in 1961.

Sade (1959–) *Nigerian-born British singer and songwriter*

Sade was one of the most successful international singing stars of the 1980s. Her early songs are distinguished by their infectious melodies and Latin rhythms; later songs are more sophisticated, while still retaining her sultry jazz style.

She was born Helen Folassade Adu in Ibadan, Nigeria. Her father was a Nigerian economics professor, and her mother was an English nurse, with whom she moved to Clacton, Essex, in 1964. She began writing songs when she was a teenager. In 1981, while studying fashion design at St. Martin's School of Art and Design in London, she joined the Latin group Arriva, which later became the soul-funk band Pride. With the band's guitarist Ray St. John, Sade wrote "Smooth Operator," Pride's most popular song.

In 1983 Sade signed with the Epic record label and, with ex-Pride members Stuart Matthewman, Paul Denman, and Andrew Hale, she recorded the album *Diamond Life* (1984). This became one of the most successful debut albums of the 1980s, selling over six million copies worldwide. In addition she had hit singles in Britain and the United States with the songs "Your Love Is King" and "Smooth Operator." Sade then released the album *Promise* (1985), which reached number one on the American charts, and had further hit singles with "The Sweetest Taboo" and "Never So Good as the First Time" (1986).

Although she temporarily retired from music between 1986 and 1988, Sade contributed to the soundtrack of the film *Absolute Beginners* (1987), in which she had a cameo role. In 1988 she went on a world tour to promote her third album, *Stronger than Pride*. She had further hit singles with "Par-adise" and "Love Is Stronger than Pride."

It was not until 1992 that Sade released her fourth album, *Love Deluxe*, with which she had further worldwide success. In 1994 she released *The Best of Sade*. Two music videos of her performances have been released: *Life Promise Pride Love* (1993) and *Live Concert Home* (1994).

Sagan, Françoise (1935–) *French writer*

> We had the same gait, the same habits and lived in the same rhythm; our bodies suited each other, and all was well. I had no right to regret his failure to make the tremendous effort required of love, and effort to know and shatter the solitude of another.
>
> —*A Certain Smile* (1956)

Françoise Sagan, a name she took from a character in Proust, is the pen name of Françoise Quoirez. She is best remembered for her highly successful novel *Bonjour Tristesse*, written when she was only 18.

Sagan was born in Cajarc, in south-central France. After attending various private schools, she studied at the Sorbonne in Paris but left without taking a degree.

Like almost all her novels, *Bonjour Tristesse* – a skilfully told story of an unhappy teenage girl set on preventing the remarriage of her widowed father – examines the transitory nature of love. It was an instantaneous success on its publication in 1954 and was awarded the Prix des Critiques that same year. It also quickly became an international bestseller and was translated into some 20 languages, as well as being made into a film. The novel appeared in English translation in 1955.

Sagan's other books include *A Certain Smile* (1956), *Aimez-Vous Brahms?* (1959), *The Wonderful Clouds* (1962), the autobiographical work *Responses* (1980), *The Painted Lady* (1983), *Incidental Music* (1984), and *Salad Days* (1984). She collaborated on a ballet, *Le Rendevous manqué*, with the composer Michel Magne, with whom she has also written such popular songs as "La Valse" and "De toute manière."

Her plays include *Château en Suède* (1959; A Castle in Sweden), *Le Cheval évanoui* (1966; The Disappearing Horse), and *Zaphorie* (1973). She has also written collections of short stories and the biography *Dear Sarah Bernhardt* (1989).

Salerno-Sonnenberg, Najda

(1961–   ) *Italian-born American violinist*

Najda Salerno-Sonnenberg rose to prominence in the 1980s as a result of her virtuosity as a violinist and her exuberant personality.

She was born in Rome, the daughter of Josephine Salerno and a Russian father, who left the family soon after her birth. Her mother remarried, and Najda adopted the second half of her name, Sonnenberg, from her stepfather (who also left the family). She showed early promise with the violin and – advised by her music teacher – she moved with her family to the United States in 1969 in order to receive further musical training. She grew up in Cherry Hill, New Jersey, and Philadelphia, Pennsylvania.

In addition to attending high school in Philadelphia, Najda also studied at the city's Curtis Institute of Music, where she was the youngest pupil. At the age of ten she made her orchestral debut with the Philadelphia Orchestra. In 1975 she transferred to the Juilliard School of Music in New York, where she was taught by Dorothy DeLay. After a troubled adolescence she won the prestigious Naumburg Competition in 1981.

She made her New York debut with the American Symphony Orchestra in 1982, the same year that she graduated from the Juilliard School. She then embarked on her professional career and has played as a soloist with most of the major orchestras in the United States and Europe. Both critics and audiences have been impressed by the passion and eloquence of her performances. Her playing is generally regarded as technically impeccable. Her exuberant manner and willingness to talk about her interests outside music – notably baseball and the cinema –

have made her a favourite with the hosts of TV chat shows.

Sallé, Marie (1707–1756) *French dancer*

Marie Sallé was the first woman to choreograph the ballets in which she danced.

She was born in Paris, the daughter of touring players. A child prodigy, she made her first appearances as a dancer in pantomime in London. After studying with François Prévost at the Paris Opéra School, she made her debut there in 1721. At the Opéra Sallé showed originality by dancing without the mask that was traditionally worn by dancers, in order to allow the audience to see her expressions during the dance.

Marie Sallé was a rival of Marie CA-MARGO, who also danced at the Paris Opéra. Frustrated by this competition, Marie Sallé moved in 1734 to London, where she was a great success in *Les Caractères de l'amour* and *Bacchus and Ariadne*. She is, however, chiefly remembered for dancing the role of Venus in *Pygmalion*, in which she wore a Grecian-style dress and loose hair instead of the usual restrictive clothing. In 1735 she appeared in several operas by Handel, who composed the ballet *Terpsichore* for her.

Marie Sallé returned to Paris in 1735 after Marie Camargo went into temporary retirement. She danced in the first performance of Jean Rameau's *Les Indes galantes* (1735) and played Hébé in *Castor and Pollux* (1737). A graceful and expressive dancer, she is regarded as one of the originators of the *ballet d'actions* in which plot and theme are more important than costumes and staging. She retired in 1740 but continued to dance at the court of King Louis XV, where she was a favourite. She was a friend of many leading thinkers and artists of the day, including Voltaire, David Garrick, and Handel.

Salome (1st century AD) *New Testament character*

Salome contrived the death of St. John the Baptist by dancing for her stepfather, Herod Antipas, the tetrarch of Galilee and Peraea.

Her story is told in the Gospels of Mark (6:14–29) and Matthew (14:1–12). Herod promised to grant Salome anything she asked for if she would dance for him and his guests at a banquet. After Salome had danced, she demanded the head of St. John the Baptist on a plate. Her reason for this cruel demand was that the prophet had angered HERODIAS, Salome's mother, by condemning her marriage to Herod Antipas as a violation of the Mosaic Law (Herodias was the divorced wife of Herod Antipas's half-brother Herod Philip). Herodias therefore persuaded Salome to ask for the Baptist's head.

Although Herod Antipas had imprisoned St. John the Baptist for his outspoken criticisms of his regime, he was reluctant to execute him because of the prophet's popularity with the people of Galilee. However, Herod had to honour his promise, and St. John the Baptist was beheaded on his orders. Salome then presented his head to her mother on a plate.

The story has endured in Western art, literature, and music. It inspired both the Italian Renaissance painter Masolino da Panicale and such 19th-century "decadents" as Gustave Moreau and Aubrey Beardsley. Oscar Wilde wrote a one-act play called *Salomé* (1893) that was later translated by Hedwig Lachmann to form the libretto for Richard Strauss's opera of the same name (1905).

Wilde and Lachmann portrayed Herod as desiring Salome, while Salome was depicted as being in love with St. John the Baptist, who had rejected her. After his execution she kisses his lips, an image that has become an icon of erotic decadence in Western art. Strauss also has Salome performing the "Dance of the Seven Veils," a striptease with which she is now commonly associated; however, there is no mention in biblical literature of her having performed such a dance.

Salomé, Lou Andreas (1861–1937)
German writer

Lou Andreas Salomé is remembered for her relationships with the great thinkers of her day as well as for her novels and her books on female sexuality.

She was born in St. Petersburg, the daughter of a German mother and a Russian army officer. A woman of great beauty and penetrating intellect, she was one of the first female students at the University of Zurich, where she studied religion and philosophy (1880–81).

After graduating, she travelled abroad and met many of the leading thinkers of the time. In 1881, while living with the philosopher Paul Ree, she met Friedrich Nietzsche, who fell in love with her. Rejecting his offer of marriage, she married instead the orientalist F. C. Andreas. In 1897 she met the poet Rainer Maria Rilke, who – although 14 years her junior – fell in love with her; their two journeys to Russia together in 1899 and 1901 had a major influence on his life and work.

Later she wrote biographies of Nietzsche – *Friedrich Nietzsche in seine Werken* (1894) – and Rilke – *Rainer Maria Rilke* (1928). Her correspondence with Rilke was published in 1952. She also knew the dramatists Gerhart Hauptmann, Frank Wedekind, and Artur Schnitzler.

Salomé wrote fiction, including *Ruth* (1896), *Fenitschka* (1896), and *Eine Ausschweifung* (1898; Wandering from the Path), which investigated the psychosexuality of women and argued for their emotional and erotic emancipation. Her more detailed views on this subject are contained in *Die Erotik* (1910). This new horizon in her life led her to study psychoanalysis, first with Alfred Adler and then with Sigmund Freud, with whom she is believed to have had a sexual relationship. She herself later practised as a psychoanalyst. She wrote about this period in her life in *Mein Dank an Freud* (1931; My Gratitude to Freud) and *Grundriss einiger Lebenserinnerungen* (1933; Sketches for a Memoir).

Samuelson, Joan Benoit (1957–)
American marathon runner

Joan Benoit Samuelson will be remembered as the winner of the first Olympic marathon for women in 1984.

Joan Benoit was born in Cape Elizabeth, Maine. She ran 12 marathons, winning the Boston marathon twice in record times before taking the gold medal in the first women's marathon at the 1984 Olympic Games in Los Angeles, California. Her achievement in winning the Boston marathon of 1983 in a world record time of 2 hours, 22 minutes, 43 seconds had been tarnished by allegations of pacing. However, she overcame criticism and injury to win the Olympic race in 2 hours, 24 minutes, 52 seconds. Her tactic of going out fast, running her own race, and not worrying about the rest of the runners paid off. She beat one of the finest fields of women distance runners ever assembled. In 1984 she received the Sullivan Memorial Trophy and the U.S. Sportswoman of the Year Award (which she shared with Mary Lou Retton) from the Women's Sports Foundation.

A knee injury forced her to give up marathon running after the 1984 Olympics, and she concentrated instead on 10,000-metre running for the rest of her career. She married in 1984 and now lives in Freeport, Maine.

Sand, George (1804–1876) *French writer*

> Liszt said to me today that God alone deserves to be loved. It may be true, but when one has loved a man it is very different to love God.
> —*Intimate Journal*

Although considered a great writer by many contemporary critics, George Sand outraged bourgeois society with her unconventional ways – which included wearing trousers and smoking cigars in public – and her many love affairs with prominent artistic figures.

Born Amandine Aurore Lucie Dupin in Paris, she spent her early childhood at the chateau of Nohant with her grandmother, a cultured woman with royal ancestors, who embodied the spirit of the old aristocracy. After a convent school education, she married Casimir, Baron Dudevant, in 1822 and bore him two children. Bored by the restrictions of marriage, she left him in 1831, taking her children with her to Paris. There she led a bohemian life, associating with young artists and writers, flouting every convention, and embarking on a liaison with the writer Jules Sandeau. With Sandeau she collaborated on a number of stories published under the name "Jules Sand." Shortly afterwards she adopted her familiar pen name, George Sand, to publish her first novel, *Indiana* (1832; English translation, 1881), a plea for women's right to independence. Other novels followed in rapid succession – *Valentine* (1932), *Lélia* (1833), and *Jacques* (1834) all met with public opposition for protesting against current social norms and advancing the claims of romantic feminism.

Meanwhile, George Sand became involved in a turbulent love affair with the poet and playwright Alfred de Musset, who was six years her junior. Although this tempestuous affair came to an end in 1835, it was the source of much literary material, notably Musset's *Nuit de Mai* (1835–37) and *Confession d'un enfant du siècle* (1836) and Sand's *Elle et lui* (1859; published in English as *He and She*, 1900), as well as her exquisite *Lettres d'un voyageur* (1834–1836).

George Sand's next celebrated liaison, with the composer and pianist Frédéric Chopin, lasted ten years. A somewhat more tranquil relationship, it allowed Sand to turn her attention to politics and write humanitarian, broadly "socialistic" novels. *Mauprat* (1837) was followed by *Spiridion* (1838–39), *Les Sept Cordes de la lyre* (1840; The Seven Strings of the Lyre), *Le Meunier d'Angibault* (1845; The Miller of Angibault), and *Le Péché de Monsieur Antoine* (1847; The Sin of Monsieur Antoine) – each a persistent call for the reconstruction of society. She also wrote studies of rustic life, notably *La Mare au diable* (1846; published in English as *The Haunted Pool*, 1890), which are generally regarded as among her finest works. Meanwhile, she was nursing Chopin, who was suffering from tuberculosis; *Un Hiver à Majorque* (1841; A Winter on Majorca) is a description of her stay on the island of Majorca with him.

In 1848 Sand supported the revolution against the monarchy and offered her services to the provisional government, writing articles for the *Bulletin de la République* and composing her *Lettres au peuple*. However, following the violence and repression of June 1848, she returned to Nohant and wrote a series of pastoral novels, including *La Petite Fadette* (1848; *Fanchon the Cricket*, 1864), *François le champi* (1850; *Francis the Waif*, 1889), and *Les Maîtres sonneurs* (1853; The Master Bellringers). She became the "good lady of Nohant," kindhearted and hospitable to all, entertaining artists and writers and presiding over village fêtes. Her autobiography, *Histoire de ma vie* (4 vols., 1854–55), was considered a masterpiece. Later works include *Jean de la Roche* (1860), *Le Marquis de Villemer* (1861), and *Mademoiselle de la Quintinie* (1863). Her final volume, *Contes d'une grand'mère* (Tales of a Grandmother), appeared in 1873.

Sanger, Margaret (1883–1966)
American birth-control campaigner

> Women of the working class, especially wage workers, should not have more than two children at most. The average working man can support no more and the average working woman can take care of no more in decent fashion.
>
> —*Family Limitations* (1917)

> "Yes, Yes – I know, Doctor," said the patient with trembling voice, "but," and she hesitated as if it took all of her courage to say it, "*what can I do to prevent getting that way again?*" "Oh, ho!" laughed the doctor good naturedly. "You want your cake while you eat it too, do you? Well, it can't be done...I'll tell you the only sure thing to do. Tell Jake to sleep on the roof!"
>
> —*My Fight for Birth Control* (1931)

Margaret Sanger, who was a founder and leader of the birth-control movement in the United States, promoted the idea that contraception was a basic human right that should be available to all. She was also responsible for coining the phrase "birth control."

Born Margaret Louise Higgins in Corning, New York, the sixth of 11 children of a stonemason, she attended Claverack College, Hudson, before studying nursing at White Plains (New York) Hospital and at the Manhattan Eye and Ear Hospital. In 1900 she married William Sanger, an architect. After the birth of the second of their three children in 1912 she worked as an obstetrical nurse on New York's Lower East Side and also lectured to young mothers on health.

Deeply affected when a young woman died in her arms after a self-induced abortion, Sanger became determined to emancipate women from what she viewed as the servitude of unwanted pregnancy. In 1913 she went to Europe, where contraceptive knowledge was more advanced, and after returning to the United States in 1914, she founded the magazine *Woman Rebel* to advance her views. In 1916, in defiance of New York law, she opened the first birth-control clinic in the United States in Brooklyn. The clinic was soon raided and Sanger was arrested and jailed. Despite numerous other arrests and formidable opposition, she pursued her cause. Through speaking tours in the United States and in Europe, and by means of published articles, she gradually won over some influential people. In 1917, with the help of suffragists, she founded the National Birth Control League, which became the Planned Parenthood Federation of America. She was divorced from Sanger in 1920 but retained his name professionally. In 1922 she married the industrialist Noah H. Slee, who supported her work.

Sanger was instrumental in organizing the first International Birth Control Congress at Geneva in 1927. By 1932 80 clinics were operating in the United States. She retired from active leadership of the movement in 1938, following a ruling that doctors would in future be permitted to prescribe contraceptives on medical grounds. However, she continued to lecture, and the true culmination of her work came in 1952, when the International Planned Parenthood Federation was established in Bombay, India. She became its first president. Her many books include *What Every Mother Should Know* (1917), *Woman and the*

New Race (1920), and *My Fight for Birth Control* (1931).

See also STOPES, MARIE.

Sappho (*c.* 612 BC–*c.* 580 BC) *Greek poet*

What is beautiful is good, and who
                                    is good
Will soon also be beautiful.
                        —*Fragments*, No. 101

Sappho's lyric poems, only fragments of which survive, were written for her group of female admirers on the Greek island of Lesbos (from which the term "lesbian" is derived). She is the most famous woman poet of ancient Greece.

Sappho was born on Lesbos into an aristocratic family. Little is known for certain of her life, but she was married and had a daughter, whom she named Cleïs after her own mother. Stories of her love for a man called Phaon and of her suicide by leaping from a cliff into the sea off the coast of Epirus are legends. The exact date of her death is unknown.

Although Sappho's poems were apparently arranged according to type into nine books in ancient times, no continuous manuscript of her works still exists. Two poems of greater length, possibly complete, have survived through quotation by later critics, and some epigrams (of doubtful authenticity) are preserved in *The Palatine Anthology*. There are also fairly extensive papyrus fragments that have been found, some representing almost complete poems.

Despite the civil wars that are said to have disturbed her life, Sappho's short lyrics, written in the Lesbian dialect, mostly depict idyllic scenes of rural life. There are also poems to the girls in her circle whom she favoured, in which her emotions are described with great intensity, and a group of wedding poems. In other verses, however, Sappho can be bitter and sometimes terse. Sappho may well have invented several types of line and stanza, including the one named after her: the "Sapphic" stanza is a four-line stanza, the first three lines of which have 11 syllables each, and the fourth line, five syllables.

Sappho's poetry was well known in ancient Rome. Catullus translated one poem, borrowed lines elsewhere, and used some of her metres; he also took her treatment of sexual jealousy as his model in several poems. Horace used the Sapphic stanza frequently, while Ovid wrote about Sappho's legendary love for Phaon in his *Heroides*.

Sarah (early 2nd millennium BC) *Old Testament character*

Sarah or Sarai (both of which mean "princess") was the wife of Abraham and, according to the story, gave birth at the age of 90 to their son Isaac.

Following God's calling of Abraham, she travelled with him from Ur in Chaldaea to Canaan and subsequently to Egypt. A woman of great beauty, she posed as Abraham's sister, rather than his wife, so that the Egyptian men would not be tempted to kill Abraham in order to possess her. However, Pharaoh, seeing her beauty, took her into his household as one of his wives. When Pharaoh found out that Sarah was Abraham's wife, he banished them both from Egypt, and they returned to Canaan. The Bible tells a very similar story about the couple's later journey to Gerar.

God had promised Abraham that he would become the father of a great nation. Accordingly, when Sarah reached old age without having conceived, she gave her handmaid Hagar to Abraham as his second wife. Hagar soon bore him a son, Ishmael. However, after Abraham accepted the covenant of circumcision, God repeated his promise, emphasizing that Sarah would even yet become "a mother of nations" (Genesis 17:16). As Sarah was by this time 90, she greeted the promise with sarcastic laughter (Genesis 18:12). When she did, indeed, give birth to Isaac (whose name is Hebrew for "laughter"), she was overcome with joy. In biblical legend Sarah's son Isaac became the ancestor of the Jewish nation, while Hagar's son Ishmael, whom Sarah banished with his mother into the desert, became the ancestor of the Arabs. Sarah died at the age of 127 in Hebron.

In the New Testament St. Paul used the miraculous birth of Isaac as an allegory for the redemption that makes all Christians "the children of promise" (Galatians 4:22–31). St. Peter portrayed Sarah as a model wife to Abraham (1 Peter 3:6).

Sarandon, Susan (1946–) *American film actress*

> I play *unusual* moms. I'm interested in not making the transition from leading lady to mother role, to stay as a person who is sexual while still being a mom.
>
> —Commenting on her film roles

An Oscar-winning actress, Susan Sarandon is known for her screen portrayals of mature women with a strong sexuality.

Born Susan Tomalin in New York City, the eldest of the nine children of Philip and Leonara Tomalin, she studied drama and English at the Catholic University of America in Washington, D.C., from which she graduated in 1968. She married Chris Sarandon, also an actor, in 1967, but they were divorced in 1979, causing her to have a serious breakdown. She subsequently had a daughter by the writer Franco Amurri in 1985 before forming a long-term relationship with the actor and director Tim Robbins.

After making her movie debut in *Joe* (1970), Sarandon worked in the theatre and television before attracting growing attention in *The Front Page* (1974), *The Great Waldo Pepper* (1975), and especially *The Rocky Horror Picture Show* (1975). She then appeared in a string of mostly undistinguished films before she received an Academy Award nomination for her role as Sally in *Atlantic City* (1980). In 1982 she was named Best Actress at the Venice Film Festival for playing the role of Aretha in *Tempest* (1982).

In the late 1980s Sarandon took major parts in a series of successful films including *The Witches of Eastwick* (1987), *Bull Durham* (1988) – in which she played opposite Tim Robbins – *A Dry White Season* (1989), and *The January Man* (1989). This was followed by starring roles in *White Palace* (1990) and *Thelma and Louise* (1991), for which she received an Academy Award nomination, a Golden Globe Award, and a BAFTA Award for Best Actress. Further Oscar nominations followed for *Lorenzo's Oil* (1993) and *The Client* (1994) before she finally won the Best Actress Award for her role in *Dead Man Walking* (1996), a film directed by Robbins.

Sarraute, Nathalie (1902–) *Russian-born French novelist and critic*

Sarraute was a leading exponent of the *nouveau roman*, an experimental type of novel pioneered in France during the 1950s. An important figure in Parisian cultural life for over four decades, she was involved in almost continuous controversy with the writer Simone de BEAUVOIR.

Born Nathalie Tcherniak in Ivanovo, Russia, she moved with her family to France when she was three. After studying at the Sorbonne, and at Oxford University, she practised law until 1942, after which she devoted herself to writing. In 1925 she married Raymond Sarraute.

Sarraute's first work, *Tropismes*, appeared in 1939. A collection of short prose pieces, it was published in English as *Tropisms* in 1964. In 1947 her book *Portrait d'un inconnu* (1947; *Portrait of an Unknown Man*, 1958) was hailed as the first "antinovel" in a preface supplied by Jean-Paul Sartre. With its abandonment of conventional plot, characterization, and chronology, it was clearly influenced by the work of Virginia WOOLF. *Martereau* (1953; English translation, 1959) and *Le Planétarium* (1959; published in English as *The Planetarium*, 1960) further extended the experimental, fragmented structure of the *nouveau roman*. Sarraute also wrote radio plays. Her later works include *Les Fruits d'or* (1963; *The Golden Fruits*, 1964), *C'est Beau* (1973), and *Enfance* (1983; *Childhood*, 1984). In 1982 Sarraute was awarded France's prestigious Grand Prix National des Lettres for her lifetime's work.

Sarton, May (1912–1995) *Belgian-born American poet and novelist*

> There was such a thing as women's work and it consisted chiefly, Hilary sometimes thought, in being able to

stand constant interruption and
keep your temper.
—*Mrs. Stevens Hears the Mermaids
Singing* (1965)

May Sarton was a prolific writer of poetry, novels, and other works in which she explored the concepts of love and individuality in modern society.

She was born Eleanor Marie Sarton in Wondelgem, Belgium, the only child of the noted historian of science George Sarton and the artist and designer Eleanor Elwes. On the outbreak of World War I May Sarton and her parents fled Belgium for England and then emigrated to the United States, settling in Cambridge, Massachusetts, in 1918 (she became a naturalized U.S. citizen in 1924). May studied at the Shady Hill School and the High and Latin School in Cambridge. After leaving school, she started to write poetry but had a great desire to enter the theatrical profession. Overcoming her father's objections, she joined Eva LE GALLIENNE's Civic Repertory Company in New York as an apprentice in 1929. After the company collapsed in 1934, she continued to run its apprentice group, known as the Associated Actors Theater, until it too was forced to close from lack of money in 1937.

May Sarton then turned to teaching as a way of financing her travels and writing, becoming an instructor in creative writing at Stuart School, Boston, Massachusetts, from 1937 to 1942. After World War II, during which she served as a scriptwriter for the Overseas Film Unit in New York, she was the Briggs-Copel Instructor in English Composition at Harvard University (1949–52). She was a lecturer in creative writing at Wellesley College, Massachusetts, from 1960 to 1964 and also lectured extensively at universities, colleges, and writers' conferences throughout the United States. She received numerous awards, including 18 honorary degrees.

Sarton began to publish her poetry and novels in the late 1930s. Her poetry collections include *Encounter in April* (1937), *Inner Landscape* (1939), *The Lion and the Rose* (1948), *A Private Mythology* (1966), and *The Silence Now* (1988). Her novels include *The Single Hound* (1938), *Faithful Are the Wounds* (1955), and *Mrs. Stevens Hears the Mermaids Singing* (1965). As well as a play, screenplays, and children's stories, she published *At Seventy: A Journal* (1984). She died of breast cancer in York, Maine.

Saunders, Dame Cicely (1918–)
British philanthropist

Dame Cicely Saunders is the founder of the modern hospice movement. Believing that death is a natural part of life, rather than a medical failure, she has aimed to provide surroundings in which people can die with dignity.

She was born in Barnet, London, the daughter of Gordon Saunders and Mary Christian Knight. After studying at Rodean School in Sussex and St. Anne's College, Oxford, she trained as a nurse at St. Thomas's Hospital Medical School and the Nightingale School of Nursing in London. She qualified as a doctor in 1957.

In 1967 Saunders set up St. Christopher's Hospice in Sydenham, London, in order to provide sensitive nursing and effective pain control for terminally ill patients, having realized that this service did not exist in hospitals. She was medical director of the hospice from 1967 to 1985, when she became chairman. All modern hospices, including those within the National Health Service and many in the United States, are modelled on St. Christopher's.

Her pioneering work has been widely recognized. She was made a DBE in 1980 and was appointed to the Order of Merit in 1989. She has received honorary degrees from universities in Britain and the United States as well as the Gold Medal of the Society of Apothecaries of London in 1979, the Templeton Foundation Prize in 1981, and the Gold Medal of the British Medical Association in 1987. In 1980 she married Professor Marian Bohusz-Szyszko, who died in 1995.

Dame Cicely has published a number of books on terminal care, including *Care of the Dying* (1960), *The Management of Terminal Disease* (1978), *Hospice: The Living Idea* (1981), *Living with the Dying* (1983),

St. Christopher's in Celebration (1988), *Beyond the Horizon* (1990), and *Hospice and Palliative Care* (1990).

Saunders, Jennifer (1958–) *British comedienne and writer*

Jennifer Saunders is best known for writing and starring in the highly successful BBC TV series *Absolutely Fabulous*.

She was born in Sleaford, Lincolnshire, and studied at Manchester University and the Central School of Speech and Drama in London. There she met Dawn French, with whom she formed a very successful comedy act. In 1980 they joined the newly formed Comic Strip Club in London and began to appear in cabarets around Britain. With other "alternative" comedians, including Rik Mayall and Adrian Edmondson, they later appeared in the TV series *The Comic Strip Presents…*

In the mid 1980s Saunders and French cowrote and appeared in the TV series *Girls on Top*. They were then given their own TV show, *French and Saunders*, which has enjoyed five successful series. However, Jennifer Saunders's greatest success has been the TV show *Absolutely Fabulous*, in which she caricatured the world of fashion and public relations. The first series won a BAFTA award in 1993 and an Emmy when it was shown in the United States in 1995. The show, which ran for three series, costarred Joanna LUMLEY. Saunders is married to the comedian Adrian Edmondson, and they have three daughters.

Sauvé, Jeanne Benoit (1922–1993) *Canadian politician and journalist*

Jeanne Sauvé became the first woman speaker of the Canadian House of Commons in 1972 and the first woman governor-general of Canada in 1984. She was an outspoken champion of women's rights.

Born in Prud'homme, western Canada, Jeanne Benoit grew up in Ottawa. She was educated at universities in Ottawa and Paris and became president of the Jeunesse Étudiante Catholique (Young Catholic Students), a reformist group, from 1942 to 1947. In 1948 she married Maurice Sauvé, an economist who later became a member of Parliament and minister of forestry. She then spent several years in France, receiving a diploma in French civilization from the University of Paris in 1951 and working briefly as an assistant to the director of the youth section of UNESCO. In 1952 she joined the Canadian Broadcasting Corporation and began a 20-year career as a journalist and commentator. During this time she held various posts, including vice president of the Canadian Institute of Public Affairs (1962–64) and director of Bushnell Communications (1969–72).

Elected as a Liberal to the Canadian House of Commons in 1972, she served successively as minister for science and technology, minister for the environment, and minister of communications. While speaker of the House, she reformed its corruption-ridden administration. Nominated by Prime Minister Pierre Trudeau to be Canada's 23rd governor-general, she took office in 1984 and served until January 1990.

Sayers, Dorothy L(eigh) (1893–1957) *British writer*

> There is perhaps one human being in a thousand who is passionately interested in his job for the job's sake. The difference is that if that one person in a thousand is a man, we say, simply, that he is passionately keen on his job; if she is a woman, we say she is a freak.
>
> —*Gaudy Night* (1935)

> The keeping of an idle woman is a badge of superior social status.
>
> —Essay, 1957

Best known for her detective stories featuring the elegant, sophisticated, and erudite sleuth Lord Peter Wimsey, Dorothy L. Sayers also wrote religious works and an uncompleted translation of Dante's *Divine Comedy* (*Inferno*, 1949; *Purgatorio*, 1955).

Born in Oxford, Sayers studied at Somerville College there and in 1915 became one of the first women to be awarded a full degree from Oxford University. She taught briefly and then joined a London advertising agency as copywriter, producing witty slogans for such companies as Guinness. Her first detective novel, *Whose Body?* (1923), introduced Wimsey, a character modelled on an Oxford don whom she knew. Wimsey subsequently appeared in such stories as *Unnatural Death* (1927), *Strong Poison* (1930), *The Nine Tailors* (1934), and *Gaudy Night* (1935). In 1933, after she had left the agency, Sayers published the mystery *Murder Must Advertise*, which is set in an advertising company.

Sayers's other works include the verse drama *The Zeal of Thy House* (1937) and the religious plays *The Devil to Pay* (1939) and *Just Vengeance* (1946). The radio play *The Man Born to Be King* (1941) was considered controversial in its day for its treatment of the life of Jesus. A devout Roman Catholic, she also published several collections of theological essays, among them *Creed or Chaos?* (1940) and *The Mind of the Maker* (1941).

Scharrer, Berta (1906–1995) *German-born American physiologist*

Berta Scharrer is known for her extensive work on neurosecretion, the ability of certain nerve cells to function as glands and secrete hormones.

Born Berta Vogel in Munich, the daughter of Karl and Johanna Vogel, she studied at the University of Munich, where she subsequently worked as a research associate at the Research Institute of Psychiatry (1931–34). She married her fellow student Ernst Albert Scharrer in 1934, thus beginning a professional and personal relationship that lasted until his death. From 1934 until 1937 she worked at the University of Frankfurt Neurological Institute.

Since employment prospects were poor in Germany, the Scharrers moved to the United States in 1937. Berta worked first at the University of Chicago (1937–38) and then at the Rockefeller Institute, New York (1938–40). In 1940 she became an instructor and fellow of the Western Reserve University in Cleveland, Ohio, where her husband also worked. She then became a Guggenheim Fellow and later an assistant professor at the

University of Colorado (1947–55) and professor of anatomy at the Albert Einstein College of Medicine in New York (1955–77). She was elected a member of the U.S. National Academy of Sciences in 1978.

Berta and Ernst Scharrer's work on neurosecretion was of fundamental importance. Neurosecretory cells are found in the brain and other parts of the nervous system. As well as sending out nerve impulses, they secrete hormones, such as epinephrine, directly into the bloodstream. After Ernst's death in 1965, Berta continued to widen the boundaries of knowledge in this field. She died in New York.

Schiaparelli, Elsa (1890–1973) *Italian-born French fashion designer*

> So fashion is born by small facts, trends, or even politics, never by trying to make little pleats and furbelows, by trinkets, by clothes easy to copy, or by the shortening or lengthening of a skirt.
>
> —*Shocking Life* (1954)

Elsa Schiaparelli's designs always startled with some distinctive feature that rapidly became the height of fashion. Her "shocking pink" introduced a new note into fashion's colour spectrum, and her shoulder pads altered women's silhouettes in the early 1930s. Famous for her international influence on women's fashions, she was also noted for her button and jewellery designs and her perfume (called "Shocking").

Born in Rome, the daughter of a professor, she studied philosophy but had no formal design training. After working in New York as a translator and scriptwriter, she moved to Paris in 1920. There she began designing sweaters after one she had created for herself was much admired. In 1927 she set up a workshop on the Boulevard St. Germain, employing Armenian women as knitters, and a year later she opened a retail shop. Having quickly established herself in haute couture with designs for town suits and evening dresses, she moved to a showroom on the Rue de la Paix in 1929 and then to a grand salon on the Place Vendôme in 1935. She became a French citizen in 1931.

After spending World War II lecturing in the United States, Schiaparelli re-opened her Place Vendôme salon in 1945, establishing a branch in New York in 1949 to mass-produce her clothes. Always ready to try out something new and adventurous in her creations, which some have called exotic and even surrealist, she was the first couturier to use both the zip fastener and synthetic fabrics. She ended the reign of the cloche hat of the 1920s by sticking a sock sideways on her head and calling it a hat. Schiaparelli told the story of her career in her book *Shocking Life*, published in 1954.

Schreiner, Olive (1855–1920) *South African writer and political activist*

> But this one thought stands, never goes – if I might but be one of those born in the future; then perhaps, to be born a woman will not be to be born branded.
>
> —*The Story of an African Farm* (1883)

> We have always borne part of the weight of war, and the major part... Men have made boomerangs, bows, swords, or guns with which to destroy one another; we have made the men who destroyed and were destroyed!...*We pay the first cost on all human life.*
>
> —*Woman and Labour* (1911)

Widely known for her militant feminism and her attacks on conventional Christianity, Olive Schreiner set out her ideas most clearly in her first book, *The Story of an African Farm*, which was published in Britain in 1883 under the pen name Ralph Iron.

Schreiner was born in Wittebergen Reserve, Cape Colony (now part of South Africa), where her father was a Lutheran missionary. She was largely self-educated, developing a love of nature and a free spirit. She was employed for a time as a governess and began writing *The Story of an African Farm*, but finding no publisher for it in Africa, she travelled to Britain in 1881 to try her luck there. While in England she made friends with progressive intellectuals, including the psychologist Havelock Ellis.

Back in Africa she married Samuel Cronwright, a politician, in 1894. A second novel, *Trooper Peter Halket of Mashonaland* (1897), was widely criticized for its negative portrayal of Rhodesian settlers. Over the next ten years Schreiner and her husband campaigned together for racial justice, suffrage, and the Boer cause; they were interned for a while during the Boer War (1899–1902). Her brother William Philip Schreiner had by this time become prime minister of Cape Colony. Her own political views, especially concerning the place of women in society, are expressed in *Woman and Labour* (1911). An unfinished novel, on which she had worked intermittently for many years, was published after her death as *From Man to Man* in 1926, as was another earlier work, *Ondine*.

Schumann, Clara (1819–1896) *German pianist, teacher, and composer*

> I once thought that I possessed creative talent, but I have given up this idea; a woman must not desire to compose – not one has been able to do it, and why should I expect to? It would be arrogance, though indeed, my father led me into it in earlier days.
>
> —Diary entry, November 1839

> There is nothing greater than the joy of composing something oneself, and then listening to it. There are some pretty passages in the trio, and I think it is fairly successful as far as form goes...Of course, it is only a woman's work, which is always lacking in force, and here and there in inventions.
>
> —Diary entry, October 1846

The wife of the composer Robert Schumann, Clara Schumann became one of the leading concert pianists of the 19th century. A child prodigy, she was renowned throughout Europe by the time she was 16. She was also highly regarded as a teacher.

Born in Leipzig, the daughter of the composer and teacher Frederick Wieck, Clara studied piano with her father and made her debut at the age of nine. In 1831–32, accompanied by her father, she made her first concert tour throughout the musical centres of Germany and France.

Clara had known Robert Schumann since her childhood, when he had been a pupil of her father's. Despite strong opposition from her father, the couple married in 1840; they had eight children. For 16 years, until Schumann's death in 1856, she shared his struggles and successes while also continuing to perform and tour herself. After his death she pursued her public career alone. She did much to further recognition of her husband's genius, as well as that of their friend Johannes Brahms, by performing their works whenever she could.

Clara Schumann's own most notable compositions are a piano concerto (1836) and a piano trio (1847). She also wrote many songs but ceased to compose at all after 1853. With Brahms's assistance she published the first complete edition of her husband's works (1881–93) and also edited his correspondence, which was published in 1885. For many years she taught both privately and, during the 1840s, at the Leipzig Conservatory. She was appointed principal piano teacher at the conservatory in Frankfurt am Main in 1878, a post she held for some years.

Schumann, Elisabeth (1888–1952) *German-born American singer*

One of the leading sopranos of her day, Elisabeth Schumann was highly regarded for her interpretations of the operas of Mozart and Richard Strauss and of the lieder of Strauss, Schubert, and Hugo Wolf.

She was born in Merseburg, and made her opera debut with the Hamburg Opera in 1910. In 1919 she was engaged by the Vienna State Opera at the insistence of Richard Strauss, who had just become the company's conductor. She remained with the company for 23 years. Meanwhile, she sang in most of the world's leading opera houses, making her New York City debut at the Metropolitan in 1914 as Sophie in Strauss's *Der Rosenkavalier*. She appeared frequently at Covent Garden in London until 1931 and sang regularly at the Salzburg Fes-

tivals from 1922 until 1935. Her appearances in Mozart's *The Marriage of Figaro, Così fan tutte*, and *Don Giovanni* brought widespread acclaim for her acting as well as her singing. She also made a number of concert tours in which she performed Strauss songs with the composer accompanying her.

In 1938, after the Nazi takeover of Austria, Elisabeth Schumann moved to the United States and in 1944 she became an American citizen. She taught at the Curtis Institute of Music, Philadelphia, from 1938 until her death and published a book, *German Song*, in 1948.

Schwarzkopf, Dame Elisabeth (1915–) *German-born singer of dual Austrian–British nationality*

Highly acclaimed for her soprano roles in the operas of Mozart and Richard Strauss, Elisabeth Schwarzkopf was especially noted as the Marschallin in Strauss's *Der Rosenkavalier*. She also excelled in the interpretation of lieder.

Olga Maria Elisabeth Friederike Schwarzkopf was born in Jarotschin, which is now in Poland, the daughter of a classics teacher. She studied singing in Berlin and made her opera debut in 1938 at the Berlin City Opera as one of the Flower Maidens in *Parsifal*. She went on to sing Zerbinetta in Richard Strauss's *Ariadne auf Naxos* in 1942, after which she joined the Vienna State Opera.

In the years after World War II Schwarzkopf gained international fame, becoming principal singer with the Vienna State Opera. She made her London debut with that company at Covent Garden in 1947, singing Donna Elvira in Mozart's *Don Giovanni* and Marzelline in Beethoven's *Fidelio*. Following this triumph, she sang with the Covent Garden opera company until 1951. She performed regularly at the Salzburg Festival (1947–64) and at La Scala, Milan (1948–63), and sang the role of Eva in the performance of Wagner's *Die Meistersinger* that inaugurated the postwar Bayreuth Festivals in 1951. That same year she created the role of Anne Trulove in Stravinsky's *The Rake's Progress* in Venice. She gave her first American performance, a recital at Carnegie Hall, in 1953, making her operatic debut with the San Francisco Opera in 1955. She sang with the Metropolitan Opera, New York, from 1964 until 1966.

Although she retired from opera in 1972, Schwarzkopf continued to sing lieder until 1975, when she made a farewell recital tour of the United States. She also made many superb recordings, notably with her husband Walter Legge, the artistic director of EMI Records, whom she married in 1953. After his death in 1979 she published *Walter Legge: On and Off the Record* (1982), a memoir. Her master classes at the Juilliard School in the United States and on British television were widely praised. She was created a DBE in 1991 and now lives mainly in Switzerland.

Schygulla, Hanna (1943–) *German actress*

Hanna Schygulla is most often associated with the German director Rainer Werner Fassbinder, with whom she made almost 20 films.

Schygulla was born in Katowice, Poland, and grew up in Munich. She broke off her studies at Munich University in the late 1960s when she became increasingly involved with the avant-garde Action Theatre group. She made her film debut in Straub's *Der Bräutigan, die Komödiantin, und der Zuhälter* (*The Bridegroom, the Comedienne, and the Pimp*) in 1968. Between 1969 and 1972 she appeared in some 24 films, TV shows, and stage plays, about half of which were directed by Fassbinder. She was often cast in the role of the girlfriend, first supporting and then opposing the ambitious male lead.

In 1972 Schygulla stopped acting in order to resume her university studies but broke these off again in order to appear in the Fassbinder film *Effi Briest* (1974). She then hitchhiked through the United States and worked in children's theatre in Germany before returning to the screen in Wim Wenders's *Falsch Bewegung* (1974; *False Move*) and Vojtech Jasny's *Ansichten eines Clowns* (1975; *Clowns*).

This was followed by her brilliant performance in the title role of *Die Ehe der Maria Braun* (1978; *The Marriage of Maria Braun*), Fassbinder's most commercially successful film. In this and her later films Schygulla portrays independent, intelligent, yet sensitive career women.

By the time of Fassbinder's death in 1982 Schygulla had established herself as an international star, playing leading roles in a number of commercially successful films. A woman with considerable physical presence on screen, which derives mainly from her subtly expressive face, she has retained her distanced acting style and is regarded as the mistress of "exaggerated understatement."

Scott Brown, Denise (1931–) *Zambian-born American architect*

Denise Scott Brown has established an international reputation with her work in architecture and urban design.

Born Denise Lakofski in Nkana, Zambia, she went to school and college in Johannesburg, before training at the Architectural Association School in London, and the University of Pennsylvania, Philadelphia, where she taught from 1960 to 1965. She married Robert Scott Brown in 1955, but he died in 1959.

During her time at the Fine Arts School at Pennsylvania there was much conflict between the architects and the planners over civic design. Scott Brown herself took a middle position. Her understanding of the need for architects to heed social reality has influenced the planning and design of the work that she has since undertaken with the architect Robert Venturi. With Venturi, her business associate and second husband, she set up an internationally famous firm in 1967.

Scott Brown has been involved with over 25 urban planning schemes in the United States. With her husband she has also designed the extensions for the Seattle Art Museum (1981) and the National Gallery (1991) in London. A visiting professor at several universities, she has received many honorary degrees and awards and served on various advisory committees in the

United States. She has also designed furniture, fabrics, and household furnishings for international companies, such as the Fabric Workshop in Philadelphia, Alessi International in Milan, the Formica Corporation in New York, and Kroll International.

Her publications with her husband include *A View from the Campidiglio; Selected Essays 1953–84* and *Urban Concepts* (1990).

Scotto, Renata (*c.*1934–) *Italian opera singer*

A soprano, Renata Scotto sang all over Europe and was particularly acclaimed in the operas of Verdi and Puccini.

Born in Savona, she studied singing in Milan with Ghirardini and Clopart; after winning a vocal competition, she made her formal operatic debut as Violetta in *La Traviata* at the Teatro Nazionale, Milan, in 1953. She then joined La Scala company in Milan, with which she sang secondary roles until she was called on to substitute for Maria CALLAS in *La Sonambula* at the 1957 Edinburgh Festival. This launched her international career.

Scotto made her New York debut at the Metropolitan Opera in 1965, triumphing as Madame Butterfly. Her portrayal of Mimi in *La Bohème* in a 1977 "Live from Lincoln Center" television broadcast was another great success, earning her star status on the American opera scene. Her presence in televised opera was considered particularly powerful, and she recorded a long list of complete roles. Her book *Scotto: More than a Diva*, written with Octavio Roca, was published in 1984.

Scudéry, Madeleine de (1607–1701) *French novelist and poet*

> I would, without a doubt, rather be a simple soldier than be a woman, because, to be truthful, a soldier can become king but a woman can never become free.
>
> —*Clelia, An Excellent New Romance* (1654–60)
>
> In losing a husband one loses a master who is often an obstacle to the enjoyment of many things.
>
> —As above

Madeleine de Scudéry is best known for her ten-volume novel *Clelia, An Excellent New Romance* (1654–60) and for the literary salon that she opened in 1652. Molière satirized Scudéry and her salon, which was associated with the cult of *préciosité* – excessive refinement in manners and expression – in his play *Les Précieuses ridicules* (1659; The Affected Ladies).

Born in Le Havre, she joined her brother Georges in Paris in 1638. There she assisted him in his literary work and they began writing novels together, which he published under his name. Mlle. de Scudéry also became a frequenter of the famous salon of the Marquise de RAMBOUILLET, from which she drew much of the material she used in her romances. When this salon ended, Mlle. de Scudéry established her own, the Société du Samedi (so-named because it met on Saturdays).

Apart from *Clelia*, Mlle. de Scudéry's best-known novels are the ten-volume *Artamène, ou le Grand Cyrus*, (1649–53; Artamène, or Cyrus the Great) and *Amalida, ou l'esclave riche* (1660–63; Amalida, or the Wealthy Slave). In *Le Grand Cyrus* the hero, Artamène, was based on the outstanding French general of the day, the Prince de Condé, and in volume ten she introduced herself under the name "Sappho."

Seacole, Mary (1805–1881) *Jamaican nurse and war heroine*

Mary Seacole is best known for her heroic efforts to nurse wounded British soldiers during the Crimean War.

She was born Mary Jane Grant in Kingston, Jamaica, the daughter of a Scottish army officer and a black woman. Her mother, who ran a boarding house, taught her Creole medicine and hotel keeping, and she ran the boarding house after her mother's death. She was well educated and paid two visits to England, where she met and married Edwin Horatio Seacole. After his death in 1836 she returned to Jamaica, where she rebuilt her boarding house following its destruction by fire. After gaining valuable nursing experience during the cholera and yellow fever epidemics that swept the island at this time, she spent the next few years travelling in Colombia and Panama, where she did some nursing and gold prospecting, as well as setting up two hotels.

Following the outbreak of the Crimean War in 1854, Seacole went to England to volunteer her services as a nurse to the British Army. It seems that she was turned down on account of her colour. Undaunted, she travelled to the Crimea at her own expense, attempting to recoup her losses by setting up as a sutler (a merchant selling provisions to the soldiers) and establishing the British Hotel for both officers and soldiers at Spring Hill, near Balaclava. From this base she nursed the wounded on the battlefield, often under fire, and became known as "Mother" or "Aunty" Seacole.

The end of the war in 1856 found Mother Seacole out of work and in debt. But her popularity was such that *The Times*, *Punch*, and *The Illustrated News* raised funds by public subscription to help her out of bankruptcy. Her autobiography, *The Wonderful Adventures of Mrs. Seacole in Many Lands* (1857), was a bestseller. She spent the remainder of her life in London and Jamaica.

Seghers, Anna (1900–1983) *German novelist and writer*

The work of Anna Seghers was inspired by her belief in communism.

Born Netty Reilling in Mainz, the daughter of a Jewish art dealer, she studied art history at the universities of Heidelberg and Cologne. She received her doctorate in 1924 for her thesis on *Aspects of Jews and Jewishness in the Work of Rembrandt*. She married the Communist Laslo Radvanyi in 1925 and joined the Communist Party in 1929. In that same year she published her first novel, *Der Aufstand der Fischer von St. Barbara* (The Insurrection of the Fishermen of St. Barbara) to great critical acclaim; the book also won the coveted Kleist Literary Prize.

After Hitler came to power in 1933, Seghers's writings were banned, and she fled with her two children to France. Following the German invasion of France in 1940, she was forced to flee again, this time to Mexico. During her exile she wrote her best-known novels: *Das siebte Kreuz* (1942; The Seventh Cross), which was later made into a film starring Spencer Tracy, and *Transit* (1944). These established her reputation as a writer of international standing.

After World War II she returned to live in East Germany, where she became president of the Association of German Writers and a respected figure. Her later works show her unwavering support for communism and are regarded as models of socialist realism.

Seles, Monica (1973–) *Yugoslav-born American tennis player*

Monica Seles made tennis history in 1992 when, aged 19, she became the youngest number-one-ranked player in the world.

Born in Novi Sad, Yugoslavia, she was taught to play tennis by her father, who created the unusual double-fisted strokes that have proved to be her greatest weapon. By the age of eight she had won a major European tournament for players aged under 12. Four years later she was named Yugoslavia's Sportswoman of the Year. After playing in a tournament in Florida, she was talent-spotted by the American coach Nick Bollettieri and moved with her family to his tennis academy in Bradenton, Florida. She made her professional breakthrough in 1989 by winning the Virginia Slims tournament in Houston. The following year, despite an injury to her shoulder and her acrimonious departure from Bollettieri's tennis school, she won the Italian, German, and French Open championships as well as the Virginia Slims tournament in New York.

In 1991 she won the Australian, French, and U.S. Open championships but was heavily criticized and penalized for her last-minute decision not to compete at Wimbledon. A year later she again won the Australian, French, and U.S. competitions, which confirmed her standing as the top women's tennis player in the world. In 1993 tragedy struck when she was injured in a knife attack by a deranged fan at a tournament in Hamburg. The traumatic physical and mental effects of this incident meant that she was out of tennis for the next two years.

Seles made an impressive comeback in 1995, when she won every match she played in until she was narrowly defeated by Steffi GRAF in the final of the U.S. Open. She won the Australian Open in 1996 and is still a force to be reckoned with. The hallmark of her play, apart from her devastating double-fisted strokes, is the loud grunting noise that she makes when she hits the ball. She became a U.S. citizen in 1994 and lives in Sarasota, Florida, and Los Angeles, California.

Her talent and outgoing personality have brought Seles lucrative endorsements for a variety of products, making her a wealthy woman. She is a powerful advocate for women's tennis, demanding equal prize money for men and women.

Semiramis (8th century BC) *Assyrian queen*

> Nature gave me the form of a woman; my actions have raised me to the level of the most valiant men.
>
> —Quoted by Frank B. Goodrich in *Women of Beauty and Heroism*

Semiramis, who was called Sammuramat by the Assyrians, was the wife of the Assyrian king Shamshi-Adad V (reigned 823–811 BC) and the mother of Adadnirari III (reigned 810–783 BC). She was queen regent during the minority of her son (810–806 BC), and is credited with having made Babylon into a great city. Her story has been overlaid with myth and legend.

Semiramis seems to have been a Syrian princess; her name, which was originally Shemiramat ("the goddess Shemi is exalted"), is found in Hebrew as Shemiramoth. She occupied a more important place than any other known Assyrian queen, and her dates agree well with the account of her preserved by the Greek historian Herodotus. Her husband's last known triumph was the conquest of Babylonia, a fact that supports Herodotus's statement that she built earthworks at Babylon. Her armies are said to have fought in Armenia and Media. Semiramis was particularly influential during her regency, when she developed and encouraged worship of the god Nabu.

Semiramis appears as a legendary figure in the writings of the Greek historian Ctesias (about 400 BC), who calls her a daughter of the Aramaean goddess Atargatis (a form of Astarte and Ishtar) and the wife of Ninus, the legendary founder of the Assyrian empire. She herself is supposed to have had a long reign, during which she enlarged the empire enormously. At her death she left her throne to her son Ninyas and was turned into a dove.

Serao, Matilde (1857–1927) *Greek-born Italian novelist and journalist*

A prolific novelist, Matilde Serao was also the founder of several newspapers, both with her husband, Eduardo Scarfoglio, and, after their separation in 1904, alone.

She was born in Patras, Greece, the daughter of an Italian political exile and his Greek wife. Having trained as a teacher at the Scuola Normale in Naples, she began to write articles while working in a telegraph office in the late 1870s. She first attracted attention with a short-story collection, *Novelle*, following this with her first novel, *Cuore infermo* (A Sick Heart), in 1881. In the 1880s she joined a Rome newspaper and contributed to other leading journals. Success came with her romantic novel *Fantasia* (1883; *Fantasy*, 1890) and *Il ventre di Napoli* (1884; The Belly of Naples), a collection of her writings about life in Naples. Her most famous novels are *La virtú di Checchina* (1885; The Virtue of Checchina), *Il paese di cuccagna* (1891; *The Land of Cockayne*, 1901), *La conquista di Roma* (1885; *The Conquest of Rome*, 1902), and *La ballerina* (1899; *The Ballet Dancer*, 1901).

Matilde Serao married Eduardo Scarfoglio in 1885. Together they founded the Rome newspaper *Il Corriere di Roma*, which was short-lived, and then, in Naples, *Il Corriere di Napoli*. After separating from her husband in 1904, she founded the journals

Il Mattino and *Il Giorno*. She continued to write novels, including *Suor Giovanna della Croce* (1901; *Sister Giovanna of the Cross*), and *Ella non rispose* (1914; *Souls Divided*, 1916).

Sévigné, Marquise de (1626–1696)
French letter writer

> There is nothing so lovely as to be beautiful. Beauty is a gift of God and we should cherish it as such.
>
> —*Letters of Madame de Sévigné to Her Daughter and Her Friends* (1696)

> We are transfused into our children, and…feel more keenly for them than for ourselves.
>
> —As above

Madame de Sévigné's witty, eloquent, and often humorous letters to her daughter, first published after her death, earned her a prominent place in French literature. They provide a fascinating commentary on daily life during the glittering reign of Louis XIV.

The daughter of the Baron de Chantal, Marie de Rabutin-Chantal was born in Paris. Orphaned at the age of six, she was raised chiefly by her uncle, Philippe II de Coulanges, at the Abbaye de Livry in Brittany, where she received an excellent education. In 1644 she married the Marquis Henry de Sévigné, who was killed in a duel in 1651, leaving her with a son, Charles, and a daughter, Françoise-Marguerite, whom she adored. The marquise chose not to remarrry and lived in Paris among a close circle of friends that included the writers Madame de LA FAYETTE and La Rochefoucauld. In 1669 her daughter married Comte François de Grignan and accompanied him to Provence, where he had been appointed lieutenant governor. This separation resulted in the voluminous correspondence that made Madame de Sévigné famous.

Most of her 1,700 letters cover the seven-year period following her separation from her daughter in 1671. In later life they were rarely apart. The letters abound in delightful gossip and witty anecdote as well as lively descriptions of the pleasures of Parisian society. In her letters Madame de Sévigné reveals herself in several different guises – a court beauty, the brilliant wit of the salons, a religious devotee, a woman of business endeavouring to meet the demands placed on her income by her extravagant son, an appreciative student of the Latin and French classics – but above all, she appears as a devoted mother.

Sewell, Anna (1820–1878) *British children's writer*

Anna Sewell's only novel is the children's classic *Black Beauty*, which was published in 1877.

Anna Sewell was born in Great Yarmouth, Norfolk, the daughter of Mary Wright Sewell, a writer of educational ballads and verses. After an injury to her ankle in childhood she was virtually an invalid for the rest of her life. She had always loved horses, and after reading an essay pleading for their better treatment, she decided to write a story incorporating the same plea indirectly. The resulting novel, *Black Beauty: The Autobiography of a Horse*, tells of the ill treatment of horses from the animal's point of view.

Black Beauty became popular immediately, was widely translated, and eventually won acclaim as one of the most successful animal stories ever written. It has since been made into several successful films and TV series.

Sexton, Anne (1928–1974) *American poet*

> I was tired of being a woman,
>   tired of the spoons and the pots…
> I was tired of the gender of things.
>
> —*Live or Die* (1966)

Anne Sexton is known for the anguished intensity of her mainly autobiographical poetry.

She was born Anne Harvey in Newton, Massachusetts, and studied at Garland Junior College in Boston. After marrying Alfred M. Sexton in 1948, she became a fashion model and raised two daughters. She discovered poetry as a result of attending a workshop run by Robert Lowell at Boston University. Encouraged by Lowell, the writer W. D. Snodgrass, and her friend Sylvia PLATH, she broke away from the intellectualism and restraint of contemporary American poetry to write about her own life in a raw intense style. This is evident in such poems as "Those Times," which explores her tormented childhood, and "Little Girl, My String Bean," which conveys her joy in having a daughter. Like the poetry of Plath, Sexton's work shows a preoccupation with death and her own recurring mental breakdowns.

During the 1960s and early 1970s she published her poetry in such magazines as *The New Yorker* and in several collections. These include *To Bedlam and Part Way Back* (1960), *All My Pretty Ones* (1962), *Live or Die* (1966), which won the Pulitzer Prize in 1967, *Love Poems* (1969), *Transformations* (1971), *The Book of Folly* (1972), and *O Ye Tongues* (1973). As her reputation grew, she taught at several universities and was in great demand on the American college lecture circuit. She received many awards and honorary degrees for her work.

The Death Notebooks (1974), *The Awful Rowing towards God* (1975), and *45 Mercy Street* (1976) were published after the breakdown of her marriage and her suicide in 1974.

Seymour, Jane (*c.* 1509–1537) *Third wife of King Henry VIII of England*

The mother of Henry VIII's only son, the future King Edward VI Jane Seymour died in childbirth at Hampton Court Palace near London.

Jane Seymour was born at Wolf Hall, the house of her father, Sir John Seymour, in Savernake, Wiltshire. She served as lady-in-waiting to both of Henry's former wives, CATHERINE OF ARAGON and Anne BOLEYN. From the date of Henry's first meeting with Jane Seymour on September 10, 1535, he pursued her with gifts, but Jane discreetly rejected his proposals. Determined to marry Jane, Henry initiated the legal proceedings against Anne, for alleged adultery, that led to her execution. Henry married Jane on May 30, 1536, 11 days after Anne's execution.

Her portrait was painted by the German artist Hans Holbein, the Younger during his time as court painter to Henry.

See also ANNE OF CLEVES; HOWARD, CATHERINE; PARR, CATHERINE.

Shaw, Fiona (Mary) (1958–   ) *Irish-born British actress*

For the past 15 years Shaw has won the plaudits of critics and theatregoers alike in a series of classic stage roles.

Shaw was born Fiona Wilson in Cork, Ireland, the daughter of an ophthalmic surgeon. A gifted amateur musician, she graduated from University College, Cork, with a degree in philosophy before attending the Royal Academy of Dramatic Art in London. She made her theatrical debut in *Love's Labours Lost* in 1982 and immediately became a much sought-after actress, with roles that included Julia in the National Theatre's production of *The Rivals* (1983).

From 1985 Shaw was a member of the Royal Shakespeare Company, with whom she took a series of major roles including Celia in *As You Like It*, Madame des Volonges in *Les Liaisons Dangereuses*, Beatrice in *Much Ado About Nothing*, Portia in *The Merchant of Venice*, and Katharina in *The Taming of the Shrew*. In 1990 she appeared at the Old Vic as Rosalind in *As You Like It* and at the National Theatre as Shen Te/Shui Ta in Brecht's *The Good Person of Setzuan*, for which she received two awards. She also played the title roles in *Electra* (RSC, 1988) and *Hedda Gabler* (Dublin Playhouse, 1991). More controversial was her portrayal of the king in Deborah Warner's 1995 production of *Richard II*. In 1997-98 her one-woman performance of T. S. Eliot's *The Wasteland* found acclaim in both Britain and Australia. Films in which Shaw has appeared include *My Left Foot* (1990), *Super Mario Brothers* (1992), and *Jane Eyre* (1996). She has also published several books, including *Players of Shakespeare* (1987) and *Conversations with Actresses* (1990).

Shearer, Moira (1926–   ) *British ballet dancer and actress*

In the 1940s Moira Shearer danced all the major classical ballet roles at Covent Garden and on American tours. She reached a wider public when she starred in the highly successful Michael Powell and Emeric Pressburger film *The Red Shoes* (1948).

Born Moira Shearer King in Dunfermline, Fife, she attended Dunfermline High School and went on to study ballet at the Mayfair School and the Nicolas Legat Studio. In 1942 she joined London's Sadler's Wells Ballet, dancing her first role in *The Sleeping Beauty* at Covent Garden in 1946.

As a ballet dancer, she toured the United States with the Sadler's Wells Ballet in 1949 and 1950–51. In 1955 she joined the Bristol Old Vic company as an actress, playing many leading roles there and at the London Old Vic, including the title character in George Bernard Shaw's *Major Barbara*. She has also appeared on TV, lectured in America on the history of ballet, and performed regularly with her husband, the writer and broadcaster Sir Ludovic Kennedy.

A regular reviewer for London newspapers, Lady Kennedy also wrote *Balletmaster: A Dancer's View of George Balanchine* (1986).

Shearer, Norma (1900–1983) *Canadian-born American film actress*

Known especially for her roles in Hollywood films adapted from successful stage plays, Norma Shearer was billed by MGM as the "First Lady of the Screen." She won an Oscar for her role in *The Divorcee* (1930) and was nominated a further five times.

Born and raised in Montreal, Shearer settled in the United States in 1919 and became a naturalized citizen in 1931. She worked as a cinema pianist and model before entering films in the early 1920s. Her first memorable role came in the silent film *He Who Gets Slapped* (1924), in which she appeared with Lon Chaney and John Gilbert. Among her first talking pictures was *The Last of Mrs. Chaney* (1929).

In 1928 she married the leading MGM executive Irving Thalberg, and they became Hollywood's golden couple. Her best-known films of that time include *Strangers May Kiss* (1931), *Private Lives* (1931), *Smilin' Through* (1932), *Strange Interlude* (1932), *The Barretts of Wimpole Street* (1934), and *Romeo and Juliet* (1936). However, following Thalberg's sudden death in

1936, major roles became scarcer, and her popularity waned.

Shearer's later films included *Marie Antoinette* (1938), *The Women* (1939), *Idiot's Delight* (1939), and *We Were Dancing* (1942). Having turned down leading roles in *Gone with the Wind* (1939) and *Mrs Miniver* (1942), she retired in 1942 to marry a skiing instructor.

Sheba, Queen of (10th century BC)

According to Jewish and Islamic traditions, the Queen of Sheba (or Saba') ruled over a kingdom in southwestern Arabia.

In the Old Testament account she visited the court of King Solomon in Jerusalem, bearing exotic gifts, and asked him a number of riddles in order to test his legendary wisdom. In the Koran, in which she is known as the sun worshipper Bilqis, she also visited Jerusalem, where Solomon's devils warned him against marrying her by revealing that she had hairy legs and the hooves of an ass. After she was tricked into revealing her hairy legs (she did not have hooves), Solomon ordered his devils to make a depilatory cream for the queen. Islamic tradition disagrees as to whether Bilqis married Solomon or a Hamadani tribesman. Whoever she married, Sheba became a believer in the Jewish God.

The Sheba story also occurs among the Persians, who say that her father was a Chinese king, and among the Ethiopians, who believe that after marrying Solomon, she produced a son who founded the royal dynasty of Ethiopia.

Shelley, Mary (Wollstonecraft Godwin) (1797–1851) *British writer*

> Mrs. Shelley is very clever, indeed it would be difficult for her not to be so; the daughter of Mary Wollstonecraft and Godwin, and the wife of Shelley, could be no common person.
>
> —Lord Byron, quoted by the Countess of Blessington in *A Journal of Conversations with Lord Byron* (1832)

Mary Shelley is best known for her famous horror novel *Frankenstein or, the Modern Prometheus*. It first appeared in 1818, creating an immediate sensation.

She was born in London, the daughter of the philosopher William Godwin and Mary WOLLSTONECRAFT, the author of *A Vindication of the Rights of Woman*, who died a few weeks after her daughter's birth. In 1814 Mary eloped to Switzerland with the poet Percy Bysshe Shelley, whom she married after the death of his first wife Harriet in 1816. She wrote *Frankenstein* while staying near Geneva with her husband and Lord Byron, following Byron's suggestion that they each write a ghost story.

In 1818 the Shelleys went to live in Italy. Following the deaths of two of their children and Shelley's death from drowning off Lerici in 1822, Mary devoted herself to literary work, producing such novels as *Valperga* (1923), *The Last Man* (1826), *Lodore* (1835), and *Falker* (1837) in order to support her last surviving child, Percy. *Lodore* and *Falker* are both fictional defences of Shelley against his critics.

Her other works include *Journal of a Six Weeks' Tour* (1817), written with Shelley, and *Rambles in Germany and Italy* (1844). She also published editions of Shelley's poetry and miscellaneous writings (1839, 1840, 1847) and began a biography of him that remained unfinished at the time of her death.

Sherman, Cindy (1954–) *American photographer*

Cindy Sherman found international fame with her first solo exhibition, *Untitled Film Stills (1977–1980)*, at Metro Pictures in New York in 1980. Featuring herself in a variety of costumes and poses, her photographs recycle imagery from the mass media to comment on the representation of women in the 20th century.

The youngest of five children, Cynthia Morris Sherman was born in Glen Ridge, New Jersey, and grew up in suburban Huntington Beach, Long Island. Artistically inclined from an early age, she grew up with television and enjoyed dressing up in old clothes. She attended the State University of New York College at Buffalo, where she studied art, receiving her BA in 1976. She learned about pop, performance, video, and multimedia art through the work of New York artists who exhibited in Buffalo. Her work at this time shows a grasp of contemporary art theory and a fascination with pop culture, film noir, and trashy novels.

In 1976 Sherman moved to New York City, where she worked in black-and-white photography until she completed her *Untitled Film Stills* series in 1980. After this she began to work in colour, often photographing herself in front of projected backgrounds designed to evoke the lurid hues of Technicolor. In the mid 1980s she expanded her cast of characters to include increasingly bizarre creatures from her own imagination. Originally conceived for an assignment for *Vanity Fair* magazine (which ultimately fell through), these life-size images were darker and more mythical than anything she had done before. Aided by prosthetic body parts, Sherman photographed herself as scarred, disfigured, and even dead. In 1989 and 1990 she posed herself in a series of photographs designed to imitate classic works in the history of Western portraiture.

In the mid 1990s she returned to her earlier investigation of sexuality and the grotesque by arranging plastic and rubber body parts in a series of explicit poses and photographing them. Sherman, who has shown extensively in both the United States and abroad, was awarded a Guggenheim grant in 1983. She was the subject of a major retrospective exhibition at the Whitney Museum of American Art in New York in 1987.

Shields, Carol (Ann) (1935–) *American-born Canadian novelist, writer, and academic*

The fiction of Carol Shields combines wit, humanity, and great formal skill: since the early 1990s she has been internationally recognized as one of Canada's finest living writers.

Carol Warner was born in the United States at Oak Park, a prosperous suburb of Chicago, and educated at Hanover College. In 1957 she married Donald Shields, a Canadian, and moved with him to Vancouver, then Toronto. After several years raising their children (she has a son and four daughters), Carol Shields resumed her education at the University of Ottawa, where she gained an MA in Canadian literature and became a lecturer in 1976. She moved to the University of British Columbia in 1978 and in 1980 took up a professorship at the University of Manitoba in Winnipeg. Now a full-time writer, she divides her time between Manitoba and France.

Shields's earlier novels, which include *Small Ceremonies* (1976), and *A Fairly Conventional Woman* (1982), are realistic stories of marriage and family life, full of quirky humour. Her original approach to narrative became more evident in the twinned novellas published as *Happenstance* (1980) and the short-story collections *Various Miracles* (1985) and *The Orange Fish* (1987). Shields's international breakthrough came with her fifth novel *The Republic of Love* (1992), a poignant witty love story that won the Governor-General's Award for Fiction in Canada and delighted the critics when it was published in Britain and the United States. Still greater acclaim followed for *The Stone Diaries* (1995), a fictional biography that recounts the extraordinary life of an "ordinary" Canadian woman, complete with family trees, letters, and photographs: the novel was shortlisted for the Booker Prize and earned a Pulitzer Prize in America. Her most recent novel is *Larry's Party* (1996), a book about a garden designer that shows her ability to write from a male point of view. Shields has also published several collections of poetry and the mystery story *Mary Swann* (1987).

Shore, Dinah (1917–1994) *American singer*

> I earn and pay my own way as a great many women do today. Why should unmarried women be discriminated against? Unmarried men are not.
>
> —Quoted in *The Los Angeles Times*, April 16, 1974

Dinah Shore was one of America's best-known entertainers of the 1940s and 1950s.

Born Frances Rose Shore in Winchester, Tennessee, she made her singing debut on Nashville radio while she was still at school. She then moved to New York, where she made more broadcasts and appeared on stage. Although she was rejected by the Big Band leaders Benny Goodman and Tommy Dorsey, she was one of the first singers to become a star in her own right. She made her solo recording debut in 1939 and went on to make records with Ben Bernie and Xaviar Cugat in the early 1940s.

Under the name Dinah Shaw she had success with such songs as "The Breeze and I" and "Whatever Happened to You." Her low smoky voice was well suited to ballads, and she had over 80 hits between 1940 and 1957, including "Yes, My Darling Daughter," "All That Glitters Is Not Gold," "Doin' What Comes Natur'lly," "I'll Walk Alone," "The Gypsy," "Anniversary Song," and "Buttons and Bows."

Shore made a number of films, including *Thank Your Lucky Stars* (1943), *Up in Arms* (1944), *Follow the Boys* (1944), *Belle of the Yukon* (1945), *Till the Clouds Roll By* (1946), *Oh God!* (1977), and, *H.E.A.L.T.H.* (1979). From the early 1950s she appeared regularly on television, and from the 1970s she became a chat-show host; in all, she won ten Emmy Awards for her TV work. She continued to perform on the stage and to appear on television until 1991. She died in Los Angeles, California.

Shore, Jane (c. 1445–1527) *Mistress of King Edward IV of England*

Known for her beauty, charm, and wit, Jane Shore is believed to have had a beneficial influence over the king.

Born in London, she was married at an early age to the goldsmith William Shore. In 1470, after Edward IV's return from France, she became his mistress, living in luxury until his death in 1483. She then became the mistress of Thomas Grey, Marquis of Dorset, the son of Edward's widow ELIZABETH Woodville. She also later became the mistress of William, Lord Hastings, who had been Edward's chamberlain and friend.

After Edward's death a struggle for power took place between the Woodvilles and their supporters (who included Hastings) and the king's brother Richard, Duke of Gloucester, who eventually became king as Richard III. Suspecting a conspiracy, Richard had Hastings executed and arrested Jane Shore, accusing her of practising witchcraft against the king. Failing to secure a conviction, he then directed her to be tried for adultery by the Bishop of London's court, which condemned her to do public penance dressed only in a petticoat at St. Paul's. She later died in poverty.

Jane Shore's story is treated sympathetically in Sir Thomas More's *History of King Richard III*, Shakespeare's *Richard III*, *The Tragedy of Jane Shore* (1713) by Nicholas Rowe, and in many old English ballads.

Sibley, Dame Antoinette (1939–)
British ballet dancer

Noted for her grace and beauty, Antoinette Sibley was the prima ballerina of the Royal Ballet in the 1960s and 1970s.

Born in Bromley, Kent, she was educated at the Arts Educational School and trained at the Royal Ballet School in London. In January 1956, while still a student at the Royal Ballet School, Sibley gave her first performance on stage for the Royal Ballet – as a swan in *Swan Lake*. She joined the company in July of that year.

Sibley went on to dance the leading roles in all the major classical ballets, including *Swan Lake*, *Sleeping Beauty*, *Coppelia*, and *The Nutcracker*. Among her greatest performances were those in the title role of Kenneth MacMillan's *Manon* and as Titania in Frederick Ashton's *The Dream* – both roles that she created. She was particularly noted for her dancing partnership with Anthony Dowell, who became director of the Royal Ballet in 1986.

An injury to her knee forced Sibley to retire from dancing in 1976, but she made a comeback in 1981. She was appointed vice president of London's Royal Academy of Dancing in 1989 and has been the academy's president since 1991. She is also a guest coach at the Royal Ballet. Sibley was created a DBE in 1996.

Siddons, Sarah (1755–1831) *British actress*

> I have often observed, that I have performed worst when I most ardently wished to do better than ever.
>
> —Letter to Rev. Whalley, July 16, 1781

> She was the stateliest ornament of the public mind.
>
> —William Hazlitt, *The Examiner*, June 16, 1816

Sarah Siddons was hailed by her contemporaries, including the writers William Hazlitt and Leigh Hunt, as the leading tragic actress of her day. Extremely beautiful and dignified, she had a rich, resonant voice and excelled in such Shakespearean roles as Volumnia in *Coriolanus* and Lady Macbeth.

Born Sarah Kemble at Brecon in Wales, she was the eldest of 12 children of Roger Kemble, the actor-manager of a travelling theatrical company. She was the sister of the actors John Philip, Stephen, and Charles Kemble and the aunt of Frances KEMBLE. She spent her childhood in her father's company and at the age of 18, despite her parents' opposition, married William Siddons, also a member of the troupe. In 1775 David Garrick engaged her to play a part in his company's production of *The Merchant of Venice* at Drury Lane. After appearing there briefly without success, she returned to the provincial theatres, where she soon began to display the dramatic power for which she later became famous. Recalled to Drury Lane by its new manager, Richard Brinsley Sheridan, in 1782, she won acclaim as Isabella in Thomas Southerne's tragedy *The Fatal Marriage*.

In 1783, the year she played her first tragic Shakespearean roles in London, Siddons was appointed as the elocution teacher to the royal children. In 1802 she and her brother John Philip Kemble took over Covent Garden, where she appeared regularly for the next decade. She made her formal farewell to the stage in 1812, playing the role in which she was said to be perfect – that of Lady Macbeth. After this she made a number of private appearances, her last being a performance as Lady Randolph in John Home's tragedy *Douglas* on June 9, 1819. Amongst the many portraits of her by famous painters, perhaps the best known is *The Tragic Muse* by Sir Joshua Reynolds. There is a statue of her in Westminster Abbey.

Signoret, Simone (1921–1985) *French actress*

Sometimes described as having the "saddest face in French cinema," Simone Signoret is probably best known for her Oscar-winning performance as an alcoholic in *Room at the Top* (1958).

Born Simone Henriette Charlotte Kaminker in Wiesbaden, Germany, the daughter of a French army officer, she was raised in Paris. During the German occupation of France her father, a Jew, fled to Britain; the rest of the family remained in Paris, where Simone worked as a typist and a tutor in English and Latin to support her mother and two brothers. She also began to play bit parts on the French stage and screen.

One of her first important film roles was in *Macadam* (1946), which earned her the Prix Suzanne Bianchetti in 1947. She then starred in such notable films as *Thérèse Raquin* (1953), *La Ronde* (1954), and *Diabolique* (1955). In *The Witches of Salem* (1958), an adaptation of Arthur Miller's *The Crucible*, she starred with Yves Montand, who had become her second husband in 1951.

Signoret's later films include *Ship of Fools* (1965), which brought her another Oscar nomination; *The Sleeping Car Murders* (1966), in which she again starred with Montand; and *The Seagull* (1968), *Le Chat* (1971), and *Madame Rosa* (1977). Her last film was *I Sent a Letter to My Love* (1981). She published a volume of memoirs, *Nostalgia Isn't What It Used to Be* (1978), and the novel *Adieu, Volodia* (1985).

Sills, Beverly (1929–) *American opera singer and arts administrator*

> My singing is very therapeutic. For three hours I have no troubles – I know how it's going to come out.
>
> —Interviewed on CBS-TV

> I would willingly give up my whole career if I could have just one normal child.
>
> —Quoted by Winthrop Sargeant in *Divas: Impressions of Six Opera Superstars*

Regarded by many as one of the greatest sopranos of the 1960s and 1970s, Beverly Sills was also the director of the New York City Opera (NYCO) from 1979 to 1989. In 1994 she was elected chairwoman of the Lincoln Center in New York, the first woman to hold that post.

She was born Belle Miriam Silverman in Brooklyn, New York. A child prodigy, she sang on the radio at the age of three, and at 11 she began vocal studies with Estelle Liebling, who remained her only teacher. She made her opera debut at 17 with the Philadelphia Civic Opera, as Frasquita in *Carmen*. She then toured with the Charles Wagner Opera Company before making her debut with the San Francisco Opera in 1953.

Sills joined the NYCO in 1955, creating the title role in Douglas Moore's *The Ballad of Baby Doe* in 1956. That same year she married Peter Bulkeley Greenough. After the births of their two children, one of whom was born deaf and the other mentally handicapped, she was obliged to take a two-year break from her career. Although she returned to the stage in 1963, it was not until 1966, when she sang the role of Cleopatra in Handel's *Julius Caesar*, that she became a star. After this she sang in the major European opera houses in such roles as Manon, Lucia di Lammermoor, Norma, Queen Elizabeth in Donizetti's *Roberto Devereux*, and the four women in *The Tales of Hoffman*. She made her debut at La Scala, Milan, in Rossini's *The Siege of Corinth* in 1969 and at the Metropolitan Opera in New York City in 1975. Meanwhile, she remained a member of the NYCO. On July 1,

1979, she became general director of the NYCO, giving her farewell performances as a singer the following year. During her service as director of the NYCO Sills promoted American musicians and broadened the company's repertoire.

Sills also produced television programmes about opera and concert singing. She was the author of two books: *Bubbles: A Self-Portrait* (1976; revised as *Bubbles: An Encore* in 1981) and *Beverly: An Autobiography* (1987). She received an honorary doctorate from Harvard University in 1971 and the U.S. Presidential Medal of Freedom in 1980. In 1991 she became chairwoman of the New York advisory board of the Enterprise Foundation, an organization working with community groups, government, and corporations to renovate disused properties for the homeless.

Simmons, Jean (1929–) *British-born American actress*

Jean Simmons has appeared successfully in over 50 films but narrowly failed to become a Hollywood superstar.

Born in London, she trained at the Ada Foster School of Dancing and made her film debut at the age of 15 in *Give Us the Moon* (1944). By 1945 she was under contract to British film mogul J. Arthur Rank, and a year later she gave an impressive performance as the young Estella in David Lean's highly acclaimed film of Dickens's *Great Expectations*. In 1948 she was awarded the prize for Best Actress at the Venice Film Festival for her performance as Ophelia in Laurence Olivier's *Hamlet*. Her stage debut came in 1949.

After marrying the actor Stewart Granger in 1950, Simmons emigrated to the United States, becoming a U.S. citizen in 1956. In 1951–52 she was under contract to Howard Hughes at RKO. Simmons gave what was probably her best screen performance in *Elmer Gantry* (1960), the story of a corrupt evangelist. The same year she divorced Granger to marry the film's director Richard Brooks. Their marriage lasted until 1977.

Simmons made her American stage debut in 1964. Although she received an Oscar nomination for her performance in *The Happy Ending* (1969), by the 1970s her career had refocused on television miniseries. In 1983 she received an Emmy Award for her performance in *The Thornbirds* (1982), and in 1989 she played Miss Havisham (Estella's elderly guardian) in a TV version of *Great Expectations*. She has also appeared in such TV films as *People Like Us* (1990).

Simone, Nina (1933–) *American singer*

One of America's leading jazz singers, Nina Simone is known for her many protest songs. Like many African Americans she was inspired by Marian ANDERSON.

Born Eunice Kathleen Waymon in Tryon, North Carolina, she adopted the stage name Nina Simone in 1954. A gifted pianist, she trained at the Juilliard School for a year before beginning a career singing in nightclubs. Fame came in 1959 with her melodramatic version of Gershwin's "I Loves You, Porgy," and during the 1960s she toured extensively throughout the United States and Europe. Increasingly her repertoire turned from commercial material to political protest songs, such as "To Be Young, Gifted and Black," "Blacklash Blues," and "Mississippi Goddam."

In the 1970s Simone left the United States following a series of bitter disputes with agents, recording companies, and the tax authorities. After a period living in Africa, she eventually settled in the south of France but returned to the United States in 1993 to promote her album *A Woman Alone*. Her autobiography *I Put a Spell on You* was published in 1992.

Sinclair, May (1863–1946) *British writer*

In her novels May Sinclair was a pioneer of the "stream of consciousness" technique, in which the writer attempts to reproduce the disjointed flow of thoughts and sensations through the minds of her characters.

Born in Cheshire, Mary Amelia St. Clair Sinclair was the daughter of a shipowner who went bankrupt and subsequently became an alcoholic. Following the separation of her parents, she lived in London with her mother, a very dominating woman. Apart from one year at Cheltenham Ladies' College, May was educated at home, where she read very widely and developed a particular interest in philosophy. She also began to write, publishing a volume of poetry in 1887 and her first novel, *Audley Craven*, in 1896.

After the death of her mother in 1901 May Sinclair supported herself entirely by her literary work, which included numerous reviews and translations as well as fiction. Her early novels *The Divine Fire* (1904) and *The Creators* (1910) were praised for their realism and enjoyed some success. An avid supporter of women's suffrage, she published the pamphlet *Feminism* in 1912. During World War I she worked with a field ambulance unit in Belgium.

May Sinclair was one of the first English-language writers to show an awareness of the psychoanalytical theories of Freud and Jung. The influence of these ideas can be seen in her biography of the BRONTË sisters (1912) and her novel *The Three Sisters* (1914), both of which explore the repression of women within the family. In 1918 Sinclair introduced the psychological term "stream of consciousness" into literary criticism, using it to describe the experimental approach of the novelist Dorothy RICHARDSON. She herself used a similar technique in her best-known novels, *Mary Olivier: A Life* (1919) and *The Life and Death of Harriet Frean* (1922). While the former is a clearly autobiographical work based on her own successful struggle for independence, the latter gives a bleak picture of the results of female self-denial.

With the exception of *Dark Night* (1924), a novel written entirely in verse, Sinclair's later work was more conventional. In later life she developed an interest in spiritualism and the supernatural, reflected in such works as *Uncanny Stories* (1923).

After her death Sinclair's novels remained out of print and largely forgotten until the feminist publishing boom of the 1980s revived interest in her achievements.

Sirani, Elisabetta (1638–1665) *Italian painter*

Elisabetta Sirani was a greatly admired 17th-century Italian painter who opened a studio for women.

Born in Bologna, Elisabetta learned to paint in the workshop of her father, Gian Andrea Sirani, and was recognized as an accomplished artist while still in her teens. By her twenties she was successful enough to support her entire family from her earnings after her father could no longer work. She also capitalized on her reputation by opening a studio for other women artists, an entirely original idea in the 17th century.

In addition to much-praised etchings of biblical scenes Sirani also produced a painting of *The Baptism of Christ* for the Church of the Certosini in her native city and won high praise for a nave painting for the church of San Girolamo in 1658. By 1664 she was sufficiently eminent to be commissioned by Prince Leopold of Tuscany to paint his portrait and by the crown prince of Tuscany to paint a Madonna. She died suddenly at the age of 27, possibly from stomach ulcers, possibly from poison. She was given a highly elaborate civic funeral.

Sitwell, Dame Edith (1887–1964) *British poet*

> My poems are hymns of praise to the glory of life.
>
> —"Some Notes on My Poetry," *Collected Poems* (1954; 1957)

Considered by some to be one of the finest English poets of the 20th century, Edith Sitwell also had plenty of critics. A striking woman, she was six feet tall and liked to wear long flowing robes, exotic hats or turbans, and massive jewellery. She justified her rather theatrical eccentricity by describing it as "the ordinary carried to a high degree of pictorial perfection."

Edith was born in Scarborough, the daughter of Sir George Sitwell, and spent an unhappy childhood at the family's ancestral home in Derbyshire, where she was educated by a governess. In 1914 she and her governess, Helen Rootham, took a London flat together; Edith's first volume of poetry, *The Mother*, was published the following year. In 1916 she helped found *Wheels*, a yearly anthology of modernist verse, and for the next five years she and her brothers Osbert and Sacheverell were its chief contributors. Her notoreity was firmly established in 1923, when she publicly recited her eccentric poetry sequence *Façade* through a megaphone to a musical accompaniment by the young composer William Walton. *Façade* was made into a ballet in 1931.

During the 1930s Sitwell lived in Paris with Helen Rootham, who died in 1938. The poetry in *Gold Coast Customs* (1929) showed increasing depths of feeling, while *Street Songs* (1942; containing her fine poem "Still Falls the Rain") and *The Shadow of Cain* (1947) reflect her anguished response to World War II. Sitwell became a Roman Catholic in 1955. In all her poetry she sought to communicate sensations, rather than to describe them, and she avoided traditional imagery, considering it worn out and useless.

Sitwell's later volumes of poetry include *The Canticle of the Rose* (1949), *Gardeners and Astronomers* (1953), and *The Outcast* (1962). Her critical works include *Alexander Pope* (1930), *Aspects of Modern Poetry* (1934), and *A Poet's Notebook* (1943). She also wrote two books on Queen ELIZABETH I – *Fanfare for Elizabeth* (1946) and *The Queens and the Hive* (1962). *The English Eccentrics* (1933) is a collection of her essays.

Generous towards struggling artists whose work she believed in, Edith Sitwell helped, among others, William Walton and Dylan Thomas. In the 1950s she travelled to Hollywood, hoping to earn a fortune; this did not materialize, but she did meet Marilyn MONROE. In 1954 she was created a DBE. Her autobiography, *Taken Care Of*, was published in 1965.

Skinner, Cornelia Otis (1901–1979) *American actress and writer*

> These were clever and beautiful women, often of good background, who through some breach of the moral code or the scandal of divorce had been socially ostracized but had managed to turn the ostracism into profitable account. Cultivated, endowed with civilized graces, they were frankly – kept women, but kept by one man only, or, at any rate, by one man at a time.
>
> *—Elegant Wits and Grand Horizontals* (1962)

Acclaimed for her solo stage performances, Cornelia Otis Skinner was also famous for her humorous books, notably *Excuse It, Please!* (1936) and the best-selling *Our Hearts Were Young and Gay* (1942, with Emily Kimbrough), describing a European trip.

Cornelia Otis Skinner was born in Chicago, daughter of the actor Otis Skinner. After attending Bryn Mawr College, Pennsylvania, and studying acting in Paris, she appeared on the stage with her father's company in *Blood and Sand* (1921). In 1925 she wrote her first play, *Captain Fury*. She later turned to writing and performing monologues. After the 1940s she returned to full-scale plays, most notably *The Pleasure of His Company* (1958), which she wrote with Samuel Taylor.

In addition to her theatre pieces, Skinner was the author of witty essays and light verse. Collections of her work include *Tiny Garments* (1932), *Nuts in May* (1950), and *The Ape in Me* (1959). She also wrote a biography of Sarah BERNHARDT.

Skram, (Bertha) Amalie (1847–1905) *Norwegian novelist*

Amalie Skram was a pioneer of literary naturalism. Her deeply pessimistic works reflect her own troubled and unhappy life.

Bertha Amalie Alver was born in Bergen, the daughter of a failed businessman who abandoned the family when she was a child. At the age of 17 she married a sea captain, Berent Muller, and joined him in a restless wandering life that took her to several countries. In 1880, after 15 years of marriage and the birth of two sons,

Amalie left her husband. Settling in southern Norway, she began to write reviews and short stories for periodicals. Her first novel, *Madam Höjer's Tenants*, appeared in 1882; owing to its stark realistic style it is usually considered the first work of naturalism in Scandinavian literature.

In 1884 Amalie married the Danish writer Erik Skram and settled in Copenhagen, where she wrote the novels for which she is now best remembered. At the time such novels as *Constance Ring* (1885) and *Lucie* (1888) were considered shocking because of their attacks on marriage and their frank treatment of women's sexual lives. Also distressing was her autobiographical novel *At St. Joergen's* (1895), which describes her experience of depression following the birth of a daughter and her subsequent stay in a mental hospital. Her pessimistic philosophy is seen at its most relentless in the four-part novel sequence *Hellemyrsfolket* (1887–98; The People of Hellemyr), which describes the decay of a family over several generations. Skram emphasizes the role of environment and heredity in the tragedy, so that her characters seem completely trapped by fate. Although now little read, the work is considered a landmark in Scandinavian literature.

Skram's remaining years were profoundly unhappy. Following the collapse of her second marriage in 1900, she suffered a severe breakdown. Thereafter she spent long periods of time in mental hospitals.

Slessor, Mary (Mitchell) (1848–1919) *British missionary*

Mary Slessor's pioneering work with the tribes of the Calabar region of West Africa gained her a reputation as one of the most fearless and independent 19th-century missionaries.

Mary Slessor was born in Aberdeen, the daughter of a shoemaker father and a weaver mother. She was still young when the family moved to Dundee, where Mary worked part-time in a factory while continuing with her lessons. She also started to do missionary work for the United Presbyterian Church.

In 1875, when she was 27, Mary decided to work as a missionary in Africa; the following year she sailed for the Calabar coast, a region that had seen little colonial development (it is now part of Nigeria). From the first, Mary made a strong impression with her gift for befriending tribesmen and for learning their languages. After only three years in Africa she chose to live and work independently of other Europeans – a quite remarkable choice for a young woman at that time.

In 1888 Slessor decided to travel into the unexplored interior of the continent to work with the Okoyong, a little-known tribe whose trust she soon gained. Despite her strong religious beliefs, she was a very practical and down-to-earth woman. In her ten years with the Okoyong she showed herself less concerned with making converts than with stamping out such evils as human sacrifice and infanticide; she also did much to encourage education and peaceful trade. By 1892 "White Ma," as she was known, had established her personal authority so firmly that the British colonial authorities appointed her a vice-consul. She spent the last years of her life working with tribes even further inland. By the time of her death her exploits had made her a heroine in Britain.

Smart, Elizabeth (1913–1986) *Canadian novelist and poet*

Elizabeth Smart is best known for her autobiographical novel *By Grand Central Station I Sat Down and Wept* (1945), which explores the nature of romantic obsession.

Smart was born into a middle-class family in Ottawa. After attending private schools, she travelled to Britain in the early 1930s to study at King's College, London. She then returned to Canada, where she began to work as a journalist on the *Ottawa Journal*.

In 1941 Smart's life changed for ever when she met and fell in love with the British poet George Barker, a married man. Their passionate but clandestine affair provided the inspiration for her first book, *By Grand Central Station I Sat Down and Wept*. Written in lyrical prose, the book explores both the pain and the joy of an illicit all-consuming passion. Although little noticed when it was first published, the book was acclaimed as a masterpiece of modern Canadian literature when it was reissued in the 1960s.

After travelling to England with Barker in 1943, Smart supported herself for the next few decades with a mixture of reviewing, journalism, and work as an advertising copywriter. Smart's turbulent relationship with Barker produced four children and continued for the rest of her life, despite Barker's later marriage to another woman.

In 1977 Smart returned to public attention with *The Assumption of the Rogues and the Rascals*, a semiautobiographical work dealing with her later experiences in England. She also published two volumes of poetry, *A Bonus* (1977) and *Eleven Poems* (1982).

Interest in Smart's writing has continued to increase since her death. *Necessary Secrets*, a selection of her journals, appeared in 1986, and *Early Writings* in 1987.

Smedley, Agnes (1890–1950) *American radical*

A writer and political activist, Smedley was well known for her books on China, to which she first went as a foreign correspondent for a German newspaper.

Born in Missouri and brought up in the mining districts of Colorado, Agnes Smedley was only 16 when her mother died, worn out by work, the strain of poverty, and a harsh marriage. Refusing "to live the life of a cabbage" and submit to a similar fate, Smedley overcame the disadvantages of her inadequate schooling to become a teacher in Arizona and then in California, where she was dismissed for her socialist beliefs.

After a brief unsuccessful marriage she moved to New York, where she became involved in radical causes, including campaigns for birth control and Indian independence. Imprisoned for her anti-British political activities in 1918, she began to write in jail and published a book, *Cell Mates*, describing her experiences in prison. After her release she settled in Germany (1920) before moving on to China.

Her only novel, *Daughter of Earth* (1929), drew on her own experience of a nervous breakdown following an affair with an Indian revolutionary, Virendranath Chattopadhyaya. She is best known, however, for her five books describing the events and personalities of the Chinese Communist revolution, which she witnessed at first hand. These include *Chinese Destinies* (1933) and *China Fights Back* (1938). Returning to the United States in 1941, she settled in a writer's colony in New York State, publishing *Battle Hymn of China* in 1943. Forced abroad by the anti-Communist agitation led by Senator Joseph McCarthy in 1949, she died in London on her way to China. Her remains were buried in China.

Smiley, Jane (Graves) (1949–   ) *American novelist, writer, and academic*

The novels of Jane Smiley range from intense family drama to sweeping social comedy.

She was born in Los Angeles but brought up mainly in St. Louis, Missouri. After studying at Vassar College, Poughkeepsie, she took a PhD in creative writing from the University of Iowa, where she went on to hold a series of teaching posts, including professor (1989–90) and distinguished professor (from 1992). She married John Whiston in 1970, was divorced and married William Silag in 1976 (two daughters), and was again divorced before marrying Stephen Mortensen in 1987 (one son).

Smiley began to publish her fiction in the early 1980s. Her debut novel *At Paradise Gate* (1981), was followed by the thriller *Duplicate Keys* (1984), and *Ordinary Love and Goodwill* (1989). The *Age of Grief* (1987) was an accomplished collection of short stories and novellas. Smiley's best-known novel, *A Thousand Acres*, appeared in 1991 and won both the Pulitzer Prize for Fiction and the U.S. National Book Critics Award. The novel is a contemporary reworking of the *King Lear* theme set in a small agricultural community in

Idaho. This *tour-de-force* was followed by *Moo* (1995), a satirical comedy set on a campus in the Mid-West that earned comparisons with Balzac.

Smith, Bessie (1895–1937) *American blues singer*

Bessie Smith was an all-time great of jazz. As the "Empress of the Blues," she was known and loved throughout the world.

Born Elizabeth Smith into a poor African-American family in Chattanooga, Tennessee, she began her musical career as one of Ma RAINEY's Rabbit Foot Minstrels. Her extraordinary, powerful voice and dynamic stage presence soon transcended anything Ma Rainey could teach her, and her first record, "Down Hearted Blues," sold 800,000 copies when it was issued in 1923.

Over the course of the following decade and a half she recorded some 150 songs, many featuring the accompaniment of such outstanding jazz instrumentalists as Louis Armstrong and Benny Goodman. In 1929 she took the leading role in an early sound film, *St. Louis Blues*, which was banned at the time on the grounds that it was too downbeat to be shown during the Depression.

Standing 5 feet 9 inches tall and weighing over 14 stone, the statuesque Bessie Smith dominated the jazz world until her alcoholism made managements increasingly wary of booking her. During her later years the proud and successful "Empress of the Blues" lost most of her following, was frequently out of work, and saw her marriage to Jackie Gee (whom she had married in 1923) collapse.

The circumstances surrounding her death following a car accident inspired Edward Albee's play *The Death of Bessie Smith* (1960). As a black woman she was refused admission to the nearby whites-only hospital and had to be taken much further away to the African-American hospital, where she could not be saved. Had she been white, she would have received more prompt medical attention, which might have saved her life.

Smith, Delia (1941–) *British cookery writer and broadcaster*

A household name in Britain, Delia Smith is one of the most widely known and admired writers and broadcasters in the cookery field.

Delia Smith was born in Woking, Surrey. She left school at 16 to work in a hairdressing salon and a travel agency before becoming a waitress, which enabled her to move into cooking. Baffled by the bad reputation of English food, she set out to study its history and by 1969 was writing for the *Daily Mirror*, of which her future husband, Michael Wynn Jones, was the deputy editor. From 1972 to 1985 Smith wrote a cookery column for the London *Evening Standard*. In 1973 she published her first book, *How to Cheat at Cooking*.

After moving to rural Suffolk, Smith began to broadcast on BBC regional television and produced a series of books based on traditional country recipes. In 1978 she published her *Complete Cookery Course*. By 1992 this popular book had been through 27 printings, and her total sales had exceeded five million copies. Books and linked television series on special themes such as Christmas, cooking for one, and cooking on a budget, have made Delia Smith a household name. Her success is based on recipes that work even for the most unskilled cooks. When she published her *Winter Collection* (1995), her decision to feature cranberries brought about a nationwide cranberry shortage. So widespread was her influence that emergency imports by air had to be made to meet the surge in demand as Delia's frustrated devotees scoured supermarket shelves in vain.

Smith's friendly and commonsensical broadcasting style masks a degree of stage fright so severe that she refuses to do live cookery demonstrations. A devout Roman Catholic, she is an energetic campaigner for charity and has written a number of religious works, including *A Journey into God* (1980) and *A Feast for Lent* (1983). She was appointed OBE in 1995.

Smith, Dodie (1896–1990) *British writer*

Dodie Smith is remembered for her plays, which include *Autumn Crocus* and *Dear Octopus*, as well as her children's classic *The Hundred and One Dalmatians*, which was immortalized in a Disney animation.

She was born Dorothy Gladys Smith in Whitefield, Lancashire, and brought up in nearby Manchester in a home crammed with pianos, pets, and relatives. At 14 she moved to London, where she attended St. Paul's School for Girls, which she disliked for its snobbery but respected for the excellence of its teaching. An eager participant in amateur dramatics, she was accepted as a pupil by the Royal Academy of Dramatic Art (RADA), where she was a hard-working but mediocre student. For some years she struggled to establish herself on the stage, but being under five feet tall, she found herself confined to juvenile roles.

Leaving show business, she became a buyer at London's large, modern furniture store Heals, where she was highly regarded. Meanwhile, she redirected her theatrical ambitions towards writing plays, having her first success in 1931 with *Autumn Crocus*, a romance. During the 1930s she wrote five more plays, which between them ran for 1,800 performances. The most celebrated, *Dear Octopus* (1935), drew affectionately on the extended family of her Manchester childhood, with its octopus-like tentacles. It made her rich enough to own a Rolls-Royce and was made into a successful film in 1943, starring Michael Wilding and Margaret LOCKWOOD.

During World War II and for some years afterwards Smith lived in the United States. There she worked on screenplays and published a novel, *I Capture the Castle* (1949), which was intended for adults but proved a huge hit with teenagers. After returning to live in a small English market town, she wrote her children's classic, *The Hundred and One Dalmatians*, in 1956. Once again she drew on personal experience, owning up to nine Dalmatian dogs at the same time herself. A Disney cartoon film appeared in 1961, and a live-action version, starring Glenn CLOSE as Cruella de Vil, in 1996. In later life Smith published four volumes of autobiography, which revealed her affair with the designer Sir Ambrose Heal and her friendship with the writer Christopher Isherwood.

Smith, Dame Maggie (1934–) *British actress*

> She is resourceful, inventive, and she has mystery and power. Mystery in a woman is terribly important.
> —George Cukor

On stage and screen Maggie Smith is known for her versatility in both comedy and drama. She has won two Academy Awards – the Best Actress Award for her performance in *The Prime of Miss Jean Brodie* (1968) and the Best Supporting Actress Award for *California Suite* (1977); she has also been nominated on three other occasions. In 1992 she received the BAFTA Award for Lifetime Achievement.

Born in Ilford, Essex, Margaret Natalie Smith trained at the Oxford Playhouse, making her stage debut in 1952 as Viola in a production of Shakespeare's *Twelfth Night*. Her Broadway debut came in the 1956 revue *New Faces*, and a year later she appeared with Kenneth Williams in the West End revue *Share My Lettuce*. In the early 1960s she joined Sir Laurence Olivier's National Theatre company; her parts included Desdemona to Olivier's Othello in a production that also became an acclaimed film (1965). In 1976 she went to Ontario, Canada, to work with the Stratford Festival for four years.

Smith has given outstanding performances in Restoration comedy and in the plays of Noël Coward, notably *Private Lives* (London, 1972; New York, 1975). She has also excelled in plays by Shakespeare, Ibsen, Chekhov, Ionesco, Anouilh, Cocteau, and Stoppard. Some of her most successful West End roles have been repeated on Broadway, including the tour guide Lettice Douffet in Peter Shaffer's comedy *Lettice and Lovage* (London, 1987; New York 1990), which earned her a Tony Award.

Many of her most memorable roles

have been eccentric middle-aged women, as in the films *Travels with My Aunt* (1972), *A Room with a View* (1986), and *The Lonely Passion of Judith Hearne* (1989) and the one-woman television play *Bed among the Lentils*, written by Alan Bennett as part of his series *Talking Heads* (1988). In 1993 she played Lady Bracknell in a London revival of Wilde's *The Importance of Being Earnest*. Other recent work includes supporting roles in the films *Hook* (1991), *Sister Act* (1992), and *The Secret Garden* (1993).

In 1967 Smith married the actor Robert Stephens, with whom she had two sons. After divorcing Stephens, she married the playwright Beverley Cross in 1975. She was named CBE in 1970 and DBE in 1990.

Smith, Patti (1946–) *American rock singer and poet*

With her refusal to conform to any of the conventional stereotypes of the female rock performer, Smith proved an inspiration to many women musicians in the late 1970s. Her eccentric vocal style was also widely imitated.

Born in Chicago, Smith received a strict religious upbringing from her mother, who was a Jehovah's Witness. Her childhood was also marked by severe illness, which left her prone to hallucinations for years afterwards. She grew up hero-worshipping both rock idols such as Bob Dylan and poets such as Baudelaire and Rimbaud.

During the early 1970s Smith moved in the New York art world and became the girlfriend of Robert Mapplethorpe, a fashionable photographer. She also published several volumes of her avant-garde poetry, beginning with *Seventh Heaven* (1971). Her involvement with rock music began when she started to use a live rock backing to accompany some of her poetry readings. By the time she released the single "Hey Joe" in 1974, Smith had developed into a powerful if unconventional singer.

In 1975 Smith formed a band to record the album *Horses*, which was released to widespread critical acclaim. Combining partly improvised lyrics with driving aggressive rock, *Horses* was one of the most original albums of the decade and became an immediate cult success. It is seen as one of the key records in the development of the American punk sound. However, a second album, *Radio Ethiopia* (1976), was less well received, and Smith's live appearances began to be criticized for their self-indulgence. In January 1977 she fell from the stage during a concert and broke her neck. After a lengthy period of recuperation she released her most commercial album, *Easter* (1978), which included the hit single "Because the Night." Both this record and its successor, *Wave* (1979), showed a growing interest in religious themes.

After disbanding her group in 1980, Patti Smith retired almost completely from the rock world for some 15 years. During this period she lived quietly in Detroit with her husband, the guitarist Fred "Sonic" Smith, and concentrated on raising their children. However, following Smith's death in 1995, Patti made a much publicized comeback in a concert tour with Bob Dylan. *Gone Again* (1996), an elegiac album dedicated to her husband, was widely praised by the critics.

Smith, Stevie (1902–1971) *British poet and novelist*

> Marriage I think
> For women
> Is the best of opiates.
> It kills the thoughts,
> That think about the thoughts,
> It is the best of opiates.
>
> —"Marriage I Think" (1937)

> Stevie herself was so much her work…her work illustrates her grasp of the joy and absurdity of life, and simultaneously of its pain and brevity.
>
> —Kay Dick, *Ivy and Stevie* (1971)

Noted for her ironic wit, unexpected turns of phrase, and unsentimental view of the human condition, Stevie Smith wrote poetry that was as unconventional as her own character.

Florence Margaret Smith was born in Hull. Her interest in horseriding and her small build prompted friends to call her "Stevie" after the famous jockey Steve Donoghue. As a child she moved with her mother and sister to Palmers Green, a London suburb that was to become the setting for much of her writing. After her mother's death she lived with a crusty maiden aunt (whom she affectionately called the "Lion Aunt") for more than 60 years.

During this period she worked as a private secretary to Sir Neville Pearson of Newnes Publishing Company from 1923 until 1953, when she resigned after a suicide attempt. She then looked after her aged aunt. As her reputation grew in the 1950s and 1960s Smith read from her works on radio and gave public recitals. She also attended a pop-poetry festival in Brussels.

After having her early poems rejected by a number of publishers, Smith turned to fiction, achieving critical success with *Novel on Yellow Paper* (1936). She wrote two more semi-autobiographical novels, *Over the Frontier* (1938) and *The Holiday* (1949). Her first volume of poems, *A Good Time Was Had by All* (1937), was well received, and her reputation was enhanced by *Tender Only to One* (1938), *Mother, What Is Man?* (1942), and her most highly acclaimed volume, *Not Waving But Drowning* (1957). Later volumes of verse include *The Frog Prince* (1966), *The Best Beast* (1969), and *Scorpion* (1972). Her books of poetry were all illustrated with her own whimsical line drawings. Smith was awarded the Queen's Gold Medal for Poetry in 1969.

Stevie Smith's life was dramatized by Hugh Whitemore in the play *Stevie* (produced in London in 1978); a film version was released in 1981, with Glenda JACKSON playing the poet.

Smithson, Alison (1928–1993)
British architect

Alison Smithson and her husband Peter formed a partnership that has had a wide influence on international architecture.

Alison Margaret Gill was born in Sheffield, Yorkshire, and studied architecture at the University of Durham before working briefly in the architect's department of the London County Council. In 1949 she married another Durham-trained architect, Peter Smithson, with whom she established a joint practice in 1950. Together the Smithsons exerted a powerful influence on British architectural theory over the following decades.

Their first major project was a school (1954) at Hunstanton in rural Norfolk, an uncompromisingly modernist steel and concrete composition in the tradition of Mies van der Rohe. In 1956 they designed a House of the Future for Britain's annual Ideal Home Exhibition. In the 1960s their work ranged from a group of office buildings, in the St. James's area of London (completed 1965), to a low-cost housing development in the East End (1969). Their most consistent patron was the new University of Bath, to which they contributed several campus buildings.

Much more characteristic, however, were the dozens of schemes they submitted to international competitions, which were widely admired but never built. These included a British embassy building for the new Brazilian capital, Brasilia. Both Smithsons proved highly influential teachers at London's Architectural Association. They were members of the Independent Group, a group of painters, writers, and architects that met at the ICA in London, as well as leading the Team X group that organized the tenth International Congress of Modern Architecture in 1956.

Smithson, Harriet (Constance)
(1800–1854) *Anglo-Irish actress*

A striking beauty, Smithson caused a sensation when she first appeared in Paris in the late 1820s. She is now remembered as the first wife of Hector Berlioz and the inspiration for some of his greatest music.

Little is known of Smithson's early life, except that she was born in Ireland, where her father managed several theatres. By 1818 she was acting on the London stage. Although she once appeared opposite the tragedian Edmund Kean, she made no special impact during her London career.

Things proved very different when

she travelled to Paris with an English company headed by Charles Kemble. In 1827–28 she electrified French audiences with her interpretation of such Shakespearean heroines as Juliet and Ophelia. Her romantic beauty and intense delivery proved a revelation to theatregoers used to the rather artificial style of French classical tragedy. In particular she became the idol of the group of young Romantics, led by Victor Hugo and Alexandre Dumas, who went on to revolutionize the French theatre in the 1830s.

Harriet's most ardent admirer was the young composer Hector Berlioz, who developed an obsessive love for her. When she rebuffed his advances, Berlioz was inspired to compose his most famous work, the *Symphonie fantastique* (1831). According to his programme notes, the music describes the despairing love of a young musician for an unattainable beauty; when rejected, he takes refuge in opium and has various lurid visions culminating in his death.

The true outcome was more prosaic but no less tragic. After her initial triumphs, Harriet's career went into a decline, owing mainly to her poor command of French. She also lost most of her savings to a dishonest theatre producer. Accordingly, when Berlioz renewed his offers of marriage a year or two later, she responded more favourably. The couple married in 1833, set up home in Paris, and had a son. Unfortunately the marriage soon began to go wrong. In 1836, prompted by his violent jealousy, Berlioz demanded that she leave the stage. Her resentment at this, together with his neglect and infidelity, led her to become a heavy drinker, and the marriage finally broke up in 1842. She died in Paris, poor and almost forgotten.

Smyth, Dame Ethel Mary (1858–1944) *British composer, suffragette, and writer*

> This temptation to pretend that women are non-existent musically, to ignore or damp down our poor little triumphs...is a microbe that will flourish comfortably, though perhaps surreptitiously, in the male

> organism, till there are enough women composers for it to die a natural death. Whereupon men will forget it ever existed. Have they not already forgotten their frenzied opposition to "Votes for Women"?
> —*A Final Burning of Boats* (1928)

A leading suffragette and member of the Women's Social and Political Union, Dame Ethel composed *The March of the Women* for the movement. She was recognized as the first significant British woman composer after the performance of her *Mass in D* at the Albert Hall, London, in 1893.

Born in Kent, Ethel Smyth attended the Leipzig Conservatory in Germany and then continued her studies in Berlin, where her talents were noticed by Clara SCHUMANN and Johannes Brahms. In 1888 she returned to London, where several of her compositions, including the orchestral *Serenade* (1890), were performed during the next few years. Later she turned to opera with such works as *Fantasio* (1898), *Der Wald* (1902), and *The Wreckers* (1906), which all had their premieres in Germany, where opera had a more receptive audience.

Back in England Smyth became involved in the women's movement, and *The March of the Women* (1911) became an anthem sung all over London by the suffragettes. She, with others, was briefly imprisoned in Holloway, for throwing stones at a cabinet minister's window. Her fourth opera, *The Boatswain's Mate* (1916), had its premiere in London.

Smyth also wrote songs, choral pieces, and a concerto for violin, horn, and orchestra (1927). Her two-volume autobiography, *Impressions That Remained* (1919), and her other writings contain amusing anecdotes of her musical career and her many friends, including the Empress EUGÉNIE and Virginia WOOLF. She was created a DBE and received an honorary DMus from Durham University in 1922.

Smythe, Pat (1928–1996) *British showjumper*

In the 1950s and early 1960s Pat Smythe was the heroine of thousands of aspiring showjumpers, not only in

Britain but also in the United States and Germany.

Patricia Rosemary Smythe was born in Barnes, London. After her father's death the family moved to Gloucestershire, where the young Patricia helped her mother run a guesthouse. Already a keen rider, she acquired a showjumping horse on which she competed at the 1946 International Show. She did so well that she was subsequently invited to join the British showjumping team on its first postwar tour abroad. At the 1956 Games she became the first woman equestrian to compete at Olympic level and won a bronze medal in the team event. In 1957 she won the European ladies championship on her own horse Flanagan; she won the same championship a record three more times on the same horse, in 1961, 1962, and 1963.

In 1963 Pat Smythe married a Swiss businessman, Sam Koechlin. She left the British showjumping team the following year and gave up competitive riding in favour of writing and charity work. From 1986 to 1989 she served as president of the British Show Jumping Association. She wrote over 20 books, many of them for children, including *Jump for Joy: Pat Smythe's Story* (1954). In 1992 she published her autobiography, *Jumping Life's Fences*.

Söderström, Elisabeth Anna
(1927–) *Swedish opera singer*

An outstanding operatic soprano, Elisabeth Söderström was well known in opera houses throughout the world.

After studying at the Opera School in Stockholm, her native city, Elisabeth Söderström joined the Swedish Royal Opera in 1950. She performed at Glyndebourne for six seasons from 1957, and at the New York Metropolitan Opera for eight seasons from 1959, the year in which she was appointed Singer of the Court by the Swedish monarchy.

That same year Söderström sang all three leading female roles in productions of Strauss's opera *Der Rosenkavalier*. In 1965 she was awarded the Royal Swedish Academy prize for acting, and in 1966 she toured in the Soviet Union. Söderström's range ex-

tended from Monteverdi to Tchaikovsky, but she was best known for her performances in the operas of Mozart and Janáček. In 1993 she became the artistic director of the Drottningholm Court Theatre, a restored 18th-century theatre in the grounds of the Swedish royal palace near Stockholm.

Somerset, Lady Isabella Caroline
(1851–1921) *British philanthropist and temperance worker*

Lady Somerset is best known for her establishment in 1895 of a retreat for alcoholic women at Duxhurst in Surrey, the first institution of its kind in England. There she supervised enlightened humane methods of treatment. She later added a home for children from broken or impoverished families.

Isabella Somers-Cocks was born in London, the eldest daughter of Earl and Countess Somers. Educated in modern languages and other fashionable accomplishments at home by governesses, she read widely, being particularly impressed by the works of the historian Thomas Macaulay and the philosopher John Stuart Mill. She married Lord Henry Somerset in 1872, but the marriage was unhappy because of his promiscuous homosexuality. After getting a legal separation from her husband in 1878, Isabella was abandoned by polite society and devoted herself to work among the poor at Ledbury, Herefordshire. There she observed the brutalizing effects of drunkenness, and in 1887 she took the pledge and embraced the temperance movement.

Lecturing throughout England, she became known for her eloquence and charm. In 1890 she was elected president of the British Women's Temperance Association (BWTA), founding its periodical, *Woman's Signal*, in 1894. In 1891 she visited the United States, where she addressed large and enthusiastic crowds about her cause. In 1898 she succeeded Frances Willard, with whom she had worked in the United States, as president of the World's Women's Christian Temperance Union (WWCTU), serving until 1906. She also edited their paper, *The*

Woman's Herald. However, her later rejection of Prohibition made her unpopular with some temperance workers; she resigned from the BWTA in 1903 and did not seek re-election to the WWCTU in 1906.

Lady Somerset died in London. Her publications include some works of fiction and verse, notably *Our Village Life* (1884), *Under the Arch of Life* (1906), and *Beauty for Ashes* (1913), as well as numerous articles on temperance.

Somerville, Edith Oenone (1858–1949) *Irish writer*

Edith Somerville and her cousin Violet Martin were the joint authors of 14 humorous books, largely about rural Ireland.

Born on the Greek island of Corfu, the daughter of an Anglo-Irish army officer, Edith Somerville was educated in Ireland and studied art in London, Düsseldorf, and Paris. In 1886 she met her cousin Violet Martin, who wrote under the pen name Martin Ross. They became lifelong friends and co-authored 14 books as "Somerville and Ross." Some were about their travels, but most were humorous accounts of life in rural Ireland from the point of view of the Protestant landowning elite, to which they belonged.

In 1903 Edith, a fanatically keen fox hunter, became the first woman to serve as a Master of Foxhounds. *Some Experiences of an Irish RM*, published in 1899, proved an international success and inspired two sequels, *Further Experiences of an Irish RM* (1908) and *In Mr. Knox's Country* (1915). These stories became the basis of a successful British television series decades after their authors' deaths.

Although Violet Martin died in 1915, Edith Somerville carried on as though Violet were still alive, publishing over a dozen more titles under their usual style of "Somerville and Ross." The most important was the historical romance *The Big House at Inver* (1925).

In 1932 Trinity College, Dublin conferred on her the honorary degree of Doctor of Letters; Violet Martin was granted the honour posthumously. In that same year Edith Somerville published *An Incorruptible Irishman*, a biography of her great-grandfather Charles Kendal Burke, Lord Chief Justice of Ireland in the early 1800s. In 1933 she became a founder member of the Irish Academy of Letters.

Somerville, Mary (1780–1872) *British mathematician, astronomer, and physical geographer*

Mary Somerville was the author of major works on astronomy, physical science, and geography. She was also a firm believer in higher education for women.

She was born Mary Fairfax in Jedburgh, Scotland. The daughter of a naval officer, she received only one year of formal education before her marriage in 1804 to a cousin who was a captain in the Russian navy. He died in 1807, and she married another cousin, W. Somerville, an army physician, in 1812.

Somerville was unique in 19th-century British science since she was an independent female. Virtually all other women who participated in science at this time did so as the wife or sister of a husband or brother, whom they assisted, though some of them went on to make contributions of their own. Her interest in science began when, as a young girl, she first heard of algebra and Euclid; she later satisfied her curiosity as to the nature of these subjects from books she bought herself. She certainly received no encouragement from her father, nor was her first husband much more sympathetic. She was more fortunate with her second husband, who encouraged and assisted her.

Living with her husband in London from 1816, she soon became a familiar and respected figure in the scientific circles of the capital. Her first significant achievement was her treatise on the *Mécanique céleste* of Pierre Simon de Laplace. She was persuaded to undertake this difficult task by the astronomer John Herschel, and in 1831 750 copies of *The Mechanism of the Heavens* were published. The work was a great success and was used as a basic text in advanced astronomy for the rest of the century.

She followed this in 1834 with her *On the Connexion of the Physical Sciences*, a more popular but still serious work. In this she suggested that the deviations from its orbit of the planet Uranus might reveal the existence of an undiscovered planet. Somerville was of course denied such obvious honours as a fellowship of the Royal Society as a result of her work. She was, however, granted a government pension of £300 a year in 1837.

From 1840, because of the poor health of her husband, she moved to Europe, living mainly in Italy. It was there that she produced her third and most original work, *Physical Geography* (1848). Although overshadowed by the *Kosmos* of Friedrich von Humboldt, which came out in 1845, it was widely used as a university textbook to the end of the century.

She produced her fourth book, *On Molecular and Microscopic Science* (1869), at the age of 89 and was working on a second edition when she died.

When a hall was opened in Oxford in 1879 for the education of women, it was appropriately named after her. Somerville College went on to produce a multitude of talented women – disproving her own belief that genius was a gift not granted to the female sex.

Sontag, Susan (1933–) *American critic, writer, and filmmaker*

> Everyone who is born holds dual citizenship, in the kingdom of the well and the kingdom of the sick. Although we all prefer to use the good passport, sooner or later each of us is obliged...to identify ourselves as citizens of that other place.
> —*Illness as Metaphor* (1978)

With interests as diverse as politics, philosophy, film, theatre, and literature, Susan Sontag is regarded as one of America's foremost critics and cultural interpreters.

Born in New York, the daughter of an aloof father and an alcoholic mother, Susan Sontag grew up in Tucson, Arizona, and Los Angeles. Her voracious intellectual appetite enabled her to graduate from Chicago University with a bachelor's degree in philosophy in only two years. She subsequently took master's degrees in English literature and philosophy at Harvard before studying at Oxford, Paris, and Columbia University.

Although her avant-garde novel *The Benefactor* was published in 1963, Sontag's standing as one of America's leading intellectuals dates from the publication of a volume of critical essays, *Against Interpretation*, in 1966. A second novel, *Death Kit*, appeared in 1967. In 1968, at the height of the Vietnam War, she made a controversial visit to North Vietnam, and a year later she published one of her most influential books, *Styles of Radical Will*. During the 1970s she published mostly short stories while working on her definitive study *On Photography*, which won a U.S. National Book Critics' Circle Award in 1977.

Her two-year battle against breast cancer resulted in the penetrating essay *Illness as Metaphor* (1978), which earned her another NBCC award. A revised version appeared in 1989, incorporating material relating to Aids. She has also made four films – *Duet for Cannibals* (1969), *Brother Carl* (1971), *Promised Lands* (1974), and *Unguided Tour* (1983) – as well as directing for the theatre. In 1992 she published another novel, *The Volcano Lover*, and in 1993 a play, *Alice in Bed*.

Sophia (1657–1704) *Regent of Russia*

Sophia was the able and ambitious regent of Russia from 1682 to 1689. During her regency she promoted industry and encouraged foreign craftsmen to settle in Russia. She also tried to foster good relations with Poland through a treaty in 1686.

Sophia Alekseyevna was the daughter of Tsar Alexis I and his first wife, Maria Miloslavskaya. When Sophia's brother Fyodor III, Alexis's successor, died in 1682, her half-brother Peter (later called the Great) was proclaimed emperor. Sophia resented the selection of Peter, Alexis's son by Natalia Naryshkina, and schemed successfully to have her mentally handicapped brother Ivan installed as coruler and herself as regent.

Ruling under the guidance of her lover, Prince Vasily Golitsyn, Sophia sponsored his two disastrous expeditions to the Crimea in 1687 and 1689, which helped to undermine her position. She did, however, conclude peace treaties with Sweden and Denmark (1684) and China (1689). In 1689 the *streltsy* (palace guard) threw its support behind Peter, who became emperor and imprisoned Sophia in the Novodevichy Convent. When her supporters in the *streltsy* appealed to her to assume the crown in 1698, Peter crushed his opponents and forced Sophia to become a nun, which she did under the name Susanna.

Sophia (1630–1714) *Electress of Hanover*

Sophia was the granddaughter of King James I of England. It was owing to this descent that Sophia's son George became king of England in 1714, thereby founding the Hanoverian dynasty.

Sophia was born in The Hague, the twelfth child of Frederick V, the elector palatine, and his wife Elizabeth Stuart. In 1658 she married Ernest Augustus, Duke of Brunswick, who in 1692 became the first elector of Hanover. He died in 1698.

Sophia was an intelligent woman and a distinguished scholar. She was a close friend of the philosopher Leibniz and corresponded with other scholars. She also took a keen interest in English affairs.

In order to exclude the Roman Catholic descendants of James II from the English throne, Parliament passed the Act of Settlement in 1701. This placed Sophia and her heirs next in the line of succession after Queen ANNE, none of whose children had survived to adulthood. In the event, Sophia died on June 8, 1714, a few weeks before Anne. Her son George succeeded to the throne of England as George I in August of that year.

Sorel, Agnès (c. 1422–1450) *Mistress of King Charles VII of France*

The first official mistress of a French king, Agnès Sorel was known as "Dame de Beauté" after the chateau and estates of Beauté-sur-Marne, which were given to her by the king.

A minor member of the household of Isabella of Lorraine, queen of Sicily, Agnès Sorel apparently became the mistress of Charles VII in 1444, having met him the year before. She was said to have received so many gifts from the king that the royal treasury was strained.

Though she exerted great influence over the king, particularly during his campaigns against the English, she was disliked by the dauphin, the future Louis XI. Her influence made her many other enemies. Despite her reputation for immoral behaviour and wild extravagance, she is said to have been shrewd and sensible. Having settled at Loches, a forbidding fortress near the Loire, she had four daughters by Charles, and her influence over him remained supreme until her death. The public, scandalized by her behaviour, generally assumed that the dauphin had had her poisoned, though there is no proof of this. Others, with still less justification, accused the financier Jacques Coeur, who was arrested in 1451 and charged with causing her death (he subsequently escaped).

Southcott, Joanna (c. 1750–1814) *British religious fanatic*

Believing herself to be pregnant with a second Prince of Peace, Joanna Southcott persuaded tens of thousands of followers (known as Southcottians) to accept her as a prophet. The title of her book *Strange Effects of Faith* (1804) may explain some of the gullibility of the Southcottians.

The daughter of a Devon farmer, Joanna Southcott worked as a servant until about 1792, when she announced that she was the woman mentioned in the twelfth chapter of the Book of Revelation, who would proclaim the Second Coming of Jesus Christ. This event would herald the first stage of the ending of the world.

After moving to London in 1802, she spread her message through two publications, *A Warning* (1803) and *The Book of Wonders* (1813–14), and gathered a following that numbered tens of thousands. In 1814 she announced that on October 19 she would produce by a virgin birth a second Prince of Peace, who would inaugurate the last era of world history. Although she was in her sixties, she swelled visibly, probably from dropsy. Taking to her bed while her followers waited in reverent expectation, she died of a brain tumour.

Believing that their prophetess would rise from the dead, a small core of her followers was still in existence a century later.

Spark, Dame Muriel (1918–)
British writer

> Give me a girl at an impressionable age, and she is mine for life.
>
> —*The Prime of Miss Jean Brodie* (1961)

> Her prose is like a bird darting from place to place, palpitating with nervous energy; but a bird with a bright beady eye and a sharp beak as well.
>
> —Francis Hope, *The Observer*, April 26, 1963

Murel Spark is known for her witty and original novels dealing with the bizarre or eccentric in human behaviour. Her best-known work is *The Prime of Miss Jean Brodie* (1961), which was also successful as a play (1965) and a film (1969).

Muriel Sarah Camberg was born in Edinburgh and educated there at James Gillespie's School for Girls. At the age of 18 she eloped to marry and subsequently moved to Rhodesia (now Zimbabwe) with her husband. After the break-up of her marriage she returned to Britain with her son in 1944. She then worked in the political intelligence department of the Foreign Office (1944–45) before becoming a freelance writer and editor with various jobs, including editor of *Poetry Review* (1947–49). Her first books were works of literary criticism, among them *Child of Light: A Reassessment of Mary Shelley* (1951) and *John Masefield* (1953). For the last three decades she has lived mainly in Italy.

A convert to Roman Catholicism in 1954, Spark brings a Catholic orientation to much of her fiction, notably her first novel, *The Comforters* (1957), and

The Mandelbaum Gate (1965), which won the James Tait Black Prize. Among her other novels are *Memento Mori* (1959) – a study of old age and coming to terms with death – *The Ballad of Peckham Rye* and *The Batchelors* (both 1960), *The Girls of Slender Means* (1963), *The Abbess of Crewe* (1974), *The Only Problem* (1984), and *Reality and Dreams* (1996). She has also written poetry, plays, two collections of short stories (1967 and 1987), and the memoir *Curriculum Vitae* (1992). She was made a fellow of the Royal Society of Literature in 1963 and a DBE in 1967.

Spence, Catherine Helen (1825–1910) *Australian novelist, social reformer, and feminist*

Catherine Spence's first novel was published anonymously in 1854; she continued to write novels for the next 30 years. In her late forties she became involved in a number of social issues, including the care of destitute children, education, women's suffrage, and other feminist causes.

Born in Melrose, Scotland, Catherine Spence was taken by her father to South Australia in 1840 after the failure of his business ventures. In Australia she became a children's governess at the age of 17. However, some 14 years later she emerged as Australia's first successful female novelist with the anonymous publication of *Clara Morison: A Tale of South Australia during the Gold Fever* (1854) and *Tender and True: A Colonial Tale* (1856). Her many subsequent novels, which included *Mr. Hogarth's Will* (1865) and *The Author's Daughter* (1868), were published under her own name and reveal interesting social and political aspects of colonial life in mid 19th-century Australia.

Having become interested in the plight of destitute children in 1870, Spence was appointed to the State Children's Council in 1886. But her interest was not restricted to working on committees; she took three successive families of orphaned children into her own home. She was also at this time interested in improving the poor educational facilities available in South

Australia, especially for girls. Another of the causes for which she worked was the movement to introduce proportional representation into Australian politics. Her first published work on this subject was *A Plea for Pure Democracy* (1861).

The issue of votes for women was another of the causes for which Catherine Spence is remembered. In 1891 she was elected vice-president of the Women's Suffrage League of South Australia; only three years later the women of South Australia were given the vote.

Catherine Spence travelled widely in the United States, addressing a number of meetings on women's issues at the Chicago World Fair in 1893.

Springfield, Dusty (1939–) *British pop singer*

Remembered for her husky voice and extravagant bouffant hairstyles, Dusty Springfield is often considered the best British woman pop singer of the 1960s.

Born Mary O'Brien in London, she began her musical career with the Springfields, a folk trio that also included her brother Tom. The group enjoyed several hit singles in Britain, and their song "Silver Threads and Golden Needles" (1963) was also a success in the United States.

After the Springfields split up in 1964, Dusty adopted a more soulful style influenced by the Tamla-Motown sound and such contemporary "girl groups" as the Ronettes. Her strong vocals and sure taste in choosing both songs and musical associates led to a series of British hits in the mid 1960s, including "I Only Want to Be with You" and "You Don't Have to Say You Love Me." In 1969 Springfield travelled to Memphis, Tennessee, to record the album *Dusty in Memphis* with a team of American musicians and producers. The record, which included the hit "Son of a Preacher Man," is regarded as her finest achievement and one of the best pop albums of its era.

Dusty Springfield recorded little of note in the next few years and after a failed comeback attempt in 1977–78 virtually retired from music making.

Nevertheless, she remains warmly admired by many younger musicians. In 1987 she enjoyed a big hit in Britain and the United States singing with the Pet Shop Boys on their composition "What Have I Done to Deserve This?"

Spry, Constance (1886–1960) *British flower arranger and cookery expert*

Constance Spry was a perfectionist who sought to bring beauty, good food, and good wines into people's homes.

Born in Derby but brought up and educated in Ireland, Constance Spry did welfare work in London's East End in the 1920s. In 1929 she opened her first florist's shop, and in the 1930s established a school of flower arranging in London's exclusive Mayfair district. Spry's outstanding skill and creativity made her much in demand at the highest social levels; she was responsible for the floral decoration of the Royal Opera House, Covent Garden, on gala evenings and for the flower arrangements at the wedding and coronation of Queen ELIZABETH II.

Constance Spry became joint principal with Rosemary Hume of the Cordon Bleu Cookery School in London and ran a school at Winkfield Place near Windsor, where young women could learn the complete art of cookery and entertaining. Her influence on British taste and lifestyles became wider still through her 13 books on flower arranging, gardening, cookery, and wine.

Spurgeon, Caroline (1869–1942) *British educator*

Caroline Spurgeon was the first woman to hold a professorship at an English university.

Caroline Spurgeon graduated from Oxford University in 1899 and went on to become an authority on Chaucer and Shakespeare. In 1901 she began lecturing at London's Bedford College for Women, a post she held until 1906, when she joined the staff of the University of London. From 1913 to 1929 she was professor of English literature at London and head of the English department at Bedford. She also served as the first president of the International Federation of University

Women from 1920 until 1924. In 1939 she retired to Tucson, Arizona.

Spyri, Johanna (1827–1901) *Swiss writer of children's novels*

Johanna Spyri is best known as the author of *Heidi*, an internationally loved classic of children's literature. First published in 1880–81, the book was quickly translated into many languages, among them English (1884).

She was born Johanna Heusser in Hirzel, Switzerland, into a conservative, middle-class family. In 1852 she married Bernhard Spyri, a lawyer, and settled in Zurich. She wrote over 50 novels for children. The enduring popularity of *Heidi*, about an orphaned girl who lives with her grandfather, is due both to Spyri's sensitive insights into the thoughts and emotions of her young characters and to her superb descriptions of the mountainous Swiss countryside. Her other novels include *Heimatlos* (1881) and *Gritli* (1882).

Staël, Madame de (1766–1817) *French writer, critic, and feminist*

> The entire social order...is arranged against a woman who wants to rise to a man's reputation.
>
> —*De la littérature* (1800)

> I was, and I still am convinced that women being the victims of all social institutions, are destined to misery if they make the least concession to their feelings and if, in any way whatever, they lose control of themselves.
>
> —*Delphine* (1803)

Madame de Staël's famous salons were frequented by the most prominent intellectual and political figures of the period and became the centre of liberal opposition to Napoleon Bonaparte. She herself had a direct influence on literature as an important forerunner of French romanticism.

Anne Louise Germaine Necker was born in Paris, the daughter of the Swiss banker Jacques Necker, who became Louis XVI's minister of finance. Her mother was Suzanne NECKER, a Calvinist Frenchwoman, in whose famous literary salon Germaine spent her childhood. In 1786 her parents married her to Baron Eric Magnus de Staël-Holstein, the Swedish ambassador to France. The marriage was an unhappy one, and Madame de Staël had many lovers. Viscount Louis de Narbonne-Lara was the father of her sons, Auguste and Albert.

After the outbreak of the French Revolution in 1789 de Staël's salon became a focus of support for the liberal policies of her father, whom she worshipped. However, after Necker was dismissed in 1790 and her lover Narbonne was forced to flee to England, ending his short term as minister of war, she too travelled to England early in 1793. In the summer of 1793 her affair with Narbonne ended, and she went to her father's estate at Coppet, near Geneva, where she was to spend much of her life.

In 1795 Madame de Staël returned to Paris with her new lover, the French writer and political leader Benjamin Constant. (He was probably the father of her daughter Albertine, born in 1796.) When she reopened her salon, it became a centre of opposition to Napoleon, with whom she constantly quarrelled. Her first important work, *De l'influence des passions sur le bonheur des individes et des nations* (The Influence of the Passions on the Wellbeing of Individuals and Nations), appeared in 1796.

After repeated banishments by Napoleon, her exile became permanent in October 1803, when he forbade her to approach within 40 leagues of Paris. She then made Coppet, where she received the intellectual and social elite of her time, into a headquarters of anti-Bonapartist opinion. Among her major works written during these turbulent years were *De la littérature considérée dans ses rapports avec les institutions sociales* (1800; On Literature Considered in Relation to Social Institutions), and the romantic novel *Delphine* (1803).

During her exile Madame de Staël travelled widely, notably to Germany (1803–04, 1808), where she met Goethe, Schiller, and the leaders of the romantic movement, and to Italy (1805). In this period she produced two of her most important works – the novel *Corinne ou l'Italie* (1807), in which she portrayed herself, and *De l'Allemagne*, her account of Germany. *De l'Allemagne*, which introduced German romantic literature and philosophy to France, was suppressed by Napoleon in 1810 as "un-French." It was subsequently published in London (1813).

Owing to increased persecution by Napoleon's agents, Madame de Staël fled from Coppet in 1812, shortly after giving birth to a son by her lover Lieutenant John Rocca. She returned to Paris after Napoleon's abdication in 1814. Although in poor health, she remained active, opposing the reactionary tendencies of the Bourbon regime and working for the abolition of the slave trade. She also finished her *Considérations sur les principaux événements de la Révolution française* (1816; Reflections on the Principal Events of the French Revolution), in which she asserted that the French Revolution, far from destroying tradition, was the fulfilment of the true French tradition – the struggle for liberty.

Stanhope, Lady Hester (1776–1839) *British traveller*

> I am reckoned here the first politician in the world, and by some a sort of prophet.
> —Letter from Syria to Dr. Meryon, 1836

Lady Hester Stanhope became a famous eccentric, dressing as a Turkish man and living in a hill-top monastery in western Syria (now Lebanon).

Hester Lucy Stanhope, eldest daughter of Charles, 3rd Earl Stanhope, was born at Chevening in Kent. In 1803 she took over the household of her unmarried uncle, the prime minister William Pitt, and acted as hostess for him on public occasions. Following Pitt's death in 1806, Lady Hester was granted a royal pension of £1,200 in recognition of her services.

Restless after her withdrawal from public life and grieved by the death in the Peninsular War of Sir John Moore, whom she had loved, she left England in 1810 to travel in the Middle East. Having visited Jerusalem and camped with desert bedouins, she settled down to live in a monastery on Mount Lebanon in 1814 before moving to another monastery on the summit of Dar Djoun nearby. There she adopted the local dress and lifestyle, dabbled in astrology, and gained a reputation as a prophet. Held in awe by local tribes for her fearless horsemanship and her eccentricity, she frequently interfered in their rivalries and disputes.

Her reckless generosity to anyone with a hard-luck story to tell reduced her to dire poverty in the final years of her life. She died at Dar Djoun, where she was buried.

Stanton, Elizabeth Cady (1815–1902) *American reformer*

> We still wonder at the stolid incapacity of all men to understand that woman feels the invidious distinctions of sex exactly as the black man does those of colour, or the white man the more transient distinctions of wealth, family, position, place, and power; that she feels as keenly as man the injustice of disfranchisement.
> —*History of Woman Suffrage* (1881)

A leader of the U.S. women's suffrage movement, Elizabeth Cady Stanton organized, with Lucretia MOTT, the first women's rights convention at Seneca Falls, New York State, in 1848. She was the first president of the National American Woman Suffrage Association.

Elizabeth Cady was born in Johnstown, New York, and brought up in a strict Presbyterian household. By special arrangement she was admitted to Johnstown Academy, open only to boys, where she excelled in Greek, before attending Emma WILLARD's academy in Troy, New York, from which she graduated in 1832. She then studied law with her father, Judge Daniel Cady, but because of her sex could not practise as a lawyer. While working in her father's office, she became interested in the property and custody rights of women. In 1840 she married the abolitionist Henry Brewster Stanton but did not vow to "obey" him, believing that "The Bible and Church have been the greatest stumbling block in the way of woman's emancipation."

The Stantons had seven children, one of whom, Harriet Stanton Blatch, also became a suffrage leader.

In the summer of 1840 the Stantons attended the world antislavery convention in London, at which Lucrecia Mott and other women delegates were refused recognition because of their sex. On their return to Boston the Stantons became active in supporting the temperance and abolition campaigns. In 1846 they moved to Seneca Falls, and it was in this small industrial community that Elizabeth Cady Stanton was able to observe more fully the narrow lot of most women. In 1848 she, Lucretia Mott, and others called the Seneca Falls Convention, which formally launched the women's rights movement. Stanton read a "Declaration of Sentiments," which stated grievances of women against existing laws and customs.

During these years Stanton contributed regularly to the New York *Tribune* and the temperance paper *The Lily*. In 1851 she persuaded Susan B. ANTHONY to join the women's rights movement, and they worked together for the rest of her life, organizing programmes, lecturing, and appearing before legislative bodies to argue for the property rights of married women. Stanton was chosen first president of the National Woman Suffrage Association, founded in 1869, and called and addressed its first International Council of Women, held in Washington in 1888. When the two major women's suffrage groups merged in 1890, she was elected president of the new National American Woman Suffrage Association.

Because of her pioneering stand for women's suffrage and her demand that women be allowed to control their own property and to obtain divorce on grounds of brutality and drunkenness, Stanton was regarded by many as a radical. In addition to pursuing her reform work, from 1869 until 1881 she lectured regularly on family life and child care. With Susan B. Anthony and Matilda Gage she compiled the *History of Woman Suffrage* (1881–86), and with Susan B. Anthony, *The Woman's Bible* (1895, 1898). Her pam-

phlets *The Degradation of Disenfranchisement* and *The Solitude of Self* (1892) were very influential. She published her reminiscences, *Eighty Years and More* in 1898.

See also CATT, CARRIE; STONE, LUCY BLACKWELL.

Stanwyck, Barbara (1907–1990)
American film actress

> Just be truthful, and if you can fake that you've got it made.
>
> —Advice on acting given to Walter Matthau

One of the most popular film stars of the 1930s and 1940s, Barbara Stanwyck usually played assertive coldhearted women. She won four Oscar nominations and in 1944 was named as the highest-paid woman in the United States.

She was born Ruby Stevens, in Brooklyn, New York, the youngest of five children. Orphaned at the age of four, she left school at 13 to take dancing lessons. She began her career as a dancer and was discovered at the Ziegfeld Follies by theatrical producer Willard Mack, who gave her the lead in his Broadway production *The Noose* (1925) and suggested that she take the name Barbara Stanwyck. After her success in the musical *Burlesque* (1927) she received several film offers.

After making her screen debut in the silent film *Broadway Nights* (1927), Stanwyck achieved her big break with Frank Capra's *Ladies of Leisure* (1930) and *Miracle Woman* (1931). Her subsequent movies included *Union Pacific* (1939), *Golden Boy* (1939), *The Lady Eve* (1941), *The Strange Love of Martha Ivers* (1946), and *Executive Suite* (1954). She was nominated for Academy Awards for her performances in *Stella Dallas* (1937), *Ball of Fire* (1942), the classic *Double Indemnity* (1944), and *Sorry, Wrong Number* (1948). In the 1950s she made several Westerns, including Allan Dwan's *Cattle Queen of Montana* (1954). She later had her own television programme, *The Barbara Stanwyck Show* (1960–61), and appeared on the series *The Big Valley* (1965–69). Her last film was the thriller *The Night Walker* (1965), in which she costarred with her ex-husband, Robert Taylor (an earlier marriage to vaudeville star Frank Fay had also ended in divorce). She was given an honorary Academy Award in 1982.

Stark, Dame Freya (1893–1993)
British traveller and writer

> The great and almost only comfort about being a woman is that one can always pretend to be more stupid than one is, and no one is surprised.
> —*The Valley of the Assassins* (1934)

Dame Freya Stark was an expert on Arab affairs who travelled widely in the Middle East and worked for the British ministry of information in the region during World War II. Her many books tell of her experiences before, during, and after the war.

Born in Paris, the daughter of nomadic artists, Freya Madeline Stark was educated privately at her grandmother's home in Italy and grew up able to speak fluently in Italian, French, German, and English, albeit with an Italian accent. She also studied literature at Bedford College, London. During World War I she served as a nurse in Italy and then for three years endured a period of intense poverty and semi-invalidism. Recovering, she took a course in Arabic at the School of Oriental and African Studies in the University of London and in 1927 set out on the first of many journeys through the Middle East.

A tiny but supremely self-confident figure, she braved bedouins, bandits, storms, and heat and nearly died at different times from malaria, dysentery, measles, and dengue fever. She survived, however, and produced a series of books, such as *The Valley of the Assassins* (1934), *The Southern Gates of Arabia* (1938), and *A Winter in Arabia* (1940), that wove history, mythology, archaeology, and her own travels into enthralling explorations of the past and present. The Royal Geographical Society awarded her its Mungo Park Medal in 1936 and its highest honour, the Founder's Medal, in 1942.

During World War II Stark worked for the British government in the Middle East, promoting a network of cells of antifascist sympathizers. She later described her experiences in *West Is East* (1945). In 1950 she published the first of her four volumes of autobiography and began to learn Turkish by reading the Bible and detective stories in that language. For most of the last 40 years of her life she was based in the mountain town of Asola in the Italian Dolomites, but continued to travel, crossing Afghanistan in a jeep at the age of 76 and trekking through Nepal on horseback in her eighties. An outstanding photographer, she was also a brilliant letter writer and published superb books of photographs and letters. In 1972 she was created a DBE.

Starr, Belle (1848–1889) *American outlaw*

A daring rider and a crack shot, Belle Starr was a member of William Quantrill's gang of Confederate guerrillas, which also included Frank and Jesse James and the Younger brothers.

She was born in Carthage, Missouri, the daughter of Judge John Shirley. After her brother Edward joined Quantrill's gang, Belle supplied them with news of federal troop movements. When Edward was killed in 1863, she joined the band, which often took refuge on her family's farm in Texas. After giving birth to a daughter, Pearl Younger, in 1869, Belle worked for a while in Dallas saloons. In about 1872 she married Jim Reed, another member of the gang, and gave birth to their son Edward. The couple was involved in a famous stagecoach hold-up near Austin, but Reed was dead within a year, killed by lawmen.

In 1880 Belle married Sam Starr, an Irish Cherokee, and their ranch in Indian territory became a notorious outlaw hideout. Although charged four times with horse stealing, she was imprisoned only once, in 1883, managing on the other occasions to find legal loopholes. Sam was killed in 1886. On February 3, 1889, during a court hearing at Fort Smith, Belle Starr was shot in the back by an unknown gunman. Although suspicion fell on Edgar Watson, a neighbour, it was also rumoured that her son Ed was the killer.

St. Denis, Ruth (1877–1968) *American dancer, choreographer, and teacher*

One of the pioneers of modern dance, Ruth St. Denis founded (in 1915) the influential Denishawn company and school in Los Angeles with her husband Ted Shawn. As principal soloist with the company she introduced American audiences to serious ethnic dance. The school trained such great dancers as Martha GRAHAM, Doris HUMPHREY, and Charles Weidman.

Born Ruth Dennis in Newark, New Jersey, she received little formal education. Her dancing career began in vaudeville and Broadway spectaculars, and in 1898 she appeared in *The Ballet Girls*. After changing her name, she spent several seasons travelling with the impresario David Belasco in the United States and Europe. Inspired by a cigarette poster of the Egyptian goddess Isis, she began to specialize in Oriental dance. Her Hindu-based dance *Radha*, which was performed in New York in 1906, was her first success. She then toured Europe and the United States in 1909 with *The Incense* and *Cobras*. Her repertoire, including *Green Nautch*, *Egypta*, *O-Mika*, and *White Madonna*, was danced barefoot, usually in Oriental costume, and emphasized rippling arm movements and striking poses with scarves and veils.

In 1914 Ruth St. Denis married Ted Shawn, and the couple became partners, founding the Denishawn company and school the following year. Like her husband, St. Denis was interested in the religious roots of dance and believed that dancers should be trained in all traditions. In 1932 St. Denis and Shawn separated to work independently. St. Denis continued to dance, sometimes at Shawn's school in Jacob's Pillow, Massachusetts. Turning towards Christian themes in her work, she was involved in the Society of Spiritual Arts (founded 1931), founded the Church of the Divine Dance in Hollywood in 1947, and produced such works as *Freedom* (1955). She taught at several schools, including the School of Natya, which she founded with La Meri in New York City in 1940, and at Adelphi College. She also lectured and made films of her dances.

Stead, Christina (1902–1983) *Australian writer*

Christina Stead was a prolific short-story writer and novelist; although initially neglected, her 11 novels are now known throughout the English-speaking world.

Christina Ellen Stead was born in Sydney, where her father was a naturalist; her mother died when she was a baby. She trained and was employed as a teacher before taking up office work to save for her fare to Europe. After living briefly in London, where she met the American economist William Blake, she moved to Paris with him, working for five years in a Paris bank as a secretary. Her first published work, a collection of short stories entitled *The Salzburg Tales*, appeared in 1934. It was soon followed by *Seven Poor Men of Sydney* (1934), a novel that weaves together the experiences of apparently unconnected characters from the waterfront area of her native city.

From 1937 to 1947 Stead and Blake, now married, lived in the United States, where she worked in Hollywood as a screenwriter for MGM and as an instructor in novel-writing at New York University. During this period she published *House of All Nations* (1938), a novel about the world of high finance that drew on her Paris experiences, and *The Man Who Loved Children* (1940), a novel about the tensions of family life that is generally considered her finest work. After a further period of travel Stead and Blake settled in England in 1953, where she wrote a number of novels, including *A Little Tea, A Little Chat* (1948), *Cotter's England* (1956), and *Miss Herbert* (1976). *I'm Dying Laughing*, a novel about Hollywood that she started to write when she was living there, was published in 1986, after her death.

Since none of Stead's novels had been published in Australia until 1965, recognition in her native country was belated. She was even debarred from one Australian award on the grounds that, since she had lived so long overseas and many of her works were set in Paris, London, or New York, she could no longer be considered an Australian writer. Following her husband's death, she finally returned to Australia in 1974 and in that same year became the first recipient of the prestigious Patrick White Award in recognition of her lifetime's literary achievement.

Stein, Charlotte von (1742–1827)
German noblewoman

Charlotte von Stein is best remembered for her friendship with the poet Goethe and for her influence on his work.

Born Charlotte von Schardt in Eisenach, the daughter of the master of ceremonies at the Weimar court, at the age of 15 she became lady-in-waiting to Anna Amalia, the mother of the Duke of Saxe-Weimar. In 1764 she married the duke's equerry, Baron Friedrich von Stein, by whom she had seven children. The marriage, however, was an unhappy one.

Frau von Stein's association with Goethe began in 1775, when he arrived in Weimar at the duke's invitation, and lasted until his departure for Italy in 1786. He saw her as the ideal of femininity, and she inspired such characters in his work as Iphigenie in *Iphigenie auf Tauris* (1787) and Natalie in *Wilhelm Meister* (1795–96). They shared literary and philosophical interests, and their close attachment is reflected in his letters to her and such poems as "To Charlotte von Stein." After Goethe returned from Italy in 1788, he formed a relationship with Christiane Vulpius, whom he later married; this resulted in a complete break with von Stein.

Her own works include the humorous drama *Rino* (1776), which contains a portrait of Goethe and the ladies of the court, and the prose tragedy *Dido* (published posthumously in 1867), which alludes to her break with him.

Stein, Edith (1891–1942) *German philosopher*

> Come, we are going for our people.
>
> —Last words to her sister as they entered the gas chambers

A Jewish philosopher who became a Carmelite nun, Edith Stein was gassed with her sister in Auschwitz. Her subsequent beatification as a Christian martyr caused some controversy.

Born of orthodox Jewish parents in Breslau, Edith Stein renounced her family's faith at the age of 13, proclaiming herself an atheist. After studying at Göttingen University, she was awarded a PhD in philosophy at the University of Freiburg for her work in phenomenology, a new approach to philosophy that was developing there.

Stein converted to Roman Catholicism in 1922 and for the next decade taught at a Dominican girls school in Speyer. During this period she translated the works of St. Thomas Aquinas and Cardinal Newman. Shortly after she became a lecturer at the Educational Institute in Münster, the Nazi party came to power in Germany (1933) and she was dismissed on account of her Jewish origins.

In 1934 Stein entered a Carmelite convent in Cologne to become a nun, adopting the name Sister Teresa Benedicta of the Cross. Four years later she was transferred to a convent at Echt in Holland to keep her safe from persecution by the Germans. Here she worked on a biographical and phenomenological study of St. John of the Cross. In 1942, shortly after the Dutch bishops spoke out against the German persecution of Jews, she was arrested with her sister Rosa, another convert. Within weeks both perished in the gas chambers of the extermination camp at Auschwitz.

In 1955 the Edith Stein Guild for aiding converts was founded in the United States. Stein's beatification in 1987 was not without controversy. Some Jews interpreted her last words as a return to the Jewish faith, and on these grounds objected to her beatification as a Christian martyr.

Stein, Gertrude (1874–1946) *American writer*

> Reading Gertrude Stein at length is not unlike making one's way through an interminable and badly printed game book.

—Richard Bridgeman, *Gertrude
Stein in Pieces*

The Jews have produced only three
originative geniuses: Christ, Spin-
oza, and myself.

—Quoted by J. Mellow in *Charmed
Circle*

A unique and controversial figure who
lived in France from 1903 until her
death, Gertrude Stein is now remembered more for her influence on the
American expatriate writers around
her in Paris – Ernest Hemingway, F.
Scott Fitzgerald, and Sherwood Anderson – than for her own work.

Born in Allegheny, Pennsylvania,
Gertrude Stein spent her childhood in
Vienna and Paris before the family settled in Oakland, California, where her
father and her eldest brother Michael
made a fortune in street railways and
property. After attending Radcliffe
College, where she studied with the
philosopher William James from 1893
to 1897, she went to Johns Hopkins
University in Baltimore to study medicine. In 1902, abandoning a medical
career in favour of literature, she followed her brother Leo to Paris and
with him established a famous salon.
They also began to buy the paintings
of Matisse, Braque, and Picasso before
these artists were well known, thereby
enabling her to take the credit for their
later success. Although this was vehemently denied by the artists involved,
she nevertheless did much to promote
modern art, and Picasso became a
long-standing friend.

By 1903 Stein had established a relationship with her lifelong companion,
Alice B. TOKLAS, a friend from San
Francisco. Her early writings were directly influenced by the work of such
painters as Cézanne, Matisse, and Picasso. Her first important book, *Three
Lives* (1909), was followed by a series
of abstract verbal portraits of her
friends suggested by early cubist portraits. These led to the composition of
her major work, *The Making of Americans* (1925).

After World War I, during which she
and Toklas did fieldwork with the
American Fund for French Wounded,
Stein was taken up with salon life and
the support of expatriate writers. She
did not attain wide recognition until
1933, when she published her memoirs,
The Autobiography of Alice B. Toklas.
In 1934 she returned to the United
States for the opening of her opera
Four Saints in Three Acts, with a musical score by Virgil Thomson, in Hartford, Connecticut, and gave a highly
publicized lecture tour. During World
War II she remained in occupied
France, an experience she recounted in
Wars I Have Seen (1945). In her last
years Stein's kindness and generosity
made her a great favourite with American servicemen in Paris, and her last
novel, *Brewsie and Willie* (1946), is
concerned with them.

Gertrude Stein always meant to return to the United States after the war
but died of cancer before she was able
to leave Paris. *The Mother of Us All*,
an opera based on the life of Susan B.
ANTHONY, for which Stein provided
the libretto and Virgil Thomson the
score, was first produced in New York
in 1947.

Steinem, Gloria (1934–   ) *American
writer, editor, and feminist*

No man can call himself liberal, or
radical, or even a conservative advocate of fair play, if his work depends in any way on the unpaid or
underpaid labor of women at home,
or in the office.

—*The New York Times*,
August 26, 1971

I have yet to hear a man ask for advice on how to combine marriage
and a career.

—Interview on LBC radio,
April 2, 1984

One of the most forceful and articulate
campaigners in the women's movement, Gloria Steinem also took part in
the radical protest movements of the
1960s, notably those against the Vietnam War and against racial discrimination. In 1971 she helped found the
National Women's Political Caucus,
which encouraged political activity by
women, and in 1972 she founded *Ms.*,
a magazine that treated contemporary
issues from a feminist viewpoint.

Steinem was born in Toledo, Ohio,
and graduated from Smith College in

1956 with a qualification in government. She then studied in India for two years at the universities of Delhi and Calcutta, before becoming a freelance journalist in New York, where she worked for women's magazines and television. In 1968 she began writing a political column for *New York* magazine. About this time she joined the women's movement, helping to organize the National Women's Political Caucus and the Women's Action Alliance, which attacked discrimination against women in employment and other areas. Within a year of its inception *Ms.* magazine had reached a circulation of 350,000. Although she resigned as editor in 1987, she has continued with the magazine as a columnist and consulting editor. She also travels widely to raise funds for the *Ms* Foundation for Women, a charity.

Steinem's writings include *The Thousand Indias* (1957), *The Beach Book* (1963), *Outrageous Acts and Everyday Rebellions* (1983), *Marilyn* (1986) – a controversial study of Marilyn MONROE – *Revolution from Within: A Book of Self-Esteem* (1992), and *Moving Beyond Words* (1994).

Stepanova, Varara Feodorovna
(1894–1958) *Russian artist*

Varara (or Warwara) Stepanova was a leading figure in constructivism, a form of abstract art that evolved in Russia after the Revolution.

Born in Kovno, Lithuania, Varara Stepanova trained at the Karzan School of Art (1910–11) before moving on to further study at the Stroganov School of Arts and Crafts in Moscow (1912–14). Following the Bolshevik Revolution, she became deputy director of the decorative arts section of the Commissariat for Public Instruction.

Accepting wholeheartedly the new regime's conviction that art should serve the working masses in their everyday lives, she focused her own efforts on graphic design, typography, textiles, and sets for the propagandistic theatre. In 1921 Stepanova joined her husband, the artist Alexsandr Rodchenko, in founding the avant-garde First Working Group of Constructivists to promote a view of art that celebrated technology and the social and cultural revolution they believed it was bringing into being. From 1923 to 1928 they also produced the magazine *Lef*. In the 1930s and 1940s she produced a number of books in collaboration with the futurist poet Vladimir Mayakovsky. In the 1950s she continued her work on the design of posters.

Stevens, Nettie Maria (1861–1912)
American biologist

Nettie Stevens was a latecomer to biology, not attending university until she was 35. However, she made a considerable contribution to biology, in particular by identifying the role of X- and Y-chromosomes in determining the sex of organisms.

Nettie Stevens was born in Cavendish, Vermont, and began her career as a librarian. She did not take her bachelor's degree in physiology at Stanford University until she was 38. Within four more years she gained a master's degree and then a doctorate from Bryn Mawr College, Pennyslvania, where she studied under a German biologist, Theodor Boveri, and later carried out her own research.

Her most important discovery, in 1906, was that the sex of a plant, insect, or human being is determined by the operation of the Y-chromosome. This breakthrough, made in the same year by Edmund Beecher Wilson, was fundamental to the development of the science of genetics. She was also interested in the form and structure of protozoa and in cytology (the study of cells). In 1994 she was elected to the U.S. National Women's Hall of Fame.

Stevenson, Juliet (Anne Virginia)
(1956–) *British actress*

An actress of great charm and accomplishment, Juliet Stevenson is perhaps best known for playing vulnerable and introspective characters.

Stevenson was educated at Hurst Lodge School, Berkshire, St. Catherine's School, Surrey, and the Royal Academy of Dramatic Art (RADA), where she was awarded the Gold Bancroft Medal. She has one daughter (born 1994) by her former partner Hugh Brody.

Stevenson began her acting career

with the Royal Shakespeare Company in 1979. Her many roles with the company in the 1980s included Rosalind in *As You Like It*, Cressida in *Troilus and Cressida*, Isabella in *Measure for Measure* (Drama Magazine Best Actress Award), Lady Percy in *Henry IV Parts I and II*, and Octavia/Iras in *Antony and Cleopatra*. In 1989 she took the title role in a National Theatre production of Ibsen's *Hedda Gabler* and in 1992 she won the Time Out Best Actress Award for her performance as a brutalized torture victim in Ariel Dorfman's *Death and the Maiden*. More recently (1995) she took the lead in a revival of Webster's *The Duchess of Malfi*.

Stevenson's roles in the cinema include a murderess in Peter Greenaway's *Drowning by Numbers* (1988), a grieving daughter in *The Secret Rapture* (1994), and a matchmaker in the Jane Austen adaptation *Emma* (1996). However, she is probably best known for her touching performance as the newly widowed Nina in *Truly Madly Deeply* (1991) a role reputedly based on Stevenson's own slightly eccentric character and lifestyle.

Stocks, Mary, Baroness (1891–1975)
British educationalist and broadcaster

An economist by training, Mary Stocks was a lifelong supporter of liberal causes who dedicated herself to extending educational opportunities in Britain. In later life her forthright opinions made her a popular radio personality.

Mary Danvers Brinton was born in London, the daughter of a doctor, and grew up in a highly intellectual atmosphere. After attending St. Paul's Girls' School in London, she studied at the London School of Economics (LSE), where she gained a first-class degree. By this time she was already an active supporter of the women's suffrage movement, although she adhered to its moderate rather than its militant wing. In 1913 Mary married John Stocks, an Oxford academic. During their early married life she lectured on economics at the LSE and at King's College for Women, London. In 1924, however, the couple moved to Manchester, where John Stocks was appointed professor of philosophy at the university. Over the next 12 years Mary was active in educational programmes that were intended to make the university's courses and facilities available to nonmembers, including the industrial working class. She later became deputy president of the Workers' Educational Association (WEA) and wrote its history. During this time she was also involved in community work in Manchester, where she set up Britain's first birth-control clinic outside London.

Following her husband's death in 1937, Mary Stocks moved back to London, where she served as principal of Westfield College (1938–51). She also sat on a series of government committees dealing with educational and welfare issues. From the 1950s onwards she became nationally known for her appearances on BBC radio, especially on the discussion programmes *The Brains Trust* and *Any Questions?* She was created a baroness by the Labour government in 1966 but later refused to support the party in the House of Lords. Her publications include two volumes of memoirs and a biography of her friend Eleanor RATHBONE; she also wrote several plays.

Stone, Lucy Blackwell (1818–1893)
American reformer

> We want rights. The flour-merchant, the house-builder, and the postman charge us no less on account of our sex; but when we endeavour to earn money to pay all these, then, indeed, we find the difference.
>
> —"Disappointment is the Lot of Women," speech made in October 1855

> In education, in marriage, in religion, in everything, disappointment is the lot of women. It shall be the business of my life to deepen this disappointment in every woman's heart until she bows down to it no longer.
>
> —As above

A pioneer in the movement for women's rights and an eloquent speaker, Lucy Stone helped to organize the American Woman Suffrage Association in 1869 and became the editor of the *Woman's Journal* in 1872. It remained the leading journal of the U.S. women's rights movement for many years.

She was born near West Brookfield, Massachusetts. Disagreeing with her father's belief that women should be subservient to men and that they did not need to be educated, she undertook to educate herself. By working as a schoolteacher from the age of 16, she finally saved enough money to enrol at Oberlin College in 1843 (she eventually received some financial help from her father).

After graduating in 1847, she toured the country, speaking against slavery for the Anti-Slavery Society and also advocating equality for women. She was an organizer of the first national women's rights convention held in Worcester, Massachusetts, in 1850. In 1855 she married Henry Blackwell, a crusader for women's suffrage; by mutual agreement with her husband she retained her maiden name. She then concentrated on winning equality for women, generally through legislation and often in vain. She continued to be active in the cause of women's rights almost until the time of her death, giving her final lecture for the World Columbian Exposition in Chicago in 1893.

Stone's daughter, Alice Stone Blackwell (1857–1950), continued her mother's work as editor of *The Woman's Journal*.

See also ANTHONY, SUSAN B(ROWNELL); CATT, CARRIE; MOTT, LUCRETIA COFFIN; STANTON, ELIZABETH CADY.

Stopes, Marie (1880–1958) *British pioneer of birth control*

> Dr. Marie Stopes made contraceptive devices respectable in a somewhat gushing book, *Married Love*. For this she deserves to be remembered among the great benefactors of the age.
>
> —A. J. P. Taylor, *English History 1914–45*

A palaeobotanist of distinction, Marie Stopes developed her interest in birth control after her first marriage failed. It led her to found the first British birth-control clinic, which helped to get family planning recognized as a respectable and necessary activity.

Marie Charlotte Carmichael Stopes was born in Edinburgh and studied at University College, London, before taking her PhD in Munich. In 1904 she was appointed as the first-ever woman science lecturer at Manchester University after being awarded a DSc. There she specialized in palaeobotany, the study of fossilized plants. In 1907 she went to Japan to lecture and while there collaborated with Professor Sakurai in writing a book about the Noh drama. In 1911 she married Reginald Gates, but the sexual aspect of the relationship proved disastrous, and five years later the marriage was annulled on the grounds of nonconsummation. Driven by her own frustration, Marie Stopes set herself an intensive reading programme in the field of sexual relations and condensed the results of her research to produce Britain's first modern sex manual, *Married Love* (1918), which was banned in the United States.

After marrying a wealthy aircraft manufacturer, Harry Verdon Roe, who supported her propaganda work, Stopes campaigned for a wider knowledge of birth control, especially among the poor, who were often burdened with large families. Since the infant mortality rate was falling rapidly, thanks to improved nutrition and midwifery, her message was very timely, although it provoked considerable opposition from church leaders and newspaper moralists who feared it would lead to an epidemic of promiscuity.

In 1921 Marie Stopes opened her first birth-control clinic in Holloway, a deprived area of north London. To stress the serious and responsible nature of its work, she ensured that the staff wore nurses' uniform and followed a formal medical routine when giving advice. Unlike many other advocates of birth control, she was less concerned with eliminating poverty or "raising the quality of the race" (the objective of eugenicists) than with improving the quality of marriage itself. She believed that by freeing women from the fear of unwanted pregnancies and enabling them to space out births to match their economic circumstances, their own health and happiness would be improved.

By the 1930s Stopes had won over the Church of England to the cause of contraception, although the Roman Catholic Church has remained an implacable opponent. After World War II Stopes travelled the Far East to promote contraception there.

Although widely honoured in later years for her pioneering work, Marie Stopes became something of an embarrassment to the birth-control movement on account of her increasingly eccentric and quarrelsome personality. A prolific author, she wrote over 70 books, including *Wise Parenthood* (1918), *Radiant Motherhood* (1920), and a comprehensive survey of her field, *Contraception: Its Theory, History and Practice* (1923).

See also SANGER, MARGARET.

Stoppard, Miriam (1937–) *British physician, writer, and broadcaster*

Miriam Stoppard was a successful physician before writing a number of popular books on healthcare, beauty, and child and baby care. She has also presented a number of TV series on women's subjects.

Miriam Stern was born in Newcastle upon Tyne, to Sydney and Jenny Stern. After attending Newcastle Central High School, she went on to study medicine at London's Royal Free Hospital, the only medical school in London that accepted women as students at that time, where she specialized in dermatology. Subsequently she joined Syntex Pharmaceuticals Ltd., becoming medical director in 1974 and managing director from 1977 to 1981.

During this period she wrote a number of popular medical books, including *Miriam Stoppard's Book of Health Care* (1979) and *The Face and Body Book* (1980). Many more books followed after she ceased to be managing director of Syntex. They include *Your Baby* (1982), *Your Growing Child* (1983), *The Magic of Sex* (1991), and *The Menopause* (1994).

In 1972 Miriam Stern married the dramatist Tom Stoppard and subsequently used his surname in her writing. They had two sons before the marriage was dissolved in 1992.

Stowe, Harriet Beecher (1811–1896)
American writer and humanitarian

> Harriet Beecher Stowe, whose *Uncle Tom's Cabin* was the first evidence to America that no hurricane can be so disastrous to a country as a ruthlessly humanitarian woman.
>
> —Sinclair Lewis, *Henry Ward Beecher, An American Portrait*

> Women are the real architects of society.
>
> —"Dress, or Who Makes the Fashions," *Atlantic Monthly*, 1864

Harriet Beecher Stowe is best known for her immensely popular antislavery novel *Uncle Tom's Cabin*, which has been translated into at least 23 languages since its first publication in 1852.

She was born in Litchfield, Connecticut, the daughter of the clergyman and educator Lyman Beecher and his first wife Roxana Foote Beecher. Owing to the influence of their father, who was a powerful Puritan preacher, Harriet, her elder sister Catherine BEECHER, and her five brothers (who all became ministers) were used to discussing religious and moral problems from an early age. In 1832 she moved with her family to Cincinnati, Ohio, and joined Catherine as a teacher at her college there. In 1836 she married the Reverend Calvin Ellis Stowe. They had seven children.

Since Cincinnati lay close to the border with Kentucky, a slave-holding state, Harriet Beecher Stowe came in frequent contact with fugitive slaves fleeing violence and injustice. When her sixth child, her particular favourite, died of cholera in 1849, she felt that she finally understood the lot of African-American mothers separated from their children, and she vowed to do some special service on behalf of the slaves.

In 1850 the Stowes moved to Brunswick, Maine, where her husband had been appointed to the faculty of Bowdoin College. That same year her horror at the passing of the Fugitive Slave Law, which required the return of slaves who escaped their owners, prompted her to fulfil her vow by writing *Uncle Tom's Cabin, or Life Among the Lowly*. First published serially (1851–52) in the *National Era*, a Washington, D.C. antislavery paper, it appeared in book form in 1852 and within a year reached sales of 300,000 copies. The book consolidated antislavery opinion in the North, deeply angered the South, and must be counted as one of the factors bringing on the American Civil War. Many have argued about the book's literary merits, but it cannot be dismissed as mere propaganda.

After the success of *Uncle Tom's Cabin* Stowe became a full-time writer, producing 11 more works of fiction, including *Dred: A Tale of the Great Dismal Swamp* (1856) – a second antislavery novel – and several novels of New England life – *The Minister's Wooing* (1859), *The Pearl of Orr's Island* (1862), *Oldtown Folks* (1869), *Sam Lawson's Oldtown Fireside Stories* (1872), and *Poganuc People* (1878). She also continued to write for the *Atlantic Monthly* as well as producing biographies and children's books. Her collected works were published in 16 volumes in 1896.

Strachey, Ray (1887–1940) *British social reformer, feminist, and writer*

Ray Strachey is remembered for her advocacy of women's suffrage and access to the legal profession for women. Her many books include biographies of leading British and American suffragettes and a history of women's movements.

Rachel Costello was born in London, where she attended school before going on to Newnham College, Cambridge. She also studied in the United States, at Bryn Mawr College, Pennsylvania.

In 1911 Ray married Oliver Strachey, brother of the biographer and essayist Lytton Strachey. Through her sister-in-law Phillipa Strachey, a well-known suffragette, she became interested in social reform, especially in relation to women's issues.

After becoming parliamentary secretary to the London Society for Women's Suffrage, Strachey was actively involved in lobbying parliament, although she was not a supporter of the militant wing of the suffrage movement. She was also editor of the influential women's suffrage journal *Women's Leader*.

During World War I, in common with most British suffragists, she supported the war effort, making her own positive contribution to women's participation as chair of the Women's Services Bureau and as a delegate to the Paris conference on women's war work in 1917. After the war she was actively engaged on committees that worked to open the legal profession to women and to safeguard the rights of women in the civil service. At the same time, she ran unsuccessfully for parliament (1918, 1922, 1923), as an Independent.

She wrote many books, including biographies of the American suffragist Frances Willard (1912) and the leader of Britain's constitutional suffragettes, Millicent FAWCETT (1931), of whom she was a close friend. Perhaps her most important book was *The Cause: A Brief History of the Women's Movement* (1928).

Stratas, Teresa (1938–) *Canadian opera singer*

A lyric soprano noted for her dramatic stage presence, Teresa Stratas is also known as an extremely temperamental and volatile personality. She has been highly acclaimed for her performances in the operas of Verdi and Puccini and took the title role in the world premiere of Alban Berg's *Lulu* in 1979.

Born Anastasia Stataki in Toronto, Stratas was the youngest of three children of Greek immigrants. As a child she performed in the family restaurant and on radio before studying at the Royal Conservatory of Music, Toronto, with Irene Jessner (from 1956). In 1959 she made her professional debut as Mimi in a Canadian Opera Company production of *La Bohème* and won the "Auditions of the Air" held by New York's Metropolitan Opera. She made her Metropolitan debut later that year with a small part in Massenet's *Manon*.

After starring in a Hollywood film, *The Canadians*, in 1961, she concentrated on her opera career, advancing to leading roles at the Metropolitan Opera, La Scala, Covent Garden, the Salzburg Festival, and the Paris, Hamburg, and Moscow operas. Although particularly associated with the heroines of Verdi and Puccini, she has also appeared in Mozart and Tchaikovsky operas as well as contemporary works. Stratas made history at the Paris Opéra in 1979 with her performance in the completed version of Alban Berg's *Lulu*, earning enthusiastic reviews for brilliant singing and acting in the infamously difficult title role. That year she also sang Jenny in the Metropolitan Opera premiere of Kurt Weill and Bertolt Brecht's *Rise and Fall of the City of Mahagonny*.

Stratas's sudden cancellation of a live telecast of *Lulu* from the Lincoln Center in 1982 led to a four-year retirement. In 1986 she returned to the stage in a Broadway musical, *Rags*, which closed after only four performances. She then resumed her work at the "Met" while also starring as Marie Antoinette in the 1991 world premiere of *The Ghosts of Versailles* by William Hoffman and John Corigliano.

In the 1980s Stratas's dramatic gifts found a new outlet in a series of collaborations with Franco Zeffirelli, who directed her in film versions of *La Traviata*, *I Pagliacci*, and *La Bohème*. She also starred in Götz Friedrich's acclaimed video of Richard Strauss's *Salome*. Her adventurous approach to repertoire is reflected in her recordings, which include popular music selections as well as the highly successful album *The Unknown Kurt Weill* (1981).

Her many awards include three Grammys, an Emmy, and the 1986 Drama Desk Award; she was made an Officer of the Order of Canada in 1972. Stratas was the subject of Harry Rasky's film, *StrataSphere* (1983), on which his book *Stratas: An Affectionate Tribute* (1988) was based.

Streep, Meryl (1949–) *American film actress*

One of Hollywood's most respected actresses, Meryl Streep is noted for her versatility and her talent for accents.

Mary Louise Streep was born in Madison, New Jersey, the daughter of a pharmaceutical executive and a commercial artist. She began vocal training at the age of 12 and subsequently starred in several of her high school's musical productions. After studying drama at Vassar College, New York State, and touring with a Vermont repertory company, she attended the Yale School of Drama, where she gained a master's degree and played a wide range of roles at the Yale Repertory Theater. In 1975 she moved to Manhattan and joined the New York Shakespeare Festival, taking key roles in *The Taming of the Shrew* and other plays.

After making her film debut with a small part in *Julia* (1977), Streep went on to gain an Oscar nomination for Best Supporting Actress with her next role, that of a wife in *The Deer Hunter* (1978). That same year she won an Emmy Award for portraying the wife of a concentration-camp prisoner in the television miniseries *Holocaust*. In 1980 she won the Oscar for Best Supporting Actress in *Kramer vs. Kramer* (1979); a Best Actress Oscar for her role as the title character in *Sophie's Choice* followed in 1982. This film, about an Auschwitz survivor, required her to have a Polish accent.

Streep's other films of this period include *Manhattan* (1979) and *The Seduction of Joe Tynan* (1979). *The French Lieutenant's Woman* (1981), in which she demonstrated a perfect English accent, brought her another Oscar nomination and a BAFTA Award. Subsequent films included *Silkwood* (1983); *Out of Africa* (1985), in which she adopted a Danish accent to portray Isak DINESEN; *Ironweed* (1987), which brought another Oscar nomination; *A Cry in the Dark* (1988); and *Postcards from the Edge* (1990). After a run of flops in the early 1990s, she gave a *tour-de-force* performance in an uncharacteristic role in the action adventure *The River Wild* (1994). In 1995 she costarred with Clint Eastwood in *The Bridges of Madison County*.

Streisand, Barbra (1942–) *American singer, actress, producer, and director*

Barbra Streisand's exuberant stage personality and original style have made her one of the most successful performers in the modern Broadway tradition. During the 1960s and 1970s she also became a successful film actress, before branching out into direction and production during the 1980s. She has received Oscar, Tony, Emmy, and Grammy awards, including a special Tony Award in 1970 as "actress of the decade."

Barbara Joan Streisand (the middle "a" in her first name was later dropped) was born in Brooklyn, New York, and brought up by her grandmother after the early death of her father. She studied briefly at acting schools, played in off-Broadway revues, and appeared in New York nightclubs. In 1962 she made her Broadway debut as Miss Marmelstein in the musical *I Can Get It for You Wholesale*, which brought her critical acclaim. In 1963 she married the actor Elliott Gould (they have a son and were divorced in 1971) and began recording with Columbia Records. When the musical *Funny Girl*, in which she portrayed the comedienne Fanny BRICE, opened on Broadway in 1964, Streisand became a major star. She made her screen debut in the film version of *Funny Girl* in 1968, receiving an Academy Award for her performance.

Her *Barbra Streisand: The First Album* sold more than a million copies, as did several subsequent recordings, including *The Broadway Album* (1986). Her television appearances – especially the 1965 show *My Name Is Barbra* – were extraordinarily successful. Two New Year concerts (1993–94) in Las Vegas, her first live appearances in over 20 years, set a U.S. box-office record for ticket applications. In 1994 Streisand announced that she would do no more live performances as they were too stressful.

Streisand also enjoyed continuing success in the cinema with *Hello Dolly!* (1969), *What's Up Doc?* (1972), *The Way We Were* (1973), *Funny Lady* (1975), and *A Star Is Born* (1976).

With *Yentl* (1983), which is based on a story by Isaac Bashevis Singer, she became the first woman to cowrite, direct, produce, and star in a film. She then became the first woman to earn $5 million for a film appearance with *Nuts* (1987). Streisand has since directed and starred in *The Prince of Tides* (1991), which earned an Oscar nomination as Best Picture, and *The Mirror Has Two Faces* (1996).

Stuart, Arabella (1575–1615) *English noblewoman*

A claimant to the English throne, Arabella Stuart had a sad life in which she was used as a pawn in the political activities concerning the succession to Queen ELIZABETH I. As the daughter of Charles Stuart, Earl of Lennox, Arabella was the great-granddaughter of MARGARET TUDOR, daughter of Henry VII, the founder of England's Tudor dynasty. Her claim to the throne after the death of Elizabeth ranked after that of her first cousin, King James VI of Scotland; but since she had been born and brought up in England, there was a faction at court that regarded her as the preferable candidate.

Brought up from 1582 onwards in virtual seclusion by her grandmother, the Countess of Shrewsbury, Arabella Stuart became a close companion to MARY, QUEEN OF SCOTS during her imprisonment in England. As Arabella approached marriageable age, her movements became even more confined as a result of Elizabeth I's concern over the succession. Shortly before the queen's death Arabella was arrested on suspicion of planning to marry William Seymour, who was also of royal descent.

When James VI of Scotland succeeded Elizabeth in 1603, becoming James I of England, he allowed Arabella to return to court, despite the fact that she had been implicated in a plot to make herself queen by ousting him. In 1609 she was arrested again on the grounds that she was planning a forbidden marriage to Edward Seymour, William's brother. She was subsequently released and awarded a generous annual income of £1,600. In 1610 she became engaged to William

Seymour, although she formally retracted the engagement before the Privy Council, receiving more money as a reward. Then, in July of that year she went ahead and married Seymour in secret. When this was discovered, she was placed under house arrest, and William Seymour was imprisoned in the Tower of London.

Arabella eventually escaped by pretending to be ill, only to be recaptured at sea while fleeing to meet Seymour, who had also escaped and made his way safely to their rendezvous at Ostend. Arabella was then imprisoned in the Tower, where she suffered a mental breakdown and died. She is buried in the vault of Mary, Queen of Scots in Westminster Abbey.

Stuart, Miranda (1792–1865) *British doctor*

Miranda Stuart's place in history relies on the fact that she had a distinguished medical career in which she masqueraded as a man, known as Dr. James Barry.

The events of Miranda Stuart's early life are not known. She was probably born in Edinburgh, and possibly became an orphan before she entered Edinburgh College in about 1810 as a medical student. Since women were not accepted as medical students or doctors at that time, she masqueraded as a man, using the name James Barry.

After she gained a medical degree in 1812, Dr. Barry went on to have a successful career as a military surgeon in several British colonies, including Canada and the West Indies, as well as during the Crimean War.

Her real gender was not known until after her death, when an autopsy revealed the truth. It also revealed that at some time in her life she had given birth to a child.

Suchocka, Hanna (1946–) *Polish politician*

Hanna Suchocka became Poland's first woman prime minister in 1992. During her 15-month term of office she guided post-Communist Poland towards becoming a successful free-enterprise economy.

Born in Pleszew, western Poland, Hanna Suchocka became a keen student of languages, fluent in English, French, and German as well as her native Polish. She opted to study law at Adam Mickiewicz University in Poznán, later specializing in constitutional law as a postgraduate. Entering politics in 1980, she became a legal adviser to the Solidarity trade union, which was challenging Poland's Communist government.

During a major political crisis in July 1992 Suchocka was unexpectedly invited to become Poland's fifth postcommunist prime minister, at the head of a fragile coalition of seven political parties. A devout Roman Catholic, Suchocka proved sternly conservative on social issues, such as birth control, but a free-market radical on the economic front. Although her policies provoked some strikes, she had the satisfaction of seeing Polish exports boom.

She was, however, brought down in October 1993 following her failure to win support for a wide-ranging programme to privatize dozens of inefficient enterprises, which relied on government subsidies to keep going. Despite her relatively short tenure of office, her premiership was hailed by foreign observers as a decisive turning point on Poland's road to becoming a free-enterprise economy, following a period of extreme political uncertainty. Frequently compared to Margaret THATCHER, whose picture she keeps in her office, Suchocka remains a member of the Polish parliament and still commands considerable popularity.

Sullavan, Margaret (1911–1960) *American actress*

> This wonderful voice of hers –
> strange, fey, mysterious – like a
> voice singing in the snow.
>
> —Louise Brooks, quoted by David
> Shipman in *Movie Talk* (1988)

Highly regarded by her fellow actors as well as by theatre critics and audiences, Margaret Sullavan was known for her husky voice, her blonde good looks, and the candour of her acting style on both stage and screen.

Born in Norfolk, Virginia, she attended Sullins College in Bristol, Virginia, and gained stage experience with a summer theatre group at Falmouth, Massachusetts. She made her Broadway debut in *A Modern Virgin* 1931.

Sullavan first won wide acclaim for her performance in *Dinner at Eight* in 1933. Other stage successes included *Stage Door* (1936); *The Voice of the Turtle* (1943), probably her greatest triumph; *The Deep Blue Sea* (1952); and *Sabrina Fair* (1953). She made numerous films, beginning with *Only Yesterday* (1933) and ending with *No Sad Songs for Me* (1950), and appeared frequently on television. She made her London stage debut in *The Voice of the Turtle* in 1947.

Margaret Sullavan was almost as well known for her marriages as for her stage performances. Having married Henry Fonda in 1930, she later eloped with William Wyler, who was directing her in the film *The Good Fairy* (1935). In 1936 she married her agent, Leland Hayward, and in 1950, the industrialist Kenneth A. Wagg. She was appearing in New Haven, Connecticut, in a pre-Broadway tour of *Sweet Love Remember'd*, when she committed suicide with an overdose of barbiturates. Her daughter by Leland Hayward, the actress Brooke Hayward, wrote about her parents' stormy marriage in *Haywire* (1977).

Sumac, Yma (1927–) *Peruvian-born American soprano*

Yma Sumac is renowned for the power, flexibility, and incredible range (deep contralto to high soprano) of her voice. She has given concerts all over the world.

She was apparently born Emperatriz Chavarri at Ichocan, in the highlands of Peru, although her origins are somewhat mysterious. Some dispute her Peruvian background altogether, claiming that her real name is Amy Camus (Yma Sumac spelt backwards) and that she was born in Brooklyn, New York. A self-taught singer, she was apparently heard singing at a Native-American festival by a government official who spread the word about her astonishing voice. After being presented to the public in Lima, she successfully toured Latin America

and the United States, where in 1946 she sang at Carnegie Hall, New York, the Hollywood Bowl, and elsewhere.

Sumac got her big break when she made her first recording, *Voice of Xtabay*, for Capitol Records. The album sold 500,000 copies overnight. In addition to her numerous subsequent recordings she appeared in the 1954 film *Secret of the Incas* and on Broadway (as an Arabian princess) in the musical *Flahooley*. She also sang on the radio and television, in Las Vegas night clubs, and at the Roxy Theater in New York with Danny Kaye. Sumac became an American citizen in 1955. Her popularity waned at the end of the 1950s, but when she reappeared in the 1980s, her voice was as expressive – and impressive – in concert as it had been decades earlier.

Summerskill, Edith, Baroness (1901–1980) *British politician*

> In the matter of abortion the human rights of the mother with her family must take precedence over the survival of a few-weeks'-old foetus without sense or sensibility.
>
> —*A Woman's World* (1967)

Baroness Summerskill had a distinguished career as a doctor, Labour MP, and government minister.

Born in London, the daughter of a doctor with radical views, Edith Clara Summerskill followed her father in both his profession and his outlook. Although she married another doctor, she kept her maiden name, a very unusual decision for a married woman at that time. After practising as a family doctor in London, she entered local government in 1934 and became a Labour MP in 1938.

During World War II she headed the Women's Home Defence movement, taking rifle-shooting lessons herself. As a member of the reforming Labour government of 1945–51, she had the very unpopular job of administering the rationing system, which continued into the postwar period. She later became a government minister with responsibility for welfare. During 1954–55 she served as chairman of the Labour Party and in 1961 she was raised to the peerage and entered the

House of Lords as Baroness Summerskill. She was created a Companion of Honour in 1966.

Tall, handsome, and with a tough no-nonsense manner, Edith Summerskill was a fearless campaigner for better medical care, clean food, and women's rights. She considered her most important single achievement to be the legislation passed in 1949 that required all milk to be pasteurized to prevent the spread of tuberculosis. She was a passionate opponent of boxing, which she attacked in her book *The Ignoble Art* (1956). She also wrote *Babies without Tears* (1941). Her daughter Shirley Summerskill, also a doctor, followed in her mother's footsteps by becoming a Labour MP and a government minister.

Sun Ch'ing-ling (1892–1981) *Chinese stateswoman*

Sun Ch'ing-ling was the second wife of the revolutionary leader and founder of the Chinese Republic, Sun Yat-sen. After his death in 1925 she devoted the rest of her life to the furtherance of their shared ideals for a new China. She was awarded the Stalin Peace Prize in 1950. In 1981 she was named honorary president of the People's Republic of China.

Madame Sun was born in Shanghai, a member of the influential Soong family (her elder sister, Mayling Soong, became Madame CHIANG Kai-shek). Educated in the United States, she graduated from the Wesleyan College for Women in Macon, Georgia, in 1913 and returned to Shanghai. There she became Sun Yat-sen's secretary and – despite the 26-year difference in their ages – they were married in Tokyo the following year.

In May 1923 Sun Yat-sen became president of China, and Sun Ch'ing-ling began to take a more active role in politics. Sun Yat-sen died in 1925. Following the break between the Nationalists and Communists in 1927, Madame Sun claimed that her husband's policies had been violated and left for the Soviet Union. After returning in 1929, she associated with dissident political elements and opposed Chiang Kai-shek's leadership (except

during World War II). From 1937 she organized the China Defence League, which arranged medical relief and did child welfare work, especially in the Communist-controlled areas of the country.

After the People's Republic was founded in 1949, Madame Sun often undertook political and ceremonial duties, being held in high regard by the Communists because she symbolized the link between the new republic and the older revolutionary movement of Sun Yat-sen. She was also prominent in the women's movement and continued to be involved in child welfare, international relations, and peace committees. In 1957 she became honorary president of the Women's Federation of China.

Sutherland, Dame Joan (1926–) *Australian singer*

One of the leading 20th-century sopranos, Joan Sutherland was widely acclaimed for the beauty of her voice and her impeccable technique. Although a specialist in the 19th-century operas of Rossini, Donizetti, and Verdi, she was also well known for her performances of Handel.

Born and educated in Sydney, Joan Sutherland received singing and piano lessons from her mother. After leaving school, she studied singing in her spare time and made her debut in Sydney in 1947 as Dido in Purcell's *Dido and Aeneas*. Subsequent competition awards enabled her to continue her studies at London's Royal College of Music and Opera School. She made her Covent Garden debut in 1952, as First Lady in Mozart's *The Magic Flute*, In 1954 she married the Australian pianist and conductor Richard Bonynge, who coached her and persuaded her to specialize in the bel canto repertoire of the earlier 19th century. However, she also sang the title role in Handel's *Alcina* for London's Handel Opera Society in 1957.

After studying with the Italian conductor Tullio Serafin, Sutherland triumphed at Covent Garden in the title role of Donizetti's *Lucia di Lammermoor* in 1959. During the 1960s and 1970s she sang regularly at La Scala in

Milan, the Metropolitan Opera in New York, and other leading opera houses. She also made many recordings, generally with her husband conducting.

Although Sutherland and Bonynge settled in Switzerland in 1960, they continued to tour widely, including an extremely successful season in Australia (1965–66), when they worked with their own specially formed company. They were invited to appear at the opening of the South Korean cultural centre in 1978. The following year Sutherland was made a DBE. She gave her farewell operatic performance on October 2, 1990 – in *Les Huguenots* in Sydney. Her book *The Joan Sutherland Album*, which she wrote with her husband, was published in 1986.

Suttner, Bertha von (1843–1914)
Austrian novelist and pacifist

One of the first women to be a prominent pacifist, Bertha von Suttner is credited with persuading Alfred Nobel to include a peace prize among the awards for which he made provision in his will. In 1905 she became the first woman to be awarded the Nobel Peace Prize.

Born in Prague, she was the daughter of Count Franz Joseph Kinsky, a retired officer in the Austrian army. In 1874 she became governess to the children of Baron Arthur von Suttner, whose son Arthur, a novelist and engineer seven years her junior, she secretly married two years later.

Baroness von Suttner published more than a dozen novels on social issues. Her most compelling work, *Die Waffen nieder!* (1889; *Lay Down Your Arms!*, 1892), recounts the tribulations of a fictional noblewoman, Martha von Tilling, during four contemporary wars. Although the book shocked some readers with its pacifism, it proved a huge popular success and was translated into many European languages. It also aroused enthusiastic support for her Austrian Peace Society, which she had founded in 1891.

Bertha had first met the scientist and businessman Alfred Nobel in 1876, when she answered his advertisement for a housekeeper at his Paris home. Although nothing came of the appointment, she maintained a correspondence with him until his death in 1896. From 1892 to 1899 Baroness von Suttner was editor of the international pacifist journal *Die Waffen nieder!*, named after her most famous novel. She also attended various congresses on world peace, including one at Bern, Switzerland, in 1892.

Suu Kyi, Aung San (1945–   )
Burmese political leader

> I always feel that even if only five such people [imprisoned pro-democracy activists] remain we will get democracy – and there are certainly more than five.
>
> —Interview in *New Internationalist*, June 1996

Aung San Suu Kyi has been a determined opponent of Burma's military government since the late 1980s. Although she won an electoral victory, the military junta refused to relinquish power and kept her under house arrest for six years.

Suu Kyi was born in Rangoon, the daughter of General Aung San, a national hero who led the Burmese independence movement until his assassination in 1947. She was educated in Burma and India, at St. Hugh's College, Oxford, and at the University of London's School of Oriental and African Studies. In 1972 she married an Englishman, Michael Aris, and thereafter spent several years in England raising her two sons. She also spent two years (1972–74) as a visiting scholar at the University of Kyoto in Japan.

In 1988 Suu Kyi returned to her native country to care for her ailing mother and to support opposition to the Burmese military regime. That same year she founded the National League for Democracy, becoming the most articulate leader of the opposition to the military government. As a result, she was placed under house arrest in 1989. In the following year the National League for Democracy won a sweeping electoral victory, but the military junta reneged on their promise and refused to relinquish power, keeping her under house arrest until 1995. For two years of her house arrest she was forbidden to communicate with her husband or her sons.

Her refusal to be intimidated by the military and give up her demand for the restoration of free elections won her the Sakharov Prize in 1990 and both the European Parliament Human Rights Prize and the Nobel Peace Prize in 1991. Her books include *Freedom from Fear and Other Writings* (1991). Although determined and persistent in her opposition to the military, Aung San Suu Kyi has been careful not to provoke violence, emphasizing instead the need for dialogue, patience, and persistence.

Suzman, Helen (1917–) *South African campaigner for human rights*

Helen Suzman, aunt of the actress Janet SUZMAN, was a tireless opponent of apartheid in South Africa.

Born Helen Gavronsky in Germiston, Transvaal, South Africa, she trained as an economist and statistician at Witwatersrand University. She married Dr. Moses Suzman when she was 20, and had two daughters by him before returning to her university as a part-time lecturer in 1944.

After leaving academic life in 1952, Suzman entered politics and was elected to parliament as a member of the United Party in 1953. In 1961 she switched to the Progressive Party, serving as its sole representative in the South African legislature until 1974. She remained in parliament with its successors, the Progressive Reform Party and then the Progressive Federal Party, until her retirement in 1989. Throughout her long parliamentary career she campaigned fearlessly and ceaselessly against the now-discredited apartheid laws.

Her struggle was rewarded by the respect of the African National Congress and Nelson Mandela (who became president of South Africa in 1994) and was recognized internationally by the award of over 20 honorary doctorates, the United Nations Human Rights Award (1978), and two nominations for the Nobel Peace Prize. In 1989 she was made an honorary DBE. Her autobiography, *In No Uncertain Terms*, was published in 1993.

Suzman, Janet (1939–) *South African-born British actress*

An actress of great versatility, Janet Suzman has played many roles in both Shakespeare and modern plays, as well as making film and TV appearances. She is the niece of Helen SUZMAN.

Janet Suzman was born in the city of Johannesburg, South Africa, where she attended Kingsmead College before going on to the University of Witwatersrand. She then studied at the London Academy of Music and Dramatic Art, settling in London in 1960. She joined the Royal Shakespeare Company in 1963, playing many leading Shakespearean roles in the 1960s. In 1969 she married the British theatrical director Trevor Nunn, with whom she had one son; the couple divorced in 1986.

In the 1970s and 1980s Suzman acted in many West End productions, including *Hedda Gabler* (1977) and *Andromache* (1987). In 1991 she appeared in *The Cruel Grasp* at the Edinburgh Festival.

Her film appearances include *A Day in the Life of Joe Egg* (1970), *Nijinski* (1978), and *Leon the Pig Farmer* (1992). She returned to South Africa in 1987 in order to direct a highly acclaimed production of *Othello* at the Market Theatre in Johannesburg. She also directed a TV version of *Othello* in 1988. Suzman has appeared in many TV productions, including *Robin Hood* for CBS (1983) and *The Singing Detective* (1986) for the BBC.

Swanson, Gloria (1899–1983) *American film actress*

> When I die, my epitaph should read: *She Paid the Bills*. That's the story of my private life.
>
> —Quoted in *Saturday Evening Post*, July 22, 1950

As the highest paid star of the silent screen, earning a reputed $20,000 a week, Gloria Swanson epitomized the glamour of Hollywood in the 1920s. However, she is best remembered for her portrayal of the faded film star Norma Desmond in *Sunset Boulevard* (1950), which earned her an Oscar nomination.

Born Gloria May Josephine Svensson in Chicago, she worked as a shop assistant before obtaining work as an extra, at the age of 14, at the Essanay studios in Chicago. After moving to Hollywood in 1916, she played in a series of Mack Sennett comedies but soon tired of slapstick. Beginning in 1918, she starred in six films directed by Cecil B. De Mille and became identified with the opulence and sophistication of his productions. She also starred opposite Rudolph Valentino in *Beyond the Rocks* (1922).

In the mid 1920s Swanson broadened her dramatic range in such films as *Madame Sans-Gêne* (1925), which was made in France, and set up as an independent producer with Joseph P. Kennedy (father of the future president), who was rumoured to be her lover. The film *Sadie Thompson* (1928), which was produced by her own Swanson Productions, won her an Oscar nomination. Her next movie, Erich von Stroheim's *Queen Kelly*, lost her company a fortune and was never finished.

Swanson's career never really recovered, and after 1934 she virtually retired from films until her triumphant return to the screen in *Sunset Boulevard*. After two further films she restricted her appearances to television chat shows, but in 1971 made another comeback in the Broadway play *Butterflies Are Free*. She appeared as herself in *Airport 1975*.

Gloria Swanson had six husbands, including the film actor Wallace Beery and a French marquis, Henri de la Falaise. Her sixth marriage, at the age of 79, to the writer William Duffy, ended in divorce in 1981.

Szewinska, Irena (1946–) *Polish athlete*

An outstanding short-distance runner, Irena Szewinksa won three Olympic gold medals and set numerous records between 1964 and 1980.

Born Irena Kriszenstein in Leningrad (now St. Petersburg), Russia, she married her coach, Janusz Szewinski, in 1967. At the age of 18 she won a gold medal at the 1964 Tokyo Olympics in the 4 × 100-metre relay and silver medals in the 200 metres and the long jump. At the Mexico Games in 1968 she won a gold medal for the 200 metres and a bronze medal for the 100 metres. In 1974 she ran in a 400-metre race for only the second time in her career, becoming the first woman in history to run it under 50 seconds. At the 1976 Montreal Games she won a gold medal in the 400 metres, setting a new world record of 49.28 seconds.

Szewinska's competitive career spanned five Olympiads (from 1964 to 1980) and saw her accumulate 41 championship medals, including seven Olympic medals and five golds at the European Championships – an unequalled record. In addition to this she set 38 Polish records and, when at the height of her powers between 1965 and 1976, 13 world records.

Szold, Henrietta (1860–1945) *American educator, writer, and social worker*

An active Zionist, Henrietta Szold is perhaps best known for her outstanding work with Youth Aliyah, an organization that managed to rescue tens of thousands of Jewish teenagers from Nazi-dominated Europe in the 1930s and 1940s. Shortly before World War II she became the first president of the League of Jewish Women.

Henrietta Szold was born in Baltimore, Maryland, the daughter of Hungarian immigrants. Since her father was a prominent rabbi and Hebrew scholar, she received a thorough education in the Jewish faith. After graduating in 1877 from Baltimore's Western Female High School, she taught classics and modern languages at a nearby girls' school for 15 years. At the age of 19 she began to write articles for the Anglo-Jewish press. In 1889 she founded a school in Baltimore to teach newly arrived Jewish immigrants, who had escaped persecution in Russia, the language and customs of the United States. Similar institutions were then founded in other cities. In 1893 she became literary secretary of the Jewish Publication Society of America. In this post, which she held until 1916, she translated into English, rewrote, and revised a number of important Jewish scholarly works. In 1903 she moved to New

York, where she studied at the Jewish Theological Seminary.

Following a visit to Palestine in 1909, she became a committed Zionist and a year later took on the role of secretary of the Federation of American Zionists. In 1912 she had a central role in founding Hadassah, the Women's Zionist Organization of America, and five years later she organized the American Zionist Medical Unit, which went to Palestine in 1918. She herself moved to Palestine in 1920 but continued to visit America frequently. In 1927 she became the first woman member of the Executive of the World Zionist Organization; three years later she was appointed a member of the National Council of the Jews of Palestine, heading its department of social welfare. She took charge of Youth Aliya in 1934 and greatly expanded its work in response to the Nazi persecutions in Europe. She died in Jerusalem.

Szymborska, Wislawa (1923–)
Polish poet

> The joy of writing.
> Power of preserving,
> The revenge of a mortal hand.
>
> —"The Joy of Writing"

Wislawa Szymborska's poetry asserts the significance of the individual observer as a social and cultural critic.

Born in the small Polish town of Bnin, she has lived in Kraków since 1931. Between 1945 and 1948 she studied Polish literature and sociology at the Jagiellonian University, making her literary debut in 1945 with a poem appropriately entitled "I Seek the Word."

Her first volumes of verse were published in 1952 and 1954, when Communist censorship was in full force and conformity to its ideology of "social realism" was a prerequisite for publication. The thaw in government attitudes in 1956 enabled Szymborska to follow her true bent, and she subsequently repudiated her earliest work as unworthy and false. From 1953 to 1981 she worked on the staff of the weekly *Zycie Literackie* (Literary Life). Her review column, "Noncompulsory Reading," considered books on every subject from gardening to witchcraft; she also contributed numerous translations of 17th-century French poets.

During the 1980s, as popular resistance to the Communist regime strengthened, Szymborska contributed to the underground publication *Arka* and to the expatriate magazine *Kultura*, which was published in Paris, using the pen name Stancykowna. The diversity of styles employed in her poetry has presented translators with a severe challenge, but examples of her work can now be found not only in the major European languages but also in Japanese, Chinese, Arabic, and Hebrew. A selection of 100 of her poems has been translated into English by Stanislaw Baranczak and Clare Cavanagh as *View with a Grain of Sand* (1995). In 1996 she was awarded the Nobel Prize for literature.

T

Tabei, Junko (1939–) *Japanese mountaineer*

Junko Tabei was the first woman to reach the summit of Mount Everest; moreover, she achieved this by the South Col route – a feat that had previously been described as 99% impossible.

Junko Tabei was born in Miharu Machi, Japan. A slight woman under five feet tall, she developed her passion for mountaineering early in life. By the age of 30 she had founded the Japanese Ladies Climbing Club and climbed Annapurna III, a demanding peak of the Himalayas in Nepal.

In 1975, International Women's Year, Tabei and her colleague Eiko Hisano organized the first all-woman team to attempt Mount Everest. In spite of an injury sustained in an avalanche on the way up, she reached the summit on May 16 – the first woman to do so. At the time of her climb she had a three-year-old daughter. Apart from the achievement itself, Junko Tabei's expedition was remarkably cheap. Its budget was less than half that of the previous Japanese expedition, a comparable men-only venture.

Junko Tabei has now conquered the highest mountains on five continents and is an avid conservationist.

Taglioni, Maria (1804–1884) *Italian ballet dancer*

Maria Taglioni was not only an outstandingly graceful dancer but also one of the greatest innovators in the history of ballet.

Born in Stockholm, the daughter of a Swedish mother and an Italian ballet teacher, Maria Taglioni was trained by her father and made her debut in Vienna in 1822. Although she had nei-
ther a fine figure nor good looks, she became renowned for her brilliantly individual style. Her delicate performance in her father's production of *La Sylphide* at the Paris Opéra in 1832 was hailed as a landmark in the romantic era of ballet, creating the image of the dancer as an ethereal floating being.

One of the pioneers of dancing on the points of the toes, she also introduced such new movements as the arabesque. Her diaphanous white dresses, reaching only to calf-length, revealed the dancer's footwork as never before and were the forerunner of the modern tutu.

In 1832 Taglioni married the Comte de Voisins; in the 1850s she emerged from retirement to teach at the Paris Opéra. Later she moved to London and taught deportment to the children of the British royal family. Her niece, Marie Paul Taglioni (1833–91), was prima ballerina of the Berlin State opera (1848–65). Her cousin, Louise Taglioni, was principal dancer at the Paris Opéra (1848–57) and appeared in the United States in 1855.

Tailleferre, Germaine (1892–1983) *French composer*

Germaine Tailleferre was the only female member of the avant-garde group of French composers known as Les Six.

Born Germaine Taillefesse at Parc-St-Maur, near Paris, she modified her surname to escape an unfortunate pun (*fesse* means buttock in French). After training at the Paris Conservatory and studying under Maurice Ravel, she became the only woman member of Les Six, a group of like-minded composers who included Poulenc, Honegger, Auric, Durey, and Milhaud. These composers worked and performed together in the years after World War I. During World War II, after the collapse of France, Tailleferre lived in the United States.

Tailleferre's compositions, which include a concertino for harp and orchestra (1926) and *French Songs* (1930) as well as several ballets and operas, were not highly regarded at the time but have become better appreciated in recent years. Her autobiography, *Mémoires à l'emporte pièce* (Telling Memoirs), was published in 1974.

Tamiris (6th century BC) *Queen of the Scythians*

A celebrated warrior queen of the Scythians, a nomadic people from Asia Minor, Tamiris defeated and killed Cyrus the Great, the Persian king who founded the Achaemenian Empire.

Tamiris was the ruler of the Massagetae tribe of ancient Persia (now Iran). According to the account of her given by the Greek historian Herodotus in the 5th century BC, she was courted by Cyrus the Great, who was anxious to acquire her kingdom. A valiant and accomplished leader, Tamiris rebuffed his advances, being unwilling to succumb to a man – even if he was a Persian king – who was clearly more interested in her possessions than he was in her. Cyrus, swiftly abandoning the role of suitor, then mounted an invasion of her lands. Tamiris responded by sending her son, at the head of her army, to stem the invasion.

Unfortunately for both participants in this failed courtship, Tamiris's son was killed in the ensuing battle. The enraged queen took command of her army herself, and after a protracted battle defeated the army of Cyrus; to avenge her son, she killed her devious suitor.

Cyrus was entombed in the abandoned city of Pasargadae, which he had founded as his capital and where his tomb still stands. His successor, Darius I, replaced Pasargadae as the capital with Persepolis (sacked by Alexander the Great in 330 BC).

Tamiris, Helen (1905–1966) *American dancer and choreographer*

Trained in classical ballet, Helen Tam-

iris developed her own concert programme after a number of seasons with the New York Metropolitan Opera Ballet. She then spent over a decade choreographing Broadway musicals before returning to concert dancing with her husband, Daniel Nagrin.

Helen Becker was born in New York to Russian émigré parents. Her emerging talent as a young dancer was encouraged by Irene Lewisohn, who became her teacher. At the age of 15 she was taken on by the Metropolitan Opera Ballet; her four years with the company included a tour in South America. After leaving the Metropolitan she studied with the Russian dancer Michel Fokine, who had emigrated to New York in 1923. At this stage in her career she changed her name to TAMIRIS, the ancient Scythian queen who proved capable of overcoming all obstacles.

By now dissatisfied with the restrictions of traditional ballet, Tamiris joined Isadora DUNCAN's school in New York but found that this did not fulfil her needs. She therefore developed her own techniques and founded her own company, which she directed until 1945.

Although Tamiris did not invent an individual style of dancing, believing that each dance needed to create its own mode of expression, she choreographed some 135 dances in the 15 years she directed her own company. Many of these reflected her interest in social and political issues, especially the problems experienced by African Americans in the U.S. South.

After 1945 she spent most of the next 12 years choreographing Broadway shows, including *Annie Get Your Gun* (1946). She subsequently returned to concert dance performances in which she explored modern American themes. In 1960 she formed the highly successful Tamiris–Nagrin Dance Company with her husband.

Tan, Amy (1952–) *American writer*

Amy Tan's best-known novels explore family relationships within the Chinese-American community.

Born in Oakland, California, of Chinese immigrant parents, Amy Tan moved with her widowed mother to Europe when she was 15. After returning to California, she became a freelance writer in 1981. In 1987 she visited China for the first time with her mother.

Major success followed with her first novel, *The Joy Luck Club* (1989), which became a bestseller and subsequently a film. It concerns the relationship between a Chinese-born mother and her American-born daughter. The motivation for writing the book came from Tan's mother, who once said to her, "You don't know little percent of me." It was this remark that prompted Tan to take her mother back to China and to weave part of her mother's story into her novel.

The success of this first book was followed by *The Kitchen God's Wife* (1991), which is in some senses a sequel to her first book. In it the mother figure reveals the extent to which her life in China was dominated by males and by clan structures. *The Moon Lady* (1992) and *The Hundred Secret Senses* (1996) are her latest books.

Tandy, Jessica (1907–1994) *British-born American actress*

Jessica Tandy crowned a distinguished career on stage, screen, and television by winning an Oscar in her sixtieth year in the acting profession.

Born in London, the daughter of a travelling salesman, she made her West End debut in 1929 and appeared on Broadway for the first time the following year. In 1934 she played opposite John Gielgud in a celebrated production of *Hamlet*. In 1947 Tandy was chosen to play Blanche DuBois in the first production of Tennessee Williams's *A Streetcar Named Desire*; her performance in this play earned her a Tony Award. She subsequently appeared many times on Broadway, often with her second husband, Hume Cronyn.

Their successes together – which earned comparisons with the famous acting partnership of Alfred Lunt and Lynn FONTANNE – included *The Four-poster* (1951), *The Honeys* (1955), *A Delicate Balance* (1966), and *The Gin Game* (1977) and *Foxfire* (1982), for which Tandy won two more Tony Awards. The couple also performed together on radio and TV and in several films, including *The Seventh Cross* (1944) and *Cocoon* (1985).

Tandy became a U.S. citizen in 1954. Her other films included *The Desert Fox* (1951) and *The Birds* (1963), and she won a Best Actress Academy Award for her performance in the title role of *Driving Miss Daisy* (1989). Tandy and Cronyn received Tonys for Lifetime Achievement in 1994, the first time such awards had ever been bestowed.

Tate, Phyllis Margaret (1911–1987) *British composer*

Phyllis Tate's output as a composer ranged from full-scale operas to works specially designed for young performers.

At the Royal Academy of Music in London (1928–32) she studied composition under Harry Farjeon and went on to publish much light music under various pen names. In 1944 the BBC commissioned her to write a concerto for alto saxophone and strings. Her sonata for clarinet and cello (1947) was performed at the 1952 festival of the International Society for Contemporary Music.

In 1960 Tate completed a two-act opera, *The Lodger*, based on the story of Jack the Ripper. Another opera, *Dark Pilgrimage*, was finished in 1963. Her choral compositions include *A Secular Requiem* (1967) and *St. Martha and the Dragon* (1976), a major work based on a poem by Charles Causley. Determined to make serious music more accessible, she also composed two operettas for performance by young musicians, *Twice in a Blue Moon* (1969) and *Scarecrow* (1982).

In 1976 she became the first woman to be invited to become a member of the management committee of the Performing Right Society's Members' Fund, which audits and distributes royalty payments to composers.

Taussig, Helen Brooke (1898–1986) *American paediatrician*

Helen Brooke Taussig was the joint pioneer of surgical and medical techniques that saved the lives of thousands of babies; she also established a new medical speciality of paediatric heart surgery.

Born in Cambridge, Massachusetts, into an academic family, she studied at Radcliffe College and elsewhere, receiving her MD from Johns Hopkins University, Baltimore, in 1927. The major focus of her research work was the problem of "blue babies," who are born with malformed hearts and a bluish skin. This occurs because their hearts are unable to pump the blood correctly so that it is not adequately supplied with oxygen in the lungs.

Pioneering the use of x-rays and fluoroscopy (which enables x-ray images to be viewed directly) to analyse different types of heart defects, she worked with the heart surgeon Alfred Blalock to devise new surgical techniques and aftercare procedures to help blue babies. After extensive trials on dogs the techniques were successfully applied to human babies from 1944 onwards, saving thousands of lives. Her *Congenital Malformations of the Heart* (1947) became the standard textbook in its field.

In 1959 Taussig became the first woman to attain a full professorship on the medical faculty at Johns Hopkins University. In 1962–63 she played a leading role in alerting physicians to the dangers to pregnant women of the tranquillizer thalidomide, which caused the birth of thousands of malformed children in Britain and Europe. Her work prevented the birth of similarly handicapped children in the United States.

Taylor, Annie (1855–*c.*1920) *British missionary*

Annie Taylor's stoic life as a Christian missionary in Tibet was followed by a death in her native England so obscure that even its date is uncertain.

Born at Egremont in rural Cheshire, she heard a missionary give a lecture when she was 13 and decided that Christian evangelism was to be her life's work. After a missionary apprenticeship in the slums of London she set sail for China at the age of 28. For three years she worked along the Yangtze River before being relocated

to Lanzhou, far inland on the Tibetan border. In this unruly frontier area a lone woman constituted no threat to the local inhabitants – who, paradoxically, allowed her to move around more freely than a foreign man. A bout of severe illness, however, forced Taylor to spend some time in Australia recovering her strength.

From Australia she went to Darjeeling in northern India, where she studied Tibetan migrants and learned their language. Disguised as a pilgrim and accompanied only by a Tibetan convert, Pontso, she then made a hazardous journey into Tibet itself, covering some 1,250 miles over the course of seven months. In order to bring Christianity to this obscure part of the world she was obliged to brave ice, snow, wolves, and bandits. These exploits provided her with startling lecture material, making her the toast of London after her equally epic journey home.

In 1904 Taylor returned to Tibet, accompanying the official Younghusband exploration expedition as a nurse. Its bloody confrontation with Tibetan troops must have greatly dismayed Taylor, who sought only to bring Christianity to this remote land. In 1909 she returned to England, broken in health, to die in obscurity.

Taylor, Elizabeth (1912–1975) *British novelist and short-story writer*

> She belongs to a Temperance Society…of course by temperance they mean exactly the opposite – total abstinence.
>
> —*Angel* (1957)

A shrewd observer of the domestic manners of the English middle classes, Elizabeth Taylor has been hailed as the Jane AUSTEN of her day.

Born Elizabeth Coles and educated in Reading, Berkshire, she was the daughter of an insurance inspector. After working as a governess and a librarian, she married John Taylor, the director of a confectionery factory. They had two children and lived in the village of Penn, Buckinghamshire.

The first of Taylor's 12 novels, *At Mrs. Lippincote's* (1945), was written while her husband was away serving in the Royal Air Force. In 1951 *A Game of Hide and Seek* became a bestseller, and in 1957 *Angel* was selected as one of the Book Marketing Council's "Best Novels of Our Time." Her other novels include *The Wedding Group* (1968) and *Mrs. Palfrey at the Claremont* (1971).

She sometimes referred to her novels and four collections of short stories as "books in which practically nothing ever happens." In fact their focus on the everyday lives of ordinary women, set against the intimate background of an English village, enables her to illuminate moral qualities with a searching light. Generosity, she shows, can be used to manipulative ends, while apparently minor weaknesses, such as self-deceit or indulgence in nostalgia, can prove unexpectedly destructive.

Taylor, Elizabeth (1932–) *American actress*

> I don't pretend to be an ordinary housewife.
>
> —Interview, 1980

Elizabeth Taylor became as famous for her diamonds, diets, and husbands as for her beauty and acting ability.

Born in London of American parents, she moved to Los Angeles at the outbreak of World War II and made her film debut there at the age of ten in *There's One Born Every Minute*. Her fourth film, *National Velvet* (1944), based on Enid BAGNOLD's novel about a girl who wins the Grand National, made her a household name. Despite further juvenile parts in two "Lassie" films (1943, 1946) and in *Little Women* (1949), she successfully made the transition to an adult role in *The Father of the Bride* (1950). *Giant* (1956) confirmed her reputation.

Taylor's performances in *Raintree County* (1957), *Cat on a Hot Tin Roof* (1958), and *Suddenly Last Summer* (1959) all gained her Academy Award nominations. In 1960 she finally won her first Oscar for *Butterfield 8*. Her starring role in *Cleopatra* (1962), the most expensive film made to that date, boosted her to superstar status and led to a high-profile romance with the actor Richard Burton, whom she was to marry in 1964, divorce (1974), re-marry (1975), and divorce again in 1976. Together they made a number of films, including *Who's Afraid of Virginia Woolf?* (1966), for which Taylor won a second Oscar. In the 1980s she made her stage debut in New York in Lillian HELLMAN's *The Little Foxes* (1981) and also successfully worked in television. She made a hilarious big-screen comeback as the mother-in-law from hell in *The Flintstones* (1994).

Liz Taylor has also played a leading part in the campaign to assist sufferers from Aids. Both before and after Burton she has had other husbands: the hotelier Nick Hilton (1950), the British actor Michael Wilding (1952), the producer Mike Todd (1957), who was killed in a plane crash, singer Eddie Fisher (1959), U.S. Senator John Warner (1978), and a builder, Larry Fortensky (1991), from whom she separated in 1995.

Tebaldi, Renata (1922–) *Italian opera singer*

Renata Tebaldi is one of that elite band of opera stars whose name has become known to millions who know little about opera. By opera buffs she is regarded as an outstanding soprano.

Born in Pesaro and initially trained by her mother, herself a singer, Tebaldi subsequently studied at the Parma Conservatory; she made her debut in 1944. After auditioning for the conductor Arturo Toscanini, she was hired for the postwar reopening of La Scala, Milan, Italy's premier opera house.

From 1949 to 1954 she was a regular member of La Scala's company but also sang in London, Chicago, and San Francisco. From 1955 onwards she became a regular performer at the Metropolitan Opera in New York, where she was best known for her interpretations of classic roles by Verdi (Violetta, Aida, Desdemona) and Puccini (Mimi, Tosca).

Te Kanawa, Dame Kiri (1944–) *New Zealand opera singer*

Kiri Te Kanawa is one of the few opera stars to have started her career as a pop singer before making a successful transition to the status of diva.

Born in Gisborne, New Zealand, to

a Maori father and a mother of British descent, she was named Kiri Janette and adopted in infancy by Thomas and Elanor Te Kanawa, who were also of Maori and British descent respectively. She was already making recordings and appearing on radio and television as a teenager before winning several singing competitions in New Zealand and Australia. In 1966 she was given a government grant to enable her to train at the London Opera Centre in England (1966–69).

Her first major role, as the Countess in Mozart's The Marriage of Figaro at Covent Garden, came in 1971 and made her a star overnight. Her American debut at Santa Fe in the same role later that year was a similar triumph. These appearances led to international tours and recording contracts. In 1974 she made her debut at the Metropolitan Opera House in New York at three hours' notice as a stand-in and scored another major success. Her performance of Handel's Let the Bright Seraphim at the wedding of the Prince of Wales and Lady Diana Spencer (see DIANA, PRINCESS OF WALES) in 1981 was seen on television by over 600 million viewers. A decade later she again reached a worldwide audience in the satellite performance of Paul McCartney's Liverpool Oratorio.

In 1982 Kiri Te Kanawa was created a DBE and in 1990 she was invested with the Order of Australia. In 1994 a gala evening was staged in London to honour her career on the occasion of her 50th birthday. She has recorded 15 complete operas, many selections from the works of popular composers, such as George Gershwin and Jerome Kern, and such musicals as West Side Story and My Fair Lady. In 1989 she published a children's book, Land of the Long White Cloud: Maori Myths, Tales and Legends.

Tempest, Dame Marie (1864–1942) British actress

Marie Tempest successfully switched direction midway through her career, abandoning operetta to become a stylish comedy actress.

Born Mary Susan Etherington in London, she was educated on the Con-

tinent but returned to London to study singing under Manuel Garcia, tutor to the famed "Swedish Nightingale," Jenny LIND. She made her stage debut in operetta in 1885 and in 1887 became known for playing the title role in Dorothy, which ran for 931 performances.

In 1899 Tempest turned to comedy and went on to establish a new reputation by creating the role of Nell GWYN, mistress of King Charles II, in English Nell (1906). She subsequently developed other coquettish roles, including those of the 18th-century actress Peg WOFFINGTON and Becky Sharp, the central character of Thackeray's Vanity Fair. Her best-known roles were the title part of Somerset Maugham's Mrs. Dot (1908) and Judith Bliss in Noël Coward's Hay Fever (1925).

In 1935 Marie Tempest celebrated her theatrical half-century with a performance attended by King George V, at the historic Theatre Royal, Drury Lane. The proceeds from this event were donated to St. George's Hospital to fund a special ward for members of the theatrical profession. She was made a DBE in 1937 and continued to tour until a year before her death.

Temple, Shirley (1928–   ) American child star and diplomat

Shirley Temple's career has followed a brilliant but improbable path from dimpled child film star to senior American diplomat.

Born in Santa Monica, California, she proved a stunningly talented child, utterly unselfconscious on the screen. By the age of six she was a veteran performer, playing leading roles in films written specifically to exploit her unique charm and massive public appeal. The tiny curly-headed star sang, danced, and mimicked her way into the hearts of millions of cinema-goers throughout the world – many of whom were seeking escapism in the Depression years of the 1930s. Many more, no doubt, fantasized that they were a parent of this lovable source of unlimited wealth and fame.

Bright Eyes (1934), in which Temple sang the famous "On the Good Ship Lollipop," won her a special Academy

Award; for the next four years she was the top box-office attraction and the highest-paid film-star in the United States, starring in such movies as *Curly Top*, *Dimples*, *Wee Willie Winkie*, *Heidi*, *Rebecca of Sunnybrook Farm*, *Little Miss Broadway*, and *The Little Princess*.

Adolescence dimmed her appeal, however, and she retired from the cinema at the age of 21. After occasional appearances on television in the 1950s and 1960s she re-emerged into public life as the wife of California businessman Charles A. Black, a leading activist in Republican party politics. In 1967 she ran unsuccessfully for the House of Representatives, but in 1969 was appointed, as Mrs. Shirley Temple Black, as a U.S. delegate to the United Nations General Assembly. She subsequently served as U.S. ambassador to Ghana (1974–76), President Ford's White House chief of protocol (1976–77), and U.S. ambassador to Czechoslovakia (1989–92). She published an autobiography covering her early years, *Child Star* (1988).

Tencin, Claudine-Alexandrine Guerin de (1681–1749) *French writer and adventuress*

Claudine Guerin de Tencin escaped from a convent to become a courtesan, a political intriguer, and a writer.

Born in Grenoble, she was sent to a convent to become a nun at the age of 16. However, she managed to be absolved from her vows and in 1714 moved to Paris. There she exploited her beauty and wit to accumulate a string of lovers, who included the regent of France, Philippe d'Orléans, and Cardinal Dubois, formerly chief minister of the government. Through them she amassed a considerable fortune accompanied by sufficient backstairs influence to enable her to ensure that her brother, Cardinal Pierre Guerin de Tencin, became ambassador at the court of the pope in 1721. Unfortunately both the regent and Cardinal Dubois died in 1723, greatly reducing her influence.

In 1726, after one of her lovers had shot himself in her house, Madame de Tencin was jailed briefly in the Bastille and falsely charged with his murder until her brother secured her release. Somewhat chastened by this unpleasant interlude, she then turned to literature for her excitement, presiding over one of the capital's most popular salons, of which the writers Bernard le Fontenelle (another of her lovers), Pierre de Marivaux, Jean-François Marmontel, and Baron de Montesquieu were leading members.

Her published romances, included *Memoirs of the Count of Comminges* (1735), *The Siege of Calais* (1739), and *Misfortunes of Love* (1747). The renowned mathematician and philosopher Jean d'Alembert was one of her children.

Teresa, Mother (1910–97) *Yugoslavian-born Indian nun*

> I would not give a baby from one of my homes for adoption to a couple who use contraception. People who use contraceptives do not understand love.
>
> —Radio interview, 1983

Mother Teresa of Calcutta was often regarded as a living saint in an age that no longer believes in them. She was also no stranger to controversy.

Born Agnes Gonxha Bojaxhiu, the daughter of a grocer in Skopje, Macedonia, she joined an Irish religious order, the Sisters of Loretto, at 17 and was sent to Darjeeling in northern India. From there she went to the port of Calcutta, where she taught at St. Mary's, a school for well-to-do girls.

After 20 years as a teacher she came to believe that God was calling her to leave the comfort of the school to work among the very poor. After some medical training in Paris she returned to the Calcutta slums, barefoot and dressed in an Indian sari, to teach children who would otherwise never go to school and to tend the sick, the lepers, and the dying.

In 1950, the year in which Mother Teresa became an Indian citizen, the Vatican officially recognized the Order of the Missionaries of Charity, which she had founded in 1948. In 1952 she opened a House for the Dying to offer free care for those who would otherwise literally die in the streets. Her leper colony, which she called "Town of Peace" (Shanti Nagar), was opened in 1957. The Order of the Missionaries of Charity has spread to over 20 countries and enrolled almost 2,000 nuns, all dedicated to helping the poor by teaching, nursing, and charity. By the 1970s the tiny stooped form of Mother Teresa had become an internationally recognized symbol of compassion, self-sacrifice, and simple goodness: although some ventured to criticize her authoritarian style and doctrinal conservatism, this had little effect on her standing as perhaps the world's most widely admired woman. Increasingly frail, Mother Teresa finally resigned as head of the order in 1996, after undergoing several operations.

In 1979 "the saint of the gutters" was awarded the Nobel Peace Prize. Her other awards include the Pope John XXIII Peace Prize (1971), an honorary Order of Merit from Queen ELIZABETH II (1983), the Presidential Medal of Freedom (1985), and the Woman of the Year Award (1989). Her death and funeral in September 1997 were overshadowed by those of DIANA, PRINCESS OF WALES only a few days earlier – a circumstance that was inevitably seen as a last gesture of humility.

Teresa of Avila, Saint (1515–1582)
Spanish nun and religious reformer

> When thou wert in the world, Lord, thou did'st not despise women...it is not right to repel minds which are virtuous and brave, even though they be the minds of women.
> —*The Gospel According to Woman* (1570)

Teresa of Avila is chiefly remembered for the brilliant writings describing her religious experiences, which are regarded as classic expositions of the spiritual life.

Born Teresa de Cespeda y Ahumada into a noble family in Avila, she entered a local Carmelite convent in 1533 – against the wishes of her father. After a serious illness lasting three years and a long period of apathy regarding her religious commitment she re-established her faith in 1555. Rigorous meditation, prayer, fasting, and other self-imposed hardships brought her personal stability and a reputation for sanctity.

In 1562 she founded the Convent of St. Joseph, reforming the Carmelite religious order by requiring its followers to give up such luxuries as shoes and rely entirely on alms for their support. Despite frail health she spent much of the rest of her life on the move, founding another 16 convents. Her rules were widely copied by other existing convents, and the 16th-century mystic St. John of the Cross (Juan de Yepes y Alvarez) used them as the model for his male branch of the Carmelite order.

St. Teresa's surviving writings include 31 poems and 458 letters. Her most important books are *The Way of Perfection* (1583), a manual for spiritual development; *The Interior Castle* (1588), in which she compares the human soul to a fortress with many hidden rooms; the *Book of Foundations* (1610), which chronicles her struggles to found convents against the background of a brutal age; and her autobiography, *Life of the Mother Teresa of Jesus*.

She was canonized as a saint in 1622. Her works are still widely studied; in 1970 Pope Paul VI honoured her as a doctor of the Church, the first woman to be so recognized.

Tereshkova, Valentina Vladimirovna (1937–) *Russian cosmonaut and politician*

Valentina Tereshkova made history in 1963 when she became the first woman ever to fly in space.

Born near Yaroslavl, the daughter of a farmer, she worked in a cotton mill and was an avid amateur parachutist with 126 jumps to her credit. This intrepid woman was recruited as a cosmonaut in 1962, the year after Yuri Gagarin made the first-ever manned space flight.

On June 16, 1963, Tereshkova flew as solo pilot of the space capsule Vostok 6, making 48 orbits of the earth in a 71-hour flight, which covered 1,242,800 miles (776,750 km). For this exploit she was honoured with the title Hero of the Soviet Union. In the same

year she married Colonel A. G. Niko-
layev, commander of the cosmonaut
corps, who had piloted the flight of
Vostok 3.

In 1966 Valentina Nikolayeva, as
she had become, began a political career as a deputy of the Supreme Soviet.
In 1968 she was elected to the chair of
the Soviet Women's Committee, a post
she held until 1987. From 1974 until
1989 she was a member of the Supreme
Soviet Praesidium and from 1987 to
1991 was head of the USSR International Cultural and Friendship Union,
promoting links with foreign countries. In 1992 she assumed the chair of
the Russian Association of International Co-operation; the following
year she published *Valentina, First
Woman in Space*.

Terrell, Mary (1863–1954) *American
civil-rights campaigner*

Mary Terrell's life was unceasingly devoted to the struggles of both African
Americans and women to prove their
value as citizens of the United States.

Born Mary Eliza Church in Memphis, Tennessee, she was the child of
ex-slaves, both of whom prospered
through their enterprise. Her mother
moved to New York, where she ran her
own beauty parlour for over 30 years.
Her father became a property dealer
and the South's first African-American millionaire. Thanks to her parents'
farsightedness, Mary had the benefit of
an excellent education; she was usually
the only African American and often
the only girl in whatever class she was
in.

After her graduation from Oberlin
College in 1884 Mary's father expected
her to live a life of leisure, serving as
his hostess on social occasions. She
emphatically rejected this opportunity,
becoming instead a teacher of Latin in
the only high school for African Americans in Washington, D.C. Faced with
her determination, her father soon re-
lented and paid for her to undertake a
two-year tour of Europe, where she
perfected her French, German, and
Italian. Although she was tempted to
stay abroad by the absence of colour
discrimination in Europe, she finally
returned to the United States and in

1891 married Robert Heberton Terrell,
one of the first African Americans to
graduate from Harvard, who became a
school supervisor and later a federal
judge.

Serving as the first African-American member of the District of Columbia Board of Education, Mary Terrell
also became president of the National
Association of Colored Women in
1896; in 1901 she was elected its honorary president for life. An accomplished public speaker, in 1904 she
addressed the International Council of
Women on the problems and progress
of African-American women, speaking
faultlessly in both French and German. She also travelled extensively
throughout the United States to de-
liver her campaigning lectures against
lynching, disfranchisement, and discrimination in all its forms.

She became a charter member of the
National Association for the Advancement of Colored People and successfully led a drive to integrate the
American Association of University
Women. In 1940 she published her autobiography, *A Colored Woman in a
White World*. At the age of 89 she
could be seen heading a picket line to
achieve the desegregation of lunch
rooms in the nation's capital.

Terry, Dame Ellen (1847–1928)
British actress

> She has...a great deal of a certain
> amateurish, angular grace...and a
> countenance very happily adapted
> to the expression of pathetic emo-
> tion. To this last effect her voice
> also contributes; it has a sort of mo-
> notonous, husky thickness which is
> extremely touching.
>
> —Henry James in *Nation*, June 12,
> 1879

Ellen Terry was widely acknowledged
as the greatest Shakespearean actress
of her day. When the society portraitist John Singer Sargent painted
her, it was almost inevitable that he
should depict her as Lady Macbeth.

Born into a theatrical family in
Coventry, Ellen Alice Terry was acting
by the age of nine and made her adult
debut at 15. After a brief disastrous
marriage to the painter G. F. Watts,

she had a liaison with the architect Edward Godwin, by whom she had her two children. In 1875 Terry returned to the stage to triumph as Portia in *The Merchant of Venice*.

In 1878 she married the actor Charles Kelly and became the leading lady of the eminent actor-manager Henry Irving. They would remain London's leading theatrical partnership until 1902. Based at Irving's Lyceum Theatre in the West End, they also made eight hugely successful tours of the United States between 1883 and 1901.

After leaving Irving's company, Terry played occasionally in modern works by Ibsen, Barrie, and G. B. Shaw, who wrote *Captain Brassbound's Conversion* specifically for her to play the role of Lady Cicely Waynflete. In 1906 she celebrated half a century on stage with a mammoth matinée at the Theatre Royal, Drury Lane, in which she was supported by 22 members of the Terry theatrical clan. In 1907 she married for the third time, to the American actor James Carew, but the marriage lasted only two years.

After her sixtieth birthday Terry rarely acted, although she continued to lecture and give public readings in the United States and Australia. She made her last acting appearance in 1925, the year in which she became the first actress to be honoured with the title DBE. Her autobiography was published in 1908.

Ellen Terry's correspondence with George Bernard Shaw, published in 1931, revealed her discerning literary judgment. Her son, Edward Gordon Craig, became a leading theatrical designer, and her daughter, Edith Craig, became an actress and director.

Tetrazzini, Luisa (1871–1940) *Italian opera singer*

Luisa Tetrazzini's career as a great soprano is an example of success coming overnight after many years of professional perseverance.

Born and trained in Florence, she made her debut in 1895 in Meyerbeer's *L'Africaine*. For the next 12 years she toured widely, singing in places as far afield as St. Petersburg, Sao Paolo, and San Francisco. In 1907 she appeared before an apathetic audience at London's Royal Opera House, Covent Garden, and electrified it with her performance as Violetta in Verdi's *La Traviata*. This was the turning point in her career; as a result of it she was invited to the United States to sing with the Manhattan (1908–10), Metropolitan (1911–12), and Chicago (1913–14) opera companies.

Tetrazzini's light voice was allied to a phenomenal technique, which enabled her to excel at ornamentation and the interpretation of staccato passages. However, like most Italian singers of her time, she was judged a poor actress. In 1921 she published her autobiography, *My Life of Song*, and in 1923 followed it with *How to Sing*.

She retired from the concert stage in 1931. Rumour credits her third husband with squandering her vast fortune before her death in Milan. The dish "Chicken Tetrazzini" was named in her honour.

Teyte, Dame Maggie (1888–1976) *British singer*

Maggie Teyte is best remembered as an outstanding interpreter of classical French songs.

Born Margaret Tate in Wolverhampton, she was admitted to the Royal College of Music in London as a child; at 16 she moved to Paris to study singing under Jean de Reszke. Her concert debut came in 1906, and her operatic debut a year later. In 1908 Debussy chose her to play Melisande in his *Pelleas and Melisande* and later conducted her in concerts throughout Europe.

Maggie Teyte's career included performances with the leading opera companies of Boston, Chicago, New York, Paris, and London. Her 1937 recordings of works by Debussy and 1940 recordings of songs since the times of Berlioz confirmed her standing as a leading exponent of the French contribution to classical songs.

She made her last concert appearance at London's Royal Festival Hall in 1955. In 1957 she was made a Chevalier of the Legion of Honour in

France, and the following year became a DBE.

Thaïs (4th century BC) *Greek courtesan*

Although a shadowy figure of whom little is known, Thaïs has fired the imagination of several poets and writers, including John Dryden. Establishing her identity is made difficult by the fact that Thaïs was a common name for courtesans in the ancient Greek and Roman worlds.

According to the somewhat unreliable historian Cleitarchus, she was an Athenian courtesan who accompanied the army of Alexander the Great when it invaded the Persian empire and persuaded Alexander, in the course of a drunken revel, to burn down Persepolis, the Persian capital, in 330 BC. Although the city was, in all probability, fired for strictly political reasons, Dryden based his poem *Alexander's Feast* (1697) on the idea that Thaïs's intervention was the decisive factor. After Alexander's death in 323 BC, Thaïs probably became the mistress of Ptolemy, one of his comrades, who became ruler of Egypt and founder of the last dynasty of pharaohs.

There was also a Thaïs who lived in Egypt in the 4th century AD. According to tradition, she was a reformed prostitute who unwittingly tempted the saint responsible for her conversion. This story is even more likely to be entirely fictitious, although it inspired the novelist Anatole France to write his *Thaïs* (1890). This in turn inspired an opera of the same name, by Jules Massenet (1894).

Tharp, Twyla (1941–) *American choreographer*

> She has been the most visible manifestation of what is sometimes termed "crossover" dance – dance that rules out nothing, from ballet to boogaloo, from Bach to rock. Her own label for what she does is simply: dance.
>
> —Gerald Jones, *Dancing* (1992)

Twyla Tharp's inventive choreography has pioneered a fusion of the technical discipline of the classical ballet and the freedom of contemporary dance.

Born in Portland, Indiana, and brought up in San Bernardino, California, the young Twyla took after-school lessons in violin, viola, drumming, baton twirling, ballet, tap, flamenco, acrobatics, French, German, and shorthand and typing. Having entered Pomona College to study medicine, she switched to comparative literature and then transferred to Barnard College in New York, where she majored in art history while studying dance under Martha GRAHAM, Merce Cunningham, and Alwin Nikolais.

After a year with the prestigious avant-garde Paul Taylor Dance Company she left to pursue a solo career. Her first work, *Tank Dive*, was premiered in 1965. In that same year she formed her own company, which from 1973 onwards was called the Twyla Tharp Dance Foundation. Many of her early pieces were performed in unconventional places, such as parks and art galleries, without music.

Tharp's career breakthrough came in 1971 with *Eight Jelly Rolls*. Using the music of pianist Jelly Roll Morton, this was the first of a series of works based on jazz. In 1973, as a commission for the Joffrey Ballet, she choreographed music by the Beach Boys to produce *Deuce Coupe*. Her other commissions of that decade included works for the Paris Opéra Ballet, the New York City Ballet, the Boston Ballet, and John Curry, the British Olympic ice-skating champion. National recognition of her standing came in 1976 when the American Ballet Theater danced the premiere of her most celebrated creation, *Push Comes to Shove*.

In 1979 Tharp choreographed the film version of *Hair*, following this with choreography for *Ragtime* (1981), *Amadeus* (1984), and *White Night* (1985). In 1985 she directed and choreographed a Broadway production of *Singin' in the Rain* and produced a TV programme on the Russian dancer Mikhail Baryshnikov, with whom she has had a long working association. At Baryshnikov's invitation she choreographed four works for the American Ballet Theater in 1989–90. In 1991–92, while in residence at Ohio State University, she created *Octet*, *The Men's Piece*, *Grand Pas de Deux*, and a series entitled *Cutting Up*, with which she and Baryshnikov toured in 1993.

In 1995 she created a new ballet for Britain's Royal Ballet, *Mr. Worldly-Wise*, based on the music of Rossini. Her autobiography, *Push Comes to Shove*, was published in 1992.

Thatcher, Margaret, Baroness
(1925–) *British stateswoman*

> It will be years – and not in my time – before a woman will lead the party or become prime minister.
> —Speech, 1974

> In politics, if you want anything said, ask a man; if you want anything done, ask a woman.
> —Quoted by Anthony Sampson in *The Changing Anatomy of Britain* (1982)

Margaret Thatcher, Britain's first woman prime minister, decisively changed the way in which British politics had worked since the end of World War II.

Born in the small market town of Grantham, in Lincolnshire, Margaret Hilda Roberts idolized her father, a grocer, who was also a staunch Methodist and a leader of the local community. From him and from her local grammar school she absorbed the Victorian values that were later to underpin her political programmes – self-reliance, self-improvement, thrift, and a strong sense of moral certainty.

At Oxford University she studied chemistry and became president of the University Conservative Association. After graduating, she worked as a research chemist in the plastics industry before studying law. She specialized in tax law and was called to the Bar in 1953. In 1951 she married Denis Thatcher, a wealthy businessman who loyally supported her political aspirations. They had twin children – Mark, who eventually married a Texan heiress, and Carol, who became a journalist and broadcaster. After unsuccessfully attempting to enter Parliament in 1950 and 1951, Margaret Thatcher was finally elected to the House of Commons in 1959, as Conservative MP for Finchley, north London.

After serving as a junior minister in the government of Harold Macmillan, Thatcher became a member of the cabinet of Edward Heath in 1970 as secretary of state for education. Her abolition of free school milk earned her the nickname "Ma Thatcher, Milk Snatcher" and gave her a reputation as a politician who was quite willing to be unpopular if she thought she was right. Following the fall of the Heath government after a bruising confrontation with the trade unions, Thatcher became one of the challengers to Heath's leadership of the party in 1975; against all expectations, she won on the first ballot. When James Callaghan's Labour government was brought down in 1979 by a "winter of discontent," largely orchestrated by trade union leaders, Thatcher came to power as Britain's (and Europe's) first woman prime minister.

Her first aims were to reassert the authority of government, while making industry and public services more efficient by cutting their subsidies and forcing them to meet the disciplines of the market. She proclaimed herself a "conviction" politician, rather than a compromiser who would resolve conflicts by seeking consensus. Although "Thatcherism" was based as much on opportunism as on ideology, she did pursue a number of consistent aims – privatizing major government-owned enterprises, such as British Airways, the telephone system, and the service industries; curbing the powers of trade unions by legislation; fighting inflation; and encouraging popular capitalism by promoting share ownership and establishing the right of tenants in public housing to buy their homes instead of renting them.

By 1981 Thatcher's confrontational style and radical economic policies had raised unemployment to its highest level in half a century and provoked riots in deprived inner-city areas. Opinion polls showed her to be the most unpopular prime minister since 1945.

In 1982 Argentina's surprise invasion of the British-occupied Falkland Islands presented a direct external challenge that enabled Thatcher to make a comeback in political popularity. Accepting the grave risks involved in sending a hastily assembled task force 8,000 miles to face a numerically superior enemy in entrenched positions, she unhesitatingly opted to fight. This decision, vindicated by the professionalism of the armed forces, brought victory that confirmed her status as "the Iron Lady" and swept her to a landslide triumph at the polls in 1983.

Fortified by success, Thatcher prepared to take on the toughest union, that of the coal miners, which she defeated after a year-long strike (1984–85). Meanwhile, in 1984, she survived an assassination attempt by the Irish Republican Army, which blew up the hotel in which she and other cabinet members were staying during the Conservative Party conference at Brighton. Within half an hour of the blast she was calmly giving an interview to journalists. Although unemployment remained a major problem, for those in work incomes were rising fast, and in 1987 she defeated a still-fragmented opposition to win a third successive election, a unique achievement in modern British history. In 1990 Thatcher became the longest-serving prime minister since the 1820s. Her long tenure of office had by now made her a commanding figure in the international arena, a trusted confidante of Presidents Reagan and Bush, and a key figure in the politics of the European Community and post-communist eastern Europe.

Her fall from power came following a downturn in the economy, quarrels with senior colleagues over European policy, and the imposition of a deeply unpopular poll tax to fund local government, which was widely denounced as unjust and unworkable. Challenged for the leadership of the Conservative Party by Michael Heseltine in November 1990, she failed to win an outright victory in the first ballot and resigned when defeat in the second ballot appeared certain. Although overthrown by a party hierarchy that had become intolerant of her uncompromising attitudes, she remained the idol of many of the party faithful. Her successor, John Major, though more conciliatory in style, continued her policies of privatization and safeguarding national rights in the European Union.

Despite her removal from office, Thatcher could look on with satisfaction at the adoption of "Thatcherite" privatization programmes throughout most of the world and the acceptance by her lifelong opponents, Britain's Labour Party, of the superiority of the free market over state direction of the economy. In 1992 she was created Baroness Thatcher of Kesteven.

Her publications include the autobiographical *The Downing Street Years 1979–1990* (1993) and *The Path to Power* (1995).

Theodora (*c.*500–548) *Wife of Byzantine emperor Justinian I*

Theodora was the power behind the throne who kept her husband on it. Those who criticize her devious manipulations fail to recognize that intrigue was normal behaviour in the Byzantine court.

Theodora, who was probably born in the imperial capital of Constantinople, was the daughter of a circus bear tamer and an entertainer from childhood. Adept in exploiting both her beauty and her sexual skills, she became the mistress and then the wife of Justinian, heir to the throne, after he had successfully persuaded his uncle, Emperor Justin I, to suspend a law banning an alliance between a member of the senatorial class and a common showgirl. Theodora was, however, detested by court aristocrats on account of her lowly origins; she was depicted by the historian Procopius as a devious intriguer, using all her female wiles to manipulate her weak husband, who ascended the throne in 527.

Justinian, if not actually weak, was often indecisive and fearful even of his most loyal servants, such as the brilliant general Belisarius. It was almost certainly Theodora who kept her nerve in the greatest crisis of Justinian's reign, when in 532 factional riots between rival groups of chariot-racing fans, the Blues and the Greens, threatened to topple his government. Justinian considered abdicating the throne to placate the mob. Theodora, however, conceived the more direct plan of sending in Belisarius at the head of trusted troops to slaughter the dissidents.

Although she was never made a joint ruler, she was the emperor's most trusted adviser, explicitly mentioned in almost all the legal reforms for which his reign was notable. In addition, she also received foreign envoys and corresponded with foreign rulers, functions normally reserved for the emperor alone. Her efforts to enhance the status of women in Byzantine society led to strict laws against trafficking in young women and greater rights for females in cases of divorce. She was also notable for her personal generosity to the poor of her own sex.

There were, however, clear limits to her influence. Her support for the Monophysite heresy (that Christ had only a divine nature, in opposition to the orthodox belief that he was both human and divine) totally failed to budge Justinian from his firm support for orthodox theology. She did, however, persuade him to end the active persecution of the Monophysites. Theodora's death from cancer was a severe blow to Justinian, whose persecution mania worsened in her absence and whose energy as a reformer almost completely deserted him.

Thérèse of Lisieux, Saint (1873–1897) *French nun*

St. Thérèse of Lisieux's brief life of spiritual struggle has inspired millions to follow her "Little Way."

Marie-Françoise-Thérèse Martin was born in Alençon, the youngest of a watchmaker's nine children. After the death of her mother, when she was just four, Thérèse was brought up in Lisieux, Normandy, by her older sisters and an aunt in a deeply religious atmosphere. She applied to join the Carmelite convent at Lisieux when she was 14, but was refused. A year later, after making a pilgrimage to Rome, she was accepted.

Despite her struggles against doubt, depression, and a sense of guilt, she remained outwardly cheerful, unselfishly and obediently following the disciplines of her order. In 1893 she was appointed to supervise the training of novice nuns. On the instructions of her prioress she wrote an autobiographical account of her spiritual development since childhood. This *Story of a Soul* (1898) was published after her death from tuberculosis at the age of 24. It consists of a series of essays in letter form setting out her "Little Way," through which, by "trust and absolute surrender" to the teaching of the Gospels, even an ordinary and insignificant person can attain sanctity.

It immediately became hugely popular, and the burial site of the "Little Flower of Jesus" became a place of pilgrimage, which was eventually crowned in a basilica built between 1929 and 1954. Thérèse was canonized in 1925 and in 1947 was associated with JOAN OF ARC as a patron saint of France. She is also the patron saint of foreign missions and aviators. An English translation of *Story of a Soul* was produced by Father Ronald Knox in 1958.

Thirkell, Angela Margaret (1891–1961) *British novelist*

Angela Thirkell's principal literary achievement was a series of novels featuring the imagined descendants of characters created by the Victorian novelist Trollope.

Born in London, Angela Mackail was the daughter of the Oxford Professor of Poetry and a cousin of Rudyard Kipling. After the failure of an early marriage, she married her second husband, the Australian George Thirkell, in 1917 and spent the 1920s in Australia. Returning to England after the break-up of this marriage, she settled with her parents in Kensington, London, and began to write.

Her first novel, *Ankle Deep*, appeared in 1933. This was followed by *Trooper to the Southern Cross* (1934) and then over 30 novels populated by snobbish gentlefolk living in the mythical county of Barsetshire, which had been invented by Anthony Trollope. The best known include *Coronation*

Summer (1937), *Growing Up* (1943), and *The Duke's Daughter* (1951).

Thirkell's son Colin MacInnes also became a well-known novelist.

Thompson, Dorothy (1893–1961)
American journalist

At the height of her fame in the 1930s Dorothy Thompson was said to wield an influence equalled only by that of the president's wife, Eleanor ROOSEVELT.

Born in Lancaster, New York State, the daughter of an English-born Methodist minister, she attended Syracuse University (1912–14), where she became involved in the campaign for women's suffrage and began to develop her skills as a publicist. In 1920 she travelled to Europe; after living in Paris and Vienna, in 1924 she settled in Berlin, where she was appointed Central European Bureau Chief for the *Philadelphia Public Ledger* and the *New York Evening Post*.

From 1922 to 1927 she was married to a Hungarian playboy, Josef Bard. After her marriage broke up, she visited the Soviet Union, publishing a book-length account of her impressions of the country as *The New Russia* (1928). Her second marriage, to novelist Sinclair Lewis, winner of the Nobel Prize for literature in 1930, lasted from 1928 to 1942, after which she married an easy-going Austrian émigré artist, Max Kopf.

After conducting a face-to-face interview with the rising politician Adolf Hitler, she published *I Saw Hitler!* in 1932. In 1934 she became the first foreign correspondent to be expelled from Germany by the Nazis, making her a vociferous critic of their regime. Her perceptive contributions in the 1930s to the prestigious journal *Foreign Affairs* won her respect as a serious political commentator. By 1936 her "On the Record" column in the *New York Herald Tribune* was being syndicated in 170 newspapers. She was also reaching a far wider audience through her monthly column in the *Ladies' Home Journal* and broadcasts on the NBC radio network.

The outbreak of the war of which she had for so long warned led her to turn from antifascism to the plight of refugees. In the postwar period she concentrated on Middle Eastern affairs, serving as president of the pro-Arab American Friends of the Middle East from 1951 to 1957.

Thompson, Emma (1959–) *British actress*

Emma Thompson's career as an actress and screenwriter has been a cascade of successes.

Born in London, the daughter of a television director and an actress, she studied English literature at Cambridge, where she performed in its celebrated drama society, the Footlights. Thompson began her professional career as a stand-up comedienne, having her first success with her vivacious performance in the long-running musical *Me and My Girl* (1985–86). In 1987 she made the transition from stage to television with a leading role in the miniseries *Tutti Frutti*, playing a Scottish art student. In *Fortunes of War*, which appeared in 1988 and was based on the novels of Olivia MANNING, she played opposite her future husband, Kenneth Branagh. Her performance in this TV series won her awards from the Variety Club as Newcomer of the Year and from BAFTA as Best Actress. In 1988 she had her own six-part television comedy series, *Thompson*, in which she appeared with her mother, Phyllida Law, and her sister, Sophie.

Thompson joined Kenneth Branagh's Renaissance Theatre Company that same year. In 1989 she made her first big-screen appearance in Branagh's acclaimed production of Shakespeare's *Henry V*. She married Branagh that year. During the period of their marriage (1989–95) she starred in three more of his films – *Dead Again* (1991), *Peter's Friends* (1992), and *Much Ado about Nothing* (1993). It was, however, her performance in the film version of E. M. Forster's novel *Howards End*, made by Ismail Merchant and James Ivory, that won her several international awards for Best Actress in 1992, including the Film Critics' Circles of New York and Los Angeles, the U.S. National Board of Review, a Golden Globe, and an Oscar.

Another Merchant–Ivory film, of Kazuo Ishiguro's novel *The Remains of the Day*, brought Thompson an Academy Award nomination for Best Actress in 1994. In the same year she was nominated for a Best Supporting Actress Oscar for her role as a lawyer in *In the Name of the Father*. In 1996 her film adaptation of Jane AUSTEN's *Sense and Sensibility* won her Golden Globe Awards for Best Screenplay, a BAFTA Award for Best Actress, and an Oscar for Best Adapted Screenplay.

Further praise followed for her portrayal of the ambitious wife of a U.S presidential candidate in the film *Primary Colors* (1998) - her character being a thinly disguised portrait of Hillary CLINTON.

Thompson, Flora Jane (1876–1947)
British writer and social historian

Thompson's books, which are mainly concerned with her childhood memories, provide a fascinating description of Victorian country life.

Born Flora Timms in Juniper Hill, a small village on the borders of Oxfordshire and Buckinghamshire, she left school at the age of 14 and went to work in a local post office. She married a postmaster and they moved to Bournemouth to raise what was to become a large family. At the turn of the century she began to produce mass-market fiction to supplement the family's income.

Thompson did not begin serious writing until she was in her sixties, when she wrote *Lark Rise* (1939), *Over to Candleford* (1941), and *Candleford Green* (1943). The three parts of this semi-autobiographical sequence were combined as *Lark Rise to Candleford* in 1945 and have also been successfully dramatized. The work gives an elegaic but unsentimental account of life in an Oxfordshire hamlet as the development of modern industrial society swept away old customs and values. It is particularly regarded for its description of the demise of the rural aristocracy. In 1948, a year after Thompson's death, *Still Glides the Stream* was published, followed in 1979 by *A Country Calendar and other writings*.

Thorndike, Dame Sybil (1882–1976)
British actress

Sybil Thorndike was one of the best-loved theatrical dames and a stalwart of the English theatre.

Born in the market town of Gainsborough, Lincolnshire, she initially trained as a pianist but – in spite of family discouragement – decided to take up a less socially acceptable career as an actress. She made her stage debut in 1904 in Shakespeare's *The Merry Wives of Windsor* and then spent four years touring the United States, playing Shakespeare in repertory. On returning to England in 1908, she married the actor-manager Lewis Casson and became the leading female actor in Annie HORNIMAN's repertory company in Manchester. In 1914 she joined the Old Vic theatre in London, which was managed by the redoubtable Lilian BAYLIS and served as the home of Shakespearean productions in London.

The absence of young male actors, who were in the armed forces during World War I, obliged Thorndike to take on such traditionally male parts as the Fool in *King Lear*, Puck in *A Midsummer Night's Dream*, and even Prince Hal in *Henry IV*. In 1924 she played the title role in the first English performance of Shaw's *Saint Joan*. She was created DBE for her services to theatre in 1931.

During World War II she made morale-raising tours of mining areas in Britain with an Old Vic company. After the war she developed a fine range of elderly lady character roles. In 1958 she appeared with her husband in *Eighty in the Shade*, which had been specially written for them by Clemence Dane to mark their golden wedding anniversary. They appeared together again in 1962 in *Uncle Vanya* at the first Chichester Theatre Festival, after which Thorndike undertook an arduous tour of Australia. In 1969 a theatre named in her honour was opened in Leatherhead, Surrey, and at 85 she took the lead in *There Was an Old Woman*, playing a female vagrant. She collaborated with her husband in writing a biography of Lilian Baylis.

Tibbles, Susette (1854–1903) *American campaigner for the rights of Native Americans*

Half Native American herself, Susette Tibbles worked unceasingly for the rights of these dispossessed tribes. With her husband she made an important contribution to the Dawes Act, which recognized the rights of citizenship and land ownership of Native Americans.

Susette La Flèsche was born in Nebraska, the granddaughter of a French fur trader. Her father, chief of the Omaha tribe, brought her up on the tribe's reservation. She was educated in mission schools and at the Elizabeth Institute in New Jersey, which enabled her to return to the Omaha as a schoolteacher.

In 1879 the celebrated trial of the Native American known as Standing Bear took place. He had been arrested for leading his Ponca tribe (or what was left of it) back to its homelands. This caused widespread controversy, particularly in the Eastern states, which Standing Bear visited to publicize his case. Susette La Flèsche accompanied him as his interpreter. The case for the Ponca was championed by the journalist Thomas Henry Tibbles, who also accompanied Standing Bear on his tour. In 1881 Susette La Flèsche married Tibbles, and in 1886 they visited England to lecture on Native-American culture – especially on the role of women in Native-American tribes.

As a result of the campaign headed by the Tibbleses, the Native-American cause found many supporters, including the writer and reformer Helen Hunt Jackson, with whose help the 1887 Dawes Act was passed, granting citizenship to the Native Americans.

After spending some time in Washington, D.C., to ensure that their case was properly presented, the Tibbleses returned to the Omaha in Nebraska.

Tilley, Vesta (1864–1952) *British entertainer*

Vesta Tilley was the greatest male impersonator of her time.

Born Matilda Alice Powles, the daughter of a provincial theatre manager, she made her stage debut at three and by seven was appearing regularly as "The Great Little Tilley." By the age of nine she had begun to appear in male dress and was playing in three theatres in London every night. To her real name she added Vesta, from the trade name "Swan Vesta" – a widely used brand of matches named after the Roman goddess of fire. As a personal name it was unique, but at the same time instantly recognizable to the working classes, who were to become her greatest fans.

Dressed as a dandy for her famous numbers, such as "Burlington Bertie" and "Following in Father's Footsteps," she stylishly mocked the foppish manners of the rich to the delight of the adoring poor, who saluted her as no less than "The London Idol." She also toured successfully on the vaudeville circuit in the United States.

During World War I Tilley threw herself into recruiting men for the armed forces, singing such songs as "Jolly Good Luck to the Girl Who Loves a Soldier," "The Army of Today's All Right," and "Six Days' Leave." For this effort she became known as "England's Greatest Recruiting Sergeant." In 1919 her husband, an MP who composed many of her songs, was knighted as Sir Walter de Frece. She retired from the stage the following year and published *Recollections of Vesta Tilley* in 1934. On her retirement she was presented with a set of books that contained the signatures of some two million fans. She died in Monte Carlo.

Tizard, Dame Catherine (1931–   ) *New Zealand public official*

Catherine Tizard spent some 25 years in local government in New Zealand before becoming the country's first female governor-general.

Born in Auckland, Catherine Anne McLean was educated at Matamata College and the University of Auckland, where she taught zoology from 1967 to 1984. In 1951 she married Robert James Tizard, a New Zealand MP, who later became minister of defence, science, and technology. With him she had one son and three daughters, but the marriage was dissolved in 1983.

An Auckland city councillor from 1971, Tizard resigned from the university after becoming mayor in 1983. In 1984 she was created a DBE. During her period of office she oversaw the completion of the long-planned Aotea Centre performing arts complex.

When she ceased to be mayor in 1990, Dame Catherine was appointed the first woman governor-general of New Zealand. Outspoken and popular, with passions for scuba diving and cryptic crossword puzzles, she completed her term of office in 1996.

Toklas, Alice B. (1877–1967) *American literary hostess*

Alice B. Toklas is remembered as the long-term companion of the writer Gertrude STEIN.

Born in San Francisco, she met Stein in Paris in 1907. Together they hosted a salon that attracted expatriate American writers, such as Ernest Hemingway and Sherwood Anderson, and avant-garde painters, including Picasso, Matisse, and Braque. Acting as Stein's cook, secretary, and general organizer, Toklas remained a background figure until Stein published her memoirs in 1933 under the teasing title *The Autobiography of Alice B. Toklas*.

After Stein's death in 1946 Toklas published her own literary memoir, which mixed reminiscences and recipes under the title *The Alice B. Toklas Cook Book* (1954). In 1963 she published her autobiography, *What Is Remembered*.

Torvill, Jayne (1957–) *British ice skater and dancer*

Jayne Torvill became famous as the female half of Torvill and Dean, a partnership that gave ice dancing an entirely new standard of artistic achievement.

Born in Nottingham, she started skating at ten, becoming British junior pairs figure-skating champion at 13. Partnered by Christopher Dean from 1975 onwards, she went on with him to win a record six successive British ice-dance championships (1978–83), four European championships (1981, 1982, 1984, 1994), and four world championships (1981–84). At the Los Angeles Olympic Games in 1984 they won the gold medal for their unique interpretation of Ravel's *Bolero*. In 1985 they retired from amateur competitive skating and for the next nine years performed professionally in their own ice shows.

In 1994 Torvill and Dean returned to competitive skating at the Olympics in Lillehammer, Norway, where they won a bronze medal. Disappointed with this award, they returned to professional skating in 1995. The story of the Torvill and Dean partnership was published in 1994 as *Fire on Ice*. Although the relationship between Torvill and Dean was the subject of much media speculation, Jayne married Phil Christiansen, a sound engineer, in 1990. Torvill was honoured as the Sports Writers' Sportswoman of the Year in 1981 and BBC Sports Personality of the Year in 1984.

Toumanova, Tamara (1919–) *French dancer*

Toumanova's dancing career has been both highly praised and very varied – ranging from the Ballets Russes to Broadway musicals and from prima ballerina roles in New York and London to Hollywood films.

Tamara Toumanova was born in Shanghai, China, to Russian émigré parents. A talented dancer at an early age, she went to Paris to study ballet, making her debut at the Paris Opéra in 1928, when she was only nine years old.

Four years later she was taken on by the Ballets Russes de Monte Carlo, which had been founded by Sergei Diaghilev in 1911. Here she became one of their three celebrated "baby ballerinas," making her name in *La Concurrence*, a ballet by George Balanchine. In 1936 Toumanova danced with the choreographer Léonide Massine in his *Symphonie fantastique*. Two years later she moved with Massine to the company founded by René Blum, the French ballet impresario, who had also defected from the Ballets Russes.

In the late 1930s Toumanova moved to Broadway, dancing in such musicals as *Stars in Your Eyes*. However, she soon returned to classical ballet, appearing in 1941 in *Balustrade*, which had been especially choreographed for her by Balanchine. Later in the 1940s she was guest ballerina with several companies, including the Paris Opéra, to which she returned to dance the title role of Cocteau's *Phèdre*; she also appeared at the American Ballet Theater, the London Festival Ballet, and La Scala in Milan.

Toumanova danced in several successful Hollywood films, including Gene Kelly's *Invitation to the Dance* (1956) and the Hitchcock thriller *Torn Curtain* (1966).

Travers,   P(amela)   L(yndon)
(1906–   ) *Australian writer*

P. L. Travers is best known as the creator of the immortal nanny Mary Poppins.

Born in Queensland, Australia, she moved to England, where she acted, wrote poetry, worked as a journalist, and became drama critic for the *New English Weekly*. In 1934, the year in which she visited Moscow, she published a children's story about a cheerful miracle-working nanny, *Mary Poppins*. It was an international success, inspiring seven more books and a film (1964), starring Julie ANDREWS in the title role.

In 1941 Travers published *I Go By Sea, I Go By Land*, a diary recounting the experiences of a British child evacuated from his city home to avoid wartime bombing. In her later years she taught at Smith, Radcliffe, and Scripps colleges in the United States. Through such books as *About Sleeping Beauty* (1975) and *What the Bee Knows* (1989) she became widely acknowledged as an expert on mythology.

Trimmer, Sarah (1741–1810) *British educationalist*

A mother of 12 children who educated all of them at home, Sarah Trimmer became an authority on church Sunday schools as well as being a writer of children's books.

Sarah Kirby was born in Ipswich, Suffolk, the daughter of the artist John Kirby. After attending local schools, she married James Trimmer at the age of 18. The 12 children of the

marriage were all educated by their mother at home. This experience gave Sarah Trimmer a taste for education, which was encouraged by the achievements of her contemporary Anna BAR-BAULD, who had written a number of popular educational books for children.

In 1782 Trimmer published her first book, *An Easy Introduction to the Knowledge of Nature*, and a subsequent volume providing a guide to the Bible. She also organized a number of Sunday schools for poor children and advised Queen Charlotte on setting up Sunday schools.

A strong advocate of maintaining the influence of the church in secular education, she wrote two influential books on the subject, *Reflections Upon the Education of Children in Charity Schools* (1801) and *The Economy of Charity* (1801). She also edited educational magazines and wrote children's books, including *Fabulous Histories* (1786).

Tristan, Flora (1803–1844) *French political writer and feminist*

Flora Tristan was one of the first feminist socialists. For her the establishment of equal rights for women was an inextricable part of the emancipation of the working classes.

Tristan was the illegitimate daughter of a Spanish Peruvian army officer and a French woman. Although her father's family was wealthy and influential (her uncle later became president of Peru), Flora was brought up in poverty in Paris. At the age of 18 she made a fateful marriage to her employer, the painter and lithographer André Chazal. After three years of ill-treatment she left him in 1824 but was unable to get a divorce; a long battle to get custody of their children began. In 1830 her dire financial position prompted her to travel to Peru, where she made a vain appeal for assistance to her uncle.

By the time she returned to France in 1834, Flora Tristan's experiences had made her a convinced feminist and radical. During the next few years she became active in left-wing groups and wrote several political pamphlets. Her first major work, the autobiographical *Pérégrinations d'une paria* (1838; Travels of an Outcast), described her journey to Peru and her indignation at the low status of women in that country. It also contained some bitter reflections on her married life that so enraged her husband that he attempted to kill her. As a result he spent over 20 years in jail.

On recovering from this trauma, Flora Tristan travelled to London to study the conditions of the English working class. Her book *Promenades dans Londres* (1840; Walks in London) describes the squalid conditions of the urban poor with special emphasis on the hardships of working women. In 1843 Tristan published her most substantial book, *L'Union ouvrière* (The Workers' Union), a major work of socialist theory that called on workers' organizations in all countries to make common cause against capitalism. The book proposes the total reorganization of society on co-operative lines and the establishment of complete equality between the sexes.

Flora Tristan was engaged in a lecture tour to promote these views when she contracted typhoid and died at Bordeaux in France. Her grandson was the painter Paul Gauguin.

Trollope, Frances (1780–1863) *British writer*

> I certainly believe the women of America to be the handsomest in the world, but as surely do I believe that they are the least attractive.
>
> —*Domestic Manners of the Americans* (1832)

The mother of the novelist Anthony Trollope, Fanny Trollope was herself a writer, who supported her family by the proceeds of her many travel books and novels.

She was born Frances Milton in Stapleton, near Bristol. After the death of her mother and her father's remarriage she moved to London to become housekeeper for her brother. In 1809 she married Thomas Trollope, who failed successively as a lawyer, a professor, and a farmer but succeeded in fathering their seven children. In an attempt to recoup the family fortunes,

Fanny sailed to the United States in 1827 with her husband and their three youngest children. The Trollopes helped to found the model community of New Harmony, Memphis, Tennessee, which failed, and then bankrupted themselves trying to run a bazaar in Cincinnati, Ohio. On returning to England with her family, Fanny took up yet another career – as a writer.

Her caustic *Domestic Manners of the Americans*, which appeared in 1832, gave an account of America as a nation of boasters and spitters; this amused the British but not all Americans. Nevertheless, the book was a tremendous success, bringing her offers to write similar books on Britain's continental neighbours. *Paris and the Parisians* appeared in 1835, and *Vienna and the Austrians* in 1838.

After the death of her husband Fanny settled in Florence, where she produced her book *A Visit to Italy* (1842). She also wrote a series of novels. A number of these were semi-autobiographical, featuring a character named Widow Barnaby, whose adventures predictably included a stay in the United States; they include *The Widow Barnaby* (1839), *The Widow Married* (1840), and *The Barnabys in America* (1843). Of her other books, the best known are the antislavery novel *The Life and Adventures of Jonathan Jefferson Whitlaw* (1836) and *The Vicar of Wrexhill* (1837). Fanny Trollope eventually produced over 100 volumes in a writing career that only began in her fifties. She died in Florence.

Her son Anthony Trollope became one of the most outstanding novelists of the Victorian era. Another son, Thomas Adolphus, wrote books about Italian life and history.

Trollope, Joanna (1943–) *British novelist*

Joanna Trollope, a distant relative of the 19th-century novelist Anthony Trollope, has been hailed as "queen of the Aga Saga" – a type of novel that explores the domestic tensions likely to occur in a contemporary English village. She is also the author of a series of well-researched historical novels.

Born in rural Gloucestershire, she studied English at St. Hugh's College, Oxford; after graduating, she worked as a researcher in the Foreign Office for two years. For most of the 1970s Joanna Trollope worked in education, teaching classes ranging from young children to adults, while supplementing her earnings with contributions to such magazines as *Harper's* and *Vogue*.

Success as a novelist came with *Parson Harding's Daughter*; set in 18th-century India, it won the Romantic Historical Novel of the Year award in 1980. It was followed by *Charlotte*, which tells the story of the disastrous British retreat from Kabul in 1842. *The City of Gems* (1981) is set in Burma in the 1880s, and *The Steps of the Sun* (1984) is a novel of the 1899–1902 Boer War in South Africa. In 1983 Trollope published a well-received nonfiction work, *Britannia's Daughters: Women of the British Empire*.

In Trollope's historical novels the plot usually revolves around a flawed heroine who must overcome her shortcomings to find fulfilment. In her contemporary novels the heroine is less often flawed than frustrated by circumstances, often a loveless marriage. *The Choir* (1987) explores the infighting between families involved in the life of a great English cathedral. *A Village Affair* (1989) deals with the reactions of a small community when confronted with a lesbian relationship in its midst. *The Rector's Wife* (1991) is the story of the long-suffering partner of a village priest who finally rebels against a life of self-sacrifice, which she is expected to accept without question or regret. All three novels have been made into highly successful television series. Her later novels include *The Men and the Girls* (1992), *A Spanish Lover* (1993), *The Best of Friends* (1995), and *Next of Kin* (1996).

Joanna Trollope was appointed OBE in 1996. She has two daughters by her first husband and is now married to the television scriptwriter Ian Curteis.

Truth, Sojourner (c. 1797–1883)
American reformer

> If the first woman God ever made was strong enough to turn the world upside down all alone, those [American] women together ought to be able to turn it back, and get it right side up again.
>
> —Speech, Ohio, 1851

Sojourner Truth was born a slave; from the age of about 30, when she was freed, she devoted her life to the abolition of slavery, the emancipation of women, and the education of freed slaves.

Born in Ulster County, New York State, and christened Isabella, she was sold on from her family at an early age and passed through the ownership of several masters, during which time she gave birth to five children. In 1827, when the New York State Emancipation Act freed all slaves within its territory, Isabella left for New York City, where she undertook domestic work to support herself and two of her children and became a member of a fringe religious sect.

By 1843 Isabella was convinced that she had been divinely commanded to proclaim the need to abolish slavery and grant equal rights for all women. Adopting the name Sojourner Truth, she set out – with only a bag of clothes and 25 cents – to travel the roads and preach. Although she was illiterate and unpolished in speech, she dominated audiences by the sheer force of her personality. In 1850 she dictated her autobiography, *The Narrative of Sojourner Truth*, to a man called Oliver Gilbert; its sales supported her evangelism.

During the Civil War she carried supplies to African-American volunteer soldiers in the Federal army. In 1864 President Lincoln appointed her as counsellor to the freedmen of Washington. After the Civil War she campaigned for adequate opportunities for education and employment to be provided for freed slaves entering the labour market. She finally retired in 1875.

Sojourner Truth's prose poem, "Ain't I a Woman," has inspired successive generations of African-American women. In 1997 the wheeled robot that was sent on the expedition to Mars to explore the surface of the planet was named after her.

Tsvetaeva, Marina Ivanovna (1892–1941) *Russian poet*

Marina Tsvetaeva has, since her tragic suicide, become widely recognized as one of the greatest 20th-century Russian poets. She was also the author of verse plays, short stories, and memoirs.

Born in Moscow, the daughter of an art professor and a pianist, she spent much of her childhood in western Europe, where she attended the Sorbonne in Paris. Her first volume of verse, *Evening Album*, was published in 1910 to considerable critical acclaim, although it is now regarded as technically competent but somewhat pallid beside her later work.

In 1912 she married Sergei Yakovlevich Efron, who became an officer in the imperial army and later joined the White Russians to fight the Bolsheviks in the civil war that followed the Revolution. Tsvetaeva loathed the revolutionaries and devoted an entire cycle of poems, *The Encampment of the Swans*, to praising the counter-revolutionary forces. She was, nevertheless, allowed to leave the newly established Soviet Union after the civil war and rejoined her husband, whom she had thought dead, in Prague.

Publication of more of Tsvetaeva's poetry in Berlin and Moscow in 1922 confirmed her reputation and led her into an extended correspondence with the poets Rainer Maria Rilke and Boris Pasternak. Between 1922 and 1925 she wrote some of her greatest poetry, which appeared as the collections *Craft* (1923) and *After Russia* (1928). Moving to Paris in 1925, she found herself increasingly estranged from her fellow exiles and forced into great poverty. Her husband had now become pro-Soviet, to the extent of assassinating a Soviet defector on the orders of the secret police, after which he departed for the USSR. Ostracized completely by the émigré community as a result of her husband's betrayal, in 1939 Tsvetaeva reluctantly decided

to follow him, only to be shunned on arrival by her former friends.

Later that same year her daughter Ariadna was arrested, and Ariadna's husband was arrested and shot. After the outbreak of World War II Tsvetaeva was sent to the remote Tatar Autonomous Republic in Central Asia, where she hanged herself in despair. Since 1961 much of her work has been republished in her native country, and English translations, notably by Elaine Feinstein, have also been published.

Tubman, Harriet (1821–1913) *American abolitionist*

Through aiding slaves to escape from the U.S. South, Harriet Tubman became known as "the Moses of her people." The abolitionist John Brown described her as "one of the best and bravest persons on this continent – *General* Tubman as we call her."

Born into slavery on a Maryland plantation, she was set to work as a field hand as a child and remained illiterate all her life. In 1844 she was forced to marry a fellow slave, John Tubman, but five years later she escaped to the North, leaving her husband behind and changing her name from Araminta to Harriet.

From then until the outbreak of the Civil War in 1861 Tubman devoted herself to working on the "Underground Railroad," by which slaves were secretly smuggled to freedom. Helped by Quaker sympathizers, she undertook 20 missions back to the South, rescuing more than 300 people, including her own parents. Although an enormous reward of $40,000 was offered for her capture, she was never taken and reportedly never lost a "passenger," being quite prepared to threaten death to the faint-hearted if their resolution failed en route.

Between missions Tubman worked as a cook and spoke at antislavery meetings. During the Civil War she was attached to the Union Army in South Carolina, serving as cook, nurse, laundress, scout, and spy. After the war she settled in Auburn, New York State, where she had set her parents up in a house of their own. She continued her work for freedmen, founding a home for the destitute although she was scarcely better off herself.

A biography by Sarah Bradford first appeared in 1869, and a revised version, *Harriet Tubman: The Moses of Her People*, was published in 1886. Despite her wartime service, she was denied a federal pension until 1897. When she died, the citizens of Auburn erected a monument to her memory, and she was buried with full military honours.

Tuchman, Barbara (1912–1989)
American historian

Barbara Tuchman's work as a historian has shown that in spite of a trend for professional historians to abandon narrative for analysis, there is still a place for story telling. By incorporating graphic detail and the compelling presentation of personalities in her books, Tuchman has managed to combine readability and sustained interest with high academic standards.

She was born Barbara Wertheim in New York City. After graduating from Radcliffe College, she worked as a researcher at the Institute of Pacific Relations before becoming a staff writer for the *Nation* magazine. In 1940 she married Dr. Lester Tuchman, with whom she had three daughters.

Her first major success came in 1958 with *The Zimmermann Telegram*, which explored Germany's attempts to persuade Mexico to attack the United States during World War I. *The Guns of August* (1962), which dealt with the outbreak of World War I, won her a Pulitzer Prize. In 1971 she gained a second Pulitzer Prize for *Stilwell and the American Experience in China*.

A Distant Mirror: The Calamitous Fourteenth Century (1978) represented a drastic shift of focus to medieval France, and her last book, *The First Salute* (1988), was concerned with the Revolutionary War. Her best-selling *The March of Folly* (1984) presented four case studies of governmental mismanagement, ranging from the Trojan Horse to the Vietnam War.

Tucker, Sophie (1884–1966) *American entertainer*

Sophie Tucker had a career as a singer that lasted over 60 years. In World War II she toured widely to entertain the troops.

The child of Russian Jewish immigrants, Sonia Abuza was born while her parents were travelling to the United States. She began her career as a child singer in her father's kosher restaurant in Hartford, Connecticut, and made her stage debut in New York in 1906 as a comedienne in blackface. A brief marriage to a brewer's driver, Louis Tuck, helped to suggest her stage name.

Blues and jazz greatly influenced her singing style, and throughout her career Sophie Tucker remained close to such African-American musicians as Shelton Brooks, who wrote her theme song, "Some of These Days." In 1909 she appeared briefly in the *Ziegfeld Follies*. In 1911 her jazzy version of Irving Berlin's "Alexander's Ragtime Band" made this song a national craze.

By 1914 Tucker had become a leading entertainer in her own right. In 1925 Jack Yellen wrote "My Yiddisher Mama" for her. For the next 40 or so years she sang it to great effect in vaudeville, burlesque, nightclubs, and English music halls. Her other songs were sometimes raucous, sometimes romantic, and often risqué. She was a great favourite with both young and old, stalwartly providing entertainment into her late seventies. Her autobiography, *Some of These Days*, appeared in 1945.

Tuckwell, Gertrude (1861–1951)
British trade-union official and social reformer

An active trade unionist and an early member of the Labour Party, Gertrude Tuckwell played a prominent part in improving the lot of working women.

Gertrude Tuckwell was born in Oxford, where her father, the master of New College School, educated her at home. After teaching in several London state schools, she became secretary to her aunt, Lady Emily Dilkes, who was president of the Women's Trade Union League. This experience made her aware of the abuses suffered by women who were forced by poverty to work in poor or dangerous conditions for low pay. In 1906, with several collaborators, she organized the Sweated Goods Exhibition, and in 1908 she published her book *Women in Industry*. Her exhibition and her book, together with her campaign against poisoning by white lead, led to the Trade Boards Act (1909), which restricted the worst of these abuses.

After World War I Gertrude Tuckwell became involved with the Labour Party and campaigned for many social reforms. She was appointed in 1924 to membership on the Royal Commission on National Health Insurance and in 1927 to the Maternal Mortality Committee. During her later years she was also a Justice of the Peace in London, president of the National Association of Probation Officers, and a member of the Central Committee on Women's Training and Employment.

Turishcheva, Lyudmila Ivanovna
(1952–) *Russian gymnast*

Lyudmila Turishcheva was, at her peak, the world's greatest female Olympic gymnast.

Born in Grozny, now capital of the Russian republic of Chechnia, she did not take up gymnastics until she was 13. A year later she became a member of the Soviet team. She won team gold medals at the 1968, 1972, and 1976 Olympic Games. At the 1972 Olympics she won a gold medal in the all-around competition, as well as a silver medal for the floor exercises and a bronze medal for vaulting. In 1976 she won silver medals for the floor exercises and vaulting and a bronze medal in the all-round competition, bringing the total of her Olympic medals to nine.

At the first World Cup competition in 1970 Turishcheva won all five individual events. In 1971 she won the European championship and in 1973 at the same competition took the gold medal in every event. In 1974 she was again world champion and in 1975 again took the World Cup. In 1977 she retired from competitive gymnastics, becoming coach to the Soviet team.

Turner, Kathleen (1954–) *American actress*

Kathleen Turner's film career has seen her progress from a husky-voiced seductress to a character actress with a talent for comedy.

Born in Springfield, Missouri, the daughter of a diplomat, she travelled the world as a child. She attended Southwest Missouri State University and the University of Maryland before undergoing professional training at the Central School of Speech and Drama in London. After playing on stage with the Manitoba Theatre Company and Baltimore Arena Players, she made her Broadway debut in 1976; by 1977 she was appearing in a television soap opera, *The Doctors*.

Turner's big-screen debut came in *Body Heat* (1981), an erotic thriller that won her immediate attention. Still greater success came playing opposite Michael Douglas in the comedy thriller *Romancing the Stone* (1984), which won her the Los Angeles Film Critics' Circle Best Actress award. She reprised the part of novelist Joan Wilder, again with Douglas, in the sequel *The Jewel of the Nile* (1985). In the same year she showed her comic powers by portraying a hired killer, opposite Jack Nicholson, in *Prizzi's Honor*.

Kathleen Turner's role in *Peggy Sue Got Married* (1986), in which she played both a mature woman and the same character as a teenager, gained her an Academy Award nomination for Best Actress. Having provided the husky voice of Jessica Rabbit in the animated feature *Who Framed Roger Rabbit?* (1988), she took the title role in the thriller *V. I. Warshawski* (1991), based on a novel by Sara PARETSKY. She returned successfully to her comic style playing a suburban housewife killer in the black comedy *Serial Mom* (1994).

Turner, Lana (1920–1995) *American actress*

Lana Turner was a classic example of the small-town girl who becomes a glamorous Hollywood film star.

Born Julia Jean Mildred Frances Turner in Wallace, Idaho, she was the daughter of a mine foreman who was murdered when she was nine. While still a teenager she moved with her mother to Los Angeles, where she was "discovered," working as a waitress; as a result, she made her screen debut at 17 playing a bit part as a girl sipping a soda in a drug store in *They Won't Forget*. Her casual skirt-and-sweater style was soon seized upon by Hollywood publicists, who made her famous as the "Sweater Girl."

Director Mervyn LeRoy was sufficiently impressed by what he saw to get Turner a contract with MGM, which enabled her to appear as an extra in *A Star is Born* (1937). The studio initially traded on her glamour in such films as *Dancing Co-Ed* (1939) and *Ziegfeld Girl* (1941), but in *The Postman Always Rings Twice* (1946) she proved that she could act as well as look decorative. In this film she played a seductive murderess – possibly her most memorable role. She also gave an impressive performance as the alcoholic girlfriend of Kirk Douglas in *The Bad and the Beautiful* (1952).

Turner's performance as a neurotic mother in *Peyton Place* (1957), a sensationalized melodrama of small-town sleaze and sex, won her an Academy Award nomination. *Imitation of Life* (1959) proved to be her greatest box-office success, but in her later career she reverted to the undemanding roles with which she had begun, making her last film, *Witches' Brew*, in 1978. She then appeared on stage and in the TV soap opera *Falcon Crest* (1982–83).

Married seven times, Lana Turner often attracted more publicity for her personal life than for her professional abilities. She responded in her autobiography *Lana: The Lady, The Legend, The Truth* (1982).

Turner, Tina (1938–) *American pop singer*

Tina Turner survived a turbulent marriage and a career that appeared to be coming to an end by relaunching herself as the world's sexiest rock 'n' roll grandmother.

Born Annie Mae Bullock in Nutbush, Tennessee, she met Ike Turner in a nightclub in St. Louis, Missouri, joined his Revue Band, and married him in 1956. Together they recorded several hits, including "River Deep, Mountain High" (1966) and "Nutbush

City Limits" (1973), before divorcing in 1976.

By this time Turner had taken refuge in Britain, having been written off as a spent force in the United States. She gave a strong performance in the film of Pete Townshend's rock opera *Tommy* (1975), and in the same year Townshend produced her album *Acid Queen*. However, there were lean years ahead before her album *Private Dancer* (1984), which was also produced in Britain, shot her to superstardom – a status that she consolidated with an outrageous cameo performance in the sci-fi fantasy *Mad Max Beyond Thunderdome* (1985), starring Mel Gibson.

Turner's hit singles include "What's Love Got To Do With It," "We Don't Need Another Hero," and "Simply the Best." Among her later solo albums are *Break Every Rule* (1986), *Foreign Affair* (1989), and *Simply the Best* (1990). She collected one Grammy Award in 1972, three more in 1985, and another in 1986. France has honoured her with the rank of Chevalier of Arts and Letters.

Tussaud, Marie (1761–1850) *Swiss waxwork modeller*

A century and a half after her death, "Madame Tussaud's" exhibition of waxworks is still one of London's most successful tourist attractions.

Marie Grosholtz was born in Strasbourg, France, and grew up first in Bern, Switzerland, and then in Paris, where she learned the art of modelling portraits in wax in the studio of her uncle, Philip Curtius. After he was guillotined in 1794, she inherited the business. Among her first subjects were Jean-Jacques Rousseau and Benjamin Franklin. Suspected of royalist sympathies during the French Revolution, she was forced to model the severed heads of victims of the guillotine, including those of King Louis XVI and his queen, MARIE ANTOINETTE. She also modelled the head and body of the politician Marat as his corpse lay in the bath in which he had been assassinated by Charlotte CORDAY.

In 1795 Marie married the military engineer François Tussaud, by whom she had two sons. The marriage having failed, in 1802 she took advantage of a temporary peace to flee to England with some of her best models and her younger son, Francis. After touring Britain, exhibiting a gallery of heroes and villains, she eventually took permanent premises in London's Baker Street in 1835. Although best known for its Chamber of Horrors, featuring notorious murderers and torturers, Madame Tussaud's Exhibition was highly regarded as an educational institution and enthusiastically patronized by such influential figures as Charles Dickens and the Duke of Wellington.

At the age of 81 Madame Tussaud produced what was generally agreed to be her most accomplished work, a self-portrait. Her Exhibition moved to its present site in Marylebone Road, off Baker Street, in 1884. Fire ravaged the premises in 1925, but the original moulds were saved, and the range of models has been constantly added to ever since; the Exhibition now includes a panoramic history of London, called "The Spirit of London," which opened in 1993. After her death Madame Tussaud left the Exhibition to her two sons. The business remained in the hands of her descendants until the death of her great-great-grandson Bernard Tussaud in 1967.

Tutin, Dorothy (1931–) *British actress*

Dorothy Tutin's acting career has successfully embraced both classical and contemporary roles, ranging from Shakespeare to Ibsen and Harold Pinter.

Born in London and trained at the Royal Academy of Dramatic Art (RADA), she made her debut in 1949. As a member of the Old Vic company, she extended her range to include such modern roles as Rose in Graham Greene's *The Living Room* (1953) and Sally Bowles in *I Am a Camera* (1954). Her first major success came in 1958 when she appeared in the Stratford Shakespeare Festival and toured the Soviet Union with the Shakespeare Memorial Theatre company. In 1960 the London *Evening Standard* gave her its Best Actress Award. In the follow-

ing year she scored a notable success in the role of Sister Jeanne in John Whiting's *The Devils*. She played VICTORIA in *Portrait of a Queen* in 1965, taking the role to Broadway three years later.

Tutin gave many memorable performances in the 1970s, notably as Kate in Harold Pinter's *Old Times* (1971) at London's Aldwych Theatre and as Madam Ranevsky in *The Cherry Orchard* (1978) at the National. In the same year she won the Society of West End Theatres Award for her performance as Lady Plyant in *The Double Dealer*. Tutin's successes in the following decade included the part of Hester in a revival of Terence Rattigan's *The Deep Blue Sea* (1981) and her performance in Pinter's *A Kind of Alaska* (1985). More recently she has appeared in *Henry VIII* (1991) and Shaw's *Getting Married* (1993), both at Chichester.

Tutin has also made a number of films, including *The Importance of Being Earnest* (1951), in which she played the part of Cicely. In 1972 she received the Variety Club of Great Britain's award as Best Film Actress for her performance as Sophie Breska in *Savage Messiah*. Her more recent films include *The Shooting Party* (1992).

In 1963 she married Derek Waring, by whom she has one son and one daughter. In 1967 she was appointed CBE.

Twiggy (1949–) *British model*

In the 1960s Twiggy – so called because of her extreme thinness – was a supermodel with an international reputation. She later became an actress and singer.

Born Lesley Hornby in an unfashionable part of northwest London, she was launched as a model in 1966 by the self-publicizing Justin de Villeneuve (whose real name was Johnny Davies). For the ensuing decade she dominated the emerging youth fashion scene, rising to adorn the pages of *Elle* in France and *Vogue* on both sides of the Atlantic.

Her sticklike legs, their length often accentuated by a miniskirt, won her the nickname Sticks, which became

Twigs and ultimately Twiggy. Her almost emaciated figure, boyish Vidal Sassoon haircut, exquisite face, and down-market Cockney accent embodied a combination of attributes that made her irresistible to the style-crazy pundits of London's "Swinging Sixties."

In 1971 Twiggy made her film debut in a screen version of Sandy Wilson's 1920s pastiche musical *The Boy Friend*. A competent talent as a singer and dancer earned her Golden Globe Awards as Most Promising Newcomer and Best Actress. She went on to make several other films in the 1970s and 1980s and also appeared on stage.

Twiggy has remained a household name and appears from time to time on television. After the death of her first husband, by whom she had a daughter, she married Leigh Lawson in 1988, now being known as Lesley (or Twiggy) Lawson. She published an autobiography, *Twiggy*, in 1975 and *An Open Look* in 1985. Her many awards and honours include being made an Honorary Colonel of the Tennessee Army.

Twining, Louisa (1820–1912) *British social reformer*

The two main areas of concern for Louisa Twining were Poor Law reform, especially as it applied to workhouses, and the role of women in local government.

Louisa Twining was born in London into an old-established family of tea importers and purveyors whose name is still widely known. Her father, the head of the firm, was also a manager of King's College Hospital. This connection brought Louisa into contact with many families less fortunate than her own. She began her work among London's poor in 1840 and continued to be active throughout her long working life.

Among her priorities was a concern for the inhabitants of workhouses, not only in London but throughout the country. She was appointed secretary of the Workhouse Visiting Society and in 1858 published *Workhouses and Women's Work*; her second book on the subject, *Workhouses and Pau-*

perism, appeared 40 years later. Having helped her father to establish a local church nursing sisterhood in the 1840s, in 1879 she established a nursing association to improve standards in workhouse infirmaries. She also founded a hostel for girls from workhouses who were employed as domestic servants.

From 1884 to 1890 she was Poor Law Guardian for the London borough of Kensington, and after moving to Sussex in 1893, she fulfilled the same role in Tunbridge Wells.

Apart from her philanthropic work, Louisa Twining was an active social scientist and a member of the National Association for the Promotion of Social Science. She was also president of the Society for Women in Local Government and a lifelong women's suffrage supporter.

In *Recollections of Life and Work* (1895) Twining gave an account of her achievements in social work.

Tyler, Anne (1941–) *American novelist*

Anne Tyler's highly acclaimed novels make use of witty colloquial dialogue to reveal the tensions and tragedies underlying everyday life in Baltimore and the small communities of the American South.

Born in Minneapolis, Minnesota, she was brought up in Raleigh, North Carolina, and graduated from Duke University when she was only 19, having twice won the Anne Flexner Award offered there for creative writing. She has worked as a Russian bibliographer and as assistant to the librarian at McGill University Law Library. In 1963 she married a physician, Tughi Modarressi, by whom she has two daughters.

Her literary debut came in 1964 with *If Morning Ever Comes*. Later titles include *Dinner at the Homesick Restaurant* (1982) and *The Accidental Tourist* (1985), which was made into a film in 1988. For *Breathing Lessons* (1988), she won the Pulitzer Prize for fiction. Her more recent novels include *Saint Maybe* (1991), and *Ladder of Years* (1995).

Tyson, Cicely (1933–) *American actress*

> Cicely Tyson is not a great black actress. She is a great actress who, quite incidentally, just happens also to be black.
> —Rex Reed, *The New York Daily News*, January 18, 1974

Cicely Tyson has commanded considerable respect in the theatrical profession by her scrupulous refusal to play any roles demeaning to an African American's cultural identity.

Born in East Harlem, New York, she was the daughter of immigrants from Nevis in the West Indies. Her childhood, though greatly impoverished, was enriched by her involvement in St. John's Episcopal Church. After graduating from high school, she began work as a secretary with the Red Cross.

A chance opportunity to serve as a model in a hair-styling contest inspired Tyson to pay for a modelling course; as a result, she soon became one of the top ten African-American models in the United States. After studying at New York University and the Actors' Studio, she made her film debut in 1957 in *Twelve Angry Men*; her stage debut came two years later in an off-Broadway production. In 1962 she received a Vernon Rice Award for her stage acting and in 1963 became the first African-American actress to be given a continuing role in a television drama series.

A decade later her performance as a sharecropper's wife in the film *Sounder* (1972) won Tyson an Academy Award nomination and the Best Actress awards of the National Society of Film Critics and the Atlanta Film Festival. In 1974 her portrayal of an ex-slave in a television special, *The Autobiography of Miss Jane Pittman*, was highly acclaimed. During the 1980s her career focused increasingly on television work, though she did give a notable performance in the 1989 film *Fried Green Tomatoes*.

She was briefly married to the jazz trumpeter Miles Davis and was a cofounder of the prestigious Dance Theater of Harlem.

Tz'u-hsi (1835–1908) *Chinese empress dowager*

The efforts of Tz'u-hsi (or Cixi), "the Dragon Empress," to preserve imperial China by resisting reform helped to ensure that she was its last effective ruler.

Born in Beijing, the imperial capital, she was a member of the Manchu family of Yehonala and thus one of the empire's ruling elite. At the age of 16 she was chosen to serve as a concubine to Emperor Hsieng-feng (or Xianfeng). When she gave birth to his only heir, Tsai-ch'un, five years later, she was promoted to the rank of second-class imperial consort. In 1860 the capital was attacked by British and French troops, and the imperial family fled to Jehol in Manchuria, where the emperor died in 1861. Tz'u-hsi became joint regent for her son with the senior widow, Dowager Empress Hsiao, but proved much the stronger of the two.

Returning to Beijing, she purged the administration, replacing key officials with her own appointees and suppressing large-scale peasant uprisings. During the 1860s she tolerated attempts to introduce Western-style technology and reforms in the military and education. In 1875 the young emperor died. To retain her power Tz'u-hsi violated the strict law of succession to replace him with her three-year-old nephew, Kuang-hsü. The death of the senior consort, Hsiao, in 1881 further strengthened her hand, and in 1889 she was confident enough of her ability to manipulate Kuang-hsü to allow the young emperor to assume nominal rule, after marrying him to one of her nieces.

China's disastrous defeat at the hands of Japan in 1894–95, caused in part by Tz'u-hsi's own diversion of naval funds for her personal use, led to demands for further reforms, which she feared would undermine her influence. When the emperor threw his weight behind the reformers, she had him imprisoned. Leading reformers were banished or executed, and the fanatically anti-Western outbursts led by the secret society known as the Boxers were given covert encouragement.

When the diplomatic community

was besieged by Boxer rebels advancong on Beijing, an international expeditionary force was despatched to their rescue, forcing Tz'u-hsi to flee the city. Agreeing to reforms too late, she was gravely weakened by a stroke and almost certainly ordered the simultaneous deaths by poisoning of the young emperor and empress the day before she died in 1908. The dynasty finally fell in 1911, yielding to a chaotic republic.

U

Ulanova, Galina Sergeyevna
(1910–1998) *Russian ballerina*

Ulanova was one of the great figures of classical ballet in the 20th century. A poetic dancer, she had a magical ability to live her roles instead of merely acting them.

Galina Sergeyevna Ulanova was born in St. Petersburg, to parents who were both dancers and dance teachers. Her mother became her first teacher at the city dance school, and Professor Agrippina Vaganova taught her for the remaining four years that she studied there.

Ulanova spent the first half of her career at the Kirov Ballet (1928–44), where she created the role of Marie, a tragic Polish aristocrat, in *The Fountain of Bakhchisarai* in 1934. She also performed many principal roles in classic ballets. Delicate and pale, Ulanova brought something almost spiritual to her roles, using her body with great expression to create each character.

After dancing as a guest with the Bolshoi Ballet in Moscow, Ulanova joined the company in 1944 and remained with it until her retirement in 1962. With the Bolshoi, Ulanova danced in the premieres of the ballets *The Red Poppy* (1950) and *The Stone Flower* (1954). She became well known for her performances in *Swan Lake*, *Raymonda*, *Don Quixote*, and especially *Giselle*. Many people view her Giselle as the most perfectly danced and best acted of the 20th century.

In addition to her stage performances Ulanova danced in numerous films, including *Stars of the Ballet* (1946), *Ballerina* (1947), *Trio Ballet* (1953), *Romeo and Juliet* (1954), and *The Bolshoi Ballet* (1957). Her famous interpretation of Giselle has also been recorded on film. After her retirement Ulanova was chairman of the jury in the International Ballet Competitions from 1964 to 1972. She also continued her association with the Bolshoi by coaching young dancers in important roles.

Ullmann, Liv
(1939–) *Norwegian actress and film director*

Ullman was the most brilliant actress to emerge from the ensemble maintained by the film director Ingmar Bergman. She had her greatest successes in Bergman's films, making much less of an impact in Hollywood.

Liv Johanne Ullmann was born in Tokyo, where her Norwegian father was working as an engineer. During the Nazi occupation of Norway her family lived in Canada. After the war and her father's death Ullman returned to Norway with her mother and sister. Missing her father, she found comfort in reading and religion. She decided to become an actress and, after leaving school, studied drama for eight months in London.

On returning to Norway, Ullmann made her first stage appearance at Stavanger in the title role of *The Diary of Anne Frank*. After three years with the same company she joined the National Theatre and the Norwegian Theatre in Oslo, where she played Juliet, Ophelia, Nora in *A Doll's House*, and other classic roles.

Ullmann made her Norwegian film debut in 1957. In the early 1960s she began a relationship with Ingmar Bergman, who cast her in his film *Persona* (1966). Ullmann demonstrated her remarkable acting ability by playing a character unable to speak and won great praise for her performance. Co-starring with the Swedish actor Max von Sydow, Ullmann then appeared in Bergman's films *Hour of the Wolf* (1968), *Shame* (1968), and *The Passion of Anna* (1969). In 1971 she received the New York Film Critics' Award for her performance in Bergman's harrowing masterpiece *Cries and Whispers*. Bergman wrote the television film *The Six Faces of a Woman* especially for her in 1972.

After breaking her link with Bergman, Ullmann starred with von Sydow in Jan Troell's *The Emigrants* (1972). A success in the United States, the film won Ullmann an Oscar nomination and a Golden Globe Award. She then went to Hollywood, but the films she made there – for example, *Lost Horizon* and *Forty Carats* (both 1973) – were unsuccessful.

Ullmann returned to Bergman's guidance to star in the brilliant *Scenes from a Marriage* (1974) and *Autumn Sonata* (1979). In the late 1970s she appeared on Broadway as Nora in *A Doll's House*, in the title role of O'Neill's *Anna Christie*, and in the musical *I Remember Mama*. She has also directed the films *Sofie* (1993) and *Private Confessions* (1997). Married twice, Ullmann has written two autobiographies, *Changing* (1978) and *Choices* (1984).

Undset, Sigrid (1882–1949) *Norwegian novelist*

Undset's work was at its finest when she combined a concern for the experiences of women with a colourful interpretation of history, most notably in *Kristin Lavransdatter* (1929).

Born in Kallundborg, Denmark, Undset had a Danish mother. Her father, a noted Norwegian archaeologist, died when she was 11. There was no money to pay for a college education, and Sigrid had to earn her living. While she was working in a law office, she began to write. Her first success was *Jenny* (1911), a story of art students in Rome. In 1912 Undset married an artist, Anders C. Svarstad.

Undset was received into the Roman Catholic Church in 1924. Two years later she was separated from her husband. Undset's interest in the Middle Ages led to the writing of her most famous work, *Kristin Lavransdatter*. A

study of a medieval woman's life from girlhood to old age, it was originally published in three volumes: *The Bridal Wreath* (1920), *The Mistress of Husaby* (1921), and *The Cross* (1922). It was widely praised and translated into many languages. In 1928 it won Undset the Nobel Prize for literature. Her religious and historical preoccupations were reflected in further novels, which included the two-part *Master of Hestviken* (1934), *The Faithful Wife* (1937), and *Madame Dorthea* (1940). She also wrote *Saga of the Saints* (1934), a religious history of Norway.

When the Germans invaded Norway, Undset escaped to the United States and spent several years there, returning to Norway in 1945. Her experiences are told in *Return to the Future* (1942). Other notable works include the children's tale *Sigurd and His Brave Companions* (1943) as well as short stories, essays, and poems. Undset died in Lillehammer, Norway.

Upshaw, Dawn (1960–) *American singer*

Dawn Upshaw combines great stylistic gifts with a pleasant if not spectacular soprano voice. Her intelligent appealing interpretations have helped win audiences for relatively obscure modern works, and she has breathed fresh life into some of the standard light operatic roles.

Upshaw was born in Nashville, Tennessee, and was raised near Chicago. She graduated from Illinois Wesleyan University in 1982 and obtained a master's degree from the Manhattan School of Music in 1984. Later studies at the Aspen Music School focused on the performance of contemporary music. In 1984 Upshaw was chosen for the New York Metropolitan Opera's "Young Artists" programme, leading to her "Met" debut in a small role later that year. In 1989 Upshaw won a Grammy Award for *Knoxville, Summer of 1915*, a recording of a collection of American works.

By the 1991–92 season Upshaw was well established at the "Met," appearing that year in four Mozart roles (Despina in *Così fan tutte*, Pamina in *The Magic Flute*, Susanna in *The Marriage of Figaro*, and Ilia in *Idomeneo*). In 1992 she won her second Grammy for her recording *The Girl with Orange Lips*, a collection of songs by Ravel, Stravinsky, Delage, and Kim. That summer she also received excellent reviews in Messiaen's *Saint Francis of Assisi* at the Salzburg Festival and performed in Stravinsky's *The Rake's Progress* at the Aix-en-Provence festival in France.

Upshaw's large enthusiastic following owes much to the fact that she has recorded popular and Broadway songs in addition to making extensive concert and opera appearances in the United States and abroad. She typifies the new-era prima donna with her emphasis on musical and linguistic versatility rather than on sensationalism. She is equally at home in popular and classical music. Though successful in light operatic roles, Upshaw is considered by some critics as better suited to concert work than to the opera house because of her subtle intimate style.

Ursins, Princesse des (1642–1722) *French noblewoman*

As lady-in-waiting to Queen María Luisa, Ursins became the most influential member of the Spanish court during the first 14 years of Philip V's reign.

The daughter of a French duke, Marie-Anne de la Tremoille was born in Paris. She moved to Italy after her marriage, and when her first husband died, she married Flavio Orsini, Duke of Bracciano. They lived in Rome until Orsini's death in 1698, when his widow adopted the French form of his family name, Ursins.

After Philip V ascended the Spanish throne in 1700, the Princesse des Ursins helped arrange his marriage to María Luisa of Savoy. Philip's grandfather, Louis XIV of France, then sent the princess to Spain as María Luisa's chief lady-in-waiting. A sharp-witted woman, the princess began to have great influence over the royal couple. With the French economist Jean Orry she also carried out important reforms in Spain's administration. It was the princess who chose ELIZABETH FARNESE as Philip's second wife after María Luisa's death in 1714, but this was her undoing. The new queen took an immediate dislike to her and banished her from Spain. She died in Rome.

Ursula, Saint (late 3rd or early 4th century) *Christian martyr*

According to a 9th-century legend, Ursula, a British king's daughter, made a pilgrimage to Rome accompanied by 11,000 virgins. All of them were massacred by Huns on the way home.

Casting aside later myths, very little is known about Ursula. She may have been one of 11 (rather than 11,000) girls martyred near Cologne. Her feast, October 21, was removed from the Church calendar in 1969 because of the uncertainty about her life. The 15th-century painter Carpaccio produced a series of panels, now in the Accademia, Venice, depicting the Saint Ursula legend.

Uttley, Alison (1884–1976) *British writer of children's books*

Alison Uttley published over 100 books but is best known for the ever-popular Little Grey Rabbit stories for young children.

Alison Taylor was born and brought up on a remote farm in the Peak District of Derbyshire. She went to Bakewell Grammar School and then Manchester University, where she gained an honours degree in physics. After studying education for a year at Cambridge University she worked as a teacher in London, where she became active in the suffragette movement. She married James Uttley, a scientist, in 1911 and they had a child; following her husband's death in 1930 she took to writing to support herself and her son.

Uttley used her first-hand knowledge of the countryside and its creatures – she spent most of her later life in rural Buckinghamshire – to write fascinating stories for children. Her first book *The Country Child* was published in 1931, with illustrations by the wildlife artist C. F. Tunnicliffe. She is best known, however, for her stories for younger children featuring such well-loved characters as Sam the pig, Brock the badger, Fuzzypeg the hedgehog,

Little Red Fox, and Little Grey Rabbit. Most of these books were illustrated by either Margaret Temple or Katherine Wigglesworth. Ghosts and the supernatural had a place in her books for older children, notably the evocative *A Traveller in Time* (1939). She also wrote two novels for adults and several nonfiction books about the countryside.

V

Valadon, Suzanne (1867–1938)
French painter

Suzanne Valadon's career as an artist and model typifies the bohemian life associated with Paris in the late 19th and early 20th centuries.

Marie Clémentine Valadon was born in Bessines, near Limoges, to working-class parents – her mother was a laundress. First, she became a circus acrobat and then, at 15, an artists' model, posing for Toulouse-Lautrec, Puvis de Chavannes, Renoir, and Degas. At 16 she gave birth to an illegitimate son, who became the well-known painter of Parisian life Maurice Utrillo (1883–1955). About this time Valadon began to draw and was encouraged by Toulouse-Lautrec – who advised her to change her name to Suzanne – and, especially, by Degas, who was amazed that a person of her background, without training, had such a masterly touch. After a while she gave up modelling altogether and concentrated on painting – mainly landscapes, still lifes, and nudes.

Although Valadon's work shows some influence of Gauguin, in general it is very personal, displaying simplicity and an earthy realism. She painted with a strong line, but her colour was heavy and sometimes crude. At their best her paintings are vigorous and reflect her keen observation. Valadon died in Paris.

Vanderbilt, Gloria (1924–   ) *American artist and actress*

> If she has not yet made of herself a living work of art, she's come...as close as anyone I'd ever want to meet.
>
> —Wyatt Cooper, Introduction to *Gloria Vanderbilt Book of Collage* (1970)

Rich, beautiful, and four times married, Gloria Vanderbilt also became famous as a painter, actress, writer, and designer.

The great-great-granddaughter of the multimillionaire Cornelius Vanderbilt, Gloria was born in New York. A year later, on her father's death, she inherited $4,000,000, and her mother took her to live in Europe. After her return to the United States, the ten-year-old Gloria became known to newspaper readers as the "poor little rich girl" when her paternal aunt fought her mother for custody and won. Gloria was sent to expensive schools but left at 17 to marry the actors' agent Pasquale di Cicco. Three years later she ran off with the conductor Leopold Stokowski, who was then over 60.

Vanderbilt married Stokowski in 1945 and had two sons. Based in New York, she took up painting and writing poems. She gave her first one-woman show of oil paintings and pastels in 1948, and other successful shows followed.

In 1954 Vanderbilt ventured into acting. She appeared in various productions, including Noël Coward's *Tonight at 8:30* on television (1954) and *The Time of Your Life* on Broadway (1955). By this time she and Stokowski had agreed to divorce, and in 1956 Vanderbilt married the film director Sidney Lumet. A fourth marriage (in 1963), to Wyatt Cooper, produced two more sons.

In the late 1960s Vanderbilt turned to designing greetings cards and other items. By the time of Cooper's death in 1978 she had moved on to fabrics and fashion design, giving her name to the well-known brand of jeans. Vanderbilt's published writings include poems, stories, articles, and an autobiography.

Varda, Agnès (1928–) *French film director*

> Women have to make jokes about themselves, laugh about themselves, because they have nothing to lose.
>
> —Interview, *Saturday Review*, 1972

Varda's work belongs to the "New Wave" of French cinema that emerged in the late 1950s. An original director with an eye for detail, she has written the screenplays for all her films.

Born in Belgium to a French mother and a Greek father, Varda was raised and educated in the south of France. After World War II she studied in Paris at the Sorbonne and the Louvre and took a diploma in photography. From 1951 to 1961 Varda was a professional photographer. Her first film, *La Pointe courte* (1954), was named after its setting, a fishing village she had known as a child. Despite her lack of experience as a director, the film's innovative technique (it had two interwoven plots) made it influential in the emerging "New Wave".

Varda's next feature, *Cleo from 5 to 7* (1962), was released in the year she married the film director Jacques Demy. It focuses on two hours in the life of a singer, whose outlook on life changes as she waits to find out whether or not she has cancer. More controversial was *Le Bonheur* (1965). This story of marital infidelity and suicide, set in the idyllic France of the impressionist painters and accompanied by Mozart's music, was seen by some as tasteless and immoral, though it was pronounced Best Film at the Cannes Festival. In the late 1960s Varda made three films in the United States, including the feature *Lions Love* (1969). Her later works include the feminist film *One Sings, the Other Does Not* (1977); *Vagabond* (1985), which won the Golden Lion at the Venice festival; *Jacquot of Nantes* (1991), a tribute to her late husband; and *The Hundred and One Nights* (1995).

Vaughan, Dame Janet (1899–1993) *British medical doctor and academic*

Janet Vaughan's most important contribution to medicine was in the field of haematology.

Born and brought up in Bristol, Vaughan studied medicine at Somerville College, Oxford, and completed her clinical training at University College Hospital, London (1927–29). The scenes of poverty she witnessed in London made her a socialist.

After taking up a scholarship to study in Boston, Massachusetts, for a year, Vaughan married David Gourlay in 1930, and they had two daughters. She held several academic posts in the early 1930s and in 1934 published a book on anaemias. In the late 1930s she set up an emergency blood transfusion service in London, based on techniques developed during the Spanish Civil War. During World War II Vaughan directed a blood-supply unit in northwest London, and after the war she was given the difficult task of rehabilitating half-starved victims of German concentration camps.

As principal of Somerville, her old Oxford college, from 1945 to 1967, Vaughan was popular for her strong character, energy, organizational skills, and warm personality. She was also a member of a number of public committees, including one that promoted equal pay for women (1944–46). Continuing her own research, she wrote several books and articles on the medical effects of radiation. Vaughan received many honours from Oxford, Cambridge, and other universities. She was made a DBE in 1957.

Vaughan, Sarah (1924–1990) *American jazz singer*

> Is that child singing or am I crazy?
>
> —Earl Hines, on first hearing Vaughan, *c.* 1942

Sarah Vaughan had a deep rich voice with a prodigiously wide range, and although she could hit any note dead on, she was always varying and embellishing what she sang. Her many popular recordings include "It's Magic," "Banana Boat Song," "Broken-Hearted Melody," and "Send in the Clowns."

Vaughan grew up in her birthplace, Newark, New Jersey. Her parents were both musical, and at the age of seven

Sarah joined her mother in their local church choir. She also learned piano and organ and helped out locally as an accompanist.

Furtive visits to a local bar taught Vaughan to love jazz, and at 18 she won a talent contest at the famous Apollo Theater, Harlem. Spotted by the trumpeter Billy Eckstine, she was recruited into the band of Earl Hines (1943). A year later she joined Eckstine's own breakaway band. With her fluid vocal variations Vaughan made a big contribution to Eckstine's pioneering "bebop" style, before she left to pursue a solo career.

Vaughan married George Treadwell, the first of her four husbands, in 1947. He became her manager and spent his savings on making her a star. She began to make recordings and in 1949 signed with Columbia. A year later her records were selling in huge numbers.

In the 1950s and 1960s Vaughan enjoyed international fame. Nicknamed "Sassy," she travelled widely and made numerous recordings (from 1953 with Mercury). Her popularity suffered during the rock 'n' roll era, but in the 1970s she re-emerged as a sophisticated pop singer, usually accompanied by a small backing band. After signing up with Mainstream records in 1972, she made further albums and in 1982 won a Grammy Award.

Veil, Simone (1927–) *French stateswoman*

> If this [European] parliament has a Jew, a woman, for its president, it means everyone has the same rights.
> —Remark, 1979

A survivor of the German concentration camps, in 1979 Simone Veil was voted president of the first directly elected European parliament.

The fourth child of a Jewish architect, Simone Jacob was born in Nice. In 1944, when Simone had just left school, she and her mother and sister were deported to Auschwitz concentration camp. Her mother died there, and Simone and her sister were moved to Belsen. When that camp was liberated by the Allies in 1945, the sisters found no trace of the rest of their family. Picking up the pieces of her life,

Simone studied law and political science at the Paris Institute for Political Studies, where she met Antoine Veil; they married in 1946.

For the next ten years Simone Veil was busy with her family of three sons, but in 1956 she became a magistrate. Soon afterwards she joined the French ministry of justice, where she dealt with issues concerning prisoners and children. She rose within the ranks and became the first female French secretary of state in 1970.

In 1974 Veil was chosen as the minister for health in Giscard d'Estaing's government. In a Catholic country she was a controversial minister, passing legislation to promote contraception and legalize abortion. Nevertheless, she was admired for her courage, self-control, and sincerity.

In 1979 Veil ran for the European parliament and was not only elected but also voted its president. After serving for three years, she decided not to run for re-election. Instead, she became chair of the parliament's legal affairs committee and, later, of the Liberal and Democratic Reformist Group. After leaving the European parliament, Veil served as the French minister of social affairs from 1993 to 1995. She has won many prizes and awards.

Verdy, Violette (1933–) *French ballet dancer and dance director*

A significant figure in 20th-century ballet, Verdy has performed widely, notably with the American Ballet Theater and the New York City Ballet, and has directed the Paris Opéra Ballet.

Born Nelly Guillerm in Pont-l'Abbé, Brittany, Verdy studied dance with Madame Rousanne and Victor Gsovsky in Paris. A child prodigy, she first appeared with the Ballets of the Champs-Elysées before she was 12, and she remained with the company until 1949. In that year she appeared in the film *Ballerina* and changed her name to Verdy. In 1950 and again in 1953–54 she danced with Roland Petit's Ballets de Paris. Her most famous role with the company – and one that was specially created for her – was the bride in *Le Loup* (1953). In 1954 she was again on screen in *The Glass Slipper*. Verdy performed with the London Festival Ballet (1954–55) before moving to New York, where she became a leading dancer with the American Ballet Theater (1957–58) and appeared in the title role of *Miss Julie*.

From 1958 until 1977 Verdy was principal dancer with the New York City Ballet, where she danced lead roles created for her by George Balanchine. Some of her other important ballet roles were in *Romeo and Juliet* (1955), *Cinderella* (1955), *Episodes* (1959), *Jewels* (1967), *Dances at a Gathering* (1969), and *Pulcinella* (1972).

From 1977 until 1980 Verdy was director of the Paris Opéra Ballet, where she added a number of modern works to the repertoire. She was then associate artistic director of the Boston Ballet until 1984. While there she staged Nureyev's *La Sylphide*, introduced new ballets, choreographed several works, and improved the classical training at the ballet school.

In 1984 Verdy became a teaching associate with the New York City Ballet. She has served as a guest teacher with the Paris Opéra Ballet and other companies, a guest choreographer for regional and college companies, and an artistic consultant for the Royal and San Francisco ballet companies, among others. She has also won several awards and honours, and is the author of *Giselle: A Role for a Lifetime* (1977) and *Of Swans, Sugarplums, and Satin Slippers: Ballet Stories for Children* (1991).

Vestris, Madame (1797–1856) *British actress and singer*

Famous for such songs as "Cherry Ripe" and "I've Been Roaming" and for her excellence in light comedy, Madame Vestris may also have been the first woman in the history of the stage to lease and run a theatre.

Born Lucia Elizabeth Bartolozzi in London, she married Auguste-Armand Vestris in 1813 but separated from him a few years later. She began her 40-year stage career as Proserpina in an opera by Peter von Winter and might have had a great future in opera if she had troubled to train her contralto voice. As an actress, she scored great successes as Phoebe in *Paul Pry* and, in male costume, as Macheath in *The Beggar's Opera*. She also appeared as Cherubino in *The Marriage of Figaro*. Having become rich by 1830, Madame Vestris leased the Olympic Theatre, London, which she managed until 1837. She later managed Covent Garden (1839–42) and the Lyceum (1847–55). Despite constant financial difficulties, she was an excellent manager and improved scenery, costume, and staging. In 1838 she married Charles James Mathews, a noted actor.

Viardot-García, Pauline (1821–1910) *French opera singer*

A mezzo-soprano, Pauline Viardot-García was one of the most famous and distinguished operatic singers of the 19th century.

Michelle Ferdinande Pauline García was born in Paris, a daughter of the famous tenor Manuel García. Her sister was the well known contralto Maria Malibran (1808–36). Having sung at concerts in Belgium, Germany, and France, she gave her first operatic performance as Desdemona in Rossini's *Otello* in London in 1839. In 1841 she married Louis Viardot, a journalist and director of the Italian Theatre in Paris. After this she toured Europe with her husband.

At the Paris Opéra, Pauline Viardot created the role of Fidès in Meyerbeer's *The Prophet* (1849) and the title role in Gounod's *Sappho* (1851). In 1859 she appeared in a revival of Gluck's *Orpheus and Eurydice*, prepared for the Paris Opéra by Berlioz. She sang the role of Orpheus more than 150 times.

Pauline Viardot had a wide vocal range, taking both soprano and contralto roles. She was also known for her dramatic skill and intellectual distinction. After retiring from the stage in 1863, she took up composing and teaching. Her opera *Le Dernier Sorcier*, to a libretto by her close friend (and possible lover) Ivan Turgenev, was performed at Weimar in 1869. Viardot died in Paris. The autographed score of Mozart's *Don Giovanni*, which she owned, was willed to the library of the Paris Conservatory.

Victoria (1819–1901) *Queen of the United Kingdom*

> It is impossible to imagine a *politer* little woman.
>
> —Thomas Carlyle, letter, 1869

> Nowadays a parlour-maid as ignorant as Queen Victoria was when she came to the throne would be classed as mentally defective.
>
> —George Bernard Shaw

Spanning 63½ years, Queen Victoria's reign was the longest in British history and saw greater change than had ever previously been known. It was an age of industrialization, invention, scientific advancement, and imperialist expansion. But it was also a time when the problems of a "modern" society first became evident. Urbanization, unemployment, and pollution are among the 20th-century problems with roots in the Victorian era.

Known in infancy as Drina, Alexandrina Victoria was the only child of Edward Augustus (1767–1820), Duke of Kent, and his wife Victoria Mary Louisa (1786–1861). Her father, the fourth son of King George III, had married her mother (the daughter of the Duke of Saxe-Coburg-Saalfeld and the widow of the Prince of Leiningen-Dachsburg-Hardenburg) to produce an heir. Shortly before her birth the future queen's parents left their home in Franconia, Germany, so that she could be born in London, in Kensington Palace. However, her father died in debt before she was a year old, and there were few luxuries during her lonely childhood at Kensington. The young princess was distressed by quarrels between her mother and the royal family. She became greatly attached to her governess, the Hanoverian baroness Louise Lehzen, who provided her with a somewhat limited education. When she was 13, Victoria began to keep a journal, which she maintained to the end of her life. In it she recalled that she had not been allowed to walk downstairs without someone

holding her hand until she came to the throne.

Victoria became queen on the death of her uncle, William IV, in 1837 and was crowned in Westminster Abbey the following year. Almost unknown by the official world, the young girl impressed everyone with her poise and grace. She took a liking to her prime minister, the Whig Lord Melbourne, who tutored her in politics and worldly wisdom. Having become a faithful Whig herself, Victoria obstructed Sir Robert Peel's attempt to form a Conservative government in 1839 when she refused to replace the ladies of her bedchamber appointed during the Whig administration. Another rumour that she had been unkind to the Tory lady-in-waiting Lady Flora Hastings began to make the queen unpopular.

Victoria's popularity was restored through marriage. Her mother and her uncle, King Leopold of the Belgians, had long thought of her cousin, Prince Albert of Saxe-Coburg-Gotha, as a suitable consort. The handsome prince captured Victoria's heart, and she proposed to him at Windsor Castle in 1839. They were married the next year. Albert was a popular choice, and the marriage was a very happy one. Victoria was greatly influenced by her husband in all aspects of her life. The couple had nine children: Victoria, the Princess Royal, later Empress of Germany (1840–1901); Albert Edward, Prince of Wales, later Edward VII (1841–1910); Alice, later Grand Duchess of Hesse-Darmstadt (1843–78); Alfred, Duke of Edinburgh, later Duke of Saxe-Coburg-Gotha (1844–1900); Helena, later Princess of Schleswig-Holstein (1846–1923); Louise, later Duchess of Argyll (1848–1939); Arthur, Duke of Connaught (1850–1942); Leopold, Duke of Albany (1853–84); and Beatrice, later Princess of Battenberg (1857–1944).

The responsibilities of a large family allowed the queen little time for society. Under her husband's influence she grew to dislike fashionable life and to enjoy country pursuits. There was no shortage of money. In addition to the £385,000 per year paid by Parliament throughout her reign, Victoria received from the Duchy of Lancaster £60,000 per year, and in 1852 she also gained £500,000 in a bequest from the eccentric John Camden Neild. In 1845 Victoria acquired Osborne, a seaside estate on the Isle of Wight, and in 1848 she leased the estate of Balmoral in the Scottish highlands, which she purchased in 1852. New royal residences, largely designed by Prince Albert, were built on these estates, and Victoria afterwards spent less time in her official residences, Buckingham Palace and Windsor Castle, both of which she disliked.

During Victoria's reign the monarchy developed a new ceremonial function in relation to the public and to state affairs. The queen paid several visits to the large industrial towns. In 1851 she opened the Great Exhibition, a showcase for Britain's technological supremacy planned by Prince Albert, and in 1855 she paid an official visit to Napoleon III of France. Guided by Albert, she also intervened in politics. She promoted the repeal of the Corn Laws (1846) to relieve the famine in Ireland but strongly opposed attempts by the foreign secretary, Lord Palmerston, to build up new democratic nationalistic forces in Europe. She and Albert were on friendly terms with the rulers of Belgium, Prussia, Portugal, and France and had a knowledge of foreign affairs that was in some ways better and more current than that of the government. Their disapproval of Palmerston was a major factor in his dismissal by the prime minister, Lord John Russell, in 1851. A year later Victoria welcomed Lord Aberdeen's formation of a coalition government, which she had helped to engineer. Although Victoria and Albert failed to prevent the outbreak of the Crimean War in 1853, Victoria won public approval by organizing relief for the wounded and visiting hospitals. She also distributed medals and instituted the Victoria Cross (VC), the highest British award for military bravery.

When Albert died from typhoid fever in 1861, the queen was devastated. She dressed in full mourning and used writing paper with a mourning band for the rest of her days. For years she lived in seclusion, appearing only to unveil memorials to her "prince consort," as she had named him in 1857, and in 1866 to open Parliament. She tried to continue her former involvement in public affairs but found it increasingly difficult.

Victoria had intense prejudices, which she never attempted to hide. In particular she loathed the Liberal statesman William Gladstone; in 1880 she tried to prevent him becoming prime minister, and in 1885 she publicly blamed him for the death of General Charles Gordon at Khartoum. On the other hand, she doted on the Tory Benjamin Disraeli, who as prime minister in 1876 gave her the title Empress of India. But despite her prejudices, the queen showed a devotion to duty that touched the public and helps to explain the almost frenzied celebrations that marked her golden jubilee of 1887, her diamond jubilee in 1897, her appearances during the Boer War from 1899, and her appearance in Dublin in 1900.

Victoria was a short plain woman, though graceful and in her youth very fair. She had a beautiful speaking voice and spoke German, French, and late in her life even a little Hindustani. She was shy in public, especially in the presence of those she thought cleverer than herself. She enjoyed drama, music, dancing, poetry (especially Tennyson's *In Memoriam*, which comforted her during her widowhood), and writing journals and letters. Though hastily written and sometimes ungrammatical, her writings provide some of the most vivid material for a study of 19th-century Britain. Some extracts from her journals were published during her lifetime in *Leaves from the Journal of Our Life in the Highlands* (1868) and *More Leaves* (1883).

After Albert's death she spent many months in the seclusion of Balmoral, where she formed some kind of relationship with a manservant, John Brown, whom she promoted to a position enabling him to attend to her in London and the Isle of Wight. The exact nature of this relationship has never been discovered. After her death at Osborne House passages from her journals were burnt by her youngest daughter, who was her literary executor.

Vieira da Silva, Maria Helena
(1908–1992) *Portuguese-born French abstract painter*

Although she became a French citizen in 1956 and lived in Paris until her death, Vieira da Silva is generally considered Portugal's most important contemporary painter. Her paintings, often resembling mazes or mosaics, reflect the sense of confusion often experienced in modern cities.

Vieira da Silva was born in Lisbon. From 1928 she studied sculpture in Paris with two followers of Auguste Rodin, Charles Despiau and Emile-Antoine Bourdelle, whose works had an abstract element. She also studied printmaking and painting with Othon Friesz and Fernand Léger. From Léger she gained an interest in cubism and in the theme of modern technology. In 1930 she married the Hungarian artist Arpad Szenés.

Vieira da Silva produced a controlled type of abstraction in her works, using mainly earth tones. Characteristic oil paintings, such as *The Dream* (1949; private collection, Finland) and *Invisible Walker* (1951; Museum of Modern Art, San Francisco), are made up of linear patterns that suggest perspective and space from different viewpoints. Two superb oils on canvas, *Chess Game* (1943; Pompidou Centre, Paris) and *Card Players* (1947; private collection, Neuilly), include half-disguised figures that magically and playfully reveal themselves through wavy chessboard patterns.

After 1946, the year she first exhibited in New York, Vieira da Silva attracted the interest of the American abstract expressionist painters. In 1988 a major exhibition of her past work was held in Lisbon and Paris. Her paintings can be seen in many permanent collections, including the Guggenheim Museum, New York; the Tate Gallery, London; and the National Museum, Amsterdam. She died in Paris.

Vigée-Lebrun, Marie Anne Elisabeth
(1755–1842) *French portrait painter*

One of the first women ever to become famous as an artist, Vigée-Lebrun specialized in portraits of royalty, painted in a somewhat sentimental style.

Born in Paris, Elisabeth Vigée was trained in painting by her father and encouraged by Gabriel François Doyen and Joseph Vernet. In 1776 she married the painter Jean Baptiste Pierre Lebrun; they had a daughter but later separated.

In 1779 Mme. Vigée-Lebrun painted Queen MARIE ANTOINETTE, marking the beginning of her lifelong career as a painter of royalty. Benefiting from the fashionable new idea that women should be taken seriously, she was elected to membership of the French Royal Academy in 1783.

At the outbreak of the French Revolution in 1789 Vigée-Lebrun fled to Rome with her daughter. The next year she went to Naples, where she painted the queen and her children, as well as Emma HAMILTON. She then travelled through Austria and Russia, receiving commissions from CATHERINE II (the Great) and other royal figures. She returned to France in 1801 and a year later went to England, where she painted the Prince of Wales (later George IV). Vigée-Lebrun returned to Paris from her long exile in 1805 and painted Napoleon's sister, Mme. Marie Murat.

Most of the numerous portraits that Vigée-Lebrun painted were of women. The aim was to make the sitters look as pretty as possible and to show off their fine costumes. But although she had to do what was fashionable and therefore profitable, Vigée-Lebrun had the talent of a great painter. Towards the end of her life she spent much of her time at her country house Louveciennes, and in 1835 she wrote her memoirs. Some of her paintings are on display in the Metropolitan Museum, New York; the Louvre, Paris; and the National Gallery and Wallace Collection, London. Portraits of Marie Antoinette and her children are in the Versailles Museum, and a self-portrait is in the Uffizi Gallery, Florence.

Vionnet, Madeleine (1876–1975)
French fashion designer

Vionnet was responsible for the complete change in women's fashion that occurred after 1918, when the rigid clothing of the 19th century was replaced by the more fluid modern style of dress. Viewing clothes as a natural wrap, almost another skin, for the body, she liked to give them shape by means of their stretchable elements (bias, pleats, etc.) rather than by such features as darts.

Born in Aubervilliers, France, Vionnet was apprenticed at the age of 12 to a dressmaker and spent the rest of her life in the trade. She worked for the London dressmaker Kate Reilly from about 1896 to 1901, then returned to Paris to work for the house of Callot Soeurs and afterwards for Jacques Doucet. She opened her own fashion house in Paris in 1912.

Vionnet believed clothing should be comfortable and supple. Discarding boned structures and heavy undergarments, she cut clothes on the bias, producing both fluidity and style. This revolutionized clothing, since the fabric was able to stretch slightly to match the shape of the body. She introduced halter and cowl necklines; new lingerie finishes (especially the type of frilly pleating called crimping and a technique of embroidering over gathers called fagoting); hook-and-eye and wrap-over fastenings; soft fabrics, such as crêpe-de-chine; and such features as bouncy hems, pleating, and exposed seaming. Vionnet's dresses were daring, even in the liberal 1920s and 1930s, because the light unstructured fabric would cling to the body, showing off the wearer's figure. Her dresses moved gently with the wearer's movements to create a dancelike effect.

Except for a brief interruption during World War I, Vionnet continued to design until she officially retired in 1940, becoming a legend in her long lifetime. Numerous American and European designers studied or were influenced by her work. She retained her interest in fashion almost until her death.

See also CHANEL, COCO.

Von Stade, Frederica (1945–)
American opera singer

Von Stade has been consistently successful in opera, concerts, and recordings thanks to her strong vocal technique and lively manner. Her light agile singing and sunny personality have come across especially well in the comic operas of Mozart and Rossini, while her mastery of language and sense of style have served her well in performing subtle French art songs.

Frederica Von Stade was born in Somerville, New Jersey. After studying at the Mannes College of Music in New York and the Mozart School in Paris, she reached the semi-finals in auditions for the New York Metropolitan Opera and won a contract with the "Met" in 1969. She made her debut at the "Met" a year later and was soon performing leading roles there and in other American theatres. From 1973 Von Stade made many appearances as the boy Cherubino in Mozart's *The Marriage of Figaro* in both the United States and Europe. As well as singing at American venues, including performances with the Houston Grand Opera and the San Francisco and Boston operas, she appeared at Covent Garden, La Scala (Milan), the Spoleto in Italy, and the Vienna State Opera.

In addition to the standard roles for lighter mezzo-sopranos, Von Stade sang in several world premieres, starting in 1971 with a leading part in Villa-Lobos's opera *Yerma* at Santa Fe. She created the role of Nina in *The Seagull* by Thomas Pasatieri at the Houston Grand Opera in 1974; was the original Tina in *The Aspern Papers* by Dominick Argento at the Dallas Opera in 1988; and starred as the Marchioness of Merteuil in the world premiere of *The Dangerous Liaisons* by Conrad Susa at the San Francisco Opera in 1994. The Metropolitan Opera celebrated her 25th anniversary season by featuring her in a new production of Debussy's *Pelléas and Mélisande* in 1995.

In the latest phase of her career Von Stade has extended her concert and recital repertoire to include modern song cycles and other less familiar works. She has also ventured into operetta and has recorded Broadway musical comedies, including *Showboat* and *The Sound of Music*.

von Trotta, Margarethe (1942–)
German film director, screenwriter, and actress

Margarethe von Trotta's thoughtful films about the lives and relationships of women have made her one of Germany's most respected directors.

Born into an upper-class family in Berlin, Margarethe von Trotta studied German and Latin literature at universities in Munich and Paris. She subsequently trained as an actress and began to appear on the German stage from the mid 1960s.

In 1969, the year she made her film debut in Rainer Werner Fassbinder's *Gods of the Plague*, von Trotta married Volker Schlöndorff, a young director who had recently emerged at the forefront of the so-called "New German Cinema." For the next five years the couple collaborated on a series of well-received films, including *The Sudden Fortune of the Poor People of Kombach* (1971) and *Summer Lightning* (1972), which were directed by Schlöndorff but starred and were cowritten by von Trotta. In 1975 they codirected and cowrote one of the best-known German films of the 1970s, *The Lost Honour of Katharina Blum*; the movie concerns an ordinary woman who is ruthlessly persecuted by the media after being falsely labelled a communist conspirator.

Subsequently von Trotta chose to work independently of her husband. Her films, which she usually scripts as well as directing, include *The Second Awakening* (1977), *Sisters, or the Balance of Happiness* (1979), *The German Sisters* (1981), and *Rosa Luxemburg* (1986), a biography of the Polish-born revolutionary. Admirers of von Trotta's work have praised the subtle way in which she explores political issues through the personal lives of her mainly female characters. In the 1990s she directed several films in Italy, including *Paura e amore* (1990; Fear and Love) and *I lungo silencio* (1992; The Long Silence).

Vreeland, Diana (c. 1902–1989)
American fashion journalist

> She became news by creating an image so bizarre that it was instantly recognizable. She was "seen" wherever she went, listened to whenever she spoke, and quoted endlessly.
>
> —Ingeborg Day, *Ms.*, 1975

A colourful personality who was famously meticulous about her appearance, Diana Vreeland exerted a huge influence on the fashion of this century through the pages of *Vogue* and *Harper's Bazaar*.

Born in Paris, the daughter of a stockbroker, Diana took her mother's surname, Dalziel. In 1914 she was taken to live in the United States, and after marrying the banker Thomas Vreeland in 1924, she took U.S. citizenship. By the time she became a journalist in the late 1920s, she already had two sons.

In 1936 Vreeland began writing the famous "Why Don't You...?" column for *Harper's Bazaar*, in which she made frivolous suggestions, such as "Why don't you cut your old ermine wrap into a bathrobe?" As fashion editor of the journal from 1937 to 1962, she was enormously influential.

In 1962 Vreeland joined the staff of *Vogue*, serving as chief editor from 1963 to 1971. Reshaping the magazine to reflect her own tastes and attitudes, she led the way in promoting such 1960s trends as see-through shirts and the bikini, which she called "the most important thing since the atom bomb." A distinctive figure, Vreeland was the embodiment of her editorial style – she loved red, dressed in chic clothes, and spoke in a manner described as "all capitals and italics."

From 1971 Vreeland served as consultant editor to *Vogue*. A year later she became the costume specialist at New York's Metropolitan Museum of Art, where she mounted a series of successful exhibitions. Vreeland contributed to various exhibition catalogues and books on fashion. She also invented the word "pizzazz."

W

Wade, (Sarah) Virginia (1945–)
British tennis player

Virginia Wade dominated British women's tennis in the late 1960s and 1970s. She was inaugurated into the International Tennis Hall of Fame in 1989.

The daughter of Canon Eustace Wade, a former archdeacon of Durban in South Africa, Virginia Wade was born in Bournemouth. A dedicated amateur player from the age of 17, she turned professional after completing a science degree at the University of Sussex (1968).

While still an amateur, Virginia Wade was chosen to represent Britain in the Wightman Cup competition of 1965. She went on to make a record 20 appearances for her country, captaining both the Wightman Cup and the Federation Cup teams for most of the 1970s. As well as winning the British hard-court championships in 1967, 1968, 1973, and 1974, she scored international triumphs in both the U.S. Open (1968) and the Australian Open (1972). However, the climax of her career came in 1977 when she won the ladies' singles championship at Wimbledon in the tournament's centenary year: her victory coincided with the silver jubilee celebrations of Queen ELIZABETH II and was greeted with a wave of patriotic euphoria.

Since her retirement from tennis in 1981 Virginia Wade has worked as a BBC sports commentator and a tennis administrator. She was appointed an MBE in 1979 and an OBE in 1986.

Wagner, Cosima (1837–1930) *German writer and musical director*

Cosima Wagner devoted most of her adult life to her second husband, the composer and conductor Richard Wagner, supporting and promoting his work through the annual Bayreuth Festival.

The daughter of the composer and pianist Franz Liszt and the writer Countess Marie d'AGOULT, Francesca Gaetana Cosima Liszt was born at Bellaggio on Lake Como in Italy. Her parents' relationship ended in 1844, and Cosima had an unsettled childhood; she was educated in Paris and moved to Berlin in the 1850s to live with the family of the German musician Hans von Bülow. From an early age she showed signs of musical and literary talent inherited from her parents, particularly in playing the piano.

In 1857 Cosima married von Bülow, who was a great admirer of the work of Richard Wagner. During the years that followed Cosima found herself increasingly drawn to Wagner, despite the fact that he was nearly twice her age. They began a relationship that resulted in the birth of two daughters – Isolde in 1865 and Eva in 1867 – and a son, Siegfried, in 1869. Wagner's estranged wife, Minna, died in 1866, and in 1868 Cosima left her husband to live with her lover in Switzerland. Von Bülow agreed to a divorce, and the couple were finally married in 1870.

Cosima devoted the rest of her life to helping Wagner and his music gain the international recognition that she and many others – including her ex-husband – knew they deserved. An opera house was built at Bayreuth in Bavaria for the performance of Wagner's works, opening in 1876, and an annual festival was established. After the death of her husband in 1883 Cosima continued to direct all the productions at the Bayreuth Festival, insisting that her interpretation of the composer's wishes be followed in every detail. This often led to friction, but Cosima's strong will and dominant personality usually won the day. In 1906 her son Siegfried took over the festival.

Cosima also helped shape Wagner's public image through the publication of her diaries and his autobiography *Mein Leben* (1911). She kept a collection of his correspondence, and her own letters to Friedrich Nietzsche were published in 1940.

Waitz, Grete (1953–) *Norwegian athlete*

In the 1970s and 1980s Grete Waitz was one of the fastest female distance runners in the world. Of the 19 marathons she entered between 1978 and 1990 she lost only six, and she won the World Cross-Country Championships a record five times between 1978 and 1983.

She was born Grete Andersen in Oslo, and changed her name to Grete Waitz on her marriage to Jack Nilsen in 1975. As a child she showed a talent for athletics, particularly running, and in 1971 she set a European junior record for the 1500 metres. She took part in the 1972 Olympic Games in Munich and went on to compete internationally in the 1500 metre- and 3000-metre events, breaking world records for the longer distance in 1975 and 1976.

Encouraged by her husband, who was also her coach, Waitz entered the New York marathon in 1978 and won, setting a new women's record at 2 hours, 32 minutes, and 30 seconds. In the following year's race she cut her winning time down by nearly five minutes, and in 1980 she finished in 2 hours, 25 minutes, and 41 seconds. She went on to shave a further 12 seconds off the world record in the 1983 London marathon. The Olympic Games held in Los Angeles in 1984 were the first to include a women's marathon, but Waitz managed only second place, losing to the American runner Joan Benoit SAMUELSON. In the 1986 London marathon she achieved a personal best time of 2 hours, 24 minutes, and 54 seconds.

Walburga, Saint (710–779) *English abbess*

For the last 18 years of her life Walburga had sole charge of a double monastery of monks and nuns at Heidenheim in southern Germany.

Walburga, also known as Waldburg or Walpurgis, was born in Wessex. Her brothers Willibald and Winebald were also destined to become saints, and all three took part in St. Boniface's mission to Germany in the 8th century. Willibald became the first bishop of Eichstätt in Bavaria, and Winebald and Walburga were made abbot and abbess of a new monastery at Heidenheim. A double monastery with monks and nuns in adjoining buildings on the same site, it was the first of its kind in Germany, though there were many similar establishments in Anglo-Saxon England.

When Winebald died in 761, Walburga took charge of the whole monastery, which gained a reputation as a centre of education. She remained there until her death and was buried there, but her body was moved to Eichstätt in the second half of the 9th century. A miraculous oil with healing properties was said to flow from a rock at her new shrine, which became a place of pilgrimage.

St. Walburga's feast day is February 25, but the night of April 30 has also become associated with her name (possibly because her body was moved to Eichstätt on May 1). Known as Walpurgis Night, it is a time when witches are said to congregate on the Brocken, the highest peak in the Harz mountains in central Germany. In other parts of Europe it is celebrated as a springtime festival with music and dancing.

Wald, Lillian D. (1867–1940) *American social worker*

Lillian D. Wald is best known as the founder of the Henry Street Settlement in New York, the first nonsectarian, public-health nursing system in the world. By 1913 the service had 92 nurses making 200,000 visits annually.

Wald was born and grew up in Cincinnati, Ohio, the third of four children. At the age of 22, after meeting a nurse who had been sent to care for her sister during childbirth, she decided to become a nurse herself. She studied medicine at the New York Hospital Training School for Nurses and the Women's Medical College in New York. In 1893 she and another nurse, Mary Brewster, enlisted the financial support of several wealthy friends and established a small settlement on Rivington Street, New York, before moving to the famous settlement at 265 Henry Street, which was Wald's home for nearly 40 years. In 1902 she set up in New York the first municipal nursing service for schools in the world. Wald also originated both the plan for town and country nursing adopted by the American Red Cross and the Federal Children's Bureau, which was set up by Congress in 1908. A bitter opponent of slums and child labour, she was a strong advocate of more parks and play areas.

In 1915 Wald became the first president of the American Union against Militarism. However, after the United States entered World War I, she became a subcommittee member of the Council of National Defense. After the war she represented the Children's Bureau at international conferences in Europe and founded the League of Free Nations Association; she was also chairman of the Nurses Emergency Council during the 1918 influenza epidemic. During the 1920s and 1930s Wald served on numerous state and city commissions in the interest of public health and became first president of the National Organization for Public Health Nursing. In 1933 she resigned as president of the Henry Street Settlement's board of directors.

In addition to a number of popular magazine articles and pamphlets, Wald wrote two books: *The House on Henry Street* (1915) and *Windows on Henry Street* (1934).

Walker, Alice (1944–) *American novelist, poet, and social activist*

> We will be ourselves and free, or die in the attempt. Harriet Tubman was not our great-grandmother for nothing.
>
> — *You Can't Keep a Good Woman Down* (1981)

Underlying most of Alice Walker's

fiction and poetry is the struggle of African-American women for self-fulfilment and public recognition.

The youngest of eight children in a family of sharecroppers, Alice Walker was born in Eatonton, Georgia, and attended Spelman College in Atlanta, where she took part in civil-rights demonstrations. A gifted student, she won a scholarship to Sarah Lawrence College, from which she graduated in 1965. She then became a caseworker in the New York City Welfare Department and taught black studies at Jackson State College (1968–69) before becoming a full-time writer. Her marriage in 1967 to Melvyn Rosenman Leventhal, a white civil-rights lawyer, ended in divorce in 1976.

Walker's first volume of poems, *Once* (1968), was inspired by a tour of Africa in 1964; it was praised for its penetrating treatment of African culture, racial politics, love, and despair. Subsequent collections, which were generally well received for their originality and lyrical grace, include *Revolutionary Petunias and Other Poems* (1973), *Goodnight, Willie, I'll See You in the Morning* (1979), and *Horses Make a Landscape More Beautiful* (1984).

In her debut novel, *The Third Life of Grange Copeland* (1970), Walker analysed the plight of African-American men who fail in their family relationships, partly because of social constraints but also because of their inability to treat women as equals. Her second novel, *Meridian* (1976), draws heavily on her own experiences of the civil-rights movement. *The Color Purple* (1982), about a resolute African-American woman who finds success and happiness in her life despite physical and psychological abuse from the men around her, won the 1983 Pulitzer Prize and the American Book Award. The highly acclaimed 1985 film version starred Whoopi GOLDBERG.

Walker's collections of short stories include *Love and Trouble: Stories of Black Women* (1973) and *You Can't Keep a Good Woman Down* (1981). Her essays are represented in the collection *In Search of Our Mother's Gardens: Womanist Prose* (1983). Other works include *To Hell With Dying* (1980), and *Her Blue Body Everything We Know* (1991). *Possessing the Secret of Joy* (1992) is a controversial novel about an African-American woman who undergoes ritual female circumcision in a misguided attempt to get back to her African roots.

Walter, Lucy (*c.* 1630–1658) *English courtesan*

Mistress of the future King Charles II while he was in exile in Holland and France, Lucy Walter bore him a son, James Scott, Duke of Monmouth.

Lucy Walter (also known as Lucy Walters or Waters) was born at Roch Castle near Haverfordwest in Wales, the daughter of a Welsh family who supported Charles I during the Civil War. In 1648, after the Parliamentarians had captured and burned Roch Castle, Lucy travelled to The Hague in Holland. There she met the future Charles II, whose mistress she became for some three years. In 1649 she bore him a son, who was acknowledged by Charles and made Duke of Monmouth in 1663.

In 1651, after her liaison with Charles had ended, Lucy Walter fell into a life of promiscuity and bore a daughter, Mary, whose father was said to be Henry Bennet, Earl of Arlington. (Mary later married William Sarsfield, the brother of Patrick Sarsfield, Earl of Lucan.) In 1656 Lucy was briefly imprisoned in the Tower of London on suspicion of being a spy but was soon released and deported to France. She also used the alias of Mrs. Barlow (or Barlo) and was referred to by the contemporary diarist John Evelyn as "beautiful and bold." She died in Paris.

Shortly before the death of Charles II in 1685 Lucy's son, the Duke of Monmouth, became involved in a failed attempt by Whig noblemen to put forward a Protestant claimant to the throne in preference to the Catholic James, Duke of York (later James II). It was said at the time that proof that Charles had married Lucy resided in a mysterious black box, but Charles himself always denied they were married. Monmouth was banished, but returned to lead a rebellion after James became king. He was defeated at the battle of Sedgemoor and beheaded.

Walters, Julie (1950–) *British actress and comedienne*

A versatile actress, Julie Walters excels in roles that blend comedy with drama or tragedy. She is also a talented comedienne, known for her long-standing partnership with Victoria WOOD on British television.

Julie Walters was born in Smethwick, near Birmingham. She wanted to be an actress, but her mother persuaded her to go into nursing, a more secure profession. Still drawn to the stage, she took a teaching certificate in English and drama at Manchester Polytechnic and joined the Everyman Theatre in Liverpool. In 1980 she starred in the play *Educating Rita*, as a hairdresser determined to better herself by studying at the Open University, and won two best newcomer awards. In the 1983 film version she played the same role opposite Michael Caine, earning a BAFTA award and an Oscar nomination for her performance.

By this time Walters had made her name as a performer in television comedy, working with Victoria Wood in *Wood and Walters* (1980–82) and many subsequent series. In her television appearances, as in her roles on stage and screen, she demonstrated her ability to play women of all ages and social backgrounds. Of her repertoire of accents she once remarked, "I can do Irish, Welsh, Manchester, Liverpool, Birmingham, Cockney, and New York Jewish lesbian." Her roles include a brothel-keeper in the film *Personal Services* (1987), the wife of one of the Great Train Robbers in *Buster* (1988), the ageing mother of an ambitious local politician in the TV drama serial *GBH* (1991), and a dying woman in *Wide Eyed and Legless* (1993).

Among Walter's stage credits are *Macbeth* (1985), *Frankie and Johnny in the Clair de Lune* (1989), and *The Rose Tattoo* (1991). The birth of her daughter inspired the book *Baby Talk*, published in 1990. She has appeared most recently on the big screen in *Sister My*

Sister (1995) and *Intimate Relations* (1996).

Ward, Dame Barbara (1914–1981)
British economist and journalist

Barbara Ward was acknowledged on both sides of the Atlantic as one of the most influential commentators on economic and political subjects in the postwar era.

Barbara Ward was born in York and educated at Somerville College, Oxford, where she gained an honours degree in 1935 and was a lecturer from 1936 to 1939. In 1939 she joined the staff of *The Economist*, Britain's leading financial weekly, becoming its foreign editor in 1940.

In 1942 she began lecturing in the United States and later became visiting scholar at Harvard (1957–68) and Schweitzer Professor of International Economic Development at Columbia University (1968–73). In 1967 she was appointed to the Vatican Commission for Justice and Peace, becoming the first woman to address the Vatican Council in 1971. From 1973 until 1980 she was president of the International Institute for Environment and Development, remaining its chairman from 1980 to 1981. Her husband, Commander (later Sir) Robert Jackson, an Australian whom she married in 1950, was a UN official.

Barbara Ward's publications include *The International Share-Out* (1938), a study of the colonial system; *The West at Bay* (1948); *Faith and Freedom* (1954); *Five Ideas That Change the World* (1959); *India and the West* (1961); and *The Rich Nations and the Poor Nations* (1962). She was an early advocate of European economic union and urged the establishment of a broad Western policy to counter that of the Communist bloc in dealing with emergent nationalism in underdeveloped areas. Throughout her career she argued for a fairer balance between the developed nations and the Third World and for a more rational use of the world's natural resources. She wrote *Spaceship Earth* (1966) and *Only One Planet* (1972, with René Dubos), to bring these views to a wider public. She was also instrumental in instigating the UN's programmes for clean water and sanitation.

Barbara Ward was created a DBE in 1974 and raised to the peerage in 1976, taking the title Baroness Jackson of Lodsworth.

Ward, Mrs. Humphry (1851–1920)
British novelist and social worker

Mrs. Humphry Ward is remembered for her bestselling novel *Robert Elsmere* (1888) and for her outstanding achievements as a social worker. In 1890 she founded a settlement house in a poor district of London, from which grew the famous Passmore Edwards Settlement.

Born Mary Augusta Arnold in Hobart, Tasmania, she was the granddaughter of Dr. Thomas Arnold, the founder of Rugby School, and a niece of the poet Matthew Arnold. Returning to England in 1856, soon after her father's conversion to Roman Catholicism, she was brought up mostly in Oxford, where she became influenced by the liberal social philosophy of T. H. Green. In 1872 she married Thomas Humphry Ward, a fellow of Brasenose College, Oxford.

In 1881 the Wards moved to London, and Mrs. Ward began her career as a writer with the publication of a children's story, "Millie and Olly." Her first important literary work was a translation (1884) of Henri Frederic Amiel's *Journal Intime*. Her second novel, *Robert Elsmere*, dedicated to T. H. Green, proved an instant success and was translated into several languages. It expressed her strongly held conviction that the Christian Gospel could best be served by minimizing its mystical qualities and striving towards fulfilment of its social ideas.

Many of her novels of the next few years, namely *The History of David Grieve* (1892), *Marcella* (1894), *Sir George Tressaday* (1896), *Helbeck of Bannisdale* (1898), *Eleanor* (1900), and *Lady Rose's Daughter* (1903), are concerned with the need to help the poor. Sensitive to the plight of women, particularly poor ones, she pressed for women to become more involved in social work but nonetheless opposed the franchise movement, becoming in 1908 the first president of the Anti-Suffrage League. She criticized women's suffrage campaigners in several of her novels, notably *The Testing of Diana Mallory* (1908), *Delia Blanchflower* (1915), and *Cousin Philip* (1919). In 1911 she founded the Local Government Advancement Committee to promote the charitable activities of women.

After the death of her sister in 1908, Mrs. Ward devoted much of her time to the care of her nephews Julian Huxley (later Sir Julian Huxley, the well-known biologist and writer) and Aldous Huxley (the future novelist). In 1918 she published *A Writer's Recollections*, which contains interesting accounts of her family and friends (including the novelist Henry James). She was appointed one of the first seven women magistrates in 1920. Altogether she wrote 25 novels, three plays, and nine nonfiction works. Her daughter, Janet Penrose Trevelyan, published *The Life of Mrs. Humphry Ward* in 1923.

Warner, Marina (Sarah) (1946–   )
British novelist, historian, and feminist

In both her fiction and her nonfiction Marina Warner has questioned the powerful images of women conveyed by art, mythology, and popular convention.

Warner was born in London. After receiving a Roman Catholic education at St. Mary's Convent, Ascot, she studied at Lady Margaret Hall, Oxford, and gained a degree in modern languages. She married the journalist William Shawcross in 1971 and they had a son before divorcing in 1980. In 1981 she married the painter John Dewe Mathews. From 1987 to 1988 she was the Getty Scholar at the Paul Getty Center for the History of Art and the Humanities, California, and in 1990 she became the Tinbergen Professor at Erasmus University, Rotterdam. She has also held other fellowships and visiting professorships as well as being a board member of numerous organizations and pressure groups, including Charter 88 and the National Council for One-Parent Families (both from 1990).

Warner's literary talent was first recognized by the Young Writer of the Year Award in 1969. Her first major publication *The Dragon Empress*, a biography of TZ'U-HSI, the formidable empress dowager of China, followed in 1972. As a writer of nonfiction Warner is best known for three books in which she studies some of the most famous representations of women in Western culture: *Alone of all her Sex: The Myth and Culture of the Virgin Mary* (1976), *Joan of Arc: the Image of Female Heroism* (1981), and *Monuments and Maidens: the Allegory of the Female Form* (1985). The last-named book is an impressively wide-ranging study of the use of the female form to represent such allegorical figures as Truth, Justice, and Britannia that earned its author the Fawcett Prize in 1986. A similar approach informs her book *Managing Monsters* (1994), based on her Reith Lectures of the same year, which is subtitled 'Six Myths of Our Time,' and *From the Beast to the Blonde* (1994), a multilayered study of some well-known fairytales.

Marina Warner is also known for her novels, which explore similar themes of sexuality, power, and myth. These include *In a Dark Wood* (1977), *The Skating Party* (1983), and the semi-autobiographical *The Lost Father* (1988), which was shortlisted for the Booker Prize. Her more recent works of fiction include *Indigo* (1992), an exploration of colonialism that reworks themes from *The Tempest*, and the short-story collection *Mermaids in the Basement* (1993). She has also written children's books and opera libretti, including *In the House of Crossed Desires* (1996).

Warner, Sylvia Townsend (1893–1978) *British novelist, short-story writer, and poet*

Acclaimed as a subtle and imaginative writer, Sylvia Townsend Warner was also one of the editors of a ten-volume collection of Tudor church music and a well-known authority on supernatural matters. She took an active part in left-wing politics and served for a while in Spain during the Civil War (1936–39).

Born at Harrow-on-the-Hill, near London, Sylvia Townsend Warner was educated privately and began her literary career as a poet with the collection *The Espalier* in 1925. Her first novel, *Lolly Willowes*, which had the distinction of being the first Book of the Month Club selection, appeared the following year. Subsequent novels, such as *The Corner That Held Them* (1948), set in a medieval convent, and *The Flint Anchor* (1954), about a 19th-century English family, confirmed her critical reputation.

Warner's other novels include *Mr. Fortune's Maggot* (1927) and *Summer Will Show* (1936), while her collections of short stories include *A Garland of Straw* (1943), *A Spirit Rises* (1962), and *A Stranger with a Bag* (1966). *Sketches from Nature* (1963) are childhood reminiscences. She also wrote a biography of the writer T. H. White (1967). Her *Collected Poems* appeared in 1982.

Warnock, (Helen) Mary (1924–)
British philosopher and university administrator

Mary Warnock is a moral philosopher with a particular interest in educational matters; she is also well known for her work on government bodies dealing with some of the most complex ethical issues of our time.

Mary Wilson was born in Winchester, the daughter of a master at the famous boys' school there, who died before she was born. She was educated at St. Swithun's, Winchester, and Lady Margaret Hall, Oxford, where she graduated in classics. In 1949 she married the Oxford philosopher Geoffrey Warnock; they have two sons and three daughters. After 16 years (1949–66) as tutor in philosophy at St. Hugh's College, Oxford, during which she established her reputation with several books on existentialism, she was appointed headmistress at Oxford High School (1966–72). She then returned to Lady Margaret Hall as Talbot Research Fellow and in 1976 became senior research fellow at St. Hugh's College. From 1985 to 1991 she was the mistress of Girton College, Cambridge. She became a DBE in 1984 and a year later was created a life peer as Baroness Warnock of Weeke in the City of Winchester.

Mary Warnock's expertise in dealing with complex moral questions, together with her personal qualities of candour and open-mindedness, have made her much in demand as a member of government inquiries and advisory bodies. Since the late 1970s she has led several high-profile committees of inquiry, notably those concerned with animal experimentation (1979–86), environmental pollution (1979–84), and human fertilization (1982–84). The report produced by this last committee, known as the *Warnock Report* (1984), attempted to lay down ethical guidelines for the freezing and storage of human embryos and their use in scientific research. Most of its recommendations were incorporated in the Human Fertilization and Embryology Act (1990).

Many of Warnock's later publications reflect her interest in the related areas of education, psychology, and the creative arts; they include *Imagination* (1976), *Education: A Way Forward* (1979), *Memory* (1987), *A Common Policy for Education* (1988), *The Uses of Philosophy* (1992), and *Imagination and Time* (1994). In 1996 she edited the volume *Women Philosophers*.

Warwick, Dionne (1940–) *American pop and soul singer*

Dionne Warwick made her name in the 1960s with a series of hits by Burt Bacharach and Hal David and is still producing successful albums three decades later.

Marie Dionne Warwick was born into a musical family in East Orange, New Jersey. Her aunt was the gospel singer Cissy Houston, whose daughter Whitney HOUSTON became a successful pop and soul singer in the late 1980s. At the age of six Warwick joined the choir of the New Hope Baptist Church in Newark, and in her teens she formed a group called the Gospelaires. She was working as a backing vocalist when her talent was discovered by the songwriting team Burt Bacharach and Hal David in the early 1960s. They became her producers and wrote numerous hits for her, including "Anyone Who Had a Heart," "Walk On By," and "I Say a Little Prayer". From 1964 to 1973 she released two or three albums every year, including *Here I Am* (1966) and *Windows of the World* (1968).

In the early 1970s she changed her name to Warwicke for a short time. She also changed her record company and sang with the Spinners on "Then Came You" (1974), the first of her singles to top the charts in the United States. After a major dispute with Bacharach and David in the mid 1970s her career declined for a time, but by 1979 she was back on form with the album *Dionne*, which earned her two Grammy Awards. Her success continued through the 1980s and into the 1990s with such albums as *Heartbreaker* (1982); *Friends* (1985), on which she was joined by Gladys Knight and Stevie Wonder among others; *Reservations for Two* (1987); and *Friends Can Be Lovers* (1993), which also featured her cousin Whitney Houston. In 1986 she joined 44 other singers to make the hit single "We Are the World," the proceeds of which were used to fight famine in Africa.

Warwick has appeared in a handful of films, including *Slaves* (1969) and *Rent-a-Cop* (1988), and in a number of TV shows. In 1986 she launched a perfume called "Dionne."

Washington, Martha (1731–1802)
Wife of President George Washington

As the wife of the first president of the United States, Martha Washington performed her social duties – which included entertaining distinguished visitors – with generous hospitality, dignity, and reserve.

Martha Dandridge was born in New Kent, Virginia, the daughter of John and Frances Jones Dandridge, who both belonged to respected New England families. In 1794 Martha, an attractive capable girl, married Daniel Parke Custis, son of John Custis, a wealthy planter. The couple lived in the "White House" on a plantation on the Pamunkey River and had four children, two of whom died in infancy. On the death of her husband on July 8, 1757, Martha inherited a sizable fortune.

This fortune enabled her to take her pick of many suitors, so by choosing George Washington, she was indicating her strong feelings for him. They were married on January 6, 1759, and in the following spring Washington took Martha and her children, John Parke Custis and Martha Parke Custis, to his estate, Mount Vernon, which they started to rebuild after its neglect during Washington's service in the French and Indian War.

Martha was a cheerful companion, good-natured and with abundant common sense. During the American Revolution she spent her winters with General Washington and supervised Mount Vernon during the remainder of the year. They had no children of their own, and the death of Martha's daughter in 1773 was a grievous blow. Her son John had four children, and after his death in 1781 George and Martha helped to raise them.

After Washington died in 1799, Martha lived in seclusion at Mount Vernon until her death.

Waters, Ethel (1896–1977) *American actress and jazz singer*

Ethel Waters won acclaim for her performances on radio, television, stage, and screen and was still performing at the age of 80.

Born Ethel Howard in Chester, Pennsylvania, she spent her childhood in conditions of extreme poverty in the slums in and around Philadelphia. After working for a time as a hotel chambermaid, she began her career as a vocalist in a theatre in Baltimore, Maryland. She made her first recordings in 1921, when she was backed by the Fletcher Henderson orchestra. She first appeared in New York in 1925 at the Plantation Club in Harlem and later worked with Duke Ellington, Benny Goodman, and others. After appearing on Broadway in 1927 in an African-American revue, *Africana*, Waters combined nightclub work with the theatre. She appeared in the Irving Berlin hit *As Thousands Cheer* (1933), costarred with Beatrice LILLIE in *At Home Abroad* (1935), and in 1938 gave a concert recital at Carnegie Hall in New York.

Waters's first straight dramatic role, in *Mamba's Daughters* (1939), was a success; she went on to act and sing in the hit *Cabin in the Sky* (1940–41), also appearing in the film version (1943). Her greatest artistic success was as the wise and patient cook in Carson MC-CULLERS's *The Member of the Wedding* (1950), which received the New York Drama Critics' Circle Award. She repeated this role in the film version of 1953. She also appeared extensively on radio and television.

In 1951 Ethel Waters brought out her autobiography (cowritten with Charles Samuels), *His Eye Is on the Sparrow*, which was widely acclaimed for its candour and sensitivity. In it she describes how she was sustained by her religious faith through years of racial prejudice. Beginning in the late 1950s, she participated as a gospel singer in the crusades of the evangelist Billy Graham. She died in Chatsworth, California.

In both her acting and her singing Ethel Waters showed a freshness, exuberance, and warmth that captivated audiences. Popular songs with which she is identified include "Dinah," "Having a Heat Wave," and "Stormy Weather." Ella FITZGERALD was greatly influenced by her vocal improvisations.

Weaver, Sigourney (1949–) *American actress*

A tall intelligent-looking woman with a commanding presence on the screen, Sigourney Weaver rocketed to stardom as the astronaut Ellen Ripley in the movie *Alien* (1979) and its sequels. The $5 million she earned for *Alien 3* (1992), which she also coproduced, made her one of the highest-paid actresses of the early 1990s.

She was born Susan Alexandra Weaver in New York, the daughter of Sylvester ("Pat") Weaver, the president of NBC broadcasting. In the early 1960s she decided to adopt the name Sigourney, from a character in F. Scott Fitzgerald's *The Great Gatsby*. After studying English at Stanford University and drama at Yale, she

began acting in stage plays, making her debut in *Watergate Classics* (1973). She was first seen on the big screen – very briefly – in the Woody Allen film *Annie Hall* (1977).

In 1979 Weaver made her first appearance as Ellen Ripley, the tough heroine of the science-fiction classic *Alien* and its sequels. Having made her name as such a strong character, there was a risk that she would be typecast, but she proved her versatility by playing a haunted cellist in the comedy *Ghostbusters* (1984), a double-dealing boss who gets her comeuppance in *Working Girl* (1988), and a nervous wreck in *Copycat* (1995). She took up the role of Ellen Ripley again in *Aliens* (1986), earning an Academy Award nomination for her performance. In *Alien 3* (1992) Ripley finally met her death, but fans of what had become a cult series were relieved to learn that the character had been cloned for a fourth movie, *Alien Resurrection* (1997). Her other major film roles include that of the naturalist Dian FOSSEY in *Gorillas in the Mist* (1988), which brought her a second Best Actress Oscar nomination.

Weaver continued to act on stage in her early career, appearing in such plays as *A Flea in Her Ear* (1978), *As You Like It, Beyond Therapy* (1981), and *Hurly Burly* (1984). After *The Merchant of Venice* (1986–87) she took a break from the theatre, returning in 1996 to star in the Broadway play *Sex and Longing*. Having waited until her mid thirties to marry and start a family, she once remarked, "Whether it was work, marriage, or family, I've always been a late bloomer."

Webb, Beatrice (1858–1943) *British economist and socialist*

> When a man said to Beatrice Webb, "Much of this talk about feminism is nonsense; any woman would rather be beautiful than clever," she replied, "Quite true. But that is because so many men are stupid and so few are blind."
>
> —*The Daily Express*, October 14, 1947

> If I ever felt inclined to be timid as I was going into a room full of

people, I would say to myself, "You're the cleverest member of one of the cleverest families in the cleverest class of the cleverest nation in the world, why should you be frightened?"

—Quoted by Bertrand Russell in *Portraits from Memory* (1956)

In partnership with her husband, Sidney Webb, Beatrice Webb produced over 100 books and articles, and the Webbs became the leading researchers and propagandists for the Labour movement in Britain. Their first major works were a *History of Trade Unionism* (1894) and *Industrial Democracy* (1897). They were involved in the founding of the London School of Economics in 1895 and the left-wing journal *The New Statesman* in 1913.

Born Martha Beatrice Potter at Standish House near Gloucester, she was the eighth daughter of a railway and industrial magnate. Beatrice was educated privately and became a close business associate of her father after her mother's death in 1882. Moving in liberal intellectual circles, she became interested in reform and began to do social work in London. She investigated working-class conditions as part of the survey *Life and Labour of the People in London* (1891–1903), directed by her cousin Charles Booth. In 1891 she published *The Co-operative Movement in Great Britain*. It was while she was working on this that she met Sidney Webb, a member of the socialist Fabian Society, whom she married in 1892.

Sidney and Beatrice Webb served on many royal commissions and wrote widely on economic problems. After a tour of the United States and the Dominions in 1898, they embarked on their massive ten-volume work, *English Local Government* (1906–29). Mrs. Webb also served on the Poor Law Commission (1906–09) and was joint author of its minority report, which awakened public interest in the principles of social insurance. The Webbs' London house became a socialist salon, and they played an increasingly influential role in guiding the intellectual development of the Labour Party.

During World War I Beatrice Webb wrote *Wages of Men and Women – Should They Be Equal?*. She was a member of the War Cabinet committee on women in industry (1918–19) and served on the Lord Chancellor's advisory committee for women justices (1919–20), being a justice of the peace herself from 1919 to 1927. Her *Constitution for the Socialist Commonwealth of Great Britain* was published in 1920. Sidney Webb became an MP in 1922 and held ministerial office in both the early Labour governments. In 1932, after he had left office, the Webbs visited the Soviet Union, where they were greatly impressed by the workings of the socialist state. They recorded their views in *Soviet Communism: A New Civilization* (1935). The Webbs retired to their home in Hampshire in 1928. Beatrice Webb produced two volumes of autobiography: *My Apprenticeship* (1926) and *Our Partnership* (1948), which was published after her death.

Webb, Mary (1881–1927) *British novelist*

Webb is best remembered for the novel *Precious Bane* (1924), set in the rural Shropshire where she spent much of her life.

She was born Gladys Mary Meredith in Leighton, Shropshire, the daughter of a schoolteacher. Through her mother she had family connections with the writer Sir Walter Scott; from her father she inherited a love of nature and the countryside. She was educated at home and began writing poems and stories as a child. In 1912 she married Henry Webb, and together they worked as market gardeners, growing fruit and vegetables for sale at Shrewsbury market. The Webbs left Shropshire for London in 1921, but Mary, whose health had never been good, died six years later.

Her first novel, *The Golden Arrow*, was published in 1916. It was followed by *Gone to Earth* (1917), *The House in Dormer Forest* (1920), *Seven for a Secret* (1922), and *Precious Bane* (1924). In all her writings she painted a vivid picture of life in the Shropshire countryside, developing a passionate and melodramatic style of writing that was satirized by Stella Gibbons in *Cold*

Comfort Farm (1932). Critical opinions of her work vary, but some have compared her novels with those of Thomas Hardy or D. H. Lawrence.

Webb found little fame in her lifetime, but a speech of praise made in 1928 by one of her admirers – the prime minister Stanley Baldwin – led to a sudden demand for her work that the libraries and bookshops were unable to satisfy. Her novels were reprinted in 1928 with introductions by Baldwin and such noted writers as John Buchan and G. K. Chesterton. The following year saw new editions of Webb's poems and *The Spring of Joy* (a collection of nature essays originally published in 1917), as well as the first appearance of her unfinished historical novel, *Armour Wherein He Trusted*, and a number of short stories.

Webster, Margaret (1905–1972)
British actress, director, and producer

With Eva LE GALLIENNE and Cheryl CRAWFORD Margaret Webster was a cofounder of the American Repertory Company in 1946. In 1948 she formed the Margaret Webster Shakespeare Company, a troupe that brought exciting swift-moving drama to most of the United States and many Canadian provinces.

Margaret Webster was the daughter of Ben Webster, a well-known English Shakespearean actor, and Dame May Whitty, a popular stage and film actress. Her great-grandfather was the actor, manager, and playwright Benjamin Nottingham Webster. She was born in New York, where her father was performing at the time, but the family soon returned to England. Margaret made her first professional appearance in the chorus of Euripides's *Trojan Women* in 1924. The following year she made her Shakespearean debut with John Barrymore in *Hamlet*. From 1929 she acted with John Gielgud's Old Vic company in London, appearing in such productions as *Musical Chairs* (1932) and *Richard of Bordeaux* (1933).

Webster's distinguished career as a director began in 1937, when the actor Maurice Evans invited her to stage his *Richard II* on Broadway. Paul Robe-

son's *Othello* (1943) was another of her major directorial successes. She continued to act and in 1944 also emerged as a producer as well as director. In 1950 she directed her first opera, *Don Carlos*, at the Metropolitan Opera House in New York. Her acting successes of the 1950s included *An Evening with Will Shakespeare* (1952) and *Measure for Measure* (1957). She also worked in England during this period, directing *The Merchant of Venice* at Stratford-upon-Avon and *Measure for Measure* at the Old Vic. In 1960 she directed Noël Coward's *Waiting in the Wings* at the Duke of York's Theatre in London.

Margaret Webster wrote the books *Shakespeare without Tears* (1942) and *The Same Only Different* (1969), which chronicled five generations of her theatrical family.

Wedgwood, Dame Veronica (1910–1997) *British historian*

Wedgwood wrote about the 17th century, especially the period of the English Civil War, in a scholarly but readable style, with the aim of encouraging others to share her passion for the past.

Cicely Veronica Wedgwood was born in Northumberland, a direct descendant of the 18th-century potter Josiah Wedgwood. As a child, she was happier among her father's history books than playing with friends, and after a private education with a Swiss governess she went to Oxford University to read history. She graduated in 1931 with a first-class honours degree and joined the editorial staff of *Time and Tide*, a weekly review of arts and politics. She continued to work for the paper for many years, researching and writing her history books in her spare time.

In 1935 her first work, a biography of the Earl of Strafford, was published. Strafford was the chief adviser to King Charles I before the Civil War, and this period of history became Wedgwood's speciality. Her books on the "Great Rebellion" include *Oliver Cromwell* (1939), *The King's Peace* (1955), *The King's War* (1958), and *The Trial of Charles I* (1964). She also produced historical and biographical works about other political figures and events of the 17th century, notably *The Thirty Years' War* (1938) and *Richelieu and the French Monarchy* (1949). For her biography of William the Silent (1944) she was awarded the James Tait Black Memorial Prize. In the latter part of her career she embarked on an ambitious new project – a history of the world – but completed only one volume, *The Spoils of Time* (1984).

Wedgwood was not an academic historian – she wrote for the general reader in an elegant narrative style, describing what happened rather than analysing why it happened. Her biographies are well-rounded portraits of their subjects, which do not neglect the human angle. She also wrote about art and literature and published three collections of essays: *Velvet Studies* (1946), *Truth and Opinion* (1960), and *History and Hope* (1987). In 1968 she was honoured with the title DBE. The numerous awards and other honours she received during her lifetime included honorary degrees from universities in Britain and the United States.

Weil, Simone (1909–1943) *French philospher and mystic*

> The word "revolution" is a word for which you kill, for which you die, for which you send the laboring masses to their death, but which does not possess any content.
>
> —*Oppression and Liberty* (1958)

> Learn to reject friendship, or rather the dream of friendship. To want friendship is a great fault. Friendship ought to be a gratuitous joy, like the joys afforded by art, or life (like aesthetic joys). I must refuse it in order to be worthy of it.
>
> —*First and Last Notebooks* (1970)

One of the first women to be admitted to the prestigious Ecole Normale Supérieure in Paris, where she studied philosophy, Simone Weil was an active socialist in the 1930s. After a mystical experience in 1938 she became a Roman Catholic, and during World War II she worked for the Free French Resistance in London.

Born in Paris into a well-to-do Jewish family, Simone Weil studied under the philosopher Alain (the pen name of Emile-Auguste Chartier) before attending the Ecole Normale Supérieure, from which she graduated in 1931. Although deeply influenced by the teachings of Karl Marx, she did not join the Communist Party. She taught philosophy at a girls' school at Le Puy, and later at Bourges and St. Quentin, but interspersed this with periods of manual labour on farms and on the shop floor at the Renault motor works to experience the life of the working classes. In 1936 she joined the International Brigade to fight against Franco in the Spanish Civil War.

After the first of her mystical experiences Weil embraced Roman Catholic doctrine but was never baptized, preferring to identify herself with the powerless outside the Church. Following the defeat of France by Nazi Germany, Jews were forbidden to teach by the Vichy government, so Weil became a farm servant near Marseilles. In 1942 she and her family escaped to the United States, but after a few months she returned to Europe to work in London for the Free French Resistance. Never healthy, she refused to eat more than the official ration allotted to the citizens of occupied France. Ravaged by pleurisy, she was admitted to the Middlesex Hospital in London and then to a sanatorium at Ashford in Kent, where she died at the age of 34.

Weil's writings were all collected and published after her death. They include *La Pesanteur et la grâce* (1948; English translation, *Gravity and Grace*, 1952), a collection of religious and philosophical guidelines; *L'Enracinement* (1949; English translation, *The Need for Roots*, 1952), an essay on the obligations of the individual and the state; *L'Attente de Dieu* (1950; English translation, *Waiting for God*, 1951), a spiritual autobiography; *La Source grecque* (1953; The Greek Source), translations and studies; *Oppression et liberté* (1955; English translation, *Oppression and Liberty*, 1958), political and social papers on war, factory work, and language; and three volumes of *Cahiers* (1951, 1955, 1956; translated as *Notebooks*, 2 vols., 1956). Her writings have made her widely known as one of the great advocates for religion in our time, one of the subtlest psychologists of the spiritual quest, and a genuine analyst of force, violence, terror, and death, who found in suffering a source of purity and grace.

Weir, Judith (1954–) *British composer*

Judith Weir has produced a wide range of compositions, including orchestral and choral works and many pieces for small groups of voices or instruments.

She was born in Cambridge, of Scottish parents, and studied musical composition under John Tavener and Olivier Messiaen amongst others. After her graduation from Cambridge University in 1976, she spent three years as composer-in-residence at the Southern Arts Association before taking up a teaching fellowship at Glasgow University (1979–82). She went back to Cambridge in 1983, moving to London two years later. From 1988 to 1991 she was composer-in-residence at the Royal Scottish Academy of Music.

Weir's early works include a number of pieces for small instrumental groups, such as the wind quintet *Out of the Air* (1975), *Between Ourselves* (1978) for seven players, and *Music for 247 Strings* (1981) for violin and piano. In 1981 she also produced two orchestral compositions, *Isti Mirant Stella* and *Ballad*, and *Thread!*, a humorous piece for narrator and eight instruments inspired by the Bayeux Tapestry. Her *Spij döbrze* ("Pleasant Dreams"), for double bass with recorded electronic sound, had its first performance in 1983 as part of the International Society for Contemporary Music festival in Poland.

Her other compositions include the operas *The Black Spider* (1984), *A Night at the Chinese Opera* (1987), and *The Vanishing Bridegroom* (1990); choral works, such as *Heaven Ablaze in His Breast* (1989); and the piano pieces *Ardnamurchan Point* (1990) and *Roll off the Ragged Rocks of Sin* (1992). In 1994 she received the Critics' Circle Award for her outstanding contribution to British musical life.

Welch, Raquel (1940–) *American actress*

Raquel Welch made her name as a voluptuous sex symbol in the 1960s, and in late middle age was still considered one of the most beautiful women in the world. Rarely praised for her acting ability, she nevertheless won a Golden Globe Award for her performance in the film *The Three Musketeers* (1973).

She was born Raquel Tejada in Chicago, Illinois. In her late teens and early twenties she worked as a model and cocktail waitress; by the age of 24 she had married and divorced her first husband, James Welch, and had given birth to two children. She made her film debut with a small part in *A House Is Not a Home* (1964). The press agent Patrick Curtis, who later became her second husband, marketed her as a sex symbol, and she gained international stardom with such films as *One Million Years B.C.* (1966), *Bedazzled* (1967), and *Lady in Cement* (1968). She also appeared in a number of European movies, including the French–German–Italian coproduction *The Oldest Profession* (1968), about prostitution in the past, present, and future.

Welch continued to make regular big screen appearances throughout the 1970s, notably in the swashbuckler *The Prince and the Pauper* (1978). During the 1980s she concentrated on stage and television work, appearing in the Broadway musical *Woman of the Year* (1982) and such TV movies as *Right to Die* (1987). She also produced exercise books and videos, notably *The Racquel Welch Total Beauty and Fitness Program* (1984). In 1994 she returned to the big screen in *Naked Gun 33⅓: The Final Insult*, and in 1997 she took over the title role in the Broadway production of *Victor/Victoria*.

Weldon, Fay (1931–) *British writer*

The author of many novels and plays for the theatre, radio, and television, Weldon is perhaps best known for the novel *The Life and Loves of a She-Devil* (1983), which she adapted for British television in 1985 (it was also filmed in 1989 with Roseanne Arnold in the title role). It is the story of an unattractive wife's terrible revenge on her unfaithful husband and his beautiful lover, a bestselling writer.

Born Fay Birkinshaw in Worcestershire, she emigrated to New Zealand with her parents and was educated at Christchurch Girl's High School. After World War II the family returned to Britain, and Fay went on to study at the University of St. Andrews in Scotland. She subsequently worked as an advertising copywriter, creating such memorable slogans as "Go to work on an egg," used by the Egg Marketing Board in 1958. In 1962 she married Ron Weldon, who died in 1994.

In the 1960s Weldon began writing for radio and television, and among her early credits is the first episode of the TV drama series *Upstairs Downstairs* (1970). Since then she has produced numerous plays, scripts, and adaptations, including a dramatization of Jane AUSTEN's *Pride and Prejudice* in 1980. Her first novel, *The Fat Woman's Joke* (1967), was followed by such works as *Down among the Women* (1971), *Female Friends* (1975), *Puffball* (1980), *The President's Child* (1982), *The Heart of the Country* (1987), *The Cloning of Joanna May* (1989), *Affliction* (1994), and *Big Women* (1998). *Praxis* (1978), about a woman who has killed a baby, was nominated for the Booker Prize. She has also written short stories, published in *Watching Me, Watching You* (1981) and other collections. Weldon's writings present a feminist view of the world, centring on women's relationships with men, family members, and each other. Although her novels show a skilful blend of realism with fantasy and tragedy with comedy, the dominant tone is set by the caustic witty voice of the author herself. Her books are popular with readers of both sexes and all ages.

In the later part of her career Weldon has been an active campaigner for the rights of authors, supporting such causes as the Public Lending Right (by which writers receive a small payment every time one of their books is borrowed from a public library).

Wells-Barnett, Ida Bell (1862–1931)
American journalist and civil-rights activist

Elected the first president of the Negro Fellowship League in 1900, Ida Wells-Barnett went on to become a cofounder of the National Association for the Advancement of Colored People (NAACP) in 1909 and the chairman of the Chicago Equal Rights League in 1915.

The daughter of slaves, Ida Bell Wells was born in Holly Springs, Missouri, and educated at the local freedmen's school. At the age of 14 she became a teacher to support herself when her parents and three of her seven brothers and sisters died in a yellow fever epidemic. She briefly attended Fisk University in Nashville. In 1883 she moved to Memphis, Tennessee, where she continued to teach and started writing. She was dismissed from her teaching position in 1891, after she had brought an uᵣ successful lawsuit challenging Tennessee's racist Jim Crow laws (1887) and, under the pen name "Iola," criticized the inadequate educational opportunities open to African Americans.

Wells became part-owner of an African-American weekly newspaper, the *Memphis Free Speech*, and in 1892 began an antilynching crusade by denouncing the lynching in Memphis of three of her friends. After the office of the *Memphis Free Speech* was destroyed by a white mob, she went to New York, where she became a reporter on the newspaper *Age*. She wrote and lectured against lynching, both in northern U.S. cities and, between 1893 and 1894, in Britain. In 1895 she married Ferdinand Lee Barnett, a lawyer and editor, and settled in Chicago. They had four children.

Wells-Barnett organized antilynching societies and African-American women's clubs in Chicago and elsewhere and was active in the National Afro-American Council. She also organized protests against the exclusion of African Americans from the World Columbian Exposition. She generally supported the militant views of W. E. B. Du Bois and in 1895 published *A Red Record*, a statistical study of lynching. From 1913 until 1916 she was a probation officer for the Chicago city courts and organized legal aid for the victims of the 1918 Race Riots and similarly oppressed people. Wells-Barnett also organized and demonstrated on behalf of women's suffrage. Her autobiography, *Crusade for Justice*, was published in 1970.

Welty, Eudora (1909–   ) *American novelist and short-story writer*

One of the most distinguished American writers of the mid 20th century, Eudora Welty explored the nuances of human behaviour through a wide range of characters, rich and poor, black and white, from her native Mississippi delta. She was awarded the U.S. National Medal for Literature and the Presidential Medal of Freedom in 1980. In 1984 she received the Commonwealth Award for Distinguished Service in Literature.

Eudora Welty was born in Jackson, Mississippi, and attended Mississippi State College for Women before graduating in 1929 from the University of Wisconsin. From there she went to New York, where she attended the Columbia School of Advertising (1930–31), but with the deepening Depression was unable to find work and returned to Jackson. She then took a job travelling throughout Mississippi as a publicity agent for the Works Progress Administration, a role that brought her into contact with many different kinds of people. One result of this work was a series of photographs of the people and places she encountered, a selection of which she published in 1971 as *One Time, One Place: Mississippi in the Depression: a Snapshot Album*.

Welty published her first short story, "Death of a Traveling Salesman," in 1936; her first collection of stories, *A Curtain of Green*, followed in 1941. For one of these stories, "The Worn Path," Welty won the first of several O. Henry Memorial Contest Awards. *The Robber Bridegroom*, a fairytale novel set in Mississippi in 1798, appeared in 1942, and a second collection of stories, *The Wide Net*, in 1943. These and her first full-length novel,

Delta Wedding (1946), were highly acclaimed by the critics.

Although Welty has lived virtually her entire life in Jackson, her themes are universal. She manages to capture the essential isolation of the individual and the way this can conflict with the responsibilities of family and community bonds. Her writing is distinguished by extensive use of both monologue and dialogue and an unfailing ear for Southern dialect.

Eudora Welty won the William Dean Howells Medal of the American Academy in 1955 for her novel *The Ponder Heart* (1954). Both it and *The Robber Bridegroom* were produced on Broadway. In 1973 she received the Pulitzer Prize for *The Optimist's Daughter* (1972), another novel. Her other works include *The Golden Apples* (1943), a group of interrelated stories; the novel *Losing Battles* (1970); and *Collected Stories* (1981). *One Writer's Beginnings* (1984) is an autobiographical sketch based on a series of Harvard lectures.

Welty is also an accomplished reviewer and critic. During World War II she was on the staff of *The New York Times Book Review*. Her selected essays and reviews were reprinted in *The Eye of the Story* (1978). Two further collections of book reviews were published in 1994 as *A Writer's Eye* and *Monuments to Interruption*.

Wertmuller, Lina (1928–   ) *Italian film director and screenwriter*

Wertmuller's films are often controversial, dealing with sexual relationships in an explicit manner. Her husband and business partner is the artist Enrico Job, who has worked as set designer on many of her productions.

Arcangela Felice Assunta Wertmuller von Elgg was born in Rome. After working as a teacher for a time, she studied at the Theatre Academy in Rome and went on a tour of Europe with a puppet show. In the 1950s she worked as a stage actress, writer, and director. She broke into the Italian cinema when the actor Marcello Mastroianni introduced her to Federico Fellini, who gave her a job as assistant on his Oscar-winning movie *8½*

(1963). In the same year Wertmuller wrote and directed *The Lizards*, her first film.

She gradually built up her reputation in Europe with such films as *The Seduction of Mimi* (1972), for which she was named Best Director at the Cannes Film Festival; *Love and Anarchy* (1973); and *Swept Away* (1974). Her fame spread to the United States and elsewhere with *Seven Beauties* (1976), set in a Nazi concentration camp, which earned her an Academy Award nomination and a contract with Warner Brothers for a series of films in English. Only one of these, *The End of the World in Our Usual Bed in a Night Full of Rain* (1977), was made. Starring Candice BERGEN as an American photographer and Giancarlo Giannini as her Italian lover, the film received poor reviews, and the contract was terminated.

Wertmuller's subsequent films include *Revenge* (1979), *Softly, Softly* (1985), *Saturday, Sunday, and Monday* (1990), *The Nymph* (1996), and *An Interesting State* (1997), a film about Bosnia-Herzegovina starring Harvey Keitel. As well as writing the scripts for all her pictures – and often making drastic changes in the middle of shooting – she has also collaborated on the screenplays of other directors' films. In 1993 she published her memoirs.

Wesley, Mary (1912–) *British novelist*

Success came to Mary Wesley rather late in life: she was in her seventies when she began writing her novels about love and sex in the British upper middle classes, such as *The Camomile Lawn*.

She was born Mary Aline Mynors Farmar in Berkshire. The youngest of three children, she felt unloved and unwanted by her parents. Her father was an army officer, and the family frequently moved, so Mary had few friends of her own age. She married Lord Swinfen in 1936 and bore him two sons, but the relationship was not a happy one and ended in the early 1940s. During World War II she fell in love with the journalist Eric Siepmann and lived with him for several years before their marriage. Mary's parents showed their disapproval by cutting her out of their wills; when Siepmann died in 1970, she was left almost penniless, with a teenage son to support. Life was hard for the next 12 years, until Mary found her voice as a writer.

Wesley had written two books, *Speaking Terms* and *The Sixth Seal*, in the late 1960s, but she was 70 years old when her first major novel, *Jumping the Queue*, was published. It was followed by such works as *The Camomile Lawn* (1984), which was subsequently adapted for television; *Harnessing Peacocks* (1986), about a young unmarried mother who turns to prostitution to pay for her son's education; and *The Vacillations of Poppy Carew* (1986). Her stories often feature a female character who resembles the author's younger self – a shy misfit surrounded by self-assured and independent women.

Wesley's novels became bestsellers, and money was no longer a problem. By writing about the upper-middle-class world she had grown up in, she regained the wealth she had lost when she turned her back on it to "live in sin" with her lover. She continued writing well into the 1990s, producing such works as *A Sensible Life* (1990), *A Dubious Legacy* (1993), *An Imaginative Experience* (1994), and *Part of the Furniture* (1997).

West, Mae (1893–1980) *American actress and writer*

Mae West raised the spirits of cinemagoers during the Depression of the 1930s with her unique blend of comedy and sexuality. She is credited with a host of comic one-liners full of sexual innuendo, such as "Is that a gun in your pocket, or are you just glad to see me?," "It's not the men in my life that counts – it's the life in my men," and, most famously, "Come up and see me sometime." Her generous curves inspired American airmen to nickname the inflatable life jacket issued to them during World War II a "Mae West."

Born in Brooklyn, New York, she began performing in vaudeville as a child, appearing as "The Baby Vamp" at the age of 14. Four years later she married the actor Frank Wallace and made her debut on Broadway. In 1926 she wrote, produced, directed, and starred in a Broadway show of her own. Its title was *Sex*, and it led to West's arrest and imprisonment for obscenity. Her next play, *Drag* (1927), was banned on Broadway because it dealt with the issue of homosexuality. She continued to write and perform on stage, returning to Broadway in triumph with the hugely successful *Diamond Lil* (1928).

In 1932 West made her first appearance on the big screen in *Night after Night*, in what should have been a supporting role. The star of the film, George Raft, later remarked, "She stole everything but the cameras." The following year West starred in *She Done Him Wrong*, a film version of *Diamond Lil*, which broke box-office records. This was followed by starring roles in *I'm No Angel* (1933), *Belle of the Nineties* (1934), *Goin' to Town* (1935), and *Klondike Annie* (1936), all of which were written or cowritten by West, making her one of the highest paid women in the United States. However, censorship rules were being tightened, and she was forced to tone down the risqué style and content of her films to such an extent that they lost their appeal.

After retiring from the cinema in the early 1940s, West continued to write and perform in plays and shows on stage, notably *Catherine Was Great* (1944), and toured with a cabaret act. Her autobiography, *Goodness Had Nothing to Do with It*, was published in 1959. (The title is a line from the film *Night after Night*, uttered by West in response to the remark "Goodness, what beautiful diamonds!") Having turned down the role of Norma Desmond in Billy Wilder's film *Sunset Boulevard* (1950), West was eventually lured back to the cinema for *Myra Breckinridge* (1970), after rewriting most of her dialogue. Her last appearance on the big screen, in *Sextette* (1978), was not a great success. She suffered a serious stroke in 1980 and died three months later.

West, Dame Rebecca (1892–1983)
British writer, journalist, and critic

> God forbid that any book should be banned. The practice is as indefensible as infanticide.
> —*The Strange Necessity* (1928)

> She regarded me as a piece of fiction – like one of her novels – that she could edit and improve.
> —Her son, Anthony West, *Heritage*

One of the 20th century's most outspoken writers, Rebecca West found greater fame as a critic and a journalist than as a novelist.

She was born Cicily Isabel Fairfield in County Kerry, Ireland, the daughter of a soldier and war correspondent. After attending George Watson's Ladies College, Edinburgh, she appeared for a short time on the London stage, notably in Ibsen's *Rosmersholm*; she took her pen name from the heroine of this play. From 1911 West became involved in women's suffrage campaigns and turned to journalism; throughout her life she continued to contribute to leading British and American periodicals, beginning with the feminist *Freewoman* (which her mother had forbidden her to read). She joined *The Clarion* the following year as a political writer and later reviewed novels for *The New Statesman* and contributed to *The Daily Telegraph*.

In about 1913 Rebecca began a ten-year affair with the novelist H. G. Wells. Their son, Anthony West, who also became a writer, was born in 1914. In 1916 her first full-length book appeared, a critical study of Henry James. Her first novels, *The Return of the Soldier* (1918), about the effects of shell shock, and *The Judge* (1922), a study of the Oedipus complex, show the impact of Freudian psychology on her thinking. All her later novels, which appeared at irregular intervals, show this same psychological interest. They include *Harriet Hume* (1929), *The Harsh Voice* (1935), *The Thinking Reed* (1936), and, after a gap of 20 years, *The Fountain Overflows* (1956) and *The Birds Fall Down* (1966).

In 1923, after breaking with Wells, West went to the United States and began contributing to the prominent American journals *The New Republic* and *The New Yorker*. After travelling in 1937 to Yugoslavia with her husband, Henry Maxwell Andrews, a banker whom she had married in 1930, she produced *Black Lamb and Grey Falcon* (1941). A controversial two-volume travel diary that expands into a cultural and political examination of Balkan history, it is generally considered her greatest work. During World War II she supervised BBC broadcasts to Yugoslavia. In 1945 she was highly acclaimed for her coverage in *The New Yorker* of the trial of William Joyce ("Lord Haw-Haw"), who was tried for treason for broadcasting Nazi propaganda to Britain and subsequently executed. This was later published as *The Meaning of Treason* (1949) and expanded and updated in 1965 to include material on the communist traitors Burgess, Maclean, Philby, and Blake. Her reports on the Nuremberg trials of German war criminals were collected in *A Train of Powder* (1955).

Rebecca West's other nonfiction works include *D. H. Lawrence* (1930), *St. Augustine* (1933), *The Modern Rake's Progress* (1934), *McLuhan and the Future of Literature* (1969), and *1900* (1982). She was created an OBE in 1949 and DBE in 1959.

Westwood, Vivienne (1941–)
British fashion designer

> The English aristocracy is now only the middle class with knobs on.
>
> —Quoted in *The Guardian*, February 22, 1997

Vivienne Westwood is best known for her punk fashions of the 1970s but has continued to shock – and inspire – with her subsequent outrageous collections.

She was born Vivienne Isabel Swire in Glossop, Derbyshire. Her father came from a long line of cobblers, and her mother worked in the local cotton mills. When she was 17, the family moved to Harrow, where they bought a post office. Vivienne attended a teacher-training college and became a primary-school teacher for some years, during which time she married Derek Westwood.

Retaining her husband's surname after their divorce (the marriage lasted three years), Vivienne Westwood began her fashion career by designing jewellery, which she sold in a London street market. She did not begin designing clothes until 1971, when she met the entrepreneur Malcolm McLaren, who became her lover. In that year Westwood and McLaren opened Let It Rock, a shop in the King's Road, Chelsea, where they sold 1950s-style clothing. By 1974 the shop was called Sex and emphasized themes of bondage, sadomasochism, and body fetishes. During the mid 1970s McLaren was the manager of the punk rock band the Sex Pistols, and Westwood became enthralled by the punk movement's anarchic style. Her designs gave commercial form to what was originally a wholly improvised street style, retaining the torn edges, safety pins, and combinations of fabrics popular in punk. Her shop was renamed Seditionaries in 1977 and World's End in the 1980s.

Westwood's early 1980s collections – Pirates (1981–82), Savages (1982), Buffalo Girls (1982–83), Punkature (1983), and Witches (1983) – helped to create the fashionable "New Romantic" look of the era. In 1985 she showed hoop skirts – based on 19th-century crinolines – that critics immediately denounced as unwearable. Nevertheless, this "Mini Crini" collection turned out to anticipate styles popular later in the 1980s. In 1991 Westwood added a made-to-order bridal line to her output, producing traditional white and ivory dresses but also an outrageous design in her own tartan. This is now displayed with all the traditional tartans in the Lochcarron Museum of tartan in Scotland. It is called MacAndreas in honour of her second husband, Andreas Kronthaler, also a designer, whom she married in 1992. Her Café Society collection (1994) was inspired by turn-of-the-century Paris and featured dresses with long trains and bustles.

Westwood continues to tease the British establishment: her trademark combines the orb, which represents the power of the sovereign, with a satellite, symbolizing the future. Nevertheless, she supports the clothing industry in her homeland: her Gold Label clothes are produced in Britain and make ample use of such traditional regional fabrics as tartans, Harris tweeds, and Irish linen. (Her Red Label designs are made in Italy.) She has a longstanding interest in exposing "innerwear as outerwear" and bringing historical lingerie and corsets to street clothes, as in the 1990–91 Portrait collection, in which she created corsets featuring photo-printed details from Old Master paintings. After an absence of six years Vivienne Westwood returned to the London fashion shows in 1997 with her Vive La Bagatelle collection.

Westwood's designs show her prodigious knowledge of fashion and social history and her equally acute awareness of contemporary trends. One of her ambitions has been to establish a "salon" in the spirit of the 19th-century establishments where artists, writers, and assorted intellectuals gathered. Her designs have inspired a host of younger designers, including Jean-Paul Gaultier, Alexander McQueen, John Galliano, and Helmut Lang.

Westwood was the recipient of the British fashion industry's Designer of the Year Award an unprecedented two years in a row (1990, 1991). In his book *Chic Savages* (1989) John Fairchild, editor of *Women's Wear Daily*, named her one of the six best fashion designers in the world. From 1989 to 1991 Westwood was professor of fashion at the Vienna Academy of Applied Arts, and in 1993 she became professor of fashion at the Berlin Hochschule. In 1992 the Royal College of Art, London, named her an honorary senior fellow. She was created an OBE in 1997.

Wexler, Nancy (1946–) *American clinical psychologist*

Following the death of her mother from Huntington's disease, Nancy Wexler has devoted most of her time to a search for the gene responsible for the condition.

Wexler was born in New York, the daughter of the well-known psychoanalyst Milton Wexler. She was educated at Harvard and the University of Michigan, where she completed her doctorate. In 1968 her mother developed Huntington's disease (HD), an untreatable and incurable hereditary condition that leads inevitably to the destruction of the mind. The disease usually appears between the ages of 35 and 50, and Nancy and her sister had a 50% chance of inheriting it. Milton Wexler's response was to set up the Hereditary Disease Foundation to stimulate and organize research into Huntington's disease and other hereditary complaints.

After completing her doctorate, Nancy Wexler moved to Columbia University as professor of clinical psychology. Following the death of her mother in 1978, she began to devote more of her time to work on HD. In 1981 she heard from a Venezuelan biochemist, Americo Negrette, of an extended family on the shores of Lake Maracaibo in which HD was rife. Wexler sought to trace the gene through the family tree, which began with Maria Concepcion in about 1800. Of her 9,000 living descendants, Wexler traced 371 with HD and found 1,200 with a 50% chance of contracting the disease and a further 2,400 with a 25% chance. Wexler realized that the material she had gathered could be used to identify the gene responsible for HD.

The key step in this process had been the discovery by Ray White and his colleagues of isolated fragments of DNA that could be used as genetic markers. Blood samples were taken and sent immediately to James Gusella at Massachusetts General Hospital, and he began what he thought would be a lengthy search for the appropriate DNA fragment. But Gusella was extremely lucky and soon identified a fragment that seemed to be linked with HD. Further work established that the gene for HD was located on chromosome number 4.

Wexler and Gusella announced their results in 1983. They continued to home in on the gene and by 1992 had restricted it to a particular stretch of DNA in the chromosome in which a series of three particular bases (the chemicals making up DNA) was repeated. In people without HD there seem to be 11–34 copies of this series, while those affected by HD have 42–86 copies.

Wharton, Edith (1862–1937) *American novelist*

Edith Wharton's best-known works are her novels about the changing face of New York society at the turn of the century. These include *The House of Mirth* (1905), *Ethan Frome* (1911), and *The Age of Innocence* (1920), for which she won the Pulitzer Prize in 1921. In 1930 she was elected a member of the American Academy of Arts and Letters and in 1923 she became the first woman to receive an honorary LittD from Yale.

Born Edith Newbold Jones in New York, a descendant of wealthy and socially prominent New England families, she was educated at home by governesses. In 1885, after her debut in society, she married Edward Wharton, a Boston banker. They spent much time in Europe, moving to France in 1907. The marriage was a disaster, and after her husband's mental breakdown the couple separated and were divorced in 1913. Wharton never remarried. She maintained a residence in the United States but continued to live in France, where she became an important figure in the American expatriate community. During World War I she organized American relief for refugees, running the Children of Flanders Rescue Committee, which helped 600 orphans to escape from Belgium. She received the Cross of the Legion of Honour in 1916 and the Order of Leopold in 1919.

Edith Wharton had written since her lonely and isolated childhood; a book of her verse appeared when she was 16. In the 1890s she began to contribute stories and poems to magazines and by the turn of the century she was publishing short-story collections and novels. Her first popular success came with *The House of Mirth* (1905), which deals with the plight of a young woman who lacks the financial means to maintain her high position in New York society. It was followed by several other novels with similar themes, the most successful of which was *The Age of Innocence*. (In 1993 Martin Scorsese directed a film adaptation of this novel starring Daniel Day-Lewis, Winona RYDER, and Michelle PFEIFFER.) The moral hypocrisy of the New England social world is also explored in her novelette *Ethan Frome*, a stark and tragic story set in an imaginary town reminiscent of the region around Lenox, Massachusetts, where Wharton had often spent her summers. *Ethan Frome* achieved enormous popularity.

Wharton's other novels reveal a wide range of interests. The first, *The Valley of Decision* (1902), had an 18th-century European setting. *The Fruit of the Tree* (1907) treats an American executive's conflicts of love and business, while *Summer* (1917) returns to the New England realism of *Ethan Frome*. She explored Americans in France in *The Reef* (1912) and *The Custom of the Country* (1913); war themes in *The Marne* (1918) and *A Son at the Front* (1923); international manners in *The Glimpses of the Moon* (1922); parent and child relationships in *The Mother's Recompense* (1925), *Twilight Sleep* (1927), and *The Children* (1928); and Midwestern versus New York society in *Hudson River Bracketed* (1929) and its sequel *The Gods Arrive* (1932). Her final novel, *The Buccaneers* (1938), was left unfinished, but has since been adapted for a highly successful British TV series.

Wharton was also a master of the novelette and short story. Besides *Ethan Frome* her novelettes include *Sanctuary* (1903); *Madame de Treymes* (1907), contrasting French and American ideals; and her Old New York series (1924) comprising *False Dawn*, *The Old Maid*, *The Spark*, and *New Year's Day*. Her short-story collections include *The Greater Inclination* (1899), *Crucial Instances* (1924), *The Hermit and the Wild Woman* (1908), *Xingu and Other Stories* (1916), *Here and Beyond* (1926), *Human Nature* (1933), *The World Over* (1936), and *Ghosts* (1937).

Wharton is often compared to another expatriate writer, Henry James. Their work has much in common.

Both depict an orderly mannered world of delicate scruples and quiet heroism, but she pays more attention to the details of social gradation and custom. She was a close friend of James during the last 12 years of his life, a significant period in her own creative development, and sometimes read her work aloud to him for criticism. However, she was no slavish imitator of his and viewed with suspicion his preoccupation with pure artistic technique. At one point, hearing that he was in financial difficulties, she arranged for some of her own royalties to be transferred to his account, handling the transaction so that James never knew, a gesture befitting some of her fictional heroines.

Altogether Wharton wrote some 46 books, including travel books and a critical volume, *The Writing of Fiction* (1925). Her autobiography, *A Backward Glance*, appeared in 1934.

Wheatley, Phillis (*c*. 1753–1784) *African-American poet*

A slave, Phillis Wheatley was acclaimed as a poet in America and in England and even received a favourable mention from Voltaire. Nevertheless, her life ended in tragedy and poverty.

Phillis Wheatley was born in Africa, possibly Senegal, and was brought to Boston as a slave while still a child. There she was bought by John Wheatley, a tailor, as a servant for his wife. In the Wheatley household she learned to read English and the rudiments of Latin and became acquainted with mythology, ancient history, and the contemporary English poets. Beginning to write her first verses when she was 13 years old, she published her first poem in 1770. When she was about 20 years old, she was sent to England with the Wheatley's son Nathanial for her health. She was cordially received and became a popular figure in London society because of her personality and her easy conversation.

The first bound volume of her verse, published in 1773 and dedicated to Selina Hastings, Countess of HUNTINGDON, was *Poems on Various Subjects, Religious and Moral, by Phillis Wheatley, Negro Servant to Mr. John Wheatley of Boston, in New England*. After her return to America she published several poems, including an address to George Washington. In 1778, after the death of the Wheatleys and the granting of her freedom, she married John Peters, a free African American, but the marriage was an unhappy one. She lost touch with her old circle of friends, and two of her three children died. When her husband was imprisoned for debt, Phillis took work as a servant and died alone in poverty in Boston, her last child dying with her.

In 1834 Margaretta M. Odell published the *Memoir and Poems of Phillis Wheatley*, and *The Letters of Phillis Wheatley, the Negro Slave-Poet of Boston* appeared in 1864.

Whitbread, Fatima (1961–) *British athlete*

Whitbread set new records for throwing the javelin in 1985 and 1986 and won the World Championship title the following year. A popular figure, she was voted BBC Sports Personality of the Year, British Sports Writers Sportswoman of the Year, and British Athletics Writers Woman Athlete of the Year in 1987.

Born Fatima Vedad in London, she was abandoned by her parents and raised in a children's home until the age of 12, when she was adopted by Margaret Whitbread, a former British athlete who had competed internationally in javelin throwing. Margaret felt that Fatima could do well in the same sport, despite her comparatively small stature, and trained her for international competition. Fatima's first major success came in 1979, when she won the javelin event at the European Junior Championships. She was voted Woman Athlete of the Year in 1983, after coming second in the World Championships and first in the European Cup, and took the bronze medal in the Olympic Games the following year. Her team-mate Tessa Sanderson, who was to become her closest rival, won the gold.

In 1985 Whitbread broke the women's 76-metre record for javelin throwing, and in 1986 she set a new record of

77.44 metres at the European Athletics Championships. She was consistent in her achievement, regularly exceeding the throw of 69.56 metres that had earned Sanderson the Olympic gold in 1984. After winning the 1987 World Championships, Whitbread had a second attempt at the Olympic title in 1988, but the coveted gold medal still eluded her, and she had to be content with the silver. A series of back and shoulder injuries brought her career in competition to an end, and in the 1990s she became involved with a variety of sporting and other organizations, including Thurrock Harriers Athletic Club and the Eastern Region Sports Council.

White, Antonia (1899–1980) *British novelist and translator*

Antonia White is best remembered for *Frost in May* (1933) and other autobiographical novels.

Antonia Botting was born in London, where her father taught at St. Paul's Girls' School. Her parents, who were fervent Roman Catholics, sent Antonia to a strict convent school in Roehampton, London, where she displayed a precocious literary talent and a strong rebellious streak. When her secret writings about the school and its teachers were discovered, she was expelled. She finished her education at the more liberal St. Paul's Girls' School.

During her twenties Antonia worked variously as a teacher, an actress, and an advertising copywriter. She also made two disastrous short-lived marriages: in each case her husband turned out to be homosexual, and the marriage was annulled without having been consummated. It was during the earlier of these marriages that Antonia suffered the first of the mental breakdowns that would recur throughout her life; in 1920 she was certified insane and confined to an asylum for nine months. A third marriage, to the journalist H. T. Hopkinson, proved more satisfactory and provided the stability that enabled her to complete her first novel, *Frost in May*. This largely autobiographical work (published under the name Antonia White) was praised for its brilliant bitter account of life at a Catholic girls' school in the 1910s. Despite this success, further literary work was held up by recurrent mental problems and the breakdown of her marriage to Hopkinson in 1938.

During the 1930s and 1940s Antonia White worked as a freelance journalist, as the fashion editor of a daily newspaper, and for the BBC. Her remaining novels appeared in the 1950s. Although the central character of these three works has a different name from the heroine of her first novel, *The Lost Traveller* (1950), *The Sugar House* (1952), and *Beyond the Glass* (1954) are effectively sequels to *Frost in May*. They describe the various mental and marital difficulties of one "Clara Batchelor," who is clearly a stand-in for White herself.

In her later years White published books on subjects ranging from her pet cats to her reasons for returning to the Catholic faith of her youth (described in *The Hound and the Falcon*, 1966). She also translated prolifically from French authors, especially COLETTE.

After White's death her daughter Susan Chitty edited a selection from her diaries – writings that present a frank picture of her bohemian lifestyle and numerous love affairs. Chitty also caused controversy with *Now to My Mother*, a bitter memoir in which she accused her mother of neglect and emotional cruelty.

Whitelaw, Billie (1932–) *British actress*

Billie Whitelaw is best known as a stage actress, especially in the plays of Samuel Beckett, although she is also a familiar face on television and in the cinema.

She was born in Coventry and educated at Thornton Grammar School, Bradford. Having begun her career as a child actor on radio, she later worked as assistant stage manager at a provincial theatre. In 1954 she made her London debut in Feydeau's *Hotel Paradiso*. This was followed by the Theatre Workshop's production of *Progress to the Park* (1960), which transferred to the West End in 1961, the revue *England, Our England* (1962), and *A Touch of the Poet* (1962).

Whitelaw subsequently joined the newly formed National Theatre company, with whom she appeared at the Old Vic in her first Beckett work, the one-act *Play* (1964); over the next year she appeared at the Chichester Festival Theatre in *The Dutch Courtesan*, at the Old Vic as Maggie in *Hobson's Choice*, and at Chichester once again in *Trelawney of the 'Wells'*. In 1971 she moved to the Royal Shakespeare Company to play Clare in David Mercer's *After Haggerty*. Her association with Beckett continued in *Not I* (1975), *Footfalls* (1976), *Happy Days* (1979), and *Rockaby* (1981) – all intensely demanding works for a solo (or effectively solo) actress. Beckett is thought to have written the roles in *Footfalls* and *Rockaby* with Whitelaw in mind, though she was embarrassed to hear herself described as one of the leading interpreters of his work. In the 1980s and 1990s she gave lectures on the playwright in Britain and the United States.

Whitelaw's film credits include *No Love for Johnnie* (1961), *The Omen* (1976), *The Dressmaker* (1988), and *Jane Eyre* (1996). She won a British Film Academy award as Albert Finney's ex-wife in *Charlie Bubbles* (1968). On television she has been seen in numerous plays, films, and serials, such as *Lena, O My Lena* (1960), *Sextet* (1972), *Napoleon and Love* (1974), *Jamaica Inn* (1983), *A Murder of Quality* (1991), and *Born to Run* (1997). Her autobiography, *Billie Whitelaw – Who He?* was published in 1995.

Whiteread, Rachel ((1963–   ) *British sculptor*

Whiteread's provocative sculptures and installations have made her one of the best-known of Britain's younger artists.

Whiteread was born in London and educated at Brighton Polytechnic and the Slade School of Art, London. Since 1987 she has exhibited in Britain and overseas, including one-woman shows in London (1988, 1990, 1991, 1994), New York and Barcelona (1992), Paris, Chicago and Berlin (1993), Philadelphia (1995) and Liverpool (1996–97). Her works often make use of everyday objects such as baths, sinks, and beds, and some are on a very large scale indeed – most notably her 'Untitled (Room)' (1993) and 'House', a concrete cast of an entire terraced house that was shown in London from 1993. This unignorable work provoked mixed responses from both critics and the general public, as did the local council's decision to demolish it in 1994. Whiteread was a controversial choice as winner of the Turner Prize in 1993 and a contributor to the Royal Academy's "Sensation" exhibition in 1997.

Whitlock,   Elizabeth   Kemble (1761–1836) *British actress*

Although somewhat overshadowed on the London stage by the brilliant successes of her sister Sarah SIDDONS, Elizabeth Whitlock was herself an accomplished actress who found acclaim in both England and the United States.

Born Elizabeth Kemble in Warrington, north-west England, she was the fifth child of Roger and Sarah Kemble, who ran a well-known touring theatre company. After gaining some stage experience in local towns, she went with her two elder sisters, Sarah Siddons and Frances KEMBLE, to London, where she first appeared at Drury Lane in 1783 as Portia in *The Merchant of Venice*. In 1785 she married Charles Edward Whitlock, a local theatre manager and actor, and seven years later accompanied her husband to the United States, where they performed for many years in the principal cities. Elizabeth Whitlock became the most popular actress of the day in the United States and frequently performed before President Washington and other distinguished persons in Philadelphia.

She returned to England to an enthusiastic reception at Drury Lane in 1807 but retired from the stage shortly afterwards.

Whitney, Anne (1821–1915) *American sculptor*

Anne Whitney received important public commissions for historical figures but is also remembered for works reflecting her lifelong interest in social justice. Notable examples of these include *Lady Godiva* (1864) and *Africa* (1865), which relate to the liberation of women and African Americans, respectively.

Whitney was born in Watertown, Massachusetts, the youngest of seven children. Educated mostly at home, she ran a school in Salem from 1847 to 1849. A keen abolitionist and feminist, she was also a writer, publishing her poems in 1859. Largely self-taught as an artist, she began to sculpt in her thirties. In 1858 she went to study art and sculpture in New York and Philadelphia and anatomy in a Brooklyn hospital.

Whitney first began showing her work in 1860, when she exhibited a marble bust of a child at the National Academy of Design in New York. In 1867 she went to Rome for four years, during which time she studied and travelled extensively, visiting (among other places) Munich and its noted bronze foundry. Her piece *Roma* (1989) personified Roman society as a beggar woman and caused such outrage at the papal court that it had to be moved to France.

On her return to Boston in 1873, Massachusetts commissioned Whitney to create a full-length figure of the patriot Samuel Adams for Statuary Hall in the Capitol, Washington, D.C. Her statues of Leif Ericsson (1887; Boston) and Charles Sumner (1902; Cambridge) are also major works, although the commission for the latter was initially withdrawn when it was realized that the sculptor was a woman. She also created a large marble statue of the English reformer Harriet MAR-TINEAU, which the Boston abolitionist Maria Weston Chapman commissioned in 1878 to represent the emancipation of women (it was on view at Wellesley College, Massachusetts, until 1914, when it was destroyed by a fire). Other important subjects were Lucy STONE, Harriet Beecher STOWE, and Frances WILLARD.

Whitney, Gertrude Vanderbilt
(1875–1942) *American sculptor and patron of the arts*

Gertrude Vanderbilt Whitney founded the Whitney Museum of American Art in 1930 in Greenwich Village, New York, where she had first opened a studio in 1907. It is now housed in a building on Madison Avenue designed by Marcel Breuer.

Gertrude Vanderbilt was born in New York into a wealthy and socially prominent family. Her father was the financier and art patron Cornelius Vanderbilt (1843–99), and her great-grandfather was Commodore Cornelius Vanderbilt (1794–1877), the steamship and railway magnate and philanthropist. In 1896 Gertrude married the financier and sportsman Harry Payne Whitney. She studied sculpture in New York and Paris, where she was inspired by Auguste Rodin.

In 1908 she won her first prize, for a sculpture of *Pan*. During World War I she established a hospital and worked as a nurse. Her feelings of horror for war are expressed in many of her works, including *Victory Arch* (1918–20) and the *Washington Heights War Memorial* (1921), both in New York. Among her other important works are the *Titanic Memorial* (1914–31), which illustrates the words in Revelation 20:13: "The sea gave up its dead," and the terracotta *Aztec Fountain* (1912), both in Washington, D.C.; the *Peter Stuyvesant Memorial* (1936–39) in New York; the *Columbus Memorial* (1928–33) in Palos, Spain; the *St.-Nazaire War Memorial* (1924) in St.-Nazaire, France; *Spirit of Flight*, for the 1939–40 New York World's Fair; and numerous equestrian statues. All her works are striking and inspired by a traditional simplicity. She was equally well known as a sponsor of aspiring artists, and much of her effort and wealth was directed towards developing and encouraging a national artistic taste.

In 1929 Gertrude Whitney offered to donate her collection of about 500 works by modern American artists to the Metropolitan Museum of Art, in the belief that such artists needed recognition. However, the museum's director, a traditionalist, turned her offer down, and she set about establishing her own institution, which was founded in 1930 and opened in November 1931. She also helped fund the Whitney Wing of the American Museum of Natural History in New York.

Wightman, Hazel (1886–1974) *American tennis player*

Hazel Wightman won 47 tennis titles between 1909 and 1954. She also donated a trophy for international women's team competition; Great Britain and the United States began competing for the Wightman Cup in 1923 and have continued ever since.

Hazel Hotchkiss was born near Healdsburg, California, and began playing tennis at the age of 16. She had to get up at dawn to play because the courts were reserved for men after 8 a.m. Entering her first major competition in 1909, she won the national singles title and played in the victorious doubles and mixed-doubles teams. She gained nationwide fame when she repeated this performance in 1910 and 1911. She and her women's doubles partner, Helen WILLS, were never beaten when they played together. They won the Wimbledon doubles in 1924 and the American title six times. In 1919 Hazel won her fourth national singles title.

She married George Wightman and had five children. Hazel Wightman continued to play competitively until she retired from the veterans' competitions at the age of 74. In her book *Better Tennis* (1934) she referred to the game as "a channel of intensified life." She died at Chestnut Hill, Massachusetts.

Wilcox, Ella Wheeler (1850–1919) *American poet*

> Laugh, and the world laughs with
>   you.
> Weep, and you weep alone.
>
> —"Solitude"

Ella Wheeler Wilcox was probably the best-known poet of her day, writing verses that appeared in more than 250 newspapers across the United States.

Ella Wheeler was born in Johnstown Center, Wisconsin, and claimed that she was a descendant of Princess POCA-HONTAS. Encouraged by her mother, she began composing verses even before she could write. By the age of seven Ella was a "professional" poet, having received payment for her poems from the publishers of the magazines in which they appeared. She continued to versify prolifically for the rest of her life, producing at least one or two poems every day, and was soon able to support her family on her income. In 1884 she married the journalist Robert M. Wilcox. The couple travelled widely, using their wealth to indulge their passion for collecting: she collected dolls and necklaces, and he collected musical instruments. Ella also made several visits to Britain, where she had almost as many fans as in the United States; her hard work there during World War I may have contributed to her death from nervous exhaustion.

Wilcox's verses were first published in book form in the collection *Drops of Water* (1872). A later volume, *Poems of Passion* (1883), contained some mildly erotic verses that were condemned by the church but did nothing to affect her popularity. Her simple sentimental poetry, with its message of hope and comfort, touched the hearts of readers of all ages and classes, though it failed to impress the literary critics. Wilcox also wrote novels, short stories, essays, and two autobiographical works: *Story of a Literary Career* (1905) and *The World and I* (1918).

Wilder, Laura Ingalls (1867–1957) *American writer*

Laura Ingalls Wilder is best known as the author of the popular "Little House" series of novels for children, based mainly on her own pioneering experiences between the ages of five and 18.

She was born in Pepin, Wisconsin, and lived on a farm all her life. At 15 she became a teacher to pay for her blind sister's special schooling. A few years after her marriage in 1885 Laura moved to Florida with her husband and daughter, Rose Wilder Lane (who also became a writer). In 1894 the family settled in the Ozark country. There she began to write a newspaper column, "As a Farm Woman Thinks," and was the editor of the *Missouri Ruralist* for 12 years.

It was not until the age of 65, at the suggestion of her daughter, that she began to write her series of novels. The first of her "Little House" novels, *Little House in the Big Woods* (1932), is about the pioneering spirit and frontier life in Wisconsin. It was followed by *Farmer Boy* (1933), based on the early childhood experiences of her husband Almanzo. *Little House on the Prairie* (1935) continues her story into Kansas and is followed by five other novels in chronological sequence: *On the Banks of Plum Creek* (1937), set in the Minnesota wheat country; *By the Shores of Silver Lake* (1939), set in Dakota territory; *Long Winter* (1940), reintroducing the Wilder brothers of *Farmer Boy*; *Little Town on the Prairie* (1941), again in Dakota; *These Happy Golden Years* (1943), based on her experiences of pioneer schoolteaching, which she began at the age of 15, and marriage; and finally *The First Four Years* (1971), which covered the early years of Laura's marriage and was published after her death.

In 1954 the series won a special Newberg-Caldecot Award, and in the 1970s it was adapted for television as "The Little House on the Prairie," a show that also became extremely popular in Britain. In 1954 the American Library Association established the Laura Ingalls Wilder Award for lasting contributions to children's literature.

Wilhelmina (1880–1962) *Queen of the Netherlands*

Queen Wilhelmina's reign, which lasted for 50 years, was characterized by her shrewd and practical judgment. Despite her wish to remain neutral during World War II (as she had during World War I), after the Netherlands was invaded by Germany she headed the Dutch government in exile in England from May 1940 until July 1945.

Wilhelmina Helena Pauline Maria was born in The Hague, the daughter of King William III by his second wife, Emma of Waldeck. On her father's death in 1890 the ten-year-old Wilhelmina became queen under the regency of her mother until she was 18. On September 6, 1898, soon after her 18th birthday, she was crowned at Amsterdam. On February 7, 1901 she married Henry Wladimir Albert Ernst, Duke of Mecklenburg-Schwerin, who died in 1934. Their only child, JULIANA, was born in 1909.

Queen Wilhelmina received popular support in her public activities and respected the powers of Parliament under the constitutional monarchy, maintaining the traditional peace and neutrality of her country until the outbreak of World War II. She oversaw a programme of extensive social reform that was introduced to resolve an economic crisis resulting from World War I. At the same time, the development of industry and foreign trade under Wilhelmina's rule brought prosperity to an expanding population.

After Germany's invasion of the Netherlands on May 10, 1940, Queen Wilhelmina escaped to England with her family and leading government officials. She broadcast constantly to the Netherlands during her exile. In 1942 she visited Canada and the United States, where she addressed a joint meeting of Congress, and the following summer she visited President Franklin D. Roosevelt.

After the invasion of France by Allied armies in 1944 Queen Wilhelmina remained in London until March 1945, when she visited liberated areas of her kingdom and began to apply herself to the problems of reconstruction. Her daughter, Crown Princess Juliana, had by then rejoined her in London after spending a few years in Canada. After the celebration of the 50th anniversary of the queen's reign in 1948 Wilhelmina, exhausted by illness and stress, abdicated in favour of Juliana. Her memoirs, *Lonely but Not Alone*, were published in 1958.

Wilkinson, Ellen (1891–1947) *British politician*

Known as "Red Ellen" (as much for her red hair as her politics), Ellen Wilkinson became the first woman Labour MP when she won a seat for Middlesbrough East in 1924. As the

Labour MP for Jarrow (from 1935), she was one of the leaders of the famous hunger march to London. She was appointed minister for education in 1945.

Ellen Cicely Wilkinson was born in Manchester, the third of four children of a millworker. She was educated with the aid of secondary school scholarships and, after winning a history scholarship, graduated with an MA from Manchester University in 1913. Like her mother and grandmother before her, she became a member of the Manchester and Salford Co-operative Society. In 1912 she joined the Independent Labour Party, becoming an organizer of the National Union of Women's Suffrage Societies in 1913 and of the National Union of Distributive and Allied Workers in 1915. She was also a founder of the Communist Party of Great Britain in 1920. Failing to win a parliamentary seat in 1923, she was elected as a Communist to the Manchester City Council that same year.

After severing her Communist connections and joining the Labour Party, she was elected to Parliament in 1924, retaining her Middlesbrough seat until 1931. In 1939, after the Jarrow hunger march, she published *The Town That Was Murdered*, describing the appalling conditions brought about by unemployment in Jarrow. A passionate critic of the Conservative government's policies on appeasement and unemployment, she also became known for sponsoring a bill to protect hire-purchase buyers.

Wilkinson joined Winston Churchill's wartime coalition government in 1940, first as parliamentary secretary to the ministry of pensions, then as parliamentary secretary to the ministry of home security. After the sweeping Labour Party victory in the general election of 1945 she was appointed by the new prime minister, Clement Attlee, to the post of minister of education, with the job of translating the 1944 Education Act into practical reality. She was a member of the British delegation to the 1945 United Nations Conference in San Francisco. Her writings include *Why War?* (1934) and, with Edward Conze, *Why Fascism?* (1934).

Wilkinson, Jemima (1752–1819)
American religious leader

Jemima Wilkinson, who called herself the "Universal Public Friend," convinced her followers of her own resurrection from the dead.

Born into an affluent Quaker family in Cumberland, Rhode Island, Jemima Wilkinson was powerfully impressed as a girl by the sermons of the Methodist George Whitefield and later by Ann LEE, the founder of the Shakers. During her early twenties, after a severe attack of fever that was followed by a prolonged coma, Jemima claimed that she had been raised from the dead and that her body was occupied by the "Spirit of Life," sent by God to warn the world of his impending wrath. She preached widely throughout Rhode Island and Connecticut and pretended to work miracles. She induced many intelligent people to become her followers, and churches were established by her adherents in Greenwich, Rhode Island, and New Milford, Connecticut. However, she was forced to leave New England when she began to advocate the Shaker practice of celibacy, and some of her disciples claimed that she was the Messiah.

In 1790, accompanied by two "witnesses," Sarah Richards and Rachel Miller, Wilkinson established a colony of Universal Friends at Jerusalem Township in Yates County, New York, near Seneca Lake. She exacted from the group complete submission and the most menial services, her influence over them being practically supreme. When her rules were broken, the punishment that followed often gave rise to dissension. Wilkinson also taught mystical dream interpretation and professed that she was a divine messenger from God, even perhaps that she was Christ reincarnated.

Although she never abandoned her claims, after some years her influence began to wane, she lost her physical beauty, and the latter part of her life was embittered by illness, jealousies, annoyances, and controversies between herself and her followers. She ended her days living alone, away from the other houses in the community. The sect broke up after her death.

Willard, Emma (1787–1870) *American educationalist*

The first woman to prove the value of higher education for women, Emma Willard provided the inspiration for the founding of many high schools for girls and colleges for women. The seminary that she herself founded in 1821 became the Emma Willard School in 1895. In 1854 she represented the United States at the World's Educational Convention in London.

Born Emma Hart in Berlin, Connecticut, into a large and influential family, she attended Berlin Academy from 1802 to 1803. In 1807 she took charge of the Female Academy at Middlebury, Vermont, but left in 1809 to marry Dr. John Willard. Continuing her own studies, she completed the curriculum at the all-male Middlebury College but was not allowed to attend classes or obtain a degree. In 1814 she opened a school for young ladies in her own home, introducing mathematics and philosophy, subjects previously not taught to women.

In 1818, anxious to further the cause of women's education, Willard sent the governor of New York State, DeWitt Clinton, her *Plan for Improving Female Education* (1819) and pleaded for it herself before the state legislature. She asked that state aid be provided for female seminaries and that women be given the same educational opportunities as men. In 1819 she moved her school to Waterford, New York, and in 1821, with the help of local citizens but without state aid, she established the Troy Female Seminary, effectively the first women's college. Here she continued her policy of teaching traditionally "male" subjects, including science. She evolved new methods of teaching geography and history, published many best-selling textbooks, and trained hundreds of teachers whom she sent into the South and West, making her seminary a model in the United States and Europe.

After a trip to Europe in 1830 Willard published a volume of poems (1831), which included "Rocked in the Cradle of the Deep," as well as her *Journal and Letters from France and Great Britain* (1833), the proceeds of which she used to help found a training school for teachers in liberated Greece in 1833. In 1838 she handed the seminary over to her son and his wife and devoted herself to campaigning for improved state schools, travelling widely to demand that women be given equal opportunities as teachers. That same year she married Dr. Christopher Yates (her first husband had died in 1825), but they were divorced in 1843. She continued to publish textbooks, among them *Last Leaves of American History* (1849).

Emma Willard's other published works include *Nineteen Beautiful Years* (1864), a life of her sister; *How to Win: A Book for Girls* (1886); and *Glimpse of Fifty Years* (1889).

Williams, Betty (1943–) *Northern Irish peace activist*

With Mairéad Corrigan, Betty Williams founded the Northern Ireland Peace Movement and shared the Nobel Prize for Peace in 1976.

Born in Belfast, Betty Williams was living there with her husband and two children when she witnessed an incident that sparked off her campaign to end the violence in the province. In 1976 three children from the Maguire family were accidentally killed by a car whose driver had been involved in a terrorist shooting, and the horror-struck Williams immediately began to gather support among her neighbours for a peace movement. Mairéad Corrigan, aunt of the Maguire children, was one of the first to join the campaign, and the following week more than 10,000 Catholics and Protestants came together in a march for peace through Belfast.

The movement spread throughout Northern Ireland and gained support from far and wide, including the United States. A Peace Assembly was set up, with small local groups working within the community. Williams was on the executive committee until

1978 and remained involved with the movement until 1980, travelling around the British Isles and abroad to speak about the Troubles. She was awarded an honorary doctorate from Yale University in 1977. After her first marriage ended in divorce, she married James Perkins in 1982 and settled in Florida.

Williams, Esther (1923–) *American swimmer and film actress*

A former swimming champion, Esther Williams was the star of numerous aquatic MGM musicals and other films of the 1940s and 1950s.

Born in Inglewood, near Los Angeles, Esther Jane Williams showed an early talent for swimming. She would have competed in the 1940 Olympic Games had they not been cancelled because of World War II; instead she joined an aquacade in San Francisco, where she was spotted by a Hollywood talent scout. Her first film appearance, with Mickey Rooney in *Andy Hardy's Double Life* (1942), was followed by a string of films in which her swimming skills were exploited to the full. *Bathing Beauty* (1944), a story about a water pageant at a girls' school, made her a star and a major box-office attraction. Most of her films were romantic or spectacular musicals, such as *Neptune's Daughter* (1949), in which she and Ricardo Montalban sang the Oscar-winning song "Baby, It's Cold Outside," and *Dangerous When Wet* (1953). In the biopic *Million Dollar Mermaid* (1952) she took the part of Annette Kellerman, the Australian swimmer turned actress who pioneered the one-piece bathing costume.

Williams came out of the water to play a more serious role in *The Unguarded Moment* (1956). Her dramatic skills were limited – the comment "Wet she's a star, dry she ain't" has been attributed to various people, including Fanny BRICE, who appeared with Williams in *Ziegfeld Follies* (1945), and the producer Joe Pasternak, who worked on some of her films. After retiring from the cinema in the early 1960s, Williams became a successful businesswoman, designing swimwear and marketing Esther Williams Swimming Pools. In 1967 she married her third husband, the actor Fernando Lamas, who died in 1982.

Williams, Shirley, Baroness (1930–) *British politician*

Shirley Williams was one of the founder members of the Social Democratic Party, which broke away from the Labour Party in 1981; she remained its president until 1988, when it merged with the Liberals.

Shirley Vivien Teresa Brittain was born in Chelsea, London, the daughter of the writer and feminist Vera BRITTAIN and Sir George Catlin, a professor of political science. She was educated in London (apart from a period during World War II when she was evacuated to the United States) and went on to study at Oxford. After a year in New York at Columbia University she returned to Britain and worked as a journalist while trying to gain a seat in Parliament. In 1955 she married her first husband, Bernard Williams, a professor of philosophy.

Shirley Williams had been involved with Labour politics since her teens, when she belonged to the Labour League of Youth. She was elected Labour MP for Hitchin in 1964 and remained in Parliament for the next 15 years. During that time she served in various ministerial positions, including minister of state for the Home Office (1969–70) and secretary of state for education and science (1976–79). She played a major role in the reorganization of the state secondary education system in Britain, campaigning for the replacement of selective grammar and secondary modern schools with comprehensive schools.

When the Conservative Party was returned to power in the general election of 1979, Williams lost her seat in Parliament. After a series of disagreements with the more left-wing elements of the Labour Party she left in 1981 to form the Social Democratic Party (SDP) with three other ex-Labour politicians. With her victory in a by-election later that year she became the new party's first MP, but she lost her seat in 1983. The SDP merged with the Liberal Party to form the Social and Liberal Democrats in 1988; in the same year Williams moved to the United States with her new husband, Harvard professor Richard Neustadt, to become professor of elective politics at the John F. Kennedy School of Government, Harvard. In 1993 she was raised to the peerage as Baroness Williams of Crosby.

Wills, Helen Newington (1905–1988) *American tennis player*

The greatest woman tennis player of her time, she was known as Helen Wills Moody during the years of her marriage to Frederick S. Moody, Jr. She won 31 titles, a record only broken by the Australian player Margaret COURT in the early 1970s.

Helen Wills was born in Centerville, California, the daughter of a doctor who taught her to play tennis. She was educated at the Anna Head School and the University of California and later studied art, exhibiting her work in New York.

She joined the Berkeley Lawn Tennis Club at the age of 14 and entered the National Singles Championships for the first time when she was 16. Although unsuccessful that year, she went on to win the U.S. singles title seven times (1923–25, 1927–29, 1931), the Wimbledon singles eight times, the French singles four times, and the Wightman Cup singles 18 times.

Helen Wills retired from major tournament play in 1938 to spend her time painting. She wrote and illustrated the books *Tennis* (1928) and *Fifteen-Thirty* (1937). In 1939 she married Aidan Roark.

Winchilsea, Anne Finch, Countess of (1660–1720) *British poet*

Anne Finch, Countess of Winchilsea, is remembered for her nature poetry and satirical verses.

Born Anne Kingsmill near Southampton, she was the daughter of a country landowner. Although educated entirely at home, she was clearly a woman of some learning. In 1683 she became a maid of honour to MARY OF MODENA, the second wife of James, Duke of York, the future King James II (from 1685). Interestingly, Anne's fellow maids of honour included Anne Killigrew, another young woman who became known as a poet.

In 1684 Anne married Colonel Heneage Finch, who in 1712 became the Earl of Winchilsea. Following the Glorious Revolution of 1688, in which James II was forced to flee abroad, Anne Finch and her husband left court and settled on their estates in Kent. It was during this period that she began to write poems and verse dramas, which she circulated among friends.

In 1701 Anne Finch found a wider audience when her poem "The Spleen" was printed and received praise from several critics. The poem is a satirical ode describing the symptoms of melancholy, a condition to which she seems to have been prone. During the 1710s she mixed in literary circles, winning the friendship of such leading contemporaries as Alexander Pope and Jonathan Swift. Her chief publication, *Miscellany Poems on Several Occasions*, appeared in 1713.

The Countess of Winchilsea's poems have interested later critics mainly because of their descriptions of nature, which are unusually observant and sensitive for their time. In particular, such poems as "A Nocturnal Reverie" show an awareness of how the observing mind projects its own moods onto the landscape. This aspect of her work was to win special praise from William Wordsworth. Her work also includes a number of lively satirical pieces in which she defends women's rights to education and literary expression and contrasts the liberties allowed to married men with the restrictions imposed on their spouses.

Windsor, Duchess of (1896–1986) *American socialite*

As Mrs. Wallis Simpson, a divorcée, she was the woman for whom King Edward VIII gave up the British throne in 1936 with the historic announcement: "I have found it impossible...to discharge my duties as King as I would wish to do without the help and support of the woman I love."

Bessie Wallis Warfield was born at Blue Ridge Summit, Pennsylvania. Her father died when she was just a few months old, leaving the family with little money, but a wealthy uncle provided for Wallis's education and enabled her to enter Baltimore society in 1914. Although she was not a great beauty, her lively personality and her elegant sense of fashion won her many admirers. In 1916 she married Lieutenant Earl Winfield Spencer, but this first marriage was not a happy one and ended in divorce in 1927. The following year Wallis married Ernest Simpson, an American-born British subject, in England.

The couple set up home in London, and in 1931 Mrs. Simpson was introduced to Edward, Prince of Wales, at a country house party. During the following years the Simpsons were frequent weekend guests at the prince's home. In 1934 Wallis joined Edward and his friends on a Spanish holiday without her husband; it was probably at this time, in her own words, that she and the future king "crossed the line that marks the indefinable boundary between friendship and love." Her second marriage ended in divorce in 1936.

Earlier the same year the Prince of Wales had succeeded his father to the British throne as Edward VIII. His relationship with Wallis was condemned by the royal family and the British government: as a divorcée of common birth, Wallis was not considered to be a fit wife for the new king. Forced to choose between the crown and the woman he loved, Edward abdicated in December 1936 and married the former Mrs. Simpson six months later. They were given the titles Duke and Duchess of Windsor, but they were not welcome at court.

The Windsors lived in France for most of their married life, apart from a period during World War II when the duke served as governor of the Bahamas. After the war they travelled widely in Europe and the United States, and in 1956 Wallis published her memoirs, *The Heart Has Its Reasons*. The Windsors' estrangement from the royal family came to an official end in 1967, when they were invited by Queen ELIZABETH II to attend the unveiling of a memorial to Queen MARY (OF TECK), the duke's mother. Five years later, when Edward was seriously ill and close to death, the queen and the Duke of Edinburgh visited the couple at their Paris home. After Edward's death in 1972 the Duchess of Windsor lived as a recluse.

Winfrey, Oprah (1954–) *American chat-show host, actress, and producer*

With a television talk show watched by millions in more than a hundred countries, Oprah Winfrey was the highest paid entertainer in the United States in 1997. Such was her influence over the viewing public that most of the books she recommended on her book-club slot headed straight for the bestseller lists.

Oprah Winfrey was born in Kosciusko, Mississippi. Her teenage parents were unmarried, and she was raised in poverty by her grandmother. After moving to Milwaukee to live with her mother in the mid 1960s, she was sexually abused and raped by relatives and gave birth to a baby – her only child – at the age of 14. The baby did not live long, and Oprah moved on again, this time to her father's home in Nashville. He insisted that she have a proper education, and she went on to study at Tennessee State University, gaining a BA in speech and performing arts. During this time she began working as a broadcaster, first at a Nashille radio station and then on TV. At the age of 24 she hosted her first chat show at Baltimore's WJZ-TV station, and in 1984 she moved to *A.M. Chicago*. It was there that she discovered the secret of success as a chat-show host – by coming across as everybody's best friend and talking freely about her own problems, she encouraged her guests to open up and talk about themselves.

In 1985 Winfrey made her first appearance on the big screen in the Steven Spielberg movie *The Color Purple*, based on Alice WALKER's novel of that name, and earned an Academy Award nomination for her performance. In the same year her TV talk show was relaunched nationally as *The Oprah Winfrey Show* She became a famous and influential figure, debating controversial topics on daytime television, and established her own production company, Harpo Productions. One of the personal issues Oprah shared with her audience was her obesity: for many years she was seriously overweight, but with a combination of diet and exercise she managed to slim down from over 12 stone (91 kg) to around 7½ stone (55 kg).

Winfrey's other acting credits include the films *Native Son* (1986) and *Throw Momma from the Train* (1987) and a starring role in the American TV mini-series *The Women of Brewster Place* (1989). She has received numerous awards, including three Emmys for her chat show, and has used her great wealth to further the work of a number of charitable causes. Her attempt to help the poor in Chicago, which began in 1994 with the Families for a Better Life Foundation and swallowed nearly $1 million of her own money, ended in failure after two years.

Witt, Katerina (1965–) *German ice skater*

After winning the gold medal at the 1984 Olympic Games in Sarajevo, Katerina Witt became the first female figure skater for 50 years to retain the Olympic title by winning a second gold at the Calgary Olympics in 1988.

Katarina Witt was born in Karl-Marx-Stadt, which was then in East Germany, and began skating at the age of five. Her talent was spotted in the mid 1970s by Jutta Mueller, who coached her for international competition. In 1979 Katarina entered the European championships for the first time and came 14th; by 1983 she had worked her way up to first place, a position she held for six years. During the same period she also won the World Championships four times – in 1984, 1985, 1987, and 1988 – and took the gold medal at the 1984 and 1988 Olympic Games. At that time her career was dependent on her success – the Communist government would support her only as long as she continued winning.

Following the reunification of Germany in 1989, Witt took advantage of her greater freedom to perform professionally in ice shows and on television in the United States and elsewhere. She bought an apartment in New York and won an Emmy Award for her performance in *Carmen on Ice* (1991). After a brief and disappointing return to international competition in the 1994 Olympics at Lillehammer, she went on tour with the ice show *Discover Card Stars on Ice.* In 1996 she took first place in the Legends Championship.

Woffington, Peg (*c.* 1714–1760) *Irish actress*

Peg Woffington was renowned for her beauty and for her portrayal of "breeches parts" (male roles played by actresses). She dominated the stage in London and Dublin from 1740 to 1757. A woman of uncertain temper, she had tempestuous relationships with many other actresses, one of whom she actually stabbed during a performance.

Born Margaret Woffington in Dublin, she first appeared on the stage at the age of ten in a children's production of *The Beggar's Opera.* Her role in this play attracted attention and launched her career as an actress. She went on to appear in Dublin's Smock Alley Theatre, where she played Ophelia in *Hamlet* and Silvia in *The Recruiting Officer.* In 1740 she moved to London, where she took the part of Sir Harry Wildair in George Farquhar's *The Constant Couple* at Covent Garden. It was phenomenally successful. She also played opposite David Garrick in many leading roles there and was openly acknowledged as his mistress.

Peg Woffington was particularly admired in such comic roles as Millimant in Congreve's *The Way of the World* and Lady Betty Modish in Colley Cibber's *The Careless Husband*, but the audiences preferred her male impersonations. She continued to star at Drury Lane until 1746, then spent seven years in Dublin (1747–54) before returning to London to perform at Covent Garden. On May 3, 1757, she collapsed during a performance of *As You Like It*, in which she was playing Rosalind. Amid thunderous applause she left the stage, never to return. She died three years later, the same year as her *Memoirs* were published.

Wolf, Christa (1929–) *German writer*

Many of Christa Wolf's novels and short stories were inspired by the political situation in East Germany and examine the effect that totalitarian systems of government have on the individual. In 1964 she received the National Prize for Art and Literature of the German Democratic Republic.

Christa Wolf was born in Landsberg (now Gorzów in Poland). She grew up in Nazi Germany and the aftermath of World War II, later studying at the universities of Leipzig and Jena. After graduation she worked as an editor and critic on various literary journals and other publications. She made her name as a writer in her homeland with such novels as *Moskauer Novelle* (1961; Moscow Novella); *Der geteilte Himmel* (1963; *Divided Heaven*, 1976), about an East German woman whose lover moves to West Berlin; and *Nachdenken über Christa T.* (1968; *The Quest for Christa T.*, 1982), which was initially banned because of its central theme of disillusionment. However, her work was little known in the outside world until the 1970s, when her novels began to be translated into English.

Wolf's other writings include a collection of critical essays, *Lesen und Schreiben* (1972; *The Reader and the Writer*, 1978), and several short-story collections, such as *Unter den Linden* (1974; Under the Linden). The internationally successful *Kassandra* (1983; published in English as *Cassandra*, 1984) combined a short novel with a series of essays on feminist themes. The novel *Kindheitsmuster* (1976), published in English as *A Model Childhood* (1982), is partly autobiographical, being inspired by her own early years. Following the collapse of the East German regime, Wolf published *Was bleibt* 1989; What Remains), a memoir describing her harassment by the state authorities.

Wollstonecraft, Mary (1759–1797) *British writer and pioneer of the women's rights movement*

> The *divine right* of husbands, like the divine right of Kings, may, it is hoped, in this enlightened age, be contested without danger.
>
> —*A Vindication of the Rights of Woman* (1792)

Mary Wollstonecraft is best known as the author of *A Vindication of the Rights of Woman*, which argued for equal opportunities for both sexes in education and society.

Born at Hoxton, near London, Mary had an unhappy childhood. Her father was an alcoholic and a wife beater, and she had little education. After working for two years as a lady's companion, she became a teacher in a school she established with her sister Eliza and a childhood friend, Fanny Blood. She then spent a year in Ireland as a governess. These experiences inspired her *Thoughts on the Education of Daughters* (1787), which was published by the radical London publisher Joseph Johnson and gave her access to a London circle of literary and radical figures, including Thomas Paine, William Blake, and William Godwin. Johnson employed her as a translator and continued to publish her work, including *Mary (A Fiction)* (1788), *The Female Reader* (1789), and *A Vindication of the Rights of Man* (1790), her reply to Edmund Burke's *Reflections on the French Revolution.*

In 1792 Wollstonecraft went to Paris to witness the aftermath of the French Revolution at first hand. Her observations were published in her *Historical and Moral View of the French Revolution* (1794). While in Paris she met Gilbert Imlay, an American émigré writer with whom she had an affair that led to the birth of a daughter, Fanny, in 1794. She returned to England with Imlay, but his infidelity caused her to attempt suicide. She nevertheless found brief happiness with the radical philosopher William Godwin, whom she married in March 1797. She died in London in September of that year, shortly after giving birth to a daughter, Mary, the future wife of Percy Bysshe Shelley and, as Mary SHELLEY, the author of *Frankenstein* (1818).

Mary Wollstonecraft's major work was *A Vindication of the Rights of Woman* (1792), now regarded as one of the earliest feminist classics. Many of its ideas, such as the opening of the professions to women, were shocking to her contemporaries and were linked by her critics to her unconventional lifestyle. By demonstrating the equality of the sexes and demanding equal education, she hoped to bring forward the day when the relationship of women to men might be a "rational fellowship instead of slavish obedience."

Wood, Mrs. Henry (1814–1887)
British novelist

A prolific writer who was also a devout and deeply conservative Anglican Christian, Mrs. Henry Wood is now best remembered for her second novel, *East Lynne* (1861). It became a bestseller and by 1900 had sold more than 500,000 copies. Since then it has often been dramatized and has also been translated into many languages.

She was born Ellen Price in Worcester, the daughter of a prosperous glove manufacturer. From her girlhood she suffered from curvature of the spine, which made her a partial invalid and required her to be educated at home. After she married Henry Wood, a banker and consular official, in 1836, she lived on the French Riviera for most of the following 20 years. She began her literary career by contributing stories to *Bentley's Miscellany* and the *New Monthly Magazine*.

In 1860 Mrs. Wood returned to England with her husband and settled in Norwood, south of London. She published almost 50 volumes of fiction; the most popular of her early novels were *East Lynne*, *Mrs. Halliburton's Troubles* (1862), and *The Channings* (1862). In 1867 she became editor and proprietor of *Argosy* magazine, in which her "Johnny Ludlow" stories appeared. Of her later novels *Within the Maze* (1872) and *Edina* (1876) were the most popular. Mrs. Wood's works owed their popularity to their ingeniously melodramatic plots and their vivid depiction of character.

Wood, Victoria (1953–) *British comedienne and writer*

Victoria Wood's sharply observed humour and cheerful personality made her a popular figure on British television in the 1980s and 1990s. In 1995 she received a British Comedy Award as Top Female Comedy Performer.

Victoria Wood was born in Prestwich, near Manchester. While she was a drama student at Birmingham University, she made her first broadcasts on local radio and television, singing comic songs she had written herself. In 1975 she appeared on the television talent show, *New Faces*, and the following year she was given a regular spot as one of the comic turns on the Esther RANTZEN consumer programme *That's Life*. She teamed up with Julie WALTERS for the television comedy series *Wood and Walters* (1981–82), and in 1985 she made her first solo series, *Victoria Wood – As Seen on TV*. This was followed by a number of award-winning TV series and specials, such as *An Audience with Victoria Wood* (1988) and *Victoria Wood's All Day Breakfast* (Christmas, 1992). Most of her shows combine stand-up monologues and sketches (often featuring Walters and other regulars, such as the actresses Celia Imrie and Susie Blake) with the occasional comic song. The main subjects of her humour are incidents from everyday life and such popular institutions as package holidays, health farms, chat shows, and soap operas.

As well as originating most of the material for her shows, Wood has also written stage plays and television screenplays, including *Talent* (1978) and *Happy Since I Met You* (1981). In 1994 she wrote and costarred with Julie Walters in a film for television, *Pat and Margaret*. Her books include *Up to You, Porky* (1985), *Barmy* (1987), *Mens Sana in Thingummy Doodah* (1990), and *Chunky* (1996). In 1980 she married the magician Geoffrey Durham. She was appointed an OBE in 1997.

Woodward, Joanne (1930–) *American actress*

Woodward starred in many films of the 1950s and 1960s, sometimes with her husband Paul Newman, and has remained a familiar face in the cinema and on television. She also became known as a social and political activist, who campaigned for a variety of causes. In 1990 she received the New York Critics' Award for Best Actress, as well as an Oscar nomination, for her portrayal of a discontented lawyer's wife in the film *Mr. & Mrs. Bridge*.

Joanne Woodward was born in Thomasville, Georgia, and began her career as a stage and television actress. In 1955 she made her film debut in the Western *Count Three and Pray*. Her performance in *The Three Faces of Eve* (1957), as a woman suffering from a multiple personality disorder, earned her an Academy Award for Best Actress. In *The Long Hot Summer* (1958), based on a story by William Faulkner, she costarred with Paul Newman, whom she married the same year. Their marriage was to become one of the most durable in show business, spanning four decades during which they frequently appeared on screen together.

Woodward's films of the 1960s include *The Stripper* (1963), *A Fine Madness* (1966), and *Rachel, Rachel* (1968). In the last of these, directed by her husband, she gave a moving Oscar-nominated performance as an unmarried schoolteacher. *Summer Wishes, Winter Dreams* (1973), in which she played a middle-aged housewife devastated by the sudden death of her mother, brought her another Academy Award nomination. This was followed by four more films with Newman: *The Drowning Pool* (1975), *Harry and Son* (1984), *The Glass Menagerie* (1987) – in which her husband remained on the director's side of the camera – and *Mr. & Mrs. Bridge* (1990), with the famous couple in the title roles. From the mid 1970s onwards Woodward was also seen in a number of TV movies, winning Emmys for *See How She Runs* (1978) and *Do You Remember Love* (1985).

Woolf, Virginia (1882–1941) *British writer*

> I do not believe that she wrote one word of fiction which does not put out boundaries a little way; one book which does not break new ground and form part of the total experiment.

> —Susan Hill, *The Daily Telegraph*,
> May 5, 1974

> It would be a thousand pities if women wrote like men, or lived like men, or looked like men, for if two sexes are quite inadequate, considering the vastness and variety of the world, how should we manage with one only? Ought not education to bring out and fortify the differences rather than the similarities?
>
> —*A Room of One's Own* (1929)

> If you do not tell the truth about yourself you cannot tell it about other people.
>
> —*The Moment and Other Essays* (1947)

Virginia Woolf was a central figure in the so-called Bloomsbury Group – an informal association of writers and artists who first met during the 1900s in London's Bloomsbury district and strove to explore new freedoms both in personal relationships and in art. In 1917 she and her husband, the writer Leonard Woolf, founded the Hogarth Press. Her own novels, notably *Mrs. Dalloway* (1925), *To the Lighthouse* (1927), and *The Waves* (1931), are highly innovative in style and structure.

Born Adeline Virginia Stephen in London, the second daughter of the writer Sir Leslie Stephen and Julia Duckworth, she was 13 when her mother died. She was educated through "the free run of a large and unexpurgated library," owned by her father. When he died in 1904, she moved, together with her sister Vanessa, a painter (see BELL, VANESSA), and her brothers Adrian and Thoby, to Gordon Square, Bloomsbury. The first of her many reviews for *The Times Literary Supplement* appeared in 1905. The death of her brother Thoby in 1906 was a further shock to her delicate health, already affected by the death of her parents. In 1907 she settled in Fitzroy Square, London, with her brother Adrian after her sister had married the art critic Clive Bell. The meetings of the Bloomsbury Group began at this time. Its members included Clive and Vanessa Bell, the writers Lytton Strachey and E. M.

Forster, the art critic Roger Fry, and the economist J. M. Keynes. It was in this environment that Virginia started to formulate the critical ideas and theories that so influenced her creative career. In 1912 she married Leonard Woolf, and together they launched the Hogarth Press, which was to publish some of the most interesting literature of the 20th century, including the works of T. S. Eliot and Katherine MANSFIELD as well as Virginia's own novels.

The Woolfs divided their time between London and the house they had bought at Rodmell in Sussex. Virginia's first novel, *The Voyage Out* (1915), is comparatively conventional and autobiographical. However, her second novel, *Night and Day* (1919), reveals her growing tendency to describe the "arrows of sensation striking strangely through the envelope of personality which shelters us so conveniently from our fellows." This approach is further developed in the impressionistic study of a talented young man's world, *Jacob's Room* (1922), and in *Mrs. Dalloway*, which presents a complex picture of life through the thought and action of a single day in London. Virginia's next novel, *To the Lighthouse*, often considered her finest, is set on the Isle of Skye in Scotland but draws on her childhood memories of summers spent with her family in St. Ives in Cornwall. In it she makes extensive use of a stream of consciousness technique – recording the flow of thoughts and feelings as they pass through her characters' minds. After the extravagant fantasy biography *Orlando* (1928), a remarkable work deriving from her love for Vita SACKVILLE-WEST, and the symbolism of *The Waves* (1931) her creative urge declined. *The Years* (1937) is more traditional in technique.

In addition to her novels Virginia Woolf produced a great variety of other work – short stories, criticism, and biography – despite recurring bouts of depression, which had begun early in life after her mother's death. Her best critical essays are contained in *The Common Reader* (1925; second series, 1932). *A Room of One's Own*

(1929) and *Three Guineas* (1938) are feminist classics. Her other works include *Flush* (1933), a fanciful biography of Elizabeth Barrett BROWNING's dog, and *Roger Fry* (1940), a friendly tribute.

In the end Virginia could no longer cope with her depression, made worse by the oppressive news of World War II. She committed suicide by drowning herself in the river running close to her Sussex home. Leonard Woolf wrote movingly about his relationship with her in his autobiography and edited several volumes of her criticism, published after her death. He also printed her final novel, *Between the Acts* (1941) and a collection of short stories, *A Haunted House* (1943). Her letters and journals appeared in a series of volumes during the 1970s and 1980s.

Woolsey, Sarah Chauncey
(1835–1905) *American writer*

Sarah Chauncey Woolsey is best known under her pen name, Susan Coolidge, as the author of popular stories for girls, notably *What Katy Did* (1872) and its sequels *What Katy Did at School* and *What Katy Did Next*. These books describe the adventures and trials of their heroine in a natural unsentimental style.

Born in Cleveland, Ohio, she grew up in a comfortable home there before moving with her family to New Haven, Connecticut, where her uncle, Theodore Dwight Woolsey, was president of Yale. After her father's death in 1870, she began to write verse and prose under her pen name. Her first girls' novel, *The New Year's Bargain* (1871), was followed over the next two decades by the "Katy" series and other popular stories.

In addition to her girls' story books Woolsey published three volumes of verse (1880, 1889, 1906), wrote *A Short History of the City of Philadelphia* (1887), and edited numerous literary papers and letters. She died in Newport, Rhode Island.

Wootton, Barbara, Baroness
(1897–1988) *British social scientist*

Barbara Wootton made major contributions to academic life at a time when there were few openings for gifted intelligent women like herself; she went on to become a prominent public figure.

Barbara Frances Adam was born into an intellectual family in Cambridge. Her father, the son of a Scottish farm worker, had graduated in classics from Cambridge University and was a tutor there until his death in 1907. Her mother was also a classicist and encouraged Barbara to embark on a university course in the same subject. Barbara dutifully followed her mother's wishes but eventually abandoned Greek and Latin to take a degree in economics. In 1917 she married Jack Wootton, a research student, but he died in World War I just five weeks after their wedding. The early loss of her father and her husband, as well as a schoolfriend and a brother, contributed to Barbara's rejection of religion in later life.

Having graduated from Girton College, Cambridge, in 1919, Wootton returned to Cambridge the following year as director of social studies and lecturer in economics. In 1922 she joined the research department of the Labour Party and the Trades Union Congress, and from 1927 to 1944 she was director of studies for adult education at the University of London. Her second husband, George Percival Wright, whom she married in 1935, was persistently unfaithful to her, but they remained together for nearly 30 years until he died from cancer.

In 1948 Wootton became professor of social studies at the University of London, and from 1950 to 1956 she was a governor of the BBC. In 1958 she was raised to the peerage as Baroness Wootton of Abinger and took her place in the House of Lords. As a socialist, she disagreed in principle with the existence of the upper chamber, but she respected the antiquity of the institution, commenting: "no one in his senses would invent the present house if it did not already exist...but... ancient monuments are not light-heartedly to be destroyed."

Wootton wrote or contributed to many academic texts, notably *Lament for Economics* (1938), *Freedom under Planning* (1945), *Social Science and So-cial Pathology* (1959), and *Crime and the Criminal Law* (1963). Towards the end of her career she was regarded as an authority on social work and the criminal justice system; in her seventies she served on advisory councils for the penal system (1966–74) and the misuse of drugs (1971–74).

Wordsworth, Dorothy (1771–1855)
British diarist

Devoted to her brother, the poet William Wordsworth, Dorothy served as his housekeeper-companion both before and after his marriage to Mary Hutchinson in 1802. He called her the "sister of my soul" (in *The Prelude*, XIII), and her *Grasmere Journal* was a direct inspiration to him for such poems as "Daffodils" and "Resolution and Independence."

Dorothy Wordsworth was born in Cockermouth, Cumberland, but was sent away to live with a succession of relatives after her mother's death in 1778. In 1795 a legacy enabled William to take a house at Racedown in Dorset, which he shared with Dorothy. There they met the poet Samuel Taylor Coleridge and in 1797 moved to live nearer to him, beginning a long and close friendship. The period between 1798 and 1799 was spent in Germany before they finally settled at Grasmere in the Lake District.

Dorothy is a prominent figure in many of William's poems, including "Tintern Abbey" and *The Prelude*, and is the probable original of his "Lucy" and "Emma." It was she who sustained him during his period of breakdown following the failure of his hopes for political revolution, which he writes about in *The Prelude* (X).

Although William printed a few of Dorothy's poems with his own, her talent found its fullest expression in her journals. The most elaborate is *Recollections of a Tour Made in Scotland* (1874), which she started soon after returning from a tour with her brother and Coleridge in September 1803 and finished in May 1805. Her miscellaneous diaries kept at Alfoxden (January to May 1798) and Grasmere (May to December 1800, October 1801 to January 1803) range from mere trivia to exquisite descriptions of light, lake-water, and the wild flowers growing on the hillsides; these are interspersed with lively observations of country life and country people and poignant personal comments. Dorothy's journals were first published 30 years after her death. She was also an excellent letter writer.

In April 1829 she became ill (it is possible she had a nervous breakdown) and never quite recovered, becoming increasingly confused and agitated. The shock of William's death in 1850 brought about a period of relative calm before her own death five years later.

Workman, Fanny (1859–1925) *American explorer and mountaineer*

With her cycling, her sensible clothes, and her belief in women's suffrage, Fanny Workman personified the "New Woman" at the turn of the 20th century. In 1906 she established an altitude record for women of 23,300 feet on one of the peaks of Nunkun in Kashmir.

Born Fanny Bullock, in Worcester, Massachusetts, the daughter of Governor Alexander Hamilton Bullock, she married a prominent physician, William Hunter Workman, in 1881. Between 1895 and 1899 they undertook several cycling tours in Europe, North Africa, and the Far East, which they then wrote about in such books as *Sketches Awheel in Fin de Siècle Iberia* (1897) and *Through Town and Jungle: 14,000 Miles Awheel among the Temples and Peoples of the Indian Plain* (1904), which were illustrated with their photographs. From 1899 to 1912 they explored and mapped parts of the Himalaya and Karakoram ranges, making several first ascents of peaks over 20,000 feet.

The Workmans collaborated on other books describing their travels, notably *Ice-Bound Heights of the Mustagh* (1908), *Peaks and Glaciers of Nun Kun* (1909), *The Call of the Snowy Hispar* (1910), and *Two Summers in the Ice Wilds of Eastern Karakoram* (1917). Fanny Workman also gave many lectures about her travels and in November 1905 was the first woman to address the Royal Geographical Society since Isabella BISHOP, the British explorer, in 1897.

Wray, Fay (1907–) *American film actress*

Chiefly remembered as the screaming heroine of *King Kong* (1933), Fay Wray starred in a number of other films of the 1930s and made a brief comeback as a character actress in the 1950s.

Fay Wray was born in Alberta, Canada, grew up in Los Angeles, and made her screen debut in 1919. After playing minor roles for several years, she costarred with director Erich Von Stroheim in the silent film *The Wedding March* (1928). This was followed by an early silent version of *The Four Feathers* (1929) and a Western, *The Texan* (1930), with Gary Cooper. In the early 1930s Wray began to be cast in horror films, such as *Doctor X* (1931), *The Most Dangerous Game* (1932), and *The Vampire Bat* (1933). Most of these films are long forgotten, but the classic original version of *King Kong* (1933) has lived on (even after the inferior 1976 remake). Its spectacular special effects included shots of Wray screaming and writhing in the hand of the giant ape at the top of the Empire State Building, and this image was to remain with her forevermore: as she later commented, "At the premiere of *King Kong* I wasn't too impressed... I didn't realize then that King Kong and I were going to be together for the rest of our lives, and longer."

Wray's other films of the 1930s include the costume drama *The Affairs of Cellini* (1934), *The Clairvoyant* (1935), with Claude Rains, and *Murder in Greenwich Village* (1937). She retired from the cinema in 1942 but returned in the 1950s to appear in such films as *Small Town Girl* (1953), *Queen Bee* (1955), and *Crime of Passion* (1956). After her second retirement in 1958 she made just one television appearance, in the TV movie *Gideon's Trumpet* (1980). In 1989 she published her autobiography, *On the Other Hand*. She also wrote a number of plays and stories.

Wright, Frances (1795–1852) *Scottish-born American social reformer*

> The prejudices still to be found in Europe...which would confine...female conversation to the last new publication, new bonnet, and *pas seul* are entirely unknown here. The women are assuming their places as thinking beings.
>
> —*Views of Society and Manners in America* (1821)

Following the publication of her book *Views of Society and Manners in America* (1821), Frances Wright became a close friend of the French general, the Marquis de Lafayette, who fought against the British in the American Revolution, and she and her sister Camilla accompanied him on his triumphal tour of the United States in 1824–25. Afterwards Frances was determined to work at the problem of slavery in the United States; she was also active in the causes of women's rights, education, and reform.

Frances (known as Fanny) Wright was born in Dundee, Scotland. Her parents died when she was two years old, and she became heir to a substantial fortune. She was educated in London and then returned to Scotland. Wright first visited the United States with her sister in 1818–20; having decided to settle there, she bought a few slaves and 2,000 acres of woodland, which she called Nashoba, in western Tennessee. She was not an immediate abolitionist but hoped to demonstrate that slaves could use their labour to buy their freedom (ultimately, perhaps, to set up colonies outside the United States) while their children were being schooled for liberty. Her *Plan for the Gradual Abolition of Slavery* (1825) won the approval of Thomas Jefferson and James Madison. She was also impressed by the socialist community in New Harmony, Indiana, started by Robert Owen and his son Robert Dale Owen; she therefore resolved to make Nashoba a co-operative community. However, one of her radical recruits published a report that Nashoba advocated free love and racial interbreeding; the scandal had little basis, but it destroyed the community. Wright eventually settled her slaves in Haiti.

Meanwhile, she had become America's first woman lecturer, denouncing the influence of the church in politics and demanding rights for women and workers. With Robert Dale Owen she edited the *Free Enquirer* in New York (1829–30), which opposed imprisonment for debt and proposed free public education. In this paper Wright also advocated birth control, which the public found particularly scandalous; mobs threatened her, and the newspapers attacked her. Nevertheless, the "Fanny Wrighters" polled 6,000 votes in the New York election of 1829. She also published her *Course of Popular Lectures* and joined the Working Men's Club.

From 1829 to 1835 Fanny Wright lived in Europe. After Camilla's death in 1831 she married Guillaume Phiquepal D'Arusmont, a Frenchman who had worked with her in the United States. Her return to lecturing in the United States in 1835 led to the break-up of her marriage, but she nevertheless embarked on a lecture tour, speaking out against monopolies, the banking system, and slavery. She also wrote for the Boston *Investigator* and became the editor of the *Manual of American Principles*. After 1838 she became still more controversial, returning to the subject of birth control as well as advocating equal distribution of property and the social and legal emancipation of women. She died in Cincinnati, Ohio, after breaking her hip in a fall.

Wright, Judith (1915–) *Australian poet*

> Brought up in a landscape once of extraordinary beauty, but despised by its settlers because of its unfamiliarity, I have I suppose been trying to expiate a deep sense of guilt over what we have done to the country, to its first inhabitants of all kinds, and are still and increasingly doing.
>
> —Describing an important source of inspiration for her work

Judith Wright's love and concern for the natural heritage of Australia is reflected in her poems, essays, and other writings. She was awarded the Queen's Medal for Poetry in 1993.

Judith Arundell Wright was born in New South Wales and grew up in a rural sheep-farming area. After studying at Sydney University, she travelled around Europe for a year, returning to Australia in 1938 to work as a secretary. In the early 1940s she moved to the mountains of Queensland, where she found inspiration for her poetry. Her first collection, *The Moving Image*, was published in 1946. She continued to write poetry and essays, lectured occasionally at Australian universities, and became an active conservationist. Her subsequent volumes of poetry include *Woman to Man* (1949), *The Gateway* (1955), *Birds* (1962), *The Other Half* (1966), *Alive* (1973), *The Double Tree* (1978), *Journeys* (1982), *A Human Pattern* (1990), and *Collected Poems 1942–1985* (1994). She also wrote about other poets and their verse in such works as *Charles Harpur* (1963) and *Preoccupations in Australian Poetry* (1965). In 1956 she edited *A Book of Australian Verse* for Oxford University Press; a revised edition was published in 1968.

Wright's research into Australian history, including her own family background and the effect that her pioneering ancestors had on the Aboriginal way of life, emerges in such works as *The Generations of Men* (1959), *The Cry for the Dead* (1981), *We Call for a Treaty* (1985), and *Born of the Conquerors* (1991). Among her other writings are the collection of short stories *The Nature of Love* (1966), essays on environmental issues, and four books for children. In the 1970s she was president of the Wildlife Preservation Society of Queensland, and in the 1980s she became involved with the peace movement and with organizations supporting the rights of Australian Aborigines.

Wrinch, Dorothy (1894–1976) *American mathematician and biochemist*

Dorothy Wrinch was one of the many scientists who, in the 1930s, sought to find a chemical model for the passing on of genetic information from one generation to the next. Although the model she devised was not correct, it was a positive step towards the discovery of genetics.

Wrinch was born at Rosario in Argentina of British parents and educated at Cambridge University, where she held a research fellowship from 1920 to 1924. She then taught physics at Oxford until 1939, when she moved to the United States to take up an appointment as lecturer in chemistry at Johns Hopkins University. In 1942 she moved to Smith College, Massachusetts, where she remained until her retirement in 1959.

In 1934 Wrinch tackled the important problem of identifying the chemical carriers of genetic information. In common with other scientists at that time, she argued that chromosomes consisted of sequences of amino acids; these were the only molecules thought to possess sufficient variety to permit the construction of complex molecules. She proposed a model of the gene in the form of a T-like structure with a nucleic-acid stem and a sequence of amino acids as the cross bar.

In fact many such models were proposed in the 1930s. If it was not accepted that genes consisted of specific sequences of amino acids, then it became very difficult to visualize what they could consist of. The trouble with all these models was that the experimentalists quickly found serious defects in them. Thus W. Schmidt in 1936 was able to show that Wrinch's model was incompatible with the known optical properties of nucleic acid and the chromosomes. The first suggestion that there might be an alternative to the protein structure of the gene came with the famous experiment of Oswald Avery in 1944.

Wu, Chien-Shiung (1912–1997) *Chinese-born American physicist*

An outstanding experimental physicist, Chien-Shiung Wu overcame the traditional Chinese reluctance to permit women to take part in higher education. She was greatly respected by many of the leading American physicists of the 20th century.

Wu, who was born in Shanghai, gained her BSc from the National Central University of China before moving to the United States in 1936. There she studied under Ernest O. Lawrence at the University of California, Berkeley. She gained her PhD in 1940 then went on to teach at Smith College, Massachusetts, and later at Princeton University. In 1946 she became a member of staff at Columbia University, where she advanced to become professor of physics in 1957.

Her first significant research work was on the mechanism of beta disintegration (electron emission in radioactive decay). In particular, she demonstrated in 1956 that the direction of emission of the electrons is strongly correlated with the direction of spin of the emitting nucleus, showing that parity is not conserved in beta disintegration (i.e., more than half the electrons can spin in one direction). This experiment confirmed the theories advanced by Tsung Dao Lee of Columbia and Chen Ning Yang of Princeton that in the so-called "weak" nuclear interactions the previously held "law of symmetry" was violated. Yang and Lee later received the Nobel prize for physics for their theory, and the discovery overturned many central ideas in physics.

In 1958 Richard Feynman and Murray Gell-Mann proposed the theory of conservation of vector current in beta decay. This theory was experimentally confirmed in 1967 by Wu, in collaboration with two other Columbia University physicists.

Wu's other contributions to particle physics include her demonstration that the electromagnetic radiation from the annihilation of positrons and electrons is polarized – a finding in accordance with Dirac's theory, proving that the electron and positron have opposite parity. She also undertook a study of the x-ray spectra of muonic atoms. Later in her life she became interested in biological problems, especially the structure of haemoglobin (the pigment of red blood cells).

Chien-Shiung Wu was married to another Chinese physicist who had emigrated to the United States, Yuang Chia-liu (who later Americanized his name to Luke Yuan).

Wu Zhao (625–705) *Chinese empress*

Wu Zhao ruled the vast Chinese empire for 50 years, first as Emperor Gao Zong's wife and then as China's first female sovereign. During this period she brought peace, prosperity, and unity to the country.

Wu Zhao was just 13 or 14 years old when she was called to the palace of Emperor Tai Zong and became one of his young concubines. When Tai Zong died in 649, the new emperor, Gao Zong, allowed Wu Zhao to remain at the palace because he had fallen in love with her. After giving birth to Gao Zong's son, Wu Zhao took the place of his chief wife, who had borne him no children, and became empress. Throughout the remainder of Gao Zong's reign she was a powerful influence at court, and all those who opposed her or stood in the path of her ambition were either removed from office or killed. The emperor, weakened by illness in 660, gave her a free hand in running the country, and she played a major role in the conquest of Korea.

In 683 Gao Zong died and was succeeded by his eldest son, Zhong Zong. Fearing that her authority would be weakened, Wu Zhao deposed Zhong and made his younger brother Rui Zong the official emperor. After continuing to govern through Rui for some years, she finally claimed the throne for herself in 690 and ruled the country until her death. Her long reign saw the introduction of a number of social reforms, including greater freedom for women and better care for the sick. She was also a patron of the arts and literature and was responsible for the building of many magnificent pagodas and temples.

Wylie, Elinor Morton (1885–1928) *American poet and novelist*

During the 1920s Elinor Wylie established herself as a poet and novelist of sensitivity and elegance.

Born Elinor Hoyt in Somerville, New Jersey, she was educated at the Baldwin School, Pennsylvania, and the Holton Arms School, Washington, D.C. In 1905 she married Philip Hichborn but five years later she eloped with Horace Wylie, whom she married in 1916. The Wylies were divorced in 1923, and Elinor then married William Rose Benét, the poet and critic.

Apart from *Incidental Numbers*, which was published anonymously in 1912, Elinor Wylie's main work consists of nine books – four novels and five volumes of verse – in which she made wide use of the lore of history and literature. Well acquainted with the work of 17th-century metaphysical poets, Wylie was also familiar with the earlier Scottish, Irish, and English ballads; she sang these – as well as her own verses – to tunes that she composed herself. Her *Nets to Catch the Wind* (1921) is a collection of poems about animals and birds.

Wylie's first novel, *Jennifer Lorn* (1923), set amongst the Anglo-Indian aristocracy of the 18th century, was immediately recognized as possessing a rare and delicate satire. Her collection of poems *Black Armor* appeared that same year. Her second novel, *The Venetian Glass Nephew* (1925), is a fable of the marriage of Christian art and pagan nature; while her third, *The Orphan Angel* (1926; British title *Mortal Image*, 1927), explores the fantasy that Percy Bysshe Shelley was rescued by an American ship instead of drowning off the coast of Italy. Shelley's subsequent adventures on the American frontier give Wylie scope for witty and sensitive analysis of both the poet and the times. In *Mr. Hodge and Mr. Hazard* (1928) she describes England after the deaths of Shelley and Byron.

Wylie's final volumes of verse were *Trivial Breath* (1928), the posthumous *Angels and Earthly Creatures* (1929), which includes the interesting sonnet sequence "One Person," and *Last Poems* (1943). She died in New York. After her death her husband edited her *Collected Poems* (1932) and *Collected Prose* (1933) and wrote a brief critical study of her work, *The Poetry and Prose of Elinor Wylie* (1934).

Wylie, Ida Alexa Ross (1885–1959)
British writer

Wylie's novels, with their mainly political themes, show her understanding of the national and social characteristics of her time.

Wylie was born in Melbourne, Australia, but soon afterwards her family moved to England, where her mother died. From her tenth year she was accustomed to travelling unaccompanied through Europe at her father's expense; until the age of 14 she received no formal education, although she read widely. After attending schools in Belgium and England, she continued her education in Germany, where she remained for eight years (1903–11); it was here that her first stories were published. In 1911 she became active in the suffrage movement in England, and in 1917 she visited the United States, where she spent her later years. She never married.

Towards Morning (1920), Wylie's first mature novel, was based on her time in Germany as a young woman. *To the Vanquished* (1934) is set during the rise of Nazism. After a visit to the Soviet Union in 1934 she wrote *Furious Young Man* (1935), in which a young Englishman is converted to communism. *Where No Birds Sing* (1947) is set in Germany under the American occupation after World War II, while *Candles for Thérèse* (1951) concerns a quest to revenge the betrayal of French Resistance fighters during the war. Her last novel, *The Undefeated* (1957), tells of the efforts made by members of a guilt-ridden community in post-Vichy Provence to exonerate themselves. Wylie also wrote more than 200 short stories, some screenplays, and an amusing autobiography, *My Life with George* (1940), George being her unconscious mind. She died in Princeton, New Jersey.

Wynette, Tammy (1942–) *American country singer*

In her long and successful career Tammy Wynette has had many hits – 20 of her records have made it to the top of the U.S. country charts – and she has been called "the First Lady of country music."

Born Virginia Wynette Pugh in Tupelo, Mississippi, she grew up on her grandparents' cotton farm in Alabama. She married her first husband in 1959 and had three children in the three years they spent together. After their separation she worked as a beautician to pay for her youngest daughter's medical treatment for spinal meningitis. Wynette had always wanted to become a singer and began performing on local radio and television to earn more money. In 1966 she made her first recording, "Apartment No. 9." Two hits followed in 1967 – "Your Good Girl's Gonna Go Bad" and "I Don't Wanna Play House" – and in 1968 she recorded one of her most famous songs, "D-I-V-O-R-C-E." The success of this record brought her the Country Music Association Award for Female Vocalist of the Year. Her next major hit, "Stand by Your Man" (1969), made her one of the bestselling female country singers of all time.

In 1969 Wynette married the country singer George Jones, but their relationship was a particularly turbulent one, and they divorced in 1975. Together they made a number of recordings in the early 1970s, including "Take Me" and "We're Gonna Hold On," and performed on stage at the Grand Ole Opry in Nashville and elsewhere. In 1978 Wynette married the songwriter George Richey. She has continued singing and recording through the 1980s and 1990s, releasing hit singles, such as "Crying in the Rain" (1981) and "Sometimes When We Touch" (1985), and such albums as *Higher Ground* (1987). Her autobiography, *Stand By Your Man*, was filmed in 1982.

X

Xanthippe (5th century BC) *Greek matron*

> ...in Xanthippe's society [I] shall learn to adapt myself to other persons.
>
> —Socrates, quoted by Diogenes Laertius in *Lives and Opinions of Eminent Philosophers*

Xanthippe has become notorious as the nagging and scolding wife of Socrates.

The great Athenian philosopher made his wife famous by comparing her with a spirited horse. Socrates claimed that just as horsemen who have mastered difficult horses have no trouble with tamer ones, Xanthippe had taught him how to handle any person, good-natured or not.

Socrates himself was apparently unattractive, with a turned-up nose and a beer belly, but despite this Xanthippe bore him a son.

Y

Yalow, Rosalyn Sussman (1921–)
American physicist

Rosalyn Yalow shared the Nobel Prize for physiology or medicine in 1977 for her work in developing the technique known as radioimmunoassay, which enables the detection of extremely small amounts of hormone.

Born in New York, Yalow was educated at Hunter College there and then at the University of Illinois, where she obtained her PhD in nuclear physics in 1945. Since 1947 she has worked at the Veterans Administration Hospital in the Bronx as a physicist and since 1968 she has also held the post of research professor at the Mount Sinai School of Medicine.

In the 1950s, while working with Solomon Berson, Yalow developed radioimmunoassay. The technique involves taking a known amount of radioactively labelled hormone, together with a known amount of antibody against it, and mixing it with human serum containing an unknown amount of unlabelled hormone. The antibodies bind to both the radioactive and normal hormone in the proportions in which they are present in the mixture. It is then possible to calculate with great accuracy the amount of unlabelled hormone present in the original sample.

It wasy this technique that enabled Roger Guillemin and Andrew Schally to detect hormones released from the hypothalamus in the brain.

Yates, Dame Frances (Amelia) (1899–1981) *British historian*

Frances Yates was known for her highly original studies of the history and culture of the Renaissance. Her works shed light on many obscure aspects of the period, especially in the fields of symbolism, ritual, and occult beliefs.

Yates's father was a naval architect who frequently moved with his family to various locations around Britain. As a result, Frances attended a number of schools, including Laurel Bank High School, Glasgow, and Birkenhead High School, and also spent much time educating herself. She later gained a degree in French from University College, London.

During the 1920s and 1930s Yates worked entirely outside the academic system, publishing a study of Shakespeare's *Love's Labour Lost* and a biography of John Florio, an Italian who lived in England in the time of ELIZABETH I. During the early years of World War II she worked as an ambulance attendant and became (1941) a research assistant at the Warburg Institute, London; she eventually became reader in the history of the Renaissance (1956–67) at the Warburg. Her publications of the 1940s and 1950s include *The French Academies of the Sixteenth Century* (1947) and *The Valois Tapestries* (1959). Mystical and occult influences on a famous Renaissance figure were described in *Giordano Bruno and the Hermetic Tradition* (1964), the work that first made her known outside specialist circles. This was followed by another brilliantly original book, *The Art of Memory* (1966), which exhumed the lost mnemonic techniques that had played an important role in Renaissance ideas of learning. Her interest in the secret traditions of the occult came to the fore again in such later works as *The Rosicrucian Enlightenment* (1971), *Astraea: the Imperial Theme of the Sixteenth Century* (1975) and *The Occult Philosophy in the Elizabethan Age* (1979).

Frances Yates was appointed OBE in 1972 and DBE in 1977.

Yonge, Charlotte M(ary) (1823–1901) *British novelist*

Yonge wrote about 160 novels and other books for children and adults. Reflecting her own Christian beliefs, her works reinforced the firm moral values of Victorian society.

Born in Otterbourne, Hampshire, Yonge was educated at home by her father, a country gentleman. Under the influence of John Keble, vicar of the neighbouring village of Hursley, she became interested in the Anglo-Catholic movement in the Church of England, which promoted a return to a more dogmatic theology, together with a more mystical and aesthetic style of worship. She remained in Otterbourne for the rest of her life.

As Yonge's talent as a writer developed, Keble encouraged her to promote her religious views in her work. Her first full-length novel, *The Heir of Redclyffe* (1853), was immediately successful, partly because it was sentimental and somewhat pious. Her other stories of contemporary life include *Heartsease* (1854), *The Daisy Chain* (1856), and *The Clever Woman of the Family* (1865). Yonge branched out into historical romances with *The Lances of Lynwood* (1855), *The Prince and the Page* (1865), and *The Dove in the Eagle's Nest* (1866). She also produced biographies, popular history, and Bible study material. From 1851 until 1890 she edited *The Monthly Packet*, a children's magazine.

Young, Loretta (1913–) *American film and television actress*

A glamorous leading lady, Loretta Young enjoyed a highly successful Hollywood career before giving up the big screen for a TV career.

Loretta Young's real name was Gretchen Michaela Young. Born in Salt Lake City, Utah, she moved to Hollywood with her mother at the age of four after her parents' marriage broke up. With the help of an uncle she, her two sisters, and her brother found parts in silent films when they were still young children. Later, when she was 14, Gretchen was given a part first offered to her sister (who was too busy) in the silent picture *Naughty but Nice* (1927). The film company First National put her under contract and changed her name to Loretta.

After this Young played leading roles in nearly 100 pictures with Warner Brothers (1927–34), with 20th Century-Fox (1934–40), and as a freelance (from 1940). She received the Academy Award for Best Actress for her performance in *The Farmer's Daughter* (1947), a Cinderella tale in which Young played a Swedish servant who runs for her employer's Congressional seat. Later films included *Come to the Stable* (1949), in which she played a nun and earned an Oscar nomination, *Cause for Alarm* (1951), and *It Happens Every Thursday* (1953).

Young subsequently became one of America's favourite television actresses in the *Loretta Young Show*, which won Emmy Awards in 1954, 1956, and 1959. Years later she won a Golden Globe Award for her work in the television film *Christmas Eve* (1986). She also appeared on stage in *An Evening with Loretta Young* (1989). Married twice, Young had an illegitimate daughter by Clark Gable. Her autobiography, *The Things I Had to Learn*, was published in 1961.

Young, Rida (*c.* 1875–1926) *American playwright and librettist*

> Sure I love the dear silver that
> shines in your hair,
> And the brow that's all furrowed
> and wrinkled with care...
> Oh God bless you and keep you,
> Mother Machree.
> —"Mother Machree" (1911)

Rida Young is remembered for her successful plays, song lyrics, and librettos for musical comedy. Some of her most popular works drew on Irish traditions.

Born in Baltimore, Maryland, Young travelled to New York as an aspiring young playwright. Having been a society beauty in Baltimore, she spent several years as a minor actress, as well as writing popular song lyrics for a music publisher, before completing her first satisfactory play, *Glorious Betsy*. Her first real success, *Brown of*

Harvard (1906), gave an idealized view of a Harvard undergraduate. It was followed by *The Boys of Company B* (1907) and *The Lottery Man* (1909).

In 1910 Young prepared the book and lyrics for Victor Herbert's operetta *Naughty Marietta*. For the entertainer Chauncey Olcott she wrote the lyrics for the musical *Barry of Ballymore* (1911), including the words of the popular song "Mother Machree." This was followed by *Isle of Dreams* (1912) and *Shameen Dhu* (1913). Later Young undertook the dramatic adaptation for Sigmund Romberg's first great success, the musical *Maytime* (1917), the book and lyrics for Rudolf Friml's musical *Sometime* (1918), and other librettos. Her comedies *Captain Kidd Junior* and *Her Soldier Boy* were produced in 1916; *Little Old New York* was staged in 1920.

Yourcenar, Marguerite (1903–1987)
Belgian-born French–American writer

> She feels she is linked to everything, to the past as well as the present, to human beings but also to animals, landscapes, buildings.
>
> —Jacqueline Piatier in *Les Yeux ouverts* (1984)

In 1980 Marguerite Yourcenar became the first woman member of the French Academy. The winner of many awards, this scholarly writer was not only a historical novelist but also a poet, essayist, playwright, and translator.

Yourcenar's real name was Marguerite de Crayencour. She was born in Brussels to a Belgian mother (who died a few days after her birth) and a French father. Educated at home, near Lille, she could read French, English, Latin, and Greek at an early age.

Displaced by World War I, Marguerite and her father settled in Paris. She wrote poetry from the age of 14, and in 1921–22 her father helped her publish two volumes under the name Yourcenar – a near anagram of her real name. When her father died in 1927, Yourcenar took comfort in travel and writing novels. Among her earliest were *Dénier du rêve* (1934; *A Coin in Nine Hands*, 1982) and *Coup de grâce* (1939; published in English in 1957).

Having visited the United States in 1937, Yourcenar decided to move there at the outbreak of World War II. Staying with her friend Grace Frick, she found a teaching job in Bronxville, New York State, and in 1947 took U.S. citizenship. In 1950 Yourcenar and Frick set up home in Maine, and a year later Yourcenar's masterpiece, *Les Mémoires d'Hadrien* (1951; *Memoirs of Hadrian*, 1954), was published. Constructed as a letter written by the emperor Hadrian on his deathbed, it gives a remarkably full portrait of his character, including his homosexual love for a young man. Equally complex but less real was Zeno, the character at the centre of Yourcenar's Renaissance novel *L'Oeuvre en noir* (1968; *The Abyss*, 1976).

In her two autobiographical volumes, *Souvenirs pieux* (1974; Pious Memories) and *Archives du nord* (1977; Northern Archives), Yourcenar used her skills as a historical novelist to describe the dramatic events of the 20th century.

Z

Zaharias, Babe Didrikson (1914–1956) *American athlete*

An all-round sportswoman, Zaharias was chosen by an Associated Press poll in 1950 as the outstanding woman athlete of the first half of the 20th century.

Mildred Ella (known as "Babe") Didrikson was born in Port Arthur, Texas, the daughter of Norwegian immigrants, and grew up in Beaumont, Texas. She began her sports career in basketball with an insurance company team.

In 1932 Didrikson became famous when she won eight of ten events in the Amateur Athletic Union's national women's track and field championships, including the 80-metre hurdles, baseball throw, shot put, long jump, and javelin. Later that year at the Olympic Games she set two world records – for the javelin (143 feet 4 inches, or 43.68 metres) and the 80-metre hurdles (11.7 seconds). After this Didrikson became a professional athlete playing basketball and baseball, as well as revealing her talent for billiards, swimming, diving, and other sports. In 1938 she married George Zaharias, a professional wrestler.

Zaharias started her championship record in golf in 1940 and won every available women's title at least once during the next decade. However, her career was tragically cut short when she was stricken with cancer in 1953. She died in Galveston, Texas, a year after the publication of her autobiography, *This Life I've Led* (1955).

Zasulich, Vera Ivanovna (1851–1919) *Russian revolutionary*

A revolutionary activist from her teens, Zasulich was seen as a heroine by many Russians after she shot and wounded a much disliked general.

Born in Mikhailovka, Smolensk, Zasulich belonged to a family of the lesser nobility. Her early revolutionary activities led to a two-year prison sentence when she was 18. In 1878 the military governor of St. Petersburg had a political prisoner flogged for no good reason, which created a great stir in revolutionary circles. On February 5 Vera Zasulich shot and seriously wounded the general in his office, making no attempt to escape. When she was acquitted at her trial, there was widespread public delight, although the authorities were alarmed and had the verdict set aside. Vera Zasulich escaped abroad and did not return to Russia until the amnesty of 1905.

In 1900 Zasulich joined Lenin and other political exiles in founding the Marxist newspaper *Iskra*. When the Russian Social Democratic Party split into the Bolsheviks and Mensheviks in 1903, she became associated with the Menshevik wing. Subsequently she opposed the October Revolution of 1917, in which the Bolsheviks seized power.

Zauditu (1876–1930) *Empress of Ethiopia*

Zauditu (whose name is a variant of Judith) had an eventful life during troubled times in Ethiopia.

Born in Addis Ababa, Zauditu was the daughter of Emperor Menelik II. Already a widow at the age of 12, she was widowed again in her twenties; she was married a third time, to Ras Gugsa Wolie, in 1902. Zauditu ascended the throne as "queen of kings" in 1917 after Menelik's grandson, Lij Yasu, was deposed and on condition that she renounce her third husband. At the same time, Ras Tafari Makonnen (later Haile Selassie) was made regent.

Zauditu came into conflict with Ras

Tafari over his efforts to liberalize and modernize the country and to arrange its membership of the League of Nations (achieved in 1923). In 1928 he forced Zauditu to name him emperor. After this, in spite of an unsuccessful attempt by her former husband to restore her authority through a revolt, she had little political influence, although she kept her title until her death.

Zenobia (late 3rd century) *Queen of Palmyra*

Beautiful and ruthless by reputation, Zenobia was a powerful figure who for a short time ruled both Egypt and Asia Minor.

Septima Zenobia was probably of Arab descent. She married the bedouin Odenathus, who was lord of the Syrian city of Palmyra, an outpost of the Roman Empire. In 264 her husband was given the title "governor of all the east," but three years later he and his son (Zenobia's stepson) were murdered. Zenobia's own son Wahballat was named ruler of Palmyra, but she ruled for him as queen.

Ambitious to have an empire independent of Rome, Zenobia invaded and conquered Egypt and much of Asia Minor in 269. However, the Roman emperor Aurelian defeated her armies in 271 at Antioch and Emesa. After a siege Aurelian captured Palmyra and took Zenobia and Wahballat back to Rome as prisoners. When the people of Palmyra revolted again in 273, their city was completely destroyed.

Meanwhile Zenobia fared surprisingly well. With two of her other sons she joined Aurelian's triumphal procession in Rome in 274, subsequently marrying a Roman senator, at whose villa in the summer resort of Tivoli, in central Italy, she ended her days.

Zetkin, Clara (1857–1933) *German Communist leader*

Zetkin was one of the founders of the German Communist Party. She also wrote about women's issues and was well known as a passionate speaker.

Born Clara Eissner in Wiederau, Saxony, she began her career as a schoolteacher. After joining the German Social Democratic Party in 1881, she became its outstanding spokesperson on women's rights and edited the paper *Die Gleichheit* from 1892 until 1916. Married to the revolutionary Ossip Zetkin from 1881, she led the revolutionary Spartacus movement with Rosa LUXEMBURG.

After World War I Zetkin was a joint founder of the Communist Party in Germany (1919). From 1920 to 1932 she was a Communist deputy in the Reichstag, although during much of this period she had disagreements with the Soviet leadership.

From the early 1930s Zetkin lived in Soviet Russia. In addition to writing a number of books on women's problems, she published *Reminiscences of Lenin*, based on her experiences as a close friend of the Communist leader; it appeared in English translation in 1929.

Zetterling, Mai (1925–1994) *Swedish actress and director*

Although she began her career on stage and screen in Sweden, Zetterling was especially popular in films made in Britain. From the 1960s she enjoyed success as the director of her own powerful and sensuous films – often about the position of women.

Zetterling was born in Vasteras, Sweden, into a poor family. Her first appearance on stage at 16 led to a place at the Royal Dramatic Theatre School in Stockholm. She enjoyed her first major success on screen playing a schoolgirl harassed by a sadistic teacher in Alf Sjöberg's *Hets* (1944; *Torment*).

After this Zetterling was invited to Britain where she appeared in numerous films, including *Frieda* (1947), in which she played the German wife of a British wartime airman, *Quarter* (1948), and the biopic *The Bad Lord Byron* (1949). She also appeared in films in Sweden and the United States. In the American movie *Knock on Wood* (1954) Zetterling played opposite Danny Kaye, and in *Only Two Can Play* (1961) she costarred with Peter Sellers. As a stage actress, she continued to act in works by Ibsen, Chekhov, and Anouilh.

Zetterling's first venture into directing came in 1963, when she and her second husband, David Hughes, made the documentary *The War Game*. The film won her the Golden Lion at the Venice Film Festival. Zetterling's subsequent films included *Loving Couples* (1964), a tale of sexual hypocrisy; *Night Games* (1966), based on a novel of her own; *Vincent the Dutchman* (1972), about Van Gogh, and *Scrubbers* (1982), a brutal film set in a girls' borstal.

Returning to acting in 1989, Zetterling took the role of a grandmother in *The Witches* (1990), a film based on a Roald Dahl children's story, and appeared in *Hidden Agenda* (1990), a controversial film about Northern Ireland.

Zia, Khaleda (1944/45–) *Bangladeshi politician*

From 1991 to 1996 Begum Khaleda Zia served as the first woman president of Bangladesh. Although she came to power promising the country economic improvements, her period in office saw mounting disorder and ended amidst constitutional chaos.

The daughter of Iskander and Taiyaba Majumder, Khaleda Zia studied at Surendranath College, Dinajpur. In her teens she was married to Major General Ziaur Rahman, with whom she had two sons. Her husband became leader of the centre-right Bangladesh Nationalist Party (BNP).

Zia was held captive for a time during the Bangladeshi civil war (1971), following which Mujibur Rahman, the leader of a party called the Awami League, established himself as the country's first prime minister. He was assassinated in 1975, and after the resulting struggles Zia's husband took control of the country; he served as president from 1977 until his own assassination in 1981. For the next 16 years Bangladesh was ruled by the military leader President Ershad. During this period Khaleda Zia was persuaded to take over the deputy leadership (1982) and then the leadership (1984) of the BNP.

In 1990 Ershad was deposed because of charges of corruption, and elections were held the following year. The BNP

and Awami League each won 32% of the vote, but the BNP had many more seats and therefore set up a minority government with Khaleda Zia as prime minister. She was also responsible for information, energy, establishment, and mineral resources. The opposition was led by Mujibur Rahman's daughter, Hasina Wajed, of the Awami League.

Zia's period of office began badly with a disastrous cyclone, which killed 139,000 people and caused damage amounting to billions of pounds. Her opponents criticized her handling of the international aid offered. That same year Zia visited several Arab states, China, and Thailand. She also reformed the parliamentary system.

From early 1994 onwards, however, her attempts to implement unpopular privatization policies led to strikes and protests across the country. The opposition also accused her government of vote-rigging in by-elections, and finally resigned en masse from parliament (December 1994) in an attempt to paralyse the political process. Growing violence and disorder led to the calling of an early general election in February 1996, but this was boycotted by the opposition and much of the electorate. Zia finally resigned in March, precipitating a second general election that was won by the opposition under Hasina Wajed.

Zoë (*c.* 978–1050) *Byzantine empress*

Zoë was empress of the Eastern Roman Empire for over 30 years, sharing the throne at various times with her husbands, stepnephew, and sister.

A daughter of Emperor Constantine VIII, Zoë shared the throne after her father's death in 1028 with her husband Romanus III Argyrus, banishing her sister Theodora to a nunnery. When her husband began to neglect her, Zoë had an affair with her chamberlain, Michael the Paphlagonian. In 1034 Romanus died, probably poisoned by Zoë and her lover, and the couple then married and ruled jointly.

Michael (now Michael IV) died in 1041 and was succeeded as coruler by his nephew, Michael V Calaphates, whom Zoë had adopted. Michael V imprisoned the empress and seized sole power, but he was deposed in a revolt in 1042. Zoë then reigned briefly with her sister Theodora. The same year she took another husband, who as Constantine IX Monomachus ruled the empire jointly with both sisters until Zoë's death. Constantine then ruled with Theodora alone until his own death in 1055.

Index of Women by Occupation

Mae 679; Whitelaw, Billie 685; Williams, Esther 692; Winfrey, Oprah 694; Wood, Victoria 697; Woodward, Joanne 697; Wray, Fay 701; Young, Loretta 709; Zetterling, Mai 712

heroism

Arundell, Blanche 28; Calamity Jane 110; Corbin, Margaret 158; Darling, Grace (Horsley) 175; Hallowes, Odette 288; Jael 325; Joan of Arc, Saint 331; Judith 339; MacDonald, Flora 404; Pocahontas 514; Ricard, Marthe 539; Sacagawea 560; Seacole, Mary 575; Tubman, Harriet 643

journalism

Adie, Kate 6; Ayer, Harriet Hubbard 38; Bly, Nellie 76; Brown, Helen Gurley 98; Chase, Edna Woolman 135; Croly, Jane 166; Didion, Joan 189; Dix, Dorothy 192; Faithfull, Emily 220; Faludi, Susan 221; Foster, Hannah Webster 240; Frederick, Pauline 245; Fuller, Margaret 250; Gellhorn, Martha (Ellis) 257; Graham, Katharine Meyer 274; Hopper, Hedda 309; Ibárruri Gómez, Dolores 318; Kael, Pauline 342; Luce, Clare Boothe 397; Manley, Mary de la Rivière 412; Mitford, Jessica (Lucy) 450; Monroe, Harriet 454; Parker, Dorothy 499; Parsons, Louella 501; Popp, Adelheid 516; Quindlen, Anna 524; Rayner, Claire (Berenice) 533; Sauvé, Jeanne Benoit 570; Serao, Matilde 577; Steinem, Gloria 607; Thompson, Dorothy 636; Vreeland, Diana 663; Ward, Dame Barbara 668; Wells-Barnett, Ida Bell 677; West, Dame Rebecca 680

law

Abzug, Bella 2; Allen, Florence Ellinwood 14; Butler-Sloss, Dame Elizabeth 106; Clinton, Hillary Rodham 149; Ginsburg, Ruth Bader 261; Heilbron, Dame Rose 296; Kennedy, Helena (Ann), Baroness 351; Lockwood, Belva Ann 391; O'Connor, Sandra Day 485; Reno, Janet 537; Robinson, Mary 546

mathematics and computing

Agnesi, Maria 8; Byron, Augusta Ada, Countess of Lovelace 108; Germain, Sophie 259; Hopper, Grace Murray 309; Kovalevsky, Sonya Vasilievna 361; Noether, Amalie 478; Somerville, Mary 596; Wrinch, Dorothy 703

medicine

Agnodice 8; Anderson, Elizabeth Garrett 15; Baker, Josephine 44; Barnes, Dame Josephine 48; Barton, Clara 50; Blackwell, Elizabeth 71; Blackwell, Emily 72; Cavell, Edith 129; Dick, Gladys Henry 188; Elion, Gertrude Belle 207; Hamilton, Alice 288; Jacobi, Mary Putnam 324; Jex-Blake, Sophia Louisa 328; Kenny, Elizabeth 352;

Kitzinger, Sheila (Helen Elizabeth) 358; Marsden, Kate 424; Montessori, Maria 457; Nightingale, Florence 475; Pelletier, Madeleine 505; Pitt-Rivers, Rosalind 512; Pye, Edith Mary 522; Sabin, Florence Rena 559; Sanger, Margaret 566; Seacole, Mary 575; Stopes, Marie 610; Stoppard, Miriam 611; Stuart, Miranda 615; Taussig, Helen Brooke 624; Vaughan, Dame Janet 656; Wexler, Nancy 682

music (classical)

Alboni, Marietta 12; Anderson, Marian 16; Bacewicz, Grazyna 40; Baillie, Dame Isobel 42; Baker, Dame Janet (Abbott) 43; Bartoli, Cecilia 50; Battle, Kathleen 52; Beach, Amy Marcy 54; Berganza, Teresa 63; Bori, Lucrezia 86; Boulanger, Nadia (Juliette) 86; Brico, Antonia 91; Bumbry, Grace (Melzia) 102; Butt, Dame Clara 107; Caballé, Montserrat 109; Caldwell, Sarah 111; Callas, Maria 111; Calvé, Emma 111; Carreño, Maria Teresa 117; Chaminade, Cécile Louise Stéphanie 132; Cher 136; Chin Kieu 139; Crawford Seeger, Ruth 165; Crespin, Régine 166; Cross, Joan 166; Curtin, Phyllis 171; de los Angeles, Victoria 180; Demessieux, Jeanne-Marie-Madeleine 180; Destinn, Emmy 185; du Pré, Jacqueline 199; Farrar, Geraldine 222; Farrell, Eileen 222; Ferrier, Kathleen 227; Flagstad, Kirsten 235; Fremstad, Olive 246; Galli-Curci, Amelita 253; Gipps, Ruth 262; Glanville-Hicks, Peggy 264; Gluck, Alma 266; Grisi, Giulia 282; Gruberová, Edita 283; Hammond, Dame Joan 289; Hess, Dame Myra 302; Hildegard, Saint 303; Horne, Marilyn 310; Jeritza, Maria 327; Joyce, Eileen 338; Kurz, Selma 363; Landowska, Wanda 367; Larrocha, Alicia de 371; LeFanu, Nicola 378; Lehmann, Lilli 379; Lehmann, Lotte 380; Lind, Jenny 388; Lutyens, Elisabeth 400; Lympany, Dame Moura 401; Maconchy, Dame Elizabeth 405; Melba, Dame Nellie 441; Midori 444; Milanov, Zinka 444; Monk, Meredith 454; Musgrave, Thea 467; Mutter, Anne-Sophie 467; Nilsson, Birgit 477; Norman, Jessye 479; Patti, Adelina (Juana Maria) 502; Pons, Lily 516; Popp, Lucia 517; Price, Leontyne 520; Resnik, Regina 538; Salerno-Sonnenberg, Najda 563; Schumann, Clara 572; Schumann, Elisabeth 573; Schwarzkopf, Dame Elisabeth 573; Scotto, Renata 575; Sills, Beverly 584; Smyth, Dame Ethel Mary 594; Söderström, Elisabeth Anna 595; Stratas, Teresa 612; Sutherland, Dame Joan 617; Tailleferre, Germaine 622; Tate, Phyllis Margaret 624; Tebaldi, Renata 626; Te Kanawa, Dame Kiri 626; Tetrazzini, Luisa 631; Teyte, Dame Maggie 631; Upshaw,

Dawn 652; Vaughan, Sarah 656; Viardot-García, Pauline 658; Von Stade, Frederica 662; Wagner, Cosima 664; Weir, Judith 676

music (popular)

Armatrading, Joan 26; Baez, Joan 41; Bailey, Pearl 42; Baker, Josephine 44; Brice, Fanny 91; Brightman, Sarah 93; Bush, Kate 104; Cline, Patsy 149; Devi, Kanan 186; Faithfull, Marianne 220; Fields, Dame Gracie 229; Fitzgerald, Ella 233; Franklin, Aretha 243; Garland, Judy 255; Guilbert, Yvette 284; Holiday, Billie 307; Horne, Lena (Calhoun) 310; Houston, Whitney 312; Jackson, Mahalia 323; Joplin, Janis 336; Kitt, Eartha 357; Laine, Dame Cleo 366; lang, k d 368; Lawrence, Gertrude 374; Lennox, Annie 382; Lenya, Lotte 383; Lillie, Beatrice 387; Lloyd, Marie 390; Lynn, Dame Vera 401; Madonna 406; Makeba, Miriam 409; Matthews, Jessie 432; Merman, Ethel 442; Minnelli, Liza 446; Mitchell, Joni 448; O'-Connor, Sinead 485; Paige, Elaine 493; Parton, Dolly 502; Piaf, Edith 510; Rainey, Ma 528; Ross, Diana 551; Russell, Lillian 555; Sade 562; Shore, Dinah 582; Simone, Nina 585; Smith, Bessie 590; Smith, Patti 592; Springfield, Dusty 600; Streisand, Barbra 614; Sumac, Yma 616; Tilley, Vesta 638; Tucker, Sophie 644; Turner, Tina 646; Warwick, Dionne 670; Waters, Ethel 671; Wynette, Tammy 705

noblewomen

Aelgifu 6; Agrippina the Elder 8; Agrippina the Younger 9; Beaufort, Lady Margaret 56; Berry, Duchesse de 67; Borgia, Lucrezia 85; Cenci, Beatrice 130; Chevreuse, Duchesse de 137; Cornelia 161; Dashkova, Yekaterina Romanovna 175; d'Este, Isabella 184; Diane de France 187; Diane de Poitiers 188; Domitilia, Saint Flavia 193; du Barry, Countess 196; Francesca da Rimini 242; Galla Placidia 252; Godiva 267; Jacqueline of Bavaria 324; Lamb, Lady Caroline 367; La Vallière, Louise, Duchesse de 372; Longueville, Duchesse de 393; Maintenon, Marquise de 408; Marlborough, Sarah Churchill, Duchess of 423; Messalina, Valeria 442; Montespan, Marquise de 457; Octavia Minor 486; Pompadour, Marquise de 515; Rambouillet, Marquise de 529; Stein, Charlotte von 606; Stuart, Arabella 614; Ursins, Princesse des 653

philanthropy

Barnett, Dame Henrietta Octavia (Weston) 48; Barton, Clara 50; Burdett-Coutts, Angela Georgina, Baroness 103; Cabrini, Saint Frances Xavier 109; Carpenter,

Mary 116; Chisholm, Caroline 140; Diana, Princess of Wales 187; Dodge, Grace Hoadley 192; Drexel, Katharine 195; Hale, Clara 287; Saunders, Dame Cicely 569; Somerset, Lady Isabella Caroline 595; Teresa, Mother 628

philosophy

Agnesi, Maria 8; Arendt, Hannah 24; Beauvoir, Simone de 56; Davis, Angela 176; Hypatia 317; Irigaray, Luce 319; Kristeva, Julia 362; Murdoch, Dame Iris 466; Rand, Ayn 530; Stein, Edith 606; Warnock, (Helen) Mary 670; Weil, Simone 675

photography

Abbott, Berenice 1; Arbus, Diane 24; Arnold, Eve 27; Bourke-White, Margaret 86; Cameron, Julia Margaret 112; Cunningham, Imogen 168; Dahl-Wolfe, Louise 173; Käsebier, Gertrude 344; Lange, Dorothea 368; Leibovitz, Annie 380; Miller, Lee 445; Model, Lisette 452; Modotti, Tina 453; Norman, Dorothy Stecker 479; Riefenstahl, Leni 543; Sherman, Cindy 581

politics and diplomacy

Çiller, Tansu 144; Abbott, Diane (Julie) 1; Abzug, Bella 2; Adams, Abigail 3; Albright, Madeleine Korbel 12; Aquino, Corazon 23; Arteaga, Rosalia 28; Ashrawi, Hanan 31; Asquith, Margot 32; Astor, Nancy, Viscountess 33; Bandaranaike, Sirimavo (Ratwatte Dias) 46; Beckett, Margaret (Mary) 57; Belgioioso, Cristina, Princess of 59; Bell, Gertrude (Margaret Lowthian) 59; Bhutto, Benazir 68; Blackstone, Tessa (Ann Vosper), Baroness 71; Bloor, Ella Reeve 75; Bondfield, Margaret Grace 79; Bonham Carter, (Helen) Violet, Lady Asquith 80; Bonner, Yelena 81; Boothroyd, Betty 84; Braddock, Bessie 89; Breshko-Breshkovskaya, Yekaterina Konstantinovna 90; Brundtland, Gro Harlem 99; Caraway, Hattie (Ophelia) Wyatt 114; Castle, Barbara, Baroness 122; Chamorro, Violetta Barrios de 132; Charles, Dame (Mary) Eugenia 134; Chiang, Mayling Soong 137; Clinton, Hillary Rodham 149; Davis, Angela 176; Deng Yingchao 182; Feinstein, Dianne 224; Felton, Rebecca Ann 225; Ferraro, Geraldine (Anne) 226; Figner, Vera 230; Finnbogadóttir, Vigdís 230; Firestone, Shulamith 231; First, Ruth 231; Flynn, Elizabeth Gurley 237; Gandhi, Indira 253; Goldman, Emma 268; Gonne, Maud 269; Grasso, Ella 275; Hobby, Oveta Culp 305; Ibárruri Gómez, Dolores 318; Jackson, Glenda 323; Jiang Qing 329; Joseph, Helen 336; Kelly, Petra 349; Khan, Ra'ana Liaquat Ali 354; Kirkpatrick,

Jeane 357; Kollontai, Aleksandra Mikhailovna 360; Kumaratunge, Chandrika Bandaranaike 363; Lee, Jennie 377; Luce, Clare Boothe 397; Luxemburg, Rosa 400; McAliskey, Bernadette 433; Makeba, Miriam 409; Mandela, Winnie 411; Marcos, Imelda (Romualdez) 414; Markiewicz, Constance, Countess 422; Meinhof, Ulrike Marie 439; Meir, Golda 440; Mercouri, Melina 441; Michel, Louise 443; Mistral, Gabriela 447; Modotti, Tina 453; Mowlam, Marjorie (Mo) 464; Myrdal, Alva 468; Naidu, Sarojini 469; Ngoyi, Lilian Masediba 474; Pandit, Vijaya Lakshmi 495; Pauker, Ana 503; Perón, Eva 506; Perón, Isabel 507; Perovskaya, Sophie 508; Qiu Jin 524; Rankin, Jeannette 530; Rathbone, Eleanor (Florence) 531; Robinson, Mary 546; Roland (de la Platière), Marie-Jeanne 548; Roosevelt, Eleanor 549; Sauvé, Jeanne Benoit 570; Suchocka, Hanna 615; Summerskill, Edith, Baroness 616; Sun Ch'ing-ling 617; Suu Kyi, Aung San 618; Suzman, Helen 619; Temple, Shirley 627; Tereshkova, Valentina Vladimirovna 629; Thatcher, Margaret, Baroness 633; Tizard, Dame Catherine 638; Veil, Simone 657; Wilkinson, Ellen 689; Williams, Shirley, Baroness 692; Zasulich, Vera Ivanovna 711; Zetkin, Clara 712; Zia, Khaleda 713

publishing
Beach, Sylvia (Woodbridge) 54; Cunard, Nancy (Clara) 167; Faithfull, Emily 220; Graham, Katharine Meyer 274; Hobby, Oveta Culp 305; Monroe, Harriet 454; Serao, Matilde 577; Steinem, Gloria 607

religion
Abigail 2; Adelaide, Saint 5; Aethelthryth, Saint 6; Agatha, Saint 7; Agnes, Saint 7; A'isha 10; Alacoque, Saint Margaret Mary 11; Askew, Anne 31; Aylward, Gladys 38; Baldwin, Monica 45; Barton, Elizabeth 51; Bernadette of Lourdes, Saint 65; Blackwell, Antoinette Brown 71; Blavatsky, Helena Petrovna 73; Booth, Catherine 82; Booth, Evangeline 83; Bora, Katharina von 84; Bourignon, Antoinette 86; Bridget of Sweden, Saint 92; Brigid of Ireland, Saint 94; Cabrini, Saint Frances Xavier 109; Catherine de' Ricci, Saint 125; Catherine of Alexandria, Saint 125; Catherine of Bologna, Saint 126; Catherine of Genoa, Saint 127; Catherine of Siena, Saint 127; Catherine of Sweden, Saint 128; Cecilia, Saint 130; Chantal, Saint Jane Frances de 134; Clare, Saint 146; Clotilda, Saint 151; Deborah 178; Domitilia, Saint Flavia 193; Dyer, Mary 201; Eddy, Mary Baker 204; Elizabeth of Hungary, Saint 214; Eulalia, Saint 218;

Fatimah 223; Foster, Jodie 240; Fox, Margaret 241; Frideswide, Saint 247; Geneviève, Saint 258; Gertrude of Helfta, Saint 260; Guyon, Jeanne-Marie 284; Heck, Barbara Ruckle 296; Helena, Saint 297; Héloïse 298; Hilda, Saint 303; Hildegard, Saint 303; Huntingdon, Selina Hastings, Countess of 315; Hutchinson, Anne 316; Joan, Pope 330; Joan of Arc, Saint 331; Juana Inés de la Cruz 338; Julian of Norwich 340; Kempe, Margery 350; Khadijah 354; Lee, Ann 377; Lucy, Saint 398; McPherson, Aimée Semple 437; Margaret, Saint 416; Mary Magdalene, Saint 428; Mary of Bethany 428; Mary the Virgin, Saint 430; O'Hair, Madalyn Murray 487; Olga, Saint 488; Porete, Marguerite 517; Rose of Lima, Saint 550; Ruth 556; Sarah 567; Slessor, Mary (Mitchell) 588; Southcott, Joanna 598; Stein, Edith 606; Taylor, Annie 625; Teresa, Mother 628; Teresa of Avila, Saint 629; Thérèse of Lisieux, Saint 635; Ursula, Saint 653; Walburga, Saint 665; Weil, Simone 675; Wilkinson, Jemima 690

royalty
Adelaide, Saint 5; Aethelthryth, Saint 6; Alexandra 13; Alexandra Fyodorovna 13; Amalsuntha 15; Anastasia 15; Anne, the Princess Royal 19; Anne of Bohemia 20; Anne of Brittany 21; Anne of Cleves 21; Anne of Denmark 21; Augusta 36; Beauharnais, Hortense de 56; Berengaria 62; Berenice 62; Berenice I 63; Berenice II 63; Blanche of Castile 72; Boleyn, Anne 78; Bonaparte, Caroline 79; Bonaparte, Elisa 79; Bonaparte, Pauline 79; Brunhilde 100; Carlota 114; Caroline of Ansbach 115; Caroline of Brunswick 116; Catherine of Aragon 126; Catherine of Braganza 126; Catherine of Valois 128; Clotilda, Saint 151; Désirée 184; Diana, Princess of Wales 187; Eleanor of Aquitaine 206; Eleanor of Castile 206; Eleanor of Provence 207; Elizabeth, the Queen Mother 213; Elizabeth 210; Elizabeth 210; Elizabeth Farnese 214; Elizabeth of Hungary, Saint 214; Emma 215; Eudocia 217; Eudocia Macrembolitissa 217; Eudoxia 217; Eugénie 217; Fredegund 245; Grey, Lady Jane 280; Henrietta Anne, Duchesse d'Orléans 299; Henrietta Maria 299; Herodias 301; Howard, Catherine 313; Isabella 320; Isabella of Bavaria 321; Isabel of Angoulême 322; Joan of Navarre 333; Joséphine 337; Juana la Beltraneja 339; Julia the Elder 340; Kelly, Grace 349; Kent, Joan of 352; Livia 389; Margaret, Maid of Norway 415; Margaret, Princess 415; Margaret, Saint 416; Margaret of Anjou 416; Margaret Tudor 417; Marguerite de Valois 418;

Marguerite of Navarre 418; Marie Antoinette 420; Marie de Médicis 421; Marie Louise 421; Mary of Modena 429; Mary of Teck 429; Matilda 431; Montpensier, Duchesse de 459; Nefertiti 472; Octavia 486; Parr, Catherine 501; Philippa of Hainault 510; Pulcheria 521; Seymour, Jane 579; Sophia 598; Theodora 634; Windsor, Duchess of 693

rulers

Aelgifu 6; Aethelflaed 6; Anna Ivanovna 18; Anna Leopoldovna 19; Anne 19; Anne of Austria 20; Anne of France 21; Arsinoë II 27; Artemisia I 28; Artemisia II 28; Athaliah 34; Beatrix 56; Boadicea 77; Catherine de' Médicis 124; Catherine I 123; Catherine II 124; Charlotte 134; Christina 142; Cleopatra 148; Elizabeth 210; Elizabeth I 210; Elizabeth II 212; Hatshepsut 292; Irene 319; Isabella I 320; Isabella II 321; Jezebel 328; Jingo 329; Joanna I 330; Joanna the Mad 330; Juliana 339; Liliuokalani, Lydia Kamekeha 386; Margaret I 415; Margaret of Austria 417; Margaret of Parma 417; Margrethe II 418; Maria Theresa 419; Mary, Queen of Scots 427; Mary I 426; Mary II 427; Matilda of Tuscany 431; Olga, Saint 488; Olympias 489; Semiramis 577; Sheba, Queen of 580; Sophia 598; Tamiris 623; Tz'u-hsi 649; Victoria 659; Wilhelmina 689; Wu Zhao 704; Zauditu 711; Zenobia 712; Zoë 713

science

Agassiz, Elizabeth 7; Anning, Mary 22; Arber, Agnes 23; Bell Burnell, (Susan) Jocelyn 61; Burbidge, (Eleanor) Margaret 102; Cannon, Annie Jump 113; Carson, Rachel (Louise) 119; Châtelet, Emilie, Marquise du 136; Cori, Gerty Theresa Radnitz 160; Curie, Marie (Skłodowska) 169; Fell, Dame Honor Bridget 225; Fleming, Williamina Paton 236; Fossey, Dian 240; Franklin, Rosalind (Elsie) 244; Geller, Margaret Joan 257; Goodall, Jane 270; Herschel, Caroline Lucretia 301; Hodgkin, Dorothy Crowfoot 306; Hogg-Priestly, Helen Battles Sawyer 307; Hyman, Libbie Henrietta 317; Joliot-Curie, Irène 335; Karle, Isabella Helen 343; Kendrick, Pearl 351; Kirch, Maria Margarethe 356; Klumpke, Dorothea 358; Lavoisier, Marie (Anne Pierrette) 373; Leakey, Mary 375; Leavitt, Henrietta Swan 376; Lehmann, Inge 379; Levi-Montalcini, Rita 385; Lonsdale, Dame Kathleen 393; McClintock, Barbara 435; Manton, Sidnie Milana 413; Maury, Antonia Caetana (de Paiva Pereira) 432; Mayer, Maria Goeppert 433; Meitner, Lise 440; Mitchell, Maria 449; Needham, Dorothy (Mary Moyle) 472; Nice, Margaret Morse 474; Noddack, Ida

(Eva Tacke) 478; North, Marianne 480; Nüsslein-Volhard, Christiane 482; Perey, Marguerite Catherine 506; Pitt-Rivers, Rosalind 512; Ray, Dixy Lee 532; Rothschild, Miriam Louisa 552; Rubin, Vera Cooper 553; Scharrer, Berta 571; Somerville, Mary 596; Stevens, Nettie Maria 608; Wrinch, Dorothy 703; Wu, Chien-Shiung 703; Yalow, Rosalyn Sussman 708

social reform

Addams, Jane 5; Anthony, Susan B(rownell) 22; Ashby, Dame Margery Corbett 29; Baez, Joan 41; Baker, Josephine 44; Balch, Emily Greene 44; Barnett, Dame Henrietta Octavia (Weston) 48; Beard, Mary Ritter 55; Beauvoir, Simone de 56; Besant, Annie 67; Blackwell, Antoinette Brown 71; Bloomer, Amelia Jenks 74; Bloor, Ella Reeve 75; Booth, Catherine 82; Booth, Evangeline 83; Bremer, Fredrika 90; Bright Eyes 93; Brittain, Vera Mary 94; Butler, Josephine 106; Catt, Carrie (Lane Chapman) 128; Child, Lydia Maria 139; Chisholm, Caroline 140; Claflin, Tennessee 145; Claflin, Victoria Woodhull 145; Cobbe, Frances Power 152; Croly, Jane 166; Cunard, Nancy (Clara) 167; Davies, (Sarah) Emily 176; Davison, Emily 177; Despard, Charlotte 184; Ding Ling 191; Dix, Dorothea 191; Dworkin, Andrea 201; Faithfull, Emily 220; Fawcett, Dame Millicent 224; Felton, Rebecca Ann 225; Firestone, Shulamith 231; Flynn, Elizabeth Gurley 237; Friedan, Betty 247; Fry, Elizabeth 249; Gilman, Charlotte Perkins (Stetson) 261; Gore-Booth, Eva (Selina) 272; Greer, Germaine 277; Grimké, Angelina Emily 281; Grimké, Sarah Moore 281; Hale, Clara 287; Hill, Octavia 303; Holtby, Winifred 308; Howe, Julia Ward 313; Joseph, Helen 336; Keller, Helen 348; Key, Ellen 353; King, Coretta Scott 355; Kuzwayo, Ellen 364; Lytton, Lady Constance 402; Martineau, Harriet 425; Marx, Eleanor 425; Millett, Kate 445; More, Hannah 461; Mott, Lucretia Coffin 464; Myrdal, Alva 468; Nation, Carry 469; Ngoyi, Lilian Masediba 474; Noonuccal, Oodgeroo Moongalba 479; Norman, Dorothy Stecker 479; Norton, Caroline 481; O'Hair, Madalyn Murray 487; Olsen, Tillie 489; Pankhurst, Dame Christabel (Harriette) 495; Pankhurst, Emmeline 496; Pankhurst, (Estelle) Sylvia 497; Parks, Rosa 500; Paul, Alice 503; Pelletier, Madeleine 505; Perkins, Frances Coralie 506; Pethick-Lawrence, Emmeline 508; Pizzey, Erin 512; Popp, Adelheid 516; Qiu Jin 524; Ramabai, Pandita 528; Rankin, Jeannette 530; Rathbone, Eleanor (Florence) 531; Ricard, Marthe 539; Roosevelt, Eleanor 549; Russell, Dora 554; Sanger, Margaret 566; Schreiner, Olive 572; Smedley, Agnes 589; Spence, Catherine Helen 599; Stanton, Elizabeth Cady 602; Stone, Lucy Blackwell 609; Stopes, Marie 610; Stowe, Harriet Beecher 611; Strachey, Ray 612; Suttner, Bertha von 618; Suzman, Helen 619; Szold, Henrietta 620; Terrell, Mary 630; Tibbles, Susette 638; Tristan, Flora 640; Truth, Sojourner 642; Tubman, Harriet 643; Tuckwell, Gertrude 644; Twining, Louisa 648; Wald, Lillian D. 665; Ward, Mrs. Humphry 668; Webb, Beatrice 672; Wells-Barnett, Ida Bell 677; Williams, Betty 691; Wollstonecraft, Mary 696; Wright, Frances 702; Zasulich, Vera Ivanovna 711; Zetkin, Clara 712

social sciences

Çiller, Tansu 144; Anna Comnena 18; Arendt, Hannah 24; Beard, Mary Ritter 55; Benedict, Ruth (Fulton) 61; Blackstone, Tessa (Ann Vosper), Baroness 71; Douglas, Mary 193; Freud, Anna 247; Gimbutas, Marija 261; Han Suyin 290; Hawkes, Jacquetta 293; Hite, Shere D. 304; Horney, Karen 311; Irigaray, Luce 319; Johnson, Virginia E(shelman) 334; Kenyon, Dame Kathleen 352; Kimura, Doreen 355; Klein, Melanie 358; Kristeva, Julia 362; Leakey, Mary 375; Macaulay, Catherine 403; Martineau, Harriet 425; Mead, Margaret 438; Mitchell, Juliet 448; Oakley, Ann 483; Pan Chao 494; Robinson, Joan 545; Rowbotham, Sheila 552; Salomé, Lou Andreas 564; Tuchman, Barbara 644; Ward, Dame Barbara 668; Warner, Marina (Sarah) 669; Webb, Beatrice 672; Wedgwood, Dame Veronica 674; Wootton, Barbara, Baroness 699; Yates, Dame Frances (Amelia) 708

sport

Berg, Patty 63; Blankers-Koen, Fanny 73; Brough, Louise 97; Budd, Zola 101; Bueno, Maria 102; Chadwick, Florence 131; Connolly, Maureen 157; Court, Margaret Smith 162; Decker, Mary 178; Devers, Gail 186; Ederle, Gertrude Caroline 205; Ender, Kornelia 215; Evans, Janet 219; Fleming, Peggy 236; Fraser, Dawn 244; Gibson, Althea 260; Goolagong, Evonne 270; Graf, Steffi 273; Gunnell, Sally 284; Hard, Darlene Ruth 290; Henie, Sonja 299; Jacobs, Helen Hull 324; King, Billie Jean 355; Koch, Marita 359; Korbut, Olga 360; Lenglen, Suzanne 382; Lloyd, Chris Evert 390; Lopez, Nancy 394; Loroupe, Tegla 395; McColgan, Liz 435; Maillart, Ella 407; Marble, Alice 414; Navratilova, Martina 470; Pérec, Marie-José 505; Peters, Mary 508; Quirot, Anna

525; Rankin, Judy 531; Rodnina, Irina Konstantinovna 547; Sabatini, Gabriela 559; Samuelson, Joan Benoit 564; Seles, Monica 576; Smythe, Pat 594; Szewinska, Irena 620; Torvill, Jayne 639; Turishcheva, Lyudmila Ivanovna 645; Wade, (Sarah) Virginia 664; Waitz, Grete 665; Whitbread, Fatima 684; Wightman, Hazel 688; Williams, Esther 692; Wills, Helen Newington 693; Witt, Katerina 695; Zaharias, Babe Didrikson 711

theatre

Achurch, Janet 3; Adams, Maude 4; Aidoo, Ama Ata 9; Anderson, Dame Judith 15; Anderson, Mary Antoinette 16; Andrews, Julie 17; Ashcroft, Dame Peggy 29; Atkins, Eileen 34; Bagnold, Enid 42; Bailey, Pearl 42; Baillie, Joanna 43; Bancroft, Anne 45; Bankhead, Tallulah Brockman 46; Barry, Elizabeth 49; Baum, Vicki 53; Baylis, Lilian 53; Behn, Aphra 59; Bell, Marie 60; Bernhardt, Sarah 66; Bonstelle, Jessie 82; Booth, Shirley 84; Bracegirdle, Anne 88; Brice, Fanny 91; Brightman, Sarah 93; Campbell, Mrs. Patrick 113; Carter, Mrs. Leslie 120; Casarès, Maria 121; Centlivre, Susanna 130; Champmeslé, Marie 132; Channing, Carol 133; Churchill, Caryl 143; Cixous, Hélène 144; Clairon, Mademoiselle 146; Clive, Kitty 150; Collier, Constance 155; Collins, Joan 156; Cooper, Dame Gladys 158; Cornell, Katharine 161; Cowl, Jane 162; Crabtree, Lotta 163; Crawford, Cheryl 164; Crothers, Rachel 167; Cushman, Charlotte (Saunders) 171; Delaney, Shelagh 179; Dench, Dame Judi 181; Draper, Ruth 194; Dressler, Marie 195; Dumesnil, Marie-Françoise 198; Duse, Eleonora 200; Evans, Dame Edith 218; Fenton, Lavinia 226; Ferber, Edna 226; Feuillière, Edwige 228; Fiske, Minnie Maddern 232; Flanagan, Hallie 235; Fontanne, Lynn 239; Gish, Dorothy 263; Gish, Lillian 263; Glaspell, Susan 265; Gordon, Ruth 271; Gregory, Isabella Augusta, Lady 279; Grenfell, Joyce 279; Gwyn, Nell 285; Hagen, Uta 286; Hansberry, Lorraine 290; Harris, Julie 291; Hayes, Helen 294; Haywood, Eliza 294; Hellman, Lillian 297; Hepburn, Katharine 300; Hiller, Dame Wendy 304; Horne, Lena (Calhoun) 310; Horniman, Annie 311; Hrosvitha 314; Inchbald, Elizabeth 318; Jackson, Glenda 323; Johnson, Dame Celia 334; Johnson, Pamela Hansford 334; Jordan, Dorothy 336; Keene, Laura 347; Kemble, Frances 349; Kendal, Felicity 350; Langtry, Lillie 369; Lawrence, Gertrude 374; Lecouvreur, Adrienne 376; Lee, Gypsy Rose 377; Le Gallienne, Eva 378; Leigh, Vivien 381;

Lenya, Lotte 383; Lillie, Beatrice 387; Littlewood, Joan 388; Lloyd, Marie 390; Luce, Clare Boothe 397; McKenna, Siobhán 437; McKenna, Virginia 437; MacLaine, Shirley 404; Malina, Judith 410; Manley, Mary de la Rivière 412; Marlowe, Julia 424; Matthews, Jessie 432; Merman, Ethel 442; Mirren, Helen 447; Mistinguett 447; Mnouchkine, Ariane 451; Modjeska, Helena 453; Nazimova, Alla 470; Neagle, Dame Anna 470; Ouspenskaya, Maria 491; Page, Geraldine 492; Paige, Elaine 493; Palmer, Lilli 494; Plowright, Joan 514; Rachel 526; Rame, Franca 529; Redgrave, Lynn 534; Redgrave, Vanessa 535; Reid, Beryl 536; Richardson, Miranda 541; Rigg, Dame Diana 543; Robins, Elizabeth 545; Robson, Dame Flora 546; Russell, Lillian 555; Russell, Rosalind 556; Rutherford, Dame Margaret 557; Shaw, Fiona (Mary) 579; Shearer, Moira 579; Siddons, Sarah 583; Skinner, Cornelia Otis 587; Smith, Dodie 591; Smith, Dame Maggie 591; Smithson, Harriet (Constance) 593; Stevenson, Juliet (Anne Virginia) 608; Sullavan, Margaret 615; Suzman, Janet 619; Tandy, Jessica 624; Tempest, Dame Marie 627; Terry, Dame Ellen 630; Thorndike, Dame Sybil 637; Tilley, Vesta 638; Tutin, Dorothy 647; Tyson, Cicely 649; Vestris, Madame 658; Walters, Julie 667; Waters, Ethel 671; Webster, Margaret 674; West, Mae 679; Whitelaw, Billie 685; Whitlock, Elizabeth Kemble 686; Woffington, Peg 695; Young, Rida 709

travel and exploration

Aylward, Gladys 38; Bell, Gertrude (Margaret Lowthian) 59; Bishop, Isabella Bird 70; Bly, Nellie 76; Cobbe, Frances Power 152; d'Angeville, Henriette 174; Digby, Jane 190; Duff-Gordon, Lady Lucy 197; Eberhardt, Isabelle 204; Grimshaw, Beatrice 281; Hahn, Emily 286; Kingsley, Mary 356; Maillart, Ella 407; Marsden, Kate 424; Mitchison, Naomi 450; Montagu, Lady Mary Wortley 456; Peck, Annie Smith 504; Sacagawea 560; Stanhope, Lady Hester 602; Stark, Dame Freya 604; Tabei, Junko 622; Taylor, Annie 625; Trollope, Frances 641; Workman, Fanny 701

writing (fiction)

Agoult, Marie, Comtesse d' 8; Aguilar, Grace 9; Aidoo, Ama Ata 9; Alcott, Louisa May 12; Allende, Isabel 14; Atherton, Gertrude 34; Atwood, Margaret (Eleanor) 35; Aulnoy, Comtesse d' 36; Austen, Jane 37; Avellaneda y Arteaga, Gertrudis Gómez de 38; Bachmann, Ingeborg 40; Bagnold, Enid 42; Barnes, Djuna (Chappell) 47; Baum, Vicki 53; Bentley, Phyllis

62; Blume, Judy (Sussman) 76; Blyton, Enid 76; Böhlau, Helene 77; Bowen, Elizabeth 87; Boyle, Kay 88; Braddon, Mary Elizabeth 89; Bremer, Fredrika 90; Bridge, Ann 92; Brontë, Anne 95; Brontë, Charlotte 95; Brontë, Emily 96; Brookner, Anita 96; Brooks, Gwendolyn 97; Bryher 100; Buck, Pearl S. 101; Burnett, Frances Hodgson 103; Byatt, A(ntonia) S(usan) 107; Caballero, Fernán 109; Carter, Angela 119; Cartland, Dame Barbara 120; Castro, Rosalía de 122; Cather, Willa 123; Charrière, Isabelle Agnès Elisabeth de 135; Child, Lydia Maria 139; Chopin, Kate 140; Christie, Dame Agatha 141; Colet, Louise 154; Colette 154; Collett, Camilla 155; Collins, Jackie 155; Compton-Burnett, Dame Ivy 157; Corelli, Marie 159; Cornwell, Patricia 161; Craik, Dinah Maria 163; Deland, Margaret Wade 179; Deledda, Grazia 180; Desai, Anita 183; Dickens, Monica 188; Didion, Joan 189; Dinesen, Isak 191; Drabble, Margaret 194; Droste-Hülshoff, Annette Elisabeth von 196; du Maurier, Dame Daphne 197; Duras, Marguerite 200; Dutt, Toru 201; Edgeworth, Maria 205; Eliot, George 207; Emecheta, Buchi 215; Esquivel, Laura 216; Fauset, Jessie Redmon 223; Ferber, Edna 226; Ferrier, Susan (Edmonstone) 228; Fielding, Sarah 229; Fisher, Dorothy Canfield 231; Fitzgerald, Penelope 233; Fitzgerald, Zelda 234; Foster, Hannah Webster 240; Frame, Janet (Paterson) 241; Freeman, Mary E. Wilkins 245; French, Marilyn 246; Gaskell, Elizabeth Cleghorn 256; Gellhorn, Martha (Ellis) 257; Genlis, Comtesse de 258; Ginzburg, Natalia Levi 262; Glasgow, Ellen 264; Glaspell, Susan 265; Glendinning, Victoria 265; Glyn, Elinor 266; Godden, Rumer 266; Gordimer, Nadine 271; Goudge, Elizabeth 272; Grau, Shirley Ann 276; Green, Anna Katherine 276; Hall, (Marguerite) Radclyffe 287; Handel-Mazzetti, Enrica von 289; Han Suyin 290; Haywood, Eliza 294; Head, Bessie 295; Highsmith, Patricia 302; Holtby, Winifred 308; Huch, Ricarda 314; Hurston, Zora Neale 315; Ibarbourou, Juana de 318; Inchbald, Elizabeth 318; James, P(hylis) D(orothy), Baroness 325; Jhabvala, Ruth Prawer 328; Johnson, Pamela Hansford 334; Jong, Erica 335; Kaye, M(ary) M(argaret) 345; La Fayette, Madame de 365; Lagerlöf, Selma (Ottiliana Louisa) 366; Lamb, Lady Caroline 367; La Roche, Sophie von 371; Lavin, Mary 373; Lehmann, Rosamond (Nina) 380; Lennox, Charlotte (Ramsay) 383; Lessing, Doris 384; Lidman, Sara 386; Lively, Penelope 389; Loos, Anita 394;

writing (nonfiction)

writing (poetry)

Index of Women by Nationality

Shirley 627; Turner, Kathleen 645; Turner, Lana 645; Tyson, Cicely 649; Weaver, Sigourney 672; Welch, Raquel 676; West, Mae 679; Williams, Esther 692; Winfrey, Oprah 694; Woodward, Joanne 697; Wray, Fay 701; Young, Loretta 709

heroism

Calamity Jane 110; Corbin, Margaret 158; Pocahontas 514; Sacagawea 560; Tubman, Harriet 643

journalism

Ayer, Harriet Hubbard 38; Bly, Nellie 76; Brown, Helen Gurley 98; Chase, Edna Woolman 135; Croly, Jane 166; Didion, Joan 189; Dix, Dorothy 192; Faludi, Susan 221; Foster, Hannah Webster 240; Frederick, Pauline 245; Fuller, Margaret 250; Gellhorn, Martha (Ellis) 257; Graham, Katharine Meyer 274; Hopper, Hedda 309; Kael, Pauline 342; Luce, Clare Boothe 397; Mitford, Jessica (Lucy) 450; Monroe, Harriet 454; Parker, Dorothy 499; Parsons, Louella 501; Quindlen, Anna 524; Steinem, Gloria 607; Thompson, Dorothy 636; Vreeland, Diana 663; Wells-Barnett, Ida Bell 677

law

Abzug, Bella 2; Allen, Florence Ellinwood 14; Clinton, Hillary Rodham 149; Ginsburg, Ruth Bader 261; Lockwood, Belva Ann 391; O'Connor, Sandra Day 485; Reno, Janet 537

mathematics and computing

Hopper, Grace Murray 309; Wrinch, Dorothy 703

medicine

Baker, Josephine 44; Barton, Clara 50; Blackwell, Elizabeth 71; Blackwell, Emily 72; Dick, Gladys Henry 188; Elion, Gertrude Belle 207; Hamilton, Alice 288; Jacobi, Mary Putnam 324; Sabin, Florence Rena 559; Sanger, Margaret 566; Taussig, Helen Brooke 624; Wexler, Nancy 682

music (classical)

Anderson, Marian 16; Battle, Kathleen 52; Beach, Amy Marcy 54; Brico, Antonia 91; Bumbry, Grace (Melzia) 102; Caldwell, Sarah 111; Cher 136; Crawford Seeger, Ruth 165; Curtin, Phyllis 171; Farrar, Geraldine 222; Farrell, Eileen 222; Fremstad, Olive 246; Glanville-Hicks, Peggy 264; Gluck, Alma 266; Horne, Marilyn 310; Lehmann, Lotte 380; Monk, Meredith 454; Norman, Jessye 479; Pons, Lily 516; Price, Leontyne 520; Resnik, Regina 538; Salerno-Sonnenberg, Najda 563; Schumann, Elisabeth 573; Sills, Beverly 584; Upshaw, Dawn 652; Vaughan, Sarah 656; Von Stade, Frederica 662

music (popular)

Baez, Joan 41; Bailey, Pearl 42; Baker, Josephine 44; Brice, Fanny 91; Cline, Patsy 149; Fitzgerald, Ella 233; Franklin, Aretha 243; Garland, Judy 255; Holiday, Billie 307; Horne, Lena (Calhoun) 310; Houston, Whitney 312; Jackson, Mahalia 323; Joplin, Janis 336; Kitt, Eartha 357; Madonna 406; Merman, Ethel 442; Minnelli, Liza 446; Parton, Dolly 502; Rainey, Ma 528; Ross, Diana 551; Russell, Lillian 555; Shore, Dinah 582; Simone, Nina 585; Smith, Bessie 590; Smith, Patti 592; Streisand, Barbra 614; Sumac, Yma 616; Tucker, Sophie 644; Turner, Tina 646; Warwick, Dionne 670; Waters, Ethel 671; Wynette, Tammy 705

philanthropy

Barton, Clara 50; Cabrini, Saint Frances Xavier 109; Dodge, Grace Hoadley 192; Drexel, Katharine 195; Hale, Clara 287

philosophy

Arendt, Hannah 24; Davis, Angela 176; Rand, Ayn 530

photography

Abbott, Berenice 1; Arbus, Diane 24; Arnold, Eve 27; Bourke-White, Margaret 86; Cunningham, Imogen 168; Dahl-Wolfe, Louise 173; Käsebier, Gertrude 344; Lange, Dorothea 368; Leibovitz, Annie 380; Miller, Lee 445; Model, Lisette 452; Norman, Dorothy Stecker 479; Sherman, Cindy 581

politics and diplomacy

Abzug, Bella 2; Adams, Abigail 3; Albright, Madeleine Korbel 12; Bloor, Ella Reeve 75; Caraway, Hattie (Ophelia) Wyatt 114; Clinton, Hillary Rodham 149; Davis, Angela 176; Feinstein, Dianne 224; Felton, Rebecca Ann 225; Ferraro, Geraldine (Anne) 226; Flynn, Elizabeth Gurley 237; Goldman, Emma 268; Grasso, Ella 275; Hobby, Oveta Culp 305; Kirkpatrick, Jeane 357; Luce, Clare Boothe 397; Rankin, Jeannette 530; Roosevelt, Eleanor 549; Temple, Shirley 627

publishing

Beach, Sylvia (Woodbridge) 54; Graham, Katharine Meyer 274; Hobby, Oveta Culp 305; Monroe, Harriet 454; Steinem, Gloria 607

religion

Blackwell, Antoinette Brown 71; Blavatsky, Helena Petrovna 73; Booth, Evangeline 83; Cabrini, Saint Frances Xavier 109; Dyer, Mary 201; Eddy, Mary Baker 204; Foster, Jodie 240; Fox, Margaret 241; Heck, Barbara Ruckle 296; Hutchinson, Anne 316; McPherson, Aimée Semple 437; O'Hair, Madalyn Murray 487; Wilkinson, Jemima 690

royalty

Kelly, Grace 349; Windsor, Duchess of 693

science

Agassiz, Elizabeth 7; Cannon, Annie Jump 113; Carson, Rachel (Louise) 119; Cori, Gerty Theresa Radnitz 160; Fleming, Williamina Paton 236; Fossey, Dian 240; Geller, Margaret Joan 257; Hyman, Libbie Henrietta 317; Karle, Isabella Helen 343; Kendrick, Pearl 351; Klumpke, Dorothea 358; Leavitt, Henrietta Swan 376; McClintock, Barbara 435; Maury, Antonia Caetana (de Paiva Pereira) 432; Mayer, Maria Goeppert 433; Mitchell, Maria 449; Nice, Margaret Morse 474; Ray, Dixy Lee 532; Rubin, Vera Cooper 553; Scharrer, Berta 571; Stevens, Nettie Maria 608; Wrinch, Dorothy 703; Wu, Chien-Shiung 703; Yalow, Rosalyn Sussman 708

social reform

Addams, Jane 5; Anthony, Susan B(rownell) 22; Baez, Joan 41; Baker, Josephine 44; Balch, Emily Greene 44; Beard, Mary Ritter 55; Blackwell, Antoinette Brown 71; Bloomer, Amelia Jenks 74; Bloor, Ella Reeve 75; Booth, Evangeline 83; Bright Eyes 93; Catt, Carrie (Lane Chapman) 128; Child, Lydia Maria 139; Claflin, Tennessee 145; Claflin, Victoria Woodhull 145; Croly, Jane 166; Dix, Dorothea 191; Dworkin, Andrea 201; Felton, Rebecca Ann 225; Flynn, Elizabeth Gurley 237; Friedan, Betty 247; Gilman, Charlotte Perkins (Stetson) 261; Grimké, Angelina Emily 281; Grimké, Sarah Moore 281; Hale, Clara 287; Howe, Julia Ward 313; Keller, Helen 348; King, Coretta Scott 355; Millett, Kate 445; Mott, Lucretia Coffin 464; Nation, Carry 469; Norman, Dorothy Stecker 479; O'Hair, Madalyn Murray 487; Olsen, Tillie 489; Parks, Rosa 500; Paul, Alice 503; Perkins, Frances Coralie 506; Rankin, Jeannette 530; Roosevelt, Eleanor 549; Sanger, Margaret 566; Smedley, Agnes 589; Stanton, Elizabeth Cady 602; Stone, Lucy Blackwell 609; Stowe, Harriet Beecher 611; Szold, Henrietta 620; Terrell, Mary 630; Tibbles, Susette 638; Truth, Sojourner 642; Tubman, Harriet 643; Wald, Lillian D. 665; Wells-Barnett, Ida Bell 677; Wright, Frances 702

social sciences

Arendt, Hannah 24; Beard, Mary Ritter 55; Benedict, Ruth (Fulton) 61; Gimbutas, Marija 261; Hite, Shere D. 304; Horney, Karen 311; Johnson, Virginia E(shelman) 334; Mead, Margaret 438; Tuchman, Barbara 644

sport

Berg, Patty 63; Brough, Louise 97; Chadwick, Florence 131; Connolly, Maureen 157; Decker, Mary 178; Devers, Gail 186; Ederle, Gertrude Caroline 205; Evans, Janet 219; Fleming, Peggy 236; Gibson, Althea 260; Hard, Darlene Ruth 290; Jacobs, Helen Hull 324; King, Billie Jean 355; Lloyd, Chris Evert 390; Lopez, Nancy 394; Marble, Alice 414; Navratilova, Martina 470; Rankin, Judy 531; Samuelson, Joan Benoit 564; Seles, Monica 576; Wightman, Hazel 688; Williams, Esther 692; Wills, Helen Newington 693; Zaharias, Babe Didrikson 711

theatre

Adams, Maude 4; Anderson, Mary Antoinette 16; Bailey, Pearl 42; Bancroft, Anne 45; Bankhead, Tallulah Brockman 46; Baum, Vicki 53; Bonstelle, Jessie 82; Booth, Shirley 84; Brice, Fanny 91; Carter, Mrs. Leslie 120; Channing, Carol 133; Cornell, Katharine 161; Cowl, Jane 162; Crabtree, Lotta 163; Crawford, Cheryl 164; Crothers, Rachel 167; Cushman, Charlotte (Saunders) 171; Draper, Ruth 194; Dressler, Marie 195; Ferber, Edna 226; Fiske, Minnie Maddern 232; Flanagan, Hallie 235; Fontanne, Lynn 239; Gish, Dorothy 263; Gish, Lillian 263; Glaspell, Susan 265; Gordon, Ruth 271; Hagen, Uta 286; Hansberry, Lorraine 290; Harris, Julie 291; Hayes, Helen 294; Hellman, Lillian 297; Hepburn, Katharine 300; Horne, Lena (Calhoun) 310; Keene, Laura 347; Lee, Gypsy Rose 377; Luce, Clare Boothe 397; MacLaine, Shirley 404; Malina, Judith 410; Marlowe, Julia 424; Merman, Ethel 442; Modjeska, Helena 453; Page, Geraldine 492; Robins, Elizabeth 545; Russell, Lillian 555; Russell, Rosalind 556; Skinner, Cornelia Otis 587; Sullavan, Margaret 615; Tandy, Jessica 624; Tyson, Cicely 649; Waters, Ethel 671; West, Mae 679; Young, Rida 709

travel and exploration

Bly, Nellie 76; Hahn, Emily 286; Peck, Annie Smith 504; Sacagawea 560; Workman, Fanny 701

writing (fiction)

Alcott, Louisa May 12; Atherton, Gertrude 34; Barnes, Djuna (Chappell) 47; Baum, Vicki 53; Blume, Judy (Sussman) 76; Boyle, Kay 88; Brooks, Gwendolyn 97; Buck, Pearl S. 101; Cather, Willa 123; Child, Lydia Maria 139; Chopin, Kate 140; Cornwell, Patricia 161; Deland, Margaret Wade 179; Didion, Joan 189; Fauset, Jessie Redmon 223; Ferber, Edna 226; Fisher, Dorothy Canfield 231; Fitzgerald, Zelda 234; Foster, Hannah Webster 240; Freeman, Mary E. Wilkins 245; French, Marilyn 246; Gellhorn, Martha (Ellis) 257; Glasgow, Ellen 264; Glaspell, Susan 265; Grau, Shirley Ann 276; Green, Anna Katherine 276; Highsmith, Patricia 302; Hurston, Zora Neale 315; Jong, Erica 335; Loos, Anita 394; Lurie, Alison 399; McCarthy, Mary (Therese) 434; McCullers, Carson 436; MacInnes, Helen 404; Mitchell, Margaret 449; Morrison, Toni 463; Nin, Anaïs 477; Oates, Joyce Carol 484; O'Connor, Flannery 485; Olsen, Tillie 489; Paley, Grace Goodside 493; Paretsky, Sara 498; Parker, Dorothy 499; Porter, Katherine Anne 517; Rand, Ayn 530; Sarton, May 568; Smiley, Jane (Graves) 589; Stowe, Harriet Beecher 611; Tan, Amy 623; Tyler, Anne 648; Walker, Alice 666; Welty, Eudora 678; Wharton, Edith 683; Wilder, Laura Ingalls 688; Woolsey, Sarah Chauncey 699; Wylie, Elinor Morton 704; Yourcenar, Marguerite 710

writing (nonfiction)
Adams, Abigail 3; Angelou, Maya 17; Arendt, Hannah 24; Atherton, Gertrude 34; Barney, Natalie 49; Barrymore, Ethel 49; Beard, Mary Ritter 55; Bright Eyes 93; Brown, Helen Gurley 98; Buck, Pearl S. 101; Calderón de la Barca, Fanny 110; Child, Lydia Maria 139; Claflin, Tennessee 145; Claflin, Victoria Woodhull 145; Dworkin, Andrea 201; Fisher, Dorothy Canfield 231; French, Marilyn 246; Friedan, Betty 247; Fuller, Margaret 250; Gellhorn, Martha (Ellis) 257; Gilman, Charlotte Perkins (Stetson) 261; Gimbutas, Marija 261; Goldman, Emma 268; Hahn, Emily 286; Hite, Shere D. 304; Keller, Helen 348; Lorde, Audre Geraldine 394; McCarthy, Mary (Therese) 434; MacLaine, Shirley 404; Millett, Kate 445; Mitford, Jessica (Lucy) 450; Nin, Anaïs 477; Norman, Dorothy Stecker 479; Paglia, Camille 492; Post, Emily 518; Skinner, Cornelia Otis 587; Smedley, Agnes 589; Sontag, Susan 597; Stein, Gertrude 606; Steinem, Gloria 607; Toklas, Alice B. 639; Tuchman, Barbara 644

writing (poetry)
Angelou, Maya 17; Bishop, Elizabeth 70; Bogan, Louise 77; Bradstreet, Anne 89; Brooks, Gwendolyn 97; Dickinson, Emily 189; Doolittle, Hilda 193; Howe, Julia Ward 313; Jong, Erica 335; Lazarus, Emma 375; Levertov, Denise 384; Lorde, Audre Geraldine 394; Lowell, Amy 396; Millay, Edna St. Vincent 444; Moore, Marianne (Craig) 459; Plath, Sylvia 512; Rich, Adrienne 539; Riding, Laura 542; Rukeyser, Muriel 554; Sarton, May 568; Sexton, Anne 578; Smith, Patti 592;

Walker, Alice 666; Wheatley, Phillis 684; Wilcox, Ella Wheeler 688; Wylie, Elinor Morton 704

miscellaneous
Bridgman, Laura Dewey 92; Lincoln, Mary Todd 388; Madison, Dolley 406; Oakley, Annie 483; Onassis, Jacqueline Kennedy 490; Reagan, Nancy 533; Washington, Martha 671

Anatolian women
Artemisia I 28; Artemisia II 28

Arab women
A'isha 10; Fatimah 223; Khadijah 354; Sheba, Queen of 580; Zenobia 712

Argentinian women
Perón, Eva 506; Perón, Isabel 507; Sabatini, Gabriela 559

Assyrian women
Semiramis 577

Australian women
film and television
Anderson, Dame Judith 15; Armstrong, Gillian 26

medicine
Kenny, Elizabeth 352

music (classical)
Glanville-Hicks, Peggy 264; Joyce, Eileen 338; Melba, Dame Nellie 441; Sutherland, Dame Joan 617

philanthropy
Chisholm, Caroline 140

social reform
Chisholm, Caroline 140; Greer, Germaine 277; Noonuccal, Oodgeroo Moongalba 479; Spence, Catherine Helen 599

sport
Court, Margaret Smith 162; Fraser, Dawn 244; Goolagong, Evonne 270

theatre
Anderson, Dame Judith 15

writing (fiction)
Praed, Rosa 519; Prichard, Katharine (Susannah) 520; Richardson, Henry Handel 540; Spence, Catherine Helen 599; Stead, Christina 605; Travers, P(amela) L(yndon) 640

writing (nonfiction)
Greer, Germaine 277; Noonuccal, Oodgeroo Moongalba 479

writing (poetry)
Wright, Judith 702

Austrian women
Bachmann, Ingeborg 40; Baum, Vicki 53; Elizabeth 210; Elssler, Fanny 214; Freud, Anna 247; Handel-Mazzetti, Enrica von 289; Klein, Melanie 358; Kurz, Selma 363; Lenya, Lotte 383; Maria Theresa 419; Marie Antoinette 420; Marie Louise 421; Meitner, Lise 440; Model, Lisette 452;

music (classical)

Baillie, Dame Isobel 42; Baker, Dame Janet (Abbott) 43; Butt, Dame Clara 107; Cross, Joan 166; du Pré, Jacqueline 199; Ferrier, Kathleen 227; Gipps, Ruth 262; Hess, Dame Myra 302; LeFanu, Nicola 378; Lutyens, Elisabeth 400; Lympany, Dame Moura 401; Maconchy, Dame Elizabeth 405; Musgrave, Thea 467; Patti, Adelina (Juana Maria) 502; Schwarzkopf, Dame Elisabeth 573; Smyth, Dame Ethel Mary 594; Tate, Phyllis Margaret 624; Teyte, Dame Maggie 631; Weir, Judith 676

music (popular)

Armatrading, Joan 26; Brightman, Sarah 93; Bush, Kate 104; Faithfull, Marianne 220; Fields, Dame Gracie 229; Laine, Dame Cleo 366; Lawrence, Gertrude 374; Lennox, Annie 382; Lillie, Beatrice 387; Lloyd, Marie 390; Lynn, Dame Vera 401; Matthews, Jessie 432; Paige, Elaine 493; Sade 562; Springfield, Dusty 600; Tilley, Vesta 638

noblewomen

Aelgifu 6; Beaufort, Lady Margaret 56; Godiva 267; Lamb, Lady Caroline 367; Marlborough, Sarah Churchill, Duchess of 423; Stuart, Arabella 614

philanthropy

Barnett, Dame Henrietta Octavia (Weston) 48; Burdett-Coutts, Angela Georgina, Baroness 103; Carpenter, Mary 116; Chisholm, Caroline 140; Diana, Princess of Wales 187; Saunders, Dame Cicely 569; Somerset, Lady Isabella Caroline 595

philosophy

Murdoch, Dame Iris 466; Warnock, (Helen) Mary 670

photography

Cameron, Julia Margaret 112

politics and diplomacy

Abbott, Diane (Julie) 1; Asquith, Margot 32; Astor, Nancy, Viscountess 33; Beckett, Margaret (Mary) 57; Bell, Gertrude (Margaret Lowthian) 59; Blackstone, Tessa (Ann Vosper), Baroness 71; Bondfield, Margaret Grace 79; Bonham Carter, (Helen) Violet, Lady Asquith 80; Boothroyd, Betty 84; Braddock, Bessie 89; Castle, Barbara, Baroness 122; Jackson, Glenda 323; Lee, Jennie 377; Mowlam, Marjorie (Mo) 464; Rathbone, Eleanor (Florence) 531; Summerskill, Edith, Baroness 616; Thatcher, Margaret, Baroness 633; Wilkinson, Ellen 689; Williams, Shirley, Baroness 692

publishing

Cunard, Nancy (Clara) 167; Faithfull, Emily 220

religion

Aethelthryth, Saint 6; Askew, Anne 31; Aylward, Gladys 38; Baldwin, Monica 45; Barton, Elizabeth 51; Booth, Catherine 82; Booth, Evangeline 83; Frideswide, Saint 247; Hilda, Saint 303; Huntingdon, Selina Hastings, Countess of 315; Julian of Norwich 340; Kempe, Margery 350; Lee, Ann 377; Margaret, Saint 416; Slessor, Mary (Mitchell) 588; Southcott, Joanna 598; Taylor, Annie 625; Walburga, Saint 665

royalty

Aethelthryth, Saint 6; Alexandra 13; Anne, the Princess Royal 19; Anne of Bohemia 20; Anne of Cleves 21; Anne of Denmark 21; Berengaria 62; Boleyn, Anne 78; Caroline of Ansbach 115; Caroline of Brunswick 116; Catherine of Aragon 126; Catherine of Braganza 126; Catherine of Valois 128; Diana, Princess of Wales 187; Eleanor of Aquitaine 206; Eleanor of Castile 206; Eleanor of Provence 207; Elizabeth, the Queen Mother 213; Elizabeth 210; Emma 215; Grey, Lady Jane 280; Henrietta Anne, Duchesse d'Orléans 299; Henrietta Maria 299; Howard, Catherine 313; Isabella 320; Isabel of Angoulême 322; Joan of Navarre 333; Kent, Joan of 352; Margaret, Maid of Norway 415; Margaret, Princess 415; Margaret, Saint 416; Margaret of Anjou 416; Margaret Tudor 417; Mary of Modena 429; Mary of Teck 429; Matilda 431; Parr, Catherine 501; Philippa of Hainault 510; Seymour, Jane 579; Windsor, Duchess of 693

rulers

Aelgifu 6; Aethelflaed 6; Anne 19; Boadicea 77; Elizabeth I 210; Elizabeth II 212; Mary, Queen of Scots 427; Mary I 426; Mary II 427; Victoria 659

science

Anning, Mary 22; Arber, Agnes 23; Bell Burnell, (Susan) Jocelyn 61; Burbidge, (Eleanor) Margaret 102; Fell, Dame Honor Bridget 225; Franklin, Rosalind (Elsie) 244; Goodall, Jane 270; Herschel, Caroline Lucretia 301; Hodgkin, Dorothy Crowfoot 306; Leakey, Mary 375; Lonsdale, Dame Kathleen 393; Manton, Sidnie Milana 413; Needham, Dorothy (Mary Moyle) 472; North, Marianne 480; Pitt-Rivers, Rosalind 512; Rothschild, Miriam Louisa 552; Somerville, Mary 596

social reform

Ashby, Dame Margery Corbett 29; Barnett, Dame Henrietta Octavia (Weston) 48; Besant, Annie 67; Booth, Catherine 82; Booth, Evangeline 83; Brittain, Vera Mary 94; Butler, Josephine 106; Chisholm, Caroline 140; Cobbe, Frances Power 152; Cunard, Nancy (Clara) 167; Davies, (Sarah)

Manning, Olivia 412; Mitchison, Naomi 450; Mitford, Nancy 451; Murdoch, Dame Iris 466; Nesbit, E(dith) 473; Oakley, Ann 483; Oliphant, Margaret 488; Orczy, Baroness 490; Ouida 491; Pargeter, Edith Mary 498; Pizzey, Erin 512; Potter, (Helen) Beatrix 518; Pym, Barbara 522; Radcliffe, Ann 526; Rayner, Claire (Berenice) 533; Renault, Mary 536; Rendell, Ruth, Baroness 537; Rhys, Jean 538; Richardson, Dorothy M. 540; Sayers, Dorothy L(eigh) 570; Sewell, Anna 578; Shelley, Mary (Wollstonecraft Godwin) 580; Sinclair, May 585; Smith, Dodie 591; Spark, Dame Muriel 599; Taylor, Elizabeth 626; Thirkell, Angela Margaret 635; Trollope, Frances 641; Trollope, Joanna 641; Uttley, Alison 653; Ward, Mrs. Humphry 668; Warner, Marina (Sarah) 669; Warner, Sylvia Townsend 669; Webb, Mary 673; Weldon, Fay 676; Wesley, Mary 679; West, Dame Rebecca 680; White, Antonia 685; Wood, Mrs. Henry 697; Woolf, Virginia 698; Wylie, Ida Alexa Ross 705; Yonge, Charlotte M(ary) 709

writing (nonfiction)

Adamson, Joy 4; Aguilar, Grace 9; Asquith, Margot 32; Astell, Mary 32; Baldwin, Monica 45; Barbauld, Anna Letitia 47; Behn, Aphra 59; Bell, Gertrude (Margaret Lowthian) 59; Bishop, Isabella Bird 70; Brittain, Vera Mary 94; Burney, Fanny 104; Carlyle, Jane (Baillie Welsh) 115; Carter, Elizabeth 119; Cavendish, Margaret, Duchess of Newcastle 129; Cobbe, Frances Power 152; Craik, Dinah Maria 163; Cunard, Nancy (Clara) 167; Duff-Gordon, Lady Lucy 197; Garnett, Constance 256; Gaskell, Elizabeth Cleghorn 256; Glendinning, Victoria 265; Godden, Rumer 266; Harrison, Jane Ellen 292; Johnson, Pamela Hansford 334; Kemble, Frances 349; Kempe, Margery 350; Kennedy, Helena (Ann), Baroness 351; Kingsley, Mary 356; Macaulay, Catherine 403; Macaulay, Dame Rose 403; Martineau, Harriet 425; Meynell, Alice 442; Mitchell, Juliet 448; Mitchison, Naomi 450; Mitford, Jessica (Lucy) 450; Mitford, Mary Russell 451; Mitford, Nancy 451; Montagu, Elizabeth 455; Montagu, Lady Mary Wortley 456; More, Hannah 461; Morrell, Lady Ottoline 462; Murdoch, Dame Iris 466; Norton, Caroline 481; Oliphant, Margaret 488; Piozzi, Hester Lynch 511; Rowbotham, Sheila 552; Russell, Dora 554; Sackville-West, Vita 561; Sinclair, May 585; Stark, Dame Freya 604; Stoppard, Miriam 611; Strachey, Ray 612; Thompson, Flora Jane 637; Warner, Marina (Sarah) 669; Wedgwood, Dame

Veronica 674; West, Dame Rebecca 680; White, Antonia 685; Wollstonecraft, Mary 696; Woolf, Virginia 698; Wordsworth, Dorothy 700; Yates, Dame Frances (Amelia) 708

writing (poetry)

Baillie, Joanna 43; Barbauld, Anna Letitia 47; Brontë, Emily 96; Browning, Elizabeth Barrett 99; Carter, Elizabeth 119; Cornford, Frances (Crofts) 161; Hemans, Felicia Dorothea 298; Ingelow, Jean 319; Jennings, Elizabeth (Joan) 327; Meynell, Alice 442; Raine, Kathleen (Jessie) 527; Rossetti, Christina Georgina 551; Sackville-West, Vita 561; Sitwell, Dame Edith 586; Smith, Stevie 592; Winchilsea, Anne Finch, Countess of 693

miscellaneous

Fitton, Mary 232; Fitzherbert, Maria 234; Hamilton, Emma, Lady 289; Hathaway, Anne 292; Jekyll, Gertrude 326; Keeler, Christine 347; Shore, Jane 582; Walter, Lucy 667

Burmese women

Suu Kyi, Aung San 618

Byzantine women

Anna Comnena 18; Eudocia 217; Eudocia Macrembolitissa 217; Eudoxia 217; Irene 319; Kassia 345; Pulcheria 521; Theodora 634; Zoë 713

Canadian women

Arden, Elizabeth 24; Atwood, Margaret (Eleanor) 35; Carr, Emily 117; Crawford, Isabella Valancy 164; Firestone, Shulamith 231; Hayden, Melissa 293; Hogg-Priestly, Helen Battles Sawyer 307; Kimura, Doreen 355; lang, k d 368; Mitchell, Joni 448; Montgomery, L(ucy) M(aud) 458; Munro, Alice 465; Roy, Gabrielle 553; Sauvé, Jeanne Benoit 570; Shields, Carol (Ann) 581; Smart, Elizabeth 588; Stratas, Teresa 612

Chilean women

Allende, Isabel 14; Mistral, Gabriela 447

Chinese women

Aylward, Gladys 38; Chiang, Mayling Soong 137; Deng Yingchao 182; Ding Ling 191; Han Suyin 290; Jiang Qing 329; Jung Chang 340; Pan Chao 494; Qiu Jin 524; Sun Ch'ing-ling 617; Tz'u-hsi 649; Wu, Chien-Shiung 703; Wu Zhao 704

Cuban women

Quirot, Anna 525

Czech and Slovak women

Destinn, Emmy 185; Gruberová, Edita 283; Jeritza, Maria 327; Navratilova, Martina 470

Danish women

Dinesen, Isak 191; Grahn, Lucile 275; Lehmann, Inge 379; Margaret I 415; Margrethe II 418

Dominican women

Charles, Dame (Mary) Eugenia 134

Dutch women

Beatrix 56; Bijns, Anna 69; Blankers-Koen, Fanny 73; Charrière, Isabelle Agnès Elisabeth de 135; Jacqueline of Bavaria 324; Juliana 339; Leyster, Judith 386; Margaret of Austria 417; Margaret of Parma 417; Mata Hari 431; Peeters, Clara 504; Ruysch, Rachel 557; Wilhelmina 689

Ecuadorian women

Arteaga, Rosalia 28

Egyptian women

Arsinoë II 27; Berenice I 63; Berenice II 63; Cleopatra 148; Hatshepsut 292; Nefertiti 472

Ethiopian women

Zauditu 711

French women

art and crafts

Bonheur, Rosa 81; Delaunay, Sonia 179; Goncharova, Natalia Sergeyevna 269; Labille-Guiard, Adelaide 365; Laurencin, Marie 372; Morisot, Berthe 462; Valadon, Suzanne 655; Vieira da Silva, Maria Helena 661; Vigée-Lebrun, Marie Anne Elisabeth 661

crime

Corday, Charlotte 159

dance

Camargo, Marie (Anne de Cupis de) 112; Caron, Leslie 116; Sallé, Marie 563; Toumanova, Tamara 639; Verdy, Violette 657

education

Cixous, Hélène 144; Maintenon, Marquise de 408

espionage

Ricard, Marthe 539

fashion and beauty

Chanel, Coco 133; Schiaparelli, Elsa 571; Vionnet, Madeleine 662

film and television

Aimée, Anouk 10; Arletty 25; Bardot, Brigitte 47; Caron, Leslie 116; Casarès, Maria 121; Deneuve, Catherine 182; Duras, Marguerite 200; Feuillière, Edwige 228; Huppert, Isabelle 315; Moreau, Jeanne 461; Signoret, Simone 584; Varda, Agnès 656

heroism

Hallowes, Odette 288; Joan of Arc, Saint 331; Ricard, Marthe 539

mathematics and computing

Germain, Sophie 259

medicine

Pelletier, Madeleine 505

music (classical)

Boulanger, Nadia (Juliette) 86; Calvé, Emma 111; Chaminade, Cécile Louise Stéphanie 132; Crespin, Régine 165; Demessieux, Jeanne-Marie-Madeleine 180; Tailleferre, Germaine 622; Viardot-García, Pauline 658

music (popular)

Guilbert, Yvette 284; Piaf, Edith 510

noblewomen

Berry, Duchesse de 67; Chevreuse, Duchesse de 137; Diane de France 187; Diane de Poitiers 188; du Barry, Countess 196; La Vallière, Louise, Duchesse de 372; Longueville, Duchesse de 393; Maintenon, Marquise de 408; Montespan, Marquise de 457; Pompadour, Marquise de 515; Rambouillet, Marquise de 529; Ursins, Princesse des 653

philosophy

Beauvoir, Simone de 56; Irigaray, Luce 319; Kristeva, Julia 362; Weil, Simone 675

politics and diplomacy

Michel, Louise 443; Roland (de la Platière), Marie-Jeanne 548; Veil, Simone 657

religion

Alacoque, Saint Margaret Mary 11; Bernadette of Lourdes, Saint 65; Chantal, Saint Jane Frances de 134; Clotilda, Saint 151; Geneviève, Saint 258; Guyon, Jeanne-Marie 284; Héloïse 298; Joan of Arc, Saint 331; Porete, Marguerite 517; Thérèse of Lisieux, Saint 635; Weil, Simone 675

royalty

Anne of Brittany 21; Beauharnais, Hortense de 56; Berengaria 62; Blanche of Castile 72; Bonaparte, Caroline 79; Bonaparte, Elisa 79; Bonaparte, Pauline 79; Brunhilde 100; Clotilda, Saint 151; Eleanor of Aquitaine 206; Eugénie 217; Fredegund 245; Henrietta Anne, Duchesse d'Orléans 299; Henrietta Maria 299; Isabella of Bavaria 321; Isabel of Angoulême 322; Joan of Navarre 333; Joséphine 337; Margaret of Anjou 416; Marguerite de Valois 418; Marguerite of Navarre 418; Marie Antoinette 420; Marie de Médicis 421; Marie Louise 421; Montpensier, Duchesse de 459

rulers

Anne of Austria 20; Anne of France 21; Catherine de' Médicis 124; Joanna I 330

science

Châtelet, Emilie, Marquise du 136; Curie, Marie (Skłodowska) 169; Joliot-Curie, Irène 335; Lavoisier, Marie (Anne Pierrette) 373; Perey, Marguerite Catherine 506

social reform

Beauvoir, Simone de 56; Pelletier,

READ MORE IN PENGUIN

In every corner of the world, on every subject under the sun, Penguin represents quality and variety – the very best in publishing today.

For complete information about books available from Penguin – including Puffins, Penguin Classics and Arkana – and how to order them, write to us at the appropriate address below. Please note that for copyright reasons the selection of books varies from country to country.

In the United Kingdom: Please write to *Dept. EP, Penguin Books Ltd, Bath Road, Harmondsworth, West Drayton, Middlesex UB7 ODA*

In the United States: Please write to *Consumer Sales, Penguin Putnam Inc., P.O. Box 999, Dept. 17109, Bergenfield, New Jersey 07621-0120.* VISA and MasterCard holders call 1-800-253-6476 to order Penguin titles

In Canada: Please write to *Penguin Books Canada Ltd, 10 Alcorn Avenue, Suite 300, Toronto, Ontario M4V 3B2*

In Australia: Please write to *Penguin Books Australia Ltd, P.O. Box 257, Ringwood, Victoria 3134*

In New Zealand: Please write to *Penguin Books (NZ) Ltd, Private Bag 102902, North Shore Mail Centre, Auckland 10*

In India: Please write to *Penguin Books India Pvt Ltd, 210 Chiranjiv Tower, 43 Nehru Place, New Delhi 110 019*

In the Netherlands: Please write to *Penguin Books Netherlands bv, Postbus 3507, NL-1001 AH Amsterdam*

In Germany: Please write to *Penguin Books Deutschland GmbH, Metzlerstrasse 26, 60594 Frankfurt am Main*

In Spain: Please write to *Penguin Books S. A., Bravo Murillo 19, 1° B, 28015 Madrid*

In Italy: Please write to *Penguin Italia s.r.l., Via Benedetto Croce 2, 20094 Corsico, Milano*

In France: Please write to *Penguin France, Le Carré Wilson, 62 rue Benjamin Baillaud, 31500 Toulouse*

In Japan: Please write to *Penguin Books Japan Ltd, Kaneko Building, 2-3-25 Koraku, Bunkyo-Ku, Tokyo 112*

In South Africa: Please write to *Penguin Books South Africa (Pty) Ltd, Private Bag X14, Parkview, 2122 Johannesburg*

READ MORE IN PENGUIN

BIOGRAPHY AND AUTOBIOGRAPHY

Freedom from Fear Aung San Suu Kyi

Aung San Suu Kyi, human-rights activist and leader of Burma's National League for Democracy, was detained in 1989 by SLORC, the ruling military junta. In July 1995 she was liberated from six years' house arrest. *Freedom From Fear* contains speeches, letters and interviews, as well as forewords by Archbishop Desmond Tutu and Václav Havel and gives a voice to Burma's 'woman of destiny'.

Lucie Duff Gordon Katherine Frank

'What stays in the mind is a portrait of an exceptional woman, funny, wry, occasionally flamboyant, always generous-spirited, and firmly rooted in the social history of her day' – *The Times Literary Supplement*

Cleared for Take-Off Dirk Bogarde

'It begins with his experiences in the Second World War as an interpreter of reconnaissance photographs ... His awareness of the horrors as well as the dottiness of war is essential to the tone of this affecting and strangely beautiful book' – *Daily Telegraph*

Mrs Jordan's Profession Claire Tomalin

The story of Dora Jordan and her relationship with the Duke of Clarence, later King William IV. 'Meticulous biography at its creative best' – *Observer*. 'A fascinating and affecting story, one in which the mutually attractive, mutually suspicious, equally glittering worlds of court and theatre meet, and one which vividly illustrates the social codes of pre-Victorian Britain' – *Sunday Times*

In Harm's Way Martin Bell

'A coruscating account of the dangerous work of a war correspondent, replete with tales of Bell dodging, and in one case not dodging, bullets across the globe in order to bring us our nightly news' – *Independent*

READ MORE IN PENGUIN

WOMEN'S INTEREST

Killing Rage: Ending Racism bell hooks

Addressing race and racism in American society from a black and a feminist standpoint, bell hooks covers a broad spectrum of issues in these twenty-three essays, including: the psychological trauma of racism; anti-Semitism; friendship between black women and white women; and the internalized racism of the media.

The New Our Bodies, Ourselves Angela Phillips and Jill Rakusen
A Health Book by and for Women

Rewritten and expanded to meet the needs of women and men in the 1990s, *The New Our Bodies, Ourselves* has influenced the thinking of a generation.

The Well Woman Handbook Suzy Hayman

Practical and informative, *The Well Woman Handbook* will enable you to learn more about your body and put the responsibility for its health back into your own hands.

Nine Parts of Desire Geraldine Brooks
The Hidden World of Islamic Women

'She takes us behind the veils and into the homes of women in every corner of the Middle East ... It is in her descriptions of her meetings – like that with Khomeini's widow Khadija, who paints him as a New Man (and one for whom she dyed her hair vamp-red) – that the book excels' – *Observer*

Banishing the Beast Lucy Bland
English Feminism and Sexual Morality 1885–1914

'Fascinating ... Her work is a timely reminder that balancing social responsibility and individual rights in sexuality and maternity is far from being a new debate ... This is scholarly history with a contemporary relevance' – Sheila Rowbotham

READ MORE IN PENGUIN

WOMEN'S INTEREST

Mixed Messages Brigid McConville

Images of breasts – young and naked, sexual and chic – are everywhere. Yet for many women, the form, functions and health of our own breasts remain shrouded in mystery, ignorance – even fear. The consequences of our culture's breast taboos are tragic: Britain's breast-cancer death rate is the highest in the world. 'Lively, gutsy, fast-paced and information-packed' – Sheila Kitzinger

Against Our Will Susan Brownmiller
Men, Women and Rape

Against Our Will sheds a new and blinding light on the tensions that exist between men and women. It was written to give rape its history. Now, as Susan Brownmiller concludes, 'we must deny it a future'. 'Thoughtful, informative and well researched' – *New Statesman & Society*

The Courage to Raise Good Men Olga Silverstein and Beth Rashbaum

Why are women raising sons who later in life neglect, abuse, undermine and patronize them? Calling for change, Olga Silverstein, a working therapist and an early member of the family therapy movement in the USA, offers a sane and considered plea to reassess our parenting.

Understanding Women Luise Eichenbaum and Susie Orbach

Understanding Women, an expanded version of *Outside In . . . Inside Out*, is a radical appraisal of women's psychological development based on clinical evidence. 'An exciting and thought-provoking book' – *British Journal of Psychiatry*

Doubly Deviant, Doubly Damned Ann Lloyd
Society's Treatment of Violent Women

A ground-breaking examination of the way society treats violent women, *Doubly Deviant, Doubly Damned* points out the failures, omissions and weaknesses of a system designed by men for men. Based on a wealth of research, it is a clear, informative work that exposes the injustice of a society that labels violent women as either 'mad or bad'.

READ MORE IN PENGUIN

REFERENCE

The Penguin Dictionary of Literary Terms and Literary Theory
J. A. Cuddon

'Scholarly, succinct, comprehensive and entertaining, this is an important book, an indispensable work of reference. It draws on the literature of many languages and quotes aptly and freshly from our own' – *The Times Educational Supplement*

The Penguin Dictionary of Symbols
Jean Chevalier and Alain Gheerbrant, translated by John Buchanan-Brown

This book draws together folklore, literary and artistic sources and focuses on the symbolic dimension of every colour, number, sound, gesture, expression or character trait that has benefited from symbolic interpretation.

Roget's Thesaurus of English Words and Phrases
Edited by Betty Kirkpatrick

This new edition of Roget's classic work, now brought up to date for the nineties, will increase anyone's command of the English language. Fully cross-referenced, it includes synonyms of every kind (formal or colloquial, idiomatic and figurative) for almost 900 headings. It is a must for writers and utterly fascinating for any English speaker.

The Penguin Guide to Synonyms and Related Words
S. I. Hayakawa

'More helpful than a thesaurus, more humane than a dictionary, the *Guide to Synonyms and Related Words* maps linguistic boundaries with precision, sensitivity to nuance and, on occasion, dry wit' – *The Times Literary Supplement*

The Penguin Book of Exotic Words   Janet Whitcut

English is the most widely used language today, its unusually rich vocabulary the result of new words from all over the world being freely assimilated into the language. With entries arranged thematically, words of Saxon, Viking, French, Latin, Greek, Hebrew, Arabic and Indian origin are explored in this fascinating book.

READ MORE IN PENGUIN

REFERENCE

Medicines: A Guide for Everybody Peter Parish

Now in its seventh edition and completely revised and updated, this bestselling guide is written in ordinary language for the ordinary reader yet will prove indispensable to anyone involved in health care – nurses, pharmacists, opticians, social workers and doctors.

Media Law Geoffrey Robertson QC and Andrew Nichol

Crisp and authoritative surveys explain the up-to-date position on defamation, obscenity, official secrecy, copyright and confidentiality, contempt of court, the protection of privacy and much more.

The Penguin Careers Guide
Anna Alston and Anne Daniel; Consultant Editor: Ruth Miller

As the concept of a 'job for life' wanes, this guide encourages you to think broadly about occupational areas as well as describing day-to-day work and detailing the latest developments and qualifications such as NVQs. Special features include possibilities for working part-time and job-sharing, returning to work after a break and an assessment of the current position of women.

The Penguin Dictionary of Troublesome Words Bill Bryson

Why should you avoid discussing the *weather conditions*? Can a married woman be celibate? Why is it eccentric to talk about the aroma of a cowshed? A straightforward guide to the pitfalls and hotly disputed issues in standard written English.

The Penguin Dictionary of Musical Performers Arthur Jacobs

In this invaluable companion volume to *The Penguin Dictionary of Music* Arthur Jacobs has brought together the names of over 2,500 performers. Music is written by composers, yet it is the interpreters who bring it to life; in this comprehensive book they are at last given their due.

READ MORE IN PENGUIN

DICTIONARIES